PSYCHOLOGY

PSYCHOLOGY
THE DISCOVERY EXPERIENCE

Stephen L. Franzoi
Marquette University

ATOMIC**dog**PUBLISHING

Cincinnati, Ohio
www.atomicdog.com

Library of Congress Control Number: 2002117418

ISBN 1-59260-037-9

Printed in the United States of America by Atomic Dog Publishing,
1203 Main Street, Third Floor, Cincinnati, OH 45202.

10 9 8 7 6 5 4 3 2 1

To

the women in my life,
Cheryl, Amelia, and Lillian;
To my parents, Lou and Joyce;
And to my brother and sister,
Randy and Susie:
Together, and singly, they influence
the essential elements of my life.

Brief Contents

Contents

4   Human Development   73

5   Sensation and Perception   115

Discovery Boxes

Preface

In teaching introductory psychology, professors are essentially trying to persuade you—the student—that the information presented in the course is a valuable way to understand behavior and the process of living on this planet. There are compelling arguments in the message of psychology, and most professors believe that, if they can get you to spend some time thinking about and evaluating the message, you will become more competent in dealing with future life events. The distinct advantage that a psychology course has in stimulating student interest is that its subject matter is the "study of the mind." As such, introductory psychology offers you the hope that course material will help you not only better understand other people, but also yourself. Seeking such knowledge is a distinguishing feature of young adulthood, and the college experience is specifically designed to foster this quest.

To help you in your quest to better understand yourself and others, this text presents the science of psychology as a journey of discovery—a journey undertaken both by researchers in their search for knowledge over the past century and by students over the course of the term. The text explains how psychology has expanded our understanding of how people think, feel, and behave, while also motivating you to apply this knowledge to better understand yourself and others. By regularly encouraging you to consider how psychological knowledge relates to your own life, the text places your learning experience within a personally relevant context that benefits retention of course material, while also fostering self-insights that can be applied to your daily living.

The history of psychology is infused with compelling stories of how researchers' intense interest in learning about the nature of human and animal behavior led them on a journey of discovery that eventually culminated in important new knowledge. The fundamental difference between our often informal, anecdotally based personal journeys of discovery and the journeys of discovery found in psychology is that the vehicle employed in the latter journeys is the scientific method. Throughout *Psychology: The Discovery Experience*, I tell selected discovery stories in psychology so that you will appreciate both the human element and the ever-evolving nature of scientific knowledge and insight.

Following chapter 1's introduction to psychology, which covers the field's history and areas of specialization, chapter 2 is devoted to the vehicle for psychological discovery—research methodology. This chapter provides a solid base for understanding the scientific enterprise of psychology. Each chapter also includes *Discovery Boxes* that discuss selected studies in detail. This emphasis on the scientific enterprise encourages a healthy, scientific skepticism of the many, often contradictory, commonsense truisms we learn from others.

Encouraging Self-Discovery

While encouraging you to analyze the scientific journey of discovery in psychology, the text also facilitates a personal journey of discovery by including over 20 self-report questionnaires that ask you to consider how the specific text material relates to your own life. The self-report questionnaires are those that researchers currently use, and the results of studies employing them are part of the text material. Thus, as you learn about various psychological theories and relevant research findings, you also learn something about yourself.

Applying Psychology to Everyday Experiences

Beyond self-report questionnaires, the text also presents a *Psychological Applications* section at the end of each chapter that demonstrates how psychology can be applied to your life. In these sections, you learn how the theories and research in a particular chapter can be applied to real-world settings. Topics covered in the *Psychological Applications* sections include developing critical thinking skills, learning how to exercise self-control in your academic and personal life, improving everyday memory, understanding test anxiety, coping with jealousy, and many others.

Encouraging Critical Thinking

You can develop an understanding of yourself and others by reading astrological predictions, internalizing the varied messages of popular culture, and uncritically accepting the advice and "wisdom" of friends, family, and (yes!) college professors. Yet, what is the value of this understanding if it is not subjected to critical cognitive analysis? Critical evaluation is an important component of *Psychology: The Discovery Experience*. Questions in the main body of the text encourage critical thinking by inviting you to guess a study's hypotheses, results, or alternative interpretation of findings. In addition, questions that appear in the captions of figures, tables, and photos inspire further analysis of text material. Each chapter also features *Journey of Discovery Questions*, which require critical analyses of current discussion topics. Possible answers to these questions are provided in an *Appendix* in the print version of the text and are "clickable" in the online version. Strategically placed *Info-bits* in each chapter provide additional information on selected topics. Last, but certainly not least, is a feature unique to the online version of this text: *QuickCheck* interactive questions. These questions test your knowledge on various topics and provide immediate feedback on the extent of your understanding.

Recognizing the Diversity and Unity of People

Integrated within this book's journey of discovery theme is the encouragement to recognize the ways in which people are both similar to and different from one another. *Psychology: The Discovery Experience* tells the story of the science of psychology in such a way that you will recognize the "yin-yang" of unity and diversity, whether you are trying to understand the thoughts, emotions, and behavior of your college roommates or those of people from other cultures.

The text not only analyzes how culture and our individual developmental experiences influence the way we think, feel, and behave, but also examines how humans, as a species, often respond similarly to their physical and social surroundings. The "yin" in this diversity-unity analysis is the sociocultural perspective, while the "yang" is the evolutionary perspective. The text explains that the culture of a people is based on their relationship with the environment, and the evolution of our species is a story of how we have adapted to our surroundings. Thus, just as our bodies and brains are products of evolutionary forces, so, too, is our culture. Yet, cultural change occurs much more rapidly than genetic change. This is why the world's cultures vary greatly, despite little meaningful genetic variation among cultural groups.

Two belief systems that explain how individuals relate to their groups and that are important to understanding the psychology of human behavior are individualism and collectivism. Individualism is a philosophy of life stressing the priority of personal goals over group goals, a preference for loose-knit social relationships, and a desire to be relatively independent of others' influence. In contrast, collectivism is a philosophy of life stressing the priority of group needs over individual needs, a preference for tightly knit social relationships, and a willingness to submit to the influence of one's group. Although we know that cultures differ in their individualist-collectivist orientations, we do not know whether one is better than the other in any ultimate evolutionary sense. *Psychology: The Discovery Experience* periodically examines how the psychology of people from different cultures differs due to their individualist-collectivist bents. For those chapter topics where the individualist-collectivist analysis is not especially relevant, other more relevant cultural factors are highlighted.

Pedagogical Aids

Psychology: The Discovery Experience enhances learning with the following pedagogical devices:

1. Each chapter opens with a *chapter outline*.

2. *Short-sentence headings* compactly summarize the content of chapter sections and facilitate recall of text topics.

3. A *bulleted summary* at the end of each major chapter section reviews the section's most important concepts.

4. Beautifully rendered four-color illustrations throughout the text clarify and enhance chapter concepts.

5. In both the print and online versions of the text, *key terms* and concepts are highlighted and defined on first appearance. In the print version, key terms are also defined in the text margins and listed in alphabetical order with page references at the end of each chapter. A *Glossary* at the end of the print book presents all of the definitions alphabetically. The online version of the text has "pop-up" definitions of key terms, as well as a key term matching quiz in each end-of-chapter Study Guide.

6. *Journey of Discovery Questions* within each chapter require critical analyses of current discussion topics. Possible answers are found online, as well as in an appendix at the end of the print book.

7. *Info-bits* briefly describe the results from psychological studies that enhance text material.

8. *Quotes* from famous individuals in other fields illustrate text material.

9. *Discovery Boxes* within each chapter enhance your understanding of a variety of topics. See the list of *Discovery Boxes* on page xvi.

10. *Psychological Applications* sections help you to apply each chapter's psychological concepts to real-world situations.

11. *Suggested Websites* at the end of each chapter are online sources that you can access to obtain a better understanding of chapter material.

12. *Review Questions* at the end of each chapter allow you to check your comprehension of the chapter's major concepts.

Online and in Print

Psychology: The Discovery Experience is available online as well as in print. The online chapters demonstrate how the interactive media components of the text enhance presentation and understanding. For example,

- Animated illustrations help to clarify concepts.

- Self-report questionnaires show you how specific text material relates to your own life. (Due to copyright restrictions, not all of the questionnaires appear in the online text.)

- *QuickCheck* interactive questions and chapter quizzes test your knowledge of various topics and provide immediate feedback.

- Clickable glossary terms provide immediate definitions of key concepts.

- Highlighting capabilities allow you to emphasize main ideas. You can also add personal notes in the margin.

- The search function allows you to quickly locate discussions of specific topics throughout the text.

You may choose to use just the online version of the text, or both the online and print versions together. This gives you the flexibility to choose which combination of resources works best for you. To assist those who use the online and print versions together, the primary heads and subheads in each chapter are numbered the same. For example, the first primary head in Chapter 1 is labeled 1-1, the second primary head in this chapter is labeled 1-2, and so on. The subheads build from the designation of their corresponding primary head: 1-1a, 1-1b, etc. This numbering system is designed to make moving between the online and print versions as seamless as possible.

Finally, next to a number of figures, tables, and boxes in the print version of the text, you will see icons similar to those on the left. These icons indicate that this figure, table, or box in the online version of the text is interactive in a way that applies, illustrates, or reinforces the concept.

Ancillary Materials

A test item file is available in the ExamView® Pro format. ExamView® Pro enables you to quickly create printed tests for your course using either a Windows or Macintosh computer. You can enter your own questions and customize the appearance of the tests you create. Each chapter has 100 carefully constructed questions, five of which are essay and 95 of which are multiple-choice.

A complete instructor's manual contains learning objectives, lecture suggestions, articles of interest, critical thinking questions, video suggestions, and additional web resources for each chapter. PowerPoint® presentations (over 200) are available for classroom use of text materials.

Acknowledgments

While I was writing this text, many people provided me with invaluable assistance and understanding. I first want to thank my family for not only supporting my writing efforts and forgiving my memory lapses during this time, but also for providing me with wonderful examples of psychological principles that I used throughout the text. I also apologize to my daughters, Amelia and Lillian, for any future embarrassment I may cause them by retelling some of their life experiences in the book!

I owe a big debt of gratitude to the students in my introductory psychology courses at Marquette University, who are the first to be exposed to my new stories of the psychological journey of discovery. I also wish to thank three colleagues who provided their expertise during the writing of five of the chapters in this book. My departmental colleague, Dr. Michael Wierzbicki, provided important content in the early drafts of chapters 13 (Psychological Disorders) and 14 (Therapy), Dr. Jeffrey Ratliff-Crain at the University of Minnesota–Morris did the same for chapters 11 (Motivation and Emotion) and 15 (Stress, Coping, and Health), and Dr. Karl Stukenberg at Xavier University contributed important information to chapter 12 (Personality). Their help was greatly appreciated and provided added depth to the book content.

Finally, I would like to warmly thank the people at Atomic Dog Publishing for not only providing me with the opportunity to make my book a reality, but also for making the entire publishing experience so thoroughly enjoyable. First, I would like to thank Alex von Rosenberg, Founder of Atomic Dog, who has provided the necessary resources at all stages of development and production to make this a first-rate text. Second, I would like to thank some Atomic Dog people whom I have known for a number of years: Tom Doran, Vice President, Business and Product Development; Edgar Laube, Publisher in Psychology; and Victoria Putman, Director of Production. I had previously worked with Tom, Ed, and Vickie when I was an author at Brown & Benchmark Publishers in the 1990s, and it is great to be working with them again. While completing this book, I worked most closely with Ed, and he did a great job of coordinating and organizing numerous book tasks, tracking down reviewers and resources, allaying my anxieties about deadlines, and keeping me focused. Ed, I owe you! I was also very fortunate to work with Production Coordinator Mary Monner, who kept me on track during copyediting and page proofing, and even budgeted in my vacation time! Design Coordinator Christine Abshire did a super job in taking my scrawled drawings and half-baked ideas and turning them into highly polished interactive learning devices for students. Thanks are also extended to Copy Editor Laurie McGee, who patiently cleaned up my manuscript prior to it going into production, and to Permissions Coordinator Karyn Morrison, who adeptly secured the rights to a great deal of valuable material that is included in this text.

Numerous reviewers, who obviously care very much about psychology and the art and craft of teaching, generously provided feedback during the writing of this text. I would like to thank:

Paul Bell, *Colorado State University*
Trey Buchanan, *Wheaton College*
Robert Caldwell, *Michigan State University*
James R. Cook, *University of North Carolina–Charlotte*
Wendy Domjan, *University of Texas–Austin*
Natalie Dove, *Purdue University*
Gary D. Fisk, *Georgia Southwestern State University*
Donelson R. Forsyth, *Virginia Commonwealth*
Susan M. Frantz, *Highline Community College*
Traci Giuliano, *Southwestern University*
Wind Goodfriend, *Purdue University*
Judith Harackiewicz, *University of Wisconsin–Madison*
Robert M. Hessling, *University of Wisconsin–Milwaukee*
Scott F. Madey, *Shippensburg University*

Michael S. Ofsowitz, *University of Maryland, European Division*
Daniel Osherton, *Rice University*
Ellen Peters, *University of Oregon*
Laura Richardson, *University of Guam*
Leland Swenson, *Loyola Marymount University*
Alan Swinkels, *St. Edward's University*
Kris Vasquez, *Alverno College*
Brian T. Yates, *American University*

And Finally . . .

I welcome your comments and feedback. Thanks to the online learning environment for Atomic Dog texts, I'll be in a position to incorporate appropriate suggestions several times a year. The prospect of being able to develop a robust exchange of ideas with current users, both students and faculty, is truly exciting. You can reach me at:

stephen.franzoi@marquette.edu.

Very best wishes,
Steve Franzoi

Stephen L. Franzoi is Professor of Psychology at Marquette University in Milwaukee, Wisconsin. Born and raised in Iron Mountain, Michigan, he received his B.S. in both psychology and sociology from Western Michigan University and his Ph.D. from the University of California at Davis. He also worked as a postdoctoral fellow at Indiana University in the Self Program sponsored by the National Institute of Mental Health and served as the assistant editor of *Social Psychology Quarterly*. At Marquette University, Professor Franzoi teaches introductory psychology courses and is also the author of the textbook *Social Psychology* (third edition). He is an active researcher in the areas of body esteem and self-awareness, and is currently the associate editor of the journal *Social Problems*. Over the years, Dr. Franzoi has discussed his research in *The New York Times* and *USA Today*, and on National Public Radio and the "Oprah Winfrey Show." Because of his desire to apply psychological knowledge to real-world problems, Dr. Franzoi regularly provides gender equity and multicultural workshops, including NAACP-sponsored programs, to schools and organizations. He and Cheryl Figg are the proud parents of Amelia, age 16, and Lillian, age 13.

Introduction to Psychology

1

Chapter Outline

If there truly are decisive moments in life that set people onto a clear course, then one of mine came in the fall of 1972 when I was a college sophomore. My roommate, Ted, showed me a university brochure announcing awards of $1,000 to undergraduate "scholars" who designed innovative projects in their respective majors. Ted, an English major, announced that he was going to apply for this award and then embark on a grand adventure: a cross-country trip in his pickup truck and camper, writing an account of his road experiences along the lines of John Steinbeck's *Travels with Charley*. As Ted described all the places he planned to visit on his journey, I first thought of the factory job waiting for me back home, and then my thoughts shifted from assembly lines to the empty passenger seat in Ted's truck. In no time, I began to devise a plan to be the person riding in that very seat. While Ted wrote the great American novel, his roommate and new traveling companion—me—would conduct a nationwide psychological study.

But of what? Even I, with only one scientific methods course under my belt, realized that an aspiring psychologist should have a specific research topic in mind before setting out to collect data. Wait. Cross-country. The term itself gave me an idea. In the early 1970s, many young adults, carrying backpacks and sleeping bags, hitchhiked from destination to destination, sometimes for months at a time. When describing these dropouts from the mainstream culture, news reporters used such phrases as "hippies on the move" and "modern-day hobos." Yet, who were these people? Did they share a common set of personality traits? There it was—the basis for my first psychological study!

Surprisingly, we both obtained awards for our respective projects. Perhaps it was because enough members on the university selection committee found it humorously appealing to subject unsuspecting summer travelers to a pair of Steinbeck-Freud "wannabes." Whatever the reason, the following June we began our adventure, traveling 13,000 miles through 23 states in 10 weeks' time. When we picked up cross-country hitchhikers, I would first interview them and then they would answer a personality questionnaire as we bounced around in the truck's camper. Although neither Ted nor I set the literary or scientific communities buzzing with the products of our summer excursion, my analysis of hitchhikers' personalities was eventually published in a scientific journal (Franzoi, 1985) and, more important, the experience created in me a passion for the discipline of psychology.

Many of you reading this textbook will also feel a similar intensity of interest in learning as much as possible about the science of psychology. For others, whose passions burn for different life pursuits, this text and the course in which it is offered can still provide valuable knowledge that will serve you well while following those desires. At its heart, the science of psychology is a *journey of discovery* undertaken both by researchers in their search for knowledge over the past one hundred-odd years and by you, the student, over the course of the term. Throughout this text, as you learn how psychology has expanded our understanding of how people think, feel, and behave (the discipline's journey of discovery), I will encourage you to apply this knowledge to better understand yourself and others (your own journey of discovery). With this thought in mind, let's begin.

A journey of a thousand miles starts from beneath one's feet.

—Lao-Tzu, 6th century B.C., Chinese philosopher

1-1 WHAT IS PSYCHOLOGY?

A basic necessity to any successful journey is to know how to read the road signs, and for you, the reader of this textbook, this means understanding the terminology. Throughout this book, I will define important concepts that will help you navigate your understanding of the discipline of psychology.

1-1a Psychology Is the Scientific Study of Mental Processes and Behavior

The term *psychology* comes from the Greek words *psyche,* meaning "mind," and *logos,* meaning "study." In its broadest sense, **psychology** is the scientific study of mental processes and behavior. This means that psychologists are interested in using scientific methods (see chapter 2) to understand how we and other living creatures think, feel, and act.

> **Psychology:** The scientific study of mental processes and behavior.

People often confuse psychology with **psychiatry,** which is a branch of medicine concerned with the diagnosis and treatment of psychological disorders, practiced by physicians. Psychology also deals with the diagnosis and treatment of such disorders (see chapters 13 and 14), but this interest represents only one area of specialization in a discipline that has a much broader scope than psychiatry.

> **Psychiatry:** A branch of medicine concerned with the diagnosis and treatment of psychological disorders. The roughly comparable specialty area in psychology is known as *clinical psychology.*

1-1b Most Psychologists Believe That There Are Lawful Patterns of Behavior

In trying to understand the means by which we "operate" in our life's journey, psychologists have struggled with the following fundamental question: Do we freely choose our actions or are they determined beforehand by factors beyond our awareness and control?

During the fourth century B.C., the Greek philosopher Democritus, a proponent of *determinism,* contended that human behavior is no different from any other physical action—it is caused by lawful patterns that can be understood and predicted. If this is true, then all human decisions, from our clothing preferences to our career choices, are controlled—and ultimately determined—by our genetics, present environment, and past experiences (Sappington, 1990). In contrast to this perspective, the seventeenth-century French philosopher and mathematician, René Descartes, rejected determinism and argued instead that people—but not other animals—have *free will,* meaning they have absolutely no limitations on their power of free choice. If this is true—that such choices are really free—then human behavior itself would be random and impossible to understand or predict (Slife & Fisher, 2000).

Although the free will versus determinism debate is still a topic of discussion in psychology, most social scientists believe in what could be called *probabilistic determinism* (Gillett, 2001; Harris, 1999). This means that although psychological phenomena cannot be predicted with 100 percent certainty, they do occur with a regularity that is not random and can be reasonably understood using scientific methods.

SECTION SUMMARY

- Psychology is the scientific study of mental processes and behavior.
- Probabilistic determinism asserts that psychological phenomena occur with a regularity that is not random and can be reasonably understood using scientific methods.

Wilhelm Wundt, the founder of psychology.

Structuralism: An early theory in psychology that sought to identify the components of the conscious mind.

1-2 EARLY PIONEERS

Any brief history of psychology will exclude some of those who made valuable contributions. However, let me introduce you to the individuals who were ranked by prominent historians as some of the most important psychologists of all time and the schools of thought that they spawned (Korn et al., 1991; Skokal, 2002).

1-2a Wilhelm Wundt and Structuralism Sought to Identify the Components of the Conscious Mind

Most historians call Wilhelm Wundt (pronounced "Vill-helm Voont," 1832–1920) the "world's first psychologist." In 1879, Wundt established the first institute for research in experimental psychology at the University of Leipzig in Germany. Although in the early years there were no formal psychology courses offered at the institute, many students from Europe and the United States traveled to Leipzig to study the psychology of consciousness (Schlesinger, 1985). Wundt's method for studying the mind was known as *introspection*, a research technique in which trained observers would report on the contents of their own immediate states of consciousness. His model of consciousness, which his student Edward Titchener later named **structuralism,** sought to identify the components of the conscious mind.

Between 1876 and 1919, more than 100 students obtained doctoral degrees studying psychological topics under Wundt's supervision (Fernberger, 1933; Tinker, 1932). Some of his more illustrious students were Titchener (1867–1927, named and popularized structuralism in America), G. Stanley Hall (1844–1924, founded the American Psychological Association in 1892), Hugo Münsterberg (1863–1916, America's first industrial psychologist), James McKeen Cattell (1860–1944, a pioneer in the study of individual differences), and Viktor Henri (collaborator with Alfred Binet in developing the first intelligence tests). Wundt's influence on the first generation of psychologists was so great that most contemporary psychologists can probably trace their historical lineage back to him (Blumenthal, 2002; Hothersall, 1995).

1-2b William James and Functionalism Analyzed How the Conscious Mind Helps Us Adapt to Our Environment

One of the first American students to visit Wundt in Leipzig was William James (1842–1910), but he quickly concluded that Wundt's structuralist approach to psychology was not to his liking. Although both men studied consciousness, James's desire was to understand how the mind affects what people do rather than merely identifying its components. In addition, his approach to psychology had very little to do with laboratory studies and, instead, relied heavily on his own rich ideas and eloquent writing (Leary, 2002). Because of his interest in how the conscious mind helps humans survive and suc-

William James, the first major American psychologist.

Journey of Discovery Question
At the beginning of the twentieth century, Hermann Ebbinghaus (1850–1909), one of psychology's pioneers, stated that "Psychology has a long past, but only a short history." What do you think he meant by this statement?

We take issue . . . with every treatment of psychology that is based on simple self-observation or on philosophical presuppositions.

—Wilhelm Wundt, 1832–1920

I wished, by treating Psychology like a natural science, to help her to become one.

—William James (1892)

cessfully adapt to their environment—that is, how the mind functions—his approach to psychology came to be called **functionalism.** James's theory of emotion (discussed in chapter 11, section 11-5d), his contention that there are two different kinds of memory, and his analysis of the psychology of religion are still highly regarded today.

In 1890, James published a brilliant two-volume text entitled *Principles of Psychology,* which quickly established its author as America's foremost psychologist and is still considered today to be a classic among classics. In addition to his superb writing and brilliant ideas, James was a masterful teacher at Harvard University and even wrote a popular book, *Talks to Teachers* (1899), in which he offered practical advice to teachers. Unlike Wundt, James had a relatively small group of students, but among them were such luminaries as James Angell (1869–1949, further developed functionalism), Mary Calkins (1863–1930, pioneer in memory research), Edward Thorndike (1874–1949, investigated trial-and-error animal learning), and Robert Woodworth (1869–1962, pioneer in motivation and drive theory).

Functionalism: An approach to psychology that studied how the conscious mind helps humans survive and successfully adapt to their environment.

1-2c Sigmund Freud and Psychoanalysis Examined How the Unconscious Mind Shapes Behavior

The third prominent founder of psychology was Sigmund Freud (1856–1939), an Austrian physician trained as a neurologist. Actually, because Freud was a physician, his proper title is "psychiatrist" and not "psychologist." Despite this technicality, psychology still claims him as an important founder of one of the early schools of thought in the discipline.

Instead of working in the lab (like Wundt) or teaching at the university (like James), Freud developed his approach to psychology through clinical practice. Based on his work with patients who suffered from ailments that had no known physical causes, Freud developed a theory that all human behavior is determined by hidden or unconscious motives and desires that are sexual in nature. In a very real sense, he contended that part of our personality never matures, and the "adult" side of our personality struggles to control the "infant" side, with only limited success.

Freud's emphasis on the unconscious mind stood in sharp contrast to Wundt and James's study of conscious experience. It was this belief that most of the mind was inaccessible to a person's conscious awareness that led Freud and his followers to develop therapy techniques and personality tests designed to reveal this hidden domain. This approach to psychology, which Freud called **psychoanalysis,** influenced the study of such diverse topics as dreams, childhood development, aggression, sexuality, creativity, motivation, personality, and psychotherapy (Kafka, 2002).

Freud's writings attracted many followers to psychoanalysis; yet, he was intolerant of disagreement or dissent. Among the brightest of this group were Alfred Adler (1870–1936, founder of individual psychology), Carl Jung (1875–1961, founder of analytic psychology), and Karen Horney (1885–1952, one of the first psychologists to emphasize social rather than biological determinants of gender differences). When each of these

Sigmund Freud, the founder of psychoanalysis.

Psychoanalysis: An approach to psychology that studies how the unconscious mind shapes behavior.

I am actually not at all a man of science, not an observer, not an experimenter, not a thinker. I am by temperament not but a conquistador—an adventurer, if you want it translated—with all the curiosity, daring, and tenacity of a man of this sort.

—Sigmund Freud

people developed ideas of their own that challenged some of Freud's cherished concepts, they either left or were expelled from the psychoanalytic inner circle (Roazen, 1975). In response to these challenges, Freud established a committee of loyal followers whose job was to repulse critics of psychoanalysis. Although no other psychologist comes close to matching the impact that Freud has had on popular culture, his reluctance to submit psychoanalysis to critical examination stunted its development as a scientific theory. In chapter 12, section 12-2, we will examine Freud's theory of personality and its influence on contemporary psychological theories.

1-2d John Watson and Behaviorism Investigated Observable Behavior

Behaviorism: An approach to psychology that studies observable behavior, rather than hidden mental processes.

Just as psychoanalysis is closely associated with Sigmund Freud, so is **behaviorism** intimately intertwined with John Watson (1878–1958). His research with rats, dogs, and other animals caused him to question the three current schools of psychology that analyzed the structure, content, and function of the mind. His subjects couldn't talk or introspect, and thus, there was no hope that they could reveal the seeming mysteries of the mind. Perhaps partly because of this very fact, Watson came to believe that psychology should study observable behavior rather than hidden psychological processes. In 1913, Watson published an article entitled "Psychology as the Behaviorist Sees It," in which he challenged his fellow psychologists to abandon the other schools of thought because their focus of study, consciousness, was neither a definable term nor a usable concept. His opening paragraph spelled out the direction for this new school:

> Psychology as the Behaviorist sees it is a purely objective, experimental branch of natural science. Its theoretical goal is the prediction and control of behavior. Introspection forms no essential parts of its methods, nor is the scientific value of its data dependent upon the readiness with which they lend themselves to interpretation in terms of consciousness. The behaviorist, in his efforts to get a unitary scheme of animal responses, recognizes no dividing line between man and brute. The behavior of man, with all its refinement and complexity, forms only a part of the behaviorist's total scheme of investigation. (Watson, 1913, p. 158)

John Watson, the founder of behaviorism.

© Underwood & Underwood/CORBIS.

Watson's radical behaviorism struck a responsive chord among many American psychologists who shared his impatience with what they considered to be the "fuzziness" of the other schools within psychology (Schnaitter, 1987). Underlying behaviorism was a philosophy known as *logical positivism*, which contended that all knowledge should be expressed in terms that can be verified empirically or through direct observation. These "new" psychologists sought to describe, explain, predict, and control behavior. Behaviorism dominated psychology in North America from the 1920s through the 1950s (Innis, 1992).

1-2e Max Wertheimer and Gestalt Psychology Studied How the Mind Organizes Stimuli into Coherent Wholes

Gestalt psychology: An approach to psychology that studies how the mind actively organizes stimuli into coherent wholes.

During the first decades of the twentieth century, **Gestalt psychology** gained prominence primarily as a critique of—and an alternative to—structuralism. *Gestalt* is a German word that means shape or form. The founder of this school of psychology, Max Wertheimer (1880–1943), criticized Wundt's structuralism for attempting to understand the conscious mind by identifying and analyzing its components. Instead, Wertheimer contended that "the whole is different from the sum of its parts." That is, our perceptions are not to be understood as the mind passively responding to a simple combination of individual elements, but rather, the mind actively organizing stimuli into coherent wholes. Wertheimer and his colleagues Wolfgang Köhler (1887–1967) and Kurt Koffka (1886–1941) produced many demonstrations of the unity of perceptual processes.

An example of how our perceptions emerge as wholes, not parts, is the experience of the four dots in figure 1-1a. Most people perceive the dots as corners of an invisible square rather than as separate, discrete objects. Do you? When three of the dots are increased in

FIGURE 1-1
Gestalt Psychology Stressed That Perception Strives toward a Complete Form

(a) These four dots are likely to be perceived as a square. *(b)* If three of the dots become twice as big, however, while the fourth remains the same size, the four dots are likely to be perceived as a triangle (of larger dots) and a single dot.

size in figure 1-1b, most people see a configuration of a triangle and a separate dot. Do you? This dot example illustrates the *laws of grouping*, which describes how people tend to group discrete stimuli together into a meaningful whole (see chapter 5, section 5-5a).

Besides creating new ways of thinking about perception, Wertheimer, Koffka, and Köhler also analyzed learning, problem solving, and brain disorders, but they always treated these topics as whole phenomena (Sarris & Wertheimer, 2001). Later, one of their colleagues, Kurt Lewin (1890–1947), applied the Gestalt approach to understanding social behavior, and he and his students were instrumental in shaping the development of a new area of specialization, social psychology (Ash, 2002).

1-2f Despite Discrimination, Many Women and Ethnic Minorities Were Pioneers in Psychology

During the first 75 years of its existence, women and minorities were generally excluded from graduate education due to the prejudice and discrimination of the times (Kimmel, 1992). Those who were fortunate enough to be granted the opportunity to pursue a career in psychology often had a substandard environment in which to conduct their research (Furumoto & Scarborough, 2002). Even with such impediments, many women and ethnic minorities made valuable contributions to the development of psychology.

A good example of the prejudice and discrimination faced by women is the career of Mary Calkins, who completed all requirements for a Ph.D. at Harvard University in 1895. William James described her defense of her dissertation as being "the most brilliant examination for the Ph.D. that we have had at Harvard." Yet, despite being enthusiastically recommended for her doctoral degree by James and her other professors, it was denied because the university did not grant degrees to women. Harvard, like most universities at the time, only allowed women to attend graduate classes as "hearers," and thus, they were not considered full-fledged graduate students. Can you imagine how you might react to such blatant discrimination? Keep in mind, excluding women from most professions was the accepted practice throughout society. Would you fight it? If so, how would you fight it?

In 1902, Harvard offered Calkins a Ph.D. from their "sister college," Radcliffe, but she declined, stating that accepting it would mean that she also accepted the college's discriminatory policies. Pursuing the few career paths open to her, Calkins became a non-Ph.D. professor at all-female Wellesley College. There, she established one of the first psychology laboratories in the United States, pioneered research in short-term memory, and in 1905 became the first woman president of the American Psychological Association. Despite this distinguished career, in 1930 Harvard again rejected a petition presented by several famous alumni to award Calkins her previously earned Ph.D. (Madigan & O'Hara, 1992).

The first woman to actually receive her doctorate in psychology was Margaret Washburn (1871–1939) in 1894 at Cornell University (Furumoto, 1992). During her

Mary Calkins, the first female president of the American Psychological Association.

Archives of the History of American Psychology—The University of Akron.

Journey of Discovery Question
Consider the five early perspectives in psychology. What contribution did each make to our understanding of thinking and behavior?

Margaret Washburn, the first woman to receive a Ph.D. in psychology.

Archives of the History of American Psychology—The University of Akron.

Kenneth and Mamie Clark's scientific findings that racial segregation had a negative impact on Black children's self-concept were instrumental in shaping the U.S. Supreme Court's 1954 decision to integrate the nation's educational institutions. In 1971, Kenneth Clark became the first African American to be elected president of the American Psychological Association.

distinguished career, Washburn was a research pioneer in comparative psychology and served as president of the American Psychological Association in 1921 (Dewsbury, 1992). Like Calkins, but unlike most of her male colleagues, Washburn never married, for a woman's decision to marry generally required her to not work outside the home.

In addition to this discrimination, even when women found a place within psychology, often their contributions went unrecognized by contemporaries. One such example is Bärbel Inhelder, a student of developmental psychologist Jean Piaget (see chapter 4, section 4-3a). Despite collaborating with the pioneer of cognitive development on eight books and providing significant insights into cognitive processes and mental retardation, Inhelder never became widely known for her work (DeAngelis, 1996).

Similar obstacles also impeded the careers of ethnic minorities. The first African American to receive a Ph.D. in psychology was Gilbert Jones, who obtained his degree from the University of Jena in Germany in 1901 (Guthrie, 1976). Thirty-two years later, Inez Prosser, after teaching many years with a master's degree, became the first African American woman to receive her doctorate in psychology. Despite the discrimination faced by African Americans during these early years, many made significant contributions to this budding science. In the 1930s, for example, Mamie Phipps Clark and Kenneth Clark's groundbreaking research on the self-concept of Black children provided the scientific justification for the U.S. Supreme Court to end the practice of racially segregated education in the 1954 *Brown vs. Board of Education* decision (Benjamin & Crouse, 2002; Lal, 2002). In 1971, Kenneth Clark became the first African American to be elected president of the American Psychological Association.

As you can see from this brief overview, women and minorities in psychology had to overcome considerable social obstacles before they could position themselves to contribute to the development of the new science of psychology. During the past quarter century, career opportunities for women and ethnic minorities in psychology have expanded, and this greater diversity has challenged old assumptions of human behavior and spurred the study of previously overlooked populations. Despite these advances, more work is needed (Sonnert & Holton, 1995). For example, while in graduate school, women still receive less financial assistance from their institutions than do men (Cohen & Gutek, 1991), and once they gain employment, female psychologists earn 15 percent less than their male counterparts (National Science Foundation, 1994). It is also true that there are still far too few ethnic minorities in the field of psychology (Cervantes, 1987; McShane, 1987; Myers et al., 1991). Thus, although women and ethnic minorities have begun to share more of the center stage with their white male colleagues (Howard et al., 1986; Vasquez, 1991), the dawning of the twenty-first century still awaits a more diverse cast of characters in this ever-changing science. Some of you reading this textbook will be part of this new generation of psychologists. What would you do to encourage this greater diversity without unfairly limiting the opportunities of young white males?

SECTION SUMMARY

- Wilhelm Wundt and structuralism sought to identify the components of the conscious mind.
- William James and functionalism studied how the conscious mind helps humans survive and successfully adapt to their environment.
- Sigmund Freud and psychoanalysis studied how the unconscious mind shapes behavior.
- John Watson and behaviorism considered only observable behavior to be legitimate topics of scientific inquiry.
- Max Wertheimer and Gestalt psychology studied how the mind actively organizes stimuli into coherent wholes.
- Despite discrimination, many women and ethnic minorities made valuable contributions to the development of psychology.

1-3 CONTEMPORARY PERSPECTIVES AND AREAS OF SPECIALIZATION

Of the five early schools of psychology, only psychoanalysis and behaviorism have survived as contemporary perspectives, although even they have been significantly altered from their original form. There is a contemporary approach to psychotherapy known as Gestalt therapy (see chapter 14, section 14-5b), but this has little more than the name in common with the early German school of Gestalt psychology. Instead, Gestalt psychology's influence is seen today in the specialty areas of cognitive and social psychology. It is also true that even elements of the now defunct structuralist and functionalist schools continue to shape psychology as it enters the twenty-first century. Let us now briefly examine seven contemporary perspectives within psychology that shape current psychological theory and research and its application in everyday settings.

1-3a The Psychoanalytic and Behaviorist Perspectives Still Influence Theory and Research

Many psychoanalysts today downplay Freud's emphasis on sexual drives and, instead, emphasize cultural experiences in explaining personality. Despite this shift in focus, the unconscious mind and early childhood experiences are still central areas of attention within this perspective. Yet, many contemporary psychoanalysts, influenced by Erik Erikson's (1902–1994) writings, have rejected Freud's view that personality development, for all practical purposes, is complete by age 5. Instead, contemporary psychoanalysis generally accepts Erikson's (1980) view that personality continues to be shaped and changed throughout life.

The central figure who shaped contemporary behaviorism was B. F. Skinner (1904–1990), who stressed the role of consequences in controlling behavior (Malone & Cruchon, 2001). His research—which we will discuss in chapter 7—found that people and other animals tend to repeat behaviors that are followed by positive consequences and avoid behaviors that bring negative consequences. For example, if you are rewarded for being helpful, you are likely to repeat such actions in the future, but you are unlikely to do so if your helpfulness is punished. In addition, this psychological perspective also played a key role in insisting that psychologists precisely define and objectively measure the concepts they study. Although behaviorism does not exert the influence over psychology that it once enjoyed, you will recognize its footprints throughout this text as you examine various psychological topics (Smith, 2002).

Erik Erikson, a neo-Freudian whose personality theory encompasses the entire life span.

© Ted Streshinsky/CORBIS.

1-3b The Humanistic Perspective Highlights Personal Growth and Conscious Decision Making

Arising out of many psychologists' dissatisfaction with both the psychoanalytic and behavioristic views of human nature, a third force exerted its influence on psychology in the 1950s. This **humanistic perspective** emphasizes people's innate capacity for personal growth and their ability to consciously make choices. Carl Rogers (1902–1987) and Abraham Maslow (1908–1970) were the primary architects of this perspective, and both contended that—like William James before them—psychology should study people's unique subjective mental experience of the world.

Although the humanistic approach has been criticized for being the least scientifically based of all contemporary perspectives within psychology, its emphasis on conscious experience and the essential goodness of people has promoted the scientific study of previously neglected topics such as self-awareness, love, helping behavior, and positive personality growth. These are all issues that we will explore in this text.

Humanistic perspective:
An approach to psychology that emphasizes human beings' innate capacity for personal growth and their ability to consciously make choices.

1-3c The Cognitive Perspective Analyzes How the Mind Organizes and Interprets Experiences

Cognitive perspective:
An approach to psychology that attempts to understand behavior by studying how the mind organizes perceptions, processes information, and interprets experiences.

Accompanying the criticism of behaviorism by humanistic theorists was the fact that laboratory research was finding some interesting phenomena that were difficult to explain without reintroducing the concept of consciousness. In the 1960s, when this evidence had reached a sufficient "critical mass," the theoretical center of gravity in psychology shifted from behaviorism to cognitive psychology (Hilgard et al., 1991). The word *cognitive* comes from the Latin for "to know." The **cognitive perspective** is a psychological approach that attempts to understand behavior by studying how the mind organizes perceptions, processes information, and interprets experiences. For example, how do you remember a new friend's phone number? Or how do you decide whether a defendant is guilty or innocent while serving on a jury? Cognitive theories provide insights into these kinds of mental processes.

The ascendancy of the cognitive perspective coincided with the development of a new form of technology, namely, the computer. Cognitive psychologists argued that the mind was like a computer (Harnish, 2002). Like a computer, the mind receives input from the environment, which it then transforms, stores, and later retrieves using a host of "programs," ultimately leading to specific response outputs. The computer is not only a useful metaphor for the mind, but as new generations of computers are developed to actually work like the human brain, they have become invaluable subjects of study, simulating human thought. Today, behaviorist John Watson's description of the brain as "a black box forever mysterious" is no longer true, thanks largely to the discoveries of cognitive psychologists. This perspective provides valuable insights into many of the topics we will examine throughout this text.

1-3d The Biological Perspective Studies Physiological Processes, Especially Those Occurring in the Brain

Biological perspective:
An approach to psychology that attempts to understand behavior by examining physiological processes, especially those occurring in the brain.

In recent years, as new techniques and instruments have been developed to examine the brain and how it reacts under different circumstances, psychologists have become increasingly interested in biological mechanisms. The resulting attempts to understand behavior by examining physiological processes, especially those occurring in the brain, came to be known as the **biological perspective.** In its study of how the brain communicates with itself and other bodily organs, as well as its attempt to understand elementary biochemical processes, this approach to psychology is focused on the most precise microscopic levels of analysis (Posner, 2002; Rosenzweig et al., 2002).

Although biological psychologists do study humans, they conduct a good deal of their research using animals with simpler brains, hoping that the knowledge gained in these studies will lead to greater understanding of the brain's building blocks. For example, in attempting to better understand memory loss in Alzheimer's disease (the most common form of dementia in the elderly), a researcher might graft tissue from the brains of rat fetuses into the brains of elderly rats. If such a procedure improves the older rats' memory, this finding may provide a crucial clue to curing this disease in humans. Chapter 3 will introduce you to some of the discoveries uncovered by this biological approach, and Discovery Box 1-1 will introduce you to a recurring debate in psychology related to biological explanations of behavior.

1-3e The Evolutionary Perspective Studies How Behavior Can Be Explained by Natural Selection

Evolutionary psychology:
An approach to psychology based on the principle of natural selection.

Fueled by the growing belief in the social sciences that behavior is at least partly influenced by the effects of *evolution,* a perspective known as **evolutionary psychology** is increasingly being incorporated into psychological theories (Barrett et al., 2002). Yet, what is evolution? The evolutionary perspective is partly based on the writings of biolo-

DISCOVERY BOX 1-1

What Is the Nature-Nurture Debate?

Have you ever wondered why we, as individuals, often differ in our thinking and behavior? Are we born this way or do these differences develop based on our life experiences? Philosophers have endlessly debated the degree to which individual differences are due to inborn biological processes versus environmental influences. For example, in the fourth and third centuries B.C., Plato argued that individual differences are largely inborn and due to heredity (*nature*), while Aristotle stressed the importance of environmental factors (*nurture*) and described the mind as a *tabula rasa*, or blank slate, that was later filled by life experiences. Which perspective on human nature makes more sense to you? Is there possibly a middle-ground position on this issue?

This **nature-nurture debate** has been a classic controversy in psychology. Followers of the "nature" position point toward the greater behavioral similarities found between identical twins (genetically the same) than between fraternal twins (genetically not the same) as evidence for the influence of heredity. They further contend that similar behaviors found among humans and other animals suggests the operation of similar biological processes. In contrast, advocates of the "nurture" position emphasize how people's thoughts, feelings, and behavior are shaped by the rewards and punishments they receive from their immediate surroundings. According to the "nurturists," it is this type of learning, combined with the values and beliefs of the larger culture, that forms the basis for differences in the way we live our lives. As you will discover, the different perspectives within psychology tend to emphasize either nature or nurture points of view in their analysis of psychological events. However, what you will also learn is that most contemporary psychologists believe that human beings, like all other animals, are a product of *both* nature and nurture. Thus, instead of being opposing explanations of behavior, biological and environmental explanations often complement one another, adding a depth of understanding that cannot be achieved by only considering one alone (Gottlieb, 2002a; Rutter, 2002).

Nature-nurture debate: The question of whether individual differences in behavior are primarily due to inborn biological processes or environmental factors.

gist Charles Darwin (1809–1882), who theorized that changes in the population of a species occur over many generations due to the interaction of environmental and biological variables.

According to evolutionary theory, living organisms struggle to survive and, within each species, there is a great deal of competition and biological variation between individuals (Darwin, 1859; Nielsen, 1995). Those members of a species with genetic traits best adapted for survival in their environment will produce more offspring and, as a result, their numbers will increase in frequency in the population. As the environment changes, however, other members within the species possessing traits better suited to the new conditions will flourish. In this way, the environment *selects* which genetic traits will be passed on to future generations. As this process of **natural selection** continues, and as the features best suited for survival change again and again, the result is **evolution,** which is the gradual genetic changes that occur in a species over generations. *Reproduction* is central to natural selection; the essence of the natural selection process is that the characteristics of some individuals will allow them to produce more offspring than others.

Natural selection: The process by which organisms with inherited traits best suited to the environment reproduce more successfully than less well-adapted organisms over a number of generations. Natural selection leads to evolutionary changes.

Evolution: The genetic changes that occur in a species over generations due to natural selection.

It may metaphorically be said that natural selection is daily and hourly scrutinising . . . the slightest variations; rejecting those that are bad, preserving and adding up all that are good; silently and insensibly working, whenever and wherever opportunity offers, at the improvement of each organic being in relation to its organic and inorganic conditions of life. We see nothing of these slow changes in progress, . . . we see only that the forms of life are now different from what they formerly were.

—Charles Darwin, 1859, *The Origin of Species*, pp. 90–91

1-3f The Sociocultural Perspective Studies How Behavior Is Shaped by Social and Cultural Forces

Sociocultural perspective:
An approach to psychology that emphasizes social and cultural influences on behavior.

Culture: The total lifestyle of people from a particular social grouping, including all the ideas, symbols, preferences, and material objects that they share.

While the evolutionary perspective examines how the behavior of humans and other living creatures are shaped due to inherited genes, the **sociocultural perspective** emphasizes the role that social and cultural factors play in explaining behavior (Gripps, 2002; Haight, 2002). **Culture** is the total lifestyle of people from a particular social grouping, including all the ideas, symbols, preferences, and material objects that they share. It is a shared system of ideas about the nature of the world, and consists of rules governing how people should think, feel, and act within this world.

Many countries contain a number of distinct cultures. For example, in the United States you can identify many cultural heritages, among them Native American, Hispanic, European, African, Asian, and Middle Eastern. In analyzing culture, it's important to understand that lifestyle changes over time. Thus, Native American culture today is not the same as Native American culture of the 1800s or even of the mid-1900s. This attention to social and cultural factors as a means to explain human thought and behavior is a central element in many psychological theories.

Are the sociocultural and evolutionary perspectives compatible? Yes, say a growing number of psychologists who believe that these cultural and evolutionary forces operate simultaneously in shaping behavior (Gottlieb, 2002b; Plomin & McClearn, 1993). The argument they make is that the culture of a people is based on their relationship with the environment, and the evolution of our species is a story of how we have adapted to our environment. Thus, just as our bodies and brains are a product of evolutionary forces, so too is our culture. Yet, culture change occurs much more rapidly than genetic change. This is the reason there is a great deal of variation in the world's cultures, but little meaningful genetic variation between cultural groups. In this textbook, the evolutionary perspective will provide insight into how we, as a species, got to where we are with our biological structure and behavioral traits, and the sociocultural perspective will suggest how culture can reinforce, or attempt to change these evolutionary-based tendencies and patterns (see Discovery Box 1-2).

INFO-BIT: Some historians believe that the scientific concept of evolution can be traced back at least 2,500 years, to the Greek philosopher Anaximander who contended that life arose in water and that simpler life-forms preceded more complex ones. However, the more influential Greek philosopher Aristotle held that species are fixed and do not evolve. Aristotle's views, combined with the Judeo-Christian beliefs that all species were individually designed by God and that the earth is, at most, only about 6,000 years old, dominated scientific and intellectual debate until the mid-1800s. To what degree has your own thinking been shaped by these contrasting views?

DISCOVERY BOX 1-2

Do Cultures Differ in How Members Relate to Their Groups?

One aspect of culture that has a great deal of importance to the understanding of the psychology of human behavior is the belief system concerning how individuals relate to their groups (Triandis, 1995). The human species has evolved within a social group sphere. One of the fundamental dilemmas we have faced throughout our existence is that each individual's inherent desire to pass their genes on to the next generation pushes her or him toward selfish, self-serving actions that can potentially threaten the survival of the individual's group, and thus, the individual's own survival. Somehow through the process of natural selection, we have struck a delicate balance between these conflicting tendencies. Today, the cultural belief systems known as individualism and collectivism are products of this evolutionary-based tension between the desire to selfishly maximize one's reproductive fitness and the need to cooperate with others in order to survive (Kågitçibasi, 1994; Oyserman et al., 2002).

Individualism is a philosophy of life stressing the priority of personal goals over group goals, a preference for loosely knit social relationships, and a desire to be relatively autonomous of others' influence. In contrast, *collectivism* is a philosophy of life stressing the priority of group needs over individual needs, a preference for tightly knit social relationships, and a willingness to submit to the influence of one's group (Tower et al., 1997; Triandis, 1989). Currently, 70 percent of the world's population lives in cultures with a collectivist orientation, which is a much older cultural belief system than individualism (Singelis et al., 1995). Individualism developed out of collectivism and is largely a manifestation of the mind-set of people living in industrialized societies where cooperation is not as critical to individual survival as in most preindustrialized societies.

Although we know that cultures differ in their individualist-collectivist orientations, we do not know whether one is better than the other in any ultimate evolutionary sense. In this text, we will periodically examine how the psychology of people from different cultures differs due to their individualist-collectivist bents. For example, in the chapter on human development, you will discover that within collectivist societies, child-rearing practices tend to emphasize conformity, obedience, and knowing one's proper place, while within more individualist societies, independence and self-reliance are stressed. One consequence of these differing views is that in an individualist society, people develop a belief in their own uniqueness and diversity. This sense of individuality is nurtured and fostered within the educational system and its manifestation is considered to be a sign of maturity. On the other hand, in a collectivist society, uniqueness and individual differences are often seen only as impediments to proper self-growth. Instead, the person becomes most meaningful and complete when she or he is closely identified with—not independent of—the group.

1-3g Psychology's Subfields Can Be Distinguished by Their Emphasis on Research Versus Application

Now that you have learned something about the different schools of thought within psychology, you might be wondering who employs psychologists and what they do in these jobs. About one-fourth of all psychologists who received their Ph.D.s during the past 25 years are employed at colleges, universities, or institutes where they teach and conduct research in their areas of specialization (see figure 1-2). Their goals are to acquire psychological knowledge through scientific methods and to teach this knowledge to students. Seven areas of specialization for these research psychologists are as follows:

1. *Psychobiology* (also called *biopsychology, behavioral neuroscience, physiological psychology*)—Studies behavior by examining physiological processes, especially those occurring in the brain.

2. *Developmental psychology*—Studies how people mature and change physically, cognitively, and socially throughout the life span.

3. *Experimental psychology*—Studies basic psychological processes such as sensation, perception, learning, motivation, emotion, and states of consciousness.

4. *Comparative psychology*—Studies similarities and differences in the physiology, behavior, and abilities of different species, including humans.

5. *Cognitive psychology*—Studies all aspects of thinking, including problem solving, decision making, memory, reasoning, and language.

6. *Personality psychology*—Studies how people are influenced by relatively stable internal traits.

7. *Social psychology*—Studies how people are influenced by others.

In addition to psychologists within these seven areas, a little over half of the psychologists who received their Ph.D.s during the past 30 years have careers in specialty

FIGURE 1-2
The Percentage of Ph.D.s Awarded in Psychology by Specialty Area

Source: Based on data from the Summary Report: Doctorate Recipients from U.S. Universities, National Research Council, reported in the *APA Education Directorate,* 1995, p. 12.

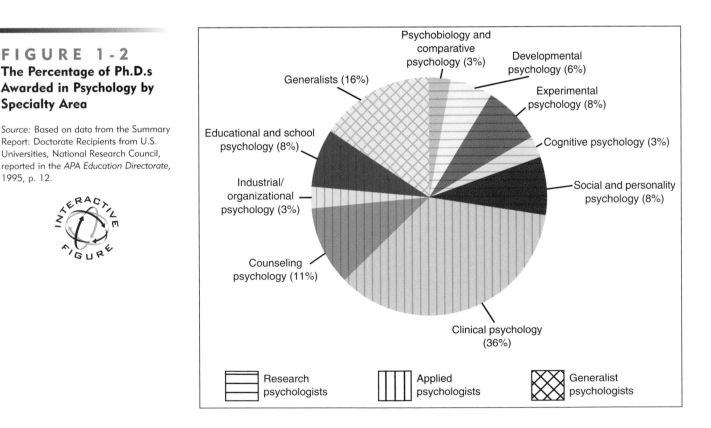

areas where they use existing psychological knowledge to solve and prevent problems (see figure 1-2). These **applied psychologists** most often work in mental health centers, schools, industries, governmental agencies, or private practice. Four major applied specialties are as follows:

> **Applied psychologists:**
> Psychologists who use existing psychological knowledge to solve and prevent problems.

1. *Clinical psychology*—Diagnose and treat people with psychological disorders, such as depression and schizophrenia.
2. *Counseling psychology*—Diagnose and treat people with personal problems that do not involve psychological disorders, such as marriage counseling, social skills training, and career planning.
3. *Industrial-organizational psychology*—Focuses on ways to select, motivate, and evaluate employees, as well as improving the management structure and working conditions.
4. *Educational and school psychology*—Assessment and treatment of both students and the educational environment in order to facilitate children's learning and adjustment in school.

SECTION SUMMARY

- Of the five early schools of psychology, only psychoanalysis and behaviorism survived as contemporary perspectives.
- The humanistic perspective emphasizes human beings' capacity for personal growth and their ability to consciously make choices.
- The cognitive perspective attempts to understand behavior by studying how the mind organizes perceptions, processes information, and interprets experiences.
- The biological perspective attempts to understand behavior by examining physiological processes, especially those occurring in the brain.
- The evolutionary perspective assumes that all species have evolved in ways that maximize the chances of their genes being passed on to their offspring.
- The sociocultural perspective emphasizes social and cultural influences on behavior.
- Seven primary areas of specialization for research psychologists include: psychobiology, developmental psychology, experimental psychology, comparative psychology, cognitive psychology, personality psychology, and social psychology.
- Four primary areas of specialization for applied psychologists include: clinical psychology, counseling psychology, industrial-organizational psychology, and educational and school psychology.

SUGGESTED WEBSITES

Note: These websites were functional when we went to press. Please access the online text for the most up-to-date URLs.

American Psychological Association
http://www.apa.org
Official APA site provides access to many APA-sponsored websites related to various psychological issues.

American Psychological Society
http://www.psychologicalscience.org
Official website of the APS provides access to many psychology-related websites and APS journals.

The History of Psychology
http://www.usca.sc.edu/psychology/histor~1.html
This site provides information on the history of psychologically related topics from ancient to modern times.

Psychweb
http://www.psychweb.com
This website provides psychology-related material for both students and instructors of psychology.

PSYCHOLOGICAL APPLICATIONS
From What Psychology "Is" to How Psychology "Works"—A Prelude

There is a famous fable from India about several blind men who happen upon an elephant. None of the men had ever encountered this sort of creature before, so each reached out to explore a different part of the animal. The man who grabbed the tail exclaimed, "An elephant is like a rope!" The man who touched one of the elephant's ears shouted, "An elephant is as thin as a leaf!" "No!" marveled another who was holding the trunk. "This animal is surely related to the snake!" "You are all mistaken," said the man grasping one leg. "An elephant is shaped like the trunk of a tree!" What resulted was a heated argument over whose description accurately captured the essence of the elephant. The mistake these men made was that they tried to understand their subject by only examining one aspect of it.

In many respects, this is the problem that we face on our journey of discovery in psychology. Each of the psychological perspectives previously discussed attempts to understand the thoughts and behavior of humans and other animals by focusing on different psychological processes. Like the blind men—who would have come to a more accurate understanding of the elephant if they had tried to reconcile their seemingly conflicting discoveries—we too can better understand our subject matter if we consider multiple perspectives. Alone, none provides an adequate understanding of the human condition. Together, they provide us with an ever-clearer portrait of ourselves.

In closing this introductory chapter, allow me to turn your thoughts again to the chapter-opening story in which I shared how my passion for psychology was kindled as I traveled cross-country conducting my first research study. Prior to experiencing the excitement of actually investigating my group of hitchhikers, there was a great deal of background preparation necessary to make this research project possible. In addition, while I collected information on these people, and while I later analyzed this information, there were specific scientific guidelines I followed to increase the value of my findings. This background preparation, combined with the process of data collection and analysis, will be the subject matter of chapter 2, "The Vehicle for Psychological Discovery."

KEY TERMS

applied psychologists (p. 15)
behaviorism (p. 6)
biological perspective (p. 10)
cognitive perspective (p. 10)
culture (p. 12)
evolution (p. 11)

evolutionary psychology (p. 10)
functionalism (p. 5)
Gestalt psychology (p. 6)
humanistic perspective (p. 9)
natural selection (p. 11)
nature-nurture debate (p. 11)

psychiatry (p. 3)
psychoanalysis (p. 5)
psychology (p. 3)
sociocultural perspective (p. 12)
structuralism (p. 4)

REVIEW QUESTIONS

1. Which of the following statements is *true* of psychology?
   a. It does not implement scientific methods.
   b. It is a small branch of psychiatry.
   c. Psychological phenomena can be predicted with 100 percent certainty.
   d. It is incompatible with free will.
   e. none of the above

2. In what year was the first institute for research in experimental psychology opened?
   a. 1879
   b. 1890
   c. 1921
   d. 1940
   e. 1960

3. Which of the following was *true* of Sigmund Freud?
   a. He contended that our personality matures slowly but surely over the years.
   b. He emphasized the study of the conscious experience.
   c. He had no direct experience working with patients.
   d. He was technically not a psychologist, but a psychiatrist.
   e. He is closely associated with behaviorism.

4. Which of the following founders of psychology believed psychology should study observable behavior rather than hidden psychological processes?
   a. Sigmund Freud
   b. William James
   c. John Watson
   d. Wilhelm Wundt
   e. Max Wertheimer

5. Which of the following is *true* of William James?
   a. He wrote a classic book, titled *Principles of Psychology.*
   b. He wanted to understand how the mind affects what people do, rather than merely identifying its components.
   c. He did very little lab work; rather, he relied on his ideas and writings.
   d. His approach to psychology became known as functionalism.
   e. all of the above

6. Gestalt psychology produced
   a. logical positivism.
   b. laws of grouping.
   c. psychoanalysis.
   d. pragmatism.
   e. introspection.

7. Of the five early schools of psychology, which perspectives survived as contemporary perspectives?
   a. psychoanalysis
   b. behaviorism
   c. Gestalt psychology
   d. functionalism and structuralism
   e. *a* and *b*

8. Who were considered the architects of the perspective that emphasized people's innate capacity for personal growth and their ability to make choices?
   a. William James and Wilhelm Wundt
   b. Carl Rogers and Abraham Maslow
   c. Mary Calkins and Mamie Phipps Clark
   d. Sigmund Freud and B. F. Skinner
   e. none of the above

9. Which of the following is *true* of the cognitive perspective?
   a. It emphasized the essential goodness of people.
   b. It coincided with the development of the computer.
   c. It is the least scientifically based of the contemporary perspectives.
   d. It promoted the scientific study of love.
   e. none of the above

10. Which of the following is *true* of the biological perspective?
   a. A good deal of its research is done on humans.
   b. It does not believe that research on animals can benefit humans.
   c. It is focused on the most precise microscopic levels of analysis.
   d. It is based on the writings of the biologist Charles Darwin.
   e. all of the above

11. Which of the following statements is *true*?
   a. A central element in many theories is that social and cultural factors can help explain human thought and behavior.
   b. The sociocultural and evolutionary perspectives are not compatible.
   c. Genetic change occurs more rapidly than cultural changes.
   d. There is a great deal of genetic variation among cultural groups.
   e. all of the above

12. Which of the following statements is *true*?
   a. Thirty percent of the world's population lives in cultures with a collectivist orientation.
   b. The cultural belief system of individualism is older than collectivism.
   c. From an evolutionary perspective, individualism is better than collectivism.
   d. all of the above
   e. none of the above

13. Which of the following is an applied specialty?
   a. clinical psychology
   b. counseling psychology
   c. industrial psychology
   d. school psychology
   e. all of the above

14. Which psychological perspective does the author feel best explains human thought and behavior?
   a. cognitive
   b. biological
   c. psychoanalysis
   d. evolutionary
   e. all of the above

The Vehicle for Psychological Discovery

C h a p t e r   O u t l i n e

How do people react when they learn that you are enrolled in a psychology course? Based on our society's voracious appetite for "pop psychology" talk-radio shows and self-help books, I'm sure that some of your friends and family members are intrigued—and perhaps a bit envious—about what you might learn in the coming months. Others, in contrast, might dismiss what psychology has to offer as merely "warmed-over common sense." One reason some people think of psychology as simply rephrasing what we already know is because its subject matter is so personal and familiar: We all informally think about our own thoughts, feelings, and actions and those of others. Why would such informally attained knowledge be appreciably different from what psychologists achieve through their scientific observations? This chapter examines how the scientific inquiry adopted by psychology is different from the much more casual analysis we employ in our everyday thinking.

2-1 IS PSYCHOLOGY JUST COMMON SENSE?

In the course of our everyday lives, we spend considerable time and energy trying to understand our world and the people who inhabit it. An important product of this informal journey of discovery is the development of certain belief systems about how we function on the psychological level.

2-1a We Often Understand Our World Based on a "Naive" Psychology

The belief systems that we develop are best characterized as being embedded within a *naive psychology*, because, instead of being based on careful scientific analysis, they develop from everyday experiences and uncritical acceptance of other people's views and opinions. Although these commonsense psychological beliefs often result in good decision making, they can also produce distorted judgments. To illustrate some of the pitfalls of this naive psychology, let's briefly examine how we typically judge other people's personalities and how we generally overestimate our knowledge of how people and the world operate.

Common Mistakes in Assessing Personality

Research indicates that the first bits of information we learn about a person carry more weight in forming an overall impression than information learned later. Thus, if a stranger was described to you as intelligent, industrious, impulsive, critical, stubborn, and envious, your overall impression of her might be more favorable than if she was described as envious, stubborn, critical, impulsive, industrious, and intelligent. Although the information contained in these two descriptions is identical, a person described in the first manner is typically thought to be competent and ambitious, while a person described in the reverse order is more likely considered to be overemotional and socially maladjusted (Asch, 1946). One possible explanation for this *primacy effect* (see chapter 8, section 8-1a) is that the early bits of information provide a mental outline in memory, which we then use to process later information. If the later information contradicts this outline, we are more likely to ignore it. The primacy effect is particularly strong when people are given little time to make judgments and are not under a great deal of pressure to be correct (Kruglanski & Freund, 1983).

Much of what we take to be true is seriously wrong.

—Gore Vidal, U.S. author, b. 1925

Our everyday personality judgments are not only shaped by the order in which we learn information about others, but also by our prior set of beliefs about which personality traits go together. These assumptions or naive belief systems that we have about the associations among personality traits have been called an **implicit personality theory.** In this unscientific theory of personality, there is a strong tendency for us to assume that all good things occur together in persons and that all bad things do so as well, with little overlap between the two (Leyens, 1991; Schneider et al., 1979). Thus, we are likely to believe that someone whom we perceive as being warm and outgoing could not also be prone to violence. In an implicit personality theory, there appears to be operating a principle of *evaluative consistency*—a tendency to view others in a way that is internally consistent. Even when contradictory information is provided, we often ignore it and persist in viewing people as either consistently good or bad.

> **Implicit personality theory:** Assumptions or naive belief systems people make about which personality traits go together.

Implicit personality theories affect how young adults make sexual choices. For example, surveys find that many young adults have a well-developed set of ideas—an implicit personality theory—regarding which potential sexual partners are safe and which are not (Kimble et al., 1992). Who are these sexually "safe" persons? People whom one knows and likes are perceived not to be a risk, while risky people are those one does not know well, who are older, and are overanxious for sex. These young adults' tendencies not to practice safe sex with partners they know and like is due to their reluctance to link the risk of disease with loving or caring relationships. Unfortunately, these criteria used to judge AIDS risk are completely unrelated to a person's HIV status. People who use such a belief system run the very real risk of exposure to AIDS.

The Hindsight Bias

If you did indeed develop an intervention program informing people about faulty decision making regarding safe sex and AIDS, one likely response you would get from participants is that you are not telling them anything they didn't already know. In other words, your psychological findings are likely to be seen as simply reflecting obvious commonsense notions of life. Yet, is it really true that most young adults already understand the psychological dynamics of how they judge other people and, thus, realize that they cannot assume that others are "safe" sexual partners simply because they are likable? As we have already seen, the available evidence certainly does not support this conclusion. What else might explain this "I-knew-it-all-along" response?

Research suggests that, when recalling past events, we tend to believe that we "knew all along" how things would turn out. For example, after learning the results of a local election, you might think, "I knew this would be the outcome long ago." Or after your favorite sports team narrowly defeats its archrival for the first time in years, you exclaim, "All week I could sense that my team was going to win!" This after-the-fact overestimation of your ability to have foreseen the outcome is known as the **hindsight bias** (Fischoff, 1977; Hawkins & Hastie, 1990). It occurs because in thinking about a past event, we selectively remember information in constructing a plausible story that is consistent with the now-known outcome (Harvey & Martin, 1995). This "rewriting" of how events occurred allows us to insert missing causal connections so that everything conforms with the outcome. Although we actively rewrite these life stories, we generally do not realize that we are doing so (Wasserman et al., 1991). The outcome now seems obvious—one that we would have easily predicted.

> **Hindsight bias:** The tendency, once an event has occurred, to overestimate our ability to have foreseen the outcome.

Of course, not all "I-knew-it-all-along" claims are due to the hindsight bias. Because we all observe and analyze the world in which we live, we are sometimes accurate in foreseeing how events unfold. This is true for both personal and historical happenings, as well as the findings of psychological research. But there are other times when the

Life is lived forwards, but understood backwards.

—Søren Kierkegaard, Danish philosopher, 1813–1855

scientific findings of psychology are considerably distant from anything we would have predicted based on our casual observations. This is one fact that you will be regularly reminded of as you read this textbook: Many commonsense ideas are simply a product of wrongheaded thinking. One of the objectives of psychological research is to identify and dispel these faulty commonsense beliefs.

2-1b Scientific Methods Minimize Error and Lead to Dependable Generalizations

There is no magic formula to erase these mental quirks and glitches so that our minds run with computer-like precision. Even if there was such a formula, who would be so foolhardy as to "cure" themselves in this manner? As you will discover in your journey through psychology, the quirks and glitches in our everyday thinking are important elements in what it means to be human.

While it is true that psychologists are not immune to error-prone thinking, they do use special methods to minimize these problems when conducting research. These **scientific methods** consist of a set of procedures used to gather, analyze, and interpret information in a way that minimizes error and leads to dependable generalizations. Remember my cross-country hitchhiking research described in chapter 1? When I collected my data, I did so using the scientific method of survey research (see section 2-3a), interviewing and administering personality questionnaires to more than 100 cross-country hitchhikers in many different locations throughout the country. With this number of participants in my study collected over such a wide geographic area, I could be more confident that my hitchhiking sample accurately represented the population of cross-country hitchhikers in the United States. In research, a **sample** is a group of subjects who are selected to participate in a given study, while a **population** consists of all the members of an identifiable group from which a sample is drawn. The closer a sample is in representing the population, the greater confidence researchers have in generalizing their findings beyond the sample.

In my attempt to understand their personalities, instead of simply asking my hitchhiking participants questions that I thought of at the moment, I had them all respond to the same set of questions that other researchers had previously developed to measure specific aspects of personality. I then compared their responses to one another as well as to those of other young adults who were not cross-country hitchhikers using a series of statistical computations. These statistical analyses allowed me to determine whether and how these groups differed from one another.

Based on my brief description of scientific methodology, you can see that the guidelines psychologists follow when conducting research are far more stringent than those typically employed in everyday thinking. Psychologists also approach the study of the mind by engaging in **critical thinking,** which is the process of deciding what to believe and how to act based on a careful evaluation of the evidence. An important aspect of critical thinking is ruling out alternative explanations. Can a hypnotized person be induced to commit murder? Is there compelling evidence that psychics can predict future events? Can subliminal tapes improve memory and increase self-esteem? These are a few of the fascinating questions we will examine in our journey of discovery. And we will do so while using critical thinking skills. The *Psychological Applications* section at the end of this chapter will discuss how you can develop critical thinking skills to aid you in your journey. In the meantime, let's examine the research process itself, and then scrutinize more thoroughly the structure of the various scientific methods psychologists use in their research.

Scientific method: A set of procedures used in science to gather, analyze, and interpret information in a way that minimizes error and leads to dependable generalizations.

Sample: A group of subjects who are selected to participate in a research study.

Population: All of the members of an identifiable group from which a sample is drawn.

Critical thinking: The process of deciding what to believe and how to act based on a careful evaluation of the evidence.

Since the beginning of the 20th century, people's innate desire to understand themselves— and the human condition—has found a new avenue toward the answer: the scientific method.

—Jacqueline Swartz, contemporary Canadian journalist

SECTION SUMMARY

- Faulty belief systems that make up our naive psychology can produce distorted judgments.
- The primacy effect is the tendency for the first bits of information we learn to carry more weight in forming an overall impression than information learned later.
- Implicit personality theories are the assumptions people make about which personality traits go together.
- Hindsight bias is the tendency, once an event has occurred, to overestimate our ability to have foreseen the outcome.
- To minimize these human biases when conducting research, psychologists employ scientific methods.

2-2 WHAT IS THE PROCESS IN CONDUCTING RESEARCH?

For psychologists to effectively study the mind and behavior, they must carefully plan and execute their research projects employing scientific methods. This process occurs in a series of four sequential stages, which are summarized in figure 2-1. Let's examine each in turn.

2-2a The First Research Stage Involves Selecting a Topic and Reviewing Past Research

In most instances, the research process begins by selecting a topic worth exploring. Scientists get their ideas from many sources. Inspiration could come from someone else's research, from an incident in the daily news, or from some personal experience in the researcher's life. Psychologists generally investigate topics that have relevance to their own lives and culture. For example, in 1964 people were stunned to learn of the brutal murder of a woman outside her New York City apartment building. The victim, Kitty Genovese, was repeatedly attacked by her assailant over a period of 45 minutes. Despite the fact that Ms. Genovese obviously needed help, none of her neighbors came to her aid. Later, the question everyone was asking was "Why were these bystanders so callous to her suffering?" Two people who discussed this disturbing event in detail were social psychologists John Darley and Bibb Latané. The *model of bystander intervention* that emerged from this discussion (Darley & Latané, 1968), and the subsequent research it spawned, provided valuable insights into the complex decision making that occurs among bystanders in emergency situations (see chapter 16, section 16-4d). Had this murder not received such wide coverage, perhaps Darley and Latané would have directed their research activities in a different direction.

Once a topic has been selected, researchers need to search the scientific literature to determine whether prior investigations of the topic exist. The findings from these previous studies generally shape the course of the current investigation. Today, psychologists can vastly accelerate literature searches by using a number of computer-based programs that catalog even the most recently published studies. In addition, psychologists can often instantly obtain unpublished articles from researchers at other universities either through

FIGURE 2-1

Stages in the Psychological Research Process

Stage 1: Selecting a Topic and Searching the Literature

Ideas come from a variety of sources, including existing theories, past research, current social events, and personal experiences. Once a topic has been selected, psychologists must not only become knowledgeable about past research findings in their area of interest, they must also keep abreast of recently published studies and those reported at scientific meetings.

Stage 2: Developing a Theory and Formulating Hypotheses

Once the research literature has been digested, a theory is formulated and hypotheses that can be empirically tested must then be developed.

Stage 3: Selecting a Scientific Method and Submitting the Study for Ethical Evaluation

Research can be conducted in the laboratory or in the field, and the psychologist can employ a variety of methods, including correlational, experimental, and case study. All institutions seeking federal research funding must establish institutional review boards to evaluate the potential benefits and risks of proposed studies.

Stage 4: Collecting and Analyzing Data and Reporting Results

The three basic techniques of data collection are self-reports, direct observations, and archival information. Data can be analyzed using either descriptive or inferential statistics, with the latter mathematical analysis being the more valuable because it allows researchers to generalize their findings to the population of interest. Psychologists principally report their results at professional meetings and by publishing articles in scientific journals.

computer networks or fax machines. Keeping abreast of other colleagues' discoveries and insights is a necessity during all stages in the research process. For this reason, searching the research literature may be thought of as a never-ending endeavor.

2-2b The Second Research Stage Involves Theory and Hypothesis Development

Theory: An organized system of ideas that seeks to explain why two or more events are related.

The basic motivation underlying research is the desire to find answers to questions. The question of interest usually revolves around whether some event can be explained by a particular theory. A **theory** is an organized system of ideas that seeks to explain why two or more events are related. Put simply, a theory provides a picture of reality concerning some phenomena. Theory development is an important aspect of the second stage of the research process. What makes a good theory depends on a number of factors, some of which are listed in table 2-1 (Kuhn, 1977; McMullin, 1983).

The most salient factor in determining the value of a theory is its *predictive accuracy*. In other words, can it reliably predict behavior? A second factor is that it should have *internal coherence*—there shouldn't be any logical inconsistencies or unexplained coincidences among the theoretical principles and concepts. A third characteristic of a good theory is that it should be *economical*, meaning that it includes the minimum number of principles or concepts necessary to adequately explain and predict the phenomena in question. Finally, a fourth and equally important quality in a good theory is *fertility*—the ability to generate sufficient interest in other scientists so that the theory is tested and extended to a wide variety of behavior.

TABLE 2-1

Predictive accuracy—Can the theory reliably predict behavior?

Internal coherence—Are there logical inconsistencies between any of the theoretical ideas?

Economy—Does the theory only contain what is necessary to explain the phenomenon in question?

Fertility—Does the theory generate research, and can it be used to explain a wide variety of behavior?

What Makes a Good Theory?

One of the most serious problems confronting psychology is that of connecting itself with life. . . . Theory that does not someway affect life has no value.

—Lewis Terman, U.S. psychologist, 1877–1959

The way that scientists determine the predictive accuracy of a theory is by formulating hypotheses. **Hypotheses** are specific propositions or expectations about the nature of things derived from a theory—they are the logical implications of the theory. The researcher asks, "If the theory is true, what observations would we expect to make in our investigation?" An example of a hypothesis developing from a theory is William Dement's interest in dreaming. Following other researchers' (Aserinsky & Kleitman, 1953) discovery that dreaming was associated with periods of rapid eye movement (REM sleep), Dement (1960) developed a theory that dreaming was a fundamental requirement for all humans. He hypothesized that if people were not allowed to dream over a series of nights (by waking them when they entered REM sleep), they would experience some kind of pressure to increase their "dream time" on subsequent nights. This hypothesis was a logical extension of Dement's theory that there was something basic in our need to dream (refer to chapter 6, section 6-2d, for the results of Dement's research).

Hypotheses: Specific propositions or expectations about the nature of things derived from a theory.

2-2c The Third Research Stage Involves Selecting a Scientific Method and Obtaining Approval to Conduct the Study

When a theory and hypotheses have been developed, researchers must next select a scientific method that allows the hypotheses to be tested. In all scientific methods, psychologists seek to determine the nature of the relationship between two or more factors (called *variables* because people vary on them), but the way this is accomplished differs. We will examine these differences in greater detail a bit later in the chapter (see section 2-3).

To ensure the health and safety of participants in psychological studies, all research-oriented institutions have *institutional review boards (IRBs)* to monitor and evaluate research proposals involving both human and animal subjects (Blass, 2000). To guard against harm to participants, the guidelines followed by IRBs focus on the *risk/benefit ratio*, which weighs the potential risks to those participating in a study against the benefits that the study may have for advancing knowledge about humanity (Hayes, 2002). In assessing proposed studies involving human participants, priority is always given to the welfare of the participants over any potential benefits of the research (Colombo, 1995; Rosenthal, 1994, 1995). With such standards and monitoring agencies in place, human psychological research is a very low risk activity, and participants usually enjoy their experience, even if they were initially deceived about the study's true purpose (Christensen, 1988; Smith & Richardson, 1983). Table 2-2 lists some of the guidelines followed when conducting research involving human participants (American Psychological Association, 1992).

TABLE 2-2

Guidelines for Conducting Research with Human Participants

In assessing proposed studies involving human subjects, priority is always given to assuring their welfare over any potential benefits of the research (Saks et al., 2002; Street & Luoma, 2002). The guidelines also urge researchers to:

1. Provide enough information to possible participants about the activities they will perform in the study so they can freely give their *informed consent*.
2. Be truthful whenever possible. *Deception* should be used only when absolutely necessary and when adequate debriefing is provided.
3. Allow participants the *right to decline* to be a part of the study or to discontinue their participation at any point without this decision resulting in any negative consequences (for example, not receiving full payment for their participation).
4. *Protect participants* from both physical and psychological harm. If participants suffer any undesirable consequences, the researcher must do as much as possible to remove the damaging effects.
5. Ensure that any information provided by individual participants is kept *confidential*.
6. *Debrief* individuals once they have completed their participation. Explain all aspects of the research, attempt to answer all questions and resolve any negative feelings, and make sure they realize that their participation contributes to better scientific understanding.

IRBs also evaluate animal research, which accounts for about 5 percent of all research published in psychology journals (Kiple & Ornelas, 2001). The vast majority of these studies involve little more than slightly modifying the environment of animals and observing how these changes affect their behavior. A minority of studies, however, involve painful and dangerous experimental procedures that would never be attempted on human participants. For example, research investigating the effect that drugs have on the functioning of the brain or investigations into the treatment of brain disorders and brain damage often begin with animal studies.

Do such benefits outweigh the costs in the harm caused to the animal subjects? Many animal rights activists do not think so, and they have strenuously opposed such research, regardless of the resulting benefits (Erwin et al., 1994; Plous, 1998). Moderates among animal rights activists recognize the need for some of this research, but they argue that other research inflicts needless pain and suffering on animals. Within the field itself, although the majority of psychology Ph.D.s and psychology majors support animal studies involving observation or confinement, most disapprove of studies involving pain or death (Plous, 1996a, 1996b).

In response to such criticism, virtually all scientists who conduct animal research state that they support the humane treatment of animals, but they deny that animals have the same rights as people (Cohen, 1994). Instead, they contend that every advance in science must sooner or later be tried on a living creature. If animals are not substituted for humans in studies that pose significant health risks, then, we must either (1) place human participants at serious risk in these studies, or (2) simply abandon the research altogether. Because neither of these options is acceptable to most people, animal research continues, as does the debate (Baldwin, 1993). Table 2-3 lists some myths and facts about animal research.

Journey of Discovery Question

For every dog or cat used in a laboratory experiment, 10,000 dogs and cats are abandoned by their owners (Miller, 1985). When these abandoned animals are brought to local humane societies and are not adopted, should they be made available as subjects for scientific research? Upon what values would you base your decision?

TABLE 2-3

Some Myths and Facts about Animal Research

Myth: Most animal research is unnecessary.

Fact: There are strong economic pressures against the unnecessary use of animals in research. The extremely limited funds available to conduct animal research minimize the possibility that animals will be used for trivial purposes.

Myth: Other research methods can be used so that animals are not needed in behavioral research.

Fact: In most cases, no good alternatives exist. For example, computerized models of complex behavior still do not truly mimic actual behavior.

Myth: Most research animals are dogs, cats, and nonhuman primates.

Fact: Dogs and cats account for less than 1 percent of the total animal subjects. The same is true of nonhuman primates. Nearly 90 percent of the animals used in research are rats, mice, and other rodents.

Myth: Most animals in research suffer great pain and distress.

Fact: The vast majority of behavioral and biomedical research (over 90%) does not cause pain or significant distress to the animal. In only 6 percent of experiments are anesthesia or painkillers withheld. In such instances, researchers withhold pain relief because it would interfere with the objectives of the research (for example, studying the effects of pain).

Myth: Animal research only benefits humans.

Fact: Animal research benefits both humans and animals. For example, knowledge of animal sexual and feeding behavior has helped to save a number of species from extinction. Further, insights gained through animal research on taste aversion have been used by both ranchers and conservationists to condition animal predators in the wild to avoid killing livestock and endangered species (see chapter 7, section 7-1c).

2-2d The Fourth Research Stage Involves Data Collection, Analysis, and Reporting Results

When approval has been granted by the IRB, it is time to collect the data. There are three basic techniques of data collection: (1) *self-reports*, (2) *direct observations*, and (3) *archival information*. Collecting data using self-reports allows researchers to measure important subjective states such as people's perceptions, emotions, or attitudes. However, because people may not always be able to accurately describe these internal states (Greenwald et al., 1998), many researchers prefer to directly observe people's behavior, recording its quantity and direction of change over time. Finally, researchers will sometimes examine existing documents, or archives, to gather information. These accumulated records come from a wide variety of sources (for example, census information, court records, newspaper articles) and can provide researchers with a great deal of valuable information.

Once the data has been collected, the researcher must analyze it. Such data analysis generally requires extensive knowledge of statistical procedures and computer software packages. The two basic kinds of statistics employed by psychologists are descriptive and inferential. **Descriptive statistics** simply summarize and describe the behavior or characteristics of a particular sample of participants in a study, while **inferential statistics** move beyond mere description to make inferences about the larger population from which the sample was drawn. Inferential statistics are used to estimate the likelihood that a difference found in the groups studied would also be found if everyone in the population participated in the study. Psychologists generally accept a difference as statistically significant if the likelihood of it having occurred by chance is less than 1 in 20—that is, a probability of less than 5 percent (Nickerson, 2000). Because one of the main objectives of psychological research is to generalize research findings to the population of interest, inferential statistics are the more valued type of statistic. (See Discovery Box 2-1.)

Descriptive statistics: Numbers that summarize and describe the behavior or characteristics of a particular sample of participants in a study.

Inferential statistics: Mathematical analyses that move beyond mere description of research data to make inferences about the larger population from which the sample was drawn.

DISCOVERY   BOX 2-1

How Can Meta-Analysis Improve Our Understanding of Multiple Studies?

One of the problems in science is that of contradictory findings from one study to the next. If, for example, seven studies find that one type of psychotherapy is effective in treating depression, while four studies find that it is ineffective, what conclusions should be drawn? In the past, researchers often used the "majority rules" approach to resolve such controversies. That is, they merely counted up the number of studies that found or did not find a particular psychological effect and then concluded that the effect existed if it occurred in the majority of studies. To better assess the findings from numerous studies, during the past 20 years researchers have increasingly relied on a more sophisticated comparison procedure called meta-analysis (Hall & Brannick, 2002; Stamps, 2002). **Meta-analysis** is the use of statistical techniques to sum up a body of similar studies in order to objectively estimate the reliability and overall size of the effect (Chalmers et al., 2002; Rothstein et al., 2002). Because many studies may find small differences between groups that do not reach statistical levels of significance, meta-analysis can determine whether these small effects are indeed "real" or merely measurement error.

Meta-analysis: The use of statistical techniques to sum up a body of similar studies in order to objectively estimate the reliability and overall size of the effect.

The final task in the fourth stage of the research process is to report results. By informing fellow scholars of their discoveries, researchers build upon and refine one another's work, and the understanding of psychology is enriched. Yet, a psychologist's research findings are not uncritically accepted by others. At scientific conventions where research is often first reported and in scientific journals where studies are ultimately published, all stages in the research process are scrutinized for possible errors and oversights. It is through such critical analysis that psychological knowledge is advanced.

SECTION SUMMARY

- The process of scientific inquiry occurs in stages.
- Stage 1 involves selecting a topic and searching the research literature.
- Stage 2 involves the development of theories and hypotheses.
- Stage 3 involves selecting a scientific method and submitting a proposed study for ethical evaluation.
- Stage 4 involves data collection, analysis, and reporting results.

2-3 COMMONLY USED SCIENTIFIC METHODS

One of the most important factors in determining whether a study will ultimately add to our knowledge of psychology is the method used to collect data. Let us now examine the most commonly used scientific methods employed by psychologists, which can be placed into three broad categories: *observational methods*, which seek to describe behavior; *correlational methods*, which try to understand the relationship between two or more behaviors; and *experimental methods*, which attempt to explain the causes of behavior.

2-3a Description Is the Goal of Observational Research

To understand behavior so that it can be predicted and controlled, a scientist must first describe it accurately. Scientific methods that have description as their primary goal fall under the category of observational research (Heyman et al., 2001). Within this category, there are the methods of *naturalistic observation, participant observation,* and *case study.*

Naturalistic Observation

Naturalistic observation is an observational method that investigates behavior in its natural environment (Crabtree & Miller, 1992; Martin & Bateson, 1993). Settings for such research range from day-care centers, where developmental psychologists might record the play behavior of children, to the jungles of Africa, where comparative psychologists might study how a troop of baboons defends itself against predators. In all such naturalistic studies, behavior is merely observed and recorded—it is not manipulated.

One example of a naturalistic observation study was Robert Levine and Ara Norenzayan's (1999) analysis of the pace of everyday life in 31 cultures. Some of the data they collected were measurements of people's average walking speed on city sidewalks, the speed at which postal clerks responded to a simple request, and the accuracy of clocks in public settings. Notice that all of these measurements simply involve the researchers observing how people behave in their natural surroundings. Their findings indicated that the pace of life was faster in colder and more economically productive cultures (such as Switzerland and Japan) than in those that were hotter and less economically energetic (such as Mexico and Indonesia).

Naturalistic observation:
A descriptive scientific method that investigates behavior in its natural environment.

Participant Observation

Another type of observational method is **participant observation.** Here, as in naturalistic observation, a researcher records behavior as it occurs in its natural environment, but does so as a participant of the group being studied. One of the chief benefits of this research strategy is that it allows investigators to get closer to what they are studying more than does any other method.

An excellent example of this method was Leon Festinger's study of a doomsday cult in the 1950s (Festinger et al., 1956). The leader of the cult, Mrs. Keetch, claimed that aliens from outer space had told her the world would come to an end on a specific date, December 21. She also stated that the only survivors of this catastrophe would be members of her group. When Festinger and his coworkers learned of Mrs. Keetch, they became interested in measuring the psychological changes that would occur within the group when the doomsday came and passed with the world still intact. To accomplish this task, over a period of several weeks, these researchers infiltrated the group as participant observers and began describing its dynamics. This descriptive study was one of the first tests of a very influential theory in psychology called cognitive dissonance theory (see chapter 16, section 16-2c).

The following are four advantages of both naturalistic and participant observation research (Hong & Duff, 2002; Weick, 1985):

Participant observation:
A descriptive scientific method where a group is studied from within by a researcher who records behavior as it occurs in its natural environment.

1. Researchers are able to watch behavior in its "wholeness," providing the full context in which to understand it.
2. Researchers are able to record rare events that may never occur in a controlled laboratory environment.
3. Researchers are able to systematically record events that were previously observed only by nonscientists.
4. Researchers are able to observe events that would be too risky, dangerous, or unethical to create in the laboratory.

> *Every journey into the past is complicated by delusions, false memories, false namings of real events.*
>
> —Adrienne Rich, U.S. poet, b. 1929

Despite these benefits, there are also some problems in using naturalistic and participant observation methods. First, because of the absence of control that researchers have in such studies, conclusions must be drawn very carefully. Second, researchers must be mindful that their participation in or even observation of events can significantly alter the participants' behavior and thus taint the data. Although researchers assume that after a period of time those who are being observed become accustomed to their presence, it is difficult to evaluate to what degree this actually occurs. Finally, more than any other scientific method, observational methods pose the most ethical problems involving invasion of others' privacy.

Case Study

Case study: A descriptive scientific method involving an in-depth analysis of a single subject, usually a person.

Another form of observational research is a **case study,** which involves an in-depth analysis of a single subject. This method of inquiry is common in clinical work, in which psychotherapists provide an extensive description of a person suffering from a particular psychological disorder to illustrate the factors that lead to and influence it (Morgan & Morgan, 2001). Sigmund Freud's work is perhaps the most famous example of this method (Gedo, 2001).

The advantage of the case study is that it produces a more detailed analysis of a person than any other method. One disadvantage is that researchers must be extremely cautious in generalizing from a single case to the population as a whole. Another problem is that this method often depends on people's memories of the past, which all too often are both selective and inaccurate (see chapter 8, section 8-3c).

2-3b Correlational Research Analyzes the Direction and Strength of the Relationship between Variables

Besides simply describing a phenomenon under study, often psychologists want to also know whether two or more variables are related, and if so, how strongly. When changes in one variable relate to changes in another variable, we say that they *correlate.* **Correlational research** assesses the nature of the relationship between two or more variables that are not controlled by the researcher. The importance of correlational research for psychologists is prediction: It allows them to predict a change in one variable by knowing the value of another variable.

Correlational research: Research designed to examine the nature of the relationship between two or more naturally occurring variables.

Using Surveys When Conducting Correlational Research

Surveys: Structured sets of questions or statements given to a group of people to measure their attitudes, beliefs, values, or behavioral tendencies.

Although studying the relationships among variables can be done by directly observing behavior, it is often accomplished by asking people carefully constructed questions. **Surveys** are structured sets of questions or statements given to a group of people to measure their attitudes, beliefs, values, or behavioral tendencies (Bradburn & Sudman, 1988; Lavrakas, 1993). Obtaining information using surveys is generally relatively easy, but its main disadvantage is that it relies on people's self-reports, which are often faulty. My hitchhiking study involved the use of surveys.

Surveys are often used to gather information on behavior or other psychological processes that are difficult, if not impossible, to observe directly. For example, imagine that you are a psychologist interested in learning the degree to which people pay attention to their private thoughts and feelings and the degree to which they self-disclose these private thoughts and feelings to others. You might ask them to complete a survey questionnaire similar to the one in Discovery Box 2-2 that measures both the personality trait known as *private self-consciousness* and the behavioral tendency to *self-disclose.* Before reading further, spend a few minutes answering these items and check how your responses compare with those of other adults.

If you simply used survey data to determine how people compare on various personality and behavioral measures, this type of research would involve observational methods in which description is the primary goal. However, returning to our example, imagine that you are interested in discovering whether there is a relationship between private self-consciousness and willingness to self-disclose. That is, do people who regularly attend to their private thoughts and feelings disclose this private side of themselves more than those who do not habitually self-reflect? Now, you are seeking information on whether these two variables are *correlated*. That is, can you predict whether people are likely to self-disclose based on their level of private self-consciousness, or vice versa? In correlational research, as in observational research, you would not try to influence how often people in your study actually spent thinking about themselves. Instead, you would merely gather information on how often they attend to their own thoughts and feelings and the degree to which they self-disclose to others.

The Correlation Coefficient

Correlational research aids in prediction by providing information on the *direction* and *strength* of the relationship between two variables. The direction of the relationship between variable A and variable B tells the researcher how they are related (positively or negatively). The strength of the relationship can be thought of as the degree of accuracy with which you can predict the value of one variable by knowing the value of the other variable. The direction and strength of the relationship between two variables is described by the statistical measure known as the **correlation coefficient (r).** This correlation coefficient can range from −1.00 to +1.00.

Returning to the example of self-consciousness and self-disclosure, a correlation at or very near zero indicates the absence of a *linear relationship* between these two variables. This zero correlation may mean one of two things: (1) regularly self-reflecting has no association with self-disclosing, or (2) there is a *curvilinear relationship* between self-reflection and self-disclosing. One can easily determine the meaning of a zero correlation by plotting the pairing of these two variables on a graph, as is illustrated in figure 2-2. In marked contrast to a zero correlation, one that is near +1.00 would suggest that people who regularly attend to their private thoughts and feelings are much more likely to self-disclose than those who engage in little self-reflection. In contrast, a correlation near −1.00 indicates that those who regularly self-reflect are much less likely to self-disclose to others than those who engage in little self-reflection.

Regarding the strength of a relationship, researchers seldom find a perfect or near perfect (r = +1.00 or r = −1.00) correlation between variables. For example, a study investigating the relationship between young adults' private self-consciousness and their degree of self-disclosure to their romantic partners found a correlation of .36 for men and a correlation of .20 for women (Franzoi et al., 1985). Due to the direction of the correlation, you might predict that high private self-conscious men would be more likely to self-disclose to their romantic partners than low private self-conscious men. For women, you would make the same prediction, but you would be less confident due to this correlation's lower strength.

Although these correlations might seem small to you, in social science research correlations seldom exceed .60. Correlations of .50 to .60 are regarded as strong, those between .30 and .50 are moderately strong, and those below .30 or .20 are considered rather weak. The reason correlations rarely exceed .60 is that many variables determine human behavior. In the example of self-disclosing to someone, many variables will influence people's degrees of self-disclosure. In addition to the disclosers' own levels of private self-consciousness, we must also consider their partners' willingness to listen, the closeness of the relationship, as well as the amount of time they actually spend together. Furthermore, even if researchers could isolate all the important variables that influence self-disclosing, because of the nature of our subject—humans with minds of their own—it's unlikely they would be able to predict with perfect reliability people's actions.

> **Correlation coefficient (r):** A statistical measure of the direction and strength of the linear relationship between two variables, which can range from −1.00 to +1.00.

DISCOVERY BOX 2-2

How Do Psychologists Measure Self-Consciousness and Willingness to Self-Disclose?

Measuring Private Self-Consciousness

The personality trait of private self-consciousness is measured by items on the Self-Consciousness Scale (SCS: Fenigstein, Scheier, & Buss, 1975). To obtain information on the degree to which you attend to your own private thoughts and feelings, read each item below and then indicate how well each statement describes you using the following response scale:

0 = extremely uncharacteristic (not at all like me)
1 = uncharacteristic (somewhat unlike me)
2 = neither characteristic nor uncharacteristic
3 = characteristic (somewhat like me)
4 = extremely characteristic (very much like me)

___ 1. I'm always trying to figure myself out.
___ 2. Generally, I'm not very aware of myself.*
___ 3. I reflect about myself a lot.
___ 4. I'm often the subject of my own fantasies.
___ 5. I never scrutinize myself.*
___ 6. I'm generally attentive to my inner feelings.
___ 7. I'm constantly examining my motives.
___ 8. I sometimes have the feeling that I'm off somewhere watching myself.
___ 9. I'm alert to changes in my mood.
___10. I'm aware of the way my mind works when I work through a problem.

Two of the items are reverse-scored; that is, for these items a lower rating actually indicates a greater tendency to attend to private thoughts and feelings. Before summing the items, recode those with an asterisk ("*") so that 0 = 4, 1 = 3, 3 = 1, and 4 = 0. To calculate your private self-consciousness score, simply add up your responses to the ten items. The average, or mean, score for college students on private self-consciousness is about 26. The higher your score is above this value, the greater is your tendency to reflect upon your private

The major disadvantage of the correlational study is that it cannot definitively determine the cause of the relationship between two variables. That is, besides knowing the strength and direction of a relationship, another piece of information that is extremely valuable when conducting an empirical study is knowing which variable caused a change in the other. Does attending to their own thoughts and feelings make people more eager to self-disclose, or does self-disclosing make people more attentive to these thoughts and feelings? This methodological disadvantage can result in the *reverse-causality problem*, which occurs whenever either of the two variables correlated with one another could just as plausibly be the cause or the effect (see figure 2-3).

A second problem resulting from the inability to confidently determine causality is that it is possible that a third, unmeasured variable causes changes in both variables under study. This is known as the *third-variable problem* (see figure 2-3 again). Regarding our previous example, it's possible that what looks like a positive correlation between private self-consciousness and self-disclosing is really an illusion because it is really another variable—perhaps parental upbringing or inherited traits—that is causing both those changes.

thoughts and feelings compared with the average American college student. The lower your score is below this value, the less likely is your tendency to regularly engage in this sort of private self-awareness compared with other students.

Measuring the Tendency to Self-Disclose

Indicate for the topics listed below the degree to which you have disclosed to a close romantic partner using the following scale:

Discussed not at all   0   1   2   3   4   Discussed fully and completely

1. My personal habits   _____
2. Things I have done which I feel guilty about   _____
3. Things I wouldn't do in public   _____
4. My deepest feelings   _____
5. What I like and dislike about myself   _____
6. What is important to me in life   _____
7. What makes me the person I am   _____
8. My worst fears   _____
9. Things I have done which I am proud of   _____
10. My close relationships with other people   _____
    Total score

You can determine your overall self-disclosure score by adding up the scores in the column. The higher the score, the greater your willingness to self-disclose.

Sources: Self-Consciousness Scale: From "Public and Private Self-Consciousness: Assessment and Theory" by Allan Fenigstein, Michael F. Scheier, and Arnold H. Buss in JOURNAL OF CONSULTING AND CLINICAL PSYCHOLOGY, 1975, 43, pp. 522–527 (Table 1, p. 524). Copyright © 1975 by the American Psychological Association. Adapted with permission. Self-Disclosure Scale: From "Openers: Individuals Who Elicit Intimate Self-Disclosure" by L. C. Miller, J. H. Berg, and R. L. Archer in JOURNAL OF PERSONALITY AND SOCIAL PSYCHOLOGY, 1983, 44, pp. 1234–1244 (Table 2, p. 1236). Copyright © 1983 by the American Psychological Association. Adapted with permission.

The invalid assumption that correlation implies cause is probably among the two or three most serious and common errors of human reasoning.

—Stephen Jay Gould, *The Mismeasure of Man* (1981), p. 242

2-3c Experimental Research Determines Cause-Effect Relationships

Due to the fact that correlational studies cannot conclusively tell us why variables are related to one another, psychologists conduct **experimental research** to examine cause-and-effect relationships (Crano & Brewer, 2002). In an experiment, the psychologist manipulates one variable by exposing research participants to contrasting levels of it (for example, high, medium, low, no exposure), and then observes what effect this manipulation has on the other variable that has not been manipulated. The variable that is

Experimental research: Research designed to test cause-effect relationships between variables.

FIGURE 2-2

Plotting the Relationship between Variable X and Variable Y on a Graph

The points on the graphs represent a pairing of variable X with variable Y for each participant in the study. As you can see in the curvilinear relationship graph, the zero correlation is hiding a meaningful relationship, where both high and low levels of X are associated with high levels of Y, but moderate levels of X are associated with low levels of Y. Can you think of variables that would have a curvilinear relationship?

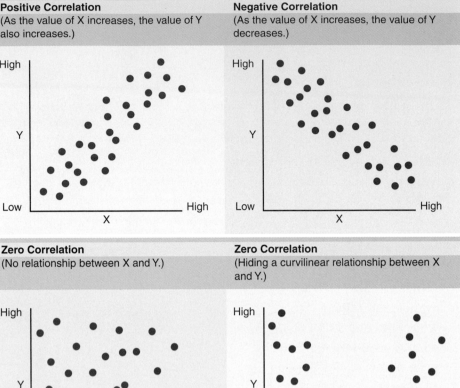

Positive Correlation
(As the value of X increases, the value of Y also increases.)

Negative Correlation
(As the value of X increases, the value of Y decreases.)

Zero Correlation
(No relationship between X and Y.)

Zero Correlation
(Hiding a curvilinear relationship between X and Y.)

Independent variable: The experimental variable that the researcher manipulates.

Dependent variable: The experimental variable that is measured because it is believed to depend on the manipulated changes in the independent variable.

Random assignment: Placement of research participants into experimental conditions in a manner that guarantees that all have an equal chance of being exposed to each level of the independent variable.

manipulated is called the **independent variable,** and it is the one the experimenter is testing as the possible cause of any changes that might occur in the other variable. The variable whose changes are considered to be the effect of the manipulated changes in the independent variable is called the **dependent variable.** Once participants have been exposed to the independent variable, their behavior is carefully monitored to determine whether it changes in the predicted fashion with different levels of the independent variable. If it does, the experimenter concludes that the independent variable is the cause of the changes in the dependent variable.

A key feature of most experiments is that participants are randomly assigned to the different levels of the independent variable. In such **random assignment,** the experimenter, by some random procedure, decides which participants are exposed to which level of the independent variable. Due to this procedure, the experimenter can be reasonably confident that the participants in the different experimental conditions don't differ from one another.

One of the better-known experiments in psychology is Albert Bandura's Bobo doll studies, in which he and his colleagues studied whether children would imitate the behavior of an aggressive adult (Bandura et al., 1961). In one of these experiments, a child was first brought into a room to work on an art project. In another part of the room, an adult who was a *confederate*—meaning she was an accomplice of the experimenter—was playing quietly with some Tinker Toys. Near these toys was a mallet and a Bobo doll, which is a big, inflatable clownlike toy that is weighted down so that when it is pushed or punched down it will bounce back to an upright position. For half of the children in the

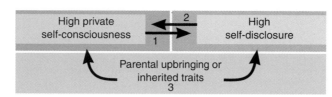

High private self-conscious individuals tend to be more willing self-disclosers than those low in the personality trait of private self-consciousness. Thus, you might conclude that being high in private self-consciousness causes increased self-disclosing in people (arrow 1). However, an alternative explanation is that what is really going on is that the act of regular self-disclosing causes an increase in people's level of private self-consciousness (arrow 2). What is this methodological problem of correlation interpretation called? Now look at arrow 3. What if parental upbringing or their inherited genes were causing the changes in both private self-consciousness and self-disclosing? Of what correlation problem is this an example?

study, after playing with the Tinker Toys for a minute, the adult stood up, walked over to the Bobo doll, and began to attack it. She punched the doll, kicked it, hit it with the mallet, and even sat on it. As she pummeled the clown doll, she yelled out, "Sock him in the nose! . . . Kick him! . . . Knock him down!" For the other children, the adult simply played quietly and nonaggressively with her toys for 10 minutes.

In Bandura's study, the independent variable (remember, that is the variable that is manipulated) was the aggressiveness of the adult's play behavior. After witnessing either the aggressive or nonaggressive adult confederate, the child was led into another room filled with many interesting toys. However, before the child could play with them, the experimenter aroused frustration by saying that these were her best toys and she must "save them for the other children." The child was then led to a third room, containing both aggressive and nonaggressive toys, including a Bobo doll. What children did in this third room was the essential question of the study, for their level of aggressive play here was the dependent variable. The children who had observed the aggressive adult were in what is called the **experimental condition,** which is the condition where participants are exposed to different levels of the independent variable (in this case, the adult's aggression). In contrast, the children who had observed the nonaggressive adult were in what is called the **control condition,** which is the condition where participants are not exposed to the independent variable. Because the only difference between the experimental and control conditions in this study was whether or not they had been exposed to an aggressive adult (the independent variable), any subsequent differences in the children's aggression (the dependent variable) could be explained as being caused by the manipulation of the independent variable.

So what happened in the third room? Children in the control condition tended to play nonaggressively with the toys, while those in the experimental condition tended to beat up the Bobo doll, often shouting the same things at the clown as the previous aggressive adult. Based on this experiment and others like it, Bandura concluded that observing adult aggression can teach children to act more aggressively themselves. Figure 2-4 provides an overview of the elements in an experiment, using Bandura's study as an example.

Now that you have learned about the different scientific methods used by psychologists, which is the best? Actually, what I hope you take from this overview is that there is no one best method in all research settings. In each investigation, the psychologist must decide what method would provide the best test of the hypotheses under consideration. The best overall strategy for psychologists to take is a multimethod approach—employing different methods to study the same topic, thereby capitalizing on each method's strengths and controlling for their weaknesses.

Experimental condition: The condition in an experiment where participants are exposed to different levels of the independent variable.

Control condition: The condition in an experiment where participants are not exposed to the independent variable.

SECTION SUMMARY

- Observational research describes behavior as it occurs in its natural setting.
- Correlational research assesses the direction and strength of the relationship between two or more variables.
- Experimental research involves manipulation of one or more independent variables to determine what effect this has on nonmanipulated dependent variables.

FIGURE 2-4
**The Basic Elements
in an Experiment**

As illustrated in the Bandura study, the power of experimental research is based on treating the experimental and control groups exactly alike except for the manipulation of the independent variable. Any later observed differences in the dependent variable between the two groups can be confidently attributed to the effects of the independent variable.

Hypothesis		
Children will imitate the behavior of an aggressive adult.		
Random Assignment	Subjects randomly assigned to experimental and control conditions.	
Manipulation of Independent Variable	Experimental condition: Child observes an aggressive adult.	Control condition: Child observes a nonaggressive adult.
Measurement of Dependent Variable	Experimental group later engaged in greater aggressive behavior than did the control group.	
Conclusion		
Observing an aggressive adult model increases the aggressive behavior of children.		

SUGGESTED WEBSITES

Note: These websites were functional when we went to press. Please access the online text for the most up-to-date URLs.

Critical Thinking and Psychology Links
http://www.kcmetro.cc.mo.us/longview/ctac/
psychlink.htm
This website contains critical thinking exercises specifically related to psychological issues and research.

Animal Welfare Information Center
http://www.nal.usda.gov/awic/
This website provides information on the ethical treatment of animals in government-sponsored research programs.

PSYCHOLOGICAL APPLICATIONS
How Can You Develop Critical Thinking Skills?

In this last section of chapter 2, I would like to discuss the kinds of critical thinking skills that not only are necessary in conducting scientific research, but also are important in making you both a wise consumer of psychological knowledge and a capable decision maker in your own journey of discovery (Halonen, 1995; Stanovich, 1996).

What Is Critical Thinking?

A few years ago, my oldest daughter, Amelia, was in a toy store trying to decide which new bicycle to pick for her birthday present. The colors, names, and styles of the bikes were clearly aimed at steering girls and boys toward different choices. Yet, Amelia ignored these gender labels and tested all the bikes. At the end of this process, she knew which bike felt the best riding-wise—the blue "Huffy Hyper Force" boy bike. She also knew, however, that if she picked a boy's bike, some of the neighborhood kids would tease her. Amelia realized she could avoid the negative comments by picking her second choice, the pink "Barbie Fashion Fun" girl bike. All of this she explained to me as we stood in the store scanning the array of possibilities before us. Perhaps she was hoping that I would draw upon that mystical "father knows best" wisdom that I had sometimes alluded to and simply tell her which bike to choose.

Instead I said, "Amelia, this is your decision. Think about what's most important to you." After carefully evaluating the evidence and weighing the possible consequences of her two choices, she picked the Hyper Force boy bike.

This Amelia example illustrates an important type of problem-solving skill known as critical thinking. As defined earlier in the chapter, critical thinking is the process of deciding what to believe and how to act based on a careful evaluation of the evidence. In picking a bike, Amelia could have uncritically followed the color designations and bike styles that her culture designates for girls, but instead, she decided that these gender labels unnecessarily restricted her choices. By challenging the assumption that a bike's color and style restricted who could ride it, Amelia could now entertain many more bike possibilities. Once she had gathered her own information by riding all the bikes, she also could have ignored the evidence of her senses and chosen the gender-appropriate but less rider-worthy bike. Again, based on careful reflection of her options, she made her choice. That is one hallmark of critical thinking.

What if Amelia had decided, after going through this entire process, that the benefits of the better-riding boy bike were not enough to justify the social hassles associated with it? Would this decision to pick the girl bike not be based on critical thinking? The answer is no. The choice does not determine whether critical thinking took place. Rather, it is the type of cognitive process that one engages in that is crucial. What we know is that thinking critically about the arguments that you make to yourself, or that others make to you, can greatly improve your own decision making (Anderson, 1993; McBride et al., 2002).

Guidelines for Critical Thinking

The following are some general guidelines on how to critically think (Halpern, 1995; Ruggerio, 1988):

1. *Be willing to ask questions*—Knowledge begins with questioning the nature of things. Think of the process of questioning as a sign of inquisitiveness, not a lack of intelligence.
2. *Analyze assumptions*—Instead of passively accepting assumptions as facts, think about possible exceptions and contradictions.
3. *Examine the evidence*—Instead of accepting a conclusion without evidence, ask for and analyze the evidence that supports and contradicts the various positions.
4. *Be cautious of emotional decisions*—Although there is certainly nothing wrong with being emotionally involved with a particular decision, avoid basing your decision on what you would like to be true, versus what you know to be true.
5. *Avoid oversimplifying issues*—It can be comforting to make simple generalizations about complex events, but resisting glib explanations provides the opportunity for creative complexity.
6. *Tolerate ambiguity*—By rejecting simple answers, you must learn to develop a tolerance for ambiguity. Don't be afraid to admit that you don't know the correct answer when the evidence doesn't suggest one correct solution, but many possible ones.

Critical thinking can be fostered through many activities, but the study of psychology is particularly helpful in promoting this type of cognitive activity (Lehman et al., 1988; Smith, 2002). In this instance, knowledge really is power. Hopefully, one of the benefits of taking this course is that your increased knowledge of how people think and behave will allow you to make more intelligent decisions in your everyday life.

Using Critical Thinking While Reading This Textbook

Although greater knowledge of psychology may ultimately benefit future decision making, one of your more immediate concerns may be how critical thinking can improve your study skills in college.

This is certainly a legitimate concern. Let me briefly describe how you can use a critical thinking strategy known as PRQR while reading the textbook.

The PRQR Technique

Before reading each chapter, *preview* (P) the material by first reading the chapter-opening story and outline, as well as the section summaries and *Journey of Discovery Questions*. This will provide you with a general understanding of what you are about to read so that you can better organize the text material in memory. Next, *read* (R) an entire chapter section, and, as you do, *ask questions* (Q) that focus your attention on the topics. Regularly ask yourself how the text material supports or calls into question any prior beliefs you may have had on the topic. Further, how can the material you are reading help you better understand your own life and events in your world? In writing this text, I attempted to facilitate your critical thinking by regularly asking you questions in the main body of the text and in the captions accompanying the tables, figures, and photographs. Finally, once you have read the chapter, *review* (R) the material so that the information is more securely stored in memory.

In addition to this reading technique, I also recommend that you read text material before your professor talks about it in lecture. By staying slightly ahead of lecture content, you will better comprehend and remember the material presented in class because you already have information in memory upon which you can "hang" this new lecture material. Also, spend time answering the *Journey of Discovery Questions* contained within each chapter. These focused questions encourage you to analyze psychological concepts, provide alternative explanations for research findings, and explore the implications of the text material.

In summary, to be an efficient consumer of psychological knowledge and a capable decision maker in your everyday activities, you need to be willing to exercise your mind like athletes exercise their bodies. You must condition yourself to actively question and scrutinize not only course material but also life events. If you learn to think critically, you will retain something of value long after this textbook and your psychology course are distant memories.

We do not live to think, but, on the contrary, we think in order that we may succeed in surviving.

—José Ortega y Gasset, Spanish philosopher, 1883–1955

KEY TERMS

REVIEW QUESTIONS

1. Research on how young adults judge potential sex partners illustrates the concept of
   a. primacy effect.
   b. evaluative consistency.
   c. implicit personality theory.
   d. all of the above
   e. b and c

2. Which of the following statements is *true?*
   a. Psychologists have developed special formulas to eliminate biases and errors in human judgment.
   b. Statistical analysis is useful in comparing samples to the population.
   c. Psychologists are immune to error-prone thinking.
   d. It is not important that a sample represents the population.
   e. Psychologists cannot make dependable generalizations.

3. Dement's claim that there is something basic in our need to dream would be considered
   a. a hypothesis.
   b. a theory.
   c. a case study.
   d. a correlational coefficient.
   e. topic selection.

4. Institutional review boards (IRBs)
   a. monitor and evaluate research proposals involving only human subjects.
   b. focus on risk/benefit ratio.
   c. never allow participants to be deceived about a study's true purpose.
   d. claim that human psychological research is a high-risk activity.
   e. *a* and *b*

5. Which of the following statements is *true* of animal research?
   a. Most animal research is unnecessary.
   b. Other methods could be used so that animals are not needed in behavioral research.
   c. Nearly 90 percent of animals used in research are rodents.
   d. Ninety percent of behavioral and biomedical research causes pain and significant distress to animals.
   e. Animals do not benefit from animal research.

6. Which of the following statements is *true?*
   a. Descriptive statistics are a more valued type of statistic than inferential statistics.
   b. A difference is considered statistically significant if the likelihood of it having occurred by mere chance is less than 1 in 5.
   c. Contemporary psychology does not require extensive knowledge of statistics.
   d. Meta-analysis is the technique of counting the number of studies that find or do not find a particular effect.
   e. Reporting results is an important stage of research.

7. Leon Festinger's study of a doomsday cult used which form of observational research?
   a. naturalistic
   b. participant
   c. case study
   d. correlational
   e. survey

8. All of the following are advantages of naturalistic and participant observation research *except*
   a. absence of control.
   b. provides a full context for behavior.
   c. opportunity to record events difficult to replicate in a laboratory.
   d. can observe events too risky to create in a laboratory.
   e. can record events previously only observed by nonscientists.

9. Correlational studies cannot determine the cause of the relationship between two variables because
   a. of the third-variable problem.
   b. of the reverse-causality problem.
   c. research correlation rarely exceeds .60.
   d. all of the above
   e. *a* and *b*

10. In Bandura's Bobo doll study, the level of aggressive play of the child in the third room was the
    a. experimental condition.
    b. control condition.
    c. dependent variable.
    d. independent variable.
    e. random assignment.

11. The author claims that the best scientific method for psychologists to use would be
    a. laboratory experiments.
    b. field experiments.
    c. multimethod.
    d. participant and natural observation.
    e. surveys.

12. Considering the Amelia example, which of the following choices illustrates critical thinking?
    a. buying the boy bike
    b. buying the girl bike
    c. not buying a bike at all
    d. asking her dad's advice
    e. none of the above

13. According to the author, which of the following is a guideline to help in critical thinking?
    a. Ask questions.
    b. Base decisions on what you would like to be true.
    c. Don't make issues seem too complex; keep it simple.
    d. Avoid ambiguity.
    e. Never be wrong.

14. The PRQR technique suggests you
    a. preview the material by first reading the chapter-opening story and outline.
    b. read an entire section.
    c. ask questions that focus your attention on the topics.
    d. review the material so that the information is more securely stored in memory.
    e. all of the above

Biological Bases of Behavior

It's like waking up, sort of like waking up in the world. You're waking, trying to push things together yourself, reaching back. And you wonder at times yourself just, well, what it is and what it isn't. (Hilts, 1995, p. 239)

Have you ever had the experience of waking from a dream feeling disoriented, not quite sure where you are or what's happening? If so, then perhaps you can relate in some small way to the life of an extraordinary man— Henry M.

Up until the morning of his 16th birthday, Henry M.'s life had been relatively normal and uneventful. Then, while en route to a birthday party celebration, Henry experienced his first major grand mal epileptic seizure. Over the next 11 years, the seizures increased to as many as 10 minor blackouts and one major grand mal per week. Faced with a future filled with such incapacitating convulsions, Henry's doctors recommended that he undergo a radical operation that they believed would cure his epilepsy.

In August of 1953, Henry's physician drilled two holes into his skull above the eyes and inserted metal spatulas into the holes to lift the frontal lobes of the brain slightly. With the front of the brain raised, the physician next inserted a silver straw deep into Henry's brain and sucked out a fist-sized piece of it containing nearly the entire mass of the *hippocampus* and the regions leading up to it. What is all the more horrifying about this event was that Henry was awake the entire time, being anesthetized only on his scalp. Because the brain has no sensory receptors, Henry felt no pain.

In the 1950s, the purpose of the hippocampus was not known, but the physician who performed the surgery believed that the removal of this portion of the brain would stop the seizures (Corkin, 1984; Milner et al., 1968). But at what price? The surgery did indeed lessen the frequency and intensity of Henry's epileptic seizures, but by removing the hippocampus, the physician had also unwittingly removed Henry's ability to form new memories (see section 3-3b). Commenting on Henry's sorry state of mind, this physician later sadly noted, "Guess what, I tried to cut out the epilepsy of a patient, but took his memory instead! What a trade!" (Hilts, 1995, p. 100).

Today, for Henry, as for all of us, the events of the moment are full and rich. His memories of people and events prior to his surgery also remain largely intact. Yet, unlike us, when Henry stops thinking about something that has just happened to him, the memory of these events disappears entirely, leaving him stuck in a constantly changing, meaningless present. With this inability to create new memories, almost everything he encounters is a surprise to him, regardless of how many times he has been exposed to it. In describing his state of mind, Henry says it is like perpetually waking from a dream and not knowing what day it is or what he should be doing on that day. With this confusion comes a tug of fear and concern. As he confided on one occasion to the scientists who were studying him:

> Right now, I'm wondering, have I done or said anything amiss? You see, at this moment everything looks clear to me, but what happened just before? That's what worries me. (Hilts, 1995, p. 138)

During the past 50 years, Henry M. has remained ignorant of all the changes and advances in the world around him. Not only does he not know that his parents have died or that people have walked on the moon, he also has no realization that his tragic life circumstances have dramatically increased the scientific community's understanding of the neuropsychology of memory. Indeed, over the years, psychobiologists and other neuroscientists have learned a great deal about the functioning of the human brain by studying Henry and other people like him who have had their brains damaged in some manner (Calvin & Ojemann, 1994; Feinberg, 2001). This organ of our body, which comprises only about 2 percent of our total body weight, controls most of the complex aspects of our behavior and mental life. In this chapter, we continue our journey of discovery by examining this most marvelous organ—the brain. But before analyzing the brain's larger structures and functions, we need to first examine the complex network of nerve cells, or *neurons,* that account for all human thought and action. After investigating the basic structure and function of these nerve cells, we will see how they are organized in our *central nervous system* and *peripheral nervous system.* Finally, we will end our analysis of the biological bases of behavior by examining the genetic basis for behavior.

3-1   THE NEURON

In the late nineteenth and early twentieth centuries, scientists were struggling to identify the basic structural units of the brain and how they connect and interact. Today we know that the nervous system has specialized cells, called **neurons,** that send and receive information throughout the body. They are the nervous system's building blocks. One of the first persons to discover that neurons were separate and distinct units and not simply a thick clump of cell matter was Spanish neuroanatomist Santiago Ramón y Cajal (1852–1934). The amazing thing about Cajal's discovery was that he made it while working in a makeshift laboratory in his attic with a $25 microscope and a single box of slides! His resulting theory on how the brain processes information earned him the Nobel Prize for Physiology and Medicine in 1906.

> **Neurons:** Specialized cells in the nervous system that send and receive information.

The human nervous system contains anywhere from 90 to 180 billion neurons, with 98.8 percent residing in the brain and the remaining 1.2 percent (over 1 billion neurons) distributed throughout the spinal cord (Rosenzweig et al., 2002; Williams & Herrup, 1988). On average, each neuron transmits information to about a thousand other neurons, which means that there are trillions of different neural connections in the brain (Beatty, 2001). Although these elementary units of the nervous system come in thousands of different shapes and sizes, researchers have identified three basic kinds. *Sensory neurons* detect stimuli inside the body (for example, a headache or strained muscle) or in the world (for example, another person's voice) and send this information from sensory receptors to the brain. In the opposite direction, *motor neurons* send commands from the brain to glands, muscles, and organs to do, cease, or inhibit something. Finally, the vast majority of neurons are *interneurons,* which connect other neurons to one another. One of their most important functions is to link up the sensory neurons' *input* signals with the motor neurons' *output* signals.

3-1a   A Neuron Consists of a Soma, Dendrites, and an Axon

As illustrated in figure 3-1, most neurons have three basic parts (Levitan & Kaczmarek, 1991). The central part of the neuron is the **soma,** which is the Latin word for "body." This cell body contains the *nucleus,* or control center of the neuron, and other components of the cell that preserve and nourish it. Attached to the soma are branchlike extensions, known as **dendrites** (the Greek word for "trees"), that receive information from other neurons and bring it to the soma. As previously noted, each neuron may have hundreds or thousands of dendrites. After integrating this information, the soma transmits it to a tubelike extension called an **axon** (Greek for "axle"), which carries the information from the soma to the other end of the axon in the form of an electrochemical impulse (Hille, 1984). Axons can range in length from 1/32 of an inch to more than three feet. To give you some idea of the relative size and length of the soma, dendrites, and the axon of some of the longer neurons, visualize a tennis ball with a number of shoelaces attached to one side of it and a thin rope 14 miles long attached to the other side. The tennis ball

> **Soma:** The cell body of the neuron that contains the nucleus and other components that preserve and nourish it.
>
> **Dendrites:** Branchlike extensions of the soma that receive information from other neurons.
>
> **Axon:** An extension of the soma that sends information in the form of electrochemical impulses to other neurons.

FIGURE 3-1
Structure of a Neuron

The primary components of the specialized cell known as the neuron are the soma, dendrites, and axon. The soma contains the nucleus of the cell, while the dendrites receive information from other neurons, and the axon passes this information to other neurons. Do you know the range in length of our axons?

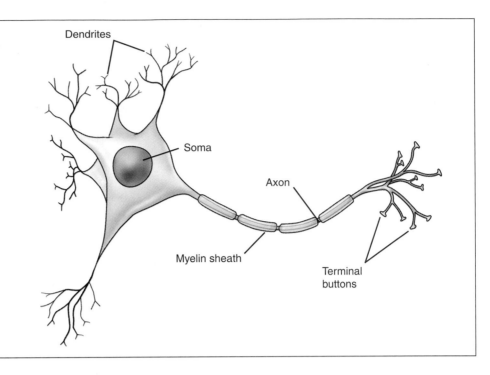

INFO-BIT: Scientists believe that the myelin sheath developed in humans as our brains evolved and became larger, making it necessary for information to travel faster over longer distances in the nervous system. Part of the reason that children cannot learn and respond as fast as adults on many cognitive and motor tasks is because their axons have not yet been fully covered by these neural speed-enhancing fatty cells.

Myelin sheath: A protective coating of fatty cells around an axon that hastens the transmission of the electrochemical charge.

Synapse: The entire area composed of the terminal button of one neuron, the synaptic cleft, and the dendrite of another neuron.

Glial cells: Non-neuron cells that supply the neurons with support, nutrients, and insulation.

is the soma, the shoelaces are the dendrites, and the long rope is the axon. Many axons are covered with a protective coating of fatty cells known as a **myelin sheath** that hasten the transmission of the electrochemical charge. In certain diseases, such as multiple sclerosis, the myelin sheath is slowly destroyed, causing impairment of brain to muscle communication and the loss of muscle control (Adams & Victor, 1993).

At the end of each axon are branches with knoblike tips called *terminal buttons* that closely approach, but do not touch, the dendrites of other neurons. The space between the axon's terminal buttons and the dendrites is less than a millionth of an inch wide and is known as the *synaptic cleft*. The entire area composed of the terminal button of one neuron, the synaptic cleft, and the dendrite of another neuron is known as the **synapse,** which in Greek means "to clasp." In a later section, we will see how neurons communicate at this synapse through a complex process of electrical and chemical (electrochemical) changes.

This brief outline of the neuron's structure is greatly simplified. In fact, there are some neurons with many axons and some without any axons at all. In addition, some neurons do not synapse on dendrites but do so on axons or somas. Despite these exceptions, in general, dendrites receive information from other neurons and pass it through the soma, then along the axon to the dendrites of other neurons at junction points called synapses. In this capacity as the receiver, integrator, and transmitter of neural information, the neuron truly earns its reputation as the workhorse of the nervous system.

One last important point. Santiago Cajal also discovered that the brain and spinal cord are not solid masses of neurons. Nerve tissue throughout the body is composed of two kinds of cells: neurons and supporting **glial cells,** which supply the neurons with support, nutrients, and insulation. Glial cells have no axons or dendrites. If you think of the brain as a house, then the glial cells are the floors, walls, and supporting beams, while the neurons are the electrical wiring. In essence, the glial cells hold the brain together, while the neurons send and receive information throughout the brain structure. The myelin sheath that covers most axons is made up of glial cells. Glial cells also help form the *blood-brain barrier*, which is a semipermeable membranelike mechanism that prevents certain chemicals in the bloodstream from reaching the brain. Interestingly, there are ten times more glial cells in the nervous system than there are neurons, although they are much smaller than neurons and constitute about half of the brain's total mass (Travis, 1994). Now that you understand the makeup of neurons and their supporting glial cells, let's examine how information travels within a single neuron.

3-1b A Neuron Is Either in a Resting or a Firing State

A neuron is always either in a resting or a firing state—there is no in-between condition. Whether the neuron fires an electrochemical impulse depends on whether the combined stimulation received by the dendrites exceed a certain minimum intensity, or *threshold*. If the threshold is exceeded, the neuron's membrane transmits an electrochemical impulse. If the threshold is not exceeded, nothing happens. This effect is known as the *all-or-none law*.

One useful way to think about a neuron is that it is like a liquid-filled balloon surrounded by a slightly different kind of liquid. The axon part of this "balloon" is stretched to form a very long, thin tube. A neuron's electrochemical impulse results from positively and negatively charged particles, called *ions*, moving back and forth through the axon's membrane walls. The important ions in the inside and outside liquids are positively charged sodium and potassium ions and negatively charged chlorine ions. When the neuron is in a resting state, the ions floating inside the axon are mostly negatively charged, while those outside the axon's membrane are mostly positively charged. The reason why there are more negative ions inside is that, in its resting state, the cell membrane of the axon does not let positive ions pass through its "gates." In this stable resting state, there is a tiny negative electrical charge—about one-twentieth of a volt, or −70 millivolts—within the axon, making it a storehouse of potential energy (Koester, 1995). When the inactive neuron is in this chemical balancing state—more positive ions outside of the membrane and more negative ions inside—its tiny electrical charge is known as the **resting potential** of a neuron.

Resting potential: The stable, negative charge of an inactive neuron.

How is this resting potential changed? As previously stated, in its resting state the axon's cell membrane does not allow positive ions through its gates. Yet, just as the negative pole of a magnet attracts the positive pole of another magnet (an event called *polarization*), the negative ions inside the axon attract positive ions along the external wall of the cell membrane. As illustrated in figure 3-2, when a neuron receives sufficient stimulation through its dendrites from other neurons, the neural membrane nearest where the axon emerges from the soma opens its gates, allowing the clustered positive sodium ions to rush in. For an instant, the charge inside this part of the axon switches from negative to positive (an event known as *depolarization*), eliminating the resting potential and sending a brief electrochemical charge or impulse down to the next section of the axon farther away from the soma. This electrical disturbance—which transpires in about one-thousandth of a second—is called the **action potential** and is analogous to a pulse of electricity traveling along a wire. As soon as the resting potential has been eliminated, the axon membrane gates in this area again open, but this time, they pump the positive

Action potential: The brief shift in a neuron's electrical charge that travels down the axon.

[The neuron is] the aristocrat among the structures of the body, with its giant arms stretched out like the tentacles of an octopus to the provinces on the frontier of the outside world, to watch for the constant ambushes of physical and chemical forces.

——Santiago Ramón y Cajal, 1852–1934,
Spanish scientist credited with first discovering the neuron

FIGURE 3-2
**Structure and Operation
of the Neuron**

When the combined stimulation received by the dendrites exceeds a certain minimum intensity, or threshold, an electrochemical impulse is transmitted down the axon. This impulse results from positively and negatively charged ions moving back and forth through the axon's membrane walls. Can you describe how depolarization occurs? How does the diameter of the axon and the myelin sheath covering it affect the speed of the impulse?

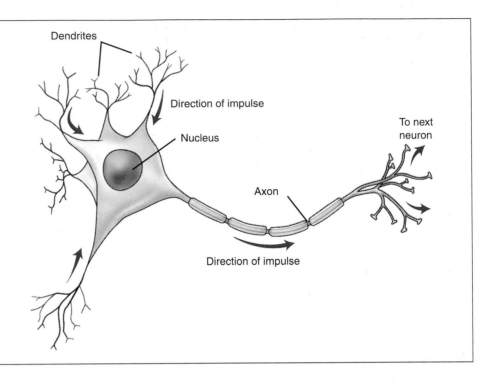

sodium ions back out, restoring the positive-outside and negative-inside polarization. At the same time this is transpiring, the action potential has traveled farther down the axon, causing the gates there to open in the next axonal section so that it too depolarizes, setting off a domino-like chain reaction down the entire length of the axon (Hall, 1992).

It is this flood of electrically charged ions in and out of each section of the axon that constitutes the neural impulse—which, remember, was all started by stimulation to threshold at the dendrite side of the neuron. In different neurons, the speed of the impulse varies from two to over two hundred miles per hour, but its speed is always constant *within* a given neuron. The larger the diameter of the axon, and the more myelin surrounding its outer surface, the faster the impulse. Although this neural impulse speed may seem fast, consider that the speed of an electric current passing through a wire is three million times faster. The fact that electrical wire transmission is so much faster than neural impulse speed explains why we can build machines that respond faster than our bodies.

Besides neurons differing in the speed at which the impulse moves down the axon, neurons also differ in their potential rate of firing. Some neurons can reachieve their action potential within milliseconds after firing and can fire as many as one thousand times per second. Other neurons take a great deal longer to recover their action potential. Thus, while it is true that a bright light or a loud sound causes a higher rate of firing in neurons than less intense stimulation, some neurons will not fire as rapidly as others due to their slow recovery rate.

3-1c Neurons Communicate with One Another by Releasing Chemicals

Now that you understand the basic operation of a single neuron, how do the billions of neurons in the nervous system work together to coordinate the body's activities? To explore this process, you need to examine how neural impulses get from one neuron to another.

As noted earlier (see section 3-1a), at the end of each axon are *terminal buttons* that closely approach, but do not touch, the dendrites of other neurons. Most of these *terminal buttons* contain a number of tiny round sacs called *synaptic vesicles*. When an action potential arrives at the axon's terminal buttons, it causes these vesicles to release varying

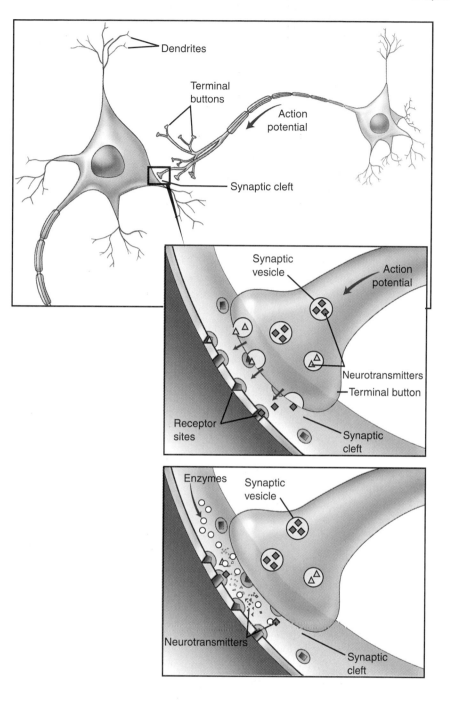

FIGURE 3-3
Synaptic Transmission

The axon's terminal buttons contain synaptic vesicles that contain chemical messengers called neurotransmitters. These neurotransmitters travel across the synaptic cleft to the receiving neuron's dendrites, where they fit into receptor sites. Excitatory neurotransmitters increase the likelihood that the receiving neuron will transmit an electrochemical impulse, while inhibitory neurotransmitters decrease this likelihood. After locking into these receptor sites, the neurotransmitters are either repackaged into new synaptic vesicles (reuptake), or they are broken down by enzymes and removed from the synaptic cleft.

amounts of chemical messengers, called **neurotransmitters,** that travel across the synaptic cleft. As the neurotransmitters arrive at the other neuron's dendrites—within 1/10,000th of a second of being released by the synaptic vesicles—they fit into *receptor sites* like keys fit into locks. Just as specific keys can fit into only specific kinds of locks, each kind of neurotransmitter has a unique chemical configuration that allows it to fit into only one specific kind of receptor site on the dendrites of the receiving neuron. This neural communication process, which is known as *synaptic transmission,* is illustrated in figure 3-3.

Once a neurotransmitter fits into a receptor site, it unlocks tiny channels that permit either positively or negatively charged ions to enter the receiving dendrite. *Excitatory* neurotransmitters increase the probability that the neuron will fire, while

Neurotransmitters: Chemical messengers released by the synaptic vesicles that travel across the synaptic cleft and either excite or inhibit adjacent neurons.

inhibitory neurotransmitters reduce the likelihood of neural firing. Because the dendrites of a neuron receive both excitatory and inhibitory messages simultaneously, whether the neuron fires will depend on which type of message is in greater abundance. If a neuron receives many more excitatory than inhibitory messages, it will fire. However, if the number of inhibitory messages is greater than the excitatory ones, the neuron will remain in a resting state.

What happens to the neurotransmitters after they lock into the receptor sites and either excite or inhibit the firing of the dendrites of the receiving neuron? This is an important question because if the neurotransmitters are not quickly removed from the synaptic cleft, they will block the transmission of any additional signals to the receiving neuron other than their own excitatory or inhibitory messages. The primary way in which the synapse is cleared is by taking the neurotransmitters back into the terminal buttons from which they came, repackaging them into new synaptic vesicles, and using them again. This recycling process, which is called *reuptake*, is also used on many of the neurotransmitters that fail to reach the receptor sites (Schwartz, 1995). When neurotransmitters are not recycled they are broken down and removed from the synaptic cleft by enzymes. Both of these means of clearing the synapse are depicted in figure 3-3.

To date, about 75 neurotransmitters have been identified, but neuroscientists believe that many more will be discovered in the future (Fishbach, 1992; Rosenzweig et al., 2002). One of the most prominent neurotransmitters identified so far is **acetylcholine (ACh),** which is an excitatory transmitter found throughout the nervous system (Cooper et al., 1991). ACh is the chemical key that transmits excitatory messages to our skeletal muscles. Its continuing presence at the appropriate receptor sites enables us not only to walk, talk, and blink our eyes but also to breathe. If it is either prevented from reaching receptor sites or too much of it floods the synapses between motor neurons and muscles, the results can be disastrous. For example, the botulin bacteria, a poison found in improperly processed food, blocks the ACh receptors, which leads to respiratory paralysis and suffocation. In contrast, the venom from a black widow spider—if of sufficient dosage—causes these same receptors to be flooded, triggering severe muscle contractions, convulsions, and even heart failure. Besides its central role in the functioning of skeletal muscles, ACh also appears to play a critical role in cognition and the formation of new memories (Hasselmo & Bower, 1993). Researchers believe that the memory loss exhibited in the degenerative brain disorder known as Alzheimer's disease—which afflicts 11 percent of people over the age of 65—is caused by a sharp reduction in the supply of this neurotransmitter (Goldman & Coté, 1991).

Another important neurotransmitter is **dopamine (DA),** which promotes and facilitates movement, as well as influencing thought and emotion. Too much or too little dopamine in the brain results in a wide variety of debilitating effects, ranging from jerky muscle movements to psychotic hallucinations (Barr, 2001). Researchers have found that degeneration of dopamine-producing neurons in the brain causes *Parkinson's disease*, a disorder affecting many elderly adults. The main symptoms of this disease are uncontrollable tremors, slowness of movement, altered body posture, and depressed mood (Rao et al., 1992). When Parkinson patients are given the L-dopa drug, their brains convert it to dopamine, and this helps them regain control over their muscles (Parkinson Study Group, 2002). Although the destruction of the brain's dopamine-producing system appears to be the cause of Parkinson's disease, increasing evidence shows that an overactive central dopamine system may be the root cause of *schizophrenia*, a psychological disorder we will examine more closely in chapter 13, section 13-3d. Drugs that block the reception of dopamine have proven effective in reducing schizophrenic symptoms in those suffering from this disorder (Julien, 1998).

One group of neurotransmitters that is important in the experience of pleasure and the control of pain are chemical substances known as **endorphins** (Hughes et al., 1975; Pert & Snyder, 1973). The brain produces endorphins in response to injury and many forms of physical stress, such as intense exercise and the labor of childbirth (Akil, 1982;

Acetylcholine (ACh):
A neurotransmitter involved in muscle contractions and memory information.

Dopamine (DA):
A neurotransmitter that promotes and facilitates movement, as well as influencing thought and emotion.

Endorphins: A family of neurotransmitters that are similar to morphine and that play an important role in the experience of pleasure and the control of pain.

Neurotransmitters	Involved in
Acetylcholine (ACh)	Stress, wakefulness, mood
Dopamine (DA)	Voluntary movement, schizophrenia, cognition, mood
Endorphins	Pain suppression, pleasure
Epinephrine	Blood pressure, heart rate
GABA (gamma-amino-butyric acid)	Relaxation, anxiety
Norepinephrine (NE)	Stress, wakefulness, mood
Serotonin	Sleep, arousal, depression, schizophrenia

TABLE 3-1

Major Neurotransmitters

Vives & Oltras, 1992). During such times of bodily stress, the increase in endorphins not only temporarily provides the body with a natural painkiller, but it may also explain the state of euphoria many runners experience following a strenuous workout, as well as the pain-reducing effects of *acupuncture*, an ancient Chinese medical technique that involves inserting needles in the body (Harte et al., 1995; Pert, 1999).

As you will discover in later chapters, other neurotransmitters play important roles in controlling aggression, sexual activity, blood pressure, sleep cycles, food and water intake, as well as learning and immune responses (see table 3-1). The mysteries of neurotransmitter functioning revealed to date will no doubt be overshadowed by the discoveries yet to come as neuroscientists continue their studies of these key factors in synaptic transmission.

SECTION SUMMARY

- Neurons are specialized cells in the nervous system that send and receive information throughout the body.
- The soma is the central part of the neuron.
- Dendrites are branchlike extensions at one end of the soma that receive electrical impulses from other neurons.
- The axon is a tubelike extension at the other end of the soma that carries impulses to other neurons.
- A neuron fires if it receives many more excitatory than inhibitory messages from other neurons.
- Neurotransmitters are chemicals that deliver excitatory or inhibitory messages to neurons.

3-2 NEURAL AND HORMONAL SYSTEMS

Now that we have examined the structure and function of neurons, let's inspect the structure and function of the nervous system that neurons combine to form. The nervous system is our body's primary information system and is divided into two major portions, the *central nervous system* and the *peripheral nervous system* (figure 3-4). One thing you will notice as you study these two divisions is that they too consist of a series of systems of twos. In addition to exploring the nervous system, we will also explore a second communication system within the body that is interconnected with the nervous system, namely the *endocrine system*.

FIGURE 3-4
The Central and Peripheral Nervous Systems

The human nervous system is divided into two major portions, the central nervous system, which consists of the brain and spinal cord, and the peripheral nervous system, which consists of the remaining nerves in the body.

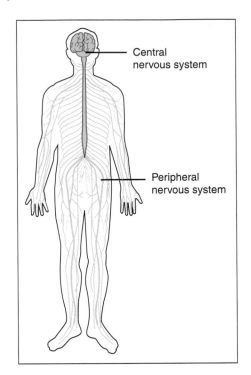

Central nervous system

Peripheral nervous system

3-2a The Peripheral Nervous System Connects the Brain and Spinal Cord with the Organs and Tissues of the Body

Peripheral nervous system: That portion of the nervous system containing all the nerves outside the brain and spinal cord.

The **peripheral nervous system** consists of all the nerves located outside the brain and spinal cord. Its function is to connect the brain and spinal cord with the organs and tissues of the body. It accomplishes this task by conducting neural impulses into and out of the central nervous system.

Because the peripheral nervous system is made up of a network of nerves, you might be wondering whether nerves are the same thing as neurons. The answer is no. While a neuron is a single cell, a **nerve** is a bundle of axons from many neurons that are routed together in the peripheral nervous system. Just as a single telephone line from your home is bundled together with thousands of other users' lines to form a telephone cable, so too are thousands of axons from many neurons bundled together to form a single nerve. Due to their sheer number, many neurons in this bundle could be destroyed without adversely affecting the nerve function, but the destruction of the entire nerve—for example, the optic nerve controlling vision—would certainly be much more problematic.

Nerve: A bundle of axons from many neurons that are routed together in the peripheral nervous system.

The peripheral nervous system is also composed of two major divisions: the somatic nervous system and the autonomic nervous system. The **somatic nervous system** transmits commands to the voluntary skeletal muscles by way of the *motor neurons* and receives sensory information from the muscles and the skin by way of the *sensory neurons* (refer back to section 3-1). The commands to the skeletal muscles control our movement, while the messages received from the muscles and the skin provide us with the sense of touch, the sense of position in our surroundings, and the perception of temperature and pain. As you read these words on the computer screen, for example, the movement of your eyes is being controlled by the somatic nervous system. Likewise, your ability to actually *see* the words and *feel* the "mouse" that is controlling what you see on the computer screen is aided by this same division of the peripheral nervous system.

Somatic nervous system: A division of the peripheral nervous system that transmits commands to the voluntary skeletal muscles and receives sensory information from the muscles and the skin.

Autonomic nervous system: A division of the peripheral nervous system that controls movement of nonskeletal muscles, such as the heart and lung muscles, over which people have little or no voluntary control.

The word *autonomic* means "self-governing." Thus, the **autonomic nervous system** commands movement of *involuntary*, nonskeletal muscles—such as the heart, lung, and stomach muscles—over which we have little or no control. The primary function of this self-governing system is to maintain *homeostasis*, the body's steady state of normal functioning.

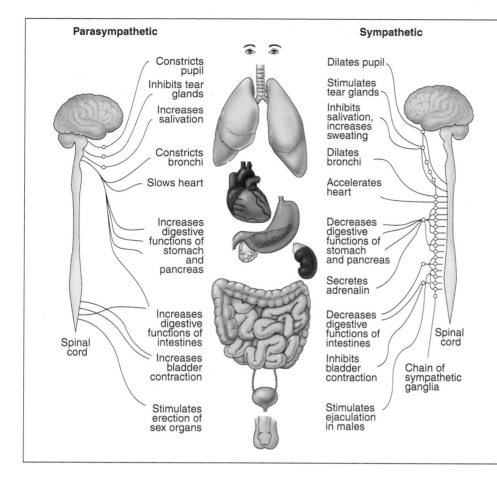

Parasympathetic

- Constricts pupil
- Inhibits tear glands
- Increases salivation
- Constricts bronchi
- Slows heart
- Increases digestive functions of stomach and pancreas
- Increases digestive functions of intestines
- Increases bladder contraction
- Stimulates erection of sex organs

Spinal cord

Sympathetic

- Dilates pupil
- Stimulates tear glands
- Inhibits salivation, increases sweating
- Dilates bronchi
- Accelerates heart
- Decreases digestive functions of stomach and pancreas
- Secretes adrenalin
- Decreases digestive functions of intestines
- Inhibits bladder contraction
- Stimulates ejaculation in males

Spinal cord

Chain of sympathetic ganglia

FIGURE 3-5

The Dual Functions of the Autonomic Nervous System

The sympathetic and parasympathetic divisions of the autonomic nervous system often stimulate opposite effects in the body's organs. The sympathetic nervous system prepares your body for action, while the parasympathetic nervous system calms the body. Can you explain how these two systems respond to threat?

The autonomic nervous system is further divided into two separate branches—the *sympathetic* and *parasympathetic* systems (figure 3-5)—that tend to work in opposition to each other in regulating many of our body functions. In general, the **sympathetic nervous system** activates the body's energy resources to deal with threatening situations. If something angers or frightens you, the sympathetic system will prepare you for "fight or flight" by slowing your digestion, accelerating your heart rate, raising your blood sugar, and cooling your body with perspiration. In contrast, the **parasympathetic nervous system** acts to conserve and maintain the body's energy resources. Thus, when the threat ceases, parasympathetic nerves slow the autonomic system back down to its normal levels of functioning.

In summarizing this discussion, it is important to emphasize that although the sympathetic and parasympathetic systems produce opposite effects, together they keep the nervous system as a whole in a steady state of normal functioning. In this case, opposites are indeed attractive . . . to our overall health (see Discovery Box 3-1).

3-2b The Spinal Cord Connects the Peripheral Nervous System to the Brain

The **central nervous system** is that portion of the nervous system located in the bony central core of the body and consists of the brain and spinal cord. Besides being encased in bone and swaddled in three protective membranes (called *meninges*), the central nervous system is further cushioned and shielded from injury by a clear solution, known as **cerebrospinal fluid,** which is secreted by the brain. The **spinal cord,** which is a bundle of nerves with the thickness of a pencil, connects the brain to the rest of the body through the peripheral nervous system (Waxman, 2001). Encased within the vertebrae of the spinal column and bathed in cerebrospinal fluid, the nerves of the spinal cord transmit information from sensory neurons up to the brain, and from the brain down to

Sympathetic nervous system: The part of the autonomic nervous system that activates the body's energy resources to deal with threatening situations.

Parasympathetic nervous system: The part of the autonomic nervous system that acts to conserve and maintain the body's energy resources.

Central nervous system: That portion of the nervous system located in the bony central core of the body and consisting of the brain and spinal cord.

Cerebrospinal fluid: A clear, cushioning fluid secreted by the brain and circulated inside and around the brain and spinal cord.

Spinal cord: The slender, tube-shaped part of the central nervous system that extends from the base of the brain, down the center of the back, and is made up of a bundle of nerves.

DISCOVERY BOX 3-1

Do You Notice the Activation of Your Sympathetic Nervous System?

The sympathetic nervous system triggers your energy resources to better respond to threatening situations. Try the following exercises to help you better notice when this aspect of your nervous system is activated:

Exercise 1: Ask someone who spends a good deal of time with you to plan a surprise in which she or he startles you while you are engaged in some quiet, relaxing, or thought-absorbing activity. For example, a startle response could be elicited by making a very loud noise while you are studying or settling down to take a nap. However it transpires, when it does occur, take note of your body's reaction. Has your heart rate accelerated? Does your stomach feel queasy? Are you perspiring? Is your mouth dry? Have your pupils dilated? How long does it take for your parasympathetic system to return your body to a steady state?

Exercise 2: Again enlist a friend to be the instigator of a specific stressor: tickling you. Lie on the floor with your eyes closed after giving your friend the following instructions: "Hover over me, and periodically tickle me. Sometimes, do so without warning, while at other times, let me know that the tickling is about to commence." While this good-natured torturing is taking place, your own instructions are to notice how your body is reacting to this situation. When this tickling session ends, how long does it take for your body to return to its normal state? Next, reverse roles with your friend and compare physiological reactions.

> **INFO-BIT:** The protective cerebrospinal fluid, which circulates inside and around the brain and spinal cord, has a specific gravity that is slightly greater than that of the brain, allowing the brain to literally float inside the skull. In this floating state, the brain's 3-pound "air weight" is reduced to only a few ounces, significantly reducing the pressure it exerts on the spinal cord. The importance of the cerebrospinal fluid in supporting and cushioning the brain is dramatically demonstrated when patients have it drained away during brain surgery. Until the brain replenishes this fluid, the patients suffer terrible headaches and experience intense pain whenever they move their heads abruptly.

motor neurons that initiate movement. Every voluntary action, such as walking and moving one's arms, requires a message from the brain to the spinal cord, and from the spinal cord to the muscles.

The spinal cord extends from the base of the brain to slightly below the waist. By and large, the upper segments of the spinal cord control the upper parts of the body, while the lower segments control the lower body. If a segment of the spinal cord is ever severed, the person loses all sensation and muscle control below the injury. Some 11,000 Americans injure their spinal cords each year. The higher along the spine an injury occurs, the greater the extent of paralysis. Thus, when actor Christopher Reeve—who played the role of Superman in several 1970/80s films—severed his spinal cord just below the base of his neck in a horse-riding accident, he not only lost the ability to breathe on his own and to move any part of his body below the injury point, but he also lost feeling in these areas as well. When such injuries occur, the central nervous system cannot repair itself. However, recent advances in medical science provide hope that the neural circuitry of the spinal cord can be regenerated. With the benefit of these advances, Reeve has recovered some sensation and muscle control below his injury.

In addition to transmitting information to and from the brain, the spinal cord also controls some automatic, involuntary responses to sensory stimuli. These **reflex** actions, of which the *knee-jerk response* is one example, involve no interaction with the brain. Thus, when you accidentally place your hand on a hot stove and immediately pull it away, your ability to respond so quickly is because your action involves no thinking—that is, no input from the brain. The pain message does continue traveling up the spinal cord to the brain, so that within a second you will respond with a cry of pain, but the action of removing your hand off the burner is achieved by the spinal nerves. Such quick reflexive responses by the spinal cord enable the body to avoid serious injury.

3-2c The Endocrine System Communicates by Secreting Hormones

The **endocrine system** is interconnected with—but not actually part of—the nervous system. It consists of a network of glands in various parts of the body that manufactures and secretes chemical messengers, known as **hormones,** directly into the bloodstream (see table 3-2). Because these hormones are carried by our blood throughout the body, and because the membrane of every cell has receptors for one or more hormones, these chemical messengers have a direct effect on many different body organs, including the brain (Elmquist, 2001; Kravitz, 1988). Hormones effecting the brain influence our interest in food, aggression, and sex. However, unlike neural impulses, which rely on electrochemical transmission and can be measured in thousandths of a second, hormonal communications traveling through the bloodstream often take minutes to reach their destinations. Although the endocrine system generally affects bodily organs more slowly than the nervous system, the effects of hormonal stimulation typically have a longer duration than that of neurotransmitters.

The most influential endocrine gland is the **pituitary gland,** a pea-sized structure located in the base of the brain and controlled by a nearby brain area called the *hypothalamus* (see section 3-3b). The pituitary is often referred to as the "master gland" because it releases about ten different hormones that stimulate and regulate the rest of the endocrine system. The pituitary gland also releases another hormone that influences growth. At puberty, the pituitary gland increases its secretion of this *growth hormone,* which acts directly on bone and muscle tissue to produce the adolescent growth spurt.

Another hormone released by the pituitary gland is *oxytocin,* which causes the uterus to contract during childbirth and the mammary glands to produce milk. Besides the role

Reflex: An automatic, involuntary response to sensory stimuli, many of which are facilitated by the spinal nerves.

Endocrine system: A network of glands in various parts of the body that manufactures and secretes hormones directly into the bloodstream.

Hormones: Chemical signals manufactured and secreted into the blood in one part of the body and that affect other parts of the body.

Pituitary gland: The body's "master" gland, located in the base of the brain, whose hormones stimulate and regulate the rest of the endocrine system.

Gland	Hormone	Effects
Pituitary gland	Growth hormone	Stimulates growth (especially bones) and metabolic functions
	Oxytocin	Stimulates contraction of uterus and mammary gland cells; may possibly promote prosocial behavior
Thyroid gland	Thyroxin	Stimulates and maintains metabolic processes
Adrenal glands	Epinephrine and norepinephrine	Increase metabolic activities and blood glucose; constrict certain blood vessels
Gonads (male testes and female ovaries)	Androgens (males), estrogens (females)	Support male sperm formation; stimulate female uterine lining growth; development and maintenance of secondary sex characteristics, such as chest hair growth in men and breast development in women

TABLE 3-2

Major Endocrine Glands and Some of Their Hormones

it plays in childbirth and nursing, animal research indicates that this hormone also influences social and sexual behavior, as well as parental behavior (Caldwell, 2002; Pedersen & Boccia, 2002). Animals who have higher levels of oxytocin more strongly desire companionship, are more sexually active, and take better care of their young than those with lower levels (Leckman & Herman, 2002; Young, 2002).

Thyroid gland: The gland, located just below the larynx in the neck, that controls metabolism.

Other notable glands in the endocrine system are the *thyroid gland*, the *adrenal glands*, and the *gonads* (see table 3-2). The **thyroid gland,** located just below the larynx in the neck, produces the hormone *thyroxin,* which controls metabolism; that is, the rate at which the food we eat is transformed into energy. People with an underactive thyroid—a condition known as *hypothyroidism*—tend to be lethargic and depressed, while those with an overactive thyroid tend to be very excitable, easily agitated, and have short attention spans (Haggerty et al., 1993).

Adrenal glands: Two glands, located near the kidneys, that secrete epinephrine and norepinephrine, which activate the sympathetic nervous system.

The **adrenal glands,** located near the kidneys, secrete *epinephrine* (also called adrenaline) and *norepinephrine* (also called noradrenaline) when you feel anxious or threatened (Thompson, 2000). These hormones complement and enhance the effects of the sympathetic nervous system, making the heart beat faster, slowing digestion, and increasing the rate at which the body uses energy. Interestingly, epinephrine and norepinephrine also act as neurotransmitters, stimulating neural firing in the sympathetic nervous system (Raven & Johnson, 1999). The fact that epinephrine and norepinephrine levels remain high following stressful events explains why it takes considerable time to calm down from such experiences.

Gonads: The two sex glands, called ovaries in females and testes in males.

Finally, the **gonads** are the two sex glands. The two male gonads are called *testes,* and they produce sperm cells, while the two female gonads are known as *ovaries,* and they produce ova, or eggs. The gonads also secrete hormones that not only are essential in sexual arousal but also contribute to the development of secondary sexual characteristics, such as chest hair growth in men and breast development in women.

SECTION SUMMARY

- The central nervous system consists of the brain and spinal cord.
- The peripheral nervous system encompasses all the nerves outside the central system.
- The two major divisions of the peripheral nervous system include the following: the somatic nervous system (transmits commands to the voluntary skeletal muscles by way of the motor neurons and receives sensory information from the muscles and the skin by way of the sensory neurons) and the autonomic nervous system (controls movement of involuntary, nonskeletal muscles, such as the heart and lung muscles).
- The autonomic nervous system is divided into two separate parts: sympathetic system—activates body's energy resources in threatening situations and the parasympathetic system—conserves and maintains body's energy resources.
- The endocrine system is a network of glands throughout the body that manufactures and secretes hormones directly into the bloodstream.

3-3 THE BRAIN

Imagine how Henry M.'s life would have been different if he was undergoing medical treatment today rather than in the 1950s when neuroscientists knew so little about the brain. One of the primary reasons we now know so much more about brain function is that contemporary neuroscientists have the ability to eavesdrop on the brain without causing it harm (Moses & Stiles, 2002; Toga & Mazziota, 1999). In this section of the chapter, before exploring specific brain regions, let us examine the different technologies used to study the brain.

3-3a Modern Technology Can Measure the Brain's Electrical Activity, Structure, Blood Flow, and Chemistry

The most widely used technique is the **electroencephalograph (EEG),** which records "waves" of electrical activity in the brain using metal electrodes placed on a person's scalp. EEG measurement has provided researchers with invaluable information on brain functioning, especially in the areas of sleep, different states of awareness, and brain disease (Russo et al., 2001). The one drawback of the EEG is that it measures the overall electrical activity of many different areas of the brain at once, making it difficult to pinpoint the exact location of specific brain wave activity.

A more revealing look at the functioning brain is obtained by *brain imaging techniques* that provide pictures—or scans—of this bodily organ. One such technique is the **computerized axial tomograph (CAT) scan,** which takes thousands of X-ray photographs of the brain while the person lies very still on a table with her or his head in the middle of a doughnut-shaped ring. Using a computer, these many X-ray images are combined to construct a cross-sectional brain picture. CAT scans are particularly helpful in detecting brain abnormalities, such as swelling and enlargement of certain areas.

Another brain imaging technique is **magnetic resonance imaging (MRI),** which produces three-dimensional images of the brain's soft tissues by detecting magnetic activity from nuclear particles in brain molecules (Senior et al., 2002). MRI provides greater accuracy in the diagnosis of diseases of the brain than does the CAT scan, and this has led to some groundbreaking discoveries. For example, as we will discuss more fully in chapter 13, section 13-3d, MRI researchers have found that there may be an association between enlarged ventricles (hollow, fluid-filled cavities) in the brain and schizophrenic disorders (Suddath et al., 1990).

Unlike CAT or MRI scans, which document the brain's structure, the **positron emission tomography (PET) scan** measures the amount of brain *activity*. Neural activity in different brain regions is measured by showing each region's consumption of glucose, a sugar that is the brain's chemical fuel. These readings are obtained by injecting a person with a safe level of radioactive glucose liquid and then monitoring its consumption in the brain. PET scans can reveal which parts of the brain are most active in such tasks as talking or listening to others, reading, listening to music, and solving math problems (Nyberg et al., 2002; Schluter et al., 2001). As such, this technique has been especially useful in revealing localization of brain function.

One disadvantage with the PET scan is that the picture of brain activity it provides is an average of the activity that occurs over several minutes. Another disadvantage is that it exposes people to small amounts of radioactivity, making extensive scanning somewhat risky. A newer technology, called **functional magnetic resonance imaging (fMRI),** does not suffer from these drawbacks (Barinaga, 1997; Georgopoulos et al., 2001). It can produce a picture of neural activity averaged over seconds, not minutes, and it measures fluctuations in naturally occurring blood oxygen levels, not fluctuations in ingested radioactive glucose. The images produced by fMRI scans are also much sharper, and thus, they can be used to identify much smaller brain structures than those of PET scans.

As you can see, all of these brain-imaging techniques are providing researchers with the means to make new discoveries about our most important body organ. Improvements in neuroscientists' ability to "peek" into the brain provides them with the necessary information to better prevent the type of surgical calamity experienced by Henry M.

Electroencephalograph (EEG): An instrument that records "waves" of electrical activity in the brain using metal electrodes placed on a person's scalp.

Computerized axial tomograph (CAT) scan: A brain-imaging technique in which thousands of X-ray photographs of the brain are taken and then combined to construct a cross-sectional brain picture.

Magnetic resonance imaging (MRI): A brain-imaging technique that produces three-dimensional images of the brain's soft tissues by detecting magnetic activity from nuclear particles in brain molecules.

Positron emission tomography (PET) scan: A brain-imaging technique that measures over several minutes the average amount of neural activity in different brain regions by showing each region's consumption of sugar glucose, the brain's chemical fuel.

Functional magnetic resonance imaging (fMRI): A brain-imaging technique that measures over a few seconds the average neural activity in different brain regions by showing fluctuations in blood oxygen levels.

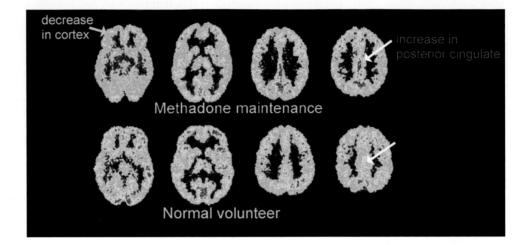

(Right) Color-coded PET scans showing rates of glucose use, a measure of brain activity in a patient treated with methadone and a normal volunteer. Methadone is a synthetic morphinelike drug used to treat drug addicts as a substitute. The patient shows the typical morphinelike lowering of brain metabolism in some cortical areas, but normal metabolic rates in many other brain areas and increased metabolic rate in the posterior cingulate, part of the brain's limbic system. Individuals may vary in their response to methadone. *(Below)* Three-dimensional image of the living brain, based on computer-enhanced MRI and PET scans highlighting the cingulate gyrus.

Photos courtesy of Monte S. Buchsbaum, M.D., Mount Sinai School of Medicine, New York, NY.

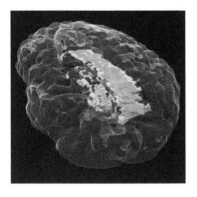

3-3b Three Major Brain Regions Are the Hindbrain, Midbrain, and Forebrain

The names for the three major brain regions—*hindbrain, midbrain,* and *forebrain*—come from their physical arrangement in the developing human embryo. In the embryo, the central nervous system begins its development as a long, hollow *neural tube,* but within five weeks, this tubular cluster of neurons changes its shape into these three distinct regions (see figure 3-6). The forebrain is the farthest forward, near where the face will develop. The midbrain comes next, just above the hindbrain, which is near the back of what will become the neck. The remainder of the neural tube develops into the spinal cord. In this section of the chapter, I first briefly describe each of these major brain regions and then focus attention on that part of the forebrain that dominates the rest of the brain, namely, the *cerebrum.*

FIGURE 3-6
Development of the Brain

During the course of embryonic development, the neural tube forms distinct regions called the forebrain, midbrain, and hindbrain. In the photograph of a five-week embryo on the right, you can see the long, hollow neural tube from which these three brain regions develop.

Photo: © Science Pictures Limited/CORBIS.

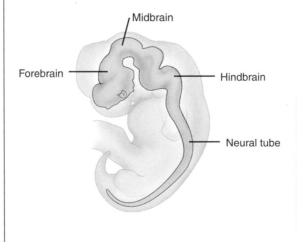

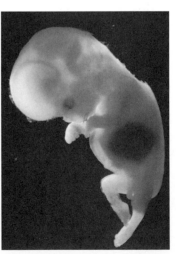

The Hindbrain

In figure 3-7, you see that located directly above the spinal cord is the **hindbrain,** which consists of the medulla, pons, and cerebellum. The **medulla,** which looks like a swelling at the top of the spinal cord, controls our breathing, heart rate, swallowing, and digestion. It also allows us to maintain an upright posture. Besides these functions, the medulla is also the place in the brain where the nerves from the left side of our body cross over to the right side of the brain, and nerves from the right side of the body cross over to the left side of the brain (Yes! We are cross-wired!). The **pons,** located just above the medulla, is concerned with sleep and arousal. Behind the medulla and pons is the **cerebellum** (meaning *little brain*), which is not only important in the regulation and coordination of body movement, but also appears to play a role in learning (Daum et al., 1993; Leiner et al., 1989). Damage to this area of the brain not only results in jerky, poorly coordinated muscle functioning, but it also causes severe disturbances in balance, gait, speech, and the control of eye movement. The *cerebellum* is also one of the first brain structures affected by alcohol, which explains why intoxicated individuals are uncoordinated and have slurred speech.

The Midbrain

The **midbrain** (see figure 3-7) is a small neural area located above the hindbrain. The most important structure in the midbrain is the **reticular formation,** a finger-shaped network of neurons involved in the regulation and maintenance of consciousness, including sleep. Actually, the reticular formation extends into the hindbrain where it makes up a portion of the pons. When you are startled by a loud noise, it is the reticular formation that causes your heightened state of arousal (Steriade et al., 1980). Likewise, when you sleep through familiar sounds in your surroundings, it again is the reticular formation that filters out these background noises. The reticular formation's ability to respond to incoming stimuli can be shut down. This is exactly the function of anesthetics used in surgery. *Anesthetics* are chemicals that prevent certain "locks" from being opened at the synaptic level. Also, if the reticular formation is damaged, it can result in a permanent coma.

Hindbrain: Region of the brain above the spinal cord that contains the medulla, pons, and cerebellum.

Medulla: A part of the hindbrain that controls breathing, heart rate, swallowing, and digestion, as well as allowing us to maintain an upright posture.

Pons: A part of the hindbrain that is concerned with sleep and arousal.

Cerebellum: A part of the hindbrain that regulates and coordinates basic motor activities and may also play a role in learning.

Midbrain: Region of the brain above the hindbrain that contains the reticular formation.

Reticular formation: A part of the midbrain involved in the regulation and maintenance of consciousness.

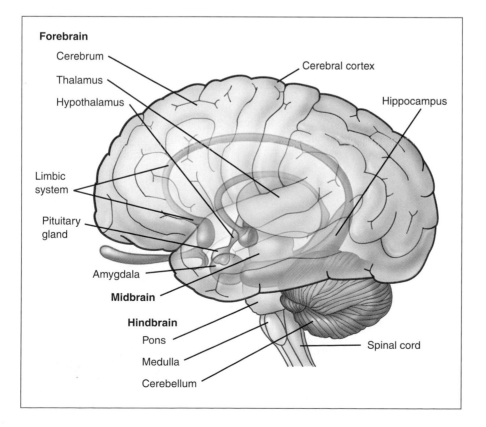

F I G U R E   3 - 7
Main Parts of the Human Brain

You have probably heard the following statement many times: "We use only 10 percent of our brain." Based on what you have learned about brain functioning, do you think that this statement is true? In pondering the merits of this expression, consider another type of human functioning: athletic performance. Do athletes use only 10 percent of their muscles when competing?

INFO-BIT: Would it surprise you to learn that about 200,000 neurons in your brain die each day of your life? It's true. Fortunately, because you are born with so many neurons and because some neurons are replenished, you will only lose about 6 percent of your original supply over 80 years (Dowling, 1992).

The Forebrain

As we move up past the first two brain regions, we come to the most interesting—and the most evolutionarily recent—region, namely, the **forebrain.** The forebrain allows us to engage in complex emotional reactions, cognitive processes, and movement patterns. It consists of such important structures as the *thalamus, hypothalamus,* and *limbic system.* On top of them is the *cerebrum,* the most complex part of the brain.

The **thalamus,** looking like a joined pair of eggs, is the brain's sensory relay station, sorting and sending messages from the eyes, ears, tongue, and skin to the cerebral cortex. The thalamus, working closely with the reticular formation, also plays an important role in the control of sleep and wakefulness. The **hypothalamus** (*hypo* means "beneath") is located under the thalamus and is less that one-tenth its size (less than one cubic centimeter). One of its most important functions is to provide *homeostasis*—the maintenance of a constant internal body state. Your relatively steady body temperature is a direct result of the hypothalamus. This small brain structure also regulates several motivated behaviors, including eating, drinking, and sexual activity. Last but not least, the hypothalamus regulates the release of hormones from the pituitary gland. All in all, this is one cubic centimeter of the brain that you cannot function without.

A series of interrelated doughnut-shaped neural structures, located at the border of the brain's older parts and the soon-to-be-discussed *cerebral cortex,* is the **limbic system.** Its two main structures are the *amygdala* and *hippocampus.* The amygdala (which means "almond" in Greek) consists of two almond-shaped neural clusters that influence fear and aggression. Damage to—or electrical stimulation of—this part of the brain can result in either intense fear or uncontrollable rage, depending on what part of the amygdala is activated. Such damage can also short-circuit these feelings: For example, monkeys with destroyed amygdalas lose their fear of natural predators. The other limbic structure, the hippocampus, is central in the acquisition and consolidation of new information in memory (Gabrieli, 1998; Gluck & Myers, 2001). This is exactly the part of the brain that was surgically removed in Henry M. to control his seizures, leaving him unable to form new memories.

As you have learned, many vital functions are controlled and regulated by the hindbrain, midbrain, and selected parts of the forebrain. Yet, despite the complexity of these different brain areas, what sets us apart from all other animals and makes us "humans" is the forebrain structure known as the *cerebrum,* which is the subject of the next chapter section.

3-3c The Cerebrum Is the Crowning Achievement of Human Evolution

Among primates, there are five different groups, including prosimians, new-world monkeys, old-world monkeys, apes, and hominids. *Homo sapiens* (or humans) are the only surviving species of the hominid line (Andrews, 1986; Gould, 1991). Approximately 5 to 7 million years ago, hominids and apes diverged in their evolutionary lineage when hominids became *bipedal,* that is, developed the habit of walking on two legs (Lemonick

Forebrain: Region of the brain above the midbrain that contains the thalamus, hypothalamus, and limbic system.

Thalamus: A part of the forebrain that is the brain's sensory relay station, sending messages from the senses to higher parts of the brain.

Hypothalamus: A part of the forebrain involved in regulating basic biological processes, such as eating, drinking, sexual activity, emotion, and a stable body temperature.

Limbic system: A part of the forebrain consisting of structures that influence fear and aggression (amygdala) and the acquisition and consolidation of new information in memory (hippocampus).

My own brain is to me the most unaccountable of machinery—always buzzing, humming, soaring, roaring, diving, and then buried in mud. And why? What's this passion for?

—Virginia Woolf (1882–1941), British novelist

INFO-BIT: Mammals are about 10 times brainier than reptiles and amphibians. Two orders of mammals have significantly larger brains than the rest: primates and toothed whales. Among the primates, the brain of humans is three times bigger than that of an ape of the same body size (Lewin, 1993).

& Dorfman, 2002). Besides the ability to walk erect, the second important adaptation in the evolution of our species was the increase in our brain size (Eccles, 1989). The most dramatic differences between humans and other animals can be seen in the relative sizes of the brain stem—which includes the hindbrain and midbrain—and the cerebrum. As previously discussed, the brain stem regulates basic life processes, while the **cerebrum,** located at the uppermost portion of the forebrain, is the "thinking" center of the brain. What coordinates and integrates all other brain areas into a fully functioning brain unit is the thin outer surface of the cerebrum, known as the **cerebral cortex.**

The *cerebral cortex* contains about 80 percent of the brain's total mass (Kolb & Whishaw, 1990). Its name is derived from two Latin words, *cerebrum*—meaning "brain"— and *cortex*—meaning "bark." Basically, this is the part of the brain that looks like the bark of a tree. It has a gray appearance because it primarily contains gray nerve cell bodies and unmyelinated fibers. Although it is only one-eighth of an inch thick, this densely packed system of interneurons is mostly responsible for our ability to plan, reason, remember, speak, and analyze ourselves. As you can see in figure 3-7, the cortex in humans has a great number of *convolutions* (folds), allowing a greater volume of it to fit into the skull cavity.

The relative sizes of the cerebrum and brain stem of species with different evolutionary ages indicates that most of the growth has occurred in the cerebrum. Not only do humans have a larger cerebrum than other species, but a human's cerebrum also has a great deal more convolutions on the cerebral cortex. About 90 percent of our cerebral cortex is of relatively recent evolution.

3-3d   The Cerebral Cortex Consists of Specialized, Interactive Regions or "Lobes"

The cerebral cortex is divided into two rounded halves, called the **cerebral hemispheres.** These hemispheres are connected together at the bottom by the **corpus callosum,** a thick band of over 200 million white nerve fibers that transmit information between the two hemispheres (figure 3-8). As mentioned earlier, our brain is cross-wired, meaning that the right hemisphere controls movement and feeling of the left side of the body, and the left hemisphere controls the right side of the body.

Both hemispheres can be divided into four major sections called *lobes:* the frontal, parietal, temporal, and occipital (see figure 3-9). Thus, you have a right and a left lobe of each of these hemispheric divisions. These lobes are not distinct, independent parts of the cortex, but rather, are convenient regions named for the bones of the skull covering them. The **occipital lobes,** located at the back of the cerebral hemispheres, are the visual regions of the brain. Here, we experience shapes, color, and motion in our world. Damage to the occipital lobes can cause blindness, even if our eyes and optic nerves are healthy. The **parietal lobes,** situated in front of the occipital lobes, are involved in touch sensation and in monitoring the body's position in space. Damage to these brain regions can destroy people's sense of touch, making it impossible for them to feel objects placed in their hands. The **temporal lobes** are located below the parietal lobes, near the temples

Cerebrum: The uppermost portion of the forebrain, which is the "thinking" center of the brain.

Cerebral cortex: The thin, outer surface of the cerebrum, containing about 80 percent of the brain's total mass; largely responsible for higher-order mental processes.

Cerebral hemispheres: The two main parts of the cerebral cortex.

Corpus callosum: A thick band of nerve fibers connecting the right and left cerebral hemispheres that transmits information between them.

Occipital lobes: One of the four major sections of the cerebral cortex, located at the back of the cerebral hemispheres, that is primarily responsible for visual processing.

Parietal lobes: One of the four major sections of the cerebral cortex, situated in front of the occipital lobes, that is involved in touch sensation and in monitoring the body's position in space.

Temporal lobes: One of the four major sections of the cerebral cortex, located below the parietal lobes and near the temples, that is important in audition and language.

FIGURE 3-8
The Corpus Callosum

The corpus callosum is the dense band of nerve fibers connecting the right and left cerebral hemispheres. What would happen if this transmission bridge were cut?

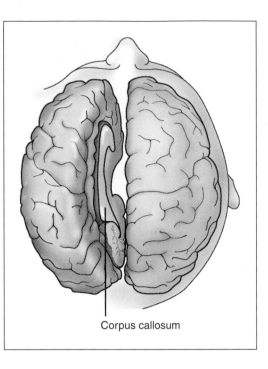

Corpus callosum

FIGURE 3-9
The Lobes of the Cerebral Cortex

Each hemisphere of the cerebral cortex can be divided into four lobes: the occipital lobe, the parietal lobe, the temporal lobe, and the frontal lobe. Do these lobes represent distinct, independent parts of the cortex?

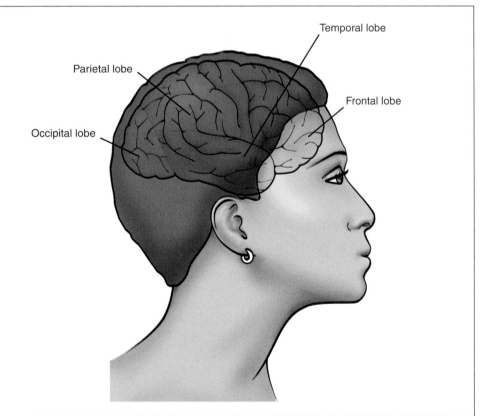

Temporal lobe

Parietal lobe

Frontal lobe

Occipital lobe

Frontal lobes: One of the four major sections of the cerebral cortex, situated in the front of the cerebral hemispheres and behind the forehead, that is involved in the coordination of movement and higher mental processes.

(hence, the name). These regions of the cerebral hemispheres are important in audition (hearing) and language. Damage to what is called *Wernicke's area* in the left temporal lobe can cause difficulty understanding what words and sentences mean. People with such damage may speak smoothly and expressively, but their sentences consist merely of "word salad," which is meaningless words strung together. Finally, the largest lobes in the human brain are the **frontal lobes,** which are situated in the "front" of the cerebral hemispheres,

Using measurements of Phineas Gage's skull and modern neuroimaging techniques, Hanna Damasio and her coworkers (1994) reconstructed Gage's accident and the likely path taken by the metal tamping rod as it traveled through his brain.

AP/Wide World Photos.

just behind the forehead. These regions of the cerebral cortex are involved in the coordination of movement and higher mental processes, such as planning, social skills, and abstract thinking (Goldberg, 2001).

Damage to the frontal lobes can result in dramatic personality changes, as was first discovered in 1848 when a Vermont railroad worker named Phineas Gage suffered severe damage to this area of his brain. While using an iron tamping rod to pack gunpowder into a boulder, Gage accidentally ignited the gunpowder, rocketing the tamping rod up into his left cheek, through the frontal lobe of his brain, and out the top of his head. Unbelievably, Gage survived this accident and was pronounced cured in less than two months. Yet, despite his outward recovery, Gage no longer possessed the same personality. Before the accident, he was a friendly, popular, hardworking, and emotionally mature adult. Following the accident, he was irresponsible, disrespectful, profane, and unable to control his own impulses. In later studies of patients with similar frontal damage, researchers found that they not only are unable to make sound decisions in their personal lives, but they also lack the ability to experience strong emotions (Damasio, 1994; Russell & Roxanas, 1990). Although these people might have been warm, loving, considerate, and responsible individuals prior to their illness or accident, they are now uniformly cold, distant, inconsiderate, and irresponsible. This decline in their reasoning and emotional abilities does not affect basic attention, memory, intelligence, and language ability. But now they are no longer who they once were.

This link between the frontal lobes and emotional expression was further explored in an interesting set of studies conducted by Richard Davidson and his colleagues (Henriques & Davidson, 1990; Tomarken et al., 1990). Testing both infants and adults, they found that the left frontal lobe governs more positive feelings, while the right frontal lobe controls more negative moods, even as early as 10 months of age. They also discovered that people with more active left frontal lobes tend to be happier, more cheerful, optimistic, sociable, and self-confident than those with more active right frontal lobes.

3-3e The Right and Left Cerebral Hemispheres Function Differently

Beyond damage to the lobes of the cerebral cortex, what would happen if these brain regions were healthy but the right and left hemispheres could not transmit information to each other through the bundle of nerves that make up the corpus callosum? This was exactly the question asked by psychologists Roger Sperry (1964, 1968) and Michael Gazzaniga (1970, 1989) when they began studying *split-brain patients*. These were patients who, in most cases, had the nerves of their corpus callosum surgically cut in a now-outmoded treatment for severe epileptic seizures. The technique was drastic, but the patients did improve rapidly, and their personality and behavior did not undergo major changes. However, now these patients had two brain hemispheres acting more or less independently. What Sperry and his colleagues found was that these patients essentially had two brains that controlled different cognitive and behavioral functions. The degree to which the right or left hemispheres control various cognitive and behavioral functions is known as **cerebral lateralization** (Morin, 2001; Spence et al., 2001).

The practical problem with a severed corpus callosum for split-brain patients is that sometimes one hemisphere will initiate a behavior that conflicts with the other hemisphere's intentions. Now, without a direct line of communication between the right and left hemispheres, each has its own separate and private sensations, perceptions, and impulses to act (Bogen, 2000). For example, shortly following surgery, split-brain patients were often surprised to find that while dressing, their right hands (controlled by the left hemisphere) would reach for one article of clothing only to be brushed aside by their left hands (controlled by the right hemisphere), which had a different choice in mind. Despite these occasional hemispheric conflicts, split-brain patients generally behave normally (Iaccino, 1993).

When split-brain patients are studied in the laboratory, certain interesting effects have provided scientists with a clearer understanding of the right and left hemispheres' abilities (Gazzaniga & Miller, 2000; Walsh, 2000). For example, in one experiment, Gazzaniga (1967) had split-brain participants stare at a dot while the word *HEART* was flashed across their visual field, with *HE* in the left visual field of each eye (which is processed by the right hemisphere) and *ART* in the right visual field (which is processed by the left hemisphere). The word could be seen for only about 150 milliseconds, providing insufficient time for the eyes to move and process the entire word in each hemisphere. Participants were first asked to report verbally what they saw, and then to indicate with their left hands what they saw. When people with intact corpus callosums perform this task, the right and left hemispheres pass the different information between them and the word *HEART* is seen and reported. Yet, with split-brain persons, something very interesting occurs. As depicted in figure 3-10, split-brain individuals said they saw the word *ART*, but their left hands pointed to the word *HE*.

Cerebral lateralization: The degree to which the right or left hemispheres control various cognitive and behavioral functions.

FIGURE 3-10
Testing the Split Brain

When the word HEART flashes across the visual field of split-brain patients, they verbally report seeing the portion of the word transmitted to their left hemispheres (ART). However, when asked to indicate with their left hands what they saw, they point to the portion of the word transmitted to their right hemispheres (HE).

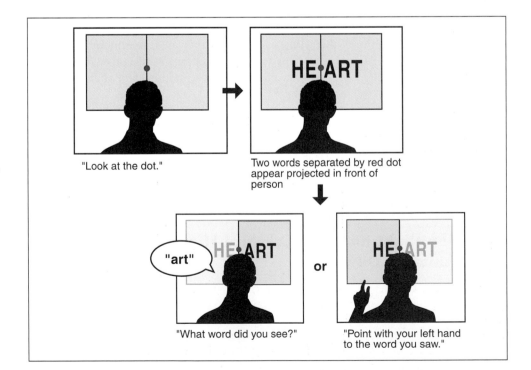

"Look at the dot."

Two words separated by red dot appear projected in front of person

"art"

"What word did you see?"

or

"Point with your left hand to the word you saw."

On another task in this same study, when the word *PENCIL* was flashed in their right visual field, the split-brain participants could easily read aloud the word, but not when it was flashed in their left visual field. What Gazzaniga discovered was that the right hemisphere did perceive and comprehend the word *PENCIL,* but the participants could not verbalize what they saw. However, using the left hand—which was controlled by the right hemisphere—the split-brain participants could easily pick out a pencil from a host of unseen objects.

Further research on the intact brain using brain imaging techniques examined in greater detail the question of cerebral lateralization (Berninger et al., 2002; Federmeier & Kutas, 2002). Although generalizations should be made with caution, it appears that the right hemisphere is superior to the left in visual and spatial tasks, recognizing nonlinguistic sounds (such as music and environmental noise), identifying faces, and perceiving and expressing emotions (Keenan et al., 2001; McAuliffe & Knowlton, 2001). In contrast, the left hemisphere excels at language, logic, and providing explanations for events (Best & Avery, 1999; Hellige, 1993). Indeed, Gazzaniga (1988) describes the left hemisphere as being the brain's "interpreter," always striving to assign some rational meaning to behavior, even when there is none. Thus, when reading a map, listening to music, looking for a friend in a crowd, or laughing and crying at life's ups and downs, it's likely that there is more neural firing occurring in your right hemisphere than in your left hemisphere. In contrast, when talking on the phone, balancing your checkbook, or explaining to your parents why you need extra money for your spring vacation, your left hemisphere is probably the most active.

Having made the case that the two hemispheres appear to be more in control of certain functions than the other, it is important to add that these different specialized abilities are almost always relative differences, not absolute differences (Reuter-Lorenz & Miller, 1998). That is, whatever task we work on, both hemispheres are activated to some extent. (See Discovery Box 3-2.) It is this literal "side-by-side" exchange of information that is the hallmark of the healthy brain (Banich, 1998; Gazzaniga, 2000).

3-3f There May Be Sex Differences in Hemispheric Organization

Try two simple tasks. First, mentally run through the alphabet and count as quickly as possible the number of letters, including the letter *e,* that when silently pronounced contain the sound "ee." Next, and again as quickly as possible, mentally count the number of letters that contain curves when they are printed as capitals. Writing or speaking out loud is not permitted.

Which task was harder for you, counting sounds or counting curves? Your answer may partly depend on whether you are a woman or a man. Women tend to be more accurate and slightly faster in the sound task, while men tend to do better in the shape task, which suggests that there are sex differences in verbal and spatial abilities (Coltheart et al., 1975; Kimura, 1992). Because language abilities are more associated with the left hemisphere and spatial abilities are more closely aligned with right hemispheric functioning, researchers wondered whether women and men differ in hemispheric dominance.

If the cerebral hemispheres function somewhat differently in women and men, it is likely that these differences will be reflected in the effects of brain injury. Support for this reasoning comes from studies of damage to the left hemisphere following stroke. A stroke causes damage to the brain by starving it of needed oxygen when its blood supply is temporarily interrupted. Men are three times more likely than women to develop **aphasia,** which is the inability to recognize or express language (McGlone, 1978). Some studies suggest that the reason women are less susceptible to aphasia is that their brains are more *bilateralized* for language—that is, they are more likely than men to use both hemispheres for this cognitive function (Bryden, 1979; Reuter-Lorenz & Miller, 1998). For instance, when women and men were asked to process and compare sounds, PET scans indicated that an area of the left hemisphere was activated in both sexes. However, in a majority of

Aphasia: The inability to recognize or express language as a result of damage to brain tissue, such as after a stroke.

DISCOVERY BOX 3-2

Do You and Your Friends Use Different Patterns of Brain Activity to Recognize One Anothers' Faces?

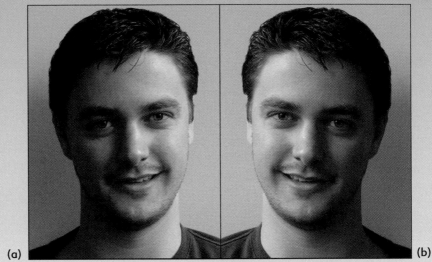

(a) (b)

Which of these faces looks happier to you?

If you are like most people, you perceive the face in photo (b), with the smile on the left, as the happier face. This is so because most people tend to be more accurate in recognizing visual stimuli presented to the left visual field, which is processed first in the right hemisphere. Exercises like this one suggest that the right hemisphere generally plays a larger role in recognition of facial expression than the left hemisphere (Levy et al., 1983). Of course, because virtually everybody has an intact corpus callosum, after a very brief interval, both hemispheres will share this information. Yet until they do, the right hemisphere will exert greater influence in recognizing facial features.

Is right hemispheric dominance for facial expression true for everyone? No. Some people fail to show a left visual field advantage, while others actually demonstrate an advantage for the right visual field. To demonstrate individual differences in the lateralization of brain function, ask as many people as possible to complete this exercise. Are there any of them who do not show this right-hemisphere preference?

the women—but in none of the men—the same area in the right hemisphere was also activated (Shaywitz et al., 1995). This study's finding that women's language functions are less likely to be located solely in the left hemisphere of the brain (less lateralized) may explain why women experience fewer language deficits than men when their left hemispheres are damaged by stroke. It may also partly explain why women tend to be less adept at spatial tasks than men. Put simply, because the right hemisphere tends to control spatial functioning, and because women are more likely than men to also use part of this hemisphere for language functioning, this bilaterality in language function may result in less proficient processing of spatial tasks (Sanders et al., 2002).

Not only is there evidence that women's brains are less lateralized, but some studies further suggest that their left hemispheres may be organized differently than men's. Although it is still not known *why* the left hemisphere might be organized differently for women and men, some researchers have focused attention on hormonal influences during brain development and early childhood (Gerschwind & Galaburda, 1987; Hines, 1982). A few studies even suggest that during high-estrogen periods of the menstrual cycle, women's spatial abilities are not as acute as at other times (Kimura, 1987; Kimura & Hampson, 1994). In assessing these possible sex differences, one thing to keep in mind is that they not only appear to be very small, but the similarities in brain function between women and men far outweigh the differences (Riger, 1992; Rogers, 2001). What might explain these differences?

Although scientific inquiry has yet to yield a widely accepted explanation for why women's and men's brains appear to be organized somewhat differently, Jerre Levy (1972) suggests that evolutionary pressures may have played a decisive role. That is, because our species evolved with women being principally responsible for raising the young, verbal bilateralization may have given them a more developed communication system that fostered their survival. In contrast, because men have historically been more involved in the hunting and gathering of food and other resources, having male spatial functioning clearly separate from verbal functioning in the brain may also have benefited their survival. Levy states that although this different hemispheric arrangement between women and men may no longer provide any survival value for us, we still inherit and exhibit these biological differences.

Despite the fact that there is evidence of sex differences in brain organization, no one knows what these differences mean for the general abilities and behavior of women and men in their daily lives (Hoptman & Davidson, 1994). It is also true that culture profoundly shapes people's skills and interests, and the different manner in which girls and boys are typically socialized often has an important impact on what specific abilities are nurtured. The greater verbal abilities of females, for example, may have nothing at all to do with evolutionary factors, and more to do with the fact that girls receive greater encouragement to talk during infancy and early childhood (Brody & Hall, 1993; Lewis & Weintraub, 1979). It's possible that this relatively high amount of verbal attention relative to boys may foster greater elaboration of neural interconnections in certain areas of the brain.

Are There "Left-Brain" and "Right-Brain" People?

As previously discussed, it appears that the left hemisphere exerts a greater influence on verbal skills such as reading, writing, math, and logic, while the right hemisphere exercises greater control over nonverbal activities such as spatial tasks, music, art, and face recognition. These findings of hemispheric specialization have led a number of popular writers to claim that some people are logical and scientific because they rely mostly on their left hemispheres ("left-brainers"), while others are creative and artistic because they mostly use their right hemispheres ("right brainers"). Armed with such a simple explanation, these same writers have written popular books with such titles as *Educating the Right Brain*, *Drawing on the Right Side of the Brain*, and *The Other Side of the Mind*, in which they give advice on how to increase creative thinking by both tapping into unused right brain potential and suppressing left brain activity. Despite the simplistic appeal of these books, there is no sound evidence that individuals significantly differ in their sheer reliance on one hemisphere over the other (Hellige, 1990; Springer & Deutsch, 1998). In addition, these books are based on the incorrect assumption that various cognitive functions are completely localized within the left and right hemispheres. Yet, what you have learned in this chapter is that, while certain tasks may activate one hemisphere somewhat more than the other, both hemispheres are involved in the completion of any task a person might perform. Thus, the idea that a given person significantly relies more on one hemisphere than on the other, or that you can train yourself to activate and suppress hemispheric functioning, remain interesting, but wholly unconfirmed, hypotheses (Corballis, 1999).

3-3g The Brain Can Alter Its Neural Connections

What happens when one part of the brain is severely damaged or destroyed? Are the cognitive functions associated with that brain area lost forever? The answers to these questions are partly being found by following the remarkable lives of children who have undergone *hemispherectomies*—having one of their cerebral hemispheres surgically removed to control life-threatening epileptic seizures. Although this surgery may appear even more foolhardy than the procedure performed on Henry M. 50 years ago, because of the advances made in neuroscience, we now know a great deal more about how the brain functions (Gazzaniga, 2000). Specifically, we understand that although normal functioning is not possible without a hippocampus, it is possible to live a relatively normal life even following the loss of an entire cerebral hemisphere (Battro, 2001). For example, in the case of hemispherectomies of the left cerebral hemisphere, although half the skull is now filled with nothing but cerebrospinal fluid, the only visible effects of the operation are often a slight limp, limited use of one of the hands and arms, no right peripheral vision in either eye, and some language deficits (Curtiss et al., 2001). In fact, brain scans indicate that the remaining healthy hemisphere takes over many of the functions of the removed hemisphere (Rossini & Pauri, 2000; Swerdlow, 1995).

This transferring of neural function is probably due to the accelerated growth of dendrites that provide the connections between neurons. Just like other children with normal brains, these children's production of dendrites are at a peak level from about age 4 to age 10. Besides neural connections being caused by inherited growth patterns, they are also fostered by environmental challenges, which is exactly why children who undergo this procedure are pushed so hard during their weekly speech and language therapy sessions. As more connections are made among the billions of neurons in their remaining brain regions, the end result is a better-functioning brain. Indeed, children who have had one of their brain hemispheres removed have later earned college degrees and are currently leading successful and productive lives as adults (Battro, 2001; Vining et al., 1997).

These children's extraordinary recovery from such a dramatic loss of brain tissue demonstrates what neuroscientists call *plasticity*—the remarkable flexibility of the brain to alter its neural connections (Stein et al., 1995). Through such *collateral growth* (figure 3-11), branches from the axons of nearby healthy neurons grow into the pathways previously occupied by the axons of damaged neurons (Bach-y-Rita, 1990). This ability to transfer brain functions from one part of the brain to the other is highest in childhood, during the peak years of dendrite growth (Leonard et al., 1996; Scharff, 2000). Yet, it is also true that limited transfer of function can occur in older adults, when certain brain areas are destroyed by strokes or accidents (Cotman, 1990; Kempermann & Gage, 1999). (See Discovery Box 3-3.) One of the important lessons learned in this chapter is simple, yet profound: Exercising the brain at all stages of life increases its ability to adapt to and overcome life's challenges and hard knocks.

Journey of Discovery Question

In the case of limbs that have been amputated, amputees often feel excruciating pain in the area of their lost limb. How might the brain's plasticity play a role in this pain?

The brain is wider than the sky.

—Emily Dickinson (1830–1886), U.S. poet

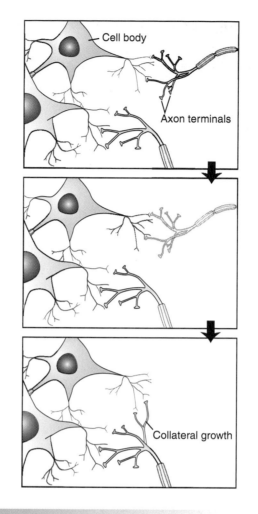

FIGURE 3-11
Collateral Growth

The brain's plasticity is demonstrated by the way in which neural connections are altered when neurons are damaged. This collateral growth is highest in childhood, when dendrite growth is at its peak.

SECTION SUMMARY

- Technology allows us to examine the brain's electrical activity, structure, blood flow, and chemistry.

- There are three major brain regions: the hindbrain, located above the spinal cord and consisting of the medulla, pons, and cerebellum; the midbrain, which contains the reticular formation and is located above the hindbrain; and the forebrain, which consists of the thalamus, hypothalamus, limbic system, and the cerebrum and is located above the midbrain.

- The cerebral cortex is the thin outer surface of the cerebrum, which coordinates and integrates all other brain areas and is mostly responsible for our ability to plan, reason, remember, speak, and analyze ourselves.

- The cerebral cortex is divided into two rounded halves, called the cerebral hemispheres.

- The left and right cerebral hemispheres are both divided into four major sections: frontal lobe, parietal lobe, temporal lobe, and occipital lobe.

- The right hemisphere is superior to the left in visual and spatial tasks, recognizing nonlinguistic sounds, identifying faces, and perceiving and expressing emotions.

- The left hemisphere excels at language, logic, and providing explanations for events.

- Women's brains may be less lateralized—less likely to have various brain functions located in only one of the hemispheres—than men's brains.

- The brain can alter its neural connections to compensate for damage.

DISCOVERY BOX 3-3

How Can You Keep Your Brain Healthy As You Age?

Scientists once believed that brain structures ceased any positive physical development by early adulthood. Yet, this thinking changed following a series of studies that suggested a very different developmental pattern. In this research, rats with an age equivalent to that of 75 human years were moved from the impoverished physical environment they had lived in all their lives (bare cage, simple food containers) to an enriched environment (spacious home, interesting playthings). By the time they reached the equivalent of 90 human years, these rats showed significant increases in brain growth and synaptic interconnections (Diamond, 1988). These findings, which mirror the results of studies with baby rats, adult monkeys, and other species, suggest that environmental enrichment significantly enhances brain functioning, even among the elderly (Gould et al., 1999; Rosenzweig, 1984). What this means is that although we may not be able to train one side of the brain to turn on and off like a light switch, we can make life choices that will improve the longevity of the 3-pound neural network enclosed within our skull (Drachman, 1997; Mahoney & Restak, 1998).

Neuroscientific research suggests the following lifelong strategies to maintain a healthy brain at any age:

1. *Avoid harmful substances:* Drug abuse and alcohol abuse damage brain cells (Kish, 2002; Torvik et al., 1982).
2. *Exercise on a regular basis:* People who engage in strenuous physical activity throughout their lives are not only more likely to stay physically healthy, but they are also more likely to maintain high cognitive functioning (Rowe & Kahn, 1998). The type of exercise that has the greatest benefit to brain longevity is that which requires the use of complex motor skills and focused attention, rather than the repetition of simple motor skills (Kolb & Whishaw, 1998). Thus, playing tennis or soccer might be better for your brain than simply doing jumping jacks or running on a treadmill.
3. *Eat sensibly:* Dietary factors are associated with the incidence of stroke, which is the largest single cause of brain disabilities. In your diet, decrease the intake of saturated fat, and eat more fruits and vegetables (Bidlack, 1996).
4. *Challenge yourself mentally:* When it comes to the brain, the old adage "Use it or lose it" really does apply. People with more formal schooling tend to maintain higher mental functioning in their seventies than those with less schooling (Jacobs et al., 1993). Staying mentally active by reading regularly and learning new skills strengthens neural connections in a similar manner as regular physical exercise strengthens the heart (White et al., 1994).

Phenotype: The visible and measurable traits of an organism.

Genotype: The underlying genetic composition of an organism.

3-4 GENETIC INFLUENCES ON BEHAVIOR

Having examined the neural basis of human functioning, let us now turn our attention to the influence of genetics on human functioning. The primary question I want to address in this section of the chapter is how the visible and measurable traits (**phenotype**) of an organism reflect its underlying genetic composition (**genotype**).

3-4a The Basic Biochemical Unit of Inheritance Is the Gene

In 2003, geneticists are expected to complete the Human Genome Project, which is identifying all the genetic material in humans. The focus of this project is the **gene,** which is the biochemical unit of inheritance (Johnston & Edwards, 2002). Genes are located on and transmitted by **chromosomes,** which are threadlike structures found in every cell of the body, with the exception of red blood cells. All chromosomes contain strands of the molecule **deoxyribonucleic acid,** commonly known as **DNA,** which contains thousands of different genes, located at fixed positions (see figure 3-12).

DNA structural similarity between species provides scientists with important clues concerning how closely related they are on the evolutionary tree. For example, humans and chimpanzees share 98 percent of the same DNA structure, humans and gorillas share a bit less than 98 percent, and humans' and monkeys' DNA similarity is only about 90 percent. Coupled with the fossil record studies of these species, the DNA evidence indicates that monkeys diverged from humans much earlier in their evolutionary past than did chimps and gorillas.

All humans possess 99.9 percent of the same genes, which is why we have the capacity to do many of the same things, such as walking, talking, and engaging in abstract thought (Plomin & Crabbe, 2000; Wade, 1999). Despite this genetic similarity, there also is a great deal of genetic variation across individuals in that final one-tenth of 1 percent of genetic material. As you have already discovered in the chapter 1, section 1-3e discussion of the evolutionary process, the genetic makeup of organisms not only determines their ability to survive in their environment, but it also influences their ability to reproduce and pass their genes on to the next generation.

How did you inherit your particular genotype? Putting it simply, each sperm cell of a human male and egg cell of a human female contains 23 chromosomes. Upon the union of your father's sperm and your mother's egg at conception, all body cells that developed from this new cell (called the *zygote*) contained 46 chromosomes, or 23 pairs. Each of these body cells contained your genetic blueprint, or genotype, with half the genetic material coming from each parent. Among the 23 chromosomal pairs, one pair, known as the **sex chromosomes,** determined your sex. You inherited an X chromosome from your mother and either an X or Y chromosome from your father. XX pairings result in the embryo developing female physical characteristics, while XY pairings lead to male physical characteristics. Because it is only the father's sex chromosome that varies, it is your father's genetic contribution that determined your sex.

Just as you share 50 percent of the same genes with each of your parents, you also share that same percentage with your brothers and sisters. This is true even for **fraternal twins**

Gene: The basic biochemical unit of inheritance that is located on and transmitted by chromosomes.

Chromosomes: Threadlike structures carrying genetic information and found in every cell of the body.

Deoxyribonucleic acid (DNA): The complex molecular strands of a chromosome that contains thousands of different genes, located at fixed positions.

Sex chromosome: One of 23 pairs of chromosomes that determines whether someone is male or female.

Fraternal twins: Twins who develop in the womb from the union of two separate sperms and eggs (also known as dizygotic twins).

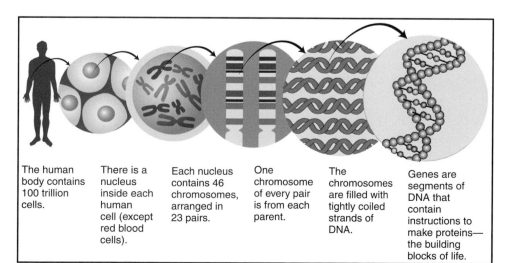

| The human body contains 100 trillion cells. | There is a nucleus inside each human cell (except red blood cells). | Each nucleus contains 46 chromosomes, arranged in 23 pairs. | One chromosome of every pair is from each parent. | The chromosomes are filled with tightly coiled strands of DNA. | Genes are segments of DNA that contain instructions to make proteins—the building blocks of life. |

FIGURE 3-12
Genetic Building Blocks

Chromosomes are contained in the nucleus of each of the cells in our bodies. Each chromosome contains tightly coiled strands of DNA. Genes are DNA segments that are the biochemical units of inheritance.

Identical twins: Twins who develop from the union of the same egg and sperm, and thus, share exactly the same genotype (also known as monozygotic twins).

(also known as *dizygotic twins*), who develop in the womb from the union of two separate sperms and eggs. The exception to this rule, of course, are **identical twins** (also called *monozygotic twins*), who develop from the union of the same egg and sperm. Identical twins share exactly the same genotype. In contemplating the genetic makeup of identical twins, one question you might ask is whether identical twins are truly identical. The answer is that they are identical genetically, but they may not express these identical genes in identical ways. That is, their phenotype may not be identical. Environmental factors, such as stress and nutrition, can actually cause certain genes to become activated or deactivated, resulting in even identical twins not having the same *active* genetic makeup (Lytton & Gallagher, 2002; McClearn, 1993).

3-4b Both Heredity and Environment Can Influence Physical and Behavioral Traits

Behavior genetics: The study of how the genotype and the environment of an organism influence the organism's behavior.

What you have learned so far is that we not only inherit our genes from our parents, but the interaction of genotype (our underlying genetic composition) with the environment can produce changes in our phenotype (our visible and measurable traits). The field of **behavior genetics** studies how the genotype and the environment of an organism influence its behavior (Dick & Rose, 2002; Looren de Jong, 2000; Plomin & McClearn, 1993).

One example of how heredity and environment can influence phenotype is obesity, a condition afflicting many adults (Kuczmarski et al., 1994). What causes obesity? Overeating is certainly an important cause of weight gain, but some people can consume many calories without gaining a pound (Rodin, 1981). What accounts for these individual differences? Research suggests that obesity is partly related to the number and size of fat cells in the body, with the number being determined by our genes and the size being determined by our eating habits (Grinker, 1982). When people overeat beyond their bodily needs, the number of fat cells does not increase, but the size of the fat cells does (Rodin & Wing, 1988). Adoption and twin studies indicate that heredity is an important factor in determining both how many fat cells you have and how efficiently you utilize your intake of calories (Bouchard et al., 1990; Stunkard et al., 1990). Apparently, some people are born with an overabundance of fat cells, while others are born with a tendency to burn excess calories by turning them into muscle tissue rather than fat. Thus, regardless of whether they are raised together or apart, identical twins—whose genes are the same—have virtually the same weight. In contrast, the weight of fraternal twins—whose genes are different—differs greatly. In addition, the body size of children adopted from birth resembles more the body size of their biological parents, who share 50 percent of the children's genes, than that of their adoptive parents. What this example illustrates is that both heredity and environment can influence a specific phenotypic characteristic, namely body size. Although the nature of the gene-environment interaction is still not clearly understood, what is clear is that neither genes nor environment alone can account for how we live our lives.

SECTION SUMMARY

- Genes are the biochemical units of inheritance located on and transmitted by chromosomes.

- Chromosomes are threadlike structures found in human body cells containing strands of DNA.

- Behavior genetics studies how the genetic makeup of an organism and the environment influence its behavior.

SUGGESTED WEBSITES

Note: These websites were functional when we went to press. Please access the online text for the most up-to-date URLs.

Society for Neuroscience
http://apu.sfn.org
This official website for the Society for Neuroscience provides brochures and newsletters on a number of relevant topics.

Neurosciences on the Internet
http://www.neuroguide.com
This website provides a wealth of information on the brain and nervous system. You will find facts on brain disorders and neurosurgery, as well as the disciplines of psychology and psychiatry.

Brain Model Tutorial
http://pegasus.cc.ucf.edu/~Brainmd1/brain.html
This is a "teaching" website devoted to the various parts and functions of the brain.

The Whole Brain Atlas
http://www.med.harvard.edu/AANLIB/home.html
This website produced by the Harvard Medical School provides a great deal of information and animated graphics of the brain, neuroimaging techniques, and brain disorders, such as strokes and Alzheimer's.

Human Genome Project Information
http://www.ornl.gov/hgmis/
The Human Genome Project is a 13-year effort coordinated by the Department of Energy and the National Institutes of Health to accelerate understanding of dynamic living systems. This website provides updates on the project and research findings.

PSYCHOLOGICAL APPLICATIONS
If You Are Left-Handed, Is Your Brain Organized Differently Than That of Right-Handers?

Are you a "lefty" or a "righty"? Actually, people rarely use the same hand for all manual activities. Instead, one hand tends to be preferred for more tasks than the other. One of the most commonly employed questionnaires to assess a person's direction and degree of handedness is the *Edinburgh Handedness Inventory* (Oldfield, 1971), reproduced in table 3-3. Before reading further, complete this questionnaire to determine your laterality quotient.

What Makes You Right-Handed or Left-Handed?
If you are predominantly left-handed, you are among the 7–8 percent minority of people who live in a right-handed world (Iaccino, 1993). What determines hand preference in the first place? Both environmental and genetic theorists have proposed opposing explanations.

Environmental theorists argue that very powerful cultural pressures are brought to bear on many natural left-handers to use their right hand (Ashton, 1982; Coren & Halpern, 1991). For example, many tools, material, and equipment—such as power saws, can openers, fishing reels, bowling balls, scissors, and school desks—are designed for right-handed persons. Given this right-handed bias, left-handers can function most effectively only if they learn to use their nondominant hand for most tasks. Due to this process of nurtural (rather than natural) selection, a number of left-handers gradually convert to the right hand. Although this *Right-Sided World Argument* (Porac & Coren, 1981) may explain the conversion of some left-handers, it cannot explain the consistency in the prevalence of right- and left-handedness across cultures that differ in their tolerance of left-handedness. That is, even though conventional schooling in Germany, Greece, Asia, and Russia discourages left-handed writing, manifestations of left-handedness are comparable to what is observed in more tolerant countries such as the United States and Canada (Annett, 1985).

Genetic theorists point to a variety of different sources to support their contention that handedness is determined by our biology. For example, when the human figures depicted in more than 1,000 drawings, paintings, and engravings spanning thousands of years are analyzed regarding their handedness, 90 percent are right-handers (Coren, 1989). Likewise, ultrasound studies of fetal thumb-sucking indicate the same percentage of left-right hand preferences, further suggesting that handedness may be an inherited trait (Hepper et al., 1990). Yet, one problem with a simple genetic explanation of handedness is that 54 percent of the children of two left-handed parents are right-handed (Coren, 1992). What we know about genetics would lead us to expect more left-handed children in this case. Even more troublesome is the fact that identical twins are no more likely to prefer the same hand than are fraternal twins (Coren & Halpern, 1991; Sicotte et al., 1999).

Faced with these problems, some genetic theorists have proposed that handedness is related to the lateralization of the brain. They argue that although there may be no specific gene for left- or right-handedness, there is a dominant gene responsible for the development of speech in the left hemisphere, and it is this gene that also predisposes people toward right-handedness (Annett, 1985). Support for this view comes from studies indicating that while over 95 percent of right-handers have speech localized to the left hemisphere, only about 65 percent of left-handers show this same pattern (Loring et al., 1990; Springer & Deutsch, 1998). The remaining 35 percent of left-handers tend to process speech using either the right hemisphere or both hemispheres. These findings suggest that, for left-handers, the two hemispheres are less specialized than they are for right-handers. Due to this difference, left-handers experience less language loss following damage to either

TABLE 3-3   What Is Your Direction and Degree of Handedness?

Instructions: Consider each of the 10 activities listed below and indicate which hand you prefer using when engaged in each of these different tasks by placing an "x" in either the "left" or "right" box.

	Left	Right
1. Writing	❑	❑
2. Drawing	❑	❑
3. Throwing	❑	❑
4. Scissors	❑	❑
5. Toothbrush	❑	❑
6. Knife (without fork)	❑	❑
7. Spoon	❑	❑
8. Broom (upper hand)	❑	❑
9. Striking match (match)	❑	❑
10. Opening box (lid)	❑	❑

Scoring: Once hand preferences for all 10 activities have been identified, your *laterality quotient* is found by subtracting the number of left x's from right x's, and then multiplying by 100. The quotient's range extends from +100 for extreme right-handedness to −100 for extreme left-handedness, with 0 representing ambidextrous activity (that is, equal use of both hands). About 50 percent of right-handers who completed this questionnaire had laterality quotients greater than 80, while 50 percent of left-handers had quotients less than −76. What these findings indicate is that (1) people tend to exhibit a preference for one hand over the other rather than being ambidextrous, and (2) right-handers are stronger hand dominant than left-handers.

Source: From "The assessment and analysis of handedness: The Edinburgh Inventory" by R. C. Oldfield in *NEUROPSYCHOLOGIA,* 9, 1971, pp. 97–114. Copyright © 1971, with permission from Elsevier Science.

hemisphere and recover more quickly than right-handers, because their healthy hemisphere is better equipped to assume the speech functions (Provins, 1997).

Is Being Left-Handed Hazardous to Your Health?

Some scientific studies have found a weak association between left-handedness and a variety of pathological conditions, including mental retardation, reading disabilities, epilepsy, alcoholism, schizophrenia, and allergies (Bryson, 1990; Ostatnikora et al., 2000). Although the percentage of left-handers who have such problems is very small, researchers have speculated as to possible explanations for even this weak association.

One explanation is that because some left-handers show evidence of language ability in both hemispheres, this duplication of language functions may impede other cognitive functions in the right hemisphere, such as visuospatial ability, resulting in cognitive deficits (Levy, 1969). Does this hypothesis sound familiar? It is exactly the same hypothesis given for why women—who also tend to be bilateral for language proficiency—generally are less adept than men at spatial tasks. Surprisingly, although both left-handers and women tend to be bilateralized for language, women are not more likely than men to be left-handed.

Another explanation contends that prenatal hormonal imbalances or birth stress may cause neurological disturbances in the left hemisphere, which, in turn, causes the right hemisphere to become dominant (Coren & Halpern, 1991). According to this hypothesis, these right hemisphere dominant individuals not only begin favoring their left hands, but the neurological problems in their left hemisphere make them more susceptible to the previously mentioned mental and physical health problems.

At present, we are not sure why left-handers are slightly more susceptible to these problems than right-handers. What we do know is that just as left-handers are somewhat more likely to experience certain health problems, they are also more likely to emerge as gifted and creative individuals (Benbow & Stanley, 1983). Indeed, the incidence of left-handedness is much higher in artists than in the population as a whole (Mebert & Michel, 1980). Although the meaning of these findings is still unclear, it certainly poses problems for the hypothesis that left-handedness is caused by some sort of cognitive defect. Thus, taking everything into account, it doesn't appear that either right-handers or left-handers can claim to hold a decided advantage over the other when it comes to adaptiveness to their world.

KEY TERMS

acetylcholine (ACh) (p. 46)
action potential (p. 43)
adrenal glands (p. 52)
aphasia (p. 61)
autonomic nervous system (p. 48)
axon (p. 41)
behavior genetics (p. 68)
central nervous system (p. 49)
cerebellum (p. 55)
cerebral cortex (p. 57)
cerebral hemispheres (p. 57)
cerebral lateralization (p. 60)
cerebrospinal fluid (p. 49)
cerebrum (p. 57)
chromosomes (p. 67)
computerized axial tomograph
    (CAT) scan (p. 53)
corpus callosum (p. 57)
dendrites (p. 41)
deoxyribonucleic acid (DNA) (p. 67)
dopamine (DA) (p. 46)
electroencephalograph (EEG) (p. 53)

endocrine system (p. 51)
endorphins (p. 46)
forebrain (p. 56)
fraternal twins (p. 67)
frontal lobes (p. 58)
functional magnetic resonance
    imaging (fMRI) (p. 53)
gene (p. 67)
genotype (p. 66)
glial cells (p. 42)
gonads (p. 52)
hindbrain (p. 55)
hormones (p. 51)
hypothalamus (p. 56)
identical twins (p. 68)
limbic system (p. 56)
magnetic resonance imaging (MRI) (p. 53)
medulla (p. 55)
midbrain (p. 55)
myelin sheath (p. 42)
nerve (p. 48)
neurons (p. 41)

neurotransmitters (p. 45)
occipital lobes (p. 57)
parasympathetic nervous system (p. 49)
parietal lobes (p. 57)
peripheral nervous system (p. 48)
phenotype (p. 66)
pituitary gland (p. 51)
pons (p. 55)
positron emission tomography
    (PET) scan (p. 53)
reflex (p. 51)
resting potential (p. 43)
reticular formation (p. 55)
sex chromosome (p. 67)
soma (p. 41)
somatic nervous system (p. 48)
spinal cord (p. 49)
sympathetic nervous system (p. 49)
synapse (p. 42)
temporal lobes (p. 57)
thalamus (p. 56)
thyroid gland (p. 52)

REVIEW QUESTIONS

1. The story of Henry M. illustrates that
   a. the hippocampus is responsible for emotional expression.
   b. the brain has sensory receptors.
   c. the brain is a complex organ that scientists are only beginning to understand.
   d. neurons account for all human thoughts and action.
   e. none of the above

2. All of the following make up a synapse *except*
   a. myelin sheath.
   b. terminal button.
   c. synaptic cleft.
   d. dendrite of another neuron.
   e. *a* and *b*

3. Which of the following statements is *true*?
   a. Neurons never synapse on somas.
   b. Neurons receive, integrate, and transmit information of the nervous system.
   c. The brain and spinal cord are solid masses of neurons.
   d. Glial cells make up a very small percentage of the brain's mass.
   e. *b* and *d*

4. The speed of neuron impulses
   a. is always constant within a given neuron.
   b. can vary.
   c. increases with the diameter of the axon.
   d. is slower than an electrical impulse.
   e. all of the above

5. Neuroscientists believe that neurotransmitters such as ACh, DA, and endorphins are responsible for
   a. convulsions and severe muscle contractions.
   b. cognition and the formation of new memories.
   c. influencing thought and emotion.
   d. *a* and *b*
   e. *a, b,* and *c*

6. What causes a neuron to fire?
   a. dendrites
   b. inhibitory neurotransmitters
   c. a flood of electrically charged ions that exceeds the threshold
   d. *a* and *b*
   e. *a, b,* and *c*

7. The peripheral nervous system consists of the
   a. somatic and endocrine systems.
   b. somatic, sympathetic, and parasympathetic nervous systems.
   c. brain and spinal cord.
   d. *b* and *c*
   e. none of the above

8. The autonomic nervous system plays a part in which of the following bodily functions?
   a. blood pressure, heart rate
   b. digestion
   c. breathing
   d. all of the above
   e. *a* and *b*

9. Which of the following statements is *true?*
   a. The central nervous system cannot repair itself.
   b. All body actions require interaction between the brain and spinal cord.
   c. If a section of the spinal cord is severed, a person loses all sensation and muscle control above the injury.
   d. none of the above
   e. *a* and *c*

10. The hindbrain is involved in controlling
    a. breathing, heart rate, swallowing, and digestion.
    b. sleep and arousal.
    c. learning and body movement.
    d. all of the above
    e. *b* and *c*

11. If I am unable to remember new skills, which region of my brain is likely damaged?
    a. occipital lobe
    b. parietal lobe
    c. temporal lobe
    d. none of the above
    e. *a* and *c*

12. Which of the following statements is true?
    a. Women's brains tend to be more bilateralized for language.
    b. Women tend to be less adept at spatial tasks than men.
    c. Similarities in brain function between men and women far outweigh any differences.
    d. all of the above
    e. *a* and *b*

13. The brain cannot function
    a. without both of the cerebral hemispheres.
    b. if there is damage to the cerebellum.
    c. with a cut corpus callosum.
    d. all of the above
    e. none of the above

14. Which of the following statements is *true?*
    a. You receive half of your genetic blueprint from each parent.
    b. Of all the human genes, 50 percent are identical in all humans.
    c. There are chromosomes in every cell of the body.
    d. The environment does not influence phenotype.
    e. all of the above

15. If you wanted to study the blood flow or chemical makeup of the brain, you would use
    a. an EEG.
    b. a CAT scan or MRI.
    c. a PET.
    d. an fMRI.
    e. *c* and *d*

16. Which of the following diseases may result from too much or too little of a neurotransmitter?
    a. Parkinson's disease
    b. schizophrenia
    c. botulism
    d. all of the above
    e. none of the above

Human Development

Chapter Outline

When I was in fourth grade, there was a period of time where I spent a good deal of the school day leaning forward so that I put almost all my weight on the front right leg of my desk. Why? Because that desk leg was balancing on top of a lump of coal about the size of my fist. I had found the lump of coal on the school playground. While Mrs. Rahm talked about math, science, and U.S. history, I earnestly pressed down on that black rock at my feet. Why? Because I had a plan. In the latest issue of Superman comics, the Man of Steel had taken a piece of coal, squeezed it in his superhand for a few seconds, and transformed it into a valuable diamond. I knew I was no Superman, but I also knew I was only 9 years old and had a lot of years left in me. If the Man of Steel could use his superhuman strength to turn a lump of coal into a precious diamond in only a few seconds, then maybe I could do the same thing if I desk-pressured my coal from now until high school graduation. So at the end of each school day, I would pull my project out from under that desk leg and inspect it carefully, looking for any signs of crystal growth.

Needless to say, I never witnessed any mineral transformation during Mrs. Rahm's class that year. Yet, while that lump of coal remained essentially unchanged, the child sitting in the desk above it was undergoing many different transformations. Indeed, every child in that classroom was changing and becoming something different during the course of that school year. Some of these changes could be attributed to the "mind pressure" that Mrs. Rahm exerted on us every school day, while other transformations were due to "peer pressure," "parental pressure," and, yes, the "biological pressure" changing us from within. Unlike the hands of Superman, which can take sole credit for turning coal into diamond, in the real world the **development** of a child is the result of many different forces working simultaneously. In our journey of discovery concerning human development, it is our job to analyze these forces so that we better understand their role in shaping not only who we are now, but who we will become.

Development: The systematic physical, cognitive, and social changes in the individual occurring between conception and death.

4-1 PHYSICAL AND PRENATAL DEVELOPMENT

Look at the period at the end of this sentence. That's approximately the single-cell size of all human beings shortly after conception. Compare that dot to your current size. How did such an incredible transformation take place? Don't look to Superman for an answer to this question; instead, let's go back to before you were even a dot.

4-1a Prenatal Development Occurs in Three Stages

Every month, an egg is released by one of a woman's two ovaries and travels down to her fallopian tubes. During this time period, if she has sexual intercourse with a man without the use of birth control, and if any of his seminal fluid is deposited into her vagina, she could become pregnant. During sexual intercourse, a man ejaculates between 200 and 500 million sperm into a woman's vagina, but only a few thousand will actually complete the 6- or 7-inch journey to the fallopian tubes. If the egg is present and one of the sperm successfully fertilizes it, a new cell is formed. If all goes well, about 38 weeks later a baby is born. During that period of time, the many changes that transform the fertilized egg into a newborn baby is known as **prenatal development.** Prenatal development can be divided into the stages of the *zygote,* the *embryo,* and the *fetus.*

Prenatal development: The many changes that transform a fertilized egg into a newborn baby.

> **INFO-BIT:** Consistent with gender stereotypes, biologists once described male sperm as the active participant in conception, with the female egg as being passive. Yet, today, we know that conception is more accurately described as due to the egg "grabbing" the sperm rather than the sperm "penetrating" the egg.

Zygote Stage

As you recall from chapter 3, section 3-4a, in humans, each male sperm cell and each female egg cell contains 23 chromosomes. When the sperm fertilizes the egg, this new cell, the zygote, contains 46 chromosomes, or 23 pairs, with half the genetic material coming from each parent. The zygote travels down the fallopian tubes toward the uterus, dividing into an ever more complex multicelled ball every 12 hours. On rare occasions, the zygote splits into two separate clusters that will eventually become identical (monozygotic) twins. Fraternal (dizygotic) twins develop when two eggs are released by the ovaries and fertilized by different sperm cells. The **zygote stage** lasts two weeks, from conception until the zygote implants itself in the wall of the uterus. By the end of the second week, the zygote is about one millimeter in diameter and consists of a few thousand cells.

Zygote stage: The first two weeks of prenatal development, from conception until the zygote implants itself in the wall of the uterus.

Embryonic Stage

Mainly due to abnormalities in the chromosomes, about 30 percent of all zygotes are spontaneously aborted (Plomin et al., 1997). If the zygote successfully embeds itself in the uterine wall, this living tissue is considered to be an embryo. The **embryonic stage** lasts from the third week through the eighth week of prenatal development. During this stage, the head develops before the rest of the body, and arms and legs develop before hands and feet. Between the fourth and eighth weeks, the gonads of the genetically male embryos secrete the hormone testosterone, and this stimulates the development of male sex organs. Otherwise, the embryo develops into a female. By the end of the eighth week, the embryo has facial features, fingers, toes, and a functioning heart that pumps blood, yet it still is only an inch long and weighs a tenth of an ounce!

Embryonic stage: The second stage of prenatal development that lasts from the third week through the eighth week of pregnancy.

Fetal Stage

The last and longest stage in prenatal development is the **fetal stage,** which extends from the ninth week after conception until birth. In the third month, identifiable sex organs appear, bones and muscles develop, and the fetus begins to move. At four months, the fetus is large enough (4 to 8 ounces) for the mother to feel its movements. By the seventh month, all the major organs are working and the fetus has a chance of surviving outside the womb, though not without enormous high-tech medical intervention. Premature babies born this early have trouble breathing because their lungs are not fully developed, and they also cannot adequately regulate their body temperature because insulating body fat doesn't form until the eighth month.

Fetal stage: The last and longest stage in prenatal development that extends from the ninth week after conception until birth.

4-1b The Fetus Can Be Harmed by a Number of Parental and Environmental Factors

Among the risk factors that can harm a developing fetus are a parent's age, maternal nutrition, and harmful environmental agents.

Parental Age and Maternal Nutrition

Both the ages of the mother and father can affect prenatal development. The safest ages for women to bear children are from about age 17 or 18 to age 35 (Campbell & Wood, 1994; Kessner, 1973). Mothers younger and older than this age range run a greater risk that spontaneous abortions will occur due to chromosome abnormalities or that their babies will be born with birth defects (Culp et al., 1988; Strigini et al., 1990). For men, as they enter their 30s and 40s, there is a slightly greater risk that a damaged sperm will fertilize an egg and cause chromosome damage.

Because the mother is the fetus's only source of nutrition, her diet is extremely important to its health and development. Inadequate maternal nutrition can cause premature births, underweight babies, higher infant mortality, and, in some cases, permanent intellectual deficits (Campbell et al., 1996; Huffman et al., 2001). Such negative effects are most likely when the malnutrition occurs during the last three months of pregnancy, for this is the time when the fetus gains most of its weight and new brain cells are rapidly growing (Keen et al., 1993; Tanner, 1990).

Teratogens

Teratogen: Any disease, drug, or other noxious agent that causes abnormal prenatal development.

A **teratogen**—which in Greek means "monster maker"—is any disease, drug, or other noxious agent that causes abnormal prenatal development. Many drugs administered during pregnancy can pose serious risks to the developing fetus, especially during the first three months of development (Brennan et al., 1999). Table 4-1 lists several drugs that are known teratogens (Jacobson & Jacobson, 2001). For example, women who drink large quantities of alcohol while pregnant are 30 percent more likely to give birth to babies with **fetal alcohol syndrome,** which is characterized by mental retardation, motor deficits, and heart problems (Barr et al., 1990; Schneider et al., 2002). Children with fetal alcohol syndrome also suffer from facial deformities, such as a small head, a short nose, and widely spaced eyes (Julien, 1992). Because of evidence indicating that even small amounts of alcohol may cause minor cognitive deficits, most medical experts recommend that expectant mothers drink no alcohol at all during pregnancy (Kaufman, 1997; Streissguth et al., 1993).

Fetal alcohol syndrome: Physical and cognitive abnormalities in children caused by pregnant women consuming large quantities of alcohol.

Besides drugs, maternal infections such as rubella (German measles), chicken pox, mumps, and syphilis are another class of teratogens that can be hazardous to the fetus (Isada & Grossman, 1991). Two sexually transmitted diseases, *genital herpes* and *acquired immune deficiency syndrome (AIDS)*, are especially dangerous. Genital herpes is typically transmitted to newborns during the birth process when they come into contact with their mothers' genital lesions. Herpes can cause blindness, serious brain damage, paralysis, and even death to the newborn. For these reasons, mothers with active herpes have cesarean

TABLE 4-1

Teratogenic Drugs and Their Consequences on Prenatal Development

Drug	Potential Consequences
Alcohol	Heavy drinking can cause fetal alcohol syndrome (facial deformities, heart damage, mental retardation), while moderate drinking may cause small cognitive deficits
Aspirin	Deficits in intelligence, attention, and motor skill
Antibiotics	Cataracts, retarded skeletal growth, and premature delivery
Anticonvulsants	Heart problems and cleft palate
Caffeine	Premature births, lower birth weight, abnormal reflexes, and decreased muscle tone
Cocaine and heroin	Retarded growth, brain damage, sluggishness, poor attention span, and heart abnormalities
Codeine, morphine, and methadone	Addicted baby, withdrawal symptoms (fever, tremors, convulsions, breathing problems)
Marijuana	Lower birth weight and less motor control
Nicotine	Increased risk of miscarriage, retarded growth, irritability in newborns, chronic respiratory problems, and facial deformities
Thalidomide	Abnormalities in arms and legs
Tranquilizers (other than thalidomide)	May produce respiratory distress in newborns

deliveries to avoid infecting their babies through contact with the vaginal tract (Hanshaw et al., 1985). Of even greater concern to the fetus is AIDS, the fatal disease caused by the virus HIV. AIDS can be transmitted prenatally if the virus passes through the *placenta,* which is the thick membrane that passes nutrition and oxygen from the mother to fetus. The disease also can be transmitted during birth, when there may be an exchange of blood between mother and newborn as the umbilical cord separates from the placenta, or after birth, when the virus may be passed through the mother's milk during breast feeding (Kaufman, 1997). Of the 30 percent of babies who receive AIDS from their HIV-infected mothers, few live longer than three years (Gabiano et al., 1992; Valleroy et al., 1990).

4-1c A Child's Brain Grows at an Immense Rate

As discussed in chapter 3, section 3-1, the basic unit of the nervous system is the neuron, or nerve cell. You might be surprised to learn that the brain of an 8-month-old human fetus has more than twice as many nerve cells as an adult brain (Kolb, 1989) and produces new neurons at a rate of hundreds of thousands per minute! This excess neural production is an adaptive means of adjusting neuron number, for as babies grow, the billions of neurons are shaped by their environment, with many being destroyed (Cicchetti, 2002). Each sight, sound, and touch the baby experiences activates and strengthens specific neurons and their connections, while other neurons that are not regularly activated grow weak and die (see figure 4-1). Such brain "sculpting" also occurs with other animals, including insects (Kolb & Whishaw, 1998; Strausfeld, 2001). What this means is that, although an animal's brain is generally programmed by genetics, it is more specifically shaped by life experiences.

Neural development during the early years of life results in the brain's weight ballooning from a modest three-quarters of a pound to about two and a third pounds by age 4. Most of this added mass is due to (1) the growth of new dendrites that increase the connections between neurons, and (2) the growth of the protective coating of fatty cells—known as a *myelin sheath*—around neural axons (Bower, 1994). To understand the importance of brain growth for the overall development of the individual, consider these facts: Although the

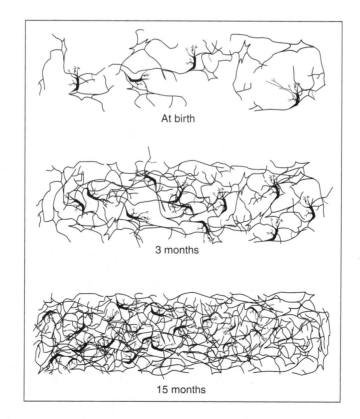

At birth

3 months

15 months

FIGURE 4-1
Neural Network Growth during Infancy

As infants mature and interact with their physical and social environment, the neural connections in their brains grow increasingly complex. Depicted here are drawings of an infant's cerebral cortex sections during the first 15 months of life.

rest of a newborn's body weighs only about 5 percent of what it will weigh as an adult, its brain is already 25 percent of its adult weight. By age 2, the brain is at 75 percent of its adult weight while the body has only grown to 20 percent. At age 5, the brain/body adult percentages are at 90 percent and 35 percent, respectively. The most likely reason why the brain grows so much more quickly than the rest of the body is that it plays a major role in coordinating the physical and perceptual development of the body as a whole.

4-1d Physical Growth and Motor Development Occur Hand in Hand

Although the brain grows faster than the rest of the body, infant body growth is by no means slow. During the first year of life, the body almost triples in weight (from about 7 pounds to 20 pounds) and increases in length by about one-third (from about 20 inches to 29 inches). After this initial surge, the rate of childhood growth slows to about 2 to 3 inches and 4 to 7 pounds per year. Middle childhood is a time when bones continue to grow and harden, and muscles grow in strength. The height of a child is largely determined by heredity, with tall parents generally having tall children and short parents generally having short children (Plomin, 1984).

Accompanying the physical growth of the body is motor development. Basic motor skills develop from the head downward to the trunk and legs. In North American culture, infants first lift their heads at about 2 months of age. By 6 months, they can sit up without support, and by the end of the first year, they begin walking. Although this pattern is mirrored in many other cultures, variations do occur. For example, at 10 months of age—when North American infants are only beginning to learn how to stand alone—Ugandan infants are already walking. One possible explanation for this cultural difference is that, in Uganda, babies are carried upright on their mother's backs, which helps to develop their trunk and leg muscles at a faster rate than occurs in most North American infants (Bril, 1986).

Newborns also enter the world with a number of reflexes. (See Discovery Box 4-1.) As mentioned in chapter 3, section 3-2b, a reflex is an automatic, involuntary response to sensory stimuli. Some reflexes are called *survival reflexes* because they are essential for survival; others are known as *primitive reflexes* because they are believed to be holdovers from our evolutionary history that have outlived their usefulness. Examples of survival reflexes are the eye-blink reflex, which protects us from bright lights and foreign objects, and the sucking reflex, which allows us to receive necessary nourishment. The swimming reflex, which is an active movement of the arms and legs and an involuntary holding of the breath when immersed in water, is an example of a primitive reflex. Table 4-2 lists some reflexes that are easily observed in normal newborns. Many of these reflexes—such as the rooting, grasping, and Babinski reflexes—eventually disappear, but others—such as the eye-blink, pupillary, and breathing reflexes—are permanent.

SECTION SUMMARY

- Prenatal development consists of three stages: the zygote, embryonic, and fetal stages.
- Possible risk factors during the fetal stage include parental age, maternal nutrition, and teratogens.
- As the brain grows, some neurons are strengthened through repeated stimulation, while others grow weak and die.
- Infants are born with a number of reflexes.
- Basic motor skills soon develop from the head downward to the trunk and legs.
- Prior to birth, the fetus is capable of hearing sounds and being sensitive to touch.
- Newborns can both taste and smell, but they do not see as clearly as normal-sighted people.

TABLE 4-2

Reflexes of the Newborn Baby

Reflexes	Developmental Course	Significance
Survival Reflexes		
Breathing reflex	Permanent	Provides oxygen and expels carbon dioxide
Eye-blink reflex	Permanent	Protects eyes from bright lights and foreign objects
Pupillary reflex (constriction and dilation of pupils due to the amount of light)	Permanent	Protects eyes from bright lights and adapts vision to darkness
Rooting reflex (turning of cheek in direction of a touch in search of something to suck on)	Gradually weakens during the first six months of life	Orients child to mother's breast
Sucking reflex (sucking on anything placed in the mouth)	Gradually modified by experience	Allows child to receive nourishment
Swallowing reflex	Permanent, but modified by experience	Allows child to receive nourishment and protects against choking
Primitive Reflexes		
Babinski reflex (splaying outward and then inward of toes)	Disappears within the first year of life	Presence at birth and later disappearance indicates normal neurological development
Grasping reflex (curling of fingers around objects that touch the palm)	Disappears by fourth month of life	Presence at birth and later disappearance indicates normal neurological development
Moro or "startle" reflex (throwing arms out and arching of back due to loud noise or sudden movement of baby's head)	Disappears by seventh month of life but is replaced by adult startle reflex	Presence at birth and later disappearance indicates normal neurological development
Swimming reflex (active movement of arms and legs and involuntarily holding of breath when immersed in water)	Disappears by sixth month of life	Presence at birth and later disappearance indicates normal neurological development
Stepping reflex (walking movements when held upright so that feet just touch the ground)	Disappears by second month of life	Presence at birth and later disappearance indicates normal neurological development

DISCOVERY BOX 4-1

Are the Senses Functional Prior to Birth?

William James (see chapter 1, section 1-2b) once described a newborn's perceptual world as being a "blooming, buzzing confusion" of sights, sounds, and other sensations with no distinguishing patterns. Is his description accurate?

Audition

There is evidence that even before birth—during the final two months of pregnancy—the fetus is not only capable of hearing sounds, but of recognizing them as well. These facts were uncovered due to an ingenious series of studies conducted by Anthony DeCasper and his colleagues. In the most famous of these studies, the researchers had 16 women read aloud Dr. Seuss's *The Cat in the Hat* twice a day during the last six weeks of their pregnancy (DeCasper & Spence, 1986). Three days after birth, the babies sucked on artificial nipples that activated a tape recording of their mothers' voice either reading the familiar Dr. Seuss story or some other unfamiliar story. Thirteen of the 16 babies sucked to hear a tape of their mother reading *The Cat in the Hat* but not to hear the other story. Similarly, DeCasper and his colleagues found that newborn infants preferred their mother's voice or a heartbeat to that of an unfamiliar male voice (DeCasper & Fifer, 1980; DeCasper & Sigafoos, 1983). What these studies indicate is that hearing is not only functional prior to birth, but learning begins in the womb. That is, the newborns were already capable of distinguishing one pattern of sounds (mother's voice) from another pattern of sounds.

Vision

At birth, vision is not as well developed as hearing, but newborns can follow slowly moving objects, and, within a day, they begin to show a preference for their mother's face (Field et al., 1984). Although newborns can see, they cannot see very clearly (Courage & Adams, 1990): They see objects at 20 feet as clearly as normal-sighted people—that is, those with 20/20 vision—see objects at between 400 and 600 feet (thus, their visual acuity ranges from 20/400 to 20/600). By 6 months of age, as the visual cortex in the back of the brain and retina in the back of the eye mature, infants' vision improves so that it approaches normal adult levels.

Newborns are particularly attentive to facial features (see figure 4-2). Faces and objects with qualities similar to faces are attended to more than are other objects (Field, 1982; Mondloch et al., 1999). In fact, a number of studies have found that newborns exposed to an adult making a happy, sad, or surprised face are able to imitate the corresponding expression (Meltzoff & Moore, 1977, 1989; Reissland, 1988). Evolutionary psychologists believe that this innate ability to respond to the expressed emotions in others' facial expressions is a survival reflex (Gould, 1993; Izard et al., 1995). How might imitating facial gestures help infants survive? One possibility is that infants' attentiveness to their mothers' faces and even their imitation of the mothers' facial gestures helps to establish an emotional bond between the two, making it

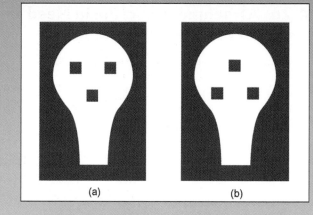

(a)   (b)

FIGURE 4-2
Newborns' Preference for Faces

In studies of newborns, when shown stimulus *(a)* and stimulus *(b)*, babies spent almost twice as much time looking at stimulus *(a)*, which mimics the facial features of a human (Mondloch et al., 1999; Morton & Johnson, 1991). Why might this apparent innate ability to attend to the human face foster an infant's survival?

more likely that the newborn will be nurtured and protected. Another possibility is that this early attentiveness to others' facial expressions may provide infants with the necessary foundation to later develop social interaction skills that will increase the likelihood that they will successfully mate and reproduce (Phillips et al., 1990).

Taste and Smell

At birth, infants have the ability both to taste and smell, making positive and negative facial expressions in response to various odors and preferring sweetness over other tastes (Bartoshuk & Beauchamp, 1994; Steiner, 1979). This sweet tooth persists during childhood, and, for some people, sweets maintain their top ranking throughout life. Regarding smell, not only can babies discriminate between various odors, but within six days of birth they recognize their mother's scent from that of other women (Macfarlane, 1975) and prefer the breast odor of a nursing female to that of a non-nursing female (Makin & Porter, 1989).

Touch

As we will discuss in chapter 5, section 5-4b, touch consists of several senses: temperature, pain, and pressure. The sense of touch is functional well before birth, although pain receptors may be less developed than the other skin senses (Porter et al., 1988). Infants' sensitivity to touch explains why they can be comforted by being rocked and held.

As you can see from this brief overview, William James's description of the newborn's perceptual world was very much mistaken. Today, we know that infant perception is not a meaningless jumble, but rather, a number of different sensations can be meaningfully perceived (Gopnik et al., 1999).

4-2 SOCIAL DEVELOPMENT

Although physical and perceptual development provides us with the necessary biological infrastructure to survive in the world, there is more to survival than simple biology. In this section, we examine some of the social and cultural forces that shape our essential humanity, beginning with the development of an emotional attachment to our caregivers.

4-2a Attachment Is a Basic Need in Humans and Many Other Animals

Attachment: The strong emotional bond a young child forms with its primary caregiver.

Attachment is the strong emotional bond a young child forms with its primary caregiver; it is considered to be the cornerstone for all other relationships in a child's life (Belsky & Cassidy, 1994; Field, 1996). This bond is not unique to humans but can also be observed in most species of birds and mammals (Mason, 1997). Based on his analysis of both orphaned children and other species, British psychiatrist John Bowlby (1969, 1988) proposed that attachment is part of many species' genetic heritage, and its evolutionary function is to keep immature animals close to their parents so that they are protected from predators.

The Development of Attachment

An important ingredient in developing attachment is receiving *contact comfort*—that is, direct contact with soft objects (Harlow & Harlow, 1962; Harlow & Zimmerman, 1959). This is why toddlers enjoy stroking and being stroked by their parents. It also explains why children often clutch or stroke soft objects when they feel anxious or tired (Passman & Weisberg, 1975). As a youngster, my daughter Lillian always needed her favorite blanket to hold close to her body and rub between her fingers when settling down for a nap. One afternoon, she apparently could not find this most cherished object as fatigue settled in and thus chose a convenient substitute—an unopened bag of disposable diapers (see photo). When loved ones are not available, children bond to other cuddly objects.

Newborn humans are equipped with a number of attachment behaviors, such as smiling, cooing, and clinging, that adults seem to naturally respond to with care and atten-

The need for contact comfort is a basic ingredient in attachment and explains why children clutch or stroke soft objects when they feel anxious or tired. When my daughter Lillian could not find her favorite blanket, she found a suitably soft substitute, a bag of diapers. Have you observed this need for contact comfort in other species?

tion. Because newborn babies' attachment behaviors are not directed toward a specific person, they not only will coo, smile, and cling to their caregivers, they also will engage in these behaviors in response to strangers and even inanimate objects. If the infants' attachment behaviors are not responded to by adults, these bonding signals decrease in frequency (Ainsworth et al., 1978). Infants' initial attachment bond usually is with their mothers because mothers provide most of the early care.

Between the ages of 3 to 6 months, infants show a clear preference for their primary caregivers but do not yet become upset when separated from them. In contrast, between 7 and 9 months, the child forms an attachment bond toward a specific caregiver and usually becomes extremely upset following separation. The fear and distress that infants display when separated from their primary caregiver is known as **separation anxiety,** and it usually persists until they are about 2 or 3. Also during this time, children develop a fear of strangers called **stranger anxiety.** Stranger anxiety develops at about 6 or 7 months of age, peaks at about 1 year, and gradually subsides during the second year. Neither separation anxiety nor stranger anxiety are unique to Western culture but are found throughout the world (Super, 1981; van Bakel & Riksen-Walraven, 2002).

Individual Differences in Attachment Style

As infants mature and as they interact with their parents, they develop either optimistic or pessimistic beliefs about human relationships (Meins, 1999). Infants who form a *secure attachment style* believe that they are worthy of others' love and that people can be trusted to care for them. In contrast, those who develop an *insecure attachment style* believe that they are unworthy love objects, and that others cannot be relied upon. Attachment style remains quite stable throughout childhood, unless the family experiences a major disruption, such as divorce, illness, or death.

About 60–65 percent of babies in the United States are securely attached, while the remaining 35–40 percent have an insecure attachment style (Lamb et al., 1992). Secure attachment promotes psychological adjustment and health, while insecure attachment typically fosters problematic social relationships. Infants who are securely attached at 1 year of age tend to mature into popular, independent, socially skilled, and self-assured children (Cummings & Cummings, 2002; Kagan et al., 1992). In contrast, insecurely attached infants tend to become children who lack curiosity, perform poorly in school, and are emotionally withdrawn. They also often exhibit contradictory social behavior, sometimes initiating social contact but then unexpectedly spurning others' social advances. This vacillating pattern of approach-avoidance invites social rejection from peers, which then serves to confirm the child's original sense of insecurity and distrust about the world outside.

Despite the sharply contrasting consequences of secure and insecure attachment, these findings by no means imply that secure attachment makes a child invulnerable to later problems in life, or that insecure attachment dooms one to a life of loneliness and misery. Instead, the research suggests that children with a secure attachment history have an understanding of themselves ("I am worthy of love") and their relationship with others ("People can be trusted") that makes it easier for them to form satisfying social attachments than those who have an insecure attachment history (Cassidy & Shaver, 1999).

4-2b Parenting Style, Initial Temperament, and Culture All Influence Attachment Style

A number of factors influence children's attachment style toward their parents. Three of the more important factors are the parents' behavior toward the child, the child's inborn temperament, and the family's culture.

Separation anxiety: The fear and distress that infants display when separated from their primary caregiver.

Stranger anxiety: The fear and distress that infants often display when approached by an unfamiliar person.

Parenting Style

Parents who are sensitively responsive to their children's needs and emotional signals, and provide a great deal of contact comfort, tend to foster secure attachment (NICHD Early Child Care Research Network, 2002; Teti et al., 1991). In feeding, for example, they pay attention to the infant's verbal and nonverbal behavior to determine when to start and stop. They also respond promptly to the baby's cries and behave affectionately when holding her or him. In marked contrast, parents of infants who show insecure attachment pay less attention to their infants' moods and respond more on the basis of their own needs and desires (Bretherton, 1985; Pederson et al., 1990). For example, they will feed the baby when it is convenient for them to do so, and they will cuddle the baby when they themselves desire contact comfort but will avoid the baby at other times. Mothers with insecurely attached babies seem to derive less pleasure out of contact comfort and will often refuse to console the baby when it is crying.

Temperament

Another factor that influences the quality of the parent-child attachment is the initial temperament of the newborn (Putnam et al., 2002). Infants with an *easygoing temperament* generally react positively to new situations or stimuli, such as food, people, or toys, while those with a *difficult temperament* tend to react to these situations by crying or fussing. Temperament appears to be significantly shaped by inherited biological factors (DiLalla et al., 1994; Schmidt & Fox, 2002), and temperament, in turn, appears to partly influence the quality of parent-child attachment. Infants who develop a secure attachment style tend to be naturally easygoing, while those who develop an insecure attachment style are more likely to be rather difficult (Chess & Thomas, 1987).

Of the two factors, most studies suggest that parenting style has a greater impact than the child's temperament in shaping the quality of the attachment (Rosen & Rothbaum, 1993; Seifer et al., 1996), For example, in one experiment, Dutch researchers randomly assigned 6- to 9-month-old temperamentally difficult babies to either one of two conditions. In the experimental condition, mothers received training in how to respond sensitively to their child's needs, while in the control condition, they received no training. When the children reached the age of 1, 68 percent of those in the experimental condition were securely attached—right at the national average—versus only 28 percent in the control condition.

Culture

The nature of attachment also appears to be significantly shaped by culture and the ideologies of individualism and collectivism (Harwood et al., 1995). For example, both U.S. and German children, who are raised in individualist cultures, are far more likely than Japanese children, who are raised in a collectivist culture, to develop a type of insecure attachment style characterized by avoiding intimacy with the mother (Cole, 1992). The reason for these cultural differences in attachment are probably partly due to different views on how to raise children. Parents in the United States and Germany try to foster independence at an earlier age, and thus, they discourage their children from staying near them and are more likely to give them toys or food when they cry rather than picking them up. In contrast, Japanese parents do not promote independence, and thus, they rarely leave their children alone and quickly pick them up when they cry.

Another consideration when studying attachment is that in certain ethnic groups in North America (for example, Hispanic and Filipino families) and in various cultures around the world (for example, Israeli kibbutzim and the Hausa culture in Nigeria), the existence of extended families results in many people sharing in the rearing of a child. In such instances, the child develops attachments to many people, without adverse consequences (Lynch, 1994; Sagi et al., 1985). Figure 4-3 summarizes some of the possible causes of children's attachment style.

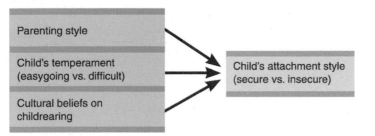

| Parenting style |
| Child's temperament (easygoing vs. difficult) |
| Cultural beliefs on childrearing |

→ Child's attachment style (secure vs. insecure)

FIGURE 4-3
Possible Causes of Children's Attachment Style
Research suggests that whether children develop a secure versus an insecure attachment style is determined by a variety of factors, including parenting style, children's temperament, and cultural beliefs on childrearing. Parents who are sensitively responsive to their children's needs tend to foster secure attachment, while parents who are inattentive to their infants' needs and desires tend to foster insecure attachment. Regarding children's initial temperament, easygoing infants tend to develop secure attachment, while difficult infants tend to develop insecure attachment. Finally, cultures that try to foster independence at an early age tend to teach parents to remain less close to their children, which tends to promote higher levels of insecure attachment than in cultures that do not promote independence.

4-2c Children Can Handle Parental Separation under Certain Conditions

The notion of multiple caregivers raises the question of what effect day care has on the formation of attachment. A related question is whether the physical separation of one parent from the child caused by divorce disrupts the attachment process.

Day Care and Attachment

Given the fact that only 40 percent of infants and toddlers in the United States are regularly cared for by their parents during the day (Hofferth, 1996), understanding the effects of nonparental care has become an important priority for researchers, as well as parents. Some studies (Belsky & Rovine, 1988; Lamb et al., 1992) suggest that infants who spend many hours in nonparental care before the age of 1 are slightly less likely to be securely attached to their parents than those children cared for primarily by their parents (65% versus 71% securely attached). However, most research indicates that infants who attend high-quality day-care centers are no less securely attached than infants raised at home (Belsky, 1990; Booth et al., 2002; Harvey, 1999). The key ingredient here is "high-quality" care, regardless of who provides it (Clarke-Stewart & Allhusen, 2002; Ghazvini & Mullis, 2002). Table 4-3 lists the important characteristics of high-quality day-care programs.

Divorce and Attachment

A little over half of all marriages in the United States end in divorce, while in China its occurrence is less than 15 percent. Yet, regardless of how common it is, divorce generally negatively affects the children involved (Dong et al., 2002). For example, a meta-analysis of over 90 studies indicates that children of divorce feel less emotionally secure and grow up feeling less happy than those who come from intact families (Amato &

TABLE 4-3

Characteristics of High-Quality Day-Care Programs

- A low child-to-caregiver ratio:

  3-to-1 infant-to-adult ratio
  4-to-1 toddler-to-adult ratio
  8-to-1 preschooler-to-adult ratio

- Caregivers who are warm, emotionally expressive, and responsive to children

- Age-appropriate planned activities

- Low staff turnover, so that children feel comfortable and can emotionally bond with their caregivers

Keith, 1991). Further, a 23-year **longitudinal study** of over 17,000 infants born in Great Britain during one week in 1958 found that parental divorce had a moderate, long-term negative impact on about 12 percent of the grown-up children's mental health (Chase-Lansdale et al., 1995). Some studies find that the emotional turmoil surrounding divorce has a greater impact on younger children than on their older peers (Allison & Furstenberg, 1989; Lowery & Settle, 1985).

Another factor that can negatively affect children is the change in parental child-rearing that often accompanies divorce (Madden-Derdich & Leonard, 2002). In most divorces, mothers retain primary custody of the children, while fathers obtain considerably fewer parental rights. In this environment, overburdened custodial mothers may be less warm and less consistent in their discipline, whereas noncustodial fathers may become overly permissive. The lack of parental structure resulting from these contrasting types of childrearing can heighten children's sense of emotional insecurity (Hetherington & Stanley-Hagen, 2002).

Despite these potential negative consequences, children of divorce tend to be psychologically healthier than children who come from conflict-ridden two-parent families (Cherlin et al., 1991). In fact, the emotional stress that children from troubled intact families experience can often be substantially reduced by the termination of the marriage (Barber & Eccles, 1992).

4-2d Self-Concept Is the Primary Social Achievement of Childhood

While the primary social achievement of infancy is attachment, the primary social achievement of childhood is **self-concept,** which is the "theory" or "story" that a person constructs about herself or himself through social interaction. How does self-concept develop?

Self-Awareness: An Essential Ingredient

Stop reading for a moment and think about those personal aspects that you are most proud of and those that you are least proud of. In doing this, you engaged in **self-awareness,** a psychological state where you take yourself as an object of attention. You are not born with this ability, but rather, you develop it. Psychologists discovered this developmental fact by unobtrusively placing a spot of rouge on babies' noses and then placing them in front of a mirror (Lewis & Brooks, 1978). If babies have mental images of their own faces and can recognize their mirror images as their own, they should notice the rouge mark and reach for or wipe their noses rather than the nose of the mirror image. When tested in this manner, infants between 9 and 12 months treat their mirror image as if it was another child, showing no interest in the unusual rouge spot. Yet, those around 18 months exhibit self-recognition—and thus, self-awareness ability—by consistently staring in the mirror and touching the mysterious spot on their own noses, not the ones in the mirror. Recognizing the image in the mirror as their own, they realize that they look different from how they looked before. Based on such studies, it appears that self-awareness develops at about 18 months of age (Amsterdam, 1972; Butterworth, 1992).

Self-Esteem Development

Once children engage in self-awareness, they begin to develop a self-concept. Before reading further, go to table 4-4 and spend a few minutes answering the question, Who am I?

Self-concept is not a dispassionate self-theory, but rather, consists of numerous evaluations of self as being good, bad, or mediocre. This evaluation of the self-concept is called **self-esteem.** In the early years, children's self-concepts display little organization and little negativity, and they have not yet developed a recognizable sense of self-esteem (Harter, 1988). During middle childhood, however, children have the cognitive maturity to integrate others' evaluations of them and their own self-assessments into a global sense of self-esteem (Marsh et al., 1991). A number of studies indicate that high self-esteem individuals generally are more happy and optimistic, and they tend to take greater

TABLE 4-4

Who Am I?

Take out a sheet of paper and write the numbers 1–20 down the left column of the page. Then, beginning each sentence with the statement "I am," list up to 20 different responses to the question "Who Am I?" Respond as if you were giving the answers to yourself, not to someone else. When finished, learn how to evaluate your responses by reading the following classification scheme devised by social scientists who conduct self-concept research.

A commonly used classification scheme for analyzing the "Who Am I?" exercise (see Hartley, 1970) is to code each response into one of the following four categories:

1. *Physical self-descriptions*—This is where you identify yourself in terms of physical qualities that do not imply social interaction (e.g., "I am a male"; "I am a brunette"; "I am overweight").
2. *Social self-descriptions*—This is where you identify yourself in terms of social roles, institutional memberships, or other socially defined statuses (e.g., "I am a student"; "I am a daughter"; "I am a Jew").
3. *Attributive self-descriptions*—This is where you identify yourself in terms of psychological/physiological states or traits (e.g., "I am intelligent"; "I am assertive"; "I am boring").
4. *Global self-descriptions*—This is where you identify yourself in a manner that is so comprehensive or vague that it doesn't distinguish you from any other person (e.g., "I am a human being"; "I am alive"; "I am me").

Code each of your responses into one of these four categories. Which category occurs most frequently for you? People in individualist cultures write more attributive self-descriptions, which highlight their differences with other people, while collectivists write more social self-descriptions, which highlight their connections to their social groups.

achievement risks in their lives than those with low self-esteem (Diener & Lucas, 2000; Shepperd et al., 1996).

Given our previous discussion of attachment, it shouldn't surprise you to learn that children with high self-esteem tend to come from families where parents are warmly expressive toward their children (Maccoby & Martin, 1983). In addition, high self-esteem children usually have *authoritative parents:* parents who exert control not merely by imposing rules and consistently enforcing them, but also by allowing their children a fair amount of freedom within the rules, and by discussing the rationale behind their decisions (Baumrind, 1991; Scott et al., 1991). This research indicates that children need love combined with a set of boundaries to structure their behavior. In contrast, parents who impose many rules and expect strict obedience (*authoritarian parents*) and those who make few demands and submit to their children's desires (*permissive parents*) tend to raise children who are less confident in their abilities and have lower self-esteem (Grolnick & Ryan, 1989).

The detrimental effect that authoritarian parenting has on children's self-esteem is most apparent in Caucasian-American families, where this parental style is often used to "break the child's will." However, in many ethnic-minority families, greater value is placed on authoritarian parenting as a positive socialization tool (Lynch, 1994; Parke & Buriel, 1998). For example, Chinese-American parents use authoritarian discipline to "train" (*chiao shun*) and "govern" (*guan*) children so that they will know what is expected of them (Chao, 1992). In such a cultural context, authoritarian parenting is not associated with lower self-esteem or lower levels of achievement (Steinberg et al., 1992).

4-2e Self-Concept Is Shaped by Culture

Our self-concept is shaped by loved ones. It is also shaped by culture. Two important cultural influences are the belief systems concerning the relationship between the individual and the group (individualism versus collectivism), and the beliefs about what it means to be a man or a woman in society (gender).

Individualism and Collectivism

As discussed in chapter 1, section 1-3f, the United States, Canada, and many Northern European cultures cultivate *individualism*, which is a philosophy of life stressing the importance of the individual over the group (Hofstede, 1980). In this cultural belief system, the person is thought of as being independent and having unique attributes. In contrast, many Asian, African, and Central and South American cultures nurture *collectivism*, which is an older philosophy of life stressing the priority of group needs over individual needs. Collectivist cultures tend to value similarity and conformity rather than uniqueness and independence. About 70 percent of the world's population lives in cultures with a collectivist orientation.

Research suggests that the differing cultural perspectives of individualism and collectivism affect the degree to which people identify with groups within the society, and this identification process is reflected in basic differences in the nature of self-concept (Kanagawa et al., 2001; van den Heuvel et al., 1992). When asked to describe themselves, the self-concepts of people from collectivist cultures are primarily defined by their social roles and group identifications, while individualists' self-concepts are defined mostly in terms of their personal attributes and psychological characteristics.

These cultural differences in the structure of self-concept are rooted in the way children are socialized (Pratt, 1991). Within collectivist societies, child-rearing practices emphasize obedience and knowing one's proper place. In collectivist China, for example, educational theories and practices emphasize shaping children's personalities to best meet societal needs and goals (Greenfield, 1994; Shweder, 1984). In contrast, individualist societies encourage independence and self-reliance, and children develop a belief in their own uniqueness and diversity.

A few years ago, my daughter Amelia came home from third grade with a library book that nicely illustrated how North American culture socializes children to value independence and uniqueness. The book, *The Upside-down Boy* (Palazzo-Craig, 1986), is about a child who was different because he liked to do everything upside down. Despite everyone trying to get the boy to stand right-side-up, he didn't comply. Instead, his persistence in being different led to him foiling a bank robbery and, thereby, becoming a local hero. Such stories convey values of independence and uniqueness that are different from children's literature in collectivist cultures, which stress fulfilling group goals, doing one's duty, and bringing pride to one's family, not one's self. Can you think of similar stories from your own childhood? Table 4-5 outlines how cultural differences regarding individualism-collectivism may influence self-concept. In addition, Discovery Box 4-2 discusses how different culturally based child-rearing practices in the United States may have different effects on children's self-concept and self-esteem.

TABLE 4-5 **Differences between Collectivist and Individualist Cultures**	**Collectivist**	**Individualist**
	Identity is based in the social system and given by one's group.	Identity is based in the individual and achieved by one's own striving.
	People are socialized to be emotionally dependent on organizations and institutions.	People are socialized to be emotionally independent of organizations and institutions.
	Personal and group goals are generally consistent, and when inconsistent, group goals get priority.	Personal and group goals are often inconsistent, and when inconsistent, personal goals get priority.
	People explain others' social behavior as being more determined by social norms and roles than by personal attitudes.	People explain others' social behavior as being more determined by personal attitudes than by social norms and roles.
	Emphasis is on belonging to organizations and membership.	Emphasis is on individual initiative, individual achievement, and leadership.
	Trust is placed in group decisions.	Trust is placed in individual decisions.

DISCOVERY BOX 4-2

Are There Cultural Differences in What Determines Self-Esteem?

Several studies demonstrate that, among African-American and Caucasian-American children, high self-esteem is associated with competitiveness (Peplau & Taylor, 1997; Rosenberg, 1965). In other words, children's feelings of self-worth are likely to be bolstered if they adopt a competitive approach to others. This orientation conforms to the individualist values of mainstream American culture. Yet in contrast to this association, researchers have found that among second-generation Mexican-American children, high self-esteem is associated with cooperativeness, not competitiveness (DeVoe, 1977; Kagan & Knight, 1979). For these children, their parents teach them to value and conform to the cooperative cultural norms of their collectivist Mexican homeland. For them, the growth and enhancement of self-concept and self-esteem do not appear to depend on a competitive comparison process with others. This same research indicates that as Mexican-American children become more acculturated to mainstream American culture this association between cooperativeness and self-esteem weakens. These findings and additional studies suggest that as Mexican-American youth strive to "fit in" to the larger American society they adopt a more competitive approach to life (Delgado-Gaitan, 1994; Uribe et al., 1994).

Journey of Discovery Question

If you were to tell someone to "just be yourself," what would that mean to that person, depending on whether he or she was from an individualist or a collectivist culture?

Gender Socialization

Shortly after children develop self-awareness—by the age of 2—they begin to develop an understanding of themselves as being either a "boy" or a "girl" (Katz, 1986). This knowledge is called **gender identity,** and it is one of the basic elements in self-concept. Once children identify with the girl or boy label, they learn to differentiate a wide variety of objects, activities, games, careers, and even basic personality traits as either being "natural" or "unnatural" for them (Etaugh & Liss, 1992; Fagot et al., 1986). In some societies, these gender expectations are clearly defined, nonoverlapping, and rigidly enforced, while in other societies, there are many shared expectations, with subtle and inconsistent social enforcement. In North American culture, we teach girls to express their emotions—including fear—and we teach boys to hide their emotions, especially if they are of the nonmasculine variety (Becht & Vingerhoets, 2002).

Gender identity: The knowledge that one is a male or a female and the internalization of this fact into one's self-concept.

In learning the "right way" to think about gender, children often segregate themselves into boy and girl play groups and adopt a fairly rigid set of gender beliefs (Maccoby, 1990; Maccoby & Jacklin, 1987). However, during the later elementary years, this gender inflexibility often declines as children become more aware of nontraditional gender views and exhibit greater cognitive complexity (Serbin & Sprafkin, 1986). Yet, even with this tendency toward greater gender flexibility in later childhood, traditional gender expectations significantly shape many adult social relationships (see sections 4-5c and 4-5d).

What can adults do to encourage children not to limit their potential by conforming to narrow social definitions of male and female? The following are five recommendations to counter gender stereotypes in the larger culture:

1. *Teach by example.* As we will discuss in chapter 7, section 7-3a, people often learn how to think and act by listening to the thoughts and observing the actions of others, especially those important to them. Children who see their mother and father taking turns doing laundry, making dinner, driving the car, and mowing the lawn are less likely to attach gender labels to these activities.

2. *Monitor your use of pronouns such as he and she.* As we will discuss in chapter 9, section 9-1f, children associate men and women with certain occupations by listening to the gendered pronouns adults use in referring to those occupations. For example, when telling children what a police officer does on the job, using only the male pronoun ("He arrests people who break the law") conveys to the child that this is an occupation for men, not women. A more inclusive way to describe occupations is to use the plural pronoun *they* and provide concrete examples of both men and women who occupy these jobs.

3. *Monitor children's entertainment.* Many forms of children's entertainment contain messages that boys and girls inherently engage in different kinds of social behavior. Often the message is that boys are aggressive and born to be adventurers, while girls are helpless and born to offer support to boys. For example, when reading fairy tales, researcher Sandra Bem (1983) suggests that adults can make such comments as, "Isn't it interesting that the person who wrote this story seems to think that girls always need to be rescued?" If not heavy-handed, such discussions can provide children with the idea that gender beliefs are relative and not fixed.

4. *Provide a cross-cultural and historical view of gender.* Because children will be exposed to gender stereotypes, they need to understand that beliefs about gender vary not only from household to household and from culture to culture, but also over time. For instance, you could let them know that in certain North African societies, decorating and beautifying the face and body is a sign of masculinity, not femininity. Or you could talk about anthropologist Margaret Mead's observations of the New Guinea Tchambuli society, where males were expected to be passive, emotionally dependent, and socially sensitive, while females were characterized as dominant, independent, and aggressive.

5. *Teach children about sexism.* Cultural relativism is a valuable lesson to learn, but children should also be taught that preventing people from engaging in certain behaviors simply because they are a member of one sex and not the other is wrong. This means that you should be prepared to let children know that these sexist practices should be opposed and corrected. Further, by telling them how sexism has been successfully opposed in the past, children will realize that this aspect of their social reality can be redefined and altered by their own future actions.

4-2f Erikson Asserted That Social Development Occurs in Stages, Each Marked by a Crisis

Erik Erikson (1902–1994) believed that people's social development occurs in identifiable stages. Each stage is marked by a crisis or conflict related to a specific developmental task. The more successfully people overcome these crises, the better chance they have to develop in a healthy manner (Erikson, 1950). Table 4-6 summarizes this eight-stage theory of psychosocial development.

Developing a sense of *trust versus mistrust* is the crisis of the first psychosocial stage, which corresponds to our previous discussion of attachment (refer back to section 4-2b) and occurs during the first year of life. Trust is established when an infant's basic needs for comfort, food, and warmth are met. If these needs are not adequately satisfied, the infant develops a mistrust of others.

Erik Erikson, a neo-Freudian whose personality theory encompasses the entire life span.

© Ted Streshinsky/CORBIS.

Identity Stage	Crisis	Description of Crisis
Infancy (birth–1 year)	Trust vs. mistrust	If basic needs are met, infants develop a sense of trust. If these needs are not adequately satisfied, infants develop a mistrust of others.
Toddlerhood (1–2 years)	Autonomy vs. shame and doubt	If toddlers can control their own actions and act independently, they develop a sense of autonomy. If they fail, they experience shame and doubt their own abilities.
Preschooler (3–5 years)	Initiative vs. guilt	If preschoolers can get what they want while acting responsibly, they develop a sense of initiative. If their impulses are not kept in check by a sense of guilt, they become undisciplined. If they are made to feel overly guilty, this will inhibit their initiative.
Elementary school (6–12 years)	Competence vs. inferiority	If children master the knowledge and skills necessary for adult life, they develop a sense of competence. If they are unable to achieve competence, they feel inferior and develop low self-esteem.
Adolescence (13–18 years)	Identity vs. role confusion	Teenagers struggle to develop a sense of identity by experimenting with different roles and integrating them into a single identity. If they fail to develop their own personal identity, they become confused about who they are.
Young adulthood (19–45 years)	Intimacy vs. isolation	If young adults successfully develop close relationships, they gain a sense of intimacy. If they are unable to develop such relationships, they feel socially isolated.
Middle adulthood (46–65 years)	Generativity vs. stagnation	If the middle-aged believe that they are contributing to the world and the next generation, they develop a sense of generativity. If they fail to do so, they experience a sense of stagnation.
Late adulthood (66 years and up)	Integrity vs. despair	If the elderly have successfully managed the previous crises in their lives, they will feel a sense of integrity. If they regret many of their life choices, they will feel a sense of despair.

TABLE 4-6

Erikson's Stages of Psychosocial Development

The second crisis, *autonomy versus shame and doubt,* occurs during the second year of life. Here, toddlers attempt to control their own actions and act independently. If successful, they develop a feeling of confidence or sense of autonomy, but if they fail or are restrained too severely, they may experience shame and doubt their own abilities.

During the third stage of development, which occurs between the ages of 3 and 5 (the preschool years), children struggle with *initiative versus guilt.* This stage deals with learning how to initiate plans, set goals, and attain them without breaking rules of proper behavior. If children can successfully get what they want while acting responsibly, this increases their initiative. Trouble arises, however, when initiative and guilt are not properly balanced. If children's impulses are not adequately kept in check by a sense of guilt over social transgressions—as is common in permissive parenting—they become undisciplined. In contrast, if children are made to feel overly guilty—as is common in authoritarian parenting—this will inhibit their initiative.

Between the ages of 6 and 12, children face the conflict of *industry versus inferiority,* where they attempt to master the knowledge and intellectual skills necessary for adult life. Children who are successful in this type of learning develop a sense of competence and achievement, while those who do poorly feel inferior and develop low self-esteem.

During adolescence (ages 13 to 18), children face the most crucial stage in Erikson's theory: *identity versus role confusion* (Erikson, 1968). Although knowing who you are and where you're headed is a lifelong task, adolescence is the first time that individuals make a concerted effort to consciously form their own identity or self-concept. One of the primary ways teenagers create their identity is by experimenting with many different roles—the nonconformist, the obedient son or daughter, the thrill-seeker, and so forth. Through such experimentation, adolescents gradually construct a theory about who they are that prepares them for adulthood. Often, this identity is an integration of many of the roles

Teenagers work at creating a personal identity. In so doing, they often define themselves in opposition to their parents. Why do you think that identity search and opposition to one's parents are more likely in individualist cultures than collectivist cultures?

A race of people is like an individual man; until it uses its own talent, takes pride in its own history, expresses its own culture, affirms its own selfhood, it can never fulfill itself.
—Malcolm X, U.S. Muslim and Black nationalist, 1925–1965

with which they previously experimented and serves as a guide for future life choices. According to Erikson, if adolescents cannot settle upon an identity they suffer role confusion and may feel "lost."

Regarding personal identity search, what might happen if you live in a society where the ethnic group to which you belong is devalued by the larger culture? In such circumstances, your search for personal identity may also encompass a search for **ethnic identity,** which is your sense of personal identification with a particular ethnic group (Hutnik, 1991; McAdoo, 2002). Discovery Box 4-3 describes the process of ethnic identity search.

Ethnic identity: A person's sense of personal identification with a particular ethnic group.

The sixth psychosocial stage involves the struggle with the main crisis of young adulthood, *intimacy versus isolation* (ages 19 to 45). Intimacy refers to sharing that which is inmost with others (McAdams, 1988). As we learned earlier in our review of research on attachment (see section 4-2b), those who do not feel a sense of security and trust in their social relationships have a difficult time achieving intimacy. Without close, loving relationships, Erikson contends that people will live in emotional isolation.

During middle adulthood (ages 46 to 65), the person faces the crisis of the seventh stage, namely *generativity versus stagnation.* For middle-aged adults, generativity involves teaching and nurturing the next generation, as well as creating something of substance in the world of work. Those who fail to contribute and produce something that they feel is worthy of their efforts experience a sense of stagnation, or lack of purpose in their lives.

Finally, during the last stage in psychosocial development (ages 66 and on), Erikson believes that the crisis revolves around the issue of *integrity versus despair.* As elderly adults look back on their lives, they ask themselves, "Did my life have meaning?" If they have successfully managed the crises in the previous seven stages, they will feel a sense of integrity (Holman, 2001). However, if they regret many of their important life choices, they will likely experience a sense of despair.

One of the primary strengths of Erikson's theory is its ability to draw connections between important psychosocial developments throughout a person's life (Friedman, 2001). For example, as predicted by Erikson's theory and confirmed by attachment researchers, failing to develop a sense of trust in one's caregivers early in life can have a detrimental effect on one's ability to develop satisfying romantic relationships in adulthood (Hazan & Shaver, 1987; Mikulincer & Erev, 1991). In addition to the stage connections, Erikson's highlighting of the identity search in adolescence has generally been supported, although research also indicates two important qualifications. First, identity development is not reserved solely for the adolescent years but, rather, continues at least into young adulthood (Hill, 1993). Second, as Erikson himself readily admitted, his theory best describes psychosocial development in Western industrialized cultures and does not accurately depict development in nonindustrialized or in collectivist societies. Indeed, the need to search for one's identity is a foreign notion for most collectivists because one's identity is often simply provided by the social group (Kroger, 1996).

There are three things extremely hard. Steel, a diamond, and to know one's self.
—Benjamin Franklin, U.S. statesman and scientist, 1706–1790

DISCOVERY BOX 4-3

What Does It Mean to "Search" for Your Ethnic Identity?

In a very real sense, ethnic identity is a state of mind, and acquiring it often requires considerable effort (Peters, 2002). This effort is especially important for people who experience prejudice in the larger culture due to their ethnicity. Faced with such intolerance, how might you search for your own ethnic identity?

Sociologist Jean Phinney (1993) has developed a three-stage model of ethnic identity formation (see table 4-7). In stage 1, the *unexamined ethnic identity* stage, you have not examined ethnic identity issues and may have incorporated negative ethnic stereotypes from the dominant culture into your own self-concept. One consequence of internalizing these derogatory social beliefs into your self-concept is that you may experience low self-esteem and feelings of inadequacy (Clark & Clark, 1939; Phinney & Kohatsu, 1997).

In stage 2, *ethnic identity search*, a personal experience with prejudice or your more general search for personal identity may kindle an interest in your ethnicity (Kelman, 1998; Roberts et al., 1999). Whatever the initial spark, this stage often entails an intense period of searching, in which you passionately consume ethnic literature and participate in cultural events. During stage 2, you may also develop an *oppositional identity*, in which you actively reject the values of the dominant culture and denigrate members of the dominant group.

The third stage and culmination of this process is a deeper understanding and appreciation of your ethnicity—what Phinney labels *achieved ethnic identity*. Confidence and security in a newfound ethnic identity allows you to feel a deep sense of ethnic pride along with a new understanding of your own place in the dominant culture. You are able to identify and internalize those aspects of the dominant culture that are acceptable and stand against those that are oppressive. In this manner, the development of a positive ethnic identity functions not only to protect you from continuing intolerance, but it also allows you to use this positive social identity to pursue mainstream goals and participate in mainstream life.

A number of studies support Phinney's view of the mental health benefits of ethnic identity development, among them being high self-esteem and a stable self-concept (Phinney et al., 1997; Phinney & Kohatsu, 1997). These findings indicate that it is our commitment and attitudes toward our ethnic group, rather than the evaluations of our group by the larger society, that influence our self-esteem. Such positive ethnic identities can short-circuit the negative effects that prejudice can inflict on self-esteem (Branscombe et al., in press).

TABLE 4-7

Stages in Ethnic Identity Formation

Stage 1: *Unexamined ethnic identity*. Lack of exploration of ethnicity, due to lack of interest or due to having merely adopted other people's opinions of ethnicity

Stage 2: *Ethnic identity search*. Involvement in exploring and seeking to understand the meaning of ethnicity for oneself, often sparked by some incident that focused attention on one's minority status in the dominant culture

Stage 3: *Achieved ethnic identity*. Clear and confident sense of one's own ethnicity; able to identify and internalize those aspects of the dominant culture that are acceptable and stand against those that are oppressive

SECTION SUMMARY

- Attachment is the primary social achievement of infancy.

- Infants who receive tender and loving care develop secure attachment, which fosters psychological adjustment and health.

- Infants who receive neglectful or abusive care develop insecure attachment, which fosters problematic social relationships.

- Self-concept is the paramount social achievement of childhood, and it is predicated on the development of self-awareness.

- Collectivist cultures foster group-oriented self-concepts, whereas individualist cultures foster self-focused self-concepts.

- Gender identity is one of the basic elements in self-concept.

- Erikson's theory of psychosocial development explains the social conflicts encountered in eight life stages.

4-3 COGNITIVE DEVELOPMENT

Cognition is the activity of knowing and the processes through which knowledge is acquired and problems are solved. How does cognition, or thinking, emerge and develop in the mind of a child? For a good start in answering this question, let's turn to the pioneering work of Jean Piaget, the person to have the single most important impact on developmental psychology (Flavell, 1996; Siegler & Ellis, 1996).

4-3a Piaget's Theory of Cognitive Development Has Four Distinct Stages

Eighty years ago, young Swiss psychologist Jean Piaget (1896–1980) was intrigued by the fact that children of different ages made different kinds of mistakes while solving problems. Based on his observations, he argued that children are not like "little adults" who simply know less, but instead, they think about the world in a very different way. Piaget's subsequent research led him to conclude that as children mature, they move through four chronological cognitive stages, each distinguished by a qualitatively different type of thinking, and each building upon the stages preceding it (see table 4-8). Perhaps influenced by his culture's individualist beliefs concerning self-reliance, Piaget also conceived

Jean Piaget (1896–1980).

© Bettmann/CORBIS.

TABLE 4-8

Piaget's Stages of Cognitive Development

Typical Age Range	Description of Stage	Developmental Phenomena
Birth–2 years	*Sensorimotor*—Experiencing the world through actions (grasping, looking, touching, and sucking)	• Object permanence • Stranger anxiety
2–6 years	*Preoperational*—Representing things with words and images but no logical reasoning	• Pretend play • Egocentrism • Language
7–11 years	*Concrete operational*—Thinking logically about concrete events; understanding concrete analogies and performing arithmetical operations	• Conservation • Mathematical transformations
12 through adulthood	*Formal operational*—Abstract reasoning	• Abstract logic

of cognitive development as being a relatively solitary process, something children achieved by actively interacting with the world. Later in this chapter (see section 4-3c), you will be introduced to a theorist from a collectivist culture who proposed a more "group-oriented" view of cognitive development.

Schemas

According to Piaget, children's cognitive development is made possible by them organizing their own structures of knowledge, called schemas, to better adapt to their environment. A **schema** is an organized cluster of knowledge that people use to understand and interpret information. For example, when teaching my daughters how to play "catch," I had them hold out their arms about 6 inches apart and then gently tossed them a stuffed bear. When it landed on their arms, they pulled it to their chests, mission accomplished. By repeating this activity, they developed a schema for "catching."

Schema: An organized cluster of knowledge that people use to understand and interpret information.

Assimilation and Accommodation

In using schemas, people's acquisition of knowledge occurs through the two complementary processes of assimilation and accommodation (Piaget & Inhelder, 1969). **Assimilation** is the process of absorbing new information into existing schemas, while **accommodation** is the process of changing existing schemas in order to absorb new information. Once my daughters learned how to catch a stuffed bear, I began throwing other things to them: a beach ball, a pillow, a Ping-Pong ball. For the ball and pillow, they were able to use their bear-catching schema quite nicely, so they engaged in assimilation. However, trying to assimilate the Ping-Pong ball didn't work—it fell right between their outstretched arms. So they had to accommodate—they adjusted their catching posture, using their cupped hands more than their outstretched arms to cradle the ball. Throughout life, the major dilemma in learning and problem solving is whether one will attempt to assimilate new information into existing schemas or change those knowledge structures so that the new information can be better handled and understood. Generally, people first try to assimilate, but if that fails, they accommodate their schemas in an attempt to deal with the situation.

Assimilation: The process of absorbing new information into existing schemas.

Accommodation: The process of changing existing schemas in order to absorb new information.

Sensorimotor Stage

As you can see from table 4-8, the first stage in Piaget's theory of cognitive development is the **sensorimotor stage** (birth to age 2), a period of time where infants develop the ability to coordinate their sensory input with their motor actions. One of the major accomplishments at this stage is the development of **object permanence,** which is the realization that an object continues to exist even if you can't see it or touch it. For infants who lack a schema for object permanence, out of sight is quite literally out of mind. Although Piaget's research suggested that children do not exhibit memory for hidden objects prior to 8 months, later studies indicated that infants as young as 3 or 4 months have at least some understanding of object permanence (Baillargeon & DeVos, 1991; Diamond, 1985).

One quick and easy way to determine whether infants have a clear understanding of object permanence is to try to engage them in a game of peekaboo. If they wait for your face to emerge from behind your hands, out of sight is definitely not out of mind for them; they have the capacity to retain a mental image of you in their minds. Piaget stated that object permanence marks the beginning of *representational thought,* which is the ability to use mental imagery and other symbolic systems, such as language. It also is associated with the onset of separation anxiety (refer back to section 4-2a). Babies who cry when their mothers leave them are demonstrating that they have a schema for object permanence—they know she exists when she is out of sight, and this knowledge creates anxiety.

Sensorimotor stage: The first stage in Piaget's theory of cognitive development (birth to age 2) in which infants develop the ability to coordinate their sensory input with their motor actions.

Object permanence: The realization that an object continues to exist even if you can't see it or touch it.

There are two ways of meeting difficulties. You alter the difficulties or you alter yourself to meet them.

—Phyllis Bottome, English author, 1884–1963

Preoperational Stage

Between the ages of around 2 to 7, children are in the **preoperational stage,** a maturational period marked by the full emergence of representational thought that started at the end of the sensorimotor stage. Not only do they think in terms of language, but they also begin to engage in make-believe play, in which they act out familiar activities, such as eating or sleeping. This stage is called preoperational because children have difficulty performing what Piaget called *operations*, which are mental manipulations of objects that are reversible (Piaget, 1972a). For example, a preoperational child might know that adding 7 plus 2 equals 9 but find that of no value in trying to figure out its reverse, namely, what 9 minus 2 equals.

Another important limitation of preoperational thinking is **egocentrism,** which is the tendency to view the world from one's own perspective without recognizing that others may have different viewpoints. Piaget demonstrated preoperational egocentrism in his famous *three-mountains problem* (Piaget & Inhelder, 1956). In this task, children were seated at a table with three model mountains like those depicted in figure 4-4, and with a doll sitting in another chair opposite to them. When asked to choose a picture that corresponded to the doll's view of the mountains, preoperational children often chose the picture depicting their own view instead. Although preoperational children are not egocentric in every situation, they are much more likely to make egocentric mistakes than older children (Ford, 1979). This is why 3-year-olds might play hide-and-seek by simply closing their eyes. As far as they're concerned, they've found a pretty good hiding place because they can't see a thing!

Another limitation at this stage can be traced back to our earlier discussion of preoperational children's difficulty in reversing operations. Due to this inability to reverse thinking, children do not understand **conservation,** which is the understanding that certain physical properties of an object remain unchanged despite superficial changes in its appearance. A 5-year-old, Jason, illustrated his lack of understanding of conservation when I poured each of us the same amount of soda into two identical glasses and then poured his soda into a third glass that was wider than the other two:

After pouring the same amount of soda into two identical glasses:

S.F.: "Do I have more soda than you? Do you have more soda than me? Or do we have the same amount of soda?

Jason: "We've both got the same."

S.F.: "OK, now I'm going to take your soda and pour it into here (wider glass). Now, look at your soda. Do I have more soda than you? Do you have more soda than me? Or do we have the same amount of soda?"

Jason: "You've got more than me."

S.F.: "Why is that?"

Jason: "Because it's put into a bigger glass, so my soda is lower."

Preoperational stage: The second stage in Piaget's theory of cognitive development (ages 2 to 7), marked by the full emergence of representational thought.

Egocentrism: The tendency to view the world from one's own perspective without recognizing that others may have different points of view.

Conservation: The understanding that certain physical properties of an object remain unchanged despite superficial changes in its appearance.

What does the doll see?

FIGURE 4-4
The Three-Mountains Problem

In the three-mountains problem, preoperational children typically do not understand that the doll "sees" the mountain from a perspective different from their own. This is an example of egocentrism.

FIGURE 4-5
Conservation of Liquid, Mass, and Number

Preoperational children cannot mentally reverse a sequence of events (an operation) back to the starting point. Further, because of centration, preoperational children cannot simultaneously consider two features of an object (for example, the height and width of liquid in a glass). As a result of these problems of reversibility and centration, they are not yet able to comprehend the principle of conservation.

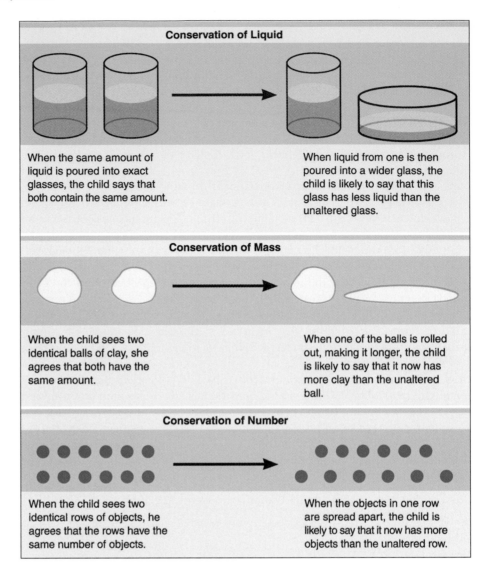

Conservation of Liquid

When the same amount of liquid is poured into exact glasses, the child says that both contain the same amount.

When liquid from one is then poured into a wider glass, the child is likely to say that this glass has less liquid than the unaltered glass.

Conservation of Mass

When the child sees two identical balls of clay, she agrees that both have the same amount.

When one of the balls is rolled out, making it longer, the child is likely to say that it now has more clay than the unaltered ball.

Conservation of Number

When the child sees two identical rows of objects, he agrees that the rows have the same number of objects.

When the objects in one row are spread apart, the child is likely to say that it now has more objects than the unaltered row.

S.F.: "Can you make it so that we have the same amount of soda?"

Jason: "Just pour it back into the first glass."

After pouring the soda back into the original glass:

S.F.: "Do we have the same amount again?"

Jason: "Yes."

Jason's inability to mentally reverse the operation of pouring contributed to his inability to understand the conservation of liquid. Another factor that hindered Jason's inability to understand the conservation of liquid was that he paid attention to only one feature of the liquid in the glass–its height. Like other preoperational children, Jason engaged in *centration*, which is the tendency to focus (or center) on one feature of an object and ignore other relevant features. By noticing only the height of the liquid in the glass—which was lower than the original—and not noticing that its width was greater, Jason falsely concluded that he had lost some soda in the transfer. Preoperational children have difficulty with conservation tasks because they not only cannot reverse operations, but they tend to pay attention to only one feature of the object. Figure 4-5 lists a number of conservation tasks that preoperational children have difficulty performing.

Do you see something that egocentrism and centration have in common? In egocentrism, children only see things from one perspective (their own), and in centration, children consider only one feature of an object. Thus, in both mental activities, when judging reality, preoperational children can only think about events or objects in one way.

Concrete Operational Stage

Around the age of 5, children advance to what Piaget called the **concrete operational stage,** a time in which they can perform mental operations and gradually begin to engage in logical reasoning. During this stage, children develop an understanding of the principle of conservation, usually first in relation to number and liquid (ages 6–7), followed by mass and length (ages 7–8), and finally area (ages 8–10). Piaget called this stage *concrete* operational because children's thinking and their use of logic is limited to concrete reality, not abstract or hypothetical concepts. If it is not something that can be directly experienced, concrete operational children have difficulty thinking about it. For example, ask a 7-year-old to explain the concept of friendship. Instead of defining it abstractly, by saying that it is the emotional attachment we have toward someone based on affection, she or he is likely to say that "friendship is when you play with someone." For the concrete operational child, friendship is understood only from actual everyday experiences.

Concrete operational stage: The third stage in Piaget's theory of cognitive development (ages 7 to 11), a time in which children can perform mental operations on tangible objects or events and gradually engage in logical reasoning.

Formal Operational Stage

The **formal operational stage,** beginning sometime around 11 years or later, is the fourth and final stage in Piaget's theory of cognitive development. Here, early adolescents are able to reason abstractly and make predictions about hypothetical situations, much like a scientist does. Whereas problem solving in earlier stages often tends to occur using trial-and-error methods, formal operational thinking involves much more systematic and reflective strategies. A demonstration of these different problem-solving modes was provided in one of Piaget's own experiments (Inhelder & Piaget, 1958). In this study, youngsters were presented with several flasks containing clear liquids and told that their task was to determine which liquid combinations would produce a blue liquid. Concrete operational children haphazardly poured one liquid in with another, trying to stumble upon the correct solution. In contrast, formal operational children tended to step back and contemplate their choices prior to acting, and then kept track of each liquid combination until they solved the problem. Such reflective thought and abstract reasoning is necessary for teenagers to competently study such subjects as philosophy, theology, politics, and science (Renner et al., 1990).

Formal operational stage: The fourth and final stage in Piaget's theory of cognitive development (ages 11 or beyond), during which a person is able to reason abstractly and make predictions about hypothetical situations.

Although Piaget initially believed that all children eventually attained formal operations sometime during adolescence, later research found that many older adolescents and even some adults have yet to attain this ability (Piaget, 1972b). For example, only 25 percent of all first-year college students and 50 percent of all college students are at the formal operation stage (McKinnon, 1976; McKinnon & Renner, 1971).

4-3b Some of Piaget's Conclusions about Children's Mental Capabilities Are Incorrect

No theory comes close to matching the impact that Piaget's cognitive developmental theory has had on the field of developmental psychology (Beilin & Pufall, 1992; Gopnik, 1996), and numerous studies have supported many of Piaget's central propositions (Lourenço & Machado, 1996). Yet, despite Piaget's continuing influence, an increasing number of studies are questioning certain aspects of his work.

First, it appears that children are more cognitively advanced and adults are less cognitively sophisticated than outlined by Piaget (Spelke et al., 1992; Thomas, 2001). For example, although still egocentric, preschoolers develop a **theory of mind,** meaning a theory of other people's mental states—their beliefs, feelings, and desires—that allow them to predict how others will behave in specific situations (Flavell, 1999; Wellman, 1990).

Theory of mind: A theory of other people's mental states—their beliefs, feelings, and desires—that allows them to predict how these people will behave in specific situations.

Second, cross-cultural research suggests that cognitive development is more influenced by social and environmental factors than Piaget thought. For example, in nomadic societies where quantifying objects is not very important, the development of the conservation of number occurs later than in Western cultures (Dasen, 1994). In contrast, the fact that these nomadic societies move frequently from place to place probably explains why their children's spatial abilities—the ability to orient themselves in their environment—develop more rapidly.

Perhaps the most serious criticism of the theory is that cognitive development doesn't occur in the sequential manner Piaget described; that is, children progressing through qualitatively distinct stages of thinking. Instead, an increasing number of researchers contend that mental growth is more accurately characterized by continuous and gradual changes that are less distinct from one another than Piaget described (Case, 1992; Flavell, 1982). Further, it is also now known that people who have the ability to engage in formal operations often will fall back on concrete operational reasoning when they are dealing with an unfamiliar task (Flavell, 1992). Thus, just because you progress to a more sophisticated type of thinking doesn't mean that you will always engage in that type of thinking in all instances.

Despite these criticisms, most developmental psychologists still agree that Piaget has generally outlined an accurate view of many of the significant changes that occur in mental functioning with increasing childhood maturation. They also credit Piaget with highlighting the fact that children are not passive creatures merely being molded by environmental forces, but that they are actively involved in their own cognitive growth. Not only has his work advanced our understanding of childhood development, but Piaget's insights have profoundly influenced how and what we teach our children in elementary and secondary schools.

4-3c Vygotsky's Theory of Cognitive Development Stresses Instruction and Guidance

One implication of Piaget's theory for educators is that children's level of cognitive development should first be determined so that they can be taught material appropriate to that level. According to Piaget, trying to accelerate children's learning beyond their current stage of mental functioning is not only a waste of time, it can undermine their confidence due to the inevitable failure they will experience. Standing in sharp contrast to this view is the work of Russian psychologist Lev Vygotsky (1896–1934). Perhaps influenced by his culture's collectivist beliefs concerning cooperation or its Marxist beliefs emphasizing the role of experience, Vygotsky argued that children's mental development can be accelerated if they are given instruction and guidance by someone who is more mentally mature. Where Piaget stressed the biological limits of learning due to age, Vygotsky emphasized how social environmental factors can assist and nurture cognitive development (Vygotsky, 1934/1986). Whereas Piaget conceived of cognitive development proceeding "from the inside out" and being relatively asocial, Vygotsky viewed it as proceeding "from the outside in" and being inherently social (Cornejo, 2001; Matusov & Hayes, 2000).

Private Speech and Internalization

According to Vygotsky, learning occurs through the social instrument of language. They listen to people, observe their actions, and then they internalize this knowledge and make it their own through private speech. **Private speech** is part of a larger cognitive process, known as **internalization,** in which people absorb knowledge from their social surroundings. Internalization is one of the key mechanisms through which children's environments influence their cognitive development.

Zone of Proximal Development

In assessing cognitive development, Vygotsky maintained that you need to identify children's **zone of proximal development (ZPD).** The ZPD is the cognitive range between

Private speech: Overt language that is not directed to others but, rather, is self-directed.

Internalization: A process of cognition in which people absorb knowledge from their social surroundings.

Zone of proximal development (ZPD): The cognitive range between what a child can do on her or his own and what the child can do with the help of adults or more-skilled children.

what a child can do on her or his own and what the child can do with the help of adults or more-skilled children. The lower limit of the ZPD is the level of problem solving the child can successfully accomplish working alone, while the upper limit of the ZPD is the child's untapped cognitive capacity, which is realized only through working closely with an instructor. According to Vygotsky, one of the most important jobs of educators is identifying each child's ZPD and then pushing each of them toward that upper limit (DeVries, 2000). Once the child can problem-solve at that upper limit alone, it becomes the foundation for a new and more-advanced ZPD.

Private speech plays an important role in reaching the upper limit of the ZPD. By engaging in cooperative dialogues with their instructors, children can incorporate their instructors' language into their own private speech, and later use this speech when working on the task alone (Berk, 1994). By internalizing the instructor's language and making it their own, children become less dependent on direct assistance regarding the task at hand (Rogoff, 1984). The use of private speech to work at the upper limit of the ZPD is not only employed by children, but by adults as well. For example, the next time you study for an exam, try to catch yourself incorporating your instructors' language into your own private speech. According to Vygotsky, engaging in this internal dialogue is an essential part of the learning process at all age levels.

Although Vygotsky's theory of cognitive development has profoundly shaped Russian and East European developmental psychology since the 1920s, his work remained relatively unknown in the West until the easing of international tensions between the East and the West in the late 1980s and the dismantling of the Soviet Union in the early 1990s (Kozulin, 1990; Wertsch & Tulviste, 1992). However, since then his ideas have helped psychologists and educators in the West better understand how learning new cognitive skills is often very much a social activity (see the *Psychological Applications* section at the end of the chapter).

4-3d The Information-Processing Approach Examines Age-Related Differences in How Information Is Organized and Manipulated

Another perspective on cognitive development that has become influential during the past 35 years is the *information-processing approach*, which examines age-related changes in the way information is processed, stored, and actively manipulated (Demetriou, 1988; Siegler, 1998). According to this perspective, a number of important changes occur in children's information-processing system that directly affect their ability to learn. For example, the speed of processing information increases throughout childhood as some abilities become more automatic (Kail, 1991). This increase in performance speed appears to be due to the maturation of the brain. As the brain matures, children also become less easily distracted (Jensen & Neff, 1993; Siegler, 1996). Because human's information-processing capacities are rather limited (refer to chapter 8, section 8-1d), this increasing ability to focus attention greatly aids learning.

The types of memory strategies children employ changes with age as well. Prior to age 5, most children don't use any memory strategies. At the age of 5, however, children develop the ability to use rehearsal to remember information, but they use it much less frequently than older children (Flavell et al., 1966). Older children also employ more complex rehearsal strategies, such as categorization and imagery (Alexander & Schwanenflugel, 1994; Moely et al., 1969).

One reason older children employ more sophisticated memory strategies than younger children is because they have developed **metacognition,** an awareness and understanding of their own cognitive processes. Cognitive psychologists believe that this ability to "think about thinking" allows older children and adults to acquire new and more complex strategies for increasing their cognitive efficiency (Moses & Chandler, 1992).

Metacognition: An awareness and understanding of one's own cognitive processes.

The information-processing approach is not necessarily incompatible with either Piaget's or Vygotsky's theories of cognitive development. In fact, some theorists have combined the insights from all three perspectives into what are called neo-Piagetian theories. These theories tend to view development as occurring gradually, with later cognitive structures developing from earlier ones due to children's interaction with their environment (Case, 1985, 1991). As continuing studies provide us with a better understanding of the child's developing mind, it is likely that Jean Piaget's work will still serve as the fundamental springboard for new theories.

SECTION SUMMARY

- According to Piaget, children move through the following four cognitive stages: sensorimotor, preoperational, concrete operational, and formal operational.
- Vygotsky believes that by instructing children within their zone of proximal development and encouraging internalization of knowledge, mental development can be pushed beyond the cognitive limits proposed by Piaget.
- The information-processing approach examines age-related changes in the way information is processed, stored, and actively manipulated.
- Neo-Piagetian theories combine the insights from all three of these perspectives.

4-4 MORAL DEVELOPMENT

Consider the following hypothetical situation:

> In Europe, a woman is dying from a special kind of cancer. The one drug that the doctors think might save her is a form of radium recently discovered by a local druggist. The drug is expensive to make, costing $200, and the druggist is charging 10 times his cost, or $2,000, for a small dose. The sick woman's husband, Heinz, goes to everyone he knows asking to borrow money to buy the drug, but he is only able to scrape together $1,000. He tells the druggist that his wife is dying and asks him to lower the price or let him pay the balance later, but the druggist says, "No, I discovered the drug, and I'm going to make money from it." In desperation, Heinz breaks into the druggist's office and steals the drug for his wife.

Do you agree or disagree with his course of action? What are the reason(s) for your answer?

4-4a Kohlberg Maintained That There Are Three Levels of Moral Development

According to Lawrence Kohlberg (1981, 1984), the reasons you give concerning the correctness of Heinz's behavior—and not simply your agreement or disagreement—provide insights into your level of moral development. Influenced by Piaget's theory of cognitive development, Kohlberg maintained that people pass through three levels of moral development, each containing two stages. Each successive level is a less egocentric and more mature analysis of moral choices (refer to figure 4-6).

At level one, **preconventional morality,** children's sense of moral reasoning centers on avoiding punishment (stage 1) or seeking concrete rewards (stage 2). Due to their egocentrism, people operating at the preconventional level focus on how their moral choices will affect them and not others. Thus, a preconventional person might reason either that Heinz should not steal the drug because he could end up in jail, or that he should steal the drug because his wife might make him something nice.

As children cognitively mature and become more aware of others' perspectives and the conventions of society, many begin to engage in **conventional morality.** Here, people define what is right and wrong in terms of societal norms and laws, and they are motivated to conform to these rules in order to gain the approval or avoid the disapproval of others. According to Kohlberg, most people will remain at this level of moral reasoning the rest

Preconventional morality: The first level of moral reasoning in Kohlberg's theory of moral development, characterized by avoiding punishment and seeking rewards.

Conventional morality: The second level of moral reasoning in Kohlberg's theory of moral development, characterized by conforming to societal norms and laws.

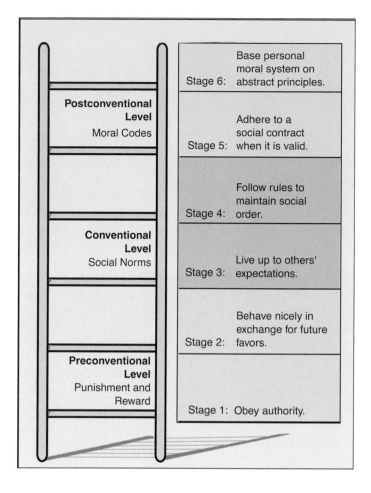

FIGURE 4-6
Kohlberg's Levels of Moral Development

According to Kohlberg, we move through six stages of moral development, reflecting three different levels of moral reasoning. Each successive level represents a more mature analysis of moral choices. Which level do you think you are on?

of their lives, basing their moral choices either on seeking acceptance and approval of others (stage 3) or conforming to authority to maintain the official social order (stage 4). The reason Kohlberg considered social order conformity more advanced than interpersonal approval-seeking is that stage 4 reasoning is based on attention to rules made by representatives of the larger society rather than merely by a person's immediate peer group. In the Heinz dilemma, a person at the stage 4 conventional level might argue that Heinz should not steal the drug because it is illegal.

Postconventional morality involves moving beyond mere acceptance of interpersonal norms and societal rules, to basing moral judgments on abstract principles and values that may conflict with self-interest and contemporary thinking. A basic requirement of postconventional moral reasoning is the ability to engage in formal operational thought. Yet, to attain this third level of moral development, abstract thinkers must either base their moral decisions on democratically agreed upon individual rights (stage 5) or on universal ethical principles (stage 6). An adult at stage 6 might say that Heinz should steal the drug because saving a life is a principle that is more important than any law.

Postconventional morality: The third and final level of moral reasoning in Kohlberg's theory of moral development, characterized by making moral judgments based on abstract universal principles.

4-4b Kohlberg's Theory Has Been Criticized As Being Male-Oriented

One intriguing finding reported in several studies employing Kohlberg's theory is that women tend to be classified at a lower level of moral reasoning than men. Carol Gilligan (1982, 1990) believes that the reason for this gender difference is not that women are less sophisticated moral thinkers than men, but rather, that Kohlberg's theory emphasizes values more often held by men, such as independence and rationality, while de-emphasizing

DISCOVERY   BOX 4-4

Is Moral Reasoning Shaped by a Culture's Individualist-Collectivist Tendencies?

Cross-cultural research confirms that children in diverse societies progress from the preconventional to the conventional levels, but the postconventional level is typically reached only by those raised in individualist cultures where personal rights and privileges are given priority over those of the group (Al-Ansari, 2002; Eckensberger, 1994; Snarey, 1985). Based on these findings, critics claim that Kohlberg's theory is not equipped to explain the development of moral reasoning in collectivist societies (Shweder et al., 1990).

Whereas Kohlberg's individualist theory of moral development considers the abstract principles of individual rights and social justice as the basis for the most "mature" moral reasoning, the religious and philosophical teachings from collectivist China and India, for example, emphasize social cohesion and group welfare (Ma, 1988; Miller, 1994). Here, morality is associated with an adherence to many rules and fits most closely with Kohlberg's conventional morality. Yet, why should those cultures that emphasize social harmony and the good of the group ahead of the good of the individual be thought of as having a less-sophisticated sense of morality? What cross-cultural research teaches us is that moral development may vary considerably from society to society, and what stands for mature moral reasoning in one culture may not be recognized as such in another culture.

values more associated with women, such as concern for others and belonging. Gilligan proposed that females in many cultures, including our own, are socialized to analyze moral dilemmas based on these values. According to Gilligan, the end result is that women's moral reasoning is more influenced by a desire to relieve distress and promote social welfare, while men's moral reasoning is more influenced by a desire to uphold individual rights and privileges.

Despite some empirical support for Gilligan's position (Baumrind, 1986; Gilligan & Attanucci, 1988), other studies have not found the earlier reported gender differences in moral development (Al-Ansari, 2002). Instead, they have found evidence indicating that most women and men, as well as boys and girls, consider both justice and caring values when making moral judgments (Thoma, 1986; Walker, 1989). Thus, while Gilligan's assertion that men and women engage in different styles of moral reasoning appears questionable, her work has led to the realization that Kohlberg's theory is incomplete, and that people's concern for the welfare of others must be considered when evaluating their level of moral development (Dawson, 2002; Galotti et al., 1991). (See Discovery Box 4-4.)

SECTION SUMMARY

- According to Kohlberg, people pass through three levels of moral development, with each successive level being a less egocentric and more mature analysis of moral choices.

- Questions remain concerning how well Kohlberg's stages accurately describe moral development in both women and in collectivist cultures.

4-5 ADOLESCENCE AND ADULTHOOD

Are you an adult or an adolescent? If you are between the ages of 16 and 22, you may not know the answer to this question. Adolescence, as a stage in life, is a relatively recent phenomenon (Ben-Amos, 1994). Most societies have always viewed young people as needing instruction and time to develop. However, as societies industrialized, they had a greater need for workers with more specialized skills. To adequately train these workers, it was necessary to extend education beyond puberty and to delay adulthood—hence **adolescence,** the transition period between childhood and adulthood. In preindustrialized societies, such as the Sambia of Papua New Guinea or many African hunter-gatherer tribes, there is little need for this transition period (Turnbull, 1989). Instead, following sometimes painful and demanding ritualistic ceremonies, children are ushered into adulthood and expected to take on the responsibilities associated with their new social status. For such groups, there is no adolescence.

In our culture, instead of going through one rite of passage where everyone recognizes you as an adult, you go through many formal and informal rituals that make you more "adultlike." Perhaps the best way to describe adolescence is that it is a time when you are en route to becoming an adult, and people differ on when they arrive at the adult designation (Steinberg, 1999).

4-5a Puberty Signals the Onset of Adolescent Physical Development

Most people would agree that adolescence begins at the onset of **puberty,** when the pituitary gland's increased secretion of the growth hormone triggers a growth spurt lasting about two years. Children vary a great deal on when they experience this growth spurt, but in North America, girls generally start at age 10+, while boys begin at 13 (Tanner, 1990). Accompanying height and weight gains are the maturation of both the primary and secondary sex characteristics. **Primary sex characteristics** are the reproductive organs; **secondary sex characteristics** are the nonreproductive physical features that distinguish the two sexes from one another. Examples of developing secondary sex characteristics in pubescent females are breast enlargement, a widening of the hips, and an increase in fat deposits. In adolescent males, the development of facial hair, deeper voices, and greater upper body strength are some of the more noticeable secondary sex characteristics. Figure 4-7 lists the average sequence of puberty for the two sexes.

In girls, puberty's landmark event is the first menstrual period, called **menarche,** which occurs about the age of 13. If parents or other adults have adequately prepared girls for menarche, they generally experience it as a positive life transition, although they still may respond with both pride and embarrassment (Greif & Ulman, 1982). The most significant pubertal event for boys is their first ejaculation, which also occurs at about age 13.

The timing of pubertal growth can have different psychological effects on girls and boys (Faust, 1977; Simmons et al., 1979). Because our culture tends to judge female bodies in terms of beauty and sexuality (Franzoi, 1995), early maturing girls receive greater attention from boys than later maturing girls, and they also tend to date and engage in sexual relations earlier (Phinney et al., 1990). For some, this generally unwanted attention causes early maturing girls to feel awkward and anxious in social situations and suffer from low self-esteem. In contrast, our culture tends to judge male bodies by athletic ability and strength (Franzoi & Chang, 2000). Because early maturing boys are physically superior to their peers, they tend to be popular, have high self-esteem, and feel relaxed and in control socially. What about late maturing adolescents? The opposite effects are found. While slow maturing girls are often pleased by the delay in the onset of puberty and tend to be more popular and socially poised, slow maturing boys are distressed, feel physically inferior, and may become attention-seeking. Fortunately, the stress sometimes

Adolescence: The transition period between childhood and adulthood.

Puberty: The growth period of sexual maturation, during which a person becomes capable of reproducing.

Primary sex characteristics: The body organs that make sexual reproduction possible.

Secondary sex characteristics: The nonreproductive physical features that distinguish the two sexes from one another.

Menarche: The first menstrual period.

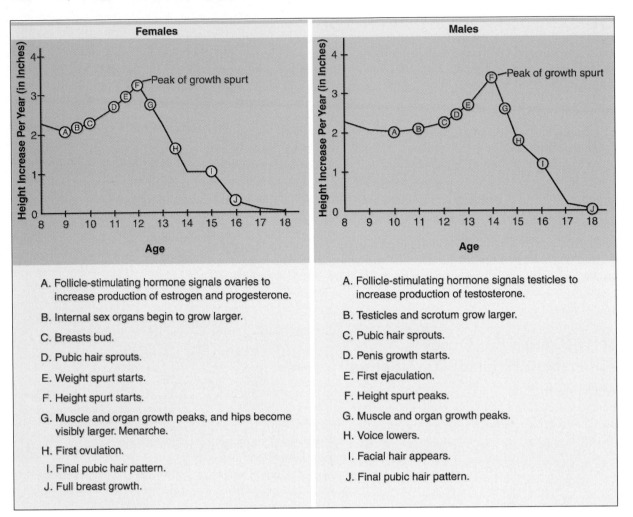

A. Follicle-stimulating hormone signals ovaries to increase production of estrogen and progesterone.

B. Internal sex organs begin to grow larger.

C. Breasts bud.

D. Pubic hair sprouts.

E. Weight spurt starts.

F. Height spurt starts.

G. Muscle and organ growth peaks, and hips become visibly larger. Menarche.

H. First ovulation.

I. Final pubic hair pattern.

J. Full breast growth.

A. Follicle-stimulating hormone signals testicles to increase production of testosterone.

B. Testicles and scrotum grow larger.

C. Pubic hair sprouts.

D. Penis growth starts.

E. First ejaculation.

F. Height spurt peaks.

G. Muscle and organ growth peaks.

H. Voice lowers.

I. Facial hair appears.

J. Final pubic hair pattern.

FIGURE 4-7
Sequences of Puberty in Adolescent Females and Adolescent Males

Imaginary audience: Adolescents' belief that their thoughts, feelings, and behavior are constantly being focused on by other people.

Personal fable: The tendency for adolescents to believe that their experiences and feelings are unique.

experienced by early maturing girls and late maturing boys does subside, and the experience tends to result in these females entering adulthood with good coping skills and the males having a strong sense of identity.

4-5b Heightened Self-Consciousness Is a Hallmark of Adolescence

At the same time adolescents are physically maturing, they are also further developing their reasoning abilities. Teenagers begin to think in greater depth about their place in the social world. With these cognitive advances comes a greater tendency to focus on the self, and this greater self-attention often results in a heightened sense of self-consciousness.

One way that adolescents' self-consciousness is manifested is by the **imaginary audience,** a belief that other people are constantly focused on their thoughts, feelings, and behavior (Elkind, 1985). For example, a teenager may be so convinced that everyone will notice a minor blemish on his face, or the fact that he is infatuated with a particular person, that he may actually refuse to leave the house until he believes this unwanted attention has subsided.

Being so self-absorbed often results in the development of the **personal fable,** which is the tendency for teenagers to believe that no one has ever felt or thought as they do (Elkind & Bowen, 1979). Thus, teenagers in love may believe that no one has ever felt the intense emotions they feel. When relationships end, they may believe that no one can understand what they are going through—least of all their parents.

Despite these self-focused tendencies, as adolescents mature, they become more sophisticated in their social judgments. In assessing others, they not only recognize that people possess distinct and sometimes inconsistent personality traits, but they also integrate these discrepant traits into personality profiles that are considerably more complex than those provided by children (O'Mahony, 1986). Like many teens, perhaps you recall spending hours analyzing your friends and family members' personalities, trying to figure out what made them tick. These attempts to understand the hidden world of personality is just one example of how teenagers exercise their emerging formal operational thinking. In a sense, during adolescence, there is a cognitive-emotional "push-pull." On one side, the emergence of formal operational thinking gives teenagers greater capability for deep thinking, but this is often accompanied by learning how to cope with new emotions that often side-track cognition into egocentrism.

4-5c Friendship Is an Important Emotional Bond throughout Life

Beyond the intimacy of family relationships, friendships provide important sources of social and emotional support throughout our lives (Elbedour et al., 1997). However, largely due to competing time demands, adults typically have fewer friends than do adolescents (Norris & Tinsdale, 1994).

Although both men and women value friendship, research suggests certain gender differences in heterosexual friendship patterns from childhood through adulthood (Felmlee, 1999; Felmlee & Sprecher, 2000). The most notable gender difference involves the level of emotional expressiveness within same-sex friendships. Put simply, women's friendships tend to be more intimate and involve more emotional sharing than men's friendships (Veniegas & Peplau, 1997; Way et al., 2001). The general consensus among social scientists is that these intimacy differences between men and women are not rooted in biology but, rather, are due to gender socialization.

What is it about gender socialization that leads to less friendship intimacy? Research suggests that men in North American culture appear to be governed by a more rigid set of gender rules than women, especially regarding expressions of tender emotions and physical touching (Timmers et al., 1998). This social injunction against intimacy expression among males appears to be the result of men being socialized to conform to *heterosexual masculinity*, which entails valuing masculine traits related to power and control, while devaluing feminine traits related to the expression of tenderness and vulnerability (Shields, 1987). This perspective on manhood especially denigrates male homosexuality because it is perceived to be the antithesis of masculinity. For a man to express warmth, nurturance, or caring toward another man is often interpreted as an indication of homosexuality, which was once also considered to be a sign of psychological maladjustment (see chapter 11, section 11-2c). Thus, to be masculine requires men to avoid acting in ways that might indicate homosexuality, including expressing warmth, tenderness, and affection in friendships with other men.

The contemporary conception of masculinity as not encompassing tenderness and affection in male friendships is a fairly recent historical development in Western culture, and one not shared by many non-Western societies (Williams, 1992). As we enter the twenty-first century, the changes in gender roles may eventually lead men to feel less constrained in their expression of tenderness and affection toward other men. Until that time, however, male heterosexual friendships will generally lack the emotional intensity and gratification of the average female friendship.

4-5d Parenting and Job Responsibilities Often Provide Conflicts

As previously discussed in section 4-2f, most adults devote tremendous time and effort pursuing careers and/or raising children (generativity). Unlike many of their mothers and grandmothers, young women today are encouraged to work outside the home. Despite this historical shift toward gender equity, young women are much more likely than young men to receive mixed messages from their social environment concerning their ability to juggle these dual responsibilities. Such mixed messages occur because career opportunities often conflict with the traditional feminine role of child nurturer (Yoder & Schleicher, 1996). Due to this conflict, young women learn that their plans for work and family will be inter-dependent, with a great deal of trade-off occurring in how best to balance both roles.

Interestingly, this fear of conflict between occupational and family goals is less of an issue among Black than White college women (Bridges & Etaugh, 1994). One likely rea-son for this racial difference is that, out of economic necessity, African-American women have a longer history of maternal employment than do White American women. Because Black female college students are more likely to have mothers who worked outside the home, juggling these two roles seems more natural and less stressful for young African-American women.

In contrast to women's tendency to perceive conflict in their career and family roles, young men generally learn to view work and family decisions as independent issues (Silverstein, 1996). This is so because in industrialized societies, many generations of fathers have spent long periods of time away from their families, resulting in many fathers being emotionally distant from their children (Masson, 1999). Despite this father-absent tendency, many men today are becoming more involved in the care of their children, largely due to the fact that over two-thirds of all mothers are now working outside the household (Adler, 1996).

Yet, even with this increasing father involvement, mothers in all ethnic groups con-tinue to have far more direct physical contact with infants (such as holding, hugging, and kissing them) and spend far more time with their children than fathers do (Lamb et al., 1987; Wyche, 1993). In addition, wives still perform two-thirds of household work, or about 15 more hours each week of child care and housework than husbands (Steil, 1994). These statistics suggest that, while modern society has succeeded in encouraging women to expand their social responsibilities outside the household, it has failed to adequately encourage men to expand their responsibilities within the household.

What are the possible societal benefits of expanding the male gender role to include greater household and child care responsibilities? Research suggests that when families have actively involved and caring fathers, everyone benefits: The children exhibit higher cognitive and social skills than children of less involved fathers, working mothers' stress levels decrease, the fathers gain greater confidence in their parenting abilities, and the couple's happiness with each other increases (Atkinson, 1995; Hoffman, 1989; Lamb, 1987). Although increased involvement in child care and household work can sometimes lead to increased stress for men in the short run, in the long run, it tends to strengthen marriages (Gilbert, 1994). Fathers who are most likely to break from the traditional father role and take on more nurturing child care responsibilities are those who are older rather than younger, perhaps because they are more emotionally mature and secure in the parental role (Cooney et al., 1993; Neville & Parke, 1997).

4-5e Aging Is the Progressive Deterioration of the Body

Aging: The progressive deterioration of the body that culminates in death.

During adolescence and young adulthood, the body operates at its peak efficiency and strength. But, beginning in the twenties, it begins to burn calories at a slower rate, caus-ing many people to add extra pounds. Hearing also declines somewhat by the late 20s, especially for high-pitched tones. By the 30s and 40s, outward signs of **aging** become much

---

INFO-BIT: A widely held belief in many cultures is that mothers are much more important to child development than fathers. As a result of this belief, a father's rela-tionship with his children has historically been defined in the context of a bond with the mother. If that bond is broken by divorce or is not legitimized (as in the case of unmar-ried teens), the father's relationship with his children is often seriously undermined.

INFO-BIT: Men in African-American, Mexican-American, and Puerto Rican dual-earner families share a greater percentage of household chores than their White counterparts, but it still is not equal to the women's contributions (Herrera & DelCampo, 1995; John et al., 1995). In fact, the only household where a woman's romantic partner tends to equally share chores with her is a lesbian household (Kurdek, 1995).

Journey of Discovery Question

Why do you think it might be easier to encourage women to expand their gender roles to include work outside the household than it is to encourage men to expand their gender roles to include domestic child care responsibilities?

more noticeable, with hair thinning out and becoming gray, wrinkles developing, and visual acuity declining. Less noticeable aging effects are the loss of bone mass, which not only makes bones weaker and more brittle but can actually cause them to compress slightly. Due to bone compression in the spinal column and changes in posture, by the age of 70, people have shrunk 1 to 2 inches.

The most significant biological sign of aging in women is **menopause,** which is the ending of menstruation. The onset of menopause varies, but usually occurs within a few years of 50, and is accompanied by a reduction in the hormone estrogen. Although menopause is often thought to cause depression and other psychological problems in women, survey studies that have tracked middle-aged women's mental health over 10 years have found them no more depressed during menopause (Busch et al., 1994; Matthews, 1992). Indeed, over two-thirds of American women who have experienced menopause generally feel better than they have for years after going through "the change," and the vast majority recalled "only relief" when their periods stopped (Goode, 1999; Neugarten et al., 1963).

Unlike women, middle-aged men do not experience a cessation of fertility or even a sharp drop in sex hormones. However, they do undergo a more gradual reduction in sperm count, testosterone level, and overall sex drive, which can cause depression, insomnia, and impotence (Sternbach, 1998).

With advancing age, the power and strength of our mind can begin to degenerate as well (Finucane et al., 2002; Schmitter-Edgecombe & Nissley, 2002). After the age of 50, people begin losing neurons at an accelerated rate, so that at death they may have between 5 to 30 percent less brain mass than in young adulthood (Selkoe, 1992). More neural loss occurs in the association areas of the cortex involved with thought or in the brain stem, which controls basic physiological functions (Whitbourne, 1985). This neural death in old age, combined with reduced blood flow to the brain and decreased levels of important neurotransmitters, can result in a significant loss of cognitive skill.

No one knows for sure why we age, but rest assured that there is more to aging than mere deterioration. Just as the brains of children can alter their neural connections following injury (refer to chapter 3, section 3-3g), as more neurons die during advancing age, the dendrites of surviving neurons can grow longer and bushier and take over many of the dead neurons' functions. What this means is that, at the same time that the aging brain

Menopause: The ending of menstruation.

Through our great good fortune, in our youth our hearts were touched with fire.
—Oliver Wendell Holmes, Jr., American poet, 1841–1935

Age in a virtuous person, of either sex, carries in it an authority which makes it preferable to all the pleasures of youth.
—Sir Richard Steele, 1672–1729

is degenerating, it can also exhibit remarkable plasticity (Kempermann & Gage, 1999). The aging brain is not as flexible as the young brain, but if adults live in an "enriched environment"—that is, one that is intellectually stimulating—their brains may actually form more new neural connections than they lose (Nelson, 1999). Surprisingly, this later-life "rewiring" of the brain can actually result in improved cognitive functioning with age—at least until very advanced age.

4-5f There Is No Clear Understanding of How We Cope with Dying

The most inescapable thing in life is death. Perhaps it is this knowledge that gives life its meaning. Yet, how do people typically cope with their own impending death and the loss of loved ones?

Psychological Stages of Dying

In her studies of how people cope with their own impending death, Elisabeth Kübler-Ross (1969, 1981) has developed a five-stage theory: First, there is *denial* that one is going to die; then *anger* ("Why me?"); followed by *bargaining* with God for an extension or second chance; next, *depression* when the illness can no longer be denied and what will be lost sinks in; and, finally, *acceptance* of the inevitable.

Although Kübler-Ross's stage theory has been accepted by many professionals and laypeople who have daily contact with the dying, critics have argued that little evidence shows that people generally follow this five-stage sequence (Schulz & Alderman, 1974; Shneidman, 1992). For example, counter to the theory, people who are old do not typically view death with a good deal of fear and anger (Wass et al., 1978–1979). Additionally, there is no empirical evidence that terminally ill people become calmer or happier as death approaches (Aronoff & Spilka, 1984–1985). Thus, despite the appeal of Kübler-Ross's theory, it probably needs to be revised to more adequately account for the differing reactions people have to death.

Communicating with the Dying Person

Despite the fact that some people believe it is best not to discuss death and the terminal circumstances of the illness with a dying person, research indicates that open discussion and disclosure of dying is almost always beneficial (Kalish, 1985; Wright & Flemons, 2002). Richard Kalish (1981) identifies some benefits of this open awareness of death for the dying:

1. Dying persons have more understanding of what is happening to their bodies and what the medical staff is doing.

2. They can complete some plans and projects, make provisions for survivors, and participate in decisions about their funeral.

3. They have the opportunity to reminisce with loved ones and to tie up emotional loose ends.

In the final analysis, what dying individuals need most are caring, loving relationships, with communication directed toward internal processes, important memories, and personal successes (Bowes et al., 2002; Coppola & Trotman, 2002).

Even the seasons form a great circle in their changing, and always come back again to where they were. The life of a person is a circle from childhood to childhood and so it is in everything where power moves.

—Black Elk, Native American, 1863–1950

SECTION SUMMARY

- Adolescence is marked by a heightened sense of self-consciousness and a greater sophistication in rendering social judgments.

- Young adulthood is the time in which our bodies operate at their peak efficiency and strength.

- Male-male friendships are not as intimate as female-female friendships.

- Women are more likely than men to experience conflict in their family and career roles.

- The aging process ultimately leads to death.

- Kübler-Ross asserts that people pass through five stages in preparing to die: denial, anger, bargaining, depression, and acceptance.

4-6 A FINAL NOTE

Quest—An act or instance of seeking; an adventurous journey.

The theme of this book is that both the science of psychology and your own life is a journey of discovery. I began this chapter relating an incident from my childhood in which I earnestly tried to turn a lump of coal into a diamond. Throughout our lives, we will undertake many quests, and a substantial number of these will be irreparably flawed from the outset and, thus, doomed to fail. Others, however, will be fabulously successful due to a combination of factors, including good planning, skill, effort, fortunate circumstances, and the assistance of others. Certainly, one very important lesson in life is to learn how to recognize the foolish from the profound quests. Yet, perhaps an even more important lesson to learn is that it is absolutely essential for us to undertake quests regularly, however small they may sometimes be. For it is in such quests—both the large and the small variety—that we develop new ways of looking at ourselves and the world around us. And it is the "pressure" of the many quests we undertake throughout our lives that transforms us into what we ultimately become.

SUGGESTED WEBSITES

Note: These websites were functional when we went to press. Please access the online text for the most up-to-date URLs.

Attachment
http://www.psychology.sunysb.edu/attachment/
This website provides information on Bowlby-Ainsworth attachment research.

Birth Psychology
http://www.birthpsychology.com/
A website devoted to information on life before birth, birth traumas, and literature on birth psychology.

American Academy of Child and Adolescent Psychiatry
http://www.aacap.org/
This website offers information about adoption, bedwetting, teenage suicide, divorce, and other developmental issues.

The Jean Piaget Society
http://www.piaget.org/
A website covering Piaget's life and theory, with student links and information about the society.

Kohlberg's Theory of Moral Development
http://snycorva.cortland.edu/~ANDERSMD/KOHL/CONTENT.html
A website that has information about Kohlberg's theory, including applications.

Adult Development & Aging
http://www.aging.ufl.edu/apadiv20/apadiv20.htm
An APA-related website for Division 20 devoted to information on adult development.

PSYCHOLOGICAL APPLICATIONS
Using Effective Tutoring Strategies to Facilitate Cognitive Development

When Zinacanteco Mexican girls learn traditional weaving skills from more experienced women in their community, they first spend most of their time simply watching the women weave. Next, the girls begin to weave by cooperating with their teachers, starting with easy activities and then progressing to more challenging tasks. At each stage of learning, their teachers provide the girls with just the right amount of instruction to successfully complete the task (Greenfield & Lave, 1982). This example of informal learning is typical of how *tutors* play a crucial role in the learning of new skills. To better understand how tutoring figures into cognitive development and what tutoring strategies are most effective, let's take a second look at the work of the Russian psychologist Lev Vygotsky.

Tutoring and the Zone of Proximal Development
One of Vygotsky's central concepts is the zone of proximal development (ZPD), which is the cognitive range between what people can do on their own and what they can achieve through guided collaboration with those who already have the knowledge and skills (DeVries, 2000). In teaching a young would-be weaver her craft, a more experienced adult first assesses the child's cognitive range of weaving skills—her weaving ZPD—and then slowly moves her from the lower limit to the upper limit of that range. The upper limit of the girl's ZPD can only be reached through working closely with her tutor, yet once this upper limit is reached, it becomes the lower limit for a more challenging ZPD.

There is no one single "best" strategy in tutoring, but research indicates that the most effective instructors are those who combine general and specific interventions according to the learner's progress (Wood et al., 1976). In this two-pronged tutoring approach, the teacher begins with general instructions and stays at that level of advice until the learner runs into difficulties. The teacher then switches to a more specific type of instruction or demonstration. An example of this combined instruction strategy is the way my wife often teaches social studies to her fourth-grade class. First, she gives students general instructions, telling them to read that day's lesson and then answer a series of questions at the end. If any students have problems answering the questions, her instructions become more specific: Preread the questions before reading the lesson; look for bold-faced words in the reading related to question material. This two-pronged style allows children considerable latitude in making their own learning choices, while still providing careful guidance when they reach the upper limits of their abilities.

In providing assistance to the learner, effective tutors engage in their own problem solving: They modify their approach based on how the learner responds to instruction (Rogoff, 1990; Wood & Middleton, 1975). Good tutors also provide instruction that involves one extra operation or decision beyond the level at which their instructees are currently performing so that they are pushed to the upper limit of their ZPD. In trying to determine whether learners are "stuck" on a task, observant tutors will not only listen to what they say but also closely monitor their nonverbal behavior, such as pauses, sighs, and nervous laughter (Fox, 1988).

Obstacles to Effective Tutoring
One complicating factor that all tutors must bear in mind is that their tutoring should never so dominate the lesson that it demotivates the learner, causing him or her to lose interest in the task altogether (Deci et al., 1993). This problem generally occurs when the tutor attempts to exercise control over a task that is within the learner's ability to perform—that is, at the lower limit of the learner's ZPD. For example, in trying to teach a child how to play a new computer game, a parent might take over the entire operation of the game instead of simply providing occasional hints. Before the parent realizes what he has done, his child has lost interest and is off doing something else.

Another potential problem faced by tutors is trying to teach a skill to someone who is not interested in learning it. A prime example of such reluctant learning occurs in the arena of household chores (Goodnow, 1988). Am I mistaken, or didn't all of us learn in childhood that if we acted wholly incompetent at, say, washing the dishes or sweeping the floor, that our parents would do it themselves? At that young age we already intuitively grasped Vygotsky's notion of ZPD and were banking on our parents believing that these chores were so beyond our present skill levels that even guided collaboration was fruitless!

KEY TERMS

accommodation (p. 96)
adolescence (p. 105)
aging (p. 108)
assimilation (p. 96)
attachment (p. 82)
concrete operational stage (p. 99)
conservation (p. 97)
conventional morality (p. 102)
development (p. 74)
egocentrism (p. 97)
embryonic stage (p. 75)
ethnic identity (p. 93)
fetal alcohol syndrome (p. 76)
fetal stage (p. 75)
formal operational stage (p. 99)

gender identity (p. 89)
imaginary audience (p. 106)
internalization (p. 100)
longitudinal study (p. 86)
menarche (p. 105)
menopause (p. 109)
metacognition (p. 101)
object permanence (p. 96)
personal fable (p. 106)
postconventional morality (p. 103)
preconventional morality (p. 102)
prenatal development (p. 74)
preoperational stage (p. 97)
primary sex characteristics (p. 105)
private speech (p. 100)

puberty (p. 105)
schema (p. 96)
secondary sex characteristics (p. 105)
self-awareness (p. 86)
self-concept (p. 86)
self-esteem (p. 86)
sensorimotor stage (p. 96)
separation anxiety (p. 83)
stranger anxiety (p. 83)
teratogen (p. 76)
theory of mind (p. 99)
zone of proximal development (ZPD) (p. 100)
zygote stage (p. 75)

REVIEW QUESTIONS

1. Which of the following statements is *true* of a zygote?
   a. It is created at conception.
   b. It contains 46 cells.
   c. It spontaneously aborts 10 percent of the time.
   d. It is developed during the longest stage of prenatal development.
   e. It can survive outside of the womb.

2. A child's brain
   a. has fewer nerve cells than an adult brain.
   b. is not shaped by environment.
   c. is 75 percent of its adult weight by age 2.
   d. does not grow new dendrites.
   e. none of the above

3. Which of the following statements is *true* of physical growth and motor development of children?
   a. Motor development is not affected by culture.
   b. Basic motor skills develop from the legs up.
   c. Reflexes are permanent.
   d. There is a surge in height and weight during middle childhood.
   e. Primitive reflexes have outlived their usefulness.

4. There is evidence that
   a. the fetus is not capable of recognizing sounds.
   b. newborns can see very clearly.
   c. infants prefer sour tastes to sweet.
   d. the sense of touch is not functional before birth.
   e. none of the above

5. Which of these characteristics has been attributed to securely attached babies?
   a. invulnerable to later problems in life
   b. lack curiosity
   c. popular
   d. independent and socially skilled
   e. *c* and *d*

6. Which of the following is supported by studies on attachment style?
   a. Temperament is not significantly shaped by inherited biological factors.
   b. Parenting style has a greater impact than the child's temperament.
   c. Attachment style is not shaped by culture.
   d. Multiple attachments can cause adverse consequences.
   e. all of the above

7. Which of the following statements is supported by studies?
   a. The quality of day care is irrelevant when considering impact on attachment.
   b. Children who come from conflict-ridden two-parent families tend to be psychologically healthier than children of divorce.
   c. Mothers in all ethnic groups spend more time with their children than fathers.
   d. There is no long-term impact on children of divorce.
   e. none of the above

8. The study by Lewis and Brooks that put babies in front of a mirror with rouge on their noses illustrated the concept of
   a. attachment.
   b. self-awareness.
   c. contact comfort.
   d. self-esteem.
   e. temperament.

9. Studies have indicated that children with high self-esteem tend to have
   a. authoritarian parents.
   b. permissive parents.
   c. authoritative parents.
   d. all types of parents.
   e. There have been no such studies.

10. What recommendation does the author give to counter gender stereotypes in the larger culture?
   a. Mothers and fathers should take turns doing household activities.
   b. Provide concrete examples of both men and women in all types of occupations.
   c. Engage in conversations about stereotypes with children.
   d. Monitor children's entertainment.
   e. all of the above

11. According to Erikson, the crisis that occurs when a person discerns whether he or she has contributed or produced something worthy of his or her efforts is called
   a. trust vs. mistrust.
   b. autonomy vs. shame and doubt.
   c. initiative vs. guilt.
   d. competence vs. inferiority.
   e. generativity vs. stagnation.

12. Piaget's three-mountain problem demonstrated the notion of
   a. object permanence.
   b. representational thought.
   c. egocentrism.
   d. conservation.
   e. assimilation.

13. Which of the following is *true* of Vygotsky's theory of cognitive development?
   a. The cognitive development stage should first be determined so that children can be taught material appropriate to that level.
   b. Children's mental development cannot be accelerated.
   c. Cognitive development is relatively asocial.
   d. Learning occurs through the social instrument of language.
   e. Internal dialogue is detrimental to the learning process.

14. Which of the following statements is *true* of aging?
   a. The body operates at its peak efficiency during a person's late twenties.
   b. Middle-aged men experience a cessation of fertility in their fifties.
   c. Older brains may form more new neural connections than they lose.
   d. No studies have been done on how people cope with their impending death.
   e. Research indicates that open discussion and disclosure of dying is rarely beneficial.

Sensation and Perception

The Dassanetch people of southwestern Ethiopia have two principal livelihoods: prestigious cattle-raising or lowly fishing (Almagor, 1987). In Dassanetch culture, the smell of everything associated with cattle is considered good, and cattle-raisers go out of their way to highlight those valued smells. Women smear liquid butter—*ghee*—on their bodies to ensure fertility and attract suitors, while men do the same with cow manure. In contrast, the odor of fish is considered noxious in Dassanetch. It is not surprising, then, that Dassanetch fishermen abstain from any fish-smearing activities over their own bodies.

Whereas the Dassanetch identify social status through the use of smells, the agricultural Tzotzil people of the Chiapas highlands of Mexico—descendants of the ancient sun-worshiping Maya—structure their social order according to heat. Everything in the world is thought to contain a different quantity of heat, with heat conveying power. Although men are considered to possess greater heat than women, both sexes accumulate heat throughout their lives, reaching their thermal peak just before death (Vogt, 1976).

Finally, the Desana of the Colombian Amazon organize their world according to visual color. Color is a vital life force created by the sun, with each color imbued with a specific energy (Reichel-Dolmatoff, 1971). Yellow is associated with male procreative power, red with female fertility, green with growth, and blue with communication. The distribution of color energies is very important to growth, and an imbalance in one's color energies is believed to cause illness.

What these cultural vignettes demonstrate is that the dominant sensory medium organizing life experiences may differ from culture to culture. The Tzotzil organize meaning in life primarily through the temperature of their bodies and the objects in their world. The Desana make sense of their world through the perception of colors, while the Dassanetch use smell. Of course, this does not mean that these people ignore their other senses, or that the sense that they most value is the one of most practical importance. Instead, what is demonstrated here is that people's social world significantly shapes which senses they emphasize in organizing and understanding the others. What we have here are not just different worldviews, but different worlds of sense (Classen, 1993).

In this chapter, we continue our journey of discovery in psychology by examining two interrelated processes, namely sensation and perception. **Sensation** is the process that detects stimuli from our bodies and our environment; **perception** is the process that organizes those stimuli into meaningful objects and events (d'Y'dewalle, 2000; Ross, 2000). Normally, we experience sensation and perception as one process, but they can be distinguished. For example, consider the contents of figure 5-1. Initially, you may have a hard time seeing anything meaningful. If this is the case, you can *sense* different patterns and shapes but you cannot perceive a meaningful pattern.

I will begin our analysis of these two interrelated processes by examining some basic principles that apply to all sensory systems. Next, I will individually discuss the six senses of *vision*, *audition* (hearing), *olfaction* (hearing), *gustation* (taste), *touch*, and *proprioception* (the sense of body position and movement). From there, I will examine how the brain organizes sensations into perceptions.

Sensation: The process that detects stimuli from our bodies and our environment.

Perception: The process that organizes sensations into meaningful objects and events.

5-1 BASIC PRINCIPLES OF SENSATION

Psychophysics: The study of how physical stimuli are translated into psychological experience.

Can you sometimes overhear others' quiet conversations when you are considerably distant from them? Or do you sometimes "tune out" distracting sensations around you? These are the sorts of questions of interest to the field of **psychophysics,** the study of how physical stimuli are translated into psychological experience.

5-1a Our Senses Vary in Their Sensitivity Thresholds

German scientist Gustav Fechner (1801–1887), who was a pioneer in psychophysics, introduced the term **absolute threshold** to explain such instances of detecting minimal stimuli (Fechner, 1966). Absolute threshold is the lowest level of intensity of a given stimulus that a person can detect half the time. Psychologists measure absolute thresholds by presenting a stimulus (for example, a light or a sound) to a person at different intensities and determining what is the lowest level detectable 50 percent of the time. Some examples of absolute thresholds for various senses are listed in table 5-1.

A number of studies have found that the absolute threshold for a given sense varies between people (Rabin & Cain, 1986). For instance, due to the damaging effects that tobacco smoke has on nasal cavities, smokers or people regularly exposed to tobacco smoke have a less sensitive sense of smell than nonsmokers (Richardson & Zucco, 1989). As people age, their absolute thresholds for all senses increase, meaning that greater stimulation is necessary to detect stimuli (Schiffman, 1997; Stevens, 1989).

The assumption underlying the absolute threshold concept is that there is a minimum intensity level at which a stimulus is consistently detected. However, according to **signal-detection theory,** the detection of a stimulus is also influenced by the observer's decision-making strategy or criterion (Gesheider, 1985; Swets, 1992). Two important factors that shape this decision making are (1) the observer's expectations about the probability that the stimulus will occur, and (2) the rewards and costs associated with detecting or not detecting the stimulus (Harder et al., 1989). For example, suppose you were looking for shooting stars on a night in which you mistakenly thought there was a meteor shower. Due to your false expectation, you probably would detect more faint, fleeting flashes of light in the sky than if you expected no meteor shower. Detecting these flashes might also be affected by how important this task was to you. If astronomy was your favorite hobby, you might "see" more flashes than if star-gazing was merely a lark.

One major contribution of signal-detection theory is that it points out that we do not have a single absolute threshold for a given sense. Whether or not we perceive a particular stimulus depends on the situation, and what expectations and motives we bring to it.

Absolute threshold: The lowest level of intensity of a given stimulus that a person can detect half the time.

Signal-detection theory: The theory that explains how detection of a stimulus is influenced by observers' expectations.

Stimulus	Absolute Threshold
Vision	A candle seen at 30 miles on a dark, clear night
Hearing	The tick of a watch at 20 feet under quiet conditions
Taste	One teaspoon of sugar in 2 gallons of water
Smell	One drop of perfume diffused into a 3-room apartment
Touch	The wing of a fly falling on your cheek from a distance of 0.5 inch

TABLE 5-1

Examples of Absolute Thresholds

Source: Adapted from Galanter, 1962.

Such knowledge is important because many signal-detection tasks carry life-and-death implications. Consider the task of a medical technician who is screening numerous X rays every hour for possible signs of disease. Are those faint markings on the lungs normal or do they indicate the early stages of cancer? Studies demonstrate that when people try to judge whether a faint stimulus is present or absent, their vigilance diminishes after about 30 minutes due to fatigue. Although such fatigue effects won't cause any serious consequences when looking for shooting stars, it could prove disastrous in the medical lab.

Just-noticeable difference (JND): The smallest difference in the amount of stimulation that a specific sense can detect.

Besides detecting a weak stimulus, we often must detect changes in the intensity of a stimulus or discriminate between two similar stimuli. A **just-noticeable difference (JND)** is the smallest difference in the amount of stimulation that a specific sense can detect. For example, what is the minimum amount of difference in the sweetness of two soft drinks that you can detect? In 1834, Ernst Weber (1795–1878), Fechner's brother-in-law, discovered that the amount of change in stimulation necessary to produce a JND is a constant proportion of the original stimulus. Like the absolute threshold, the JND for a particular sense varies from person to person and from situation to situation. According to **Weber's law,** a weak or small stimulus does not require much change before a person notices that the stimulus has changed, but a strong or large stimulus requires a proportionately greater change before the change is noticed (Laming, 1985; Norwich, 1987). Thus, lighting the second candle on a birthday cake in an otherwise darkened room will be more noticeable than lighting the eighty-first candle.

Weber's law: The principle that a weak or small stimulus does not require much change before a person notices that the stimulus has changed, but a strong or large stimulus requires a proportionately greater change before the change is noticed.

The values of these proportions vary a great deal for the different senses. While we can detect a change in sound of 0.3 percent (one-third of 1 percent) and a change in brightness and weight of about 2 percent, it requires a 7 percent increase to detect a JND in smell, and a whopping 20 percent increase in taste! This means that our sense of hearing is much more sensitive than our sense of taste.

5-1b Our Sensory Receptors Adapt to Unchanging Stimuli

During my first year in graduate school, I attended City College of New York and rode the subway to school each day. At first, the noise was so distracting that I not only had difficulty reading, but I invariably came home with a headache. Yet, within a few days, the subway noise appeared to diminish, and I was comfortably reading and headache-free. This example illustrates **sensory adaptation,** the tendency for our sensory receptors to have decreasing responsiveness to stimuli that continue without change. The most common explanation for sensory adaptation is that it is caused by our nerve cells firing less frequently after high levels of stimulation.

Sensory adaptation: The tendency for our sensory receptors to have decreasing responsiveness to stimuli that continue without change.

From an evolutionary perspective, sensory adaptation makes sense. Animals that tune out constant unchanging stimuli that provide no new information should be better able to detect more useful information for survival. However, sensory adaptation is occasionally disadvantageous. For example, while tuning out subway noises increased my ability to study for exams, I sometimes didn't hear the conductor call out my stop, causing me to arrive late for class!

Auditory adaptation occurs much more slowly than adaptation to odors, tastes, and skin sensations (Scharf, 1983). For example, we adapt to smells very quickly, with the perceived magnitude of odor decay occurring at the rate of about 2.5 percent each second (Cain, 1978). Within one minute, odor adaptation is essentially complete, and the per-

> **INFO-BIT:** Synesthesia is a rare and extraordinary sensory condition in which people perceive stimuli in other senses, such as tasting color or feeling the sounds of musical instruments on their bodies. The most common form of synesthesia is colored hearing: sounds, music, or voices seen as colors. Brain scans of synesthetics who report colored hearing indicate that visual areas of their brains show increased activation in response to sounds (Carpenter, 2001).

ceived magnitude of the smell is about 30 percent of the initial magnitude. We still smell it, but not as intensely. Try a little demonstration on yourself. Place a substance with a strong odor—perhaps an onion, perfume, or shaving lotion—near your nose for a few minutes. Its odor will seem less intense over time. Next, remove the substance for five minutes and then smell it again. Now it should smell as strong as it did when you first smelled it.

SECTION SUMMARY

- Absolute threshold is the lowest level of intensity of a given stimulus that a person can detect.

- According to signal-detection theory, detection of a stimulus is influenced both by stimulus intensity and the observer's decision-making strategy.

- Just-noticeable difference (JND) is the smallest difference in the amount of stimulation that a specific sense can detect.

- Sensory adaptation refers to our sensory receptors' decreasing responsiveness to an unchanging stimulus.

5-2 VISION

Due to the fact that scientific inquiry has discovered more about the visual system than any of the other senses, I will not only examine this sense first, but I will later use the visual system to explain the major principles of perception.

5-2a We See Only a Narrow Band of Electromagnetic Energy

Electromagnetic energy is all around us and travels in waves of different lengths, created by the vibration of electrically charged particles. A **wavelength** is the distance between two peaks of adjacent waves. Our eyes can detect the wavelengths of *visible light*, which ranges from 400 to 750 nanometers, with a nanometer being one-billionth of a meter. Within this range of visible light, the colors we see are determined by the size of the wavelength (refer to figure 5-2). The shorter wavelengths are experienced as violet, the intermediate ones as blue, green, and yellow, and the longer ones as red. Other forms of electromagnetic energy that our eyes cannot detect because they fall outside this 400- to 750-nanometer range are radio, infrared, ultraviolet, and X-ray radiation.

Wavelength: The distance between two peaks of adjacent waves.

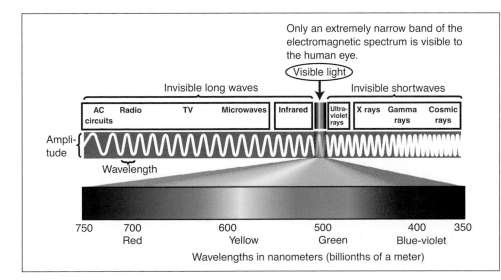

FIGURE 5-2

The Electromagnetic Spectrum

Humans sense only a narrow band of electromagnetic energy, ranging from 400 to 700 nanometers. Within this narrow band, light at different wavelengths is experienced as different colors.

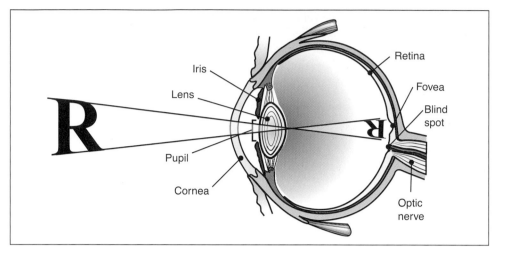

FIGURE 5-3
Major Structures of the Human Eye

Light first passes through the cornea, pupil, and lens and is then focused on the retina at the back of the eye. The point of sharpest vision on the retina is at the fovea. To observe the pupillary response to light, first look in a mirror under high-light conditions and notice the size of your pupils. Now, turn out the light for 30 seconds and then flick it back on while gazing into the mirror. Notice how much larger your pupils have become in response to the lack of light and how quickly they constrict as they respond to the added light.

Cornea: A clear membrane covering the front of the eyeball that aids in visual acuity by bending light that falls on its surface.

Iris: A ring of muscles that range in color from light blue to dark brown.

Pupil: A hole in the center of the iris that regulates how much light enters the eye.

Lens: An elastic, disc-shaped structure that focuses light.

Retina: A light-sensitive surface at the back of the eye.

5-2b Light Passes through the Cornea, Pupil, and Lens before Focusing on the Retina

Light enters the eye through the cornea, a clear membrane covering the front of the eyeball (see figure 5-3). The cornea bends the light falling on its surface just enough to focus it at the back of the eye. From the **cornea,** light passes through a pocket of fluid known as the *aqueous humor,* which carries oxygen and other nutrients to the cornea and lens. Next, light passes through a hole in the **iris,** called the **pupil,** which is a ring of muscles that functions much like the diaphragm of a camera. In dim light, muscle fibers in the iris dilate (open) the pupil, letting in more light, while in bright light the pupil constricts, letting in less light. Pupil size is not only affected by light. When psychologically aroused or interested in something, your pupils dilate (Hess, 1975).

After passing through the pupil, light enters a clear, elastic, disc-shaped structure called the **lens,** which refocuses the light with the aid of muscles attached to it. A clear image of distant objects is achieved by these muscles stretching and flattening the lens, while relaxing the lens and making it more spherical results in a clear image of near objects. Because the lens changes shape without any willful action, people often mistakenly assume that everything, near and far, is always in focus. To demonstrate to yourself that this is not the case, close one eye and look at a distant object, and then, while still focusing on this object, begin moving a pencil toward you while attending to—but not focusing on—the pencil point. As the pencil gets closer, notice that the point becomes blurred and is seen double. When the pencil is about 12 inches away, focus on the point and you will notice that the faraway object becomes blurred. As you move the pencil within a couple of inches to your eyes, you will no longer be able to bring the point into focus because the lens has reached its maximum curvature and cannot get any fatter. This distance at which your lens can no longer accommodate to bring the pencil point into focus is called the *near point.* As you get older (past the age of 45), the distance of the near point will increase because aging causes a loss in the elasticity of the lens.

After being focused by the lens, light travels through the *vitreous humor,* which is a clear jellylike liquid that occupies the space behind the lens, and is then projected onto a light-sensitive surface at the back of the eye known as the **retina.** A common problem afflicting humans is that abnormalities in the cornea's outer membrane wall and abnormalities in the lens can affect *visual acuity,* which is the sharpness of the visual image at the retina. My*opia,* or nearsightedness—which is decreased acuity for distant objects—occurs when the cornea and lens focus the image in front of the retina. In contrast, *hyperopia,* or farsightedness—which is blurred vision for near objects—occurs when the eye focuses the image on a point beyond the retina. These defects in the eye can be easily corrected by fitting people with glasses or contact lenses that alter the eye's focus. More

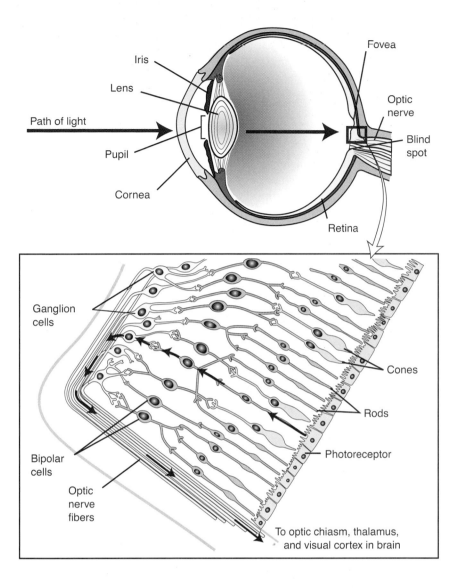

Iris
Lens
Path of light
Pupil
Cornea
Fovea
Optic nerve
Blind spot
Retina

Ganglion cells
Cones
Rods
Photoreceptor
Bipolar cells
Optic nerve fibers
To optic chiasm, thalamus, and visual cortex in brain

FIGURE 5-4
How Light Travels through the Eye

Light passing through the eye activates the rods and cones, which are located below the surface of the retina. The resulting neural impulses from these photoreceptors activate bipolar cells which, in turn, activate the ganglion cells. The axons of these ganglion cells converge to form the optic nerve, which sends information to the brain.

modern medical procedures, such as laser surgery, can also restore visual acuity by shaving off minute portions of the cornea and restoring proper curvature so that light striking the eye is bent correctly.

The retina is actually a piece of the brain that migrates to the eye during early fetal development (Gregory, 1998). Below its outer layer of cells reside a layer of two basic kinds of receptor neurons, or *photoreceptors*, called **rods** and **cones** (see figure 5-4). The rods, located at the edges of the retina, are extremely sensitive to light and are central to the detection of patterns of black, white, and gray. The rods function best under low-light conditions, and thus, are most useful at night. In contrast to the rods, the cones require much more light to be activated and play a key role in color vision. Most cones are concentrated in a small area near the center of the retina known as the **fovea,** which is the area of central focus. A human retina contains about 125 million rods and 7 million cones (Pugh, 1988). As you would expect, animals that are most active at night, such as owls and rats, have all-rod eyes, whereas daytime animals, such as lizards and chipmunks, have mostly cone-dominant retinas (Tansley, 1965; Wagner, 2001).

When activated by light energy, rods and cones generate neural signals that activate adjacent *bipolar cells*, which in turn activate neighboring ganglion cells (see figure 5-4). The axons of the *ganglion cells* converge like the strands of a rope to form the optic nerve, which carries information from the retina to the brain. Before being sent on to the brain,

Rods: Receptor neurons in the eye located at the edges of the retina that are sensitive to the brightness of light.

Cones: Receptor neurons in the eye located near the center of the retina that mediate color vision.

Fovea: The retina's area of central focus.

You can experience your own blind spot by closing your right eye and lining up the cross with your left eye. Now, slowly move your head back and forth. When the image is between 6 to 18 inches away from your eye, the image of the happy face falls on your blind spot and it disappears from sight. One reason you are not more aware of your blind spot is that when an image falls on the blind spot of one eye, it falls on the receptors of the other, and thus, you detect the image. Another reason you don't often see the blind spot, even with one-eyed vision, is that it is located off to the side of your visual field, and thus, objects near this area are never in sharp focus. Finally, perhaps the most important reason that you don't see the blind spot is that your visual system somehow "fills in" the place where the image disappears. Thus, when you try the blind spot demonstration, the place where the happy face used to be wasn't replaced by a "hole" or by "nothingness," but rather, by the white surrounding it.

Optic nerve: The bundle of nerve cells that carries information from the retina to the brain.

Blind spot: The area on the retina where the optic nerve leaves the eye and that contains no receptor cells

Feature detectors: Cells in the visual cortex that respond only to a highly specific feature of a visual stimulus, such as a straight edge, an angle, movement of a spot, or brightness.

however, a great deal of complex information processing takes place in the retina (Slaughter, 1990). This processing occurs in the bipolar and ganglion cells, where information from the rods and cones is integrated and compressed so that it can be more easily transmitted along the **optic nerve.** On the retina where the optic nerve leaves the eye, there are no rods or cones, which means that images falling here are not seen (Ramachandran, 1992). For this reason, this area is called the **blind spot** in the field of vision (see figure 5-5).

5-2c Visual Information Is Transmitted to Both Brain Hemispheres

After they leave the eyes, the axons of the ganglion cells that make up the optic nerve separate, and half of them cross to the other side of the head at the *optic chiasm.* As illustrated in figure 5-6, the axons from the right side of each eye are connected to the right hemisphere of the brain and those from the left side of each eye are connected to the left hemisphere. Thus, visual information in a person's *left visual field,* which is the area to the left of the person, will go to the right hemisphere, while the exact opposite will be true for information in the person's *right visual field.* This splitting and crossing over of the optic nerve is important because it ensures that signals from both eyes go to both brain hemispheres.

A short distance after leaving the optic chiasm, the optic nerve fibers diverge along two pathways. Eighty percent of the nerve fibers are connected to the lateral geniculate nucleus of the thalamus, while most of the rest of the nerve fibers are attached to the *superior colliculus* in the midbrain. The superior colliculus is the evolutionarily older of the two brain structures and is the primary area for visual processing in less developed animals, like frogs. In humans, the superior colliculus is involved in controlling eye movements. In contrast to this more primitive brain structure, the lateral geniculate nucleus is a kidney-bean-shaped cluster of neurons that performs much more detailed visual analysis. Six different layers of cells in the *lateral geniculate nucleus* not only organize information about color and other aspects of the visual field reaching it from the retina, but they also create a "map" of visual space in the retina where each location on the lateral geniculate nucleus corresponds to a location on the retina (Mollon, 1990).

From the lateral geniculate nucleus, visual information is sent to areas in the occipital lobe that make up the visual cortex. To understand how cells in the visual cortex communicate with one another, in the late 1950s David Hubel and Tortsen Wiesel placed microelectrodes in this area of a cat's brain to record action potentials from individual neurons. To stimulate action potentials, the researchers projected spots of light onto a screen with a slide projector, but they were initially unable to get the neurons to fire with any regularity. Then, quite by accident, as they were inserting a glass slide containing a spot stimulus into their projector, a neuron began firing like crazy. What Hubel and Wiesel discovered was that the rapid neural firing was not in response to the image of the spot, but to the image of the straight edge of the slide as it moved downward on the projector screen! They proposed that cells in the visual cortex known as **feature detectors** respond only to a highly specific *feature* or characteristic of a visual stimulus, such as a straight edge, an angle, movement of a spot, or brightness (Hubel & Wiesel, 1965a, 1965b). This information is then passed on to other cells that, in turn, respond only to more complex features. Through this interaction among many different type of visual

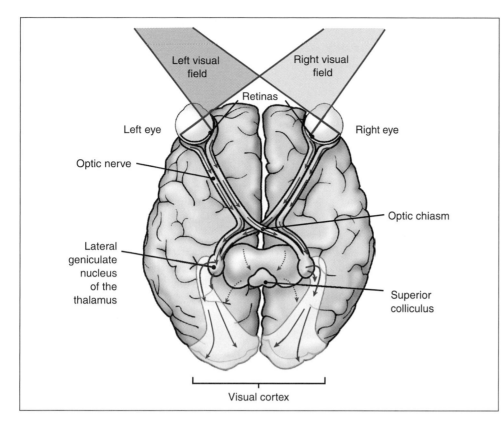

FIGURE 5-6
The Brain's Visual Pathways

This is a view of the visual system of the brain, showing how the optic nerve carries visual information from the retina to the optic chiasm, where the optic nerve splits. Information from the right half of the visual field strikes the left side of each retina and is sent to the left hemisphere. Information from the left half of the visual field strikes the right side of each retina and is sent to the right hemisphere. After reaching the optic chiasm, a minor pathway goes to the superior colliculus in the midbrain, but the major visual pathway is to the lateral geniculate nucleus of the thalamus. From the lateral geniculate nucleus, visual information is sent to the occipital lobe or visual cortex.

neurons, each responsible for specific tasks, our brain is provided with the basic building blocks of visual perception that it then assembles into a meaningful whole (Hubel, 1996; Jiang et al., 2002; Rolls & Deco, 2002). This groundbreaking research by Hubel and Wiesel earned them the Nobel Prize in physiology in 1981.

5-2d Colors Are Created in Our Visual System

What does it really mean when we say that a leaf is green? Does the leaf actually *possess* the color we perceive? The answer is "no." An object appears a particular color because it absorbs certain wavelengths of light and reflects others. The color green is not actually *in* the leaf, nor is it in the light waves reflected from it. Instead, the color resides in our own visual system. The leaf absorbs all the wavelengths of light except those that *evoke* the sensation of green in our minds. There is nothing inherently "blue" about short wavelengths or "red" about long wavelengths. These wavelengths are simply energy. Colors are *created* by our nervous system in response to these wavelengths.

Because the experience of colors is created by the nervous system, species differ in what they see when looking at the same object (Smith et al., 2002). For example, although honeybees have trichromatic vision like us, their three kinds of color receptors are spread out over a much wider band of the spectrum than our own, and thus, they are sensitive to light in the ultraviolet range (Menzel & Backhaus, 1989). Pigeons have color vision based on five kinds of receptors (*pentachromatic* vision), and thus, they undoubtedly see the world differently than do we (Varela et al., 1993).

Astonishingly, our difference threshold for colors is so low that the average person can discriminate about two million different colors (Abramov & Gordon, 1994; Gouras, 1991). Cross-cultural research indicates that there is a universally shared physiological basis for experiencing color among humans (Pokorny et al., 1991). Thus, although cultures like the Desana of the Amazon emphasize color perception more in their daily practices than many other cultures, and although they have more terms to describe different colors, they do not have different abilities to detect color.

5-2e The Trichromatic Theory and the Opponent-Process Theory Explain Different Aspects of Color Vision

Trichromatic theory: A theory of color perception that proposes that there are three types of color receptors in the retina that produce the primary color sensations of red, green, and blue.

As illustrated in figure 5-7, any color can be created by combining the light wavelengths of three basic colors—red, green, and blue. To explain how mixing these three colors of light gives us all colors, in the nineteenth century two scientists—first English physician Thomas Young (1773–1829) and later German physiologist Hermann von Helmholtz (1821–1894)—hypothesized that the retina has three types of color receptors with differing sensitivities to the different light waves associated with these three colors. According to what came to be called the Young-Helmholtz **trichromatic theory,** light of a particular wavelength stimulates these three types of receptors to different degrees, and the resulting pattern of neural activity among these receptors results in color perception.

Over 100 years after the trichromatic theory was offered as an explanation for color vision, George Wald verified the existence of three different types of cones in the retina (Brown & Wald, 1964; Wald, 1964), a discovery that earned him a Nobel Prize. As trichromatic theory proposed, each cone is most sensitive to a particular wavelength of light. Long-wavelength cones (L-cones) are most sensitive to wavelengths of about 555 nanometers, which are perceived as red. Middle-wavelength cones (M-cones) produce the sensation of green and are most sensitive to wavelengths of about 525 nanometers. Finally, short-wavelength cones (S-cones), which produce the sensation of blue, are most sensitive to wavelengths of about 450 nanometers. By combining different stimulation levels from these three kinds of cones, our visual system produces a multitude of different color sensations. The trichromatic theory provides a partial explanation for **color blindness,** which is a deficiency in the ability to distinguish among colors (see figure 5-8 in Discovery Box 5-1). Approximately 1 in 50 people are color-blind, with about 90 percent of these being male because the defect is genetic and carried on the X chromosome. A male who inherits the trait on his single X chromosome will be color-blind, but a female must inherit the trait on both of her X chromosomes to be color-blind.

Color blindness: A deficiency in the ability to distinguish among colors.

Actually, the term *color blindness* is misleading because most people classified as color-blind are *dichromats*—they can see two primary colors but are insensitive to the third because the cone that is sensitive to that color is nonfunctional (Gouras, 1991; Ladd-Franklin, 1929). In contrast, only about 10 people out of one million have the rare form of color blindness where they have no functioning cones. These *monochromats* see everything in shades of white, gray, and black. Thus, while the relatively rare monochromats are truly color-blind, color *deficiency* is a more accurate term to describe the much more prevalent dichromats.

Afterimage: A visual image that persists after a stimulus has been removed.

At roughly the same time that Helmholtz was championing the trichromatic theory, German physiologist Ewald Hering (1834–1918) proposed a competing theory. His ideas were sparked by the observation of **afterimages,** which are visual images that persist after

FIGURE 5-7
The Three Primary Colors of Light

The three primary colors of red, green, and blue combine to create all the other colors. For example, red and green make yellow, while all three together create white.

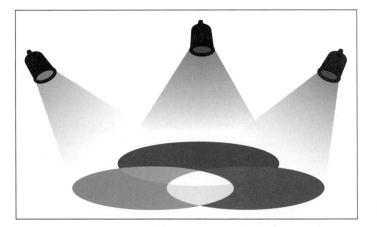

DISCOVERY BOX 5-1

Are You Color-Blind?

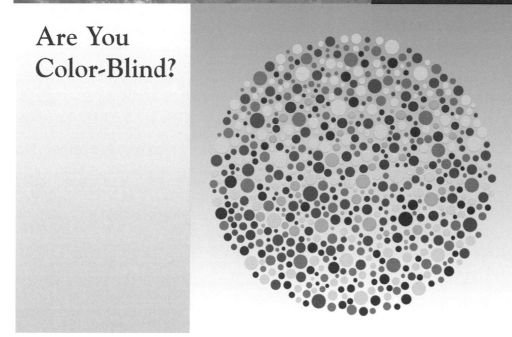

FIGURE 5-8
Color Blindness

In this test for red-green color blindness, a red 26 is presented against a background of green dots. People who are red-green color-blind do not perceive the number 26, but instead see only a random array of dots.

The best work of artists in any age is the work of innocence liberated by technical knowledge. The laboratory experiments that led to the theory of pure color equipped the impressionists to paint nature as if it had only just been created.

—Nancy Hale, U.S. writer, b. 1908

a stimulus has been removed (figure 5-9). Pointing out that the trichromatic theory could not explain this visual phenomenon, Hering proposed a theory that could, namely his **opponent-process theory.** This theory argues that all colors are derived from three opposing color processes: black-white, red-green, and blue-yellow. The black-white opponent process determines the brightness of what we see, while the other two processes determine color perception. Stimulation of one color inhibits its opposing color. When stimulation stops, the opposing color is seen as an afterimage.

A century after Hering proposed his theory, research by Russell de Valois and his colleagues (1966) supported its basic propositions. After leaving the cones, visual information is processed in terms of the opposing colors by certain bipolar and ganglion cells in the retina and certain cells in the thalamus, which are collectively known as *opponent cells.* These opponent cells respond to light at one end of the spectrum with an increase in nerve firing, and to light at the other end of the spectrum with an inhibition of spontaneous activity. Opponent cells that are inhibited from firing by a particular wavelength (which we experience as a particular color) produce a burst of firing as soon as that wavelength is removed. Similarly, cells that fire in response to a particular wavelength stop firing when that wavelength is removed (de Valois & Jacobs, 1984; Zrenner et al., 1990). The end result of this inhibition and firing of opponent cells is that we experience *negative afterimages* due to a "rebound effect" in opponent cells.

Opponent-process theory:
A theory proposing that color perception depends on receptors that make opposing responses to three pairs of colors.

FIGURE 5-9
Afterimage

Gaze steadily for about a minute at the lower right corner of the yellow field of stars, and then look at the white space above or beside the flag. What do you see? The "Old Glory" you see is composed of the complementary colors in your visual system. Why do these colors reverse in this manner?

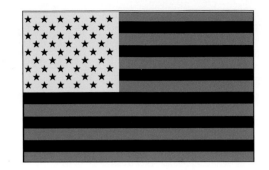

Opponent-process theory explains why people who are color-blind to red are also color-blind to green. The opponent-process cells responsible for perceiving red are also responsible for perceiving green. Thus, when these opponent cells are nonfunctional, a person cannot perceive red *or* green. The same is true for those opponent cells responsible for blue-yellow perception.

Although Hering formulated his theory in opposition to trichromatic theory, research indicates that *both* theories accurately represent the process of color perception, but at two different stages in the visual process. In the first stage of color processing, the trichromatic theory explains how the retina's red, green, and blue color-sensitive cone receptors match the wavelength of the light stimulus. In the second stage, the opponent-process theory explains how opponent cells both in the retina and in the thalamus of the brain are either stimulated or inhibited from firing by wavelengths of varying sizes. Put more simply, trichromatic theory explains most of the visual processing occurring in the eye, while opponent-process theory explains the processing occurring between the eye and the brain.

5-2f Color Constancy Demonstrates That We Perceive Objects in Their Environmental Context

Try the following demonstration. First, find two sheets of paper, one blue and the other yellow. Next, hold these papers near a window and look at them carefully. Then look at them when illuminated by a fluorescent or tungsten light. Although you may have noticed some small change in color as you changed the illumination, the blue sheet didn't change to yellow and the yellow to blue, did they? No, certainly not. Yet, you might be surprised to learn that the wavelengths reflected from a blue color chip by an indoor light bulb match the wavelengths reflected from a yellow color chip by sunlight (Jameson, 1985). Despite the fact that the blue paper under tungsten light and the yellow paper under sunlight reflect the same wavelength pattern, we still perceive one as blue and the other as yellow. Further, when we bring the blue paper outside and the yellow paper indoors, they still retain their same colors to us even though they now reflect different wavelength patterns. This relative constancy of perceived color under different conditions of illumination is known as **color constancy.**

Color constancy: Perceiving objects as having consistent color under different conditions of illumination.

The fact that our perception of an object's color remains relatively unchanged despite changes in the wavelengths reflected from it is proof that our experience of color is based not only on stimulation coming from the object but also on the stimulation coming from other objects in the environment. Research indicates that color constancy works best when an object is surrounded by objects of many different colors, suggesting that our brain perceives color partly based on computations of the light reflected by an object relative to the light reflected by surrounding objects (Land, 1986; Pokorny et al., 1991). This finding that we perceive objects in their environmental context has long been recognized and utilized by artists, clothes designers, and interior decorators in their work.

- Light passes through the cornea, pupil, and lens, and then is projected onto the retina.

- Below the retina's outer layer of cells reside two kinds of photoreceptors, called rods—which function best under low light conditions—and cones—which require much more light to be activated and play a key role in color vision.

- Rods and cones generate neural signals that activate adjacent bipolar cells, which activate ganglion cells.

- Behind the eyes, ganglion cell axons of the optic nerve separate, with half crossing to the other side of the head at the optic chiasm.

- Most optic nerve fibers run to the lateral geniculate nucleus, which performs detailed visual analysis.

- Trichromatic theory explains most of the visual processing occurring in the eye.

- Opponent-process theory explains visual processing occurring between the eye and the brain.

- Our perception of color of an object remains relatively unchanged despite changes in wavelength reflected from it.

5-3 HEARING

Stop reading for a minute, look around and notice what your sense of vision tells you about your surroundings. Next, close your eyes, listen carefully, and notice what your sense of hearing, or **audition,** tells you.

> **Audition:** The sense of hearing.

When I did this exercise, looking around my den I noticed my computer screen, my desk, a lamp, an antique clock, a phone, two windows, and many stacks and shelves of books and journal articles. When I closed my eyes and listened, my experience changed dramatically. Now I noticed the clock ticking, the computer fan whirring, the robins in our yard chirping and the geese in the nearby woods honking. I also heard the soft rustle of my daughter's papers as she did her homework in the kitchen and the sound of a plane flying high overhead. Although these sensations were present when I looked around the room, I did not notice them.

This exercise demonstrates that hearing is an important, though sometimes unrecognized, sense. From an evolutionary perspective, hearing was essential for our ancestors' survival, helping them detect the approach of predatory animals, locate food, and communicate with others (Nathan, 1982). Yet, how exactly does hearing take place?

5-3a Sound Is the Stimulus for Hearing

Sound depends on a wave of pressure created when an object vibrates. The vibration causes molecules in an elastic medium—such as air, water, or solid material—to move together and apart in a rhythmic fashion. Like ripples on a pond, these pulsations move away from the vibrating object as **sound waves,** growing weaker as they travel farther from their source. Although sound waves weaken with increased distance, their speed remains constant, about 1,070 feet (or 330 meters) per second in air and about 4,724 feet (or 1,440 meters) per second in water. The number of sound waves that pass a given point in one second is its **frequency.** Sound frequency is measured in *hertz* (Hz), which is named after the nineteenth-century German physicist Heinrich Hertz (1857–1894). One Hz equals one cycle per second. The physical quality of sound frequency roughly corresponds to the psychological experience of *pitch*. Although people are most sensitive to sounds at frequencies between 2,000 and 5,000 Hz (Gulick et al., 1989), young adults can typically hear tones with frequencies as low as 20 Hz and as high as 20,000 Hz (Gelfand, 1981). As

> **Sound waves:** Pressure changes in a medium (air, water, solids) caused by the vibrations of molecules.
>
> **Frequency:** The number of sound waves that pass a given point in one second; corresponds to the psychological experience of pitch.

Amplitude: The height of a sound wave; corresponds to the psychological experience of loudness.

people age, their lower limit of hearing changes very little, but the upper range falls steadily from adolescence onward.

The height of a sound wave is its **amplitude** and corresponds to the psychological experience of the *loudness* of a sound. Amplitude is measured in *decibels* (*dB*). The greater the amplitude, the louder the sound, with perceived loudness doubling about every 10 decibels (Stevens, 1955). A whisper has an amplitude of about 20 dB, normal conversation occurs at about 60 dB, and a jet aircraft taking off nearby has an amplitude of about 140 dB. Exposure to sounds over 120 dB can be painful and may cause hearing damage (Henry, 1984). Prolonged exposure to sounds over 90 dB, such as those found in industrial settings, subway trains, and rock concerts, can contribute to permanent hearing loss.

Complexity: The extent to which a sound is composed of waves of different frequencies; corresponds to the psychological experience of *timbre*.

Most sounds are actually a combination of many different waves of different frequencies. This **complexity** corresponds to the psychological experience of *timbre*. Just as we can differentiate the sounds of different musical instruments because of the different frequencies of sound they blend together, we can also recognize the voices of different people over the telephone due to their unique sound-frequency blending. To experience a simple example of timbre perception, first clap your hands together while holding them flat, and then clap them again when they are cupped. Cupped hand-clapping produces a greater combination of low-frequency sound waves than flat hand-clapping, and thus, it is a more complex sound.

5-3b The Auditory System Consists of the Outer Ear, Middle Ear, and Inner Ear

The evolution of the modern mammalian ear can be traced back to the primitive internal ears found in some types of fish that consist of a system of looping passages filled with fluid (Békésy, 1960; Stebbins, 1980). Mammals, birds, and some reptiles have a more complex system of looping passages that contain a **cochlea,** which is a coiled, fluid-filled tube in the inner ear that contains the hairlike auditory receptors. The ears of mammals differ from those of birds and reptiles in that mammalian ears have three small bones to transmit vibrations to the cochlea, while the other species have only one bone.

Cochlea: The coiled, fluid-filled tube in the inner ear that contains the hairlike auditory receptors.

Operation of the Ear

The ear can be divided into three major parts: the *outer ear, middle ear,* and *inner ear* (see figure 5-10). The most visible part of the outer ear is the *pinna*, which is the skin-covered cartilage visible from the outside. Only mammals have pinnae, and its funnel shape is useful for channeling sound waves to the other part of the outer ear known as the *auditory canal*. This passageway is about an inch long, and as sound waves resonate in the auditory canal, their amplification is doubled.

Eardrum: A thin, flexible membrane at the end of the auditory canal that vibrates in sequence with sound waves.

At the end of the auditory canal is a thin, flexible membrane, known as the **eardrum,** which vibrates in sequence with the sound waves. Beyond the eardrum is the middle ear. As the eardrum vibrates, it sets in motion those three tiny, interconnected bones—the hammer, anvil, and stirrup—known collectively as *ossicles*. The ossicles, which are the tiniest bones in the body, further amplify the sound waves two or three times before transmitting them to the liquid-filled inner ear.

The main parts of the inner ear are the *oval window, cochlea,* and the *organ of Corti*. The stirrup is attached to the oval window, which is a thin membrane that transmits the sound waves from the stirrup to the cochlea. As mentioned earlier, the cochlea is a coiled, fluid-filled tube. The vibrations of the oval window cause pressure waves in the cochlear

---

INFO-BIT: Because sound travels almost one million times slower than light, when lightning flashes in the sky during a storm, you can roughly calculate how far away the lightning is by counting how many seconds it takes the sound of the thunder to reach you, with a 5-second delay indicating about a distance of 1 mile.

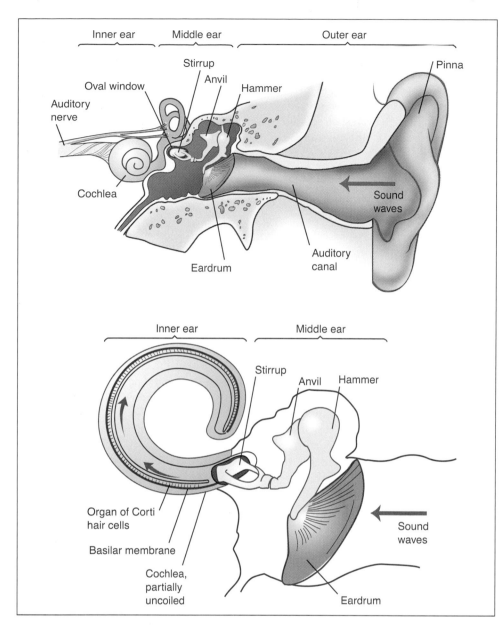

F I G U R E   5 - 1 0
The Human Ear

The ear consists of the outer, middle, and inner sections, which have different functions. First, the outer ear directs the sound to the eardrum. From there, the bones of the middle ear (hammer, anvil, and stirrup) greatly amplify the sound through the oval window to the inner ear. The vibrations of the oval window cause pressure waves in the cochlear fluid, which, in turn, cause the basilar membrane to move, bending the hair cells on its surface. This stimulation triggers action potentials in bundles of sensory neurons forming the auditory nerve, which sends information to the brain.

fluid. Running down the middle of the cochlea is a rubberlike membrane, known as the **basilar membrane,** which moves in a wavelike fashion in response to these pressure waves. Lying on top of the basilar membrane is the organ of Corti, which contains 15,000 receptors for hearing, called *hair cells.* When these hair cells are stimulated by movement of the basilar membrane, this stimulation triggers action potentials in bundles of sensory neurons forming the *auditory nerve,* which transmits auditory information to the brain. Which of the hair cells are stimulated determines which neurons fire and how rapidly they fire, and the resulting pattern of firing determines the sort of sound we hear.

Perceiving the Location of Sound

The ability to locate objects in space solely on the basis of the sounds they make is known as **sound localization.** People with only one functioning ear have difficulty accurately locating sounds. To demonstrate this auditory fact, close your eyes and ask a friend to make a noise from somewhere in the room. Point to your friend's location and then open your eyes to determine your accuracy. Next, place your index finger in one

Basilar membrane: A membrane that runs down the middle of the cochlea that contains the auditory receptor.

Sound localization: The ability to locate objects in space solely on the basis of the sounds they make.

ear and repeat this exercise. The reason two ears are better than one is that sounds coming from points other than those equidistant between your two ears reach one ear slightly before they reach the other. Sounds reaching the closer ear may also be slightly more intense because the head blocks some of the sound waves reaching the ear on the other side of the head. Because your ears are only about 6 inches apart, the time lag between the sound reaching your two ears and the different intensities of the sounds are extremely small. Yet, even such small differences provide your auditory system with sufficient information to locate the sound (Middlebrooks & Green, 1991; Phillips & Brugge, 1985).

5-3c Different Theories Explain Different Aspects of Pitch Perception

How does the auditory system convert sound waves into perceptions of pitch? Like our understanding of color perception, our current understanding of pitch perception is based on two theories that were once considered incompatible.

Place theory: A theory that pitch is determined by which place along the cochlea's basilar membrane is most activated.

Place theory contends that we hear different pitches because different sound waves trigger the hair cells on different portions, or *places*, on the cochlea's basilar membrane. The brain detects the frequency of a tone according to which place along the membrane is most activated. Place theory was first proposed by Herman von Helmholtz (1863), the codeveloper of trichromatic color theory, and later tested and refined by Hungarian scientist Georg von Békésy (1947, 1957), who won a Nobel Prize for this work in 1961. Békésy's research indicated that high-frequency tones trigger the greatest activity at the beginning of the cochlea's basilar membrane, where the oval window is located.

Frequency theory: A theory that pitch is determined by the frequency with which the basilar membrane vibrates.

Although place theory explains how we hear high-frequency tones, it cannot account for how we perceive very low-frequency tones. The problem is that at very low frequencies the entire basilar membrane vibrates uniformly, so that no one place is more activated than another. One theory that can explain the perception of low-frequency tones is **frequency theory,** which was first proposed by English physicist Ernest Rutherford (1861–1937) in 1886. According to frequency theory, the basilar membrane vibrates at the same frequency as the incoming sound wave, which, in turn, triggers neural impulses to the brain at this same rate. Thus, a sound wave of 800 Hz will set the basilar membrane vibrating 800 times per second, which will cause neurons to fire at 800 times per second.

Volley theory: A theory of pitch that neurons work in groups and alternate firing, thus achieving a combined frequency corresponding to the frequency of the sound wave.

One important problem with frequency theory is that individual neurons cannot fire more than 1,000 times per second. Because of this fact, frequency theory cannot explain people perceiving sounds with frequencies above 1,000 Hz. A revision of frequency theory, namely psychologist Ernest Wever's **volley theory,** contends that neurons work in groups and alternate firing, thus achieving a combined frequency of firing well above 1,000 times per second (Wever, 1949; Wever & Bray, 1937). Studies indicate that such alternate firing of groups of auditory nerves can generate volleys of up to 5,000 impulses per second (Zwislocki, 1981).

Based on what we now know, it appears that frequency theory, place theory, and volley theory account for different aspects of pitch perception. Place theory best explains high-frequency sounds, while frequency theory can better explain the perception of low-frequency sounds. For sounds between 1,000 and 5,000 Hz, pitch perception seems to be best explained by volley theory, which is a revision of frequency theory.

When music fails to agree to the ear, to soothe the ear and the heart and the senses, then it has missed its point.

—Maria Callas, Greek soprano, 1923–1977

SECTION SUMMARY

- Frequency refers to the number of sound waves that pass a given point in one second and corresponds to the experience of pitch.

- Amplitude is the height of a sound wave and corresponds to the experience of loudness.

- Complexity is the extent to which a sound is composed of different frequencies and corresponds to the experience of timbre.

- Sound localization is the ability to locate objects in space due to their sound.

- Place theory best explains high-frequency sounds.

- Frequency theory better explains low-frequency sounds.

- Volley theory best explains intermediate sounds.

5-4 YOUR OTHER SENSES

Through natural selection, animals come to possess the sensory mechanisms they need to survive in their specific environment. This is why animals that inhabit similar environments have similar sensory mechanisms. Our own human senses share the most similarity to those species that are our closest cousins on the evolutionary tree, namely other primates (Hodos & Butler, 2001). Like all primates, we primarily rely on our vision, with hearing being our distant second sense. These two sensory systems are classified as *higher senses* in humans, meaning they are extremely important to our survival. In contrast, the senses of taste, smell, touch, and proprioception are classified as *minor senses* because they are not considered as crucial to sustaining life.

5-4a Smell and Taste Represent "Far" and "Near" Chemical Senses

As life evolved from the sea to the land, two anatomically separate chemical sensory mechanisms developed. These two distinct senses, namely taste and smell, came to serve different functions. The sense of taste became a "near" sense, providing the last check on the acceptability of food, while the sense of smell became a "far" sense, able to detect stimuli from a much farther distance.

Smell

Olfaction is the sense of smell, and its stimuli are airborne molecules. When you smell fresh-brewed coffee (see figure 5-11), you are sensing molecules that have left the coffee and have traveled through the air to your nose. These molecules then enter your nasal passages and reach tiny receptor cells at the top of the nasal cavity. These olfactory receptors are located on a thin, dime-sized, mucous-coated layer of tissue known as the **olfactory epithelium.** The odor molecules from the coffee are then trapped and dissolved in the mucus of the epithelium, and this causes the olfactory receptor cells to transmit a neural impulse directly to the olfactory bulb at the base of the brain. From here, the signals are processed before being sent to the *primary olfactory cortex*, which is located in the frontal lobes (Dade et al., 2002; McLean & Shipley, 1992). Olfaction is the only sensation that is not relayed through the thalamus on its way to the cortex. Once processed by the brain, you appreciate the coffee's wonderful fragrance.

Olfaction: The sense of smell.

Olfactory epithelium: A thin layer of tissue at the top of the nasal cavity that contains the olfactory receptor cells.

INFO-BIT: Studies of various languages around the world reveal that between two-thirds and three-fourths of all words applying to the senses describe the two higher senses of vision and audition (Wilson, 1997).

FIGURE 5-11
The Olfactory System

The sense of smell depends on odor molecules in the air reaching the nose and traveling up the nasal passages to the receptor cells in the olfactory epithelium. The odor molecules are trapped and dissolved in the olfactory mucus, and this triggers the receptor cells to send a neural impulse to the olfactory bulb. From there, information is sent to the primary olfactory cortex in the frontal lobes.

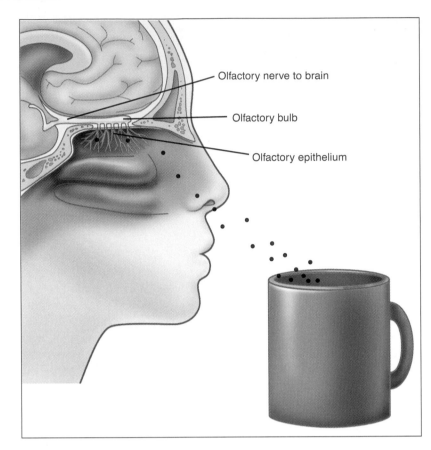

- Olfactory nerve to brain
- Olfactory bulb
- Olfactory epithelium

INFO-BIT: Olfactory sensitivity is substantially determined by the number of receptors present in the epithelium. Animals that have more receptors have much keener senses of smell. While we have about 10 million olfactory receptors, dogs have an astounding 200 million receptors, putting us at the lower end of the scale of smell sensitivity.

Humans have at least a hundred different types of olfactory receptor cells, with each type responding to only a limited family of odor molecules (Buck & Axel, 1991; Ressler et al., 1994). This large number of different types of receptors stands in sharp contrast to the three basic receptors involved in vision. Although it is not yet known exactly how the brain processes all these different types of olfactory information, together these receptors allow us to distinguish among about 10,000 different smells (Malnic et al., 1999). Having so many different types of olfactory receptors may mean that a great deal of the processing necessary for odor perception occurs in the nose itself. Despite the staggering number of odors that we can distinguish, for some unknown reason, we have a hard time correctly identifying and attaching names to specific odors. Thus, you may have a hard time correctly distinguishing the smell of smoke from that of soap.

Although our sense of smell is not as highly refined as that of dogs and cats, we are drawn toward perfumelike fragrances, such as flowers, and repulsed by foul and sulfurous odors (Miller, 1997). Yet, cross-cultural research indicates that the smells we pay most attention to are those that help us adapt and survive in our immediate surroundings (Classen et al., 1994). This is why the Dassanetch people (refer back to chapter-opening story) are especially sensitive to the smells associated with their cattle. These cattle-raisers identify the time of year by predictable changes in surrounding smells, such as the decaying and burning odors during the dry season, and the fresh smell of new plant growth during the rainy season.

> **INFO-BIT:** The attention we pay to others' smells probably harkens back to our ancestors' reliance on scent messages to regulate their sexual behavior. Even today, vestiges of this earlier reliance on olfactory cues can be demonstrated in people's ability to detect the sex of others reasonably well, based on the smell of their breath, hands, and clothing (Doty et al., 1982; Wallace, 1977).

Like many animals, we can recognize one another by our body odor. For example, in one study, blindfolded mothers were able to identify with close to 95 percent accuracy the clothing worn by their own children by smell alone (Porter & Moore, 1981). Odors can also evoke memories and feelings associated with past events (Richardson & Zucco, 1989). The smell of freshly cut grass or the scent of a specific perfume can mentally transport us back to a time in our lives when these odors were associated with specific memorable events.

Taste

As mentioned earlier, taste, or **gustation,** is a near sensation, occurring when a substance makes contact with about 10,000 special receptor cells in the mouth (Bartoshuk, 1991; Miller, 1995). Most of these receptors are located on the tongue, but some are also in the throat and on the roof of the mouth. The surface of the tongue contains many bumps, called **papillae** (Latin for pimple), most of which contain taste buds. Each taste bud has 50 to 150 receptor cells (Margolskee, 1995). Because of their constant contact with the chemicals they are designed to sense, as well as their exposure to bacteria, dirt, and dry air, these receptor cells wear out and die within 10 days (Pfaffmann, 1978). Fortunately, new cells emerge at the edge of the taste bud and migrate inward toward the center, replacing the old cells. Although this cycle of death and replacement of taste cells operates throughout our lives, it occurs more slowly among the elderly, which is one reason their taste sensitivity becomes less acute (Cowart, 1981).

When these taste cells absorb chemicals dissolved in saliva, they trigger neural impulses that are transmitted to one of two brain areas. One pathway involves information first being sent to the thalamus and then to the primary gustatory cortex, where taste identification occurs. The second pathway leads to the limbic system and allows one to quickly respond to a taste prior to consciously identifying it, such as when you reflexively spit out sour milk (Sekuler & Blake, 1994).

Cross-cultural research indicates that while people from different cultures may differ in their taste preferences, everyone can detect only four primary tastes: sweet, sour, salty, and bitter (Laing et al., 1993). As depicted in figure 5-12, sensitivity to sweet and salty substances is best near the front of the tongue, sour is best along the sides, and bitter is best at the back. If you ever have to swallow an unpleasant-tasting pill, place it in the center of the tongue because there are few taste cells here.

Unlike vision, hearing, and olfaction, which have different types of sense receptors, most taste receptor cells appear to respond to all of the four basic kinds of taste stimuli, but with different sensitivities (Arvidson & Friberg, 1980). Although no taste receptors seem to respond to only one of the four basic taste qualities, different gustatory *nerve fibers* do seem to be especially sensitized to certain taste stimuli (Pfaffman et al., 1979). While each nerve fiber does respond somewhat to all four basic tastes, it is most responsive to one. Thus, it is not an exaggeration to state that there are some "sweet" nerve fibers, and others that are primarily salty, sour, or bitter. These specialized nerve fibers transmit information to the brain that signals a particular flavor. The pattern of activation *across* these four different types of nerve fibers provide us with the many different tastes that we experience (Smith, 1985).

Although the taste of a particular substance depends on whether one or more of the four basic taste sensations is activated, the *flavor* of this substance is a combination of both its smell and taste (Mozell et al., 1969). To personally experience the role that olfaction plays in flavor perception, pinch your nostrils closed before approaching a particular food. Then place the food in your mouth and swish it around while paying attention to the

Gustation: The sense of taste.

Papillae: Taste receptors on the tongue.

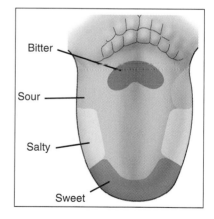

FIGURE 5-12
The Four Primary Tastes

Different areas of the tongue are most sensitive to the four primary qualities of taste: sweet, salty, sour, and bitter.

flavor. Next, release your nostrils, open your mouth slightly, and breathe in gently through both your mouth and nose. You should experience a significant increase in the food's flavor.

5-4b Touch Is Determined by the Skin Senses of Pressure, Temperature, and Pain

Every living thing has a "skin" of some sort that defines its boundaries with the environment, and every living creature has a sense of touch. Indeed, the skin is the largest sensory organ, with the average adult having more than two square yards of skin receptors covering her or his body. Our sense of touch is actually a combination of three skin senses: *pressure, temperature,* and *pain* perception (Craig & Rollman, 1999). Although the 5 million sense receptors in our skin consist of a variety of different types, like our taste receptors, there is no one type of skin receptor that produces a specific sensory experience. Instead, it appears that the skin's sensory experiences are due to the pattern of stimulation of nerve impulses reaching the somatosensory cortex of the brain.

Pressure

The stimulus for pressure is physical pressure on the skin. Although the entire body is sensitive to pressure, most of the cells in the somatosensory cortex are devoted to processing neural impulses coming from the fingers, lips, face, tongue, and genitals because these areas of the skin have the greatest concentration of receptors. That's why you are so much more sensitive to objects that come into contact with these skin areas than other regions of the skin.

Try the following exercise. First, touch your two index fingers together. Most people report about equal pressure intensity from both fingertips. Now lightly touch one fingertip repeatedly to your upper lip. Most people report sensations mostly on the lip and little or none from the fingertip. The reason your lip is more pressure sensitive than your finger when these two skin areas touch has to do with the relative lengths of their neural pathways to the brain. When touched simultaneously, neural impulses from the lip reach the brain 1 millisecond faster than those coming from the finger. Apparently, even when two places on the skin are being equally stimulated, the impulses that reach the brain first dictate where the sensation will be primarily experienced.

Temperature

In 1927, Karl Dallenbach discovered that we have two different kinds of temperature receptors in the skin, one sensitive to warm and the other to cold. Interestingly, the "hot" sensation is triggered by simultaneous stimulation of both the warm and cold receptors. Thus, if you ever grasp two braided pipes—one containing warm water and the other containing cold water—you will quickly pull away because the pipes will feel scalding hot.

Although temperature sensations depend on which type of receptor is stimulated, whether more warm or cold receptors are stimulated will depend on the difference between the temperature of the skin and the object you are feeling. This is why washing your hands in 60-degree water feels warm after coming in from the cold, but chilly when in a hot environment.

Pain

Although pain is an unpleasant experience, it is important to survival because it serves as a warning system that signals danger and the risk of injury (Wall, 2000). Pain also has the effect of forcing people to cope appropriately with an injury by both inducing them to seek treatment and to be still to promote healing. The importance of this sense is dramatically demonstrated by those rare individuals who are born with an insensitivity to pain due to improperly functioning nerve pathways that normally transmit pain signals to

For we are born in other's pain, and perish in our own.

—Francis Thompson, English poet, 1859–1907

the brain (Sternbach, 1963). In one such case of this type, a woman called Ms. C died at the age of 29 from massive infections caused by a lifetime of abrasion and unhealed injury (Melzack & Wall, 1982a).

Pain is induced through tissue damage or intense stimulation of sensory receptors (Gatchel & Turk, 1999). Light that is too bright, noises that are too loud, or pressure that is too great will all trigger the pain experience. Yet, overstimulation can sometimes occur without eliciting pain, as demonstrated when you eat something that is too sweet for your sense of taste. The too-sweet substance has certainly overstimulated your taste receptors, but there is no pain.

The sensation of pain appears to originate in *free nerve endings* in the skin, around muscles, and in internal organs. When intense stimuli cause cell and tissue damage, the damaged cells release chemicals—including a neurotransmitter called *substance P* (for pain)—that stimulate the free nerve endings, which in turn transmit pain signals to the brain (Beyer et al., 1991). People with the previously discussed rare disorder that makes them insensitive to pain have extremely low levels of substance P in or near the nerve endings (Pearson et al., 1982).

Two distinct peaks of pain are experienced upon suffering an injury, differing in quality and separated in time. For example, when you sprain your ankle or pound your thumb with a hammer, you experience what is known as *double pain* (Cooper et al., 1986; Willis, 1985). The first is a sharp, stinging pain caused by large-diameter nerve fibers (called *L-fibers*) in the spinal cord that transmit pain information very quickly to the brain, while the second is a dull or burning pain arising from small-diameter and slower-operating nerve fibers (called *S-fibers*) in the spinal cord. Most pain signals are transmitted by the small, slower-operating S-fibers.

The most widely accepted theory of pain is Ronald Melzack and Patrick Wall's (1982b) **gate-control theory,** which proposes that the L-fibers and S-fibers open and close "gateways" for pain in the spinal cord. According to this theory, the fast-transmitting, large L-fibers not only carry information about sharp pain to the brain, but they also carry information about most other forms of tactile stimulation. Once their information is transmitted to the brain, they close the pain gate by inhibiting the firing of neurons with which they synapse. The slower-transmitting, thin S-fibers, which carry information about dull and burning pain to the brain, also synapse with these same neurons, and thus, their pain information may arrive at a closed gate due to the faster operation of the L-fibers. When this happens, the pain information from the S-fibers cannot be sent to the brain.

Gate-control theory explains why rubbing, massaging, or even pinching a bruised or sore muscle can ease the pain. These actions activate the large and fast-transmitting L-fibers, which then close the pain gate to the stimuli transmitted by the thin and slower-operating S-fibers. Because most pain information is transmitted by the S-fibers, blocking these signals significantly reduces the pain experience. This also explains why placing ice on a sprained ankle eases pain. The ice not only reduces swelling, but, by triggering cold messages transmitted by the L-fibers, it also closes the gate on the S-fibers' pain signals.

Besides explaining normal pain, gate-control theory can also provide an explanation for a type of pain that has baffled science for years, namely, *phantom limb pain*. Phantom limb pain occurs when an amputee feels pain in a missing limb (Gagliese & Katz, 2000; Melzack, 1992). According to gate-control theory, when L-fibers are destroyed by amputation, the pain gates remain open, which permits random neural stimulation at the amputation site to trigger the experience of pain in the missing limb (Melzack, 1973).

Research indicates that the brain can also send messages to the spinal cord to close the pain gate, thus preventing pain messages from reaching the brain (Melzack, 1986; Whitehead & Kuhn, 1990). In such instances, the brain's messengers are a class of substances known as *endorphins*. Apparently, the ancient Chinese healing technique of *acupuncture*, which inserts long, thin needles into the skin at specific points, stimulates the release of endorphins (Takeshige, 1985). Similarly, a more modern pain-relief procedure, known as *transcutaneous electrical nerve stimulation* (*TENS*), which electrically stimulates painful body regions, also stimulates the release of endorphins (Barbaro, 1988). (See Discovery Box 5-2.)

Gate-control theory: A theory of pain perception that proposes that small and large nerve fibers open and close "gateways" for pain in the spinal cord.

DISCOVERY BOX 5-2

Can You Use Psychology to Reduce Pain?

More than any of our other senses, our experience of pain can be significantly influenced by a variety of psychological factors (Kotzer, 2000). For example, diverting people's attention away from painful stimulation to some other stimulus, such as soothing music or a pleasant image ("Imagine yourself on a warm, sunny beach"), is an effective strategy to alleviate pain (Fernandez & Turk, 1989; McCaul & Malott, 1984). Recognizing the benefits of distraction, dentists and other health care workers provide music, videos, and a constant flow of conversation while performing painful procedures in order to divert patient's attention away from the source of the pain. Another psychological technique to reduce pain is to give someone a placebo, which is an inert substance that the person believes will produce a particular effect, such as pain relief. Studies indicate that up to 35 percent of patients with chronic pain get relief from taking placebos (Weisenberg, 1977). The reason these patients feel less pain is that, unlike those who do not experience relief, their brains produce higher levels of endorphins in response to the placebos (Lipman et al., 1990). Quite literally, their brains are "fooled" into releasing pain-relieving chemicals because they expect pain relief from the fictitious drug in the placebos!

INFO-BIT: Neuroscientists recently discovered that we have a special set of thin nerves that are especially sensitive to the soft touches generated by tender caresses and reassuring hugs but not to rough touches, pinches, or jabs. These nerves stimulate the same brain areas activated by romantic love and sexual arousal, and appear to provide the emotional aspects of touch. Researchers speculate that these nerves may have evolved to guide humans toward tenderness and nurture.

5-4c The Proprioceptive Senses Detect Body Movement and Location

Besides the traditional five senses of vision, hearing, smell, taste, and touch, there are two additional sources of sense information, called *proprioceptive senses*, which detect body position and movement. If you've ever observed someone who was intoxicated with alcohol unsuccessfully trying to control their own body movements and sense of balance, you have witnessed the malfunctioning of the proprioceptive senses.

One type of proprioception, namely, the **kinesthetic sense,** provides information about the movement and location of body parts with respect to one another. Kinesthetic information comes from receptors in muscles, joints, and ligaments (Gandevia et al., 1992). Without this feedback about where our body parts are located, we would have trouble with any voluntary movement. You sometimes experience partial disruption of your kinesthetic sense when your leg "falls asleep" and you have trouble walking, or when a dentist numbs your jaw and you have difficulty talking.

While the kinesthetic sense provides feedback on the position and movement of body parts, the **vestibular sense (or equilibrium)** provides information on the position of the body—especially the head—in space by sensing gravity and motion. Vestibular sense information comes from tiny hairlike receptors located in the fluid-filled *vestibular sacs*

Kinesthetic sense: A type of proprioceptive sense that provides information about the movement and location of body parts with respect to one another.

Vestibular sense (or equilibrium): A type of proprioceptive sense that provides information on the position of the body—especially the head—in space.

and the *semicircular canals* in the inner ear, above the cochlea (refer back to figure 5-10). Whenever the head moves, these receptors send messages through a part of the auditory cortex that is not involved in hearing, and this information helps us maintain our balance. Perhaps you recall how much fun it used to be—and maybe still is—to twirl yourself around on a swing at the park until you were silly with dizziness. What happened in these instances was that when you stopped twirling, the fluid in your semicircular canals and your vestibular receptors did not immediately return to a normal state, and thus, you experienced the illusion of spinning while standing still. The vestibular imbalance caused by this twirling exercise is very similar to the vestibular imbalance caused by drunkenness.

SECTION SUMMARY

- Humans have at least a hundred different types of olfactory receptor cells, with each type responding to only a limited family of odor molecules.
- Most taste receptors are located on the tongue, in bumps called papillae.
- Humans detect four primary tastes: sweet, sour, salty, and bitter.
- The skin is the largest sensory organ.
- Touch is a combination of three skin senses: pressure, temperature, and pain perception.
- Pain is induced through tissue damage or intense stimulation of sensory receptors.
- According to gate-control theory, small and large nerve fibers open and close "gateways" for pain in the spinal cord.
- Kinesthetic sense provides information about the movement and location of body parts with respect to one another.
- Vestibular sense provides information on the position of the body in space by sensing gravity and motion.

5-5 PERCEPTION

As defined at the beginning of the chapter, perception is the process that organizes sensations into meaningful objects and events. For some of our senses, such as taste and smell, the distinction between sensation and perception is so fine that it is virtually impossible to distinguish one from the other. For others, such as hearing and vision, psychologists have been able to make sufficiently clear distinctions between these two processes so that greater insight has been gained into how we assign meaning to sensory stimuli.

5-5a Sensory Stimuli Are Organized into a Gestalt

In the summer of 1910 while gazing out the window of a moving train, German psychologist Max Wertheimer noticed that close, stationary objects—such as fences, trees, and buildings—appeared to race in the opposite direction of the train, while distant objects—such as mountains and clouds—seemed to slowly move along with the train. Wertheimer became so enthralled with understanding the psychological origins of what later came to be called *motion parallax* that he began conducting experiments that ultimately led to the development of a new school of thought in psychology: *Gestalt psychology* (see chapter 1, section 1-2e). According to Gestalt psychologists, our perceptions are not to be understood as the mind passively responding to a cluster of individual sensations, but rather, as the mind actively organizing sensory stimuli into a coherent whole, or **gestalt.**

Form Perception

Form perception is the process by which sensations are organized into meaningful shapes and patterns. One basic rule of form perception, known as the **figure-ground relationship,** states that when people focus on an object in their perceptual field, they automatically

Gestalt: An organized and coherent whole.

Form perception: The process by which sensations are organized into meaningful shapes and patterns.

Figure-ground relationship: The Gestalt principle that when people focus on an object in their perceptual field, they automatically distinguish it from its surroundings.

FIGURE 5-13
Reversible Figure and Ground

Danish psychologist Edgar Rubin (1915/1958) designed *reversible figure-ground* patterns like the one illustrated here distinguishing characteristics of figure and ground. When the white vase is perceived as the figure, it appears to be in front of the black ground, yet when the black faces are figure, black switches position with white. Can you keep one image in mind without the other intruding? No. Because the ground is perceived as unformed material, when you see the vase as figure, it is impossible to simultaneously see the faces, and vice versa. Because the stimuli in this vase-faces figure are ambiguous, the figure-ground relationship continually reverses, changing what you perceive. Rubin's vase-faces exercise nicely illustrates how the same stimulus can trigger more than one perception.

Depth perception: The ability to perceive objects three-dimensionally.

Binocular cues: Depth cues that require information from both eyes.

Monocular cues: Depth cues that require information from only one eye.

distinguish it from its surroundings. (See figure 5-13.) What they focus on is the *figure*, and everything else becomes the *ground*. For example, the words you are reading are the figures in your perceptual field, while the white surrounding the text is the ground. When there are not enough cues to reliably distinguish a figure from its ground, it is difficult to perceive the sought-after object. Objects blending into their surroundings is the basic principle behind camouflage (Regan & Beverley, 1984).

The figure-ground relationship applies to all the senses, not just vision. For example, I can distinguish the sound of my daughters' singing voices against the ground of the rest of the school chorus, the taste of cinnamon in pumpkin pie, and the smell of barbecued chicken at a county fair. In all instances, I perceive one object as the figure and the other sensory information as the background.

Once distinguishing figure from ground, we must next organize the figure into a meaningful form. To give meaning to these sensations, Gestalt psychologists identified the following additional principles, known collectively as the *laws of grouping*, that describe how people group discrete stimuli together into a meaningful whole:

Similarity—We tend to group together stimuli that are similar.

Proximity—We tend to group nearby stimuli together.

Continuity—We tend to perceive the contours of straight or curving lines as continuous flowing patterns.

Closure—We tend to close gaps in a figure and perceive it as a whole.

Depth Perception

In addition to organizing sensations into meaningful shapes and patterns, another aspect of visual perception involves organizing sensations in terms of the distance they are to us. To judge distance, our brains must transform the two-dimensional images that fall on our retinas into three-dimensional perceptions. This ability to perceive objects three-dimensionally is known as **depth perception** and depends on the use of both *binocular cues* and *monocular cues* (Jacobs, 2002).

Binocular cues are depth cues that require information from both eyes. Because our eyes are about 3 inches apart, they receive slightly different images on their retinas when looking at the same scene. This degree of difference between the two images—which is greater when objects are closer to us—is known as the binocular cue of *retinal disparity*. Our brains automatically fuse these two images into one and use the cue of retinal disparity to judge the distance of objects. You can see the difference between the views of your eyes by holding both forefingers vertically in front of you, one at a distance of 6 inches and the other at arm's length. Now alternately close each eye while looking at both fingers. Notice that the closer finger appears to move further side to side than the farther finger. If you focus on one finger with both eyes, you will see two images of the other finger. Stereoscopes and 3-D movies create the illusion of depth by presenting to each eye slightly different views of the same image.

Another binocular distance cue is *convergence*, which is the degree the eyes turn inward as an object gets closer. By receiving information on the angle of convergence from the muscles of your eyes, your brain automatically calculates the distance at which you are focusing. The eye strain you experience after staring at a near object for a long time, such as a book or computer terminal, is caused by continuous convergence (Tyrrell & Leibowitz, 1990).

While binocular cues result from both eyes working together, **monocular cues** are depth cues that require information from only one eye. Some of the more important monocular cues—some of which are illustrated in figure 5-14—are as follows:

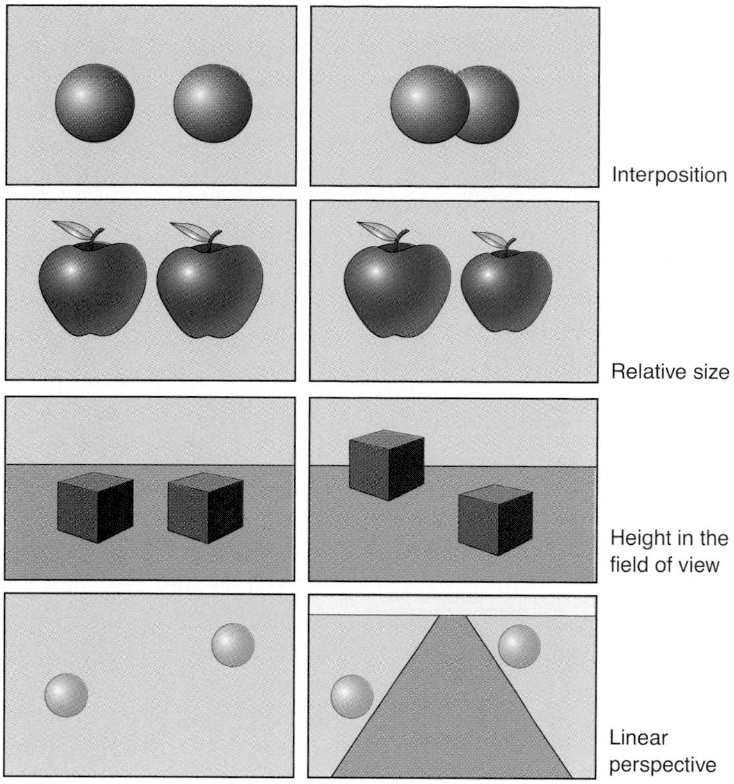

Interposition

Relative size

Height in the field of view

Linear perspective

FIGURE 5-14
Monocular Cues

Monocular cues are depth cues that require information from only one eye. Close one eye and test this depth perception principle for yourself.

Interposition—When one object partially blocks our view of another, we perceive the partially obscured object as more distant.

Familiar size—When we see a familiar object, we perceive it as near or distant based on the size of its retinal image. Familiar objects that cast small retinal images are perceived as distant, while familiar objects that make large retinal images are perceived as near.

Relative size—If we assume that two objects are similar in size, we perceive the object with the larger retinal image as being closer.

Linear perspective—When we see the converging of what we assume are parallel lines, we perceive this convergence as indicating increasing distance.

Texture gradients—When we see a change in the surface texture of objects from coarse, distinct features to fine, indistinct features, we perceive increasing distance.

Aerial perspective—When we see objects that appear hazy, we perceive them as being farther away than sharp, clear objects.

Height in the field of view—When we see objects, those closer to the horizon are perceived as farther away. Thus, terrestrial objects will be perceived as farther away when higher in our visual field, while aerial objects will be perceived as farther away when lower in our visual field.

Relative brightness—When objects reflect more light to our eyes than other objects, we perceive the brighter objects as being closer.

The eye sees only what the mind is prepared to comprehend.

—Henri Bergson, French philosopher, 1859–1941

One last important monocular cue deals with movement. *Motion parallax* refers to the fact that as you move your head sideways, objects at different distances appear to move in different directions and at different speeds (Ichikawa & Saida, 2002; Ujike & Ono, 2001). *Parallax* means a change in position, so motion parallax is a change in the position of an object caused by motion. It was Wertheimer's attention to this perceptual phenomenon that led to the founding of Gestalt psychology. The next time you ride in a car, bus, or train, experience what Wertheimer experienced by focusing on a distant object to your side. Notice how the speed and direction of motion depends on distance. Closer objects appear to speed by in the opposite direction of your own movement, while farther objects seem to move more slowly and in your same direction. It is this motion parallax that causes many children to believe that the moon or clouds they see through their side windows are actually following them.

Perceptual Constancy

Thus far, you have learned how we organize sensations into meaningful shapes and patterns, and how we also organize them in space. A third aspect of perceptual organization involves **perceptual constancy,** which is the tendency to perceive objects as relatively stable despite continually changing sensory information. Once we form a stable perception of an object, we can recognize it from almost any distance, angle, and level of illumination. We have already examined *color constancy* earlier in the chapter, and thus, let us now turn our attention to size and shape constancy.

Size constancy is the tendency to perceive objects as stable in size despite changes in the size of their retinal images when they are viewed from different distances. This form of perceptual constancy explains why you don't perceive people approaching you from a distance as midgets who are mysteriously growing in stature before your eyes. Likewise, **shape constancy** is the tendency to perceive an object as the same shape no matter from what angle it is viewed. Thus, when you look at your hand, this book, or a door from different angles, you still perceive them as retaining their original shapes despite changes in the shape of their retinal images.

5-5b Perceptual Sets Create Expectations for How to Interpret Sensory Stimuli

Just as expectations can influence whether we detect the *presence* of a stimulus (refer back to section 5-1a), the expectations we bring to a situation can also influence *how* we perceive the stimulus object. These expectations, known as **perceptual sets,** create a tendency to interpret sensory information in a particular way. For example, look at the drawing of the duck in figure 5-15 and then read the figure caption. Based on your initial expectation of seeing a duck, you most likely organized the stimuli in this drawing so that

Perceptual constancy: The tendency to perceive objects as relatively stable despite continually changing sensory information.

Size constancy: The form of perceptual constancy in which there is a tendency to perceive objects as stable in size despite changes in the size of their retinal images when they are viewed from different distances.

Shape constancy: The form of perceptual constancy in which there is a tendency to perceive an object as the same shape no matter from what angle it is viewed.

Perceptual sets: Expectations that create a tendency to interpret sensory information in a particular way.

FIGURE 5-15
What Kind of a Duck Is This?

Now that you have seen the duck, look again at this drawing, but now, see the rabbit.

Source: From MINDSIGHTS: ORIGINAL VISUAL ILLUSIONS, AMBIGUITIES AND OTHER ANOMALIES, WITH A COMMENTARY ON THE PLAY OF MIND IN PERCEPTION AND ART by Roger N. Shepard, ©1990 by Roger N. Shepard. Reprinted by permission of Henry Holt and Company, LLC.

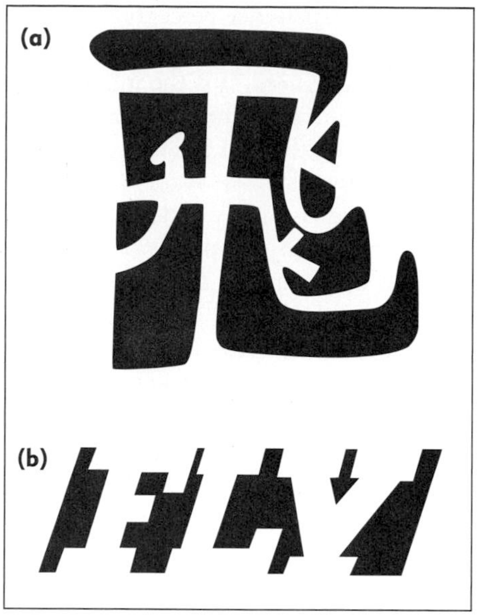

FIGURE 5-16
Cultural Influence on Perception

(a) Why does this figure appear to be a confusing pattern of black figures to most English-speaking Westerners, but not to people who are familiar with Chinese? *(b)* Why is the exact opposite probably true for this figure?

your expectation was realized. Yet, now ask a friend to look at this same drawing (cover up the caption), but tell them to "look at the rabbit." This is a demonstration of how people can develop different perceptions of the same stimuli based on the situational context that creates different perceptual sets.

Perceptual set can also be influenced by culture. For example, look at figure 5-16a. Most of you will see a rather confusing pattern of black shapes that may look somewhat like a boot. However, when you look at figure 5-16b, most of you readily perceive the word *FLY* in the white spaces. Your experience with the English language causes you to focus attention on the white spaces of figure 5-16b, while the black regions serve as background. Yet, if you were a native Chinese, you would readily perceive the white spaces in figure 5-16a as depicting the Chinese calligraphic character for the word *FLY*, and it would be figure 5-16b that would likely look confusing (Coren et al., 1987).

Our perceptual sets can influence what we hear and taste as well as what we see. One incident from my childhood that has become family lore is the time we invited Great-Aunt Edith over for dinner. After the meal, as my sister was trying to coax our finicky dog to eat table scraps, she blurted out in exasperation, "Oh eat it, you dumb dog!" However, what our aunt heard was, "Oh Edith, you dumb dog!" Needless to say, my sister had to do some quick explaining! Regarding taste expectations, during White House parties, President Richard Nixon occasionally instructed waiters to refill empty bottles of fine and expensive wine with cheaper and less-quality brands as a cost-saving measure. Nixon was counting on the expensive bottle's label creating a perceptual set of fine taste in his guests. The psychological phenomenon of perceptual set is yet another illustration that what we perceive is much more than just a matter of detecting sensory stimuli in the world—perception has to do with what's going on in our minds.

5-5c Perceptual Illusions Represent a Misperception of Physical Reality

Because perception depends on how the perceiver interprets sensory stimuli, errors or *mis*perceptions are bound to occur (Glover & Dixon, 2002; Logvinenko et al., 2002). For example, have you ever been sitting behind the driver's wheel of a parked car when the car parked next to you begins to back up, and you mistakenly perceive your car moving forward? I know that when this happens to me, I slam on my brakes before realizing that I have just experienced a **perceptual illusion** called **induced movement.** The reason we

Perceptual illusion:
A misperception of physical reality often due to the misapplication of perceptual principles.

Induced movement: The illusory movement of a stationary object caused by the movement of another nearby object.

sometimes experience perceptual illusions is because we misapply one or more of the perceptual principles previously examined in this chapter (see section 5-5a). In the case of induced movement, it is the misapplication of the principle of motion parallax. That is, instead of your movement forward causing close objects to appear as though they are moving backward, the movement backward of the car close to you makes you feel like you are moving forward.

Because vision is our dominant sense, we know more about *visual* illusions than any other sensory misperceptions. Thus, in this section, the type of perceptual illusions we will focus on will be mostly of the visual variety. Yet, let me mention one *auditory* illusion I am hearing right now as I type this sentence. As mentioned previously, I have an antique clock in my den. Although I know it is making a steady click-click-click-click sound as the pendulum swings back and forth, what I more often hear is an accented CLICK-click-CLICK-click. The reason for this auditory illusion is that people tend to group the steady clicks of a clock into patterns of two clicks, with one of the clicks—usually the first—being misperceived as slightly louder than the other. Check out Discovery Box 5-3 on how culture may affect visual illusions.

The most important visual illusion you experience when watching movies and playing video games is **stroboscopic movement,** which is the illusion of movement produced by a rapid pattern of stimulation on different parts of the retina (Anstis, 1978). In motion pictures, stroboscopic movement is created by rapidly passing a series of still pictures (or film frames) past a light source, which projects these images onto a screen. For this illusion of movement to occur, each film frame must replace the previous one 24 times per second. During the early days of motion pictures, the frame rate was only 16 per second, resulting in jerky and disjointed movement, and a noticeable flickering of light. In television and video games, the static frames change about 30 times per second.

One visual illusion that was popular with movie audiences during the 1950s was 3-D photography, which relies on the binocular cue of retinal disparity to fool the brain into perceiving a three-dimensional scene (McCarthy, 1992; McGee, 1989). The modern-day version of the 3-D movie is the *virtual environment*, in which 3-D images and sounds can be experienced while wearing a relatively light visor. The visor sends clear, full wrap-around 3-D images to each eye, and the ears receive digital stereo sound. The images and sounds transmitted by the visor are controlled by a computer that takes into account the head movements of the wearer. Thus, whenever the wearer's head turns, the scene shifts accordingly. Virtual environment visors and helmets are not only used to train airline pilots, police officers, surgeons, and soldiers in their various environments, but they are quickly becoming an integral part of the equipment used by computer game players.

Finally, one last illusion that may be affected by the perception of depth is the **moon illusion,** in which the moon appears larger when near the horizon than when high in the sky despite both objects casting the same-sized retinal image. One explanation of the moon illusion, known as the *apparent-distance theory*, is that an object near the horizon is viewed across the filled space of the terrain, which contains much depth information. In contrast, an object that is elevated in the sky is viewed through empty space, which

---

Stroboscopic movement: The illusion of movement produced by a rapid pattern of stimulation on different parts of the retina.

Moon illusion: A perceptual illusion in which the moon appears larger when near the horizon than when high in the sky.

However, no two people see the external world in exactly the same way. To every separate person a thing is what he thinks it is—in other words, not a thing, but a think.

—Penelope Fitzgerald, British author, b. 1960

INFO-BIT: One troubling fact about most of the virtual environment computer games is that they involve violence. Despite the denials from the video-game industry, a meta-analysis of 33 video-game studies involving over 3,000 participants found that high video-game violence is associated with heightened aggression in the real world among young adults and children (Anderson & Bushman, 2001).

DISCOVERY BOX 5-3

Do Perceptual Illusions Differ Cross-Culturally?

The most famous and extensively studied illusion is the **Müeller-Lyer illusion** shown in figure 5-17. Notice that the vertical line *b* to the right appears longer than line *a* to the left. Yet, if you measure the lines with a ruler, you will find that they are equal in length. The generally accepted explanation for this illusion is that it is due to the misapplication of size constancy (Gregory, 1998; Nijhawan, 1991). That is, because figure *a* bears a likeness to the outside corner of a building and figure *b* resembles the inside corner of a room, the vertical *b* line appears farther away than the vertical *a* line. As a result of this distance cue, the application of size constancy enlarges the perceived length of *b* relative to *a*. Interestingly, cross-cultural research indicates that the Müeller-Lyer illusion is most likely to occur in cultures where straight lines, right angles, and rectangles are common design elements in buildings (Segall et al., 1966, 1990). People who live in curved buildings without straight lines and right angles, such as the Zulu of southeastern Africa, are much less susceptible to this particular perceptual illusion.

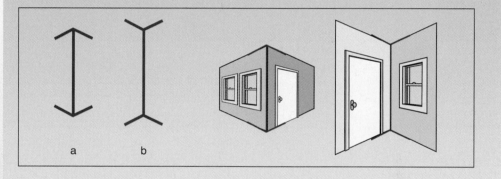

FIGURE 5-17
The Müeller-Lyer Illusion

In the Müeller-Lyer illusion, lines of equal length are perceived as unequal. Research indicates that this illusion is more commonly experienced in cultures where straight lines, right angles, and rectangles are common building design elements. What monocular distance cue is misapplied in this illusion?

FIGURE 5-18
The Ponzo Illusion

Although the two horizontal lines are the same length, our experience tells us that a more distant object can create the same-sized retinal image only if it is larger. What monocular distance cue is being misapplied here?

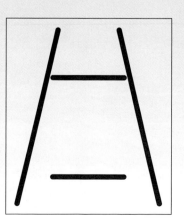

Another perceptual illusion caused by the misapplication of size constancy is the **Ponzo illusion** depicted in figure 5-18. Most people see the line on top as longer than the one on the bottom. As in the Müeller-Lyer illusion, these two lines cast the same-sized retinal image, and thus, the illusion occurs due to the top line appearing farther away than the bottom line because people misapply the monocular distance cue of linear perspective. This illusion is also less likely to be experienced by people who live in cultures where they aren't exposed to many straight lines and right angles (Deregowski, 1989; Segall et al., 1966).

Müeller-Lyer illusion: A perceptual illusion in which the perceived length of a line is influenced by placing inward or outward facing wings on the ends of lines.

Ponzo illusion: A perceptual illusion in which the perceived lengths of horizontal lines are influenced by their being placed between vertical converging lines that serve as distance cues.

The modern film tries too hard to be real. Its techniques of illusion are so perfect that it requires no contribution from the audience but a mouthful of popcorn.

—Raymond Chandler, U.S. author, 1888–1959

contains little depth information. Due to the greater depth information available when looking at a horizon moon, it should appear to be farther away, and thus, it is viewed as larger than the less-distant-appearing sky-high moon (Kaufman & Rock, 1962).

Although the apparent-distance theory has been the most popular explanation for the moon illusion, one problem with it is that when people are asked to judge which moon appears to be closer (Coren & Aks, 1990), some report that the horizon moon looks closer, not farther away! Of course, this directly contradicts apparent-distance theory. Currently, the moon illusion is still not fully understood, but, consistent with apparent-distance theory, it does seem to be related to size constancy and the number and strength of depth cues in the perceiver's visual field (Coren, 1989; Reed, 1989).

5-5d Certain Aspects of Perception Are Innate, While Others Are Learned

The principles of Gestalt psychology describe how we transform sensory information into meaningful perceptions. Gestalt psychologists believe that we are born with these principles for organizing sensory information. Yet, to what extent is perception based on inborn abilities versus experience-based learning?

The Visual Cliff

To study the ability to perceive depth, Eleanor Gibson and Richard Walk (1960) designed the *visual cliff*. This apparatus consists of a glass-covered table top with a "shallow" checkerboard on one end and a "deep" checkerboard on the other end that appears to drop off like a cliff (see figure 5-19). When infants between 6 and 14 months were placed in the middle of this table, their mothers were instructed to try to coax them into crawling to one side or the other. Although the mothers had little problem getting their children to crawl toward them on the shallow end, most refused to crawl past the visual cliff onto the deep end (Walk & Gibson, 1961). It's possible that by the time they learned to crawl, these children had also learned to perceive depth, yet newborn animals that can walk the day they're born—such as lambs, chicks, kittens, pigs, and rats—also avoid the deep end of the visual cliff (Walk, 1981). In addition, later studies using the visual cliff

FIGURE 5-19
The Visual Cliff

The visual cliff consists of a glass-covered tabletop with a "shallow" checkerboard on one end and a "deep" checkerboard on the other end that appears to drop off like a cliff. Most 6-month-old infants won't crawl across the "deep" side.

found that when younger noncrawling infants were physically moved from the shallow end of the table to the deep end, their heart rates slowed down, which is a typical reaction when people try to orient themselves in new situations (Campos et al., 1970). In other words, although these younger babies may not have known precisely how to react, they did *perceive* something different between the shallow and deep ends of the table.

Newly "Sighted" People and Animals

Further evidence that some perceptual abilities are inborn comes from case histories of people who have gained sight after a lifetime of blindness. Most gained their vision by having *cataracts*—clouded lenses that allow only diffused light to enter the eye—surgically removed. Following this procedure, these newly sighted individuals could distinguish figure from ground, scan objects, perceive colors, and follow moving objects with their eyes (Gregory, 1998). Unfortunately, they often could not recognize objects until they touched them.

Seeking to study this same phenomenon under more controlled conditions, Tortsen Wiesel (1982) either stitched closed the eyelids of newborn kittens and monkeys or placed goggles over their eyes that enabled them to see only diffused light. Following infancy, when these visual impairments were removed, the animals exhibited similar perceptual limitations observed in the human cataract patients. Further studies with cats found that the first three months of life are a critical period in the development of their ability to detect horizontal and vertical lines (Hirsch & Spinelli, 1970; Mitchell, 1980). If kittens don't get the necessary exposure to this visual stimuli, they experience a permanent deficit in visual perception even after years of living in a normal environment. Together, these studies suggest that although certain aspects of visual perception may be inborn, others require experience-based learning during critical periods in infancy. If this critical period is missed, certain perceptual deficits cannot be corrected through later learning.

5-5e There Is Little Scientific Evidence for Extrasensory Perception

Besides the types of perception we have already discussed, some people believe that we can also perceive events in the world without using the normal sensory receptors. This **extrasensory perception (ESP)** is a controversial topic within psychology, with only a minority of psychologists believing in its possible existence (Hoppe, 1988; Hyman, 1994). The field that studies ESP and other paranormal phenomena is known as **parapsychology.**

Parapsychologists study a variety of extrasensory abilities. Mental telepathy is the alleged ability to perceive others' thoughts, while clairvoyance is the alleged ability to perceive objects or events that are not physically present. For example, telepathists might claim they can "read" your mind, and clairvoyants might claim they can find your lost jewelry. Unlike telepathy and clairvoyance, which involves perception of things in the present, precognition is the alleged ability to perceive events in the future—that is, before they happen. Thus, you might consult a fortune teller who claims to use precognition to reveal an impending love interest. Finally, psychokinesis is the alleged ability to control objects through mental manipulation, such as causing a chair to move or a flipped coin to land either "heads" or "tails."

One of the main reasons for skepticism in the scientific community regarding ESP claims is that whenever one study discovers evidence for paranormal abilities, these findings generally cannot be replicated in subsequent research (Alcock, 1989; Hines, 1988). Similarly, after 20 years of testing "psychic spies," the Central Intelligence Agency concluded in a 1995 report that ESP claims were not supported by any reliable evidence (Hyman, 1996).

Another reason to doubt paranormal claims is that many published ESP studies have employed flawed research methodologies or have failed to detect outright fraud by those they were testing. In one famous case, the alleged psychic Uri Geller, who is also a

Extrasensory perception (ESP): The ability to perceive events without using normal sensory receptors.

Parapsychology: The field that studies ESP and other paranormal phenomena.

magician, claimed to be able to bend spoons using psychokinesis. However, upon closer inspection by another trained magician, it was discovered that Geller's powers were well short of anyone's definition of miraculous (Randi, 1980). Like any good magician, he used sleight-of-hand techniques to distract people's attention, and then quickly bent the spoons using normal physical force!

Although there is little evidence indicating that ESP is a viable means of gathering information about our world, the vast majority of people believe in its existence (Messer & Griggs, 1989). In most cases, the evidence that laypersons base their beliefs on comes from anecdotal accounts, not scientific studies. Yet, these accounts could simply be due to unusual coincidences, exaggerated gossip, or—as we have seen—outright fraud. Until the phenomena known as ESP can be reliably replicated in carefully controlled scientific studies, it will remain only a highly speculative "extra-sense" to most practitioners of science.

SECTION SUMMARY

- Form perception is the process by which sensations are organized into meaningful shapes and patterns.

- Figure-ground relationship is a Gestalt principle stating that when people focus on an object or "figure" in their perceptual field, they automatically distinguish it from its surroundings.

- Depth perception is the ability to perceive objects three-dimensionally.

- Perceptual constancy is the tendency to perceive objects as relatively stable despite continually changing sensory information.

- Perceptual set refers to the expectations an observer brings to a situation that influence what is perceived.

- Perceptual illusion is a misperception of physical reality due to the misapplication of perceptual principles.

- Certain aspects of visual perception may be inborn, while others require experience-based learning during critical periods in infancy.

- Extrasensory perception is the ability to perceive events without using normal sensory receptors.

SUGGESTED WEBSITES

Note: These websites were functional when we went to press. Please access the online text for the most up-to-date URLs.

Experimental Psychology Lab
http://www.genpsy.unizh.ch/Ulf/Lab/WebExpPsyLab.html
This website has links to numerous psychology experiments, including those related to sensation and perception.

PsychExperiments
http://psychexps.olemiss.edu/
This website contains demonstrations and experiments in perception and cognition.

Grand Illusions
http://www.grand-illusions.com/
This website has many optical and sensory illusions and interactive demonstrations and puzzles.

PSYCHOLOGICAL APPLICATIONS
Can You Improve Your Memory and Self-Esteem through Subliminal Persuasion?

As discussed earlier in the chapter, we know that we do not consciously experience many events because they are below our absolute threshold. Stimulation just below the absolute threshold for conscious awareness is known as **subliminal stimulation.** As with extrasensory perception, many astounding claims have been made over the years about the powerful influence that subliminal messages can have on our minds and actions. For example, popular author Wilson Bryan Key warns about the dangers that cleverly hidden subliminal messages can have on our lives (Key, 1989). As Key states:

> Every person . . . has been victimized and manipulated by the use of subliminal stimuli directed into his unconscious mind by the mass merchandisers of media. The techniques are in widespread use by media, advertising and public relations agencies, industrial and commercial corporations, and by the Federal government itself. (Key, 1973, p.1)

The views expressed by Key are widely held by the American public, and thus, it isn't surprising that many companies are trying to profit from this cultural belief in the power of subliminal stimulation (Zanot et al., 1983). Today, in stores throughout the country, you can buy subliminal audiotapes to improve memory, stop smoking, lose weight, or increase self-esteem. Is there any evidence that such tapes are effective? Should you spend your money on such products?

Although some studies have found that people can respond to stimuli without being aware that they are doing so, these effects have only been obtained in laboratory studies and last only a fraction of a second (Bornstein et al., 1987; Krosnick et al., 1992). If subliminal effects last less than a second, they will have little practical impact on everyday attitudes and behavior. Yet what about those people who have used subliminal tapes and swear that their lives have been changed? Isn't this evidence that subliminal persuasion can be effective at least some of the time?

This was the question that Anthony Greenwald and his colleagues (1991) were interested in answering when they conducted a study of such self-help tapes. Participants were first pretested for their level of self-esteem and memory recall ability and then given an audiotape containing various pieces of classical music. The tape manufacturers claimed that embedded within these self-help tapes were subliminal messages designed either to increase self-esteem (e.g., "I have high self-worth and high self-esteem") or to increase one's memory (e.g., "My ability to remember and recall is increasing daily."). Half of the tapes were purposely mislabeled by the researchers, leading the participants who received them to believe they had a memory tape when they really had a self-esteem tape, or vice versa. The rest of the tapes, with correct labels, were distributed to the remaining participants. During the next five weeks, these volunteers listened daily to their respective tapes at home. After this exposure period, they were again given self-esteem and memory tests and were also asked whether they believed the tapes had been effective. Results indicated no self-esteem or memory increases: The subliminal tapes were utterly ineffective. Despite these null findings, participants who thought they had received the self-esteem tape tended to believe their self-esteem had increased, and those who thought they had received the memory tape believed their memory had improved. This was true even if they had received a mislabeled tape!

These results, combined with other subliminal tape studies, suggest that whatever benefits people derive from such self-help products have little to do with the content of the subliminal messages (Pratkanis & Aronson, 1992). Instead, people's expectations (the **placebo effect**), combined with their economic and psychological investment ("I invested a lot of time and money in this tape, it must be good!"), appear to be the sole means of influence operating here. Thus, even though people can perceive stimuli at thresholds below their conscious awareness, there is no evidence that subliminal messages have anything even remotely close to the power that many people believe.

Subliminal stimulation: Stimulation just below the absolute threshold for conscious awareness.

Placebo effect: A situation where people experience some change or improvement from an empty, fake, or ineffectual treatment.

KEY TERMS

absolute threshold (p. 117)	*cones (p. 121)*	*gate-control theory (p. 135)*
afterimage (p. 124)	*cornea (p. 120)*	*gestalt (p. 137)*
amplitude (p. 128)	*depth perception (p. 138)*	*gustation (p. 133)*
audition (p. 127)	*eardrum (p. 128)*	*induced movement (p. 141)*
basilar membrane (p. 129)	*extrasensory perception (ESP) (p. 145)*	*iris (p. 120)*
binocular cues (p. 138)	*feature detectors (p. 122)*	*just-noticeable difference (JND) (p. 118)*
blind spot (p. 122)	*figure-ground relationship (p. 137)*	*kinesthetic sense (p. 136)*
cochlea (p. 128)	*form perception (p. 137)*	*lens (p. 120)*
color blindness (p. 124)	*fovea (p. 121)*	*monocular cues (p. 138)*
color constancy (p. 126)	*frequency (p. 127)*	*moon illusion (p. 142)*
complexity (p. 128)	*frequency theory (p. 130)*	*Müeller-Lyer illusion (p. 143)*

REVIEW QUESTIONS

1. Which of the following statements is *true?*
   a. To determine absolute threshold, a stimulus must be detectable 90 percent of the time.
   b. We have many thresholds for a given sense.
   c. Our sense of taste is more sensitive than hearing.
   d. Sensory adaptation occurs with vision without any special equipment.
   e. none of the above

2. Which of the following types of energy can our eyes detect?
   a. radio
   b. ultraviolet and infrared
   c. X-ray radiation
   d. none of the above
   e. *a* and *c*

3. Pupil size is affected by
   a. light.
   b. psychological arousal.
   c. interest.
   d. all of the above
   e. *a* and *b*

4. Which of the following animals have all-rod eyes?
   a. lizards and chipmunks
   b. rats
   c. bears
   d. owls
   e. *b* and *d*

5. Which of the following statements is *true?*
   a. Visual information in the right visual field goes to the left hemisphere of the brain.
   b. Visual information in the left visual field goes to the right hemisphere of the brain.
   c. Axons from the right eye are all connected to the right hemisphere of the brain.
   d. The optic nerve is the retina's area of central focus.
   e. *a* and *b*

6. Color is
   a. energy.
   b. created by our nervous system.
   c. the same for humans and animals.
   d. *a* and *b*
   e. all of the above

7. The theory that best explains color blindness is
   a. trichromatic theory.
   b. opponent-process theory.
   c. vision theory.
   d. *a* and *b*
   e. none of the above

8. The main parts of the inner ear include the
   a. oval window, cochlea, and organ of Corti.
   b. hammer, anvil, and stirrup.
   c. pinna, cochlea, and basilar membrane.
   d. basilar membrane, oval window, and hammer.
   e. none of the above

9. What theory best explains how we can hear sounds at frequencies of 5,000 Hz?
   a. volley
   b. place
   c. frequency
   d. *a* and *b*
   e. none of the above

10. Which of the following statements is *true?*
   a. Sensitivity to sweet and salty substances is best along the sides of the tongue.
   b. If your L-fibers are destroyed, you will be insensitive to pain.
   c. The inner ear is responsible only for our sense of hearing.
   d. Our tongue is the largest sensory organ.
   e. none of the above

11. Which of the following statements is *true?*
   a. Our sense of smell is as refined as that of a cat or dog.
   b. Our ears appear to have evolved from our sense of touch.
   c. We cannot recognize each other from body odor alone.
   d. all of the above
   e. none of the above

12. The areas of the skin with the greatest concentration of receptors are the
   a. fingers, lips, face, tongue, and genitals.
   b. fingers, lips, bottom of feet, and genitals.
   c. toes, elbows, and eyes.
   d. knees, wrists, and neck.
   e. none of the above

13. Gestalt psychology is based on the principle
   a. that our mind responds to individual sensations.
   b. that our mind actively organizes stimuli into a whole.
   c. of motion parallax.
   d. *a* and *b*
   e. none of the above
14. Depth perception depends on
   a. binocular cues.
   b. monocular cues.
   c. convergence.
   d. retinal disparity.
   e. all of the above

15. To fool the brain into seeing in three-dimensions, 3-D movies rely on
   a. monocular cues.
   b. retinal disparity.
   c. amplitude.
   d. *a* and *b*
   e. none of the above
16. How have scientists tried to determine what aspects of perception are innate?
   a. studying human infants
   b. studying newborn animals
   c. studying blind people with eyesight surgically restored
   d. all of the above
   e. *a* and *c* only

Consciousness

Chapter Outline

The discovery that helped change the course of sleep research from a relatively mundane area of inquiry into an intensely exciting journey occurred in 1952. A young graduate student working in the physiology department's sleep lab had been assigned by his professor, Nathaniel Kleitman, to watch their sleep participants' slow rolling eye movements as they fell asleep. Despite these instructions, his student, Eugene Aserinsky, soon noticed another kind of eye movement occurring well after the participants had fallen asleep. About every 90 minutes, their eyes began darting about behind their closed lids. Aserinsky was astonished because these seemingly searching eye movements had all the characteristics associated with someone who was wide awake! How could this be happening? Wasn't sleep the time when the brain was supposed to be quiet and resting?

Is sleep really a time when the brain is sedentary? Are there perhaps two kinds of sleep, one quiet and the other active? As we continue our psychological journey of discovery through the landscape of consciousness, these are some of the questions we will tackle. Similarly, can you recall ever being surprised by unusual states of awareness occurring while you were awake? When labeling one state of mind an unusual or "altered" state, how well do you understand the state with which you compare it? Are these normal and altered states the same for everyone, or do you inhabit your own unique experiential world? Luckily for us, researchers have also explored these areas of consciousness and their discoveries will become ours as we follow their footprints in this part of our journey.

6-1 THE NATURE OF CONSCIOUSNESS

Despite the fact that almost everyone would agree that consciousness is highly important for our survival, scientists and philosophers still argue about its essential characteristics (Dennett, 1994; Revonsuo et al., 1994; Roth, 2001; Searle, 1994).

6-1a Consciousness Is Personal, Selective, Divided, Continuous, and Changing

Consciousness: Awareness of ourselves and our environment.

Consciousness is our awareness of ourselves and our environment. Such consciousness is highly complex. It is *personal*—you cannot share it with another person; it is *selective*—you can be aware of some things while ignoring others; it is *divided*—you can pay attention to two different things at once; it is *continuous*—each moment of consciousness blends into the next moment; it is *changing*—what you are aware of now will normally shift to awareness of other things within seconds; and it consists of *many levels*—from an alert and focused awareness to the relative stupor of deep sleep. These qualities of consciousness allow human beings to negotiate a complex social world (Crook, 1980; Kreitler, 1999).

Selective Attention

Selective attention: The ability to focus awareness on a single stimulus to the exclusion of all others.

The ability to focus awareness on a single stimulus to the exclusion of all others is known as **selective attention,** and it is one of the defining characteristics of consciousness. (See Discovery Box 6-1.) In reading this chapter, you are employing selective attention. Yet, while ignoring all the background noise around you, certain stimuli will find it easier to penetrate your concentration. For instance, you may be able to ignore another person in the room, but what if that person turns toward you with a threatening expression on her

DISCOVERY BOX 6-1

How Do Psychologists Study Selective Attention?

One way psychologists study selective attention in the laboratory is through dichotic listening tasks. They place earphones on research participants and deliver different messages to each ear simultaneously but instruct them to listen only to one of the messages. To ensure they do this, participants are asked to repeat the message, a process known as *shadowing*. Typically in such studies, participants are able to completely ignore the nonshadowed information in the other ear (Cherry, 1953). Participants are usually so good at shadowing the message that if it is switched between the two ears, they continue to shadow it, following the content rather than the ear. However, if the participant's name is mentioned in the nonshadowed message, or if it contains sexually explicit words, she or he is likely to notice this at least some of the time (Nielsen & Sarason, 1981; Wood & Cowan, 1995).

Although participants in most shadowing studies show no ability to recall or recognize any of the nonshadowed information, they do appear to process it to some degree (Nisbett & Wilson, 1977; Schacter, 1992). For example, if the word *Wisconsin* is part of the unattended message, the person may not remember it but may be more likely to say "Madison" when asked to name a state capital than someone for whom "Wisconsin" was not part of the unattended message. Similarly, less time will be needed to answer the question, "What state is known as the 'Dairy' state?"

face? You are likely to take notice because we automatically divert our attention to threatening faces (Mogg & Bradley, 1999). This ability to override attentional focus and notice signs of impending danger is a useful trait and undoubtedly was of great survival value to our human ancestors.

Divided Attention

This evidence of some processing of unattended messages suggests that it is possible to attend to different stimuli at the same time. You demonstrate such *divided attention*—which is a second characteristic of consciousness—when you drive a car while listening to music or walking while talking. Performing these tasks simultaneously is relatively easy because at least one of them is so well learned that you can do it automatically (Schneider, 1985). Yet, how can you simultaneously listen to a lecture and take notes when both tasks require substantial attention? Research suggests that you can divide your attention in such instances because each task requires different kinds of attentional brain resources (Wickens, 1992a, 1992b). In listening to the lecturer's words, your primary attentional resources are devoted to perceiving this incoming stimuli, while others handle note taking.

Although we all are capable of engaging in both selective and divided attention, the efficiency of each person's nervous system determines the upper limit of individual attention abilities (Hoptman & Davidson, 1994). As people age, their nervous system becomes less efficient, which weakens their ability to sustain either selective or divided attention (Madden, 1992; Rutman, 1990). Children who have attention-deficit hyperactivity disorder (ADHD), which appears to be biologically based (Solanto, 2002), also are unable to concentrate for any extended time periods. Yet, even among these children and among the elderly, strategies to improve attention can be learned, even in complex tasks (Kramer et al., 1995; Pashler, 1992).

Because daydreaming involves thinking about internal thoughts and imaginary situations, what effect do you think television viewing might have on daydreaming? Do you think people who watch a lot of television would daydream more or less than those who watch little television? Why?

The Stream of Consciousness

Psychologists have long recognized that consciousness is continuous and changing. Indeed, over 100 years ago, William James (1902/1985) described this continuous, altering flow of thoughts, feelings, and sensations as being a *stream of consciousness*. To understand James's viewpoint, reflect on your own awareness as you read these words—are there other things passing through your mind? Try to pay attention only to these words on the page. This is not easy because irrelevant thoughts often interrupt and distract you.

Daydreaming: A relatively passive state of waking consciousness that involves turning attention away from external stimuli to internal thoughts and imaginary situations.

One interesting stream of consciousness is **daydreaming,** which is a relatively passive waking state in which attention is directed away from external stimuli to internal thoughts and imaginary situations (Morley, 1998). Almost everyone daydreams on a daily basis, yet daydream frequency and intensity decreases with age in adulthood (Giambra, 1989, 2000). Despite the common belief that daydreaming is an inconsequential part of daily consciousness, at least one study estimated that college students spend about one-third of their waking hours daydreaming (Bartusiak, 1980)! Although 95 percent of us admit to daydreaming about sex (Klinger, 1990; Leitenberg & Henning, 1995), most daydreams deal with practical, daily concerns and tasks, future goals, and interpersonal relationships (Greenwald & Harder, 1997; Zhiyan & Singer, 1997).

Why do we daydream? Several possibilities have been suggested (Klinger, 1999). Fantasizing about actual people, events, or problems in our lives may help us formulate useful future plans of action. For example, imagining how to tell your professor that you slept through her exam may help when you actually explain the situation to her. Second, daydreams may help us regulate our behavior by either providing a safe avenue to imaginatively act out certain desires, or by helping us consider the possible outcomes of our actions. For example, your fantasy of kissing your best friend's boyfriend or girlfriend may not only temporarily soothe your sexual desires, but it may also inhibit you acting on this impulse as you imagine the damage it could cause to your friendship. Finally, when our external surroundings are providing insufficient stimulation, we may daydream as a way to escape boredom and stay mentally aroused. Perhaps this is why college students spend so much classtime daydreaming!

Fantasy-prone personality: A person who has regular, vivid fantasies and who sometimes cannot separate fantasy from reality.

One disadvantage of daydreaming is that we become much less attentive to our surroundings, and thus, our effectiveness in the world is diminished. About 4 percent of the adult population daydream so much they are called **fantasy-prone personalities** (Lynn et al., 1996; Lynn & Ruhe, 1986). Not surprisingly, due to the amount of time spent daydreaming, and the intensity of these experiences, fantasy-prone individuals occasionally have trouble separating their daydreams from their memories of real events (Nickell, 1996; Wilson & Barber, 1983).

6-1b Consciousness May Provide Us with Survival Advantages

According to the evolutionary principle of natural selection (see chapter 1, section 1-3e), members of a species with inborn traits best adaptive for survival in their environment will produce more offspring and, as a result, their numbers will increase in frequency in the population. What advantage might the emergence of consciousness have given to our ancestors?

One possibility is that consciousness provided our ancestors with a mental representation of the world that allowed them to more effectively plan future activities (Cairns-

Evolution is an ascent towards consciousness.

—Pierre Teilhard de Chardin, French priest and cosmic evolutionist, 1881–1955

Smith, 1996; Fetzer, 2002). That is, by mentally manipulating events and reflecting on possible behavioral choices *before* acting, our ancestors were able to greatly reduce the sort of aimless and impulsive behavior that is likely to cause death. Another related explanation is that consciousness may have evolved as a means of categorizing and making sense of primitive emotions (Dennett, 1991; Humphrey, 1992). According to this perspective, each of the primitive emotions came to be associated with a different state of consciousness, and, as a result, these states of consciousness provided our ancestors with information that aided their survival. For instance, the negative emotions caused by a snake bite or a fall from a tree became associated with a specific state of consciousness that led our ancestors to avoid similar situations in the future, thus lowering injury and death. Similarly, the positive emotions resulting from eating, drinking, and having sex became associated with states of consciousness that led our ancestors to seek out similar situations, which again benefited them. Although both of these explanations sound plausible, we currently have no way of knowing whether they accurately account for the emergence of consciousness.

SECTION SUMMARY

- Consciousness is personal, selective, divided, continuous, changing, and consisting of many levels.

- In daydreaming, attention is directed away from external stimuli to internal thoughts and imaginary situations.

- Consciousness and evolution may have allowed our ancestors to plan future activities and/or to categorize and make sense of emotions.

6-2   SLEEP

Sleep is a nonwaking state of consciousness characterized by minimal physical movement and minimal responsiveness to one's surroundings. To understand this state of consciousness, in this section we examine the sleep-wake cycle, sleep stages, possible reasons for sleep, and different dream theories.

> **Sleep:** A nonwaking state of consciousness characterized by minimal physical movement and minimal responsiveness to one's surroundings.

6-2a   Daily Body Rhythms Regulate Our Activities

While typing this sentence, I noticed how tired I feel. It is almost midnight, and I am ready for a good night's sleep. Yet, as my day winds down, I know somewhere in the nearby woods, there is a great-horned owl whose day is in full swing. Mammals can be classified into two categories based on their sleep cycles. *Diurnal mammals* are awake during the day and asleep at night, while *nocturnal mammals* are asleep during the day and awake at night. These sleep-wakefulness cycles have evolved because they permit a species the maximum adaptation to its environment (Moore, 1990).

The behavioral cycle of sleep and wakefulness that we naturally follow throughout our lives corresponds to physiological changes, such as body temperature, blood pressure, and hormone levels. Together, these daily behavioral and physiological changes are known as **circadian rhythms** (in Latin, *circa* means "about" and *diem* means "day"). Some of these circadian rhythms help to regulate the sleep-wake cycle. For instance, as you can see in figure 6-1, body temperature rises in the early morning, peaks midday, and then

> **Circadian rhythms:** Internally generated behavioral and physiological changes that occur on a daily basis.

FIGURE 6-1
Circadian Rhythms

As you can see in the graph, as core body temperature changes, a person's level of alertness also changes. Based on what this graph tells you, what happens to your alertness as your core body temperature drops?

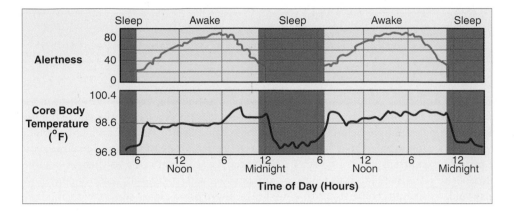

begins to drop 1 to 2 hours prior to sleep. Because body temperature influences feelings of arousal, you generally feel most alert late in the afternoon or early evening (Broughton et al., 1990). Thus, if you've ever pulled an all-nighter, you probably felt most tired around 4:00 A.M. when your body temperature was lowest, but you probably began to perk up just before your normal waking time as your temperature began to rise.

One way that circadian rhythms have been studied is by eliminating any environmental cues that would indicate the time of day. This has been accomplished by isolating people in a lab without windows or clocks, or by having them live underground in specially built "houses." Findings from such studies initially suggested that in the absence of daylight and time cues, circadian rhythms drifted toward a 25-hour cycle (Welsh, 1993; Wever, 1979). Indeed, for almost 30 years, sleep researchers believed these findings meant that humans were off-kilter with the natural world! Recently, however, researchers discovered that all the previous research testing the 25-hour cycle hypothesis had inadvertently created the effect (Shanahan et al., 1999). In these studies, the artificial light that participants relied on to see while deprived of natural sunlight was sufficiently intense to reset their sleep-wake cycle. Further, because participants often left lights on well after the sun had set in the outside world, this caused their brains' circadian pacemaker to keep them alert and awake longer than normal. Over the course of many days, their sleep-wake cycle appeared to drift to 25 hours. However, when researchers subsequently reduced light levels, they discovered that participants' true circadian cycle was about 24 hours. This research provides a valuable lesson in the way that the scientific method is self-correcting. In the journey of discovery, scientists sometimes follow false paths, but the critical analysis that drives this search eventually reveals past missteps.

How does the brain reset this aspect of our biological clock? A small area of the hypothalamus known as the *suprachiasmatic nucleus* and the hormone *melatonin*, which is produced by the pineal gland, appear to be crucial in readjusting the body's sleep-wake cycle (Brown, 1994; Sorokin et al., 2000). Chronic insomniacs who receive synthetic forms of melatonin sleep better and feel more alert than those who are given placebos (Garfinkel et al., 1995; MacFarlane et al., 1991). This finding prompted researchers to refer to this hormone as "nature's sleeping pill." Even more important, scientists have isolated a gene in the suprachiasmatic nucleus that, along with perhaps 10 other genes, actually controls our internal clock (Katzenberg et al., 1998; Vitaterna et al., 1994). The discovery of this gene—which has been named "clock"—may eventually lead to more effective treatment of ailments related to disruptions in circadian rhythms, such as insomnia and depression.

Disruptions in circadian rhythms also occur when you travel by jet through a number of time zones. The severity of this jet lag depends on whether you fly westward or eastward (see figure 6-2). When flying westward—say from London to Detroit—your regular sleep cycle is pushed back five hours (a *phase delay*), so that your 24-hour day is stretched to 29 hours. The jet lag resulting from such east-west travel is easier to adjust to —and thus, less severe—than eastward-induced jet lag. Why? Perhaps because phase

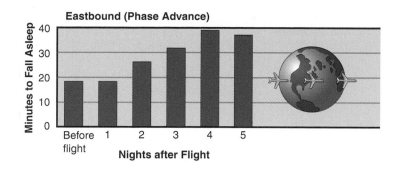

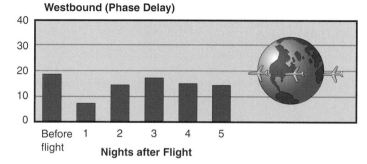

FIGURE 6-2
Circadian Rhythms and Jet Lag

One way jet lag can be assessed is by determining whether it is harder for people to fall asleep after flying to a different time zone. In one study, people who flew eastward through five time zones had increased difficulty falling asleep following their arrival, whereas travelers who flew westward through five time zones experienced no sleep difficulties (Nicholson et al., 1986).

delays coincide with the tendency in modern times to habitually stretch waking time out to the limits of the 24-hour, 11-minute sleep-wake cycle. In contrast, flying eastward across five time zones results in your day being shortened to 19 hours (a *phase advance*), which is not only farther away from your natural 24-hour sleep-wake cycle but also is inconsistent with your day-stretching habits. Consistent with this explanation, in the study depicted in figure 6-2, travelers who flew eastward from Detroit to London had increased difficulty falling asleep following their arrival, while travelers who flew westward from London to Detroit experienced no sleep difficulties (Nicholson et al., 1986).

Shift workers, who work during their normal sleeping hours, experience a similar problem (Goh et al., 2000; Khaleque, 1999). Of the 7 million Americans who work at night, 75 percent are regularly sleepy, and 20 percent have actually fallen asleep on the job, factors that lead directly to higher accident rates and lower productivity than any other work schedule (Akerstedt, 1991; Smith et al., 1995). In an attempt to correct this work-related health problem, sleep researchers recommend that employers schedule workers on rotating shifts in a "clockwise" direction (from days to evenings to nights), so that changes are phase delays rather than phase advances (Monk, 2000; Monk & Folkard, 1992). For example, if you are working an evening shift (4:00 P.M. to midnight), it would be easier for you to move forward to a night shift (midnight to 8:00 A.M.) rather than backward to a day shift (8:00 A.M. to 4:00 P.M.) because moving backward (a phase advance) forces you to try to sleep during the time you had previously been working. Phase-delayed work schedules promote greater worker health, productivity, and satisfaction than phase-advanced schedules (Czeisler et al., 1982; Scott, 1994).

The readjustment of circadian rhythms can be speeded up by light-treatment therapy (Ando et al., 1999). In such therapy, workers are exposed to bright lights mimicking the daylight sun during the first few days of their night shift. They are also exposed to eight hours of total darkness at home during the day (Bougrine et al., 1995; Czeisler et al., 1990). NASA ground personnel who worked on shifted schedules during two Space Shuttle missions reported better sleep, performance, and physical and emotional well-being if they received light-treatment therapy during the prelaunch week and during the mission itself (Stewart et al., 1995).

FIGURE 6-3
EEG Brain Wave Patterns

The regular beta and alpha waves associated with normal waking consciousness are very different from the brain wave patterns typical of the stages of NREM and REM sleep.

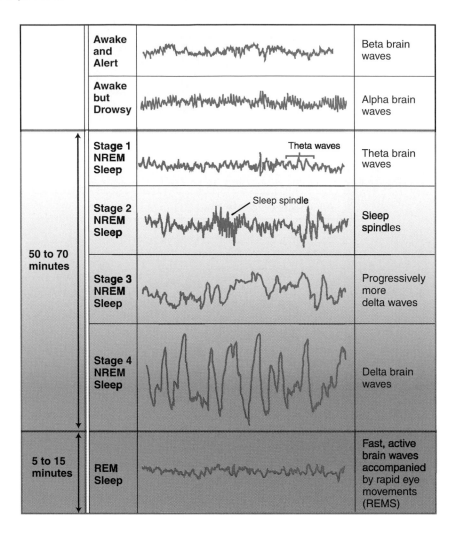

	Awake and Alert		Beta brain waves
	Awake but Drowsy		Alpha brain waves
50 to 70 minutes	**Stage 1 NREM Sleep**	Theta waves	Theta brain waves
	Stage 2 NREM Sleep	Sleep spindle	Sleep spindles
	Stage 3 NREM Sleep		Progressively more delta waves
	Stage 4 NREM Sleep		Delta brain waves
5 to 15 minutes	**REM Sleep**		Fast, active brain waves accompanied by rapid eye movements (REMS)

6-2b There Are Five Stages of Sleep

Just as you have circadian rhythms regulating your sleep-wake cycle, you also follow a biological rhythm during sleep. This was one of the important discoveries that followed in the wake of the 1952 discovery—described at the beginning of the chapter—that rapid eye movements occurred in predictable cycles during the course of a night's sleep. In sleep studies using electroencephalograms (EEGs), investigators such as Nathaniel Kleitman and Eugene Aserinsky discovered that about every 90 or 100 minutes we cycle through five distinct sleep stages, each associated with a different pattern of brain activity (Aserinsky & Kleitman, 1953). These EEG brain wave patterns are depicted in figure 6-3. The two most common EEG patterns that people experience while awake are **beta waves,** associated with an active alert state of mind, and **alpha waves,** indicating relaxed wakefulness.

As you gradually enter the light sleep of *stage 1,* your alpha-wave EEG pattern changes to the smaller, more rapid, irregular **theta waves.** Stage 1 sleep is a brief transitional state between wakefulness and sleep usually lasting only a few minutes. Heart rate and breathing slow as body temperature drops and muscles begin to relax. Typical experiences reported during stage 1 sleep are sensations of falling (hence the term, "falling asleep") or floating, as well as visual and auditory hallucinations (Mavromatis, 1991). You can be easily awakened during stage 1 sleep.

Beta waves: Very fast, low-amplitude brain waves associated with an active, alert state of mind.

Alpha waves: Fast, low-amplitude brain waves associated with a relaxed, wakeful state.

Theta waves: Irregular, low-amplitude brain waves associated with stage 1 sleep.

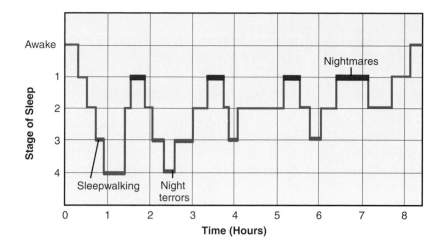

FIGURE 6-4
The First 90 Minutes of Sleep

Most people follow a rather consistent sleep cycle during the night, each lasting about 90 minutes and consisting of four NREM stages followed by REM sleep. Nightmares and other dreams occur during REM sleep, but sleepwalking and night terrors (see the *Psychological Applications* section at the end of the chapter) typically occur in stages 3 and 4, respectively. Based on this figure, what can you conclude about the duration of REM sleep as the night progresses?

Stage 2 sleep lasts about 20 minutes and is characterized by **sleep spindles,** which are bursts of rapid, rhythmic brain-wave activity. Muscle tension is now greatly reduced. Although sleeptalking can occur at anytime during sleep, it is most likely to occur during stage 2.

In *stage 3*, you begin to move into the deeper form of *slow-wave sleep* in which your brain waves become higher in amplitude and slower in frequency. These **delta waves** become much more pronounced during the even deeper sleep of *stage 4*. It is difficult to arouse a person at this stage of the sleep cycle.

From the time you enter stage 1 and progress to stage 4, between 50 and 70 minutes usually passes. These first four stages make up *NREM sleep,* or non-rapid-eye-movement sleep. Now the sleep cycle reverses itself, and you move back up through the stages to stage 2 (where you spend about half your night). NREM sleep is often called "quiet sleep" because of the slow, regular breathing, the general absence of body movement, and the slow, regular brain activity exhibited in the EEG. Actually, the term "quiet sleep" is a bit misleading because snoring is most likely to occur during NREM sleep.

As you can see in figure 6-4, once you reach stage 2, you do not fully enter stage 1, but rather, you enter a fifth stage marking an entirely different kind of sleep. In this fifth stage, your brain waves become rapid, somewhat like waking alpha waves and stage 1 theta waves, your heart rate and breathing also increase, and your eyes begin darting back and forth behind your closed eyelids. This phase of "active sleep," which completes the sleep cycle, has come to be known for these quick eye movements and is called **REM (rapid eye movement) sleep.** During the night, you will go through about four or five sleep cycles, each lasting about 90 minutes (Anch et al., 1988). As also depicted in figure 6-4, after the first few sleep cycles, you do not usually pass through all of the sleep stages. (See Discovery Box 6-2.)

Sleep spindles: Bursts of rapid, rhythmic electrical activity in the brain characteristic of stage 2 sleep.

Delta waves: Slow, high-amplitude brain waves most typical of stage 4 deep sleep.

REM (rapid eye movement) sleep: A relatively active phase in the sleep cycle, characterized by rapid eye movements, in which dreaming occurs.

6-2c Sleep Habits Vary Individually and Culturally

How much sleep you need partly depends on your age. The amount of total time spent sleeping declines throughout the life cycle: Newborns sleep approximately 16 hours, children average between 9 and 12 hours, and adolescents average about 7.5 hours. In adulthood, both the quantity and quality of sleep usually decrease, especially among the elderly (Almeida et al., 1999; Monane, 1992). Less time is spent in slow-wave stage 4 deep sleep and a greater proportion of stage 1 sleep occurs, resulting in more nighttime awakenings (Bliwise, 1989). Although stage 4 sleep declines, the percentage of REM sleep remains fairly constant throughout most adulthood, only diminishing in later life (Moran & Stoudemire, 1992).

DISCOVERY BOX 6-2

Why Do We Sleep?

A number of theories have been proposed about why we sleep. One widely held theory is that sleep allows the body to restore itself following the rigors of daily activity (Flanagan, 1996). Research supporting this view finds that people sleep longer and spend more time in deep sleep (stages 3 and 4) after vigorous physical exercise (Vein et al., 1991). Testosterone levels depleted in males during the day are also restored during sleep. In addition, deep sleep promotes new cell growth by triggering the pituitary gland to release a growth hormone (see chapter 3, section 3-2c). As people advance from childhood to adulthood, less of this growth hormone is released, and they spend less time in deep sleep (Mancia, 1981; Pekkanen, 1982). Studies also suggest that children aged 2 to 5 who fail to get sufficient sleep at night or during daytime nap periods are at greater risk for behavior problems (Dement, 1999).

Another theory contends that sleep is simply a product of our evolutionary heritage: It prevents us from moving about and being injured (or eaten) during a time of the day (darkness) in which our bodies are not well adapted. Sleep also conserves energy for that part of the day (daylight) in which our bodies are most efficient. Thus, sleep may have been selected for because of its value in promoting both physical safety and energy conservation (Webb, 1992). Today, although we no longer need sleep for the same reasons as our ancestors, sleep mechanisms still have a significant influence on our lives.

Which of these theories provides the best explanation for why we sleep? It may well be that both provide part of the answer to this puzzle. In the coming years, further research will undoubtedly shed greater insight into the ultimate function of sleep.

We also differ in when we typically go to sleep and awaken. Have you ever heard of "morning" and "night" people? Morning people wake up early, with a good deal of energy and alertness, but are ready to retire before 10:00 P.M. Night persons, on the other hand, stay up much later in the evening and have a hard time getting up early in the morning (Thoman, 1999). About 25 percent of us are "night persons," 25 percent are "morning persons," and the remaining 50 percent fall somewhere between these two extremes. This different sleep pattern appears to be related to differences in circadian body temperatures. Morning persons' body temperature quickly rises upon awakening and remains high until about 7:30 P.M. The body temperature of night persons, in contrast, rises much more gradually when they wake, peaks midday, and only begins dropping late in the evening. Not surprisingly, in one study, college students identified as morning persons obtained better grades in early-morning classes than in evening classes. The opposite effect was found for students classified as night persons (Guthrie et al., 1995). Complete the questionnaire in Discovery Box 6-3 to determine whether you are more a night person or a morning person.

Besides these individual differences in sleep patterns, cultural differences have also been documented. For example, in tropical cultures, midday naps, or *siestas*, are common because they allow people to avoid strenuous activity during the hottest time of the day. Interestingly, as these "siesta" cultures industrialize, they abandon this practice (Kribbs, 1993). This change in napping patterns is probably due to the greater comfort that can be achieved with air conditioning, combined with the greater emphasis on productivity in industrialized settings.

DISCOVERY BOX 6-3

Are You a Morning or a Night Person?

Respond to the following items by circling either "Day" or "Evening."

1. I prefer to work during the		Day	Evening
2. I enjoy leisure-time activities most during the		Day	Evening
3. I feel most alert during the		Day	Evening
4. I get my best ideas during the		Day	Evening
5. I have my highest energy during the		Day	Evening
6. I prefer to take classes during the		Day	Evening
7. I prefer to study during the		Day	Evening
8. I feel most intelligent during the		Day	Evening
9. I am most productive during the		Day	Evening
10. When I graduate, I would prefer to find a job with _____ hours.		Day	Evening

If you answered "Day" to eight or more items, you are probably a morning person. However, if you answered "Evening" to eight or more items, you are probably a night person.

Source: From "Day persons, night persons, and variability in hypnotic susceptibility" by B. Wallace in JOURNAL OF PERSONALITY AND SOCIAL PSYCHOLOGY, 1993, 64, 827–833 (Appendix, p. 833). Copyright © 1993 by the American Psychological Association. Adapted with permission.

With industrialization also comes less nighttime sleep. As with the gradual disappearance of napping in industrialized siesta cultures, the lower overall sleep time found in industrialized settings can undoubtedly be traced to the development of a stronger work ethic. Yet, another related factor is electricity and the ability to literally light up the night and thereby extend the time people can be active and productive. People who live in cultures without electricity generally retire shortly after the sun sets and sleep about 10 hours. In contrast, the average length of sleep for North American and European adults is less than 7.5 hours, about 20 percent lower than what it was a hundred years ago (National Sleep Foundation, 2002). Because all humans still possess the physiology that evolved to fit the ecological niche of a hunter-gatherer culture, our lower sleeping average suggests that many of us are sleep-deprived (Benbadis et al., 1999; Coren, 1996). To determine whether you are getting enough sleep, answer the questionnaire in Discovery Box 6-4.

INFO-BIT: While studying for exams, many college students get little or no sleep. Yet results from sleep deprivation experiments indicate that people lose their ability to concentrate and think creatively after only a couple days of sleep deprivation (Dinges et al., 1997; Webb, 1992). These findings suggest that engaging in long hours of continuous studying before final exams may actually lower academic performance. If all-night studying cannot be avoided, however, research indicates that grabbing a few hours of nap time during the day can offset some of the negative effects of sleep deprivation (Batejat & Lagarde, 1999). Remember this *Info-bit* when preparing for your next exam!

DISCOVERY BOX 6-4

Are You Getting Enough Sleep?

Psychologist James Maas (1998) has developed the following questionnaire to measure people's sleep needs. To determine whether you might be suffering from sleep deprivation, answer true or false to the following items regarding your current life experiences.

True False

1. It's a struggle for me to get out of bed in the morning.
2. I need an alarm clock to wake up at the appropriate time.
3. Weekday mornings I hit the snooze bar several times to get more sleep.
4. I often sleep extra hours on weekend mornings.
5. I often need a nap to get through the day.
6. I have dark circles around my eyes.
7. I feel tired, irritable, and stressed out during the week.
8. I have trouble concentrating and remembering.
9. I feel slow with critical thinking, problem solving, and being creative.
10. I often fall asleep in boring meetings or lectures or in warm rooms.
11. I often feel drowsy while driving.
12. I often fall asleep watching TV.
13. I often fall asleep after heavy meals or after a low dose of alcohol.
14. I often fall asleep while relaxing after dinner.
15. I often fall asleep within five minutes of getting into bed.

If you answered "true" to three or more items, you probably are not getting enough sleep. Keep in mind that we differ in our individual sleep needs. If this questionnaire suggests that you may be sleep deprived, Maas recommends that you go to bed 15 minutes earlier every night for a week. Continue adding 15 more minutes each week until you are waking without the aid of an alarm clock and without feeling tired during the day. Encourage your family and friends to also try this exercise, and compare your experiences over the next few weeks to see if your daily alertness and energy level improves.

Source: From THE SLEEP ADVANTAGE by James B. Maas, PhD, copyright © 1998 by James B. Maas, PhD. Used by permission of Villard Books, a division of Random House, Inc.

6-2d Dreaming Often Occurs during REM Sleep

As previously mentioned, at the end of each sleep cycle you enter REM sleep. The fact that the brain and other physiological functions are almost as active during REM sleep as in the waking state has led some to describe this phase of sleep as *paradoxical sleep*. Accompanying rapid eye movements are **dreams,** which are storylike sequences of visual images. This association between rapid eye movement and dreaming was first discovered by Eugene

Dreams: Storylike sequences of vivid visual images experienced during sleep.

Aserinsky when he awakened sleepers as their eyes darted about behind closed lids (see chapter-opening story). Subsequent research found that people awakened from REM sleep report dreaming 78 percent of the time versus only 14 percent of the time during NREM sleep (Antrobus, 1991; Schwartz & Maquet, 2002). This discovery led some researchers to speculate that sleepers moved their eyes as they "watched" their dream activities (Dement, 1978). The problem with this *scanning hypothesis*, however, is that most research has not found a strong correlation between rapid eye movement and dream content. Instead of dreaming causing rapid eye movement, it is more likely that both are caused by the brain's relatively high level of activation during REM sleep (Chase & Morales, 1983).

Although your ability to respond to external cues is diminished during REM sleep, it is not entirely absent (Arkin & Antrobus, 1991). Research indicates that unexpected sounds or other sensory stimulation may be incorporated into dreams, thus allowing the dreamer to continue sleeping. For example, in one experiment, sleeping volunteers who were sprayed with a mist of water and then awakened were more likely to report dreams of being squirted by someone, experiencing a sudden rainfall, or standing under a leaking roof than were volunteers who were not sprayed (Dement & Wolpert, 1958).

How important is REM sleep? When participants in sleep studies were partially deprived of REM sleep by being awakened whenever they began exhibiting rapid eye movements, they reported feeling more tired and spent more time in REM sleep the next night than those who were not deprived of REM sleep (Dement et al., 1966). This extra time spent in REM sleep following such deprivation is known as REM *rebound*. When REM sleep deprivation is prolonged, people become anxious and irritable, have difficulty concentrating, and exhibit poorer recall of recently learned material than those not deprived of REM sleep (May & Kline, 1987; Tilley & Empson, 1978).

All mammals except the Australian anteater have REM sleep, as do some birds, but fish, reptiles, and amphibians do not. It is possible that those animals that engage in REM sleep also have dreams, but it is unlikely that most of them possess the cognitive ability required to distinguish dream events from real events. This inability to separate the dream world from the real world would pose a serious threat to animals if they remembered their dreams upon awakening. For instance, what if your cat "Tabby" had a dream that the vicious dog next door was replaced by a family of fat, juicy mice? If Tabby remembered this dream, she would likely saunter over for a nutritious breakfast and quickly become the dear-departed Tabby. Thinking about Tabby's situation from an evolutionary perspective, it's plausible that animals that remembered their dreams as real events were less likely to survive to pass their genes onto the next generation.

In humans, REM sleep is greatest early in life, accounting for at least 50 percent of all sleep time in normal newborns and as high as 80 percent among premature infants (Hobson, 1989). This finding suggests that prior to birth, REM sleep makes up virtually the entire mode of existence of the late-developing fetus. Within 6 months of birth, REM sleep declines to about 30 percent of all sleep time, and by early childhood its 20 percent level remains unchanged until diminishing once again later in life.

6-2e No Consensus Exists on the Cause or Meaning of Dreams

I'm at the ocean on a beautiful summer day, standing on a wooden pier jutting out from shore. The sky is a clear blue. I begin walking to the end of the pier where an old woman is sitting. When I reach her, I notice an unattended fishing pole nearby. As soon as I look at the pole, I realize a fish has taken the bait at the other end. Without thinking, I grab the pole and begin reeling in the line. About a quarter mile from shore, a huge beautiful blue fish jumps high out of the water. This is what is at the end of the line! I have to use all my strength to keep from being pulled into the ocean. The old woman gives me advice, but I am confident I know what I am doing. As I struggle with the fish, I learn about its life. After an hour of labor, I have the fish next to the pier. At the moment when I should get it in place to be hoisted up, a thought comes to me that what is important is the struggle, not the victory. I throw the pole down and the fish swims away. The woman looks up at me and nods. She knows too. I walk back to shore.

Lucid dreams: Dreams in which the dreamer is aware of dreaming and is often able to change the plot of the dream.

Perhaps like the college student who had this dream while preparing for an important exam, you too may have pondered whether these sleep experiences are worth analyzing. The simple fact is that we all dream, whether we remember doing so or not. While dreaming most people are not aware they are dreaming: The dream is experienced as "real." Exceptions to this rule are the 10 percent who occasionally experience **lucid dreams,** in which they are aware that they are dreaming *while* they are dreaming (LaBerge, 1992). Such dreams can be very enjoyable because the lucid dreamer is often able to shift the dream plot while it is in progress (Tart, 1988).

In some cultures, people believe you should be held accountable for your dreams. Thus, among the New Guinea Arapesh, if you hurt someone in your dreams, you must try to undo the harm in your waking life. In other cultures, dreams are believed to foretell the future. Although belief in *precognitive dreams* is held by some people in Western cultures, most do not place such importance on the stories generated by our unconscious minds.

Dreams As Wish Fulfillment

Manifest content: The dream that is remembered by the dreamer.

Latent content: The true meaning of the dream that is concealed from the dreamer through the symbols that make up the manifest dream content.

The most famous dream theory in psychology is that proposed by Sigmund Freud (1900) and *psychoanalytic theory* (see chapter 12, section 12-2). According to Freud, dreams are disguised wishes originating in the unconscious mind. The dream that is remembered by the dreamer represents only the surface or **manifest content.** The true meaning of the dream—the "disguised" or **latent content**—is concealed from the dreamer because it would not only arouse great anxiety but also disrupt sleep. So dreams are constructed to express these wishes in a confusing symbolic manner so that the dreamer's peace of mind—and her or his sleep—are protected. In the student's "fish" dream, the struggle with the fish is the manifest dream content, perhaps symbolically representing the student's attempt to better understand, but not destroy, some unconscious desire (the latent content) dredged up by his studies.

Dreams As Problem Solving

Problem-solving theory: A theory that dreams provide people with the opportunity to creatively solve their everyday problems.

Another view of dreaming is that it is a form of problem solving. According to Rosalind Cartwright's (1977, 1989) **problem-solving theory,** dreams provide people with the opportunity to creatively solve their everyday problems because what we think about in dreams is not hampered by logic or realism. From this perspective, the fish dream might reflect the student's dawning recognition that he should be more confident in his own intellectual abilities and rely less on others' advice (the old woman in the dream).

In support of problem-solving theory, Cartwright (1991) has found that for people going through a divorce, the first dream of the night often occurs sooner, lasts longer, and is more emotional and storylike than it is for other people. In addition, those who frequently dreamed about divorce-related problems made a better adjustment to single life than those who did not dream much about their problems. Beyond empirical findings, there are numerous historical anecdotes of people using dreams as a problem-solving strategy. For example, one evening in 1857, German chemist Friedrich Kekulé fell asleep in front of a fire while trying to solve the mystery of how the benzene molecule was constructed. In a dream, he saw the carbon atoms of the benzene molecule twisting and twining like snakes, when suddenly, one of the snakes seized hold of its own tail. Upon awakening, he realized that the carbon atoms bonded with one another in a "closed chain," just like a snake biting its tail!

I do not know whether I was then a man dreaming I was a butterfly, or whether I am now a butterfly dreaming I am a man.

—Chuang-tzu, Chinese philosopher, 369–286 B.C.

Dreams As Information Processing

In contrast to conceiving of dreams as being caused by unconscious wish-fulfillment or problem-solving attempts, the **off-line dream theory** contends that the cognitive processing that occurs during dreaming consolidates and stores information gathered during the day, thus allowing us to maintain a smaller and more efficient brain (Pavlides & Winson, 1989; Winson, 1990). The term *off-line* is a computer phrase, referring to the fact that computers need time when data are not being input but instead are being analyzed and stored into memory. According to the off-line theory, dreaming is the time when the brain—our computer—goes off-line to somehow integrate the new information from the day with our older memories and experiences (Titone, 2002).

Evidence that dreaming may indeed serve an integrating function and be instrumental to learning comes from research demonstrating that both humans and other animals spend more time in REM sleep after learning difficult material than after learning easy material, and if denied REM sleep, memory retention suffers (Karni et al., 1994; Smith, 1985, 1995; Smith & Lapp, 1986). Winson believes that if we didn't dream—that is, have off-line time—we would need much larger forebrains to handle our daily learning experiences. This may explain why the Australian anteater—the only known mammal that does not engage in REM sleep—has such a large forebrain compared with the rest of its brain (Hawkins, 1986).

Off-line dream theory:
A theory that the cognitive process of dreaming consolidates and stores information gathered during the day, thus allowing us to maintain a smaller and more efficient brain.

Dreams As Interpreted Brain Activity

Although the previous theories believe that dreams either fulfill wishes, solve problems, or maintain brain efficiency, J. Allan Hobson and Robert McCarley argue that dreaming has no particular significance other than that it is a by-product of brain activity. This **activation-synthesis theory** states that a dream is the forebrain's attempt to interpret the random neural activity initiated in the midbrain during sleep (Hobson, 1994; Hobson & McCarley, 1977). As you recall from chapter 3, section 3-3b, the uppermost portion of the forebrain is the brain's "thinking" center and consists of the left and right cerebral hemispheres. According to activation-synthesis theory, the more verbal left hemisphere strives to assign some rational meaning to behavior, even when there is none. It is just this sort of thinking that appears to be involved in creating the plots of our dreams. Similarly, the right hemisphere may help construct most of the dream's visual features (Antrobus, 1987). The resulting dream constructed from this random brain activity will have a personal touch unique to the dreamer because it is based on available memories, but the dream has no hidden meaning (Kahn & Hobson, 1993).

Activation-synthesis theory:
A theory that dreaming is a by-product of random brain activity, which the forebrain weaves into a somewhat logical story.

The various dream theories discussed here are summarized in table 6-1. Currently, there is no consensus on the cause or meaning of dreams. Yet, whatever the ultimate answer, all of the theories agree that the specific content of dreams is associated with the life experiences of the dreamer. This may mean that exploring our unconscious world can help us better understand our conscious lives (Epstein, 1999).

Journey of Discovery Question

Have you ever had a dream that later seemed to come true? Many people who have had this experience, or who hear of it from a close friend or family member, believe that dreams can predict the future. What other potential explanations could there be for a dream that comes true?

TABLE 6-1

Dream Theories

Theory	Explanation	Meaning of Dream	Is Meaning of Dream Hidden?
Psychoanalytic	Dreams are anxiety-producing wishes originating in the unconscious mind.	Latent content of dream reveals unconscious wishes.	Yes, by manifest content of dreams
Off-line	Dreaming consolidates and stores information input during the day, thus allowing us to maintain a smaller and more efficient brain for survival.	Previous day's experiences are reprocessed in dreams.	Not necessarily
Problem solving	Dreams provide the opportunity to creatively solve everyday problems.	Possible solutions to everyday problems are signaled.	Not necessarily
Activation-synthesis	Dreams are the forebrain's attempt to interpret random neural activity.	Dream content is only vaguely related to the dreamer's life experiences; thus, there is little, if any, meaning in the dream.	No real meaning to hide

SECTION SUMMARY

- Circadian rhythms closely align with the 24-hour rotation of the earth.
- Jet lag and shift work can disrupt normal circadian rhythms.
- Every 90 to100 minutes, we cycle through five sleep stages.
- As people age, the quantity and quality of sleep decreases.
- Individuals and cultures differ in their sleeping patterns.
- REM sleep is where most dreaming occurs.
- According to psychoanalytic dream theory, dreams are disguised wishes originating in the unconscious.
- According to problem-solving dream theory, dreaming is where we creatively solve everyday problems unencumbered by logic or realism.
- According to off-line dream theory, dreaming allows us to maintain a smaller and more efficient brain by consolidating and storing information gathered during the day.
- According to activation-synthesis theory, dreaming is the forebrain's attempt to interpret the random neural activity initiated in the midbrain during sleep.

6-3 OTHER ALTERED STATES OF CONSCIOUSNESS

Altered state of consciousness:
An awareness of oneself and one's environment that is noticeably different from the normal state of consciousness.

Sleep is our most familiar **altered state of consciousness.** By *altered state*, I mean an awareness of ourselves and our environment that is noticeably different from our normal state of consciousness. In this section, we examine the altered states associated with *hypnosis, religious experiences, meditation,* and *drugs.*

6-3a Hypnosis Has Been Practiced for Thousands of Years

Imagine you attend a group demonstration of hypnosis. As you sit with friends and strangers in an auditorium, the hypnotist begins talking:

> I want you to get comfortable and begin to relax. Ignore what is going on around you and pay attention only to my words. . . . You can become hypnotized if you are willing to do what I tell you to do. . . . Just do your best to pay close attention to my words, and let happen whatever you feel is going to take place. Let yourself relax. . . . Sometimes you experience something very similar to hypnosis when driving along a stretch of highway and your concentration becomes narrowed so that you don't notice landmarks along the road. . . . As you continue to listen to my voice, your eyes are growing heavy. . . . Heavy and tired. . . . Droopy. . . . You are beginning to feel drowsy and sleepy. . . . Sleepy and drowsy. . . . Relax. . . . You're becoming more and more relaxed . . . and tired. . . . Tired and sleepy . . . As your eyes become heavier, it's getting harder and harder to keep them open. . . . They feel so heavy, like lead. . . . You may feel you want to close them. That's all right. . . . Let your eyes close as your muscles relax more and more.

During this *hypnotic induction*, although you may begin to feel tired, you probably won't fall asleep. Hypnosis was named after the Greek god of sleep, Hypnos, but these two altered states bear only a superficial resemblance to one another. Sleep is characterized by minimal responsiveness to one's surroundings, while **hypnosis** is a state of altered attention and awareness in which a person is unusually responsive to suggestions. In our culture, hypnosis is typically induced using suggestions for deep relaxation while the person remains relatively passive and motionless. However, this altered state can be achieved with many varied techniques, including the use of an active, alert induction, such as inducing hypnosis while a person pedals a stationary bicycle (Banyai & Hilgard, 1976).

In various forms, hypnosis has been practiced for thousands of years. For example, in 2600 B.C., the father of Chinese medicine, Wang Tai, described a hypnotic-like medical technique involving incantations and the passing of hands over patients. Similar descriptions of trance-states also appear in ancient Hindu and Egyptian medical writings (c. 1600 B.C.). More recently, in the eighteenth century, Austrian physician Franz Anton Mesmer (1734–1815) used hypnosis—which he called *animal magnetism*—to restore the balance of supposed magnetic fluid in people's bodies and, thus, cure them of disease. In the nineteenth century, French neurologist Jean Marie Charcot (1825–1893) used it to treat hysteria. Interestingly, it was partly Sigmund Freud's lack of success in using hypnosis as a therapeutic tool in the treatment of psychological disorders that led him to develop psychoanalysis in the 1890s. Freud's rejection of hypnosis slowed the development of research and theory on this altered state of consciousness for many years (Baker, 1990).

Hypnosis: A psychological state of altered attention and awareness in which a person is unusually receptive to suggestions.

What Are the Characteristic Features of Hypnosis?

When hypnotized, people's awareness is characterized by the following features (Bowers & Woody, 1996; Bryant et al., 1999; Comey & Kirsch, 1999; Lynn & Neufeld, 1996):

Enriched fantasy—The hypnotized person can readily imagine situations dissociated from reality.

Cognitive passivity—Instead of planning actions, the hypnotized person waits for the hypnotist to suggest thoughts or actions.

Hyperselective attention—The hypnotized person will focus attention on the hypnotist's voice and ignore other stimuli. Even pain that a person would find unbearable during their normal waking state can be tolerated through the hypnotically induced focused attention.

Reduced reality testing—The hypnotized person tends to uncritically accept hallucinated experiences suggested by the hypnotist.

Posthypnotic amnesia—When instructed by the hypnotist, the hypnotized person will often forget all or most of what occurred during the hypnotic session. These memories are restored when the hypnotist gives a prearranged signal. Hypnotically induced amnesia does not appear to be due to deliberate thought suppression on the part of the hypnotized person.

What Are Common Misconceptions about Hypnosis?

Hypnosis has long been used as a form of entertainment, and this history has led to certain myths about the capabilities of the hypnotized person. A list follows of some of these misconceptions accompanied by the discoveries made by scientific research (Dywan & Bowers, 1983; Gibson, 1991; McConkey, 1992; Nash, 1987; Newman & Thompson, 1999):

- *Hypnotized people can be forced to violate their moral values*—There is no evidence that hypnosis causes people to act against their will.

- *Memory is more accurate under hypnosis*—Although hypnosis may help people to recall forgotten events, it often results in people recalling events that never happened.

- *While hypnotized, people are much stronger than normal*—Hypnosis has no effect on strength.

- *Hypnosis acts like a truth serum, compelling people to avoid deception*—Hypnotized people can lie and keep secrets if they so desire.

- *Hypnotized people can be age-regressed, thus allowing them to relive childhood experiences*—Although hypnotized people may believe they have regressed to an earlier age, they typically display cognitive abilities far beyond those of a child.

Individual Differences in Hypnotizability

Hypnotizability: The degree to which a person can enter a deep hypnotic state.

People differ in their **hypnotizability,** which is the degree to which they can enter a deep hypnotic state (Hilgard, 1965; Kumar et al., 1996). Children are the most hypnotizable, which is not surprising, given the fact that being able to engage freely in fantasy is an important predictor of hypnotizability (Kihlstrom, 1985; Silva & Kirsch, 1992).

Although the ability to suspend ordinary reality facilitates entrance into the hypnotic state, highly hypnotizable persons are not more gullible or more conforming than their less hypnotizable counterparts (Fromm & Shor, 1979). Among adults, about 10 percent cannot be hypnotized at all, approximately 15 percent are very susceptible, and the rest fall somewhere in between (Barber, 2000). Research also indicates that hypnotizability is a fairly stable trait during adulthood (Piccione et al., 1989).

6-3b   Some Psychologists Doubt That Hypnosis Is an Altered State

In contrast to the sleep state, the brain wave activity (EEG) of hypnotized individuals differs only slightly from that of their normal waking states (Crawford & Gruzelier, 1992; De Pascalis, 1999; Graffin et al., 1995). This lack of any clear physiological difference between the normal and the hypnotic state has fueled suspicion that hypnosis is not really an altered state at all. One such "nonstate" theory proposes that the hypnotized person is simply playing a role (Barber, 1979; Spanos & Chaves, 1989). This *role-playing* explanation contends that hypnosis is a normal waking state in which suggestible people behave as they think hypnotized people are supposed to behave. The proponents of this view do not necessarily believe that hypnotized people are consciously faking an altered state. Instead, they argue that, because of the misguided cultural beliefs about the powers of hypnosis, people get caught up in the hypnotic role and often unwittingly confirm these beliefs by demonstrating hypnotic behavior (Gorassini, 1996; Spanos & Coe, 1992).

INFO-BIT: College students answered questions concerning their beliefs about hypnosis before either watching a stage hypnotist or attending a lecture on hypnosis. When later questioned, both groups were now more likely to correctly believe that hypnotizability does not reflect lower intelligence. However, while those students who heard the lecture were less likely to believe that a hypnotized person is robotlike and automatically acts on all suggestions, the reverse was true for those who watched the stage hypnotist (Echterling & Whalen, 1995). Why might students who saw the stage hypnotist be more likely to believe such false descriptions of hypnosis?

In support of this role-playing interpretation of hypnosis, research indicates that people's responsiveness to hypnotic suggestions can be influenced by their expectations and their desire to please the hypnotist. For example, when previously low hypnotizable individuals take *active training* programs to enhance their attitudes and expectations about hypnosis, they subsequently exhibit large gains in hypnotizability (Spanos, 1986). These gains are much more likely to occur when rapport with trainers is high rather than low. Yet, merely liking one's trainer is generally not sufficient to increase hypnotizability. When low hypnotizable persons were given *passive training*, in which their well-liked trainers told them that hypnotic responses just "happened by themselves," their level of hypnotizability did not increase (Spanos et al., 1989–1990).

Despite evidence indicating that hypnosis is influenced by social expectations and a desire to please the hypnotist, many hypnosis researchers contend that there are enough special features of hypnosis to legitimately call it an altered state. For example, people who are hypnotized often report a *dissociation* in consciousness, in which they process perceptual information on two levels simultaneously (Hilgard, 1986, 1992; Zamansky & Bartis, 1985). Based on this research, Ernest Hilgard proposed his **neodissociation theory,** which contends that the hypnotized person has two streams of consciousness operating at once. One stream responds to the hypnotist's suggestions, while the other stream, called the *hidden observer,* remains concealed from conscious awareness and merely observes what is going on.

> **Neodissociation theory:** A theory that hypnotized persons enter an altered state in which two streams of consciousness operate simultaneously, one actively responding to suggestions and the other passively observing what is going on.

Based on our previous discussion of selective and divided attention (see section 6-1a), Hilgard's theory of a *divided consciousness* is not that unusual. While engaging in normal daily activities, you can literally "split" your attention. Sometimes, you might even engage in an activity without any memory of having done so. For instance, have you ever been so engrossed in dinner conversation that you forgot what your meal tasted like or that you even ate it? This common experience during the normal waking state is not that different from Hilgard's explanation of hypnosis.

This debate about hypnosis being an altered state is still a matter of ongoing scientific inquiry (Raz & Shapiro, 2002). Although many of the more bizarre or peculiar effects observed during hypnosis might be explained by people's expectations about hypnosis and their desire to please the hypnotist, other effects—such as hypnotized patients being able to undergo surgery without pain (Hornyak & Green, 2000; Schafer, 1996)—suggest a truly altered state of consciousness. However, many researchers suggest that even if hypnosis is ultimately determined to be a legitimate altered state, it should also be thought of as a product of common principles of social influence and an extension of ordinary splits in consciousness (Chaves, 1999). For our present purposes, we can safely conclude that the power of hypnosis does not reside in any mysterious qualities of the hypnotist, but rather, in the mind of the hypnotized.

6-3c Meditation Provides Relaxation and Reduces Arousal

Meditation refers to a variety of mental exercises that alter the normal flow of consciousness in order to enhance self-knowledge. (See Discovery Box 6-5.) Although some forms of meditation encourage emptying the mind of all content, more common forms of meditation, such as *Zen, transcendental meditation,* and the *relaxation response,* teach people to

> **Meditation:** A variety of mental exercises that alter the normal flow of consciousness in order to enhance self-knowledge.

DISCOVERY BOX 6-5

How Can You Meditate?

To get some sense of what meditation is all about, try the following exercise derived from Herbert Benson's relaxation response (Benson, 1975; Benson & Klipper, 1988).

> Sit quietly in a comfortable position, close your eyes, and relax your muscles. Choose some word or short phrase (a mantra) that you can focus your attention on. It should be something that is calming to you, such as "love," "serenity," or "I am at peace." Don't concentrate too hard on the mantra; it could become only a faint idea at times. As you repeat this mantra silently to yourself, breathe through your nose and pay attention to your breathing. Continue this exercise for 10 to 20 minutes and maintain a passive attitude throughout. When your attention is distracted away from your mantra, don't get upset, but simply and gently refocus your mind. If you find this to be a pleasant experience, practice it once or twice daily.

focus attention on a single sound, image, or object, and to effortlessly ignore any intruding sensations (Sheikh, 2002). Still other techniques emphasize body movement, such as the Sufi whirling dervishes, a religious brotherhood in Turkey that seeks mystic experiences through dance (Deikman, 2000).

Although most practitioners of meditation and many researchers believe that it involves an altered state of consciousness that can open the mind to profound truths and a feeling of oneness with the universe, more skeptical observers contend that it is simply an effective relaxation technique. Meditation has indeed been found to be useful in promoting relaxation and reducing physiological arousal (Deepak et al., 1994; Walsh, 1996). Accomplished meditators exhibit high-amplitude alpha waves and theta waves while meditating, the type of brain waves associated with relaxation and stage 1 light sleep, respectively (Kasamatsu & Hirai, 1969; Kjaer et al., 2002). Meditation also tends to reduce oxygen consumption, slow heart rate, and increase blood flow in the arms and forehead (Fenwick, 1987; Wallace & Benson, 1972).

Beyond fostering relaxation, some studies suggest that meditation can be an effective treatment for insomnia, anxiety, depression, and drug abuse (Gelderloos et al., 1991; Miller et al., 1995; Shapiro et al., 1998). Other studies even suggest that it may increase longevity among the elderly (Alexander et al., 1989; Goldberg, 1995). Despite these impressive therapeutic findings, skeptics claim that meditation is effective simply because it leads to relaxation, and perhaps because it serves as a placebo to those who want to believe in its benefits (Shapiro, 1987).

Although it is still unclear whether meditation is merely a mild alteration of normal consciousness (relaxation) or something more profound, there seems to be little dispute that it is a useful relaxation technique. Until more is learned about how meditation produces its effects, scientific conclusions regarding its other possible benefits would be premature.

When someone in his own mind recalls the original condition of his Mind, then all deceptive thoughts dissolve away on their own into the realm of the ultimate reality.

—Milarepa, Tibetan Buddhist saint and poet, 1040–1123

No one can see their reflection in running water. It is only in still water that we can see.

—Taoist proverb

6-3d Intense Religious Experiences May Involve Altered States

One night I awoke gasping for breath—I thought I was dying and felt like I was—Just about to give up—I saw a vision of Jesus at the foot of my bed—the complete figure—He stretched out His hand and said, "No—not yet—Be not afraid." At that moment I felt a *peace* and *joy* come over me—such as I have never experienced in my life. (Stark, 1965)

Like this individual in Rodney Stark's study of religious experiences, have you ever had the feeling of being close to a powerful spiritual force that seemed to lift you out of yourself? When 5,420 Americans were asked this question, 40 percent answered yes (Yamane & Polzer, 1994). Similar findings have been obtained in England and Australia and are common experiences in religions throughout the world (Scharfstein, 1973). A century ago, William James (1902/1985) described such intense religious experiences as creating a sense of peace and inner harmony, in which the self and the world is perceived as having undergone a dramatic transformation, and where important truths are revealed. Regardless of the ultimate insights that people might receive from these intense religious experiences, do they qualify as true altered states of consciousness?

One of the more interesting religious experiences studied by scientists is that of the Holy Ghost people of Appalachia. In this fundamentalist Christian sect, anointment by the Holy Ghost is believed to occur when the spirit of God possesses a person. While anointed and presumably protected by the Holy Ghost, these people handle poisonous snakes, drink strychnine poison, and touch flames to their bodies (Schwarz, 1960; Wilson, 1970). Although observations of individuals during anointment suggest they are having profound religious experiences, their brain activity doesn't significantly differ from someone in an aroused, waking state. For instance, EEG recordings taken of one well-known serpent handler indicated a sudden shift from alpha to beta waves when anointment began, with beta activity predominant throughout the experience (Woodruff, 1993). Overall, the EEG pattern was not similar to the slower patterns recorded by meditating Zen monks.

Currently, there is an ongoing debate about whether altered states of consciousness are necessary for certain religious experiences (Fenwick, 2001; Godby, 2002). Similar to the hypnosis debate (refer back to section 6-3b), some researchers believe that many religious experiences are not precipitated by altered states but, rather, are the result of *role-playing* (Holm, 1991, 1995; Hood, 1991). As with the explanation of hypnosis, these researchers contend that people learn how to play the religious role, and it is within this social role context that their religious experiences can be best understood.

Although there may be debate about whether certain religious experiences are induced by altered states, there is no such controversy about religious experiences induced by mind-altering drugs. For example, to facilitate the "vision quest" among certain Native American tribes, psychoactive drugs are commonly used along with ritualistic fasting. Research indicates that under the influence of psychedelic drugs, religious imagery is quite common (Masters & Houston, 1966; Pahnke, 1970). Such findings have led some researchers to make the controversial claim that all religions in the world originated from the use of mind-altering drugs (Kramrisch et al., 1986).

So what part do altered states play in religious experiences? The answer may depend on the type of religious experience analyzed. It is important to keep in mind that religious experiences occur within the context of a set of cultural traditions and social expectations (Hood, 1995). As pointed out by social-role theorists, participants in religious exercises play identifiable roles learned from their social group. The group also provides participants with a sense of identity and a feeling of security in having shared values and beliefs. Within this group context, it is not unusual that participants often feel as though the psychological boundaries between self and nonself have dissolved. The accompanying states of consciousness may appear no different from the normal waking state, or they may be profoundly altered. Whatever the case, altered states should not be thought of as the essence of the religious experience. Theodore Roszak has argued that focusing only on the altered state component distorts the essence of the religious experience:

The temptation, then, is to believe that the behavior which has thus been objectively verified is what religious experience is *really* all about, and—further—that it can be appropriated as an end in itself, plucked like a rare flower from the soil that feeds it. The result is a narrow emphasis on special effects and sensations: "peak experiences," "highs," "flashes," and such. Yet, even if one wishes to regard ecstasy as the "peak" of religious experience, that summit does not float in midair. It rests upon tradition and a way of life; one ascends such heights and appreciates their grandeur by a process of initiation that demands learning, commitment, devotion, service, sacrifice. To approach it in any hasty way is like "scaling" Mount Everest by being landed on its top from a helicopter. (Roszak, 1975, p. 50)

6-3e Psychoactive Drug Use Can Lead to Dependence

As already discussed, **psychoactive drugs**—which are chemicals that modify mental processes and behavior—are often used to deliberately alter consciousness. The way in which they alter consciousness is by attaching themselves to synaptic receptors and thereby either blocking or stimulating neural activity. Although psychoactive drugs are sometimes used in religious ceremonies, they are mostly taken for medicinal and recreational purposes. When people persist in taking drugs even when impaired behavior or social functioning results, this is known as **drug abuse** (see table 6-2). One effect of drug abuse is **tolerance,** meaning that greater amounts of the drug are necessary to produce the same effect once produced by a smaller dose (Julien, 1992). For example, an infrequent

Psychoactive drugs: Chemicals that modify mental processes and behavior.

Drug abuse: Persistence in drug use even when impaired behavior or social functioning results.

Tolerance: An effect of drug abuse in which greater amounts of the drug are necessary to produce the same effect once produced by a smaller dose.

TABLE 6-2

Are You Abusing a Drug?

Instructions: Listed below are eight criteria that the American Psychiatric Association uses to diagnose drug abuse (also known as *substance dependence*). If three or more of the following criteria describe your own behavior, you may have a problem with substance abuse.

	Yes	No
1. The substance is often taken in larger amounts or over a longer period than intended.	___	___
2. There is a persistent desire or one or more unsuccessful efforts to cut down or control substance use.	___	___
3. A great deal of your time is spent in activities necessary to get the substance (for example, theft), taking the substance (for example, chain smoking), or recovering from its effects (for example, alcohol "hangovers").	___	___
4. You experience frequent intoxication or withdrawal symptoms when you either are expected to fulfill obligations at work, school, or home, or when substance use is physically dangerous (for example, driving when intoxicated).	___	___
5. You give up or reduce in frequency important social, occupational, or recreational activities because of substance use.	___	___
6. You continue to use the drug despite recognizing its harmfulness to your life.	___	___
7. You need increased amounts of the drug (at least 50% more) to achieve the desired effect and/or you experience a decreased effect with continued use of the same amount (tolerance).	___	___
8. You often take the drug to relieve or avoid withdrawal symptoms.	___	___

Source: Adapted from the American Psychiatric Association (1994).

drinker might become intoxicated after only two beers, but an alcoholic might have to consume two six-packs to receive the same effect.

Often accompanying tolerance is the development of *physical dependence*. A person who is physically dependent on a drug needs it to function normally. How do you determine whether someone is physically dependent? By withdrawing the drug and watching for the appearance of unpleasant physical symptoms—known as *withdrawal symptoms*—as the body reacts to its absence (Littleton & Little, 1989; Piasecki et al., 1997). Among heroin addicts, for example, common withdrawal symptoms are chills, fever, diarrhea, and a runny nose. What makes it difficult for drug abusers to stop their abuse is that readministering the drug can terminate the symptoms of withdrawal.

Besides physical dependence, many drugs produce an immediate pleasurable effect that, through continued use, leads to *psychological dependence*, in which the person experiences intense mental and emotional desires for the drug (Carroll, 1997). Many drugs of abuse cause both physical and psychological dependence. Importantly, psychological dependence can persist even when a person is no longer physically dependent on a drug.

Abuse of psychoactive drugs is one of our most serious and costly social problems, accounting for a third of all hospital admissions, a quarter of all deaths, and a majority of serious crimes. In the United States alone, its combined medical and social costs exceed $240 billion per year (Nash, 1997). Table 6-3 lists and classifies three types of psychoactive drugs: **depressants**, which slow down—or depress—the nervous system and decrease mental and physical activity; **stimulants,** which speed up—or stimulate—the nervous system and increase mental and physical activity; and **hallucinogens,** which distort perception and generate sensory images without any external stimulation. We will discuss each of these in turn.

Depressants: Psychoactive drugs that slow down—or depress—the nervous system and decrease mental and physical activity.

Stimulants: Psychoactive drugs that speed up—or stimulate—the nervous system and increase mental and physical activity.

Hallucinogens: Psychoactive drugs that distort perception and generate sensory images without any external stimulation.

TABLE 6-3

Psychoactive Drugs

Drug	Main Effects	Potential for Physical/ Psychological Dependence
Depressants		
Alcohol	Relaxation, anxiety reduction, sleep	High/High
Opiates ("narcotics")	Euphoria, relaxation, anxiety reduction, pain relief	High/High
Stimulants		
Caffeine	Alertness	Moderate/Moderate
Cocaine	Alertness, euphoria	Moderate to high/High
Nicotine	Alertness	High/(?)
Amphetamines	Alertness, euphoria	Moderate to high/High
MDMA (Ecstasy)	Blissfulness, increased sociability	Low
Ritalin	Increased concentration	Moderate/Moderate
Hallucinogens		
LSD	Hallucination, altered perceptions	Low/Low
Marijuana	Mild euphoria, relaxation, altered perceptions	Low/Moderate

6-3f Depressants Slow Bodily Functions and Induce Relaxation

In low doses, depressants induce a relaxed state, while in higher doses, they induce sleep. By far, the most widely consumed and abused depressant in the world is alcohol. Surveys indicate, for example, that 85 percent of college students consume alcohol, and nearly half (44 percent) drink heavily. Besides slowing bodily functions, depressants like alcohol also reduce awareness of both internal and external stimuli. When intoxicated with alcohol, those areas of your brain that control judgment and inhibitions are impaired, making it more likely that you will act on your impulses (Ito et al., 1996). Some researchers believe that this weakening of restraints, or *disinhibition*, is caused by an interruption of our ability to process and respond to the meaning of complex and subtle situational cues (Johnson et al., 2000; Steele & Josephs, 1988). For example, when provoked, people who are drunk are much less attentive than those who are sober to such inhibiting cues as the provocateur's intentions and the possible negative consequences of violence. This impairment of judgment partly explains why alcohol is the leading cause of domestic violence and highway deaths in the general population, and why college students who drink heavily are two to five times more likely to argue, fight, damage property, get injured, and engage in unplanned or unprotected sex (Holcomb & Anderson, 1983; O'Farrell & Murphy, 1995).

Alcoholism is the occurrence of tolerance and physical dependence resulting from the prolonged abuse of alcohol (O'Brien et al., 1995). In the United States, over 20 million people abuse alcohol, thus putting their health at risk (Cooper, 2000). Among the health problems associated with chronic alcohol abuse are liver disease *(cirrhosis)*, heart disease, stroke, memory loss, cancer, malnutrition, and loss of sexual interest (Cloninger et al., 1989; Yelena, 2002). Although these health risks certainly highlight the dangers of alcohol abuse, recent studies indicate that one possible long-term benefit of moderate alcohol consumption is reduced coronary heart disease (Criqui & Ringel, 1994; Fuchs et al., 1995). However, having stated this potential health benefit, it must be emphasized that this is far outweighed by the risks associated with *heavy* drinking.

Another category of depressants are the **opiates** (also called *narcotics*), which include such drugs as *opium, morphine,* and *heroin.* For centuries, opium extracted from the seed pods of poppy has been used to relieve pain and suffering by mimicking the effects of the brain's own naturally produced pain-relieving neurotransmitter, *endorphins* (see chapter 3, section 3-1c). Opiates not only depress the nervous system and relieve pain, but they also produce a relaxed, dreamlike state that is highly pleasurable. However, such pleasure comes at a cost—users quickly develop a strong physical and psychological dependence, and their withdrawal symptoms are extremely intense and painful. The reason withdrawal symptoms are so severe is due to the opiates' effects on the brain's production of endorphins. Regular use of opiates overloads endorphin receptors within the brain, thereby causing the brain to cease its endorphin production. When the drugs are withdrawn, the brain has an insufficient supply of these pain-relieving neurotransmitters, and this is the primary cause of the person's severe withdrawal symptoms.

Alcoholism: The occurrence of tolerance and physical dependence due to the prolonged abuse of alcohol.

Opiates: A category of depressant drugs, including opium, morphine, and heroin, that depress the nervous system, temporarily relieve pain, and produce a relaxed, dreamlike state.

6-3g Stimulants Speed Up Bodily Functions

Are you a person who needs a cup of coffee in the morning to "get going" or a cigarette to curb your appetite or relieve stress? Because stimulants speed up body functions and reduce appetite (due to blood sugar rising), people often use them to stay awake, lose weight, enhance athletic performance, or elevate mood. Two of the most commonly used stimulant

> **INFO-BIT:** The proportion of men who have been physically violent toward their wives is at least four times higher among married men in treatment for alcoholism than among demographically similar nonalcoholic men (O'Farrell & Murphy, 1995).

substances are *caffeine* and *nicotine*. Caffeine is found in coffee, tea, cocoa, and the cola nut (which is used to flavor cola beverages), while tobacco is the only natural source of nicotine. Although moderate doses of caffeine can fight off drowsiness, large doses can make a person feel jittery and anxious (Griffiths & Mumford, 1995). In addition, as previously discussed in chapter 3, habitual heavy users of caffeine can become physically dependent, experiencing headaches and depression when deprived of the drug (James, 1997).

The effects of nicotine on the nervous system are complicated. While it increases heart rate, respiration, and blood pressure, it also has a calming effect on smokers, often relieving stress. In addition to these effects, nicotine reduces blood flow to the skin, causing a drop in skin temperature, which makes blushing less common in smokers than in nonsmokers. This reduced blood flow is probably why the skin of smokers tends to wrinkle and age faster than that of nonsmokers (Daniell, 1971). Nicotine also appears to produce a decrease in hand steadiness and fine motor control (Frankenhauser et al., 1970).

Prolonged use of tobacco—primarily in cigarettes, cigars, and chewing tobacco—is a serious health hazard. It also is the single most important *preventable* risk to human health in developed countries, and an important cause of premature death worldwide (Peto et al., 1992). About 21 million people died from smoking-related illnesses in the decade 1990–1999. In addition, among nonsmoking adults, exposure to secondary smoke doubles the risk of heart disease and increases the risk of lung cancer by 30 percent (White et al., 1991). Such exposure also increases the risk of respiratory diseases and other health problems in nonsmoking children (White et al., 1991). Unfortunately for casual tobacco users, a greater percentage of them become addicted to this drug than do casual users of cocaine, morphine, or alcohol (Henningfield et al., 1990, 1995).

Despite its danger to health, nicotine-laced tobacco products—and caffeine—are only mild stimulants. Much stronger stimulants are *cocaine* and *amphetamines* (also known as "speed"). Cocaine is a natural substance that comes from the cocoa plant, while amphetamines are synthetic drugs. When cocaine is smoked (*crack*), sniffed (*snorting*), or injected directly into the bloodstream (*mainlining*), users experience a 15- to 30-minute "high" during which they feel energized, excited, and confident. Although cocaine is not generally considered to create physical dependence, due to its highly pleasurable effects it often produces strong psychological dependence (Bonson et al., 2002). In contrast, amphetamines, which also produce a high similar to cocaine, result in both psychological and physical dependence in high dose users.

One stimulant that has become popular among adolescents and young adults as an alternative to cocaine is "ecstasy" or MDMA (short for methylenedioxymethamphetamine). Taken as a pill, MDMA primarily affects brain cells that produce serotonin, a neurotransmitter that is the body's primary regulator of mood (see chapter 3, section 3-1c). The massive release of serotonin by these cells may be responsible for ecstasy users often experiencing a feeling of blissfulness and a greater closeness to others, as well as significant increases in body temperature, heart rate, and blood pressure (Green et al., 1995). Although MDMA is not physically addictive, it is a dangerous drug. When ecstasy users take several doses over the course of a few hours, their body's natural ability to control its temperature can be severely impaired. Dozens of deaths have occurred due to overheating when users have engaged in strenuous physical activity (Cloud, 2000). Findings from recent animal and human studies also raise the possibility that MDMA use can cause permanent damage to the axons of the serotonin-containing brain cells, resulting in memory and concentration problems (Gerra et al., 2000; Hatzidimitriou et al., 1999; Kish, 2002; Reneman et al., 2000).

> **INFO-BIT:** Fear of gaining weight is the primary reason many women give for not quitting smoking. Yet research indicates that women who exercise regularly while trying to "kick the habit" not only limit their weight gain, but they are twice as likely to stop smoking and to stay smoke free than nonexercisers (Marcus et al., 1999). Similar benefits are also likely for male smokers.

> *To cease smoking is the easiest thing I ever did. I ought to know because I've done it a thousand times.*
>
> —Mark Twain, U.S. author, 1835–1910

Another disturbing cultural trend has been the increased abuse of *Ritalin* (methylphenidate), a stimulant drug prescribed to treat attention-deficit hyperactivity disorder (ADHD) in children. Ritalin is effective in treating the disorder because it decreases distractibility and improves concentration (Roehrs et al., 1999). Yet, some adults—among them college students—who do not have the disorder ingest the drug to increase their concentration and productivity while working or studying for exams (Beck et al., 1999). They also more quickly develop a tolerance for the drug than those without ADHD and experience withdrawal symptoms when the dosage is reduced.

6-3h Hallucinogens Induce Profoundly Altered States

The psychoactive drugs that produce the most profound alterations in consciousness are the *hallucinogens*. As the name implies, these drugs often create hallucinations, in which sensations and perceptions occur without any external stimulation. Many hallucinogenic drugs are naturally derived from plants, such as the peyote cactus that contains *mescaline*, or the Mexican mushroom that contains *psilocybin*. These natural hallucinogens have been used for thousands of years in the religious rites of the Aztecs and other Mexican Indians and still today play an important role in the religious practices of the Native American Church of North America. As a religious sacrament—similar to the bread and wine used in Christianity—members of the Native American Church seldom abuse these hallucinogens.

LSD: The most potent of the hallucinogens, which is synthesized and induces hallucinations, distortions, and a blending of sensory experiences.

The most potent of the hallucinogenic drugs, **LSD** (technically known as *lysergic acid diethylamide*), is not found in nature, but instead, is synthesized. Following its discovery in 1938 by Swiss chemist Albert Hoffman, LSD was sometimes given to patients in psychotherapy because its mind-expanding properties were thought to facilitate the recovery of repressed memories. During the 1960s, LSD became a recreational drug on college campuses, championed by former Harvard lecturer Timothy Leary, who believed that it could be used as a vehicle to spiritual discovery.

When taken orally, LSD's effects are felt within 30 minutes to an hour and persist for about 10 to 12 hours. Although the physiological effects of LSD are minor—a slight increase in heart rate, blood pressure, blood glucose, body temperature, dizziness, drowsiness, and nausea—the psychological effects are intense. The exact nature of the psychological experience is difficult to predict because it is influenced by a host of factors, including the user's personality and expectations, the persons with whom the user interacts during the LSD experience, and the setting in which the drug is administered. However, the principal psychological effects involve hallucinations and distortions. There may also be a blending of sensory experiences known as synesthesia, where colors may be felt or heard, and sounds may be seen. Subjective time is also altered, where a few seconds might seem like many minutes, and people often feel as though they are detached from their bodies. For some, these experiences are enjoyable and even insightful; for others, they are unpleasant and even terrifying. Importantly, unpleasant experiences are relatively frequent, and "flashbacks"—recurrences of drug effects without the drug—occur in more than 15 percent of LSD users (Jaffe, 1990). Most important, there is no way to predict reactions to the drug. The same person may react positively during one experience and negatively during another.

LSD users do not become physically dependent, even after prolonged use. In fact, most people discontinue using LSD because they tire of it or have no further need for it. The lack of a physical dependence, however, does not mean that this is a "safe" drug. Although LSD has never been definitely linked to even one human overdose death, fatal accidents and suicides have occurred when people are intoxicated by LSD. For this reason, LSD is considered a dangerous drug and should be avoided.

Marijuana, which is sometimes classified as a mild hallucinogen, is a preparation of leafy material from the hemp, or *Cannabis*, plant. The earliest reference to marijuana is in a pharmacy book written in 2737 B.C. by the Chinese emperor Shen Nung, in which he called it the "Liberator of Sin," due to its ability to induce a sense of giddiness or euphoria in users. This pleasurable effect probably accounts for the fact that marijuana continues to be the most frequently used illegal drug in the world: for example, 47 percent of American adults have tried it at least once and about 3 percent are daily users (Kingery et al., 1999; Martin, 1995). Although its use is widespread, marijuana appears to be a "maturational drug" for most people, meaning that they begin using it during the exploratory years of adolescence and stop using it in early adulthood as they work to secure their career and family relationships (Mitchell et al., 1999).

The major psychoactive ingredient in marijuana is **THC,** short for the complex organic molecule delta-9 tetrahydrocannabinol. THC is concentrated in the resin of the hemp plant, with most of the resin in the flowering tops (from which the stronger form of marijuana, known as *hashish*, is made), less in the leaves, and little in the stems. When smoked, THC is quickly absorbed into the blood and reaches the brain within 7 seconds; however, when eaten in such foods as brownies or cookies, the effect is delayed.

What are the effects of marijuana? Physiologically, it produces mild arousal in the form of increased heart rate and blood pressure, and dryness of the mouth and throat. Psychologically, users often experience an increased sense of well-being and relaxation, spontaneous laughter, as well as a heightened sensitivity to various stimuli, such as tastes, sounds, colors, and smells. In addition, people often experience a distortion of time and a disconnected flow of ideas, which may be caused by a temporary impairment of short-term memory, leading users to confuse past, present, and future (Schwartz, 1993). Like alcohol, moderate marijuana use can impair coordination, attention, and reaction time, and has been linked to accidents and traffic fatalities (Chait & Pierri, 1992; Earleywine, 2002). Research further suggests that, as with tobacco, marijuana use increases susceptibility to throat and mouth cancers due to its high tar content (National Academy of Sciences, 1999). There is also sufficient evidence to recommend that the drug not be used during pregnancy, due to possible negative prenatal effects (Szeto et al., 1991; Tashkin, 1999; Wu et al., 1988). Regarding possible psychological and social effects, consistent use of *high* quantities of marijuana does appear to have negative effects on motivation and interpersonal skills, and thus, may impede the normal development of adolescents and young adults (Martin, 1995). In addition, the more heavily individuals use marijuana, the greater the probability that they will use other drugs. Given all these possible negative effects, marijuana is definitely not a risk-free drug.

6-3i Biological and Sociocultural Factors Influence Drug Use

Twin studies provide evidence that drug abuse vulnerability may have a biological link (Goldberg et al., 1993; Pickens et al., 1993). For example, the shared incidence of alcoholism is more common among identical twins than among fraternal twins (McGue et al., 1992). Similarly, twin studies in the United States and Scandinavia not only indicate a genetic contribution to risks of smoking and marijuana use, but also in *resistance* to using these substances (Carmelli et al., 1992; Kendler et al., 2002). These findings suggest that the closer the genetic makeup between people, the more similar the drug use pattern (Bierut et al., 2002; Uhl et al., 1995).

Regarding personal or social factors, although personality problems do not predict drug use in adolescents, a teenager's degree of rebellion against parents and societal norms is a good predictor of drug use: Those teens who are religious, attend school regularly and get good grades, have good relationships with their parents, and do not break the law are least likely to drink alcohol and use other drugs (Oetting & Beauvais, 1987, 1990).

Marijuana: A mild hallucinogen derived from the leafy material of the hemp, or *Cannabis*, plant that often induces a sense of giddiness or euphoria, as well as a heightened sensitivity to various stimuli.

THC: The major psychoactive ingredient in marijuana.

Rebellious adolescents, in contrast, often have closer emotional ties to their friends than to their parents, and these friends are also likely to be drug users. In other words, the nonusing teenagers are more influenced by their parents, while the drug-using teenagers are more influenced by their friends.

Finally, one question that scientists have tried to answer is how culture might influence drug dependence. Regarding alcohol abuse, studies of industrialized Western societies find that a culture's attitudes and beliefs about alcohol are strong predictors of whether or not it is abused. For example, *temperance cultures*—cultures that maintain activist approaches to combating drinking problems—consume less alcohol than nontemperance cultures (Levine, 1992; Peele, 1993). Further, alcohol consumption is more "socialized" in temperance cultures (Peele, 1996). That is, in such cultures alcohol is more likely to be integrated into mixed-sex social settings (such as family meals and cafés), whereas in nontemperance cultures it is more likely to be a part of male-dominated settings devoted exclusively to drinking (such as taverns). The drinking that occurs in these relatively isolated settings is much more likely to be excessive and to lead to alcoholism than that which takes place in the more integrated social arenas.

SECTION SUMMARY

- People differ in their hypnotizability, with children being the most hypnotizable.
- Role-playing explanation maintains that hypnosis is a normal waking state in which suggestible people behave as they think hypnotized people are supposed to behave.
- According to neodissociation theory, hypnosis is an altered state, with the hypnotized person having two streams of consciousness operating at once.
- Meditation may involve an altered state of consciousness, but skeptics claim that it simply leads to relaxation.
- Religious experiences may be precipitated by altered states but may result from role-playing and shared expectations.
- Depressants induce a relaxed state when taken in low doses but induce sleep when taken in higher doses.
- Stimulants speed up the nervous system and increase mental and physical activity.
- Psychoactive drugs that produce the most profound alterations in consciousness are the hallucinogens.
- Drug abuse occurs when people persist in taking drugs even when impaired behavior or social functioning results.

SUGGESTED WEBSITES

Note: These websites were functional when we went to press. Please access the online text for the most up-to-date URLs.

Center for Consciousness Studies

http://www.consciousness.arizona.edu/

This website for the Center for Consciousness Studies at the University of Arizona offers on-line papers on consciousness as well as information on conferences, bibliographical references, and related websites.

National Institute on Drug Abuse

http://www.nida.nih.gov

This website provides valuable information and national statistics on drug use and related web links.

Sleepnet.com™

http://www.sleepnet.com

This website provides information on the psychology and physiology of sleep, including sleep disorders, dreams, and the addresses of sleep labs around the country.

Working (and Playing) with Dreams

http://www.rider.edu/users/suler/dreams.html

This website offers information on various theories and methods of dream interpretation.

PSYCHOLOGICAL APPLICATIONS
How Can You Deal with Sleep Disorders?

Problems related to sleep are among the most common psychological disorders, but they are often underdiagnosed and undertreated (Mindell, 1999; Schenck & Mahowald, 2002). In the United States alone, approximately 40 million people suffer from some form of chronic sleep problem, accounting for about $50 billion a year in medical costs and lost labor (Holden, 1993). Some of the more common disorders of sleep are *night terrors, sleepwalking, narcolepsy, sleep apnea,* and *insomnia.*

Night Terrors

A type of sleep disorder most common among children between the ages of 3 and 8 is a **night terror,** which is a panic attack that generally occurs during early night stage 4 NREM sleep (Kahn et al., 1991). Victims sit up in bed, let out a terrified scream, stare into space, and talk incoherently, but they seldom wake up and recall little or nothing of the event the next morning. It is important to distinguish night terrors from the far more common *nightmares,* which are anxiety-arousing dreams that occur during REM sleep and are as likely to occur among adults as children. It is also important to note that night terrors are not necessarily indicative of emotional disturbance. Although those who suffer from night terrors are somewhat more likely to suffer from mood disorders (Ohayon et al., 1999), night terrors may also be caused by an immature nervous system, which would explain why it is far more common among younger children than adults.

When I woke up this morning, my girlfriend asked me, "Did you sleep well?" I said, "No, I made a few mistakes."

–Steven Wright, American comedian

Sleepwalking

Sleepwalking, also known as *somnambulism,* is a sleep disorder in which a person arises and wanders about while remaining asleep. Like night terrors, sleepwalking occurs during early night NREM sleep (Keefauver & Guilleminault, 1994). Thus, contrary to popular thinking, sleepwalkers are not acting out a dream. Also contrary to popular belief, it is not dangerous to wake a sleepwalker— although it may be difficult, due to them being in deep stage 4 sleep. This disorder is more common among children (10 percent) than adults (2 percent), and more common among boys than girls (Spielman & Herrera, 1991).

Narcolepsy

A more serious form of sleep disorder than the ones discussed thus far is **narcolepsy,** which is characterized by uncontrollable REM sleep attacks during normal waking hours (Vgontzas & Kales, 1999). About 250,000 Americans—one in every thousand—suffer from this disorder. Narcolepsy can strike at any time, even when a person is driving a car or otherwise engaged in activities where inattentiveness is dangerous, but unconsciousness can be fatal. Fortunately, stimulant drugs can usually control the symptoms of this disorder (Godbout et al., 1990; Guilleminault, 1976). The cause of narcolepsy is unknown, but people who have the disorder in their families are 50 times more likely to develop it than others, which suggests that possible genetic factors underlie this disorder.

Sleep Apnea

Another disorder with a possible hereditary cause is **sleep apnea,** in which sleeping individuals briefly stop breathing several times an hour, interrupting their sleep without their knowledge. About 12 million Americans suffer from this disorder, with overweight men older than 40 being the most common victims (Ingbar & Gee, 1985). Apnea sufferers report daytime sleepiness, morning headaches, and even occasional heart and lung problems. The loss of sleep experienced by apnea sufferers has been shown to affect their waking reaction time, making them as slow to respond as someone who is legally intoxicated (Kayumov et al., 2000; Ulfberg et al., 2000). Apnea may be treated by a number of methods, including weight loss, changing sleeping positions, hormone therapy, and even surgery to open constricted airways.

Insomnia

The most common sleep disorder is **insomnia,** which is the chronic inability to fall or stay asleep (Zorick, 1989). Approximately 30 percent of adults complain of insomnia to some degree, and it is a recurring problem for about 15 percent of the population (Gillin, 1993; Mellinger et al., 1985). The elderly and women are more likely to suffer from insomnia than the young and men. Some of the more common causes of this disorder are daily hassles and life stress, physical illness or discomfort, loneliness, depression, jet lag, shifting work schedules, menopause, and drug abuse (Cacioppo et al., 2002). Although many insomniacs rely on sleeping pills and alcohol to alleviate insomnia, both reduce REM sleep and can cause lowered moods the next day (Pagel, 1994). Instead, sleep experts suggest the following guidelines for getting a good night's sleep (Empson, 1993; Hauri, 1992; Landolt et al., 1995; Morin et al., 1999):

1. Establish a solid circadian rhythm by going to bed and getting up on a regular schedule.
2. Do not take naps during the day, especially after a bad night's sleep.
3. Relax before going to bed and get into the habit of setting up presleep rituals such as soft music or a warm bath. A warm bath is not only relaxing, but it also promotes deep sleep by raising your core body temperature.
4. Greatly reduce or eliminate entirely the use of coffee, tea, or other sources of caffeine during the entire day because it affects sleep. Also, avoid alcohol, nicotine, and chocolate in the late afternoon and evening. Instead, drink a glass of milk before retiring, because it contains the sleep-inducing amino acid *tryptophan.*
5. Being very hungry or very full prior to retiring will disrupt sleep. Eating a light snack before going to bed will reduce nighttime restlessness and increase sleep time.
6. Regular exercise promotes slow-wave sleep, but do not exercise within three hours of bedtime because its arousing effect can delay sleep.
7. Condition yourself so that you associate your bed with sleeping. Thus, don't use your bed for anything but sleep and sex.
8. If you're still awake, but relaxed, after about 20 minutes, stay in bed. If you're anxious, get out of bed and do something relaxing, such as listening to soothing music or reading. Return when you feel sleepy. Still maintain your regular waking time.

Night terrors: A sleep disorder involving panic attacks that occur during early night stage 4 NREM sleep.

Sleepwalking: A sleep disorder in which a person arises and wanders about while remaining asleep.

Narcolepsy: A sleep disorder characterized by uncontrollable REM sleep attacks during normal waking hours.

Sleep apnea: A sleep disorder in which a person repeatedly stops breathing during sleep.

Insomnia: A common sleep disorder involving the chronic inability to fall or stay asleep.

KEY TERMS

activation-synthesis theory (p. 165)
alcoholism (p. 174)
alpha waves (p. 158)
altered state of consciousness (p. 166)
beta waves (p. 158)
circadian rhythms (p. 155)
consciousness (p. 152)
daydreaming (p. 154)
delta waves (p. 159)
depressants (p. 173)
dreams (p. 162)
drug abuse (p. 172)
fantasy-prone personality (p. 154)
hallucinogens (p. 173)

hypnosis (p. 167)
hypnotizability (p. 168)
insomnia (p. 180)
latent content (p. 164)
LSD (p. 176)
lucid dreams (p. 164)
manifest content (p. 164)
marijuana (p. 177)
meditation (p. 169)
narcolepsy (p. 180)
neodissociation theory (p. 169)
night terrors (p. 180)
off-line dream theory (p. 165)
opiates (p. 174)

problem-solving theory (p. 164)
psychoactive drugs (p. 172)
REM (rapid eye movement) sleep (p. 159)
selective attention (p. 152)
sleep (p. 155)
sleep apnea (p. 180)
sleep spindles (p. 159)
sleepwalking (p. 180)
stimulants (p. 173)
THC (p. 177)
theta waves (p. 158)
tolerance (p. 172)

REVIEW QUESTIONS

1. According to the author, consciousness
   a. can be shared with other people.
   b. requires that you focus on one specific thing.
   c. never changes.
   d. has only one level.
   e. is important for our survival.

2. Which of the following statements is *true*?
   a. Strategies to improve attention cannot be learned.
   b. Experience-sampling methods are used to study stream of consciousness.
   c. Research indicates few people daydream on a daily basis.
   d. There are no advantages to daydreaming.
   e. TV viewing appears to encourage more creative thinking.

3. Which of the following are diurnal mammals?
   a. humans
   b. owls
   c. bats
   d. opossum
   e. none of the above

4. The study of circadian rhythms
   a. indicates that humans drift toward a 25-hour cycle.
   b. used natural light.
   c. provides a valuable lesson in the way that the scientific method is self-correcting.
   d. discovered how to relieve insomnia.
   e. none of the above

5. Which part of the brain appears to be responsible for the body's sleep-wake cycle?
   a. hypothalamus
   b. suprachiasmatic nucleus
   c. pineal gland
   d. all of the above
   e. *a* and *b*

6. Which of the following statements is *true* about stages of sleep?
   a. You spend half your night at stage 1.
   b. It is difficult to arouse a person from sleep during stage 4.
   c. You only go through one sleep cycle a night.
   d. The first four stages make up REM sleep.
   e. Alpha waves are associated with an active, alert state of mind.

7. Which of the following statements describes a theory in this chapter about why we sleep?
   a. Sleep occurs due to the activation of the hippocampus in the brain.
   b. It allows the body to restore itself.
   c. Children aged 2 to 5 who fail to get sufficient sleep at night or during naps have greater behavior problems.
   d. all of the above
   e. *a* and *c*

8. Which of the following statements is *true* of dreaming?
  a. Dreams occur only during REM sleep.
  b. You cannot respond to external cues while dreaming.
  c. REM sleep does not appear to be important.
  d. All animals have REM sleep.
  e. In humans, REM sleep is greatest early in life.

9. In the student's "fish" dream, the latent content would be
  a. the struggle with the fish.
  b. the old woman.
  c. the lake.
  d. letting the fish go.
  e. none of the above

10. Which dream theory believes dreams have no particular significance other than they are by-products of brain activity?
  a. off-line dream
  b. problem-solving
  c. psychoanalytic
  d. activation-synthesis
  e. none of the above

11. Which of the following statements is *true* of hypnosis?
  a. Brain wave activity under hypnosis is radically different than during normal waking states.
  b. Hypnosis compels people to avoid deception.
  c. Everyone is hypnotizable.
  d. A hypnotized person tends to uncritically accept hallucinated experiences suggested by the hypnotist.
  e. Hypnotized people can be forced to violate their moral values.

12. Research on meditation has found
  a. high-amplitude alpha waves while meditating in accomplished meditators.
  b. that it is useful in promoting relaxation.
  c. that it reduces physiological arousal.
  d. a reduction in oxygen consumption, slower heart rate, and increased blood flow in the arms and forehead.
  e. all of the above

13. The most widely consumed and abused depressant in the world is
  a. opium.
  b. alcohol.
  c. morphine.
  d. heroin.
  e. caffeine.

14. Which of the following statements is *true*?
  a. There are no naturally occurring hallucinogens.
  b. LSD creates physical dependence after prolonged use.
  c. Seventy percent of American adults have tried marijuana at least once.
  d. Marijuana does not appear to have any negative effects when used in high quantities.
  e. All drug users become addicted.

15. Sleep disorders
  a. are among the most common psychological disorders.
  b. do not occur in children under age 5.
  c. occur only during NREM sleep.
  d. *a* and *b*
  e. none of the above

Learning

Chapter Outline

Dear Frederic,

Your very interesting letter has been read and discussed by mother and me. We naturally are deeply interested in your future.... In no circumstances would we want to say or do anything to discourage you in following out your ambition....

On the other hand, we want to give you the benefit of our observation and experience. You will find that the world is not standing with outstretched arms to greet you just because you are emerging from a college—that the real rough and tumble world is not the world pictured by college professors who are constantly dealing with the theoretical and not the practical affairs of life. I am yet to be convinced that it is possible for you to make a living as a writer of fiction.

... Let's go slow and sure.... Let us arrange some plan whereby you can support yourself, get married when the fever strikes you, have a good home life, and when these things are provided for, then go to it, and if your talents enable you to do something big and startle the world, no one of course will rejoice more than your mother and I, who have our whole life centered in you and your success.

With love,

Father

What do you want to do when *you* graduate? Fred wanted to be a famous writer. Following this letter from his father, Fred spent a year after college working on his writing skills. He even submitted samples of his writing to the poet Robert Frost, asking whether he should persevere in his chosen profession. Frost replied that the young man had twice as much talent as anyone else he had read that year, but that only Fred himself could know whether his future lay in writing. At the end of this yearlong odyssey, which he later called his "dark year," Fred was frustrated with writing and began casting about in search of an alternative career path. But what path should he choose?

The year was 1927. In his searching, Fred read psychologist John Watson's (1924) recently published book, *Behaviorism*. Watson presented a perspective on learning and the future of the young science of psychology that was novel for the time, in that his focus was not on people's internal states and unconscious drives, but on the outward behavior that people exhibit. Fred had always been interested in observing the behavior of people, a useful talent for a writer, and this approach to the human condition appealed to him. He applied and was accepted to Harvard University for graduate studies in psychology, where his own personal journey of discovery quickly became wedded to psychology's scientific discovery journey.

Although Fred never "startled the world" with his fiction writing, his subsequent extensions and refinements of Watson's behaviorism rocked the field of psychology and made him one of the best-known psychologists of all time. Outside his circle of family and friends, people knew and referred to Fred by his formal name, Burrhus Frederick ("B. F.") Skinner. Throughout his career, Skinner looked for ways in which his operant conditioning principles of learning (which are discussed in section 7-2) could be used to improve daily life.

In this segment of our journey of discovery, we will focus, as Skinner did, on the outward behavior that people (and other organisms) exhibit. We will review three basic learning perspectives: *classical conditioning, operant conditioning,* and *observational learning.* First, we will discuss classical conditioning, a type of learning in which one stimulus comes to serve as a signal for the occurrence of a second stimulus. Next, we will explore operant conditioning, a form of learning in which we discover the consequences of behav-

B. F. Skinner, 1904–1990

© Bettmann/CORBIS.

Learning is a treasure that will follow its owner everywhere.

—Chinese proverb

ior. Finally, we will investigate observational learning, which deals with how we learn by observing the behaviors—and the behavioral consequences—of those around us.

7-1 CLASSICAL CONDITIONING

In science, as in other areas of life, researchers sometimes need time to realize that they have actually discovered a new scientific principle. Would you believe that one discovery that profoundly shaped the course of psychology was initially only viewed as an annoyance?

7-1a Pavlov Stumbled upon Classical Conditioning

In 1904, Russian physiologist Ivan Pavlov (1849–1936) won the Nobel Prize for his research on digestion in dogs (Pavlov, 1997). In conducting his studies, Pavlov would place meat powder on a dog's tongue to elicit reflexive salivation. One thing he noticed was that, over time, dogs began salivating *before* any food reached their mouths and even before they smelled the food. For example, they might salivate simply by seeing the food dish or by merely hearing the feeder's approaching footsteps. At first, Pavlov considered this phenomenon an irritating development because he could no longer control the beginning of the dog's salivation. However, his annoyance turned into excitement when he realized that he had stumbled upon a simple but important form of learning, which came to be known as classical conditioning (Todes, 1997).

Ivan Pavlov, 1849–1936

Classical conditioning is a type of learning in which a neutral stimulus acquires the capacity to elicit a response after being paired with another stimulus that naturally elicits that response. In his experiments investigating classical conditioning, Pavlov would place a hungry dog in an apparatus similar to the one depicted in figure 7-1. Just before injecting meat powder into the dog's mouth, Pavlov would present an initially neutral stimulus to the dog, such as the ticking of a metronome.[1] At first, this ticking would produce no response in the dog. However, the food powder that was presented right after the ticking sound naturally triggered the dog's salivary reflex. Because this act of drooling was unlearned, Pavlov called it an **unconditioned response (UCR),** and he called the food that elicited this automatic response an **unconditioned stimulus (UCS).**

Although the neutral stimulus initially had no effect on the dog, after several pairings of metronome and food, the dog began to salivate in response to the ticking alone. It had *learned* to associate the ticking with the presentation of the food powder (see figure 7-2). This learned response was called the **conditioned response (CR),** and the previously neutral stimulus that now triggered the CR was called the **conditioned stimulus (CS).** One way to remember the difference between stimuli and responses that are either unconditioned or conditioned is to think of these two terms in the following manner: *un*conditioned = *un*learned; conditioned = learned. (See Discovery Box 7-1.)

Classical conditioning may not be what you think of as learning. For instance, you are not using classical conditioning principles to understand the important points in this chapter. The type of learning that goes on in classical conditioning is essentially "mindless" and automatic—you do not usually set out to learn an association, and you do not usually consciously elicit the conditioned response. Your pleasure (CR) upon seeing a good friend (CS) or your anxiety (CR) upon hearing a dentist's drill (CS) is not an

Classical conditioning: A type of learning in which a neutral stimulus acquires the capacity to elicit a response after being paired with another stimulus that naturally elicits that response.

Unconditioned response (UCR): In classical conditioning, the unlearned, automatic response to an unconditioned stimulus.

Unconditioned stimulus (UCS): In classical conditioning, a stimulus that naturally and automatically elicits an unconditioned response.

Conditioned response (CR): In classical conditioning, the learned response to a previously neutral conditioned stimulus.

Conditioned stimulus (CS): In classical conditioning, a previously neutral stimulus that, after repeated pairings with an unconditioned stimulus, comes to elicit a conditioned response.

---

1. One of the mistaken "facts" often reported in psychology textbooks is that Pavlov conditioned his dogs with the sound of a bell or a tuning fork. In reality, his early experiments, which formed the basis for the theory of classical conditioning, used a metronome (Hock, 1992, p. 68).

FIGURE 7-1
Pavlov's Apparatus for Studying Classical Conditioning in Dogs

Pavlov used a device similar to this in his experiments on classical conditioning. The dog was restrained in a harness, and a tube was attached to its salivary gland to allow accurate measurement of its salivation response. A ticking metronome was often used as the conditioned stimulus (CS), and the meat powder was used as the unconditioned stimulus (UCS). In classical conditioning terms, what type of response does the saliva represent when it occurred due to the presentation of the meat powder? What type of response does the saliva represent when it was triggered by the metronome?

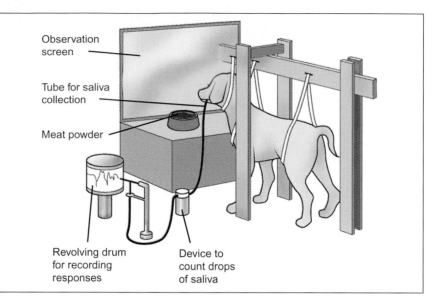

FIGURE 7-2
Classical Conditioning

Before classical conditioning, the neutral stimulus of the ticking metronome presented just before the unconditioned stimulus of the meat powder does not trigger salivation. Instead, the unconditioned response of salivation occurs only when the unconditioned stimulus is presented. However, during conditioning, through repeated pairings of the neutral stimulus and unconditioned stimulus, the neutral stimulus becomes a conditioned stimulus. Now, this conditioned stimulus produces a conditioned response.

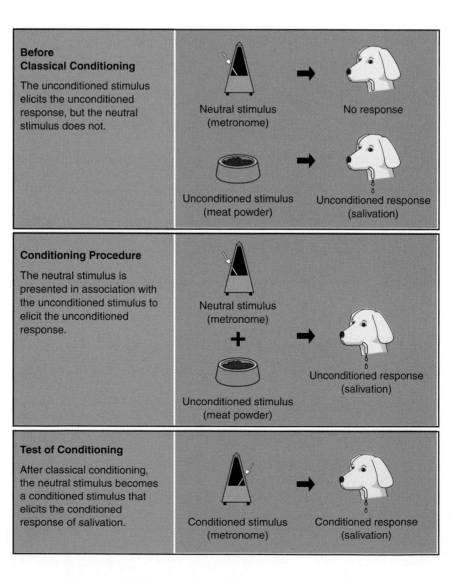

DISCOVERY BOX 7-1

Can You Classically Condition Your Own Eye-Blinking?

To experience a somewhat less arousing example of classical conditioning, try a variation of the demonstration from chapter 5 involving pupillary response to light (see section 5-2b). As you recall, when you turned out the light in your room for 30 seconds and then flicked it back on while gazing into a mirror, your pupils had become much larger in response to the lack of light. This is an example of an unconditioned response. Now, do the same demonstration, but just before turning out the light, ring a bell. Repeat the pairing of the neutral stimulus (the bell) with the unconditioned stimulus (the darkness) at least 20 times. Then, with the lights on, ring the bell while watching your eyes closely in the mirror. You should see your eyes dilate slightly even though the unconditioned stimulus is not present. The previously neutral bell sound has become the conditioned stimulus and your resulting pupil dilation is the conditioned response. Now you can truly say that classical conditioning does indeed ring a bell!

Due to the hundreds of studies that have investigated human classical eye-blink conditioning—generally conditioned by a puff of air to the eye rather than by a bell sound—scientists have almost completely identified the neural circuitry underlying this learned response (Thompson et al., 1997). Of what practical importance is this knowledge? Would you be surprised to learn that it is currently used to help determine the causes of such behavioral and brain pathologies as amnesia, mental retardation, autism, and degenerative diseases of the nervous system (Sears et al., 1994; Steinmetz, 1999)? These applications highlight how knowledge of a basic form of learning can be used to diagnose and hopefully treat serious illnesses.

intentionally learned response. They develop with no apparent effort on your part because both your friend's image and the drill noise have become associated with other stimuli that naturally evoke pleasure or pain.

Similar mindless learning permeates our lives and profoundly affects our everyday behavior, yet we often do not notice it because it is so automatic. In the sections that follow, we examine some of the principles of classical conditioning that may influence your daily life.

7-1b There Are Six Important Principles of Classical Conditioning

Besides identifying the basic mechanisms of classical conditioning, Pavlov and his coworkers also discovered six important conditioning principles: *acquisition, higher-order conditioning, stimulus generalization, stimulus discrimination, extinction,* and *spontaneous recovery*. While learning about these principles, keep in mind the following general rule about classical conditioning: A previously neutral stimulus will lead to a conditioned response whenever it provides the organism with information about the upcoming occurrence of the unconditioned stimulus (Rescorla, 1992; Rescorla & Wagner, 1972). If a metronome always ticks (CS) just before the presentation of food (UCS), the dog will begin salivating (CR) whenever the metronome ticks (CS). Conditioning occurs because the ticking provides the dog with information that food will soon be delivered.

Acquisition

How quickly and in what manner does the **acquisition,** or initial learning, of a conditioned response occur? Pavlov discovered that conditioned responses seldom occur at full strength right away (a phenomenon known as *one-trial learning*), but rather, gradually build up over a series of trials. Based on this finding, psychologists initially believed that the key to acquiring a conditioned response was the sheer *number* of CS-UCS pairings. Subsequent research, however, indicated that the *order* and *timing* of the CS-UCS pairings is also very important (Buhusi & Schmajuk, 1999; Wasserman & Miller, 1997).

Regarding order of presentation, learning seldom occurs when the CS comes after (*backward conditioning*) or at the same time as (*simultaneous conditioning*) the UCS. Instead, conditioning generally occurs only when the CS comes *before* the UCS (*forward conditioning*). This finding is consistent with the hypothesis that classical conditioning is biologically adaptive because it prepares the organism for good or bad events in the immediate future. In other words, the CS becomes a *signal* that a UCS is about to be presented. Prior to conditioning, the organism's response is dictated by the UCS appearing. However, after conditioning, the organism responds more quickly because it is now reacting to the earlier-occurring CS, not the later-occurring UCS. These quicker conditioned responses often spell the difference between life and death. For example, in the case of animals reacting to a predator's attack, those animals with prior predator experiences are more likely to quickly respond when stimuli associated with the predator (its sight, sound, or smell, for instance) are presented. Through experience, the animals that have been conditioned to respond to stimuli *preceding* the UCS are most likely to survive. Can you think of instances in your own life where conditioned responses may foster your survival?

Besides presentation order, in most cases, the UCS must follow the CS *closely in time*. In animal research, the most efficient CS-UCS interval is between 0.2 and 2 seconds. If the interval is longer, the CR is more difficult to establish because animals have difficulty recognizing it as a signal for the appearance of the UCS.

In addition to presentation order and timing of the CS-UCS pairings, the *accuracy* with which the appearance of the UCS can be predicted by the CS will also determine whether a conditioned response is formed. If the UCS reliably follows the CS but also occurs when the CS is not present, a conditioned response is unlikely to develop. For example, in one experiment (Rescorla, 1968), rats were presented with a tone (CS), followed by a mild electric shock (UCS) that caused them to jump (UCR). In one condition, the shock was given only after the tone. Very quickly, these rats began displaying a fear response, freezing (CR), after hearing the tone. In another condition, however, the shock was given both after the tone and also during times when the tone had not been presented. These rats displayed little, if any, freezing in anticipation of the coming shock. Why do you think this group of rats did not become conditioned to the tone? Because their ability to prepare for the UCS could not be accurately predicted by this event. In other words, it was a poor signal of the coming shock and thus was not used by the rats to predict its appearance. These findings are consistent with the previously stated rule that a stimulus will become "conditioned" whenever it signals to the organism that an unconditioned stimulus is about to occur.

Once a stimulus is disregarded as a poor signal for an upcoming event, it can be hard to learn a new association between the two stimuli. In a study similar to the preceding one, researchers first presented tones and shocks to rats in a random order, so that the tone did not serve as a signal of an upcoming shock (Nakajima et al., 2000). Then the researchers changed the order of presentation so that a shock always followed the tone. Because the tone was now a signal, wouldn't you expect the rats to learn the association and freeze when they heard the tone? Interestingly, they did not. Having once learned that the tone provided no information, the animals had difficulty later detecting a real association, a phenomenon called *general learned irrelevance* (Linden et al., 1997).

Overall, research on the acquisition of conditioned responses tells us that organisms are not passive in this process. They actively seek information in their environment to establish when certain events (CS) predict the occurrence of other events (UCS).

Higher-Order Conditioning

In addition to discovering how a neutral stimulus can become a conditioned stimulus, Pavlov (1927) also learned that a conditioned stimulus can be used to condition another neutral stimulus. This procedure, known as **higher-order conditioning,** greatly increases the number of situations in which classical conditioning might explain behavior. For example, do you know people who become so anxious upon entering a classroom to take an exam that it interferes with their ability to concentrate? Such anxiety is often due to higher-order conditioning. Early in their schooling, academic performance may have been a neutral event for them. However, somehow it became associated with criticism (UCS) from parents or teachers, which elicited anxiety (UCR). Through conditioning, then, academic performance (CS) acquired the ability to trigger a stress response (CR). As these people continued taking exams, this conditioned stimulus began functioning like a UCS through higher-order conditioning. That is, previously neutral stimuli immediately preceding test-taking—such as walking into a testing room or hearing test booklets being passed out—became conditioned stimuli that also elicited test anxiety. In chapter 11, I will discuss how to break this unpleasant kind of higher-order conditioning.

Fortunately, higher-order conditioning is equally effective in eliciting pleasant responses. For example, your cologne may spark romantic feelings in those who associate the fragrance with past loves. Likewise, complete strangers may respond warmly upon discovering that you are from their hometown. In both instances, a previously neutral stimulus (you) becomes a conditioned stimulus after being paired with an existing conditioned stimulus (cologne and hometown). As you see, higher-order conditioning can shape a variety of advantageous—and disadvantageous—responses. With this knowledge, are you developing a greater appreciation—perhaps, even affection—for classical conditioning principles?

> **Higher-order conditioning:** A classical conditioning procedure in which a neutral stimulus becomes a conditioned stimulus after being paired with an existing conditioned stimulus.

Stimulus Generalization

Another observation made by Pavlov was that a response triggered by the conditioned stimulus tends to generalize to other, similar stimuli. This is called **stimulus generalization.** Such generalization often fosters an organism's survival, as when a bird that becomes sick after eating a poisonous Monarch butterfly avoids eating other orange and black insects. This reaction makes good adaptive sense: Things that look, taste, feel, or sound the same often share other important characteristics. The more similar new stimuli are to the original conditioned stimulus, the greater likelihood of generalization (Balsam, 1988). Stimulus generalization may explain why you sometimes respond very warmly or coldly to strangers who look like people for whom you previously developed either positive or negative conditioned responses. In such instances, you may not realize that your emotional response is caused by the power of stimulus generalization, but it nonetheless has an impact on your social life. (See Discovery Box 7-2.)

> **Stimulus generalization:** In classical conditioning, the tendency for a conditioned response to be elicited by stimuli similar to the conditioned stimulus.

Stimulus Discrimination

When an organism gives a conditioned response to the conditioned stimulus but not to stimuli that are similar to it, you have the opposite of stimulus generalization, namely, **stimulus discrimination.** Like generalization, discrimination has survival value because slightly different stimuli can have very different consequences (Thomas, 1992). Generally, our natural tendency is to generalize, and we need experience to teach us to discriminate. This greater tendency to generalize explains why Albert in Discovery Box 7-2 reacted to the other furry objects in the same way that he had been conditioned to react to the white rat. If he had somehow been encouraged to directly experience the fact that the unconditioned stimulus did not follow the presentation of these other objects, he would have developed stimulus discrimination.

> **Stimulus discrimination:** In classical conditioning, the tendency for a conditioned response not to be elicited by stimuli similar to the conditioned stimulus.

DISCOVERY BOX 7-2

Can Fear Be Learned through Stimulus Generalization?

In 1920, John Watson, the founder of behaviorism (see chapter 1, section 1-2d), and his colleague, Rosalie Rayner, conducted the best-known study of stimulus generalization. Their subject was a 9-month-old boy whom they identified as "Little Albert B." During initial testing, Watson and Rayner presented Albert with a white rat, a rabbit, a monkey, a dog, masks with and without hair, and white cotton wool. The boy's reaction was one of interest and no fear.

Two months later, while Albert sat on a mattress placed on a table, the researchers presented him with the white rat. Just as Albert touched the rat, however, Watson made a loud noise behind him by striking a 4-foot steel bar with a hammer. This noise (the UCS) startled and frightened (the UCR) the toddler. During two sessions, spaced 1 week apart, this procedure was repeated a total of seven times. Each time, the pairing of the rat and noise resulted in a fear response. Next, the rat was presented to Albert alone, without the noise. As I'm sure you've guessed, he reacted to the rat (the CS) with extreme fear (the CR): He cried, turned away, rolled over on one side away from the rat, and began crawling away so fast that he almost went over the edge of the table before the researchers caught hold of him! Five days later, Albert showed stimulus generalization to a white rabbit:

> Negative responses began at once. He leaned as far away from the animal as possible, whimpered, then burst into tears. When the rabbit was placed in contact with him, he buried his face in the mattress, then got up on all fours and crawled away, crying as he went. (Watson & Rayner, 1920, p. 6)

In addition to the rabbit, Albert's fear response also generalized to a dog, a white fur coat, Watson's own head of gray hair, and even a Santa Claus mask! These fear responses also occurred outside the room in which the conditioned response had initially been learned. Two months later, just prior to Albert being adopted, he was tested one last time and again expressed considerable fear toward the same objects.

In addition to demonstrating stimulus generalization, an equally important reason this study is still widely discussed today is due to the serious ethical issues it raises. Essentially, Watson and Rayner induced a phobia in Albert, something that would not be tolerated by current ethical standards of psychological research. Further, the researchers made no attempt to recondition their young subject, despite knowing a month in advance that Albert's mother would be leaving the area with him. Later attempts to locate Albert to determine the long-lasting effects of his experience failed (Harris, 2002), and, as far as anyone knows, no reconditioning ever took place.

Extinction and Spontaneous Recovery

What do you think happens when a CS occurs repeatedly without the UCS? The answer is **extinction**, which is the gradual weakening and disappearance of the conditioned response. In Pavlov's experiments, when the ticking metronome (CS) was repeatedly presented to the dog without the delivery of food (UCS), the metronome gradually lost its ability to elicit salivation (CR).

This principle of extinction has been used to treat cocaine abuse, a stimulant drug (UCS) that naturally induces a sense of euphoria (UCR) in users. One problem recovering drug users must overcome is the familiar reminders associated with their addiction.

Extinction: In classical conditioning, the gradual weakening and disappearance of the conditioned response when the conditioned stimulus is repeatedly presented without being paired with the unconditioned stimulus.

Anything that has been repeatedly associated with past drug use—such as certain locations, smells, or objects—becomes a conditioned stimulus that can elicit a craving for the drug (Bonson et al., 2002). Because drug addicts use money to obtain cocaine, in one treatment program, researchers attempted to weaken the conditioned link between money and cocaine-induced euphoria by asking addicts to engage in one of two activities under the guise of a "budgetary task" (Hamilton et al., 1997). One group of addicts was given $500 in cash to hold in their hands as they explained how they would spend it, while the other group was asked to merely imagine that they had the money. Those addicts who held the actual cash initially reported a stronger craving for cocaine after handling the money than the group who imagined the money. However, repeated exposure to the cash without it being associated with cocaine use gradually reduced drug craving, as would be expected due to extinction. These results suggest that applying the principle of extinction in drug treatment programs can enhance their effectiveness.

Although you undoubtedly remember instances of conditioned responses becoming extinct in your own life, have you also noticed that occasionally a response that you thought was long ago extinguished reappears spontaneously when you happen to encounter the conditioned stimulus? This phenomenon, known as **spontaneous recovery,** is the reappearance of an extinguished response after a period of nonexposure to the conditioned stimulus. For example, former soldiers, who long ago overcame the panic attacks they experienced during combat, may later reexperience acute anxiety while viewing a movie with graphic war scenes. The practical importance of spontaneous recovery is that even if you succeed in ridding yourself of a conditioned response, it may surprise you by reappearing later.

> **Spontaneous recovery:**
> The reappearance of an extinguished response after a period of nonexposure to the conditioned stimulus.

7-1c Animals Differ in What Responses Can Be Classically Conditioned

Pavlov and other early learning theorists assumed that the principles of conditioning were similar across all species, and thus, psychologists could just as easily study rats and pigeons as people. In addition, they further assumed that associations could be conditioned between any stimulus an organism could perceive and any response it could make. Research conducted during the past 35 years indicates that neither of these assumptions is correct. Not only do animals often differ in what responses can be conditioned, but also some responses can be conditioned much more readily to certain stimuli than to others. The essential insight gained from this research is that an animal's biology steers it toward certain kinds of conditioning that enhances its survival (Hollis, 1997).

Taste Aversion

One of the most dramatic examples of a behavior being more easily conditioned by certain stimuli than others is *taste aversion*. If you have ever experienced food poisoning, you are undoubtedly familiar with this concept. When you consumed the food that ultimately made you sick, there were probably many things going on around you besides the taste of the food. But if you are like most people, the lesson you learned was to avoid whatever food you had eaten, and not (for example) the people you were talking to or the show you were watching on TV. Why is this so? Let us consider the results of an animal study that helps us better understand this behavior.

Journey of Discovery Question

Every year, thousands of drug users die from overdoses. Those who have narrowly survived such overdoses tend to report that the setting in which they took the drug that caused the problem was different from their normal drug-taking environment (Siegel, 1984). How might classical conditioning principles explain why these different settings were more likely to be associated with drug overdoses?

In a classic study of taste aversion, John Garcia and Robert Koelling (1966) allowed two groups of thirsty rats to drink flavored water from a device that produced a light flash and a loud click whenever they drank. Thus, both rat groups experienced a taste, a light, and a noise simultaneously. While they were drinking, the two groups also received a UCS: Group A received electrical shocks to their feet that immediately produced pain, while Group B received radiation in X rays that made them nauseous about 1 hour later.

According to traditional classical conditioning principles, a conditioned response occurs only if the unconditioned stimulus follows the conditioned stimulus within a very short interval. Based on this knowledge, wouldn't you predict that Group A should learn to avoid the flavored water, the light, and the sound because all three sensations immediately preceded their literally shocking UCS? Wouldn't you also predict that Group B should not learn to avoid any of these same sensations because the effects of their UCS—the radiation—were not felt until much later? As you can see from figure 7-3, what happened was something very different. Garcia and Koelling found that the rats exposed to the immediately painful shocks (Group A) learned to avoid the light and noise, but not the flavored water. In contrast, rats exposed to the delayed nausea of the radiation (Group B) learned to avoid the flavored water, but not the light and noise.

If you were the researchers, how would you explain these findings? Why would the rats have been conditioned to associate the shocks with the light and noise, but not the flavored water? Why would nausea become associated with any stimulus that preceded it so far in advance? And why did the rats learn to associate the nausea with the flavored water, but not the light and noise?

Garcia and Koelling argued that these constraints on learning were by-products of the rats' evolutionary history. Through the process of adapting to their environment, rats—like all other creatures—evolved to learn those things crucial to their survival. The sudden pain of a shock is more likely to be caused by an external stimulus than by something the rat ingests, so it is not surprising that rats are predisposed to associate shock with a sight or a sound. Similarly, nausea is more likely to be caused by something the rat drinks or eats than by some external stimulus. Thus, it makes evolutionary sense that rats are predisposed to associate nausea with a taste. It is also adaptive that in taste aversion, strong

FIGURE 7-3
Biological Constraints on Taste Aversion in Rats

Rats learned to avoid a light-noise combination when it was paired with electric shock, but not when it was followed by X rays that made them nauseous. In contrast, rats quickly learned to avoid flavored water when it was followed by X rays, but they did not readily acquire an aversion to this same water when it was followed by shock. How might these constraints on learning be by-products of the rats' evolutionary history?

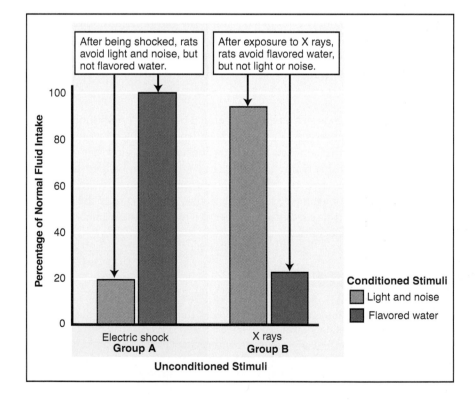

conditioning develops despite the long delay between the CS (the taste) and the UCS (the nausea). Animals biologically equipped to associate taste stimuli with illness that occurs minutes or even hours later are more likely to survive and pass their genes on to the next generation (Seligman, 1970).

With this newfound insight into conditioned taste aversion, Garcia applied this knowledge to a practical problem: controlling predators' attacks on ranchers' livestock (Garcia et al., 1977; Gustafson et al., 1974). In one study, captured wolves were fed sheep carcasses containing lithium chloride (UCS), a chemical that causes severe nausea and vomiting (UCR). After recovering from this very unpleasant experience, these same hungry predators were placed in a pen with a live sheep. At first, the wolves moved toward the sheep (CS) in attack postures. However, as soon as they smelled their prey, they backed off and avoided further contact (CR). Based on this research, today, many ranchers condition potential predators to avoid their herds by depositing lithium chloride-injected livestock carcasses near their herds. This same strategy also is used by conservationists to condition predators to avoid killing endangered species (Nicolaus & Nellis, 1987).

In a very different context, this knowledge has been applied in combating the negative effects of chemotherapy in cancer patients. During treatment, many patients lose a great deal of weight because they become nauseous when eating their normal diet. In studying this side effect, researchers discovered that it was partly due to patients eating meals prior to going in for therapy, resulting in this food (the CS) becoming classically conditioned to the nausea-producing chemotherapy (the UCS). To make such conditioning less likely, patients were told to fast before their therapy sessions to decrease the likelihood of establishing an association between food and illness. Researchers also discovered that taste aversions are more likely to develop for *unusual* rather than usual tastes (Bernstein, 1978; Broberg & Bernstein, 1987). This is so not only because usual tastes are subject to general learned irrelevance, but also because a new stimulus in your surroundings that is present about the same time as an unpleasant sensation (nausea) suggests that it is a good signal—or "cause"—of that unpleasantness.

Can you guess how they used this knowledge to develop two other useful strategies? (Hint: The key was *what* patients ate before each treatment session.) In one strategy, patients were encouraged to eat the same bland foods before every treatment. Because these foods were not part of their regular diet, if they developed a taste aversion to them, it would not adversely affect their eating habits. In the other strategy, just before receiving treatment, patients were given an unusual flavor of candy so that if they did form a taste aversion, it would more likely be to this candy rather than to their normal diet. In

---

INFO-BIT: Chemotherapy drugs are given to cancer patients to inhibit the growth of new cancer cells, but they also inhibit the growth of immune cells, which weakens our body's ability to fight off illnesses. These drugs are typically given to patients in the same room in the same hospital. Due to this fact, is it possible that these patients' immune systems become classically conditioned to negatively react in advance to stimuli in the hospital? Apparently, yes. In a study of women undergoing treatment for ovarian cancer, researchers found that, following several chemotherapy sessions, their immune systems were weakened as soon as they entered the hospital—in anticipation of the treatment (Bovbjerg et al., 1990). The hospital setting had become a conditioned stimulus, causing an inhibition of cellular activity. Armed with this knowledge, researchers are now investigating whether they can also strengthen the immune system through classical conditioning. Initial results are encouraging (Ramirez-Amaya & Bermudez-Rattoni, 1999). For example, after repeatedly pairing the taste of sherbet with shots of adrenaline—which naturally increases activity and growth in certain immune cells—researchers found that the presentation of the sherbet alone later caused an increase in people's immune response (Buske-Kirschbaum et al., 1994). These findings raise the encouraging possibility that the medical profession may be able to use classical conditioning to help fight immune-related diseases such as cancer and AIDS.

both strategies, then, patients eat something other than their usual diet just before receiving the treatment that makes them nauseous. The first strategy attempts to avoid any taste aversion from developing at all by using bland foods with few taste cues, while the second strategy introduces a new, easily recognizable—and easily discardable—taste cue that is most likely to form an association with the impending nausea.

Phobias

People who are injured in car accidents sometimes develop an intense fear of riding in all cars. These exaggerated and irrational fears of objects or situations are known as *phobias* and are discussed more extensively in chapter 13, section 13-3a. Such intense fear reactions often develop through classical conditioning (Schneider et al., 1999). Although we can develop a phobia toward anything, there is evidence that some objects or situations more easily elicit phobic reactions. For instance, people tend to develop phobias for snakes and heights quite easily, but they seldom develop phobias for knives and electrical outlets, even though these objects are often associated with painful experiences (Kleinknecht, 1991; LoLordo & Droungas, 1989). Evolutionary theorists contend that the reason people more easily develop phobias for certain objects or situations is because they once posed a real danger to our ancestors (Buss, 1995; Seligman, 1971). During that time, those individuals whose genetic makeup allowed them to quickly learn to avoid such hazards were more likely to survive and reproduce. According to this perspective, then, the reason snakes and heights make many of us unduly anxious in our modern world is because the genes that trigger such anxiety are still part of our genetic makeup.

In our modern world, fear of snakes serves very little adaptive function because very few of us are at risk of dying from poisonous snake bites. So why do we still carry the tendency to fear snakes? One reason is the time scale of evolution. Evolutionary changes are noticeable not in a single generation, or a few generations, but over hundreds of generations. A second reason is that evolutionary pressures will not remove fear of snakes until, over the long term, the fear becomes an actual *disadvantage* (Buss et al., 1998). If it is merely neutral—an annoying holdover from prehistoric times, with no effect on reproductive success—it may remain part of the human condition. In other words, the fact that something is passed on through the generations implies nothing about its value in current society.

SECTION SUMMARY

- Classical conditioning explains how organisms learn that certain events signal the presence or absence of other events; such knowledge helps them prepare for future events.
- A neutral stimulus will lead to a conditioned response whenever it provides information about the upcoming occurrence of the unconditioned stimulus.
- Conditioned responses usually gradually develop over a series of presentations.
- Higher-order conditioning is a procedure in which a conditioned stimulus is used to condition another neutral stimulus.
- Stimulus generalization is a conditioned response being elicited by stimuli similar to the conditioned stimulus.
- Stimulus discrimination is a conditioned response not being elicited by other stimuli.
- An animal's biology steers it toward certain kinds of conditioning that enhances its survival.

Chapter 7 *Learning* **195**

7-2 OPERANT CONDITIONING

The type of learning that occurs due to classical conditioning helps you prepare for future events, but it seldom allows you to change those events. Thus, when Little Albert saw a white furry animal (the CS), he began crying (CR) in anticipation of hearing a frightening sound (UCS), but his crying could not control the presentation of either the CS or UCS. Now, let us examine another type of learning in which you do learn that your actions, rather than conditioned stimuli, produce consequences.

7-2a Operant Behavior Is Largely Voluntary, Goal Directed, and Controlled by Its Consequences

A few years before Pavlov began watching hungry dogs salivate after being presented with food and a ticking metronome, American psychologist Edward L. Thorndike (1898)—a student of William James—was observing hungry cats trying to escape from a "puzzle box" to reach a bowl of food. To escape, the cats had to press a lever (the response), which, in turn, lifted a gate that allowed access to the food (the stimulus). Through trial and error, Thorndike's cats learned the correct behavior to reach the food.

The Law of Effect

How was the learning of Thorndike's cats different from the learning of Pavlov's dogs? In classical conditioning, an organism's behavior is largely determined by stimuli that *precede* it. In Pavlov's experiments, food caused the dogs to salivate. However, in Thorndike's research, behavior was influenced by stimuli that *followed* it. In addition, classical conditioning involves the learning of associations between stimuli, and the organism exerts little influence over the environment; in contrast, Thorndike's cats learned an association between behavior and its consequences and actively created a change in the environment. The cats learned to associate a response (lever pressing) with a subsequent desirable consequence (food). Gradually, the behavior that produced these desirable consequences increased in frequency and became the dominant response when the cats were placed in the puzzle box. Thorndike (1911) called this relationship between behavior and its consequences the **law of effect because** behavior becomes more or less likely based on the *effect* it has in producing desirable or undesirable consequences.

> **Law of effect:** A basic principle of learning that states that behavior becomes more or less likely based on the *effect* it has in producing desirable or undesirable consequences.

You can see how the law of effect would be very useful to survival. Evolution works by selecting those individuals whose behavior best promotes survival in their given environment. Those animals that repeat behavior that is followed by desirable consequences and terminate behavior followed by undesirable consequences (if the consequences didn't terminate the animals first) would be most likely to profit from experience with their environment, and thus, survive and reproduce.

Although Thorndike's law of effect is considered a fundamental principle of learning, it was not at first accepted by the scientific community (Iversen, 1992). Fortunately for Thorndike and psychology, in the 1930s, former frustrated writer and now new psychologist B. F. Skinner elaborated on the law of effect and made it the cornerstone for his influential theory of learning, which he called **operant conditioning.** Skinner used the term *operant conditioning* because the organism's behavior is *operating* on the

> **Operant conditioning:** A type of learning in which behavior is strengthened if followed by reinforcement and weakened if followed by punishment.

Experience is a good school, but the fees are high.

—Heinrich Heine, German poet, 1797–1856

FIGURE 7-4
Skinner Box

In studying operant conditioning, Skinner designed an apparatus, which came to be known as a "Skinner box," in which animals learned to obtain food or avoid shocks by operating on their environment within the box. In the Skinner box designed for rats depicted here, the animal learns to press the bar to obtain food pellets, which are delivered into the box down the pellet tube. If the introduction of the food pellets increases bar-pressing, what is the technical term for these pellets? The speaker and light allow the experimenter to manipulate visual and auditory stimuli, while the electric floor grid allows the experimenter control over aversive consequences (shock). Skinner also designed a new kind of bassinet for human babies, known as the "heir conditioner," and raised one of his daughters, Deborah, in it for over 2 years, leading to the false rumor that he raised her in a Skinner box. Also contrary to the false rumor that Deborah was permanently scarred by being the "baby in the box," she grew up to become a successful artist and remembers her childhood fondly.

> **Reinforcement:** The process by which a stimulus *increases* the probability of the behavior that it follows.
>
> **Reinforcer:** Any stimulus or event that *increases* the likelihood that the behavior preceding it will be repeated.

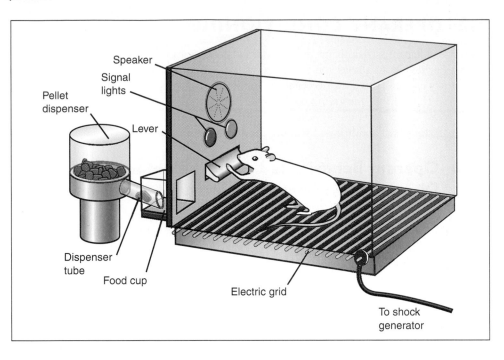

environment to achieve some desired goal.[2] Operant behavior is largely *voluntary* and *goal directed* and is controlled by its *consequences*. Thus, when a rat presses a bar in a Skinner box (see figure 7-4), it does so because it has learned that bar-pressing will lead to food pellets. Likewise, when my daughters clean their rooms, they choose to engage in this behavior because they have learned that it will provide them with something highly valued, namely, permission to play with friends.

7-2b A Reinforcer Increases the Probability of the Behavior It Follows

As you have seen, people and other animals tend to repeat behaviors that are followed by desirable consequences. This fundamental principle of behaviorism—that rewarded behavior is likely to be repeated—is known as the concept of **reinforcement**. A **reinforcer** is any stimulus or event that increases the likelihood that the behavior preceding it will be repeated. A reinforcer may be a concrete reward, such as food, money, or attention. For example, if people laugh and pay attention to you when you tell a joke, their response is likely to make your joke-telling more likely in the future. A reinforcer could also be an activity, such as allowing children to play with friends after they clean their rooms.

How do you know whether something is a reinforcer? Simple. Observe whether it increases the behavior it follows. While "friend play" reinforces my daughters' room cleaning, I have learned that allowing them to watch a football game on television with me is not a reinforcer. Sometimes, the same stimulus is a reinforcer in one situation, but not in another. For example, whereas laughter may reinforce joke-telling, my sister's laughter while teaching me to dance years ago certainly did not increase my desire to get on the dance floor! Likewise, a stimulus may be a reinforcer for one animal, but not for another. Do you think the food pellets that rats in a Skinner box work so hard to obtain would be a reinforcer for you? The lesson to be learned here is that something is a reinforcer not because of what it is, but rather, because of what it does.

---

2. Thorndike had previously called this learning *instrumental conditioning* because the behavior is *instrumental* in obtaining rewards.

Primary Versus Secondary Reinforcers

How does a stimulus become a reinforcer? Actually, some stimuli are innately reinforcing, whereas others become reinforcing through learning. **Primary reinforcers** are innately reinforcing because they satisfy some biological need. Food, water, warmth, sex, physical activity, novel stimulation, and sleep are all examples of primary reinforcers. In contrast, **secondary reinforcers** are learned and become reinforcing by being associated with a primary reinforcer. Does this sound familiar? It should because this learning involves classical conditioning. Through classical conditioning, a neutral stimulus becomes a conditioned stimulus (in our case, a secondary reinforcer) by being repeatedly paired with an unconditioned stimulus (the primary reinforcer) that naturally evokes an unconditioned response. An example of a secondary reinforcer is money. You value money because it has been repeatedly associated with a host of primary reinforcers, such as food, shelter, and entertainment. Likewise, attention becomes a secondary reinforcer for children because it is paired with primary reinforcers from adults, such as protection, warmth, food, and water. Other powerful secondary reinforcers are praise and success. Thus, an important element in operant conditioning—namely, secondary reinforcers—comes into existence not through operant conditioning, but through classical conditioning.

> **Primary reinforcers:** Stimuli that are innately reinforcing because they satisfy some biological need.
>
> **Secondary reinforcers:** Stimuli that are learned and become reinforcing by being associated with primary reinforcers.

Positive and Negative Reinforcers

The examples used thus far to describe reinforcers are known as **positive reinforcers:** They strengthen a response by presenting a positive stimulus after a response. Another type of reinforcer is a **negative reinforcer,** which strengthens a response by *removing* an aversive or unpleasant stimulus after a response. Although negative reinforcement sounds like it means reinforcing behavior with a negative consequence, in fact it refers to removing something from the environment. (Negative consequences are a form of punishment, which is discussed in section 7-2e.) In a Skinner box, a moderate electric shock administered through the floor grid often serves as a negative reinforcer. When the rat presses the bar, the shock is turned off. The removal of the shock strengthens the bar-pressing behavior.

Just as the rat learns that it can end an unpleasant sensation by responding in a specific way, you too have learned certain responses to escape negative reinforcers. The cold weather you avoid by going indoors is a negative reinforcer. Your parents nagging you to take out the garbage or to turn down the stereo are negative reinforcers. When you respond in the correct fashion, the noxious stimulus (the cold temperature or the nagging) is terminated. Similarly, when you clean your smelly refrigerator, the removal of the foul odor is also a negative reinforcer: It strengthens refrigerator cleaning in the future.

> **Positive reinforcers:** Stimuli that strengthen a response by presenting a positive stimulus after a response.
>
> **Negative reinforcers:** Stimuli that strengthen a response by *removing* an aversive or unpleasant stimulus after a response.

7-2c Different Reinforcement Schedules Lead to Different Learning and Performance Rates

Thus far in our description of the learning that occurs in operant conditioning, there has been an underlying assumption that every response is followed by a reinforcer. Although such **continuous reinforcement** leads to the fastest learning, in most instances of daily living, we are not reinforced for every response.

The biggest problem with continuous reinforcement is that when it ends, extinction occurs rapidly. For example, what happens when you put money into a vending machine and do not receive a soda? You might respond by inserting more coins, but if that still does not lead to the desired beverage, you do not continue to pump money into the machine, do you? It is unlikely because behavior that is regulated by continuous reinforcement is easily extinguished. The same is not true for responses that are reinforced only some of the time. Did you stop going to movies, visiting friends, or eating food because you had a few experiences that were not rewarding? You persist in many activities even though you are reinforced only intermittently. Thus, although continuous reinforcement allows you to *acquire* responses most quickly, once responses have been learned, **partial reinforcement**

> **Continuous reinforcement:** A schedule of reinforcement in which every correct response is followed by a reinforcer.

> **Partial reinforcement:** A schedule of reinforcement in which correct responses are followed by reinforcers only part of the time.

FIGURE 7-5
Schedules of Reinforcement

As shown in the graph, the predictability of fixed-ratio schedules leads to a high rate of responding, with brief pauses after each reinforcer is delivered. In contrast, the unpredictability of variable-ratio schedules leads to high, steady rates of responding, with few pauses between reinforcers. The predictability of fixed-interval schedules leads to a low rate of responding until the fixed interval of time approaches, and then the rate of responding increases rapidly until the reinforcer is delivered; then a low rate of responding resumes. In contrast, the unpredictability of variable-interval schedules produces a moderate, but steady, rate of responding.

Fixed-ratio schedules: Partial reinforcement schedules that reinforce a response after a specified number of nonreinforced responses.

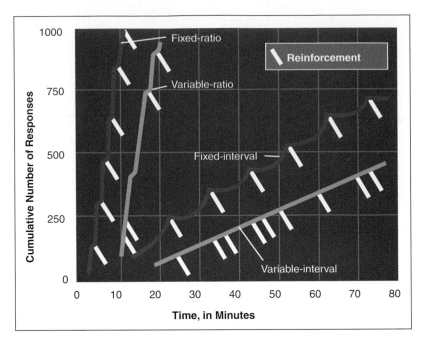

has an important effect on your continued *performance*. Being reinforced only once in a while keeps you responding vigorously for longer periods of time than does continuous reinforcement (Humphreys, 1939).

Skinner and his colleagues identified and studied several partial reinforcement schedules (Ferster & Skinner, 1957; Skinner, 1938). *Partial schedules* are defined in terms of number of responses or the passage of time. *Ratio schedules* mean that the first response after a specified number of responses is reinforced. *Interval schedules* mean that the first response after a specified time period is reinforced. In addition, some partial schedules are strictly *fixed*, while others are unpredictably *variable*.

Fixed-ratio schedules reinforce behavior after a specified number of responses. For example, students may be given a prize after reading 20 books, or factory workers may be paid a certain amount of money for every 40 machinery pieces they assemble (a system known as "piecework"). The students read their first 19 books without reinforcement, as do the workers with their first 39 machinery pieces, because they know the payoff will occur when the last book or piece is completed in the ratio. When people and animals are placed on a fixed-ratio reinforcement schedule, it produces high response rates, with only brief pauses following reinforcement (see figure 7-5)

Why do you think people and animals on fixed-ratio schedules take such short breaks before working again on their tasks? Because resting reduces rewards. In industry, this schedule is popular with management because it produces high productivity. However, it is unpopular with workers because it produces stress and fatigue. You might wonder why these employees do not exercise some self-restraint and simply slow down. According to behaviorists, this is unlikely because the source of control over their actions lies largely in the environment, not in the individual. They work themselves to exhaustion simply and solely because the fixed-ratio schedule reinforces energetic responding. The only way to reduce fatigue is to somehow turn off the reinforcement schedule eliciting these high response rates (Appel, 1963). Fortunately for workers, many employee unions in the United States, Canada, and Europe have done just that: They have pressured management to replace the fixed-ratio piecework pay with a fixed-interval hourly wage (Schwartz & Robbins, 1995).

Although fixed-ratio schedules are more resistant to extinction than continuous reinforcement, the person or animal will stop responding soon after reinforcement stops. Why? Because when the reinforcer is not delivered after the required number of responses, it quickly becomes apparent that something about the schedule has changed.

What happens when a ratio schedule is not fixed, but varies? That is, a reinforcer may be delivered after the first response on trial 1, after the fourth response on trial 2, after the ninth response on trial 3, and so on. The average ratio may be one reinforcer after every six trials, but the responder never knows how many responses are needed to obtain the reinforcer on any given trial. Schedules like this that reinforce a response after a variable number of nonreinforced responses are known as **variable-ratio schedules.** As you can see in figure 7-5, variable-ratio schedules lead to the highest rates of responding, the shortest pauses following reinforcement, and the greatest resistance to extinction. Golfing and most other sports activities are reinforced on variable-ratio schedules. Even after hitting balls into sand traps and overshooting the green all day, it only takes a few good (reinforced) shots to get most golfers excited about playing again. Most games of chance are also based on variable-ratio schedules. The intermittent and unpredictable nature of the reinforcement is why people continue pumping money into slot machines: Their concern is that as soon as they leave, someone else will win all the money.

In **fixed-interval schedules,** reinforcement occurs for the first response after a fixed time interval has elapsed. As you can see in figure 7-5, this schedule produces a pattern of behavior in which very few responses are made until the fixed interval of time approaches, and then the rate of responding increases rapidly. Researchers investigating the study patterns of college students found that they follow a fixed-interval behavior pattern when professors gave exams separated by a few weeks (Mawhinney et al., 1971). That is, when exams were given every 3 weeks, students began studying a few days before each exam, stopped studying immediately after the test, and began studying again as the next exam approached. In contrast, when professors gave daily quizzes, studying did not taper off after testing.

Unlike the predictability of fixed-interval reinforcement, **variable-interval schedules** reinforce the first response after a variable time interval has elapsed. As you can see in figure 7-5, such schedules produce relatively steady rates of responding. Have you ever taken a course where your grade is based on surprise exams that are given after a varying number of days or weeks? Because you do not know when you will be tested, you probably studied on a more regular basis in this sort of course than when exams were spread out in a fixed-interval pattern.

Variable-ratio schedules: Partial reinforcement schedules that reinforce a response after a variable number of nonreinforced responses.

Fixed-interval schedules: Partial reinforcement schedules that reinforce the first response after a fixed time interval has elapsed.

Variable-interval schedules: Partial reinforcement schedules that reinforce the first response after a variable time interval has elapsed.

7-2d Shaping Reinforces Closer Approximations to Desired Behavior

The reinforcement techniques discussed thus far describe how you can increase the frequency of behaviors once they occur. But suppose you want to train a dog to stand on its hind legs and dance, or teach a child to write the alphabet or play the piano. These behaviors are unlikely to occur spontaneously, so instead, you must employ an operant conditioning procedure that Skinner called **shaping,** or the *method of successive approximations*.

Shaping (or the *method of successive approximations*): In operant conditioning, the process of teaching a new behavior by reinforcing closer and closer approximations to the desired behavior.

INFO-BIT: In 1948, Skinner's passions for writing and for improving the world through behaviorism combined as he wrote a fictional novel, *Walden Two.* In this novel, a group of people use behaviorist principles to create a utopian society. In 1967, a group of people in Twin Oaks, Virginia, founded a community based on the vision Skinner had outlined in his novel. The community is still in existence today, although in a form somewhat different from the scientifically run community. Its core values now reflect not only issues of reinforcement, but democracy and political activism. For Skinner, it was the scientific application of behaviorist principles that would see humanity triumph over the darker impulses of human nature. In a curious irony, apparently it was more the power of Skinner's fictional writing—which he turned away from as a young man—rather than the power of his scientific research that primarily inspired the creation of this real-life utopian community.

TABLE 7-1	
How to Shape Behavior	1. Identify what the respondent can do now. 2. Identify the desired behavior. 3. Identify potential reinforcers in the respondent's environment. 4. Break the desired behavior into small substeps to be mastered sequentially. 5. Move the respondent from the entry behavior to the desired behavior by successively reinforcing each approximation to the desired behavior.

Source: Adapted from Galanter, 1962.

In shaping, you teach a new behavior by reinforcing behaviors that are closer and closer approximations to the desired behavior (see table 7-1). For example, when my brother, Randy, taught his son, Spencer, to write the letter "Q," he first identified what Spencer was initially capable of writing. Spencer's first attempt at the letter "Q" was a circular scrawl. Randy reinforced this response with praise. After several similar reinforced responses, Randy next raised the criterion for reinforcement to a circle with any straight line, then to a circle with an intersecting straight line placed anywhere, and finally, he only reinforced Spencer when he drew the correct "Q" letter. During this shaping process, when Spencer encountered difficulty at any point, Randy lowered the criterion for reinforcement to a level at which his son could perform successfully. Like Randy, all of us use praise and other reinforcers to shape successively closer approximations of desirable behavior in others. Whether it's teaching people to correct their tennis serve or improve their grammar, shaping will figure prominently in this learning process. In chapter 14, we will examine how shaping is used in therapy to change maladaptive thoughts and behavior, thus allowing people to lead more normal and happier lives.

Using shaping techniques, Skinner trained pigeons to play Ping-Pong with their beaks and to bowl in a miniature alley. During World War II, he even devised a plan to train pigeons to guide missiles toward enemy targets! Thankfully for the pigeons, this plan was never implemented, but two former students of Skinner, Keller and Marion Breland, went into business training animals for advertising and entertainment purposes. "Priscilla, the Fastidious Pig," for example, was trained to push a shopping cart past a display case and place the sponsor's product into her cart. Today, when you go to a circus or marine park and see elephants balancing on one leg or sea lions waving "hello" to you with their flippers, you are seeing the results of shaping. (See Discovery Box 7-3.)

7-2e Punishment Should Only Be Used under Certain Circumstances

Punishment: The process by which a stimulus *decreases* the probability of the behavior that it follows.

The opposite consequence of reinforcement is **punishment.** While reinforcement always increases the probability of a response—either by the presentation of a desirable stimulus or by the removal or avoidance of an aversive stimulus—punishment always *decreases* the probability of a response that it follows.

Do not confuse punishment with *negative reinforcement* (see section 7-2b). Although both involve an aversive stimulus, remember that a reinforcer strengthens behavior. Negative reinforcement strengthens behavior by removing the aversive stimulus, while punishment weakens behavior by presenting an aversive stimulus. Table 7-2 highlights the differences between these two operant processes.

Skinner, who was enthusiastic about using reinforcement to shape behavior, was equally adamant in opposing punishment. One reason he did not recommend the use of punishment is that, in most instances, its use must conform to some very narrow guidelines to be effective. There appears to be three conditions that must be met for punishment to

DISCOVERY *BOX 7-3*

Can Accidental Reinforcement Lead to Superstitious Behavior?

As a teenager, when I first began asking girls out for dates, I used the phone so that I could read what I wanted to say from a prepared script. One day I received a phone acceptance right after I had sunk 10 consecutive free throws in my driveway basketball court. For a few months after that coincidental juxtaposition of these two events, I only phoned girls for a date after shooting 10 baskets in a row. This superstitious behavior was learned simply because it was followed by a reinforcer (the girl accepting my offer!), even though my free-throw shooting was not the cause of the accepted offer.

In 1948, Skinner (1948b) trained **superstitious behavior** in hungry pigeons by reinforcing them with food every 15 seconds regardless of what they were doing. Skinner reasoned that when reinforcement occurred, it would be paired with whatever response the pigeons had just performed. Although this response had not caused the reinforcer, the fact that the reinforcer was delivered after the response would be sufficient to strengthen the response. Then, the next time food was delivered, the pigeons would be more likely to be engaging in that particular behavior than before, thereby strengthening it even further. This chain of events would continue until each individual pigeon would be spending most of its time engaging in its own particular superstitious behavior. This is exactly what happened for six out of eight pigeons. One pigeon repeatedly pecked at the floor, another turned counterclockwise, another tossed its head about, and so on. Subsequent research found that some of the behaviors Skinner observed in the pigeons are instinctive responses that pigeons make in preparation for food, and thus, were not examples of superstitious behavior (Staddon & Simmelhag, 1971). Nevertheless, Skinner's initial reasoning still bears repeating: When you are accidentally reinforced after engaging in a particular behavior, you may come to associate that desirable outcome with the preceding behavior, and thus, begin performing superstitious actions in the belief that this will help you receive another reinforcer.

Although superstitious actions do not directly influence the delivery of a reinforcer, they may sometimes have an indirect beneficial effect by helping the superstitious person cope with anxiety and stress (Matute, 1995). That is, by engaging in a ritual that you believe increases your chance of achieving success, you may gain a sense of personal control over the situation, which helps you perform better. Thus, while shooting 10 consecutive free throws did not magically cause girls to go out with me, it did lower my anxiety so that I read my prepared script without stammering and thus appeared more poised than desperate! Can you think of any of your own past or present behavior that might fit into Skinner's definition of superstitious behavior?

Superstitious behavior: A behavior learned simply because it happened to be followed by a reinforcer, even though this behavior was not the cause of the reinforcer.

TABLE 7-2

What Is the Difference between Punishment and Negative Reinforcement?

It is true that punishment and negative reinforcement both involve an aversive stimulus, but they are two very different processes.

Negative reinforcement is the process by which *escaping* or *avoiding* an aversive or unpleasant stimulus *strengthens* the response that it follows.

Escape Behavior	**Avoidance Behavior**
Organisms respond in ways that allow them to escape or terminate an aversive event that has already occurred. For example, after spraining your ankle while playing basketball, you may take ibuprofen and apply an ice pack to reduce the swelling and pain. Taking the drug and putting ice on the ankle are both negative reinforcers because they allow you to escape a painful and unpleasant set of stimuli.	Organisms respond in ways that allow them to avoid an aversive event before it occurs. For example, seeing a police car alongside the highway provides you with advance warning and allows you to respond by slowing down and, thus, avoid a speeding ticket. The police car is the negative reinforcer. Recognizing this fact, some police departments place mannequins in squad cars along troublesome roads to control speeding.

Punishment is the process by which *presenting* a stimulus *weakens* the response that it follows.

Following your sprained ankle, you may stop playing basketball, and instead, choose some other form of exercise and recreation that is less likely to lead to injury. Your previous sprained ankle was a punisher because it reduced the likelihood of your basketball playing in the future. Regarding your highway driving, slowing down when seeing a police car may likely be because you were once given a speeding ticket, and thus you have learned about the negative consequences of speeding in the presence of the police. Upon receiving the speeding ticket, you probably drove significantly slower for a period of time afterward. The ticket weakened your speeding behavior, and thus it was a punisher.

---

have a chance of being effective in reducing unwanted behaviors (Baron, 1983; Bower & Hilgard, 1981). First, the punishment must be *prompt*, administered quickly after the unwanted action. Second, it must be *relatively strong* so that its aversive qualities are duly noted by the offender. And third, it must be *consistently applied* so that the responder knows that the likelihood is high that punishment will follow future unwanted actions. Yet, even if these conditions are met, reduction of the undesirable behavior is not guaranteed. For instance, punishment is often used to curb aggressive behavior. Yet, if potential aggressors are extremely angry, threats of punishment preceding an attack frequently fail to inhibit aggression (Baron, 1973). Here, the strength of the anger overrides any concerns about the negative consequences of aggression. Likewise, the use of punishment following aggression may actually provoke counteraggression in the aggressor-turned-victim because such punishment would probably be frustrating and anger-producing.

In further considering the effectiveness of using punishment to reduce unwanted behaviors, you should be even more wary of using physical punishments, such as spankings. As you will learn in section 7-3 on observational learning, research indicates that employing physical punishment as a remedy for aggression and other undesirable

---

Violence and injury enclose in their net all that do such things, and generally return upon him who began.

—Lucretius, Roman philosopher and poet, 99–55 B.C.

> **INFO-BIT:** One alternative to punishment of undesirable behavior proposed by Skinner is to allow undesirable actions (such as a child's temper tantrum) to continue without either positive or negative consequences until they are extinguished (Schunk, 1996). In other words, ignore the unwanted behavior. Then, immediately reinforce desirable responses when they are made. Another useful extinction technique is the "time-out" in which misbehaving children are removed for a short period of time from sources of positive reinforcement (Erford, 1999; Turner & Watson, 1999). Have you ever used these techniques? Were they effective?

behaviors may simply teach and encourage observers to copy these aggressive actions. That is, the person using physical punishment may serve as an aggressive model. This is exactly the process underlying the continuing cycle of family violence found in many societies—observing adult aggression appears to encourage rather than discourage aggression in children (Hanson et al., 1997; Olweus, 1980).

Taking these factors into account, even though punishment may reduce unwanted behaviors under certain circumstances, it does not teach the recipient new desirable forms of behavior. The unwanted behaviors are not being replaced by more productive kinds of actions but are most likely only being temporarily suppressed. It is for this reason that punishment, by itself, is unlikely to result in long-term changes in behavior (Seppa, 1996).

Finally, one other unfortunate consequence of punishment is that it may unexpectedly shape behavior other than the target behavior. For example, the repeated rejections young Skinner received from publishers during his "dark year" not only sharply reduced the amount of time he subsequently spent writing fiction, but they also had an unintended effect. He stopped reading fiction and poetry and even avoided the theater for three years! As he put it, "Literature had been the great love of my high school and college years, but when I risked a year after college to test myself as a writer and failed, I turned rather bitterly against it" (Skinner, 1979, p. 90). Although the editors who "punished" young Skinner with their rejections may well have intended to stop his manuscript submissions, they would not have wanted him to give up reading the works they were publishing for their own profit. The lesson to be learned here is that although you can use punishment to reduce a targeted response, you may "throw the baby out with the bathwater" by also reducing desirable behavior.

7-2f Operant Conditioning Theory Overlooks Biological Predispositions and Cognitive Processes

As a traditional behaviorist, Skinner focused on observable stimulus-response relationships and overlooked the impact that inborn biological predispositions and cognitive processes have on learning. Thus, it became the task of other investigators to test and revise aspects of operant conditioning that related to these two factors.

Biological Constraints on Learning

One of the early assumptions underlying operant conditioning was that animals could be trained to emit any response that they were physically capable of making. However, as with classical conditioning, it was soon learned that an animal's biology can restrict its capacity for operant conditioning. Remember the animal trainers Keller and Marion Breland? Although they could train pigs to push shopping carts past display cases and raccoons to dunk basketballs in hoop, they could not train these animals to reliably deposit silver dollars into a piggy bank (Breland & Breland, 1961). Instead, the pigs threw the coins onto the ground and pushed them about, while the raccoons in the experiment continually rubbed them between their paws. Both behaviors illustrate how species-specific behavior patterns can interfere with operant conditioning, a biological constraint that the Brelands called **instinctive drift** (Breland & Breland, 1961). Through evolution, pigs

Instinctive drift: Species-specific behavior patterns that interfere with operant conditioning.

have developed a foraging behavior pattern of rooting for food in the ground with their snouts, whereas raccoons' foraging behavior involves washing food objects with their paws before eating them. These instincts inhibit the learning of new operant responses. Thus, just as certain species can be classically conditioned to learn certain responses more easily than others, operant learning is similarly constrained by an animal's evolutionary heritage (Gould & Marler, 1987).

Latent Learning

In the journey of discovery chronicled in this book, psychologists sometimes head down wrong paths due to misguided assumptions or failure to take notice of others' discoveries. Such was the case with Skinner. Despite evidence to the contrary, he died refusing to admit that an understanding of cognitive processes was necessary to fully understand human and animal behavior (Skinner, 1990). Yet, even as Skinner was developing his learning theory in the 1930s based on reinforced behavior, Edward Tolman's research (1922, 1932) with rats indicated that learning can occur without any reinforcement, something that the theory of operant conditioning assumed was not possible.

In one of Tolman's experiments, one group of rats wandered through a maze once a day for 10 days without being reinforced (Tolman & Honzik, 1930). Meanwhile, another group of rats spent the same amount of time in the maze but were reinforced at the "goal box" with food in each of their 10 trials. These reinforced rats quickly learned to accurately run the maze to reach the food reward, but the nonreinforced rats made many errors, suggesting little maze learning. On the 11th day, the nonreinforced rats were suddenly rewarded with food at the goal box, and they immediately thereafter made as few errors as the other rats. A third group of control rats that still received no food reward continued making many errors (see figure 7-6).

How would you explain these findings using operant conditioning theory? You could not because you would have to discuss cognition. However, not being constrained in this manner, Tolman suggested that, through experience, even the rats that had received no reinforcement had formed a *cognitive map*, or mental image, of the maze. They formed these maps prior to being conditioned, which meant that learning could occur without

FIGURE 7-6
Latent Learning

Rats that were rewarded for their maze running made fewer errors than rats that were not rewarded. However, on day 11, when these previously unrewarded rats were rewarded, they immediately made as few errors as the other rats. This experiment demonstrated the principle of latent learning. Can you think of examples of latent learning in your own life?

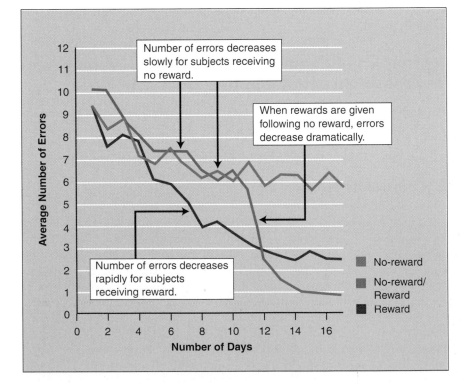

Many of the studies that have explored the principles of classical conditioning and operant conditioning were performed on animals, such as rats and pigeons. How can scientists make generalizations about the way people behave based on these studies? Why not just study people?

reinforcement. The learning of these rats remained hidden or *latent* because there was no incentive to engage in the behavior that would demonstrate it until that behavior was reinforced. Tolman called such learning that is not currently manifest in behavior and occurs without apparent reinforcement **latent learning.** Based on this research and more recent studies, psychologists now overwhelmingly believe that internal cognitive processes must be considered when explaining human, as well as animal learning (Keith & McVety, 1988; Smith, 1994).

Latent learning: Learning that occurs without apparent reinforcement and is not demonstrated until sufficient reinforcement is provided.

Learned Helplessness

In the 1960s, a group of researchers were studying *avoidance learning* caused by negative reinforcers when they stumbled upon an interesting and puzzling phenomenon. In these experiments, a dog was placed on one side of a box with a wire grid floor. Next, a light came on signaling that the animal's feet would be shocked in 10 seconds unless it jumped a hurdle and crossed to the other side of the box. This jumping response to the light was the avoidance learning, and the animals quickly learned to avoid the electrical shock by jumping the hurdle. In one experiment, prior to placing dogs in the box, the researchers first classically conditioned them to fear the light by repeatedly pairing it with a mild electrical shock while the dogs were strapped down in a harness. To the researchers' surprise, when these dogs were later placed in the box, they did not learn the simple escape response, but instead, passively laid down, whimpered, and accepted the shock (Overmier & Leaf, 1965).

Why do you think exposure to inescapable shock later caused the dogs not to learn a very simple escape response? Two young graduate students, Martin Seligman and Steven Maier, offered an answer (Maier et al., 1969; Seligman & Maier, 1967). When shock is inescapable, dogs learn that they are helpless to exert control over the shock by means of any voluntary behaviors, and they expect this to be the case in the future. Because the dogs have developed the *expectation* that their behavior has no effect on the outcome in the situation, they simply give up trying to change the outcome. Seligman and Maier called this reaction **learned helplessness.** Here again, in contradiction to behaviorist theory, research demonstrated that mental processes play a significant role in learning. This type of learning explains why, for example, many unemployed workers eventually give up trying after repeatedly being passed over for new jobs. Unfortunately, by concluding that there is nothing they can do to change their job status, these individuals often overlook real employment possibilities. In chapter 14, we will examine the role that learned helplessness plays in depression (Peterson et al., 1993).

Learned helplessness: The passive resignation produced by repeated exposure to aversive events that cannot be avoided.

SECTION SUMMARY

- Law of effect states that behavior becomes more or less likely based on the effect it has in producing desirable or undesirable consequences.

- Operant conditioning refers to learning in which behavior is strengthened if followed by reinforcement and weakened if followed by punishment.

- A reinforcer is any stimulus or event that increases the likelihood that the behavior preceding it will be repeated.

- Primary reinforcers are innately reinforcing because they satisfy some biological need.

- Secondary reinforcers are learned through classical conditioning.

- Positive reinforcers strengthen a response by presenting a positive stimulus.

- Negative reinforcers strengthen a response by removing an aversive stimulus.
- Continuous reinforcement results in the fastest learning.
- Partial reinforcement maintains vigorous responding for longer periods of time.
- Partial reinforcement schedules are defined in terms of number of responses (ratio) or the passage of time (interval): fixed-ratio; variable-ratio; fixed-interval; variable-interval.
- The steps in shaping behavior are (1) identify what the respondent can do and identify the desired behavior; (2) identify potential reinforcers; (3) break desired behavior into small substeps; (4) move respondent to desired behavior by successively reinforcing each approximation to desired behavior.
- Due to accidental reinforcement, superstitious behavior may develop.
- The opposite consequence of reinforcement is punishment.
- For punishment to effectively shape behavior, it must be promptly administered, relatively strong, and consistently applied.
- As with classical conditioning, learning in operant conditioning is limited by an animal's evolutionary heritage.
- Cognitive processes are necessary to fully understand operant conditioning principles.

7-3 OBSERVATIONAL LEARNING

Classical and operant conditioning are two ways in which we and other animals learn from experience. Both of these conditioning processes involve *direct* experience with desirable and undesirable outcomes. Yet, what about the learning that occurs without direct experience? Have you ever noticed that people and many animals learn by watching and imitating others? For example, by observing their mothers, jaguar cubs learn basic hunting techniques, as well as which prey are easiest to kill. Similarly, today, while shopping, I couldn't help but notice a mother with her son, who looked about 4 years of age. She was yelling at the top of her lungs, "How many times have I told you not to yell at people?!!! I've told you, YOU HAVE TO BE POLITE!!!" Where do you think the child learned his misbehavior?

7-3a Learning Often Occurs by Observing and Imitating Others' Behavior

Observational learning:
Learning a behavior by observing and imitating the behavior of others (models).

Social learning theory:
A theory that contends that people learn social behaviors mainly through observation and cognitive processing of information.

Vicarious conditioning:
The process by which one learns the consequences of an action by observing its consequences for someone else.

Just as nonreinforced learning cannot be explained within the framework of either classical or operant conditioning, neither can the fact that people and other animals learn simply through observing the behavior of others. Instead, a third form of learning, observational learning, must be introduced. **Observational learning** is learning by observing and imitating the behavior of others. These others whom we observe and imitate are called *models*.

Observational learning is the central feature of Albert Bandura's (1986) **social learning theory,** which contends that people learn social behaviors mainly through observation and cognitive processing of information, rather than through direct experience. According to this theory, when you watch others engage in some activity with which you are not familiar, a great deal of cognitive learning takes place before you yourself perform the behavior. For instance, consistent with the law of effect discussed earlier, you are most likely to imitate a model whose actions you see rewarded, and you are least likely to imitate behavior that is punished. This observational learning mechanism—in which you learn the consequences of an action by observing its consequences for someone else—is known as **vicarious conditioning.** As you can see, the only difference between this and the conditioning that occurs in operant learning is that, here, the behavior of others is being reinforced or punished rather than your own.

7-3b Children Can Learn Aggressive Behavior through Observation

Research suggests that widespread media coverage of a violent incident is often followed by a sudden increase in similar violent crimes (Berkowitz & Macaulay, 1971; Phillips, 1983, 1986). Apparently, reading and watching news accounts of violence can trigger some people to "copy" the aggression. This dangerous manifestation of observational learning was dramatically illustrated following the 1999 shootings and bombings at Columbine High School in Littleton, Colorado, that left 17 people dead and many wounded. Over the next year, copycat threats and actions became a common occurrence in schools throughout the United States and Canada. What insights do you think that psychology can bring to bear on this type of learning?

The first set of experiments demonstrating the power of observational learning in eliciting aggression were the famous *Bobo doll* studies (Bandura et al., 1961) described in chapter 2, section 2-3c. Likewise, another classic study conducted by Albert Bandura and his coworkers (1963) had young children watch a short film of an aggressive adult model named Rocky take food and toys from someone named Johnny. In one condition, children observed Johnny respond by punishing Rocky, while in another condition, children saw Rocky sing "Hi ho, hi ho, it's off to play I go," as he pranced off with Johnny's belongings in a sack. Not surprisingly, those children who saw Rocky rewarded for his aggression behaved more aggressively than those who saw Rocky punished.

Although these findings might leave you with the impression that aggressive models who are punished have little negative impact on children's later behavior, this is not really the case. The research demonstrates that children are less likely to *imitate* the actions of punished aggressors. Does this mean these children fail to learn the aggressive behavior, or does it mean they simply inhibit the expression of these behaviors?

To answer this question, in one study, Bandura (1965) offered children a reward if they could imitate the aggressive behavior of the model that they had previously observed. Every single one of the participants could mimic the model's aggressive actions, even those who had seen the punished model. Thus, simply observing someone being punished for aggression does not prevent the *learning* of aggression—it simply inhibits its *expression* in certain circumstances.

Bandura (1979) believes children observe and learn aggression through many avenues, but the three principal ones are the family, the culture, and the media. First, in families where adults use violence, children grow up being much more likely to use it themselves (Herrenkohl et al., 1983; Hunter & Kilstrom, 1979). Second, in communities where aggression is considered to be a sign of manhood, learning aggressive behaviors are eagerly and consciously transmitted from generation to generation, especially among males (Cohen & Nisbett, 1997; Rosenberg & Mercy, 1991). Finally, the media—principally television and the movies—unceasingly convey images of violence and mayhem to virtually all segments of society on a daily basis (Gerbner & Signorielli, 1990; Murray, 1980). Do you think such viewing can produce antisocial behavior?

Numerous experimental studies indicate that exposure to media violence significantly enhances children's and adolescents' aggression (Liebert & Sprafkin, 1988; Wood et al., 1991). Further, longitudinal research conducted in a number of countries including

INFO-BIT: Research suggests that observing peers who smoke influences adolescents' decisions to start smoking (Hawkins et al., 1992). Which teens do you think are most susceptible to such influence? The answer is those who are "outsiders," meaning they have not yet been accepted into a teen group they desire to join. If those in the group smoke, the outsiders imitate these teens and begin smoking (Aloise-Young et al., 1994). Can you think of ways that this knowledge could be used in developing effective antismoking ads for teenagers?

Journey of Discovery Question

Why are the studies on observational learning now mostly based on human populations? And why does observational learning make evolutionary sense for human beings?

the United States indicates that the early TV habits of children significantly predicted their later aggressive behavior, even after statistically controlling for their initial aggressiveness. What appears to influence children's later aggressiveness is their *identification* with aggressive TV and movie characters. That is, children who watch a lot of media violence when they are young and identify with aggressive media characters are most likely to become highly aggressive later in life (Huesmann & Hasbrouck, 1996; Huesmann & Miller, 1994). Of course, these findings do not mean that all or even most children who view violent TV programs or movies will begin terrorizing their schools and neighborhoods. However, while observing such violence is not the *primary* cause of aggression in children, social scientists believe that it may be the one factor that is easiest to control and reduce (Wilson et al., 1998). Indeed, research indicates that aggressive behavior in children is significantly reduced when they spend less time watching violent television shows and playing violent video games. One such study examined third- and fourth-grade students at two comparable schools over a 6-month period (Robinson et al., 2001). In one of the schools, TV and video-game exposure was reduced by one-third by encouraging students and parents to engage in alternative forms of home entertainment, while in the other school no effort was made to reduce exposure. The researchers found that children at the intervention school were subsequently less aggressive on the playground than students at the control school, especially those students who were initially rated as most aggressive by their classmates.

SECTION SUMMARY

- Observational learning refers to learning by observing and imitating the behavior of others.
- Watching violence on television may encourage children to become more aggressive.
- Children are less likely to imitate the actions of punished aggressors.

SUGGESTED WEBSITES

Note: These websites were functional when we went to press. Please access the online text for the most up-to-date URLs.

Neuroscience: Learning and Memory

http://www.brembs.net/learning

This website presents information describing and distinguishing between classical and operant conditioning principles.

Marine Mammal Training at SeaWorld

http://www.seaworld.org/infobooks/Training/mmtrain.html

This Sea World website contains information about animal behavior and the training of marine animals at Sea World.

Albert Bandura

http://www.emory.edu/EDUCATION/mfp/bandurabio.html

This website at Emory University provides a biography of Albert Bandura, an overview of his theory of observational learning, and his research on modeling violence.

PSYCHOLOGICAL APPLICATIONS
Learning How to Exercise Self-Control
in Your Academic and Personal Life

- Do you have trouble getting out of bed in the morning to attend an early class?
- Do you procrastinate in studying for exams and end up cramming the night before?
- Do you tend to spend money quickly, thereby leaving you with little to live on until your next pay period?
- Are you having difficulty exercising on a regular basis?
- Would you like to stop smoking or cut down on your consumption of alcohol?

If you answered yes to any of these questions, the bad news is that you are struggling with issues of self-control. The good news, however, is that what you have learned in this chapter can help you regain control over those troubled aspects of your academic and personal life. In most self-control issues, problems arise because we choose *short-term reinforcers* that provide immediate gratification instead of choosing *long-term reinforcers* that provide delayed gratification. For instance, we sacrifice a chance at a good grade at the end of the semester for the luxury of getting an extra hour's sleep each class session. Likewise, we choose to continue smoking because doing so gives us an immediate nicotine high, even though smoking significantly lowers our life expectancy. Why do short-term reinforcers have greater incentive value than long-term reinforcers?

The Relative Value of Short-Term and Long-Term Reinforcers

Let's consider this question by examining the problem of early morning class attendance. When resolving to change your habit of skipping class, you consider the incentive value of both the short-term and long-term reinforcers. In most cases, such resolutions are made when both reinforcers are relatively distant, such as just before you go to bed the night before class. At that time, the incentive value of getting a good grade is usually greater than the value of getting extra sleep, so you set your alarm for an early rising. However, as the availability of a reinforcer gets closer, its incentive value increases (Ainslie, 1975). Thus, when the alarm interrupts your sleep in the morning, the short-term reinforcer—extra sleep— is now immediately available, while the long-term reinforcer—a good grade—is still distant. Now, it will be much harder to maintain your resolve and forgo the short-term reinforcement of extra sleep. If the thought of staying in your warm, comfy bed has greater incentive value than getting a good grade, you will break your nighttime resolution.

Strategies to Modify Troublesome Behavior

Now that you understand the process of shifting incentive values, what can you do to counteract the allure of these resolution-breaking short-term reinforcers? You can adopt the following six strategies to modify your problem behavior and regain self-control.

1. *Set realistic goals:* Punishment weakens the behavior it follows. Because failure to reach your goals will punish your efforts, it is important that you set goals that you can realistically achieve.
2. *Shape your behavior:* As previously noted, the delay in receiving a long-term reinforcement can weaken your resolve to change

your troublesome behavior. One strategy to increase the incentive value of the long-term reinforcer is to shape your behavior. That is, give yourself modest reinforcers for achieving successive steps toward your ultimate desirable goal. For example, after going for a week without missing class, reward yourself by going to a movie or spending time with friends. Similarly, if you were smoking a pack a day and wanted to stop, during the first week, you might reward yourself if you smoked only a half pack per day. Remember, a reinforcer strengthens the behavior it follows, not the behavior it precedes. Only reinforce yourself *after* you have performed the desired behavior, not before. If you reward yourself before attending class, or before lowering your cigarette consumption, you are not reinforcing the desired behavior.

3. *Chart your progress:* To give yourself feedback on how well you are progressing toward meeting your goals, keep a chart of your progress. For example, to support your efforts to stop smoking, the chart would track how many cigarettes you smoked each day. Place the chart in a place where you will regularly see it. Charting your progress in this manner will bring into play both positive and negative reinforcement: You will praise yourself after reaching your daily goals, and you will also work harder to remove the guilt—a negative reinforcer—that follows a day in which you fail to meet your goals.

4. *Identify environmental cues that trigger undesirable behavior:* Environmental stimuli can serve as signals that we are about to have access to certain desirable, yet harmful, situations or substances. For example, if you regularly smoked after meals or when in taverns, those situations will likely trigger your urge to "light up" during the time that you are trying to quit smoking. If you can identify these environmental cues, you can try to avoid putting yourself in those situations while you are trying to change your behavior (stay away from taverns for a while). If you cannot avoid the tempting situations (as will be the case in eating meals), take steps to countercondition yourself. Instead of smoking after meals, eat a favorite dessert or beverage.

5. *Keep focused on the long-term reinforcer:* As previously stated, the undesirable short-term reinforcers are generally more salient than the desirable long-term reinforcers. Thus, when tempted by these more salient and troublesome reinforcers, take advantage of the cognitive aspects of learning and selectively focus on the long-term reinforcers. For example, instead of succumbing to temptation and grabbing an extra hour of sleep, imagine how good you will feel at the end of the semester when you receive a good grade in your course. Such imagining can subjectively close the gap between the present and the future goal, increasing its incentive value in the present.

6. *Select desirable role models:* Observational learning teaches us that we can learn by observing and imitating the behavior of others. Just as you may have acquired your undesirable behavior by imitating others, change your behavior by identifying people who possess traits and skills that you desire. By observing these individuals, you will not only learn how to behave differently, but you will also receive inspiration by seeing someone successfully doing what you ultimately want to do.

KEY TERMS

acquisition (p. 188)
classical conditioning (p. 185)
conditioned response (CR) (p. 185)
conditioned stimulus (CS) (p. 185)
continuous reinforcement (p. 197)
extinction (p. 190)
fixed-interval schedules (p. 199)
fixed-ratio schedules (p. 198)
higher-order conditioning (p. 189)
instinctive drift (p. 203)
latent learning (p. 205)
law of effect (p. 195)

learned helplessness (p. 205)
negative reinforcers (p. 197)
observational learning (p. 206)
operant conditioning (p. 195)
partial reinforcement (p. 197)
positive reinforcers (p. 197)
primary reinforcers (p. 197)
punishment (p. 200)
reinforcement (p. 196)
reinforcer (p. 196)
secondary reinforcers (p. 197)
shaping (p. 199)

social learning theory (p. 206)
spontaneous recovery (p. 191)
stimulus discrimination (p. 189)
stimulus generalization (p. 189)
superstitious behavior (p. 201)
unconditioned response (UCR) (p. 185)
unconditioned stimulus (UCS) (p. 185)
variable-interval schedules (p. 199)
variable-ratio schedules (p. 199)
vicarious conditioning (p. 206)

REVIEW QUESTIONS

1. The person associated with classical conditioning is
   a. B. F. Skinner.
   b. Ivan Pavlov.
   c. John Watson.
   d. Martin Seligman.
   e. *b* and *c*

2. Which of the following is *not* an example of higher-order conditioning?
   a. A perfume sparks romantic feelings.
   b. A new acquaintance likes you because she knew and liked your sibling.
   c. Upon entering a room to take an exam, you experience test anxiety.
   d. You dislike Pringles™ potato chips because you once got sick from eating too many.
   e. none of the above

3. Which of the following was *missing* from the experiment on Albert?
   a. extinction
   b. stimulus generalization
   c. punishment
   d. all of the above
   e. *a* and *c*

4. Which of the following is *true*?
   a. Classical conditioning involves "mindless" automatic learning.
   b. Humans are passive in learning conditioned responses.
   c. Learning occurs when the conditioned stimulus comes after or at the same time as the unconditioned stimulus.
   d. *b* and *c*
   e. none of the above

5. Which of the following is *true*?
   a. Animals do not differ in what responses can be conditioned.
   b. Associations can be conditioned between all stimulus and response situations.
   c. *a* and *b*
   d. none of the above

6. Which of the following can be used to protect endangered species from predators?
   a. conditioned taste aversion
   b. extinction
   c. spontaneous recovery
   d. *b* and *a*
   e. none of the above

7. Which of these is *true* of operant conditioning?
   a. Behavior is determined by stimuli that *precede* it.
   b. Associations between behavior and consequences are learned.
   c. Behavior is largely goal oriented.
   d. *b* and *c*
   e. all of the above

8. Which of the following would likely be a reinforcer for students to study more?
   a. money
   b. less homework
   c. studying with someone you enjoy being with
   d. good grades
   e. all of the above

9. Which of the following is a primary reinforcer?
   a. food
   b. water
   c. warmth
   d. sex
   e. all of the above

10. The type of reinforcement that has the greatest long-term effects is
    a. continuous reinforcement.
    b. fixed-ratio schedule.
    c. variable-ratio schedule.
    d. punishment.
    e. none of the above

11. What is the term for something that weakens behavior by presenting an aversive stimulus?
    a. negative reinforcement
    b. shaping
    c. punishment
    d. avoidance behavior
    e. none of the above

12. Which of the following is a drawback of punishment?
  a. It doesn't teach new desirable forms of behavior.
  b. It can lead to more aggression.
  c. It encourages aggressive behavior.
  d. all of the above
  e. none of the above

13. B. F. Skinner
  a. assumed that latent learning was not possible.
  b. overlooked the impact of inborn biology on learning.
  c. elaborated on the law of effect.
  d. was named Burrhus Frederick Skinner.
  e. all of the above

14. Social learning theory
  a. contends that people learn social behavior through direct experience.
  b. is inconsistent with the law of effect.
  c. requires cognition.
  d. all of the above
  e. none of the above

15. Which of the following is *true?*
  a. Media are the primary cause of aggression in children.
  b. Observing someone being punished for behaving aggressively does not prevent the learning of aggression.
  c. Less time watching violent TV diminishes aggressive behavior.
  d. *b* and *c*
  e. all of the above

16. Applying the learning principles in chapter 7, which of the following would be helpful in modifying troublesome behavior?
  a. Identify environmental cues that trigger undesirable behavior.
  b. Keep focused on long-term reinforcers.
  c. Select desirable role models.
  d. Chart your progress.
  e. all of the above

Memory

8

At the Russian newspaper where reporter S. V. Shereshevskii worked, he was surprised to learn that his editor was upset with him for never writing down assignments. Shereshevskii informed his editor that he didn't need to write down assignments because he remembered everything people told him, word for word. Didn't everybody have this ability, he naively asked?

Following that innocent question, Shereshevskii soon found himself in the office of psychologist Alexander Luria, who proceeded to test his memory. Over the years, Luria discovered there was virtually no limit to what this reporter could remember. For example, he could memorize a list of 70 words in 4 minutes. Although this feat is not that unusual, what was extraordinary was that whenever Shereshevskii created an image in his mind, it became so vivid that he never forgot it. Fifteen years after memorizing this word list, Luria asked him if he could recall it. Shereshevskii closed his eyes, paused, and then replied, "Yes, yes . . . this was a series you gave me once when we were in your apartment. . . . You were sitting at the table and I in the rocking chair. . . . You were wearing a gray suit and you looked at me like this. . . . Now I can see you saying . . . ," and then he recited the words in the exact order they were read to him so long ago (Luria, 1968).

While Shereshevskii stands out because of his amazing memory, "Ben" is noteworthy for his limited ability to remember information and events. Ben, a middle-aged businessman, happened to sit next to me during a plane trip and noticed an early draft of this memory chapter lying on my lap. "You know," he said nonchalantly, "I have no short-term memory." With that attention-grabbing opening line, Ben proceeded to tell me how 4 years ago he suffered damage to his short-term memory when he received insufficient oxygen during minor knee surgery. Now, he has to repeat information many times before he can remember it. If he doesn't repeat information over and over, or if he doesn't write it down immediately, it will disappear. By his own admission, Ben's moods are now much more even-keeled than before the accident. Why? Because, when he does experience emotions such as happiness, sadness, or anger, they now last only until his attention is distracted, and then quickly fade from consciousness, and from memory.

Despite this substantial memory handicap, Ben recently became the public relations director for a major industrial manufacturing firm. Perhaps what is most surprising about Ben's new job situation is that no one there is apparently aware of his disorder. When he was first hired, it took him a number of months to memorize the names of his office staff, and he still occasionally calls the company president "Prez" and the chief financial officer "Chief" when their names escape him. Thus far, Ben's bosses have interpreted this informality as simply an example of his winning personality.

Ben and Shereshevskii represent opposite ends of the memory spectrum. In most of us, memory—the mental process by which information is encoded and stored in the brain, and later retrieved—operates somewhere between these two extremes. There is a close link between the subject matter of chapter 7, learning, and the subject matter of this chapter (Healy & Bourne, 1995; Schacter & Scarry, 2000). Memory involves the retention of what we learn. The lesson learned from Ben's current predicament is that without a well-functioning memory, learning becomes extremely problematic.

How extensive is our memory system? One memory researcher estimated that by your early seventies you will have memories equal to about 500 times the amount of information contained in the entire *Encyclopaedia Britannica* (Hunt, 1982). Of course, a good deal of the information stored in memory would never appear in an encyclopedia (for exam-

The amount of information you have in memory could fill thousands of books. How does this information get into memory? How is it stored and organized? Can you "lose" this information? These are some of the important memory questions researchers try to answer.

ple, I have unintentionally memorized the *CatDog* and *SpongeBob Squarepants* TV theme songs). Despite the fact that some of our memories appear redundant, we could not function properly without the ability to encode, store, and later recall our life experiences.

8-1 THE NATURE OF MEMORY

Up until the late 1950s, most psychologists viewed **memory** as a single system (Melton, 1963). This perspective was largely due to the influence of behaviorism, in which remembering something was conceived of as simply due to the strength of stimulus-response pairings (see chapter 7, section 7-2a). If a person or animal consistently responded in the same way to the same stimulus, this meant they had formed a strong memory for the response. According to behaviorists, this single conditioning process was the extent of memory. Discussing unobservable events, such as cognition, were considered off-limits to the science of psychology. Then, due to technological advances outside the discipline and scientific discoveries within, psychologists dramatically changed their views of memory.

8-1a The Computer's Information-Processing System Has Been a Useful Model of Human Memory

The event outside of psychology that served as a catalyst in changing psychologists' thinking on memory was the advent of the computer age (Dodwell, 2000). Like us, computers have memories. As psychologists adopted the terms and concepts of computer scientists, they began to view memory as a kind of information-processing system that depended on three basic processes (Lewandowsky & Murdock, 1989; Searle, 1995). According to this **information-processing model,** in both computer and human memory, there are three basic processes that information goes through: an input or *encoding* process, a *storage* process, and a *retrieval* process.

Information Processes

Encoding refers to the first memory process, in which incoming information is organized and transformed so that it can be entered into memory. In the computer, typing on the keyboard transforms information into electronic language. In the brain, sensory information from our surroundings is transformed into neural language. For example, imagine that

Memory: The mental process by which information is encoded and stored in the brain, and later retrieved.

Information-processing model: A memory model concerning the sequential processing and use of information, involving *encoding, storage,* and *retrieval.*

Encoding: The first memory process, in which information is organized and transformed so that it can be entered into memory.

you are presented with the sentence "Sporminore is a town in northern Italy." If you encode the image of the letters as they appear on your computer screen, you are using *visual encoding*, and the information is represented in memory as a picture. If you encode the sound of the words as if they were spoken, you are using *acoustic encoding*, and the information is represented in memory as a sequence of sounds. Finally, if you encode the fact that this sentence is referring to the birthplace of your grandfather (which for me is true), you are using *semantic encoding*, and the information is represented in memory by its meaning to you. The type of encoding used—visual, acoustic, or semantic—can influence what is remembered. As you will discover in section 8-1d, semantic encoding yields much better memories than visual and acoustic encoding. However, because semantic encoding involves the processing of the general, underlying meaning of information, it often ignores details of the information.

> **Storage:** The second memory process, in which information is entered and maintained in memory for a period of time.

The second memory process is **storage,** which involves entering and maintaining information in memory for a period of time. Just as the computer can store information for either brief periods (in random access memory) or indefinitely (on a floppy or hard disk), we too have similar memory capabilities. The human memory systems that store information for relatively brief time periods are known as *sensory memory* and *short-term memory,* while the more permanent system is known as *long-term memory.*

> **Retrieval:** The third memory process, which involves recovering stored information from memory so that it can be used.

Finally, the third memory process is **retrieval,** which involves recovering stored information from memory so that it can be used. In both computers and humans, this means pulling information out of long-term memory storage and placing it into a much smaller working memory. To demonstrate how the retrieval process works yourself, recall the name of your best friend from sixth grade. In doing so, perhaps memories of your hometown come to mind, along with images of your sixth-grade classroom and activities you engaged in with this person. Each of these memories can serve as a stimulus to help you remember your best friend's name. When the correct memories come to mind, you retrieve the name (Valentine et al., 1996).

In a nutshell, these are the three memory processes. Encoding gets information into memory, storage keeps it in, and retrieval takes it out, just like a computer. Although the computer is by far the most popular metaphor for our memory system, as already noted, it is not perfect. Indeed, as we will discuss in section 8-2c, the human brain often does not operate like a typical computer (Gabrieli, 1999; McClelland, 1994). Despite this limitation, as of this writing, the computer is still the most convenient metaphor for organizing the major findings on memory (Tulving, 1997). With this caveat in mind (no pun intended), let us examine how psychologists, operating within this information-processing perspective, began questioning old assumptions about how we form memories.

The Identification of Three Memory Systems

A series of studies in the 1950s indicated that if people are distracted from rehearsing a small amount of information given to them, in a matter of seconds, this information is often completely forgotten (Brown, 1958; Peterson & Peterson, 1959). In trying to make sense of these findings, researchers "remembered" the findings from one of the earliest memory studies. In 1885, German psychologist Hermann Ebbinghaus (1850–1909), using himself as his own subject, studied a list of nonsense syllables (such as *BIW* or *SUW*) and measured how many he later recalled. As illustrated in figure 8-1, Ebbinghaus discovered that nonsense syllables near the beginning and end of the list were more easily remem-

> **INFO-BIT:** Did your parents tell you that "first impressions" are important? If so, they were right. In general, the first bits of information we learn about people during initial encounters have a bigger impact on our overall impression of them than later information (Asch, 1946). This is so, probably because the first bits of information are more likely to make their way into long-term memory. Another way to state this "first impressions effect" is that the *primacy effect* has more influence on impression formation than does the *recency effect*.

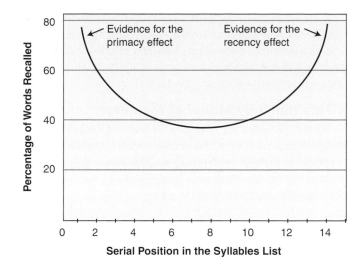

FIGURE 8-1
The Memory Curve
Hermann Ebbinghaus (1885) found that memory is better for the first few and last few items in a string of nonsense syllables. These two memory effects were respectively called the *primacy* and *recency effects*. In the 1950s, memory researchers argued that the primacy effect suggested the existence of a long-term memory system, while the recency effect suggested that there is a short-term memory system. What was the reasoning behind these assertions?

bered than the ones in the middle. The resulting "U-shaped" pattern was referred to as the *serial-position effect,* with the increased memory for items near the beginning called the **primacy effect** and the increased memory for the last few items called the **recency effect.** In the 1950s, these serial-position findings were reinterpreted as providing evidence for the existence of two distinct memory systems, not just one. Memory researchers argued that the primacy effect occurs because people have more time to think about the earlier items than the later items, and thus the earlier ones are more likely to be stored in a memory system that can hold information for a long time. This memory system was labeled **long-term memory.** Memory researchers further contended that the recency effect occurs because the last items are still in a memory system that holds information only for relatively short periods of time, up to about 18 seconds. This memory system was called **short-term memory.** Whatever you are currently thinking about or conscious of is contained within short-term memory, and some of the information that is actively processed here makes its way into the considerably more durable long-term memory, which has an immense capacity for information. Long-term memory is the memory system containing the name of your sixth-grade friend.

One important point that needs to be made about the relationship between short-term and long-term memory is that information flows in both directions. Not only does information from short-term memory go to long-term memory (for further encoding and storage), but a great deal of information stored in long-term memory is sent back to short-term memory (this is the retrieval process). The reason it is so hard for Ben to memorize new information is because his short-term memory system has trouble working with this information and sending it on to long-term memory. In contrast, the reason you are able to answer the question about your sixth-grade friend is because the correct information can be retrieved from long-term memory and sent to short-term memory.

The last memory system that scientists discovered is the first memory system typically coming into play in the memory process. A few years after identifying short-term and long-term memory, additional research demonstrated that a **sensory memory** also exists, containing a vast amount of information from the senses that decays even more quickly than short-term memory. Apparently, the purpose of this memory system is to retain for a split second a highly accurate record of what each of our senses has just experienced in the environment. Thus, sensory memory is like a "snapshot" of our surroundings concerning specific sensory information. Some of this sensory information is then transferred to short-term memory where we become aware of it, and all the remaining sensory information not transferred fades away. This process repeats itself each moment, with sensory memory continuously supplying short-term memory with new information to process.

Primacy effect: The increased memory for the first bits of information presented in a string of information.

Recency effect: The increased memory for the last bits of information presented in a string of information.

Long-term memory: A durable memory system that has an immense capacity for information storage.

Short-term memory: A limited-capacity memory system where we actively "work" with information.

Sensory memory: A memory system that very briefly stores the sensory characteristics of a stimulus.

Sensory memory happens automatically, without effort and without conscious awareness. Further, unlike the two-way processing that occurs between short-term and long-term memory, information does not travel back from short-term memory to sensory memory. In other words, sensory memory is not involved in the retrieval process of memory. Thus, we cannot analyze or intentionally review a sensory memory.

Is This the Only Model of Memory?

Figure 8-2 provides an overview of the information-processing model, depicting how information is transferred between these three memory systems and how they are related to encoding, storage, and retrieval. This model has dominated research on memory for about four decades. Although psychologists traditionally divide memory up into these three systems, it is important to mention that these are *abstract* memory systems and do not actually exist as physically identifiable brain areas. It should also be noted that this model does not explain all memory processes, and there are competing memory system theories (Weldon, 1999). Later in the chapter, we discuss a more recent approach, the *parallel distributed processing model,* in which memory is represented as a weblike network of connections that operate simultaneously rather than sequentially. For now, however, let us examine in greater detail each of these three memory systems from the traditional memory model.

8-1b Sensory Memory Preserves Detailed Sensory Information for a Few Moments

Sensory memory is the doorway to memory. It serves as a holding area, storing information just long enough for us to select items for attention from the multitude transmitted from our senses every moment. Those items that are not transferred to short-term memory are quickly replaced by incoming stimuli and lost (Martindale, 1991).

Sensory information is not actually stored all together in one system, but instead, consists of separate memory subsystems, each related to a different source of sensory information. The duration of sensory memory varies depending on the sense involved, but none lasts more than a few seconds. Visual sensory memory is referred to as *iconic memory* because it is the fleeting memory of an image, or *icon.* Auditory sensory memory is referred to as *echoic memory* because this brief memory is often experienced like an echo.

FIGURE 8-2
Overview of the Information-Processing Model of Memory

The information-processing model of memory likens human memory to computer information processing. In this model, there are three basic processes that information goes through: encoding, storage, and retrieval. There are also three memory systems: sensory memory, short-term memory, and long-term memory.

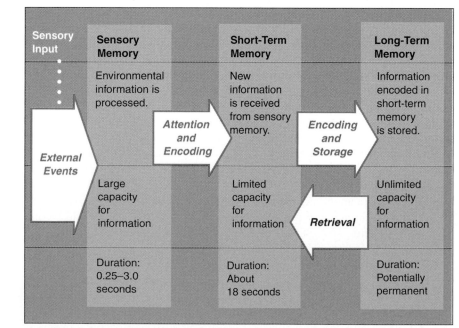

You cannot directly access sensory memory. Try the following demonstration. Move your forefinger back and forth in front of your face. The blurred images of many fingers that you see are not the actual sensory-memory images. They are gone. What you are consciously aware of is the end result of the sensory information reaching short-term memory. How do psychologists study something that cannot be consciously accessed? The groundbreaking research in this area was conducted by George Sperling (1960), who presented participants with different displays of letters, consisting of three rows of four letters each. These displays were presented for only one-twentieth of a second and looked like this:

W   K   L   P

R   B   C   U

X   V   T   D

Presenting the letters so briefly meant that participants could get only a glance at them, and most people could recall only 4 or 5 of the 12 letters. They knew they had seen more, but the fleeting image faded before they could report more than the first few letters. With this feedback, Sperling slightly modified his experiment to determine whether his participants were really seeing more of a fleeting image than they could report. The main modification involved assigning a different tone to each row of the display and then sounding one of these tones immediately after the letter pattern disappeared from view. Participants were told to report the letters in the top row if they heard a high tone, the middle row if they heard a medium tone, and the bottom row if they heard the low tone. Because the tone was not sounded until after the letter pattern disappeared, participants had to rely on their visual sensory memory, or iconic memory, to report the correct row.

With this modification, participants now correctly identified three or four letters from any given line, indicating that they had stored a fairly complete pattern of the letters in sensory memory. However, if the tone was delayed for half a second, only one or two letters were still available. At a 1-second delay, the information in their iconic memory had completely disappeared, and they could report nothing of what they saw. Now remember, as we just discussed, the participants were not directly perceiving the letters in sensory memory. What they "saw" was what had been sent to short-term memory from sensory memory. Subsequent research indicated that iconic memory lasts no more than four-tenths of a second (Van der Heijden, 1981). However, the brighter the visual image, the slower it fades (Long & Beaton, 1982).

Sensory memory studies of hearing, or *echoic memory*, indicate that auditory echoes last longer than visual fleeting images—up to a few seconds (Cowan et al., 1990). The longer duration of echoic memory explains why we hear a series of musical notes as a melody, or perceive speech as a "string" of continuous words rather than as disjointed sounds. Of course, here again, we are not directly accessing echoic memory, but instead, we are aware of what has been transferred from echoic memory to short-term memory.

8-1c Short-Term Memory Is Conceived of As a "Working Memory" System

While sensory memories are brief replicas of environmental information, to make sense of this information and to retain it for a longer time, it has to be transferred to the second memory system, namely, short-term memory. Although short-term memory was once conceived of as a relatively passive storage area that simply held information until it faded or was transferred to long-term memory, it is now thought of as the memory area where we actively "work" with information that comes from either sensory or long-term memory. This more complex and expanded view of short-term memory is referred to as **working memory** (Baddeley, 1992; Goldman-Rakic, 1995).

Working memory: The term used to describe short-term memory as an active memory system that contains a "central executive" processor and two subsystems for temporarily storing auditory and visual-spatial input.

FIGURE 8-3
Short-Term Memory as Working Memory

"Working memory" is an updated conceptualization of short-term memory. This short-term memory system is active rather than passive and contains a central executive processor and two subsystems of temporarily storing auditory input (phonological rehearsal loop) and visual-spatial input (visuospatial sketchpad).

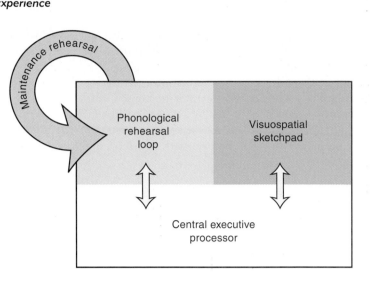

As depicted in figure 8-3, working memory has three basic components. The first is the *phonological loop*, which temporarily stores auditory input such as spoken words and meaningful sounds and is also used to generate and decode language. It can be "refreshed" through rehearsal. When you recite a phone number to yourself while trying to find a pen to write it down, you are relying on the phonological loop. This component of working memory represents all of what we originally thought of as short-term memory. The second component is the *visuospatial sketchpad*, which temporarily stores visual and spatial images. When an architect envisions a new building design, when a choreographer imagines a dancer's movements, or when you recall what your favorite stuffed animal from childhood looked like, all of these cognitive tasks rely on the visuospatial sketchpad. Finally, the third aspect of working memory is the *central executive* that supervises and coordinates the other two components.

As you can see, the two original defining characteristics of short-term memory—small capacity and short duration—still exist in the concept of working memory. However, this new view of short-term memory assumes that it handles many more functions and that it is an active, rather than a passive, process (Nyberg et al., 2002). Despite the fact that some researchers make distinctions between short-term memory and working memory (Squire & Kandel, 1999), in this introduction to the psychology of memory, I use these terms interchangeably.

Encoding in Short-Term Memory

Encoding information in short-term memory is much more complex than what occurs in sensory memory (Brandimonte et al., 1992; Richardson et al., 1996). The two storage systems in working (short-term) memory encode information either acoustically (the phonological loop) or visually (the visuospatial sketchpad), but acoustic encoding seems to dominate (Wickelgren, 1965). In one study, for example, participants were presented with a list of letters and then asked to immediately repeat them (Conrad, 1964). Even though the letters were presented visually, the mistakes made in remembering the letters were overwhelmingly of an acoustic nature. That is, a correct letter (such as V) was much more likely to be substituted with a similar-sounding letter (such as E) than with a similar-looking letter (such as U). This research suggests that, although we can store information in short-term memory using both visual and acoustic codes, we rely more on acoustic encoding, perhaps because it is easier to rehearse by mentally talking to ourselves rather than mentally imaging.

Storage Capacity of Short-Term Memory

Before reading further, complete the exercises in table 8-1 to test the storage capacity of your short-term memory. In the 1950s, George Miller tested many people's ability to remember various lists of letters, words, and digits. He found that the capacity of short-

TABLE 8-1

Testing Your Short-Term Memory Capacity

Task 1

Directions: Ask someone to read you the letters in the top row at the rate of about one per second. Then, try to repeat them back in the same order. Repeat this for the next row, and the one after that, until you make a mistake. How many letters could you repeat back perfectly?

Q M R

H Z X E

X D P Q F

G N M S W R

D H W Y U N J

E P H E A Z K R

N R E F D T O Q P

U H V X G F N I K J

H F R D S X A W U G T

H E Q L I M Y D J R N K

Task 2

Directions: Read the following string of letters and then try to write them down in correct order:

CNNA   BCCBSNB   CMCIC   IA

---

term memory is quite limited: about seven items or *chunks* of information (plus or minus two) can be retained at any one time (Miller, 1956). Cross-cultural research indicates that this seven-item limit to short-term memory is universal (Yu et al., 1985).

What happens when new information is presented to you when your short-term memory capacity is filled? Often, new information simply displaces the currently held information. However, what if you combine many discrete bits of information into a small number of meaningful groupings? This memory strategy, known as **chunking,** can greatly increase the amount of information held in short-term memory. Remember that long list of letters presented in task 2 of table 8-1? If you examine the pattern of letters closely, you will be able to chunk those 18 individual items into the following six chunks: CNN ABC CBS NBC MCI CIA. Encoding these six chunks should not exceed your short-term memory capacity.

Chunking is one of the important memory strategies that we learn in childhood, and these information chunks can be quite complex (Servan-Schreiber & Anderson, 1990). For example, you probably can repeat the following 66-letter, 14-word sentence very easily after reading it only once: *On Tuesday, three-fisted boys run after four-legged girls to compare extra limbs.* Here, you might represent this information as the following four manageable chunks: (1) "On Tuesday" (2) "three-fisted boys" (3) "run after four-legged girls" (4) "to compare extra limbs." In this case, the reason your short-term memory is so good is because you possess a great deal of knowledge about the material, namely, the English language. The ability to create meaningful chunks largely depends on how much you know

Chunking: Organizing items of information into a meaningful unit, or chunk, that can be stored in short-term memory.

INFO-BIT: In the 1950s, when the telephone company learned of George Miller's findings that people can hold only about seven items of information in short-term memory at a time, they instituted a new policy in assigning phone numbers: all numbers would consist of only seven digits. The hope was that this new standard would reduce customers' need to use operator assistance (Ellis & Hunt, 1993).

about the material that needs to be remembered (Chase & Simon, 1973; Egan & Schwartz, 1979). Thus, for chunking to effectively increase short-term memory capacity, it often requires the retrieval of information from long-term memory (Ericsson & Kintsch, 1995).

Maintenance Rehearsal

Although information is stored in short-term memory for only about 18 seconds, this time can be extended through **maintenance rehearsal,** which is the process of repetitively verbalizing or thinking about information. Reciting a phone number until you write it down is an example of maintenance rehearsal. If you are distracted before finding a pen, you will likely forget the number because it is no longer in the phonological loop of short-term memory and was not transferred to the more durable long-term memory system. Maintenance rehearsal is also important in helping you transfer information to long-term memory. This is the method you often rely on when memorizing dialogue in a play, multiplication tables, or foreign language vocabulary.

8-1d We Often Encode Information into Long-Term Memory Using Elaborative Rehearsal

One problem with using maintenance rehearsal to transfer information to long-term memory is that information learned this way has few retrieval cues and is often not strongly integrated into long-term memory. As a result, such information is often hard to retrieve from long-term memory. A different way to encode information utilizes **elaborative rehearsal,** which involves thinking about how new information relates to information already stored in long-term memory. This rehearsal is referred to as *elaborative* because, rather than merely repeating the information over and over to yourself, you *elaborate* on how it is related to something you already know. Can you still recite many—or all—of those 18 individual letters in task 2 of table 8-1? If so, it is most likely because you elaborated on how certain of these clusters of letters represent the names of previously learned organizations (CNN, ABC, CBS, NBC, MCI, and the CIA). Similarly, one way I remember phone numbers is by associating them with the jersey numbers of former football players from the Green Bay Packers (information that is in my long-term memory). So, 242-1504 becomes 242-"Bart Starr" and "Brett Favre." Organizational strategies such as this one are called *mnemonics* (pronounced "neh MON ix"), which are discussed in greater detail later in this chapter's *Psychological Applications* section.

"Shallow" Versus "Deep" Processing

Psychologists Fergus Craik and Robert Lockhart (1972) propose that elaborative rehearsal is a more effective way of encoding new information than maintenance rehearsal because it involves a deeper level of cognitive processing. The more you think about how new information is related to existing knowledge that you possess, the "deeper" the processing and the better your memory of it becomes. Craik and Lockhart believe that *shallow* processing typically involves encoding information in terms of its superficial perceptual qualities, such as its sights and sounds, while *deep* processing often involves encoding information in terms of its meaning, or *semantics* (refer back to section 8-1a). For instance, look at each of the adjectives listed below for 5 seconds and mentally note which contain the letter *e*:

> curious
>
> humorous
>
> sensitive
>
> daring
>
> quiet
>
> introspective
>
> ambitious
>
> responsible

Maintenance rehearsal: The process of repetitively verbalizing or thinking about information to either extend the usual 18-second duration of short-term memory or transfer the rehearsed information to long-term memory.

Elaborative rehearsal: Rehearsal that involves thinking about how new information relates to information already stored in long-term memory.

Journey of Discovery Question

The finding that deep processing leads to more effective encoding and better retention of new information has many practical applications for you as a student. In your own studying, how can you process new information at a deep, rather than a shallow, level?

Now, instead of scanning these words for the letter *e*, note which of these adjectives describe you as a person. Research indicates that this semantic exercise, in contrast to the previous perceptual exercise, not only triggers more activity in a part of the frontal cortex of the left cerebral hemisphere associated with language, but it also leads to a greater likelihood of long-term memory storage (Gabrieli et al., 1996). What largely explains the more permanent memory storage in semantic exercises versus perceptual exercises is that semantic exercises create more associations between new memories and existing memories (Lockhart & Craik, 1990). Further, in the semantic exercise just described, you were asked to process the adjectives by associating them with a very important set of existing memories: your self-concept. When new information is processed in terms of its relevance to ourselves, we process it at a deeper level and better remember it at a later time (Rogers et al., 1977; Symons & Johnson, 1997). Indeed, Craik and Lockhart contend that the distinction between short-term memory and long-term memory is simply a matter of the depth of the encoding process. Instead of describing two distinct memory systems (short and long), they prefer to describe a continuum of processing ranging from shallow to very deep. Information processed at a shallow level can be retained only briefly (in what is conventionally called short-term memory), while information processed at a deeper level can be kept indefinitely (in what is traditionally called long-term memory). Whether Craig and Lockhart's hypothesis is supported by future studies, their research is important because it informs us that the most important determinant of memory is how extensively information is encoded or processed when it is first received. Elaborative rehearsal, which relies extensively on semantic encoding, provides a much deeper level of processing than maintenance rehearsal, which relies primarily on acoustic encoding.

Semantic Encoding Errors

Because semantic encoding is the dominant encoding process for long-term memory, the type of errors we make in remembering information are often associated with the unique qualities of semantic encoding. For instance, semantic encoding often ignores details and instead encodes the general underlying meaning of information. Consider figure 8-4. Can you identify the correct drawing of a U.S. penny?

When Americans are asked this question, most are unsuccessful, as are people from Great Britain who are asked to identify their country's coins (Nickerson & Adams, 1979; Richardson, 1993). The reason most of us are so bad at correctly identifying a familiar object like a penny is because we never encoded all of its specific details into long-term memory. Our tendency to encode the general meaning of visual stimuli rather than its specific details is what counterfeiters depend on when "passing" fake currency. To reduce this problem, the U.S. Treasury is now using more distinctive drawings on paper money so that people will more easily recognize counterfeit currency when they see it.

8-1e There Is More Than One Type of Long-Term Memory

Although the traditional information-processing model describes long-term memory as one solitary system, it is now clear that there is more than one type of long-term memory. Thus, unlike a computer, which has one hard drive to store information for long periods of time, the brain has multiple "hard drives" (Noice & Noice, 2002; Tulving, 1997).

FIGURE 8-4
Which Is the Real Penny?

Among all these coins, can you correctly identify the "real" penny? Our failure to encode the details of coins and other currency into long-term memory is what counterfeiters rely on in plying their trade.

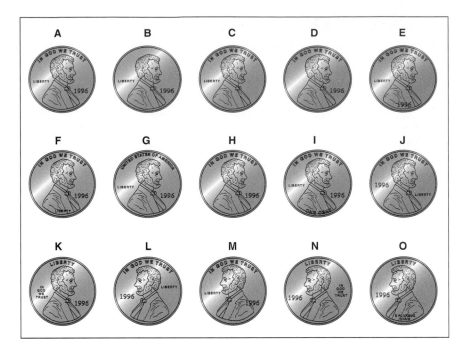

Episodic memory: Memory for factual information acquired at a specific time and place.

Semantic memory: Memory for general knowledge about the world that is not associated with a time and place when the information was learned.

Procedural memory: Memory of how to perform skilled motor activities.

Episodic memory is memory for factual information acquired at a specific time and place, such as your first romantic kiss or your first day attending college classes. Do you remember what you had for dinner last night? If so, this is an episodic memory. In contrast to the specific information stored in episodic memory, **semantic memory** is of a more general nature. It stores general knowledge about the world that we do not typically remember acquiring at a specific time and place (Menson et al., 2002; Tulving & Lepage, 2000). For example, do you remember when or where you learned that George Washington was the first president of the United States? Or when you learned that Santa Claus had a reindeer with a big red nose? All the countless facts that you have learned during the course of your life generally fit into this category of memory. Finally, **procedural memory** retains information of how to perform skilled motor activities, such as how to ride a bike, drive a car, do a cartwheel, or even walk. It is often difficult to describe in words how to actually perform these actions. For example, when I'm occasionally asked to describe how to drive a stick shift on a car, I am often at a loss for words. After a few failed attempts at verbally describing how one should depress the clutch pedal while simultaneously repositioning the shifter, I typically sit in a nearby chair and demonstrate the procedure by imagining myself in the driver's seat.

Countless everyday situations and activities require you to use all three types of long-term memory. For example, when driving a car you rely on procedural memory to steer, shift, speed up, and slow down. Remembering the rules of driving, such as stopping at red lights, yielding to pedestrians, and driving on the right side of the road would be examples of relying on semantic memory. Finally, recalling that you were ticketed for speeding on a particular stretch of road on your 19th birthday would be an example of episodic memory.

Studies of brain-injured patients and brain scans of healthy individuals indicate that the frontal lobes are important in accessing both episodic and semantic memories (Squire & Kandel, 1999). However, recalling semantic memories tends to activate the left frontal lobe more than the right, while the exact opposite effect occurs for episodic memories (Cabeza & Nyberg, 1997). These findings provide further evidence that long-term memory consists of multiple systems.

SECTION SUMMARY

- Computer information-processing serves as a rough working model for human information-processing.

- In the three basic information processes, the encoding stage transfers information into memory, the storage stage organizes and maintains information in memory for a period of time, and the retrieval stage recovers stored information from memory so that it can be used.

- The three different memory systems have the following characteristics: sensory memory stores information just long enough for us to select items for attention; short-term memory (or working memory) actively works with about seven bits of information; long-term memory has immense information capacity and durability.

- Information can be kept in short-term memory longer through rehearsal.

- There are multiple long-term memory systems, among them episodic, semantic, and procedural.

8-2 HOW IS KNOWLEDGE ORGANIZED IN MEMORY?

Quickly, recite the 12 months of the year. Barring any physical problems with your brain, I'm sure that you knew all the names. I'm also willing to bet that you recited them in the following order: January, February, March, April, May, June, July, August, September, October, November, December. Am I right about your recitation? Now, recite these same months again as fast as you can, but this time, recite them in alphabetical order. Why did this second task take you so much longer to complete than the first task?

8-2a Some Information in Long-Term Memory Is Organized into Networks

In an early study of how information is organized in long-term memory, William Bousfield (1953) asked people to memorize 60 randomly presented words that came from four semantic categories: names, animals, vegetables, and professions. Despite the random order of presentation, people later tended to recall the words in clusters corresponding to the four categories. Subsequent research indicated that even when items on a list have little in common, we still try to impose a semantic structure (Mandler & Pearlstone, 1966; Tulving, 1962). These findings suggest that, possibly due to both experience and genetic predispositions, we develop the habit of organizing information into meaningful patterns to facilitate encoding, and hence long-term memory.

In attempting to understand how knowledge is often semantically organized in long-term memory (see section 8-1e), a number of theorists have proposed that information is stored in a vast network of interrelated concepts (Anderson, 1990; Ratcliff & McKoon, 1994). One of the most influential of these theories is called the **semantic network model** (Collins & Loftus, 1975). According to this theory, there are many kinds of associations we can make between concepts. A *concept* consists of a cluster of objects, ideas, or events that share common properties and are linked to other concepts in the long-term memory network. Some concepts in this network are more strongly linked than others.

A small semantic network is depicted in figure 8-5 and represents how it might look right after you think of the concept *Santa Claus*. According to the semantic network model, when you think of a concept, your thoughts naturally go to related concepts stored in long-term memory. In figure 8-5, this network of possible associations is represented by

Semantic network model:
A theory that describes concepts in long-term memory organized in a complex network of associations.

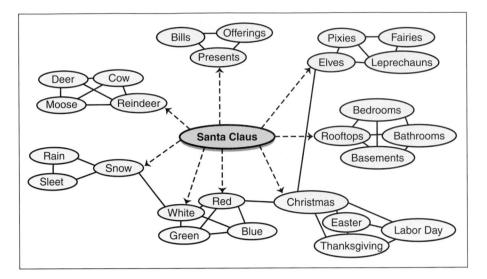

FIGURE 8-5
A Semantic Network Model

According to the semantic network model, information in long-term memory is organized in a complex network of association. The shorter the link between concepts, the more likely it is that retrieving one concept will also trigger the retrieval of the other concept.

lines connecting the concepts. *Santa Claus* activates associations with the following concepts: *red* and *white* because Santa has a red suit and a white beard; *snow* and *Christmas* because he visits during a specific night in winter; *reindeer* and *rooftops* because these animals fly him to the top of houses; and *elves* and *presents* because his elf-helpers make presents that he delivers. The length of the lines indicates the strength of the association between the concepts. Shorter lines imply stronger associations, meaning that you will more easily recall concepts with these stronger associations. Thus, when you hear *Santa Claus*, you are more likely to think of the words *Christmas, red,* and *reindeer* than the words *elves* and *white*. Similarly, you are much more likely to think of the words *elves, white, snow,* and *presents* than the words *leprechauns, blue, sleet,* and *offerings.*

Although the semantic network model assumes that semantic networks are a universal way of organizing information, cross-cultural studies indicate that the way people use these networks is influenced by experience and education. Research in rural Liberia and Guatemala, for example, found that children who receive more schooling are more likely to use semantic categories in recalling lists of concepts than children with less schooling (Cole & Cole, 1993). This finding makes sense because semantic grouping allows for the quick learning of a lot of information, a basic requirement in academic settings. Children with less schooling have less need to memorize large amounts of information and, thus, are less likely to organize information semantically. These findings do not mean that school-educated children have better memories than those with no schooling. Instead, it means that people tend to organize information in long-term memory that is consistent with their life experiences and the demands of their surroundings.

8-2b Information in Long-Term Memory Can Be Organized around Schemas

The tendency to encode information by semantic categories doesn't mean that all stored memories are arranged in semantic networks. Semantic networks are less helpful in explaining how information is clustered into coherent wholes, called *schemas*. As discussed in chapter 4, section 4-3a, schemas are organized, repeatedly exercised patterns of thought or behavior. Regarding encoding and memory, research indicates that people are more likely to remember things that can be incorporated into existing schemas than things that cannot (Marshall, 1995).

John Bransford and Marcia Johnson (1972) conducted a memory experiment that demonstrated the importance of having the right schema at the right time. To understand the importance yourself, read the following story read by Bransford and Johnson's participants, and then, like them, try to recall as much of it as you can:

If the balloons popped, the sound wouldn't be able to carry, since everything would be too far away from the correct floor. A closed window would also prevent the sound from carrying, since most buildings tend to be well insulated. Since the whole operation depends on the steady flow of electricity, a break in the middle of the wire would also cause problems. Of course, the fellow could shout, but the human voice is not loud enough to carry that far. An additional problem is that the string could break on the instrument. Then there would be no accompaniment to the message. It is clear that the best situation would involve less distance. Then there would be fewer potential problems. With face-to-face contact, the least number of things could go wrong.

After reading this passage, take a little break, look around your immediate surroundings, and make a mental note of ten different objects that you can see. What color are each of them? What are their sizes in relation to one another?

Now that I have distracted you from thinking about the Bransford and Johnson story for over 18 seconds, how much of it can you now remember? Experimental participants who, like you, were given *no schema* in which to understand the story, remembered less than 4 of its 14 ideas. However, those who were given a schema in which to understand the story—by being shown a cartoon similar to the one in figure 8-6 *before* reading the story—recalled twice as many ideas (about 8 out of 14). Interestingly, participants who were given the schema *after* the reading remembered no more than those not shown the picture at all. Apparently, seeing the picture beforehand allowed participants to make sense of what they were reading. This suggests that it is crucial to have the right schema during the encoding stage in order to understand and remember complex material. Further studies indicate that schemas help us to remember and organize details, speed up processing time, and fill in gaps in our knowledge (Fiske & Taylor, 1991; Hirt, 1990). The fact that schemas can fill in gaps in our knowledge explains why they sometimes contribute to memory distortions (see section 8-3c.)

Because schemas develop from our experiences, it is reasonable to assume that they are significantly shaped by culture. In one study, students in the United States and the Pacific island nation of Palau read separate descriptions of funerals in the two cultures and were later asked to recall everything they could about them (Pritchard, 1991). It was hypothesized that students would better remember the funeral description from their own culture because it would more closely match their cultural schema for funerals. Results supported this hypothesis. Further cross-cultural research indicates that *cultural utility* plays an important role in what kind of schemas develop and, thus, what is remembered (Hunn, 1982, 1990; Mistry & Rogoff, 1994). For example, the Fore people of New Guinea have highly elaborate schemas for many different bird species, but they tend to group all butterflies together under one schematic category (Diamond, 1966). The reason for this schematic difference is that birds are a valued food source for the Fore, while butterflies are of little use to them. This research suggests that culture shapes schema formation and thus plays an important role in what we attend to, process, encode, and later recall from long-term memory (Malt, 1995).

8-2c Memory May Involve Parallel Processing of Neural Units

Do you realize that while reading these words, you are performing some amazing memory feats? You are recognizing the patterns that make up the letters of the alphabet while simultaneously recognizing how sets of these letters make up words in the English language and how these word strings make up meaningful sentences. How can you execute these different memory tasks at the same time?

The traditional information-processing model assumes that the brain works sequentially, like a computer (Ioannides et al., 2002). Yet, we know that the human brain performs many tasks simultaneously—that is, in parallel. It apparently accomplishes such *parallel processing* of information because millions of neurons are active at once, and each neuron is communicating with thousands of other neurons. This simultaneous neural

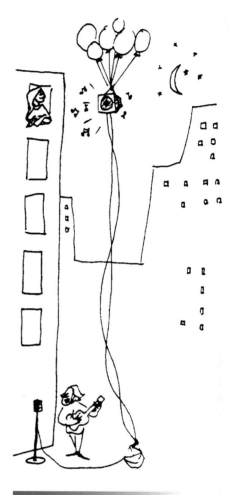

FIGURE 8-6
Man Serenading a Woman

Source: Figure from "Contextual prerequisites for understanding: Some investigations of comprehension and recall" by John D. Bransford and M. K. Johnson in JOURNAL OF VERBAL LEARNING AND VERBAL BEHAVIOR, 11, pp. 717–726, copyright © 1972 by Academic Press, reproduced by permission of the publisher. This material may not be reproduced in any form or by any means without the prior written permission of the publisher.

Parallel distributed processing models: Models of memory in which a large network of interconnected neurons, or processing units, distributed throughout the brain simultaneously work on different memory tasks.

communication produces the type of cognitive complexity necessary for parallel processing. Building on this idea, **parallel distributed processing models** of memory contend that what we call memory is knowledge distributed across a dense network of neural associations (McClelland, 1994; Raffone & Leeuwen, 2001; Smolensky, 1995). When this neural network is activated, different areas of the network operate simultaneously, in a parallel fashion. Such parallel processing allows us to quickly and efficiently utilize our storehouse of knowledge.

A parallel distributed processing system consists of a large network of interconnected neurons called *processing units,* which are distributed throughout our brains. Each unit is designed to work on a specific type of memory task. For example, one model suggests that for comprehending written English there might be individual processing units for 16 different letter patterns, for each of the 26 letters in the English alphabet, and for thousands of words (McClelland & Rumelhart, 1981). When you look at a book written in English, these processing units are activated at the same time. The letter-related units recognize letters while the word units recognize words from letter combinations, and presto, you're comprehending the words on the page with amazing speed.

Parallel distributed processing models believe that information in memory is not located in a specific place in the brain, but instead, resides in connections between the involved processing units in the neural network (Nadeau, 2001). Parallel distributed processing models better represent the actual operation of the brain, and they have been used to also explain perception, language, and decision making. However, the information-processing approach is still better at explaining memory for single events, as well as why learning new information can sometimes cause you to forget previously learned information (see section 8-4b). In sizing up these two approaches, memory expert Endel Tulving (1999) advises that, at least for the present, they are both necessary for a fuller understanding of memory.

SECTION SUMMARY

- In the semantic network model, information is organized in long-term memory in a vast network of interrelated concepts.
- Schemas help us remember and organize details, speed up processing time, and fill in knowledge gaps.
- Parallel distributed processing models contend that memory is a large network of interconnected neurons, or processing units, that simultaneously work on different memory tasks.

8-3 HOW DO WE REMEMBER?

Encoding, storing, and organizing information in long-term memory are important cognitive processes, but they would be of no use to us if we could not later retrieve this information when we needed it. Remembering involves retrieving information from long-term memory so that it resides in consciousness, or short-term memory. To appreciate firsthand the power and imperfection of memory retrieval, try answering the following questions:

Did Abraham Lincoln ever fly in an airplane?

Which two states begin with the letter K?

How many days are there in the month of April?

What did you eat for breakfast last Monday?

In Mexico, which national hero is considered the "father" of his country?

In answering these questions, it's likely that some were easier for you than others. For instance, you probably quickly answered that Lincoln never flew in a plane, but it probably took you a bit longer to remember that Kansas and Kentucky are the two states that start with the letter K, and that there are 30 days in April. Did you remember what you ate for breakfast last Monday, and were you able to recall that Benito Juárez, Mexico's first president of Indian descent, was his country's national hero?

As these questions hopefully illustrate, although memory retrieval can be effortless and automatic, it can also be difficult and unreliable. The effortful nature of some retrieval tasks might have been demonstrated when you tried to answer the "April" question. Perhaps you had to recite a rhyme learned in childhood to aid your recall: "Thirty days hath September, April, June, and November . . . ." Likewise, in identifying the "K" states, you might have had to visualize a map of the United States and then "looked" for the two right answers. By the way, if you could not answer the "Mexican national hero" question, it may have been because the Benito Juárez information was not stored in long-term memory. In this section of the chapter, we examine various cognitive strategies that facilitate remembering stored information.

8-3a Remembering Can Be Either Explicit or Implicit

As you have learned throughout this textbook, experience affects how we behave. However, what is surprising is that remembering these previous experiences can occur either consciously or relatively unconsciously (Nelson et al., 1992; Underwood & Bright, 1996).

Explicit Memory

For many years, psychologists primarily studied the conscious recollection of previous experiences, known as **explicit memory.** Explicit remembering can be either intentional or unintentional. For example, you might intentionally recall an argument, or this memory might spontaneously enter consciousness. Both instances involve explicit memory because conscious recollection takes place.

Psychologists measure explicit memory by testing a person's *recall* ability and their *recognition* ability. Although **recall** requires a person to retrieve and reproduce information from memory, **recognition** simply requires a person to decide whether or not something has been previously encountered. In most cases, recall is harder than recognition because it requires more extensive mental processing (Watkins & Tulving, 1975). This is the main reason why you will often *recognize* a person's face as being familiar, even though you cannot *recall* her or his name.

To directly test the explicit remembering of faces versus names, researchers first asked young and old high school graduates to write down the names of as many former classmates as they could remember (Bahrick et al., 1975). For all age groups, recall was poor. Recent graduates could recall only a few dozen names, and those who graduated over 40 years earlier recalled fewer than 20 names. Next, researchers asked these same individuals to identify the face of a former classmate from a card containing five photographs. In this recognition task, recent graduates and those who had graduated up to 35 years earlier correctly recognized classmates 90 percent of the time! Even those who graduated 48 years earlier still recognized classmates three-fourths of the time.

In analyzing these findings, it is important to realize that they do not suggest that we are better at remembering faces than names. Instead, they indicate that recall is more difficult than recognition. Remembering faces becomes much more difficult when we have to *recall* each facial feature rather than simply *recognizing* it as familiar. Similarly, our ability to recognize familiar names is equal to our ability to recognize familiar faces (Faw, 1990).

The greater difficulty of recall tasks compared with recognition tasks is one reason many students prefer true-false and multiple-choice exams over essay and fill-in-the-blank exams. The former exams only require recognition of the correct answer, while the latter

Explicit memory: Memory of previous experiences that one can consciously recollect.

Recall: A measure of explicit memory in which a person must retrieve and reproduce information from memory.

Recognition: A measure of explicit memory in which a person need only decide whether or not something has been previously encountered.

> *INFO-BIT:* Recent studies indicate that the cognitive capacity for recalling information from long-term memory emerges late in the first year of life, well before children have the verbal ability to describe past experiences (Bauer, 2002).

exams require the retrieval and reproduction of information (Kroll et al., 2002). The different remembering required in these exams, however, doesn't necessarily mean that recognition tests are easy. As you undoubtedly know from personal experience, multiple-choice tests can be extremely challenging (you might even say "tricky") if the alternatives are very similar to the correct response. Sometimes, the correct answer feels like it is on the "tip of your tongue," so close you can almost taste it. Read Discovery Box 8-1 for a better understanding of this memory problem.

Implicit Memory

Implicit memory: Memory of previous experiences without conscious recollection.

Remembering does not always involve conscious recollection. Sometimes, information is retained and influences our thoughts and actions without us consciously remembering it (Dovidio et al., 2001; Schacter et al., 1993). This psychological process is known as **implicit memory.** How might implicit memory affect your thoughts and behavior? If you were traumatized by a horse as a youngster, you might feel anxious when around horses as an adult, even though you have no conscious memory of the childhood incident (see the discussion of repression in section 8-4c). Similarly, feeling immediately at ease and happy around a new acquaintance because they unconsciously remind you of a cherished person from your past is another example of the power of implicit memory.

A great deal of cognitive activity involving implicit memory is not that unusual. For example, while reading these words, you are unconsciously remembering their meaning. To study this type of memory, psychologists often use word-completion tasks. In such tasks, a participant completes word stems, such as the following: part_ _ _ _ _ _. Because you just saw the word *participant* earlier in the sentence, you would be more likely to think of this word than the word *partnership*. This method of activating implicit memories is known as **priming.** The fact that a previous experience (seeing the word *participant*) makes you more likely to respond in a certain way demonstrates that you can retain more implicit knowledge about the past than you realize (Roediger, 1990). Discovery Box 8-2 discusses another way in which prior experiences can affect later thoughts and behavior without conscious knowledge.

Priming: A method of activating implicit memories in which a recently presented bit of information facilitates—or "primes"—responses in a subsequent situation.

8-3b Retrieval Cues Help Trigger Recall of Stored Memories

Retrieval cue: A stimulus that allows us to more easily recall information from long-term memory.

One of the most effective ways to facilitate remembering is to use retrieval cues. A **retrieval cue** is a stimulus that allows us to more easily recall information from long-term memory. The reason similar stimuli help us remember is because many elements of the physical setting in which we learn information are also simultaneously encoded into long-term memory (Tulving & Thomson, 1973). The helpfulness of the physical setting in fostering retrieval is also the reason students perform better on exams when tested in the same classroom in which they learned the material than in a different setting (Saufley et al., 1985; Smith et al., 1978).

If you think of a memory as being held in storage by a web of associations like in the semantic network model (see section 8-2a), then retrieval cues would be the individual strands in the web that lead to the memory (Anderson, 1983). The more retrieval cues you have for a particular memory, and the better learned these cues are, the more accessible the memory. You are likely to retrieve the sought-after memory if you can activate one or more of those strands.

DISCOVERY BOX 8-1

What Do We Know about the Tip-of-the-Tongue Phenomenon?

In explicit memory, we often can retrieve some features but not enough to identify an entire concept. For example, try to recall the names of all the dwarfs from the movie *Snow White and the Seven Dwarfs*.

How did you do? If your retrieval attempt resulted in incomplete recall, you are in good company—most people cannot recall all seven names without assistance (Miserandino, 1991). Now, try to pick out the seven dwarf names from among the 14 names listed in alphabetical order below:

Angry, Bashful, Crummy, Doc, Dopey, Father, Grumpy, Happy, Leafy, Sleepy, Sneezy, Snowy, Sweaty, Windy

I'm guessing that this task was easier than the first because it involved recognition rather than recall. In the first task, you may have felt that the names were just about to enter consciousness, but you were having trouble pulling them out of long-term memory. This frustrating retrieval problem of being unable to remember something you know is known as the **tip-of-the-tongue phenomenon** and is another demonstration of how recognition is easier than recall (Brown, 2000; Schwartz, 2001, 2002).

Listed next are some basic facts about the tip-of-the-tongue phenomenon (Brown, 1991; James & Burke, 2000; Vigliocco et al., 1999):

- It appears to be universal, occurring in all cultures and age groups.

- It increases in frequency with age.

- It is most often triggered by names of personal acquaintances.

- When trying to remember the sought-after word, related words come to mind. These words usually have a similar meaning (*favoritism* instead of *nepotism*) or sound (*Greg* instead of *Craig*).

- Usually, people can guess the first letter of the sought-after word about half of the time.

- About half of the time, the person remembers the sought-after word within the first minute.

By the way, if you are still wondering about those dwarf names, they are *Sleepy, Grumpy, Dopey, Sneezy, Happy, Bashful,* and *Doc*.

Tip-of-the-tongue phenomenon: The temporary inability to remember something you know, accompanied by the feeling that it is just beyond your conscious state.

I cannot at the present moment recall what the General's Christian name was. Your poor dear mother always addressed him as "General." That I remember perfectly.

—Lady Bracknell in *The Importance of Being Earnest*
by Oscar Wilde, Irish author and satirist, 1854–1900

DISCOVERY BOX 8-2

How Might Memory Illusions Be Formed?

When prior experiences affect thoughts and behavior without being consciously remembered, it can lead to certain kinds of interesting memory illusions. These memory illusions are believed to be a direct result of implicit remembering.

A common type of memory illusion is **déjà vu,** in which you subjectively feel a sense of familiarity in a situation that you objectively know you have never encountered before (Sno, 2000). An example of déjà vu would be walking into a house for the very first time and yet having a strong feeling of having been there before. About 60 percent of American adults experience déjà vu at least once in their lives. Such experiences occur most often among people who daydream a great deal. It is also most likely to occur when you are in a state of heightened sensitivity or anxiety, and when you are overly tired (Reed, 1979). Although a popular belief is that déjà vu occurs because people are experiencing previous lives (reincarnation), a more cognitive—and less extraordinary—explanation is that people are simply implicitly remembering similar, but unidentifiable, situations they have previously seen in their present lives.

Another type of memory illusion is **cryptomnesia,** which is also known as *unintended plagiarism* (Searleman & Herrmann, 1994). In cryptomnesia, a person honestly believes that some work she or he has done is a novel creation, when, in reality, the work is not original (Brown & Murphy, 1989; Taylor, 1965). This type of memory illusion is common when people collaborate on a project. In such instances, group members recall ideas they heard from others, but they forget where and from whom they originally heard it. After a while, everyone believes it was they who came up with the brilliant idea that made the project a success. If you think of cryptomnesia as an instance where someone else's old idea becomes your new idea, then cryptomnesia is almost the opposite of déjà vu, in which something new seems old. With cryptomnesia, as with déjà vu, previously learned information is retained and influences our thoughts and actions without us consciously remembering it.

Accusations of cryptomnesia usually arise only after someone publicly presents the unintentionally plagiarized work as her or his own. A number of the more famous incidents—and even scandals—resulting from such public presentations have involved such well-known individuals as Sigmund Freud (founder of psychoanalysis), Helen Keller (educator and lecturer who was both deaf and blind), Friedrich Nietzsche (German philosopher and poet), Eddie Murphy (comedian and movie star), and George Harrison (former member of the Beatles). The frequency of cryptomnesia occurrence is difficult to estimate, but it is probably not a rare product of implicit memory.

Déjà vu: A memory illusion in which people feel a sense of familiarity in a situation that they know they have never encountered before.

Cryptomnesia: A memory illusion in which people believe that some work they have done is a novel creation, when, in fact, it is not original.

Thus far, I have only mentioned retrieval cues originating in our external world. Yet, our internal psychological environment can also be encoded and become part of our memory strands. For example, when people learn information while in an altered state of consciousness induced by alcohol, marijuana, or some other drug, they may later recall it better when tested under the same altered state (Eich, 1989). Similar effects have been found for positive and negative moods. When in a positive mood, we tend to recall positive memories, while negative memories are more accessible when we are depressed (Ehrlichman & Halpern, 1988; Lewinsohn & Rosenbaum, 1987). This tendency for retrieval from memory being better when our state of mind at the time of retrieval matches our state at the time of initial encoding is known as **state-dependent memory.**

Although many studies have found evidence for state-dependent memory, others have not (Bower & Mayer, 1991; Kihlstrom, 1989). Two factors that appear to influence the strength of state-dependent memory are *self-awareness* and the *presence of other retrieval cues*. That is, evidence for state-dependent memory is strongest when people are self-aware (and thus, attentive to their internal state of mind), and when other retrieval cues are weakest (Rothkopf & Blaney, 1991; Singer & Salovey, 1988).

As previously mentioned, the best retrieval cues come from associations formed when we encode information into long-term memory. This rule of retrieval, known as the **encoding specificity principle,** is supported by a large body of evidence (Mantyla, 1986; Tulving & Thomson, 1973). For instance, in one study, participants were shown a long list of words and then were asked either a semantic (meaning) or a rhyming question about each word (Morris et al., 1977). Thus, if the word was *dairy*, they might be asked if *"dairy products come from cows"* or if *"dairy rhymes with fairy."* Later, participants were asked to identify from a list those words they had been shown before. Results indicated that participants did much better at recognizing words for which semantic questions had previously been asked rather than rhyming-word questions. The fact that semantically coded retrieval cues worked better than rhyming codes is not surprising, because, as was previously mentioned (section 8-1d), long-term memories are often encoded semantically. However, when asked to identify words that *rhymed* with the ones that they had previously seen (for example, *berry*, which rhymes with *dairy*), participants did much better at recognizing words that rhymed with words for which they had been asked a rhyming question rather than a semantic question.

The importance of having the right retrieval cues for a memory task is something that strikes close to home for every college student. In what you might perceive to be a cruel classroom demonstration of the encoding specificity principle, half the students in a college class were told that an upcoming exam would be multiple-choice (a recognition task), while the other half expected an essay exam (a recall task). Only some of the students, however, were given the exam they expected. Consistent with the encoding specificity principle, those students did much better on the exam than those who received an unexpected type of exam (d'Ydewalle & Rosselle, 1978). These results, combined with the previous study's findings, clearly indicate that the best retrieval cues are those that closely match up with the original encoding process.

8-3c Memories Are Often Sketchy Reconstructions of the Past

Based on the chapter 5 discussion of perception, you understand that errors or misperceptions are bound to occur because our beliefs and expectations significantly influence how we perceive sensory stimuli. Similarly, our previous discussion of schemas (see section 8-2b) demonstrated that beliefs and expectations can significantly shape what we encode and later retrieve from memory. How does this reconstructive process take place?

State-dependent memory: The tendency for retrieval from memory being better when our state of mind during retrieval matches our state during encoding.

Encoding specificity principle: A retrieval rule stating that retrieving information from long-term memory is most likely when the conditions at retrieval closely match the conditions present during the original learning.

The scientific belief in the reconstructive nature of memory was first proposed about 70 years ago by English psychologist Sir Frederic Bartlett (1932). By testing people's memories of stories they had read, Bartlett found that accurate recollections were rare. Instead, people reconstructed the material they had learned, shortening and lengthening different aspects, and overall, changing details to better fit their own beliefs and expectations. These memory distortions became more pronounced over time, yet people were largely unaware that they had reconstructed the past. In fact, the reconstructed memories were often those aspects of the story that people most adamantly claimed to be true. Based on these findings, Bartlett concluded that information already stored in long-term memory strongly influences how we both encode and later remember new information.

One factor that influences the reconstruction of memory is age-related differences in encoding and retrieval. That is, an adult's mind is organized differently than a 2-year-old's mind, and thus, the encoding and retrieval operations are different. According to the previously discussed *encoding specificity principle,* the effectiveness of a retrieval operation is determined by how well it re-creates the conditions present at the time of the original encoding. As a result, it is highly questionable whether a childhood experience that was encoded using a 2-year-old's sensorimotor schemes can be accurately retrieved using an adult's formal operational schemes (Ceci, 1995; Perris et al., 1990; Simcock & Hayne, 2002). This **infantile amnesia** is one of the primary problems surrounding claims by adults concerning their recently "remembered" memories of early childhood sexual abuse (see Discovery Box 8-3).

Infantile amnesia: The inability to remember events that occurred during the early part of life (usually, before the age of 3).

In addition to age effects, people's social expectations and stereotypes can significantly shape what they remember about an event. For example, in a set of classic studies conducted by Gordon Allport and Leo Postman (1945, 1947), White participants were first shown a picture (see figure 8-7) of a White man holding a razor while gesturing at a Black man. They were then instructed to describe the scene to another participant, who in turn described it to another, and so on until there had been six tellings. Consistent with the social expectations and stereotypes of many White Americans in

---

INFO-BIT: Infantile amnesia is not reserved solely for human memory. This inability to remember events from early infancy has also been observed in dogs, wolves, rats, mice, and even frogs (Spear, 1979). As with humans, the most accepted explanation is that infantile amnesia is due to retrieval failure.

FIGURE 8-7
Negative Stereotypes Can Reshape Memory

In the 1940s, when White Americans were briefly shown this picture of a White man holding a razor while gesturing at a Black man, they remembered it in a manner that was consistent with their racial stereotypes. What implications does this study have for eyewitness testimony?

Source: THE PSYCHOLOGY OF RUMOR, 1st edition, by G. W. Allport and L. Postman. Copyright 1947. Reprinted with permission of Wadsworth, an imprint of the Wadsworth Group, a division of Thomson Learning. Fax 800/730-2215.

DISCOVERY BOX 8-3

How Accurate Are Flashbulb Memories?

When discussing the reconstructive nature of memory, many people bring up the fact that certain experiences in their lives seem to be remembered in amazing detail, as if they were literally frozen in time. For example, do you remember where you were and what you were doing when you learned about the terrorist attacks of September 11, 2001? These detailed and vivid memories of surprising and emotion-provoking events are known as **flashbulb memories** (Brown & Kulik, 1977). Flashbulb memories are often formed when you learn of the death of a loved one or a national tragedy.

Research suggests that self-relevance is a critical factor that interacts with surprise and emotion in producing such memories (Conway, 1995). Strong emotional reactions at the time of the event activate the amygdala—which plays a key role in emotions—which in turn influences the hippocampus to create a memory (Cahill et al., 1996; Pillemer, 1984). Age is also important. When researchers asked people who were between 1 and 7 years old in 1963 to recall how they heard about the Kennedy assassination, they found that these flashbulb memories steadily increased as age at encoding rose (Winograd & Killinger, 1983). Whereas all those who were 7 years old at the time had flashbulb memories for this event, only 50 percent of the 4-year-olds had such memories. Also, those who were older at encoding had more elaborate and detailed memories. The likely reason for this increase is that a 7-year-old's encoding process is more similar to that of an adult's, and thus, their childhood memories are more accessible for adult retrieval.

Although people tend to express high confidence in the accuracy of their flashbulb memories, substantial evidence indicates that changes and reconstructions do occur (Neisser, 1982; Terr, 1988; Wagenaar & Groeneweg, 1990). For example, one day after the Space Shuttle *Challenger* explosion in 1986, college students were asked to describe exactly how they heard the news. Then, 3 years later, many of these same students were again asked to recall their experiences (Neisser & Harsch, 1992). Despite expressing confidence in the accuracy of their memories, only about 7 percent of the students demonstrated a high degree of agreement in their two reports. For instance, although 21 percent initially reported they learned the news from television, 3 years later this figure had risen to 45 percent. Those who had produced false memories during the 3-year period were surprised, if not amazed, when they were shown the handwritten reports they had produced right after the explosion. These findings suggest that flashbulb memories are not burned into our minds and fully retained, but instead, are subject to considerable change and reconstruction over time (Schmolck et al., 2000). Despite the susceptibility of flashbulb memories to error, they still tend to be more accurate than other types of memories, perhaps due to their emotional content (Schacter, 1996).

Flashbulb memories: Detailed and vivid memories of surprising and emotion-provoking events.

If it is necessary to rearrange one's memories or to tamper with written records, then it is necessary to forget that one has done so.

—George Orwell, English author and social satirist, 1903–1950

Ten thousand different things that come from your memory or imagination—and you do not know which is which, which was true, which is false.

—Amy Tan, 1991

Misinformation effects:
Distortions and alterations in witnesses' memories due to them receiving misleading information during questioning.

the 1940s, the final story described in this chain-of-telling usually had the razor in the Black man's hand.

Not only can people's expectations affect their memory of events, but the *way* they are questioned about what they witnessed can also alter their memories. These distortions and alterations in memory are known as **misinformation effects.** The altered memories generated by such misinformation not only feel real to those who hold them, but they also often look real to observers (Schooler et al., 1986). In a famous study, Elizabeth Loftus and John Palmer (1974) demonstrated misinformation effects when they showed participants a short film of two cars colliding. Afterward, some of the participants were asked, "About how fast were the cars going when they *contacted* each other?," while others were asked, "About how fast were the cars going when they *smashed* into each other?" Those who heard the word *smashed* estimated the cars' speed at 41 miles per hour, while those who heard the word *contacted* gave a 31 mile per hour estimate. In addition, a week later when questioned again, the "smashed" participants were more than twice as likely as the "contacted" participants to recall seeing broken glass at the accident scene, despite the fact that no broken glass was visible in the film.

Further research indicates that altered memories are more likely to be created when misleading information is subtly introduced and when original memories have faded with the passage of time (Jaschinski & Wentura, 2002; Loftus, 1992). For example, during criminal trials, eyewitness memory distortions may occur in response to misleading questions posed by lawyers. A witness might be asked whether a mugger's glasses had plastic or wire frames, suggesting that the mugger wore glasses. The witness may not remember glasses, and the mugger may not have worn glasses, but this question may lead the witness to now "remember" seeing glasses on the mugger's face. Currently, it is unclear whether misleading information permanently alters memory or whether true memories can be retrieved under the right conditions (Dodson & Reisberg, 1991; Weingardt et al., 1995). Children are particularly susceptible to misinformation effects, and this fact has made the prosecution of alleged child sexual abuse cases problematic (Ceci & Bruck, 1993, 1995). That is, if children's memories can be literally altered through skillful questioning, then how trustworthy is their testimony? Until more is learned about misinformation effects, distinguishing between the true and false memories of witnesses of any age—but especially those of children—will be one of the major challenges of the courts.

Have these studies concerning the reconstructive nature of memory surprised you? Does it cause you to doubt your recollection of important life events? What about those events from your past that seem "frozen in time"? How accurate are these memories? Check out Discovery Box 8-3 concerning what we know about these so-called flashbulb memories.

SECTION SUMMARY

- Explicit memory is conscious recollection of previous experiences.
- For explicit memory, recall is more difficult than recognition.
- Implicit memory is unconscious remembering.
- Memory illusions related to implicit memory are déjà vu and cryptomnesia.

- According to the encoding specificity principle, retrieving information from long-term memory is most likely when the conditions at retrieval closely match the conditions present during the original learning.

- Information stored in long-term memory influences both encoding and later remembering of new information.

- The way people are questioned about their memories can cause memory reconstruction.

- Flashbulb memories are not as accurate as we think.

8-4 HOW DOES FORGETTING OCCUR?

What would happen if you did not forget? Wouldn't this be an overwhelming experience? Shereshevskii, the Russian reporter whose story you read at the beginning of this chapter, could answer this question. Over the years, as his memories piled up, they began to overwhelm him. Eventually, the slightest stimulus evoked so many memories that Shereshevskii could no longer hold a job, read, or even follow a simple conversation.

8-4a Most Forgetting Occurs Soon after Learning

Unlike Shereshevskii, much of what the normal person learns is quickly forgotten. Do you remember Herman Ebbinghaus's research from the late 1800s discussed in section 8-1a? After learning more than 1,200 lists of nonsense syllables and then measuring how much he recalled when relearning the list from 20 minutes to 30 days later, he discovered that most forgetting occurs during the first 9 hours after learning. As you can see in his "forgetting curve" depicted in figure 8-8, more than 40 percent of the material was forgotten after just 20 minutes. By 9 hours, over 60 percent was lost, but then the course of forgetting leveled off. These findings, combined with later research, indicate that the greatest amount of forgetting occurs in the first few hours after learning, with progressively less memory loss as time marches on (Wixted & Ebbesen, 1991).

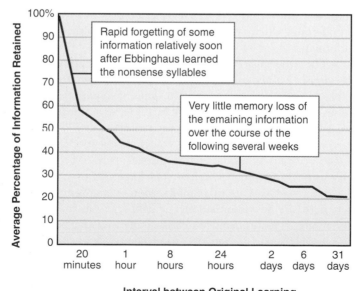

Interval between Original Learning
of Nonsense Syllables and Memory Test

F I G U R E 8 - 8
Ebbinghaus's Forgetting Curve

Ebbinghaus discovered that most forgetting occurs (over 60 percent) during the first 9 hours after learning. After 9 hours, the course of forgetting levels off. What else did Ebbinghaus learn about information that is forgotten? Is the "relearning" of this information generally difficult or easy, relative to information that was not previously learned?

A second important discovery made by Ebbinghaus was that although you may forget information that you previously learned, this does not necessarily mean that you have forgotten everything about that information. He discovered that it took less time to relearn a list of nonsense words than it did to initially learn the list. The implication of these findings is that most forgetting is not complete: You may forget something if you do not rehearse it for a period of time, but it is much easier to relearn it in the future (MacLeod, 1988). This is good news for all of us who have not practiced our French or algebra since high school graduation!

8-4b Forgetting Often Occurs Due to Interference

Now that you understand the *course* of forgetting, it is time to explore why forgetting occurs in the first place. Based on Ebbinghaus's findings on forgetting, the popular early view was that, unless periodically rehearsed, the simple passage of time caused memories to fade and eventually **decay** (Thorndike, 1914). Although decay contributes to forgetting in short-term memory, research strongly suggests that decay does not significantly influence forgetting in long-term memory (Cowan, 1995).

> **Decay:** Forgetting due to the passage of time.

An important study that discredited the decay theory of forgetting in long-term memory was conducted in 1924 by John Jenkins and Karl Dallenbach. They had college students learn lists of nonsense words either just after waking in the morning or just before going to sleep at night, and then tested their recall after 1, 2, 4, or 8 hours. For the sleeping students, this meant waking them. Despite the same amount of time passage, much more forgetting occurred when students were awake and involved in other activities than when they were asleep.

If forgetting is not due to the simple passage of time, then what is its cause? Actually, the key to this answer is contained within Jenkins and Dallenbach's findings. Do you see it? The reason more forgetting occurred early in the morning rather than late in the evening was because of the greater *interference* of other information students encountered during their daytime activities. In instances like this, the learning of new information acts backward in time to interfere with the remembering of older information (Koutsaal et al., 1999; Windschitl, 1996). This forgetting due to interference from newly learned information is known as **retroactive interference.** For example, you experience retroactive interference when learning information in this chapter interferes with your memory of information learned in a previous chapter.

> **Retroactive interference:** Forgetting due to interference from newly learned information.
>
> **Proactive interference:** Forgetting due to interference from previously learned information.

The other major type of interference is **proactive interference,** which occurs when previously learned information acts forward in time to interfere with the remembering of more recently learned information. Thus, if your memory of information learned in a previous chapter of this textbook interferes with your learning of information in the present chapter, you are experiencing proactive interference. Another common example of proactive interference—that is often embarrassing—occurs when you call your current girlfriend or boyfriend by a previous partner's name. Of the two types of interference, proactive interference probably causes more forgetting than retroactive interference because we have stored up a great deal of information in long-term memory that can potentially interfere with any new information we might try to learn. Luckily, the greater potential ability of proactive interference to cause forgetting may be offset by the fact that we can also use already-stored information to elaboratively encode new information (refer back to section 8-1d) and thus *improve* our memory.

For both types of interference, one important factor in determining how much interference will occur is the degree of *similarity* between the old and new information. The

---

Memories are hunting-horns whose noise dies away in the wind.

—Guillaume Apollinaire, French poet and art critic, 1880–1918

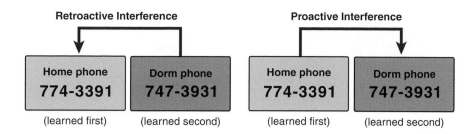

Retroactive Interference		Proactive Interference	
Home phone **774-3391**	**Dorm phone** **747-3931**	**Home phone** **774-3391**	**Dorm phone** **747-3931**
(learned first)	(learned second)	(learned first)	(learned second)

greater the degree of similarity, the greater the likelihood of interference (McGeoch & McDonald, 1931; Riccio et al., 1994). For example, as illustrated in figure 8-9, if your new phone number at the college dorm is very similar to your old phone number at home, you may well experience retroactive interference when you call home and proactive interference when you call your dorm room.

8-4c We Are Sometimes Motivated to Forget Information

Beyond the influence of interference, sometimes people forget things because they want to forget them. This is called **motivated forgetting,** and it usually occurs because a memory is unpleasant or disturbing. Sigmund Freud (1946, 1949) is generally credited with providing the theoretical framework for understanding this type of self-protective forgetting. In Freud's psychoanalytic theory, there are two types of motivated forgetting: *suppression* and *repression*.

Suppression occurs when a person *consciously* tries to forget something. For example, while preparing to execute a complicated routine during an important performance, a dancer is likely to suppress the memory of being sprawled on stage when she last attempted this number. In this situation, although the performer is aware that she failed in her previous attempt, she consciously chooses not to think about it. Unlike this conscious forgetting, Freud believed that *repression* occurs when a person *unconsciously* "pushes" unpleasant memories out of conscious awareness. Although these memories are no longer "remembered" in the conventional sense, they continue to unconsciously influence the person's thoughts, feelings, and behavior. According to psychoanalytic theory, repression plays a key role in both the formation of personality and in the development of psychological disorders (as you will see in chapters 12 and 13). Despite the assumption by psychoanalysts that repression shapes human thought and behavior, it remains a controversial topic (Loftus, 1993; Yapko, 1994). To better understand the issues underlying this controversy, read Discovery Box 8-4.

SECTION SUMMARY

- Most forgetting occurs during the first 9 hours after learning.
- It is much easier to relearn forgotten information.
- Most forgetting is caused by interference (retroactive and proactive).
- Two types of motivated forgetting are suppression and repression.

Journey of Discovery Question

Do you think you could falsely reconstruct a childhood memory based on your *beliefs* about how memory works? That is, do you think that your beliefs about how memory works could affect your recollection of past events?

FIGURE 8-9
Interference in Memory

Retroactive interference occurs when newly learned information interferes with previously learned information. Proactive interference occurs when previously learned information interferes with newly learned information. Thus, after learning your new college dorm phone number, you may have trouble remembering your parents' number at home (retroactive interference). However, your memory of your parents' phone number may also interfere with you remembering your new dorm number (proactive interference). For both types of interference, the degree of similarity between the old and new information will significantly determine how much interference occurs. More similar information causes greater interference than less similar information. Can you think of other examples of retroactive and proactive interference in your life?

Motivated forgetting: Forgetting due to a desire to eliminate awareness of some unpleasant or disturbing memory.

Suppression: Motivated forgetting that occurs consciously.

DISCOVERY BOX 8-4

Should We Trust Repressed Memories?

In 1990 George Franklin, Sr., stood trial for the brutal murder of an 8-year-old child, Susie Nason, that occurred in 1969. The major evidence provided against Franklin was the eyewitness testimony of his own daughter, Eileen, who had been Susie's best friend. What made this case so unusual was that Eileen's memory of witnessing the murder had been repressed for 20 years. Then one day, while playing with her own young daughter, she had a brief flashback of the murder—the look of betrayal in Susie's eyes just before the murder. Later, more flashbacks occurred, including the memory of Susie begging for mercy, the image of her father sexually assaulting Susie in the back of a van, and her father raising a rock above his head just before smashing Susie's skull.

One of the problems with Eileen's memory of the murder was that it changed across various tellings. First, she told police that the murder occurred in the morning while driving to school. However, when reminded that Susie had not been missing until after school was out, Eileen said it was in the late afternoon. Initially, she also reported that her sister, Janice, was riding in the van but then was dropped off when Susie was picked up. Later, that detail disappeared from her testimony. Despite these inconsistencies, the jury was so impressed with Eileen's detailed and confident memory of the murder that it returned a guilty verdict after only a day of deliberations. This case marked the first time that the return of a repressed memory proved to be the deciding factor in convicting someone of a crime in the United States. Did Eileen really witness the murder of her best friend 20 years earlier? Could such a traumatic event be forgotten for so long and then suddenly be remembered?

Many memory researchers believe that it is naive to assume that people can accurately recover memories that were previously unconsciously repressed. They further contend that people can unknowingly manufacture false memories. For ethical reasons, psychologists cannot attempt to implant false memories of murder or sexual assault in research participants. However, Elizabeth Loftus and James Coan (1995) successfully implanted less traumatic false childhood memories in five research participants ranging in age from 8 to 42. Following Loftus and Coan's instructions, trusted family members told these five individuals that, at age 5, they had been lost in a shopping mall for an extended time before being rescued by an elderly man. Following these suggestions, all participants became convinced that they indeed had been lost. One of these individuals, a 14-year-old named Chris, received this false

8-5 WHAT IS THE BIOLOGICAL BASIS FOR MEMORIES?

As mentioned at the beginning of the chapter, memory has been likened to the computer's information-processing system. In this regard, while cognitive psychologists have studied our memory "software," neuroscientists have focused their attention on its "hardware"—the biological underpinnings of memory.

account from his older brother. Two days later, Chris could remember the incident with strong feelings: "That day, I was so scared that I would never see my family again. I knew that I was in trouble." Within 2 weeks, he remembered that the man who rescued him was bald and wore glasses and a flannel shirt. When debriefed and told that his memory was false, he replied, "Really? I thought I remembered being lost . . . and looking around for you guys. I do remember that. And then crying, and Mom coming up and saying 'Where were you? Don't you ever do that again.'"

These and other studies have demonstrated that false memories can be implanted into the minds of both children and adults (Ceci et al., 1994, 1995; Johnson & Raye, 2000). In fact, research indicates that simply repeating imaginary events to people causes them to become more confident that they actually experienced these events (Begg et al., 1992; Zaragoza & Mitchell, 1996). Once constructed, these false memories may feel as real as—or even more real than—genuine memories (Brainerd et al., 1995). How are these false memories constructed? Loftus suggests that people may combine actual personal experiences—or witnessed experiences of others—with their memories of the location selected by the family member in which the alleged incident occurred (Loftus et al., 1995). Although people may first be confused when others first tell them about the false incidents, they soon combine previously unconnected bits of information into new—yet thoroughly false—memories.

Of course, this research does not tell us whether George Franklin's daughter, Eileen, recalled a false memory of sexual assault and murder rather than an authentic repressed memory. But it does raise the possibility that her repressed memory, and those of others who have come forward with similar claims, may not be real. Psychologists who conduct research on false memories readily acknowledge that childhood abuse is a major societal problem. Indeed, Elizabeth Loftus is herself a survivor of such trauma, having been molested at 6 years of age (and not forgetting). Yet many memory researchers are concerned that some cases involving repressed memories may reflect something other than real experiences. One antidote to naively accepting recovered memories of childhood trauma is to educate the public about the reconstructive nature of memory, and how they can be tricked into "remembering" things that never happened (Kassin et al., 2001).

8-5a Long-Term Potentiation May Be the Neural Basis for Memory

When a memory is made, what happens physiologically? The search for this memory trace, or *engram*, has been the focus of neuroscientists for more than 50 years (Lashley, 1950). Although there still is no scientific consensus on what an engram is or where it is located in the brain, it appears that memories begin as electrical impulses traveling between neurons, and that the establishment of long-term memories involves changes in these neurons. Eric Kandel and James Schwartz (1982) observed such neuronal changes when studying learning in the California sea slug, *Aplysia,* which has a small number (about 20,000) of large-sized neurons. By repeatedly giving sea slugs a squirt of water (the CS) followed by a mild electric shock to the tail (the UCS), Kandel and Schwartz were able to classically condition them to reflexively withdraw their gills when only squirted with the water (the CR). Kandel and Schwartz discovered that when the sea slug forms a new memory for this classically conditioned response, significant changes occur in both the *function* and *structure* of its affected neurons (Kandel, 1995). Regarding function, an increase occurs in the amount of the neurotransmitters released at the synapses—the communication points—of the neurons. Regarding structure, not only does the number of synapses increase, but so does the number of interconnecting branches between neurons. These structural changes make communication along this new neural circuit more efficient.

> **Long-term potentiation:** The long-lasting strengthening of synaptic transmission along a specific neural circuit, which is believed to be the neural basis for long-term memory.

This strengthening of synaptic transmission, which is known as **long-term potentiation,** has also been found in the brains of more complex animals. For example, when rats are raised in "enriched" environments containing many objects with which they can play and learn from, their brains develop more elaborate neural connections than rats raised in impoverished environments (Black et al., 1990; Chang et al., 1991). Additional research supporting long-term potentiation as the neural basis for memory has found that the formation of long-term memories can be blocked if animals are given drugs that inhibit long-term potentiation (Lynch & Staubli, 1991; Mathies, 1989). Finally, when researchers have altered the genes of mice so that long-term potentiation was enhanced in the hippocampus and other areas of the brain used in memory, they remembered new information over longer time periods than normal mice (Manabe et al., 1998; Tang et al., 1999). Although not all memory researchers agree, it is looking increasingly likely that long-term potentiation is the physiological key to memory.

8-5b Several Brain Regions Are Involved in Memory Formation and Storage

During the first half of the twentieth century, neuroscientists believed that a specific memory could be found in a specific place in the brain (Lashley, 1950; Penfield, 1958). Although we now know that a specific memory cannot be tied to a specific brain site, certain types of memories appear to be stored in certain brain areas (McCarthy, 1995). Short-term memory, the type of memory where we actively "work" with information, appears to involve prefrontal regions of the cerebral cortex (Fuster, 1989; Goldman-Rakic, 1992). In long-term memory, a number of different brain regions have been identified. The neocortex, striatum, and amygdala play important roles in the type of long-term memory previously identified as implicit memory (Tulving & Schachter, 1990). Regarding the sort of memory consolidation necessary for explicit memory, both animal and human studies reveal that several brain regions are involved, including the hippocampus and nearby portions of the cortex and the thalamus (Squire, 1992). Of these brain regions, the hippocampus appears to be most important in the encoding of new memories and the transfer of them from short-term to long-term memory (Squire & Knowlton, 1995). Do you remember the tragic story of Henry M. from chapter 3? Because this entire brain region was surgically removed in Henry M. to control his epileptic seizures, he lost the ability to form explicit long-term memories.

> **Anterograde amnesia:** The inability to form long-term memories due to physical injury to the brain.

This inability to form new memories due to the brain experiencing physical injury is called **anterograde amnesia.** Henry M.'s short-term memory ability is fine, and he is still capable of forming implicit memories and can remember events stored in long-term memory prior to his surgery. Similar memory deficits occur in monkeys when their hippocampus is surgically removed (Zola-Morgan & Squire, 1993). These findings suggest that although the hippocampus is critical for long-term memory formation, it is not involved in short-term memory activities or in the storage and retrieval of long-term memories.

INFO-BIT: Black-capped chickadees can remember not only the location of up to 6,000 sites where they have stockpiled food during the winter, but they can also recall what kind of food they put at a particular site and when they put it there (Clayton & Dickinson, 1998). Anatomical studies indicate that these birds have a much larger hippocampus than birds that do not stockpile food (Clayton, 1998). If the hippocampus is surgically removed, chickadees lose this memory ability.

Another type of amnesia is **retrograde amnesia,** which is the loss of information previously stored in long-term memory. People who have automobile accidents or who experience some other kind of blow to the head often cannot remember the events leading up to their physical injury (Levin et al., 1984). For example, Princess Diana's bodyguard, who was the sole survivor of the car crash that claimed her life, retained no memory of the accident. In more severe cases, the person may not remember events that occurred years before. However, in most cases, such memory loss of "distant events" is only temporary (Russell, 1971).

When researchers discovered the role played by the hippocampus in long-term memory formation, it also helped them better understand the biological basis for infantile amnesia (refer back to section 8-3c), which is a special form of retrograde amnesia (Newcombe et al., 2000). That is, the hippocampus does not fully develop until about 2 years of age (Nadel & Zola-Morgan, 1984). It's likely that whatever memory encoding that is performed by the immature hippocampus is inaccessible for later conscious remembering by the mature brain.

As you see from this brief overview of the biological basis of memory, neuroscientists' insights into our memory "hardware" provide a more complete understanding of the entire memory system. As we learn more about the biopsychology of memory, we will be in a better position to treat memory deficits caused by illness and trauma, as well as enhance the memory of healthy individuals.

Retrograde amnesia: The loss of information previously stored in long-term memory due to physical injury to the brain.

SECTION SUMMARY

- When a new memory is formed, changes may occur in both the function and structure of affected neurons.
- There is no specific location in the brain associated with a specific memory.
- Certain types of memories appear to be stored in certain brain areas.

SUGGESTED WEBSITES

Note: These websites were functional when we went to press. Please access the online text for the most up-to-date URLs.

American Psychological Association
http://www.apa.org
At the American Psychological Association website, you can search for press releases and other information about recent memory research.

Mind Tools
http://www.mindtools.com
This website contains memory techniques and mnemonics for use in everyday living, as well as links to other related websites.

Eyewitness Identification Research Laboratory
http://eyewitness.utep.edu/
This website discusses research on eyewitness testimony and provides recommendations on how to correctly design and conduct police lineups and photospreads for eyewitnesses.

PSYCHOLOGICAL APPLICATIONS
Improving Everyday Memory

Mnemonics are strategies to make it easier to encode, store, and/or retrieve information. This chapter has described current research and theory on memory. How can you use this knowledge to improve your ability to remember facts and other information? What follows is not an exhaustive guide, but research indicates that these nine techniques can improve your everyday memory:

1. *Focus your attention*—When you don't pay close attention to something, you are unlikely to remember it. Distracting stimuli, such as having the television on while studying, significantly interferes with the encoding of information into long-term memory (Armstrong & Greenberg, 1990). Thus, to better remember something, eliminate distractions by finding a quiet place to concentrate. If you cannot escape annoying distractions, reading aloud what you need to remember can help to focus your attention (Hertel & Rude, 1991).

2. *Space your practice sessions*—One of the most common mistakes students make is waiting until a day before an exam to study. Yet Ebbinghaus's (1885) famous research on forgetting (see section 8-4a) revealed another important truth about learning new material: Don't try to memorize by swallowing all your information in one big gulp. Studying new information over several days results in better learning than cramming one's studying into 1 day (Bahrick et al., 1993; Naveh-Benjamin, 1990). Such distributed practice is most effective if the interval between practice sessions is about 24 hours. Thus, four separate 1-hour study sessions spread out over 4 days will lead to better retrieval than one 4-hour session.

3. *Construct information in a hierarchy*—One of the most effective ways to remember information is to arrange it in a series of categories, from the most general to the most specific. For example, the topics in this textbook are organized hierarchically: first, with very general chapter topics (such as Memory); next, with more focused chapter "A" sections (such as The Nature of Memory); contained within these "A" sections are even more specific chapter "B" headings (such as The Computer's Information-Processing System Has Been a Useful Model Human Memory); and finally, within these "B" headings are very specific subsection "C" headings (such as Information Processes, The Identification of Three Memory Systems, and Is This the Only Model of Memory?). Hierarchical systems can double the amount of information you can recall (Bower et al., 1969).

4. *Use visual imagery*—In studying the amazing Shereshevskii, Alexander Luria discovered that he habitually and automatically used visual imagery to encode information into long-term memory. Although we are unlikely to come close to matching Shereshevskii's memory skills, research indicates that we can better remember information if we associate it with vivid mental images (Kline & Groninger, 1991). One well-known visual mnemonic technique is the method of *loci* (pronounced "low-sigh"), which requires you to mentally place items to be memorized in specific locations well known to yourself, such as rooms in your house. When you want to recall these items, you simply take a mental "walk" by these locations and "see" the memorized items. Shereshevskii would often mentally place items he wanted to remember at different locations on Gorky Street in Moscow. Later, he could even recall these items in reverse order by mentally "walking" down Gorky Street in the opposite direction. In using the method of loci, choose extremely familiar memory locations so they provide a vivid context for organizing the information to be memorized (Hilton, 1986).

5. *Use verbal mnemonics*—The use of verbal mnemonics can facilitate recall by providing extra meaning to concepts. One effective verbal mnemonic is an *acronym*, which is a word that consists of all the first letters of the items to be memorized. For example, you can remember the names of the Great Lakes (Huron, Ontario, Michigan, Erie, Superior) by remembering the acronym HOMES. Similarly, an *acrostic* is a phrase in which the first letters of each word are used to remind you of something. My daughters recite the phrase, "My Very Educated Mother Just Sold Us Nine Pizzas" to remember the names of the planets (Mercury, Venus, Earth, Mars, Jupiter, Saturn, Uranus, Neptune, Pluto). Finally, another verbal mnemonic that provides an organizational structure to information is a *rhyme* (Rubin & Wallace, 1989). Often-used rhymes are "I before E except after C," and "Thirty days hath September . . . ."

6. *Use external mnemonics*—External mnemonics play a leading role in helping us fortify our memories (Park et al., 1990). What are examples of such memory aids? The alarm clock that reminds you to get up in the morning. Your lecture notes that facilitate your retrieval of classroom material. The rubber band worn on your wrist that reminds you to visit a sick friend. The grocery list that helps you purchase the ingredients for your next meal. To effectively use these external memory aids, you must first recognize your need to use them, and then you must select an appropriate aid for the task at hand (Intons-Peterson & Newsome, 1992). Ben, the public relations director with a severe short-term memory deficit, could not have survived in his job without heavily relying on external memory devices. For example, before walking into meetings, Ben would discreetly hold in his hand the business cards of those in attendance. This external memory aid helped Ben remember their names and relevant details of previous meetings. Immediately following meetings, he would write down or tape-record his recollections before they disappeared. Although Ben could not properly function without constantly relying on these external aids, his case is merely an extension of what most of us do to bolster our fairly efficient memory systems.

7. *Overlearn*—Studying information even after you think you already know it is one of the most effective ways to firmly embed it in memory. Any information that is well learned is more likely to survive a case of the jitters than information that is only minimally learned (Martens, 1969).

8. *Use sleep to your advantage*—As you recall from chapter 6, section 6-2e, there is evidence that the cognitive processing that occurs during nighttime dreaming consolidates and stores information gathered during the day (Pavlides & Winson, 1989; Winson, 1990). In this chapter, you also discovered that, due to lack of interference, things learned just before sleep are

retained better than information learned earlier in the day. Together, these findings suggest that your parents' advice about getting a good night's rest before a big exam—and to study just before going to sleep—is well worth heeding.

9. *Cultivate close relationships*—Finally, an intriguing way to expand your memory is to form a partnership with someone else's memory! Research reveals that people in close relationships have a shared memory system that is greater than either of their individual memories (Andersson & Rönnberg, 1997; Wegner et al., 1991). In such collaborative memory, each person enjoys the benefits of the other's memory by taking responsibility for remembering just those items that fall clearly to him or her. For two people living together, this may involve one person assuming responsibility for remembering where the tools in the basement workroom are located, while the other assumes responsibility for remembering where the special dinnerware and napkins are stored. If you learn in a general way what the other person knows in detail, you can significantly improve your overall ability to remember things. Through updating one another on what is in each other's knowledge area, each of you will further embellish your collaborative memory.

Mnemonics: Strategies to make it easier to encode, store, and/or retrieve information.

KEY TERMS

anterograde amnesia (p. 242)
chunking (p. 221)
cryptomnesia (p. 232)
decay (p. 238)
déjà vu (p. 232)
elaborative rehearsal (p. 222)
encoding (p. 215)
encoding specificity principle (p. 233)
episodic memory (p. 224)
explicit memory (p. 229)
flashbulb memories (p. 235)
implicit memory (p. 230)
infantile amnesia (p. 234)
information-processing model (p. 215)

long-term memory (p. 217)
long-term potentiation (p. 242)
maintenance rehearsal (p. 222)
memory (p. 215)
misinformation effects (p. 236)
mnemonics (p. 245)
motivated forgetting (p. 239)
parallel distributed processing models (p. 228)
primacy effect (p. 217)
priming (p. 230)
proactive interference (p. 238)
procedural memory (p. 224)
recall (p. 229)
recency effect (p. 217)

recognition (p. 229)
retrieval (p. 216)
retrieval cue (p. 230)
retroactive interference (p. 238)
retrograde amnesia (p. 243)
semantic memory (p. 224)
semantic network model (p. 225)
sensory memory (p. 217)
short-term memory (p. 217)
state-dependent memory (p. 233)
storage (p. 216)
suppression (p. 239)
tip-of-the-tongue phenomenon (p. 231)
working memory (p. 219)

REVIEW QUESTIONS

1. When you encode information into memory using its personal meaning, you are using
   a. visual encoding.
   b. acoustic encoding.
   c. semantic encoding.
   d. information processing.
   e. *c* and *d*

2. If, in trying to memorize an alphabetical list of Russian states, you can remember the last two states on the list better than the middle two states on the list, you have experienced the
   a. serial-position effect.
   b. primacy effect.
   c. recency effect.
   d. *a* and *c*
   e. *b* and *c*

3. Sensory memory
   a. requires conscious awareness.
   b. exists in the hippocampus.
   c. can be studied in the laboratory.
   d. exists in one system.
   e. can be directly accessed.

4. Short-term memory
   a. stores spoken words and visual and spatial images.
   b. seems to be dominated by visual encoding.
   c. has an unlimited capacity.
   d. does not retrieve information from long-term memory.
   e. *a* and *d*

5. When I remember my first day as a college student, I am relying on
   a. episodic memory.
   b. semantic memory.
   c. procedural memory.
   d. short-term memory.
   e. working memory.

6. Which of the following statements is *true*?
   a. School-educated children have better memories than those with no schooling.
   b. All stored memories are stored in semantic networks.
   c. Bransford and Johnson's research suggests that it is crucial to have the right schema during the encoding stage.
   d. Cultural utility does not play a role in how schemas develop.
   e. Parallel distributed processing models believe information in memory is located in a specific part of the brain.

7. Research on recognition and recall of high school classmates suggests
   a. that we are better at remembering faces than names.
   b. that recognition is more difficult than recall.
   c. that recall is more difficult than recognition.
   d. *a* and *b*
   e. *a* and *c*

8. If I don't like my professor because he unconsciously reminds me of a high school teacher I disliked, which type of memory am I using?
   a. explicit
   b. recognition
   c. recall
   d. implicit
   e. priming

9. Tip-of-the-tongue phenomenon
   a. is another demonstration of how recognition is easier than recall.
   b. increases in frequency with age.
   c. appears to occur in all cultures and age groups.
   d. has to do with explicit memory.
   e. all of the above

10. Which of the following statements is *true*?
    a. Implicit memories cannot be activated.
    b. Cryptomnesia is a type of tip-of-the-tongue phenomenon.
    c. Memory illusions are believed to be a direct result of implicit memory.
    d. When in a negative mood, we tend to recall positive memories.
    e. According to the encoding specificity principle, there is little problem in believing a claim by an adult that he or she recently remembers being sexually abused as a child.

11. Which of the following statements is *true* of forgetting?
    a. The greatest amount of forgetting occurs in the first few hours after learning.
    b. Research indicates that decay significantly influences forgetting in long-term memory.
    c. Jenkins and Dallenbach's research indicates that decay causes greater memory loss than interference.
    d. Proactive interference does not improve our memory.
    e. *a* and *d*

12. Memories of past events
    a. can be consciously or unconsciously forgotten.
    b. can be falsely implanted in children and adults.
    c. can be influenced by our beliefs about how memory works.
    d. are more likely to be well remembered than completely forgotten if there is strong emotion and self-relevance.
    e. all of the above

13. The following brain regions are involved in memory formation and storage:
    a. cerebral cortex and amygdala.
    b. striatum and neocortex.
    c. long-term memory, short-term memory, and sensory memory systems.
    d. all of the above
    e. *a* and *b*

14. Considering Ebbinghaus's research, how could you best use four hours to study for an exam?
    a. four straight hours the night before the exam
    b. two separate 2-hour sessions the day of the exam
    c. four 1-hour sessions, each 24 hours apart
    d. one 4-hour session, 24 hours before the exam
    e. none of the above

15. According to research on memory, which of the following statements is *true*?
    a. Hierarchical systems can double the amount of information you can recall.
    b. It is not helpful to use the method of loci when trying to recall information.
    c. Do not waste time studying information you already know.
    d. It is a myth that studying before you go to sleep will improve your recall.
    e. Individual memories are greater than collaborative memories.

Language and Thinking

Chapter Outline

We walked down the path to the well-house, attracted by the fragrance of the honeysuckle with which it was covered. Someone was drawing water, and my teacher placed my hand under the spout. As the cool stream gushed over one hand, she spelled into the other the word "water," first slowly then rapidly. I stood still, my whole attention fixed upon the motion of her fingers. Suddenly, I felt a misty consciousness as of something forgotten—a thrill of returning thought; and somehow the mystery of language was revealed to me. I knew then that "w-a-t-e-r" meant the wonderful cool something that was flowing over my hand. That living word awakened my soul, gave it light, hope, joy, set it free! (Percy, 1976, pp. 34–35)

Having lost both her sight and hearing by a fever at 18 months of age, Helen Keller (1880–1968) lived for the next 5 years in a world not only without sight and sound but also without language. Then, at 7, by connecting the word *water* with the sensation that was running through her fingers, she suddenly realized the foundation of human language. In her own words, at that moment, she was transformed from being a mere "phantom" to being a person who could now converse with others (Keller, 1903). In addition to earning her college degree, Keller became a successful and inspirational author, lecturer, and educator.

Although Helen Keller's discovery of language is noteworthy due to her relatively advanced age, in essence, everyone who learns to speak passes through a similar experience, though in a less dramatic fashion. Understanding the psychology of language will be our first objective in this chapter. Our second objective will be to understand how we think through problems and how we make decisions. The manner in which Keller discovered the solution to the language problem, for instance, represents one product of thinking, or *cognition*, which we will examine later in the chapter. For our purposes, **cognition** will be defined as the mental activity of knowing and the processes through which knowledge is acquired and problems are solved. Yet, first, let us explore how our world is transformed by being able to share the meaning of these markings on the page and the vocal utterances we emit. We will begin this journey by stepping into the past and examining the evolution of language.

Helen Keller suddenly realized the meaning of language when her teacher placed one of Keller's hands into water while signing the word *water* in the other. This moment in Keller's remarkable life wonderfully illustrates both how language is acquired and how problems are often solved.

Cognition: The mental activity of knowing and the processes through which knowledge is acquired and problems are solved.

Communication: The sending and receiving of information.

Language: A systematic way of communicating information using symbols and rules for combining them.

Speech: The oral expression of language.

9-1 LANGUAGE

Communication is the sending and receiving of information. Every day of our lives, we communicate hundreds, if not thousands, of bits of information to others. Some of these messages are intended, while others are not. **Language,** which is the primary mode of communication among humans, is a systematic way of communicating information using symbols and rules for combining them. It is a complex and sophisticated skill and is the principal tool for building human culture. **Speech** is the oral expression of language. Yet, how did the approximately 5,000 spoken languages that exist today come into being?

9-1a The Evolution of Language Had Both Social and Cognitive Advantages for the Human Species

The search for the origins of language begins in the brain. As noted in chapter 3, section 3-3e, PET scan studies indicate that the major neural mechanisms for language are located in the left hemisphere, even in most left-handed people (see figure 9-1). A small

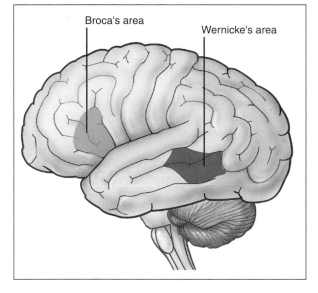

Broca's area

Wernicke's area

FIGURE 9-1
Broca and Wernicke's Areas of the Cerebral Cortex

Traditionally, two brain areas have been associated with language function—namely, Broca's area and Wernicke's area. These brain areas are usually located in the left cerebral hemisphere.

clump of neurons near the front of the brain, known as *Broca's area,* influences brain areas that control the muscles of the lips, jaw, tongue, soft palate, and vocal cords during speech. Connected by a nerve bundle to Broca's area is *Wernicke's area,* which appears to be responsible for the content and comprehension of speech. Although we can identify the major brain areas associated with language, answering the "when" and "why" questions of language evolution have proven to be bigger problems (Botha, 1997; Maestripieri, 1997).

Scientists disagree on whether human language evolved gradually or suddenly (Elman, 1999; Lewin, 1993a). The *gradual increase theory* contends that human language is the product of a very long period of biological evolution, spanning millions of years (Deacon, 1989). Evidence for this view has been obtained from examinations of fossilized skulls: A small lump on the left inside surface (near the temple) where Broca's area is located suggests that some sort of primitive spoken language could have existed about two million years ago (Falk, 1991; Holloway, 1983). In contrast to the view that language evolved gradually, the *threshold theory* asserts that human language is more a product of sudden cultural evolution (Davidson & Noble, 1989). Proponents of this theory believe that language is no older than 50,000 years and is closely tied to the development of tools, imagery, and art (Isaac, 1983).

Scientists have also examined the change in position of various parts of our vocal tract, most notably the larynx. In all mammals except humans, the larynx is high in the neck. Although this allows animals to breathe and drink at the same time, it severely restricts the range of sounds they can produce. Because our larynx is much lower in the neck, it can be much larger, allowing us to produce the wide range of sounds necessary in a language. Anthropologists who study the fossilized skulls of our ancestors have discovered that the earliest time that our ancestors had a larynx low enough in the neck to allow for something similar to humanlike speech was about 1.6 million years ago (Laitmann, 1983; Lewin, 1993b). Yet, it wasn't until about 300,000 to 400,000 years ago that our ancestors' vocal tract was essentially the same as our own. Thus, based on all the available evidence, it is still unclear whether human language evolved gradually or suddenly. Our best guesstimates are that its origins date back somewhere between 40,000 and 1.5 million years—quite a time span!

> **INFO-BIT:** Anatomically, the evolutionary descent of the larynx in the human vocal tract increased the range of sounds that we could make. The "cost" of this anatomical change is that we now have an increased risk of choking when we eat or drink (Smith & Szathmáry, 1995).

Asking an archeologist to discuss language is rather like a mole being asked to describe life in the tree-tops.

—Glynn Isaac, American archeologist, d. 1985

INFO-BIT: German scientists recently found evidence that bolsters the threshold theory of language evolution (Enard et al., in press). Their work, which involved genetic testing of different species, suggests that roughly 200,000 years ago, mutations in the FOXP2 gene may have caused changes in the brains of primitive humans, providing them with much finer control over their mouth and throat muscles. Within 1,000 generations, or about 20,000 years, this mutation may have played a central role in the development of modern humans' ability to speak and, therefore, to eventually develop language about 50,000 years ago. The human and chimpanzee FOXP2 genes differ by only two out of their 715 amino acids, but this small difference may partly explain why chimps cannot speak.

One possible reason why language evolved is due to its social significance to humans (Oda, 2001). That is, it provided a way for our ancestors to more efficiently communicate in such cooperative ventures as hunting and gathering food. Support for this view comes from contemporary cross-cultural studies indicating that language is mostly used today for establishing, maintaining, and refining social relationships (Burling, 1986; Dunbar, 1993). It is also possible that language evolved because of its cognitive significance. Throughout human evolutionary history, brains have been shaped to facilitate reflective thought and imagery, abilities essential for complex decision making and problem solving (Jerison, 1975, 1991). From this perspective, language use evolved as a means to facilitate the construction of an inner reality that we call consciousness.

It's likely that both of these explanations for the evolution of consciousness—one social, the other cognitive—are true. As discussed in chapter 6, section 6-1b, consciousness may have evolved because it provided our ancestors with a mental representation of the world that allowed them to more effectively plan future activities. Language may have evolved because it facilitated the construction of consciousness at the same time that it facilitated the cooperative efforts of individuals living in groups. Thus, consciousness and language may have coevolved because they helped us understand and survive in an increasingly complex social environment.

9-1b Language Capabilities May Not Be Unique to Humans

Beyond searching for the reasons why we became language users, scientists have also wondered whether language and speech are uniquely human abilities. Austrian biologist Karl von Frisch (1950, 1967) discovered that honeybees can communicate the exact location of food sources by engaging in an elaborate dance. All bees appear to have the same basic communication system, but in some kinds of bees, the dance is more elaborate than others, which sometimes causes miscommunication (Frisch, 1962). For example, although Italian and Austrian bees can live and breed together, they misinterpret each other's communications. The Italian bees never go far enough to look for food in response to an Austrian bee's dance, while the Austrian bees overshoot the food source that Italian bees report.

This and other research indicates that animals of the same species communicate—and sometimes miscommunicate—with one another. However, in many species, this communication appears to be completely determined by the "collective memory" genetically passed on from one generation to the next. These within-species communication patterns are extremely functional, often associated with mating, taking care of young, displaying dominance and submission, and setting territorial boundaries (Forstmeier & Balsby, 2002; Wich et al., 2002). For example, a European robin will vigorously attack a patch of red feathers tied to a tree limb in its territory, just as if it were a male intruder. Likewise, the chirping of turkey chicks stimulates brooding behavior in turkey hens, even if these sounds are tape-recorded and coming from inside a stuffed skunk—a natural enemy of the turkey! In both instances, the feathers and chirps act as stimuli that trigger biologically programmed responses (Wardhaugh, 1993). Most researchers do not label this communication a "conversation" because it appears to be based on instinctive responses.

Not all animal communication is based solely on biologically programmed responses. For instance, hummingbirds, parrots, and many songbirds (including perhaps the European robin) share with humans the ability to learn new vocalizations through imitation (Jarvis et al., 2000; Pepperberg, 2002). Thus, humans are not unique in their ability to learn new communication skills. So what makes a communication system a language?

Linguists have traditionally asserted that for a communication system to qualify as a language, it must have certain features (Hockett, 1960; Hockett & Altmann, 1968). Of the many features that have been proposed over the years, the following three might be described as most important (Hulit & Howard, 1993):

1. *Meaningfulness*—Language conveys meaningful messages, with words or signs having relatively stable relationships with the things they represent. By combining words into meaningful sentences, humans can carry on extensive conversations with one another. Other species can also convey meaningful messages, but this appears to involve fairly general messages or a limited number of specific messages (Brudzynski, 2001). For example, when a beaver slaps its tail on the water, other beavers understand this as a danger message, but the danger could be an approaching bear, a mountain lion, or a fire. Although vervet monkeys have separate warning calls for certain predators, this naming system is much more limited than human language (Cheney & Seyfarth, 1985; Seyfarth & Cheney, 1992).

2. *Displacement*—Language permits communication about things that are displaced in time or space, meaning they are not present in the here and now. Although humans can discuss what happened long ago, what may happen in the future, or what is currently happening far away, animal communication is generally considered to lack this property (Yule, 1996). When a dog says *GRRR*, it means *GRRR* right now, not *GRRR* last week by the pond in the park.

3. *Productivity*—Language allows us to communicate things that have never been communicated before. Following a set of grammatical rules, we can convey this novel message to anyone who shares our language. In contrast, most nonhuman communication appears to have considerably less novelty or flexibility. Although the honeybee's dance appears productive because it conveys information about new food sources, it has no signal for *up*, and thus, bees cannot tell other bees about food located directly above their hive (Frisch, 1967).

Based on these criteria, it is doubtful that any nonhuman species has its own language. However, since the 1930s, a number of attempts have been made to teach language to a few select species, such as chimpanzees, bonobos, gorillas, dolphins, and parrots (Hayes, 1951; Herman & Uyeyama, 1999; Kellogg & Kellogg, 1933). Perhaps the most famous case is that of Washoe, a young female chimpanzee who was raised at home by Allen and Beatrix Gardner (1969) and taught sign language as though she was a deaf human child. Within four years, Washoe was using more than 100 signs, ranging from *baby, banana,* and *airplane* to *window, woman,* and *you.* She could also combine words to produce sentencelike phrases such as *gimme banana* and *open food drink.* Some of these phrases appeared to be novel constructions by Washoe, as in her combination of *water bird* to refer to a swan. Even more impressive was Washoe's apparent ability to engage in simple conversations, prompting a visiting reporter for *The New York Times* to declare,

"Suddenly I realized I was conversing with a member of another species in my native tongue."

During the 1970s and 1980s, research with other chimps and gorillas using sign language or plastic shapes representing words provided further evidence of ape language ability (Premack & Premack, 1983). One female gorilla named Koko learned more than 600 words and demonstrated even more spontaneous and productive use of language than Washoe (Patterson, 1978). In one memorable incident, Koko created a new word for an object she had previously never encountered, calling a ring a *finger bracelet*. Yet, is this truly evidence of language ability?

One argument against accepting the achievements of Washoe as evidence of language development was offered by Herbert Terrace (1979)—a student of B. F. Skinner— who taught sign language to a male chimpanzee, named Nim Chimpsky (after the linguist Noam Chomsky). Over a two-year period, Nim's achievements in producing many single-word signs and two-word combinations at first suggested that he was developing an ability to use language in much the same way as human children. However, a closer inspection of videotapes of Nim's classroom activities indicated that, unlike human children, his two-word combinations were simply repetitions of simpler structures, not an expansion into more complex structures (Terrace et al., 1979). Also unlike human children, Nim rarely initiated signing, but instead, used sign language only in response to others' signing and tended to repeat the signs they used. Based on these findings, Terrace concluded that chimp use of sign language is not much different from pigeons pecking a sequence of keys to get food; in neither case should such behavior be confused with language acquisition.

Although Terrace's research with Nim and his skepticism of ape language ability received a great deal of initial attention, it soon came under critical scrutiny. One of the most serious criticisms was that Nim's learning environment was lacking in the sort of natural social interaction that typifies normal language development (Cantfort & Rimpau, 1982; Lieberman, 1984). When other researchers allowed Nim to socialize under more natural conditions, his spontaneous signing increased dramatically, leading some linguists to suggest that the chimp's earlier language deficit was caused by Terrace's rigid training procedures (O'Sullivan & Yeager, 1989).

Subsequent research with bonobos (or "pigmy chimps"), which are close genetic relatives of both chimpanzees and humans, provided further evidence that apes could use language. In particular, one young male bonobo, Kanzi, began using symbols at the age of $2\frac{1}{2}$ years to communicate with humans without any special training (Rumbaugh, 1990; Rumbaugh & Savage-Rumbaugh, 1986). Like human children, Kanzi learned to use symbols early in life by observing his adoptive mother use language (while she was in a training study). Eighty percent of the time, this communication occurred spontaneously, without prompting by the researchers. Kanzi not only learned how to "talk" by using hand signals and typing geometric symbols on a keyboard, he also learned to comprehend the semantic nuances of spoken English. Although dogs, cats, horses, and many other species can sometimes guess what we mean when we talk to them by attending to various situational cues (for example, our tone of voice and gaze direction), Kanzi's understanding of spoken English was much more complex. For instance, when listening through earphones to a list of words spoken by a person in another room—thus eliminating situational cues— Kanzi was able to select the correct picture from among a pile of pictures. In another testing situation, when he was told to "Give the dog a shot," Kanzi picked up a toy hypodermic syringe from among a host of objects and "injected" his stuffed toy dog.

Over the years, scientists have observed Kanzi (a bonobo), Washoe (a chimp), Koko (a gorilla), and other apes not only sign spontaneously but also use their signing to let others know their likes and dislikes, just as humans do. Although these apes have not mastered human language, a growing number of researchers now believe that these animals are able to communicate with humans and even with others of their own species using a form of human language (Fouts, 1997; Jensvold & Gardner, 2000; Savage-Rumbaugh et al., 1998). In contrast to humans, their vocabulary is small and their sentences are simple, similar to those of a 2-year-old child. Further, it takes substantially longer and requires more effort for them to learn a language than it does human children. This suggests that the human brain must have something at birth that is more ready to acquire language than do the other ape brains. Despite these qualifications, they may indeed possess the ability to learn language, an ability that we once thought was unique to humans.

Not all scientists agree with this assessment (Povinelli & Bering, 2002). Acknowledging that some apes may have the capacity to use symbolic thought under the right conditions, these skeptics still contend that this does not mean that these animals are actually using language (Pinker, 1994). Although researchers remain divided over whether animals can use language, it does appear that apes have the capacity to learn some of the basic elements of language. Perhaps the most appropriate conclusion to draw at this time is that, although nonhuman species show no capacity to produce language on their own, as a result of human intervention, certain species can be taught to produce *languagelike* communication.

9-1c Human Languages Have a Hierarchical Structure

As depicted in table 9-1, all human languages have a hierarchical structure, in which elementary sounds are combined into meaningful units to form words. In turn, these words are then combined to form phrases, which are also combined to form sentences. The system of rules that determine how this structure is created is known as **grammar.** The rules of grammar inform us about which combinations of sounds and words are permissible within the language we are using (Bybee & Fleischman, 1995). Grammar has three major components: (1) **phonology,** which refers to the rules for combining basic sounds into words; (2) **syntax,** which refers to the rules for combining words into sentences; and (3) **semantics,** which refers to the rules for communicating the meaning of words, phrases, and sentences.

Regarding phonology, all human languages are composed of **phonemes,** which are the smallest significant sound units in speech. To say *men,* you use three phonemes: *m, ĕ,* and *n. The* uses the phonemes *th* and *ŭ,* and the word *angry* has five phonemes: *a, ng, g, r,* and *ē.* As you can see, there isn't a one-to-one correspondence between a given letter of the alphabet and a phoneme. In the provided examples, the letter *e* has a different kind of speech sound in *men* than it does in the word *the,* and the *ē* sound in *angry* is made by the letter *y,* not the letter *e.*

Linguists estimate that humans have the capacity at birth to produce about 100 phonemes, but because no language uses all of these phonemes, this number is reduced to a much smaller set as children learn to speak. The English language consists of about 40 phonemes and the Polynesian language uses only 11. Because one language might not include all the phonemes found in another language, people who learn to speak another language often have difficulty pronouncing the novel phonemes in their second language.

Grammar: The system of rules that determines the proper use and combination of language symbols.

Phonology: The rules used in language to combine basic sounds into words.

Syntax: The rules used in language to combine words into sentences.

Semantics: The rules used in language to communicate the meaning of words, phrases, and sentences.

Phonemes: The smallest significant sound units in speech.

TABLE 9-1

The Hierarchical Structure of an English Sentence

Human language has a hierarchical structure, ranging from the basic fundamental sounds known as phonemes to the more complex levels of sentences. Phonemes are combined to form the smallest units of meaning, known as morphemes, and morphemes are combined to form words. Syntax rules determine how words can be combined to form phrases, and how phrases can be combined to form sentences.

Sentence	The angry men shouted at the boxers
Phrases	The angy men shouted at the boxers
Words	The angry men shouted at the boxers
Morphemes	The angry men shout ed at the box er s
Phonemes	th ŭ a ng g rē m ĕ n š ow t i d a t th ŭ b o k s e r s

Morphemes: The smallest units of language that carry meaning.

This is why Japanese who learn to speak English often fail to distinguish between *r* sounds and *l* sounds. Similarly, native English speakers have difficulty coughing up the guttural Arabic *ch* or rolling the *r* sound of German.

One step above phonemes in the spoken language hierarchy are **morphemes,** which are the smallest units of language that carry meaning. A few morphemes, such as *a* and *I*, are also phonemes, and most morphemes are themselves words. Morphemes include prefixes and suffixes, such as the *re* in *replay* or the *s* in *plans*. The word *tourists* contains three morphemes—*tour, ist* (meaning "person who does something"), and *s* (indicating plural)—each of which adds to the meaning of the morpheme it precedes. The average English speaker uses the available 40 phonemes to build between 50,000 and 80,000 morphemes.

Beyond the simple structural elements of phonemes, morphemes and their phonological rules, we also rely on syntax rules to build proper phrases and sentences. For instance, you can easily recognize that the phrase *the angry men* is a correctly formed piece of English, but the phrases *men the angry* and *angry the men* are not correct. These last two phrases violate the English syntax rules that articles (*the*) and adjectives (*angry*) precede nouns (*men*). Another simple rule of syntax is that a declarative sentence (a sentence that makes a statement) must have both a subject (what is being talked about) and a predicate (a statement about the subject). Thus, while *The angry men* is not a sentence because it lacks a predicate, *The angry men shouted at the boxers* is a sentence. The way people happen to combine words into a sentence is known as the *surface structure* of language, and it is based on syntax rules.

Although syntax rules shape proper sentence construction, the rules of semantics determine the meaning of sentences. This underlying meaning is known as the *deep structure* of language (Chomsky, 1957, 1965). Based on your knowledge of semantics, you realize that while the following sentence does not violate any syntax rules, it conveys no obvious meaning: *Silent music questions winter.* How can music—especially *silent music*—question anything, let alone winter? This sentence illustrates the fact that syntax and meaning don't always go together.

As you can see from figure 9-2, two sentences can have the same surface structure but two different deep structures ("Visiting relatives can be a nuisance"), and they can also have different surface structures but the same deep structure ("Jaelyn broke the window"; "The window was broken by Jaelyn"). People are more likely to store information in memory based on deep structure rather than surface structure. For this reason, while you probably won't remember whether someone told you that "Jaelyn broke the window" or "The window was broken by Jaelyn," you will probably remember that Jaelyn caused the window breakage.

How you understand the meaning of a sentence often depends on context, and this is especially so when a sentence is perceived to have two or more deep structures. When a sentence is unclear—as in "Visiting relatives can be a nuisance"—people automatically try to choose one deep structure over the other (Warren, 1970). The art of poetry and writing often involves forcing the reader to simultaneously consider multiple deep structures in language. An example of this "semantic stretching" can be seen in Heather McHugh's poem *Language Lesson, 1976* in table 9-2. After reading this poem, check out Discovery Box 9-1 to see what happens sometimes when our grammar usage "slips."

9-1d Infants Appear to Be Born Prepared to Learn Language

As in other areas of psychological inquiry, researchers have debated the degree to which language acquisition is simply due to experience and learning, and the degree to which it naturally unfolds due to inborn capacities (Sealey, 2000; Snow, 1999).

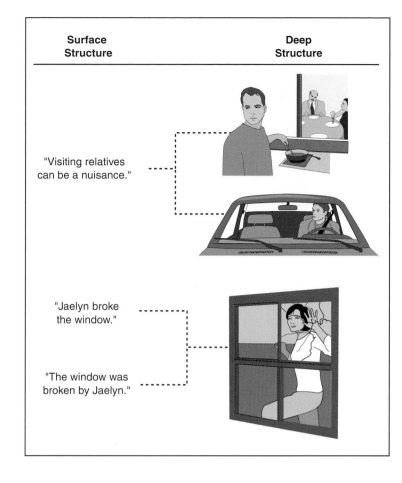

Surface Structure	Deep Structure

"Visiting relatives can be a nuisance."

"Jaelyn broke the window."

"The window was broken by Jaelyn."

FIGURE 9-2
Surface Structure Versus Deep Structure

The surface structure of a sentence consists of its word arrangement, while deep structure refers to its underlying meaning. Sometimes, the same surface structure can reflect two different deep structures ("Visiting relatives can be a nuisance"). Similarly, two sentences can have different surface structures but the same deep structure ("Jaelyn broke the window").

TABLE 9-2

Language Lesson, 1976

Poetry often forces the reader to simultaneously consider multiple deep structures in language. Such "language lessons" stretch the meaning of phrases. Do you enjoy being cognitively challenged in this manner?

When Americans say a man
takes liberties, they mean
he's gone too far. In Philadelphia
today a kid on a leash ordered
bicentennial burger,
hold the relish. Hold
is forget, in American.
On the courts of Philadelphia
the rich prepare
to serve, to fault.
The language is a game in which
love means nothing, doubletalk
means lie. I'm saying
doubletalk with me. I'm saying go
so far the customs are untold,
make nothing without words
and let me be
the one you never hold.

DISCOVERY   BOX 9-1

What Explains Slips of the Tongue?

As language users, we sometimes have difficulty in getting the brain and speech production to work together smoothly. One of the most noticeable—and often humorous—speech errors is **slips of the tongue**. These types of speech errors take a number of forms, including *tangled expressions* ("to make a long shory stort"), *word reversals* ("life is a chair of bowlies"), or *word substitutions* ("I have the breast of intentions toward your daughter, sir"). Word reversals are also known as *Spoonerisms*, after the English clergyman William Spooner, who was famous for these kind of tongue slips. Spooner once chastised a frequently absent student by exclaiming, "You have hissed all my mystery lectures and tasted the whole worm!" He meant to say, "You have missed all my history lectures and wasted the whole term." Word substitutions that appear to reveal hidden thoughts or motives are known as *Freudian slips*, after psychoanalyst Sigmund Freud.

Cognitive and psychoanalytic theorists offer different explanations for "tips of the slung" (Chen, 2000; Marx, 1999). One cognitive theory states that tongue slips may result from "slips of the brain" as it tries to organize linguistic messages (Dell, 1986, 1988). According to this *spreading-activation theory*, constructing a sentence involves the brain activating both phonemes and morphemes from memory. If activation of a particular phoneme or morpheme spreads too quickly to a similar phoneme or morpheme, a slip of the tongue occurs. For example, try reciting the following tongue twister five times in rapid succession:

She sells seashells by the seashore.

Because the *sh* sound is so highly activated by the *sh* in *she* and *shells*, during one of your recitations, it's likely that you will say *shells* instead of *sells*, *sheashells* instead of *seashells*, and/or *sheashore* instead of *seashore*.

In contrast to this cognitive view, psychoanalytic theorists argue that slips of the tongue are caused by unconscious thoughts and desires slipping past conscious censorship. Yet the findings from one experiment suggest that these unconsciously motivated *Freudian slips* may be caused by a similar cognitive process as the previously described spreading activation of phonemes and morphemes. In this study, slips of the tongue were artificially induced in male participants by setting up expectations for certain word patterns of sound (Motley & Baars, 1979). Thus, after pronouncing a series of word pairs like *ball doze*, *bell dark*, and *bean deck*, a participant was more likely to say *barn door* when he saw *darn bore*. In the first experimental condition, prior to responding to the word pairs, participants were told that they would receive random shocks during the experiment. In the second experimental condition, other participants interacted with a provocative female experimenter prior to responding to the word pairs. Results indicated that participants in the first condition produced more tongue slips related to fear of being shocked (for example, *shad bock* became *bad shock*), while individuals in the second condition produced more sexual slips (for example, *past fashion* became *fast passion*). These results not only suggest an unconscious contribution to the production of speech errors, but also that emotionally charged situations can interfere with conscious word choice just as morphemes and phonemes do (Motley, 1985).

Slips of the tongue: Inadvertent speech errors that occur when sounds or words are rearranged.

Behaviorism's Language Theory

Due to the influence of behaviorism, until about 1960, most psychologists assumed that the development of language ability in children was simply a learned response. Championing this perspective in his 1957 book *Verbal Behavior,* B. F. Skinner asserted that people speak as they do because they have been reinforced for doing so. Children, according to the behaviorists, begin life with a blank "language blackboard," and it is slowly filled by the experiences provided by people in their social environment. Throughout this learning process, behaviorists assumed that children were relatively passive; parents and other speakers were given credit for shaping their younger charges' utterances into intelligible words by selectively reinforcing correct responses.

The problem with this explanation is that it does not fit the evidence (James, 1990). For instance, it cannot explain how Helen Keller acquired language because it cannot account for her ability to move beyond merely imitating her teacher's sign language to initiating her own conversations. Behaviorism also cannot explain how children often produce sentences they have never heard before (Brown, 1973). Instead of saying "Mommy went to work" or "That is my cookie"—which would be correct imitations of adult speech—children typically say "Mommy goed to work" and "That mine cookie." Perhaps more important, children's imitation of adult speech drops dramatically after the age of 2, despite the fact that language development continues. How could children continue to learn language if imitation is at the core of their learning? Selective reinforcement and punishment also cannot explain language development; not only do parents rarely provide negative feedback when their young children make grammatical errors, but children's speech usually is not significantly influenced by such corrections when they do occur (Gordon, 1990; Morgan & Travis, 1989). This does not mean that operant conditioning principles do not play a role in learning language; for example, anyone who remembers learning when to use "who" and when to use "whom" can attest to the influence that learning principles can have in language acquisition. Yet, contrary to earlier behaviorist assumptions, operant conditioning principles do not play the primary role in language development.

The Nativist Perspective

Standing in sharp contrast to the behaviorist's view of language development is the *nativist* perspective, which contends that normal development proceeds according to an inborn program that is not significantly influenced by environmental factors. A nativist theory of language acquisition would suggest that we learn language for the same reason that we learn to walk—because we're biologically equipped for it (Bates & Dick, 2002; Ramus et al., 2001).

Linguist Noam Chomsky (1957) proposed that humans are born with specialized brain structures or neural prewiring, called the **language acquisition device,** that facilitate the learning of language. According to Chomsky, with this inborn capacity to acquire language, if children are exposed to it, they will learn to talk even if they are not reinforced for doing so. His hypothesis is certainly consistent with infants' ability to categorize words into appropriate grammatical classes, such as differentiating nouns from verbs in normal conversation (Nelson, 1981). It would also explain why children quickly learn words and grammar, and why language development unfolds at the same rate throughout the world (Slobin, 1985). Although the existence of a language acquisition device is still speculative, existing evidence does strongly suggest that we are biologically predisposed to acquire language.

Language acquisition device: According to Chomsky's linguistic theory, an innate mechanism that facilitates the learning of language.

INFO-BIT: Researchers have found that when adults learn a language, they speak with a more nativelike accent if they overheard the language regularly during childhood than if they did not (Au et al., 2002). Consistent with Chomsky's notion of a language acquisition device, these findings suggest that early exposure to a language may establish a long-lasting mental representation of it.

Interactionist Perspectives

In the debate on language acquisition, while behaviorists emphasize environmental factors and nativists champion inborn predispositions, a middle ground view has been taken by a number of *interactionist* theories (Bates & MacWhinney, 1982). As the name implies, interactionists assume that environmental and biological factors interact together to affect the course of language development.

The cognitive theory of Jean Piaget discussed in chapter 4, section 4-3a, is an example of a *cognitive-interactionist* perspective. In a 1975 debate with Chomsky, Piaget argued that the structures of language might be neither innate nor learned. Instead, they may emerge as a result of the continuing interaction between children's current level of cognitive functioning and environmental input.

While Piaget's cognitive-interactionist perspective emphasizes how children learn language by interacting with their environment, it downplays the role that other people—specifically adults—play in this process. In contrast, the *social interactionist* perspective, which is strongly influenced by Lev Vygotsky's writings (chapter 4, section 4-3c), stresses the point that while children may have an innate capacity for language, they cannot acquire it until they are immersed within social conversation with adults. Adults, especially parents, supply a "scaffold" or supportive communicative structure that allows children to begin learning language (Bates et al., 1983; Hirsh-Pasek & Golinkoff, 1993). The role of adults in providing this supportive structure is most clearly illustrated, again, in the case of Helen Keller, who came to understand the meaning of language only through the tutelage of her teacher.

Adult interaction does appear to be critical in the development of language. Studies of abused and neglected children who received little adult attention found that they had impaired speech comprehension and verbal expression when compared with children who received normal adult attention (Allen & Oliver, 1982; Culp et al., 1991). Unlike these language deficits, no differences were found in the children's cognitive development, leading to the conclusion that language development is particularly vulnerable in an environment lacking normal parent-child verbal interaction.

Evidence that verbal interaction—not just language exposure—is the crucial ingredient in normal language development comes from a case study of a young boy, named Jim, who was raised by deaf parents (Sachs et al., 1981). Using their extremely limited language skills, Jim's parents tried to teach their son spoken English. At the age of 4, when he was enrolled in a preschool program, Jim produced no spontaneous utterances and few intelligible words, despite the fact that he regularly watched television at home. In spite of his serious language deficit, after only a few months in preschool, and with speech therapy, Jim showed marked improvement. Within a few years his language usage became normal. In this case, at least, being exposed to language in a nonsocial context (watching television) did not foster language acquisition. What was necessary was actual engagement in conversation with competent language users. Luckily for Jim, corrective therapy occurred early enough so that there were no long-term negative effects. Unfortunately, when children are isolated from normal language interaction beyond their middle childhood, they develop irreversible language deficits (Gill, 1997; Ouellet et al., 2001; Rymer, 1993). Taken together, these studies suggest that a critical component in the development of language is supportive social interaction with competent language users.

In assessing these three perspectives on language acquisition, the general consensus is that behaviorists place too much emphasis on conditioning principles, while nativists don't give enough credit to environmental influences. Currently, the dominant opinion within the field is that the possible solution to the controversy between the behaviorist and nativist approaches lies in the contribution of the various interactionist approaches (Gleason, 1997). By attending to how biology interacts with social and environmental factors, we may more fully understand the language acquisition process.

9-1e Language Development Occurs in Distinct Stages

Regardless of the exact process by which language acquisition occurs, we do know that it begins shortly after birth and involves a number of distinct stages that move from simplicity to complexity.

Phonemes and Their Combination

Language development begins with children using primitive-sounding phonemes. In every culture throughout the world, by 3 to 5 weeks of age, newborns begin a vocalization pattern known as *cooing*, in which they produce phoneme sounds such as *ooooh* and *aaaah*. Between the fourth and sixth months, infants can read lips and distinguish between the phonemes that comprise their language (Cohen et al., 1992). They also begin *babbling*, in which they spontaneously repeat phoneme combinations like *ahh-goo* and *baa-baa* (Plaut & Kello, 1999). This sequence of cooing, then babbling, even occurs among babies born deaf (Oller & Eilers, 1988). Further, the early babbling of children from different cultures sounds the same because it includes the phonemes in all existing languages. However, by about 10 months of age, phonemes not in the child's native language drop out, and babbling takes on a more culture-specific sound (deBoysson-Bardies et al., 1989).

Single-Word Use

At about 1 year of age, most children begin uttering morpheme sounds that can be identified as words, like *mama*, *papa*, and the ever-popular *no*. This period in language acquisition is typically called the *one-word stage* because children can only use one-word phrases. These words usually relate to specific objects or concepts that children regularly encounter or use in their world. Because they still possess a fairly small vocabulary, young children often don't have words for many of the objects they want to talk about. Consequently, they *overextend* their words to these yet unnamed objects. Thus, an 18-month-old child might use the word *wawa* not only for water, but also for milk, juice, and any other liquid. Similarly, anything sweet might be called a *cookie*. Overextension is an application of the process of *assimilation* to children's words. As you recall from chapter 4, section 4-3a, assimilation is the process of using existing schemas to deal with information encountered in the world. When children call all liquids *wawa*, they are assimilating these objects into their *wawa* schema. However, when they begin calling liquids by their specific names—for example, milk is no longer *wawa*, but *milk*—this is an application of the process of *accommodation*, which involves the creation of new schemas.

From Primitive to Complex Sentences

By the age of 2, children enter the *two-word stage*, in which they begin using two separate words in the same sentence. During this two-word stage, a phase of **telegraphic speech** begins, in which children use multiple-word sentences that leave out all but the essential words, like in a telegrammed message (*BABY BORN. MOTHER FINE*). Thus, instead of saying "I want to go outside," children will say "Want outside." Even when using this basic telegraphic speech, youngsters demonstrate an elementary knowledge of syntax: Words are almost always spoken in their proper order ("Want outside" instead of "Outside want").

Telegraphic speech: An early speech phase in which children use short, multiple-word sentences that leave out all but the essential words, like in a telegrammed message.

Journey of Discovery Question

Research indicates that infants have an inborn ability to detect phoneme sounds that are not a part of their culture's language repertoire. Given that you cannot ask infants questions, how do you think psychologists tested this ability in newborns? That is, how did they design an experiment to test children's inborn ability to detect phoneme sounds?

> **INFO-BIT:** During childhood, we learn almost 5,000 words per year, which translates to about 13 new words per day. The vocabulary of high school graduates includes about 80,000 words, while adults with excellent vocabularies retain upward of 200,000 words (Just & Carpenter, 1987; Miller & Gildea, 1987)!

Once children move beyond using two-word sentences, they quickly produce longer phrases, and telegraphic speech is used less frequently by age 3 (Riley, 1987). By the time children reach the age of 4, they are using plurals, and the present and past tense in sentences, but they often *overgeneralize* grammatical rules. For example, in using the past tense, they will incorrectly say things like "I goed outside" or "I rided my bike." Because "goed" and "rided" are words children would not have heard from adults, it suggests that they are naturally predisposed to pick up grammatical rules and then apply them generally (Marcus, 1996). Children also don't seem to be especially attentive to adult corrections, as illustrated in the following dialogue (quoted in Cazden, 1972):

Child:	"My teacher holded the baby rabbits and we patted them."
Mother:	"Did you say your teacher held the baby rabbits?"
Child:	"Yes."
Mother:	"What did you say she did?"
Child:	"She holded the baby rabbits and we patted them."
Mother:	"Did you say she held them tightly?"
Child:	"No, she holded them loosely."

This does not mean that adults are irrelevant to children's language acquisition. As noted earlier, especially during the early stages of language development, the day-to-day verbal feedback that infants receive from their caregivers plays an important role in the learning process. This adult feedback—known as *motherese* (or *parentese*)—is characterized by exaggerated intonations, high pitch, repetition, and slow speech (Sachs, 1989). This exaggerated adult speech may help infants recognize specific language forms and understand where utterances begin and end, skills necessary for future language learning (Barnes et al., 1983; Morgan, 1986).

9-1f The Linguistic Relativity Hypothesis Asserts That Language Determines Thought

Linguistic relativity hypothesis: The proposal that the structure of language determines the structure of thought, meaning that people who speak different languages also think differently.

In this chapter, in addition to examining our language system, we also analyze how we think. Yet, how strong is the connection between cognition and language? Linguist Benjamin Lee Whorf's (1897–1941) **linguistic relativity hypothesis** proposed that the structure of language *determines* the structure of thought (Whorf, 1956). He used the term *linguistic relativity* to emphasize his belief that thought is relative to the particular language used. The implications of this hypothesis are profound. First, if language shapes your conception of reality, without a word or phrase to describe an experience, you literally cannot think about it. Second, if language shapes reality, then no two cultures share the same understanding of the world.

The idea that language determines thinking has been the subject of considerable debate and research over the years (Lucy, 1997; Penny, 1996). In a critical test of Whorf's hypothesis, Eleanor Rosch (1973) compared the color perceptions of the Dani people of New Guinea—who use only two words for color (*bright* and *dark*)—with those of English-speaking people who use many different color terms. Despite these large language differences, Rosch found no differences in the way the two groups perceive color: Dani speakers made as fine discriminations among colors as English speakers. Other cross-cultural

Every country has its own language, yet the subjects of which the untutored soul speaks are the same everywhere.

—Tertullian, Roman theologian, 160–240

studies using different languages have also failed to support the hypothesis that language determines thinking (Davies, 1998; Gumperz & Levinson, 1996). Thus, counter to the linguistic relativity hypothesis, just because a language lacks terms for various stimuli does not mean that the users of the language cannot perceive the various features of the stimuli. The truth is that when we encounter something novel, we change our language to accommodate the need to refer to it. We manipulate our language much more than our language manipulates us.

Although the hypothesis that language determines thought in some sort of lockstep fashion has no empirical support, most psychologists do believe in a weaker version of Whorf's hypothesis—that language can *influence* thinking (Hardin & Banaji, 1993; Lau & Hoosain, 1999; Lucy, 1992). This idea—that language can influence your thoughts and perceptions—may not seem that unusual to you if you speak two dissimilar languages, like English and Japanese or English and Chinese (Brown, 1986). English, rooted in an individualist cultural context, has many self-focused words, while the collectivist-based Japanese and Chinese languages have many interpersonally focused words. Bilingualists report that the way they think about themselves and others is influenced by which language they happen to use (Dinges & Hull, 1992; Hoffman et al., 1986). For instance, when speaking English, bilingualists are more likely to attend to their own personal needs and desires, while social obligations are more salient in their thoughts when they speak Japanese (Matsumoto, 1994).

Another way that language can influence thinking is in the way it calls attention to a person's gender. In English, you cannot avoid specifying gender when using pronouns like *his* or *her*. Yet, traditionally in the English language, masculine pronouns and nouns have been used to refer to all people, regardless of their gender. Although the **generic masculine** is meant to include women as well as men, it does not do so in reality. For example, a number of studies indicate that people learn to associate men and women with certain activities and occupations by listening to the gendered pronouns used to describe these activities and occupations (McConnell & Fazio, 1996; Miller & Swift, 1991). When telling children what a physician does on the job, for instance, using the generic masculine ("He takes care of sick people") conveys to the child that this is an occupation for men, not women. Similarly, after reading a paragraph describing psychologists with the generic masculine *he*, both women and men rated psychology as a less attractive profession for women than students who read a gender-neutral (*they*) description (Briere & Lanktree, 1983). Based on this research, the American Psychological Association recommends that gender-neutral language be used to reduce gender bias in people's thinking. Reading time studies indicate that using gender-neutral terms instead of gendered terms is cognitively efficient and does not reduce reading comprehension (Foertsch & Gernsbacher, 1997). Table 9-3 lists some suggestions for avoiding gendered terms in your own language.

In summary then, although research does not support the original strong version of the linguistic relativity hypothesis—that language determines what we can (and cannot) think about—it does appear that language can make certain ways of thinking more or less likely. This weaker version of the original hypothesis tells us that while language is not the sole determinant of thought, it does influence thought in some meaningful ways. Now that you have learned how language might influence thinking, check out Discovery Box 9-2 to see how language and thinking might sometimes operate in a somewhat different manner.

Generic masculine: The use of masculine nouns and pronouns to refer to all people, instead of just males.

TABLE 9-3	Gendered Terms to Avoid	Alternative Gender-Neutral Terms
Suggestions for Reducing Gendered Terms in Language	He, his, him	He or she, she or he, her or his, his or her, him or her, her or him, or they, their, them
	Man, mankind	Humanity, people, human beings, the human species
	Man-made	Handmade, synthetic, fabricated, constructed
	Coed	Student
	Freshman	First-year student, frosh
	Manpower	Workers, human resources, personnel, work force
	Businessman	Businessperson
	Career girl	Business woman
	Chairman, chairwoman	Chairperson, head, chair
	Saleswoman, salesgirl	Salesclerk
	Foreman	Supervisor
	Policeman, policewoman	Police officer
	Waitress	Server
	Man-to-man	One-to-one, person-to-person
	Forefathers	Ancestors
	Housewife, househusband	Homemaker
	Mothering	Parenting, caregiving, nurturing

SECTION SUMMARY

- According to the evolutionary perspective on language, it may have evolved because it facilitated the construction of consciousness and the cooperative efforts of group living.

- Three features of language include meaningfulness, displacement, and productivity.

- Certain species can be taught languagelike communication.

- Three theories of how language develops in humans maintain the following: Behaviorists stress the role played by operant conditioning; nativists contend that humans are born with a capacity to acquire language; and interactionists assert that environmental and biological factors interact together.

- Language has a hierarchical structure, in which elementary sounds are combined into meaningful units to form words.

- Grammar has three major components: (1) phonology (the rules for combining basic sounds into words); (2) syntax (the rules for combining words into sentences); and (3) semantics (the rules for communicating the meaning of words, phrases, and sentences).

- The smallest significant sound units in speech are phonemes, followed by morphemes, which are the smallest language units that carry meaning.

- Children progress through distinct stages in language development.

- Language can shape the way we think.

9-2 THINKING

As previously defined, thinking, or *cognition*, is the mental activity of knowing and the processes through which knowledge is acquired and problems are solved. While chapter 4 examined how cognition develops in children, in this chapter we begin by examining the building blocks of cognition, namely, *concepts*.

9-2a Concept Formation Is a Basic Element of Cognition

A **concept** is a mental grouping of objects, ideas, or events that share common properties (Markman, 1999). For example, the concept insect stands for a class of animals that have three body divisions (head, thorax, abdomen), six legs, an external skeleton, and a rapid reproductive system. As you recall from our discussion of the semantic network model in chapter 8, section 8-2a, concepts enable us to store our memories in an organized fashion. When one concept in our long-term memory is activated, other closely related concepts are also activated, or *primed*.

> **Concept:** A mental grouping of objects, ideas, or events that share common properties.

The process of forming concepts is called **categorization.** As a species, we spontaneously categorize things we experience. Categorization is adaptive because it saves time and helps in making predictions about the future. I know, for example, that if I give my daughters an object from the concept *candy*, they are likely to be pleased. I also know that if I need medical attention, I will likely receive it by seeking out people from either the concepts *physician* or *nurse*. Like the heart that pumps life-giving blood throughout the body, or the lungs that replenish oxygen to this blood, the general scientific consensus is that humans could not survive without engaging in categorization.

> **Categorization:** The process of forming concepts.

We form some concepts by identifying *defining features*. For instance, if an animal has three body divisions, six legs, an external skeleton, and a rapid reproductive system, I would say it was an insect; if it lacks one or more of these features, I would not think of it as an insect (Medin, 1989). The problem with forming concepts by definition is that many familiar concepts have uncertain or *fuzzy boundaries*. This fact makes categorizing some members of familiar concepts more difficult than others. To illustrate this point, consider the objects included in the fuzzy boundary of the concept cup in figure 9-3. In one experiment, when people were individually shown objects like this and asked to name them, they were more likely to abandon the "cup" label and identify the object as a "bowl" as its width increased relative to its depth (Labov, 1973). However, the point at which this shift occurred was gradual, not fixed.

Findings like these suggest that categorizing has less to do with the features that define all members of a concept and has more to do with the features that *characterize* the *typical* member of a concept. This is the reason some members of familiar concepts are easier to categorize than others; they are better representatives of the concept (Rosch, 1978). The *most* representative members of a concept are known as **prototypes.** For example, most people consider a German shepherd more "doglike" than a Chihuahua, a robin more "birdlike" than a penguin, and an undergraduate more "studentlike" when she is 20 years of age versus 65 years. For most of us, German shepherds are "doggier," robins are "birdier," and 20-year-olds are "studentier," because they more closely resemble our prototypes for their respective concepts than the alternative choices. In fact, the Chihuahua might be mistakenly categorized as a rat because it looks more "ratty" than "doggy," and the elderly student might be mistaken for a college professor.

> **Prototypes:** The most representative members of a concept.

FIGURE 9-3
When Is This Object a "Cup," and When Is It a "Bowl"?

DISCOVERY BOX 9-2

Do Individualists and Collectivists Differ in Their Language Styles?

As previously described, individualism entails a focus on satisfying one's own needs and desires, while collectivism is related to a greater concern for the needs and wants of one's group. Because people from individualist cultures have been brought up to satisfy themselves, they are not only used to speaking directly to others about their needs, but they also expect that others will do the same (Brown & Levinson, 1987; Ting-Toomey et al., 1991). Thus, when they converse, individualists express themselves directly and don't look for hidden meaning in others' speech. In contrast, people with a collectivist orientation tend to use language in a very different way (Holtgraves, 1997). Because they have been socialized to satisfy other group members rather than themselves, collectivists tend to not only speak *indirectly* about their own needs, but they expect that others will do likewise. Due to this cultural mindset against expressing one's needs directly, collectivists habitually look for the hidden meaning in others' speech. In collectivist cultures like Japan, China, and Korea, it is considered virtuous to be able to quickly and accurately interpret and respond to others' vaguely expressed feelings and desires before they have to be clearly articulated (Barnlund, 1989; Doi, 1973). In this kind of cultural context, directly expressing one's desires is considered inappropriate, because others are expected to be able to "read" them through indirect means.

In general, an indirect language style is not only considered more polite than a direct style, but it also is more likely to help smooth over awkward social situations (Holtgraves, 1992; Holtgraves & Yang, 1992). For example, imagine that Sandy invites Kim over for dinner and, after the meal, asks her which dish she liked best, the tofu burger or the broccoli pasta. Kim responds with something like, "That's such a difficult choice." If Sandy interprets this as a negative comment on both dishes, and confronts Kim, her guest can now simply assert that her host misinterpreted her statement. Deniability would be harder to claim if Kim had initially responded directly and told Sandy that she did not like either dish, or that she preferred one over the other.

Our failure to correctly categorize things because they don't match our prototype for that concept can lead to errors in decision making. For instance, if certain physical symptoms don't fit our flu prototype, we may continue our normal activities, thus worsening our condition and also infecting others (Bishop, 1991). Similarly, we may turn our life savings over to a dishonest investment adviser because he looks like "Honest Abe."

9-2b We Employ a Number of Problem-Solving Strategies

Problem solving: The thought process employed to overcome obstacles.

One important way we use concepts is **problem solving,** which is the thought process you engage in to overcome obstacles to attain your goals. Typically, problem solving involves using one of several strategies, including *trial and error, algorithms, heuristics,* and *insight.*

Trial and Error

Trial and error: A problem-solving strategy that involves trying one possible solution after another until one works.

Do you remember Edward Thorndike's puzzle box experiments with hungry cats described in chapter 7, section 7-2a? Through **trial and error,** which involves trying one possible solution after another until one works, Thorndike's cats eventually learned how to escape

One implication of these findings is that misunderstandings can easily develop between individualists and collectivists due to misreading each other's conversational styles. That is, individualists might become irritated because collectivists do not clearly convey their needs and preferences, while collectivists might think individualists are insulting for directly stating their attitudes and desires. If you would like to better understand your own language style regarding direct versus indirect expression of language, spend a few minutes reading the items in table 9-4.

TABLE 9-4

Do You Have a Direct or an Indirect Language Style?

People with a direct language style tend to agree with these statements:

Most of what I say can be taken at face value, and there is no need to look for a deeper meaning.

There is usually no need for people to look below the surface to understand what I really mean.

What I mean with a remark is usually fairly obvious.

People with an indirect language style tend to agree with these statements:

There are many times when I prefer to express myself indirectly.

My remarks often have more than one meaning.

Many times, people are not totally sure what I really mean when I say something.

Source: From "Styles of language use: Individual and cultural variability in conversational indirectness" by T. Holtgraves in JOURNAL OF PERSONALITY AND SOCIAL PSYCHOLOGY, 1997, 73, pp. 624–637 (Table 1, p. 628). Copyright ©1997 by the American Psychological Association. Adapted with permission.

from the puzzle box to reach a bowl of food. In many species, trial and error often provides responses that are important to survival. Whether you are a lion cub discovering how best to attack your prey or a teenager finding the right tone of voice to use when asking someone for a date, haphazardly trying various solutions until you stumble on one that works may be time-consuming, but it is often effective.

Algorithms

Unlike trial and error, which does not guarantee success, an **algorithm** is a problem-solving strategy that involves following a specific rule or step-by-step procedure that inevitably produces the correct solution. For example, recently, I needed to contact a student named John Smith. I knew he lived in Milwaukee, but I didn't know his phone number. There are 40 John Smiths in the Milwaukee telephone directory. One available strategy was to use an algorithm; that is, simply phone all the John Smiths until I found the right one. Assuming that my John Smith has a phone, this strategy was guaranteed to work. The drawback to algorithms, however, is that they are inflexible. Further, like trial and error, they are time-consuming. Computers are based on algorithms, and that is the reason they are inflexible in their functioning.

Algorithm: A problem-solving strategy that involves following a specific rule or step-by-step procedure until you inevitably produce the correct solution.

Heuristic: A problem-solving strategy that involves following a general rule of thumb to reduce the number of possible solutions.

Insight: A problem-solving strategy that involves a sudden realization of how a problem can be solved.

Heuristics

Instead of calling all the John Smiths in the phone book, I relied on a **heuristic,** which involves following a general rule of thumb to reduce the number of possible solutions. The general rule of thumb that I used in solving my problem was that college students usually live on or near campus. Now the number of phone numbers to call was reduced to five. Heuristics have a reasonably good chance of working, and, true to form, I found my John Smith on the third call. However, unlike algorithms, they do not guarantee success. What if my John Smith lived at home with his parents? The chief advantage of heuristics is that they usually save time.

Insight

Sometimes, we are unaware of using any problem-solving strategy at all; solutions simply pop into our heads (Bowers et al., 1995; Dorfman et al., 1996). The sudden realization of how a problem can be solved is called **insight** (Sternberg & Davidson, 1999). This is exactly how Helen Keller finally came to understand the foundation of language: While the well water flowed over her one hand, her teacher signed into the other the word *water*, and in that instant, she achieved insight. Consider the following problem that is often solved by insight:

> A man walks into a tavern and asks for a glass of water. The bartender pulls a shotgun from behind the bar and points it at the man. The man says "Thank you" and walks out.

Can you explain the behavior of these two people? This story was presented to people in an insight problem-solving study, with participants being allowed to ask yes/no questions for up to two hours (Durso et al., 1994). At several points during this problem-solving period, participants were asked to rate the degree to which different pairings of 14 words were related to the problem. Some of these word pairs were explicitly stated in the story (*man, bartender*), others were implicit in the correct solution (*surprise, remedy*), and still others had no relation at all to the story (*clock, grass*). Results indicated that, at first, the implicitly related words were thought by participants to be highly unrelated to the story. However, before insight was achieved, participants slowly perceived an increased association between the story and these implicitly related words. No such increase in relatedness occurred for explicitly related words or unrelated words. These results suggest that, in insight problem solving, people gradually increase their focus on those concepts important to the solution, even though they are yet unaware of the solution itself. Thus, although insight seems to happen unexpectedly, the cognitive organization necessary for this type of problem solving is built beforehand, like the slowly gathering clouds that eventually lead to the sudden lightning flash. (The solution to the problem preceding this paragraph is that the man had the hiccups.)

9-2c A Number of "Internal" Obstacles Can Impede Problem Solving

Despite having various strategies to solve problems, psychologists have identified a number of cognitive tendencies that act as barriers to problem solving. Three of the more common internal obstacles are the *confirmation bias*, *mental set*, and *functional fixedness*.

> **INFO-BIT:** Culture plays an important role in preserving useful problem-solving techniques across generations, even among nonhuman primates. For example, for more than a century, certain bands of chimpanzees in West Africa have used a variety of crude stone hammers to crack open calorie-rich panda nuts. Using an elaborate set of procedures, the chimps establish nut-cracking stations on battered tree roots employed as anvils. The precise technique required to extract the nutrients from its outer husk takes up to seven years for the animals to learn, and it has not been observed among chimps in central Africa, where similar nuts are available.

Confirmation Bias

When you think you have a solution to a problem, you may fall victim to the **confirmation bias,** which is the tendency to seek only information that verifies your beliefs (Edwards & Smith, 1996). Unfortunately, such selective attention prevents you from realizing that your solution is incorrect. In one confirmation-bias study, college students were given the three-number sequence, 2-4-6, and told to discover the rule used to generate it (Wason, 1960). Before announcing their beliefs about the rule (which is simply any three increasing numbers), students could make up their own number sequences, and the experimenter told them whether these sequences fit the rule. They were instructed to announce the rule only after receiving feedback from enough self-generated number sequences to feel certain that they knew the correct solution. True to the confirmation bias, 80 percent of the students convinced themselves of an incorrect rule. Typically, they would begin with a wrong hypothesis (for example, adding by twos) and then search only for confirming evidence (testing 8-10-12, 20-22-24, 19-21-23, etc.). Had they tried to disconfirm this hypothesis by testing other number sequences that simply increased in value (for example, 1-2-3 or 10-19-39), they would have realized their error. Experiments like this indicate that an important barrier to problem solving is our tendency to search for information that will confirm our beliefs more energetically than we pursue information that might refute them (Klayman & Ha, 1987).

How might this tendency to seek confirming information lead to incorrect social beliefs? In one experiment, Mark Snyder and William Swann (1978) asked some participants to find out whether the person they were about to interact with was an introvert, while other participants were asked to find out whether the person was an extravert. Consistent with the confirmation bias, the questions that people asked their interaction partners were biased in the direction of the original question. If they had been asked to find out whether the person was an introvert, they asked questions such as, "What do you dislike about loud parties?" In contrast, in the extravert condition, they asked questions such as, "How do you liven things up at a party?" Because most people can recall both introverted and extraverted incidents from their past, the interaction partners' answers provided confirmatory evidence for either personality trait. As you can see, such confirmation seeking can easily lead to mistakes when forming impressions about individuals. Similarly, incorrect stereotypes of social groups can also be perpetuated by seeking confirmation of preexisting beliefs (Yzerbyt et al., 1996).

> **Confirmation bias:** The tendency to seek information that supports our beliefs, while ignoring disconfirming information.

Mental Set

Another common obstacle to problem solving is **mental set**—the tendency to persist in using solutions that have worked in the past, even though better alternatives may exist (Luchins & Luchins, 1994). The influence that mental set can have on problem solving was first demonstrated by Abraham Luchins (1942) in his "water-jar" problems study. Participants were asked to solve problems involving the filling of water jars. In the first task, using a 21-cup jar, a 127-cup jar, and a 3-cup jar, they were asked to measure out exactly 100 cups of water. With minimal effort, participants discovered that the solution was to fill the largest jar (B), and from it fill the second largest jar (A) once and the smallest jar (C) twice. Try solving the remaining problems in figure 9-4 yourself before reading further.

Like Luchins's participants, you probably ran into a mental set. That is, discovering that you could use the basic algorithm, $B - A - 2C$, to solve all the remaining problems caused you to miss the much simpler solutions for problem 6 $(B - C)$ and problem 7 $(B + C)$. Thus, although mental sets can help us solve problems, they can also lead to "mental ruts" when the situation changes and old methods are either not the most efficient or are completely ineffective (Pashler et al., 2000).

> **Mental set:** The tendency to continue using solutions that have worked in the past, even though better alternatives may exist.

If the only tool you have is a hammer, you tend to see every problem as a nail.
—Abraham Maslow, founder of humanistic psychology, 1908–1970

FIGURE 9-4
The Water-Jar Problems

In each problem, what is the most efficient way of measuring out the correct amount of water using jars A, B, and/or C?

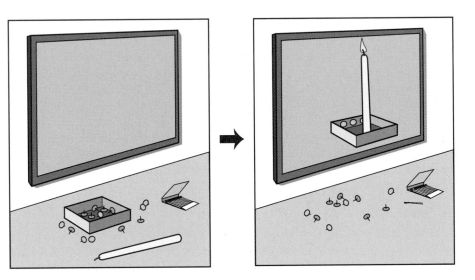

Problem	Amount Held by Each Jar			Required Amount (Cups)
	Jar A	Jar B	Jar C	
1	127	21	3	100
2	163	14	25	99
3	43	18	10	5
4	46	14	5	22
5	57	20	4	29
6	49	23	3	20
7	39	15	3	18

FIGURE 9-5
The Candle Problem

When supplied with the materials in the box on the far left, many people cannot figure out how to mount a candle on a bulletin board so that it will not drip wax when lit. How is this candle problem an example of functional fixedness?

Functional fixedness: The tendency to think of objects as functioning in fixed and unchanging ways and ignoring other less obvious ways in which they might be used.

Functional Fixedness

Finally, related to mental set is **functional fixedness,** which identifies our tendency to think of objects as functioning in fixed and unchanging ways (Furio et al., 2000). In problem solving, when you are unable to consider using familiar objects in unusual ways—for example, using a dime as a screwdriver—you are experiencing this cognitive obstacle. In one study of functional fixedness, participants were given a small cardboard box of tacks, some matches, and a candle (see figure 9-5). Their task was to mount the candle on a bulletin board in such a way that it would burn without dripping wax on the floor (Duncker, 1945). Before reading further, try solving this problem.

Many participants could not solve the problem because they thought of the box as simply a container for tacks, not as a support for a candle. Later research found that when describing the task, if the experimenter used the term *"box* of tacks" rather than just "tacks," more solutions were obtained (Glucksberg & Danks, 1968; Glucksberg & Weisberg, 1966). This suggests that when a person hears the word *box,* numerous possible encodings of *box* may be activated from memory, thus making a solution more likely. In general, the more experience a person has with an object, the greater likelihood that they will experience functional fixedness with this object.

9-2d Decision Making Involves Evaluating Alternatives and Making Choices about Them

In addition to finding solutions to problems, another aspect of everyday cognition is weighing the pros and cons of different alternatives in order to make a choice. In such decision making, there often is no one alternative that is superior to the others in every feature. To make a rational decision in such circumstances, we would systematically evaluate the features of each alternative, assigning a numerical weight to each feature according to its importance (Edwards, 1977; Reed, 1996). For example, in the chapter 2 *Psychological Applications*, I described the dilemma my oldest daughter faced when trying to decide which new bicycle to pick for her birthday present: Should she pick the better-riding "Huffy HyperForce" *boy* bike or the more socially acceptable "Barbie Fashion Fun" *girl* bike?

As illustrated in figure 9-6, Amelia placed more importance on *rideability* than *style*, and thus, rideability was assigned the highest numerical weight. She also compared additional features, such as price, color, and accessories before making her decision. According to this *weighted additive model*, you multiply the numerical weight of the feature (how important it is) by its value (how positive it is) to arrive at a weighted value. By adding all the weighted values for each alternative, you determine its weighted additive value. In Amelia's case, the Huffy Bike had a higher weighted additive value than the Barbie Bike, and thus that was the one she chose. Now, I am not contending that Amelia actually plotted out her decision in exactly this manner. What I am asserting, however, is that using the weighted additive model can greatly improve your decision making. It is an example of a type of decision-making skill known as *critical thinking*, which is the process of deciding what to believe and how to act based on a careful evaluation of the evidence (see chapter 2, *Psychological Applications*).

Research and everyday experience indicates that although we usually try to be systematic and rational in our decision making, we often fall short of this goal. Instead, we

Features (in Order of Importance)	Importance (Numerical Weight)	Huffy Hyper Force Bike		Barbie Fashion Fun Bike	
		Value	Weighted Value	Value	Weighted Value
Rideability	5	+10	50	+5	25
Style	4	+7	28	+9	36
Color	3	+8	24	+9	27
Accessories	2	+9	18	+8	18
Price	1	+10	10	+10	10
			130		116

FIGURE 9-6
Calculating the Weighted Additive Value

According to the weighted additive model of decision making, when people make systematic rational decisions, they assign numerical weights to the features of each alternative according to their importance. By multiplying the numerical weight of a feature by its value, you determine its weighted value. The final weighted additive value is determined by adding all the weighted values for each alternative. According to this model, which bike would Amelia choose to buy?

Source: Adapted from Edwards (1977).

> *To most people, nothing is more troublesome than the effort of thinking.*
>
> —James Bryce, British statesman, 1838–1922

end up using simple strategies that, while rational, focus on only a few aspects of our available options (Simon, 1957). In Amelia's case, if she had only considered the bikes' colors and accessories in making her purchase, she would have been relying on this sort of elementary decision-making strategy. By not fully analyzing the situation in which a decision is to be made, our choices are determined by what we happen to focus on.

One of the most important influences on the decision-making process is how choices are *framed*. **Framing** is the way in which alternatives are structured (Tversky & Kahneman, 1981). In one experiment, hospital physicians were presented with a hypothetical situation in which they had to choose between two forms of treatment for a lung cancer patient (McNeil et al., 1982). Half of the physicians were given the following information before making their decision:

> Of 100 patients having surgery, 10 will die during treatment, 32 will die within a year, and 66 will die within five years. Of 100 patients having radiation therapy, none will die during treatment, 23 will die within a year, and 78 will die within five years.

If you were the physician, what would you choose: surgery or radiation? The other half of the physicians received the following information:

> Of 100 patients having surgery, 90 will be alive immediately after treatment, 68 will be alive after a year, and 34 will be alive after five years. Of 100 patients having radiation therapy, all will be alive after treatment, 77 will be alive after a year, and 22 will be alive after five years.

Would your decision be different if you obtained the information in this manner? Actually, the treatment outcomes are exactly the same. The only difference is in their framing: The first description emphasizes how many people will die, while the second description stresses how many will live. You might assume that highly educated and intelligent physicians would not be swayed by simply framing information in terms of losses or in terms of gains, but this was not the case. Although surgery was the preferred choice in both framing situations, the physicians were much more reluctant to choose surgery when the choices were framed in terms of death (a loss) rather than in terms of survival (a gain). Apparently, physicians' aversion to death as an outcome in treatment made them more reluctant to perform surgery when information was framed in this manner.

The fact that decisions can be altered by the way choices are framed is not lost on advertisers. Consumers, for example, are more likely to buy ground beef when it is labeled "75 percent lean" rather than "25 percent fat" (Levin & Gaeth, 1988). To counter these framing manipulations, always make a decision only after considering both a gain frame and a loss frame. When a salesperson tells you that 82 percent of his products need no repairs during the first year, remind yourself that this also means that 18 percent of his products do need repairs. Does this reframing of the information alter your decision? Your understanding of framing can make you a better decision maker. The importance of critically analyzing options is discussed more fully in Discovery Box 9-3.

Framing: The way in which choices are structured.

9-2e Decision-Making Heuristics Often Sidetrack Everyday Cognition

When we do engage in lazy decision making, what kind of timesaving mental shortcuts do we use? Heuristics, of course! To understand how we use specific types of heuristics, and how they can sometimes lead us astray, let us examine two heuristics identified by Amos Tversky and Daniel Kahneman (1974): *representativeness* and *availability*.

The Representativeness Heuristic

Remember my example of being cheated out of your life savings because your investment adviser happened to look like an honest person? To judge the likelihood of things based on how closely they represent particular prototypes is to use a cognitive shortcut known as the **representativeness heuristic** (Tversky & Kahneman, 1974). The problem with this cognitive shortcut is that being a rapid method of decision making, it doesn't take into account other important qualifying information. The most important information of this type relates to *base rates*—the frequency with which some event or pattern occurs in the general population.

The tendency to overlook base-rate information was demonstrated in a well-known study by Tversky and Kahneman (1973). Research participants were told that an imaginary person named Jack had been selected from a group of 100 men. Some were told that 30 of the men were engineers (a base rate for engineers of 30 percent), and others were told that 70 were engineers (a base rate of 70 percent). Half the participants were given no other information, but the other half were given a description of Jack that either fit the common stereotype of engineers (for example, practical, likes to work with numbers) or did not. They were then asked to guess the probability that Jack was an engineer. Results indicated that when participants received only information related to base rates, they were more likely to guess that Jack was an engineer when the base rate was 70 percent than when it was 30 percent. However, when they received information about Jack's personality and behavior, they tended to ignore the base-rate information and, instead, focus on whether Jack fit their prototype of an engineer. The tendency to ignore or underuse useful base-rate information and overuse personal descriptors of the individual being judged has been called the *base-rate fallacy*.

> **Representativeness heuristic:** The tendency to make decisions based on how closely an alternative matches (or represents) a particular prototype.

The Availability Heuristic

Following the terrorist attacks on September 11, 2001, many Americans were afraid to fly on commercial airlines. Instead of flying, people began driving in their cars cross-country. In nixing plane travel for car travel, they based their judgments on the **availability heuristic,** which is the tendency to judge the frequency or probability of an event in terms of how easy it is to think of examples of that event. In using the availability heuristic, the most important factor for people is not the content of their memory, but the ease with which this content comes to mind (Schwarz et al., 1991). Because people could easily recall the horrible images of September 11, they decided that car travel was safer than plane travel. These judgments were made despite the fact that National Safety Council data reveal that, mile for mile, Americans are 37 times more likely to die in a vehicle crash than on a commercial flight. Indeed, if terrorists destroyed more than 50 planes per year, each containing 60 passengers, we would still be safer traveling by plane than by car. In this instance, it appears that reliance on the availability heuristic caused many Americans to actually increase their safety risks when traveling.

The ease with which we generally recall our own characteristics and opinions from memory helps to explain why we tend to believe that other people share our views and preferences to a greater extent than is actually true. This *false consensus effect* has been

> **Availability heuristic:** The tendency to judge the frequency or probability of an event in terms of how easy it is to think of examples of that event.

Journey of Discovery Question

In Olympic competition, athletes who win an event receive the gold medal, those who come in second place receive a silver medal, and third-place finishers get a bronze medal. Fourth-place finishers receive nothing. Researchers discovered that during the 1992 Olympics, bronze medalists (third-place finishers) exhibited more joy than silver medalists (second-place finishers) after their events (Medvec et al., 1995). How could this finding be explained by the availability heuristic?

DISCOVERY BOX 9-3

Do We Differ in Our Need for Cognition?

An important ingredient in competent decision making is to critically analyze your options and hazards, an approach not everyone takes. John Cacioppo and Richard Petty (1982) have designed a self-report scale measuring individual differences in the motivation to think, which they call the **need for cognition**. People high in the need for cognition (high NFC) like to work on difficult cognitive tasks, analyze situations, and make subtle cognitive distinctions. In contrast, individuals with a low need for cognition (low NFC) are more likely to take mental shortcuts and avoid effortful thinking unless they are required to do so (Nair & Ramnarayan, 2000; Sommers & Kassin, 2001). Spend a few minutes answering the need for cognition items in table 9-5 before reading further.

Researchers have studied how the need for cognition affects people's attention to political campaigns and their voting decisions. During the 1984 presidential and vice-presidential debates, for instance, voters high in the need for cognition were more likely to watch these events than were their low-NFC counterparts (Ahlering, 1987). The high-NFC voters also developed more beliefs about the candidates than did those low in the need for cognition, and their attitudes toward the candidates eight weeks before the November election were better predictors of their actual voting behavior (Cacioppo et al., 1986). This latter finding probably occurred because attitudes and beliefs formed due to critical analysis are more resistant to change than attitudes shaped by lazy thinking (Shestowsky et al., 1998).

Although high-NFC persons are more disposed to critically analyze information when making decisions than low-NFC persons, this is no guarantee that they will actually do so. Even people who enjoy intellectual stimulation will often engage in lazy thinking when the decisions have little relevance to their lives (Leippe & Elkin, 1987). Yet, it is also true that people who are typically lazy thinkers can become critical thinkers if the decision is personally compelling and relevant. Thus, while our need for cognition will generally affect how much we critically analyze our options before making a decision, when we believe that a decision is important, we all tend to take greater care in weigh-

observed in numerous contexts: We exaggerate how common our own personalities are in the general population; we overestimate how many people smoke or do not smoke, based on our own smoking habits; we assume that most people agree with our political beliefs (Alicke et al., 1996; Babad et al., 1992; Sherman et al., 1983). The ease with which we generally recall important aspects of ourselves from memory may well explain our tendency to exaggerate how common our own characteristics and opinions are in the general population. That is, the reason that we often assume others share our characteristics, habits, and opinions may be because these self-aspects are readily available in memory. As you can see, this type of thinking, brought about by the availability heuristic, can cause us to make misguided decisions.

When Do We Use Heuristics?

With what frequency do we take mental shortcuts in decision making? As you have already learned, frequency is partly determined by our need for cognition. Beyond this individual difference, Anthony Pratkanis (1989) has identified at least five conditions

ing our options. Yet, because we sometimes are not aware that a decision is "important" until after the fact, the greater overall care taken by high-NFC individuals should lead to better results than the lazier decision-making style of low-NFC persons (Cacioppo et al., 1996).

TABLE 9-5

Need for Cognition Scale: Sample Items

Directions: These are sample items taken from the Need for Cognition Scale. If you agree with items 1, 3, 5, and 7 and disagree with items 2, 4, 6, and 8, you exhibit behaviors that are indicative of a person high in the need for cognition. If your responses to these items are exactly in the opposite direction, you may be low in the need for cognition. Based on your responses, which route to persuasion do you think you tend to take?

1. I really enjoy a task that involves coming up with new solutions to problems.

2. Thinking is not my idea of fun.

3. The notion of thinking abstractly is appealing to me.

4. I like tasks that require little thought once I've learned them.

5. I usually end up deliberating about issues even when they do not affect me personally.

6. It's enough for me that something gets the job done; I don't care how or why it works.

7. I prefer my life to be filled with puzzles that I must solve.

8. I only think as hard as I have to.

Source: From "The Need for Cognition" by J. T. Cacioppo and R. E. Petty in JOURNAL OF PERSONALITY AND SOCIAL PSYCHOLOGY, 1982, 42, pp. 116–131 (Table 1, pp. 120–121). Copyright © 1982 by the American Psychological Association. Adapted with permission.

Need for cognition: A person's preference for and tendency to engage in effortful cognitive activities.

---

most likely to lead to the use of heuristics rather than rational decision making. The first condition in which these mental shortcuts will likely be used is when we simply don't have time to engage in systematic analysis. The second and third conditions are when we are overloaded with information so that it is impossible to process all that is meaningful and relevant, and/or when we consider the issues in question to be *not very important*. Finally, heuristics will often be relied on when we have *little other knowledge* or information to use in making a decision, or when something about the situation in question *calls to mind* a given heuristic, making it cognitively available.

One final note: Although basing decisions on heuristics may lead to errors, relying on them may actually be adaptive under conditions where we don't have the luxury of carefully analyzing all our options (Johnston et al., 1997; Klein, 1996). For example, reacting quickly in an emergency based only on information that is most accessible from memory (the availability heuristic) may often be the difference between life and death. Thus, although heuristics can lead to sloppy decision making, their timesaving quality may sometimes be a lifesaver.

SECTION SUMMARY

- Concept formation is a basic element of cognition.
- The process of forming concepts is called categorization.
- Failing to correctly categorize things because they don't match our prototype can lead to errors in decision making.
- Typical problem-solving strategies include: trial and error, algorithms, heuristics, and insight.
- Three common internal obstacles to problem solving include: confirmation bias, mental set, and functional fixedness.
- An aspect of everyday cognition is weighing the pros and cons of different alternatives.
- One important influence on decision making is framing.
- An important ingredient in competent decision making is critical analysis, but we often rely on mental-saving heuristics.
- People with a high need for cognition are likely to engage in critical thinking.

SUGGESTED WEBSITES

Note: These websites were functional when we went to press. Please access the online text for the most up-to-date URLs.

The Psychology of Language Page of Links
http://www.psyc.memphis.edu/POL/POL.htm
This website provides links to other websites of language researchers, organizations, journals, questionnaires, and related disciplines.

Center for the Study of Language and Information (CSLI)
http://www-csli.stanford.edu/
This website is the home page for CSLI, an independent research center at Stanford University.

Experimental Psychology Lab
http://www.psychologie.unizh.ch/genpsy/Ulf/Lab/WebExpPsyLab.html
This website contains links to a number of sites that provide people the opportunity to participate in psychological experiments.

PSYCHOLOGICAL APPLICATIONS
How Can You Change Your Language Style to Become a More Persuasive Speaker?

Imagine the following two individuals going to their separate bosses to request a raise:

Person A: "Uhm . . . excuse me, sir? . . . Uhm . . . could I speak to you for a minute? . . . This may sound a little out of the ordinary, but, I've been with the company for one year now, you know, and . . . uhm, well, I was sort of wondering if we could talk about an increase in my salary? Uhm . . . you know, since starting here, I've kind of been given a good deal of responsibilities that go beyond my job description, you know, and . . . uhm . . . I've handled this additional work efficiently and professionally, you know, without complaining and without supervision, don't you think? I'm not an expert on how to run this company, you know, but I was wondering . . . uhm . . . now that I have proven capable of handling this increased work load and responsibilities, you know, don't you think my salary should reflect this fact?"

Person B: "Excuse me, sir? Could I speak to you for a minute? I've been with the company for one year now, and I would like to talk to you about an increase in my salary. Since starting here, I've been given a good deal of responsibilities that go well beyond my job description, and I've handled this additional work efficiently and professionally without complaining and without supervision. Now that I have proven I'm capable of handling this increased work load and responsibilities, I would like to have my salary reflect this fact."

Both messages contain the same factual content, yet they differ greatly in how the content is presented. Linguists would say that Person A's presentation is an example of powerless speech, while Person B's embodies *powerful speech*. Powerless speech includes the following language forms:

1. *Hesitation Forms*—"Uh" and "You know" suggest a lack of confidence or certainty.
2. *Disclaimers*—"This may sound out of the ordinary, but . . ." and "I'm not an expert, but . . . " ask the listener to be patient or refrain from criticism.
3. *Qualifiers*—"Sort of," "kind of," and "I guess" serve to blunt the force of an assertive statement.
4. *Tag Questions*—"I've handled this additional work efficiently and professionally, don't you think?" The added-on question turns an assertive statement into a plea for agreement.

As you might guess, when people use a powerful speaking style, they are judged more competent and credible than when their style is powerless (Hosman, 1997; Erickson et al., 1978). Although the use of powerful language forms adds an assertive "punch" to messages, not everyone in society is taught to use this style of speech. Linguist Robin Lakoff (1975, 1990) asserts that because the status of women in society has been relatively powerless and marginal compared with men, they often are not socialized nor expected to express themselves as assertively and forcefully as men. As a result, in conversation, women are more likely than men to use qualifiers, ask tag questions, and use disclaimers (Coates, 1992; Mulac & Lundell, 1986).

Be skillful in speech that you may be strong.
—The Teaching for Merikare, 2135–2040, B.C.

Although a powerful speaking style generally is more persuasive than a powerless one, research suggests that women—but not men—sometimes get caught in a double bind communicatively. For a woman, adopting a powerful communication style increases her persuasive power with a female audience, but a male audience sometimes perceives her as less likable and trustworthy, which reduces her ability to persuade (Carli, 1990). Does this mean that women should adopt a powerless speaking style to improve their persuasive power with men? No. The use of such powerless language as a subtle persuasion technique will either compromise a woman's perceived competence or make it difficult for her to persuade an audience of both men and women. Instead, additional research (Carli et al., 1995) suggests that an alternative method for female persuaders to use with a male audience is to combine assertive language with a *social nonverbal style* that communicates friendliness and affiliation (relaxed forward-leaning, smiling face, moderate eye contact). In other words, men are more inclined to like and be persuaded by a competent woman when she is also sociable than when she is merely competent. For a male audience, a sociable nonverbal style appears to take the perception of threat out of a competent woman's self-presentation, making her an effective agent of persuasion.

Public speaking is done in the public tongue, the national or tribal language; and the language of our tribe is the men's language. Of course women learn it. We're not dumb. If you can tell Margaret Thatcher from Ronald Reagan, or Indira Gandhi from General Somoza, by anything they say, tell me how. This is a man's world, so it talks a man's language.

—Ursula LeGuin, U.S. author, 1983

KEY TERMS

algorithm (p. 265)
availability heuristic (p. 271)
categorization (p. 263)
cognition (p. 248)
communication (p. 248)
concept (p. 263)
confirmation bias (p. 267)
framing (p. 270)
functional fixedness (p. 268)
generic masculine (p. 261)

grammar (p. 253)
heuristic (p. 266)
insight (p. 266)
language (p. 248)
language acquisition device (p. 257)
linguistic relativity hypothesis (p. 260)
mental set (p. 267)
morpheme (p. 254)
need for cognition (p. 273)
phoneme (p. 253)

phonology (p. 253)
problem solving (p. 264)
prototype (p. 263)
representativeness heuristic (p. 271)
semantics (p. 253)
slips of the tongue (p. 256)
speech (p. 248)
syntax (p. 253)
telegraphic speech (p. 259)
trial and error (p. 264)

REVIEW QUESTIONS

1. The content and comprehension of language is associated with
   a. Broca's area.
   b. the right cerebral hemisphere.
   c. Wernicke's area.
   d. the larynx.
   e. the location of the larynx.

2. Researchers who study nonhuman language have determined that
   a. chimps' use of sign language has nothing to do with language acquisition.
   b. honeybees have flexible signals for communicating novel messages.
   c. rigid training methods, such as those used by Terrace, are the most effective way to teach spontaneous signing to chimps.
   d. Kanzi, a bonobo, learned to use symbols spontaneously by observing his adopted mother use symbols to communicate.
   e. very intelligent apes can learn to communicate at a 5- to 6-year-old human level.

3. Rules for how words are put together to form a proper phrase or sentence are referred to as
   a. semantic rules.
   b. syntax rules.
   c. surface structure.
   d. phonological rules.
   e. morpheme rules.

4. The dominant view of language currently emphasizes which of the following as a critical component of language acquisition?
   a. exposure to the language
   b. the language acquisition device
   c. selective reinforcement and punishment
   d. the nativist approach
   e. the interactionist perspectives

5. Two-year-olds' telegraphic speech involves
   a. the use of phonemes that are not part of the native language.
   b. an elementary knowledge of syntax.
   c. the use of plurals and past and present tense.
   d. learning exaggerated intonations and using a high pitch.
   e. primarily the use of slang terms.

6. A weaker version of Whorf's linguistic relativity hypothesis is supported by
   a. research showing that bilinguists focus on personal needs when speaking English and social needs when speaking Japanese.
   b. Rosch's research on cross-cultural color perception, showing that the Dani people have only two words for color.
   c. research showing that the structure of language determines the structure of thought.
   d. the finding that Chinese languages have many self-focused words.
   e. research showing that language does not influence thinking in collectivist cultures.

7. Slips of the tongue are *primarily* explained by
   a. cognitive processes such as spreading activation of phonemes and morphemes.
   b. psychoanalytic theories of unconscious thoughts and desires.
   c. Spoonerisms, tangled expressions, and word reversals.
   d. spreading activation of semantic rules.
   e. the nativist perspective.

8. The way that language calls attention to an individual's gender and the use of generic masculine pronouns and nouns supports the notion that
   a. language determines thought.
   b. cultural thinking can influence people's style of language.
   c. gender-neutral language erases females from our thinking.
   d. collectivist cultures exhibit more gender bias than individualist cultures.
   e. language influences thought.

9. Categorizing, or forming concepts, is accomplished by
   a. identifying features that define all members of a concept.
   b. learning specific concept formation rules.
   c. learning the fixed boundaries between objects' properties.
   d. identifying features that define typical members of a concept.
   e. learning the specific rules that define the meaning of fuzzy boundaries.

10. Trial and error problem-solving strategies
    a. guarantee success because you can keep guessing until you get it right.
    b. are faster and more efficient than using complex algorithms.
    c. are slower than heuristic strategies.
    d. follow a systematic and methodical step-by-step procedure.
    e. involve a gradually increasing focus on concepts important to the solution.

11. Confirmation bias leads to problem-solving errors
    a. because we seek only information that confirms our beliefs.
    b. only when we waste time testing alternative hypotheses, rather than seeking confirming evidence.
    c. only when we pursue information that disconfirms our beliefs.
    d. when we fail to rely on solutions that worked in the past.
    e. because we tend to confirm what experts tell us.

12. Rational decision-making strategies
    a. always consider all aspects of the available options.
    b. involve framing choices in multiple ways before deciding.
    c. are used less often when a decision is important to us.
    d. may involve nonsystematic or elementary strategies.
    e. are more effective than using the weighted additive value model.

13. Research on decision-making strategies and shortcuts indicates that
   a. representative heuristics are the best way to eliminate the base rate fallacy.
   b. the false consensus effect leads us to assume that our decision is wrong when we disagree with everyone else.
   c. a useful decision-making strategy that can narrow our choices is to rely on the ease with which previous examples of an event are recalled.
   d. heuristics are complex cognitive processes used primarily by those with a high need for cognition.
   e. heuristics are used more frequently when we are in a hurry than when we have time to think about our choices.

14. According to the *Psychological Applications* section concerning language style and persuasive speaking, what is the "double bind" that women, but not men, face?
   a. Women who use qualifiers in their speech are more effective in persuading women but not men.
   b. Women need to use a powerful communication style to be persuasive, but men do not need to do so.
   c. When women use a powerful communication style, they are judged to be less physically attractive than if they use a powerless style.
   d. When women use a powerful communication style, some male listeners feel threatened, and thus, are less persuaded.

15. Features of a communication system that characterize it as a "language" include all *except* which one of the following?
   a. meaningfulness
   b. signals that trigger instinctive responses
   c. displacement in space
   d. displacement in time
   e. novelty or flexibility

10

Intelligence

Chapter Outline

The Man with the Hoe

Bowed by the weight of centuries he leans
Upon his hoe and gazes on the ground,
The emptiness of ages in his face,
And on his back the burden of the world.

Who made him dead to rapture and despair,
A thing that grieves not and that never hopes,
Stolid and stunned, a brother to the ox?
Who loosened and let down this brutal jaw?
Whose was the hand that slanted back this
     brow?
Whose breath blew out the light within this
     brain?

Excerpt from "The Man with the Hoe" by Edwin
Markham, New York: Doubleday & McClure, 1899.

Jean-Francois Millet's painting *The Man with the Hoe* depicted in figure 10-1 has an interesting footnote in the history of intelligence testing. In 1899, inspired by Millet's painting, Edwin Markham wrote a poem of the same name, which was published in almost every newspaper in the United States that year and quickly became the focus of discussion and debate. For many, the weary French peasant became the symbol of how oppressive social conditions prevent people from attaining their true intellectual potential. Yet, psychologist Henry Goddard, the director of intellectual assessment at Ellis Island in New York Harbor where immigrants to the United States were processed and tested, did not agree with Markham's interpretation. Believing that he could recognize feebleminded people by sight, Goddard asserted that, as with most poor peasants, the man in Millet's painting was not the victim of bad social conditions, but rather, bad genes (Goddard, 1919). He further contended that people with very low intelligence needed to be identified so that society could prevent them from passing their feeblemindedness on to the next generation.

FIGURE 10-1
The Man with the Hoe

Source: The J. Paul Getty Museum, Los Angeles, Jean-Francois Millet, *The Man with the Hoe*, 1860–1862, oil on canvas, 31 1/2 x 39 inches.

During the first quarter of the twentieth century, Goddard and many of his colleagues used the emerging field of intelligence testing to work toward this goal. In hindsight, we can see that their research and policy recommendations—fueled by cultural prejudices in the larger society—illustrate how science can sometimes be used as a weapon of discrimination. Yet, at the dawn of a new century, psychology continues to struggle with disturbing findings from intelligence research. Persistent differences in the intelligence scores of Blacks, Whites, Hispanics, Asians, and Native Americans raise disturbing questions about what determines intelligence (Cosmides & Tooby, 2002). Do these group differences mean that the different races can be organized in a hierarchy of superior-inferior intelligence? This question threatens to further tear the social fabric of our society, which continues to be divided by race and ethnicity. But it is a question that ignoring won't dismiss.

In this chapter, we continue our discovery journey by analyzing the nature of intelligence. For our purposes, we will define intelligence as the mental abilities necessary to adapt to and shape the environment (Grossman & Kaufman, 2002; Neisser et al., 1996). What this means is that intelligence involves not only *reacting* to one's surroundings but also *actively forming them*. It also means that intelligent behavior in New York City, for example, may not be intelligent or adaptive in the jungles of South America. The mental abilities making up what we call **intelligence** are the keys to lifelong learning (Sternberg, 1997a). Yet, is intelligence something inborn or learned? Are there different types of intelligence? Are there gender differences? These are some of the issues we will grapple with as we ride the rocky road of intelligence testing and theorizing.

> **Intelligence:** The mental abilities necessary to adapt to and shape the environment.

10-1 MEASURING INTELLIGENCE

Psychometrics—which literally means "to measure the mind"—is the measurement of intelligence, personality, and other mental processes. The psychological tests developed by psychometricians assess the *individual differences* that exist between people on a wide variety of abilities, interests, and personality traits. Although the psychometric approach has been extensively employed in the study of intelligence, the results have sometimes given psychology a black eye.

> **Psychometrics:** The measurement of intelligence, personality, and other mental processes.

10-1a The Early History of Intelligence Testing Illustrates How Scientists Can Be Influenced by Cultural Stereotypes

No science is untouched by the values and politics of the culture in which it is practiced. In psychology, nowhere is this more clearly seen than in the early history of intelligence testing 100 years ago. During this time period, Western scientific thinking was heavily influenced by the cultural belief in the *natural* intellectual superiority of upper-class White men over women, the poor, and members of all other racial and ethnic groups. This mindset sometimes resulted not only in bad science but also in bad public policy.

Francis Galton: Quantifying Intelligence

As a pioneer in modern statistics, British mathematician and naturalist Sir Francis Galton (1822–1911) was so convinced that anything could be quantified that he actually tried to statistically determine the effectiveness of prayer! When cousin Charles Darwin proposed his theory of evolution, Galton decided to apply the principle of natural selection to human traits. He reasoned that if traits are inherited, then similar levels of intelligence should consistently appear in families over generations. Galton (1869) further believed that the wealthy families in society—like his own—were also the more intelligent because intelligence was assumed to result in success and wealth. He was so confident that families ended up either wealthy or poor because of their inherited traits that he founded the **eugenics** (the Greek word for "well-born") movement to improve the hereditary characteristics of

> **Eugenics:** The practice of encouraging supposedly superior people to reproduce, while discouraging or even preventing those judged inferior to do so.

Sir Francis Galton: "If everybody were to agree on the improvement of the race of man being a matter of the very utmost importance, and if the theory of the hereditary transmission of qualities in men was as thoroughly understood as it is in the case of our domestic animals, I see no absurdity in supposing that, in some way or other, the improvement would be carried into effect."

society. Eugenics not only proposed that men and women of high mental ability—meaning White and upper-middle-class individuals—should be encouraged to marry and have children, but also that those of lesser intelligence—meaning lower-class Whites and members of other races—should be discouraged (or prevented) from reproducing.

How did Galton measure intelligence? Believing that intelligence was a product of how quickly and accurately people respond to stimuli, Galton's assessment battery included measurements of sensory abilities and reaction time, as well as measurements of head size and muscular strength. Unfortunately for Galton, his tests not only did not correlate with each other, they had almost no relation to accepted criteria of intellectual functioning (Sharp, 1898; Wissler, 1901).

Alfred Binet: "Father" of Intelligence Testing

While Galton's attempts to measure intelligence failed, across the English Channel, a different type of intelligence testing was being developed by French psychologist Alfred Binet (1857–1911), whose work partly inspired Jean Piaget's theory of cognitive development (see chapter 4, section 4-3a). When the French government passed a law in 1904 that all children must attend school, Binet and physician Theophilé Simon (1905) worked to develop an inexpensive, easily administered, objective measure of intelligence that could identify lower-performing children in need of special education. In contrast to Galton's work, the resulting Binet-Simon Test measured general mental ability and emphasized abstract reasoning rather than sensory skills.

According to Binet, cognitive development follows the same course in all children, but some learn faster and more easily than others. In intelligence testing, this means that "average" children will perform similar to those their own chronological age, "dull" children will perform similar to children younger than themselves, and "bright" children will perform like older children. Binet reasoned that general mental ability can be calculated by comparing children's *mental age* with their chronological age. Thus, a 12-year-old child who performs equal to the average child her chronological age would have the mental age of 12 years. Armed with this method of intellectual comparison, testers could place children into appropriate grades in school and identify those who would benefit from additional tutoring. Unlike Galton's intelligence test, the Binet-Simon Test proved to be the first valid intelligence instrument: That is, it accurately identified lower-performing students.

In designing the Binet-Simon Test, Binet, unlike Galton, made no assumptions about why intelligence differences exist. However, he did insist that his test did not measure inborn intelligence, and he believed that intellectual ability could be increased through education. He also realized that his test merely *sampled* intelligence and did not measure all intellectual aspects. Finally, he warned that because the test was developed in France using children with similar cultural backgrounds, it may not accurately measure intelligence in other countries. Two of his fears were that his test would not be used to help slow learners receive special help, but instead, would be used to (1) limit their educational opportunities and (2) plant the idea in their own minds that they are incapable of learning (Gould, 1996). Unfortunately, both fears were realized when his test was redesigned for use in the United States (Mayrhauser, 2002).

IQ Testing in America

Henry Goddard was the first to translate and use Binet's test in the United States. Despite Binet's insistence that his test did not measure inherited intelligence, Goddard believed

Our purpose is to be able to measure the intellectual capacity of a child who is brought to us in order to know whether he is normal or retarded. . . . If we do nothing, if we don't intervene actively and usefully, he will continue to lose time . . . and will finally become discouraged. The child who loses the taste for work in class strongly risks being unable to acquire it after he leaves school.

—Alfred Binet

that it did. Also, in contrast to Binet's desire to use his scale to identify low-scoring students for special education, Goddard, a strong advocate of Galton's eugenics movement, used the test to identify the feebleminded so that they could be segregated and prevented from having children. To describe these low intelligence people, he coined the term *moron*, which is derived from a Greek word meaning foolish. Goddard (1913) later used the Binet-Simon test to assess newly arrived immigrants at Ellis Island in New York Harbor. Because these tests were biased toward native-born English speakers, many immigrants scored very low. These test results were later used by politicians to pass the Immigration Act of 1924, which dramatically restricted the admittance of certain "undesirable" ethnic groups, especially those from eastern and southern Europe (Sedgwick, 1995).

Although Goddard and most other psychologists involved in the eugenics movement later reversed their positions and argued against such discriminatory measures, this aspect of their research not only harmed the reputation of psychology as a science, but it also justified racist societal practices here and abroad. In Germany, the eugenics movement helped fan the flames of the Holocaust. Partly inspired by the success of U.S. eugenics laws, the Nazis in Germany designed deadly eugenics programs involving forced sterilization of those who supposedly had genetic defects, forbidding the marriage of Aryans and Jews, and finally, the mass execution of Jews, Gypsies, homosexuals, the mentally handicapped, and other "genetic undesirables" (Leahey, 1991). Desperate to escape the sure death awaiting them in Nazi concentration camps, millions of Jewish refugees tried to emigrate to the United States. However, in the cruelest twist to this sorry tale, few Jews were admitted, partly due to restrictions imposed by the 1924 immigration law. The indirect role that psychology played in this chapter of history chillingly demonstrates how ideas can sometimes be as destructive as guns and bombs.

10-1b　Modern Tests of Mental Abilities Measure Either Aptitude or Achievement

When describing mental abilities tests, psychologists generally place them into the two different categories of *aptitude* and *achievement*. Intelligence tests are **aptitude tests:** They predict your capacity to learn a new skill if you are given an adequate education. In contrast to predicting what you can learn, **achievement tests** measure what you have already learned. Whenever you are given an exam in a course to determine what you have learned, you are taking an achievement test.

Although the distinctions between aptitude and achievement tests seem clear-cut, they are not. For instance, suppose that two college students who have an equal capacity for learning math are given a test of mathematical aptitude. One student, however, attended a high school where he had four years of college-level math instruction, while the other student's school offered no college-level courses. Despite their equal capacity for learning math, it's likely that the student with the greater math experience will obtain a higher math aptitude score. The implication of this example is that your score on an aptitude test can be affected by your prior experience in the area being tested.

The Stanford-Binet Intelligence Test

Although Goddard introduced the Binet-Simon Test to America, Lewis Terman (1877–1956), a psychology professor at Stanford University, was responsible for revising

Lewis Terman: "The children of successful and cultured parents test higher than children from wretched and ignorant homes for the simple reason that their heredity is better. . . . The whole question of racial differences in mental traits will have to be taken up anew and by experimental methods. The writer predicts that when this is done, there will be discovered enormously significant racial differences in general intelligence, differences which cannot be wiped out by any scheme of mental culture." (1916, pp. 91–92, 115)

Aptitude test: A test designed to predict a person's capacity for learning.

Achievement test: A test designed to assess what a person has learned.

If the impression takes root that these tests really measure intelligence, that they constitute a sort of last judgment on the child's capacity, . . . then it would be a thousand times better if all the intelligence testers and all their questionnaires were sunk without warning in the Sargasso Sea.

　　　　—Walter Lippmann, 1889–1974, American journalist and social critic, comments while debating Lewis Terman

---

Stanford-Binet Intelligence Test: The widely used American revision of the original French Binet-Simon intelligence test.

Intelligence quotient (IQ): Originally, the ratio of mental age to chronological age multiplied by 100 (MA/CA × 100). Today, it is calculated by comparing how a person's performance deviates from the average score of her or his same-age peers, which is 100.

it so that it could be used on American children (Terman, 1916). The resulting **Stanford-Binet Intelligence Test** employed a new scoring system known as the **intelligence quotient (IQ).** Based on an idea by German psychologist Wilhelm Stern (1914), IQ was represented as a ratio of mental age divided by chronological age, multiplied by 100:

$$IQ = \frac{\text{Mental age}}{\text{Chronological age}} \times 100$$

With this formula, a child whose mental and chronological ages are the same had an IQ of 100. However, a 10-year-old who answers questions like a typical 8-year-old had an IQ of 80, and an 8-year-old who answers questions like a typical 10-year-old had an IQ of 125. The advantage of this ratio formula over the Binet-Simon scoring system was that it was more useful when comparing mental ages within a group of children who differed in their chronological ages.

Although the IQ ratio was adequate in representing children's intelligence, it was problematic when the Stanford-Binet was redesigned to also measure adult intelligence. Because the *rate of growth* does not occur as rapidly in adulthood as in childhood, using the IQ ratio led to the mistaken representation that intelligence *declines* with age. For example, if Raymond had the mental age of 20 at age 15, he would have an IQ of 133, which is considered mentally gifted. However, at the age of 40, if Raymond's mental age had increased to 28, his IQ would now be only 70, which is the beginning of the mentally retarded range. Raymond might have a successful career in a profession requiring above-average intelligence, but the ratio IQ would not accurately reflect this fact. Today, most intelligence tests, including the Stanford-Binet, no longer compute a ratio IQ. Instead, it has been replaced with a *deviation IQ*, which compares how a person's intelligence test score deviates from the average score of her or his same-age peers, which is 100.

The Wechsler Intelligence Scales

The person responsible for developing the deviation IQ score was David Wechsler, one of those supposedly feebleminded eastern Europeans who immigrated to this country in the early 1900s. Today's most widely used set of intelligence tests are the **Wechsler Intelligence Scales,** named after their creator. Three separate intelligence tests have been designed for adults (*Wechsler Adult Intelligence Scale*), preschoolers (*Wechsler Preschool and Primary Scale of Intelligence*), and school-age children (*Wechsler Intelligence Scale for Children*).

Wechsler Intelligence Scales: The most widely used set of intelligence tests, containing both verbal and performance (nonverbal) subscales.

For all the Wechsler tests, intelligence is measured by 11 subtests—6 verbal and 5 performance—which yield a verbal IQ score, a performance IQ score, and an overall IQ score. Figure 10-2 provides sample items from the adult test for the verbal and performance subscales. As you can see, the verbal items consist of vocabulary, general information, analogies, math, comprehension, and the recall of number strings. In contrast, the performance subscales require you to locate missing picture parts, reproduce block designs, assemble jigsaw puzzles, arrange cartoons in a logical sequence, and copy symbols on paper. Because the performance subtests rely less on familiarity with words and language, they are less likely to be affected by the test takers' education or cultural experiences. Significant differences between the verbal and performance scores alert test administrators to possible learning problems. For instance, a verbal score considerably lower than a performance score might indicate a reading or language disability (Aiken, 1996). However, as just mentioned, it could also mean that the test taker is not very familiar with the language or customs of the larger society.

Group-Administered Tests

While the Stanford-Binet and the Wechsler tests are administered individually to people, group-administered tests can assess hundreds or thousands of people simultaneously. Group aptitude and achievement tests are widely used today, including the familiar college entrance *Scholastic Assessment Test (SAT)*, which was previously known as the Scholastic Aptitude Test. The reason for this name change is because the old name's use

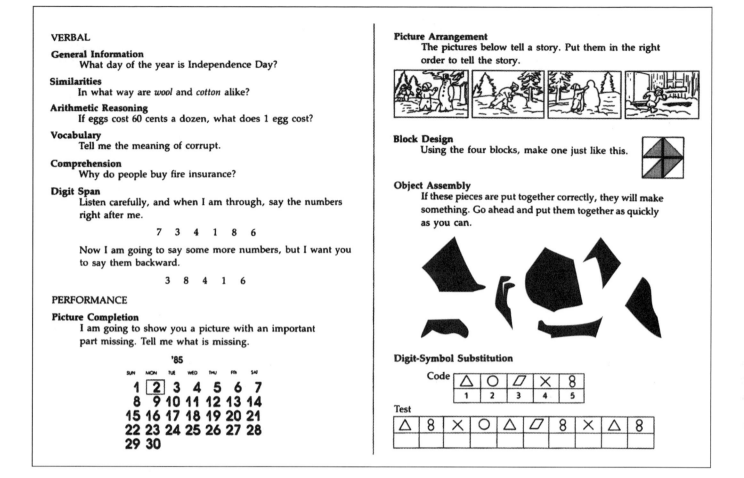

of the term *aptitude* implied that the SAT measures a person's capacity for learning. In reality, it measures learned verbal and mathematical skills; thus, it is more accurately considered an achievement test. As such, SAT scores are significantly influenced by the quality of the schools that test takers attend. Overemphasizing SAT scores in evaluating students for college admission, therefore, can disadvantage students who attended inferior schools and also those whose main academic strengths lie in such areas as music and art. Both the verbal and math sections of the SAT have an average score of 500 and a range from 200 to 800, resulting in a total score range from 400 to 1600.

Similar tests are also used to assess students' potential for postgraduate training. For graduate school in the arts and sciences there is the Graduate Record Exam (GRE), for graduate school in business there is the Graduate Management Admission Test (GMAT), medical schools use the Medical College Admission Test (MCAT), and law schools use the Law School Aptitude Test (LSAT). Like the SAT, there is sufficient evidence that these exams measure not only the potential for performing well on scholastic tasks but also achievement. The practical importance of this fact for students is that studying can improve test performance. On the SATs, extensive training or coaching on how to take the SAT can increase total scores by as many as 30 to 50 points (Kulik et al., 1984; Powers, 1993).

FIGURE 10-2

Sample Items from the Wechsler Adult Intelligence Scale (WAIS)

Source: From MEASUREMENT AND EVALUATION IN PSYCHOLOGY AND EDUCATION by A. L. Thorndike and E. P. Hagen. Reprinted by permission of Pearson Education, Inc., Upper Saddle River, NJ.

Journey of Discovery Question

Women who go to college after their mid-twenties receive better grades than what you would predict based upon their SAT scores taken just before entering college. Why might this be the case?

10-1c Psychological Tests Must Be Standardized, Reliable, and Valid

All psychological tests, including the mental ability tests discussed in this chapter, are measurement instruments that must have three basic characteristics: They must be *standardized*, *reliable*, and *valid*. The Stanford-Binet, Wechsler tests, and the scholastic tests that we have reviewed thus far all possess these characteristics.

Standardization

If you have taken the SAT or any other achievement or aptitude tests, you may recall that the testing procedures are extremely rigid. Regardless of where or when the test is administered, everyone receives the same instructions, the same questions, and the same time limits. You may also remember that when you received your test results, your individual score was compared against a previously tested group of people who had followed the same testing procedures that you followed. This comparison process allowed you to convert your "raw score" into a *percentile*, which indicates the percentage of people in the standard group who scored at or below your score. This entire process of establishing uniform procedures for administering a test and for interpreting its scores is known as **standardization.**

Standardized test results often show a roughly normal distribution, which has a bell-shaped appearance when the individual scores are placed in a graph. As you can see in figure 10-3, in a **normal distribution,** most test scores cluster around the *median*, or middle score, which has a similar value as both the *mean* (the average test score) and the *mode* (the most frequent test score). As previously mentioned, the mean score on an intelligence test is 100. As we move away—in either direction—from this mean score, we find fewer test scores. Also as depicted in figure 10-3, in a normal distribution of IQ scores, 68 percent of the scores will range between 85 and 115, and 96 percent of the scores will fall within the 70–130 point range. Only 2 percent of the population have IQ scores above 130 and only 2 percent have scores below 70.

Periodically, the Stanford-Binet and the Wechsler IQ tests are restandardized to maintain the mean score of 100. This is necessary because in every single one of the 20 countries studied worldwide, each succeeding generation intellectually outperforms the previous generation (Flynn, 1987, 1990, 1996). What this means for restandardization purposes is that test items must be made more difficult to keep the average intelligence score at 100. This tendency for people's performance on IQ tests to improve from one generation to the next is known as the **Flynn effect,** after the psychologist who first noticed it.

What accounts for this rapid increase in IQ? Evolution—which occurs slowly—cannot provide an answer, and it certainly appears inconsistent with Galton's prediction that

Standardization: The process of establishing uniform procedures for administering a test and for interpreting its scores.

Normal distribution: The bell-shaped appearance of standardized tests when individual scores are placed in a graph. Most scores cluster around the average test score, and fewer scores are found far from the average score.

Flynn effect: The tendency for people's performance on IQ tests to improve from one generation to the next.

FIGURE 10-3
The Normal Distribution

Scores on standardized aptitude tests, such as the Wechsler Adult Intelligence Scale, tend to form a normal distribution (also known as a "bell-shaped curve"). The Wechsler scale, like other IQ tests, calls the average score 100.

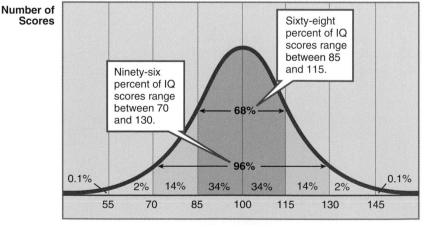

Wechsler Intelligence Score

higher birthrates observed among those with lower IQ scores would move IQ scores lower. A likely explanation is that it is the combined effects of improved education, better health and nutrition, experience with testing, and exposure to a broader range of information via television and the computer.

Reliability

The **reliability** of a test indicates the degree to which it yields consistent results. The most common technique to estimate this type of consistency is through *test-retest reliability*, which is checking to see how people score on the same test on two separate occasions. The drawback to this reliability technique, however, is that people tend to remember the test items when they take the test again, and this influences their performance. A solution is to use *alternate-forms reliability*, in which slightly different versions of the test are given to people on the two separate occasions. The items on the two-test versions are similar in format but are different enough in content so that test-takers' performance will not be influenced by familiarity. Reliability estimates for both techniques are based on correlation coefficients. As you recall from chapter 2, section 2-3b, a *correlation coefficient* (also known by the symbol r) is a statistical measure of the direction and strength of the linear relationship between two variables, and ranges from −1.00 to +1.00. In estimating both test-retest and alternate-forms reliability, the two variables are the two test scores obtained on two different occasions. If people's test scores at time 1 have a strong correspondence with their scores at time 2 (figure 10-4a), the correlation coefficient will be near +1.00, meaning that the test's reliability is high, which is good news for the test developer. However, if how people score at time 1 and time 2 does not correspond (figure 10-4b), then the correlation coefficient will be closer to 0.00, meaning that the test's reliability is low. This is bad news for the test developer. The contemporary intelligence tests described thus far have correlation coefficients of about +.90, which indicate high reliability (Kaufman, 1990; Robinson & Nagel, 1992).

> **Reliability:** The degree to which a test yields consistent results.

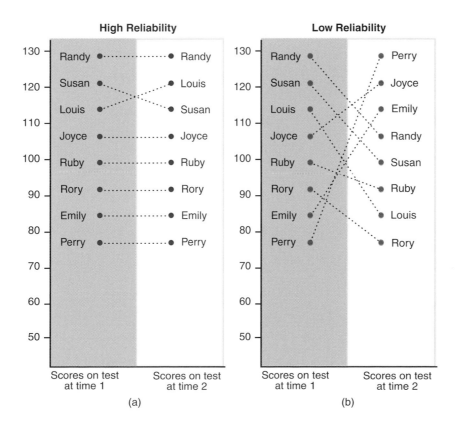

FIGURE 10-4
Determining Both Test-Retest and Alternate-Forms Reliabilities

In test-retest reliability, people take a test at time 1 and again at time 2. In alternate-forms reliability, they take one version of the test at time 1 and a slightly different version at time 2. For both of these reliability techniques, people's scores at time 1 are depicted on the left, and their scores at time 2 are depicted on the right. (a) When people obtain similar scores on both occasions, the test has high reliability. (b) If they get very different scores, the test has low reliability.

Validity

Validity: The degree to which a test measures what it is designed to measure.

Knowing that a test is reliable does not tell you anything about its validity. **Validity** refers to the degree to which a test measures what it is designed to measure. In our household, we have a weighing scale that is highly reliable: Everyone who steps on it consistently weighs 32 pounds. Although it is reliable, none of us believe it is a *valid* weight measure. While the invalidity of our household scale is a source of amusement for us, invalid intelligence tests are no joking matter.

How do researchers determine whether an intelligence test is valid? Typically, they analyze different aspects of the test (Daneman & Hannon, 2001; Ukrainetz & Blomquist, 2002). **Content validity** refers to the degree to which the items on a test are related to the characteristic the test supposedly measures. For example, if an intelligence test consisted of measuring a person's weight and height, we would probably conclude that it was low in content validity because these measurements seem completely unrelated to our conception of intelligence. However, if it contained items that measured abstract reasoning, we would be more inclined to believe that it had reasonable content validity.

Content validity: The degree to which the items on a test are related to the characteristic the test supposedly measures.

Besides content validity, tests are also analyzed in terms of **predictive validity** (also known as *criterion validity*), which is the degree to which the test results predict other observable behavior related to the characteristic the test supposedly measures. How well do contemporary intelligence tests predict behavior that is thought to be related to intelligence? It depends. The correlation between IQ scores and scholastic achievement (usually measured by students' school grades) is about +.60 to +.70 during elementary school, which is quite high. However, during the college years, this correlation drops to about +.40 to +.50.

Predictive validity: The degree to which a test predicts other observable behavior related to the characteristic the test supposedly measures. (Also known as *criterion validity*.)

Why is there this decline in predictive validity from elementary school to college? More important than the greater number of social distractions in college is that there is a greater *restricted range* of intelligence among college students than among students in elementary school. That is, regardless of whether they are low or high in intelligence, almost all children attend elementary school. In such an environment where virtually all intelligence levels are represented, it isn't surprising that IQ scores do a pretty good job predicting school grades: The cream rises to the top. However, following high school, students with above-average intelligence—the "cream" of elementary school—are the ones most likely to attend college. In this "creamy" environment, IQ scores cannot possibly predict academic performance as well as in the "milky" elementary school environment.

Do SAT scores significantly predict whether students will actually succeed or fail in college? Yes, but similar to IQ scores, they are not strong predictors: The correlation with college grades is less than +.50 (Aiken, 1996). The SAT is a better predictor of college performance for those who score at the two extremes. Very low scorers are quite likely to fail in college, while very high scorers are quite likely to succeed. A probable reason for the greater predictive power of the SAT at these two extremes has to do with the fact that college success is due to both intellectual ability *and* a desire to achieve. Most high SAT scorers have both of these personal qualities, while many of the low scorers have neither.

In summary, an intelligence test, like any other psychological test, is useful only to the extent that it is both reliable and valid. Does the test yield consistent scores and does it actually predict what it supposedly measures? In general, the reliability of intelligence tests is higher than their validity.

Journey of Discovery Question

Imagine that you wanted to develop your own intelligence test. What are some of the pitfalls in early intelligence testing you would want to avoid?

- The first useful intelligence test was developed by Alfred Binet to identify lower-performing children needing special education.

- Henry Goddard inappropriately used the Binet-Simon test to assess the intelligence of diverse groups, including immigrants.

- Intelligence tests are aptitude tests; achievement tests measure what you have already learned.

- All mental ability tests must be standardized, reliable, and valid.

- Standardization is the process of establishing uniform procedures for administering a test and for interpreting its scores.

- Test reliability indicates the degree to which test yields consistent results.

- Test validity indicates the degree to which a test measures what it is designed to measure.

- Reliability of intelligence tests is higher than their validity.

10-2 INTELLIGENCE: ONE THING OR MANY?

As you have already learned, intelligence tests were constructed to meet practical goals: to identify slow learners in school for remedial education, to weed out intellectually "deficient" immigrants and army recruits, and to select college applicants. Given this practical emphasis, relatively little research attention was initially devoted to developing theories concerning the nature of intelligence (Kaufman, 2000). During this period, Edwin Boring (1923), an early historian of psychology, wrote that "Intelligence is whatever an intelligence test measures." As researchers began to more carefully study the nature of intelligence, one of the primary questions concerned whether it was best conceptualized as a general, unifying capacity along which people vary, or whether it should be thought of as being composed of many separate and relatively independent abilities (Brody, 2000).

10-2a Early Factor-Analytic Studies Led to Conflicting Conclusions about "General Intelligence"

One of the first researchers to explore this question of how to scientifically "carve up" intelligence was British psychologist Charles Spearman (1863–1945). To aid him in his dissection of intelligence, Spearman helped develop a statistical technique called **factor analysis,** which allows researchers to identify clusters of test items that correlate with one another. By analyzing these correlations, researchers are in a better position to judge whether people's test performance can be accounted for by a single underlying ability (known as a *factor*) or whether multiple abilities (or *factors*) are needed. In essence, factor analysis helps researchers reduce the number of variables they are studying to a more manageable level by grouping together those that seem to be measuring the same thing. For example, if people who do well on reading tests also do well on writing and vocabulary tests, this suggests that there might by an underlying "verbal ability" factor that is tapped by each of the individual performance measures. Moreover, if all the different intelligence abilities are highly correlated with one another, this might suggest that intelligence can be thought of as "one thing" rather than "many things."

Based on his factor-analytic research, Spearman (1927) concluded that there indeed was a **general intelligence,** or **g,** factor underlying all mental abilities, and a set of specific factors (*s*-factors) underlying certain individual mental abilities. However, because the g-factor could predict performance on a variety of intelligence tests measuring math ability,

Factor analysis: A statistical technique that allows researchers to identify clusters of variables or test items that correlate with one another.

General intelligence (g): A general intelligence factor that Spearman and other researchers believed underlies all mental abilities.

vocabulary, and general knowledge, Spearman asserted that it was much more important than the specific factors. He and other researchers believed that this general factor, which involves the more complex, higher-level mental functions, provided the key to understanding intelligence.

Although the g-factor's relative simplicity was appealing to many researchers, others argued that a person's intellect could not be captured by a general factor. Leading this dissenting group was Louis Thurstone (1887–1955). Based on his own factor-analytic studies, Thurstone (1938) concluded that there were seven clusters of *primary mental abilities*: reasoning, verbal fluency, verbal comprehension, perceptual speed, spatial skills, numerical computation, and memory.

How could the same statistical technique, namely factor analysis, lead researchers to different conclusions? The answer is that, despite its reliance on sophisticated and objective mathematical formulas, factor analysis requires researchers to make a number of highly subjective decisions concerning how their data will be organized and interpreted. As a result, researchers with different assumptions about how intelligence is organized sometimes interpret the findings of factor analysis differently.

As of this writing, research still supports both perspectives on intelligence. There is solid evidence that we have distinct mental abilities, and there is also evidence that there may be a g-factor (Carroll, 1993, 1997; Jensen, 1992). For example, brain scans indicate that when people work on tasks requiring different intellectual abilities, the same areas of the frontal cortex are activated (Duncan et al., 2000). The fact that these different abilities rely on some of the same underlying neurological processes is consistent with the "g-factor" hypothesis. In an attempt to settle this controversy, many modern theories propose that although intelligence may encompass a general ability to deal with a wide variety of cognitive tasks and problems, it also can be expressed in many different ways (Embretson & McCollam, 2000). We can be highly "intelligent" in one or more mental abilities while being relatively "unintelligent" in others. Two recent theories that explore this diversity of intelligence will be examined in the following sections.

10-2b Gardner's Theory of Multiple Intelligences Expands the Concept of Intelligence

Multiple intelligences:
Gardner's theory contends that there are at least seven distinct and relatively independent intelligences (linguistic, logical-mathematical, spatial, musical, bodily-kinesthetic, interpersonal, intrapersonal), all of which are differently developed in each of us.

When discussing gifted athletes, musicians, or carpenters, I'm sure you've heard people say, "They may be talented, but they sure aren't rocket scientists!" The implied meaning in such declarations is that talent is not intelligence. Howard Gardner (1983, 1993) would not agree. His theory of **multiple intelligences** contends that the human brain has evolved separate systems for different adaptive abilities, and what we call "intelligence" in our culture is simply a small cluster of these abilities. Supporting Thurstone's view, Gardner proposes that intelligence consists of at least seven distinct and relatively independent intelligences, all of which are differently developed in each of us: linguistic or verbal, logical-mathematical, spatial, musical, bodily-kinesthetic, interpersonal, and intrapersonal. Whether these intellectual abilities will be developed by particular individuals largely depends on which are most highly valued in their culture (Furnham et al., 2002).

The first three intellectual abilities on this list are most highly valued in Western culture, and thus, they are the ones measured by conventional intelligence tests. A person with high *linguistic intelligence*, such as an author or public speaker, would be good at communicating through written and spoken language. A person with high *logical-mathematical intelligence*, like an engineer or scientist, would be good at solving math problems and analyzing arguments. And a person with high *spatial intelligence*, such as a carpenter or air traffic controller, would be skilled at perceiving and arranging objects in the environment. Regarding the five less conventional forms of intelligence, *musical intelligence* entails the ability to analyze, compose, or perform music. *Bodily-kinesthetic intelligence* is displayed by our gifted athletes, dancers, and surgeons, but it is also necessary in ordinary activities, such as driving a car or hammering a nail. Finally, *interpersonal intelli-*

gence identifies the ability to interact well socially and to reliably predict others' motives and behavior, while high *intrapersonal intelligence* is associated with insight into one's own motives and behavior.

Although Gardner considers that these different intelligences are separate systems located in distinct brain areas, he does believe that they often interact to produce intelligent behavior. For example, skilled politicians rely heavily on linguistic intelligence when debating issues, but they also use logical-mathematical intelligence to critically analyze these issues, and interpersonal intelligence to understand what motivates voters (Bass, 2002). By combining skills in different intellectual domains, people can become competent in certain tasks or occupations, even though they may not be particularly gifted in any specific intelligence (Gardner, 1991; Walters & Gardner, 1986).

Despite people often relying on multiple intelligences to accomplish goals, it is extremely rare to find the so-called Renaissance person who excels in all or several forms of intelligence. More frequently, a person with an extraordinary ability in one area will have normal abilities in the others. The existence of these **prodigies,** who easily master skills in one intellectual area, supports Gardner's hypothesis that various types of intelligence exist and are relatively independent of one another. Besides prodigies, an even greater intellectual variance can be found among **savants,** who demonstrate exceptional ability in one specific area, such as music or drawing, while having very limited mental abilities in all other areas (Detterman et al., 2000; Treffert, 1992). In one such case, Harriet, an autistic child who did not speak until the age of 9, could hum a classic operatic piece in perfect pitch at the age of 7 months. By age 4, she had taught herself to read music, and she had also learned to play the piano, violin, clarinet, trumpet, and French horn. As an adult, although Harriet's IQ was only 73, her proficiency in music increased dramatically. She not only could identify and provide key details about any major symphony, but she also could play a tune in the style and manner of the composers of these symphonies (Treffert, 1989). As with prodigies, the existence of savants provides dramatic evidence for multiple intelligences (O'Connor et al., 2000).

Not everyone agrees with Gardner's theory. For instance, some critics question how athletic prowess can be considered a mental ability and instead believe that it should more properly be labeled a talent (Hoberman, 1997). Others charge that the list of seven intelligences is arbitrary and that it is simply wrong to deny the existence of a general intelligence factor (Brody, 1992). As research explores these challenges to the notion of multiple intelligences, one conclusion that we can make is that how we think about intelligence has become much broader than it was even a few years ago.

> **Prodigies:** Individuals who easily master skills in one intellectual area.
>
> **Savants:** Mentally retarded individuals who demonstrate exceptional ability in one specific intellectual area.

10-2c   Sternberg's Triarchic Theory States That Intelligence Consists of Three Sets of Mental Abilities

> As an elementary-school student, I failed miserably on the IQ tests I had to take. I was incredibly test-anxious. Just the sight of the school psychologist coming into the classroom to give a group IQ test sent me into a wild panic attack. . . . For me, the game of taking the test was all but over before it even started. And the outcome was always the same: I lost. (Sternberg, 1996, p. 17)

Would you believe that the person who experienced this early academic trauma is now one of our leading intelligence experts? His name is Robert Sternberg, and his career provides a dramatic demonstration of how childhood experiences can motivate people to embark on scientific journeys of discovery that ultimately aid others in their personal journey quests. Following extensive interviewing of ordinary people, Sternberg (1985, 1997b) developed the belief that intelligence consists of much more than the abilities measured by traditional intelligence tests. Yet, while he agrees with Gardner's idea of multiple intelligences, his **triarchic theory of intelligence** (*triarchic* means "ruled by threes") asserts that human intelligence can be more simply described as comprising three sets of mental abilities, not seven (figure 10-5).

> **Triarchic theory of intelligence:** Sternberg's theory that there are three sets of mental abilities making up human intelligence: analytic, creative, and practical.

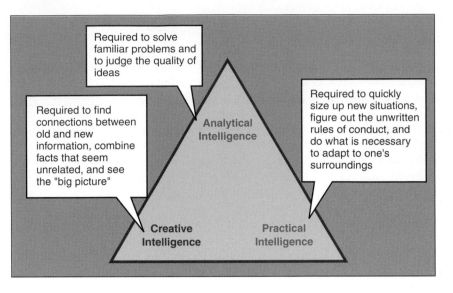

FIGURE 10-5
Sternberg's Triarchic Theory of Intelligence

According to Robert Sternberg, intelligence consists of analytical, creative, and practical abilities. You use analytical thinking in solving familiar problems, creative thinking to think about problems in new ways, and practical thinking in applying what you know to everyday situations. Of these three types of abilities, which do you think you employ most efficiently? More than one? Do you think that this self-understanding will influence your decisions about possible career paths?

One of these aspects deals with basic analytic skills. This *analytical intelligence* is required to solve familiar problems and to judge the quality of ideas. It is also the type of intelligence that is valued on tests and in the classroom, and thus people who are high in analytical intelligence tend to score high on g, or general intelligence.

Just because you can efficiently analyze information does not mean that you can develop new ways of solving problems. In such instances, what is required is creativity. People with a high degree of creative intelligence have the ability to find connections between old and new information, combine facts that appear unrelated, and see the "big picture" (Sternberg & O'Hara, 2000). Creative individuals have certain common characteristics: nonconformity, risk-taking, willingness to tolerate rejection, openness to new experiences, and at least moderate intelligence (Simonton, 2000a). During the early stages of their careers, creative people tend to rely heavily on a few close friends for advice and encouragement. However, their intense devotion to work often causes strained relationships with other people (Gardner, 1993). Discovery Box 10-1 analyzes creative intelligence in more detail, as does the end-of-the-chapter *Psychological Applications* section.

Beyond analyzing information and developing novel solutions, it is also important to apply, utilize, and implement ideas in everyday situations. People who are high in *practical intelligence* have what we call "street smarts." They are quick to size up new situations, figure out the unwritten rules of conduct, and do what is necessary to adapt to—and shape—their surroundings (Sternberg et al., 1995; Wagner, 2000).

Although some tasks require us to utilize all three intelligences, the triarchic theory does not define intelligence by how skilled we are in all three aspects. Some people are more intelligent in solving abstract, theoretical problems, while others are more intelligent when the problems are more concrete and practical. *Successful intelligence* is knowing when and how to use analytic, creative, and practical abilities. People who are successfully intelligent will seek challenges that capitalize on their intellectual strengths and downplay their weaknesses. This is exactly what personnel departments try to do when selecting employees: match people's intellectual strengths with specific jobs within the organization. Successful organizations have workers who are skilled at analyzing existing

INFO-BIT: When we say that someone is "creative," this does not mean that she or he is creative in all aspects of life. A critical aspect of creativity is having a good deal of knowledge about the subject in which you are creative (Simonton, 2000b).

DISCOVERY BOX 10-1

How Does Culture Shape Creative Expression?

Cultural values often channel creative energy into specific fields (Feldman, 1999). When a particular form of creative expression is valued, children will be encouraged to express themselves in this manner. For example, the birth of the Renaissance—a period of immense artistic creativity at the beginning of the fifteenth century in Florence, Italy—was made possible due to the generous support of artists by the entire population, especially those who had wealth and power. Cultures can also restrict creativity (Abou-Hatab, 1997). In the Omaha Indian culture, for instance, there is only one way to sing a song, and if anyone alters from that format, ritual weeping occurs (Colligan, 1983). As you might guess, this response is an effective way to prevent people from taking "creative liberties" with music. A similar social norm prevents singers in the United States from engaging in too much creative expression when performing the "Star Spangled Banner."

What is considered "creative" is also shaped by culture. An important feature of creativity in Western cultures is producing an observable product (Lubart, 1999). In contrast, the Eastern view of creativity is less product focused and has more to do with personal fulfillment or the expression of an inner sense of ultimate reality (Kuo, 1996). In Hinduism, creativity is thought of as entailing spiritual or religious expression rather than as providing an innovative solution to a problem (Aron & Aron, 1982). This Eastern sense of creativity has a great deal to do with what humanistic psychologists in the West refer to as *self-actualization*, or the process of achieving one's full potential (see chapter 11, section 11-1f).

Another distinction between Western and Eastern views of creativity is how creativity is related to traditional views. The Western approach to creativity typically involves a break with tradition (Kristeller, 1983). This is consistent with the Western philosophy of individualism, which values nonconformity and the expression of ideas that run counter to the group. In contrast, the Eastern approach to creativity is more likely to involve the reinterpretation of traditional ideas so that traditional truths come alive and become revitalized in daily activities (Hallman, 1970). This conception of creativity is consistent with the Eastern philosophy of collectivism, which values conformity and the upholding of traditional values and beliefs.

As you can see, culture has an important influence on the nature of creativity, both in how it is defined and how it is channeled. You may be born with a certain degree of creative potential, but how that potential develops and is later expressed will be significantly shaped by your social reality.

problems, others who are best at using this analysis to create new ideas, and still others who can adeptly apply these new ideas to make solutions effective.

The triarchic theory, like the theory of multiple intelligences, has not only broadened the discussion of intelligence, but it has also led an increasing number of intelligence researchers to recommend the development of new and improved tests to assess cognitive abilities (Harrison et al., 1997; Kaufman, 2000). If intelligence is more than just academic skill, then we may need to move beyond traditional tests and theories of intelligence.

10-2d Emotional Intelligence Allows Us to Understand and Regulate Our Emotional and Social Lives

If one function of intelligence is to predict what will happen next in our surroundings, and if an important part of what will happen next depends on how others behave, then we must not only predict others' behavior with some degree of accuracy but also influence their behavior in desired directions. This *social intelligence* is believed to be part of our primate evolutionary heritage (Byrne, 1995), with effective interpersonal coordination and planning increasing the survival of our ancestors.

Emotional intelligence:
The ability to recognize and regulate our own and others' emotions.

An important aspect of social intelligence is what various researchers have called **emotional intelligence,** which is the ability to recognize and regulate our own and others' emotions (Goleman, 1995; Mayer & Salovey, 1997). Individuals with high emotional intelligence are attentive to their own feelings, can accurately discriminate between them, and can use this information to guide their own thinking and actions (Mayer et al., 2000). For example, when they experience negative moods, emotionally intelligent people try to create a more positive state of mind by doing something they enjoy or by finishing a task that will bring them a reward (Tice & Baumeister, 1993). In contrast, those who are less emotionally skilled tend to be "ruled" by their emotions: They not only have quick tempers, but they also "stew in their own negative juices" when things don't go their way (Caprara et al., 1994, 1996; Salovey & Mayer, 1994). Of the two spectrums of emotional intelligence, which do you think leads to greater happiness and success?

Emotionally intelligent people are aware not only of their own emotional states but of others' as well. These are the people we seek out when we are troubled, for their emotional attentiveness makes them sympathetic listeners, and their skill at managing social conflicts often provides us with good advice on how to resolve our difficulties. Due to their ability to accurately measure the "pulse" of social relationships, emotionally intelligent people get along well with others, have many friends, and often achieve great success in their careers. Based on these findings, it isn't surprising that our skill at managing the emotional realm significantly determines the extent to which our lives are successful and fulfilling. Before reading further, spend a few minutes answering the items in table 10-1.

SECTION SUMMARY

- Spearman's factor-analytic research suggested a general intelligence, or g, factor underlying all mental abilities, and a set of specific factors (s-factors) underlying certain individual mental abilities.

- Gardner's theory of multiple intelligences proposes there are at least seven separate abilities: linguistic, logical-mathematical, spatial, musical, bodily-kinesthetic, interpersonal, and intrapersonal.

- According to Sternberg's triarchic theory, intelligence comprises three sets of mental abilities: analytical, creative, and practical.

- Emotional intelligence helps us achieve and maintain personal and career success.

10-3 THE DYNAMICS OF INTELLIGENCE

We have all heard intelligence described as "quick-witted" and "dim-witted." In this section, we not only examine individuals who substantially differ in their intelligence levels, but also analyze the degree to which IQ is fixed or changeable.

TABLE 10-1

Measuring Your Level of Empathy for Others

Instructions: One aspect of emotional intelligence is the ability to be attentive to others' feelings. *Empathy* is a feeling of compassion and tenderness toward those who encounter unfortunate life events. Research indicates that people differ in their levels of empathy. To discover your level of empathy or *empathic concern* for others, read each of the following items and then, using the following response scale, indicate how well each statement describes you.

> 0 = extremely uncharacteristic (not at all like me)
>
> 1 = uncharacteristic (somewhat unlike me)
>
> 2 = neither characteristic nor uncharacteristic
>
> 3 = characteristic (somewhat like me)
>
> 4 = extremely characteristic (very much like me)

1. When I see someone being taken advantage of, I feel kind of protective toward them.

2. When I see someone being treated unfairly, I sometimes don't feel very much pity for them.*

3. I often have tender, concerned feelings for people less fortunate than me.

4. I would describe myself as a pretty soft-hearted person.

5. Sometimes, I don't feel very sorry for other people when they are having problems.*

6. Other people's misfortunes do not usually disturb me a great deal.*

7. I am often quite touched by things that I see happen.

Scoring your responses: Three of the items on this scale are reverse-scored; that is, for these items, a lower rating actually indicates a higher level of empathic concern or personal distress. Before summing the items, recode those with an asterisk (*) so that 0 = 4, 1 = 3, 3 = 1, 4 = 0.

The mean score for female college students is about 22, while the mean score for male students is about 19 (Davis, 1996). The higher your score, the higher level of empathic concern you have for others.

Source: From EMPATHY: A SOCIAL PSYCHOLOGICAL APPROACH by Mark H. Davis. Copyright © 1996. Reprinted by permission of Westview Press, a member of Perseus Books, L.L.C.

10-3a   Neuroscientists Try to Link Differences in Intelligence to Dissimilarities in People's Brains

As previously mentioned, more than a century ago, Francis Galton believed that intelligence was related to the size of a person's head. Although his research failed to find any valid evidence to support this hypothesis, more recent studies have found a small correlation ($r = +.15$) between head size and intelligence scores (Jensen & Johnson, 1994). Yet, because there is more inside the skull than just brain tissue, skull size is not a very accurate measure of brain size. When magnetic resonance imaging (MRI) scans directly measure brain volume, the resulting brain size and IQ score correlation (adjusted for body size) increases to a moderately high +.44 (Rushton, 1995; Rushton & Ankney, 1996).

What might explain this brain size–IQ correlation? Neuroscientists are unsure. One possibility has to do with the fact that larger brains are known to have more neurons (Pakkenberg & Gunderson, 1997). The higher intelligence found among those with bigger brains may be caused by these individuals having a larger number of neural connections and a correspondingly greater cognitive capacity (Vernon et al., 2000). One problem with this "greater neuron" explanation is that men, on average, have about 4 billion

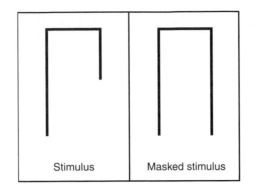

Stimulus | Masked stimulus

FIGURE 10-6
An Inspection Time Task

In a typical experiment measuring neural "quickness," researchers will often study how fast participants can process perceptual information presented to them. An incomplete stimulus is quickly flashed on a computer screen, but its lingering afterimage is immediately hidden (or *masked*) by another stimulus. The participant is then asked whether the long side of the original stimulus appeared on the left or right. Researchers determine how much time participants need to inspect the stimulus in order to answer such questions correctly 80 percent of the time. Participants who need less time to correctly answer these questions tend to score higher on intelligence tests.

(or 16 percent) more neurons than women, but they do not outscore them on IQ tests (Pakkenberg & Gunderson, 1997). Another possibility is that the brain size–IQ correlation is related to different levels of *myelin* in the brain (Miller, 1994). As you recall from chapter 3, section 3-1a, myelin is the protective coating of glial cells around an axon that hastens the transmission of the neuron's electrochemical charge.

The possibility that intelligence might be related to myelin is one of the reasons intelligence researchers have devoted a great deal of attention to the brain's processing speed. A number of studies indicate that intelligence is partly based on neural complexity, quickness, and efficiency (Vernon et al., 2000). For example, IQ scores tend to be correlated with the complexity of electrical activity in the brain: When responding to simple stimuli, high scorers have more complex brain patterns than low scorers (Barret & Eysenck, 1992; Caryl, 1994). Regarding neural "quickness," the speed at which neural impulses travel (see figure 10-6) is positively correlated with IQ—about +.40—suggesting that intelligent people are literally more quick-witted than the less intelligent (McGarry-Roberts et al., 1992; Vernon & Mori, 1992). Finally, additional studies suggest that smarter brains are not only quick and complex, they are also efficient. Using PET scans, Richard Haier and his coworkers (1992, 1995) found that people with higher intelligence tend to consume less glucose—a simple sugar required for brain activity—while working on problem-solving tasks. They also found evidence suggesting that the brains of intelligent people become more efficient with practice than the brains of those with less intelligence. That is, after practicing a relatively complex computer game, intelligent participants' brains subsequently consumed less glucose overall when playing this game, even though certain brain areas actually consumed more glucose. By concentrating the processing of information to relatively small areas of their brains, Haier and his coworkers contend that intelligent people use their brains more efficiently. Although the origins of these biological differences in brain functioning could be genetic, the fact that greater efficiency is achieved with practice suggests that these differences also develop from experience. Together, these findings suggest that intelligence is a product of both our biology (*nature*) and our experience (*nurture*).

10-3b Although Intelligence Becomes More Stable with Age, It Is Far from Fixed

Is intelligence—as measured by IQ—a stable characteristic, or does it change throughout our lives? Because infants cannot talk and have limited attention spans, studying the stability of intelligence early in life is difficult. Indeed, reliable assessments of IQ generally cannot be obtained until children reach the age of about 3 or 4. Despite this impediment, Joseph Fagan (1992) has devised an indirect intellectual assessment technique for infants that tests their preferences for visual novelty. In this test, infants are shown pairs of pictures on a screen. For each showing, one of the pictures was previously seen by the infant, while the other is new. Findings indicate that babies between the ages of 2 to 7 months who spend more time looking at the novel stimuli later tend to score higher on childhood

FIGURE 10-7
The Stabilization of IQ Scores with Age

When IQ scores obtained at age 17 are plotted with IQ scores obtained at earlier ages, the correlations before the ages of 5 or 6 are below .50, but rise in the range of .70 and .80 by the time children are 7 and 8 years old. What might account for this increased stability with age?

intelligence tests (McCall & Carriger, 1993). Fagan's test can also identify 85 percent of babies who are later diagnosed as mentally retarded. Although this simple measure of infant attention and processing is not a *true* intelligence test in the classic sense, it is useful in identifying children who are later likely to score very high or very low on conventional intelligence tests. In this sense, it provides evidence that there is some stability in intelligence even during infancy. As illustrated in figure 10-7, once children reach the age of 7 or 8, IQ scores begin to predict later IQ scores reasonably well (Bayley, 1949; Sameroff et al., 1993).

This increased stability with age, however, does not mean that IQ scores are fixed and unchanging. Many researchers believe that intelligence is pliable and that the thinking skills associated with IQ scores can be improved through learning (Halpern, 1996; Sternberg, 1996). Discovery Box 10-2 discusses this issue in more detail.

10-3c The "Challenged" and the "Gifted" Are the Two Extremes of Intelligence

One controversial area of intellectual assessment is the classification and education of individuals whose IQ scores fall at the two extremes of the normal curve. Not surprisingly, these two groups markedly differ in their abilities.

Mental Retardation

The diagnosis of **mental retardation** is given to people who not only have an IQ score below 70, but also have difficulty adapting to the routine demands of independent living (Detterman et al., 2000). According to the American Psychiatric Association (1994), only about 1 to 2 percent of the population meets both criteria, with males outnumbering females by 50 percent. Within this designation, there are four mental retardation categories, which vary in severity. As you can see in table 10-2, most retarded people are only mildly retarded.

In about 25 percent of the cases, doctors are able to identify a specific organic cause of retardation (Yeargin-Allsopp et al., 1997). Organic conditions are infections or malnutrition of the pregnant mother or infant, poisoning of the developing fetus or infant child by harmful substances (such as alcohol or lead), premature birth, and trauma to the child's head (see chapter 4, section 4-1b, discussion of teratogens).

Also included among organic causes are genetic disorders, the most common being **Down syndrome,** which is caused by an extra chromosome coming from either the mother's egg (the primary source) or the father's sperm (Gardner & Sutherland, 1996). The production of this extra chromosome is strongly related to maternal age. Among mothers under the age of 33, the rate of Down syndrome is only 0.9 per 1,000 live births.

Mental retardation:
A diagnostic category used for people who not only have an IQ score below 70, but also have difficulty adapting to the routine demands of independent living.

Down syndrome: A form of mental retardation caused by an extra chromosome in one's genetic makeup.

DISCOVERY BOX 10-2

Can Enriched Environments Enhance Intelligence?

Considerable evidence indicates that exposing children to healthy and stimulating environments can enhance their performance on IQ tests (Grotzer & Perkins, 2000). For example, in a longitudinal study of inner-city children who received a great deal of intellectual stimulation at home and in day care or school, by age 12 their average IQ scores were 15 to 30 points higher than inner-city children who were not exposed to these enriching environments (Campbell & Ramey, 1994, 1995).

How can "enriched" environments be established? The quality of interaction between adults and children is of primary importance in this regard. Following are some steps that adults can take to foster mental growth (Bradley & Caldwell, 1984; Dweck, 1990, 1992; Whitehurst et al., 1994):

- Read to young children, asking them open-ended questions about the stories ("What is the daddy doing?") rather than asking simple yes or no questions ("Is the daddy cleaning the house?").
- Talk to children in detail about many topics, and carefully answer their questions.
- Expand on children's answers, correct inaccurate responses, and emphasize the process of learning rather than its product.
- Encourage children to think through problems rather than simply guessing at solutions.

One of the more impressive intellectual-skills training programs ever developed was *Project Intelligence*, which was implemented in Venezuela during the 1980s when it had a Ministry for the Development of Intelligence. Created by a group of Harvard researchers, this program consisted of six units of instruction in analytical and creative skills comprising about 100 lessons (Adams, 1986; Perkins, 1995). A lesson on creative thinking might require students to ponder the purposes of an ordinary object, such as a pencil. What can you use it for? What features does it have? Another lesson on problem solving might emphasize various strategies, such as trial and error, heuristics, and algorithms. Each lesson included ample practice time, including individual and group exercises.

When 450 seventh-grade Venezuelan children were evaluated after being taught an abbreviated form of Project Intelligence, their IQ scores showed an increase of about seven points more than gains experienced by a control group of students. Unfortunately, a change of the political party in power in Venezuela led to such programs being available to children on only a limited basis. Due to government cutbacks in further developing and testing these programs, we do not know whether Project Intelligence enhanced the academic performance of the children whose IQ scores were raised; however, the initial findings suggest that intelligence can be raised through training (Herrnstein et al., 1986). One of the interesting footnotes to this story is that the primary author of this careful evaluation of Project Intelligence was Richard Herrnstein, an intelligence researcher who figures prominently in an ongoing controversy discussed later in this chapter.

TABLE 10-2

Degrees of Mental Retardation

Level	Typical IQ Scores	Percentage of the Retarded	Adaptation to Demands of Life
Mild	50–70	85%	May learn academic skills up to the sixth-grade level. With assistance, adults often can learn self-supporting social and vocational skills.
Moderate	35–49	10%	May progress to second-grade level. Within sheltered workshops, adults can contribute to their own support through manual labor.
Severe	20–34	<4%	May learn to talk and to perform simple work tasks under close supervision, but are generally unable to profit from vocational training.
Profound	Below 20	<2%	Limited motor development and little or no speech. Require constant aid and supervision.

Source: Reprinted with permission from the DIAGNOSTIC AND STATISTICAL MANUAL OF MENTAL DISORDERS, Fourth Edition. Copyright © 1994 American Psychiatric Association.

This rate increases to 3.8 in mothers who are 44 years of age or older (Grigorenko, 2000). Characteristic signs of Down syndrome are a small head, nose, ears, and hands; slanting eyes; short neck; and thin hair. Individuals with this disorder have IQs that place them in the mild to severe range of retardation. When given proper training and placed within a supportive family environment, many people with Down syndrome can care for themselves, hold a job, and lead happy, fulfilling lives.

Approximately 75 percent of mental retardation cases cannot be linked to any organic cause; instead, they are thought to result from unfavorable social conditions or subtle and difficult-to-detect physiological effects (Handen, 1997). Most of these cases tend to involve less severe forms of mental retardation, and poor children are 10 times more likely to be classified in this manner than those from the general population.

During the 1950s and 1960s, schoolchildren with mild retardation were placed in *special education classes* where they received instruction designed for their ability level. However, beginning in the 1970s, educational researchers recommended *mainstreaming*, which is a policy in which retarded children are educated with normal children. The goal of mainstreaming is to integrate the retarded as fully as possible into the normal educational environment, but the reality is that they are frequently teased and ridiculed by their nonretarded classmates (Marks, 1997). Although some evidence indicates that sustained in-class contact leads to more positive attitudes toward retarded children, there is also evidence that such contact leads to resentment due to the perception by some students that their retarded classmates are receiving greater attention and consideration from teachers

INFO-BIT: When Down syndrome was identified by English physician Langdon Down in 1866, it was first called "Mongolism" because the slanting eyes of Down syndrome people bore some resemblance to Asian eyes in the minds of Westerners. Consistent with existing scientific theories of White intellectual superiority, nineteenth-century European scientists claimed that Down syndrome individuals failed to develop beyond the physical and intellectual level of Asians, such as Mongolians.

> *Doing easily what others find difficult is talent; doing what is impossible for talent is genius.*
>
> —Henri-Frederic Amiel, Swiss critic, 1821–1881

(Bowers, 1997; Nabuzoka & Ronning, 1997). Given these conflicting findings, it is not currently clear whether mainstreaming is a more effective educational policy than special education, but U.S. federal law mandates mainstreaming whenever possible (Farrell, 1997; Susan, 1990).

One impediment to the mentally retarded being integrated into mainstream society is the ridicule and prejudice they often face by people with average or above-average intelligence. Have you witnessed expressions of such intolerance toward the mentally retarded? Armed with the knowledge you now possess, what information could you convey to people who express negative attitudes and beliefs toward those who are mentally handicapped?

Mental Giftedness

What does it mean to be "gifted"? For some psychologists, the term is reserved for those people with IQs above 130 or 135. Other psychologists supplement this criterion with other requirements, such as exceptional school or career achievement. Consistent with recent theories of multiple intelligences, U.S. federal law designates that giftedness should be based on superior potential in any of six areas: general intelligence, specific aptitudes (for example, math and writing), performing arts, athletics, creativity, and leadership (Callahan, 2000). Although more school districts are beginning to identify gifted students based on these broader standards, most continue emphasizing IQ scores (Fields, 1997).

Regarding the education of gifted students, one concern has been that they are not adequately challenged by the regular school curriculum (Gottfried et al., 1994; Keen & Howard, 2002). To address this concern, educators have developed two separate intervention strategies. *Acceleration* involves early admission to school and encouraging gifted students to skip grades. *Enrichment,* in contrast, keeps gifted students in their normal grade level but supplements their course work with advanced material, independent study projects, and other special learning experiences. Both intervention strategies can be effective, but many gifted students in these programs still complain that their classes move too slowly, involve too much repetition of already mastered material, and place too much emphasis on the mastery of facts rather than the use of thinking skills (Gallagher et al., 1997). One problem is that these programs are underfunded. Relative to the money provided for the education of mentally retarded students, little money is spent on education for gifted children, especially those who are poor or who live in rural areas (Winner, 1997).

One common belief about gifted individuals is that their "gift" is really a curse because it makes them social misfits who lead lonely, unsatisfied lives. Is this stereotype true? In an attempt to answer this question, in 1921 Lewis Terman began tracking the lives of over 1,500 California children with IQs above 135 (Terman, 1925). Over the course of the next 70 years, Terman and later researchers discovered that, by and large, these men and women led healthy, well-adjusted lives, with slightly more successful marriages and much more successful careers than the average person (Holahan & Sears, 1995; Terman & Oden, 1947). Other longitudinal studies of gifted individuals have replicated these findings (Janos & Robinson, 1985; Subotnik et al., 1989). Thus, counter to prevailing stereotypes, research clearly indicates that children with high IQs are *less* likely to be social misfits than their less gifted counterparts.

Children identified as extremely gifted (top 1 in 10,000) are much more likely than their nongifted counterparts to pursue doctoral degrees as adults, and many of these individuals create noteworthy literary, scientific, or technical products by their early twenties

(Lubinski et al., 2001). However, childhood giftedness does not guarantee adult eminence. For example, although the "Termanites" (as they affectionately called themselves) generally grew up to be very successful adults in their chosen careers, very few became the best and brightest members of their generation (Pyryt, 1993). Thus, although IQ is an important contributor to a person's life path, in the final analysis it is only one factor determining a person's life accomplishments. This is certainly good news to the vast majority of us who do not fall within the lofty 1 percent upper realm of the IQ normal distribution!

SECTION SUMMARY

- Intelligence is partly based on neural complexity, quickness, and efficiency.
- Stability of intelligence increases from infancy to adulthood.
- Enriched environments can increase IQ scores.
- Seventy-five percent of mental retardation cases result from harmful environment or subtle physiological effects; 25 percent are linked to organic causes.
- Gifted students are less likely to be social misfits than the nongifted.

10-4 HEREDITARY AND ENVIRONMENTAL INFLUENCES ON INTELLIGENCE

To what degree is intelligence determined by heredity, and to what degree is it determined by the physical and social environment in which we are raised? The scientific answer to this question has important social implications (Sternberg & Kaufman, 2002). For instance, in 1969, psychologist Arthur Jensen claimed that up to 80 percent of intelligence is due to heredity. Based on this claim, he argued that intellectual-skills training programs, such as Head Start, were a waste of taxpayers' money. Jensen's analysis and policy recommendations were both sharply challenged by environmentally based researchers. At the heart of this scientific debate were studies of twins and studies of adoptive families.

10-4a Twin and Adoption Studies Indicate That Genes and Environment Both Influence Intelligence

Psychologists and *behavior geneticists* who study the heritability of intelligence express the degree to which heredity determines intelligence within a particular human group in terms of a **heritability coefficient,** which ranges from 0 to 1. A coefficient of 0 would mean that heredity has no influence on intelligence, while a coefficient of 1 would mean that heredity is the only influence. As with most of the intelligence testing conducted today, heritability coefficient estimates are almost always based on standard IQ tests, which define intelligence primarily in terms of analytic and verbal ability (Petrill et al., 1996; Saudino et al., 1994). To gain a better understanding of heritability research, let us first examine studies of twins and then turn our attention to the adoption studies.

Twin Studies

Why would researchers studying the role of genetic factors in intelligence be so interested in studying identical and fraternal twins? As you learned in chapter 3, identical twins have identical genes, while fraternal twins share only about half of the same genes. The rationale for studying twins is that they normally are raised in similar environments. If the IQ scores of identical twins are more similar than those of fraternal twins, this would be presumably due to their greater genetic similarity. Or would it?

Is this your stereotype of gifted students? Does research support this stereotype? How do the lives of gifted people differ from those of the average person? Do you suppose the persistence of this stereotype might have something to do with it salving the self-esteem of those of us with merely average intelligence?

© Stockbyte/PictureQuest.

Heritability coefficient: A statistical coefficient, ranging from 0 to 1, that estimates the degree to which heredity determines intelligence within a particular human group.

FIGURE 10-8
Studies of IQ Similarity: The Nature-Nurture Debate

The results of over 100 studies correlating the IQ scores for people with different genetic and environmental backgrounds found that the most genetically similar people had the most similar IQ scores. Do these findings suggest that intelligence is partly inherited? How do the other findings reported here support the argument that intelligence is partly determined by environmental factors?

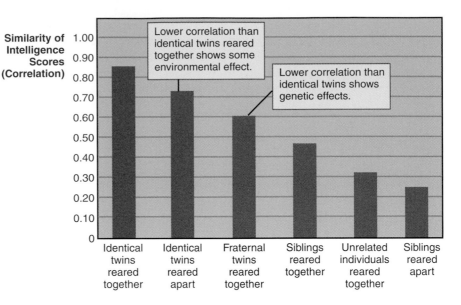

As you can see from figure 10-8, the findings of more than 100 twin studies indicate that the average correlation of identical twins' IQ scores is .86, while that of fraternal twins is significantly lower, .60 (Bouchard & McGue, 1981; McGue et al., 1993). These results seem to support the genetic contribution to intelligence. However, these same twin studies also point to environmental effects on intelligence (Lytton & Gallagher, 2002). Fraternal twins—who are genetically no more similar than regular siblings, but who are exposed to more similar experiences due to their identical ages—have more similar IQ scores than other siblings. In addition, nontwin siblings raised together have more similar IQs (*r* = .47) than siblings raised apart (*r* = .24). Together, do these findings suggest that genes and environment both contribute to intelligence, but genes have a larger influence?

That is a reasonable conclusion, but environmentally oriented researchers argue that the higher IQ correlations among identical twins than fraternal twins may be substantially caused by environmental factors. According to this argument, parents of identical twins tend to treat them more alike than parents of fraternal twins, often even dressing them identically. As a result, fraternal twins' environments often are not as similar as are the environments of identical twins. Perhaps it is this greater environmental similarity that explains the higher IQ correlations among the identical twins than among the fraternals.

Genetically oriented researchers respond that identical twins raised apart still have higher IQ correlations (*r* = .72) than fraternal twins raised together (*r* = .60). Isn't this convincing evidence for genetic effects? Maybe not, say the environmentally oriented researchers. These higher IQ correlations for identical twins reared apart may be due to *prenatal environmental factors*. About two-thirds of identical twins share the same placenta and amniotic sac in the uterus, which makes their prenatal environment more alike than that of fraternal twins, who are almost always in separate sacs (Phelps et al., 1997). Twins in the same sac share the same blood, which contains chemicals that affect brain development. Perhaps the high IQ correlations among identical twins separated at birth is due to early shared environment as well as shared genes.

Adoption Studies

Given the competing ways in which twin study findings can be interpreted as supporting either genetic or environmental effects on IQ, researchers have sought further clues among adopted children. Biological parents supply these children their genes, while adoptive parents provide them their environment. If heredity matters more than environment, the children's IQ scores should correlate higher with their biological parents' IQ scores than with their adoptive parents' scores. The reverse finding should occur if environment matters more than heredity.

A number of adoption studies have found that children who were adopted within two weeks to one year of birth were later found to have higher IQ correlations with their biological parents than with their adoptive parents (Horn, 1983; Scarr & Weinberg, 1983; Turkheimer, 1991). Furthermore, many of these same studies find that as adopted children grow up, their IQ correlation with their biological parents doesn't decrease, it increases! How could this be if environment is more important than genetics in determining intelligence? These and other findings suggest that heredity makes a somewhat larger contribution than environment (Loehlin et al., 1989, 1997; Teasdale & Owen, 1984).

Although adoption studies point toward a substantial hereditary contribution to intelligence, they also report evidence of significant environmental influences. For instance, in France, the IQ scores of lower-class children adopted by upper-class families were compared with the IQ scores of their siblings who had not been adopted (Capron & Duyme, 1989; Schiff et al., 1978). Although the average adopted children's scores in these studies ranged between 104 and 111, the average scores for their brothers and sisters reared in the original lower-class households ranged between 92 and 95, a significant difference. Furthermore, when children of upper-class parents were adopted, their later average IQ score was 120 if their adoptive parents were from upper-class families, but only 108 if they were adopted by lower-class families.

Based on the twin and adoption studies combined, the best estimate is that heredity accounts for a little over 50 percent of the variation in intelligence, with environmental factors being responsible for a little less than 50 percent. However, this does not mean that a little over half of *your* intelligence is inherited and a little less than half is environmentally influenced. It simply means that genetics and environmental factors are respectively responsible for a bit more and a bit less than about half of the differences among individuals in the population.

So how do genes and environment interact in determining intelligence? The concept of **reaction range** provides a possible answer (see figure 10-9). Our genes establish a range of potential intellectual growth, and our environmental experiences interact with our genetic makeup in determining where we ultimately fall in this reaction range (Mann, 1994). For example, children with a natural aptitude for writing are more likely to spend leisure time writing and to also select writing and literature courses in high school. If their parents and teachers further nourish this natural aptitude by offering them enrichment opportunities, their skills will be further enhanced. Their subsequently high scores on verbal aptitude tests are due to both their natural ability and their experience.

Reaction range: The extent to which genetically determined limits on IQ may increase or decrease due to environmental factors.

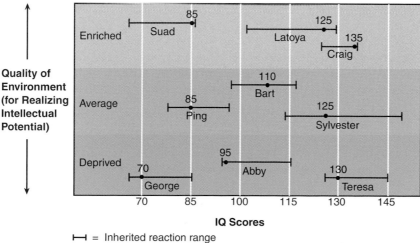

= Inherited reaction range

= Measured IQ, as shaped by the interaction of heredity and environment

FIGURE 10-9
Reaction Range

Reaction range indicates the extent to which the environment can raise or lower IQ scores, given the preexisting hereditary limits. Each person has her or his own individual reaction range. People who grow up in enriched environments should score at the top of their reaction range, while those who grow up in impoverished settings should score closer to the bottom of their range.

10-4b There Are Group Differences in IQ Scores

As discussed at the beginning of this chapter, claims about group differences in intelligence have often been used to rationalize racial, ethnic, and gender discrimination. For this reason, claims about group differences must be subjected to very careful analysis. In this section, we examine research regarding gender differences in intelligence and then focus on racial differences.

Gender Differences

Although male and female IQ scores are virtually identical, a few differences in certain aptitudes are worth mentioning (Halpern, 2000; Lynn, 1994). Females tend to do better on verbal aptitude tests, such as naming synonyms and verbal fluency, while males tend to do better on visual-spatial tests, such as mental rotation and tracking a moving object through space (Law et al., 1993; Stanley, 1993). Regarding math abilities, on the 60-item SAT math test, male high school seniors tend to average about four more correct answers than their female counterparts, and many more males score in the highest ranges (Halpern, 2000; Held et al., 1993). Although the gender differences in verbal and spatial abilities are substantial (about one standard deviation), the math differences are relatively small and are disappearing (Feingold, 1992; Hyde et al., 1990; Masters & Sanders, 1993).

As discussed in chapter 3, section 3-3f, some studies suggest that these female-male differences in verbal and spatial abilities might be linked to sex differences in the organization of those areas of the cerebral hemispheres controlling verbal and spatial abilities and to hormonal fluctuations (Gur et al., 1999; Shaywitz et al., 1995). Other studies suggest that these differences—along with the math aptitude differences—are a product of gender socialization and the different skills taught to girls and boys (Crawford et al., 1995). For example, girls not only receive greater encouragement to talk during infancy and early childhood than boys, but in school, they are more likely to be praised for their reading and writing, while boys are encouraged more often to be proficient in math and science (also refer to section 10-4d). From what we know thus far, our future understanding of these gender differences clearly will have to consider both biological and sociocultural variables—and their interactions.

Racial Differences

In the United States, African Americans score between 10 and 15 points lower on intelligence tests than White Americans and Asian Americans, whose IQ averages are about 100 (Bracken et al., 1993; Jensen, 1985; Peoples et al., 1995). Likewise, the average intelligence scores of Hispanic Americans and Native Americans falls between the Black scores and the White and Asian scores (Lynn, 1996; McShane & Plas, 1984). Although research suggests that the average IQ scores for Black children has risen over the past 20 years, these group-based IQ differences persist (Hauser, 1998; Neisser et al., 1996).

In making sense of these findings, it must be remembered that *group* differences tell us nothing about the intellectual ability of any specific person. There are tens of millions of Black, Hispanic, and Native-American individuals who have higher IQs than the average White or Asian American. Yet, if heredity influences individual differences in intelligence, does it also substantially explain these group differences?

Yes, according to psychologist Arthur Jensen. Three decades ago, he claimed that "between one-half and three-fourths of the average IQ difference between American Negroes and whites is attributable to genetic factors," such as differences in the rate of information processing (Jensen, 1973, p. 363). It was on this basis that Jensen argued, as was mentioned earlier, that training programs to enhance the IQs of Black children would have limited success. As you might guess, the social and political implications of this hypothesis landed like a bombshell in the scientific community, and many denounced its author as a racist. Fortunately, the controversy also generated a great deal of research.

Among the subsequent studies, Sandra Scarr's work is a good example of how different research methods were used to test Jensen's hypothesis. In her first line of research,

Scarr and Richard Weinberg (1976) examined the IQ of lower-class Black and White children adopted by both Black and White middle-class families. They found that adopted African-American children had an average IQ of 110, over 20 points higher than children who were raised in their original lower-class African-American families. Even when these adopted children reached adulthood, their IQ scores remained 10 points higher than those of African Americans raised in lower-class Black families (Weinberg et al., 1992). The researchers concluded that these findings suggest that Black-White IQ differences in the general population are substantially affected by environmental factors, such as unequal economic and educational conditions.

Scarr and her colleagues (1977) also examined the chemical composition of blood among African Americans. Because many African Americans have European ancestors, Scarr reasoned that if Black-White IQ differences were predominantly caused by genetics, then African Americans with a greater proportion of European ancestry in their blood should have the highest IQ scores. Counter to Jensen's genetic hypothesis, however, no correlation was found between IQ and racial ancestry. In fact, virtually all the studies that have sought to find the source of these Black-White IQ differences have failed to find evidence for genetic effects (Eyeferth, 1961; Lewontin, 1982; Loehlin et al., 1973; Nisbett, 1995). Based on these converging findings from different research avenues, Scarr and her colleagues conclude that it is "highly unlikely" that genetic differences between the races cause the observed group differences in IQ scores (Waldman et al., 1994).

10-4c Genetic Explanations of Group IQ Score Differences Remain Highly Controversial

Despite the meager evidence for a genetic explanation of racial differences in IQ, in 1994 this controversy was reignited when psychologist Richard Herrnstein and conservative political theorist Charles Murray published their book, *The Bell Curve: Intelligence and Class Structure in American Life*. Based on their review of others' research, these authors claimed that intelligence is largely inherited, that intelligence overwhelmingly determines socioeconomic status, that the nation's intelligence level is declining because low-IQ people are having more children than high-IQ people, and that intellectual-training programs will do little to help the poor. They further argued that African Americans are disproportionately poor because, as a group, they score lower on IQ tests than White Americans, and therefore, are inherently less intelligent. One thing that disturbed many scientists, social policy makers, and ordinary citizens about Herrnstein and Murray's claims were that they bore a striking similarity to the claims advanced in the nineteenth and early twentieth centuries by the eugenics movement (refer back to section 10-1a).

As with Jensen's claims in the 1970s, Herrnstein and Murray's proposals were strongly challenged by many psychologists, who claimed that a great deal of *The Bell Curve* reasoning was flawed and based on selective review of past research. For example, Robert Sternberg (1996) pointed out that the only research study related to intelligence ever conducted by Richard Herrnstein (coauthor Charles Murray has never conducted his own intelligence research) directly contradicts one of his central *Bell Curve* arguments; namely, that intellectual-skills training programs are ineffective in improving mental abilities (refer back to section 10-3b). In making this claim, Herrnstein simply ignored his own research findings!

Other critics focused on Herrnstein and Murray's contention that because *individual* differences in intelligence are strongly influenced by genetic factors, *group* differences are similarly influenced (Dorfman, 1995; Schulze et al., 1996). These critics argue that a fatal flaw in Herrnstein and Murray's group heritability estimates of racial differences in intelligence is that they are based on the heritability estimates derived from twin studies. Yet, heritability estimates for intelligence should only be made for the specific social group on which the estimate is based. In the twin studies, the heritability estimates were based on overwhelmingly White subjects, not Blacks or other ethnic groups. Why is this a problem? Consider the following analogy, which is also illustrated in figure 10-10.

FIGURE 10-10
Between-Group and Within-Group Variation

In our corn seed analogy, all of the variation in plant height within each field is due to genetics, but the overall height difference between the corn plants in the fertile field and the barren field is due to the environment. How does this analogy relate to observed Black-White IQ differences?

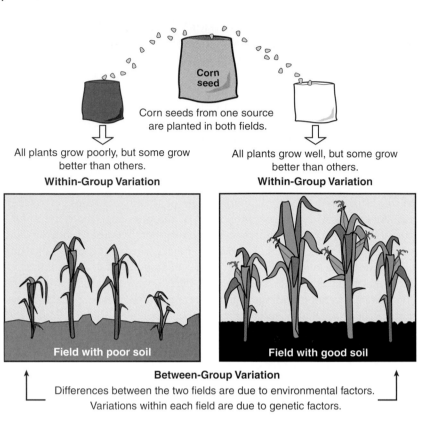

Corn seeds from one source are planted in both fields.

All plants grow poorly, but some grow better than others.
Within-Group Variation

All plants grow well, but some grow better than others.
Within-Group Variation

Field with poor soil

Field with good soil

Between-Group Variation
Differences between the two fields are due to environmental factors.
Variations within each field are due to genetic factors.

Imagine that you have a mixture of corn seeds that vary genetically. Take a handful of those seeds and plant them in fertile soil. If all conditions remain equal, some of the resulting plants will be short and some will be tall. Because the quality of your soil and care were equal for all corn seeds, the height differences of the fully grown corn can be attributed to their genetic variation. Now, fill a white bag and a black bag with this same seed mixture. However, plant the white bag of corn seeds in a rich, fertile field and the black bag of seeds in a field that is poor and barren. When the plants in these different soil conditions grow, as before, you will observe that there is considerable individual variation in the height of the plants in both fields, purely due to genetic factors. But you will also observe that the average height of the plants in the fertile field is greater than the plants in the barren field. This group difference is due entirely to environmental factors (the soil).

As this analogy illustrates, even if IQ differences *within* groups is partly or even completely caused by genetic variation, this does not mean that average IQ differences between groups is due to genetics. An important question that needs to be asked before attributing between-group IQ differences to genetics is: "Are the groups' environments the same?" In the United States, Blacks and Whites do not generally grow up in the same environments. African Americans, perhaps more than any other minority group, have endured years of economic discrimination and are overrepresented in the lower social classes. For the average child, being raised in a lower-class setting means that she or he will be less exposed to books and other learning tools, pressure to do well in school, and role models who can teach the skills and habits necessary to flourish in academic settings. Many of these same children do not receive proper nutrition, which impedes neurological development and causes attention problems at school (Brody, 1992). Singly, or together, these aspects of their impoverished environment can interfere with intellectual growth. Due to the dissimilarity in environments, critics of *The Bell Curve* correctly argue that it is a mistake to assume that IQ differences between Blacks and Whites stem from genetic factors. Although intelligence researchers generally agree that individual differences in IQ scores are substantially influenced by genetic factors, the claim by *The Bell Curve* authors that group differences in IQ are due to genetics simply does not ring true.

10-4d Cultural and Social Psychological Factors May Partly Explain Group IQ Differences

Beyond socioeconomic disadvantages accounting for lower IQ scores among Blacks and other selective minority groups, some social scientists also contend that certain cultural and psychological forces contribute to these between-group differences (Serpell, 2000).

Oppositional Identities

Anthropologist John Ogbu (1986, 1993) believes that some members of stigmatized racial and ethnic groups respond to negative ethnic stereotypes and discrimination by developing an *oppositional* ethnic identity and cultural frame of reference that defensively opposes the rejecting dominant culture (see chapter 4, section 4-2f, for a discussion of ethnic identity development). This type of reaction makes a good deal of sense, in certain respects. If you live in a society where your racial or ethnic group is devalued, developing an oppositional identity may help you cope with your hostile environment by clearly defining your racial or ethnic group in contrasting ways with the larger culture (Crocker & Major, 1989; Crocker et al., 1998). One of the most immediate benefits is that an oppositional identity can psychologically insulate you—the stigmatized person—from some of the negative effects of social injustice, such as loss of self-esteem (Helms, 1990; Parham & Helms, 1985). On the negative side, however, immersion in an identity that defines itself in terms of opposition to the larger culture will likely constrict your personal identity. For example, if you are African American and your behavior or thinking falls within the forbidden White cultural frame of reference, you may be accused by other Blacks of "acting White" or being an "Oreo" (being Black on the outside but White on the inside). These forbidden areas are those that have historically been reserved for White Americans, and where minorities have not been given an equal opportunity to excel.

How might oppositional identity development help explain racial and ethnic differences in IQ-test performance? Simply put, for many African-American youths with oppositional ethnic identities, academic tasks represent one of the forbidden White cultural domains. For these individuals, committing themselves to academic excellence and learning to follow the academic standards of the school might be perceived as adopting a White American cultural frame of reference and forsaking their ethnic identity (Ford, 1996). Unfortunately, by rejecting these academic pursuits because of their association with White culture, African Americans and other minorities are not only more likely to score lower on IQ tests than their White counterparts, but their disidentification with academics hinders them from fully taking advantage of the civil rights advances that have occurred over the past 50 years (Bankston & Caldas, 1997; Fordham & Ogbu, 1986).

Stereotype Threat

In addition to the problem that oppositional identities pose to minority students' academic achievement, social psychologist Claude Steele (1997) asserts that for those minority students who do want to excel academically, negative cultural stereotypes about their supposed inferior intellectual abilities can create feelings of anxiety and vulnerability, especially when they are in the company of people outside of their racial group. That is, if you are a student who is often one of only a few members of your race enrolled in a particular course, your individual performance is often looked upon by students not of your race as representing the "typical" student of your racial group. Accompanying this scrutiny is the added social stigma associated with your minority label, which often implies a suspicion of intellectual inferiority (Sigelman & Tuch, 1997). Because these negative stereotypes are widely known throughout society, as the target of such stereotyping, you are susceptible to developing **stereotype threat,** which is the realization that your performance on some task might confirm the negative stereotype.

According to Steele, when highly motivated African-American students take an intelligence test while simultaneously worrying that a low score will confirm that they fit the "mentally inferior" stereotype, this added pressure is often sufficient to significantly hinder their performance. To more closely analyze the stereotype threat hypothesis, let's examine a few relevant studies (see Discovery Box 10-3).

Stereotype threat: The realization that your performance on some task might confirm a negative stereotype associated with your social group.

DISCOVERY BOX 10-3

How Do Negative Stereotypes Foster Academic Under-performance?

Evidence for the stereotype threat effect among African-American college students comes from a series of experiments that Steele and Joshua Aronson (1995) conducted. In one of these studies, Black and White students were given a difficult English test. In the *stereotype threat condition*, the test was described as a measure of intellectual ability, while in the *nonstereotype threat condition*, it was described as a laboratory problem-solving task that didn't measure intelligence. Because one of the more salient racial stereotypes is that Blacks are intellectually inferior to Whites, the researchers presumed that describing the test as an intellectual measure would make this negative stereotype relevant to the Black students' performance. In turn, researchers also expected this stereotype relevance to establish for these Black students a fear of confirming the stereotype ("If I do poorly, my performance will reflect badly on my race and on me"). Steele and Aronson hypothesized that the anxiety created by such thinking would interfere with the Black students' performance. In contrast, when the task was described as not measuring intelligence, they assumed that this would make the negative racial stereotype *irrelevant* to the Black students' performance and, therefore, not arouse anxiety. As you can see in figure 10-11, consistent with the stereotype threat hypothesis, when the test was presented as a measure of ability, Blacks performed worse than Whites. However, when it was not associated with ability, no significant racial differences were found.

One common reaction to stereotype threat in academic settings is for those who feel threatened to *disidentify* with the activity that is the source of the threat; namely, academic achievement. That is, you change your self-concept so that academic achievement is no longer very important to your self-esteem (Steele, 1992). This sort of academic disidentification is much more common among African-American students than among White-American

The academic disidentification resulting from stereotype threat not only occurs among African Americans, but also among American Indians, Hispanic Americans, lower-class Whites, and female students in male-dominated majors (such as engineering and chemistry). For example, Steven Spencer and his colleagues (1999) found that women performed as well as men on a difficult English test where they suffered no social stigma, but women underachieved relative to men on a comparably difficult math test where they are more vulnerable to suspicions of intellectual inferiority. In a follow-up to this study, the researchers gave female and male college students a difficult math test but divided it into two halves and presented it as two distinct tests. Half of the students were told that the first test was one on which men outperformed women, and that the second test was one on which there were no gender differences. The other students were told the opposite—test 1 was described as exhibiting no gender differences, but men outperformed women on test 2. Consistent with the stereotype threat hypothesis, when told that the test yielded gender differences, women performed significantly worse than men. However, when the test was described as not exhibiting any gender differences, women and men performed at the same level. This dramatic change occurred even though the two tests were the same! Similar to African-American students' disidentification process described earlier, women are most likely to disidentify with math and math-related careers when negative gender stereotypes are salient (Spencer at al., 1999).

students, and it often begins in the lower elementary grades (Ambady et al., 2001; Major et al., 1998). Although such disidentification protects self-esteem and is a coping response to racial prejudice and discrimination, it also is one of the psychological factors that undermines African-American students' school achievement.

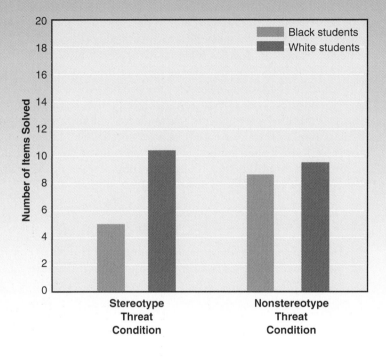

FIGURE 10-11

African-American Intellectual Test Performance and Stereotype Threat

Steele and Aronson (1995) administered a difficult English test to Black and White college students. When the test was described as a measure of intellectual ability (stereotype threat condition), Blacks performed worse than Whites. However, when it was not associated with ability (nonstereotype threat condition), no racial differences were found. How are these findings consistent with the stereotype threat hypothesis?

Considered together, these studies inform us that negative stereotypes can create damaging self-fulfilling prophecies among members of many different social groups by inducing stereotype threat. Further, these findings raise the very real possibility that stereotype threat may explain a substantial amount of the racial differences found in intelligence testing and the gender differences found in advanced math testing (refer back to section 10-4b).

Valuing Academic Achievement

Thus far, we have examined cultural and social psychological factors that might depress IQ scores among selective racial and ethnic groups. Yet, why do elementary school children in Taiwan and Japan outscore American children by about 15 points (roughly one standard deviation) in math ability and, to a lesser extent, in reading skills? Interviews with the parents of these children conducted by Harold Stevenson and his coworkers (1986) found that the Chinese and Japanese parents downplayed the importance of

---

Journey of Discovery Question

Stereotype threat in the academic area can also occur among members of privileged groups, such as White middle-class men. Can you guess what ethnic group might cause White middle-class men to experience stereotype threat in academia?

innate intellectual ability and, instead, stressed hard work. They also considered doing well in school to be the *most important* goal for their children. In contrast, the American parents were more likely to believe that intelligence is genetically determined, and they assigned academic achievement as a much lower-valued goal for their children. Following their parents' lead, when asked what they would wish for if a wizard promised to give them anything they wanted, the majority of the Asian children named something related to their education, while American children mentioned money or possessions.

Follow-up studies found that the achievement differences between these Asian and American children persisted through high school (Stevenson et al., 1993). Consistent with the different valuing of education found during their early school years, the American teenagers were much more likely than the Asian teenagers to have after-school jobs and to have time for sports, dating, and other social activities (Fuligni & Stevenson, 1995). Although engaging in such a wide variety of extracurricular activities is consistent with the American parents' goal of developing a "well-rounded" teenager, a recent study indicates that this philosophy creates a great deal of stress and academic anxiety for high-achieving American students (Crystal et al., 1994). Figuratively, they are trying to burn the candle at both ends and often simply get burned out. In contrast, high-achieving Asian students burn only one end of the candle—the academic end—and they tend to have lower stress and anxiety levels. Overall, this research suggests that intellectual growth is nurtured when parents and the larger culture stress the value of education and the importance of working hard to achieve intellectual mastery. In contrast, intellectual growth is stunted when cultural beliefs impress upon the child that their own academic success is either unlikely (due to negative cultural stereotypes) or not highly valued (due to it being incompatible with more important cultural values).

SECTION SUMMARY

- Twin and adoption studies indicate substantial hereditary contribution to individual intelligence, but also significant environmental influences.
- Females perform better on verbal aptitude tests and males do better on visual-spatial tests.
- Little scientific evidence exists to support hereditary explanations of racial differences in IQ scores.
- Racially based IQ differences are most likely due to environmental factors such as unequal economic and educational conditions, differing cultural values surrounding education, and negative effects of racial stereotypes on minority students' self-confidence.

SUGGESTED WEBSITES

Note: These websites were functional when we went to press. Please access the online text for the most up-to-date URLs.

APA Task Force Examines the Knowns and Unknowns of Intelligence
http://www.apa.org/releases/intell.html
This APA website documents what we know and don't know about intelligence.

Intelligence Theory and Testing
http://www.indiana.edu/~intell/map.html
This website discusses the history of intelligence testing and theory development.

Multiple Intelligences
http://www.thomasarmstrong.com/multiple_intelligences.htm
This website outlines Gardner's theory of multiple intelligences and how it might apply in educational settings.

Two Views of the Bell Curve
http://www.apa.org/journals/bell.html
This website contains two book reviews of Herrnstein and Murray's book, *The Bell Curve*.

IQ Tests
http://www.2h.com/iq-tests.html
This website contains a number of intelligence tests and brain teasers.

PSYCHOLOGICAL APPLICATIONS
How Can You "Create" a Creative Environment?

According to intelligence experts Todd Lubart and Robert Sternberg, to be creative you need to have a lot of things go your way (Lubart & Sternberg, 1994; Sternberg & Lubart, 1995, 1996). This sounds like creativity is a fragile and illusive form of intelligence. Fortunately, Lubart and Sternberg continue, you have the power to construct the necessary conditions that foster creative accomplishments. You can take the following six steps to increase your own creativity. Accompanying each recommendation is a qualification concerning its limits.

1. *Redefine problems*—As discussed in chapter 9, section 9-2c, a number of cognitive tendencies act as barriers to problem solving. Although certain thinking strategies may have effectively solved problems for us in the past, creative solutions often require us to look "through" and "around" problems rather than directly at them. *Warning: Don't feel that you have to "reinvent the wheel" for every new problem. Often "tried and true" problem-solving strategies are the best tools for creative products.*

2. *Make a habit out of questioning tradition*—Since childhood, we have been rewarded for conforming to the way other people think and act. Such conformity is often necessary for a society to properly function, but it does not provide a fertile environment for creative ideas. One defining characteristic of creative people is that they regularly question traditional ways of thinking and behaving (Ochse, 1990). *Warning: Defying tradition simply because it brings you attention is not the purpose of this exercise!*

3. *Find something you love to do*—Creative people, whether they are children or adults, are motivated primarily by the enjoyment, challenge, and satisfaction they derive from working on their projects, rather than from the external rewards they receive (Amabile, 1996; Amabile & Hennessey, 1992).

Warning: Being rewarded for doing things you naturally enjoy can undermine your enjoyment of those activities (see intrinsic motivation, chapter 11, section 11-1e).

4. *Become an expert in your area of interest*—Case studies of 120 creative people from diverse professions found that great accomplishments were preceded by high-quality training (Bloom, 1985). This research suggests that you will have a much better chance of being a creative success if you have developed a good base of knowledge in your chosen interest area. By tapping your accumulated learning, you will be able to generate more ideas and make more mental connections that will ultimately lead to creative problem solving. *Warning: Don't feel you need to know everything about your area of interest before you can make a creative contribution in it.*

5. *Tolerate ambiguity and take sensible risks*—Because creative ideas run against the grain of everyday thinking and often do not fit neatly into clearly defined categories, you must have sufficient confidence in your ideas so that you are not easily discouraged when others don't understand or accept what you have to offer. *Warning: Do not totally ignore feedback from others because you can profit from others' advice.*

6. *Choose friends and associates who will support your creative endeavors*—Analysis of the lives of over 2,000 successful scientists and inventors found that the most creative individuals were not isolated geniuses. Rather, they had high emotional intelligence and surrounded themselves with people who encouraged them in their work (Simonton, 1992). *Warning: Do not surround yourself with yes persons, who will agree with anything you say. Blind conformity does not foster a creative environment.*

KEY TERMS

achievement test (p. 283)
aptitude test (p. 283)
content validity (p. 288)
Down syndrome (p. 297)
emotional intelligence (p. 294)
eugenics (p. 281)
factor analysis (p. 289)
Flynn effect (p. 286)
general intelligence (g) (p. 289)

heritability coefficient (p. 301)
intelligence (p. 281)
intelligence quotient (IQ) (p. 284)
mental retardation (p. 297)
multiple intelligences (p. 290)
normal distribution (p. 286)
predictive validity (p. 288)
prodigies (p. 291)
psychometrics (p. 281)

reaction range (p. 303)
reliability (p. 287)
savants (p. 291)
standardization (p. 286)
Stanford-Binet Intelligence Test (p. 284)
stereotype threat (p. 307)
triarchic theory of intelligence (p. 291)
validity (p. 288)
Wechsler Intelligence Scales (p. 284)

REVIEW QUESTIONS

1. Eugenics, a movement founded by Sir Francis Galton, has been associated with all of the following *except*
   a. Nazi Germany's program of mass extinction of "genetic undesirables."
   b. improving the hereditary characteristics of society through sterilization.
   c. Binet's research identifying lower-performing children through intelligence testing.
   d. Galton's use of the term *moron*.
   e. intelligence test bias toward native-born English speakers.

2. Intelligence has been assessed or scored in a variety of ways since Galton's measures of sensory abilities and head size. Most intelligence tests today rely on a scoring method known as
   a. ratio IQ.
   b. deviation IQ.
   c. an intelligence quotient.
   d. mental age/chronological age (x 100).
   e. verbal IQ.

3. Standardization, or establishing rigid test administration and interpretation procedures, typically results in
   a. a reliable test.
   b. a standard test.
   c. a valid test.
   d. a normal distribution of scores.
   e. the Flynn effect.

4. Research investigating the nature of intelligence has supported all of the following *except*
   a. intelligence consists of a single general factor, referred to as *g*.
   b. intelligence consists of several specific factors.
   c. the same areas of the frontal cortex "light up" for different intellectual tasks.
   d. seven clusters of primary mental abilities are needed to explain intelligence.
   e. factor analysis consistently indicates five factors of intelligence.

5. Research evidence for multiple intelligences
   a. is lacking.
   b. is provided by the existence of savants.
   c. is negated by the existence of prodigies.
   d. contradicts Thurstone's approach to understanding intelligence.
   e. has shown that athletic ability is not a talent, but a specific type of intelligence.

6. According to Sternberg's triarchic theory of intelligence,
   a. creative intelligence is the type valued in academic settings.
   b. practical intelligence is superior to creative intelligence.
   c. intelligence is defined by how skilled an individual is in all three aspects of intelligence.
   d. successful intelligence is knowing how and when to use analytical, creative, and practical intelligence.
   e. analytical intelligence is related to nonconformity, risk-taking, and openness to new experiences.

7. The discussion of cultural differences in creativity emphasizes that
   a. creativity is an inborn characteristic having little to do with culture.
   b. creativity in Western cultures involves spiritual expression and inner growth.
   c. Eastern values emphasizing collectivism are seen in the Eastern approach to creativity.
   d. culture can shape, but not restrict, creativity.
   e. the relationship between creativity and tradition has failed to show cultural differences.

8. An individual with high emotional intelligence would likely exhibit all of the following *except*
   a. an ability to read their own emotions, but not others' emotions.
   b. a tendency to finish rewarding tasks.
   c. an ability to discriminate between different feelings.
   d. success in their career.
   e. reliance on their emotions to guide their thinking and actions.

9. Research by neuroscientists on the relationship between intelligence and the brain has shown that
   a. the strong relationship between head size and intelligence supports Galton's views.
   b. women have more neurons than men, on average.
   c. larger brains may be associated with higher intelligence because they have more myelin.
   d. there is no relationship between intelligence and mental quickness.
   e. the brains of more intelligent people use more glucose, explaining their intelligence and the larger size of their brains.

10. The stability of intelligence has been debated, with some arguing that stability is indicated
    a. by the reliability of IQ scores from infancy through old age.
    b. by the relationship of infant IQ scores to college-age IQ scores.
    c. beginning at about 7 or 8 years of age.
    d. in infants between ages 2 to 7 months.
    e. in the high correlations between ages 5 to 6 and age 17, but not in the correlations between ages 7 to 8 and age 17.

11. Enriched environments designed to enhance intelligence
    a. have improved the academic performance of hundreds of Venezuelan children through *Project Intelligence*.
    b. increased children's IQ scores by about 7 points more than control group children.
    c. emphasize the products of learning over the process of learning.
    d. have failed miserably.
    e. improved inner-city children's IQ scores more than 50 points by age 12.

12. According to the discussion on mental extremes (retardation and giftedness),
   a. the organic cause of mental retardation can be reliably identified in about 75 percent of cases.
   b. individuals with Down's syndrome suffer from severe mental retardation and must be institutionalized.
   c. malnutrition of a pregnant woman can cause mental retardation in her unborn child.
   d. giftedness interventions emphasizing acceleration show better results than interventions emphasizing enrichment.
   e. gifted children tend to be social misfits and loners as adults.

13. Research on intelligence has relied extensively on twin and adoption studies, which have indicated that
   a. identical twins raised apart have similar IQ correlations to fraternal twins raised together.
   b. "reaction range" refers to the range of similarity in twins' IQ scores.
   c. prenatal environmental factors have been discounted as a source of IQ differences among twins.
   d. heredity has a slightly larger effect on intelligence than environment.
   e. adopted infants' IQ scores are more similar to their adopted parents' IQ scores than to their biological parents' IQ scores.

14. Research on group differences in intelligence has indicated that
   a. it is highly unlikely that Black-White IQ score differences are due to genetic differences.
   b. gender differences in math abilities have been growing larger.
   c. gender socialization of boys and girls fully explains differences in verbal and spatial abilities.
   d. individual abilities can be predicted by examining group differences in ability.
   e. the strong correlation between IQ and racial ancestry supports Jensen's view of racial differences in intelligence.

15. Critics of Herrnstein and Murray's controversial book *The Bell Curve* have cited all of the following criticisms *except*
   a. Herrnstein and Murray's reasoning is flawed and based on a selective review of the literature.
   b. A fatal flaw is that group heritability estimates of Blacks are based on heritability estimates derived from the study of White twins.
   c. Within-group differences and between-group differences are presented as equivalent.
   d. Herrnstein ignores his only study of intelligence, which showed that training improves mental abilities.
   e. Herrnstein and Murray overemphasize environmental factors associated with intelligence.

16. Developing an oppositional ethnic identity may
   a. eliminate the constriction of personal identity.
   b. help explain racial and ethnic differences in IQ scores.
   c. expose the individual to increased negative effects of social injustice.
   d. cause a loss of self-esteem.
   e. lead Blacks to identify with White cultural values, thus increasing their IQ scores.

Motivation and Emotion

Chapter Outline

ould you believe that the first scientific attempt at cataloguing what it was that people actually *do* sexually was partially prompted by a university biology professor's embarrassment at not being able to answer his students' questions about people's sexual practices? It was the late 1940s, and Indiana University biologist Alfred Kinsey had been asked to teach a course on sexuality. With little advance preparation, he did his best to complete the semester, but he decided that it was time to find some answers. Thus, he and his colleague, Walter Pomeroy, began questioning 18,000 people on this most intimate subject. Using interviews and surveys to obtain participants' sexual histories, they provided evidence indicating that sexual fantasies, masturbation, premarital and extramarital sex, and same-sex sexual contacts were fairly common among Americans (Kinsey et al., 1948, 1953). Instead of greeting these research findings with praise and gratitude, a majority of the American public responded with intense disapproval, and many public officials demanded a congressional investigation into who was funding such sinful studies (Fisher, 1993). In the following years, other scientists who attempted to investigate human intimacy and sexuality endured similar accusations that they were studying something that could never be—nor should be—studied empirically.

Despite such condemnations, the undeniable facts are that sexual behavior not only affects health and happiness, but understanding human sexuality provides a means for affecting societal well-being. Consider the personal, social, and economic costs of unwanted pregnancies, sexually transmitted diseases, sexual assaults and abuse, and the negative effects of the commercial sex industry. Also, consider the positive impact that sex has on interpersonal intimacy and pleasure. Regardless of your values or your religious and social beliefs, you probably recognize that sex is a powerful motivating force in people's lives.

Sex is just one of the things that motivate us. In this chapter, we examine different approaches to the study of motivation, identifying cognitive, physiological, social, and environmental factors that shape our various needs and desires. Then we highlight three different motivational issues—namely, eating, sex, and striving for achievement. Finally, we examine the psychology of emotion, a topic that is integral to a full understanding of motivation.

11-1 MOTIVATION

We do things. Not only do we do things, we often feel irrepressible urges to initiate certain actions. Sometimes we feel "pushed" to behave, while other times we feel "pulled." This "push" or "pull" to act in certain ways or to achieve particular goals is the topic of our discovery quest in this section of the chapter.

11-1a Motivation Is a Dynamic Process

Motivation: An inner state that energizes behavior toward the fulfillment of a goal.

For our purposes, **motivation** is defined as an inner state that energizes behavior toward the fulfillment of a goal (Pittman, 1998). The study of motivation is essentially the study of motion—of what moves a person or other animals to act in a particular way. As such, motivation is best conceived of as a dynamic process where motivational states are constantly changing due to both changes outside and inside the person and due to responses made toward the motivated state itself (Reeve, 1992).

To better understand how motivation is a dynamic process, imagine that you have a strong desire to be a painter. Due to the positive feelings associated with this desire, you enroll as a student at a famous art institute. Your subsequent successes and failures at the institute, combined with conflicting goals related to your desire for wealth, romance, and children may change the intensity of your motivation toward this goal. Due to this dynamic quality of motivation, it is not easily measured or quantified. Psychologists often measure it by looking for changes in intensity and direction of desire or need—and what has caused those changes.

In making sense of this moving target, theories of motivation focus on what influences behavior at any given time and tend to either focus on internal or external sources for that influence. *Internal theories* assume that something about the organism pushes it toward (or away from) some object. In contrast, *external theories* focus more on attributes of the goal or the environment that *pull* the organism in a certain direction. Clearly, no matter which emphasis is given, both internal and external issues need to be addressed when studying motivation (DeCatanzaro, 1998; Edwards, 1999).

11-1b Genes May Shape Our Motivation

At the beginning of the twentieth century, many psychologists were fascinated by Charles Darwin's (1871) theory of evolution. Extending his theory, they proposed that humans, like other animals, have instincts (Reeve, 1992). An **instinct** is an unlearned, relatively fixed pattern of behavior that is essential to a species' survival. William McDougall (1908) was an early proponent of the view that much of human behavior is controlled by instincts, and he generated a list of 18 human instincts, including greed, self-assertion, and gregariousness. In subsequent years, other instinct theorists expanded this list into the thousands. The argument became that if a behavior is seen, it must be instinctual. Of course, one problem with such reasoning is that it is circular: An observed behavior (for example, *aggression*) is attributed to an instinct (*aggressiveness*), which, in turn, is inferred from the behavior. A second problem with instinct theory was that it could not accommodate the role of learning that early behaviorists were demonstrating in their research (see chapter 7). Simply put, many so-called instinctual behaviors are learned and shaped by experience.

Although instinct theory collapsed due to its false assumptions, we have seen in our study of other topics in psychology that genes may predispose the human species—as well as other species—to engage in certain patterns of behavior. This contemporary evolutionary perspective states that we indeed inherit adaptive genetic traits but that these traits express themselves more as predispositions for behaviors rather than as a predetermined set of actions (Barrett et al., 2002; Buss & Kenrick, 1998). For example, early instinct theorists would have explained alcoholism as being directly caused by an inherited instinct. In contrast, modern evolutionary theorists acknowledge that there may be a genetic predisposition for such behavior, but they reject the notion that some genetic code predetermines that someone will become an alcoholic. Instead, they contend that genes might affect how alcohol is responded to in the body or what emotional responses a person might have to certain environmental cues associated with drinking. Such predispositions might increase the likelihood of drinking heavily, but they would not predetermine the behavior or the addiction.

11-1c We Are Sometimes Motivated to Reduce Arousal

When the original instinct theory fell out of scientific favor, many psychologists sought to explain motivation by turning to **drive-reduction theory** (Hull, 1943), which is based on the concept of homeostasis. **Homeostasis** is the tendency for organisms to keep physiological systems internally balanced by adjusting them in response to change. An example of homeostasis is the body's temperature-regulation system: a dip or rise in body temperature causes various physiological responses (for example, constriction of blood vessels and sweating), which return the body's temperature to the desired level.

Instinct: An unlearned, relatively fixed pattern of behavior that is essential to a species' survival.

Drive-reduction theory: The idea that an imbalance in homeostasis creates a physiological need, which produces a drive that motivates the organism to satisfy the need.

Homeostasis: The tendency for organisms to keep physiological systems internally balanced by adjusting them in response to change.

FIGURE 11-1
Drive-Reduction Theory

According to drive-reduction theory, we are motivated to keep physiological systems internally balanced or in a state of homeostasis. An imbalance in homeostasis (for example, due to being deprived of liquids) creates a physiological need (for liquids), which then produces a drive that moves us to engage in behavior to find and consume liquids to satisfy the need. When the need is satisfied, the drive is reduced and homeostasis is restored.

Drive: A physiological state of arousal that moves an organism to meet a need.

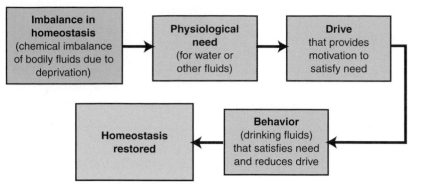

According to drive-reduction theory, an imbalance in homeostasis creates a physiological need, which in turn produces a **drive,** defined as a physiological state of arousal that moves the organism to meet the need. Once the need is met, the drive is reduced and the behavior that was initiated in response to the drive ceases. For example, as depicted in figure 11-1, if you were deprived of water or other liquids for an extended period of time, the chemical balance of your bodily fluids would become disturbed, initiating a "thirst" drive, marked by arousal and discomfort, pushing you to seek liquid to alleviate the discomfort. After you consumed a sufficient amount of liquid, homeostasis would be achieved, the drive would be reduced, and you would stop drinking.

Part of the difference between instinct theory and drive-reduction theory is that drive-reduction theory recognized the importance of learning on motivation by distinguishing between primary and secondary drives. *Primary drives* are unlearned and arise from basic biological needs such as the need for food and water. *Secondary drives* are acquired drives that are learned by being associated with primary drives. For example, the need to acquire money is a learned, secondary drive that can develop into a strong influence on behavior. By recognizing the existence of secondary drives, drive-reduction theory could explain a much wider range of behavior than instinct theory.

Despite its advantages over instinct theory, drive-reduction theory ran into problems because people engage in many behaviors, such as roller-coaster riding, watching scary movies, or drug taking, that seem designed to increase arousal, not reduce it. Due to the fact that drive-reduction theory could not account for all areas of motivation, psychologists concluded that it was incomplete.

11-1d We Are Sometimes Motivated to Achieve and Maintain an Optimal Level of Arousal

Contrary to drive-reduction theory, research indicates that levels of arousal that are too low are as uncomfortable as those that are too high (Berlyne, 1974). For example, when research participants were placed in an artificial environment that deprived them of sensory stimulation, they reported difficulties in thinking and within hours became increasingly irritable and began having vivid daydreams and hallucinations (Heron, 1957). Overall, it appears that we seek to achieve and maintain an *optimum* level of bodily arousal—not too much and not too little. This preference conforms to the *Yerkes-Dodson law,* which is named after the researchers who discovered it. As depicted in figure 11-2, this law contends that when we are underaroused or overaroused we perform below our abilities. Why? When underaroused, we tend to be bored and sluggish, while overarousal makes us nervous and tense. Our best performance occurs when we are at an intermedi-

> ***INFO-BIT:*** As you recall from chapter 7, section 7-2b, food, water, and other stimuli that satisfy primary drives are called primary reinforcers, while stimuli that satisfy secondary drives are known as secondary reinforcers.

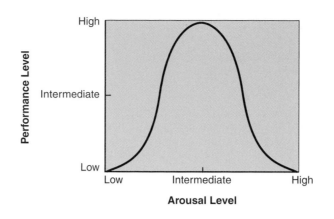

FIGURE 11-2
The Yerkes-Dodson Law

According to the Yerkes-Dodson Law, we perform best when we are at an intermediate level of arousal.

ate level of arousal (Hebb, 1955; Teigen, 1994). Thus, instead of motivation being simply tied to reducing arousal, it appears that motivation is associated with *regulating* arousal.

Not surprisingly, people differ in their optimal arousal. Those who enjoy high arousal tend to listen to loud music, socialize a great deal, eat spicy foods, drink alcohol, smoke tobacco, engage in frequent sexual activity, and do things that are risky or novel (Trimpop & Kirkcaldy, 1997; Zuckerman, 1984). Individuals with lower optimal arousal seek less intense stimulation and take fewer risks in life. Biology and blood chemistry appear to explain many of these individual differences (Shekim et al., 1989).

11-1e Incentive Theory Examines How External Factors Motivate Behavior

Unlike instinct, drive, or other physiological theories, **incentive theory** focuses on the role of external factors in motivation—how things in our environment *pull* us in certain directions (Berridge, 2001). Developed from the insights gained from classical and operant conditioning research (see chapter 7), this theory proposes that any stimulus that we learn to associate with positive or negative outcomes can serve as an incentive for our behavior. An **incentive** is a positive or negative stimulus in the environment that attracts or repels us. According to this theory, we will be motivated to behave in certain ways when we expect to gain positive incentives and/or avoid negative incentives through our actions.

The value of an incentive can change over time and across situations. For example, gaining praise from your parents may have had greater incentive value for you during different periods of your childhood and adolescence. In certain situations, such as when you were with your teenaged friends, you may have gone out of your way to avoid receiving parental praise, which was a negative incentive. Biology also influences the value of an incentive (Balleine & Dickinson, 1994). That is why food is a stronger motivator when you are hungry than when you are full.

The idea that a great deal of motivation can be explained in terms of incentives has led researchers to further distinguish between two types of motivation that are tied to whether incentives are either *intrinsic* or *extrinsic* to the behavior being performed (Sansone & Harackiewicz, 2000). A behavior or an activity that a person perceives as a valued goal in its own right represents a source of **intrinsic motivation.** On the other hand, a behavior or an activity may be valued because engaging in it leads to the receipt of a reward separate from what the act itself provides. The classic example is doing work for pay. In such instances, the work itself may not provide pleasure, but it does provide access to another outcome—money—that does bring pleasure. The type of motivation

Incentive theory: A theory of motivation stating that behavior is directed toward attaining desirable stimuli, called positive incentives, and avoiding undesirable stimuli, called negative incentives.

Incentive: A positive or negative environmental stimulus that motivates behavior.

Intrinsic motivation: Motivation to engage in a behavior or an activity because one finds it interesting or enjoyable for its own sake.

[Tom] had discovered a great law of human action . . . namely, that Work consists of whatever a body is obliged to do, and that Play consists of whatever a body is not obliged to do.

—Mark Twain, American author, in *The Adventures of Tom Sawyer* (1876)

Sometimes, when athletes are paid large sums of money to play their sport, they seem to lose their "love for the game" and become less motivated. How could this change in athletic motivation be explained by intrinsic and extrinsic motivation?

Extrinsic motivation:
Motivation to engage in a behavior or an activity because of the external rewards it can provide.

that leads a person to engage in a behavior or an activity for external reasons is known as **extrinsic motivation.**

In general, behaviors and activities that are intrinsically motivating are more highly valued than those that are extrinsically motivating. In explaining this value difference, various psychologists have proposed that intrinsic motivation is based on our need for controlling our own behavior (Deci, 1975; Ryan & Deci, 2000). From this perspective, the principal reason certain activities are intrinsically motivating—and more valued—is because engaging in them satisfies our need to feel that we are competent beings who exercise control over our lives.

It is not always possible to determine whether a behavior is engaged in because of intrinsic or extrinsic rewards. In fact, both sources of motivation often operate simultaneously. For example, a child may read a lot not simply because she enjoys the activity for its own sake, but also because doing so earns praise from adults and better grades in school.

As you undoubtedly already know, there is less need to use extrinsic motivators to convince people to do tasks that they already enjoy. Yet, did you also know that using extrinsic motivators sometimes increases or decreases people's intrinsic motivation (Deci, 1975; Deci & Ryan, 1985)? On the one hand, receiving external rewards for a task may reinforce our sense of competence and thus enhance intrinsic motivation (Harackiewicz & Sansone, 2000; Ryan & Deci, 2000). However, as we learned in chapter 7, section 7-2b, rewards are often also used to control people's behavior. If the controlling aspect of a reward is salient when it is given to us for performing a task that we enjoy, we may perceive that our behavior is more motivated by the reward (extrinsic motivation) than by our enjoyment of the task (intrinsic motivation). Discovery Box 11-1 discusses how you can use rewards without undermining intrinsic motivation.

11-1f Maslow Proposed That Some Needs Have to Be Met before Others

Hierarchy of needs: Maslow's progression of human needs, in which those that are the most basic, namely physiological needs, must be sufficiently satisfied before higher-level safety needs and then psychological needs become activated.

Another approach to understanding motives developed out of the humanistic tradition by Abraham Maslow (1970). As first discussed in chapter 1, section 1-3b, the humanistic view in general and Maslow's theory of motivation in particular assumed that people have a basic need for personal growth—to become what is possible. As illustrated in figure 11-3, Maslow proposed that we are born with a **hierarchy of needs,** meaning that basic needs must be sufficiently satisfied before we are motivated to satisfy higher-level needs. The needs further up the hierarchy are considered less basic because we can survive without satisfying them.

The most basic of these needs are *physiological,* such as hunger and thirst. Once these physiological needs are adequately satisfied, they recede into the motivational hierarchy, and the next set of needs, *safety needs,* are activated. These needs involve the striving for a sense of safety, security, and predictability in life. Regarding these first two need levels, Maslow contended that when food and safety are difficult to attain, they dominate people's lives and higher-level needs have little motivational power. Yet, if these two levels of needs are reasonably satisfied, the person becomes motivated by more social needs. The first social needs activated are the *belongingness* and *love needs,* which involve the desire for intimacy, love, and acceptance from others. Next on the hierarchy are *esteem needs,* which involve the desire for achievement, power, and gaining recognition and respect from others.

DISCOVERY BOX 11-1

How Can You Use Rewards without Undermining Intrinsic Motivation?

Many psychologists argue that American society has become so dependent on the use of extrinsic motivators (rewards and punishments) that it has seriously reduced people's intrinsic motivation for many activities (Deci et al., 1999; Eisenberger & Cameron, 1996; Kohn, 1993). For example, in one study, preschoolers, who normally chose to spend a lot of time drawing, were asked to draw a picture (Lepper et al., 1973). Preschoolers in one condition of the experiment were told that they would receive a reward for the picture, while those in another condition were not told of any reward but were given one after completing the picture. Finally, preschoolers in a third condition were not told about any rewards and not given any rewards. Results indicated that those who had expected and received a reward drew the least when later given the opportunity to do so. Other studies have found that students' involvement in math tends to decrease when rewards are emphasized at school (Turner et al., 1998), and overall academic achievement and interest decrease when parents use rewards, such as money, for good grades (e.g., Ginsburg & Bronstein, 1993; Gottfried et al., 1994).

Does this mean that external rewards always undermine intrinsic motivation? No. Although psychologists disagree on how much damage external rewards can cause to intrinsic motivation, they also can be beneficial. As previously mentioned, positive reinforcement, properly presented, can increase feelings of personal autonomy and competence, and can reduce many of the negative effects that failure inflicts on intrinsic motivation (Harackiewicz & Sansone, 2000). However, for these good effects to occur, rewards need to be given in response to specific performance standards and/or because the recipient surpasses the performance of others. Simply rewarding someone for participating in a task or for meeting some vague or meaningless objective ("Good breathing, Timmy!") will often undermine intrinsic motivation. Further, tangible rewards, such as money or treats, are much more likely to undermine intrinsic motivation than verbal praise, which often increases intrinsic motivation by bolstering our confidence that we are capable individuals. Perhaps the key ingredient in determining whether rewards enhance or undermine intrinsic motivation for a task is the degree to which the rewards convey to recipients that they are their "own masters" rather than being "pawns" of others' desires.

Up to this point in the hierarchy, Maslow believed that people are motivated by a need to overcome their feelings of being deprived of some kind of physical or psychological need. Thus, all of the needs in the first four levels of the hierarchy are *deficiency needs*, which are needs that if absent inhibit our personal growth. In contrast, the needs in the upper reaches of the hierarchy are *self-actualization needs* that move the person toward fulfilling her or his potential. **Self-actualization** is the ultimate goal of human growth, although Maslow hypothesized that it is a significant motive for very few of us. Why? The primary reason is that most of us are preoccupied throughout our lives with trying to make up for deficiencies lower in the hierarchy (Maslow, 1971).

The simplicity of Maslow's needs hierarchy made it an appealing theory of motivation in such diverse fields as philosophy, business, and education (Muchinsky, 2000). Despite this interest, the simplicity of the theory proved to be its primary problem.

Self-actualization: The ultimate goal of growth, being the realization of one's full potential.

FIGURE 11-3
Maslow's Hierarchy of Needs

Except for self-actualization, all of Maslow's needs in the hierarchy are motivated by a feeling of deprivation.

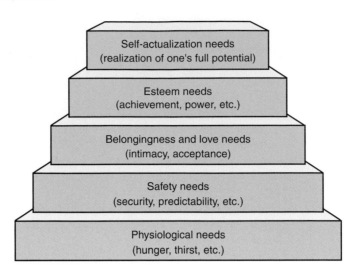

Self-actualization needs
(realization of one's full potential)

Esteem needs
(achievement, power, etc.)

Belongingness and love needs
(intimacy, acceptance)

Safety needs
(security, predictability, etc.)

Physiological needs
(hunger, thirst, etc.)

Although research generally suggests that the motives lower in Maslow's hierarchy do take precedence over those higher in the hierarchy (Baumeister & Leary, 1995), safety needs remain high in importance for all age groups and there is no clear evidence that met needs become less important than unmet needs in motivating people's behavior (Goebel & Brown, 1981; Hall & Nougaim, 1968). Despite these shortcomings, the theory provides a comprehensive and organized framework for discussing human motives.

SECTION SUMMARY

- Motivation is the study of how behavior is energized toward the fulfillment of a goal.
- According to instinct theories, motivated behaviors were genetically determined; they could not account for motivation affected through experience and learning.
- According to drive-reduction theory, motivation originated from attempts to reduce unpleasant drive states and return the body to homeostasis.
- Yerkes-Dodson Law states that people are motivated to seek an optimal level of arousal.
- In incentive theory, only externally produced consequences determine motivation, and the theory distinguishes between extrinsic and intrinsic motivation.
- Maslow's needs hierarchy reflects a prioritization of goals, ranging from basic survival goals to the ultimate goal of self-actualization.

11-2 SEXUAL MOTIVATION

Having explored some of the underlying factors in motivation, let us now turn to specific motives. As stated at the beginning of this chapter, one of the basic, primary motivated behaviors is sex. Engaging in sexual behavior is essential for the continuation of a species. From an evolutionary perspective, it would follow that reproduction would be more likely to occur if the process was pleasurable. As you already know, this is indeed the case. In fact, research suggests that the reinforcing properties of sex may well involve the same brain structures and neurotransmitter systems that are so strongly stimulated by cocaine and other addictive drugs (Melis & Argiolas, 1993; Walsh, 1993).

Motives for sexual behavior also include nonphysical factors, such as peer approval, the need to feel valued, the need for intimacy, stress reduction, the need for power, and procreation desires (Basson, 2002; Cooper et al., 1998). Understanding this powerful human motivator has proven to be a puzzle. In this section of the chapter, we try to put some of the pieces together.

Sex sells!!! If you read magazines, watch television, or go to the movies, you know that sexual content is readily available for viewing. As with other animals, humans find sex a very powerful motivating force in everyday living. Yet do men and women differ in their interest in sex?

11-2a Men Report Enjoying Greater Sexual Variety Than Women

In 1994 Edward Laumann and his coworkers reported the results from the first careful nationwide study of American sexual behaviors since Kinsey's work in the 1940s and 1950s. Based on responses from almost 3,500 adults, their *National Health and Social Life Survey* provides us with a fairly detailed look at what Americans do sexually, with whom, and how often. As you can see from figure 11-4, the most popular sexual activity among Americans is vaginal intercourse, followed by watching one's partner undress, and then oral sex. Do you notice an overall gender difference in the data? Put simply, men report enjoying every activity more than women. This is consistent with other studies indicating that men are much more likely than women to masturbate frequently and to desire more sexual partners (Fletcher, 2002; Oliver & Hyde, 1993). Why might this be so?

One possibility has to do with the different sexual scripts men and women learn while growing up and subsequently use as behavior guides (Laumann & Gagnon, 1995). A **sexual script** is a preconception about how a series of events, perceived as being sexual, is likely to occur. In North American culture and in many other cultures, the traditional sexual script taught to women is to downplay interest in sex and to resist sexual advances. Men, in contrast, are conventionally taught to freely express sexual interest, brag about sexual exploits, and sometimes even persist in sexual advances despite a partner's protests (Alksnis et al., 1996). See Discovery Box 11-2 for more discussion of sexual scripts.

Sexual script: A learned preconception about how a series of events, perceived as being sexual, are likely to occur.

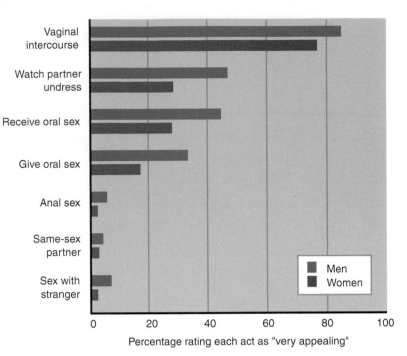

FIGURE 11-4

What Sexual Acts Do Americans Find "Very Appealing"?

A random survey of almost 3,500 U.S. adults has provided us with a better understanding of U.S. sexual practices and desires. Why do you think that men report enjoying every activity on this graph more than women do (Laumann et al., 1994)?

Instead of a sociocultural explanation, some psychologists believe that these gender differences reflect the different evolutionary pressures exerted on women and men (Buss, 1999; Pedersen et al., 2002). The argument here is that when a man and a woman have sex, the woman is most likely to bear responsibility for any resulting offspring. Further, unlike a man, a woman can only have one pregnancy at a time and her reproductive years are relatively short. These biological limitations mean that to maximize the probability that her genes will be passed on to future generations through her offspring, the best sexual strategy for a woman is to adopt a cautious approach in sexual matters. Such a strategy will better allow her to identify men with the best genes and those most likely to help care for offspring. In contrast to this cautious approach, it is to a man's advantage to establish sexual intimacy as quickly as possible in a relationship and to have frequent sexual encounters with many different women. According to evolutionary theorists, over thousands of generations, men who prefer many mates produce more offspring than men with a weaker preference for sexual variety. Thus, a preference for sexual variety has become common among men. The same preference for variety has not become widespread among women because women who prefer such variety don't necessarily produce more children.

Which of these two explanations is correct? Although I have contrasted the evolutionary and sociocultural viewpoints, they may often complement—rather than compete with—one another (Schaller, 1997). Perhaps the ultimate "best" explanation for gender differences in preferences for sexual variety may describe how evolutionary pressures faced by our prehuman ancestors shaped certain patterns of social behavior—including those related to sex—leaving modern women and men with certain *capacities* to possibly react differently to sex. Yet, the degree to which we actually manifest these inherited capacities today may be decided by how we are raised and taught to behave in our current social surroundings. In other words, culture and social learning either enhance or override these inherited capacities.

> **INFO-BIT:** Support for the evolutionary explanation of sex differences in preference for sexual variety comes from observations of other animal species. In most species, as in humans, males show more interest in more partners than do females. However, this sex difference reverses in a few species (such as the sandhill crane) in which the females abandon their eggs (and their mates) and seek other reproductive partners. In such instances, the males remain and care for the eggs and later offspring.

11-2b The Female and Male Sexual Response Cycle Is Very Similar

Although women and men may differ somewhat in their desire for sexual variety, they do not substantially differ in how they experience the sexual act itself. This fact became apparent in the mid-1960s when William Masters and Virginia Johnson (1966) published their pioneering work on the human sexual response. By monitoring 382 female and 312 male volunteers as they masturbated or had intercourse, Masters and Johnson determined that women's and men's physiological changes as they approached and achieved orgasm were not only remarkably similar, but that the physiological expression of an orgasm was similar regardless of how it was achieved.

The **sexual response cycle** that the body passes through during sexual activity involves the following four stages:

1. *Excitement*—The initial stage when the body becomes aroused (for example, the skin becomes flushed, the penis and clitoris become enlarged, vaginal lubrication increases)
2. *Plateau*—The stage of full arousal (the penis enlarges even more and the outer third of the vagina becomes engorged with blood)
3. *Orgasm*—The stage involving muscle contractions throughout the body (men ejaculate sperm-filled semen and women's vaginal contractions facilitate conception by helping propel semen from the penis up into the vagina)
4. *Resolution*—The stage when the body gradually returns to an unaroused state (muscles relax and the engorged genital blood vessels release excess blood)

> **Sexual response cycle:** The four stages of sexual responding—excitement, plateau, orgasm, and resolution—first identified by Masters and Johnson.

One thing to remember about the stages in the sexual response cycle is that they blend into one another, with no clear divisions between them. During a given cycle, a woman may experience no orgasm, one orgasm, or multiple orgasms. In contrast, men experience only one orgasm, but they can achieve orgasm again following a rest—or *refractory*—period. This refractory period can last from a few minutes up to a day or more, with the length of the rest period typically becoming longer with age. The intensity of orgasms varies, both across individuals and situations. Sometimes you might experience it as something like a sigh, while at other times it might feel like your entire body is simultaneously celebrating all the holidays of the year!

Some people cannot complete the sexual response cycle. For men, this might involve being unable to have or maintain an erection. In recent years, the drug sildenafil (trade name Viagra) has helped such men achieve and maintain an erection by increasing blood flow to the penis (Rowland & Burnett, 2000). About 10 percent of women and a few men remain at the plateau stage without experiencing orgasm, and some men experience premature ejaculation. Such sexual disorders can sometimes be traced to physiological or psychological causes, but often the cause is unknown. Although Masters and Johnson originally believed that subjective feelings of sexual arousal were directly related to specific physiological responses, later research discovered this was not the case. For example, vaginal lubrication or penile erection are not necessarily signs of sexual arousal, but instead, may be a response to a whole host of emotions, including anger or fear (Irvine, 1990).

Testosterone, a male sex hormone found in both men and women, has a positive influence on sexual desire, although the effect is stronger among men than women (Leitenberg & Henning, 1995; Reichman, 1998). Despite this positive effect, eliminating testosterone production does not eliminate desire, and heightened levels of this hormone do not affect desire to the same extent as psychological factors, such as the quality of the partners' relationship (Persky, 1983). Many other hormonal and neurological systems are involved with sexual desire, sexual responses, and behaviors, but none adequately explain, by themselves, why people are so driven to achieve sexual satisfaction nor the varied approaches sexual behaviors take. Turning sexual behaviors "on" or "off" is dramatically simpler among most animals other than humans and a few species of nonhuman primates (deWaal, 2000).

> **Testosterone:** A male sex hormone found in both men and women that has a positive influence on sexual desire. The additional testosterone in males stimulates the growth of the male sex organs in the fetus and the development of the male sex characteristics during puberty.

DISCOVERY BOX 11-2

How Might Different Sexual Scripts Lead to Acquaintance Rape?

TABLE 11-1

Rape Myth Acceptance Scale

Forced sexual intercourse that occurs either on a date or between people who are acquainted or romantically involved is known as **acquaintance rape.** On American college campuses, acquaintance rapes account for 84 percent of all rapes or attempted rapes (Koss, 1993). Further, one in five women report that they have been forced to do something sexual (Laumann et al., 1994). One factor contributing to these sexual assaults is the **rape myth,** which is the false belief that, deep down, women enjoy forcible sex and find it sexually exciting (Lonsway et al., 1998). Not surprisingly, men are much more likely to endorse this myth than are women. One consequence of men adhering to the rape myth is that they are more likely to believe that women don't really mean it when they say "no" to their sexual advances. Spend a few minutes responding to the items in table 11-1 related to the rape myth.

Directions: There are 19 items on this scale. For items 1–11, use the following 7-point scale to indicate your degree of agreement or disagreement:

Strongly disagree <u>1 2 3 4 5 6 7</u> Strongly agree

_____ 1. A woman who goes to the home or apartment of a man on their first date implies that she is willing to have sex.

_____ 2. Any female can get raped.

_____ 3. One reason that women falsely report a rape is that they frequently have a need to call attention to themselves.

_____ 4. Any healthy woman can successfully resist a rapist if she really wants to.

_____ 5. When women go around braless or wearing short skirts and tight tops, they are just asking for trouble.

_____ 6. In the majority of rapes, the victim is promiscuous or has a bad reputation.

_____ 7. If a girl engages in necking or petting and she lets things get out of hand, it is her own fault if her partner forces sex on her.

_____ 8. Women who get raped while hitchhiking get what they deserve.

_____ 9. A woman who is stuck-up and thinks she is too good to talk to guys on the street deserves to be taught a lesson.

_____10. Many women have an unconscious wish to be raped and may then unconsciously set up a situation in which they are likely to be attacked.

_____11. If a woman gets drunk at a party and has intercourse with a man she's just met there, she should be considered "fair game" to other males at the party who want to have sex with her, too, whether she wants to or not.

Note: For items 12 and 13, use the following scale to answer the questions:

1 = About 0%, 2 = About 25%, 3 = About 50%, 4 = About 75%, 5 = About 100%

_____ 12. What percentage of women who report a rape would you say are lying because they are angry and want to get back at the man they accuse?

_____ 13. What percentage of reported rapes would you guess were merely invented by women who discovered they were pregnant and wanted to protect their own reputation?

Note: For items 14–19, read the statement that follows and use this scale to indicate your response:

1 = Always, 2 = Frequently, 3 = Sometimes, 4 = Rarely, 5 = Never

A person comes to you and claims s/he was raped. How likely would you be to believe their statement if the person were:

____**14.** your best friend?   ____**17.** a young boy?

____**15.** an Indian woman?   ____**18.** a black woman?

____**16.** a neighborhood woman?   ____**19.** a white woman?

Note: Once you have indicated your response to each item, reverse the scoring for item 2 (1 = 7, 2 = 6, 3 = 5, 5 = 3, 6 = 2, 7 = 1). Then add up your total score. The higher your total score, the greater your belief in the rape myth. The mean total score in Burt's (1980) original sample of 598 American adults (average age of 42 years) was 86.6, with a standard deviation of 11.9. How does your total score compare with Burt's original sample? Are you more or less likely to believe in the rape myth than these American adults? Have your friends complete this scale as well. How do your beliefs about the rape myth compare to their beliefs?

Total score: _____

Source: From "Cultural Myths and Supports for Rape" by Martha Burt in JOURNAL OF PERSONALITY AND SOCIAL PSYCHOLOGY, 38, 1980, pp. 217–230. Copyright © 1980 by the American Psychological Association. Adapted with permission.

The rape myth and acquaintance rape are both fostered by traditional sexual scripts in which the woman's role is to act resistant to sex and the man's role is to persist in his sexual advances. In a study of acquaintance rape, researchers identified characteristics of both the victimizer and the victim that closely correspond to these sexual scripts (Allison & Wrightsman, 1993). The victim of acquaintance rape tends to have problems with forcefully conveying a clear message of "no," and the victimizer often misperceives the actions of the victim, interpreting passivity as permission.

Despite this misperception, this in no way justifies forced sex. It cannot be stressed enough that acquaintance rape occurs when a man refuses to stop his sexual aggression. Such men tend to be more sexually active than other men, and they treat women as if they are property rather than people. An acquaintance rapist also generally has a history of antisocial behavior and displays a lot of anger toward women. Because he believes that women often need a little force to enjoy sex, the victimizer does not believe that acquaintance rape is rape, even after he has committed this crime.

So what can we learn from this research? First, learning and practicing sexual scripts in which men act as "predators" and women play the "resistant" role promotes sexual aggression and acquaintance rape. Second, people who are sexually attracted to one another should put aside these traditional, limiting gender roles and engage in open, honest communication. In such exchanges, a refusal of sexual intimacy should be accepted as such.

Acquaintance rape: Forced sexual intercourse that occurs either on a date or between people who are acquainted or romantically involved. Also known as *date rape*.

Rape myth: The false belief that deep down, women enjoy forcible sex and find it sexually exciting.

11-2c Sexual Orientation Is a Continuum

Sexual orientation: The degree to which a person is sexually attracted to persons of the other sex and/or to persons of the same sex.

Heterosexuality: The sexual orientation in which a person is sexually attracted primarily to members of the other sex.

Homosexuality: The sexual orientation in which a person is sexually attracted primarily to members of the same sex.

Bisexuality: The sexual orientation in which a person is sexually attracted to members of both sexes.

Do you recall the moment when you decided that you were going to be sexually attracted to women, men, or both? It is a pretty safe bet that your answer is no. Instead of choosing what kind of person sexually attracts you, like most people, you probably discovered your sexual attractions while growing up. **Sexual orientation** is the degree to which we are sexually attracted to persons of the other sex and/or to persons of our own sex. It is usually determined by adolescence, typically about three years before one becomes sexually active (Bell et al., 1981). This finding suggests that we generally identify ourselves as "gay" or "straight," not because of our sexual behavior, but rather, because of our sexual feelings. In other words, sometime during childhood and adolescence, we typically discover that we have sexual feelings toward members of the other sex, our own sex, or both sexes. These sexual feelings—rather than actual sexual behavior—are the primary determinants of us identifying ourselves as either having a heterosexual, homosexual, or bisexual orientation.

In studying sexual orientation, contemporary behavioral scientists conceptualize it as a continuum, with **heterosexuality** at one end, **homosexuality** at the other end, and **bisexuality** somewhere in between (Haslam, 1997; Kelly, 2001). To characterize individuals' sexual orientation from this continuum perspective, Alfred Kinsey and his coworkers (1948) devised a seven-point scale, which is depicted in figure 11-5. On this scale, if you are attracted exclusively to persons of the other sex and you engage in sexual behavior only with such persons, you are at the heterosexual end of the continuum (category 0). In contrast, if you are attracted exclusively to persons of your own sex and you engage in sexual behavior only with such persons, you are at the homosexual end of the continuum (category 6). Finally, if you fall somewhere in between these two extremes (categories 2–4), you are usually defined as bisexual. This scientific viewpoint stands in sharp contrast to the conventional view that sexual orientation is an all-or-none distinction.

Many people who define themselves as heterosexual or homosexual have had sexual experiences outside of their self-labels. Indeed, cross-cultural research indicates that homosexual behavior is quite common. For example, in 22 of the 120 cultures examined in one study, over 20 percent of the men had engaged in homosexual activity, with some cultures having rates as high as 50 percent or more (Minturn et al., 1969). Another cross-cultural study found that homosexual behavior of some sort was considered normal and socially acceptable for at least some individuals in almost two-thirds of the 76 societies investigated (Ford & Beach, 1951). Even in cultures with the most restrictive views about same-sex sexual relations, homosexual behavior still takes place (Hatfield & Rapson, 1996). Yet, behavior does not equal identity. What is the prevalence of homosexual, heterosexual, and bisexual orientations in the general population?

FIGURE 11-5
Sexual Orientation as a Continuum

Instead of characterizing sexual orientation as an either-or distinction between heterosexuality and homosexuality, Kinsey et al. (1948) designed this seven-point scale to describe sexual orientation as a continuum, with heterosexuality and homosexuality at the ends and bisexuality in the middle.

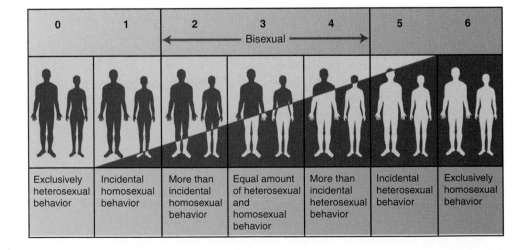

0	1	2	3	4	5	6
		←	Bisexual	→		
Exclusively heterosexual behavior	Incidental homosexual behavior	More than incidental homosexual behavior	Equal amount of heterosexual and homosexual behavior	More than incidental heterosexual behavior	Incidental heterosexual behavior	Exclusively homosexual behavior

Frequency of Different Sexual Orientations

With an estimated prevalence figure of over 90 percent, heterosexuality has been the clearly dominant sexual orientation throughout history (Bullough, 1980). Yet, it is also true that homosexuality and bisexuality have been present throughout these same time periods. Fantasies about, and sexual behaviors between, people of the same sex are far more common than identifying oneself as having a homosexual or a bisexual orientation. The National Health and Social Life Survey of American sexual behaviors found that 9 percent of men and 4 percent of women have had some form of sexual contact with a person of the same sex after puberty (Laumann et al., 1994). Further, between 7 and 8 percent of men and women either reported that the idea of having sex with a person of the same sex was "appealing," or they reported being attracted to a person of the same sex (Laumann et al., 1994). However, only about 1.4 percent of women identified themselves as lesbians and only 2.8 percent of men identified themselves as gay. About half as many women and men reported a bisexual identity. The rates in this survey are comparable to those in other recent surveys in this country and in Europe (Billy et al., 1993; Sandfort et al., 2001). Most likely these percentages underestimate the actual prevalence of homosexual and bisexual orientations. Can you guess why?

The answer is **heterosexism,** which is a system of cultural beliefs, values, and customs that exalts heterosexuality and denies, denigrates, and stigmatizes any nonheterosexual form of behavior or identity (Herek et al., 1991). How does heterosexism manifest itself? Open and blatant expressions of antigay attitudes by heterosexuals, such as someone calling another person a "faggot" or a "dyke," is certainly an example of heterosexism. However, heterosexism can also operate on a more subtle level. For instance, although heterosexuals may hardly notice a man and woman kissing in public, they often react with disgust or even hostility if the couple is of the same sex. Such condemnation of nonheterosexual behavior can make it dangerous for homosexual and bisexual individuals to do anything in public that would define them by their sexual orientation, a fact underscored by the high rate of gay hate crimes committed each year (Herek, 1990). In such an unaccepting social environment, it is likely that some gay, lesbian, and bisexual survey respondents are reluctant to tell a stranger (even anonymously) about their true sexual orientation.

Heterosexism: A system of cultural beliefs, values, and customs that exalts heterosexuality and denies, denigrates, and stigmatizes any nonheterosexual form of behavior or identity.

Historical Background of Heterosexism

Contemporary attitudes toward homosexuality have been significantly shaped by both religious and secular beliefs. In early Christianity, homosexual behavior was widely tolerated or ignored by the church, until the Middle Ages. Then, beginning in the late twelfth century in Europe, homosexual behavior was perceived as "unnatural" and officially defined as such in the writings of Christian leaders (Boswell, 1980). This religious condemnation led to the passage of laws against homosexual acts, which were often punishable by death. These harsh legal sanctions were also adopted by many of the governments in the early American colonies.

By the end of the nineteenth century, the cultural assault against homosexuality was expanded into the medical profession, when such behavior was considered an indication of mental illness (Duberman et al., 1989). In certain respects, this historical shift reflected a more humane view of homosexuality because a "sick" person is generally judged less blameful than a sinner or a criminal. Then in 1957, psychologist Evelyn Hooker published her now-famous study that examined whether homosexual and heterosexual individuals differed in their psychological adjustment. Her findings indicated that there were no significant differences between the two groups. Hooker's results were later replicated in

---

Many years ago I chased a woman for almost two years, only to discover that her tastes were exactly like mine: we both were crazy about girls.

—Groucho Marx, American comedian, 1895–1977

> ***INFO-BIT:*** Have you ever wondered about the origin of the derogatory word *faggot* that is used by bigots when referring to homosexual persons? The dictionary defines *faggot* as a bundle of sticks for firewood. During the European Inquisition, when accused "witches" were burned at the stake, people condemned to death for homosexual behavior were often set aflame ahead of time to act as kindling for the "witches" flames.

many other studies using a variety of research methods (Berube, 1990; Freedman, 1971; Gonsiorek, 1991). Confronted with this overwhelming scientific evidence, in 1973 the American Psychiatric Association removed homosexuality from their list of recognized mental disorders. Soon, the American Psychological Association endorsed the psychiatrists' actions. Additional research has disconfirmed other myths about homosexuality, such as the belief that the vast majority of child molesters are homosexual men. In reality, most molesters are male heterosexuals (Gonsiorek, 1982). Today, as in the past, the biggest threat to homosexual and bisexual individuals' mental health is not their sexual orientation, but rather, it is the hostility they experience from heterosexuals when their sexual orientation becomes public knowledge (DeAngelis, 2002).

11-2d The Causes of Sexual Orientation Are As Yet Unclear

Whenever discussion focuses on the possible causes of sexual orientation, it is often phrased in terms of "What causes homosexuality?" Yet, this question is scientifically misconceived because it falsely assumes either that heterosexuality needs no explanation or that its causes are already known. So what does cause sexual orientation?

Some researchers have examined whether specific brain areas might be associated with sexual orientation (Cohen, 2002). For example, a small part of the hypothalamus—no bigger than a grain of sand—has been found to be twice as large in the brains of heterosexual men than in homosexual men (LeVay, 1991). A similar difference has been found in a section of the fibers of the corpus collosum that connect the right and left brain hemispheres. However, here, this brain area is one-third larger in homosexual men than in heterosexual men (Allen & Gorski, 1992). Both of these brain differences are similar to the differences found between heterosexual men and heterosexual women. Together, they may indicate that brain development affects sexual orientation (LeVay, 1996). However, it is equally possible that these brain differences may not be the cause of sexual orientation, but rather, they may be the effect of behaviors associated with these two different sexual orientations (Breedlove, 1997). In other words, certain differences in the life experiences of gay and heterosexual men may cause this part of the hypothalamus to develop differently. Until further research is conducted, both of these interpretations are plausible.

The finding that all three types of sexual orientation exist throughout the world may indicate that sexual orientation is determined by our genes. As in studies on the inheritance of intelligence (see chapter 10, section 10-4a), research on the inheritance of sexual orientation has focused on twins. One study found that among gay men who were identical twins, over half of their twin brothers were also gay, compared with less than one-quarter of fraternal twin brothers (Bailey & Pillard, 1991, 1995). Similar findings were also obtained with lesbian twins (Bailey et al., 1993). Although these results suggest that sexual orientation is at least partly inherited, a more recent study failed to find this effect (Rice et al., 1999). Because of these contradictory findings, the best we can conclude at this point is that there may be a genetic influence on sexual orientation (Hamer, 2002).

Although early attempts to identify social developmental causes of sexual orientation claimed that homosexuality was caused by a smothering mother, absent father, sexual abuse, or "deviant" homosexual role models, research did not support any of these claims

(Storms, 1983). For example, sons of gay men are not more likely to become gay if they live with their father, and over 90 percent of children of lesbian mothers develop a heterosexual orientation (Bailey et al., 1995; Golombok & Tasker, 1996). Thus, unlike contagious diseases, you cannot "catch" a sexual orientation. The only early childhood experience that predicts the development of a homosexual versus a heterosexual orientation in adulthood for both women and men is *gender nonconformity*.

As depicted in table 11-2, when 1,500 homosexual and heterosexual women and men were interviewed about earlier life experiences, lesbians and gay men were significantly more likely to report that they had preferred play activities traditionally associated with the other sex and were more likely to have had other-sex friends (Bell et al., 1981). They also were less likely to have a traditional gender role (masculine for boys and feminine for girls). Describing their childhood using labels derived from a heterosexist culture, the lesbians had acted more like "tomboys" and the gay men had acted more like "sissies" than did their heterosexual counterparts.

These gender nonconformity findings have been replicated in other studies (Lippa, 2002), and a growing number of psychologists believe that they may be due to one or more of the previously discussed biological factors (Bailey & Zucker, 1995; Green, 1987). Of course, it is important to remember that we are discussing group differences here, and there are many exceptions to these general findings. In other words, many heterosexuals prefer activities traditionally associated with the other sex, and many gay men and lesbians prefer traditional gender activities. Thus, despite these findings of group differences, you cannot reliably identify people's sexual orientation based on whether they like to play baseball versus gymnastics.

So where are we in our understanding of the causes of sexual orientation? There may well be genetic or other biological influences on sexual orientation, but the nature of these influences is still an open question. It is clear that in almost all instances, we don't consciously choose our sexual orientation. Because of the strong antigay prejudice that still exists in many areas of the world, the possibility that sexual orientation is biologically

TABLE 11-2

Gender Nonconformity in Childhood among Homosexual and Heterosexual Women and Men

Gender Nonconforming Preferences and Behaviors	Men		Women	
	Gay (%)	Heterosexual (%)	Lesbian (%)	Heterosexual (%)
Did not enjoy traditional play activities for their sex	63	10	63	15
Did enjoy nontraditional play activities for their sex	48	11	81	61
Nontraditional gender role (masculinity for girls and femininity for boys)	56	8	80	24
Most childhood friends were of the other sex	42	13	60	40

Adapted from Bell, Weinberg, & Hammersmith, 1981.

determined may paradoxically lead to both a decrease and an increase in heterosexuals' intolerance of gay men, lesbians, and bisexuals. For instance, if sexual orientation is something we inherit, like skin color, than some heterosexuals may be less fearful of "catching" homosexuality through direct contact. As a result, they may interact more with non-heterosexuals and, through such contact, dispel their other misconceptions and become more tolerant (Anderssen, 2002; Tygart, 2000). However, if it is determined that genetics shape sexual orientation, it is also possible that heterosexuals with an antigay bias may try to genetically eliminate homosexuality from the human gene pool by either aborting or genetically altering fetuses with homosexual "markers." As an active creator of the social reality in which you live, you can use the information in this chapter to dispel many people's misconceptions about sexual orientation issues and thereby reduce heterosexism. Remember, in the journey of discovery, knowledge is power.

11-2e People Who Are Uncomfortable Thinking about Sex Are More Likely to Have Unprotected Sex

As a graduate student, William Fisher (1993) stumbled on a paradoxical finding that was to dominate his research career: Men and women who expressed the most negative feelings about sexual topics either had, or planned to have, the most children. In pondering this finding, Fisher began to ask a number of "what if" questions.

A set of these questions had to do with whether people with negative feelings about sex would be least able to think about intercourse in advance, to learn about birth control, to talk to their partners about it, or to effectively use contraceptives. Subsequent research did indeed find that those who were more uneasy thinking about sex tended to plan less for sexual interactions and, thus, engaged in more unprotected sex than other people. Such behavior increased their likelihood of not only having unplanned pregnancies, but also contracting sexually transmitted diseases (Fisher et al., 1977, 1979, 1988b). Fisher and his coworkers also discovered that medical students who were similarly uneasy about sexual matters were less prepared to work with patients' sexual health problems or even answer their sex-related questions (Fisher et al., 1988a). The same discomfort affected the quality of sex education offered by trained teachers (Fisher, 1993).

Having found evidence that people's discomfort with sex could actually place them at greater risk for unplanned pregnancies and sexually transmitted diseases, Fisher wondered whether he could develop an intervention program to counteract these negative outcomes. Thus, the next step in his scientific journey of discovery was to design sex-education courses that would specifically target people's discomfort in talking about contraception and sex. Subsequent evaluations of these programs indicate that they are successful in reducing unwanted pregnancies (Fisher, 1993). Fisher's work as a sex researcher nicely demonstrates how the "what if" questions in life can lead psychologists down many varied paths in the pursuit of scientific knowledge.

SECTION SUMMARY

- Evolutionary and sociocultural factors may jointly explain the greater desire that men appear to have for sexual variety when compared with women.
- Women and men similar in their sexual arousal response.
- Sexual orientation is a continuum, with heterosexuality at one end, homosexuality at the other end, and bisexuality somewhere in between.
- Heterosexism is a system of cultural beliefs, values, and customs that exalts heterosexuality and denies, denigrates, and stigmatizes any nonheterosexual form of behavior or identity.
- There may be genetic or other biological influences on sexual orientation.
- Those who are uneasy thinking about sex are most likely to engage in unprotected sex.

11-3 HUNGER AND EATING

In addition to sex, another primary motivated behavior is eating. In this section of the chapter, we explore the biological mechanisms that underlie this most basic of human needs and then we discuss various theories related to hunger, eating, and **satiety** (pronounced "sa-TY-a-tee"), which means being full to satisfaction (Pinel et al., 2002).

11-3a Various Biological Mechanisms Control Hunger and Eating

Due to its importance for survival, it is not surprising that the controls over hunger, eating, and satiety are complex and represent several independent and interacting bodily systems (Pinel et al., 2000). Three of the major control systems are the stomach, the bloodstream, and the brain.

The Stomach

It seems logical that the stomach should play some role in whether we feel hungry or full. In one early investigation of this body organ, A. L. Washburn, working with Walter Cannon, swallowed a long tube with a balloon that was then inflated (Cannon & Washburn, 1912). Whenever Washburn's stomach contracted, the corresponding changes in the balloon's air pressure were recorded. Although stomach contractions corresponded to Washburn's perceptions of hunger, later research demonstrated that these contractions do not cause hunger pangs (Rozin et al., 1998). In fact, you can still feel hungry even after your stomach has been surgically removed (Mills & Stunkard, 1976)! Although the sensation of hunger isn't caused by the stomach, the sensation of food satiety at least partly originates in this body organ. As the stomach becomes swollen from eating, sensory neural signals reflecting satiety are sent from the stomach—and the small intestine and liver—to the brain. The stomach also releases the hormone gastrin, which, among other actions, signals the pancreas to begin releasing insulin, a hormone that, among other things, decreases appetite.

The Bloodstream

The blood is the pathway for many eating-related signals that flow to the brain. The brain monitors two main types of blood signals: those dealing with the level of food nutrients that the stomach has supplied to the bloodstream, and those dealing with hormone levels in the bloodstream related to those nutrients. When the brain receives signals that the level of food nutrients in the blood is low, we feel hungry. The two major types of food nutrients are *fatty acids* and the blood sugar *glucose,* which is converted into energy that can be stored and later used by the body. The blood hormone *insulin* is essential in this conversion process. High insulin production leads to cells taking in more glucose than they can use, with the excess being converted into fat. As previously mentioned, increased levels of insulin lead to decreased hunger, while drops in the levels of insulin result in increased hunger (Nelson, 2000). Finally, one blood signal that tells the brain that eating should start or stop comes from *cholecystokinin* (CCK), which is released from the small intestine as a hormone and from the brain as a neurotransmitter. CCK not only aids digestion, it also regulates how much we eat by decreasing hunger. Administering CCK to food-deprived humans and other animals reduces hunger and eating but doesn't affect thirst or water consumption (Morley et al., 1985). If receptors in the brain for CCK are blocked, animals continue eating even after consuming their normal amount of food (Bloom & Polak, 1981).

The Brain

The *hypothalamus,* which is a small structure buried deep within the brain, plays a significant role in regulating eating behavior. As noted in chapter 3, section 3-3b, the hypothalamus is primarily responsible for homeostatic regulation. A major part of maintaining homeostasis is balancing the body's energy demands with energy availability. About 50 years ago, studies on rats suggested that two small parts of the hypothalamus were the primary centers for coordinating hunger and satiety. The lateral (side) area of the hypothalamus (LH) was thought to be the "hunger on" center (Stellar, 1954) and the ventromedial (bottom center) area of the hypothalamus (VMH) appeared to be the "hunger off" center (Hetherington & Ranson, 1942). The reason for these beliefs was the discovery that making small lesions (holes) in the VMH led to massive increases in eating, whereas lesioning the LH led to finicky eating. Although these two areas of the hypothalamus play an important role in hunger and satiety, later studies indicated that the "hunger on-off" labels were too simplistic: The LH and VMH interact with many other brain systems to produce their effects (Kalat, 1998; Pinel, 1997).

Today, scientists believe that another part of the hypothalamus, the *paraventricular nucleus (PVN)*, plays a more important role in hunger regulation by having neural circuitry that responds to various neurotransmitters (Stanley et al., 1986; Woods et al., 2000). For instance, the neurotransmitter *neuropeptide* Y has a marked effect at the PVN and greatly increases carbohydrate eating, while the neurotransmitter *serotonin* inhibits carbohydrate consumption (Woods et al., 2000). Thus, rather than describing the hypothalamus as having "hunger on" and "hunger off" areas, it is more accurate to state that it has some neurons that fire when blood nutrient levels are low, and others that fire when nutrients are at high levels and should be released. These neurons act less like "on-off" hunger switches and more like sensors that provide information to the frontal lobes of the brain, which then decides eating behavior (Winn, 1995).

11-3b Our Environment Also Controls Hunger and Eating

The fact that there is more to hunger than the operation of our physiological states was demonstrated by Paul Rozin and his colleagues (1998) when they tested two brain-damaged patients who—similar to Henry M. in chapter 3—had no recollection of events occurring more than a few minutes ago. After eating a normal meal, these patients ate a second and sometimes a third full meal when evidence of the prior meal had been cleared away. This suggests that knowing when to eat isn't simply a function of body chemistry and hypothalamic activity, but it also involves external cues and memory of when we last ate.

Anticipation is an important factor in hunger and eating. Do you recall Ivan Pavlov's digestion studies of dogs from chapter 7, section 7-1a? In conducting his studies, Pavlov (1927) would place meat powder on a dog's tongue to elicit reflexive salivation. One thing he noticed was that, over time, dogs began salivating *before* any food reached their mouths and even before they smelled the food—in other words, in anticipation of the meal (Capaldi, 1996). Since Pavlov's time many studies have shown that physiological responses that prepare the body for food (for example, a surge in insulin) occur in response to cues normally related to eating (Pinel, 1997; Woods, 1991). These cues are such things as the sight or smell of appealing food, the time of day, other people eating, and the clattering of dishes. This means that hunger is also a response to environmental cues that indicate food is on the way, rather than simply being a response to specific changes occurring within the body.

Another control over eating is related to the incentive value of food. Although the early phases of eating depend on the taste of food, as you continue eating the same food, its positive incentive value declines (Rolls, 1986). In other words, the first taste of barbecued ribs may be wonderful, but it loses its "scrumptiousness" appeal with each bite. Accordingly, you will tend to consume many more calories when there is a variety of food available rather than just one (Rolls et al., 1981). This effect cannot be explained by the body monitoring fat or glucose content (Pinel et al., 2000). Simply put, taste variety matters in how much you eat.

Finally, one other factor that affects eating behavior has to do with how you think about food in relation to yourself. If you are chronically worrying about and trying to control what and how much you eat, you are a *restrained eater* (Herman & Polivy, 1980). Restrained eaters tend to be heavily influenced by what the situation says is correct about eating rather than by what their body signals are telling them. Further, when stressed by daily events or when their self-esteem is threatened, restrained eaters are more likely than other people to go on high-calorie binges when they "let their guard down" (Green & Saenz, 1995; Heatherton et al., 1991; Polivy et al., 1994).

11-3c The Body May Be "Set" to Maintain Weight within a Limited Range

Research investigating the effects of both starvation and overeating suggest that the body has a **set point** for weight, meaning a level of body weight that it works to maintain (Keys et al., 1950; Sims, 1974; Sims & Horton, 1968). Although this physiological process is only partly understood, it appears that the body monitors fat-cell levels to keep them relatively stable (Friedman, 2000). When the body's fat cells rise above this set point, they release the hormone leptin. Leptin, which in Greek (*leptos*) means "thin," has the effect of decreasing hunger by altering neural activity in the hippocampus (Auwerx & Staels, 1998; Strobel et al., 1998). In essence, releasing leptin is the fat cells' way of telling the brain to stop eating because there is enough fat already in the body. In contrast, when fat-cell levels fall below the set point, the body compensates in the opposite direction by increasing hunger and decreasing metabolism. This constant compensation due to fluctuations in the body's fat-cell levels keeps your weight within a limited range.

> **Set point:** A level of weight that the body works to maintain.

Some set-point theorists propose that our weight and fat content are preprogrammed for us genetically and that this set point can only be altered under extreme circumstances, if at all. The practical implication of this assumption is that even after extensive dieting or overeating, we are genetically destined to eventually return to our original weight. What specifically determines our set point may have something to do with our *number* of fat cells. Research indicates that when people gain or lose weight, they do not also gain or lose fat cells. Instead, their existing fat cells increase or decrease in average *size* (Hirsch et al., 1989). According to the reasoning of set-point theorists, if you have many more fat cells than the average person, you also have a correspondingly higher set point, which greatly increases your chances of becoming overweight. On the other hand, if you have relatively few fat cells, your set point is lower, and you are likely to be relatively thin.

The idea that we have a genetically determined set point has been criticized by some researchers as being inconsistent with the increasing prevalence of obesity in countries where food supplies exceed need. For example, the percentage of Americans 30 percent or more above their ideal body weight increased from 12 percent in 1991 to 17.9 percent in 1998 (Centers for Disease Control, 2000). How can a genetically fixed set point explain this increase? It would either have to be the case that genetically programmed set points are rising at a rapid rate—which is virtually impossible—or that our natural set points are at a level that is pathologically too high—which means that they really haven't been controlling the weight levels of many people at all (Pinel et al., 2000).

Faced with this problem, the prevailing view is that set points are not genetically fixed. However, this does not mean that people don't differ in their set points or that genetics doesn't significantly shape set-point levels. What it means is that your set point can change over time. Unfortunately, the change usually is upward, not downward. Research suggests that long-term overeating can gradually raise your set point, but it is much more difficult to lower your set point (Bolles, 1980; Keesey, 1995). These results don't mean that if you are obese you have no control over your weight. Instead, they suggest that you must make permanent changes in your eating habits to lose weight and maintain it at a healthy level. Weight change is a *lifestyle* change, not just a fad diet.

SECTION SUMMARY

- The three major biological control systems in hunger and eating are the stomach, bloodstream, and brain.

- Hunger is also a response to environmental cues, anticipation, and the incentive value of food.

- The body has a set point for weight, but this set point may not be genetically fixed.

11-4 ACHIEVEMENT MOTIVATION

The motives that we have examined thus far—sex and hunger—can easily be observed in many other species. Yet, now we come to a motive that may be unique to humans: achievement motivation (Epstein, 1998). Different people seem to be more or less driven to succeed—to achieve their goals—sometimes at the expense of other pleasures. Others seem to avoid challenges out of fear of failing. Are these inborn traits? Do these tendencies develop out of experience?

11-4a There Are Individual Differences in the Need for Achievement

Need for achievement (n-Ach): A desire to overcome obstacles and to meet high standards of excellence.

Thematic Apperception Test (TAT): A test in which people "project" their inner feelings and motives through the stories they make up about ambiguous pictures.

The **need for achievement (n-Ach)** is a desire to overcome obstacles and to meet high standards of excellence (Murray, 1938). Although several different methods have been devised to study the need for achievement, researchers have traditionally measured the strength of this motive by examining people's fantasies. One of the most popular tools used to measure n-Ach in this manner is the **Thematic Apperception Test (TAT),** which we will examine again in chapter 12, section 12-6a. The TAT consists of a series of ambiguous pictures similar to the one shown in figure 11-6. Persons taking the test are asked to make up stories about the ambiguous pictures. These stories are then scored for the presence of a number of motives (for example, *need for power* and *need for affiliation*), including the n-Ach. In evaluating n-Ach, trained scorers look for the presence of achievement-related imagery and themes in the stories. For instance, if a test taker who was shown these two people sitting on a bench said the girl was talking to the adult about working harder in school or how she had just won a big part in a community play, these responses would be scored as indicating achievement desires. If the test taker's stories consistently contained such themes, she or he would be regarded as having a high n-Ach. Research suggests that the TAT does a moderately good job of measuring individual differences in n-Ach (Khalid, 1991; McClelland et al., 1953).

High n-Ach people have an intrinsic *desire to succeed*. This desire is not assumed to develop from biological or genetic sources but to come from experience and parental encouragement. David McClelland (1985) contends that n-Ach develops when children *internalize* achievement values displayed by their parents and other important role models. Such internalization comes about by children observing adults engage in achievement tasks and by themselves being placed in achievement situations that they can master. These challenges, however, cannot be so easy that the person doesn't feel some sense of satisfaction and accomplishment.

John Atkinson (1957) suggests that an important component in understanding n-Ach is the additional motivational push that we receive by *fear of failure*. That is, some people's achievement needs are less determined by a desire to achieve greatness as much as by a fear of appearing foolish, lazy, or stupid. If people's desire for success is considerably stronger than their fear of failure, they will have a high n-Ach. However, if their fear of failure is considerably stronger than their desire for success, they will have a low n-Ach.

Do high n-Ach people approach all achievement challenges with equal desire? Not at all. In fact, high n-Ach individuals are more likely to choose tasks that are moderately difficult and challenging (those with about a 50/50 chance of success) than tasks that are

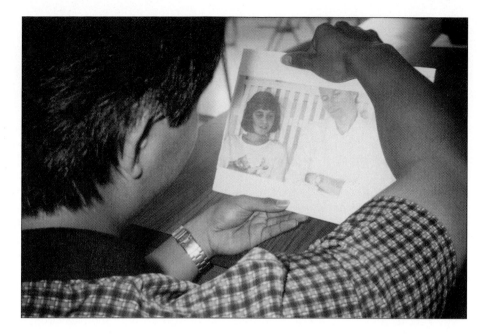

FIGURE 11-6
Measuring the Need for Achievement with the Thematic Apperception Test (TAT)

People taking the TAT tell or write stories about what is happening in a scene, such as this one showing a child and an adult sitting on a bench. The following story illustrates strong achievement motivation: "A daughter is talking to her mom about how she plans to work on a science report for the school fair. She wants to do well but is worried that she is not smart enough. Her mom is giving her some advice, but the daughter soon comes up with her own idea that is even better. Her mom is proud of her. She works really hard on the project, wins the grand prize, and is very happy. In high school, she achieves top honors in a nationwide competition, is recruited by all the prestigious universities, and grows up to become a famous scientist. Now, whenever she is faced with a difficult challenge and doubts her abilities, she thinks back to this conversation with her mom. She realizes that if she works hard, she can and will succeed."

either extremely difficult or easy (Atkinson, 1977; Slade & Rush, 1991). This is so because their desire for success is stronger than their fear of failure. Thus, these people are attracted to achievement situations that they can master if they work hard and precisely apply their skills (McClelland, 1995). When they succeed at these tasks, high n-Ach people are generally perceived as being talented, hardworking, and deserving of praise and rewards. This positive feedback serves to both satisfy and further strengthen their achievement desires. In contrast, extremely difficult and easy tasks are not nearly as appealing to those with a high n-Ach because the probability of success is either very low ("Why waste my time?") or virtually guaranteed ("Where is the challenge?"). Further, if they do succeed at a virtually impossible task, their achievement is likely to be dismissed by others as sheer "dumb luck."

What about low n-Ach individuals? Do they completely avoid achievement situations? Again, the answer is no. They tend to pick achievement situations that are either very easy so that success is guaranteed or extremely difficult so that they have a good excuse for failing (McClelland, 1985). The key fact to remember about low n-Ach people is that their fear of failure is stronger than their desire for success. As a result, they pick achievement situations that will protect them against either failing or being blamed for failing. However, such situations also virtually guarantee that they cannot take credit for any success that they achieve. Thus, while they may protect themselves from embarrassment and self-esteem loss, they have little hope of winning praise or enhancing their self-esteem. As a result, achievement situations are unlikely to ever be very rewarding to those with low n-Ach.

This desire to meet high standards of excellence in achievement situations causes many people to experience high levels of anxiety as they prepare to demonstrate their skills. Such anxiety can sabotage achievement desires. The *Psychological Applications* section at the end of this chapter examines the psychological aspects of high anxiety in academic testing situations and offers tips on how to control such anxiety.

11-4b Certain Strategies Can Increase Achievement Motivation

We are not born with a motive to achieve. Instead, we acquire it through parents and others encouraging and helping us discover the rewards of mastering challenging tasks while surviving failures (Vallerand et al., 1997). Yet, how can we foster achievement motivation in people who typically avoid achievement situations?

DISCOVERY BOX 11-3

Are There Cultural Differences in What Constitutes "Achievement"?

N-Ach was originally conceived as a motive that reflects individualist ideals of achieving personal gains in competition against others. However, a growing number of psychologists have argued that people from collectivist cultures may focus on a different type of achievement (Markus & Kitayama, 1991; Smith & Bond, 1994). Specifically, most collectivist cultures value goals that promote group harmony, loyalty, humility, and interdependence. These values are quite contrary to individualist ideals of individual achievement (Feather, 1994). Accordingly, goals that facilitate the well-being of the group will more likely be seen as a mark of achievement within collectivist cultures than within those that are individualist (Jayakar, 1994; Singhal & Misra, 1994). Even the same achievement task is often perceived as meeting different goals. For example, among collectivists, achieving success in one's career is much less likely to be viewed solely as a personal gain than it is seen as bringing honor to one's family or gaining approval from teachers and peers (Urdan & Maehr, 1995).

One effective strategy is to get people to emotionally identify with the achievement task, so that they become intrinsically motivated (see section 11-1e). If you can convince people that they are working on a task because it is something that is important to them, they will work harder and do better work, even if they are low n-Ach individuals (Cialdini et al., 1998).

In addition to fostering intrinsic motivation, you should also take steps to increase the value of achieving (for example, emphasize feelings of pride and accomplishment) while decreasing the negative effects of failing (for example, downplay feelings of shame and guilt) (Sorrentino & Hewitt, 1984). By providing realistic models of success with positive outcomes, while introducing examples of failure within a supportive environment, the emotional responses and expectations related to both can be shifted. Experience with failing—and finding that the world does not end in the absence of success—can lessen the fear and help one to cope with difficult challenges.

If people confine themselves to tasks that are too easy, they gain little satisfaction when they succeed. On the other hand, if they regularly are asked to work on tasks well beyond their capabilities, achievement situations will become associated with disappointment and a feeling of inferiority. Thus, another important factor in increasing achievement motivation is to place people in achievement situations that are moderately difficult but that they can master if they exert themselves (Locke & Latham, 1990).

Finally, a fourth factor is that you should be careful how people are given feedback when working on achievement tasks. Frequent feedback is more helpful when success is being demonstrated and something is being gained. However, less frequent feedback and keeping long-term outcomes in mind is better when progress on achieving the task goal is slow or uneven (Cochran & Tesser, 1996). This less frequent feedback shifts people's attention away from their immediate frustrations and toward the desired end state of success.

As you see, many factors shape our achievement desires. Check out Discovery Box 11-3 to see how culture can also influence how we conceive of achievement.

SECTION SUMMARY

- Need for achievement (n-Ach) is a desire to overcome obstacles and to meet high standards of excellence; it is assumed to develop from experience and parental encouragement.
- High n-Ach persons seek out achievement tasks that are moderately difficult.
- Low n-Ach persons choose either very easy or extremely difficult tasks.
- Achievement motivation can be enhanced through various intervention strategies.

11-5 EMOTION

It is difficult to imagine the push and pulls of motivation not being associated with some sort of emotion, such as fear, anxiety, love, desperation, or loathing. Likewise, it is equally difficult to think of a strong emotion that doesn't serve to either push or pull us toward or away from some goal. In many respects, motivation and emotion are two sides of the same coin, with emotions both reflecting and inciting our motives. Let us now examine the character of emotions and the various theories that have been developed to explain them.

11-5a Emotions Are Positive or Negative Feeling States

Visualize the following experiences, pausing between each one and carefully paying attention to how you would feel:

- You're walking down the street, a car comes up fast from behind, and the driver blows the horn just as it reaches you.
- You're walking down the street and you see your heart's greatest desire not just walking toward you, but looking at you and smiling.
- You're walking down the street and you see that thoroughly annoying person who makes your life miserable stumble and fall face-first into a mud puddle.

These incidents would probably induce different emotional responses. But what makes up an emotion? Choose any one of the preceding situations. In response to this change in environment, would there be changes in how your body feels? Would you feel your heart race? Muscles tense or relax? Would your attention, or what you were thinking about, change along with the emotion? What changes in body posture and/or facial expression would occur? Any changes in behavior?

Go back to the situation of seeing "your heart's greatest desire"—but now add into the vision him or her walking hand in hand with another person, gazing longingly into each other's eyes. The primary "thing" in the environment is still the Greatest Desire, but the context (and therefore meaning) has changed, and so has the way your body would feel and how you might behave.

These examples illustrate the complexity of emotions. For our purposes, we define **emotion** as a positive or negative feeling state (or *evaluative response*) that typically includes some combination of physiological arousal, cognitive appraisal, and behavioral expression. Although many theories have been developed to explain emotions (Plutchik, 1994), most consider that all emotions have the following unifying characteristics:

Emotion: A positive or negative feeling state that typically includes some combination of physiological arousal, cognitive appraisal, and behavioral expression.

INFO-BIT: The complementary relationship between emotion and motivation has been recognized for many centuries. In fact, the terms "emotion" and "motivation" share the Latin root, *movere*, which means "to move."

- Emotions involve reactions of many bodily systems.
- Expressions of emotion are based on genetically transmitted mechanisms but are altered by learning and interpretation of events.
- Emotions communicate information between people.
- Emotions help individuals respond and react to changes in their environment.

In short, an emotion is an experience that is felt as happening to the self, generated partly by a cognitive appraisal of a situation, and accompanied by reflexive physiological changes (for example, an increase in blood pressure and heart rate) and behavioral responses (for example, facial expressions and postural changes).

11-5b Emotions Facilitate Survival

Humans, like other animals, signal their readiness to fight, flee, mate, and attend to each other's needs through a variety of facial and bodily nonverbal expressions (Buck, 1984). These adaptive response patterns include emotions (Plutchik, 1994). Evolutionary theories have emphasized the survival value of emotions, not only because they tend to motivate us to avoid what is harmful and to approach what is beneficial, but also because emotional expressions and behaviors foster communication with others (Lang, 1995; Oehman, 2002).

After observing that a number of facial expressions of emotion appeared to be universal, Charles Darwin (1872) proposed that facial expressions are inborn and that the expressions we see today are those that allowed our ancestors to most effectively communicate to one another their inner states and behavioral intentions. Consistent with Darwin's evolutionary view of emotional expressiveness, cross-cultural research indicates that similar facial expressions are readily displayed and accurately interpreted by people from differing cultures (Eible-Eibesfeldt & Sutterlin, 1990; Ekman, 1970; Ekman & Friesen, 1971; Matsumoto et al., 1988). Although this research indicates substantial cross-cultural agreement in both the experience and expression of emotions, certain emotions are easier to distinguish from one another than others. For example, people from all cultures can easily tell the difference between happiness and anger, but it is harder for them to identify adoration from desire. This finding has led to the belief that certain emotions are more basic, or *primary*, than others (Ekman & Friesen, 1971; Izard, 1989). Most classification lists include the following seven primary emotions: *anger, disgust, fear, happiness, surprise, contempt, and sadness* (Ekman, 1973, 1993). The seven primary emotions are also the ones people around the world can accurately "read" by examining facial expressions (see chapter 16, section 16-1e).

This does not mean, however, that people throughout the world always express emotions in the same way. Given the important role that emotions play in human interactions, it makes abundant sense that cultures would develop social rules for when and how different emotions are expressed (Mesquita & Frijda, 1992). For example, the cultural belief systems of individualism and collectivism have shaped norms related to the acceptability of acting in ways that might threaten group harmony. That is, collectivists are much more likely than individualists to monitor their behavior so that it does not disrupt the smooth functioning of the group. Regarding emotions, research suggests that although people from collectivist and individualist cultures do not differ in publicly displaying positive emotions, collectivists are much more uncomfortable about publicly expressing negative emotions (Stephan et al., 1996).

What are the feelings of men? They are joy, anger, sadness, fear, love, disliking, and liking. These seven feelings belong to men without their learning them.

—From *The Li Chi*, first-century Chinese encyclopedia

INFO-BIT: Recent work using magnetic resonance imaging found evidence that women's brains tend to be better organized to perceive and remember emotions than men's brains (Canli et al., 2002). These results might partly explain why clinical depression is twice as common in women than in men (see chapter 13, section 13-3b).

Does this mean that people from collectivist cultures feel negative emotions differently than individualists feel them? In an attempt to answer this question, Paul Ekman (1970) unobtrusively recorded the facial expressions of Japanese and Americans while they individually watched either an emotionally neutral film or one depicting body mutilation. In this "viewing alone" condition, Ekman found a very strong, positive correlation between the Japanese and American participants' displayed facial expressions ($r = +.88$), indicating clear agreement in their expressions of such emotions as anger, disgust, surprise, and fear. However, when someone else entered the viewing room while a participant was watching a film, the Japanese, unlike the Americans, tended to display polite smiles rather than expressing their authentic emotions of the moment. These findings suggest that collectivism influences whether people publicly *express* negative feelings, but not whether they privately experience them. In other words, there is no evidence that collectivists *feel* emotions differently than do individualists.

11-5c Emotions Result in Bodily Responses

Can you imagine riding a roller coaster and not feeling your heart pounding or your blood pressure rising? What if there were no anticipatory "butterflies" in your stomach prior to an important date? The emotional impact of these events would be blunted without the physiological feedback. The *autonomic nervous system* produces the bodily responses integral to emotion. As discussed in chapter 3, section 3-2a, the autonomic nervous system is the part of the peripheral nervous system that commands movement of involuntary, nonskeletal muscles—such as the heart, lung, and stomach muscles—over which we have little or no control. The autonomic nervous system is further divided into two separate branches—the *sympathetic* and *parasympathetic* nervous systems (figure 11-7)—that tend to work in opposition to each other in order to keep the body's vital systems in a state of homeostasis (see the earlier discussion in section 11-1c).

As you recall, the sympathetic nervous system is geared toward energy expenditure—getting the body ready to respond (the "fight or flight" response) by moving blood to the muscles and releasing stored energy. This system is not only activated to meet physical demands, but it also functions when you experience strong emotions. In contrast, the parasympathetic nervous system is geared toward energy conservation and "refueling," by stimulating digestion and decreasing blood flow to the muscles. Although this system has not traditionally been associated with emotion to the same degree as the sympathetic system, its role in emotions has received more attention recently. For example, *emotional fainting* is likely a symptom of an overreaction by the parasympathetic system (Vingerhoets, 1985). In addition, *worrying* is characterized by low parasympathetic activity combined with a relatively inflexible autonomic response (Borkovec et al., 1998).

11-5d Two Theories Dispute Whether Physiological Responses Precede Emotions

In 1884, William James and Danish physiologist Carl Lange independently proposed that our subjective emotional experiences are automatically caused by specific physiological changes in the autonomic nervous system that, in turn, are caused by environmental stimuli. According to James, "we feel sorry because we cry, angry because we strike, and afraid because we tremble" (1890, p. 1066).

FIGURE 11-7

The Dual Functions of the Autonomic Nervous System

The sympathetic and parasympathetic divisions of the autonomic nervous system often stimulate opposite effects in the body's organs. The sympathetic nervous system prepares your body for action, while the parasympathetic nervous system calms the body. Can you explain how these two systems respond to threat?

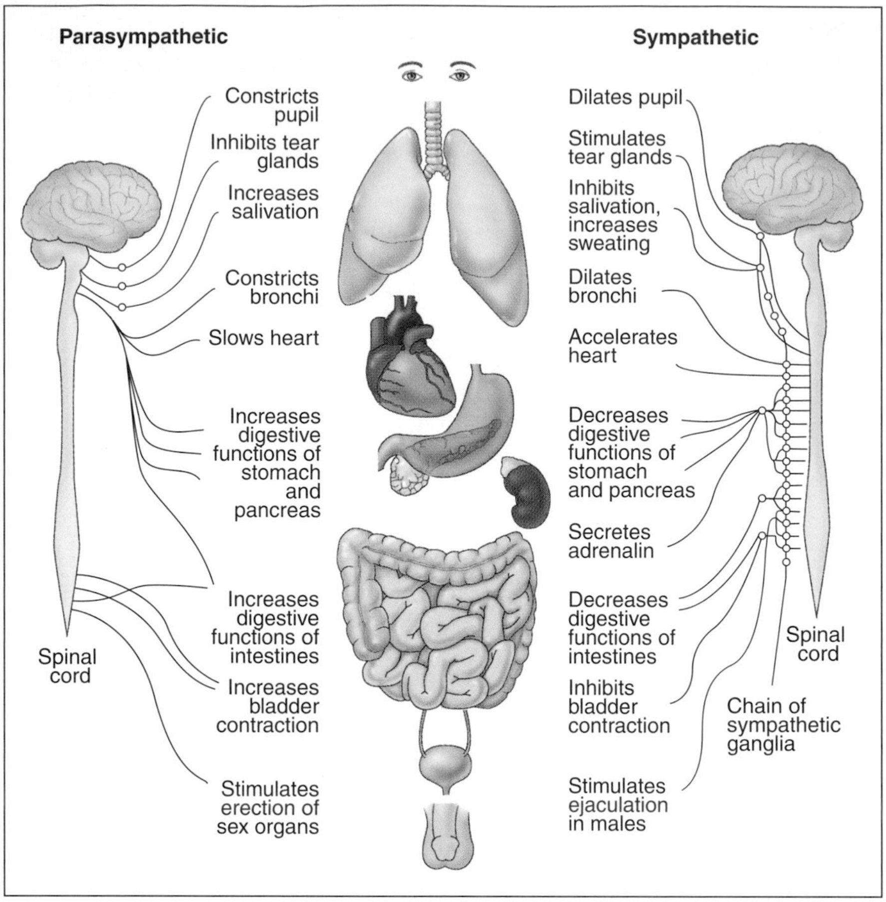

Parasympathetic

- Constricts pupil
- Inhibits tear glands
- Increases salivation
- Constricts bronchi
- Slows heart
- Increases digestive functions of stomach and pancreas
- Increases digestive functions of intestines
- Increases bladder contraction
- Stimulates erection of sex organs

Spinal cord

Sympathetic

- Dilates pupil
- Stimulates tear glands
- Inhibits salivation, increases sweating
- Dilates bronchi
- Accelerates heart
- Decreases digestive functions of stomach and pancreas
- Secretes adrenalin
- Decreases digestive functions of intestines
- Inhibits bladder contraction
- Stimulates ejaculation in males

Spinal cord

Chain of sympathetic ganglia

James-Lange theory: A theory that emotion-provoking events induce specific physiological changes in the autonomic nervous system that our brain automatically interprets as specific emotions.

Cannon-Bard theory: A theory that emotion-provoking events simultaneously induce both physiological responses and subjective states that are labeled as emotions.

Consider the example of a car honking at you unexpectedly. The **James-Lange theory** predicts that your heart would pound and your body would tremble *before* you felt fear. According to the theory, your brain would perceive the physiological responses to the horn honking as being the emotion of fear. Similarly, the palm sweating, heart fluttering, and stomach churning responses upon seeing your Greatest Desire would be perceived as "longing" or "love." All emotions are considered the product of different physiological changes that the brain automatically interprets, all of which occur in response to environmental stimuli.

In contrast to this view, physiologists Walter Cannon (1927) and Philip Bard (1934) offered what is now called the **Cannon-Bard theory,** which proposes that feedback from bodily organs cannot be the source for our emotions because autonomic processes are typically too slow (taking 1–2 seconds) to explain the almost instantaneous experience of emotions. This theory further asserts that because many different emotional states are associated with the same autonomic responses, arousal is too general to directly cause specific emotions. Instead, emotion-provoking events *simultaneously* induce both physiological responses and subjective states that we label as emotions. This occurs because information concerning the emotion-inducing event is transmitted simultaneously to the brain's cortex—which causes the subjective awareness of emotion—and to the autonomic nervous system—which causes the physiological arousal. From this perspective, then, when the car's horn sounds, this event causes your heart to race as you experience a feeling you call "fear." Figure 11-8 illustrates how these two theories view the process of emotion differently.

Which theory is more accurate? Actually, research partially supports both theories. First, the contention by Cannon and Bard that autonomic responses occur too slowly to

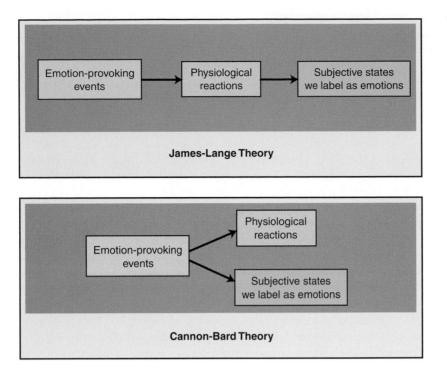

James-Lange Theory

Cannon-Bard Theory

FIGURE 11-8
Two Contrasting Theories of Emotion
While the James-Lange theory proposes that physiological reactions cause emotions, the Cannon-Bard theory contends that these two processes occur simultaneously in response to emotion-provoking events.

account for many emotional responses still appears to be valid. However, consistent with the James-Lange theory, research over the past decade suggests that different emotions do appear to be associated with distinct autonomic responses (Levenson, 1992). For example, anger and fear produce greater heart rate acceleration than happiness, and they are also automatically distinguishable from each other. Cross-cultural research further indicates that these associations between specific bodily changes and specific emotional experiences are universal, suggesting that they may be "hardwired" into the brain (Levenson et al., 1992). Although these findings suggest that emotional reactions can be generated by changes in our bodily states, most researchers agree with the Cannon-Bard proposition that our subjective experience of emotion also involves cognition. If you would like to further explore whether there is more to the experience of emotion than simply reading our physiology, check out Discovery Box 11-4 on the accuracy of lie detectors.

11-5e The Brain Coordinates Emotional Responses

Ultimately, the brain is what controls the bodily responses to emotional stimuli. Yet, no single brain region controls emotion. However, three regions are of particular importance: the hypothalamus, limbic system, and cerebral cortex. Investigations of these brain regions have provided insights into (1) how we can experience emotion before cognition (as proposed by the James-Lange theory) and (2) how the cerebral cortex interprets emotion (as proposed by the Cannon-Bard theory).

The Hypothalamus

Just as the hypothalamus is vital in the regulation of eating (see section 11-3a), it also provides a vital link between higher-order cognitive activities in the forebrain and activities controlled by more primitive areas of the lower brain and with homeostatic control of the body. It does so by converting emotional signals generated in the forebrain into autonomic and endocrine responses. Thus, when something angers or frightens you, the hypothalamus will activate the autonomic nervous system's "fight or flight" responses and the endocrine system's release of hormones.

DISCOVERY BOX 11-4

Is There Such a Thing As an Accurate Lie Detector?

An early attempt at lie detection in ancient India involved placing dry rice into people's mouths. If it was still dry when they spit it out, they were judged to be lying (Trovillo, 1939). Why? Because when someone becomes anxious (as when trying to cover up a lie), less saliva is produced due to the activation of the sympathetic nervous system.

The **polygraph** is a more typical example of a "lie detector." This mechanical device measures a variety of autonomic responses, typically respiration, heart rate, blood pressure, and Galvanic skin response (palm perspiration). Each of these physiological responses is affected by the sympathetic nervous system. Therefore, just as the inability to salivate is considered a sign of lying, so is an increase in heart rate, breathing, blood pressure, and palm sweating when responding to appropriate questions. A polygrapher will monitor physiological responses to neutral questions (for example, "What is your favorite color?") and compare those responses to ones that are being investigated ("Have you ever taken property from an employer?"). Larger responses to key questions, reflecting greater sympathetic nervous system response, are considered "consistent" with lying.

But does that make a polygraph a "lie detector"? No. It is really a sympathetic nervous system activity detector. Researcher David Lykken (1998) has made that very point when demonstrating the numerous ways in which a polygraph can lead to inaccurate conclusions about a person's guilt or innocence. It is true (I'm not lying!) that trained polygraph experts can accurately identify lying as high as 80 to 98 percent of the time. However, identifying someone as innocent still suffers under this technique, with error rates being as high as 55 percent (Honts & Perry, 1992; Kleinmuntz & Szucko, 1984; Lykken, 1984).

The Limbic System

A key component in human emotional responses is the *limbic system*, which is a set of interrelated neural structures located at the border of the brain's "older parts" and the cerebral cortex (see chapter 3, section 3-3b). Although different structures in the limbic system relate to different aspects of emotion, the structure that has received the most attention is the *amygdala*, which is thought to be the first processor of human emotional responses (Hamann et al., 2002; LeDoux, 1998).

Two distinct neural circuits involving the amygdala appear to produce emotional responses, particularly fear (Armony & LeDoux, 2000). The first circuit is very primitive and consists of the amygdala quickly evaluating incoming sensory information from the thalamus—the brain's sensory relay station—and eliciting an immediate emotional response by activating the hypothalamus. This emotional response does not entail any higher-order processing by the cerebral cortex. The fear you experience when surprised by someone jumping out at you from the shadows is an example of this first-circuit emotional response. Emotional responses acquired through classical conditioning are also a function of this primitive neural circuit. The emotional responses that the James-Lange theory best explains are those that arise through this first emotional circuit.

When the thalamus sends sensory information to the amygdala, it also simultaneously sends this information to the cerebral cortex for further processing (LeDoux, 1995). This second neural circuit involves slower processing because it requires more complex cognitive appraisal by the cerebral cortex, involving the use of acquired knowledge and con-

Further, because a polygraph is measuring sympathetic nervous system activity and not actual lying, a person being tested can also fool the machine by consciously elevating their physiological responses while answering neutral questions. This can be done by biting the tongue or squeezing the anal sphincter muscles. These falsely high physiological responses to neutral questions will later mask the elevated physiological responses to the important questions, resulting in lies being more likely to go undetected. Aldrich Ames, convicted of espionage that led to the deaths of at least 10 CIA agents, passed two polygraph tests by taking advantage of weaknesses in this area (Adams, 1995; Weiner et al., 1995).

Due to its inability to actually detect lies, the polygraph is inadmissible as evidence in almost all courts of law. However, polygraph tests are becoming increasingly common for employment screening and as part of criminal investigations. This increased use is occurring despite the fact that a majority of experts in the field of psychophysiology believe the polygraph is an invalid and theoretically unsound approach to lie detection (Iacono & Lykken, 1997). At this time, a truly accurate way to detect lying does not exist (Farwell & Donchin, 1991; Zhou et al., 1999). The polygraph, properly administered by a trained professional, can work as one possible tool for investigation but should not be regarded as providing enough evidence about guilt, innocence, or deception by itself.

> **Polygraph:** A machine that measures several of the physiological responses accompanying emotion (such as respiration, heart rate, blood pressure, and palm perspiration).

sideration of motives and goals. Following this appraisal, information is then transmitted to the amygdala, and a second emotional response occurs when the hypothalamus is activated. The subsequent changes that occur in the autonomic and endocrine systems are relayed back to the cerebral cortex for analysis and interpretation. Complex emotions such as love, happiness, sorrow, and guilt are most likely due to this second emotional circuit. The operation of this second neural circuit resembles what the Cannon-Bard theory hinted at in its proposal that the cerebral cortex causes the subjective awareness of emotion. Both neural circuits are illustrated in figure 11-9.

The Cerebral Cortex

While the limbic system is important for processing emotions, as already stated, the cerebral cortex is important for the *subjective experience* of emotions. As you recall from chapter 3, section 3-3d, the cerebral cortex is divided into two rounded halves, called the *cerebral hemispheres*. Overall, the right cerebral hemisphere seems to be more active than the left hemisphere during the expression of emotions and when processing emotional cues from others (Oatley & Jenkins, 1996). Because the right hemisphere controls the left side of the body, and the left hemisphere controls the right side, this means that the left side of the face is somewhat more involved in emotional expression than the right side.

Research further suggests that each of the two hemispheres is related to one type of emotion more than another. Activation of the left hemisphere is associated with approach-related emotions, whereas activation of the right hemisphere is associated with

FIGURE 11-9
Two Neural Circuits for Processing Emotion

Two distinct neural circuits process emotional responses, both involving the amygdala in the brain's limbic system. The activation of both circuits begins with sensory information being relayed from the thalamus. In the first circuit (blue arrows), the amygdala processes this sensory information and immediately elicits an emotional response without any higher-order processing. In the second circuit (red arrows), the cerebral cortex receives the sensory information from the thalamus and engages in more complex cognitive appraisal before transmitting a signal to the amygdala. Then, a second emotional response occurs. Both circuits ultimately activate the hypothalamus, which produces autonomic and endocrine changes. These changes are also sent back (outline red arrows) to the cerebral cortex, where they are analyzed and interpreted.

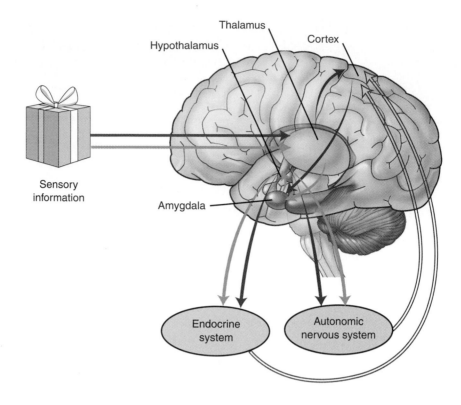

Two-factor theory: A theory of emotion suggesting that our emotional states are sometimes determined by experiencing physiological arousal and then attaching a cognitive label to the arousal.

aversion-related emotions (Sutton & Davidson, 1997). In addition, patients with damage to the left hemisphere tend to express intense negative affect, such as pathological crying, while damage to the right hemisphere often causes pathological laughing (Davidson, 1992). Together, these findings suggest that the left cerebral hemisphere is somewhat more involved in the expression of positive emotions, while the right hemisphere is more involved in expressing negative emotions (Fox & Davidson, 1991).

11-5f The Two-Factor Theory Emphasizes the Role of Cognition in Emotions

The James-Lange theory hypothesizes that physiological arousal precedes the experience of emotion. The Cannon-Bard theory hypothesizes that our emotions are physiologically similar. Taking these different hypotheses from the competing theories, Stanley Schachter and Jerome Singer (1962) proposed that if people are emotionally aroused but are not sure what they are feeling, they look for cues in their surroundings. If others are happy, they are likely to interpret their arousal as happiness. If others are anxious, they too are likely to feel anxious. In other words, they will perceive themselves experiencing the emotion that their surroundings tell them they should be experiencing. Thus, according to Schachter and Singer, emotions are based on two factors: *physiological arousal* and *cognitions* about what that arousal means. They named their theory the **two-factor theory** of emotions.

In one field experiment testing this theory, male hikers walking across a park bridge were asked by an attractive female research assistant to write an imaginative story in response to a TAT picture while standing on the bridge (Dutton & Aron, 1974). In one condition, the bridge was very sturdy and stood only a few feet above the ground. In another condition, the bridge was 5 feet wide, 450 feet long, and constructed of wooden boards attached to wire cables that were suspended 230 feet above a rocky gorge! It was assumed that the men who encountered the assistant on the high suspension bridge would be more physiologically aroused than those who met her on the low sturdy bridge. Based

Imagine that you are going out on a date with someone and you would like this person to fall in love with you. Up to this point in your relationship, this person only likes you "as a friend." Based on your knowledge of the two-factor theory of emotions, what sort of activities might you plan for the date to increase the likelihood that the object of your affections will experience a similar emotion toward you?

on the two-factor theory, it was predicted that the men on the high bridge would interpret their arousal as being caused by sexual interest toward the assistant rather than fear of heights. Consistent with the theory, the men on the high bridge not only told TAT stories with significantly higher sexual imagery than the men on the low bridge, but they were also more likely to call the assistant for a date! Additional research has demonstrated that the attributions we make concerning our physiological responses to a particular stimulus will often, but not always, determine our emotional reactions (Schachter, 1959, 1966).

11-5g One Emotion May Trigger an Opposite Emotion

As previously mentioned, once the sympathetic nervous system activates the body's energy resources in response to a threat, the parasympathetic system responds by conserving these resources. Noting how the body often responds in this counterbalancing fashion, psychologist Richard Solomon (1980) suggested that our experience of emotion often occurs in a similar manner. For example, have you experienced elation after succeeding at some task only to have that feeling soon replaced by a sense of despondency? Or have you felt angry and then afterward felt a sense of calm? Solomon's **opponent-process theory** contends that every emotion triggers an opposite emotion. In addition, the theory also proposes that repetition of an experience causes the initial emotional reaction to weaken and the opposing emotional reaction to strengthen (Solomon & Corbit, 1974).

Opponent-process theory:
A theory of emotion suggesting that every emotion triggers an opposite emotion.

Consider how the opponent-process theory would explain your emotional reaction to skydiving. During your first parachute jump, you would probably experience considerable fear as you prepared to leap from the plane. This fear would undoubtedly subside and give way to exhilaration upon landing safely on the ground. According to the theory, your "rebound" exhilaration would become greater and start earlier with each successive jump. Eventually, your fear may diminish to the point where the entire experience is pleasurable.

The opponent-process theory also provides insights into drug abuse. Initially, drug use often provides intense pleasure, which is followed by unpleasant withdrawal symptoms. With repeated drug use, these unpleasant aftereffects become stronger, while the initial pleasure diminishes. Eventually, taking the drug is motivated less by the fleeting pleasure it provides, and more by the desire to extinguish the pain of withdrawal. Table 11-3 summarizes the four theories of emotion discussed in this section of the chapter. After reviewing this table, check out Discovery Box 11-5, which examines how the social meaning of emotions may be shaped by gender.

INFO-BIT: The opponent-process theory of emotion is similar to the opponent-process principle of color vision discussed in chapter 5, section 5-2e. This principle states that when you stare at a particular color and then look away, the opposing color is seen as an afterimage due to a "rebound effect" in opponent cells. Richard Solomon believed that the same principle holds for emotions.

TABLE 11-3	Theory	Basic Assumptions
Four Theories of Emotion	James-Lange Theory	Emotion-provoking events induce physiological reactions that then cause the subjective states that we label as emotions.
	Cannon-Bard Theory	Emotion-provoking events simultaneously induce physiological reactions and subjective states that we label as emotions.
	Two-Factor Theory	Emotion-provoking events induce physiological reactions that increase arousal, which we then identify as a particular emotion based on situational cues.
	Opponent-Process Theory	Emotional reactions to an event are automatically followed by an opposite emotional reaction. Repeated exposure to the same event weakens the initial emotion while strengthening the opposing emotion.

11-5h People Differ in Their Need to Emotionally Evaluate

As we end this section of the chapter, ask yourself whether you now have a better understanding of your own and other people's emotional landscape. Emotions and evaluating people and things are an important part of everyday life. Yet, one last research finding that I would like to bring to your attention is that some people are more likely than others to base their everyday decisions on their emotional responses.

How do individuals with a high versus a low need to evaluate differ from one another? As you might expect, people with a high need to evaluate are more likely to react emotionally toward issues they have previously encountered and are more likely to describe daily events in evaluative terms than those with a low need to evaluate (Jarvis & Petty, 1996). Although research in this area is only just beginning, future studies are likely to explore how individual differences in the need to evaluate affect how people react to both positive and negative life events. For example, the impact that divorce or job loss might have on people's self-esteem or level of depression could be influenced by the degree to which they chronically evaluate these events. Insights into these possible relations await further research. W. Blair Jarvis and Richard Petty (1996) have developed a *need to evaluate scale* that measures individual differences in the tendency to engage in evaluation. Spend a few minutes responding to the items in table 11-4 to get a better idea of how your evaluation needs compare with others.

SECTION SUMMARY

- Emotions are positive or negative feeling states.
- Evolutionary theories emphasize the survival value of emotions; they motivate us to avoid what is harmful and to approach what is beneficial; emotional expressions and behaviors also foster communication with others.
- The James-Lange theory and the Cannon-Bard theory disagree on whether physiological responses precede emotions.
- Emotions reflecting approach or avoidance can occur automatically and prior to conscious interpretation.
- Three brain regions are central in controlling emotions: the hypothalamus, limbic system, and cerebral cortex.
- Cognitive appraisals help broaden the emotional experience, creating further definition and interpretation of the initial approach or avoidance response.
- One emotional experience may trigger an opposite emotional experience.

DISCOVERY   BOX 11-5

How Does Gender Shape the Social Meaning of Emotion?

As children mature, they learn an *emotion culture*, which consists of the informal norms governing what emotions are appropriate in different circumstances for particular people. These norms often vary from culture to culture (see section 11-5b).

In her book, *Speaking from the Heart: Gender and the Social Meaning of Emotion*, psychologist Stephanie Shields (2002) examines how women and men in North America negotiate the meaning of emotion. Shields describes two contrasting emotional styles that are linked to gender. Both are required of women and men, but each is expected more of one sex than the other. *Extravagant expressiveness* is an open style of experiencing and communicating emotion that is associated with femininity. It is evident in nurturing, and the form of emotion linked in our culture to intimacy. This is the kind of emotion we expect when we say "Don't just tell me that you love me, say it like you really mean it!" The second emotional style telegraphs intense emotion under control that Shields labels *manly emotion*, because of its connection to a particular version of white, heterosexual masculinity. This is the kind of emotion we have come to expect from movie heroes—think of Tom Hanks in *Saving Private Ryan* or *Road to Perdition*.

These two emotional styles convey different messages to those witnessing their expression. The strongly felt—yet controlled—emotion expressed in manly emotion conveys the message that the person is independent: "I can control my emotion (and thereby, my *self*), and I can harness it to control the situation." The underlying message of extravagant expressiveness involves nurturance: "My emotion (and thereby, my *self*) is at your service." Shields contends that in our culture manly emotion is ultimately considered more important than extravagant emotion because it is believed to express rational behavior. In contrast, whereas the feminine emotional standards underlying emotional expressiveness foster many socially desirable behaviors (such as tenderness and selflessness), they are culturally tainted because of their association with emotion out of control. Shields asserts that *control* of emotion is more central to the masculine standards because control is associated with power and dominance. Being the historical holders of power in society, men are assumed to possess greater ability to control their emotions than women.

There is no scientific evidence that there is a gender difference in emotional control—and, of course, there is more than one way to define "control." Research conducted by Shields and other emotion researchers does find that boys are encouraged to express emotions—such as anger, contempt, and pride—that reflect a sense of entitlement to power in society. In contrast, this same research suggests that girls are encouraged to express emotions associated with satisfaction, powerlessness, and service to others, such as happiness, fear, and empathy (Saarni, 1999; Shields, 1995).

To what degree does Shields' analysis fit your understanding of your own emotion culture? Can you think of situations where extravagant emotion was expected of you? Manly emotion? Do you sometimes feel locked into expressing your emotions in certain ways due to other people's (or your own) expectations about gender? What are the costs and benefits of conforming to these gender standards of emotion?

TABLE 11-4

Measuring the Need to Evaluate

Instructions: The extent to which people chronically engage in evaluation is measured by items on the Need to Evaluate Scale (NES). To take the NES, read each item below and then indicate how well each statement describes you, using the following scale:

1 = extremely uncharacteristic (very much unlike me)
2 = somewhat uncharacteristic (somewhat unlike me)
3 = uncertain
4 = somewhat characteristic (somewhat like me)
5 = extremely characteristic (very much like me)

_____ **1.** I form opinions about everything.

_____ **2.** I prefer to avoid taking extreme positions.*

_____ **3.** It is very important to me to hold strong opinions.

_____ **4.** I want to know exactly what is good and bad about everything.

_____ **5.** I often prefer to remain neutral about complex issues.*

_____ **6.** If something does not affect me, I do not usually determine if it is good or bad.*

_____ **7.** I enjoy strongly liking and disliking new things.

_____ **8.** There are many things for which I do not have a preference.*

_____ **9.** It bothers me to remain neutral.

_____**10.** I like to have strong opinions even when I am not personally involved.

_____**11.** I have many more opinions than the average person.

_____**12.** I would rather have a strong opinion than no opinion at all.

_____**13.** I pay a lot of attention to whether things are good or bad.

_____**14.** I only form strong opinions when I have to.*

_____**15.** I like to decide that new things are really good or really bad.

_____**16.** I am pretty much indifferent to many important issues.*

Directions for scoring: Several of the NES items are reverse-scored; that is, for these items, a lower rating actually indicates a higher level of evaluation need. Before summing the items, recode those with an asterisk ("*") so that 1 = 5, 2 = 4, 4 = 2, and 5 = 1. To calculate your need-to-evaluate score, add up your responses to the 16 items.

When Jarvis and Petty developed the NES in 1996, the mean score for college students was about 52. The higher your score is above this value, the greater is your motivation to evaluate objects and events. The lower your score is below this value, the less of this need to evaluate you probably possess.

Source: From "The need to evaluate" by W. B. G. Jarvis and R. E. Petty in JOURNAL OF PERSONALITY AND SOCIAL PSYCHOLOGY, 70, 1996, pp. 172–190. Copyright © 1996 by the American Psychological Association. Adapted with permission.

SUGGESTED WEBSITES

Note: These websites were functional when we went to press. Please access the online text for the most up-to-date URLs.

Thematic Apperception Test Research
http://web.utk.edu/~wmorgan/tat/tattxt.htm
At this website, you can discover the history of the TAT.

Procrastination Research Group
http://www.carleton.ca/~tpychyl/
This website contains information on the psychology of procrastination.

Emotions and Emotional Intelligence
http://trochim.human.cornell.edu/gallery/young/emotion.htm
This website provides an online bibliography covering emotions and emotional intelligence, describing current research findings and notes of interest.

Study Skills Self-Help Information
http://www.ucc.vt.edu/stdysk/stdyhlp.html
This website provides time management strategies for improving academic performance.

PSYCHOLOGICAL APPLICATIONS
Understanding Test Anxiety and Tips to Control It

As previously discussed in section 11-4a, our desire for success and our fear of failure can trigger high levels of anxiety in achievement situations. In academic achievement settings, test anxiety can seriously undermine our ability to demonstrate our intellectual skills (Hembree, 1988; Seipp, 1991). Such anxiety is generally acknowledged to be a multidimensional problem, typified by worry over performance, emotional symptoms, and distracted thoughts (Hodapp & Benson, 1997; Liebert & Morris, 1967; Sarason, 1984).

Two prevailing views about the cause of test anxiety include (1) heightened anxiety blocking retrieval of learned information (Covington & Omelich, 1987; Sarason et al., 1990) and (2) poor encoding and organizing skills leading to poorer preparation and, thus, anxiety resulting from this realization (Birenbaum & Pinku, 1997; Tryon, 1980). These two sources of performance decrements could act independently or interact. That is, poor preparation can affect performance, whether in evaluative situations or not, but worry about performance can further hinder performance under evaluative situations.

Therefore, given adequate preparation, test-anxious students have been found to perform worse than non–test-anxious students under evaluative conditions but comparably well under nonevaluative, nonthreatening conditions (Birenbaum & Pinku, 1997; Covington & Omelich, 1987). This means that when information is asked for directly—as is the case when taking exams—anxiety can interfere with performance or retrieval.

How can test anxiety, or its effects on performance, be reduced? Regardless of the source of test anxiety, adequate preparation is crucial: Students must develop good study skills. Some common suggestions for improving preparation include:

- Go to all of your classes, find out what you're expected to know, and when the exams are scheduled.
- Study and read as the course goes along to avoid "cramming" for exams.
- Have a study schedule that makes it easier to avoid more enjoyable distractions. Study where you can concentrate, get interested in the material, and give it your complete attention.
- Make flashcards and review them often.

- Learn how to take good notes by comparing your notes with others' or by going over them with your instructor. Go over them right after class and review periodically.
- Make outlines and summary sheets. Ask yourself, "What is the important information?" Reciting the material in your own words will help you encode the material more deeply.
- Being in a study group with motivated classmates is often helpful.
- Most colleges have Academic Assistance Centers to help you improve your study and test-taking skills. Free tutoring is also usually available.

To try and handle the "anxiety" aspects of preparing and taking tests, some things to keep in mind include:

- Keep tests in perspective. You're more than just a test taker or a student. Often, people with greater test anxiety will assume themselves a failure if they have not done well on an exam. A test is only a test—dwelling on past mistakes will only keep you from focusing on the current or next challenge.
- Break tasks down into more manageable bits. (Time management will help this.) By setting more realistic goals, in terms of the level and extent of what can be accomplished, the emotional response will be less severe.
- Relax. If you find yourself becoming "worked up" over an upcoming exam, find ways to counteract the emotions (for example, try progressive relaxation, described in chapter 15, section 15-3d). Your anxious emotions will interfere with encoding information. Additionally, get plenty of sleep.
- During the test, practice relaxation, taking a moment to breathe deeply and close your eyes. Read through the entire exam, just to get a sense of what's there, and begin with the "friendly" questions—the ones you readily know the answers to. Focus your attention by not allowing yourself to worry about "What if I fail this exam." Relax again and focus only on the task at hand.

Most of these suggestions require practice and time. If your anxiety about tests is disrupting your performance and is a concern to you, go to your college's counseling services center and have them assess your test anxiety and provide you with help on trying to handle it.

KEY TERMS

acquaintance rape (p. 327)
bisexuality (p. 328)
Cannon-Bard theory (p. 342)
drive (p. 318)
drive reduction theory (p. 317)
emotion (p. 339)
extrinsic motivation (p. 320)
heterosexism (p. 329)
heterosexuality (p. 328)
hierarchy of needs (p. 320)
homeostasis (p. 317)

homosexuality (p. 328)
incentive (p. 319)
incentive theory (p. 319)
instinct (p. 317)
intrinsic motivation (p. 319)
James-Lange theory (p. 342)
motivation (p. 316)
need for achievement (n-Ach) (p. 336)
opponent-process theory (p. 347)
polygraph (p. 345)
rape myth (p. 327)

satiety (p. 333)
self-actualization (p. 321)
set point (p. 335)
sexual orientation (p. 328)
sexual response cycle (p. 325)
sexual script (p. 323)
testosterone (p. 325)
Thematic Apperception Test (TAT) (p. 336)
two-factor theory (p. 346)

REVIEW QUESTIONS

1. One of the clear advantages of the drive-reduction theory of motivation over instinct theory is that it
   a. explains why people engage in behaviors that do not reduce a drive.
   b. accounts for low levels of arousal as well as high levels of arousal.
   c. explains a much wider range of behavior than instinct theory.
   d. accounts for all areas of human motivation.
   e. does not rely on the role of learning in motivation.

2. The Yerkes-Dodson law
   a. describes the fixed level of optimal arousal at which all humans respond best.
   b. claims that arousal levels vary according to environmental factors, suggesting that individuals exhibit no consistency in arousal levels.
   c. states that individuals strive to maintain consistently low levels of arousal.
   d. states that individuals strive to maintain consistently high levels of arousal.
   e. states that individuals strive to maintain intermediate levels of arousal.

3. Research on intrinsic motivation indicates
   a. that the best method for enhancing a child's motivation for doing chores is a tangible reward such as money.
   b. that rewards based on verbal praise are less likely than those based on candy treats to undermine intrinsic motivation.
   c. little support for incentive theory, which focuses on the role of internal states in motivation.
   d. that intrinsic motivation leads a person to engage in behavior to obtain incentives.
   e. that the principal reason certain activities are extrinsically motivating is that they satisfy a need to feel competent and enhance one's sense of control over one's life.

4. According to research on sexual motivation,
   a. men report enjoying different types of sexual activity more than women.
   b. women desire more frequent sexual partners than men because it helps ensure that they will bear offspring.
   c. sex is motivated exclusively by physiological needs such as the pleasure instinct.
   d. sex is motivated exclusively by socioemotional needs, including the need for intimacy.
   e. evolutionary and sociocultural explanations for sexual motivation contradict one another.

5. Sociocultural explanations for gender differences in sexual behavior emphasize traditional sexual scripts, which
   a. describe playful approaches to sexual behavior that enhance motivation.
   b. are generally the same for men and women.
   c. are learned behaviors that emphasize male dominance (e.g., bragging) and female resistance to sexual advances.
   d. have been found helpful in reducing acquaintance rape, but not the rape myth.
   e. are not harmful, and may even be beneficial, in the context of consensual sexual relations.

6. Sexual orientation has been found to be associated with all of the following *except*
   a. differences in the size of the hypothalamus and the corpus callosum.
   b. childhood preferences for same-sex or opposite-sex activities.
   c. sexual orientation of identical twins.
   d. sexual orientation of parents and/or primary caregivers.
   e. childhood gender role and same-sex or other-sex friends.

7. The regulation of eating behavior is *not* associated with
   a. the presence of CCK in the blood.
   b. a hunger on-off switch located in the hypothalamus.
   c. external cues such as the rattling of dishes.
   d. neurotransmitters such as serotonin.
   e. the self-esteem of restrained eaters.

8. Researchers studying the effects of food deprivation and overeating have found that
   a. the number of fat cells individuals have may be related to their set point.
   b. when the body's fat cells fall below a certain limit, they release leptin, which increases hunger.
   c. when people gain or lose weight, they also gain or lose fat cells.
   d. the percentage of Americans 30 percent or more above their ideal body weight has decreased since 1991.
   e. it is not possible to change your body's set point.

9. Individuals with a high need for achievement are likely to
   a. be motivated by either a fear of failure or a desire for success.
   b. approach all achievement challenges with equally strong desires for success.
   c. choose extremely difficult or challenging tasks.
   d. choose extremely easy tasks to ensure the success they desire.
   e. have an intrinsic desire to succeed.

10. Achievement motivation may be enhanced by
    a. reducing emotional identification with the achievement task.
    b. frequent feedback when progress on the task is slow.
    c. convincing people that the task is something that is important to them.
    d. protecting the individual from experience with failure.
    e. providing easy tasks that guarantee success.

11. Emotions, defined as positive or negative feeling states or evaluative responses, share all of the following characteristics *except*
    a. the expression of emotions is not altered by learning or culture.
    b. emotions communicate information between people.
    c. emotions involve a variety of physiological reactions.
    d. emotions help individuals respond to changes in the environment.
    e. emotions are partly generated by cognitive appraisals of situations.

12. Cross-cultural research on emotions indicates
    a. that collectivist cultures experience emotions differently than individualist cultures.
    b. that individualist cultures can accurately read more emotions than collectivist cultures.
    c. that ten primary emotions have been identified across all cultures.
    d. support for the notion that facial expressions of emotion vary according to cultural beliefs.
    e. no differences among cultures in the facial expression of emotions.

13. Support for the James-Lange theory of emotion is evidenced by the finding that
    a. associations between specific physiological changes and emotional experiences vary by culture.
    b. emotional changes cannot be generated by changes in bodily states.
    c. the subjective experience of emotion involves cognition.
    d. anger and fear produce greater heart rate acceleration than happiness.
    e. the experience of emotion precedes the physiological changes that automatically occur in response to environmental stimuli.

14. Support for the two theories of emotion is seen in studies of the brain's role in producing and coordinating emotional responses, which show that
    a. the left cerebral hemisphere is more involved than the right in the expression of emotion.
    b. the second neural circuit involved in producing emotion passes through the cerebral cortex before activating the hypothalamus.
    c. the amygdala is involved only in the first neural circuit.
    d. complex emotions and conflicting emotions are associated with the second neural circuit.
    e. both sides of the brain are equally involved in expressing both positive and negative emotions.

15. According to Solomon's opponent-process theory of emotion,
    a. repeating an experience weakens the initial emotional reaction and strengthens the subsequent emotional reaction.
    b. the craving associated with drug abuse is motivated by the pleasure it provides.
    c. men who encountered an attractive female on a high bridge interpreted their arousal as being caused by fear rather than sexual attraction.
    d. the interpretation of emotional arousal in ambiguous situations will be influenced by cues in the immediate environment.
    e. repeating an experience strengthens the initial emotional reaction and weakens the subsequent emotional reaction.

Personality

Chapter Outline

"It is totally me, Dad!"

This was my daughter Amelia's reaction a few years ago upon reading the "personality profile" she received from the handwriting analysis machine at Michigan's Upper Peninsula State Fair. After slipping her signature into the "data entry" slot (and paying a two-dollar fee to the cashier), the lights on the graphology machine's cardboard façade flashed furiously prior to spitting out its evaluation. As Amelia marveled at the accuracy of her personality profile, I noticed a partially hidden worker placing a fresh stack of pretyped profiles into the "Completed Profile" slot behind the machine. At that moment, a scene from *The Wizard of Oz* ran through my mind. It is the scene where Dorothy returns to Oz and presents the dead witch's broom to the all-powerful Wizard. As the huge disembodied head of the Wizard blusters and bellows at Dorothy, her dog, Toto, pulls back a curtain revealing that the Wizard is really just an ordinary man manipulating people's impressions with smoke and mirrors.

On that day at the fair, I decided not to tell Amelia about the man behind the machine. Sometime later, however, we talked a bit about the validity of handwriting analysis, palm reading, and horoscopes. Put simply, these techniques that claim to assess personality have no scientific validity (Beyerstein & Beyerstein, 1992; Kelly, 1997). They provide assessments that appear remarkably accurate in divining our unique characteristics because they are either flattering to our egos or generally true of everybody (Forer, 1949). For example, consider the following generic description of personality:

> You are an independent thinker, but you have a strong need to be liked and respected by others. At times, you are outgoing and extraverted, while at other times, you are reserved and introverted. You have found it unwise to be too frank in revealing yourself to others. While you have some personality weaknesses, you can generally compensate for them. You tend to be critical of yourself. You have a great deal of potential, but you have not yet fully harnessed it. Some of your aspirations are pretty unrealistic.

When college students were provided with personality assessments similar to this one and told that an astrologer had prepared the profiles just for them, almost all the students evaluated the accuracy of these descriptions as either "good" or "excellent" (Davies, 1997; Glick et al., 1989). Further, after receiving their assessments, students were more likely to believe that astrology was a valid way to assess personality. This tendency to accept global and ambiguous feedback about oneself—even if the source of the information lacks credibility—is known as the *Barnum effect*, in honor of master showman P. T. Barnum. Barnum credited his success in the circus industry to the fact that "there's a sucker born every minute."

Now I am not suggesting that my daughter and the majority of college students are "suckers" waiting to be fleeced of their money by unscrupulous fortune hunters. I am suggesting that there is a more accurate—and yes, more ethical—way to understand our personalities. It is through the application of the scientific method (Cervone & Mischel, 2002). In this chapter, we continue our journey of discovery through psychology by venturing behind the scientific "curtain" of personality theory and research. I think you will find that this particular journey will reveal much more than the "smoke and mirror" effects typically created by graphologists, palm readers, and astrologers.

12-1 THE NATURE OF PERSONALITY

Before reading further, spend a few minutes identifying certain recurring ways in which you respond across a variety of situations. In addition, identify ways in which you think, feel, or behave that set you apart from many other people. Is there anything on this mental list that your culture might have shaped? Do any of these personal qualities help you to successfully meet life's challenges?

12-1a Consistency and Distinctiveness Define Personality

One important quality of personality is *consistency* in thinking, feeling, and acting. We consider people to be consistent when we see them responding in the same way in a variety of situations and over an extended period of time. Of course, people are not entirely consistent, but they must be consistent enough across many different situations and over time so that we notice that they have a characteristic way of thinking, feeling, and behaving. For instance, you may have a friend who argues at the drop of a hat. This aspect of his interaction style is consistent enough that you have a pretty good idea how he will act around others, regardless of whether they are friends, relatives, or strangers.

Distinctiveness is another important quality of personality because it is used to explain why everyone does not act the same in similar situations. Returning to the example of your argumentative friend, because most people generally try to find points of agreement when interacting with others, your friend's argumentative style is *distinctive*, setting him apart from most people.

Overall then, when we study personality, we are studying how people are consistent across situations and how they differ from one another. For our purposes, **personality** is defined as the *consistent* and *distinctive* thoughts, feelings, and behaviors that an individual engages in. This definition has its roots in philosophy as much as in science. For that reason, parts of this chapter may seem like they are describing a different kind of psychology— a more speculative and less data-driven psychology—than other parts of the chapter. You will most likely notice this during the discussion of psychoanalytic and humanistic approaches to personality. During the second half of the twentieth century, the study of personality followed the rest of the field of psychology and moved away from broad theorizing to scientifically testing hypotheses about personality functioning. Modern personality theorists tend to be much more limited and narrow in their approach to the field. This more modest approach has allowed for clearer descriptions of **personality styles,** though the more overarching and comprehensive descriptions that were present earlier have been lost (Magnavita, 2002). In the later sections of the chapter, these more modern approaches to studying personality functioning are represented by the trait and social-cognitive theories. We also examine various means of assessing or describing personality.

> **Personality:** The consistent and distinctive thoughts, feelings, and behaviors in which an individual engages.

> **Personality styles:** Collection or constellation of traits that describes the functioning of the person across situations and settings.

12-1b Culture and Evolutionary Processes Shape Personality

Personality psychology was developed and has flourished in the North American and Western European social climate of *individualism*. This philosophy of life conceives of persons as being unique, independent entities, separate from their social surroundings. In contrast, *collectivism* emphasizes group needs and desires over those of the individual (Singelis et al., 1995). During the past 25 years, as psychology has become more of an international science, personality theorists in individualist societies have devoted more attention to investigating how personality is a product of the individual's interaction with her or his social settings. In adopting this approach, personality theorists are thinking about human behavior in a way similar to that of collectivists (Brislin, 1993; Triandis & Suh, 2002). This *interactionist* perspective on personality is discussed at various points in this chapter (see sections 12-4e and 12-5a).

In addition to the influence that cultural beliefs can have on the study of personality, research further suggests that cultural beliefs can actually shape personality development (Diaz-Guerrero et al., 2001). For example, people from collectivist Latin cultures are often taught to have *simpatía*, which is a way of relating to others that is empathic, respectful, unselfish, and maintains harmonious social relationships (Marín, 1994). Individuals who internalize these social norms will develop a personality style that is characteristic of their social group.

Although personality styles may be associated with particular cultures, most personality researchers strive to identify universal aspects of personality. In this regard, a growing number of social scientists are beginning to examine how certain aspects of personality have been shaped over the course of our species' evolutionary history (Buss, 1999; MacDonald, 1998). According to this viewpoint, because the evolutionary process is the only known creative process capable of producing complex organisms, all theories of human nature, including personality theories, must consider the basic principles of evolution by natural selection (see chapter 1, section 1-3e). Consistent with this viewpoint, in this chapter we periodically offer an evolutionary accounting of personality.

SECTION SUMMARY

- Personality research examines how people are consistent across situations and how they differ from one another.

- Not only does culture influence how personality is studied, but many contemporary psychologists study how cultural and evolutionary forces shape personalities.

12-2 THE PSYCHOANALYTIC PERSPECTIVE

The most recognizable person in the field of psychology is someone who was not trained as a psychologist—namely, Sigmund Freud. Freud (1856–1939) grew up in Austria, was trained as a physician in Vienna, and aspired to become a university professor (Gardner, 1993). Early in his professional career as a medical doctor, he studied the nervous system in the hope of applying newly discovered principles of physics and chemistry to the functioning of the human mind. In addition to teaching and doing laboratory work, Freud worked with patients (mostly women) who complained about problems with the functioning of their nervous systems. However, he frequently discovered that their symptoms seemed to originate from emotional trauma. Over time, Freud developed the idea that the young science of psychology held answers to many of these perplexing disorders (Freud, 1917).

An example of the kind of medical problem that set Freud on his journey of discovery into psychology was a strange neurological-like condition referred to as *glove anesthesia* (see chapter 13, section 13-3e, discussion of *conversion disorders*). In this condition, the patient had no feeling from her wrists to the tips of her fingers, but she did have feeling in her forearms. "Glove" anesthesia is not consistent with the way the nervous system functions, which suggested to Freud that its cause was not physiological, but psychological (Freud, 1950/1895). As you will see, this idea revolutionized the study of personality in the early 1900s (Stanovich, 1996; Westen, 1998).

12-2a Psychoanalytic Theory Asserts That the Unconscious Controls Behavior

When Freud suspected that some of the medical problems of his patients were, in fact, caused by emotional disturbances, he sought the advice of French neurologist Jean Charcot, who was treating such patients using hypnosis (Gay, 1998). Freud was also impressed by psychiatrist Joseph Breuer's "talking cure" therapy, in which patients with emotional problems were told to report whatever came to mind. Adapting these two techniques to his own emerging theory of the human mind, Freud encouraged his patients to talk about their symptoms and what was occurring when they emerged. As they did this, Freud developed the idea that their symptoms were psychologically related to some sort of problem or dilemma they were experiencing. For instance, the previously described glove anesthesia of one of his young patients developed soon after she became aware of her emerging sexual urges. Stimulating herself with her hand was simultaneously very pleasurable and extremely anxiety inducing. To prevent the expression of this unacceptable urge to sexually gratify herself, Freud believed that the woman unconsciously "deadened" her hand, making it unusable. Piecing together his patients' accounts of their lives while under hypnosis, Freud believed that he had discovered the unconscious mind.

Freud's model of the mind proposed that it was mostly hidden, like an iceberg (Freud, 1917). As depicted in figure 12-1, our **conscious mind** is the relatively small part of our mind that we are aware of at the moment, like the tip of the iceberg that is visible above the surface of the water. Right now, your conscious processes include (I hope!) the material from the previous sentences, perhaps an awareness of certain stimuli in your surroundings, and maybe the thought that you would like to be doing something else other than reading this book. Immediately below the surface of the conscious mind resides the **preconscious mind,** which consists of those mental processes that are not currently conscious but could become so at any moment. Examples of preconscious material might include your parents' phone number, hopefully some of the material from previous sections of this book, and a conversation you had yesterday with a friend. Below this preconscious level resides the unconscious mind, which is like the huge section of the iceberg that is hidden in the water's depths. The **unconscious mind** is driven by biological urges that have been shaped by our evolutionary history, and it contains thoughts, desires, feelings, and memories that are not consciously available to us but that nonetheless shape our everyday behavior. Examples of unconscious material are painful, forgotten memories from childhood, hidden feelings of hostility toward someone you profess to like (or even love), and sexual urges that would create intense anxiety if you became aware of them.

The significance of Freud's theory of the mind in the history of psychology cannot be overstated. Essentially, it challenged the prevailing notion that our consciousness—the part of our mind that we identify as ourselves—was the determining factor in the management and control of our lives. As you will see in later sections of this chapter, opposition to Freud's perspective on the determinants of human behavior spawned a number of competing personality theories.

Conscious mind: According to Freud, the relatively small part of our mind that we are aware of at the moment.

Preconscious mind: According to Freud, those mental processes that are not currently conscious but could become so at any moment.

Unconscious mind: According to Freud, the thoughts, desires, feelings, and memories that are not consciously available to us but that nonetheless shape our everyday behavior.

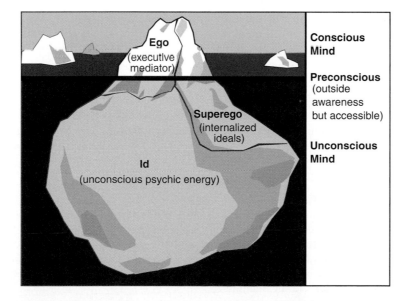

FIGURE 12-1
Freud's Model of Personality Structure

In Freud's theory of personality, the mind is likened to an iceberg, with the conscious mind being the relatively small part of the iceberg visible above the water line and the unconscious being that part of the iceberg well below the surface. In this metaphor, the ego is that aspect of the personality that includes part of our conscious mind and part of our unconscious mind. The same is true of the superego. In contrast, the id is the completely unconscious aspect of personality.

Imagine for a minute how you might behave if you had no ego and, instead, simply acted on your id desires. While walking through a park, you become hungry. Nearby, three people are eating lunch. Without hesitating, you lunge at them, fighting and clawing for all the food that you can carry. How long do you think you would survive with an unregulated id?

Id: An entirely unconscious part of the mind that contains our sexual and aggressive drives.

Pleasure principle: The process by which the id seeks to immediately satisfy whatever desire is currently active.

Ego: The part of our minds that includes our consciousness and that balances the demands of the id, superego, and reality.

Reality principle: The process by which the ego seeks to delay gratification of id desires until appropriate outlets and situations can be found.

Superego: The part of our minds that includes our conscience and counterbalances the more primitive demands of the id.

12-2b Freud Divided Personality into the Id, Ego, and Superego

As Freud continued treating patients who came to him with psychological problems, he proposed another dimension to his theory of the mind, which came to be called the *structural model* (Moore & Fine, 1990). According to Freud, personality consisted of three subcomponents or structures: the id, the ego, and the superego. Each structure has different operating principles and different goals, and frequently the goals of one component conflict with the goals of another component. This model of the mind is sometimes called a *conflict model* because it attempts to explain how psychological conflicts determine behavior.

The **id**—which in Latin means "it"—is an entirely unconscious portion of the mind. It contains the basic drives for reproduction, survival, and aggression. The id operates on the **pleasure principle,** meaning that it consistently wants to satisfy whatever desire is currently active as quickly and directly as possible. The id's agenda, as directed by the pleasure principle, might be summarized by the statement "if it feels good, do it." Freud believed that newborn infants represent the purest form of id impulses, crying whenever their needs are not immediately satisfied. He further proposed that a part of our personality continues to function like those newborns—wanting needs met immediately—throughout our lives.

One of life's realties is that our needs are very seldom immediately satisfied. Freud asserted that, as infants, whenever immediate gratification does not occur, we experience distress and anxiety. As a way to cope with this infantile stress, the **ego**—which in Latin means "I"—develops out of the id. Its function is to be the decision-making part of the personality that satisfies id impulses in socially acceptable ways. In performing this function, the ego is both partially conscious and partially unconscious. The conscious part of the ego is in contact with external reality, while the unconscious part is in contact with the id. In seeking id satisfaction, the ego is guided by the **reality principle,** which is the process by which it seeks to delay gratification of id desires until appropriate outlets and situations can be found. The ego is interested in achieving pleasure but learns that this will more likely occur if the constraints of reality are taken into account.

The **superego**—which in Latin means "over the I"—develops later in childhood, around the age of 4 or 5. The superego has several functions, including the task of overseeing the ego and making sure that it acts morally. As such, the superego is concerned not just with what is acceptable but also with what is ideal. It provides us with a conscience, making us feel guilty when we do "wrong" and instilling pride when we do "good." Essentially, the superego represents the internalization of cultural norms and values into the individual mind. Not surprisingly, the superego and the id are frequently at odds about the proper course of action in a given situation. The ego balances the demands of the id and superego, along with those of external reality, to generate behavior that will still bring pleasure.

Although this description of the three personality components appears to suggest that the ego (our conscious self) is controlling our behavior, Freud contends that this is largely an illusion. Throughout our daily activities, we are generally unaware of the unconscious compromises that our ego makes to create a particular outcome. For exam-

---

INFO-BIT: For many years, Hollywood has incorporated Freud's personality theory into many of its movies. One of the more entertaining films with a Freudian slant is the 1956 science-fiction classic, *Forbidden Planet*. In this movie, an Earth scientist living on a distant planet greatly expands the power of his mind—and unknowingly, his id—by using alien technology. When a space cruiser from planet Earth visits, his id—externalized as an invisible monster—destroys anyone who expresses sexual interest in the scientist's lovely daughter.

Journey of Discovery Question

An increasing number of contemporary personality theorists pay attention to how culture and evolutionary forces shape personality. Is there any evidence in Freud's theory of personality that he considered the impact that culture and evolution had on personality?

ple, a college sophomore may agree to spend hours tutoring a group of first-year students, unaware of how his sexual attraction to one member of the group figured in his decision. He may be conscious of feeling altruistic about helping these students, and thus his superego is satisfied, but he is largely unaware of how his ego has unconsciously allowed his id to be gratified as well.

12-2c Personality Development Occurs in Psychosexual Stages

As Freud listened to his patients during therapy, they repeatedly mentioned significant events from their childhood that left them with emotional scars. Based on his patient's reconstruction of their lives, Freud created a theory about how personality develops and how the ego and superego come into existence (Stern, 1985). Consistent with the idea that personality involves a degree of consistency, his psychoanalytic theory proposed that children pass through a fixed sequence of **psychosexual stages.** Each stage is characterized by a part of the body, called an *erogenous zone*, through which the id primarily seeks sexual pleasure. Critical elements of the personality are formed during each of these stages (see table 12-1). If children experience conflicts when seeking pleasure during a particular psychosexual stage, and if these conflicts go unresolved, they will become psychologically "stuck"—or *fixated*—at that stage. **Fixation** is a tendency to persist in pleasure-seeking behaviors associated with an earlier psychosexual stage where conflicts were unresolved. One important point to keep in mind about fixation is that the conflicts that trigger fixation can be caused by either too little or too much gratification of id desires.

Oral Stage

The first stage of psychosexual development, which encompasses the first year of life, is referred to as the **oral stage.** During this stage, infants are totally dependent on those around them to care for their needs, especially nourishment. Freud believed that the id derived intense sexual pleasure by engaging in oral activities such as sucking, biting, and chewing. Adults with fixations at the oral stage are often extremely clingy and emotionally dependent on others. In attempting to satisfy oral needs, they might smoke excessively and/or spend a great deal of time eating and thinking about eating.

Anal Stage

The **anal stage** follows the oral stage, as the focus of erotic pleasure shifts from the mouth to the process of elimination. This psychosexual stage begins at about 2 years of age when toilet training becomes an area of conflict between children and parents. Freud argued that, from the child's point of view, toilet training represents the parents' attempt at denying the child's primary pleasure by exerting control over where and when they urinate and defecate. Fixation at this stage, caused by overly harsh toilet-training experiences, produces children who too closely conform to the demands of parents and other caretakers. As adults, they will be excessively neat and orderly (this is the source of the term *anal retentive*). Overly relaxed toilet-training experiences can also cause fixation, with individuals forever being messy and having difficulty complying with authority and keeping their behavior under control (*anal expulsive*). Successful negotiation of this stage results in a capacity to engage in directed work without being dominated by the need to perform perfectly.

Psychosexual stages: The fixed sequence of childhood developmental stages during which the id primarily seeks sexual pleasure by focusing its energies on distinct erogenous zones.

Fixation: A tendency to persist in pleasure-seeking behaviors associated with an earlier psychosexual stage where conflicts were unresolved.

Oral stage: In Freud's theory, the first stage of psychosexual development during which the child derives pleasure by engaging in oral activities.

Anal stage: In Freud's theory, the second stage of psychosexual development during which the child derives pleasure from defecation.

TABLE 12-1 **Freud's Stages of Psychosexual Development**	**Stage**	**Approximate Age**	**Erogenous Zone**	**Key Tasks and Experiences**
	Oral	0–1	Mouth (sucking, biting)	Weaning (from breast or bottle)
	Anal	2–3	Anus (defecating)	Toilet training
	Phallic	4–5	Genitals (masturbating)	Coping with Oedipal/Electra conflict and identifying with same-sex parent
	Latency	6–11	None (sexual desires repressed)	Developing same-sex contacts
	Genital	Puberty onward	Genitals (being sexually intimate)	Establishing mature sexual relationships

Phallic Stage

Phallic stage: In Freud's theory, the third stage of psychosexual development during which the child derives pleasure from masturbation.

At about age 4, children enter the **phallic stage,** which is characterized by a shift in the erogenous zone to the genitals and pleasure being derived largely through self-stimulation. According to Freud, accompanying this interest in genital stimulation is the association of this pleasure with the other-sex parent. Freud asserted that boys develop an erotic attachment to their mothers and girls develop a similar attachment to their fathers. Soon, however, children realize that they are in competition with their same-sex parents for the attention and affection of their other-sex parents. Among boys, Freud related this dilemma to a character in ancient Greek literature, Oedipus Rex, who became king by unknowingly marrying his mother after murdering his father. This *Oedipus complex* arouses fear in boys that their fathers will punish them for their sexual desires for the mother. Freud asserted that this fear of the loss of genital pleasure is psychologically represented as *castration anxiety,* which is the fear that the father will cut off the penis. Among girls, instead of being afraid that their mothers will harm them, Freud believed that girls are likely to express anger because they believe that their mothers have already inflicted the harm: by removing their penis. This "mother conflict" is known as the *Electra complex,* after another Greek character that had her mother killed. Freud asserted that the *penis envy* that girls experience during this stage stems from their belief that this anatomical "deficiency" is evidence that they are inferior to boys.

Successful negotiation of the phallic stage requires that children purge their sexual desires for their other-sex parents and bury their fear and anger toward their same-sex parents. Children accomplish these dual feats by identifying with the competitive parents. According to Freud, this process of identification is critical for the development of a healthy adult personality because this is how children internalize their parents' values. This internalization of parental values—which generally mirror larger societal values—is critical in the development of the superego. Less successful negotiation of this stage can cause people to become chronically timid because they fear that they do not "measure up" to their rivaled same-sex parent.

Latency Stage

Latency stage: In Freud's theory, the fourth stage of psychosexual development during which the child is relatively free from sexual desires and conflict.

From about ages 6 to 11, children are in a psychological period of relative calm called the **latency stage.** During this time, the content of the dramatic struggles in the oral, anal, and phallic stages are forgotten by the ego. Although the ego is relatively free from interference by the id, sexual, aggressive, and other id impulses are still present and must be managed. Often this is accomplished by channeling these desires into socially acceptable activities in school, sports, and the arts.

Genital Stage

Latency is followed by puberty and the onset of the **genital stage.** During adolescence, many of the issues of the earlier stages re-emerge and can be reworked to a certain extent. Mature sexual feelings toward others also begin to emerge, and the ego learns to manage and direct these feelings. Of all the stages, Freud spent the least amount of time discussing the psychological dynamics of the genital stage. This was probably due to his belief that personality was largely determined by age 5.

> **Genital stage:** In Freud's theory, the last stage of psychosexual development during which mature sexual feelings toward others begin to emerge, and the ego learns to manage and direct these feelings.

12-2d Defense Mechanisms Reduce or Redirect Unconsciously Caused Anxiety

When Freud was first developing his theory of the mind, he proposed that people managed to move anxiety-arousing thoughts into the unconscious through the use of a very basic defense mechanism that he called **repression.** As Freud's model developed from a relatively simple one to greater levels of complexity, he developed the idea that the ego uses a variety of more sophisticated **defense mechanisms** to keep threatening and unacceptable material out of consciousness and thereby reduce anxiety (Freud, 1926). His daughter, Anna Freud (1936), later more fully described how these ego defense mechanisms reduce anxiety.

Defense mechanisms are very important features of psychoanalytic theory because they explain why humans—who Freud believed are essentially driven by sexual and aggressive urges—can become civilized (Domino et al., 2002). Furthermore, Freud asserted that the particular defense mechanisms that people rely on most often in adapting to life's challenges become distinguishing features of their personalities. Thus, Freud would tell us that although we have probably used most of the defense mechanisms described in table 12-2 at least once in our lives, our personality can be described by that configuration of defenses that we rely on most heavily. He would also say that under extreme stress, we may begin to use more powerful defenses, which are also more primitive and are associated with psychological disorders.

Rationalization is probably one of the more familiar defense mechanisms. It involves offering seemingly logical self-justifying explanations for our attitudes, beliefs, or behavior in place of the real, unconscious reasons. For instance, we might say that we are punishing someone "for her own good," when in reality the punishment primarily serves to express our anger at the person. Have you ever been romantically rejected, and

> **Repression:** In Freud's theory, a very basic defense mechanism in which people move anxiety-arousing thoughts from the conscious mind into the unconscious mind.
>
> **Defense mechanisms:** In Freud's theory, the ego's methods of keeping threatening and unacceptable material out of consciousness and thereby reducing anxiety.

> **Rationalization:** A defense mechanism in which people offer logical self-justifying explanations for their actions in place of the real, more anxiety-producing, unconscious reasons.

TABLE 12-2

Major Ego Defense Mechanisms

Repression	Pushing high anxiety-inducing thoughts out of consciousness, keeping them unconscious; this is the most basic of the defense mechanisms
Rationalization	Offering seemingly logical self-justifying explanations for attitudes, beliefs, or behavior in place of the real unconscious reasons
Reaction formation	Preventing unacceptable feelings or ideas from being directly expressed by expressing opposing feelings or ideas
Displacement	Discharging sexual or aggressive urges toward objects that are more acceptable than those that initially created the arousal
Projection	Perceiving one's own sexual or aggressive urges not in oneself but in others
Regression	Psychologically retreating to an earlier developmental stage where psychic energy remains fixated

Reaction formation: A defense mechanism allowing people to express unacceptable feelings or ideas by consciously expressing their exact opposite.

Displacement: A defense mechanism that diverts people's sexual or aggressive urges toward objects that are more acceptable than those that actually stimulate their feelings.

Projection: A powerful defense mechanism in which people perceive their own aggressive or sexual urges not in themselves, but in others.

Regression: A defense mechanism in which people faced with intense anxiety psychologically retreat to a more infantile developmental stage, where some psychic energy remains fixated.

then convinced yourself that you never really cared for the person in the first place? Freud might say that this was your ego's attempt to defend you against feeling worthless.

Reaction formation allows us to express an unacceptable feeling or idea by consciously expressing its exact opposite. Thus, if we are interested in sex (and according to Freud we all are), but are uncomfortable with this interest, we might devote ourselves to combating pornography. Such action allows us to think about sex, but in an acceptable way. Of course, there are nondefensive reasons to oppose pornography or to engage in other activities that could indicate a reaction formation. In fact, one of Freud's primary ideas is that all human actions are *multiply determined*, meaning that each behavior has many causes.

Displacement is a defense mechanism that diverts our sexual or aggressive urges toward objects that are more acceptable than the one that actually stimulates our feelings. This is commonly referred to as the "kick the dog" defense, when we unconsciously vent our aggressive impulses toward a threatening teacher, parent, or boss onto a helpless creature, such as the family pet. Similarly, we might displace sexual feelings away from a parent because that is unacceptable and, instead, date someone who is remarkably like dear old mom or dad.

Projection is one of the more powerful defense mechanisms and can involve quite serious distortions of other's motivations. In projection, we perceive our own aggressive or sexual urges not in ourselves, but in others. Thus an insecure person may falsely accuse other people of being insecure, while not recognizing this characteristic in her own personality. Freud contended that we are more likely to use projection when we are feeling strongly threatened, either by the strength of our feelings or when we are in particularly stressful situations. Soldiers in combat, for instance, may begin to see everyone around them as potential enemies who could hurt them.

Another powerful defense mechanism is **regression**, which occurs when we cannot psychologically function in our current surroundings due to anxiety, and we psychologically retreat to a more infantile developmental stage where some psychic energy remains fixated. For example, following the birth of a younger sibling that threatens an older child's sense of "place" in the family, he may lose control of bowel or bladder functions, or return to thumb sucking. When this occurs in adults, it may be a relatively contained regression, such as talking like a baby when working with an authority figure.

12-2e There Are Many Variations of Psychoanalytic Theory

In the 100 years since Freud began developing his personality theory, we have learned a great deal about human behavior, and many psychologists have worked to adapt Freud's theories to what we have learned about how people function. Yet, the process of revising Freud's ideas actually began during his lifetime. Three of his closest coworkers, Alfred Adler, Carl Jung, and Karen Horney, disagreed about the central role of sexual drives in the determination of people's personalities (Hogan & Smither, 2001; Mayer, 2002). Freud, an authoritarian individual who demanded strict obedience from his followers, reacted very negatively to such criticism. Let us briefly examine the ideas of some of those individuals who refused to follow Freud's lead. These personality theories, along with Freud's original theory of psychoanalysis, are often placed under the general label of *psychodynamic theories* (see chapter 13, section 13-1c).

Adler's Individual Psychology

In 1902, Alfred Adler (1870–1937) joined Freud's inner circle of "disciples," but he soon began developing his own ideas about how personality developed. His view of personality stressed social factors more than did Freud's theory. The Freud-Adler relationship ended in 1911 when Adler proposed his individual psychology, which downplayed the importance of sexual motivation and, instead, asserted that people strive for superiority. By this, Adler meant that children generally feel weak and incompetent compared with adults and older children. In turn, these feelings of inferiority motivate them to acquire new skills and develop their untapped potential. However, for some individuals, if the sense of inferiority is excessively strong, they simply seek to obtain outward symbols of status and power, such as money and expensive possessions. By flaunting their success, they try to hide their continuing sense of inferiority.

Jung's Analytical Psychology

Carl Jung (pronounced "Yoong"; 1875–1961), a native of Switzerland and the son of a Protestant pastor, was inspired to become a psychoanalyst after reading Freud's *The Interpretation of Dreams* (Freud, 1900/1953). In 1906, they became close friends and Freud viewed his younger protégé as the person most capable of carrying on his work. However, in 1914, after Jung challenged some of Freud's central ideas concerning personality development, their friendship abruptly ended. Jung called his psychodynamic approach *analytical psychology*. Like Adler, Jung de-emphasized the sex motive, but unlike Adler, Jung agreed with Freud that the unconscious mind had a powerful effect on people's lives. Yet, for Jung, the unconscious was less of a reservoir for repressed childhood conflicts and more of a reservoir of images from our species' evolutionary past. He asserted that besides our personal unconscious, we also have a **collective unconscious,** which is that part of the unconscious mind containing inherited memories shared by all human beings. Jung called these inherited memories **archetypes,** and he believed that they reveal themselves when our conscious mind is distracted (as in fantasies or art) or inactive (as in dreams). Jung further believed that archetypes are represented in the religious symbols found throughout the world. Key archetypal figures are *mother, father, wise old person, God,* and *the hero.*

Although Jung's idea of the collective unconscious has generally been dismissed in mainstream psychology, it has had considerably greater influence in other disciplines, such as anthropology, art, literature, and religious studies (Neher, 1996; Tacey, 2001). One aspect of his personality theory that has been incorporated into mainstream personality theories is the idea that we are born with tendencies to direct our psychological energies either into our inner self or into the outside world (Jung, 1921). **Introverts** are preoccupied with the inner world and tend to be hesitant and cautious when interacting with people. In contrast, **extraverts** are focused on the external world and tend to be confident and socially outgoing.

Horney's Neo-Freudian Perspective

German physician Karen Horney (pronounced "HOR-nigh"; 1885–1952) was the first influential female psychoanalyst. Like Adler, Horney (1945) believed that social factors played a much larger role in personality development than sexual influences. Instead of personality problems being caused by fixation of psychic energy, Horney believed that problems in interpersonal relationships during childhood created anxiety; this anxiety caused later personality problems. Developmental psychologists later expanded on these ideas by studying how parent-child emotional attachments shape children's personality (see chapter 4, section 4-2a). She was also instrumental in confronting some of Freud's assertions concerning female personality development (Gilman, 2001; Ingram, 2001). Whereas Freud proposed that gender differences in behavior were due to biological factors, Horney proposed social and cultural explanations. Although conceding that women often feel inferior to men, Horney (1926/1967) claimed that this is not due to penis envy, but rather, because of the sexism that denied women equal opportunities. What women really envied was the social power and privilege that men enjoyed in the larger society.

An Overall Evaluation of Freud's Legacy

Freud's impact on psychology cannot be dismissed. Indeed, his influence extends into other disciplines that study humans and their behavior, such as anthropology, sociology, literature, and history. Yet, a major limitation of his personality theory is that it is not based on carefully controlled scientific research (Crews, 1998). Indeed, his entire theory is based on a handful of cases from his clinical practice that do not constitute a

Collective unconscious: In Jung's personality theory, the part of the unconscious mind containing inherited memories shared by all human beings.

Archetypes: In Jung's personality theory, inherited images that are passed down from our prehistoric ancestors and that reveal themselves as universal symbols in dreams, religion, and art.

Introverts: People who are preoccupied with their inner world and tend to be hesitant and cautious when interacting with people.

Extraverts: People who are focused on the external world and tend to be confident and socially outgoing.

representative sampling of the human population. As you know from our discussion of scientific methods in chapter 2, section 2-1b, a theory's usefulness is difficult to determine if the research sample does not represent the population of interest. Further, recent reexaminations of Freud's case notes suggests that he may have distorted some of his patient's histories so that they conformed to his view of personality (Esterson, 1993). Related to these criticisms is the fact that Freud did not welcome anyone questioning or challenging his ideas (Gardner, 1993). Such a stance is typical of cult leaders, but not of those who want to advance scientific understanding.

Another criticism of Freud's theory is that many of its psychological processes—such as the id—cannot be observed, much less measured. If aspects of his theory cannot be scientifically tested, then of what use are they to the science of psychology? Further, when scientific studies have tested some of Freud's concepts, they have found little evidence to support the existence of the Oedipal/Electra complex, penis envy, or many of his ideas on sexual and aggressive drives (Crews, 1998).

Despite the inability to test certain portions of Freud's personality theory, and despite the lack of evidence for other portions that have been scientifically tested, his ideas still have an influence within psychology because a few of his general ideas concerning personality have received widespread empirical support (Lichtenberg, 1989; Pine, 1990; Westen & Gabbard, 1999). These general ideas are that (1) unconscious processes shape human behavior; (2) childhood experiences shape adult personality; and (3) learning to regulate impulses is critical for healthy development. Given these continuing contributions, psychoanalysis still deserves recognition as an important, albeit flawed, perspective on personality.

SECTION SUMMARY

- According to Freud, much of what determines human behavior takes place in the unconscious mind.

- Freud's three personality structures are the id (entirely unconscious part of the personality that contains our sexual and aggressive urges), the ego (the part of the personality that balances the demands of the id, superego, and reality), and the superego (the part of the personality that counterbalances the more primitive id demands).

- Psychosexual stages include the oral stage, anal stage, phallic stage, latency stage, and genital stage.

- The conscious part of the ego is protected from awareness of disturbing id impulses because defense mechanisms transform raw id desires into more acceptable actions.

- Alfred Adler emphasized personal striving to overcome feelings of inferiority.

- Carl Jung emphasized how our thoughts and actions are influenced by a collective unconscious.

- Karen Horney stressed how social and cultural factors influence female personality.

- Psychoanalytic theory has two major limitations: (1) it is not based on carefully controlled scientific research; and (2) many of its concepts cannot be measured.

12-3 THE HUMANISTIC PERSPECTIVE

In the early years of psychology, William James (1890) wrote freely and eloquently about what he called psychology's "most puzzling puzzle" (p. 330), the self. However, when behaviorism became the dominant perspective in psychology during the early decades of the twentieth century, anything that could not be directly observed was not considered to be a legitimate topic for psychological inquiry. As a result of this behaviorist influence, the scientific study of the self was virtually nonexistent for many decades. Then in the 1950s, a new perspective arose largely due to many psychologists' dissatisfaction with both the behaviorists' and psychoanalysts' views of human nature. This "third wave" in psychology, known as the *humanistic perspective* (see chapter 1, section 1-3b), emphasized people's innate capacity for personal growth and their ability to consciously make choices. Carl Rogers and Abraham Maslow were the primary architects of humanistic psychology, and they both contended that psychologists should study people's unique subjective mental experience of the world. This stance represented a direct challenge to behaviorism and was instrumental in focusing renewed attention on the self. Further, by emphasizing the possibilities for positive change that people can make at any point in their lives, the humanistic perspective stood in sharp contrast to the more pessimistic tone of the psychoanalytic perspective (Cassel, 2000).

12-3a Rogers's Person-Centered Theory Emphasizes Self-Realization

Carl Rogers (1902–1987) believed that people are basically good and that we all are working toward becoming the best that we can be (Rogers, 1961). Rogers asserted that, instead of being driven by sexual and aggressive desires, we are motivated by a wish to be good, and that we would achieve our potential if we were given **unconditional positive regard.** Unfortunately, according to Rogers, many of us are frustrated in our potential growth because important people in our lives often only provide us with positive regard if we meet their standards. Being the recipient of this **conditional positive regard** stunts our personal growth because in our desire to be regarded positively, we lose sight of our *ideal self,* which is the person whom we would like to become. Rogers stated that as we continue to adjust our lives to meet others' expectations, the discrepancy between our *actual self,* which is the person we know ourselves to be now, and our ideal self becomes greater.

Rogers's theory of personality is as much about how people change as it is a theory about how people are at any given moment. For him, the dilemma of personality involves how people's thwarted growth potential can be released. The answer to this dilemma is for people with damaged selves, or low self-esteem, to find someone who will treat them with unconditional positive regard. The assumption here is that when people are accepted for who they are, they will eventually come to accept themselves as well. When this self-acceptance occurs, people put aside the standards of others that are false for them, and they get back on track in developing their true selves (Truax & Carkhuff, 1967). Conveying unconditional positive regard to others involves the following three characteristics: *genuineness* (being open and honest), *warmth* (being caring and nurturant), and *empathy* (accurately identifying what the person is thinking and feeling).

Unconditional positive regard: An attitude of complete acceptance toward another person regardless of what she or he has said or done; it is based on the belief in that person's essential goodness.

Conditional positive regard: An attitude of acceptance toward another person only when she or he meets your standards.

12-3b Maslow's Self-Actualization Theory Stresses Maximizing Potential

Like Rogers, Abraham Maslow (1908–1970) was interested in people's ability to reach their full potential. As discussed in chapter 11, section 11-1f, this process of fulfilling one's potential was what Maslow (1970) called *self-actualization.* Like Rogers and Freud, Maslow used the case study method in developing his theory. However, unlike Rogers and Freud, Maslow studied healthy, creative people rather than those who were troubled and seeking therapy. He chose as his subjects people who had led or were leading rich and productive lives, including outstanding college students, faculty, professionals in other fields, and historical figures, such as Abraham Lincoln, Thomas Jefferson, and Eleanor Roosevelt (Moss, 1999; Rathunde, 2001).

Maslow found that self-actualized people were secure in the sense of who they were and therefore were not paralyzed by others' opinions. They were also loving and caring, and they often focused their energies on a particular task, one they often regarded as a life mission. Maslow also reported that these people had experienced personal or spiritual **peak experiences,** which are fleeting but intense moments of joy, ecstasy, and absorption, in which people feel extremely capable. A peak experience can occur while a person is

Peak experiences: Fleeting but intense moments when a person feels happy, absorbed, and extremely capable.

engaging in a religious activity or service, while performing athletically, listening to music, or while relating to a lover. Some women report their childbirth experiences to be peak experiences. Although anyone can have peak experiences, Maslow's group of self-actualizing people reported both more peak experiences and that the quality of those experiences was richer than the experiences reported by others whom he studied. These peak experiences have a lasting effect on those who experience them, enriching their outlook and causing them to become more open to the experiences of others.

12-3c The Humanistic Perspective Has Been Criticized As Being Overly Optimistic

Like Freud, humanistic psychologists have had a significant impact on popular culture. If you look in the self-help section in any bookstore, you will find numerous titles emphasizing the control that you have to change your life and achieve your full potential. However, in trying to correct for Freud's gloomy outlook on human nature, the humanistic perspective on personality may have overshot the mark and failed to acknowledge that many people engage in mean-spirited and even cruel behavior on a fairly regular basis. The truth is that people have the capacity to act in a wide variety of ways. Further, a wide variety of forces act to determine behavior, some of which we are aware and others that we are not.

Although humanistic psychology helped revitalize attention to the self in psychology, one of its major limitations is that it has not produced a substantial body of testable hypotheses for its personality theories. Like Freud before them, humanistic psychologists have not clearly defined their concepts and have often rejected the use of carefully controlled scientific studies to test the validity of their theories. As a result, most of the scientific investigations of the self have come from outside the humanistic perspective (Bar-On, 2001; MacDonald & Holland, 2002).

12-3d The Self Has Become an Important Area of Study in Psychology

Although humanistic psychologists' attention to the self did not generate a great deal of research, it did help to keep the concept alive in psychology during a time when behaviorism was the dominant perspective. Today, the self is one of the most popular areas of scientific study, and self-related constructs are important explanatory tools of the discipline (Robins et al., 1999). Two self topics that are central to humanistic psychology are self-concept and self-esteem. As previously discussed in chapter 4, section 4-2e, *self-concept* is the "theory" that a person constructs about herself or himself through social interaction, whereas *self-esteem* is a person's evaluation of his or her self-concept. Before reading further, spend a few minutes completing the self-esteem scale in table 12-3.

Over the years, there has been an ongoing debate regarding self-esteem and self-concept (Seta & Donaldson, 1999). *Self-enhancement theories* propose that people are primarily motivated to maintain high self-esteem, whereas *self-verification theories* assert that people are primarily motivated to maintain consistent beliefs about themselves, even when these self-beliefs are negative (Dunning et al., 1995; Swann, 1997). For those with high self-esteem, there is no conflict between these two motives because receiving positive evaluations from others verifies positive self-beliefs. However, for individuals with low self-esteem, these two motives often conflict: The need for self-enhancement causes those with low self-esteem to seek positive evaluations, but that action conflicts with their desire to verify existing negative self-beliefs. Self-enhancement theorists contend that people with low self-esteem will seek out positive social evaluations because it will bolster their self-esteem. In contrast, self-verification theorists argue that this positive feedback will create the fear in low self-esteem people that they may not know themselves after all, and therefore, they will reject it. Which of these perspectives is correct?

TABLE 12-3

Self-Esteem Scale

Instructions: Read each item below and then indicate how well each statement describes you, using the following response scale:

    0 = extremely uncharacteristic (not at all like me)
    1 = uncharacteristic (somewhat unlike me)
    2 = neither characteristic nor uncharacteristic
    3 = characteristic (somewhat like me)
    4 = extremely characteristic (very much like me)

___ **1.** On the whole, I am satisfied with myself.

___ **2.** At times, I think I am no good at all.*

___ **3.** I feel that I have a number of good qualities.

___ **4.** I am able to do things as well as most other people.

___ **5.** I feel I do not have much to be proud of.*

___ **6.** I certainly feel useless at times.*

___ **7.** I feel that I'm a person of worth, at least on an equal plane with others.

___ **8.** I wish I could have more respect for myself.*

___ **9.** All in all, I am inclined to feel that I am a failure.*

___ **10.** I take a positive attitude toward myself.

Directions for scoring: Half of the self-esteem items are reverse-scored; that is, for these items, a lower rating actually indicates a higher level of self-esteem. Before summing all ten items to find out your total self-esteem score, recode those with an asterisk ("*") so that 0 = 4, 1 = 3, 3 = 1, and 4 = 0. Your total self-esteem score can range from 0 to 40, with a higher score indicating a higher level of self-esteem. Scores greater than 20 indicate generally positive attitudes toward the self, while those below 20 indicate generally negative self-attitudes.

Source: From CONCEIVING THE SELF by Morris Rosenberg. Reprinted by permission.

As depicted in figure 12-2, self-enhancement appears to be the automatic and initially strongest response to favorable evaluations, but self-verification is the slower, more deliberate, and perhaps more lasting response (Baumeister, 1998; Sedikides & Strube, 1997). Research suggests that when people first receive favorable evaluations, they tend to automatically self-enhance ("Do I like it?"), but when they have time to critically analyze the feedback, they tend to self-verify ("Is it correct?"). Therefore, when someone tells people with low self-esteem that they are absolutely wonderful, their initial reaction is to accept this positive feedback and increase their self-esteem. However, if they engage in more complex cognitive analysis, they realize that accepting this positive feedback will require a major reassessment of their self-concept, a task they may feel ill-equipped to

Self-esteem and self-contempt have specific odors; they can be smelled.
            —Eric Hoffer, U.S. social philosopher, 1902–1983

Journey of Discovery Question

If people with low self-esteem reject attempts to increase their feelings of self-worth by others lavishly praising them, what strategy might you employ to satisfy their self-enhancement needs without triggering their need for self-verification?

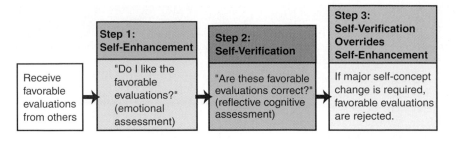

Step 1: Self-Enhancement	Step 2: Self-Verification	Step 3: Self-Verification Overrides Self-Enhancement
Receive favorable evaluations from others →	"Do I like the favorable evaluations?" (emotional assessment) →	"Are these favorable evaluations correct?" (reflective cognitive assessment) →	If major self-concept change is required, favorable evaluations are rejected.

FIGURE 12-2
How Do Low Self-Esteem People Typically Respond to Positive Evaluations?

When confronted with positive social evaluations that contradict a negative self-concept, how do people with low self-esteem resolve the conflict between self-enhancement and self-verification needs? Research suggests that people follow a three-step process in resolving this conflict. In step 1, the initial reaction is to self-enhance. However, with more time to critically analyze the feedback (step 2), self-verification dominates thinking. In step 3, if internalizing these positive evaluations will necessitate a major reassessment of their self-concept, the need for self-verification tends to override self-enhancement needs and people reject the evaluations. Why wouldn't people with high self-esteem have this same dilemma when given positive feedback from others?

Trait perspective: A descriptive approach to personality that identifies stable characteristics that people display over time and across situations.

Trait: A relatively stable tendency to behave in a particular way across a variety of situations.

accomplish. Faced with this dilemma, they often abandon self-enhancement and instead seek self-verification by rejecting the feedback and retaining their original self-concepts.

Although this is the typical response for low self-esteem individuals, it is important to add that they don't always reject positive feedback. In fact, they prefer to associate with people who make them feel better about themselves without seriously disconfirming their current self-concepts (Morling & Epstein, 1997). Discovery Box 12-1 examines another issue concerning self-enhancement.

SECTION SUMMARY

- The humanistic perspective assumes that human nature is essentially good.
- Carl Rogers proposed that providing unconditional positive regard allows a person to heal the split between their actual and their ideal selves.
- According to Abraham Maslow, people are motivated to become the best person they can be—to self-actualize.
- The humanistic perspective helped foster research on the self.
- Two important self motives are the need for self-enhancement and the need for self-verification.

12-4 THE TRAIT PERSPECTIVE

During the summer of 1919, 22-year-old psychology student Gordon Allport was traveling through Europe when he boldly decided to ask the world-famous Sigmund Freud to meet with him. Upon arriving at Freud's office, the young Allport was at a loss in explaining the purpose of his visit. In truth, he simply wanted to meet this great man. After a strained silence, Allport told a story about a boy he saw on the train to Vienna who pleaded with his meticulously dressed mother to keep dirty passengers from sitting near him. When Allport finished telling the story, Freud paused and then asked in a soft voice, "And was that little boy you?" Allport was mortified. Freud had mistakenly perceived this "ice-breaker" story as a window into the young man's unconscious. Later, after reflecting on Freud's assumption, Allport decided that psychoanalysis was not the best way to understand personality. Instead of searching for hidden, unconscious motives in people's behavior, he thought that personality psychologists should first try to describe and measure the basic factors of personality (Allport, 1967). This set him on a path of research that culminated in the development of the *trait perspective*.

12-4a Trait Theories Describe Basic Personality Dimensions

The **trait perspective** conceives of personality as consisting of stable characteristics that people display over time and across situations (Nicholson, 2002). A **trait** is a relatively stable tendency to behave in a particular way. As an approach to understanding personality,

DISCOVERY BOX 12-1

How Do You Explain Success and Failure in Your Life?

When you receive a good grade on an exam, do you usually conclude that your success was caused by your intelligence, your hard work, or a combination of the two? What if you do poorly? Are you likely to blame your failure on the unreasonable demands of your professor, or pure bad luck? Overall, this tendency to take credit for success while denying blame for failure is known as the **self-serving bias** (Campbell & Sedikides, 1999). The most agreed-upon explanation for the self-serving bias is that it allows us to enhance and protect self-esteem. If we feel personally responsible for successes or positive events in our lives but do not feel blameworthy for failures or other negative events, our self-worth is likely to be bolstered.

One thing to keep in mind, however, is that individualist cultures are much more likely than collectivist cultures to believe that high self-esteem is essential for mental health and life satisfaction (Oishi et al., 1999). This cultural difference in the importance placed on self-esteem may explain why individualists are more likely to exhibit the self-serving bias than collectivists (Heine & Lehman, 1999).

Self-serving bias: The tendency to bolster and defend self-esteem by taking credit for positive events while denying blame for negative events.

the trait perspective is more concerned with describing how people differ from one another than in explaining why they differ (Pervin, 1996). The way that psychologists typically measure traits is similar to the way that everyone assesses other people's personalities. They observe them over time and in various situations, or ask them how they typically behave. For example, if a friend is always prompt, you come to rely on that as characteristic of her. From the trait perspective, we would propose that your friend is consistently on time because of an underlying trait that predisposes her to act in this manner. This may seem a little circular, and to a certain extent it is. However, like so much else in personality psychology, traits cannot be measured directly, but instead are inferred from behavior.

In studying traits, Gordon Allport and his colleague Henry Odbert (1936) began by combing through an unabridged dictionary and making a list of words that described people's personal characteristics. From this initial list of 18,000 words, they eventually reduced it to about 200 clusters of related words, which became the original traits in Allport's personality theory (Allport, 1937). Allport's perspective on personality had a good deal in common with those of humanistic psychologists in that he emphasized that the whole human being should be the focus of study. Like humanistic psychologists, he further asserted that behaviorism was seriously mistaken when it explained human behavior as no different from that of rats and pigeons. In addition to his humanistic associations, Allport was influenced by Gestalt psychology. As you recall from chapter 1, section 1-2e, the Gestalt perspective contends that "the whole is different from the sum of its parts." Similarly, Allport (1961) argued that personality was not simply a collection of traits, but instead, these traits seamlessly fit together to form a dynamic and unique personality.

Allport's contemporary, Henry Murray (1938, 1948), was also a trait psychologist who appreciated humanistic psychology's emphasis on the total person. However, Murray's personality approach was also influenced by Jung's and Freud's theories of unconscious motivation. As a result, he focused on traits that are relatively irrational, passionate, and laden with conflict and emotion. Ironically, both men were doing their research in the same place, Harvard, at about the same time.

How can one perspective, the trait perspective, contain theorists who take such different positions about the nature of personality? Actually, the trait approach is not based on specific assumptions about human nature. Traits are viewed as the small building blocks of personality and a theorist can fit them together in a variety of ways, just as a landscaper can lay bricks into a walk in a variety of patterns. Whereas psychoanalytic and humanistic theorists have definite beliefs about whether human beings are basically rational, aggressive, or unconsciously motivated, the trait approach assumes that people differ in the degree to which they possess personality traits. For example, instead of taking a position that people are basically aggressive or nonaggressive, trait theorists contend that people differ in the degree to which they possess aggressive traits (McCrae & Costa, 1990).

12-4b Factor Analysis Is Used to Identify Personality Traits

Allport's work in identifying a list of traits was a necessary first step in the development of a scientific trait approach to personality. Yet, his list of 200-some traits needed to be reduced to a more manageable level. Researchers achieved this by relying on factor analysis. As you recall from chapter 10, section 10-2a, *factor analysis* is a statistical technique that allows researchers to identify clusters of variables that are related to—or *correlated* with—one another. When a group of traits correlate in factor analysis, this suggests that a more general trait is influencing them. For example, several studies have found that people who describe themselves as outgoing also describe themselves as talkative, active, and optimistic about the future. This cluster of traits has been identified as consisting of the more general trait of *extraversion* (Eysenck, 1973).

Raymond Cattell (1965, 1986) was one of the first trait theorists to use factor analysis to identify these general traits, which he called *source traits*. First, he collected people's ratings of themselves on many different traits, and then he identified clusters of related traits using factor analysis. Based on this procedure, Cattell concluded that you could understand an individual's personality by identifying the degree to which she or he possessed each of the 16 source traits listed in table 12-4.

TABLE 12-4	
Cattell's 16 Basic Personality Traits	

Reserved	Outgoing
Trusting	Suspicious
Relaxed	Tense
Less intelligent	More intelligent
Stable	Emotional
Assertive	Humble
Happy-go-lucky	Sober
Conscientious	Expedient
Venturesome	Shy
Tender-minded	Tough-minded
Imaginative	Practical
Shrewd	Forthright
Apprehensive	Placid
Experimenting	Conservative
Self-sufficient	Group-tied
Controlled	Casual

Cattell was a pioneer in the use of factor analysis to study personality. He also demonstrated the importance of testing personality traits in applied settings—in business organizations, in schools, in clinical work—and then using that information to better understand the traits. Testing personality theories in applied settings and then refining the theories based on what is learned has become an important part of modern trait approaches to personality (Friedman & Schustack, 1999).

British psychologists Hans Eysenck and Sybil Eysenck (pronounced "EYE-zink") also used factor analysis to describe personality functioning. However, unlike Cattell, the Eysencks believed that personality researchers should rely on other evidence besides the findings of factor analysis when identifying the basic dimensions of personality. Specifically, they believed that researchers should also consider the biological bases of personality (Eysenck, 1973; Eysenck & Eysenck, 1963, 1983). Based on thousands of studies conducted over five decades, the Eysencks concluded that there are three genetically influenced dimensions of personality: *extraversion* (which included Cattell's factors of outgoingness and assertiveness), *neuroticism* (which included Cattell's factors of emotional instability and apprehensiveness), and *psychoticism* (which included Cattell's factors of tough-mindedness and shrewdness).

12-4c The Five-Factor Model Specifies Five Basic Personality Traits

So how many basic traits are there in personality? Are there 16 source traits, as Cattell proposed, or are there a much more modest three dimensions, as the Eysencks proposed? Over the past 25 years, the consensus among most personality trait researchers is that there are five key factors or dimensions of personality, known as the *Big Five Factors*, or the **Five-Factor Model** (Endler & Speer, 1998; McCrae & Costa, 1997b; Pytlik Zillig et al., 2002). These five basic traits are *neuroticism, extraversion, openness, agreeableness*, and *conscientiousness*. As you can see in table 12-5, each of the five factors represents a clustering of more specific traits. For example, people who score high on neuroticism tend to be anxious, self-conscious, depressed, hostile, impulsive, and vulnerable. These lower-order traits are called *facets* of the Five-Factor Model (Wiggins, 1996).

With only slight variations, the five basic traits that make up the Five-Factor Model have consistently emerged in studies of children, college students, and the elderly (John & Srivastava, 1999; McCrae et al., 1999). Further, these traits have been found in societies as diverse as the United States, Bangladesh, Brazil, Japan, Canada, Finland, Germany, Poland, China, and the Philippines (Diaz-Guerrero et al., 2001; McCrae et al., 1998). This is especially impressive when you consider the wide variety of languages that have been used in these various studies to test for these traits.

Five-Factor Model: A trait theory that asserts that personality consists of five traits (neuroticism, extraversion, openness, agreeableness, and conscientiousness).

Neuroticism	Extraversion	Openness	Agreeableness	Conscientiousness
Anxious	Outgoing	Rich fantasy life	Trusting	Competent
Self-conscious	Positive emotions	Rich emotional life	Straightforward	Orderly
Depressed	Assertive	Action oriented	Compliant	Dutiful
Hostile	Full of energy	Novel ideas	Modest	Self-disciplined
Impulsive	Excitement seeking	Eccentric	Tender-minded	Deliberate
Vulnerable	Warm	Idiosyncratic	Altruistic	Achievement oriented

TABLE 12-5

The Five-Factor Model and Its Facets

Evolutionary theorists contend that the reason these five traits are found across a wide variety of cultures is because they reflect the most salient features of humans' adaptive behavior over the course of evolutionary history (Buss, 1999; MacDonald, 1998). In other words, these five traits have emerged as the basic components of personality because, as a species, we have evolved special sensitivity to variations in the ability to handle stress (neuroticism), seek out others' company (extraversion), approach problems (openness to experience), cooperate with others (agreeableness), and meet our social and moral obligations (conscientiousness).

Does this mean that these five traits compose an individual's entire personality? Most trait theorists would say no. Although almost any personality trait probably has a good deal in common with one of these five basic traits, the Five-Factor Model does not capture the entire essence of personality (Funder, 2001). Let us briefly examine each of these traits.

Neuroticism

At the core of neuroticism is negative affect (McCrae & Costa, 1987). This personality dimension, which is sometimes labeled *emotional stability*, describes people differing in terms of being anxious, high-strung, insecure, and self-pitying versus being relaxed, calm, composed, secure, and content. Neurotics can either channel their worrying into a kind of compulsive success or else let their anxiety lead them into recklessness. Many of the facets underlying neuroticism will be discussed more fully in chapter 13 when we examine psychological disorders.

Extraversion

This trait was first identified by Carl Jung (see section 12-2e) and has been included in virtually every personality system proposed in the last 50 years (Watson & Clark, 1997). Extraverts are people who seek out and enjoy others' company. They tend to be confident, energetic, bold, and optimistic, and they handle social situations with ease and grace. On the opposite end of this particular personality dimension is the introverted character. Introverts tend to be shy, quiet, reserved, and it is harder for others to connect with them (Tellegen et al., 1988).

Openness to Experience

People who are particularly open to experience are adventurous, constantly searching out new ways to do things, and they are sensitive and passionate, with a childlike wonder at the world (McCrae, 1994). They can also flout traditional notions of what is appropriate or expected in terms of their behavior or ideas (McCrae & Costa, 1997a; McCrae & John, 1992). As is the case for most of the other dimensions, openness to experience is named for the end of the pole that appears to be more desirable. In fact, many qualities of those who are more closed to experience are quite valuable. These individuals tend to be hardworking, very loyal, down-to-earth, and proud of their traditional values.

Agreeableness

Agreeableness is a personality dimension that ranges from friendly compliance with others on one end to hostile antagonism on the other (Costa et al., 1989). People who score high on agreeableness tend to be good-natured, soft-hearted, courteous, and sympathetic, whereas those who score low tend to be irritable, ruthless, rude, and tough-minded. Agreeableness is a useful way to obtain popularity, and agreeable people are better liked than disagreeable people (Graziano & Eisenberg, 1997). However, people high in agreeableness may be too dependent on others' approval and thus are ill-suited for situations requiring tough or more objective decisions. For instance, scientists, art or literary critics, and judges may be able to perform better if they are less agreeable and more "objective" in their approaches to solving problems (Graziano et al., 1996).

INFO-BIT: Agreeableness is consistent across the life span. Disagreeable boys develop into men who are described as irritable, undercontrolled, and moody (Caspi et al., 1989). Some researchers have suggested that this, in turn, may be related to the underlying temperament of individuals, and that being disagreeable may be related to an overactive sympathetic division of the autonomic nervous system (Rothbart, 1989).

Journey of Discovery Question

How do you think Freud would describe the highly conscientious person?

Conscientiousness

Conscientiousness is a measure of a person's willingness to conform to other's expectations and to follow through on what they have agreed to do, despite more tempting options that may arise. People who score high on conscientiousness tend to be well organized, dependable, hardworking, and ambitious, whereas those who score low are more likely to be disorganized, undependable, lazy, and easygoing. This dimension is very important in the workplace. Conscientious employees are good workplace citizens, while nonconscientious employees are nonproductive and undermine the organization's health (Barrick & Mount, 1991; Howard & Howard, 2000).

12-4d Both Genetic and Environmental Factors Shape Personality

Many trait theorists have long assumed that genetic predispositions influence most personality traits (Jang et al., 2001; Thomis et al., 2000). As previously discussed in chapter 10, section 10-4a, psychologists have conducted a great deal of research comparing twins reared together versus apart to better understand genetic and environmental influences on intelligence. Many of these same studies have also examined personality traits. Overall, they have found that, raised together, identical twins have more similar traits than do fraternal twins (McCrae, 1996; Tellegen et al., 1988; Viken et al., 1994). These findings indicate a moderate genetic influence on personality. However, this same research has found that the trait correlations for identical twins reared apart are considerably lower than those reared together, which suggests that environment also influences trait development (Borkenau et al., 2001). Currently, the best estimates are that personality differences in the population are between 30 and 60 percent genetically determined, with the balance attributable to the environment (Bergeman et al., 1993; Borkenau et al., 2001).

Although genetics plays an important role in shaping personality, how it does so is not clear (Beckwith & Aslper, 2002). David Buss (1995) proposes that genes most likely influence personality by their impact on physical characteristics and general predispositions toward certain temperaments associated with activity, emotionality, and sociability. These physical characteristics and temperaments then interact with environmental factors to shape personality. For example, children who inherit a healthy body and high sociability and activity levels may actively seek opportunities to play with other children. Such interactions may foster the development of important social skills and the enjoyment of social activities, which are characteristic of extraverted personalities. Of course, this does not mean that genetic predispositions will actually lead to specific personality traits for a given person. For instance, even though shyness is an inherited trait, children and older adults can consciously overcome their social inhibitions and become remarkably skilled and outgoing in a wide variety of social settings (Rowe, 1997). Thus, instead of genetics determining personality in some lockstep fashion, we appear to inherit the building blocks of personality from our parents, and then our interactions with our social

DISCOVERY BOX 12-2

Do Nonhuman Animals Have Personality Traits?

Our family dog, Maizy, is trusting, curious, very energetic, somewhat absent-minded, and extremely friendly. I would guess that she is low on neuroticism and high on agreeableness, extraversion, and openness to experience. Is my application of the Five-Factor Model to a canine based on any scientific evidence, or should it be dismissed as the whimsical musings of a dog lover?

Comparative psychologists Samuel Gosling and Oliver John believe that the Five-Factor Model can be used to describe the personality of many nonhuman animals, including dogs. In a review of 19 animal personality studies involving 12 different species, Gosling and John (1999) found that the personality traits of extraversion, neuroticism, and agreeableness were commonly observed across species. Chimpanzees, gorillas, various other primates, mammals in general, and even guppies and octopuses exhibit individual differences that are remarkably similar to these three personality traits. The researchers believe that this cross-species similarity in personality traits suggests that biological mechanisms are likely responsible.

These consistencies across species further suggest that the five factors identified by trait theorists may reflect some of the basic styles of behavior that are necessary for many species to best adapt to their environments (Gosling, 2001). For instance, an animal that is high on agreeableness may promote group solidarity by being nurturing and cooperative, whereas another animal that is low on agreeableness may force the group to make hard decisions that are ultimately beneficial. Although these two animals represent different ends of the agreeableness continuum, their habitual ways of responding foster survival, and thus the genes that influence these personality styles are likely to be passed on to future generations.

So what are the important traits in a dog's personality? I wasn't far off the mark in sizing up Maizy. Factor analyses of experts' ratings of dog breeds identified traits that closely approximated four of the five traits in the Five-Factor Model: neuroticism, agreeableness, extraversion, and openness to experience. A fifth personality dimension of "dominance-territoriality" was also identified (Gosling & John, 1999). Maizy, a golden retriever, would score very low on this dimension.

environment create the personality that we become. Check out Discovery Box 12-2 to learn how psychologists have expanded their study of the genetic contribution to personality in their analysis of personality traits among nonhuman animals.

12-4e Critics Challenge Whether Traits Reliably Predict Behavior

Personality theorists, whether they take a psychoanalytic, humanistic, or trait perspective, have all emphasized that personality is an important determinant of behavior. Yet, Walter Mischel (1968, 1984) has argued that this is a misguided belief. Instead, he asserts that the situation that we place people in can be a much stronger determinant of behavior than their personalities. In making this argument, Mischel discussed an early study conducted by Hugh Hartshorne and Mark May (1928) in which they placed children in many different situations where they had the opportunity to lie, cheat, and steal. Instead of displaying honest or dishonest traits that were consistent across many different situa-

Comparative psychologists Samuel Gosling and Oliver John (1999) believe that the Five-Factor Model can be used to describe the personality of many nonhuman animals, including dogs. Experts' ratings of dog breeds identified traits that closely approximated four of the five traits in the Five-Factor Model: neuroticism, agreeableness, extraversion, and openness to experience, as well as a fifth personality dimension of "dominance-territoriality." Which of the "Big Five" factors do you think they found only in humans and chimpanzees?

What about conscientiousness? Gosling and John's research found that chimpanzees were the only other nonhuman species that exhibited the trait of conscientiousness (it was not found among gorillas), although it was defined more narrowly in chimps than in humans. Among chimps, conscientiousness included individual behavioral variations involving lack of attention and goal directedness, unpredictability, and disorganized behavior. Because conscientiousness entails following rules, thinking before acting, and other complex cognitive functions, it is not surprising that this trait was only found in humans' closest genetic relative. These findings suggest that conscientiousness is a recent evolutionary development among hominids, the subfamily comprising humans, chimpanzees, and gorillas.

tions, Hartshorne and May found that the situation was the most important determinant of how the children behaved. If kids thought they could get away with it, most of them were likely to behave dishonestly. In Mischel's own research, he found virtually no correlation between people's traits and their behavior across situations (Mischel, 1968, 1984). In other words, personality traits were not reliably predicting behavior. Based on this evidence, Mischel argued that personality traits are a figment of trait theorists' imaginations!

As you might guess, this critique stirred up considerable controversy among personality psychologists. Seymour Epstein (1979, 1980) responded that Mischel was not seeing consistency in behavior across situations because he was not measuring enough behaviors. Using an analogy, Epstein stated that no one expects that your IQ score will predict whether you correctly answer a particular question on a particular test in a particular class during a particular semester. Predicting such a thing would be highly unreliable because so many factors exist that might influence your response (Were you rushed for time? Did you understand this information in class? Did you read the question correctly?). However,

> **INFO-BIT:** Personality traits are not only stable across situations, they are also stable across time (Block, 1971; Costa et al., 1980). A recent study suggests that our personalities are least stable during childhood (correlations in the .40s), somewhat more stable in early adulthood (correlations in the .50s), and the most stable after the age of 50 (correlations in the .70s) (Roberts & DelVecchio, 2000).

your IQ score will be much more accurate in predicting your average performance over many questions on several exams. Similarly, your score on an introversion-extraversion scale will not be very accurate in predicting whether you introduce yourself to that attractive person you see on campus tomorrow. But your score will probably be much more accurate in predicting your average sociability across many situations. By and large, research supports Epstein's argument: Personality trait scores do reliably predict how people generally behave (Funder, 2001; Paunonen & Ashton, 2001).

A second response to Mischel's critique was to acknowledge that situations do indeed shape behavior, and that an interaction of personal and situational factors often determines how we behave (Cervone & Shoda, 1999; Mischel & Shoda, 1999). In some situations, social norms may inhibit the expression of personality traits. For example, extraverts, like everyone else, are likely to be relatively quiet and subdued at a library, funeral home, or church service. The personalities of those with whom we interact also can significantly alter our own behavior. A store clerk who is low on agreeableness may treat us very rudely, which may cause us to react in a similar fashion, despite the fact that we generally are kind and considerate. Thus, although personality traits do appear to explain a good deal of our behavior, situational forces significantly influence us (see chapter 16).

The criticisms of the trait approach have helped to sharpen our understanding of the limits of personality as a determinant of behavior, but they have also increased our ability to predict behavior. Attending only to personality traits will not accurately predict behavior in most circumstances. Instead, many personality researchers have increasingly embraced **interactionism,** which is the study of the combined effects of both the situation and the person on human behavior (Magnusson & Endler, 1977).

Interactionism: The study of the combined effects of both the situation and the person on human behavior.

SECTION SUMMARY

- The trait perspective is a descriptive approach to personality that focuses on stable characteristics that people display over time and across situations.

- Trait theorists identify traits by relying on factor analysis.

- The Five-Factor Model is the most widely accepted trait theory, which contends that personality is best described by the traits of extraversion, neuroticism, agreeableness, conscientiousness, and openness to experience.

- Both genetic and environmental factors shape trait development.

- Personality traits interact with situational factors in determining behavior.

12-5 THE SOCIAL-COGNITIVE PERSPECTIVE

Social-cognitive perspective: A psychological perspective that examines how people interpret, analyze, remember, and use information about themselves, others, social interactions, and relationships.

The perspectives examined thus far all contend that personality consists of internal psychological needs or traits that shape our thoughts, feelings, and behavior. These approaches provide a good illustration of how the ideology of *individualism* has shaped the development of many personality theories. In contrast, our fourth major approach, the **social-cognitive perspective,** has a less individualist bias because it views personality as emerging through the process of the person interacting with her or his social environment. This perspective has its roots in the behavioral principles of *classical conditioning* and

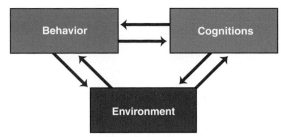

Behavior ← → Cognitions

Environment

operant conditioning, but its closest association is with the more cognitively oriented principles of *observational learning.* As you recall from chapter 7, section 7-3a, observational learning is the central feature of Albert Bandura's (1986) *social learning theory,* which contends that people learn social behaviors primarily through observation and cognitive processing of information, rather than through direct experience.

12-5a Personality Is Shaped by the Interaction of Personal Factors, Environmental Factors, and Our Behaviors

According to Bandura (1986), Skinner was only partly correct when he asserted that the environment determines people's behavior. Bandura pointed out that people's behavior also determines the environment. He further contended that people's thoughts, beliefs, and expectations determine and are determined by both behavior and the environment. As such, personality emerges from an ongoing mutual interaction among people's cognitions, their actions, and their environment. This basic principle of the social-cognitive perspective—which is depicted in figure 12-3—is known as **reciprocal determinism.** Thus, while environmental factors shape our personalities, we think about what is happening to us and we develop beliefs and expectations that will both alter our behavior and our environment (Makoul, 1998). In turn, these behavioral and environmental changes will influence our thoughts, which will then alter our personalities.

One of the most important cognitive factors in reciprocal determinism is **self-efficacy,** which is a person's belief about his or her ability to perform behaviors that should bring about a desired outcome. Perceptions of self-efficacy are largely subjective and tied to specific kinds of activities. You could have high self-efficacy for solving mathematical problems but low self-efficacy for interacting with new acquaintances. Because of these two different self-efficacies, you might approach a difficult calculus course with robust confidence, while you feign illness when invited to a new friend's party. Success in an activity heightens self-efficacy, while failure lowers it (Boudreaux et al., 1998; Lin, 1998). Further, the more self-efficacy that you have at a particular task, the more likely you will pursue that task, try hard, persist in the face of setbacks, and succeed (Bandura, 1999; Chemers et al., 2001). Success breeds self-efficacy, which, in turn, breeds further success. This mutual interaction is an illustration of reciprocal determinism.

12-5b Interactions with the Environment Can Develop Feelings of Personal Control or Helplessness

According to social-cognitive theorist Julian Rotter (1966, 1990), through the process of interacting with our surroundings we develop beliefs about ourselves as controlling, or as controlled by, our environment. The degree to which we believe that outcomes in our

FIGURE 12-3
Reciprocal Determinism
The idea that personality emerges from an ongoing mutual interaction among people's cognitions, their behavior, and their environment is known as reciprocal determinism. Reciprocal determinism is an important principle of the social-cognitive perspective and stands in sharp contrast to the strict behaviorist belief (as articulated by B. F. Skinner) that the environment is the sole determinant of people's behavior.

Reciprocal determinism: The social-cognitive belief that personality emerges from an ongoing mutual interaction among people's cognitions, their actions, and their environment.

Self-efficacy: A person's belief about his or her ability to perform behaviors that should bring about a desired outcome.

Journey of Discovery Question
Is self-efficacy the same thing as self-esteem?

Locus of control: The degree to which we expect that outcomes in our lives depend on our own actions and personal characteristics versus the actions of uncontrollable environmental forces.

lives depend on our own actions versus the actions of uncontrollable environmental forces is known as **locus of control.** People who believe that outcomes occur because of their own efforts are identified as having an *internal locus of control,* whereas those who believe that outcomes are outside of their own control are identified as having an *external locus of control.* Individuals with an internal locus of control are more likely to be achievement oriented than those with an external locus of control because they believe that their behavior can result in positive outcomes (Findley & Cooper, 1983; Lachman & Weaver, 1998). True to these expectations, internals tend to be more successful in life than are externals. Externals are less independent than internals, and they are also more likely to be depressed and stressed (Presson & Benassi, 1996). Spend a few minutes responding to the items in table 12-6 to get an idea of whether you have an internal or external locus of control.

People who believe that external events control their lives often develop a feeling of helplessness. As discussed in chapter 7, section 7-2f, Martin Seligman (1975) defined this *learned helplessness* as the passive resignation produced by repeated exposure to aversive events that are believed to be unavoidable. Because people develop the expectation that their behavior has no effect on the outcome in the situation, they simply give up trying to change the outcome, even when their actions might bring them rewards (Baum et al., 1998).

Learned helplessness is an example of the operation of reciprocal determinism. After repeatedly failing to achieve a desired outcome, people develop a belief that there is

TABLE 12-6

Do You Have an Internal or an External Locus of Control?

Instructions: For each item, select the alternative that you more strongly believe to be true. Remember that this is a measure of your personal beliefs and that there are no correct or incorrect answers.

___ **1.**   a. Making a lot of money is largely a matter of getting the right breaks.

   b. Promotions are earned through hard work and persistence.

___ **2.**   a. In my experience, I have noticed that there is usually a direct connection between how hard I study and the grades I get.

   b. Many times, the reactions of teachers seem haphazard to me.

___ **3.**   a. Marriage is largely a gamble.

   b. The number of divorces indicates that more and more people are not trying to make their marriages work.

___ **4.**   a. When I am right, I can convince others.

   b. It is silly to think that one can really change another person's basic attitudes.

___ **5.**   a. In our society, a person's future earning power is dependent upon his or her ability.

   b. Getting promoted is really a matter of being a little luckier than the next person.

___ **6.**   a. I have little influence over the way other people behave.

   b. If one knows how to deal with people, they are really quite easily led.

Scoring instructions: Give yourself one point for each of the following answers: 1(a), 2(b), 3(a), 4(b), 5(b), and 6(a). Then add up your total number of points. The higher the score, the more external you are. A score of 5 or 6 suggests that you are in the high external range, while a score of 0 or 1 suggests that you are in the high internal range. Scores of 2, 3, and 4 suggest that you fall somewhere between these two extremes.

Source: From "Generalized expectancies for internal versus external control of reinforcement" by Julian B. Rotter in PSYCHOLOGICAL MONOGRAPHS, 80 1966, Whole No. 609. Reprinted by permission of the author.

nothing they can do to alter their current conditions, so they stop trying. Even when the world around them changes so that success is now possible, they don't act on opportunities because they falsely believe that such action is futile. Learned helplessness explains why some people who have grown up in poverty don't take advantage of opportunities that, if pursued, could lead to economic rewards. Having developed the belief that they cannot change the cards that have been dealt them, these people remain mired in poverty and often instill these pessimistic beliefs in their children. Social welfare programs that have been successful in helping people pull themselves out of poverty specifically attack learned helplessness (Wanberg et al., 1999).

12-5c The Social-Cognitive Perspective Has Been Criticized for Failing to Explain the Nonrational Aspects of Personality

Traditional behavioral theories of personality that are based primarily on the operant conditioning principles of B. F. Skinner have been criticized for only assessing how environmental factors shape personality. To its credit, the social-cognitive perspective has taken a much more complex view of human personality, while still testing its theories using the scientific method. In their reliance on carefully controlled studies, social-cognitive theories have much more in common with the trait approach to personality than with the less scientifically based theories from the humanistic and psychoanalytic perspectives.

Social-cognitive personality theories have also drawn praise for emphasizing the important role that cognitions play in personality. They have quite rightly pointed out that our behavior is significantly shaped by our beliefs and expectations, including those related to ourselves as well as those related to our environment. The social-cognitive approach has also drawn praise because its scientific findings have generated useful applications in the real world concerning how to understand and help solve such problems as drug abuse, unemployment, academic underachievement, and teen pregnancy.

The social-cognitive perspective's emphasis on cognition has placed it squarely in the mainstream of contemporary psychology, and it enjoys immense popularity among many psychologists. However, by emphasizing the cognitive side of human nature, the social-cognitive perspective is best at explaining rational behavior that is "thought through." Like many cognitively oriented theories, it is less able to explain behavior that is spontaneous, irrational, and perhaps sparked by unconscious motives (Schacter & Badgaiyan, 2001). Table 12-7 provides a brief summary of the four personality perspectives that we have discussed.

SECTION SUMMARY

- In the social-cognitive perspective, personality represents the unique patterns of thinking and behavior that a person learns in the social world.

- According to the principle of reciprocal determinism, personality emerges from an ongoing mutual interaction among people's cognitions, their actions, and their environment.

- According to the concept of locus of control, by interacting with our surroundings we develop beliefs about ourselves as controlling, or as controlled by, our environment.

- Social-cognitive theories are best at explaining rational behavior but are less capable of explaining irrational behavior.

TABLE 12-7	Perspective	Explanation of Behavior	Evaluation
The Four Perspectives on Personality	Psychoanalytic	Personality is set early in childhood and is driven by unconscious and anxiety-ridden sexual impulses that we poorly understand.	A speculative, hard-to-test theory that has had an enormous cultural influence and a significant impact on psychology
	Humanistic	Personality is based on conscious feelings about oneself and is focused on our capacity for growth and change.	A perspective that revitalized attention to the self, but often did not use rigorous scientific methods
	Trait	Personality consists of a limited number of stable characteristics that people display over time and across situations.	A descriptive approach that sometimes underestimates the impact that situational factors have on behavior
	Social-cognitive	Personality emerges from an ongoing mutual interaction among people's cognitions, their behavior, and their environment.	An interactionist approach that tends to underestimate the impact that emotions and unconscious motives have on behavior

12-6 MEASURING PERSONALITY

Two basic assumptions underlie the attempt to understand and describe personality. The first assumption, which we have just examined, is that personal characteristics shape people's thoughts, feelings, and behavior. The second assumption, which we are about to examine, is that those characteristics can be measured in some manner. We will consider two kinds of personality tests: *projective* and *objective*.

12-6a Projective Tests Are Designed to Reveal Inner Feelings, Motives, and Conflicts

Projective tests: Psychological tests that ask people to respond to ambiguous stimuli or situations in ways that will reveal their unconscious motives and desires.

Projective tests are based on the assumption that if people are presented with an ambiguous stimulus or situation, the way that they interpret the material will be a "projection" of their unconscious needs, motives, fantasies, conflicts, thoughts, and other hidden aspects of personality. In other words, when people describe what they see in ambiguous stimuli, their description will be like the image that is projected on the screen at the movies. In this analogy, the film in the movie projector is like the hidden personality aspects, and the responses to the test are like the images seen on the screen. Projective tests are among the most commonly used assessment devices by psychotherapists in their clinical practices (Butcher & Rouse, 1996). The most popular projective tests are the *Rorschach Inkblot Test* and the *Thematic Apperception Test*.

The Rorschach Inkblot Test

Rorschach Inkblot Test: A projective personality test in which people are shown ten symmetrical inkblots and asked what each might be depicting.

Have you ever played the "cloud game" in which you and another person look at cloud formations and tell each other what the shapes look like? The **Rorschach Inkblot Test** has a similar format as the cloud game (Exner, 1993). Introduced in 1921 by the Swiss psychiatrist Hermann Rorschach (1884–1922), the test consists of 10 symmetrical inkblots. Five cards are black and white, and five are colored like the one in figure 12-4. Rorschach purposely varied the composition of his inkblots—some of them are essentially a large blob, others are bits of ink all over the page.

People's responses to the Rorschach are scored on three major features: the location, or part of the card mentioned in the response; the content of the response; and which aspect, or *determinant*, of the card (its color or shading) prompted the response.

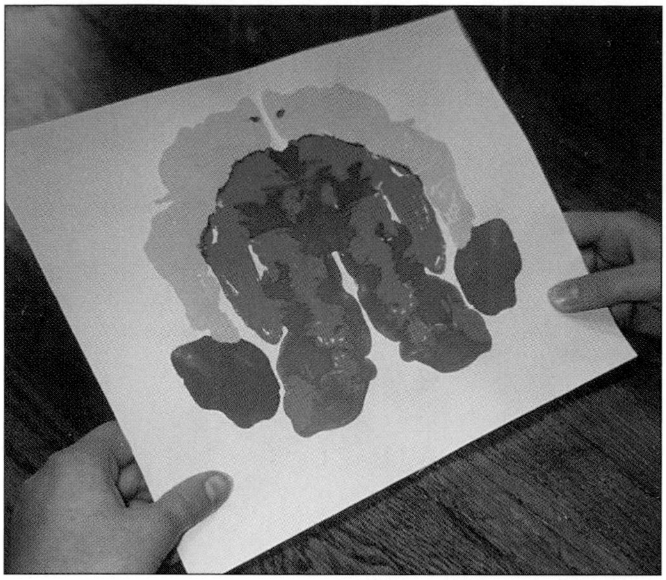

FIGURE 12-4
The Rorschach Test

Persons taking the Rorschach Inkblot test describe what they see in a series of inkblots. The assumption of this projective personality test is that the way that people interpret the inkblots will be a "projection" of their unconscious mind. What is one of the more serious validity problems with the Rorschach?

Rorschach's original system of scoring was revised by others, and by 1950, there were five separate systems for scoring and interpreting the inkblots, with none of them exhibiting good reliability or validity. To try to correct these problems, James Exner (1993) integrated the five scoring systems into one system that decreased, but did not eliminate, reliability and validity concerns (Lilienfeld et al., 2000). One of the more serious validity problems with the Rorschach is that the current scoring system tends to misidentify mentally healthy people as having psychological problems (Wood et al., 1996, 2000). Although most critics do not believe that the Rorschach is completely invalid, they believe that more valid tests are available that are also cheaper to administer, score, and interpret. Today, many users of the Rorschach administer it to clients seeking therapy as a way to start a conversation rather than as a way to measure their personality (Aronow et al., 1995).

Thematic Apperception Test

Another widely used projective measure is the *Thematic Apperception Test (TAT)*. As described in chapter 11, section 11-4a, Henry Murray developed the TAT in 1937. Administering this test involves asking a person to tell a story about several pictures that they are shown (Hunsley & Bailey, 1999). In each case the picture depicts a person or persons involved in a situation that is ambiguous. For example, in the TAT-like picture depicted in figure 12-5, are the two people happy or sad? Is this a picture of a mother and daughter, a teacher and student, or something else? The person telling the story about the TAT cards is instructed to tell about what led up to the story, what the people in the story are thinking and feeling, and how the situation resolves or comes to an end. Murray hypothesized that the issues that people are struggling with in their own lives would be perceived to be issues for the characters in the cards. He proposed that the storyteller could give the characters various needs, such as the need for nurturance or the need for achievement. There would also be an opposing pressure from the environment, such as the demand to conform or to provide nurturance to others. Murray further proposed that, across the stories people told, certain themes would emerge related to important issues in their lives.

Over several decades of research, the TAT and other variations of the test have demonstrated adequate validity in measuring need for achievement, but the test-retest reliability is relatively low (Cramer, 1999; Spangler, 1992). For this reason, it is not considered to be one of the better ways to measure personality (Lilienfeld et al., 2000). Today, as with the Rorschach, psychologists using the TAT in therapy frequently employ it to help start a conversation about a client's problems.

FIGURE 12-5
Thematic Apperception Test (TAT)

This picture of a child and an adult sitting on a bench is an illustration of a TAT-like image.

12-6b Objective Tests Ask Direct Questions about a Person's Thoughts, Feelings, and Behavior

Objective tests: Personality tests that ask direct, unambiguous questions about a person's thoughts, feelings, and behavior.

Unlike projective tests, which are designed to trick the unconscious into revealing its contents, **objective tests** are primarily designed to assess consciously held thoughts, feelings, and behavior by asking direct, unambiguous questions. The questions can be directed toward friends and family members, or toward people who have just met the person who is being assessed. When people evaluate themselves, the test is called a *self-report inventory*. This is the most common kind of objective personality test.

Like college exams, objective personality tests can be administered to a large group of people at the same time. Also similar to exams, objective tests usually ask true-false, multiple-choice, or open-ended questions. However, unlike exams in a college course, there is no one correct answer on a personality test. Each respondent chooses the answer that best describes her or him. Many objective tests measure only one specific component of personality (for example, refer to the *Self-Monitoring Scale* in the end-of-chapter *Psychological Applications* section), while other objective tests assess several traits simultaneously. One such test is the **Minnesota Multiphasic Personality Inventory (MMPI)**, which is the most extensively researched and widely used personality inventory (Butcher et al., 1989; Piotrowski et al., 1998).

Minnesota Multiphasic Personality Inventory (MMPI): An objective personality test consisting of true-false items that measure various personality dimensions and clinical conditions such as depression.

Since its development in the 1940s, the MMPI has been revised so that its language and content would better reflect contemporary concerns and a more culturally diverse population. The original test has 550 true-false items, while the second edition, MMPI-2, has 567 such items. Both versions of the MMPI measure various personality dimensions and clinical conditions such as depression. Despite the availability of the revised MMPI, many psychologists still use the original test. The MMPI is an *empirically derived* test, meaning that MMPI items were not selected for inclusion on a theoretical basis but were included only if they clearly distinguished one group of people from another (for example, patients with schizophrenia and a normal comparison group). Each item had to demonstrate its usefulness by being answered differently by members of the two groups but similarly by members within each group.

Both versions of the MMPI have 10 *clinical scales*, which are used to identify psychological difficulties or interests, so the groups that were used to choose the scale items were various groups of people with different psychological problems or interests. For example, the items that comprise the MMPI depression scale were those that depressed individuals

Scale	Description
Hypochondriasis	Abnormal concern with bodily functions and health concerns
Depression	Pessimism, feelings of hopelessness; slowing of action and thought
Hysteria	Unconscious use of mental or physical symptoms to avoid problems
Psychopathic deviate	Disregard for social customs; emotional shallowness
Masculinity/femininity	Interests culturally associated with a particular gender
Paranoia	Suspiciousness, delusions of grandeur or persecution
Psychasthenia	Obsessions, compulsions, fears, guilt, anxiety
Schizophrenia	Bizarre thoughts and perceptions, withdrawal, hallucinations, delusions
Hypomania	Emotional excitement, overactivity, impulsiveness
Social introversion	Shyness, insecurity, disinterest in others

TABLE 12-8

MMPI-2 Clinical Scales

endorsed more than did nondepressed people. People who score above a certain level on the depression scale are considered to have a difficulty with depression. Table 12-8 briefly describes the 10 clinical scales for the MMPI-2.

The MMPI also contains four *validity scales*, which are item groups that detect suspicious response patterns indicating dishonesty, carelessness, defensiveness, or evasiveness (Butcher & Williams, 2000). The interpretation of responses to these four scales can help psychologists understand the attitudes that someone has taken toward all of the test items. For example, someone who responds "true" to items such as "I like every person I have ever met" and "I never get angry" may not be providing honest answers to the other test items.

Both versions of the MMPI are easy to administer and score, and they have proven useful in identifying people who have psychological disorders (Butcher & Rouse, 1996; Butcher & Williams, 2000). Despite these advantages, it is often difficult to interpret MMPI scores when trying to diagnose specific disorders because people with different disorders score high on a number of the same clinical scales. Critics also contend that neither MMPI version has kept pace with recent advances in personality theory (Groth-Marnat, 1997).

Another objective test that is closely aligned with modern personality theory is the 243-item *Neuroticism Extraversion Openness Personality Inventory, Revised* or *NEO-PI-R* (Costa & McCrae, 1992). Unlike the MMPI, the NEO-PI-R measures personality differences that are not problematic and that are based on the Five-Factor Model (a previous version of this inventory did not measure agreeableness and conscientiousness). Although it is a relatively new personality test, the NEO-PI-R is already widely used in research and clinical therapy and represents the new wave of assessment (Katigbak et al., 2002; Stone, 2002).

SECTION SUMMARY

- Projective testing assumes that if people are presented with ambiguous stimuli, their interpretation of it will be a "projection" of unconscious needs and desires.
- The two most widely used projective tests are the Rorschach Ink Blot and the Thematic Apperception Test.
- Objective testing involves assessing consciously held thoughts, feelings, and behavior.
- The Minnesota Multiphasic Personality Inventory (MMPI) is one of the oldest and most widely used objective personality tests.
- NEO-PI-R is an objective test that measures Five-Factor Model traits.

SUGGESTED WEBSITES

Note: These websites were functional when we went to press. Please access the online text for the most up-to-date URLs.

Great Ideas in Personality
http://www.personalityresearch.org/

This is a website that deals with scientific research programs in personality psychology. It provides information about personality research from a variety of perspectives, including perspectives not covered in this chapter. It also contains a good selection of well-organized links to other personality websites.

The Society for Personality Assessment
http://www.personality.org/

This is the Society for Personality Assessment website, which is intended primarily for professional use; it contains a section outlining the requirements for personality assessment credentials and how to go about becoming a personality psychologist.

The American Psychoanalytic Association
http://www.apsa.org/

The website of the American Psychoanalytic Association is intended for both the general public and for the professional psychoanalytic community. There is information here about the current state of the psychoanalytic theoretical orientation.

Humanistic Psychology
http://www.apa.org/divisions/div32/

This is the official website of the American Psychological Association's division of humanistic psychology. This has information on upcoming APA events and information for students interested in this perspective.

QueenDom.com Complete List of Tests
http://www.queendom.com/tests/alltests.html

This website has a number of online personality tests that you can take and receive feedback on.

PSYCHOLOGICAL APPLICATIONS
Do You Have a Chameleon-like Personality?

When studying personality, we are examining how people are consistent across situations and how they differ from one another. Yet, what if I told you that personality researchers have identified a trait in which the defining characteristic is that people consistently behave inconsistently when interacting with others? Although this may sound strange to you, this trait is associated with a very normal self-presentation style that many of us exhibit. Before reading further, spend a few minutes responding to the items in table 12-9 to better understand your association with this trait.

Self-Monitoring

In social relationships, we often try to manage the impression we make on others by carefully constructing and monitoring our self-presentations (Goffman, 1959; Leary et al., 1994). Although we all monitor and adjust how we present ourselves to others depending on the situation and with whom we are interacting (Tice et al., 1995), there is a personality difference in the degree to which we make such alterations in "who we are to others." According to Mark Snyder (1987), these differences are related to a personality trait called **self-monitoring,** which is the tendency to use cues from other people's self-presentations in controlling our own self-presentations. Those of us high in self-monitoring spend considerable time learning about other people, and we tend to emphasize impression management in our social relationships (John et al., 1996).

Individuals who are high in self-monitoring are especially attuned to social cues concerning appropriate behavior in a given situation. They tend to be extraverted, good actors, and willing to change their behavior to suit others (Leck & Simpson, 1999). For example, when trying to initiate a dating relationship, high self-monitoring men and women behave in a chameleon-like fashion,

strategically and often deceptively changing their self-presentations in an attempt to appear more desirable (Rowatt et al., 1998). On the other hand, those low in self-monitoring are less attentive to situational cues, and their behavior is guided more by inner attitudes and beliefs. As a result, their behavior is more consistent across situations. Although it may appear to the casual observer that the low self-monitor has a stable personality and the high self-monitor has no identifiable personality at all, the high self-monitors' inconsistency across situations represents a stable personality trait.

Due to their greater attention to social cues, high self-monitors are more socially skilled than low self-monitors. They are better able to communicate and understand the meaning of emotions and other nonverbal behaviors. They also learn more quickly how to behave in new situations and are more likely to initiate conversations (Gangestad & Snyder, 2000). On the negative side, people high in self-monitoring have less intimate and committed social relationships, and they tend to judge people more on superficial characteristics, such as physical appearance and social activities, rather than their attitudes and values (Jamieson et al., 1987; Snyder & Simpson, 1984).

Self-Monitoring on the Job

Because high self-monitors' actions are guided by what they think are the appropriate behaviors in a given situation, some psychologists have wondered how this might affect their search for a job and their performance in that job (Snyder & Copeland, 1989). What about low self-monitors? Because they are guided more by their inner feelings and beliefs than social propriety, will they tend to gravitate toward and perform better in different jobs than their more socially sensitive counterparts?

TABLE 12-9

The Self-Monitoring Scale

The personality trait of self-monitoring is measured by items on the Self-Monitoring Scale (Snyder & Gangestad, 1986). To discover your level of self-monitoring, read each item below and then indicate whether each statement is true or false for you.

___ **1.** I find it hard to imitate the behavior of other people.

___ **2.** At parties and social gatherings, I do not attempt to do or say things that others will like.

___ **3.** I can only argue for ideas which I already believe.

___ **4.** I can make impromptu speeches even on topics about which I have almost no information.

___ **5.** I guess I put on a show to impress or entertain others.

___ **6.** I would probably make a good actor.

___ **7.** In a group of people, I am rarely the center of attention.

___ **8.** In different situations and with different people, I often act like very different persons.

___ **9.** I am not particularly good at making other people like me.

___**10.** I'm not always the person I appear to be.

___**11.** I would not change my opinions (or the way I do things) in order to please someone or win their favor.

___**12.** I have considered being an entertainer.

___**13.** I have never been good at games like charades or improvisational acting.

___**14.** I have trouble changing my behavior to suit different people and different situations.

___**15.** At a party, I let others keep the jokes and stories going.

___**16.** I feel a bit awkward in company and do not show up quite as well as I should.

___**17.** I can look anyone in the eye and tell a lie with a straight face (if for a right end).

___**18.** I may deceive people by being friendly when I really dislike them.

Directions for scoring: Give yourself one point for answering "True" to each of the following items: 4, 5, 6, 8, 10, 12, 17, and 18. Also give yourself one point for answering "False" to each of the following items: 1, 2, 3, 7, 9, 11, 13, 14, 15, and 16. Next, add up your total number of points for your self-monitoring score.

When Snyder and Gangestad (1986) developed the Self-Monitoring Scale, the mean score for North American college students was about 10 or 11. The higher your score is above these values, the more of this personality trait you probably possess. The lower your score is below these values, the less of this trait you probably possess.

Source: From "The self-monitoring of expressive behavior" by Mark Snyder in JOURNAL OF PERSONAL-ITY AND SOCIAL PSYCHOLOGY 30, pp. 526–537. Copyright © 1974 by the American Psychological Association. Reprinted with permission.

It is not whether you really cry. It's whether the audience thinks you are crying.

—Ingrid Bergman, Swedish actress, 1915–1982

Research suggests that those high in self-monitoring prefer jobs with clearly defined occupational roles. In comparison, low self-monitors tend to prefer occupational roles that coincide with their own personalities so they can "be themselves" on the job (Snyder & Gangestad, 1982). Thus, if you are high in self-monitoring, you may be more willing than those low in self-monitoring to mold and shape yourself "to fit" your chosen occupational role. You might find, for example, that occupations in the fields of law, politics, public relations, and the theater are particularly attractive to you. In these careers, you can use your social chameleon abilities to mimic others' social expectations. In contrast, if you are low in self-monitoring, and you consider yourself to be warm, compassionate, and caring, you may seek out social service or "helping" occupations such as medicine, psychology, or social work. On the other hand, if you consider yourself to be assertive, industrious, and a risk-taker, you may gravitate toward careers in business or other entrepreneurial professions.

Once having chosen and secured a job, your self-monitoring orientation may influence your work performance. One type of job that appears to be particularly suited to the skills of the high self-monitor are the so-called boundary spanning jobs in which individuals must interact and communicate effectively with two or more parties who, because of their conflicting interests, often cannot deal directly with one another. Examples of boundary spanning jobs would be the mediator in a dispute between management and labor, a real estate agent who negotiates the transfer of property from seller to buyer, or a university administrator who deals with students, faculty, and alumni. In an examination of 93 field representatives whose jobs required boundary spanning, David Caldwell and Charles O'Reilly (1982) found that high self-monitors did perform better in these jobs than low self-monitors. These findings suggest that self-monitoring skills may be particularly helpful in occupations where one must interact with people who have conflicting interests and agendas. In such work settings, high self-monitors are less likely to allow their personal feelings to affect their social interactions.

In what type of job might you perform better if you are low in self-monitoring? The job performance of low self-monitors appears to be less influenced by their leader's behavior than that of high self-monitors, who are more sensitized to such external demands. In other words, the degree of effort that low self-monitors exert on the job is less dependent on their bosses' expectations and more determined by their own intrinsic motivation. What this suggests is that if you are low in self-monitoring, you may be more effective than high self-monitors working in unsupervised settings—if you feel your work is important.

Self-monitoring: A personality trait involving the tendency to use cues from other people's self-presentations in controlling one's own self-presentations.

KEY TERMS

anal stage (p. 361)
archetypes (p. 365)
collective unconscious (p. 365)
conditional positive regard (p. 367)
conscious mind (p. 359)
defense mechanisms (p. 363)
displacement (p. 364)
ego (p. 360)
extraverts (p. 365)
Five-Factor Model (p. 373)
fixation (p. 361)
genital stage (p. 363)
id (p. 360)
interactionism (p. 378)
introverts (p. 365)
latency stage (p. 362)

locus of control (p. 380)
Minnesota Multiphasic Personality Inventory (MMPI) (p. 384)
objective tests (p. 384)
oral stage (p. 361)
peak experiences (p. 367)
personality (p. 357)
personality styles (p. 357)
phallic stage (p. 362)
pleasure principle (p. 360)
preconscious mind (p. 359)
projection (p. 364)
projective tests (p. 382)
psychosexual stages (p. 361)
rationalization (p. 363)
reaction formation (p. 364)

reality principle (p. 360)
reciprocal determinism (p. 379)
regression (p. 364)
repression (p. 363)
Rorschach Inkblot Test (p. 382)
self-efficacy (p. 379)
self-monitoring (p. 388)
self-serving bias (p. 371)
social-cognitive perspective (p. 378)
superego (p. 360)
trait (p. 370)
trait perspective (p. 370)
unconditional positive regard (p. 367)
unconscious mind (p. 359)

REVIEW QUESTIONS

1. The modern study of personality involves all of the following *except*
   a. studying how personality emerges from the interaction between the individual and his or her environment.
   b. approaches that are more limited and narrow than in the first half of the twentieth century.
   c. understanding how people may be generally predictable, yet different from others.
   d. both philosophical and scientific roots.
   e. a focus on overarching and comprehensive descriptions of personality styles.
2. Freud is perhaps best known for the significance of his theory of
   a. glove anesthesia.
   b. the nervous system.
   c. the mind.
   d. biological urges.
   e. hypnosis.

3. Regarding personality, Freud's structural model emphasized the different operating principles and goals that operated within the following subcomponents of the mind:
   a. the collective unconscious and archetypes.
   b. id, ego, and superego.
   c. id, pleasure principle, and archetypes.
   d. ego, reality principle, and the collective unconscious.
   e. id, superego, and reality.
4. Among Freud's contributions was his theory of psychosexual stages, which included an emphasis on
   a. five fixed stages of development in childhood and adolescence.
   b. fixation, which involves unresolved conflicts emerging from too little gratification of id desires.
   c. the Oedipus complex, in which children develop an attachment to their same-sex parent.
   d. the latency stage, when unconscious sexual and aggressive impulses go dormant.
   e. personality development after the age of 5.

5. The psychoanalytic theory of defense mechanisms, or ways we control anxiety-provoking thoughts and impulses, suggests that defense mechanisms
   a. protect the id from unacceptable urges.
   b. represent permanent changes in the structure of the mind.
   c. allow us to understand our unconscious motivations.
   d. explain why we can become civilized.
   e. tend to be consistent, but not distinguishing, characteristics of personality.

6. An individual with a strong desire to perform immoral acts might exhibit extremely moralistic behavior and be harshly judgmental of others, if he used which defense mechanism?
   a. rationalization
   b. reaction formation
   c. displacement
   d. projection
   e. regression

7. All of the alternative approaches to Freud's psychoanalysis have in common the notion that
   a. the collective unconscious is a fourth component of the mind's structure.
   b. social interaction is the basis for personality.
   c. the mind can only be understood through carefully controlled scientific research.
   d. the unconscious mind is less important than Freud claimed.
   e. sexual drives are not central in determining people's personalities.

8. The humanistic model of personality development differed from the predominant views of psychoanalysis and behaviorism primarily in
   a. the discrepancy between Rogers' actual and feared self.
   b. its exclusive focus on the development of psychologically healthy and creative people.
   c. the belief that individual psychological growth is predetermined.
   d. its optimistic approach to the possibilities for positive human change.
   e. the scientific and testable hypotheses it generated.

9. The trait approach to personality is primarily focused on
   a. describing how people differ from one another in specific ways.
   b. Allport's view that behavior varies across situations.
   c. relatively new ideas concerning the classification of people according to personality types.
   d. direct measurement, rather than inference, of personality characteristics.
   e. describing why people differ from one another in specific ways.

10. There is general consensus among personality researchers today that the basic personality traits
    a. are biologically or genetically determined.
    b. capture the essence of individual personality.
    c. are a result of adaptive human evolution.
    d. vary across cultures.
    e. include neuroticism, extraversion, openness to experience, agreeableness, and conscientiousness.

11. Mischel's controversial claim concerning the predictive ability of personality traits
    a. was based on limited samples of behavior.
    b. was supported by Epstein's view that traits reliably predict behavior.
    c. led to the realization that situations do not play a role in shaping behavior.
    d. generated new research but did not increase the ability to predict behavior.
    e. indicated that children are reliably honest or dishonest across situations.

12. The social-cognitive approach describes personality as primarily based on
    a. classical conditioning.
    b. operant conditioning.
    c. an individualist approach.
    d. observational learning.
    e. direct experience.

13. Bandura's *reciprocal determinism* explains that
    a. the environment plays a more important role in behavior than the individual.
    b. self-efficacy is stable and consistent across situations.
    c. personality emerges from an ongoing mutual interaction between people's cognitions, actions, and environment.
    d. individual perceptions are of little consequence in determining behavior.
    e. there is no relationship between self-efficacy and self-esteem.

14. The concept of locus of control, originated by Rotter, is associated with all of the following *except*
    a. a belief in one's ability to control the outcomes in one's life.
    b. learned helplessness.
    c. anger and acting-out behaviors.
    d. achievement orientation.
    e. success in life.

15. The primary difference between projective and objective measures of personality is that
    a. objective measures rely on ambiguous stimuli, while projective measures are more direct.
    b. projective tests assess unconscious aspects of personality, while objective tests assess conscious aspects of personality.
    c. objective tests are scored on the basis of a correct answer, while there are no correct answers on projective tests.
    d. projective tests are more reliable and valid than objective tests.
    e. objective tests are used primarily to start conversations about a client's problems.

Psychological Disorders

When I returned from my cross-country trip studying hitchhikers in the fall of 1973 (see chapter 1), my junior year in college was before me. Two of my friends and I had rented a two-bedroom apartment near campus and we needed another boarder to help pay the rent. After placing an ad in the local paper, we rashly accepted the first person who expressed an interest in the vacancy. Our new living companion was Jim, a quiet, frail-looking young man with long hair and a droopy moustache.

At first, other than being very quiet, Jim appeared to be your average college student. However, after a time, we noticed that he was lacking in virtually any kind of emotional expressiveness. He rarely smiled or laughed and his actions were slow, as if he were moving through molasses. We also soon noticed that Jim regularly repeated two specific behaviors. One behavior was flicking on and off a cigarette lighter, and the other was opening and closing a small pocketknife. Both items were always in his hand or pants pocket. Strange, we thought. But was it any stranger than our roommate Pete repeatedly playing his favorite record album (yes, record, not tape or CD), the Doors' *Soft Parade*, every single day? Was it stranger than Doug flopping down in his feather-bag chair like clockwork every day at 4 P.M.? Or stranger than me waking up every night and writing down my dreams in a notebook near my bed? Yes, we concluded, it was stranger than all those behaviors, but perhaps only by degree.

One group ritual that we quickly developed was returning to our apartment every day after classes to relax and watch reruns of the science fiction TV show *Star Trek* (with Captain Kirk and Spock). Although Jim would join us, he rarely spoke. Then one day, as an episode began, Pete burst out with an "Oh boy!!!" He was excited because he had never seen this episode before. To our surprise, the usually quiet Jim turned to Pete and asked, "Why did you call me a boy?" Utterly perplexed, Pete replied that he did no such thing, but rather, was simply excited at what he was about to watch. Not satisfied with this explanation, Jim continued, "Well, if you weren't calling me a boy, then you must have been calling him a boy." He was pointing at the television. Slowly, we realized that Jim was referring to an African-American actor on the screen. No amount of subsequent persuasion by Pete could convince Jim (who, by the way, was not African American) that his roommate was not condescending to him or to minorities. Jim was convinced that Pete was "out to get him."

That same week, Doug was in charge of preparing our evening meals. After one such culinary treat, Jim confronted Doug and accused him of putting "speed" (amphetamines, see chapter 6, section 6-3g) in his food. Again, no amount of persuasion could convince Jim that Doug wasn't trying to poison him. After all, Jim said, what else could explain the sensations he was experiencing in his body? As with Pete following the Star Trek incident, Doug was now "the enemy."

About a week following these strange incidents, Pete came home from class, put his favorite album on the turntable and settled down to relax. Yet, as the needle touched the record, it simply slid across the vinyl. No *Soft Parade*. When Pete inspected his prized record, he discovered that the vinyl grooves that produce the music had been fused together by some sort of intense heat. Immediately, the image of Jim flicking his cigarette lighter on and off popped into Pete's mind and a chill ran down his back. Just then, Doug arrived home. Before Pete could tell him about the record, Doug plopped down in his feather-bag chair and was showered by goose down that burst from hundreds of puncture holes in the chair's fabric. Doug and Pete stared dumbfounded as feathers slowly settled on the carpeting. They looked like figures in a snow-globe scene. Immediately, the image of Jim opening and closing his pocketknife popped into their minds. And like those snow globes that captivate one's attention when shaken, we soon realized that our apartment had been similarly shaken, but by a powerful, invisible force beyond our understanding. We definitely had a problem. If Jim was destroying our cherished possessions as a form of distorted and misguided retribution, what was next?

* * * * *

Jim is an example of someone who experiences severe problems in his daily living, leading him (and those around him) to experience significant distress. When exhibiting his bizarre thinking and behavior, those with whom Jim interacted were generally at a loss about how to respond. Reasoning with Jim often wasn't effective, and ignoring his destructive actions was not an option. As his apartment mates, we wondered what was causing Jim to think, feel, and behave in a manner that was so dysfunctional.

Statistics gathered by the U.S. Bureau of the Census (2001) indicate that about 2.1 million Americans are admitted to hospitals every year due to serious psychological problems, and over twice as many seek help as outpatients for less severe mental health problems. Further, it is estimated that 20 percent of all persons in the United States in any given year experience psychological problems sufficiently severe that it adversely affects their daily living, and 40 percent experience at least mild mental health problems (Kessler et al., 1994; Surgeon General, 1999). Worldwide, about 400 million people are afflicted with psychological disorders, and such problems account for 15 percent of the years of life lost due to death or disability, just below that caused by heart disease (Murray & Lopez, 1996; Phillips et al., 2002).

Many of the mental health problems addressed in this chapter are common, and so it is likely that some of the conditions discussed will remind you of someone you know, including yourself. Yet, even if you have not yet met people with serious psychological problems, you are likely to encounter them as your circle of acquaintances grows. Because you will eventually meet people with psychological problems, it is important to have a basic understanding of their types and causes. The goal of this chapter is to introduce you to the topic of psychological disorders. In doing so, you will encounter three basic questions. First, how should we *define* psychological disorders? Next, what are the important theoretical perspectives used to *understand* these disorders? Finally, how should we *classify* the major types of psychological disorders?

13-1   HOW SHOULD WE DEFINE AND EXPLAIN PSYCHOLOGICAL DISORDERS?

Based on what you have learned about Jim and his strange behavior, you probably suspect that he has some sort of psychological disorder. But how do we decide when a pattern of behavior is simply "different" or "quirky" and when it is disordered? And how do we explain such behavior?

13-1a   The Medical Model Proposes That Psychological Disorders Are Like Diseases

Many psychologists believe that a useful approach in organizing our thinking about mental health problems comes from the field of medicine. The *medical model* proposes that psychological disorders have a biological basis and can be classified into discrete categories and are analogous to physical diseases. Although not agreeing that all mental health

We do not have to visit a madhouse to find disordered minds; our planet is the mental institution of the universe.

—German philosopher Johann von Goethe, 1749–1832

Symptom: A sign of a disorder.

Diagnosis: The process of distinguishing one disorder from another.

Etiology: The initial cause that led to the development of the disorder.

Prognosis: A prediction about the likely course of a disorder.

problems have a biological basis, mainstream psychology has adopted the medical model's terminology, using such medical terms as illness and disorder when referring to troublesome behavior patterns. As in the medical profession, in psychology a **symptom** is a sign of a disorder, **diagnosis** involves distinguishing one disorder from another, **etiology** refers to a disorder's apparent causes and developmental history, and **prognosis** is a prediction about the likely course of a disorder.

Since the late eighteenth century, the medical model has reflected the dominant way of thinking about mental disorders. Yet, in the late 1800s and early 1900s, Freud and other psychologically oriented therapists challenged its assumption that biological factors were the cause of all mental illness. In the latter half of the twentieth century, some critics argued that the medical model had outlived its usefulness. One of the most forceful critics has been Thomas Szasz (1961, 1990), who contends that mental illness is a myth created by modern society and legitimated by the medical profession and their "disease" model. Szasz proposes that, instead of labeling people as "sick," a more accurate way to describe those who cannot live according to society's norms and conventions is that they have "problems in living." Although Szasz's critique is today viewed by most mental health professionals as overly simplistic and naïve, his criticisms played a role in sensitizing the society at large to the dangers in labeling people with psychological disorders as social deviants (see section 13-2a). In this respect, his ideas have promoted greater acceptance of those with psychological problems. Despite this benefit, most psychologists believe that it is still useful to think of psychological disorders as *like* diseases, although it should be kept in mind that this is only an analogy.

13-1b A Psychological Disorder Involves Atypical Behavior That Causes Personal Distress or Social Impairment

Over the years, operating from this general medical model, psychologists and other mental health professionals have developed criteria to differentiate normal from disordered behavior. Let us review the major criteria used in making such distinctions.

Atypical Behavior

One way to differentiate *disordered* from normal behavior is in terms of its statistical frequency in the general population. Behavior that is significantly above or below the average in its frequency of occurrence is atypical and thus is more likely to be classified as a psychological disorder. Jim's compulsive actions of repeatedly flicking on and off his lighter and opening and closing his pocketknife were certainly unusual, and they provided a signal of an underlying psychological disorder. However, relying only on this criterion of statistical infrequency can easily lead to false judgments. For instance, the behavioral accomplishments of Nobel Prize winners and Hall of Fame athletes are statistically infrequent, but few would label these persons as suffering from a psychological disorder. On the other hand, some disorders, such as anxiety and depression, are statistically common in contemporary society. Thus, we cannot solely rely on deviations from what is "average" in identifying psychological disorders.

Violation of Cultural Norms

Another way to differentiate between disordered and normal behavior is whether the exhibited behavior violates cultural norms. For example, in mainstream American culture,

Why do psychiatrists systematically impose themselves on persons who want to have nothing to do with them? I believe they do so because, like most people, psychiatrists love power and exult in pushing others around.

—Psychiatrist Thomas Szasz, b. 1920

reporting hallucinations is likely to raise concerns about your sanity. Yet, among various American Indian nations or the Holy Ghost worshipers of Appalachia, hallucinogenic experiences are often perceived as normal and an essential ingredient in spiritual enlightenment (see chapter 6, section 6-3d). Even within a given culture, shifts in norms can change people's perceptions of what is a mental disorder. As previously discussed in chapter 11, section 11-2c, up until 1973, homosexuality was labeled a psychological disorder by the American Psychiatric Association, not only because it was atypical, but also because it violated prevailing standards of morality. As these examples attest, simply relying on violations of cultural norms is not adequate in determining what is considered disordered.

Maladaptive Behavior

There is more to a psychological disorder than being atypical or out of sync with cultural norms. Such behavior is much more likely to be considered disordered if it is judged maladaptive—disruptive or harmful—for the person or society. The inability to perform normal activities is an indication of maladaptiveness. Not leaving your house because you fear crowds, repeatedly being fired from jobs due to excessive drinking, or losing your life savings due to compulsive gambling are all examples of maladaptive behavior. Maladaptiveness is generally considered the most important criterion in defining a disorder.

Personal Distress

Individuals who report experiencing troubling emotions are often considered to have psychological problems. They may be able to perform normal activities, such as caring for family members and holding a job, but they feel unreasonably fearful, anxious, guilty, angry, or depressed. One of the advantages in using this criterion is that it takes into account a person's own distress level rather than using the same standard for everyone. A behavior that is upsetting and extremely stressful for one person, such as the inability to maintain intimacy with others, may not be disturbing to another. The problem with this criterion, however, is that some people who suffer from psychological disorders—and who cause harm to themselves and others—are not troubled by their behavior. Further, some individuals may not be able to tell us how much distress they are experiencing because they are very young or are otherwise unable to communicate.

As you see, one of these criteria alone is usually insufficient in differentiating normal from disordered behavior. Although psychologists will sometimes rely on only one criterion in making their diagnoses, they are more confident when more than one of these indicators is present and valid. In the end, diagnoses of psychological disorders often involve *value judgments* about what behaviors cross the bounds of normality. All four criteria are useful in arriving at a diagnosis, but they are not completely objective, and thus, they can be influenced by the psychologist's value judgments (Kutchins & Kirk, 1997). Drawing a line that clearly separates normality from abnormality is often difficult because, in reality, these distinctions represent two ends of a continuum. In this chapter, a

---

INFO-BIT: In the South before the Civil War, many slaves were diagnosed with one or two forms of mental illness because their behavior violated cultural norms (Landrine, 1988). *Drapetomania* was a psychological disorder in which a slave had an uncontrollable urge to escape from bondage, and *dysathesia aethiopica* was a disorder in which a slave was disobedient to her or his owners. Although labeling the desire to be free and the resentment of human bondage as "disorders" seems ludicrous today, such labeling illustrates how culture can shape our perceptions of mental illness.

The only difference between me and a madman is that I'm not mad.

—Salvador Dali, Spanish artist, 1904–1989

psychological disorder is defined as a pattern of atypical behavior that results in personal distress or a significant impairment in a person's social or occupational functioning. Using this definition, Jim would definitely be classified as suffering from a mental disorder. He certainly was experiencing considerable anxiety and distress, his repetitive actions were definitely unusual, and his physical symptoms and the nature of his social interactions were definitely interfering with normal daily living.

13-1c Psychologists Employ Numerous Theoretical Perspectives in Explaining Mental Illness

The vast majority of contemporary psychologists believe that mental illness is real, but they do not always agree on its nature and causes. In general, psychological approaches to understanding mental illness assume that disordered behavior, like normal behavior, can be explained by people's past and present life experiences. Let us briefly review five such approaches, namely, the psychodynamic, behavioral, cognitive, sociocultural, and biological perspectives.

The Psychodynamic Perspective

As first described in chapter 12, the **psychodynamic perspective** asserts that disordered behavior, like normal behavior, is not freely chosen, but rather, is controlled by unconscious forces that have been largely shaped by childhood experiences. The founding father of the psychodynamic perspective, Sigmund Freud, contended that early traumatic events leave the individual with troubling feelings and memories. Because this material is painful, the individual represses it to the unconscious. Once this material is unconscious, the individual does not experience the anxiety that would result if the painful material were faced directly. However, although this painful material is beyond conscious awareness, it continues to influence the person's behavior and is often expressed indirectly through the action of defense mechanisms. This idea of how the unconscious mind shapes people's everyday actions formed the basis for Freud's theory of *psychoanalysis* (see chapter 12, sections 12-2a and 12-2b).

A well-known example of Freud's explanation of psychological disorders is the case of Little Hans (Freud, 1909/1963). Hans was a young boy who developed an intense fear of horses. Freud explained the child's fear as due to an unconscious fear of his father. Because fearing his father would be painful to acknowledge, the boy repressed this fear and displaced it onto a more acceptable alternative. A horse is large and strong, just like the boy's father, and so the horse became a symbolic representation of the father. According to psychoanalytic theory, the etiology of the fear was a troubling childhood experience, and the maintaining cause was the unconscious fear of father.

The Behavioral Perspective

While the psychodynamic perspective assumes that "what you see is not what you get" when you analyze mental illness, the **behavioral perspective** assumes that disordered behavior is caused by readily identifiable factors in the person's environment and is the product of learning. As you recall from chapter 7, section 7-2, behaviorists believe that learning occurs through *conditioning*. In classical conditioning, a previously neutral stimulus is paired with a stimulus that automatically elicits a reflexive response, the unconditioned stimulus. Through repeated pairing of the neutral and unconditioned stimulus, the neutral stimulus comes to elicit a response similar to the reflexive response. Classical conditioning can explain the development of several reflexive responses, including those that might lead to the development of a psychological disorder. For example, the fear response toward a white rat that John Watson and Rosalie Rayner (1920) classically conditioned in "Little Albert" (see chapter 7, Discovery Box 7-2) provided insights concerning the development of phobic disorders (see section 13-3a). Other physiological responses that occur reflexively to certain stimuli, such as allergies, nausea, and sexual arousal, may also be classically conditioned to occur in response to what had initially been neutral stimuli.

The other basic form of conditioning is operant conditioning, which is driven by reinforcement and punishment (see chapter 7, section 7-2a). As you recall, behaviors followed by reinforcement will increase in frequency, while those followed by punishment will decrease in frequency. Operant conditioning explains why some individuals develop troubling behaviors (for example, a child's misconduct is reinforced), and also why some people fail to develop appropriate behaviors (for example, a child fails to learn appropriate social skills). According to the behavioral perspective, the etiology (initial cause) of disordered behavior is conditioning, whereas the maintaining cause is either the problem behavior itself or the environment that continues to condition the behavior.

The Cognitive Perspective

Cognition is important in understanding psychological disorders, because, as you will soon learn, many disorders involve severe cognitive disturbances. Indeed, the **cognitive perspective** holds that ineffective or inaccurate thinking is the root cause of mental illness (Beck, 1991). According to this viewpoint, the person's faulty cognitive style is acquired through learning, perhaps from observing how one's parents interpret their experiences or from interpreting and attempting to understand one's own experiences. This ineffective way of thinking leads the person to experience troubling emotions or to behave ineffectively. Cognitive theorists believe that the etiology of a psychological problem is learning, and the maintaining cause is the faulty cognitive style.

Cognitive perspective: A psychological approach that attempts to understand behavior by studying how the mind organizes perceptions, processes information, and interprets experiences.

The Sociocultural Perspective

Theorists from the **sociocultural perspective** propose that mental illness is the product of broad social and cultural forces. Evidence for this viewpoint comes from a number of sources. For example, within a given culture, rates of psychological disorders are higher in poor urban settings than in other segments of the population (Kessler et al., 1994). Further, as unemployment increases, psychiatric hospital admissions and suicides tend to similarly increase (Pines, 1993). These findings suggest to sociocultural researchers that social forces, such as poverty, urbanization, and inequality, may be primary causes of many mental health problems (Lott, 2002).

Cross-culturally, although certain psychological disorders are universally encountered, others are limited to specific societies or cultural areas. For example, in only Mediterranean cultures do people suffer from *mal de ojo*, or "the evil eye," in which they experience fitful sleep, unexplained crying, diarrhea, vomiting, and fever. Similarly, only among the Arctic and sub-Arctic Eskimos do you find the *pibloktog* disorder, which involves an abrupt break with reality, violence, and hyperexcitability, followed by seizures and coma (Simons & Hughes, 1993). The existence of such *culture-bound syndromes*, along with the fluctuations that occur in mental illness rates due to socioeconomic factors, demonstrate that a complete understanding of psychological disorders must consider people's sociocultural context.

Sociocultural perspective: An approach to psychology that emphasizes social and cultural influences on behavior.

The Biological Perspective

While the perspectives on mental illness that we have reviewed so far primarily focus on the relationship between the mind and the social environment, biological researchers focus on the relationship between the mind and the body. This **biological perspective** proposes that psychological disorders are caused by biological conditions, such as genetics, hormone levels, or neurotransmitter activity in the brain. These biological irregularities are shaped by a variety of factors, including illness and response to environmental stressors, and they often can be treated through medical intervention and drug therapies (see chapter 14, section 14-7).

Biological perspective: An approach to psychology that attempts to understand behavior by examining physiological processes, especially those occurring in the brain.

All are lunatics, but he who can analyze his delusion is called a philosopher.
—Ambrose Pierce, American satirist, 1842–1914

Movement toward a Multiperspective Approach

Table 13-1 summarizes the five theoretical approaches to understanding mental illness. Over the years, as researchers have attempted to identify the origins of psychological disorders, they have discovered that adequate one-perspective explanations are rare. Further, it should be kept in mind that a perspective's emphasis on one set of symptoms does not mean that it ignores symptoms emphasized by other theoretical perspectives. For example, cognitive theorists assess social, behavioral, biological, and psychodynamic symptoms, but they emphasize the cognitions that occur prior to and simultaneously with these other symptoms. Today, many current explanations of psychological disorders combine the various perspectives into one overall account.

One such interdisciplinary approach is the **diathesis-stress model** (Kendler et al., 2002), illustrated in figure 13-1. A *diathesis* is an underlying vulnerability or predisposition that may be caused by genetic inheritance, biological processes, or early learning experiences. A person with such a diathesis is susceptible to developing a problem when experiencing later stress. Without the diathesis, stress alone may not be sufficient to produce a disorder (Zuckerman, 1999). For example, a person may have inherited neural problems that are associated with panic disorder. Further, overly protective parents may have taught the person to closely monitor his or her physiological reactions, which is also associated with panic disorder. Yet, these predispositions may be expressed as a panic disorder only when the individual is experiencing high levels of stress in life. If such stress is infrequent, or if the person has learned how to adequately cope with such stressful events, he or she may never have a panic attack, or it may be relatively mild. Thus, the diathesis-stress model proposes that it is the interaction of both the predisposition for a disorder (diathesis) and environmental stressors that cause the psychological disorder. Periodically, throughout the chapter, we discuss how the diathesis-stress model can provide additional insight into how the other perspectives might interact in explaining a particular psychological disorder.

Diathesis-stress model:
A predisposition to a given disorder (diathesis) that combines with environmental stressors to trigger a psychological disorder.

TABLE 13-1

The Etiology of Psychological Disorders by Theoretical Perspective

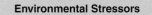

Perspective	Etiology
Psychodynamic	Unconscious conflict from childhood experiences
Behavioral	Conditioning from the environment
Cognitive	Learning ineffective or inaccurate thinking
Sociocultural	Broad social and cultural forces
Biological	Genetics, hormone levels, neurotransmitter activity

---

FIGURE 13-1
The Diathesis-Stress Model

The diathesis-stress model proposes that a predisposition to a psychological disorder (diathesis) interacts with environmental stressors to cause the disorder. According to this model, the diathesis alone and the stressors alone are unlikely to trigger the disorder.

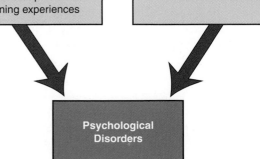

SECTION SUMMARY

- The medical model proposes that psychological disorders are like physical diseases.

- Psychologists employ multiple perspectives in studying psychological disorders.

- The diathesis-stress model proposes that it is the interaction of both the predisposition for a psychological disorder (diathesis) and environmental stressors that cause the emergence of the disorder.

13-2 HOW SHOULD WE CLASSIFY PSYCHOLOGICAL DISORDERS?

Given that the distinction between normality and abnormality is a matter of degree rather than an either-or proposition, to what extent is the diagnostic process susceptible to judgmental bias? What are the risks and benefits in diagnosing psychological disorders?

13-2a Using Diagnostic Labels Has Both Risks and Benefits

David Rosenhan (1971) demonstrated the biasing effects of diagnostic labels when he and seven of his friends and Stanford University colleagues went to various psychiatric hospitals and presented themselves as would-be patients. When asked by the hospital personnel about their problem, these pseudopatients reported that they heard voices saying "thud," "hollow," and "empty." Aside from this complaint and giving fictitious names and occupations, they answered all other questions honestly. Every single one of these individuals was admitted as a patient, most often with the diagnosis of schizophrenia. During their hospital stay, the pseudopatients acted normally, keeping records about their treatment. They remained in the hospital, on average, for about three weeks. In most cases, the discharge diagnosis stated that their schizophrenia was in remission, meaning that the "patient" no longer exhibited active symptoms of the disorder. Rosenhan concluded that the misdiagnosis of insanity by the hospital personnel was due to their general bias to call a healthy person sick.

Diagnostic labels can harm patients in several ways. First, the label may "dehumanize" patients by encouraging mental health practitioners to treat them as labels rather than as unique individuals with problems. Further, labeled individuals may experience discrimination if job, housing, or other social opportunities are limited due to negative stereotypes of the mentally ill. Such labeling may also cause people to expect those labeled to behave abnormally and thus to misperceive normal behavior as disordered. This sometimes occurred in the Rosenhan study, such as when pseudopatients' questions about their medication or their note-taking about staff interactions were interpreted by hospital personnel as further symptoms of the previously diagnosed disorder.

Despite these ethical concerns, mental health professionals continue to use diagnoses because they serve several important functions. The first benefit of a diagnostic label is that it summarizes the patient's presenting symptoms or problems. Rather than listing each patient's entire set of symptoms, clinicians can communicate a great deal of information about a patient with a single word. A second benefit is that a diagnostic label conveys information about possible causes of the disorder. For some psychological disorders, research has identified clear causal and maintaining factors, and so the diagnostic label carries with it much useful information that helps the psychologist understand the individual's condition. In other disorders where the etiology and maintaining causes are still unclear, the diagnostic label may suggest to the psychologist a range of possible causes to consider when working with the patient. A third benefit of a diagnostic label is that it conveys information about the patient's prognosis, or expected future course. An important aspect of the prognosis is the patient's likely response to treatment.

In summary, although diagnostic labels may sometimes lead to aversive consequences for those suffering from psychological disorders, they also convey important information about the nature, probable causes, and likely treatments of the problem. Psychologists continue to use diagnostic labels due to these benefits, while being mindful of the potential risks.

13-2b The *Diagnostic and Statistical Manual of Mental Disorders* Is the Most Widely Used Classification Scheme

Diagnostic and Statistical Manual of Mental Disorders (DSM): Manual of psychological disorders published by the American Psychiatric Association and used for descriptive diagnoses.

In any science, it is important to accurately and reliably classify whatever you are studying into categories. Research in the 1950s and 1960s indicated that the categories into which psychological disorders were classified were not sufficiently reliable to be useful (Wierzbicki, 1993). Responding to criticisms concerning the reliability and validity of psychological diagnoses, psychologists and psychiatrists worked to improve their classification scheme, culminating in the publication of the **Diagnostic and Statistical Manual of Mental Disorders (DSM)** by the American Psychiatric Association in 1980. This system has been since updated several times and is now in its fourth edition, text revision, or *DSM-IV-TR* (American Psychiatric Association, 2000). The *DSM's* classification system is based on the medical model, in which psychological disorders are viewed as diseases.

The *DSM* differs from previous diagnostic systems in several ways. First, this classification system is *descriptive* rather than explanatory, meaning that it is not based on a particular theory concerning what causes psychological disorders: It is *atheoretical*. Thus, diagnoses are based more on observable symptoms than on the clinician's judgment about the underlying cause of these symptoms. Second, the *DSM* provides clearer directions to clinicians concerning the number, duration, and severity of symptoms that are necessary to assign a diagnosis. By recognizing that two patients with the same disorder may substantially differ from one another, the *DSM* forces clinicians to acknowledge the uniqueness of all patients.

These improvements address many of the criticisms of diagnostic labels, and numerous studies indicate that *DSM* diagnoses are in fact more reliable than previous diagnostic systems (Blacker & Tsuang, 1999; Spitzer et al., 1979). However, critics still contend that the DSM incorrectly views many normal behaviors as indicative of a psychological disorder (Eysenck et al., 1983; Malik & Beutler, 2002). For example, an irrational fear of embarrassment is considered to be a symptom of social phobia, while a habitual tendency to violate rules at home or school is a symptom of conduct disorder (Pomerantz, 2002). In response, ongoing research seeks to improve the reliability and validity of *DSM* diagnoses, and to address criticisms of specific sections of the diagnostic system. In this respect, the *DSM* is truly a "work in progress." As research identifies new disorders or more reliable ways of diagnosing a disorder, these results are incorporated into new versions of the *DSM*.

INFO-BIT: Contrary to earlier research indicating that psychological disorders occur more often among African Americans than among White Americans, recent findings from the National Survey of American Life point to lower rates of mental illness among African Americans. This survey also found higher rates of psychological disorders in Hispanics in comparison to non-Hispanic Whites (Chernoff, 2002).

SECTION SUMMARY

- Two risks in using diagnostic labels are (1) mental health professionals may become biased in interpreting normal behavior as disordered in those labeled as mentally ill and (2) labeled individuals may be stigmatized by others and subject to discrimination.

- Using labels does have benefits; for example, diagnostic labels communicate valuable information, including possible causes of the disorder, its likely course, and possible treatment.

- Most clinicians rely on the *Diagnostic and Statistical Manual of Mental Disorders (DSM)* when diagnosing psychological disorders.

13-3 THE MAJOR CLASSES OF DISORDERS IDENTIFIED BY *DSM-IV*

The remainder of this chapter introduces you to the major classes of psychological disorders. Each class of disorders is defined according to the most severe or most prominent of the patient's symptoms. While reading about these disorders, keep in mind that you may have experienced some of these symptoms yourself at some time. In recognizing yourself, you may begin to worry that you are suffering from one (or more) of these disorders. Don't become alarmed. The truth of the matter is that many of the described symptoms are fairly common in the general population. Only when these symptoms significantly disrupt our functioning or sense of well-being are they indicative of a possible psychological disorder. In such instances, you should seek the help of a mental health professional for proper diagnosis and treatment.

13-3a Anxiety Disorders Are Characterized by Distressing, Persistent Anxiety or Maladaptive Behavior

Everybody experiences anxiety. However, what distinguishes anxiety disorders from "normal" anxiety are the severity of the emotional distress and the degree to which the anxiety disrupts daily functioning. **Anxiety disorders,** which are characterized by distressing, persistent anxiety or maladaptive behavior, are the most common psychological disorders (Hollander et al., 2002). About 25 percent of us will experience this disorder in our lifetime (Kessler et al., 1994). Anxiety disorders occur across the life span and commonly co-occur with many other disorders, such as depression and substance abuse. We discuss five major anxiety disorders in this section: panic disorder, phobic disorder, obsessive-compulsive disorder (OCD), generalized anxiety disorder (GAD), and post-traumatic stress disorder (PTSD).

Anxiety disorders: Disorders characterized by distressing, persistent anxiety or maladaptive behavior.

Panic Disorder

Maya is a 28-year-old hair stylist who has **panic disorder,** which is characterized by episodes of intense anxiety without an apparent reason. When she has these "attacks," Maya often feels dizzy, her heart races, she sweats and has tremors, and she may even faint. Besides these physiological symptoms, her psychological symptoms may include fear of dying, fear of suffocating, fear of "going crazy," and fear of losing control and doing something drastic, such as killing herself or others.

Panic episodes have a clear beginning and end and are relatively brief, usually lasting no more than a few minutes. As you can imagine, such episodes are extremely frightening, often leading sufferers like Maya to seek immediate medical attention out of concern that they are dying. Panic disorder is also relatively common, with about 3 percent of the general population worldwide experiencing it during their lifetimes (Kessler et al., 1994;

Panic disorder: An anxiety disorder characterized by episodes of intense fear and dread that usually occur suddenly and unexpectedly.

Weissman et al., 1997). In general, this anxiety disorder occurs more often in young adults than in older adults (Blazer, 1997), with about twice as many women (5 percent) suffering from it as men (2 percent).

People often take extreme steps to limit the occurrence of panic episodes. For example, Maya is embarrassed about having a panic episode in public, so she limits her social activities. She also avoids locations in which she has experienced previous panic episodes, and so she has stopped going to shopping malls and restaurants. As you can see, like many panic disorder sufferers, Maya has significantly restricted her social activities outside her home. Such restriction of activities outside the home in an attempt to limit panic episodes creates a condition called **agoraphobia,** which is a fear of going out in public or open places. As its name implies, until recently agoraphobia was classified as a phobic disorder (see next subsection). Recent studies, however, suggest that it is primarily a complication of panic disorder (Hollander et al., 1999). One reason agoraphobia was not earlier recognized as developing from panic disorder was that such sufferers rarely came to clinics for treatment due to their avoidance of outside activities.

Phobic Disorder

Another anxiety disorder is **phobic disorder,** which is characterized by strong irrational fears of specific objects or situations, called *phobias*. It is estimated that between 9 to 15 percent of adults suffer from phobic disorder, with women being about twice as likely as men to have specific phobias and to develop phobic symptoms earlier (age 10 for females and age 14 for males) (Dick et al., 1994; Kessler et al., 1994).

Different types of phobias tend to have different courses. For example, fears of strangers, doctors, storms, and the dark are more common in children than adults, whereas fears of cancer and death of a loved one are more common in adults. Interestingly, phobias have a moderate tendency to run in families, so that individuals with phobias tend to have close relatives with similar kinds of phobias (Rose & Ditto, 1983).

When analyzing phobic disorders, it is important to distinguish them from rational fears that occur in the presence of a realistic threat. For example, it is normal to experience fear when encountering a mugger or when riding in a car that skids off the road. It is also important to distinguish clinical phobias from *subclinical phobias*, which are mild irrational fears that do not interfere with daily functioning. You may experience fear when encountering a huge spider in your basement. If you continue to use the basement for normal activities despite your fear, you have a subclinical phobia. In contrast, if you are so afraid of seeing the spider that you no longer go down to your basement, than you may have a clinical phobia. Figure 13-2 lists some common phobias.

Agoraphobia: A fear of going out to public or open spaces.

Phobic disorder: An anxiety disorder characterized by strong, irrational fears of specific objects or situations.

FIGURE 13-2
Frequency of Common Phobias

Many people experience fear when exposed to these stimuli. In most of these cases, the fear represents "subclinical phobias," meaning they would not be indicative of a psychological disaster.

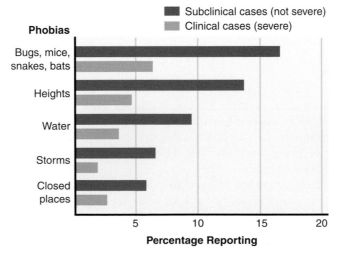

Generalized Anxiety Disorder

Generalized anxiety disorder (GAD) is characterized by a constant state of moderate anxiety. This anxiety differs from normal anxiety that occurs in response to actual stressful events or situations. For example, if you are a full-time college student who works 20 hours a week and maintains an active social life, it is normal to experience stress and anxiety throughout the semester. Further, the anxiety experienced in GAD differs from the anxiety felt in phobic disorder, because, in GAD, there is no clear object or situation that causes the anxiety. Instead, the anxiety is "free-floating." GAD also differs from panic disorder in that the anxiety does not occur in discrete, relatively brief episodes, but instead, is constant.

GAD occurs in about 5 percent of the general population in their lifetime, about twice as often in women as men, and more often among those over the age of 24 (Kessler et al., 1994). GAD often occurs in association with other problems, including other anxiety disorders and depression (Craske, 1999).

Generalized anxiety disorder (GAD): An anxiety disorder characterized by a constant state of moderate anxiety.

Obsessive-Compulsive Disorder

Obsessive-compulsive disorder (OCD) is an anxiety disorder characterized by repetitive, unwanted, and distressing actions and/or thoughts. *Obsessions* are repetitive thoughts or ideas that cause distress or interfere significantly with ongoing activity. For example, some OCD sufferers may be bothered by thoughts of killing themselves or others, even though they have no history of and are not truly at risk for suicide or homicide. *Compulsions* are repetitive actions or behaviors that cause distress or interfere significantly with ongoing activity. Most OCD rituals can be classified as cleaning or checking. Some OCD sufferers engage in hand-washing rituals, cleaning their hands hundreds of times a day, while others feel compelled to repeatedly check the locks on their doors before they can leave the house.

OCD is associated with intense anxiety. OCD patients experience many anxiety-provoking obsessions, such as fears of contamination and worries about not having taken steps to prevent harm. These obsessive thoughts are followed by compulsive rituals, which reduce the anxiety associated with the obsessions. However, the compulsive rituals lower anxiety only temporarily, and soon the individual must repeat them or add to their length.

Psychologists today recognize that this disorder is more common than had been thought in the past. The lifetime prevalence of OCD is from 2 to 3 percent, with females having a somewhat higher risk level than men (Karno et al., 1988). This disorder tends to develop in adolescence or young adulthood, although it may not be diagnosed until years later. OCD sufferers usually are embarrassed about their symptoms and try to hide them from others. Thus, it may be years before the symptoms become so intense that they can no longer be hidden. Research indicates that there is at least a moderate genetic influence on OCD (Pato et al., 2002; Pauls et al., 1995).

Obsessive-compulsive disorder (OCD): An anxiety disorder characterized by repetitive, unwanted, and distressing actions and/or thoughts.

Post-Traumatic Stress Disorder

Post-traumatic stress disorder (PTSD) occurs in some individuals who have experienced or witnessed life-threatening or other traumatic events. Following such trauma, some people experience intense emotional distress, reexperiencing of the event (say, through nightmares or flashbacks), and avoidance of situations or persons that trigger flashbacks. When these symptoms occur long after the original trauma and when these symptoms significantly interfere with normal daily functioning, then the individual is said to have PTSD (Lamprecht & Sack, 2002).

Research suggests that almost 8 percent of the general population experiences PTSD symptoms throughout their lifetime (Kessler et al., 1995). Although highly dramatic events such as warfare and natural disasters can lead to this disorder, most PTSD patients have experienced more common types of trauma, such as rape, child abuse, and witnessing violence (Bromet & Havenaar, 2002; Ullman & Brecklin, 2002). Risk varies with the nature and severity of the trauma. For example, the lifetime risk for PTSD following rape is about 35 percent (Kilpatrick & Resnick, 1993), while the lifetime risk following

Post-traumatic stress disorder (PTSD): An anxiety disorder characterized by flashbacks and recurrent thoughts of life-threatening or other traumatic events.

automobile accidents ranges from 8 to 41 percent, depending on the severity of the accident (Craske, 1999; Keppel-Benson et al., 2002). In general, as the severity of the traumatic event increases, the risk for PTSD increases. Discovery Box 13-1 explores how traumatic life events can threaten and alter our basic beliefs about life.

Etiology of Anxiety Disorders

Several biological factors appear to influence the development of anxiety disorders. As previously discussed in chapter 7, section 7-1c, our genetic heritage may predispose us to more easily develop phobic reactions toward certain objects and situations, such as snakes and heights, because they once posed real dangers to our ancestors (Buss, 1995; Kleinknecht, 1991). According to this evolutionary explanation, the reason snakes and heights make many of us unduly anxious and are the source of phobic reactions is because the genes that trigger such anxiety are still part of our biological makeup. Genetics also play a contributory role in both panic disorder and obsessive-compulsive disorder (Goldstein et al., 1997; Pato et al., 2002). For example, panic disorder is more likely to be shared by identical twins than fraternal twins (Kendler et al., 1999; Torgersen, 1983), and family, twin, and adoption studies indicate that OCD has at least a moderate genetic influence (Billett et al., 1998).

The ability of certain drugs to alleviate and of others to induce anxiety symptoms further suggests that biology plays a role in anxiety disorders (Holland et al., 1999). Brain scans also reveal that those who suffer from anxiety disorders respond differently to danger signals (Gorman, 2002). These and other findings suggest that some people are simply biologically predisposed to respond more intensely to stressful events than other people, and this stronger stress reaction puts them at greater risk for developing anxiety disorders (Buss & Plomin, 1984).

Behavioral or conditioning factors have also been implicated in anxiety disorders (Hopko et al., 2001; Watson & Rayner, 1920). In such cases, classical conditioning can produce emotional responses to previously neutral stimuli. After these conditioned emotional responses have been initiated, people's avoidance of the feared objects may be reinforced because, as they move away from the objects, their anxiety decreases. In other words, classical conditioning may be involved in instilling conditioned emotional responses, and operant conditioning may reinforce and so maintain the person's avoidance responses. This *two-process conditioning model* has been an influential and useful way to understand anxiety disorders (Mineka & Zinbarg, 1995; Mowrer, 1947). Consistent with this perspective is the finding from one study that 44 percent of sufferers of a social phobia could identify a traumatic conditioning event in their past associated with their anxiety (Stemberger et al., 1995).

Finally, cognitive factors also play an important role in anxiety disorders. Those who suffer from panic disorder often closely monitor their physiological reactions because they want to detect the onset of another panic episode. However, they often misinterpret and exaggerate the significance of their physiological symptoms, perhaps because panic episodes are so distressing. Their hypervigilance regarding the onset of panic episodes may actually contribute to what they want to avoid (Beck, 1997). This "fear of fear" is one of the fundamental problems that must be addressed in the treatment of panic disorder (Craske & Barlow, 1993).

It is easy to see how biological, behavioral, and cognitive factors interact in causing anxiety disorders. Consider again panic disorder. People with panic disorder may have a biological predisposition to this problem, and biological stressors, such as breathing a carbon dioxide rich mixture of air, can trigger panic episodes (Rapee, 1995). Through conditioning, panic is associated with certain situations so that these situations alone can eventually trigger panic attacks. Finally, panic disorder sufferers become so fearful of panic episodes that they are hypervigilant to signs of a panic attack and thus may actually frighten themselves into a panic attack. Given these possible multiple triggers, what is the ultimate cause of panic disorder? Is it biological, behavioral, or cognitive? Most likely it is some combination of all three.

DISCOVERY BOX 13-1

How Can a Traumatic Event Alter Our Basic Beliefs?

When a traumatic event happens to us, such as being assaulted or involved in a natural disaster, it can affect the deepest levels of our personality (Janoff-Bulman, 1992). One set of beliefs that is often shaken or even shattered is that our world is just and predictable. That is, most of us are taught from early childhood that the world naturally operates out of a sense of justice. Those of us who follow this *just-world belief* system perceive the world as a fair and equitable place. In a just world, hard work and clean living will be rewarded, while laziness and sinful living will be punished. According to Melvin Lerner (1980), this naive belief system is simply a defensive reaction to the sometimes cruel twists of fate encountered in life, but it is comforting because most of us conceive ourselves to be good and decent people. By believing in a just world, we have the illusion that we have more control over our lives than we actually do. Although an exaggerated sense of personal control could be dangerous if taken to extremes, in most instances, it is related to good psychological adjustment (Benassi et al., 1988; Lachman & Weaver, 1998). This fact partly explains why people who believe in a just world tend to experience less depression and stress and greater life satisfaction than those who do not believe in a just world (Dalbert & Yamauchi, 1994; Lipkus et al., 1996).

Despite these mental health advantages, there can be a downside to believing in a just world when you are the victim of unexpected trauma. Many such victims find it difficult to reconcile what happened to them with their just-world belief system. They may ask themselves, "Is the world no longer just, or did I do something wrong to cause this tragedy? If good things happen to good people and bad things happen to bad people, then what did I do to deserve this terrible thing?" Such thinking can cause victims to question their very sense of self, their beliefs about the world, and even their relationship with a Supreme Being.

Following the terrorist attacks at the World Trade Center and the Pentagon, many survivors developed post-traumatic stress disorder, which involves intense emotional distress, nightmares or flashbacks, and avoiding situations or persons that trigger flashbacks.

AP/Wide World Photos.

13-3b Mood Disorders Are Characterized by Emotional Extremes

Mood disorders: Psychological disorders characterized by emotional extremes that cause significant disruption in daily functioning.

Have you ever had "the blues"? Most people have had days when they feel sad, lethargic, and uninterested in their usual activities. These are some of the symptoms of depression, the most common **mood disorder.** In general, mood disorders are characterized by emotional extremes that cause significant disruption in daily functioning. These symptoms are relatively common: almost 30 percent of the general population reports that they have experienced depressed mood for at least two weeks at some time in their life (Weissman et al., 1991). However, to qualify as a mood disorder, such emotional extremes must persist for a long time.

Depression

Depression: A mood disorder characterized by sad mood and the inability to experience pleasure from activities one previously enjoyed.

The most common mood disorder is **depression,** which is characterized by sad mood and the inability to experience pleasure from activities one previously enjoyed (Kramlinger, 2001). Depressed individuals often experience physiological problems such as lack of appetite, weight loss, fatigue, and sleep disorders. Depressed individuals often experience behavioral symptoms, such as slowed thinking and acting (called *psychomotor retardation*), social withdrawal, and decreased rate of activity. Finally, depressed people also exhibit cognitive symptoms, such as low self-esteem, thinking about death and/or suicide, and having little hope for the future. When these symptoms are severe, persistent, and interfere with the person's daily functioning, then the person is diagnosed as having major depressive disorder. When these symptoms are mild but persistent, lasting for more than two years, then the individual is diagnosed with *dysthymia.*

Because depressive disorders are so common, they have been termed the "common cold" of mental illness (Kaelber et al., 1995). Cross-culturally, depression occurs about twice as frequently in women than in men, but there are significant variations between cultures (see figure 13-3). Depression is also associated with age (Weissman et al., 1996). In the general population, the risk of having a major depressive episode in a given year is highest (almost 4 percent) among those between the ages of 30 and 44 years (Weissman et al., 1991). Although depression does occur in children, the risk among those younger than 10 years is much lower than that among adolescents and adults (Speier et al., 1995). Table 13-2 presents a self-report questionnaire that assesses cognitive symptoms of depression.

One of the major dangers of depression is suicide (Shaffer & Greenberg, 2002). For example, one study found that as many as 30 percent of people with severe mood disor-

FIGURE 13-3
Gender and Depression

Interviews with 38,000 women and men in 10 countries found that women's risk of major depression is double that of men's. In addition, lifetime risk of depression among adults varies by culture, with a low of 1.5 percent in Taiwan and a high of 19 percent in Beirut (Weissman et al., 1996).

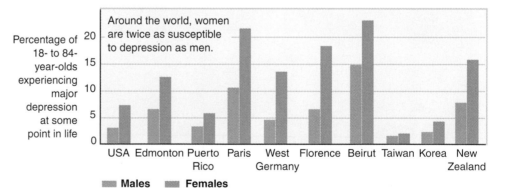

Percentage of 18- to 84-year-olds experiencing major depression at some point in life

Around the world, women are twice as susceptible to depression as men.

USA Edmonton Puerto Rico Paris West Germany Florence Beirut Taiwan Korea New Zealand

■ **Males** ■ **Females**

TABLE 13-2

The Automatic Thoughts Questionnaire

The Automatic Thoughts Questionnaire (ATQ; Hollon & Kendall, 1980) addresses common negative thoughts that occur when people are experiencing depressed mood. You may find it interesting to read the items of the ATQ and to rate your own negative thoughts. Read each thought carefully and indicate how frequently, if at all, the thought occurred to you *over the last week*. Please read each item carefully and rate yourself, using the following scale:

1 = Not at all   2 = Sometimes   3 = Moderately often   4 = Often   5 = All the time

___ **1.** I feel like I'm up against the world.
___ **2.** I'm no good.
___ **3.** Why can't I ever succeed?
___ **4.** No one understands me.
___ **5.** I've let people down.
___ **6.** I don't think I can go on.
___ **7.** I wish I were a better person.
___ **8.** I'm so weak.
___ **9.** My life's not going the way I want it to.
___ **10.** I'm so disappointed in myself.
___ **11.** Nothing feels good anymore.
___ **12.** I can't stand this anymore.
___ **13.** I can't get started.
___ **14.** What's wrong with me?
___ **15.** I wish I were somewhere else.

___ **16.** I can't get things together.
___ **17.** I hate myself.
___ **18.** I'm worthless.
___ **19.** I wish I could just disappear.
___ **20.** What's the matter with me?
___ **21.** I'm a loser.
___ **22.** My life is a mess.
___ **23.** I'm a failure.
___ **24.** I'll never make it.
___ **25.** I feel so hopeless.
___ **26.** Something has to change.
___ **27.** There must be something wrong with me.
___ **28.** My future is bleak.
___ **29.** It's just not worth it.
___ **30.** I can't finish anything.

To score the ATQ, simply add the ratings for all 30 items. According to Kendall and Hollon (1980), the average score in a college student population is about 49, whereas the average score in a depressed sample is about 80. Wierzbicki and Rexford (1989) found comparable differences in ATQ scores between depressed patients and nondepressed college students.

Source: From "Cognitive self-statements in depression: Development of an Automatic Thoughts Questionnaire" by S. D. Hollon and P. C. Kendall in COGNITIVE THERAPY AND RESEARCH, 4, 1980, pp. 383–95. Copyright © 1980. Reprinted by permission of Kluwer Academic/Plenum Publishers and the author.

ders die from suicide (Klerman, 1987). In the United States, about 30,000 people commit suicide annually (Clark, 1995), a rate of about 12 per 100,000. Suicide risk is higher in

1. males than females;
2. older adults than younger adults and minors;
3. the unemployed and retired than the employed;
4. the widowed than the married; and
5. Caucasians than African Americans (Fremouw et al., 1990).

Figure 13-4 depicts suicide rates by race and sex. Suicide risk is also associated with several psychological variables: suicide threats; prior suicide attempts; recent loss; social isolation; and substance abuse (Fremouw et al., 1990; Nock & Kazdin, 2002). The *Psychological Applications* section at the end of the chapter presents additional information about suicide.

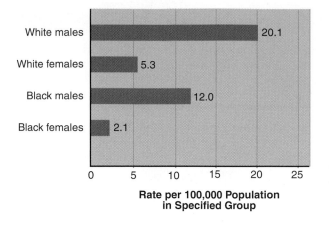

FIGURE 13-4
Suicide Rates by Race and Sex

Suicide occurs most frequently among White men and least among Black women (U.S. Bureau of the Census, 1990).

Mania: An excessively elated, active emotional state.

Bipolar disorder: A mood disorder characterized by swings between the emotional extremes of mania and depression.

Bipolar Disorder

The symptoms of depression may be familiar to you. However, you are probably less familiar with manic symptoms. **Mania** is an excessively elated, active emotional state, and its symptoms are basically the opposite of depressive symptoms. For example, persons in manic states experience buoyant, exuberant mood, and boundless energy, so that they do not feel the need for sleep. They often have increased appetites and thus overindulge in food, alcohol, drugs, and sexual activity. Manic individuals speak and move rapidly, often moving from activity to activity with endless optimism and self-confidence.

At first glance, manic symptoms may not seem very problematic. They do not appear as severe as depressive symptoms, which often are accompanied by suicidal thoughts and torturous feelings. However, a person in a manic state can engage in very destructive behavior (Dilsaver et al., 1999). For example, they may go to a casino and lose the family's life savings in a single session at the roulette wheel, or they may feel so "on top of the world" that they drive their car 100 miles per hour, oblivious to the dangers to self and others. Manic persons may also experience such an increase in physical appetites that they engage in unprotected sex with a dozen people in a day. All of these activities can destroy a person's life as decisively as a suicide attempt by a depressed person.

Individuals with high levels of manic symptoms followed by high levels of depressive symptoms that persist for weeks and that significantly interfere with daily functioning are diagnosed as having **bipolar disorder** (which was previously called *manic-depression*). Bipolar disorder is less common than major depressive disorder, occurring in about 1 percent of the population (Angst & Marneros, 2001; Weissman et al., 1991). Unlike major depression, this disorder occurs about equally in men and women and tends to occur earlier than major depression. Although bipolar disorder patients usually experience episodes of severe depression as well as bouts of mania, their depressive episodes differ from the depressive episodes in major depression in that they tend to be more severe, are accompanied by higher suicide risks, and have a distinct pattern of brain activity during sleep. This evidence suggests that bipolar disorder and major depressive disorder are distinct conditions. The symptoms of manic and depressive states are summarized in table 13-3.

Etiology of Mood Disorders

When seeking explanations of mood disorders, it is important to consider bipolar disorder and major depressive disorder separately. Bipolar disorder clearly has a genetic influence and is considered by most psychologists to have biological origins (Meltzer, 2000). Why? The risk for mood disorder in family members of bipolar disorder patients is more than 30 percent, which is very high (Sevy et al., 1995). Exactly what is inherited that may predispose an individual to develop bipolar disorder is as yet unclear. However, a growing number of researchers believe that bipolar disorders might be caused by imbalances in neural circuits that use serotonin, norepinephrine, and other neurotransmitters (Nemeroff, 1998; Thase & Howland, 1995).

Type of Symptom	Depressive State	Manic State
Emotional	Sad mood Lack of pleasure	Elated mood
Physiological	Fatigue Sleep difficulty Decreased appetite Decreased interest in sex	Increased energy Lack of need for sleep Increased appetite Increased interest in sex
Behavioral	Slowed pace Decreased activity level	Increased pace Increased activity level
Cognitive	Low self-esteem Thoughts of death Negative view of world	Increased self-esteem Lack of perception of danger Positive view of world

TABLE 13-3

Symptoms of Mood Disorders

INFO-BIT: Some researchers believe that mild fluctuations in mood may play a role in enhanced creativity (Bower, 1995). A number of well-known artists have reputedly suffered from bipolar disorders, including such classical composers as G. F. Handel, Hector Berlioz, Gustav Mahler, and Robert Schuman (Jamison, 1995). Berlioz described his two contrasting moods as "passionate" and "morose." Schuman created pieces that contrasted an impulsive and high-spirited style with one that was melancholy and inner directed.

Depression, unlike bipolar disorder, can be explained through several approaches. First, biology does have some influence on this disorder (Davidson et al., 2002; Ketter Wang, 2002). Family, twin, and adoption studies indicate that there is at least a moderate genetic influence on depression (Katz & McGuffin, 1993). Thus, some individuals may experience depression for purely biological reasons, with little relation to their psychosocial experiences. Such cases tend to be severe and are properly treated using antidepressant medications such as Prozac and Paxil.

One subtype of depression that appears to have a biological basis is **seasonal affective disorder (SAD).** SAD is characterized by symptoms of depression at particular times of the year, especially during winter (Sher, 2002b). Of course, some winter depressions may be due solely to psychosocial influences, such as decreased activity due to poor weather and increased stress due to holiday preparations. Yet, evidence that SAD is a distinct disorder comes from studies demonstrating that people with SAD have unusually high metabolic rates, as well as differ physiologically from other depressed patients (Sher, 2002a; Thase & Howland, 1995). One therapy that is quite effective in alleviating SAD is exposing sufferers to bright white fluorescent light two hours a day. Research suggests that this light therapy restores to normal brain levels the neurotransmitter serotonin, which is one of the likely biological causes of depression (Neumeister et al., 1997).

Beyond pure biological explanations, cognitive theory proposes that depression is a thinking disorder (Beck et al., 1979). Depressed persons have negative views of themselves, the world, and the future, and they misinterpret their daily experiences so that their negative outlook is supported (Beck, 1967). In contrast, the behavioral perspective holds that depression results from low social reinforcement, which may be due to skills deficits (such

Seasonal affective disorder (SAD): A subtype of depression characterized by depressive symptoms at particular times of the year, usually during winter when daylight is minimal.

Journey of Discovery Question

How could you explain seasonal affective disorder and its treatment using light therapy from an evolutionary perspective?

as the inability to solve problems or to interact successfully with others) or to decreased opportunities to interact with others (Lewinsohn & Gotlib, 1995). Consistent with the diathesis-stress model, research indicates that individuals with such predisposing cognitive and behavioral conditions are more likely to become depressed following stressful events in their lives (Peterson & Seligman, 1984; Teri & Lewinsohn, 1985).

Finally, why does depression occur more frequently among women than men? Some psychologists believe that this gender difference is due to biological factors. For example, there are modest relationships between depressed mood in women and biological factors such as stage of menstrual cycle and use of oral contraceptives (Thase & Howland, 1995). However, other psychologists contend that social and cultural factors related to sexism are the more likely cause. According to this sociocultural argument, due to the fact that women have fewer educational and occupational opportunities, receive less money for their work, and experience more violence due to their gender, the world is simply more "depressing" for them than for men (Brems, 1995). Some sociocultural theorists also contend that the reported gender difference in depression may be a statistical mistake, reflecting gender differences in help seeking and clinician bias in diagnosis. Regarding help seeking, women may seek help for depression more frequently than men, not because they suffer more from this disorder, but rather because they are more likely to seek help for their problems than men. There may also be a bias within the mental health profession so that women and men who present identical symptoms are diagnosed differently, with women labeled as depressed and men diagnosed with other conditions. Biological differences? Sociocultural differences? Gender differences in help seeking or clinician bias? Perhaps the best explanation for this gender difference involves some combination of these perspectives.

13-3c Dissociative Disorders Involve a Loss of Contact with Portions of One's Consciousness or Memory

Dissociative disorders:
Psychological disorders characterized by disruptions in consciousness, memory, sense of identity, or perception.

Anxiety disorders and mood disorders involve symptoms that are familiar to most college students. However, the next category of disorders may be less familiar. **Dissociative disorders** are characterized by disruptions in consciousness, memory, sense of identity, or perception. As the label indicates, the primary feature of this class of disorders is *dissociation*, meaning significant aspects of experience are kept separate—that is, "dis-associated"—in consciousness and memory. Dissociation usually occurs when a situation becomes overwhelmingly stressful, and the person psychologically escapes by separating their consciousness from the painful situational memories, thoughts, and feelings.

Consider what sometimes happens after a natural disaster, such as a flood or hurricane. Victims may be found wandering in a daze, only dimly aware of what is going on around them. Even though they may not have suffered any head injuries, these individuals may not remember their names, addresses, events leading up to the disaster, or other basic information that is typically available to them. Although these individuals will likely experience this dazed state only temporarily, in some cases these symptoms are prolonged and the person is diagnosed as suffering from a dissociative disorder.

Dissociative Amnesia

Dissociative amnesia:
A dissociative disorder characterized by a sudden loss of memory of one's identity and other personal information.

The type of dissociative disorder suffered by victims of natural disasters is called **dissociative amnesia,** which involves a sudden loss of memory of one's identity and other personal information. Of course, some cases of amnesia are due to organic causes, such as a head injury or a brain tumor. However, when there are no known organic causes, and the person's memory loss is isolated to information threatening to the self, the amnesia is considered *dissociative*.

Dissociative Fugue

Dissociative fugue:
A dissociative disorder characterized by a sudden departure from home or work, combined with loss of memory of identity and the assumption of a new identity.

Like amnesia, **dissociative fugue** involves loss of memory of identity. However, in fugue, the person abruptly leaves home or work and assumes a new identity without realizing that this identity is not the one that she or he had in the past. It may be hard for you to imagine how this can happen, but it does. One such case involved a "Mr. X," who experienced occasional fugue states over a period of several decades. During one episode, Mr. X married a woman, much to the chagrin of his wife, whom he did not remember. In addition to dealing with the consequences of dissociative fugue, Mr. X soon faced legal charges of bigamy.

Dissociative Identity Disorder

By far, the dissociative disorder that has received the most attention is **dissociative identity disorder (DID)**, also known as *multiple personality disorder*. This disorder is characterized by the presence of two or more distinct identities or personalities, which take turns controlling the person's behavior. At least one of the personalities will be unaware of what transpired when it was not in control. The symptoms of DID are bizarre and extreme. One personality may be that of a 6-year-old child while another may be that of an infirm grandparent. One personality may be male while another may be female. Because of the fascinating nature of its symptoms, DID has received a great deal of attention from popular culture, ranging from the 1950s book and movie titled *The Three Faces of Eve* (Thigpen & Cleckley, 1957) to the 1990s novel and film titled *Primal Fear* (Diehl, 1993).

Prior to 1980, DID was considered one of the rarest forms of psychological disorders, with only about two reported cases per decade from 1930 to 1960 (McHugh, 1995). Yet, in the 1980s, over 20,000 cases were reported! Skeptics doubted that this increase was due to better diagnosis. Instead, they suggested that it was caused both by the media coverage of multiple personalities and by the use in psychotherapy of hypnosis and other suggestive techniques that can sometimes elicit DID-like symptoms in patients. According to this argument, psychotherapists may wonder whether their patients' chaotic and unpredictable behavior is due to DID. During therapy sessions, they ask leading questions that suggest the possibility of DID. Further, they may use hypnosis to try to draw out the multiple personalities. However, one of the unfortunate consequences of hypnosis is that it can lead those hypnotized to produce "memories" that are not true (see chapter 6, section 6-3a). Because these patients are distressed and looking for ways to understand their problems, they may come to accept the multiple personality explanation (Lilienfeld et al., 1999; Nogrady et al., 1985).

Research since 1980 has shown that DID is more common than was once believed (Gleaves, 1996). Although it is possible that some cases are manufactured in therapy sessions, many psychologists believe that the research evidence suggests that this disorder is real (Ross, 1991). Patients with DID typically are female, with almost all having histories of childhood physical and sexual abuse (Ross et al., 1989).

Etiology of Dissociative Disorders

Psychodynamic theory suggests that dissociation results from the individual's attempt to repress some troubling event. If this event is associated with intense emotion, it may require a corresponding high degree of repression to keep this material in the unconscious. As the individual represses the memory of the troubling event, the individual also inadvertently represses other memories, including memory of identity. In the case of fugue and DID, individuals develop an alternative identity or identities as a way to avoid facing the stress that would occur when they recognized that they had lost memory of their identity and other personal information.

Invoking a biological explanation, some psychologists suggest that dissociative disorder patients may have a neurological problem that has not yet been detected. Research has shown that individuals with dissociative disorders have high rates of epilepsy and that those with epilepsy have high rates of dissociative disorders (Willerman & Cohen, 1990). As intriguing as this biological explanation may be, it cannot account for all cases of dissociative disorder because most DID patients do not have the hallmark abnormal brain wave patterns found among epileptic sufferers.

Another explanation of dissociative disorders comes from the cognitive perspective. This approach holds that individuals learn to dissociate as a way to cope with intense

Dissociative identity disorder (DID): A dissociative disorder characterized by the presence of two or more distinct identities or personalities, which take turns controlling the person's behavior (also known as multiple personality disorder).

distress. When a child is exposed to prolonged, intense stress (such as torturous abuse), dissociation may be used so frequently that its use becomes automatic. For example, a child who experiences repeated abuse may imagine having a superhero friend who helps them through these traumatic events (Meichenbaum & Turk, 1976). Over time, the child's use of these cognitive pain-management techniques becomes automatic, even in the presence of mild stressors. At this point, the individual's dissociation no longer serves the function of protecting her or him from stress but is a problem that interferes with daily functioning in and of itself.

13-3d Schizophrenia Involves Disturbances in Almost All Areas of Psychological Functioning

One of the most fascinating and severe forms of psychological disorders is schizophrenia. Indeed, schizophrenia is so severe that it is considered a *psychosis*, meaning that the person is out of touch with reality. Sufferers may not be aware of what is going on around them and may not be able to interact effectively in the world.

Schizophrenia is characterized by severe impairment in thinking, such as hallucinations, delusions, or loose associations. Some schizophrenic patients hallucinate, hearing or seeing things that are not there. For example, they may hear voices that they attribute to aliens or to demons. Some schizophrenic patients experience delusions, or irrational belief systems. For example, they may believe that they are Jesus, the President of the United States, a robot, and other unusual entities. Often, schizophrenic patients experience both delusions and hallucinations, which support and strengthen one another. Patients with schizophrenia may hear voices, which they attribute to God and which lead them to believe that they have been selected for a spiritual mission. Schizophrenic patients often experience loose associations, which means that their thoughts are disconnected from one another and from the world around them. Schizophrenic patients can be so disorganized in their thinking that they cannot speak in complete sentences but can only babble. Some patients are unable to speak clearly because their thoughts jump from topic to topic so rapidly that they cannot speak clearly.

Do you remember Jim in my chapter-opening story? Following the record and pillow incidents, Jim's psychological condition rapidly deteriorated. His previously quiet, sleepy demeanor gave way to episodes of whooping and hollering while he danced frenetically around the apartment jingling his ring of keys in the air. This behavior so scared us that we called his parents and only then learned that Jim had been released from a psychiatric hospital just prior to answering our ad. By the end of the day, Jim was readmitted to the hospital with a preliminary diagnosis of schizophrenia.

Schizophrenia is diagnosed when symptoms persist for at least six months, are not due to some other condition (such as substance use or severe depression), and cause significant impairment in daily functioning. Because schizophrenics experience such severe problems in thinking, they often cannot work, manage a home or apartment successfully, or care for their basic needs. Schizophrenic individuals usually require assistance to care for themselves, either from their family or a treatment center. In the absence of such assistance, many schizophrenic individuals end up living on the streets (Torrey, 1997).

Schizophrenia is relatively common, occurring in about 1 percent of the world's population (American Psychiatric Association, 2000). It occurs with roughly equal frequency

Schizophrenia: Psychological disorder characterized by severe impairment in thinking, such as hallucinations, delusions, or loose associations.

INFO-BIT: Prior to 1911, schizophrenia was called *dementia praecox* because it was thought to be a degenerative disease of the brain (dementia) that began at a young age (praecox). Swiss psychologist Eugene Bleuler (1857–1939) challenged this view, arguing that the disorder was not always degenerative. Bleuler coined the term "schizophrenia" to refer to what he regarded as the essential characteristic of the disorder—a splitting (schiz) or lack of integration among the person's normal psychological functions.

among males and females and tends to occur more often in adolescence and young adulthood than in middle and late adulthood (Zipursky et al., 2002). Although the disorder can occur in children, it is rare in those younger than age 10. Schizophrenia has been classified into several subtypes, depending on which symptoms are most prominent.

Paranoid Schizophrenia

Paranoid schizophrenia refers to cases in which the most prominent symptoms are hallucinations and delusions. Paranoid delusions do not refer simply to delusions of persecution but could also refer to grandiose delusions, such as thinking that you are the president or Jesus Christ. The afflicted individual is often anxious, angry, argumentative, and jealous, with such feelings sometimes leading to violence. One high-profile incident of violence involving a person with paranoid schizophrenia occurred in July 1998 when Russell Watson, Jr., shot and killed two police officers inside the U.S. Capitol Building. The violence sometimes exhibited by paranoid schizophrenics is not always directed against others. Of people suffering from schizophrenia, those with this subtype have the highest suicide rate (13 percent; Fenton & McGlashan, 1991). Approximately 40 percent of patients diagnosed with schizophrenia are classified as paranoid schizophrenics. One silver lining in the dark cloud of paranoid schizophrenia is that this subtype has the best prognosis for recovery.

> **Paranoid schizophrenia:** A subtype of schizophrenia characterized by hallucinations and delusions of persecution or grandeur that can sometimes lead to violence.

Disorganized Schizophrenia

Disorganized schizophrenia refers to rare cases (only 5 percent of all schizophrenics) in which the most prominent symptoms are a variety of unrelated hallucinations and delusions, incoherent speech, and strange facial grimaces. Disorganized schizophrenic patients may be unable to speak clearly but can only babble. They may act in a childlike or even infantile manner, drooling, giggling, babbling, and playing with toys.

> **Disorganized schizophrenia:** A rare subtype of schizophrenia characterized by a variety of unrelated hallucinations and delusions, incoherent speech, and strange facial grimaces.

Catatonic Schizophrenia

Catatonic schizophrenia refers to cases in which the most prominent symptom is some extreme level of motor activity. Some catatonic patients are statuelike, remaining motionless and unresponsive to the outside world, while others exhibit frenetic activity, talking and moving very rapidly. Like disorganized schizophrenia, catatonic schizophrenia is rare, occurring in only 8 percent of all schizophrenics.

> **Catatonic schizophrenia:** A subtype of schizophrenia characterized by some extreme level of motor activity.

Undifferentiated Schizophrenia

Forty percent of all patients diagnosed with schizophrenia have patterns of disordered behavior, thought, and emotion that cannot be neatly classified into any of the other three subtypes. In some cases, a patient who was previously diagnosed into one of the other subtypes is reclassified as suffering from **undifferentiated schizophrenia** because they no longer have the same set of symptoms. Such symptom shifting is not uncommon and explains why so many schizophrenic patients are classified into the undifferentiated subtype.

> **Undifferentiated schizophrenia:** A catchall category for cases that do not fall neatly into any single kind of schizophrenia.

Etiology of Schizophrenia

The current consensus is that schizophrenia has a strong genetic basis (Gottesman, 1991; Gruzelier, 2002). For example, although 1 percent of the general population develops schizophrenia in their lifetime, from 10 to 15 percent of first-degree relatives (parents, children, siblings) of a schizophrenic patient will develop schizophrenia (Willerman & Cohen, 1990). This holds true whether one is reared in the same household as the schizophrenic person or whether one is reared in an adoptive, nonschizophrenic home. Perhaps most convincing is the evidence from twin studies. Fraternal twins of schizophrenic patients have about a 15 percent risk for developing schizophrenia—about the same as for nontwin siblings—but identical twins of schizophrenic patients have about a 50 percent risk for developing the disorder (Tsuang, 2000). Figure 13-5 depicts these findings.

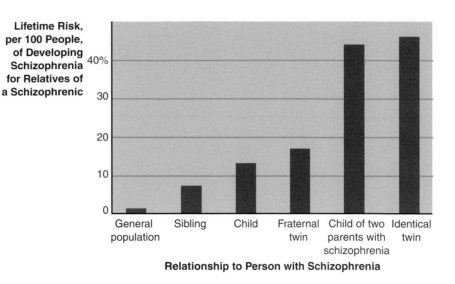

FIGURE 13-5
Risk of Developing Schizophrenia

The lifetime risk of developing schizophrenia increases with genetic closeness to relatives with schizophrenia.

Lifetime Risk, per 100 People, of Developing Schizophrenia for Relatives of a Schizophrenic

Relationship to Person with Schizophrenia

FIGURE 13-6
Structural Abnormalities in the Brains of Schizophrenics?

The hollow cavities in the brain (ventricles) are filled with cerebrospinal fluid. Brain scans of schizophrenics suggest that they may have enlarged ventricles, which means that they may have less cerebral cortex than do normal individuals.

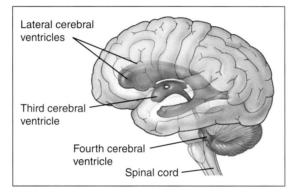

Lateral cerebral ventricles

Third cerebral ventricle

Fourth cerebral ventricle

Spinal cord

What biological condition is inherited that may predispose the development of schizophrenia? Most antipsychotic medications that control the symptoms of schizophrenia have the effect of decreasing the amount and/or activity of dopamine, a neurotransmitter that facilitates movement and influences thought and emotion (see chapter 3, section 3-1c). Amphetamines and other medications that increase the amount or activity of dopamine can induce symptoms that mimic those of schizophrenia (Green, 1998; Meltzer, 1979). Further, autopsies of schizophrenic patients reveal that they often have an unusually high number of dopamine receptors in the brain (Seeman et al., 1993). Thus, there is compelling evidence that increased dopamine activity is related to schizophrenia. Perhaps the reason why schizophrenic patients see and hear things that are not there and have racing thoughts that they cannot control is that the dopamine pathways in their brains are overactive.

There is also evidence from brain scans of schizophrenic patients (see figure 13-6) that some have an enlargement of fluid-filled brain cavities called cerebral ventricles and a corresponding shrinkage of the surrounding cerebral cortex (Raz & Raz, 1990; Wright et al., 2000). Related to these findings are studies suggesting that schizophrenia occurs at slightly increased rates in individuals who have been exposed to maternal illness that may interfere with prenatal neurological development (Torrey et al., 1997). Together, these studies may help explain such schizophrenic symptoms as lack of affect and speech, apathy, withdrawal, attention problems, and immobility.

Regarding behavioral explanations, during the 1950s, some theorists proposed that schizophrenia might directly result from disturbed family interactions that teach children how to communicate in a confusing fashion (Bateson et al., 1956; Mednick, 1958). However, by the 1970s, this "disturbed family" explanation lost much of its influence

DISCOVERY BOX 13-2

Why Are There Higher Rates of Schizophrenia among Members of the Lowest Socioeconomic Classes?

Numerous studies have found that there are higher rates of schizophrenia among people in the lowest socioeconomic classes in the United States (Gottesman, 1991). In response to such findings, sociocultural theorists proposed the *social causation hypothesis*, which contends that membership in the lowest social classes may actually cause schizophrenia. According to this explanation, the very poor receive the smallest share of the society's assets, such as quality education, employment, and health care, while receiving most of its liabilities, such as high crime and poor housing. Because many members of the lower classes are also minorities, they must also battle prejudice and discrimination. Together, these social factors create a very stressful environment that might lead to the development of schizophrenia.

This idea that social factors cause schizophrenia due to their effect on people's level of stress is not inconsistent with the diathesis-stress model. The higher stress levels found among the lower classes may interact with predisposing biological factors to elicit schizophrenic symptoms. These biological factors may exist in equal frequencies among members of higher socioeconomic classes, but they are less likely to trigger the disorder due to lower stress levels.

An alternative explanation of the relationship between socioeconomic status and schizophrenia is the *downward social drift hypothesis*, which contends that schizophrenia develops at equal rates across the social classes, but once the disorder develops, those afflicted descend into poverty. Thus, instead of highlighting the stress caused by poverty (as the social causation hypothesis does), this explanation represents a straightforward biological approach to understanding schizophrenia.

At this point, it is not clear which of these two hypotheses concerning the relationship between social class and schizophrenia is correct. Perhaps both perspectives provide one piece of the puzzle in understanding this complex disorder.

among mental health professionals because it had received very little empirical support. Although behavioral explanations do not appear to act alone in causing schizophrenia, the diathesis-stress model suggests that they may interact with biological factors in triggering the onset of the disorder (Fowles, 1992; Wearden et al., 2000). For example, poor parenting and the development of inadequate social and coping skills may influence the course of the disorder by increasing the stress level of individuals biologically predisposed for schizophrenia (Walker & Diforio, 1998). However, those who face similar environmental stressors yet do not have the necessary biological vulnerability (the diathesis) will not develop schizophrenia. Currently, the diathesis-stress model, which considers the interaction of both biological and environmental factors, provides the best explanation of this highly complex psychological disorder. Discovery Box 13-2 examines this issue in more detail.

13-3e Somatoform Disorders Are Characterized by Physical Complaints without Physical Causes

Somatoform disorders are psychological problems that involve some bodily symptom, even though there is no actual physical cause of the symptom. Thus, somatoform disorders are distinct from the *psychophysiological disorders* discussed in chapter 15, which are

> **Somatoform disorders:** Psychological disorders involving some bodily symptom, even though there is no actual physical cause of the symptom.

actual physical conditions—such as high blood pressure, migraine headaches, or asthma—that are caused or aggravated by psychological factors such as stress. Let us examine three distinct somatoform disorders, namely, *conversion disorder, somatization disorder,* and *hypochondriasis*.

Conversion Disorder

Conversion disorder:
A somatoform disorder characterized by a specific sensory or motor symptom that has a psychological rather than a physical basis.

Conversion disorder is characterized by a specific sensory or motor symptom that has no physical basis and is presumed to be due to psychological factors. Classic examples of conversion disorder include the soldier who develops paralysis in his hands so that he cannot hold or fire his weapon and the mother who sees her child killed in a traffic accident and is "struck blind" (see figure 13-7). This disorder is not very common, occurring in .01 to .5 percent of the general population (American Psychiatric Association, 2000). It occurs more frequently in women than men and occurs more often in individuals whose education, income, and understanding of medical and psychological concepts are below average (America Psychiatric Association, 2000).

Adding to the difficulty of diagnosing conversion disorder are other conditions that may be associated with medical symptoms. For example, some individuals *malinger*, which means they deliberately produce or misreport symptoms to gain some clear external incentive. A child may lie about having a stomachache to avoid going to school, a soldier may lie about being sick to avoid being shipped out to a war zone, and a person may exaggerate symptoms following an accident to gain increased insurance benefits. Malingering is not a psychological disorder, but it does make proper diagnosis of conversion disorder more difficult.

Somatization Disorder

Somatization disorder:
A somatoform disorder characterized by a series of numerous physical complaints that have a psychological rather than a physical basis.

Somatization disorder is a somatoform disorder characterized by a series of numerous physical complaints that do not have a physical basis. These symptoms include pain, gastrointestinal symptoms, sexual, and pseudoneurological symptoms, such as impaired coordination, paralysis, and hallucinations. As with conversion disorder, the physical symptoms of somatization disorder do not have a physical basis and are not being deliberately faked or misreported. However, this disorder differs from conversion disorder in that it tends to be more chronic and more associated with emotional and personality problems than conversion disorder (Willerman & Cohen, 1990). In addition, adoption studies indicate that somatization disorder has a genetic influence, whereas there is no clear family pattern in conversion disorder (Sigvardsson et al., 1984).

FIGURE 13-7
Conversion Disorder

An example of conversion disorder is "glove anesthesia," which is numbness in the entire hand, ending at the wrist. The skin areas served by nerves in the arm are shown in *(a)*. Glove anesthesia, depicted in *(b)*, cannot be caused by damage to these nerves.

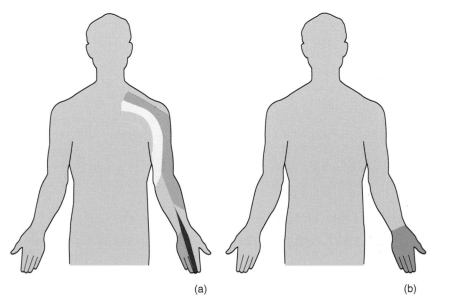

(a)　　　　(b)

Hypochondriasis

A third somatoform disorder is **hypochondriasis,** which is characterized by excessive preoccupation with or fear of developing some physical condition. This concern is not consistent with the person's actual medical condition and is resistant to reassurance from one's physician. When a physician refers such a patient to a psychotherapist, the patient often seeks out another physician rather than admit that the problem is psychological. Largely due to this fact, relatively little research has been conducted on hypochondriasis. What evidence does exist suggests that this disorder is relatively common in medical settings (from 2 to 7 percent of patients in general medical practice), it tends to occur in early adulthood, and it generally is a chronic condition throughout the person's life (American Psychiatric Association, 2000).

> **Hypochondriasis:**
> A somatoform disorder characterized by excessive preoccupation with or fear of developing some physical condition.

Etiology of Somatoform Disorders

As discussed in chapter 12, section 12-2, Freud originally developed psychoanalytic theory to explain conversion disorders. As a neurologist, he saw patients whose medical problems could not be explained by the patient's physician. One of his earliest attempts to apply psychoanalytic theory in the explanation of psychopathology was in the case of Anna O. (Breuer & Freud, 1893/1955). Anna O. was a young woman who had symptoms that defied medical explanation, including loss of feeling and motion in her limbs, loss of speech, hallucinations, and "hysterical" pregnancy. Freud suggested that Anna O. had troubling material in her unconscious related to her father (she had recently nursed her father while he had a serious illness). Because she was unable to admit this troubling material to herself, Freud believed that it was repressed to her unconscious. However, because the material was powerful, Freud further believed that it sought expression in some form. According to Freud, this material was converted to the series of physical symptoms that Anna O. developed. Freud considered these symptoms to symbolize, in some form, the nature of the underlying troubling material.

Besides this psychoanalytic explanation, more recent studies suggest that people with histrionic personality traits are more prone to develop somatoform disorders (Slavney, 1990). Such individuals tend to be self-centered, suggestible, extremely emotional, and overly dramatic: exactly the personality style that thrives on the attention received during illness.

A cognitive-behavioral explanation suggests that individuals with conversion disorder may have, in the past, been reinforced for reporting medical symptoms. For example, when sick, the individual has not had to go to school, attend work, or perform other arduous tasks. Similarly, as a child, the individual may have malingered, deliberately faking sickness to avoid going to school on the day of an exam. It is possible that, through repeated reinforcements, the individual has learned to report symptoms when stressed. This may become automatic so that the individual is not aware that the symptoms he or she is reporting are not real.

Although personality and cognitive-behavioral factors appear to account for a large portion of somatoform disorders, biological factors may account for certain cases. For example, some individuals who have been diagnosed with conversion disorder later develop a clear medical problem that probably accounted for their initial symptoms (Shalev & Munitz, 1986). The likelihood that their initial physical symptoms were caused by real medical problems demonstrates that psychologists should diagnose somatoform disorders cautiously, in conjunction with appropriate medical evaluations.

13-3f Personality Disorders Are Inflexible and Enduring Behavior Patterns That Impair Social Functioning

A final category of psychological problems is the personality disorders. **Personality disorders** differ from the other psychological disorders considered so far in that personality disorders are not associated with specific symptoms that cause distress or that interfere with daily functioning. Instead, they are characterized by general styles of living that are

> **Personality disorders:**
> Psychological disorders characterized by general styles of living that are ineffective and that lead to problems.

ineffective and that lead to problems. Personality disorders develop by adolescence or young adulthood and typically persist for a long time. They are associated with personality traits that are extreme, inflexible, and ultimately lead the person to have problems in daily functioning (Yang et al., 2002). Often, individuals with personality disorder do not consider their personality to be a problem, but, instead, they blame others for their problems. There are 10 personality disorders in the current diagnostic system of *DSM-IV-TR* (Brooner et al., 2002; Bruehl, 2002). Table 13-4 lists and briefly describes each of these personality disorders.

Three of the more common personality disorders are the paranoid personality, histrionic personality, and narcissistic personality. *Paranoid personalities* are habitually distrustful and suspicious of others' motives, and, thus, they expect their friends and family members to be disloyal. *Histrionic personalities* are excessively emotional and attention seeking, often turning minor incidents into full-blown dramas. If they are not the center of attention, they become upset and may do something inappropriate to regain the spotlight. *Narcissistic personalities* also seek attention, but what they desire is constant admiration from others. Their overblown sense of self-importance and egocentric focus makes them feel that they are entitled to special privileges without any kind of reciprocation on their part (Corbitt, 2002). As is the case with the other personality disorders, individuals with these three disorders are extremely difficult to live with on an everyday basis.

Antisocial Personality Disorder

Antisocial personality disorder: A personality disorder characterized by a persistent pattern of disregard for and violation of the rights of others.

By far, the personality disorder that has received the most attention is the **antisocial personality disorder,** which is also referred to as *psychopathy.* Psychopaths are individuals who exhibit a persistent pattern of disregard for and violation of the rights of others. They repeatedly exhibit antisocial behavior across all realms of life, often lying, cheating, stealing, and manipulating others to get what they want. When others catch them in their deceit, they fail to take responsibility and do not exhibit remorse (Harpur et al., 2002).

Good people do not need laws to tell them to act responsibly, while bad people will find a way around the laws.

—Plato, Greek philosopher, 427–347 B.C.

TABLE 13-4

Types and Symptoms of Personality Disorders

Type	Major Symptoms
Paranoid	Distrust and suspiciousness of others
Schizoid	Detachment from social relationships and restricted range of emotions
Schizotypal	Cognitive and perceptual distortions and eccentricities of behavior
Antisocial	Disregard for and violation of the rights of others
Borderline	Instability of interpersonal relationships, self-image, and emotion
Histrionic	Excessive emotionality and attention seeking
Narcissistic	Grandiosity, need for admiration, and lack of empathy
Avoidant	Social inhibition, feelings of inadequacy, and hypersensitivity to negative evaluation
Dependent	Excessive need to be taken care of, submissive and clinging behavior, and fear of separation
Obsessive-compulsive	Preoccupation with orderliness, perfectionism, and control

Although this description sounds nasty, psychopaths surprisingly are often charming and likable. They have learned how to manipulate people to get what they want, and can lie without hesitation or guilt. In the movie *Pacific Heights*, Michael Keaton portrays a psychopath who wickedly manipulates a young couple, first charming them into leasing an apartment, and then taking advantage of them for monetary gain. When the couple realizes his deceit, Keaton's character convinces the police and others in the legal system that he is in the right. Psychopathy occurs in about 3 percent of males and about 1 percent of females (American Psychiatric Association, 2000).

Etiology of Personality Disorders

Research since the 1970s suggests that personality disorders have a genetic component (Nigg & Goldsmith, 1994). For example, a large-scale adoption study found that adopted-away sons of fathers with a criminal background are themselves at increased risk for experiencing legal problems as adults, even when reared by noncriminal adoptive fathers (Hutchings & Mednick, 1977). Similarly, a large-scale twin study indicates that identical twins resemble one another with respect to various types of antisocial behavior more than fraternal twins (Lyons et al., 1995).

The current thinking about antisocial personality disorder is that both biological and environmental factors interact to cause the problem (Norden et al., 1995; Paris, 1997). For instance, there may be a biological predisposition, such as a neurological influence on impulse control. Children with this predisposition reared in chaotic households may not learn to control their impulses, and so behave in ways to maximize their benefit even if this means violating social rules. On the other hand, children with this predisposition who are reared in more stable homes may acquire self-control techniques so that they do not act to satisfy their immediate impulses.

SECTION SUMMARY

- The *DSM* lists major classes of psychological disorders.

- Anxiety disorders are characterized by distressing, persistent anxiety or maladaptive behavior.

- Mood disorders are characterized by emotional extremes that cause significant disruption in daily functioning.

- Dissociative disorders are characterized by disruptions in consciousness, memory, sense of identity, or perception.

- Schizophrenia is characterized by severe impairment in thinking, such as hallucinations, delusions, or loose associations.

- Somatoform disorders involve some bodily symptom without any physical cause of the symptom.

- In individuals with personality disorders, general styles of living are ineffective and lead to problems.

SUGGESTED WEBSITES

Note: These websites were functional when we went to press. Please access the online text for the most up-to-date URLs.

National Institute of Mental Health (NIMH)
http://www.nimh.nih.gov/
This website is for both the general public and mental health professionals and includes information on various psychological disorders.

The Anxiety Panic Internet Resource
http://www.algy.com/anxiety/
This website is a self-help network that provides information and support for those who suffer from anxiety disorders.

Depression Central
http://www.psycom.net/depression.central.html
This website provides information on mood disorders.

Dissociation, Trauma, & Recovered Memories
http://www.acsu.buffalo.edu/~jjhall/body_d_l.html
This website provides links to other websites with information on various dissociative disorders.

Schizophrenia.com
http://www.schizophrenia.com/
This website not only provides information on schizophrenia, but it also provides discussion and support groups.

PSYCHOLOGICAL APPLICATIONS
What Are Some Important Facts about Suicide?

There are many misconceptions about suicide. In this *Psychological Applications* section, we address five commonly asked questions concerning this important issue and provide information that may prove helpful to you now or in the future.

Does suicide run in families? Not exactly. People who have major mood disorders, such as severe depression and bipolar disorder, are at increased risk of suicide. It is possible to find families that have histories of suicide across generations (Egeland & Sussex, 1985); however, the genetic influence appears to be related to the mood disorder rather than suicide itself.

Is it true that people who talk about suicide never commit suicide? No!! This is a dangerous misconception. One of the best predictors of suicide risk is a stated threat to commit suicide. Psychologists therefore take every threat of suicide seriously, at least until they can conduct a thorough evaluation of risk in the individual case. Some threats may be veiled. For example, a person may give away her prized possessions or may talk about "getting away to end my problems." Observers should be sensitive to such hints of suicidal thinking and should ask direct questions about the person's intentions.

Does every person who attempts suicide truly want to die? No! Some suicide attempts are designed more to get attention and help than to die. For example, a person who takes a half-bottle of baby aspirin or who scratches his wrist with nail clippers may not truly have intended to die. Such nonlethal attempts are called "suicidal gestures" and are considered to be a cry for help. However, psychologists must be careful when working with clients who have histories of suicidal gestures. Even though a person may have made several suicidal gestures in the past, this does not mean that the person will not make a more lethal attempt in the future. Also, some persons who make suicidal gestures make a mistake and inadvertently kill themselves even though that may not have been their true intention.

Why do men have a higher suicide rate than women? Even though women attempt suicide more often than men, men have a higher suicide rate. The explanation for this gender difference is complex.

Men attempt suicide by gun use, hanging, and leaping from high places more frequently than women. Thus, men tend to use methods that are more lethal and less reversible than women, who more frequently use pills. Although you can kill yourself with pills, they take time to work, and thus, there is more time for people to change their minds or to be found and saved. Now, why do men and women use these different methods? Perhaps men have more familiarity with and accessibility to firearms than women, which leads them to select this more lethal method. Perhaps men are less willing than women to call for help, and so they are less likely to make a suicidal gesture.

What should I do if a friend is talking about suicide? It is important that you take the threat seriously. However, it is also important that you recognize that you are not a mental health professional and, thus, are not equipped to evaluate suicide risk or to provide psychotherapy. As a friend, you can listen and provide appropriate comfort and support. However, it is important to encourage your friend to seek professional help. You can convey the information that depression is not a sign of weakness or "craziness" but is instead recognized as a mental illness. You can convey the information that depression is well understood by the mental health profession and that there are effective treatments for it. However, it will be up to the mental health professional—and not you—to provide this treatment. If your friend does not take your advice, perhaps you can find someone important in your friend's life—a family doctor, a member of the clergy, a family member—who can convince your friend to see a mental health professional. As a last resort, a suicidal individual may be committed against his or her will to a psychiatric hospital for treatment. Commitment procedures vary across states, but they usually require the request of a relative and the opinion of one or more physicians that the individual is dangerous and unable to make decisions in his or her best interests. Although commitment may seem like a drastic step, it is far better to commit someone to treatment than to lose them through suicide.

KEY TERMS

agoraphobia (p. 402)
antisocial personality disorder (p. 418)
anxiety disorders (p. 401)
behavioral perspective (p. 396)
biological perspective (p. 397)
bipolar disorder (p. 408)
catatonic schizophrenia (p. 413)
cognitive perspective (p. 397)
conversion disorder (p. 416)
depression (p. 406)
diagnosis (p. 394)
Diagnostic and Statistical Manual of Mental Disorders (DSM) (p. 400)
diathesis-stress model (p. 398)

disorganized schizophrenia (p. 413)
dissociative amnesia (p. 410)
dissociative disorders (p. 410)
dissociative fugue (p. 410)
dissociative identity disorder (DID) (p. 411)
etiology (p. 394)
generalized anxiety disorder (GAD) (p. 403)
hypochondriasis (p. 417)
mania (p. 408)
mood disorders (p. 406)
obsessive-compulsive disorder (OCD) (p. 403)
panic disorder (p. 401)
paranoid schizophrenia (p. 413)
personality disorders (p. 417)

phobic disorder (p. 402)
post-traumatic stress disorder (PTSD) (p. 403)
prognosis (p. 394)
psychodynamic perspective (p. 396)
psychological disorder (p. 396)
schizophrenia (p. 412)
seasonal affective disorder (SAD) (p. 409)
sociocultural perspective (p. 397)
somatization disorder (p. 416)
somatoform disorders (p. 415)
symptom (p. 394)
undifferentiated schizophrenia (p. 413)

REVIEW QUESTIONS

1. The diagnosis of psychological disorders relies on specific criteria that distinguish normal from abnormal behavior. One of the most important of these criteria is
   a. an uncontrollable urge for freedom.
   b. behavior that is disruptive or harmful to the individual or others.
   c. behavior that is infrequent in the "normal" population.
   d. extremely odd or eccentric behavior.
   e. personal distress.

2. A variety of theories attempt to explain the etiology of psychological disorders. The cognitive approach explains mental illness primarily as
   a. behavior that has been conditioned through reinforcement and punishment.
   b. resulting from a diathesis-stress model of vulnerability interacting with environmental stressors.
   c. associated with broad sociocultural forces.
   d. a product of unconscious forces shaped by childhood experiences.
   e. a learned pattern of faulty thinking or maladaptive interpretations.

3. The use of diagnostic labels carries both risks and benefits to the patient, including all of the following *except*
   a. confirmation bias, in which expectations of certain behaviors lead to diagnoses that may not exist.
   b. the ability to summarize information concerning the patient's presenting problems.
   c. dehumanization of patients by treating them as "labels" rather than individuals.
   d. a clear association with specific and reliable etiologic and maintaining factors for all psychological diagnoses.
   e. the suggestion that researchers have identified optimal methods of treatment.

4. The *Diagnostic and Statistical Manual of Mental Disorders* is considered a work in progress primarily because
   a. ongoing research seeks to continually improve the reliability and validity of *DSM* diagnoses.
   b. the manual is currently undergoing its first classification revision.
   c. there is a lack of agreement among insurance companies concerning how the *DSM* classifies mental illness.
   d. the etiological descriptions provided by the *DSM* are considered tentative.
   e. the criteria specified for diagnosing mental disorders are vague and unclear.

5. Panic disorder is characterized *primarily* by which one of the following symptoms?
   a. extended periods of excessive fear lasting for several days at a time
   b. avoidance of places where previous attacks have or have not occurred
   c. brief attacks of intense anxiety that occur for no apparent reason
   d. strong, irrational fears of specific objects or situations
   e. subclinical phobias that do not interfere with normal functioning

6. Obsessive-compulsive disorder is unique in that two relatively distinct types of symptoms are experienced, including
   a. obsessions, which are unwanted, repetitive thoughts; and compulsions, which are repetitive behaviors that may disrupt daily functioning.
   b. obsessions, which are urges to stalk or kill others; and compulsions, which are urges to overeat.
   c. obsessions, such as repeated hand washing; and compulsions, such as fear of contamination.
   d. obsessions, which are urges to perform some type of repetitive or ritual behavior; and compulsions, which are repetitive, intrusive thoughts.
   e. obsessions and compulsions, which are rarely recognized as abnormal by the individual.

7. After the terrorist attacks on September 11, 2001, many people experienced symptoms of post-traumatic stress disorder, generally considered a "normal" or expected reaction to a trauma of such magnitude. However, a more serious disturbance might be indicated if an individual
  a. had repeated intrusive thoughts or images of the attack scene.
  b. made efforts to avoid all reminders of the attacks.
  c. experienced flashbacks or nightmares.
  d. had symptoms that continued for a long period after the attacks and if the symptoms significantly interfered with the individual's daily functioning.
  e. began to question his or her essential beliefs concerning the nature of good and evil or the just-world phenomenon.

8. Despite the similarities in many of the symptoms of anxiety disorders, a variety of different theories have been proposed to explain their causes, including
  a. conditioning explanations for the *initial onset* of generalized anxiety disorder.
  b. hypervigilance as a cause of PTSD.
  c. fear of fear explanations for generalized anxiety disorder.
  d. sociological causes of social phobia.
  e. genetic or evolutionary causes of phobias.

9. Mood disorders may involve all of the following symptoms *except*
  a. a prolonged feeling of sadness and lethargy.
  b. a change in sleep patterns.
  c. repetitive lying or dishonesty.
  d. difficulties concentrating.
  e. thoughts of suicide.

10. Less common than depression, bipolar disorder
  a. affects only about 9 percent of the population.
  b. is probably caused by the same etiological factors as depression.
  c. follows the same symptom and behavior pattern in all individuals with the disorder.
  d. involves manic behavior, which may be destructive in its consequences.
  e. involves only mild symptoms of mania and depression, but over extended periods.

11. Etiological explanations for depression and bipolar disorder tend to be quite different, although there is some degree of overlap. Bipolar disorder is typically explained by which one of the following?
  a. misinterpretations of daily experiences
  b. a genetic or biological disturbance leading to imbalances in neural circuits
  c. low social reinforcement
  d. childhood loss, with subsequent anger turned against oneself
  e. negative views of oneself, the world, and the future

12. Researchers have determined that there are distinct gender differences in the experience of depression. These have been explained by all of the following *except*
  a. a lack of social support for men, who are less intimate in their friendships than women.
  b. female hormones, which have been associated with depression.
  c. social and cultural factors related to sexism.
  d. statistical error, reflecting greater help seeking by women.
  e. clinicians' gender bias in diagnosing depression.

13. Of all the psychological diagnoses, dissociative disorder is probably the most fascinating because the symptoms tend to be so unusual. For example, some characteristic symptoms include
  a. a split personality consisting of two personalities, each of whom is aware of what occurs while the other is in control.
  b. the gradual assumption of a new identity, with no awareness by the individual involved, and no return to the previous identity, in dissociative fugue conditions.
  c. a gradual loss of memories threatening to the self, known as dissociative amnesia.
  d. a permanent "dazed" state following a trauma or tragedy.
  e. both male and female personalities in dissociative identity disorder.

14. Schizophrenia is another fascinating mental disorder, in which the affected individual may lose touch with reality, experience hallucinations and delusions, and have extremely disorganized thinking. Research investigating the etiology of schizophrenia has shown
  a. little family risk beyond that for identical twins, which is very high.
  b. that dopamine-enhancing drugs may cause schizophrenic-like symptoms, suggesting an overactive dopamine system.
  c. an enlargement of the cerebral cortex and corresponding shrinkage of cerebral ventricles.
  d. that disturbed family communication is directly responsible for some types of schizophrenia.
  e. no evidence for prenatal etiologies.

15. Personality disorders differ from the previously examined disorders in that
  a. they appear to be caused by the interaction of genetic factors, such as temperament or impulse control, and environmental influences, such as family functioning.
  b. they are almost always attributable to a single cause.
  c. they are associated with maladaptive personality traits and result in longstanding problems with living rather than extreme distress or dysfunction.
  d. individuals with personality disorders are universally unlikable.
  e. personality disorders involve affective, cognitive, and behavioral systems of functioning.

Therapy

14

magine that you were born 230 years ago. Further, imagine that you were born with an underlying vulnerability (a *diathesis*) for a specific psychological disorder (see chapter 13, section 13-1c). During the past year, you have experienced a number of very stressful life events and have found it increasingly difficult to carry out your normal daily activities. Your thinking and behavior have become so disturbed and bizarre that your family brings you to the Pennsylvania Hospital for medical attention. You are lucky because the doctor who will care for you is Benjamin Rush (1745–1813), the founder of American psychiatry and one of the signers of the Declaration of Independence.

When Dr. Rush first joined the hospital's medical staff in 1783, he was appalled by the atrocious conditions and began implementing reforms. At his urging, psychologically disturbed patients were separated from those who were physically ill and placed in a separate ward where they began receiving occupational therapy (Maher & Maher, 1985). He also stopped curiosity seekers from coming to the hospital to gawk and laugh at the mentally ill patients. At the time of your admittance, Dr. Rush was hailed throughout the country as a humane healer of the human psyche.

What sort of enlightened treatment will you receive under Dr. Rush's care? Well, he will probably puncture your skin and drain "excess" blood from your body because he believes it is the source of many psychological problems. He may also seal you in a coffin-like box and then briefly submerge you in water, strap and immobilize you in his "tranquilizer" chair, spin you rapidly in a circulating swing, and terrorize you by threatening to have you killed. The rationale behind these therapies is that fright and disorientation will counteract the overexcitement responsible for your mental illness. How lucky do you now feel to be in Dr. Rush's care?

Of course, these remedies are no longer used in mental health facilities to treat psychological disorders. What sorts of remedies are being employed today? In this chapter, we continue our journey of discovery through the mental health field by addressing this very question. As you learn about these contemporary therapies, ask yourself whether any of them seem as strange as those employed by Dr. Rush.

14-1 WHO OFFERS THERAPIES FOR PSYCHOLOGICAL DISORDERS?

Just as there are different types of psychological disorders for which people seek therapy (see chapter 13), there are many different types of therapists and therapeutic methods. In beginning our examination of the treatment of psychological disorders, let us identify two main categories of therapy and the types of therapists who are trained as mental health professionals.

14-1a There Are Psychological and Biomedical Therapies

In treating psychological disorders, there are two broad categories of therapy, one psychological and the other medical. As previously discussed in chapter 8, section 8-1a, if you think of the mind as being like a computer, then mental health problems can originate either in the brain's software or its hardware. Psychologically oriented therapies typically seek solutions for what are believed to be "software" problems, while medically oriented therapies try to repair "hardware" problems. Psychological therapy, or **psychotherapy,** employs psychological methods that include a personal relationship between a trained therapist and a client. Its focus is to change disordered thoughts, behaviors, and emotions that are associated with specific psychological disorders. In contrast, **biomedical therapies** involve the treatment of psychological disorders by altering brain functioning with physical or chemical interventions.

When Sigmund Freud developed psychoanalytic therapy in the late 1800s, only a handful of practitioners employed psychological principles to treat patients. A very limited range of psychological methods were used prior to Freud, including hypnosis, emotional support, and direct education (Ellenberger, 1970). Today, mental health experts have identified more than 400 forms of psychotherapy, with many similar variations within each of the major theoretical schools of psychology (Bergin & Garfield, 1994; Corsini, 1981). In addition to traditional Freudian psychoanalysis, there are dozens of variations of therapy that are based on Freudian concepts. Likewise, there are dozens of applications of cognitive-behavioral therapies for different psychological problems, such as panic disorder and depression.

Besides the numerous therapies within each theoretical school, there are also many formats in which psychotherapy and biomedical therapies are delivered. Whereas Freud primarily provided psychotherapy to individual adult clients, contemporary therapists provide treatment to children, groups, families, and couples. In the following chapter sections, I will introduce you to a variety of psychotherapies based on specific theoretical orientations, as well as biomedical therapies that involve surgery, electric shock, and drugs.

14-1b Three Primary Mental Health Professions Provide Therapy

The three mental health professions that provide most of the therapy to people suffering from psychological disorders are psychiatry, social work, and psychology (Peterson et al., 1996). Psychiatrists are medical doctors (M.D.s) who have been trained in treating mental and emotional disorders. As physicians, psychiatrists can prescribe medications, and thus, biomedical therapy is an important aspect of their practice. They also receive training in psychotherapy and so may provide various kinds of "talk" therapy.

Most social workers have obtained a master's degree in social work (M.S.W.) in a two-year graduate program after completing their undergraduate work, while a smaller percentage have their doctorate (D.S.W.). Clinical and psychiatric social workers provide psychotherapy and coordinate with social support agencies that may provide assistance—such as shelter, vocational training, or financial aid—to clients. They often explain problems in terms of how clients interact with their family and social surroundings.

Finally, psychologists work with either a master's or a doctoral degree. Most frequently, psychologists' doctoral degree is the doctorate in philosophy (Ph.D.). However, some doctoral degrees in psychology are the doctorate in psychology (Psy.D.) or the doctorate in education (Ed.D.). In contrast to social workers and medical doctors, psychologists who receive training in psychotherapy also receive extensive training in conducting scientific research (this is less true for the Psy.D.).

Two specialty areas in psychology—clinical and counseling—provide psychotherapy. Clinical psychology is the field that works with psychological disorders—their assessment, explanation, and treatment. Counseling psychology is the field that works with essentially "normal" individuals who experience problems in living and so could benefit from educational, vocational, or personal counseling. The fields of clinical and counseling psychology overlap somewhat in that both specialties provide outpatient psychotherapy for mildly disturbed clients (Shakow, 2002).

As you might guess, the three mental health professions have different orientations toward treating mental illness. Compared with clinical psychologists, counseling psychologists tend to place less emphasis on biological factors and more frequently adopt a holistic (or "whole person") approach (Johnson & Brems, 1991). Social workers often utilize

Psychotherapy: The treatment of psychological disorders by employing psychological methods that include a personal relationship between a trained therapist and a client.

Biomedical therapies: The treatment of psychological disorders by altering brain functioning with physical or chemical interventions.

more sociological and cultural approaches to therapy than do psychologists and psychiatrists (Wierzbicki, 1997). Finally, psychiatrists rely more on biological models when explaining disorders than do the other two professions (Kingsbury, 1987).

Despite these general differences, it is important to remember that all three mental health professions can provide various types of therapy. Training in one profession does not restrict individual practitioners from specializing in any theoretical approach to therapy. For example, there are psychiatrists who use humanistic psychotherapy, clinical social workers who are behaviorists, and counseling psychologists who have a biological orientation. Therapists who combine techniques from various theoretical perspectives in treating psychological disorders are known as having an *eclectic approach* (Stricker, 1996).

Given the reality of managed care today, mental health providers often work together as a team to treat individuals suffering from psychological disorders. An individual case is likely to be referred from a primary care physician to a psychiatrist, who then refers the client to a psychologist and/or clinical social worker. Particularly for more serious conditions, such as schizophrenia and drug addiction, a social worker is often involved in training the client in basic life skills, a psychologist will have numerous "talk therapy" sessions with the client, and the psychiatrist will monitor and adjust medications.

Other health professionals may also become involved with patients who have psychological disorders. For example, nurses, occupational therapists, physical therapists, speech therapists, and other health professionals may work in mental health settings. Although they are not primarily trained as therapists, their work with patients suffering from psychological disorders may involve basic psychotherapeutic strategies.

SECTION SUMMARY

- The two broad categories of mental health therapies are psychotherapies (which employ psychological theories in treating disorders) and biomedical therapies (which involve altering brain function with physical or chemical interventions).

- Therapy is delivered through many different approaches and with many different formats.

- Therapy is primarily provided by three mental health professions: psychology, social work, and psychiatry.

- Each profession has its own area of expertise and each can provide various forms of psychotherapy.

14-2 PSYCHODYNAMIC THERAPIES

Psychodynamic therapies:
A diverse group of psychotherapies based on the work of Sigmund Freud that assert that psychological disorders stem primarily from unconscious forces.

Psychodynamic therapies are a diverse group of therapies descended from the work of Sigmund Freud that assert that psychological disorders stem primarily from unconscious forces. All of these variations of Freudian therapy are included under the heading of *psychodynamic therapy* because, like Freud, they stress the importance of understanding the *psychological dynamics* underlying behavior.

14-2a Psychoanalysis Laid the Groundwork for Psychodynamic Therapies

Freudian therapy, as practiced originally by Freud himself, is called *psychoanalysis*. Psychoanalysis dominated the field of psychotherapy throughout the first half of the 1900s. Many of the leading figures in other theoretical schools of therapy, such as Carl Rogers, Frederick Perls, Albert Ellis, and Aaron Beck—whose ideas on therapy are discussed later in this chapter—were originally trained in psychoanalysis.

As discussed in chapters 12 and 13, Freud asserted that some traumatic childhood event, often of a sexual or aggressive nature, leaves people with troubling memories or feelings. To manage the resulting anxiety, people repress the troubling material. Although this material is now unconscious, it continues to have a powerful effect on people's functioning and eventually causes psychological symptoms. In other words, people experience problematic behaviors or feelings, without being aware of the true, underlying cause of the symptoms. According to Freud, because the cause of the patient's problem is unconscious, the goal of therapy is to bring the troubling material into conscious awareness. This process of helping clients understand their own psychological processes is called *insight* (McCabe & Quayle, 2002). For this reason, psychodynamic therapy is often called *insight-oriented*.

When clients gain insight into the underlying troubling material, they can then express the emotional energy associated with this unconscious material. This release of pent-up emotion, called *catharsis*, is an important aspect of psychodynamic therapy. In addition to discharging the emotions associated with the previously unconscious troubling material, clients can now deal with this troubling material in a conscious, rational, more effective manner.

In classical psychoanalysis, the client reclines on a couch, facing away from the therapist. This placement of the therapist and client is thought to minimize distractions, thus making it easier for the client to verbalize whatever comes to mind.

14-2b Free Association Is the Primary Psychodynamic Technique

All Freudian-based therapy techniques are directed toward helping the client gain insight. The primary technique in Freudian therapy (what Freud called the "fundamental rule" of psychoanalysis) is **free association,** in which the clients say aloud whatever comes to mind, making no deliberate attempt to inhibit their speech. According to Freud, free association gives unconscious troubling material the opportunity to come forth, perhaps allowing clients to suddenly recall important events from childhood. Free association may yield important information in other ways as well. For instance, while freely associating, clients may be unable to think of a word or finish a sentence. They may also suddenly change topics or begin to stammer. According to Freud, such responses often occur when clients are close to achieving insight concerning sensitive unconscious subjects and their defense mechanisms attempt to block this therapeutic breakthrough.

Free association: A psychodynamic therapy technique developed by Freud, in which clients say whatever comes to mind, without making any effort to inhibit their speech.

The psychodynamic therapist also draws inferences from special types of slips of the tongue (see chapter 9, section 9-1c, Discovery Box 9-1), known as *Freudian slips,* which are instances in which the client means to say one thing but actually says something else. For example, if the client means to say, "I love my wife," but actually says, "I leave my wife," the therapist would interpret this slip as communicating an unconscious desire.

The psychodynamic therapist also interprets the underlying meaning in other forms of expression: dreams, daydreams, artwork, poetry, and so on. Freud thought that almost everything we do is caused by unconscious influences. Through interpreting the symbols in the client's dreams and artwork, the therapist may come to understand the client's unconscious.

Finally, psychodynamic therapists also interpret the client's relationship with the therapist. The client may develop strong positive or negative feelings for the therapist, which is called **transference.** Feeling admiration and even romantic love for the therapist are common forms of positive transference, while feeling resentment and anger are common forms of negative transference. Freud interpreted transference as representing feelings that the client experienced toward others earlier in life. If the client becomes dependent on the therapist, this may mean that the client was overly dependent on parents during childhood. If the client resents the authority of the therapist, perhaps the client was resentful of his or her parents as a child.

Transference: Feelings the client develops for the therapist that are presumed to reflect the client's feelings for significant others early in life.

According to Freud, the client is not the only person in therapy who may project unconscious feelings from childhood on to someone. He warned therapists that they may also develop similarly strong feelings for their clients, which he called countertransference. **Countertransference** represents feelings that the therapist experienced toward others earlier in life. Freud strongly recommended that therapists should attend to these feelings so that they gain greater insight into their unconscious desires and thereby make it less likely that these feelings will interfere with their treatment of clients.

Countertransference: Feelings the therapist develops for the client that are presumed to reflect feelings the therapist had for others early in life.

Another important aspect of the client-therapist relationship in Freudian therapy is resistance. **Resistance** is anything the client does that interferes with therapeutic progress. Over the course of therapy, the client may begin to sabotage therapy by missing or coming late to sessions, talking only about trivial issues, or bringing up significant issues only at the very end of a session so that there is no time to address them. According to Freud, the cause of the client's problem is some troubling material in the unconscious. When the client starts making inroads toward identifying this troubling material, the material becomes even more threatening. Thus, even though the client wants to improve, the mind raises its defenses to keep this troubling material unconscious.

Throughout psychodynamic therapy, therapists bring clients' attention to aspects of their behavior that they are not fully aware of, and they help clients make connections between their current behavior and their childhood experiences. During this process, clients learn to examine the underlying meaning of their behavior and gain insight into their unconscious.

14-2c Psychodynamic Therapy Is Lengthy and Expensive

One of the primary criticisms of psychodynamic therapy is that it is too lengthy and expensive for all but the very wealthy. At one to three sessions a week at $150 a session, a client would pay between $40,000 to $120,000 after five years. A second criticism is that its interpretations can never be disproved. For example, if a therapist interprets a client's tardiness for an appointment as a sign of resistance, the client's attempt to disagree may be perceived as further proof of the initial interpretation.

Though still available, classic psychoanalysis is not widely practiced today. However, as previously discussed in chapter 12, section 12-2e, many followers of Freud have modified his theory and therapy. For example, Alfred Adler considered early family social interactions to be more important influences on the developing personality than unconscious sexual conflicts. As a result, Adlerian therapists place more emphasis on the ego's conscious, rational processes than on the id's unconscious processes. Similarly, Carl Jung, Freud's most cherished pupil, de-emphasized sex as the major motivation for human behavior and criticized psychoanalysis as being too negative. He also strongly disagreed with Freud that adult personality was determined by early childhood experiences and, instead, argued that behavior is primarily influenced by future goals. As a result, Jungian therapists emphasize clients' future possibilities rather than their past experiences. They also compare therapy to a spiritual exercise, in which clients must first "confess" their weaknesses before they can improve.

In general, the psychodynamic approach has had an enormous impact on how mental health professionals "do" psychotherapy. First, this perspective has helped to demythologize psychological disorders by arguing that "sane" and "insane" behaviors have their psychological roots in the same mental processes. Second, even therapists who reject Freud's theoretical basis for mental illness often still use his therapeutic technique of developing a one-to-one therapist-client relationship aimed at increasing client insight.

SECTION SUMMARY

- The goal of psychodynamic therapy is insight into unconscious troubling material.

- Free association is its primary technique.

- Psychodynamic therapy is lengthy and expensive.

- Many current variations of Freud's classic psychoanalysis de-emphasize sex as the primary motivator of behavior; they also tend to downplay the importance of the unconscious and early childhood experiences.

14-3 BEHAVIORAL THERAPIES

The behavioral perspective toward psychological disorders was addressed in chapter 13, section 13-1c. Unlike the psychodynamic perspective, behaviorists do not believe in the unconscious, and thus, insight is not important in the treatment of psychological disorders. Instead, psychological disorders and "healthy" behavior are thought to both develop through learning. Thus, in **behavioral therapies,** disordered behaviors are unlearned and replaced by more appropriate alternative behaviors.

> **Behavioral therapies:**
> Psychotherapies that apply learning principles to the elimination of unwanted behaviors.

14-3a Some Behavioral Therapies Rely upon Classical Conditioning

One category of behavior therapy employs the principles of classical conditioning first developed by Ivan Pavlov (see chapter 7, section 7-1a). As you recall, in classical conditioning, an unconditioned stimulus (UCS) automatically elicits an unconditioned response (UCR). The UCS is paired with a neutral stimulus that initially has no effect on the response. However, after repeated pairings of the two stimuli, the previously neutral stimulus, now called the conditioned stimulus (CS), elicits the response, now called the conditioned response (CR).

The most widely used form of psychotherapy that is based on classical conditioning is **counterconditioning** (Goetestam, 2002). This behavior therapy involves conditioning new responses to stimuli that trigger unwanted behaviors. Three specific counterconditioning techniques are *systematic desensitization, response prevention,* and *aversive conditioning.*

> **Counterconditioning:**
> A behavior therapy procedure based on classical conditioning that involves conditioning new responses to stimuli that trigger unwanted behaviors.

Systematic Desensitization

Systematic desensitization is a behavioral therapy technique that is commonly used to treat people suffering from phobias by gradually exposing the phobic client to the feared object without arousing anxiety and fear (Wolpe, 1958; Wolpe & Plaud, 1997). Behaviorists hold that the phobia was initially acquired through classical conditioning. That is, the phobic object was originally a neutral stimulus that was then paired with something that naturally elicited fear. A phobia conditioned in this way can be counterconditioned by pairing the feared object with relaxation or another physiological state that is incompatible with anxiety and fear.

> **Systematic desensitization:**
> A counterconditioning technique commonly used to treat phobias in which the client is gradually exposed to the feared object, while remaining relaxed.

For example, suppose a client has a fear of snakes. The client and therapist begin by constructing a *desensitization hierarchy,* which consists of a sequence of increasingly anxiety-provoking situations related to snakes (see table 14-1). The therapist then trains the client in relaxation exercises, such as slow breathing or muscle relaxation. The first step of the hierarchy is then introduced (imagining seeing a snake). If the client can handle this without experiencing anxiety, then the next step is introduced. Whenever the client experiences anxiety, the stimulus is removed and the client is given time to relax. After relaxing, a less threatening object on the hierarchy is reintroduced and the client and therapist again proceed along the hierarchy. In a relatively short time, the client often can face the highest object on the hierarchy—handling a snake—without distress (Chambless, 1990).

With advancements in computer technology, clients can now go through the hierarchy by wearing virtual reality equipment that allows them to gradually experience more intense anxiety-provoking 3-D situations without ever leaving the therapist's office (Carlin et al., 1997; North et al., 2002). This *virtual reality graded exposure* technique is especially useful in treating acrophobia (fear of heights) because it removes any danger caused by clients panicking while standing on a high structure (Rothbaum et al., 1995).

Response Prevention

A counterconditioning technique closely related to desensitization is **response prevention,** which is used to treat compulsive behaviors. Remember that in obsessive-compulsive

> **Response prevention:**
> A counterconditioning technique commonly used in the treatment of obsessive-compulsive disorder, in which clients are exposed to the situation in which they previously exhibited a compulsive behavior and are not permitted to engage in the ritual.

TABLE 14-1

A Sample Desensitization Hierarchy

The scenes in this hierarchy are typical of those used in the systematic desensitization of a fear of snakes. The numbers to the left of each item represent one patient's subjective rating of how anxiety provoking a situation is, on a scale from 0 ("Not at all anxious") to 100 ("Uncontrollable anxiety").

Fear Level	Scene
10	I imagine seeing a snake.
20	I see a line drawing of a snake.
25	I see a photograph of a small, harmless garden snake.
30	I see a photograph of a large python snake.
40	I hold a rubber snake in my hands.
50	I watch a nature video on snakes.
60	I am in the same room with a snake in a cage.
70	I am standing next to the snake cage.
80	I am looking into the top of the snake cage with the lid open.
90	I am standing next to a person holding a snake.
95	I touch a snake held by someone else.
100	I am holding a snake.

A review of 375 therapy outcome studies indicates that systematic desensitization is the most effective therapy for treating phobias (Smith & Glass, 1977). Other reviews have concluded that desensitization is also effective in treating other problems that may occur as a result of anxiety, such as sexual dysfunctions (Emmelkamp, 1986; North et al., 2002).

disorder, people experience distressing repetitive thoughts (such as worries about catching illness from exposure to germs) followed by ritualistic compulsive behaviors (such as washing one's hands hundreds of times daily). In response prevention therapy, clients are exposed to situations that trigger the distressing thoughts and feelings (for example, touching an object that fell on the floor). In the past, the clients' distress decreased after they engaged in compulsive behaviors, and so the compulsions were reinforced. However, in this treatment, clients are prevented from engaging in the compulsive behaviors, thus shutting off their usual, troublesome escape route to anxiety reduction. In all cases, response prevention causes an initial buildup of anxiety, but over time the client's distress tends to diminish. Numerous studies indicate that response prevention is effective in treating obsessive-compulsive disorder, with about 50 percent of clients showing substantial improvement and another 25 percent showing moderate improvement (Barlow & Lehman, 1996; Steketee, 1993).

> **INFO-BIT:** Mary Cover Jones (1896–1987), one of John Watson's students, was the first psychologist to demonstrate that conditioned fears could be reversed. She treated a three-year-old boy, Peter, who had a fear of furry objects very similar to Watson's famous "Little Albert." Therapy involved feeding Peter at one end of a room while a rabbit was brought in at the other end. After several sessions of slowly closing the distance between Peter and the rabbit, the boy's fear disappeared (Jones, 1924). Jones is often called "the mother of behavioral therapy."

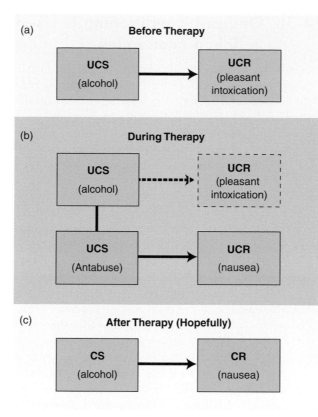

FIGURE 14-1
Aversive Conditioning for Alcoholism

(a) Before therapy, alcohol is an unconditioned stimulus for alcoholics, naturally evoking a pleasant unconditioned response. *(b)* During therapy, the Antabuse drug is mixed with alcohol given to the alcoholic, which causes severe nausea. *(c)* After repeated pairings, the alcohol becomes a conditioned stimulus, evoking the conditioned nausea response. What might weaken this conditioned response following therapy so that the treatment is ultimately ineffective in preventing abstinence?

Aversive Conditioning

One last counterconditioning technique is **aversive conditioning,** in which people are classically conditioned to react with aversion to a harmful or undesirable stimulus (Finn et al., 2001). For example, as depicted in figure 14-1, clients who abuse alcohol may be given one of their favorite drinks laced with *Antabuse,* a drug that induces severe vomiting. The objective is to replace alcoholics' positive reaction to alcohol with a decidedly negative response. After repeated pairings of alcohol with vomiting, the alcohol alone begins eliciting nausea. Alcoholics treated with this form of aversion therapy tend to achieve about a 60 percent abstinence rate up to one year after treatment (Miller & Hester, 1980; Rimelle et al., 1995; Voegtlin, 1940). However, after three years, only about one-third remain abstinent. The problem with this therapy is that alcohol is an unconditioned stimulus that naturally evokes a pleasant state of intoxication (UCR). Alcoholics know that if they drink outside of the therapist's office, they will not experience the immediate nausea but instead will experience a pleasant alcoholic "high."

Another form of aversive conditioning is *rapid smoking,* which is designed to help people stop smoking. In this treatment, the client inhales smoke from a cigarette every six to eight seconds. After only a few minutes, smokers—even those who chain smoke—become physically sick from the toxins in the tobacco. After repeated trials, the taste, smell, and even sight of cigarettes often trigger a nausea response. Rapid smoking is a fairly effective technique, with about 50 percent of clients remaining smoke-free at least three to six months after treatment (Lichtenstein & Brown, 1980).

As you can imagine, aversive conditioning is both distressing and messy, and many clients and therapists prefer other treatments. Aversive conditioning is typically used only after other methods have failed and the client provides informed consent to participate in such a difficult process. Even when this procedure is used, therapists almost always combine it with another treatment, often involving operant conditioning, which is our next topic of discussion.

Aversive conditioning: A counterconditioning technique in which a classically conditioned aversive response is conditioned to occur in response to a stimulus that has previously been associated with an undesired behavior.

14-3b Operant Conditioning Is Used in Token Economies

As you recall from chapter 7, section 7-2, *operant conditioning* involves learning through reinforcement and punishment. Because virtually every voluntary behavior can be punished or reinforced, operant conditioning is a very flexible approach to modifying behavior and has had numerous therapeutic applications.

One important therapeutic application of operant conditioning principles is the **token economy,** which uses reward and punishment to modify the behavior of groups of people who are often in institutional settings, such as psychiatric hospitals or prisons (Bellus et al., 1999). In this technique, desirable behaviors are reinforced with tokens (such as poker chips or checks on a card), and undesirable behaviors are punished by the loss of tokens (Ayllon & Azrin, 1968). People whose behavior is being modified with token economies accumulate and later exchange the tokens for other forms of reinforcement (such as television privileges or field trips). Research has shown that the token economy technique is effective in shaping desirable behavior not only in psychiatric hospitals and prisons but also in school classrooms and homes for juvenile delinquents (Ayllon & Azrin, 1968; Kazdin, 1982).

Is there a downside to using the token economy? Critics charge that this type of *behavior modification* makes people too dependent on the external rewards earned in the token economy. Why is this a problem? Well, when was the last time someone gave you a token when you did something nice or took a token from you when you behaved badly? One of the problems with token economies is that the desirable behaviors learned through this technique are likely to be quickly extinguished when people are outside the institution. Proponents of the token economy respond that such a possibility can be considerably reduced if, prior to leaving the institution, people are slowly shifted from a token-economy reward system to rewards that are more likely to be encountered outside the institution, such as social approval.

Token economy: A technique often used to modify the behavior of severely disturbed people in institutional settings that involves reinforcing desirable behaviors with tokens that can be exchanged for other forms of reinforcement, such as snacks or television privileges.

14-3c Observational Learning Is Used in Modeling and Social Skills Training

Observational learning is the central feature of Albert Bandura's (1986) *social learning theory,* which contends that people learn social behaviors mainly through observation and cognitive processing of information, rather than through direct experience (see chapter 7, section 7-3a). Specifically, *observational learning* is learning by observing and imitating the behavior of others, who are called *models*. The therapeutic application of observational learning principles is called **modeling,** and it has been especially helpful in teaching clients useful social behaviors and coping skills.

In *participatory modeling,* the therapist or someone else models more effective ways of behaving, and gradually the client is invited to participate in the behavior. For example, a person suffering from snake phobia might first watch the therapist handling snakes without expressing fear or being harmed. After a few times watching this snake handling, the client is gently coaxed into holding a snake. Participatory modeling is a very effective treatment for dealing with phobias and other fears (Bandura, 1986). It relies on *vicarious conditioning,* which is the process by which one learns the consequences of an action by observing its consequences for someone else (see chapter 7, section 7-3a).

Another therapeutic technique that involves observational learning is **social skills training,** which teaches clients who are inept or inappropriate in social situations how to interact with others more comfortably and effectively (Hersen & Bellack, 1999). For example, most schizophrenics are socially inept: They often do not directly interact with others and exhibit emotions unconnected with the situation. Thus, usually in conjunction with drug therapies (see section 14-7a), schizophrenic patients often participate in social skills training (Bellack & Mueser, 1993). Impulsive and hyperactive children, who often have problems interacting with others, are also regularly placed in such therapy programs.

Modeling: A behavioral method of psychotherapy in which desirable behaviors are demonstrated as a way of teaching them to clients.

Social skills training: A behavioral method of psychotherapy in which clients are taught how to interact with others more comfortably and effectively.

Suppose a male college student seeks therapy because he is shy and has been unsuccessful in his attempts to talk to women. He reports that he stammers and has trouble thinking of anything to say. He does not initiate conversations with women classmates, even to make small talk. When he starts to make a phone call to ask someone out, he hesitates and talks himself out of making the call. How might a behavioral psychotherapist use modeling and social skills training to treat this student's shyness?

Social skills training programs employ various learning techniques, including the previously discussed modeling of socially skilled trainers, as well as role-playing various problematic social encounters. The social skills taught in these training sessions cover such areas as initiating conversations, giving and receiving compliments, reacting nonviolently to conflict, nonverbal methods of communication, and actively listening to what others have to say in conversation (Kelly, 1997). Training is usually conducted in groups. In a typical session, the therapist might show a videotape of a model starting a conversation inappropriately or aggressively responding to a disagreement. The group might then discuss ways in which the model could have acted more appropriately. Following this discussion, another videotape might be shown in which the model performs more effectively. Each person in the training group might then role-play a conversation while others observe and then provide feedback. This role playing might even be videotaped so that group members can see exactly how they had interacted. The session might end with a homework assignment for group members to work on some specific social behavior during the following week. A number of studies indicate that those who participate in such training exercises show improvements in their social skills and an increased level of social satisfaction (Erwin, 1994; Margalit, 1995).

SECTION SUMMARY

- Behavioral therapies use conditioning and observational learning techniques to modify problem behaviors.

- Therapy techniques based on classical conditioning include systematic desensitization (gradually exposing the phobic client to the feared object without arousing anxiety and fear); response prevention (exposing clients to situations in which they previously exhibited a compulsive behavior and are not permitted to engage in the ritual); and aversive conditioning (an aversive response is conditioned to occur in response to a stimulus that, previously was associated with an undesired behavior).

- Therapy techniques based on operant conditioning are token economies (used in institutions to modify the behavior of groups of people); modeling (desirable behaviors are demonstrated as a way of teaching them to clients); and social skills training (learning how to interact with others more comfortably and effectively).

14-4 COGNITIVE THERAPIES

As discussed in chapter 13, section 13-1c, the cognitive perspective suggests that the immediate cause of psychological problems is inaccurate or ineffective thinking. Because dysfunctional thinking is considered to be the source of psychological problems, **cognitive therapies** seek to identify and then modify these faulty cognitive processes. Like behavioral therapies—and unlike psychodynamic therapies—cognitive therapies tend to be short term, problem focused, and highly directive.

Cognitive therapies: Psychotherapies that focus on identifying and then modifying dysfunctional patterns of thought.

14-4a Rational-Emotive Behavioral Therapy Confronts Clients' Irrational Assumptions

Rational-emotive behavior therapy (REBT): The cognitive therapy of Albert Ellis, in which people are confronted with their irrational beliefs and persuaded to develop a more realistic way of thinking.

Although initially trained in psychoanalysis, Albert Ellis (1962, 1999) developed a form of cognitive therapy that he now calls **rational-emotive behavioral therapy (REBT).** The basic assumption underlying Ellis's unconventional technique is that mental distress is not caused by objective events in people's lives, but by the irrational thinking people have about those events. For example, a person might say that he is depressed because he did not receive a promotion at work. However, Ellis would contend that the real cause of the depression is the person's assumption that this event means something negative about himself ("My boss does not respect me"). The goal of REBT is to help people identify problems in the way they think about their general experiences and then try to modify these cognitions.

The irrational beliefs that cause emotional problems are based on what Ellis called "all-or-none" types of thinking. For example, people who think that they must be loved or approved by everyone, or that they must be successful in everything they do are likely to feel unhappy much of the time. By setting unreachable goals, they experience frequent disappointment.

Instead of allowing clients to state their beliefs without evaluative comment (as happens in classical psychoanalysis), REBT therapists directly attack clients' irrational way of thinking, pointing out how it is inevitably self-defeating, and persuading them to develop a more realistic way of evaluating their lives. Therapists are blunt and confrontational in challenging clients' negative and unrealistic assessments of their present conditions ("So you didn't get the promotion. Where is it written that life has to be fair?").

Clients are also encouraged to "step out of character" and try new behaviors that directly challenge their irrational beliefs. For example, if a woman is afraid that others won't like her if she disagrees with them, her therapist might instruct her to forcefully disagree with five different people during the next week. The objective in such an exercise is for the woman to discover that her world doesn't end following such exchanges.

The effectiveness of REBT is difficult to determine. There are no specific psychological disorders that are best treated by REBT, and it is unclear how much clients benefit from this form of therapy (Haaga & Davison, 1993), but studies suggest that it does have some positive effects on clients' later adjustment and well-being (Engels et al., 1993; Lyons & Woods, 1991).

14-4b Cognitive-Behavioral Therapy Focuses on Depression and Other Emotional Problems

Cognitive-behavior therapy (CBT): The cognitive therapy of Aaron Beck that identifies and then changes negative thinking and behavior by using both cognitive and behavioral principles.

Like Ellis, Aaron Beck (1967) was also a psychoanalyst who developed a cognitive therapy after listening to his clients repeatedly expressing self-defeating beliefs. His **cognitive-behavior therapy (CBT)** was originally developed to treat depression—which he considers a cognitive disorder—but he later applied his treatment to anxiety and other emotional problems (Beck & Emery, 1985).

According to Beck, depressed people have negative views of themselves, the world, and their future, and they misinterpret everyday events to support these negative views (Beck et al., 1979). For example, they tend to exaggerate negative outcomes while downplaying positive outcomes, and they jump to overly pessimistic conclusions from a single event. These thinking errors may occur so frequently that they become automatic.

CBT involves identifying and then changing the client's negative thinking patterns as well as their negative behavior patterns. To do so, clients keep a diary of their thoughts before and after sad episodes. Therapists then discuss these episodes with clients and help them develop new thinking patterns that are more positive, accurate, and effective. The reason this therapy has the term "behavior" in its title is that the methods used to help clients develop new patterns of thinking often involve basic conditioning techniques. Research has shown that CBT is relatively effective in treating depression (Elkin et al., 1989), panic disorder (Craske & Barlow, 1993), bulimia (Fairburn et al., 1997), and borderline personality disorder (Linehan, 1993).

SECTION SUMMARY

- Cognitive therapy is based on the assumption that troubling emotions and behaviors result from inaccurate or ineffective thinking.

- Cognitive therapies are short term, active, and problem focused.

- In rational-emotive behavior therapy, clients are bluntly confronted with their irrational beliefs and persuaded to develop a more realistic way of thinking.

- In cognitive-behavior therapy, clients' negative thinking and behavior are modified using both cognitive and behavioral principles.

14-5 HUMANISTIC THERAPIES

As discussed in chapter 12, section 12-3, humanistic psychology focuses on positive aspects of human experience, such as love, creativity, and spirituality. Humanism was not considered in the previous chapter's discussion of psychological disorders because it generally focuses more on psychological health than on pathology. However, **humanistic therapies**—which help people get in touch with their feelings, with their "true selves," and with their purpose in life—represent an important form of treatment. Humanists believe that psychological problems develop when outside forces stifle people's natural tendency to seek personal growth. One of the primary goals of humanistic therapies is to help clients actualize their basically good nature.

Humanistic therapies:
Psychotherapies that help people get in touch with their feelings, with their "true selves," and with their purpose in life.

14-5a Client-Centered Therapy Focuses on Clients' Conscious Self-Perceptions

The psychologist who has had the strongest influence on humanistic psychotherapy is Carl Rogers (1959, 1961), developer of **client-centered therapy.** In treating psychological disorders, Rogers argued that psychotherapists should not assume the role of "detective"—as in psychodynamic therapy—nor the "active director" role—as in behavioral and cognitive therapies. Instead, he believed that therapists should be *facilitators* of personal growth by providing a supportive environment where clients can discover their "true selves." This emphasis in therapy on the client's own conscious self-perceptions rather than the therapist's interpretations of those perceptions is why Rogers's therapeutic approach is titled "client-centered."

Client-centered therapy:
A humanistic therapy in which the client and not the therapist directs the course of therapy.

A central assumption underlying client-centered therapy is that psychopathology results from people having received *conditional positive regard* from loved ones, which involves being loved and socially accepted only when meeting others' standards (Rogers, 1951). Put another way, people are not accepted as worthy individuals in their own right, but only when they meet or conform to others' wishes and desires. As previously discussed in chapter 12, section 12-3a, Rogers believed that people subjected to this conditional love fail to develop their "true selves" and, as a result, develop an array of emotional problems.

To counteract the negative effects of this conditional acceptance, Rogers proposed that psychotherapy should be built around the principle of *unconditional positive regard* (again, see chapter 12, section 12-3a). That is, clients should be accepted unconditionally—treated with warmth, kindness, and caring—regardless of what they have said or done. The assumption is that when therapists accept clients for who they are, clients will eventually accept themselves as well, put aside others' standards and develop their true selves (Truax & Carkhuff, 1967). Key ingredients in unconditional positive regard are *genuineness* (being open and honest), *warmth* (being caring and nurturant), and *empathy* (accurately identifying what the client is thinking and feeling).

In expressing unconditional positive regard, client-centered therapists typically use the techniques of *open-ended statements, reflection,* and *paraphrasing.* For instance, consider the question, "Did you have a good week?" This is a closed-ended question because it can be answered with a single word, and it suggests that the client should evaluate the week. On the other hand, "Tell me about your week" is open-ended because clients can say as much or as little about the week as they choose. Open-ended statements encourage clients to speak, without limiting the topic of conversation. With reflection, the therapist acknowledges some emotion that clients have expressed verbally or nonverbally. For example, when clients say that the week has been hard, the therapist reflects this by saying, "This has been a tough week for you." Finally, with paraphrasing, the therapist summarizes the expressed verbal content of clients. For example, when clients are distressed but do not express themselves very clearly, the therapist may summarize what the clients have said by stating, "Let me see if I am understanding the situation you faced this week. You said that. . . ."

Therapists from many theoretical schools use some or all of these client-centered techniques to build rapport with their clients. Such wide use of client-centered techniques probably explains why Carl Rogers is often identified by fellow psychotherapists as having had the biggest influence on how therapy is practiced (Smith, 1982). Further, reviews of almost 1,100 therapeutic outcome studies conducted over a 35-year period support Rogers's contention that a positive client-therapist relationship is an essential factor in determining the effectiveness of therapy (Orlinsky & Howard, 1987). Discovery Box 14-1 discusses how failure to establish rapport may partly explain the higher dropout rates among minority group members in the United States.

14-5b Gestalt Therapy Encourages Clients to Get in Touch with Their Current Feelings

Gestalt therapy: A humanistic psychotherapy that stresses awareness of feelings in the here and now.

Another influential humanistic therapy is **Gestalt therapy,** which was developed by former psychoanalyst Frederick ("Fritz") Perls, along with his wife, Laura (Perls, 1969; Perls et al., 1951). *Gestalt* is the German word for "pattern" or "whole." Perls named his approach Gestalt therapy because he said that he treated the "whole" person. For Perls, a major cause of mental illness is people's lack of awareness of their true feelings or some other important aspect of the self.

Although Gestalt therapy is most often classified as humanistic, it also has certain psychodynamic features (Kirchner, 2000). Consistent with the psychodynamic view, Perls asserted that people often are not consciously aware of their own feelings, and he sought to help clients develop their self-awareness (or gain *insight*). However, consistent with the humanistic view, in seeking self-awareness, Perls focused on the here and now rather than on childhood experiences.

In contrast to the nondirective style typical of client-centered therapists, Gestalt therapists employ a very directive approach. This approach is most clearly seen when they put clients on a figurative "hot seat" to encourage them to become aware of feelings and impulses that they have disowned and to abandon feelings and ideas that are not their own (Bowman & Brownell, 2000). For example, if clients frown following a comment by the therapist, the therapist might confront this directly by stating "Are you aware of your facial expression? What does this mean to you?" Gestalt therapists also use body awareness exercises to stimulate physical and emotional reactions. For example, if clients are having difficulty recognizing their emotions, the therapist may tell them to practice different facial expressions in front of a mirror and identify the associated feelings. The goal of such exercises is to enhance clients' awareness of their current emotional and bodily states.

Empty-chair technique: A Gestalt technique in which clients engage in emotional expression by imagining that the person to whom they would like to speak is sitting in an empty chair facing them.

Perhaps the most popular technique used in Gestalt therapy to help clients gain insight into their true feelings is the **empty-chair technique.** As depicted in figure 14-2, the therapist places an empty chair facing the client, and the client is then asked to imagine that an important person from her or his past or present—a parent, spouse, friend—is sitting in the chair. In this "safe" environment, the client can express her or his feelings by "talking" with the person and hopefully gaining insight into their feelings. Research suggests that this technique may indeed help clients deal with the emotional turmoil that initially led them to seek therapy in the first place (Paivio & Greenberg, 1995).

DISCOVERY　BOX 14-1

Why Do Certain Minorities Underutilize Therapeutic Services?

African Americans and Native Americans use mental health services as often as White Americans, but Asian Americans underutilize these services (Sue, 1991). One factor influencing willingness to seek psychotherapy is the belief systems in one's culture of origin. Most modern psychotherapies were developed in Western cultures that have an individualistic orientation, in which individuals are viewed as independent, rational creatures who seek to gratify their personal needs. However, in many collectivist Asian cultures, it is considered socially inappropriate to talk about one's personal feelings or even to focus on oneself individually (Russell & Yik, 1996). In fact, being socially non-expressive is often interpreted as an indication of emotional strength and trustworthiness in such cultures. Because of these cultural beliefs, immigrants from Asian countries are often reluctant to seek therapy.

Studies have also found that Asian Americans, Hispanic Americans, African Americans, and Native Americans drop out of therapy more often than White Americans (Wierzbicki & Pekarik, 1993). Some of these differences might be due to the fact that dropout rates are higher among poorer clients, and ethnic minorities are overrepresented in lower-income groups. Another likely factor explaining these differences is that the vast majority of therapists in the United States are White, and research indicates that clients feel more comfortable when their therapists are similar to them rather than dissimilar (Snowden & Hu, 1996). Thus, the higher dropout rates among minorities may be at least partly due to problems in establishing rapport with White therapists (Atkinson et al., 1996).

Faced with these cultural divisions that can impede therapeutic effectiveness, an increasing number of White psychotherapists have received special training to work more effectively with clients from other cultural backgrounds. Additionally, the American Psychological Association and other mental health organizations have made concerted efforts to recruit and train more ethnic minority therapists.

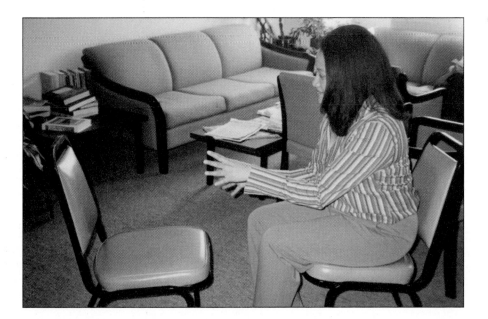

FIGURE 14-2
The Empty-Chair Technique

In the empty-chair technique, clients are asked to imagine that an important person from their past or present is sitting in the chair. Then clients engage in a conversation with this person, telling him or her things that they have been holding in for years and, as a result, presumably gaining insight into their true feelings.

14-5c Existential Therapy Helps Clients Deal with Fundamental Problems of Existence

The work of many humanistic therapists was heavily influenced by *existential psychology*, which is an outgrowth of European existential philosophy (May, 1959). *Existentialism* is an approach to philosophy that examines the fundamental problems of human existence, such as the meaning of life, the inevitability of pain and isolation, and the responsibility of self-determination. Existentialists believe that the material comforts of the modern world have caused people to fall into a pattern of conformity and to lose a sense of their "true self" (Laing, 1967). **Existential therapy** is a philosophical approach that helps clients address these existential dilemmas (May, 1990). Although some existential psychologists may not consider themselves humanists, this perspective is closer to humanistic psychology than to any of the other schools of therapy covered in this chapter, and so it will be presented here.

One important existential therapist is Viktor Frankl (1963, 1969), a student of Freud who developed a form of existential therapy called *logotherapy* ("meaning therapy"). Frankl believed that a fundamental human motive is to find meaning in life, and that emotional problems develop when such meaning cannot be found. How do you find meaning for yourself? According to Frankl, meaning can be found (1) through your life contributions (what you "give" to the world), (2) through your life experiences (what you "take" from the world), and (3) through your attitudes in facing difficult situations.

Frankl is best known for this third way of finding meaning because he himself was a survivor of Nazi concentration camps in World War II and developed logotherapy during his imprisonment. For people who find themselves in terrible situations over which they have little control, Frankl offers a philosophical—almost a religious—form of psychotherapy, in which clients are encouraged to find meaning in terms of how they face these situations. For example, in his book *Man's Search for Meaning*, Frankl (1963) described the case of an elderly man who was consumed by grief after the death of his wife. Frankl asked the man to consider the consequences if he had died before his wife. The man recognized that he would have done anything to spare her this suffering—including bearing the pain himself. Even though he continued to mourn his wife, he found meaning in her loss by seeing that his suffering had spared her.

The effectiveness of existential therapy is difficult to determine because existential therapists reject the use of conventional scientific methods to evaluate psychotherapies. Like Freud, they believe that such methods cannot accurately evaluate their techniques. Instead, they have sought to validate their therapies by solely relying on individual case studies. As a result, this therapeutic approach has very little empirical support.

Existential therapy:
A philosophical approach to treating clients who are experiencing distress principally related to a lack of meaning in their lives.

SECTION SUMMARY

- Client-centered therapy is a form of humanistic therapy based on unconditional positive regard; it focuses on the client's self-perceptions and is nondirective.
- Gestalt therapy stresses awareness of feelings in the here and now and uses active and directive techniques, such as confrontation, to enhance awareness.
- Existential therapy addresses problems that result from existential dilemmas involving a lack of meaning in life.

14-6 OTHER FORMS OF PSYCHOTHERAPY

Most forms of psychotherapy were originally developed for use with individual adult clients. However, it is important to remember that psychotherapy is often provided in other formats. In this section of the chapter, we examine *child therapy, group therapy,* and *family/couples therapy.*

14-6a Child Therapies Use Techniques Designed for Younger Minds

Approximately 12 percent of the children and adolescents in the United States experience significant behavioral or emotional problems, with about 2.5 million of them receiving some form of therapy (Weisz et al., 1992). In offering such therapy, mental health professionals must remember that children differ from adults in many ways that affect their response to psychotherapy. For instance, children's vocabulary is still fairly simple and undeveloped, making it harder for them to express their feelings. In general, their thinking is much more concrete and oriented to present events, making them less aware than adults of the possible causes of their problems. Due to these limitations, children may be less able than adults to respond to verbal and insight-oriented therapies. Thus, therapists may have to rely more on behavioral observations and the reports of third parties (such as parents or teachers) than they would with adult clients. In some cases, the parents may be recruited as "cotherapists," using at home techniques that the therapist teaches them.

A common approach therapists use when working with children is **play therapy.** Here, the child plays with puppets, blocks, crayons, and other common toys, while the therapist plays with or simply observes the child. Psychodynamic therapists consider play therapy to be a childhood form of free association, a technique that they believe allows the client's unconscious material to come forth (Klein, 1932). In contrast, client-centered therapists consider play therapy to be a perfect vehicle for them to practice their warm, nondirective approach (Axline, 1947). During play, the therapist provides the child with unconditional positive regard, thereby activating the therapeutic process. Cognitive and behavioral therapists also find play therapy useful because it provides a means of helping the child acquire new cognitive or behavioral skills. In both approaches, therapy is basically an educational enterprise. By playing with the child, the therapist can demonstrate new skills, reinforce the child's successful efforts, and modify efforts that are only partly correct.

> **Play therapy:** A therapeutic technique in which the therapist provides children with toys and drawing materials, on the assumption that whatever is troubling them will be expressed in their play.

14-6b Group Therapy Involves Clients Discussing Their Problems with One Another under a Therapist's Guidance

Thus far, the therapies that we have discussed involve individual clients. Yet, psychotherapy can also be conducted with groups of clients (Hoberman & Lewinsohn, 1985). **Group therapy** refers to the simultaneous treatment of several clients under the guidance of a therapist. Some therapy groups consist of relatively well functioning clients in outpatient settings, while other therapy groups consist of severely disturbed patients in hospital settings. Many groups are organized around one kind of problem (such as alcoholism or depression) or one kind of client (such as adolescents or police officers). The group usually consists of between 5 and 10 people who meet with a therapist about once a week for two hours. Today, all of the major theoretical schools of psychotherapy have some sort of group format (Vandervoort & Fuhriman, 1991; Wierzbicki & Bartlett, 1987; Yalom, 1995).

Although the increased use of group therapy over the past 30 years is partly due to economics—it is more cost-effective than individual therapy—there are some real advantages that the group format has over the individual format (Fuhriman & Burlingame,

> **Group therapy:** The simultaneous treatment of several clients under the guidance of a therapist.

1994; Kutash & Wolf, 1990). One advantage is that group therapy helps clients realize that others also struggle with many of the same problems that they are working to solve. A related advantage is that a group format provides clients with the opportunity to compare themselves with others and exchange information on how to become more mentally healthy. A third advantage is that group members can become an important support network, boosting self-confidence and providing self-acceptance. Finally, a fourth advantage is that the group setting allows the therapist to observe clients interacting with one another, which often helps the therapist better understand how to therapeutically treat individual members.

Self-help group: Several people regularly meeting and discussing their problems with one another without the guidance of a therapist.

One variation of group therapy is the **self-help group,** which consists of several people regularly meeting and discussing their problems with one another without the guidance of a therapist (Davison et al., 2000). One of the oldest and best-known self-help groups is Alcoholics Anonymous (AA), which has more than 70,000 chapters and more than two million members worldwide (Davison & Neale, 2001; Morganstern et al., 1997). AA was founded as a group run by and for alcoholics and provides information about the consequences of alcoholism and the opportunity to learn from the experiences of other alcoholics. AA is based on a series of 12 steps that help alcoholics attain and maintain sobriety. Many other self-help programs have been developed on the AA model, covering a wide range of problems, including mood disorders, drug addiction, compulsive gambling, childhood sexual abuse, and spouse abuse (Lieberman, 1990).

How effective are self-help groups in treating mental health problems? Lack of reliable data make an accurate assessment difficult, but such programs do appear to provide moderate to substantial benefits (Ouimette et al., 1997; Tonigan et al., 2000). Many therapists who treat clients in an individual or group format often also urge them to participate in self-help groups as part of their recovery process. The primary limitation of such groups is that the lack of guidance from a trained therapist can sometimes lead members to oversimplify the causes and remedies of their problems.

14-6c Family and Couples Therapies Try to Change Dysfunctional Interaction Patterns

Research suggests that when people who have been hospitalized for a psychological disorder return home to their families, they often suffer a relapse (Hazelrigg et al., 1987). One possible cause for such setbacks is the dysfunctional nature of their family relationships. Such an occurrence is consistent with the *diathesis-stress model* (see chapter 13, section 13-1c), which contends that stress may trigger the onset or relapse of a disorder for people who have an underlying vulnerability (a *diathesis*) for that disorder. In an attempt to prevent such relapses, all of the major theoretical schools of psychotherapy have adapted their ideas to the treatment of families. These **family therapies** are designed to constructively modify the dysfunctional relationships among family members.

Family therapies: Therapies designed to constructively modify the dysfunctional relationships among family members.

Often, family therapists base their work on *systems theory*, a theoretical approach important in biology and in cybernetics that is based on the assumption that "the whole is greater than the sum of its parts" (Ackerman, 1966; Bowen, 1960, 1966). Systems theory readily applies to families because the family itself is a system, with each family member being an interacting element in that system. According to **family systems therapy,** the family acts in specific ways to maintain itself, both in terms of the interactions among the members and in terms of how the family interacts with its outside environment (Kempler, 1974). As such, an individual family member's problems cannot be understood and treated in isolation but must be examined and treated within the family system (Clarkin & Carpenter, 1995; Levant, 1984).

Family systems therapy: A form of family therapy in which the family is treated as a dynamic system, with each member being an important interacting element in that system.

As with group therapy, family therapy allows the therapist to observe how the initially treated client interacts with other family members (Goldenberg & Goldenberg, 1995). With the therapist's guidance, family members can develop constructive communication and problem-solving skills, thereby reducing conflicts and emotional distress and improving the quality of their relationships (Alexander & Parsons, 1973; Jacobson & Margolin, 1979).

Finally, a variant of family therapy is **couples therapy,** which focuses on the problematic communication and behavior patterns of romantic partners. Over half the couples entering therapy state that their number one problem involves faulty communication (O'Leary et al., 1992). This is true for both other-sex and same-sex romantic partners (Miller, 1997; Kurdek, 1994). Due to the pervasiveness of this problem, the establishment of an honest dialogue between the two partners is crucial in virtually all couples therapies.

Couples therapists with a cognitive and/or behavioral orientation use various techniques to teach positive communication skills, including having couples keep a diary of their weekly interactions, participating in positive role-playing exercises, and even watching videotapes of themselves discussing their relationship. Humanistic therapies will often focus on getting the partners to express their emotions toward one another and reveal what kind of new relationship they would like to build (Greenberg & Johnson, 1988). Finally, psychodynamic therapists emphasize couples gaining insight into the underlying motives in their relationships and how the partners may be reacting to one another based on how they related to their parents as children.

Overall, couples and family therapies are relatively successful (Hazelrigg et al., 1987; Shadish et al., 1993). In fact, an increasing number of therapists who regularly treat married or cohabiting clients for depression on an individual basis now believe that the couples format is a more effective approach. The reason for this assessment is that research suggests that, compared with individual therapy, couples therapy is as effective in reducing depression and more effective in reducing romantic relationship problems (Beach et al., 1994). As you can see from this brief overview, psychotherapy can be administered in formats other than the one-on-one, client-therapist interaction. For an even more unconventional format, check out Discovery Box 14-2.

Couples therapy: Therapy designed to help couples improve the quality of their relationship.

A common problem addressed in couples therapy is faulty communication between partners. How effective is this form of therapy, compared with individual therapy, in reducing romantic relationship problems?

© Bill Varie/CORBIS.

SECTION SUMMARY

- Major forms of psychotherapy were originally developed for use with individual adults but have been adapted for children, families, couples, and groups.
- Alternative therapy formats are often as effective as or superior to individual therapy formats.

14-7 BIOMEDICAL THERAPIES

When compared with the 1950s, today in the United States, less than one-third the number of people are full-time residents in psychiatric hospitals. The primary reason for this sharp decrease in hospitalization is the widespread use of drug therapies in the treatment of psychological disorders such as schizophrenia and the mood disorders (Dursan & Devarajan, 2001; Schatzberg & Nemeroff, 1995). As you can see in figure 14-3, more than 90 percent of the people diagnosed with a psychological disorder currently receive drugs as part of their treatment program (Nietzel et al., 1998). This high percentage of drug therapy is not only due to its effectiveness, but also because this form of therapy is often

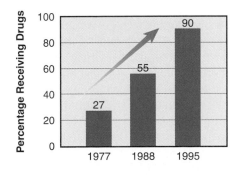

FIGURE 14-3
Use of Drugs in Treating Psychological Disorders

The percentage of people diagnosed with a psychological disorder receiving drug therapy has increased sharply since the 1970s.

DISCOVERY BOX 14-2

Can You Receive Therapy through the Internet?

You can take college courses through the Internet and you can purchase groceries and even automobiles online, but can you receive psychotherapy while sitting at your home computer? The answer is yes (King et al., 1998; Maheu & Gordon, 2000). A growing number of therapists are interacting with their clients—and providing actual therapy—through email, chatrooms, and message boards (Fink, 1999a). Although most forms of psychotherapy assume that there will be a face-to-face interaction between therapist and client, online therapy can provide help to people who are geographically isolated, extremely socially anxious, disabled, or fearful that others will discover that they are seeing a mental health professional.

One potential benefit to the relative anonymity of computer-assisted therapy is that clients may feel at ease more quickly when interacting online and, as a result, reveal their most troubling and important problems sooner and with greater honesty than when in the therapist's office (Grohol, 1998). However, one drawback to online therapy for the therapist is that all sorts of valuable information—like physical appearance, tone of voice, and body language—are missing. Without such information, accurate diagnosis and proper treatment might be more difficult to achieve than in a face-to-face setting. Another possible problem with online therapy is confidentiality (Suler, 2001). How do therapists know that the person interacting with them is, in fact, their client? If it is someone else pretending to be their client, confidentiality is destroyed. Fortunately, confidentiality problems can be addressed by using secure networks, user verification software, and video conferencing.

In 1997, the International Society for Mental Health Online was formed to promote the understanding, use, and development of online mental health technologies. In the coming years, online therapy may become commonplace as either a supplement to face-to-face therapy or as a complete treatment technique in its own right.

less expensive than psychological therapies (see section 14-8a). Let us examine some of these drugs and their effects. After this review, we discuss two controversial biomedical procedures that are sometimes used to treat severe cases of mental illness, namely, *electroconvulsive therapy* and *psychosurgery*.

14-7a Antipsychotic Drugs Affect Dopamine Neurotransmitters

Antipsychotic drugs: A group of medications that are effective in treating the delusions, hallucinations, and loose associations of schizophrenia by blocking dopamine receptors and thereby reducing dopamine activity.

One of the earliest successes in using medication to treat psychological disorders was the discovery in the 1950s that certain drugs used for other medical purposes reduced the positive psychotic symptoms of schizophrenia, such as auditory hallucinations and paranoia (Lehman et al., 1998). The first of these **antipsychotic drugs,** *chlorpromazine*, is in a class of drugs called the *phenothiazines* and is marketed under the trade name of Thorazine. As you recall from chapter 13, section 13-3d, research suggests that schizophrenia is associated with an overactive central dopamine system in the brain. Chlorpromazine and other antipsychotic medications are thought to work by blocking dopamine receptor sites in the brain, thereby reducing dopamine activity (Bernstein, 1995; Remington et al., 2001).

INFO-BIT: Delusions, hallucinations, and loose associations are sometimes called *positive symptoms* of schizophrenia because they involve the presence of symptoms that do not typically occur in other people. Schizophrenic patients also experience *negative symptoms*, which means that they do not exhibit behaviors that are present in most others.

Antipsychotic medications do not actually "cure" schizophrenia but merely help control its severe symptoms. These patients continue to have schizophrenia and often continue to have problems in living, although they can now function outside of the hospital, in their family home or in a halfway house. Because the antipsychotic drugs cannot cure the disorder, schizophrenic patients who receive these drugs must also receive appropriate aftercare services so that they do not simply move from the back wards of hospitals to our cities' back alleys.

While reducing positive schizophrenic symptoms, antipsychotic drugs do not relieve negative symptoms—such as flat affect, immobility, and social withdrawal—which may be related to structural defects in the brain (see chapter 13, section 13-3d). These drugs also have some very unpleasant side effects, including Parkinson disease-like muscular tremors, stiffness, sluggishness, and a loss of control over voluntary movements. Even the antipsychotic drug *clozapine* (Clozaril) that does not have these undesirable side effects can cause a fatal blood disorder in about 2 percent of patients who take it (LaGrenade et al., 2001). Research is currently under way on replacement drugs, such as *risperidone* (Risperdal), that do not appear to have these dangerous side effects (Ravazia, 2001; Wahlbeck et al., 1999).

14-7b Antidepressant Drugs Affect Serotonin and Norepinephrine Neurotransmitters

A second psychological disorder successfully treated with medication since the 1950s is depression. **Antidepressant drugs** include *iproniazid*, which is in a class of drugs called the *monoamine oxidase inhibitors (MAOI)* and which was the first drug used in this way. Although initially developed to treat tuberculosis, physicians observed that iproniazid significantly improved patients' mood and energy. Iproniazid and the other MAOI drugs work by inhibiting the monoamine oxidase (MAO) enzyme that is involved in breaking down the neurotransmitters of norepinephrine and serotonin. By inhibiting MAO, the available supply of norepinephrine and serotonin is increased, which has the effect of elevating mood. Despite these benefits, MAOI drugs can produce dangerous side effects, such as virtually eliminating REM sleep (see chapter 6, section 6-2d) and causing a sudden increase in blood pressure—and, thus, an increased likelihood of stroke—if mixed with certain foods, such as red wine, beer, and aged cheeses (Julien, 2001). Recently, a newer type of MAOI drug, *Maclabemide*, has become available that is less likely to have this negative food interaction (Martin, 2000).

A second class of antidepressant medications that have less severe side effects and seem to work somewhat better than the MAOI drugs is the *tricyclics* (Bernstein, 1995). These drugs increase the available supply of serotonin and norepinephrine by decreasing their reuptake at the neuron's receptor sites (see chapter 3, section 3-1c). Some of the common side effects of tricyclics are drowsiness, sleep disturbances, constipation, dry mouth, and blurred vision.

Finally, the most popular antidepressants are those that affect only serotonin, namely, the *selective serotonin reuptake inhibitors (SSRIs)*. As their name implies, SSRIs inhibit the reuptake of the neurotransmitter serotonin, which increases the available supply of serotonin in the body, making it easier for neural impulses to be transmitted along serotonin pathways in the brain (Cheer & Goa, 2001). Among the SSRIs, *fluxetine* (Prozac),

Antidepressant drugs: Drugs that relieve depression by increasing the supply of norepinephrine and/or serotonin at the neuron's receptor sites.

fluvoxetine (Luvox), *paroxetine* (Paxil), and *sertraline* (Zoloft) are all widely used. Prozac is by far the most popular, with over 1.5 million prescriptions written every month in the United States alone. Prozac is also sometimes used to treat certain anxiety disorders and eating disorders (Julien, 2001). Controlled studies indicate that the SSRIs are as effective as the tricyclics in treating depression, but they tend to have milder side effects (Fava & Rosenbaum, 1995).

Bipolar disorder, like depression, is a mood disorder that can be treated effectively with medication. Since 1969, when a mineral salt of the element *lithium* was approved for use in the United States, it has helped about 75 percent of the bipolar patients who have been prescribed the drug (Bernstein, 1995). Without lithium, bipolar patients have a manic episode about every 14 months. With lithium, manic attacks occur as infrequently as once every nine years. Despite its effectiveness, lithium can cause delirium and even death if excessive doses are taken.

Exactly how lithium works is unclear. Yet, because it takes at least a week of regular use for the drug to show any benefits, lithium's effects probably occur through some long-term adaptation of the nervous system. Although lithium has long been regarded as the "treatment of choice" for bipolar disorder, new mood stabilizers, such as *depakote*, have been developed and are now being used along with lithium (Martin, 2000).

14-7c Antianxiety Drugs Are the Most Widely Used Legal Drugs

As presented in chapter 13, section 13-3a, one of the most common types of psychological problems is anxiety. The oldest drug treatment for anxiety is alcohol, which has been available as a tranquilizer for thousands of years. However, given the recognized negative side effects of alcohol (see chapter 6, section 6-3f), physicians no longer prescribe it as an anxiety treatment. Instead, a class of **antianxiety drugs**—the *benzodiazepines*—is the most frequently prescribed anxiety medication in the United States (Roy-Byrne & Crowley, 2002). Among the benzodiazepines are *oxazepam* (Serax), *lorazepam* (Ativan), *alprazolam* (Xanax), and *diazepam* (Valium). These drugs seem to produce their effects by facilitating the action of the neurotransmitter *gamma-amino-butyric acid (GABA)*, which has an inhibitory effect on the central nervous system. That is, when GABA is taken up by receptor sites on the neuron, it becomes more difficult for the neuron to be stimulated to transmit a nerve impulse. In this way, antianxiety agents help to "slow down" the transmission of nerve impulses and so reduce the physiological and psychological changes that occur when a person is under stress.

Benzodiazepines are dangerous when combined with alcohol, and they can have such side effects as lightheadedness, slurred speech, and impaired psychomotor and mental functioning (Bernstein, 1995). These drugs can also lead to physical dependency so that, when discontinued, the patient experiences withdrawal symptoms. Because of this problem, when patients discontinue their antianxiety medication, they should do so gradually.

Table 14-2 summarizes some of the medications that are frequently used to treat psychological disorders. As you see from our overview of these drugs, they can be remarkably effective in treating serious psychological disorders. Of course, all of these drug therapies have side effects, some more serious than others.

14-7d Electroconvulsive Therapy Is Sometimes Used to Treat Depression

Another medical treatment is used to manipulate the brain, but it is much more controversial than the drug therapies (Frank, 2002). It also has been in use for a much longer period of time. **Electroconvulsive therapy (ECT)** was first used in the 1930s as a possible treatment for schizophrenia. However, subsequent research indicated that ECT does not

Antianxiety drugs: Drugs that have an immediate calming effect by facilitating the inhibitory action of the GABA neurotransmitter, thereby reducing nerve impulse transmission.

Electroconvulsive therapy (ECT): A physiological treatment for severe depression in which a brief electric shock is administered to the brain of an anesthetized patient.

TABLE 14-2

Commonly Used Drug Treatments

For Schizophrenia: Antipsychotic Drugs

Class of Medication	Drug Name	Trade Name	Effects and Side Effects
Phenothiazine	Chlorpromazine	Thorazine	Reduce hallucinations, delusions, and other positive symptoms of schizophrenia; can cause severe side effects, such as movement disorders or blood disease
Thioxanthene	Thiothixene	Navane	
Butyrophenone	Haloperidol	Haldol	
Dibenzodiazepine	Clozapine	Clozaril	

Mood Disorders: Antidepressant and Mood-Stabilizing Drugs

Class of Medication	Drug Name	Trade Name	Effects and Side Effects
MAOI	Tranylcypromine	Parnate	Act as antidepressants, but also have antipanic action; cause sleepiness and other moderate side effects; potentially dangerous if taken with alcohol
Tricyclic	Amitriptyline	Elavil	
SSRI	Clomipramine	Anafranil	
	Fluoxetine	Prozac	
	Sertraline	Zoloft	
	Paroxetine	Paxil	

Bipolar Disorder Mood Stabilizers

	Drug Name	Trade Name	Effects and Side Effects
	Lithium	Lithane	Calm mania and may reduce bipolar mood swings if taken continuously; overdose harmful, potentially deadly
	Divalproex	Depakote	

For Anxiety Disorders: Antianxiety Drugs

Class of Medication	Drug Name	Trade Name	Effects and Side Effects
Benzodiazepines	Oxazepam	Serax	Act as tranquilizers, and with regular use, can reduce symptoms of generalized anxiety disorder and panic disorder; may cause physical dependence
	Lorazepam	Ativan	
	Diazepam	Valium	
	Clonazepam	Klonopin	
	Alprazolam	Xanax	

help schizophrenia but instead is helpful in cases of severe depression, with about 80 percent of patients showing marked improvement (Coffey, 1993). Controlled treatment studies have found that ECT is about as effective as antidepressant medications in treating this mood disorder (Fava & Rosenbaum, 1995).

In a typical ECT procedure, patients are first given drugs to both render them unconscious and to induce profound muscle relaxation. Next, with an electrode placed on one side of the temple, a 70- to 130-volt charge of electricity is administered to that side of the brain for about one second. These shocks are continued until the patient has a seizure—a muscle contraction of the entire body—that lasts for at least 20 seconds (Abrams, 1993). This treatment is repeated at least once a week for two to four weeks.

Although ECT is effective in treating severe depression, no one knows for sure why it works (Coffey, 1993; Sackheim et al., 2000). Some experts believe that ECT increases the amount or activity of the neurotransmitters norepinephrine and serotonin (Noll et al., 1985). Despite ECT being as effective as antidepressant medication, it has several temporary negative side effects, including confusion, loss of memory, and impaired motor coordination (Breggin, 1979, 1991). In most instances, any memory loss for events preceding treatment is recovered within a few months (Cohen et al., 2000).

ECT is generally used only when severely depressed patients either cannot tolerate or have not responded to drug therapy. In some cases, it may also be used when severely depressed patients are at immediate risk for suicide because ECT has an almost immediate effect, while benefits from antidepressant medications usually take at least 10 days (Fink, 1999b).

14-7e Psychosurgery Involves Removing Portions of the Brain

Psychosurgery: A rarely used surgical procedure to treat psychological disorders in which brain tissue thought to be the cause of the disorder is destroyed.

By far the most radical and controversial method of treating psychological disorders is **psychosurgery,** which involves the destruction of brain tissue thought to be the cause of these disorders. In 1949, Portuguese psychiatrist Antonio Egas Moñiz received the Nobel Prize in Medicine for his psychosurgical technique known as *prefrontal lobotomy*. In this medical procedure, two small holes are drilled in the skull and a sharp instrument is inserted and moved from side to side, severing neural connections between the prefrontal lobes and the rest of the brain (Egas Moñiz, 1948). At the time that Egas Moñiz was using this technique to treat psychotic patients, it was thought that destroying the prefrontal lobes would relieve the crippling emotional reactions of many schizophrenics. The medical profession was so taken by Egas Moñiz's technique that, during the 1940s and early 1950s, over 35,000 lobotomies were performed in the United States to treat schizophrenia, aggressiveness, anxiety, and depression.

Although lobotomies did reduce the incidence of some undesirable behaviors, patients paid a very heavy price. In many cases, it profoundly altered their personalities, with some patients becoming extremely apathetic and others becoming excitable and impulsive. Due to these very negative and irreversible effects, most physicians stopped using the procedure. Then, with the advent of antipsychotic drugs in the late 1950s, lobotomies were virtually extinguished as a medical intervention (Swayze, 1995). Today, MRI-guided precision psychosurgery is performed only in extreme cases when other types of treatment have been ineffective, and it focuses on much smaller brain areas than those involved in lobotomies.

As this overview suggests, biomedical therapies—as well as psychotherapies—have made amazing strides over the past 50 years in delivering more effective treatments for psychological disorders. With this accomplishment in mind, consider again my chapter-opening story about the likely therapies you might have received had you been a patient of Benjamin Rush at the end of the eighteenth century. Viewed from the insights of the twenty-first century, Rush's methods seem primitive and appalling. Yet, before we become too smug in our assessment of how victims of psychological disorders were treated in the past, we should consider for a moment how upcoming scientific discoveries will likely change our views of current approaches to mental illness therapies.

INFO-BIT: In a strange twist of fate, psychiatrist Antonio Egas Moñiz, developer of the prefrontal lobotomy psychosurgery technique, was shot and killed by one of his lobotomized patients.

SECTION SUMMARY

- Antipsychotic drugs reduce positive schizophrenic symptoms but do not relieve negative symptoms.

- Antidepressant drugs relieve depression by increasing the supply of norepinephrine and/or serotonin at the neuron's receptor sites.

- Antianxiety drugs have an immediate calming effect by facilitating the inhibitory action of the GABA neurotransmitter, thereby reducing nerve impulse transmission.

- Electroconvulsive therapy is an infrequently used physiological treatment for severe depression in which a brief electric shock is administered to anesthetized patient's brain.

- Psychosurgery is the most radical treatment and involves destruction of brain tissue thought to cause the disorder.

14-8 CURRENT ECONOMIC TRENDS IN TREATMENT

Private insurance companies have become big economic players in the management and treatment of mental health. This system of insured health care, known as a managed care system, has had a significant impact on the treatment of psychological disorders (Alegria et al., 2001; Sharfstein, 2001). Let us briefly examine how this system works.

14-8a Managed Health Care Forces Cost Cutting in Treating Psychological Disorders

The reality of health care in the twenty-first century is that most people who have an employer-based health care plan are enrolled in some sort of **managed care system.** Typically run by health maintenance organizations, or HMOs, such managed care has both advantages and disadvantages for members. The advantage is that consumers pay lower prices for their care, but they often give up much of their freedom to make health decisions concerning who they see and what form of treatment they receive. Managed care systems have also been guilty at times of limiting or even denying access to medically necessary services in order to keep expenses down so that they can turn a profit (Duckworth & Borus, 1999).

What sort of impact has managed care had on the treatment of psychological disorders? Largely driven by cost concerns, long-term therapy is rare today, available only to those clients who can afford to continue paying for treatment once their insurance benefits have run out. In this new economic reality, treatment goals have shifted from curing mental health problems to helping clients with psychological disorders reestablish a reasonable level of functioning (Zatzick, 1999).

Another impact that cost-cutting procedures have had on psychotherapeutic care is that many patients are no longer being treated by highly trained mental health professionals, such as psychiatrists and doctoral-level psychologists. Instead, an increasing number of people suffering from psychological disorders are referred to less well trained therapists with master's degrees who may not be able to adequately diagnose and treat serious psychological disorders (Pope & Vasquez, 2001).

A further problem that cost cutting has had on treatment can be seen in the biomedical therapies. As previously discussed (see section 14-7), pharmaceutical companies are introducing new and improved drugs every year to better treat various psychological disorders. Unfortunately, psychiatrists employed by managed care providers are often required to prescribe the older, less effective drugs because they are considerably

Managed care system: A system of insured health care in which the insurance company may determine such issues as which therapists clients may choose, the number of sessions permitted, and which drugs are prescribed.

cheaper than those that have just been introduced to the marketplace (Docherty, 1999). In addition, biomedical therapies are most effective when combined with psychotherapy, especially for such disorders as major depression, bipolar disorder, and schizophrenia (Thase, 2000). However, cost management has also led to cutbacks in combining these two therapies, leading to less effective treatment for some individuals (Duckworth & Borus, 1999).

Because of these problems, many therapists and clients dislike managed care programs. Critics claim that the system rather than the trained mental health professionals is making the important decisions about how therapy should be administered to those suffering from psychological disorders. Unfortunately, there is little evidence that solutions to these problems are on the horizon. Keeping costs down to a manageable level without compromising the delivery of mental health treatment will remain a delicate balancing act for the foreseeable future.

14-8b There Are Increased Efforts to Document Treatment Effectiveness

One possible benefit of managed health care has been a renewed focus on determining which forms of psychotherapy are most effective. The first concerted attempt to determine the effectiveness of psychotherapy occurred in the 1950s when Hans Eysenck (1952) published an influential study claiming that people with psychological problems who received psychotherapy had a slightly worse outcome than those who did not receive any therapy at all. Based on these results, Eysenck concluded that there was no scientific evidence that psychotherapy is effective.

Although Eysenck's methodology was later found to be flawed, other researchers conducted their own assessments of various forms of psychotherapy using much larger samples and following more rigorous procedures. The findings from these studies demonstrated that many types of therapy "work," but they are not always effective for everyone (Orlinski & Howard, 1987; Smith & Glass, 1977). Based on these reviews of psychotherapy outcome, it appears that the following conclusions can be made (Lyddon & Chatkoff, 2001; Seligman, 1995):

1. Psychotherapy generally has a positive effect.
2. Different types of therapy are often about equally effective for many disorders.
3. Brief therapy helps many clients, with about 50 percent improving by the eighth session.
4. The more treatment clients receive, the more they improve.

The last two findings bear further comment given our previous discussion of managed care systems. Short-term psychotherapy—the format employed by most managed care systems—does result in better mental functioning for about half of all clients, but only half of these clients remain well (Westen & Morrison, 2001). Research indicates that the most effective treatments are those psychotherapies lasting more than two years (Seligman, 1995). Thus, there appears to be a positive correlation between length of therapy and long-term mental health benefits, which is not the type of therapy currently being offered by most managed care systems.

Journey of Discovery Question

Besides effective psychotherapeutic techniques being the cause for people improving during the course of therapy, what are some other factors that might explain the reduction and/or alleviation of psychological disorders?

SECTION SUMMARY

- Early review of studies of therapy outcome suggested no scientific evidence that therapy is effective.

- Later, more extensive studies on therapy outcome indicated that psychotherapy generally has a positive effect, different types of therapy are often about equally effective, and longer-term therapies are ultimately more beneficial than short-term therapies.

SUGGESTED WEBSITES

Note: These websites were functional when we went to press. Please access the online text for the most up-to-date URLs.

Psychology Information Online
http://www.psychologyinfo.com/
This site provides helpful tips for searching for a psychotherapist.

National Register of Health Service Providers in Psychology
http://www.nationalregister.com/
This site can help prospective clients find a registered psychologist in their area.

A Guide to Psychology and Its Practice
http://www.guidetopsychology.com/
This site provides information about psychology in general, including information about various forms of therapy that may be helpful for specific disorders.

PSYCHOLOGICAL APPLICATIONS
How Do You Select a Psychotherapist?

Given the variety of psychotherapies available, how should you go about selecting a therapist? Working with a therapist on a psychological problem is a sensitive and personal exercise—you can ask several important questions when considering seeing a therapist.

First, you should ask whether you actually need a therapist. As noted in the previous chapter on psychological disorders, many people experience mild or "subclinical" levels of a symptom that, in more extreme form, may define a psychological disorder. For example, many people have mild irrational fears or periods of "the blues" that would not meet diagnostic standards for a psychological disorder. When judging the severity of your symptoms, it is useful to consider the degree to which your daily functioning has been impaired. Someone whose symptoms are mildly distressing, but are not significantly interfering with daily activities, does not likely have a clinical disorder. This individual might benefit from speaking with a psychotherapist, but the therapy would likely be relatively brief. The therapist may provide information about the nature of clinical disorders, provide reassurance that this particular problem is not very severe, and make a few suggestions concerning how to better manage the symptoms.

If your symptoms are producing significant impairment, you must then judge whether you have sufficient resources to cope. Just because the symptoms are beginning to interfere with your functioning does not mean that the only way to solve the problem is through the help of a psychotherapist. If a problem is of recent origin, if you have successfully solved comparable problems before, or

if you still have many ideas about how to cope with the problem, then it may not be necessary to see a therapist. However, if you have exhausted your coping resources and no longer have confidence that you can manage the problem on your own, then it may well be appropriate to seek professional help.

When shopping for a therapist, it is useful to ask several questions. First, what is the problem you would like to change? Do you want to reduce your depression? Do you want to stop drinking alcohol? Do you want to be able to get along better with your boyfriend or girlfriend? If you can identify a clear treatment goal, then you will be in a better position to select a therapist and an approach to therapy. Clearly, many prospective clients do not have a clear idea of what they would like to change. This may be a part of the problem—they are dissatisfied with their lives but do not know what would help them feel better. In such cases, a psychotherapist can help the client clarify the goal. However, it may require some time to identify an appropriate treatment goal before therapy can begin.

Once you have identified a goal, you can then consider the kind of therapy to seek. Some prospective clients have a preference for a specific form of therapy. They may have learned, from previous therapy experiences or from other information about psychotherapy, that they would like cognitive therapy or insight-oriented therapy. In these cases, it makes sense to shop for a therapist who can provide the kind of therapy that fits this preference.

Some psychological disorders have been shown to respond well to particular treatments (Nathan & Gorman, 2002). For example, bipolar disorder is almost always treated with mood-stabilizing medication. Panic disorder has been treated very successfully using cognitive-behavioral therapy. Depression has been treated very successfully using cognitive therapy. If you are seeking help for one of these problems, it may be useful to look for a therapist who can provide the treatment that is considered most effective. Several resources are available to help you learn what therapies may be most effective for a particular kind of problem. For example, Martin Seligman (1994) has compiled a consumer guide to psychotherapy (*What You Can Change and What You Can't: The Complete Guide to Successful Self-Improvement*) that summarizes research on which therapies are generally recommended for which disorders. The National Institute of Mental Health, advocacy groups devoted to specific disorders (such as the Obsessive-Compulsive Foundation), and psychology departments at local universities can provide useful information about the current status of available therapies for a disorder.

Again, if you do not have a clear idea about the kind of problem you have or the kind of therapy that may be helpful, this should not prevent you from seeing a psychotherapist. The therapist can—following an assessment of the problem—suggest one or more possible treatments.

Given that most treatment today is paid by a third party, such as an insurance company or a social welfare agency, you should check your insurance package to determine whether there are any limits on the mental health coverage. As previously discussed, many managed care systems list preferred providers, and so your choice of professionals or agencies may be limited. Also as previously noted, most insurance plans have an upper limit on the number of therapy sessions or the total funds available for mental health services, which may dictate selecting a therapist who provides short-term forms of psychotherapy.

You should also ask some basic questions of prospective therapists: What is the therapist's degree? Is the therapist licensed in the state? Does the therapist have experience in treating problems like the one you have? Does the therapist have a particular theoretical preference? What is the cost of therapy sessions? The receptionist can usually answer these questions before you make an appointment to see the therapist. If the therapist will not allow the receptionist to answer these questions, then you might seriously consider calling another therapist.

Clearly, you can obtain referrals from many sources, such as your family doctor, clergy member, lawyer, friends, and family. Many cities have resources to refer mental health patients to psychotherapists, such as a chapter of the Mental Health Association. Local chapters of patient advocacy groups (such as CHADD—Children and Adults with Attention Deficit Disorder) can help steer individuals to experts in the area. Psychology departments at local universities often help individuals learn about practitioners in the area who may specialize in treating various disorders.

KEY TERMS

antianxiety drugs (p. 444)
antidepressant drugs (p. 443)
antipsychotic drugs (p. 442)
aversive conditioning (p. 431)
behavioral therapies (p. 429)
biomedical therapies (p. 425)
client-centered therapy (p. 435)
cognitive therapies (p. 433)
cognitive-behavior therapy (CBT) (p. 434)
counterconditioning (p. 429)
countertransference (p. 427)
couples therapy (p. 441)

electroconvulsive therapy (ECT) (p. 444)
empty-chair technique (p. 436)
existential therapy (p. 438)
family systems therapy (p. 440)
family therapies (p. 440)
free association (p. 427)
Gestalt therapy (p. 436)
group therapy (p. 439)
humanistic therapies (p. 435)
managed care system (p. 447)
modeling (p. 432)
play therapy (p. 439)

psychodynamic therapies (p. 426)
psychosurgery (p. 446)
psychotherapy (p. 425)
rational-emotive behavior
    therapy (REBT) (p. 434)
resistance (p. 428)
response prevention (p. 429)
self-help group (p. 440)
social skills training (p. 432)
systematic desensitization (p. 429)
token economy (p. 432)
transference (p. 427)

REVIEW QUESTIONS

1. Before Freud developed psychoanalysis, treatment for mental illness emphasized all of the following methods *except*
  a. hypnosis.
  b. altering the brain's functioning with chemical interventions.
  c. terrorizing the patient by threatening to have him or her killed.
  d. emotional support.
  e. draining excess blood from the body.

2. Mental health professionals who deal with psychological disorders and receive extensive training in conducting scientific research are
  a. counseling psychologists with a Psy.D.
  b. psychiatric social workers.
  c. psychiatrists.
  d. clinical psychologists.
  e. psychologists with a Ph.D. or Ed.D.

3. Although there are several varieties of psychodynamic therapies, one thing they all have in common is
   a. a disregard for insight.
   b. an emphasis on sex as the major motivation for human behavior.
   c. the view that psychological disorders stem primarily from unconscious forces.
   d. encouraging resistance as a form of free association.
   e. the view that psychotherapy requires at least five years of twice-weekly sessions to be effective.

4. Psychodynamic therapists often interpret transference, which involves
   a. feelings that the client experienced toward others earlier in life.
   b. anything the client does that interferes with therapeutic progress.
   c. only negative feelings clients develop toward their therapist.
   d. the release of pent-up emotion.
   e. free association and Freudian slips.

5. The most effective technique for treating phobias is
   a. sudden and prolonged exposure to the feared object.
   b. response prevention.
   c. reinforcement and punishment.
   d. aversive conditioning.
   e. systematic desensitization.

6. The primary techniques used in behavioral therapies are all based on
   a. unconscious learning and insight.
   b. observational learning.
   c. desensitization hierarchies.
   d. principles of learning.
   e. behavior modification.

7. Cognitive therapies may include all of the following *except*
   a. analysis of the meaning underlying dreams.
   b. confronting all-or-none types of thinking.
   c. trying new behaviors that directly challenge irrational beliefs.
   d. highly directive, problem-focused therapeutic techniques.
   e. identifying patients' negative views of themselves, the world, and their future.

8. Cognitive therapy techniques used by Beck and Ellis differ with respect to
   a. their emphasis on faulty thinking.
   b. their use of behavioral techniques as well as cognitive techniques.
   c. the therapeutic goal of modifying cognitions.
   d. their response to clients' irrational beliefs.
   e. the overall length of therapy.

9. Gestalt therapy emphasizes all of the following *except*
   a. focusing on current feelings.
   b. nondirective client-centered approaches.
   c. the empty-chair technique.
   d. body awareness exercises to stimulate emotional reactions.
   e. the development of self-awareness or insight.

10. Carl Rogers is often identified as having the biggest influence on how therapy is practiced because
   a. he emphasized the facilitation of personal growth.
   b. his client-centered techniques are widely used by therapists of many theoretical orientations.
   c. his principles of conditional positive regard are so effective.
   d. he formulated a highly directive form of therapy used by behavioral and cognitive therapists.
   e. his emphasis on closed-ended statements was already used by most therapists.

11. The humanistic technique of paraphrasing
   a. involves analyzing the meaning underlying clients' verbal statements.
   b. acknowledges a client's nonverbal emotions.
   c. is a confrontational challenge of dysfunctional thoughts.
   d. is seen in therapist responses such as "go on" and "I see."
   e. involves the therapist summarizing the expressed verbal content of clients.

12. Humanistic therapy that deals with finding meaning in life
   a. was developed by Perls.
   b. emphasizes resolving past issues.
   c. is based on Frankl's approach to existential therapy.
   d. has good empirical support.
   e. emphasizes treating the whole person.

13. Children's play therapy involves all of the following *except*
   a. a form of free association.
   b. a nondirective approach.
   c. an educational approach to learning new skills.
   d. directly challenging cognitive distortions.
   e. the use of unconditional positive regard.

14. One of the advantages of group therapy is that
   a. it is less expensive because it doesn't last as long as individual therapy.
   b. it helps clients see that others share similar problems.
   c. therapists are never used, which reduces the cost.
   d. it is based on monthly sessions rather than weekly sessions.
   e. it is more effective in reducing romantic relationship problems than couples therapy.

15. Antidepressant drugs that affect only serotonin
   a. are called SSRIs and increase the availability of serotonin by inhibiting its reuptake.
   b. are tricyclic antidepressants, a class of benzodiazepines.
   c. are part of a class of drugs called phenothiazines.
   d. include MAOIs.
   e. are useful only for depression.

16. Managed health care has affected the treatment of psychological disorders in all of the following ways *except*
   a. covered treatment is more often conducted by less well trained master's level therapists.
   b. benefits are provided only for short-term therapy, which has been found to be as beneficial as long-term therapy.
   c. reasonable functioning is emphasized rather than curing problems.
   d. both diagnoses and treatment may be less adequate.
   e. the use of psychological therapy in conjunction with biomedical therapies has been reduced.

15

Stress, Coping, and Health

Chapter Outline

I am writing this chapter in the summer of 2002, nine months after the September 11th terrorist attacks that killed over 3,000 people. As the United States and its allies continue their search for terrorists throughout the world, Americans have been repeatedly warned that new attacks are almost certain to occur in this country. Indeed, within the past month, the FBI arrested an American supporter of terrorist leader Osama Bin Laden as he returned from Pakistan. This American was planning to detonate a radioactive bomb in Washington, DC. A few months prior to this incident, businesses and government buildings in various states received letters containing deadly anthrax spores (four people died). These instances of biological terrorism further heightened the anxiety of many Americans.

Since the attacks, Californian Virginia Kostelnic has had regular headaches. Like many Americans, she was so emotionally distraught that she sought medical attention for her anxiety. In addition, like many Americans, she has rethought her travel plans, including a European trip. "I'm very scared," says Kostelnic. "You don't know where or when the next attack might occur." Steve Eisner, a Wisconsin resident, says he is not afraid to fly, but he does not want to deal with the added hassles that now accompany flying. He also realizes that the terrorist danger is not going to go away quickly or easily. "I'm much more cautious now," he says. "Look around the world. Other countries have been living like this for years. September 11th was our wake-up call."

To what degree have you been affected by these events? Is there a new sense of edginess or uncertainty in your life? Have you considered how this "war on terrorism" might affect your future? Perhaps you responded to these events like Matt Sauer of Texas, who said, "I am not changing any of my plans. Sure, I have grieved like everyone else, but I see this as a challenge that we must overcome."

In this chapter, our journey of discovery begins by examining the psychology of stress. Not just stress caused by catastrophes and war, but stress caused by everyday events. By understanding more about the causes and consequences of stress, you will be better prepared to manage major stressful events in your life as well as the hassles that are part of everyday living. This exploration of stress will lead us into a broader examination of the psychology of health. Do you know what it means to be healthy? Is health different from being disease-free?

The psychologists and physicians whose work forms the bulk of this chapter are in the interdisciplinary field of **behavioral medicine,** which integrates behavioral and medical knowledge and then applies it to health and illness. Psychologists who study the effects of behavior and mental processes on health and illness are called **health psychologists.** In studying the causes and consequences of health and illness, scientists rely on the **biopsychosocial model,** which assumes that health and overall wellness is caused by a complex interaction of biological, psychological, and sociocultural factors.

15-1 WHAT CAUSES STRESS?

The process by which Virginia Kostelnic, Steve Eisner, and Matt Sauer are perceiving and responding to the possibility of further terrorist attacks falls under the general topic that we call stress. We will define **stress** as our response to events that disturb, or threaten to disturb, our physical or psychological equilibrium. The events that disturb our equilibrium are known as **stressors.** Thus, the attacks of September 11th and many of the events that followed have been stressors for millions of people in the United States and around the world. Yet, most stressors are not of this magnitude, and not all stressors are unpleasant.

Behavioral medicine: An interdisciplinary field of science that integrates behavioral and medical knowledge and then applies it to health and illness.

Health psychologists: Psychologists who study the effects of behavior and mental processes on health and illness.

Biopsychosocial model: An interdisciplinary model that assumes that health and overall wellness is caused by a complex interaction of biological, psychological, and sociocultural factors.

Stress: Our response to events that disturb, or threaten to disturb, our physical or psychological equilibrium.

Stressors: External or internal events that challenge or threaten us.

15-1a Stressors Can Be Positive or Negative, As Well As Large or Small

Stressors come in various forms. *Major cataclysmic events*, such as the September 11th attacks or natural disasters, are easily recognized as stressors, as are *personal major events*, such as being a victim of crime or having a death in the family. Among these events, some may entail short-term, acute events (for example, surgery to remove a benign tumor), while others have a more chronic nature (for example, chemotherapy to treat cancer). Historically, these types of major events made up the bulk of early research on stress (Holmes & Rahe, 1967). Such major events can also lead to *post-traumatic stress disorder (PTSD)*, which can appear months or even years after experiencing the stressor (see chapter 13, section 13-3a). Symptoms of PTSD include anxiety, social withdrawal, survivor guilt, and flashbacks of the event (Brewin et al., 1996). PTSD is also associated with an increased risk of physical illness (Adams & Adams, 1984).

Even positive events often tax your body's resources and cause stress. For instance, the birth of a child is one of the happiest and most anticipated events in a person's life. Studies of married couples, however, have found that the arrival of a child dramatically increases stress and contributes to dissatisfaction with the relationship (Cowan & Cowan, 2000; Levenson et al., 1993). Yet, despite the ability of positive life events to increase stress levels, research indicates that negative events induce more stress than neutral or positive events (Monroe & Simons, 1991).

As disruptive as major events are to your life, they often reflect only a fraction of the stressors that affect your health and well-being. In between each of these major stressful "boulders" occur myriad *hassles* and more minor stressful "pebbles," such as losing your keys, arguing with a roommate, or getting a traffic ticket (Kanner et al., 1981; Lazarus & Cohen, 1977). The more daily hassles you experience, the more your health tends to suffer (Nelson et al., 1995). The negative effects of daily hassles, however, can be alleviated by daily positive experiences (Lazarus & Lazarus, 1994).

Which type of stressor (boulder or pebble) is worse for you? As already mentioned, both classes of events can lead to health problems. In part, accumulating pebbles can leave you more vulnerable to major events when they occur. Similarly, major events can leave you unable to deal with the daily hassles of life, resulting in them piling up and overwhelming you. Researchers have found that people who had high stress levels during the previous year were more than twice as likely to become ill as people who had lower levels of stress (Bieliaukas et al., 1995; Holmes & Rahe, 1967).

This is my father after a three-day visit with his relatives in northern Italy. Although this was a dream of a lifetime for him, he can certainly attest to the fact that pleasant events can be stressful. Yet, do positive events induce less stress than negative events?

15-1b Hans Selye Viewed Stress As a Specific Set of Responses to Demands

As discussed in chapter 3, section 3-2a, the *sympathetic nervous system* activates the body's energy resources to deal with threatening situations. If something angers or frightens you, the sympathetic nervous system will prepare you for "fight or flight" by slowing your digestion, accelerating your heart rate, raising your blood sugar, and cooling your body with perspiration. If the threatening situation does not subside, you will remain in this state of heightened arousal. Such a scenario is likely to cause serious health problems because your body will continue to divert resources away from the everyday maintenance that is essential in keeping you healthy.

One scientist who was instrumental in providing greater insight into how our bodies react to stress was physician Hans Selye (1907–1982). In the 1930s, Selye stumbled upon some of the physiological mechanisms of stress while trying to discover new sex hormones. In his experiments with rats, Selye (1936) noticed that exposing the animals to a wide range of physical stressors (cold, heat, swimming, injections) caused their bodies to respond in two ways. The first response was specific to the stressor itself, such as shivering when exposed to cold and sweating when exposed to heat. In contrast, the second response was not specific to any particular stressor but was a general response geared

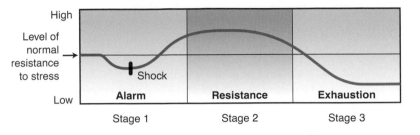

High
Level of
normal
resistance
to stress
Shock
Low
Alarm
Resistance
Exhaustion
Stage 1
Stage 2
Stage 3

FIGURE 15-1
The General Adaptation Syndrome

Hans Selye's research suggested that physical reactions to stress included three stages: initial alarm, followed by resistance, and then exhaustion. During the alarm stage, the body's resistance temporarily drops below normal due to the shock of the stressor. The body is at its highest state of resistance to stress during the resistance stage, but resistance declines as the body's resources become depleted in the exhaustion stage.

General adaptation syndrome (GAS): Selye's model of stress in which an event that threatens an organism's well-being (a stressor) leads to a three-stage bodily response: alarm, resistance, and exhaustion.

toward energizing and protecting the body from harm. This second response is what Selye (1956) called the *stress response*, and he saw it as occurring in reaction to any significant demand on the body. If the demand continues, particular changes in the body begin to occur. He referred to this stress response, and the resulting changes in the body, as the **general adaptation syndrome (GAS),** which consists of three stages: alarm, resistance, and exhaustion. Figure 15-1 depicts these three stages in the body's response to stress.

In stage 1, upon encountering a stressor, the body first reacts with *alarm*, which is essentially what was previously referred to as the "fight-or-flight" response. The alarm reaction produces an initial shock phase during which the sympathetic nervous system is activated. This phase is immediately followed by a second phase in which hormones such as cortisol and adrenalin are released into the bloodstream to meet the threat or danger. Your body's resources are now mobilized.

No organism can survive very long with the heightened arousal exhibited during the alarm stage. Homeostasis must be achieved, even if the stressor persists. During stage 2, *resistance*, the parasympathetic nervous system returns many physiological functions—such as respiration and heart rate—to normal levels, even while the body focuses its resources against the continuing stressor. Although blood glucose levels remain high, and cortisol and adrenalin continue to circulate at elevated levels, the outward appearance of the organism generally seems entirely normal. But the body remains on red alert.

If the stressor continues beyond the body's capacity, the organism exhausts its resources and becomes susceptible to disease and death. This is the third stage of the GAS, *exhaustion*. Selye described it as a "kind of premature aging due to wear and tear" (Selye, 1956, p. 31). Organs such as the heart are the first to break down during this stage.

Although this description of the GAS corresponds to Selye's original work, some researchers have recently questioned whether women typically respond with fight-or-flight tendencies in the initial alarm stage. Check out Discovery Box 15-1 for an overview of the possible gender differences that might exist in this stage of the stress response.

15-1c Cognitive Appraisal Is an Important Part of the Stress Response

Because of Selye's model, stress was catapulted into the forefront of psychological-health connections. Yet, his theory was developed before most scientists approached the study of illness from a biopsychosocial perspective. Instead, illness was considered to be a purely biological phenomenon, with any severe physiological demand triggering the GAS response pattern.. Although the GAS easily fit into accepted medical views of the time, by focusing exclusively on the body, this theory all but ignored the role of the mind in the stress response. However, as more research was conducted, evidence emerged that *psychological awareness of the stressor* was a necessary component in the stress response (Frankenhaeuser, 1975; Mason, 1975). Realizing that purely biological explanations were inadequate in explaining the stress response was an important step in the development of the biopsychosocial model.

DISCOVERY BOX 15-1

Is the "Fight-or-Flight" Response Gender Specific?

Health psychologist Shelley Taylor and her coworkers (2000) suggest that physiological responses to stress may have different consequences for females than for males. Instead of experiencing the fight-or-flight response, they assert that when women are exposed to stressors, they are more likely to experience a *tend-and-befriend response*. This response involves women taking action to protect their offspring and befriend members of their social group to reduce their vulnerability. If Taylor and her colleagues are correct in their claims, what might account for these gender differences?

Sociocultural theorists suggest that these differences are due to gender socialization. Traditionally, the way in which children are raised in North American culture fosters the construction of an *independent* self-concept among males and a *relational* self-concept among females (Cross & Madson, 1997). As such, girls are more likely than boys to be raised to think, act, and define themselves in ways that emphasize their emotional connectedness to other individuals (Cross et al., 2000). This may lead women to respond to stress with nurturance and affiliation, tending to their offspring and seeking out others for comfort and protection. In contrast, men's tendency to exhibit fight-or-flight responses to threat may be due to them being raised to be independent and self-sufficient.

An alternative explanation is that these gender differences in stress responses are the by-products of different mating strategies of males and females. According to this evolutionary explanation, males of many species, including our own, are more aggressive and have a stronger social dominance orientation than females because aggression and dominance-seeking have been the primary ways males have gained sexual access to females (Buss, 1999; Buss & Schmitt, 1993). That is, by physically intimidating—and sometimes even killing—less aggressive males, the more aggressive males became socially dominant and, thus, were more likely to sexually reproduce. Unlike males, females' reproductive success did not depend on their level of aggression, but instead on their ability to successfully nurture and protect offspring. Evolutionary psychologists contend that over many generations, the importance of aggression in male reproductive success and the importance of nurturance in female reproductive success led to genetically based differences in male and female responses to stress: Men prepare to fight or flee, while women prepare to tend and befriend.

At this point, available evidence does not clearly support one view over the other, and both perspectives could explain different aspects of gender differences in stress responses. Consistent with the evolutionary viewpoint, women and men may have evolved different stress responses due to differences in their mating strategies. In turn, consistent with the sociocultural perspective, this genetic tendency may be heightened or weakened by existing socialization patterns in contemporary society.

Cognitive Appraisal

Richard Lazarus (1993) was one of the first researchers to examine how we interpret and evaluate stressors in our lives, a process he called *cognitive appraisal*. Cognitive appraisal is essential in defining whether a situation is a threat, how big a threat it is, and what resources you have to deal with the threat (Lazarus & Lazarus, 1994). Some stressors, such as being a crime victim or undergoing surgery, are experienced as threats by almost everyone. However, many other events will be defined differently depending on the individuals, their past experiences with similar stressors, and their feelings of competence in dealing with the stressors' demands. For example, starting a new job can fill one person with excitement, while it causes someone else to feel apprehensive and overwhelmed. Context is also important. For instance, prior to the anthrax scare, you probably would not have been alarmed to find powder traces inside a letter you received in the mail. Yet, today, with so much concern about biological terrorism, powdered letters are likely to prompt a 911 call.

Lazarus identified two stages in the cognitive appraisal process: primary appraisal and secondary appraisal. *Primary appraisal* involves an initial evaluation of the situation. Here, you assess what is happening, whether it is threatening, and whether you should take some action in response to the threat. If you conclude that some action is necessary, *secondary appraisal* begins. In this second stage of the cognitive appraisal process, you assess whether you have the ability to *cope* with the stressor. The more competent you perceive yourself to be in dealing with the stressor, the less stress you will experience (Baum & Posluszny, 1999; Croyle, 1992).

Problem-Focused Versus Emotion-Focused Coping

Problem-focused coping:
A coping strategy designed to reduce the stress by overcoming the source of the problem.

Emotion-focused coping:
A coping strategy designed to manage the emotional reactions to stressors rather than trying to change the stressors themselves.

In contrast to Selye's model, which viewed the person as a passive recipient of stressors, Lazarus's model conceives of the person as an active participant in evaluating and responding to stressors. Consistent with this activist perspective, Lazarus and Susan Folkman (1984) identified two general coping strategies that people employ during secondary appraisal. **Problem-focused coping** is a strategy aimed at reducing stress by overcoming the source of the problem. If you fail your first exam in an important class, engaging in problem-focused coping might involve a number of actions such as talking to your professor about extra credit work, changing your study habits, and checking your class notes with someone who is doing well in the class. A second approach is **emotion-focused coping,** which consists of efforts to manage your emotional reactions to stressors rather than trying to change the stressors themselves (Auerbach & Gramling, 1998). Engaging in this type of coping when faced with class problems might involve trying not to cry when speaking to your professor, seeking sympathy from your friends, or immersing yourself in some other activity to take your mind off your academic troubles. By controlling how you feel, you may be better able to take control over situations, thus limiting the emotional toll of the stressor.

We tend to take the active, problem-focused approach to handling stress when we think we can overcome the problem, but we resort to an emotion-focused strategy when we believe that the problem is beyond our control (Folkman & Moskowitz, 2000; Reese et al., 1997). Of course, at times we employ both types of coping. For example, while devising a plan of action to improve your class performance, you may try to emotionally distance yourself from anxiety by reminding yourself that this is just one exam out of four in the course. Table 15-1 lists some of the specific problem-focused and emotion-focused strategies that people use (Folkman et al., 1986; Folkman & Lazarus, 1980).

Journey of Discovery Question

It is generally thought that problem-focused coping is maladaptive in situations when a person has no personal control. Yet, a situation that appears on its surface to be uncontrollable may still have controllable aspects. Consider people caring for loved ones with terminal illnesses. During the weeks leading up to death, what sort of problem-focused coping might caregivers engage in to increase their positive moods and lower stress?

Coping Skills	Example
Problem-Focused Coping	
Confronting	Standing your ground and fighting for what you want
Planful problem solving	Coming up with a plan of action and following it
Seeking social support	Talking to others to learn more about the stressor
Emotion-Focused Coping	
Distancing	Disidentifying yourself from the anxiety and fear by not thinking about it very much or trying to downplay its importance
Self-controlling	Keeping your feelings to yourself
Escape/avoidance (wishful thinking)	Wishing that the stressor would go away
Positive reappraisal	Thinking about positive aspects of yourself that are not related to the stressor
Accepting responsibility	Realizing that you brought the problem on yourself

TABLE 15-1

Problem-Focused and Emotion-Focused Coping

Source: From "Appraisal, Coping, Health Status, and Psychological Symptoms" by S. Folkman, R. S. Lazarus, R. J. Gruen, and A. DeLongis in JOURNAL OF PERSONALITY AND SOCIAL PSYCHOLOGY 50, pp. 571–579. Copyright © 1986 by the American Psychological Association. Adapted with permission.

15-1d Psychophysiological Illnesses Are Stress Related

Medical experts estimate that stress plays a role in 50 to 70 percent of all physical illnesses (Kiecolt-Glaser & Glaser, 1992). These stress-related physical illnesses are referred to as **psychophysiological disorders.** Two bodily systems that have received the most attention by researchers studying stress-related diseases are the *cardiovascular system* and the *immune system*.

Psychophysiological disorders: Physical conditions, such as high blood pressure and migraine headaches, that are caused or aggravated by psychological factors such as stress.

The Cardiovascular System

The cardiovascular system, made up of the heart and all of the blood vessels that bring blood to and from the heart, is essential for life. However, this system is also associated with the primary causes of death, namely, heart attacks and stroke. The cardiovascular system is also strongly affected by the emotional responses related to stress. People have long believed that strong emotional distress can cause sudden death from cardiac events. Converging evidence from correlational, longitudinal, and animal studies have confirmed such a connection (Kamarck & Jennings, 1991; Krantz et al., 1996). In particular, stressful events involving anger have been related to heart attacks (Mittleman et al., 1995).

High blood pressure (or *hypertension*) and diseases of the arteries that nourish the heart are primary risk factors behind heart attacks and sudden death. Increased sympathetic nervous system activity raises heart rate and blood pressure, placing more strain on the cardiovascular system and damaging arteries that nourish the heart (Krantz & Manuck, 1984; Ross & Glomset, 1976). The majority of instances of *ischemia*, a condition in which the heart does not receive sufficient blood, occur during times of daily mental strain and, in particular, following anger-inducing stressors (Ironson et al., 1992; Krantz et al., 1996). In addition to this physical strain, the emotional response to stress includes the release of *cortisol* from the adrenal cortex and *epinephrine* from the adrenal medulla (glands that sit atop the kidneys). These two hormones mobilize fats and contribute to blood clot formation, which, in turn, can ultimately lead to artery blockage and heart attacks (Muller et al., 1994).

The Immune System

Another way in which stress responses work together with other physical states to place one at greater risk for disease is through its effect on the immune system, our body's primary defense against disease. The **immune system** is made up of specialized cells, tissues, and organs that react to and destroy cells that are determined to not be part of the body. Immune system cells not only destroy these foreign cells, known as *antigens*, but they also learn the characteristics of the antigens, enabling the immune system to respond more quickly in the future.

Three important type of cells in the immune system are *B cells*, *T cells*, and *natural killer cells*. *B cells* form in the bone marrow and produce *antibodies*, which are protein molecules that attach themselves to antigens and mark them for destruction. *T cells* form in the thymus and other lymphatic tissue and attack cancer cells, viruses, and other antigens. *Natural killer cells* fight viruses and tumors (Weiss, 1992). Both acute and chronic stress can reduce the efficiency of the immune system, making the body more susceptible to disease (O'Leary, 1990).

We now know that the immune system (once thought to act independent of the nervous system) and the brain are in close communication and influence each other's actions (Keller et al., 1994). This communication means that activity of one system will affect activity of the other. One pathway is through the stress response. The release of epinephrine and cortisol into the bloodstream suppresses immune functioning, although a variety of factors, such as length and type of stressor and the aspect of immune function being considered, determine how and to what extent changes in immune function occur (Moynihan & Stevens, 2001).

The effect that immune suppression has on the body depends on how long the suppression lasts. Stress diverts energy from the immune system, making us more susceptible to disease. The longer the stress lasts, the more likely we will become ill. Chapter 13, section 13-1c, described how a predisposition for a psychological disorder can lead to the onset of the disorder following stressful events. This *diathesis-stress model* (Levi, 1974)—which is an excellent example of the biopsychosocial perspective—helps us to better understand psychophysiological illnesses. According to the model, several elements are necessary for disease to occur. In particular, a *predisposition*, or vulnerability, for a type of disease must exist. In addition, whether or not the disease is allowed to develop will be affected by exposure to something that will lower resistance—notably stress. This view can help explain not only why different people develop different illnesses following stress, but also why rates of illness change over time (Brannon & Feist, 2000). Let us briefly examine evidence concerning the causal relationship between stress and the following infectious diseases and cancers (Biondi, 2001):

- *Influenza*—Stress diminishes the immune system's response during viral infection and thus reduces the body's ability to fight the virus (Bonneau et al., 2001).

- *West Nile virus*—This mosquito-borne virus can cause encephalitis (inflammation of tissue surrounding the brain) and has been found in a growing number of regions of the United States and Canada, with numerous deaths occurring during the summer months of 2002. The virus is more likely to mutate and become more virulent when the host animal is under stress (Ben-Nathan & Feuerstein, 1990; Ben-Nathan et al., 1996).

- *The "common cold"*—When volunteers were infected with cold virus through nasal drops, they were much more likely to develop cold symptoms if they were experiencing high versus low stress in their daily lives (Cohen & Miller, 2001).

- *Cancer*—A primary defense against cancer is surveillance by the immune system against mutated cells. To date, evidence is mixed as to whether psychosocial stress leads to the development of cancer in the first place. However, the evidence is stronger (though not conclusive) that progression of the disease is greater when people experience high stress. Further, research consistently suggests that people who habitually suppress their emotions are at greater risk for both cancer development and progression, although the degree of risk is as yet unclear (Fox, 1998; Spiegel, 1999; Turner-Cobb et al., 2001).

- *HIV/AIDS*—Logic would suggest that any factor that further suppresses immune functioning, including stress, would affect the progression of HIV/AIDS. Findings from animal and human studies provide preliminary support for the hypothesis that stress negatively affects the efficiency of the body's capacity to fight HIV progression (Cole & Kemeny, 2001).

In summary, substantial evidence from both animal and human studies indicates that changes in immune function in response to stress have negative impacts on health. Clearly, psychosocial stress is one of the important factors affecting vulnerability to various diseases.

SECTION SUMMARY

- Stress is our response to events that disturb, or threaten to disturb, our physical or psychological equilibrium

- According to Selye's general adaptation syndrome, threat causes the body to first react with alarm, followed by stages of resistance and finally exhaustion as the threat continues.

- Current views of human stress maintain that it is a continually changing process determined by how a threat is cognitively appraised, what resources (both within and outside the person) are available, and how the person copes with the stressor.

- Stress can lead to decreased immune system effectiveness and can contribute to a variety of diseases.

15-2   WHAT MODERATES STRESS?

Just because you are exposed to a stressor does not mean that you will become ill. As outlined by Lazarus, the way you perceive a stressor will shape how you react to it. A number of factors moderate your reactions to stress, including the *predictability* of the stressor, *perceptions of control*, your *personality*, and the availability of *social support*.

15-2a   Predictability and Control Can Moderate the Stress Response

Whether an event will become a harmful stressor is often determined by its *predictability*. If you know that a stressor is coming but you are uncertain when it will occur, you tend to experience greater stress (Boss, 1999; Glass & Singer, 1972). This effect is especially true when the stressors are intense and occur for relatively brief periods (Parkes & Weiss, 1983).

A host of studies indicate that *perceived control* over a stressor is one of the most important factors moderating the relationship between stress and illness. If people believe that they have some control over a stressor they usually feel less stressed (Christensen et al., 1998). For example, in one study, elderly nursing home patients who were given greater control over their daily activities experienced fewer health problems and lived longer than those who were not given much control (Rodin, 1986). Similarly, people who work at demanding jobs are less likely to develop coronary heart disease when they believe they have some control over job stressors (Krantz et al., 1988, 1996).

People differ in their tendency to perceive events to be controllable (or uncontrollable). As discussed in chapter 12, section 12-5b, the tendency to assume that outcomes occur because of our *own efforts* is referred to as an *internal locus of control*, whereas an

FIGURE 15-2
Procrastination and Health

When college students who were either procrastinators or nonprocrastinators began the semester in a health psychology class, procrastinators reported slightly fewer symptoms of physical illness than nonprocrastinators. As class deadlines came due later in the semester, all students showed increases in symptoms. However, procrastinators were much more likely to miss those deadlines, and they were much more likely to report a greater increase in illness symptoms than nonprocrastinators.

Source: From "Longitudinal Study of Procrastination, Performance, Stress, and Health: The Costs and Benefits of Dawdling" by D. M. Tice and R. F. Baumeister in PSYCHOLOGICAL SCIENCE, 8, 1997, pp. 454–458. Reprinted by permission of Blackwell Publishing Ltd.

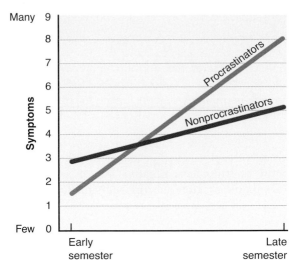

external locus of control reflects a belief that outcomes are outside of our control (Rotter, 1966, 1990). A person's locus of control appears to emerge early in life and is a fairly stable personality trait. Through experience, it is also possible to develop either a sense of mastery or a sense of helplessness toward stressors (see chapter 12, section 12-5b). By experiencing success when attempting to alleviate stressors, you are likely to become more confident that you can gain control over future challenges. Alternatively, repeated failure at trying to eliminate stressors can lead to more generalized assumptions of being helpless (Seligman, 1975). This *learned helplessness* can cause you to falsely believe that you have no control over a stressor, thus increasing the likelihood that you will take no action to reduce the threat (Baum et al., 1998).

When people doubt their ability to assert control over a stressor, they are more likely to engage in emotion-focused coping strategies (see section 15-1c). *Procrastination*, which involves delaying the start and completion of *planful problem solving*, is an example of the emotion-focused coping strategy of *escape-avoidance* (refer back to table 15-1). Approximately one out of five adults regularly procrastinate when faced with a stressor, especially when it is severe (Harriot & Ferrari, 1996). These habitually indecisive individuals are easily distracted, have low self-confidence, and have an external locus of control (Ferrari & Dovidio, 2001). Far from reducing stress, however, such delays in tackling problems tend to increase stress and lead to health problems (Ferrari & Tice, 2000). For example, at the beginning of the semester in a health psychology class, researchers identified college students who were either habitually high or low in procrastination (Tice & Baumeister, 1997). As you can see in figure 15-2, although procrastinators reported slightly fewer symptoms of physical illness than nonprocrastinators early in the semester, they had significantly greater symptoms later in the semester as term paper deadlines came due. True to form, procrastinators not only turned their assignments in later then the nonprocrastinators, but they also obtained lower grades on those papers.

15-2b Hostile and Pessimistic Persons Are More Reactive to Stressors

That stressors become less worrisome and more manageable when we perceive them as predictable and controllable highlights how our thinking about events shapes our behavioral responses. Additional research indicates that some people's consistent and distinctive ways of thinking, feeling, and behaving—that is, their personalities—cause them to react negatively to stressors, whereas others respond positively (Masten, 2001). Two personality dimensions that significantly influence stress responses are *Type A* versus *Type B behavior patterns* and *pessimistic* versus *optimistic explanatory styles*.

Type A and Type B Behavior Patterns

During the 1950s, two cardiologists, Ray Rosenman and Meyer Friedman, noted an oddity about their coronary patients—the upholstery on their waiting room chairs was worn more in the front, as if their patients were sitting on the edge of their seats. This observation, coupled with their later findings that many of these same people were also impatient workaholics, led Rosenman and Friedman to identify what they called the **Type A behavior pattern** (Rosenman, 1993; Rosenman et al., 1975). This complex pattern of behaviors and emotions—which is associated with increased risk of heart disease—is characterized by competitiveness, impatience, ambition, hostility, and a hard-driving approach to life (Boyce & Geller, 2002). The direct opposite of this personality style is the **Type B behavior pattern,** which is characterized by a patient, relaxed, easygoing approach to life, with little hurry or hostility. These individuals are only half as likely to develop coronary heart disease than their Type A counterparts (Lyness, 1993). Spend a few minutes answering the items in table 15-2 to assess yourself for Type A behavior pattern.

Based on numerous studies, *cynical hostility* appears to be the toxic component of the Type A pattern (Dembroski et al., 1985; Fredrickson et al., 2000). Specifically, people who mistrust and think the worst of others and use anger as a typical response to interpersonal problems appear to be at greatest risk for heart disease (Eysenck, 2000; Siegman et al., 1992; Vahtera et al., 2000). From a physiological point of view, cynical hostility

Type A behavior pattern:
A complex pattern of behaviors and emotions characterized by competitiveness, impatience, ambition, hostility, and a hard-driving approach to life.

Type B behavior pattern:
A pattern of behaviors and emotions characterized by a patient, relaxed, easygoing approach to life, with little hurry or hostility.

TABLE 15-2

Do You Have a Type A Personality?

Directions: Indicate how often each of the following applies to you in daily life, using the following three-point scale:

1 = Seldom or Never   2 = Sometimes   3 = Always or Usually

___ Do you find yourself rushing your speech?

___ Do you hurry other people's speech by interrupting them with "umha, umhm" or by completing their sentences for them?

___ Do you hate to wait in line?

___ Do you seem to be short of time to get everything done?

___ Do you detest wasting time?

___ Do you eat fast?

___ Do you drive over the speed limit?

___ Do you try to do more than one thing at a time?

___ Do you become impatient if others do something too slowly?

___ Does your concentration sometimes wander while you think about what's coming up later?

___ Do you find yourself overcommitted?

___ Do you jiggle your knees or tap your fingers?

___ Do you think about other things during conversations?

___ Do you walk fast?

___ Do you hate dawdling after a meal?

___ Do you become irritable if kept waiting?

___ Do you detest losing in sports and games?

___ Do you find yourself with clenched fists or tight neck and jaw muscles?

___ Do you seem to have little time to relax and enjoy the time of day?

___ Are you a competitive person?

___ **Total score**

A score of 20–34 may mean low Type A behavior, 35–44 medium Type A behavior, and 45–60 high Type A behavior.

Source: From STRESS MANAGEMENT FOR WELLNESS, 2nd edition, by W. Schafer. Copyright © 1992. Reprinted with permission of Brooks/Cole, an imprint of the Wadsworth Group, a division of Thomson Learning. Fax 800/730-2215.

> *The optimist sees the rose and not its thorns; the pessimist stares at the thorns, oblivious to the rose.*
>
> —Kahlil Gibran, Lebanese poet, 1883–1931

appears to cause chronic overarousal of the body's stress responses (Everson et al., 1997; Friedman et al., 1994). From a psychosocial point of view, cynical hostility contributes to poor health habits and tense social relationships (Smith, 1992).

Because of the health problems associated with the Type A behavior pattern, it makes sense to try to convince Type A persons to change their hostile, impatient approach to life. However, one major obstacle to orchestrating such change is that many Type A persons are not unhappy with their behavior. After all, North American culture respects and rewards this hard-driving, hostile lifestyle (Rush Limbaugh, Dr. Laura, and other radio talk-show hosts are prototypes of the Type A person). Yet, for those who are motivated to reduce their hostility and "smell the roses" in their daily lives, behavior modification and cognitive therapy (see chapter 14, sections 14-3 and 14-4) have been successful in changing Type A behavior (Forgays & Forgays, 1994; Thurman, 1985).

Pessimists Versus Optimists

Pessimistic explanatory style: The habitual tendency to explain uncontrollable negative events as being caused by one's own stable personal qualities that affect all aspects of one's life. This pessimistic style is associated with health problems and premature death.

Optimistic explanatory style: The habitual tendency to explain uncontrollable negative events as being caused by temporary factors external to oneself that do not affect other aspects of one's life. This optimistic style is associated with good health and longevity.

Another personality dimension that is related to health issues is people's *explanatory style*—their degree of pessimism or optimism—regarding negative events in their lives (Haines et al., 1999; Peterson & Seligman, 1987). Individuals with a **pessimistic explanatory style** explain uncontrollable negative events as being caused by internal factors ("It's my fault"), stable ("It won't ever change"), and global ("This affects everything"). Not surprisingly, people who fit this pattern are susceptible to depression (Alloy et al., 1999; Nolen-Hoeksma et al., 1992). In contrast, people with an **optimistic explanatory style** explain uncontrollable negative events as due to external factors ("It is not my fault"), unstable or changeable ("It won't happen again"), and specific ("This affects only one thing").

Several studies indicate that people with an optimistic explanatory style have fewer illnesses and are at lower risk for premature death than those with a pessimistic style (Peterson & Park, 1998; Scheier & Carver, 2000). Additional research suggests that these health differences may be partly explained by the fact that optimists seem to have better immune systems than pessimists. For example, one study found that optimists have higher numbers of helper T cells that mediate immune reactions to infection than pessimists (Segerstrom et al., 1998).

Fortunately, individuals with a pessimistic explanatory style can be taught to change their way of thinking through cognitive therapy (see chapter 14, sections 14-4a and 14-4b). Typically, this involves keeping a diary of daily successes and failures, and identifying how you contributed to your successes and how external factors caused your failures. Essentially, pessimists are being trained to do what most of us do naturally: take credit for our successes and deny blame for our failures! As discussed in chapter 12, section 12-3d, this beneficial way of explaining your positive and negative outcomes is known as the *self-serving bias*. In a very real sense, research on pessimists and optimists points to the important role that people's subjective interpretations of events have on their health and behavior. Check out Discovery Box 15-2 for a description of how an increasing number of psychologists are calling for greater emphasis on "positive psychology" in contemporary research and theory.

15-2c Social Support Has Therapeutic Effects

Thus far, we have discussed stress as if it is something that you must endure alone. Do you recall what you did when you first learned about the terrorist attacks on September 11, 2001? If you are like most people, during that time of anxiety, grief, and uncertainty, you sought the companionship of others who were similarly affected by this tragedy. Our desire to seek out others during times of stress and uncertainty is substantially fueled by the need

DISCOVERY   BOX 15-2

What Is Positive Psychology?

If you examine the content of this chapter, and perhaps if you look at the textbook as a whole, you might notice that the emphasis has often been on negative life events—stress and disease; drug abuse; aggression; prejudice and discrimination; anxiety, depression, and other potentially debilitating psychological disorders—rather than those that are positive. One reason for the emphasis on the negative aspects of life is that by better understanding why these events occur, psychologists believe that we may be better equipped to eliminate them from our lives. Recently, however, this "problem-focused" viewpoint has been challenged as too narrow. Instead of explaining human behavior in terms of what goes wrong in everyday functioning, many psychologists now propose a more **positive psychology** that pays an equal amount of attention to psychological processes that maximize human potentials, motives, and capacities (Sandage & Hill, 2001; Sheldon & King, 2001).

Positive psychology has a great deal in common with the humanistic perspective (see chapter 1, section 1-3b, and chapter 12, section 12-3), but it is more firmly grounded in rigorous scientific methodology. Because of this science-based approach to understanding the positive aspects of human functioning, positive psychology is in a better position to shape the future direction of psychology than humanistic psychology. Researchers in this area are currently studying what it means to be a well-adapted person (Schmuck & Sheldon, 2001). For example, when does an optimistic view of life help you overcome hurdles to success and when does it cause you to overlook impending failure? Teaching people to avoid harmful self-deceptions while still maintaining a sense of realistic optimism about life is one of the goals of this new positive psychology (Snyder, 2000). The *Psychological Applications* section at the end of the chapter examines some recent findings concerning what contributes to happiness in life.

Positive psychology: A relatively new scientific approach to studying optimal human functioning that asserts that the normal functioning of human beings cannot be accounted for within purely negative (or problem-focused) frames of reference.

to compare our emotional state with that of others ("How should I be feeling?") and to also appraise the stressful situation itself ("How much of a threat is this stressor?").

The helpful coping resources that friends and other people provide when you are confronting a stressful situation is referred to as **social support.** An overwhelming amount of evidence indicates that having supportive people in our lives provides both psychological and physical benefits (Cohen et al., 2000; Taylor, 1999). For example, in a longitudinal study of almost 7,000 residents of Alameda County, California, researchers discovered that people lived longer when they had many social and community ties (Berkman & Syme, 1979). This was true of men and women, rich and poor, and people from all racial and ethnic backgrounds. Other studies have found that being socially isolated was, statistically, just as predictive of an early death as high cholesterol or smoking (House et al., 1988; Rogers, 1995). Physiologically, having strong social support networks is associated with a stronger immune response to stress (Glaser et al., 1992; Jemmott & Magloire, 1988). For example, a meta-analysis of 81 studies found that having social support during times of stress lowers blood pressure, lessens the secretion of stress hormones, and strengthens immune responses (Uchino et al., 1996).

Social support: The helpful coping resources provided by friends and other people.

People with more extensive social support networks are happier, have stronger immune systems, and live longer than those who are socially isolated. What are some of the reasons that social connections are so therapeutic?

INFO-BIT: Owning a pet can have stress-buffering effects, resulting in fewer illnesses among people who experience negative life events (Siegel, 1990).

As previously mentioned, one common psychological benefit of social support is increased knowledge about the stressor. That is, associating with others often provides us with information about how to understand and emotionally respond to stressful events (Van der Zee et al., 1998). The people who tend to provide us with the most useful information are similar to us on some characteristic related to the stressor (Schachter, 1959). This is the rationale underlying therapeutic support groups for drug abusers, sexual assault victims, and cancer patients (see chapter 14, section 14-6b). In these therapy sessions, people who have experienced the same stressful events can compare themselves with one another while they also provide and receive emotional support.

Social support during stressful times can also provide us with opportunities to simply express our feelings, which, in turn, can lead to physical benefits (Kelly, 1999; Pennebaker et al., 1990). In one relevant experiment, college students spent 15 minutes on each of four consecutive nights writing to the experimenter about a traumatic event in their lives. These students subsequently reported fewer illnesses over the next six months compared with students who had written to the experimenter about unimportant topics (Pennebaker & Beall, 1986). In general, while "letting out" our feelings about a traumatic event can temporarily upset and arouse us, in the long run, it lowers our stress (Major & Gramzow, 1999; Smyth, 1998).

As with most things that are good for you, however, too much social support (or support given improperly) can cause negative side effects. For example, overly zealous giving of support can reduce the recipient's sense of control over a stressor and can reduce his or her self-confidence. Receiving social support can also make a person feel beholden to the giver, turning the support into a burden (Greenberg & Frisch, 1972; Gross & Latané, 1974). The key when providing support to another person is to convey caring for the recipient in a manner that provides real benefits, keeps them involved in the solution to the problem (don't "take care of" them), and avoids an inferiority-superiority relationship (Dakof & Taylor, 1990; Dunkel-Schetter et al., 1992). Discovery Box 15-3 discusses how women and men sometimes differ in providing social support in romantic relationships.

SECTION SUMMARY

- Events that are predictable and those over which we perceive to have some degree of control are less stressful.
- Hostile and pessimistic individuals are more reactive to stressors.
- Strong social support is associated with a stronger immune response to stress and better physical and psychological health.

DISCOVERY BOX 15-3

Are There Gender Differences in Providing Social Support in Romantic Relationships?

In the majority of Western cultures, most people involved in long-term romantic relationships view their partners as their best friends and the persons they would turn to in times of need (Pasch et al., 1997). Receiving such support has three important benefits: the *stress* of the partner in need decreases while her or his *satisfaction* and *commitment* to the relationship increases (Sprecher et al., 1995).

In heterosexual romance, men rely more on their partners for social support than do women, who also depend on a variety of sources, including friends, relatives, and neighbors (Cutrona, 1996). However, a woman's psychological well-being is still closely linked to the support she receives from her partner. For example, a longitudinal study of married couples found that lower levels of depression were associated with both women and men receiving a good deal of *emotional support* (tenderness and understanding) and *information support* (advice and guidance) from their partners during the previous six months (Cutrona & Suhr, 1994).

Unfortunately for women involved in heterosexual romantic relationships, their skill in providing social support during stressful times—recall the "tend-and-befriend" discussion in section 15-1b—is generally greater than that of their male partners (Vinokur & Vinokur-Kaplan, 1990). The most likely explanation for this gender difference is the greater childhood training girls receive in the caretaking role and in emotional attentiveness (Belle, 1982). While female socialization fosters the development of these *relationship-enhancing* behaviors, male socialization is more likely to promote the development of *individual-enhancing* behaviors, such as independence and control. This gender difference may explain why marriage is more beneficial to men than to women: Men marry people who, on average, have been taught to provide care and nurturance, while women marry people who, on average, have spent a lot of time learning how to be independent of others!

How does this gender socialization difference influence social support among lesbian and gay couples? A five-year longitudinal study suggests that while the "double dose" of relationship-enhancing skills that lesbians bring to romantic relationships is associated with slightly higher intimacy than that found among heterosexual couples, it doesn't lead to greater relationship satisfaction (Kurdek, 1998). For gay couples, while their "double dose" of individual-enhancing skills may explain why they tend to have a higher need for autonomy than heterosexual couples, it doesn't lower relationship satisfaction.

15-3 WHAT BEHAVIORS HURT OR HELP OUR HEALTH?

At all ages, most of the top 10 causes of death have a behavioral component. Risks for heart disease and cancer, the #1 and #2 killers, are both influenced by eating habits and exercise. Accidents, suicides, and homicides—among the top causes of death for children and young adults—are the direct result of behaviors. Death due to HIV infection, many lung diseases, and cirrhosis of the liver are influenced by sexual behaviors, smoking, and alcohol consumption, respectively. Some forms of diabetes—itself a risk factor for heart disease—are the direct result of behaviors, primarily diet.

Lifestyle differences between men and women also determine longevity. Accidents, suicides, and homicides occur two to seven times as often among boys and men than among girls and women. Additionally, men have two to three times the rate of death from HIV and cirrhosis compared with women. To get a sense of how much your own behaviors may affect how long you will live, take the Longevity Test in Discovery Box 15-4.

Am I suggesting that if you simply behave correctly, you'll never die? No—obviously that isn't true. Death is not preventable, but altering behaviors can prevent premature death and increase quality of life. In chapter 11, we analyzed sex and hunger as motivated behaviors. Now let us examine how unsafe sexual practices and disordered eating behaviors affect health and well-being.

15-3a Knowing about "Safer Sex" Is Not Enough

Do you know how HIV (the virus that causes AIDS) is passed from one person to another? Can you name at least two ways to keep from acquiring a sexually transmitted disease? If you are like most college students, you already know that HIV is spread through bodily fluids such as semen and blood, and not through casual contact (including kissing, unless open sores are present) or by mosquitoes (Langer et al., 2001). It also is probably not news to you that HIV and other sexually transmitted diseases can be prevented by abstaining from sex or, if sexually active, by practicing safer sex behaviors such as consistently using a condom (or other barrier), limiting sexual partners, and knowing the sexual histories of your partners (Coates & Collins, 1998).

The fact that nearly all college students (and the vast majority of other young adults) can correctly answer these questions speaks to the success of educational programs in informing the public about HIV over the past 20 years. However, this knowledge has little relationship with whether or not unmarried adolescents or adults remain abstinent or practice safer-sex behaviors (Bellingham & Gillies, 1993; Rimberg & Lewis, 1994). Instead, college students tend to engage in a number of risky sexual behaviors, such as high numbers of sexual partners, "one-night stands" with casual acquaintances, and frequent condomless sex (Reinisch et al., 1995; Simkins, 1995; Zimmerman & Olson, 1994). Even though 1 in 6 sexually active adults report having had at least one sexually transmitted disease (such as chlamydia, gonorrhea, genital herpes, genital warts, syphilis, or HIV), as many as 9 out of 10 do not use condoms consistently (Michael et al., 1994). Often the riskier behaviors occur in combination with use of alcohol or other drugs (Ratliff-Crain et al., 1999).

If knowledge about the risks doesn't promote safer behaviors, what does? Additionally, what motivates people to choose unsafe behaviors over those that are safer? Getting people to use safer-sex behaviors, such as using condoms, takes much more than simply telling them that condoms prevent disease and that they should use them (O'Keeffe et al., 1990). Described in the following list are some of the more common barriers to condom use:

- *Buying condoms can be embarrassing.* Buying condoms can be an embarrassing event, especially for people who are extremely uncomfortable discussing their sexuality (see chapter 11, section 11-2e). Also, the use of condoms may be inconsistent with an individual's personal or cultural values, diminishing use even further (Huff & Kline, 1999). Men and women who are comfortable talking about their sexual histories and about safer sex are about six times more likely to use condoms than those who are uncomfortable (Catania et al., 1992; Rickman et al., 1994). Programs that make condoms freely available to anyone often alleviate these barriers to safer sex.

- *Condom use education emphasizes fear and disease prevention.* Sex education programs that use fear of AIDS as the primary focus have been shown to increase awareness, but not change behaviors (Chesney & Coates, 1990). One reason such programs do not lead to safer sexual behavior is that people often associate condoms with disease, thus lowering any motivation to use them. Recently, advertisements have begun depicting condoms in a more sexual manner, treating them as a desirable part of the sexual experience rather than as something associated with disease. If condoms are not part of people's sexual scripts (see chapter 11, section 11-2a), they are less likely to be used in the "heat of the moment."

- *Riskier sexual behaviors are more likely with alcohol consumption.* Alcohol does not necessarily cause people to lose their sexual inhibitions, but it does make it less likely that they will engage in sound cognitive reasoning and think about the possible consequences of their behavior (Coates et al., 1988; Steele & Josephs, 1990). When intoxicated with alcohol, the immediate sexual arousal will be uppermost in people's minds rather than any thought that sexual activity may put them at risk for a disease.

- *Low self-esteem persons are more likely to engage in risky sexual behaviors.* Low self-esteem persons have more adverse reactions to negative events in their lives than high self-esteem persons (Smith & Petty, 1995). When experiencing these negative moods, they also have a heightened need to avoid rejection from others (Heatherton & Vohs, 2000). These reactions to negative events may explain why those with low self-esteem are more likely than high self-esteem persons to have sex without using a condom when they are in a negative mood (MacDonald & Martineau, 2002).

The research findings summarized in the preceding list suggest that effective prevention programs must focus on multiple areas of a person's life in order to increase safer sexual behaviors (Fisher & Fisher, 1992). Such programs need broader interventions, including discussions of nonsexual motivations for seeking intimacy, assertiveness training for people to feel comfortable stating their own preferences with a sexual partner, reducing barriers to obtaining condoms, and providing models and examples of situations where safer sex is still exciting sex (Coates, 1990).

15-3b Obesity and Eating Disorders Are a Function of Internal and External Forces

As discussed in chapter 11, section 11-3, eating is one of our basic, primary motivated behaviors. You also learned that feelings of hunger and eating behaviors are controlled by much more than what our stomachs tell us. A complex array of physiological, psychological, and social/environmental factors combine to create our motivation to eat.

What Is Obesity?

Recently, the Centers for Disease Control (CDC) declared that **obesity,** which is the excessive accumulation of body fat, has become an epidemic in the United States (Battle & Brownell, 1996; Mokdad et al., 1999). In diagnosing obesity, physicians calculate a *body mass index (BMI)*, which is defined as weight in kilograms divided by height in meters squared (30 kg/m^2). A ratio over 25 is considered overweight; over 30, obese; over 40, extremely obese (National Institutes of Health, 2000). Using the BMI, a 5-foot, 4-inch woman weighing 174 pounds or greater, or a 5-foot, 10-inch man weighing 207 pounds or more would be considered obese. Between 1991 and 1998, there has been about a 50 percent increase in the number of Americans who fall into this excessive body fat category (from 12.0 percent to 17.9 percent of the adult population), and the number of overweight children has doubled in the past 20 years (Yanovski & Yanovski, 1999). Similar increases in heftiness have occurred in Canada, Britain, Australia, and other countries in the developed world (Australian Bureau of Statistics, 2000; W. C. Miller, 1999; Statistics Canada, 1999).

Although being slightly overweight poses no health risks, obesity is closely related to numerous chronic health conditions, including high blood pressure, heart disease, diabetes, arthritis, and sleep disorders (Bray, 1992; Williamson, 1993; Wolf & Colditz, 1996). This is especially true for individuals with "apple-shaped" bodies, in which most of the weight resides in pot bellies, rather than "pear shaped" individuals with large hips and

Obesity: The excessive accumulation of body fat. Medically, a person with a body mass index over 30 is considered obese.

DISCOVERY BOX 15-4

How Long Will You Live?

It's possible to make a rough estimate of how long you will live based on data from population studies. It's good to remember that if you want to live a long and healthy life, you should choose your parents well. Well, aside from that "choice," many other factors contribute to how well and how long you will live—some changeable, some not. Complete the test that follows to see the influences of several different factors on how long we live.

Basic Life Expectancy

____ Start with the basic life expectancy appropriate for your gender: Males = 74 years, Females = 80 years.
____ If you're between 55 and 65, add ten years (you've shown that you're reasonably durable!). Add two more years if you're over 60 and active.

Family History

____ Two or more grandparents who lived to 80 or beyond = +5 years
____ Both parents lived to 70 or greater, with no cardiovascular problems before 60 = +2 years
____ Two or more siblings with cardiovascular problems = –2 years
____ At least one parent with cardiovascular problems or died before 60 = –1 year
____ Parents not yet 70 and in good health (or don't know family history) = +0 years

Weight

____ Subtract 1 year for every 10 pounds overweight (a body-mass index over 25)

Blood Pressure

____ Don't know it = –2 years
____ Checked regularly and it's normal = +3 years
____ High blood pressure and smoke or elevated cholesterol = –9 years
____ High blood pressure, under control with medication = –1 year
____ High blood pressure that isn't under control = –6 years

Exercise

____ Regular and moderate exercise (jogging 3 times a week) or very active = +3 years
____ Somewhat active = +0 years
____ Not active (sedentary) = –3 years

Disposition

____ You are a reasoned, practical person = +2 years
____ You are aggressive, intense, and competitive = –2 years
____ You are basically happy and content with life = +1 year
____ You are often unhappy, worried, and often feel guilty = –1 year

Driving

____ No accidents or violations in the past 3 years = +1 year

____ One to three accidents or violations in the past 3 years = +0 years

____ Four or more violations or accidents in the past 2 years = –4 years

____ Convicted of driving while intoxicated (DWI) in past 5 years = –6 years

____ Convicted of DWI more than once in the past 5 years = –12 years

Seat Belts

____ Do you always buckle up? Yes = +1 year

Smoking

____ Never smoked = +2 years

____ Quit more than 2 years ago = +1 year

____ Quit less than 2 years ago = –1 year

____ Smoke less than 1 pack per day = –4 years

____ Smoke 2 or more packs per day = –8 years

Drinking (if of Legal Drinking Age)

____ Don't drink any alcohol = –1 year

____ Never more than 3 drinks per day = +2 years

____ Five or more drinks, 1 or more times a week = –6 years

____ Two to four drinks, 3 or more times a week = –3 years

Diet

____ Light user of saturated fats (1–2 times per week) = +2 years

____ Average user of saturated fats (at least 4 times per week) = +/–0

____ Heavy user of saturated fats (7 or more times a week) = –2 years

____ Nonuser of saturated fats = +3 years

Health Care

____ Regular checkups and dental care = +3 years

____ Frequently ill = –2 years

____ Your Estimated Life Expectancy

This is just a sample of the behaviors and factors that may affect your longevity. Some of these—for example, smoking and heavy alcohol consumption—can have an effect greater than simply *adding* their effects. Many other factors can affect health and longevity, such as income, education, or living in urban or rural environments. Can you think of other things not on this list that may affect your health and longevity? Add or subtract behaviors (or change your gender!) to see the effect on your life expectancy. There are many more variables than what can be represented here, but the test can give you a glimpse of how your behaviors may be affecting your life. Women in the United States have a current life expectancy of 79.5 years and men 73.8 years.

Sources: Northwestern Mutual (2001). *The longevity game.* http://www.northwesternmutual.com/ nmcom/NM/longevitygameintro/toolbox-calculator-longevitygameintro-longevity_intro. Milwaukee, WI: Northwestern Mutual. Schulz, R. (1978). *The psychology of death, dying, and bereavement.* Reading, MA: Addison-Wesley.

FIGURE 15-3
Obesity and Mortality

A 14-year study of over 1 million Americans found that men with a BMI score of 40 were two to six times more likely to have died than were those with a BMI of 23, while women with a 40 BMI score were twice as likely to have died.

Source: E. E. Calle, M. J. Thun, J. M. Petrelli, C. Rodriguez, and C. W. Heath, Jr., "Body-mass index and mortality in a prospective cohort of U.S. adults," *New England Journal of Medicine,* 1999, 341, pp. 1097–1105.

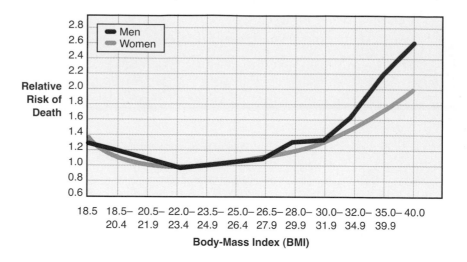

thighs (Bender et al., 1998; Greenwood, 1989). As depicted in figure 15-3, a recent 14-year longitudinal study of over 1 million Americans found that extreme obesity is a clear risk for premature death (Calle et al., 1999). Further evidence suggests that changes in weight from repeated dieting and weight-gain cycles place people at higher risk for numerous diseases (Brownell & Rodin, 1994; Rexrode et al., 1997).

What Causes Obesity?

Ample evidence shows that people are born with tendencies to be lighter or heavier. Indeed, as much as 70 percent of individual differences in weight are due to genetics (Allison et al., 1994; Stunkard et al., 1990). Yet, genetics alone cannot explain the rapid national increases in obesity. Weight gain occurs when energy intake (through food and drink) exceeds energy expenditure (through bodily functions and activity). Because the increase in obesity from 1991 to 1998 was not accompanied by a decrease in physical activity by Americans, changes in diet and eating habits probably account for a substantial portion of the national weight gain (Mokdad et al., 1999).

Weight loss through dieting is a commonly used approach for trying to control weight. Although the dieting industry receives over $30 billion dollars per year from Americans trying to lose weight, dieting is largely ineffective in achieving long-term weight loss. Several factors work against effective weight loss. First, as discussed in chapter 11, section 11-3c, it is difficult to change your weight once a set point has been established. Second, many people who diet are already at or below normal weight and therefore shouldn't be dieting. Increased activity in the form of exercise may be the best predictor for long-term weight loss, both before and after dieting (Brownell & Wadden, 1991, 1992; Foreyt et al., 1996). As with other lifestyle changes related to health, effective long-term weight loss for those who are overweight is often achieved only after much work and many failures (Jeffrey & Wing, 1983; Rzewnicki & Forgays, 1987). Yet, medical experts remind us that shedding excess weight will significantly lower our risk of premature death, chronic disease, and lower quality of life (Must et al., 1999).

On a national level, one major challenge in fighting the epidemic of obesity will be to improve the activity levels of children and adults. Television viewing, for example, has been pinpointed as a major contributor to sedentary lifestyles and obesity (Dietz & Gortmaker, 1985; Vines, 1995). One recent study suggests that simply reducing the amount of time children spend watching TV or playing video games is sufficient to greatly

---

INFO-BIT: To calculate your BMI using pounds and inches, multiply your weight in pounds by 700, divide by your height in inches, then divide by your height again.

> ***INFO-BIT:*** Healthwise, the ideal BMI differs across racial categories. For example, African-Americans' healthiest BMI score, which is around 27, is higher than that for European Americans, which is around 24 to 25 (Brannon & Feist, 2000).

reduce their weight problems (Robinson, 1999). This reduction in weight occurred even though the children did not decrease their high-fat food intake. As we will discuss in section 15-3c, encouraging increased physical activity may promote better health and well-being, not just prevent obesity and related health concerns.

Cultural Thinness Standards

Being significantly overweight is not just a health problem. In North American culture, obese individuals are often perceived as unattractive, lazy, sloppy, mean, unskilled, and slow (Crandall, 1994; Regan, 1996). In longitudinal studies of obese women and men, researchers find that they are less likely to be hired, and they tend to start at lower salaries and receive lower raises than their normal-weight counterparts (Frieze et al., 1991; Gortmaker et al., 1993). Other studies suggest that weight discrimination is more pervasive and widely condoned than race and gender discrimination (Roehling, 2000).

Underlying weight discrimination is a social climate that pressures people to reach certain body ideals (Heffernan et al., 2002). Although men are the target of some social pressure in this regard, the female ideal stresses difficult-to-attain thinness standards that actually endanger women's health if they pursue them (Posavac & Posavac, 1998; Vohs et al., in press). One consequence of this cultural obsession with female weight is that women of all age groups are more likely to view their bodies as *objects* of others' attention, and, on average, women evaluate their bodies more negatively than men (Cash & Henry, 1995; Feingold & Mazzella, 1998). By adulthood, women are more likely to habitually experience what researchers identify as *social physique anxiety*, which is anxiety about others observing or evaluating their bodies (Fredrickson et al., 1998). Spend a few minutes completing the Body Esteem Scale in Discovery Box 15-5.

Although women in North American culture generally experience less positive body esteem than men, evidence shows that minority women and lesbians feel less pressure to conform to the unrealistic standards of thinness in the larger culture than White heterosexual women feel (Franzoi & Chang, 2002; Jaramillo, 1999; Lakkis et al., 1999; Rucker & Cash, 1992). As a result, they are less concerned about dieting and weight loss (Mintz & Kashubeck, 1999). This healthier perspective appears to be partly due to a greater valuing of large body sizes in minority and lesbian cultures, but it also may be a by-product of a more general tendency to reject White and heterosexual cultural standards, respectively (Kite & Deaux, 1987; Thompson et al., 1996).

That Black heterosexual women appear to have greater body satisfaction than White heterosexual women does not mean they are unconcerned about weight issues. In general, they are still more dissatisfied with their bodies—particularly their weight—than heterosexual Black men (Harris, 1995; Pomerantz, 1979). Similar ambivalent feelings appear to describe lesbian body attitudes—interviews with young adult lesbians suggest they experience a conflict between mainstream and lesbian values about the importance of weight and overall physical appearance (Beren et al., 1997). These findings suggest that Black and lesbian cultural values are not enough to overcome the dominant White heterosexual cultural standard of female thinness.

No woman can be too slim. . . .

—Wallis Simpson, the Duchess of Windsor, 1896–1986

Besides being young, a desirable sex partner—especially a woman—should also be fat.

—Observations of the semi-nomadic Siriono Indians of Bolivia, 1946

DISCOVERY BOX 15-5

What Is Body Esteem?

A person's attitudes toward her or his body are referred to as *body esteem* (Rieves & Cash, 1996). A list of 35 body parts and body functions that make up the *Body Esteem Scale* (Franzoi & Shields, 1984) follows. Please read each item and indicate how you feel about this part or function of your own body, using the following response categories:

1 = Have strong negative feelings
2 = Have moderate negative feelings
3 = Have no feeling one way or the other
4 = Have moderate positive feelings
5 = Have strong positive feelings

____ 1. Body scent	____ 19. Arms
____ 2. Appetite	____ 20. Chest or breasts
____ 3. Nose	____ 21. Appearance of eyes
____ 4. Physical stamina	____ 22. Cheeks/cheekbones
____ 5. Reflexes	____ 23. Hips
____ 6. Lips	____ 24. Legs
____ 7. Muscular strength	____ 25. Figure or physique
____ 8. Waist	____ 26. Sex drive
____ 9. Energy level	____ 27. Feet coordination
____ 10. Thighs	____ 28. Sex organs
____ 11. Ears	____ 29. Appearance of stomach
____ 12. Biceps	____ 30. Health
____ 13. Chin	____ 31. Sex activities
____ 14. Body build	____ 32. Body hair
____ 15. Physical coordination	____ 33. Physical condition
____ 16. Buttocks	____ 34. Face
____ 17. Agility	____ 35. Weight
____ 18. Width of shoulders	

Dimensions of Female and Male Body Esteem

As you recall from chapter 10, section 10-2a, factor analysis is a statistical technique that allows researchers to identify clusters of variables that are related to—or *correlated* with—one another. In studying body esteem, researchers have asked many people to evaluate different aspects of their own bodies, such as these 35 body items. When these evaluations have been factor analyzed, the findings suggest that body esteem is not one "thing" but at least three different "things" (Franzoi & Shields, 1984). In other words, when people evaluate their bodies, they do so by evaluating different dimensions or aspects. These dimensions differ for women and men, meaning that the way in which they think about their bodies is different. For example, whereas women are more likely to think about their appetite, waist, and thighs in terms of *weight concern* (how their body looks), men are more likely to think about how these body items affect their *physical condition* (how their body moves).

The Body Esteem Scale identifies three different body esteem dimensions for both sexes. For women, the *Sexual Attractiveness* subscale measures attitudes toward aspects and functions of the body associated with facial attractiveness and sexuality (especially those that can be enhanced cosmetically), the *Weight Concern* subscale includes those body parts that can be altered by controlling functions associated with food intake, and the *Physical Condition* subscale measures attitudes toward stamina, agility, and strength. For men, the *Physical Attractiveness* subscale measures attitudes toward facial features and aspects of the physique that influence judgments of attractiveness, the *Upper Body Strength* subscale measures attitudes toward the upper body (especially those that can be enhanced through anaerobic exercise), and the *Physical Condition* subscale measures attitudes toward stamina, agility, and general body strength.

Scoring Instructions and Standards

To determine your score for each of the subscales for your sex, simply add up your responses for the items corresponding to each body esteem dimension. For example, for women, to determine self-judgments for the weight concern dimension of body esteem, add up the responses to the 10 items comprising this subscale. For men, the items of "physical coordination" and "figure or physique" are on both the upper body strength and the physical condition dimensions. The subscale items, plus the means and standard deviations for 964 college men and women (Franzoi & Shields, 1984), are listed below.

Women

Sexual Attractiveness: body scent, nose, lips, ears, chin, chest or breasts, appearance of eyes, cheeks/cheekbones, sex drive, sex organs, sex activities, body hair, face (Mean = 46.9, SD = 6.3)

Weight Concern: appetite, waist, thighs, body build, buttocks, hips, legs, figure or physique, appearance of stomach, weight (Mean = 29.9, SD = 8.2)

Physical Condition: physical stamina, reflexes, muscular strength, energy level, biceps, physical coordination, agility, health, physical condition (Mean = 33.3, SD = 5.7)

Men

Physical Attractiveness: nose, lips, ears, chin, buttocks, appearance of eyes, cheeks/cheekbones, hips, feet, sex organs, face (Mean = 39.1, SD = 5.7)

Upper Body Strength: muscular strength, biceps, body build, physical coordination, width of shoulders, arms, chest or breasts, figure or physique, sex drive (Mean = 34.0, SD = 6.1)

Physical Condition: appetite, physical stamina, reflexes, waist, energy level, thighs, physical coordination, agility, figure or physique, appearance of stomach, health, physical condition, weight (Mean = 50.2, SD = 7.7).

INFO-BIT: Fifty years ago, department-store mannequins had body shapes very similar to the average American woman. Today, mannequins are extremely thin, with an average hip circumference of 31 inches compared with the 37-inch average of young adult women. If these mannequins were real, their body fat would be so low that they would probably not menstruate (University of California, 1993). Most professional models and actresses have hardly more than half the 22 to 26 percent body fat of an average woman (Brownell, 1991).

What Are Eating Disorders?

Anorexia nervosa: An eating disorder in which a person weighs less than 85 percent of her or his expected weight, but still expresses an intense fear of gaining weight or becoming fat.

Bulimia: An eating disorder in which a person engages in recurrent episodes of binge eating followed by drastic measures to purge the body of the consumed calories.

As already noted, female body dissatisfaction is fairly common in North American culture (Cash & Henry, 1995). Sometimes this dissatisfaction is taken to such extremes that individuals develop *eating disorders* (Thompson, 1996). One eating disorder, **anorexia nervosa,** is diagnosed when a person weighs less than 85 percent of her or his expected weight but still expresses an intense fear of gaining weight or becoming fat (American Psychiatric Association, 1994). Another related eating disorder is **bulimia,** which involves recurrent episodes of binge eating—periods of intense, out-of-control eating—followed by drastic measures to compensate for bingeing, such as vomiting, use of laxatives, or excessive exercising (American Psychiatric Association, 1994). A person who is anorexic may also be bulimic. Both eating disorders occur 10 times more frequently among women than men, with about 0.5 to 1.0 percent of women in late adolescence and early adulthood being anorexic and 1 to 3 percent being bulimic (American Psychiatric Association, 1994). Because the body is being systematically starved, both disorders pose severe health risks, including death, if left untreated.

The fact that anorexia nervosa and bulimia occur mostly in women and mostly in weight-conscious cultures leads most psychologists to suspect that sociocultural factors significantly shape these disorders. Anorexia always begins as an attempt to lose weight, and the self-induced vomiting typical of bulimia almost always occurs after a person fails to follow the eating restrictions of a weight-loss diet. Further, adolescent girls who suffer from eating disorders tend to have mothers who obsess about their own weight and about their daughters' weight and appearance (Pike & Rodin, 1991).

In addition to sociocultural factors, a growing body of evidence suggests possible genetic and motivational influences. For example, identical twins are much more likely to share the disorder than fraternal twins, and evidence indicates that people with these disorders may have abnormally high levels of certain neurotransmitters that increase susceptibility to anxiety, depression, and obsessive-compulsive disorder (Kaye et al., 2000; Klump et al., 2001; Strober, 1992). The possible association of obsessive-compulsive disorder with eating disorders suggests to some psychologists that the desire to achieve *psychological control* over one's life may influence disordered eating (Bruch, 1973, 1982). That is, for some individuals suffering from eating disorders, extreme dieting may represent an attempt to control one important factor in life—weight—and this control becomes a source of power and pride. Related to this motivational explanation is the finding that eating disorders are often associated with a history of sexual, physical, or emotional abuse (Ackard & Neumarck-Sztainer, 2001; Silverman et al., 2001). Here again, disordered eating may represent abuse victims' attempts to reassert control over their own bodies and lives.

In the final analysis, what may be most important in understanding eating disorders is that they are likely determined by multiple factors (Cash, 1996; Heinberg, 1996). Successful treatment of these disorders, therefore, should involve multiple interventions, including appropriate medical attention, family therapy, individual therapy, and behavioral training (DeAngelis, 2002; Geller, 2002; Goldner & Birmingham, 1994).

15-3c Aerobic Exercise Can Increase Both Physical and Mental Health

Aerobic exercise: Sustained exercise that increases heart and lung fitness.

Thus far we have focused on harmful behaviors. What can you do to reduce the likelihood of illness while simultaneously improving your psychological health? **Aerobic exercise,** which is sustained exercise that increases heart and lung fitness, not only has a positive effect on physical health, it may also provide similar benefits to mental health (Thayer, 2001).

The image of aerobic exercise tends to be rows of sweaty people jazzercising or jogging. Yet, any activity that increases heart rate into a certain range (defined by your age and maximum possible heart rate) for at least 12 to 20 minutes fits this definition. Thus, vigorous walking, cross-country skiing, in-line skating, dancing, or even strenuous yard work all qualify as aerobic exercise. Accumulating 30 minutes of aerobic exercise three times per week has been recommended for reducing risk for chronic disease and enhancing quality of life (Pate et al., 1995). Consistent with this recommendation, physiological studies indicate that such exercise strengthens the heart, lowers blood pressure, and facilitates the metabolism of fats and carbohydrates (Simon, 1991). Further, several studies find that adults who exercise regularly live longer than those who are less active (Blair et al., 1989; Paffenbarger et al., 1986).

Does exercise also improve mental health? Based on the results from over 100 studies, most mental health experts believe that exercise can be effective in reducing tension and eliminating depressed moods (Thayer et al., 1994; van Doornen et al., 1988). For example, in one representative study, 156 adults with major depression were randomly assigned to either four months of aerobic exercise, treatment with an antidepressant medication, or a combination of both exercise and medication (Babyak et al., 2000). Although a similar number of patients in each group showed mood improvements in the first 4 months, only those in the exercise groups maintained their improvement after 10 months. One possible reason for this beneficial effect is that aerobic exercise heightens the body's supply of mood-enhancing neurotransmitters such as norepinephrine, serotonin, and the endorphins (Jacobs, 1994; Salmon, 2001). It is also possible that these mood benefits are partly a side effect of the muscular relaxation and sounder sleep that often follows aerobic exercise (Brannon & Feist, 2000).

Despite the benefits of regular exercise, it is possible to overdue a good thing. Some athletes *overtrain* to the point where they begin to experience negative effects such as fatigue and depression (O'Connor, 1997). Other people can become obsessed with exercising, feeling anxious and uncomfortable if unable to engage in the activity. Such individuals who feel compelled to exercise often have other unhealthy concerns about weight control and body image (Slay et al., 1998).

15-3d Relaxation Training Is Effective in Reducing Stress and Improving Health

Because stress is associated with physiological arousal, many psychologists recommend relaxation training as an effective stress antidote. Two effective relaxation techniques are meditation and hypnosis, which were previously discussed in chapter 6, sections 6-3b and 6-3c. However, the most basic relaxation technique is **progressive relaxation,** which was developed in the 1920s by Edmund Jacobson (1924). Jacobson started with the observation that it is not possible to be physiologically tense and relaxed at the same time. Although his original technique often required months of training, later modifications by Herbert Benson made progressive relaxation far simpler (Benson, 1975; Benson & Stuart, 1992). Once people develop some skill with this technique, they can use it to calm themselves down anywhere and anytime (Barlow & Rapee, 1991; Bernstein et al., 2000).

> **Progressive relaxation:** A stress-reducing technique that involves the successive tensing and relaxing of each of the major muscle groups of the body.

Progressive relaxation techniques have been used to help heart attack patients manage their stress. For instance, in one study, survivors of a first heart attack were randomly assigned to one of two experimental conditions (Friedman & Ulmer, 1984). In the *medical advice* condition, patients received medical advice on drugs, exercise, work, and diet, whereas in the *relaxation* condition they were also taught how to relax. Three years after this intervention, the relaxation patients had suffered only half as many repeat heart attacks as those who had only received the standard medical advice. Research suggests that one physiological benefit of relaxation training is that it may improve the effectiveness of the immune response (Hewson-Bower & Drummond, 1996; Lowe et al., 2001). In

TABLE 15-3

Progressive Relaxation Instructions

1. First, sit or lie comfortably with eyes shut, and your arms and legs bent at a comfortable angle. Take a deep breath, hold it, and exhale slowly. Repeat several times, saying the word "relax" to yourself with each exhale. Step by step, begin tensing different muscle groups one at a time—holding the tension for 5 seconds, concentrating on how that feels, followed by slowly releasing the tension.
2. Start with your arms by clenching your fists while tensing the muscles in your upper arms. Hold. Slowly release. Inhale and exhale slowly. Maintain a passive attitude and permit relaxation to occur at its own pace. When distracting thoughts occur, do not dwell on them, but simply return to repeating "relax" to yourself.
3. Next, tense the thigh and calf muscles in your legs by straightening your legs and pointing your toes downward. Hold. Slowly release. Inhale and exhale slowly.
4. Tense your stomach muscles and at the same time press your palms together over your chest in order to tighten your chest muscles. Hold. Slowly release. Inhale and exhale slowly.
5. Arch your back and pull your shoulders back (not too far) to tense these muscles. Hold. Slowly release. Inhale and exhale slowly.
6. Tense your jaw and neck muscles by drawing the corners of your mouth back. You may also want to bend your neck first to one side then the other. Hold. Slowly release. Inhale and exhale slowly.
7. Tense your forehead by pulling your eyebrows in together, wrinkling your brow. Hold. Slowly release. Inhale and exhale slowly.
8. Continue to concentrate on your breathing, breathing comfortably into your abdomen (not your chest). Think "relax" with each exhale. Continue this exercise for 10 to 20 minutes. You may open your eyes to check the time, but do not use an alarm. When finished, sit or lie quietly for a few minutes, first with your eyes closed and later with your eyes opened. With practice, you can relax very quickly with minimal effort. Practice this technique once or twice daily but not within two hours after eating a meal because digestion can interfere with the relaxation response.

Source: Adapted from THE RELAXATION RESPONSE by Herbert Benson, MD, © 1975. Used with permission of the author.

Journey of Discovery Question

Based on your readings, what tactics can you employ to manage your stress and reduce stress-related ailments?

---

one such experiment, blood samples were taken from college students one month prior to midterm exams and again on the day of the exams (Kiecolt-Glaser et al., 1985). Half of the students had been trained in progressive relaxation techniques, while the other half received no training. The students who received the relaxation training exhibited much less of a decrease in natural killer cell activity—which, as you recall, fight viruses and tumors—between the first and second measurements. Table 15-3 describes Benson's progressive relaxation procedure.

SECTION SUMMARY

- Risky sexual behaviors jeopardize overall health and well-being.
- Obesity is related to numerous chronic health conditions.
- Body dissatisfaction can lead to eating disorders.
- Aerobic exercise and progressive relaxation techniques offer many positive influences on health and well-being.

SUGGESTED WEBSITES

Note: These websites were functional when we went to press. Please access the online text for the most up-to-date URLs.

Stress by Jim's Big Ego

http://bigego.com/moodyfood/stress2000.html

For an entertaining, musical version of stress, visit this site by the Boston, Massachusetts, band, Jim's Big Ego. (A fast Internet connection is recommended.)

Something Fishy

http://www.something-fishy.com/

This website focuses on eating disorders, including anorexia, bulimia, overeating, compulsive eating, binge eating, and more, with links to the Eating Disorder FAQ, and poems and stories from others suffering from bulimia and anorexia. The site is updated frequently.

The Psych.Com

http://www.thepsych.com/

This site has links and resources related to stress, stress reduction, addictions, eating disorders, and other areas of interest.

Body Mass Index

http://www.halls.md/body-mass-index/bmi.htm

The Body Mass Index allows you to calculate your body mass index and compare yourself to other women and men of the same height and age.

PSYCHOLOGICAL APPLICATIONS
Who Is Happy and Why?

In 1776, Thomas Jefferson's penning of the Declaration of Independence was a bold assertion that individuals have the inalienable rights of life, liberty, and "the pursuit of happiness." Well over 200 years after this declaration, researchers who promote the scientific study of positive psychology have begun investigating **happiness,** which is often defined as a predominance of positive over negative emotions, and satisfaction with life as a whole (Diener, 1984; Fredrickson, 2001). Initial findings suggest that happier people tend to have high self-esteem, are optimistic and outgoing, physically healthy, and have close friendships or satisfying marriages (Diener & Lucas, 1999, 2000; Myers, 1993).

In studying happiness, psychologists have sought to determine what affects both our temporary feelings of happiness and our long-term life satisfaction. Not surprisingly, our moods brighten when we succeed at daily tasks, when others compliment or praise us, and when we feel healthy, while our moods darken when we fall short of goals, are criticized by others, or feel sick (Miley, 1999). We also tend to be happier on days associated with weekend pleasures, such as Fridays and Saturdays, rather than those associated with work, such as Mondays and Tuesdays (Larsen & Kasimatis, 1990). On average, we experience our most positive moods during the middle of the day (noon to 6 P.M.) and our most negative moods in the early morning and late evening (Watson et al., 1999). These mood fluctuations coincide with fluctuations in our circadian rhythms (see chapter 6, section 6-2a): We are happiest when at our highest levels of physiological alertness.

How is happiness affected by dramatic events? Although the death of a loved one or being the victim of a serious accident, illness, or crime can cause extreme emotional conflict, we usually recover our previous levels of day-to-day happiness within a year or two (Gerhart et al., 1994; Gilbert et al., 1998). This is also the case for dramatically positive events. After the euphoria of winning a state lottery wears off, people usually discover that their overall happiness is unchanged (Brickman et al., 1978).

Research on the happiness of lottery winners raises the following question that many people have asked over the years: Can you buy happiness? As you can see in figure 15-4, people in richer countries are happier than people in poorer countries (Myers & Diener, 1995). Yet increases in national wealth within developed nations have not, over recent decades, been associated with increases in happiness (Ryan & Deci, 2001). Further, within any given country, the happiness differences between wealthy and middle-income people are modest (Diener et al., 1999). Taken together, this research suggests that, for the most part, money only matters in increasing happiness if people do not have enough monetary resources to cover the basic needs of food, safety, and shelter (Diener et al., 1993; Niemi et al., 1989). Thus, while having adequate resources to be nourished and safe is essential for happiness, once you meet your basic needs, increasing your wealth does not make you appreciably happier.

One interesting research finding regarding wealth and happiness is that people who strongly desire wealth after satisfying their basic needs tend to be less happy than the average person (Campbell, 1981; Kasser & Ryan, 1996). This result has been confirmed in developed countries such as the United States and Germany and in less developed countries such as India and Russia (Ryan et al., 1999; Schmuck et al., 2000). Why might this be the case? One possibility is that placing too much importance on material possessions—which do not in themselves satisfy basic psychological needs—takes time and energy away from activities that do satisfy those needs. Thus, overall happiness will be lowered when people pursue their love of money rather than romantic, friendship, or familial love. In addition, people who have a high desire to accumulate wealth tend to lose their sense of personal autonomy: Their

> ***INFO-BIT:*** When researchers compared very happy people with average and very unhappy people, they found that the very happy were more extraverted, more agreeable, less neurotic, and had stronger romantic and social relationships (Diener & Seligman, 2002).

FIGURE 15-4
Gross National Product and Happiness

Does money make you happy? In a 24-nation study, happiness was strongly correlated with gross national product, which is a measure of national prosperity (Myers & Diener, 1995). Additional research suggests that money only matters in increasing happiness if people do not have enough monetary resources to cover their basic needs. After meeting basic needs, those who still strongly desire wealth tend to be relatively unhappy. So does money make you happy?

Source: From "Who Is Happy?" by D. Myers and E. Diener in PSYCHOLOGICAL SCIENCE, 6, 1995, pp. 10–19. Reprinted by permission of Blackwell Publishing Ltd.

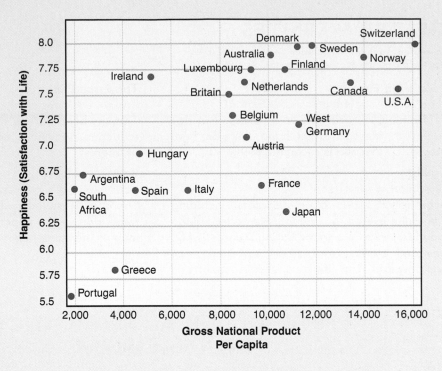

pursuit of wealth makes them feel controlled by external circumstances (Carver & Baird, 1998).

Another possible explanation for why wealth is not a better predictor of happiness—and also why dramatic life events don't permanently alter levels of day-to-day happiness—is that happiness is a fairly stable trait that is substantially determined by our biology. That is, we may each have a biologically determined baseline level of happiness toward which we gravitate (DeNeve, 1999). For example, in a study of more than 2,000 identical and fraternal twins, David Lykken and Auke Tellegen (1996) analyzed the extent to which identical twins and fraternal twins exhibited similar levels of happiness. The twins' happiness levels were measured by self-report questionnaires that asked them to respond to statements such as, "Taking the good with the bad, how happy and contented are you on the average now, compared with other people?" When twins' happiness scores were correlated, levels of happiness were much more strongly correlated (positively) for the identical twins than for the fraternal twins. Overall, it appears that happiness is more rooted in genetics than in recent life experiences.

Another predictor of happiness is strength of religious affiliation. Numerous studies indicate that as strength of religious convictions and frequency of worship rise, life satisfaction and happiness also tend to increase, especially for the elderly (Clark et al., 1999; Myers & Diener, 1995). The positive correlation between religion and happiness may be explained in a variety of ways. First, religious faith can serve as a buffer from life's stressors, especially for life-and-death issues, providing a sense of optimism that elevates happiness (Argyle, 2000). Active participation in one's religion also offers opportunities for social support and companionship and may provide a stronger source of hope and optimism that things

will turn out "all right." Perhaps because shared rituals create greater intimacy, church groups are more cohesive and provide stronger social support than most other groups (Argyle, 2000). Finally, stronger religious faith may help steer people away from harmful behaviors that cause unhappiness, such as drug and alcohol abuse (Batson et al., 1993).

Finally, some research suggests that people in certain parts of the world are happier than people in other parts. That is, numerous studies indicate that people in individualist cultures report greater levels of happiness than people from cultures with more collectivist orientations (Myers & Diener, 1995). Although some researchers have speculated that these differences are due to quality of life factors, others point out that Japan, an economically powerful collectivist country, reports much lower happiness levels than Ireland, an individualist country with a much lower gross national product (Inglehart, 1990). Other researchers speculate that individualists may have been raised to better identify personal, positive feelings that do not rely on the group's well-being (Diener & Diener, 1995). Still others contend that this difference is simply due to the fact that happiness measures have been operationally defined according to individualist standards, such as self-esteem and perceived control over one's life (Lu et al., 2001). Luo Lu and his colleagues (in press) have found that in collectivist cultures happiness is related more to collectivist values, such as harmony, social integration, and human heartedness, which is less likely the case in cultures that are individualist. So which types of cultures are happier? The answer may well depend on how the questions are asked.

Happiness: A predominance of positive over negative affect (emotion), and satisfaction with life as a whole.

KEY TERMS

aerobic exercise (p. 476)
anorexia nervosa (p. 476)
behavioral medicine (p. 454)
biopsychosocial model (p. 454)
bulimia (p. 476)
emotion-focused coping (p. 458)
general adaptation syndrome (GAS) (p. 456)
happiness (p. 480)

health psychologists (p. 454)
immune system (p. 460)
obesity (p. 469)
optimistic explanatory style (p. 464)
pessimistic explanatory style (p. 464)
positive psychology (p. 465)
problem-focused coping (p. 458)
progressive relaxation (p. 477)

psychophysiological disorders (p. 459)
social support (p. 465)
stress (p. 454)
stressors (p. 454)
Type A behavior pattern (p. 463)
Type B behavior pattern (p. 463)

REVIEW QUESTIONS

1. Stressors are events that have been associated with all of the following *except*
   a.   threats to our equilibrium.
   b.   positive events such as childbirth.
   c.   major cataclysmic events, such as the September 11, 2001, terrorist attacks.
   d.   strengthening our ability to maintain equilibrium over time.
   e.   daily hassles.

2. Selye's general adaptation syndrome describes
   a.   the fight-or-flight response.
   b.   emotional responses to stress.
   c.   a three-stage physical reaction to stress.
   d.   the reduction in cortisol that occurs in response to stress.
   e.   the body's ability to successfully adapt to stress over time.

3. The biopsychosocial perspective
   a.   was favored by medical researchers in the 1940s.
   b.   fails to consider the role of cognitive appraisal in stress.
   c.   was the foundation of Selye's GAS.
   d.   was discounted by research showing that psychological awareness of stressors is a necessary component in the stress response.
   e.   assumes that stress-related illness is caused by a complex interaction of factors.

4. Research on stress responses has shown that cognitive appraisal of stressful events
   a.   is an unconscious decision-making process.
   b.   involves both primary and secondary appraisal processes.
   c.   is universal and is not affected by individuals' feelings of competence.
   d.   occurs after having determined that a threat exists.
   e.   results in taking appropriate action in threatening or stressful situations.

5. The success of a particular coping strategy depends on
   a.   the stressor's controllability.
   b.   using a problem-focused strategy rather than an emotion-focused strategy.
   c.   taking an active approach to removing the source of the threat.
   d.   controlling one's emotional response first, followed by controlling one's cognitive response.
   e.   its consistency; that is, you should choose one strategy and seek to perfect it.

6. Research on stress-related disease has indicated all of the following *except*
   a.   stress can reduce the efficiency of the immune system.
   b.   strong emotional distress can cause sudden death from heart attacks.
   c.   suppression of the immune system during stress makes your response less efficient.
   d.   anger-inducing stressors may contribute to ischemia.
   e.   both vulnerability and stress are required components of the diathesis-stress model of illness.

7. Perceived controllability over a stressor may influence an individual's response
   a.   less than predictability, especially with intense, long-lasting stressors.
   b.   by leading to procrastination, which is beneficial in the long-term.
   c.   very little when the individual is an elderly nursing home patient.
   d.   through learned helplessness, in which you expect or believe you have no control, and thus fail to act to reduce the threat.
   e.   by discouraging procrastination, a relatively effective problem-focused coping strategy.

8. Research on stress and personality has found that
   a.   optimistic explanatory styles are detrimental because they lead to denial of real threats.
   b.   mistrust of others is more harmful to one's health than anger.
   c.   there is no difference in functioning between optimists' and pessimists' immune systems.
   d.   pessimists explain uncontrollable negative events as due to external factors and positive events as due to internal factors.
   e.   Type A behavior patterns are toxic because they often include a component of cynical hostility.

9. Having a strong base of social support has been associated with all of the following *except*
   a.   beneficial effects on self-esteem related to being taken care of by others.
   b.   a stronger immune response to stress.
   c.   gaining information concerning how to understand and emotionally respond to stressors.
   d.   reduced control over the stressor due to increased dependence on others.
   e.   benefits related to expressing our feelings.

10. Research on condom use education has found that
   a. the fear and disease prevention approach has been effective in reducing the spread of HIV.
   b. enhancing individuals' awareness of sexual risks is associated with a reduction of HIV and AIDS.
   c. people often associate condom use with disease, which reduces motivation to use condoms.
   d. focusing on broad interventions across multiple areas of an individual's life has not been helpful in reducing HIV/AIDS.
   e. assertiveness training is not helpful in promoting safer sex.

11. According to the CDC and obesity research, obesity
   a. is indicated by a body mass index greater than 25.
   b. is not associated with arthritis.
   c. is defined as weighing more than 174 pounds (women) and 207 pounds (men).
   d. is the leading cause of death in western society.
   e. has become an epidemic in the United States.

12. Eating disorders such as anorexia nervosa and bulimia
   a. occur three times more often in women than men.
   b. both involve the body being systematically starved.
   c. are associated more with low self-esteem than with sociocultural factors.
   d. represent learned behaviors; there is no evidence to suggest a genetic component.
   e. are completely separate disorders; they never occur together in the same individual.

13. Physiological methods of decreasing stress
   a. are less effective than relaxation, meditation, or hypnosis.
   b. are effective only if they contain an aerobic exercise component.
   c. include relaxation, associated with a huge decrease in natural killer cell activity.
   d. such as moderate aerobic exercise and progressive relaxation are highly effective.
   e. do not work as well as standard medical advice in reducing heart attacks.

14. Research on positive psychology and happiness has found that
   a. the pursuit of wealth may decrease one's sense of autonomy.
   b. happiness is a highly unstable characteristic, substantially determined by our environment.
   c. dramatic life events permanently alter one's characteristic level of happiness.
   d. people in collectivist cultures report greater levels of happiness than those in individualistic cultures.
   e. happiness is based on biological factors; thus, faith and optimism do not generate greater levels of happiness.

15. In general, stress-related research has found all of the following *except*
   a. the negative effects of stress are cumulative.
   b. men and women generally have different responses to stress.
   c. individuals with low self-esteem are likely to use a problem-focused coping strategy.
   d. focusing on the controllable aspects of uncontrollable situations such as caregiving helps reduce stress.
   e. communication between the immune system and the brain plays a major role in the response to stressful events.

Social Behavior

Chapter Outline

Think back to the first few class sessions in your psychology course. What characteristics were most important in shaping your first impressions of fellow students? If you are like most people, your impressions early in the semester emphasized their behavior and appearance (for example, "has her tongue pierced," "laughs a lot") rather than personality traits (for example, kind, intelligent). In other words, in forming impressions, you initially relied upon people's more noticeable and superficial personal qualities (Park, 1986). Have the important characteristics changed over time? Again, if you are like most people, as you became better acquainted you probably judged fellow students more in terms of their personalities.

Whom in your class have you grown to like? I would be willing to wager that these "likable" students either sit near you in class, have similar interests as you, or are physically attractive. Do certain students exert greater influence in class than others? What determines these differences in social power?

Insights into all these questions can be found in the discipline of **social psychology,** which is the scientific study of how people's thoughts, feelings, and behavior are influenced by others. Perhaps more than any other leg of this discovery journey in psychology, here you can seek answers to a number of questions that you probably have pondered on your own personal journey of discovery. First, you will examine how we judge our social world (social perception). Second, you will study how we develop attitudes toward people and events. Third, you will analyze how we are shaped by those around us (social influence). Fourth, you will learn about the factors that either strengthen or weaken our antisocial and prosocial behavior (aggression and helping). And finally, you will be introduced to some of the scientific insights of interpersonal attraction and romantic love. Let's begin.

Social psychology: The scientific discipline that attempts to understand and explain how the thoughts, feelings, and behavior of individuals are influenced by others.

16-1 SOCIAL PERCEPTION

Social perception (also known as social cognition): The way we seek to know and understand other persons and events.

The way we seek to understand other people and events is known as **social perception,** which can be roughly classified into two areas: impression formation and attribution. In this section, you will examine both of these social perception processes.

16-1a The First Step in Impression Formation Is Categorizing People into Groups

Imagine that you are walking down a dark deserted city street at night when suddenly you notice a person walking toward you, three blocks ahead. At a distance of one block, you can tell that this person is a man. In less than a minute, your paths will cross. Are you in danger?

Impression formation: The process of integrating various sources of information about a person into an overall judgment.

Every day, you judge people based on very little information. How do you "size up" others during initial encounters? As in the hypothetical situation of the dark street, the process of gathering information about others can be of the most vital importance to your health and safety. **Impression formation** is the process by which you combine various sources of information about a person into an overall judgment. It is like developing a theory of a person and then using this theory as a guideline in your actions toward her or him.

Labels are devices for saving talkative persons the trouble of thinking.
—John Morley, English statesman and author, 1838–1923

In our hypothetical nighttime dilemma, the way you respond to the person approaching you will be determined by how you categorize him (Clement & Krueger, 2002). As previously discussed in chapter 9, section 9-2a, human beings are categorizing creatures. That is, we identify objects— including other people—according to features that distinguish them from other objects (Hampson, 1988; Taylor, 1981). In social categorization, physical features such as race, sex, age, and attractiveness are the most common ways to classify people, especially during first encounters (Park, 1986). Because they are used so often, labeling others by these superficial physical features becomes automatic, often occurring without conscious thought or effort (Brewer, 1988; Fiske & Neuberg, 1990).

16-1b Categorizing People into Groups Can Lead to Stereotyping

Not only do we group people into different categories, but we also develop beliefs about them. These social beliefs, which are often learned from others, are stereotypes (Hilton & Hippel, 1996; Vonk & Knippenberg, 1995). **Stereotypes** are fixed ways of thinking about people that put them into categories and don't allow for individual variation. In a very real sense, stereotypes are "shortcuts to thinking" that provide us with information about individuals we do not personally know (Dijker & Koomen, 1996; Macrae et al., 1994). Returning to our nighttime example, your stereotypical beliefs about encountering a strange man on a dark, deserted city street would probably result in greater apprehension than if the stranger were a woman or a child.

Stereotypes: Fixed ways of thinking about people that puts them into categories and doesn't allow for individual variation.

Although stereotyping people can speed up our social judgments, these cognitive shortcuts also can inhibit our thinking. For example, in one study, Galen Bodenhausen (1988) asked mostly white college students to act as mock jurors in a court case. Some students were told the defendant was named Carlos Ramirez, and others were told that his name was Robert Johnson. Half of the students in each of these experimental conditions were given information about the case before learning the defendant's name, whereas the other half were given the information afterward. Bodenhausen predicted that hearing the Hispanic-sounding name "Carlos Ramirez" before receiving the evidence would activate students' ethnic stereotypes and that this activation would bias their processing of the information. In other words, instead of "weighing the facts," these students were expected to pay more attention to stereotype-consistent information than to stereotype-inconsistent information. This is exactly what Bodenhausen found. The imaginary Carlos Ramirez was found guilty more often than the imaginary Robert Johnson only when students learned the name before receiving the evidence. Bodenhausen also found that stereotypes influence information processing by increasing the amount of attention and rehearsal to stereotype-consistent information.

This study, along with others (Dijksterhuis & Knippenberg, 1996), suggests that one of the important reasons stereotyping often results in fast social judgments is that filtering social perceptions through a stereotype causes us to ignore information that is relevant but inconsistent with the stereotype. Thus, although stereotyping may often be helpful when we need to make quick decisions, the cost appears to be that we may also often make faulty judgments about whomever we stereotype (Nelson et al., 1996).

INFO-BIT: When stereotypes are evoked from memory, they can lead to the creation of false memories consistent with the stereotypes (Lenton et al., 2001). Thus, besides inhibiting thinking, stereotypes can also promote thinking that leads to false judgments.

> **INFO-BIT:** The physical attractiveness stereotype also occurs in collectivist cultures, but its content is shaped by somewhat different cultural values (Chen et al., 1997). For example, Ladd Wheeler and Youngmee Kim (1997) found that, as in individualist cultures, physically attractive Koreans are perceived to be more sexually warm, mentally healthy, intelligent, and socially skilled than unattractive Koreans. However, consistent with the greater emphasis on harmonious relationships in collectivist cultures, physically attractive Koreans are also assumed to have higher integrity and to be more concerned for others than those who are physically unattractive.

16-1c There Is a Physical Attractiveness Stereotype

As mentioned earlier, when we first meet someone, their physical appearance is generally the first thing we notice, especially if they somehow look different from the average person (McArthur, 1982; Roberts & Herman, 1986). Despite the frequently quoted folk saying that "You can't judge a book by its cover," we tend to ignore the wisdom contained within this phrase. Instead, research indicates that we perceive physically attractive people as being more sociable, dominant, sexually attractive, mentally healthy, intelligent, and socially skilled than those who are unattractive (Dion et al., 1972; Feingold, 1992; Jackson et al., 1995). This **physical attractiveness stereotype** is not reserved solely for adults but is found in all age groups (Karraker & Stern, 1990; Vaughn & Langlois, 1983). As a species, we seem to be drawn to physically attractive people, like bees to honey (Buss, 1987; Davis, 1990). This is especially true for males.

Within a given culture and during a given time period, people generally agree about what defines physical attractiveness. What is beautiful also often conforms to the current standards of the dominant social group. For example, fine facial features and light skin have been standards for physical attractiveness in North American culture for many generations, and ethnic minority groups have generally mirrored these larger cultural preferences (Bond & Cash, 1992; Neal & Wilson, 1989).

What shapes beauty standards besides dominant cultural values? Evolutionary theorists believe that what is valued as desirable and attractive in men and women is that which increases their ability to produce offspring (Buss, 1988; Kenrick & Trost, 1989). Researchers have identified two beauty standards that may be related to reproductive fitness: Weight influences perceptions of female attractiveness, and facial features influence both sexes, but in different ways (see Discovery Box 16-1).

Physical attractiveness stereotype: The belief that physically attractive individuals possess socially desirable personality traits and lead happier, more fulfilling lives than less attractive persons.

16-1d Stereotyping Can Cause Prejudice and Discrimination

The physical attractiveness stereotype illustrates how we treat people differently based on how closely their physical appearance matches beauty standards. When the stereotypes associated with a particular group of people—such as the physically unattractive—are negative and condescending, they can form the basis for prejudice and discrimination. **Prejudice** is a negative attitude directed toward people because they are members of a specific social group. In other words, people are disliked or hated simply because they are members of the stigmatized group. Although prejudice is an attitude of aversion, **discrimination** is a negative action toward members of stigmatized groups.

Discrimination can be manifested in many ways (Brewer & Brown, 1998; Hebl et al., 2002). Mild forms may simply involve an avoidance of those toward whom we hold prejudicial attitudes. As its intensity heightens, however, discrimination may produce actions resulting in violence and death (Hepworth & West, 1988).

Prejudice: A negative attitude directed toward people because they are members of a specific social group.

Discrimination: A negative action toward members of a specific social group.

Why Do Stereotypes Persist?

Have you ever described people of the other sex as being all alike regarding certain negative characteristics? If you have, this gender stereotype was held despite the fact that you proba-

DISCOVERY   *BOX 16-1*

Are There Universal Beauty Standards?

Regarding weight, Judith Anderson and her colleagues' (1992) study of 54 cultures found that female standards of beauty partly vary as a function of the reliability of the food supply. Not only were heavy women strongly favored in cultures where the availability of food was highly unpredictable (71 percent preference), but across all cultures, heavy women were preferred to slender women by a margin of two to one. The researchers believe that this preference for heavy women has fostered the survival of our species because heavy women carry a built-in food supply, making it more likely that they not only would survive famines but also would remain fertile and produce offspring.

The findings from this study suggest that female body "heftiness" may have once been a universal standard of beauty. Traces of this universal standard can still be observed today in societies where food is not abundant. Yet, in our own culture, this evolutionary based beauty standard no longer has as much influence, especially among White Americans (Cogan et al., 1996). This change in perceptions of weight among well-fed people is another example of how changes in a group's relationship with their environment produce changes in their cultural beliefs that override long-held patterns of behavior.

Although female heftiness is no longer a universal standard of beauty, further cross-cultural research suggests that there may be universal standards of facial attractiveness (Zebrowitz & Rhodes, 2002). Among heterosexuals, women tend to be judged more attractive when they have youthful or immature facial features (large eyes, a small nose, and large pupils), whereas male attractiveness is increased with mature facial characteristics related to social dominance (square jaw, thick eyebrows, small eyes, and thin lips).

Due to women's shorter reproductive time span relative to men's, evolutionary theorists contend that men have evolved to perceive women who look young as being more desirable (that is, more physically attractive), because youth implies high reproductive potential (Alley & Cunningham, 1991; Cunningham et al., 2002). Using this same logic, evolutionary theorists also contend that heterosexual women will not be as interested in youthful characteristics in men, but instead will favor male traits indicating an ability to provide resources for them and their offspring. Thus, instead of youth being valued, when women judge male attractiveness, they should place more importance on status, ambition, and other signs of social dominance (Buss, 1989, 1990).

Interestingly, a somewhat similar attractiveness pattern has been observed in homosexual relationships (Cunningham et al., 1995). First, as with heterosexual men, gay men place more importance on "good looks" than do lesbians. Second, while lesbians do not appear to have a preference for immature- or dominant-looking faces in potential partners, gay men are similar to heterosexual men in being attracted to immature faces. Combined with the attractiveness preferences of heterosexuals, this research suggests that what we consider physically attractive is a result of the effects of both evolution and culture.

If we accept and acquiesce in the face of discrimination, we accept the responsibility ourselves and allow those responsible to salve their conscience by believing that they have our acceptance and concurrence. . . . We should, therefore, protest openly everything . . . that smacks of discrimination.

—Mary McLeod Bethune, U.S. educator and civil rights activist, 1875–1955

bly had friends and loved ones of the other sex whom you didn't categorize in this manner. Why didn't these friends and lovers automatically serve as a catalyst to alter your stereotype?

One likely explanation for why global stereotypes often resist such disconfirming evidence is that they consist of a number of more limited stereotype subcategories (Devine & Baker, 1991; Hewstone et al., 1994). These subcategories give us a place to categorize those individuals whose personal characteristics don't fit the global stereotype (Lambert, 1995). For example, Kay Deaux and her colleagues (1985) found that American college students distinguish at least five different subcategories of women: housewives, career women, athletes, feminists, and sex objects. When a man with strong gender stereotypes meets and learns to respect a woman who does not fit his stereotype, he may retain his prior gender beliefs by concluding that this woman is "different" from other women. Instead of revising his global stereotype of women, the man merely creates a new subcategory for this woman. Although subcategories often are more flattering and desirable than many global stereotypes, their very creation allows us to retain more rigid and unflattering views of the social group in question, which can form the basis for discrimination (Kunda & Oleson, 1995).

Can We Control Our Prejudicial Attitudes?

The research discussed thus far suggests that stereotyping and prejudice are difficult to change. Yet, change can and does occur for those of us who want to reduce our prejudicial responding. For example, imagine that Virginia, a young White woman, has grown up being taught that Black people are intellectually inferior to Whites and has developed prejudicial views based on this upbringing. However, during the course of her life, Virginia has also been exposed to a number of people who do not fit this racial stereotype. Because of these experiences, she may begin to adopt a more accepting view of Blacks. Although Virginia no longer accepts this negative racial stereotype, she has not eliminated it from her memory. Quite the contrary. During her relearning process, this stereotype may well be more frequently activated from memory than her newly adopted beliefs (Devine, 1989). In a very real sense, for a person like Virginia who wants to be less prejudiced, censoring the negative stereotype and guarding against prejudicial thinking takes conscious and deliberate attention—like breaking a bad habit.

Take a look at figure 16-1, which outlines how self-awareness and self-regulation may play a role in reducing prejudiced responses. Whenever Virginia encounters a Black person, the racial stereotype is likely to be involuntarily activated. If she does not consciously monitor her thoughts, she may automatically slip back into acting as though Blacks were intellectually inferior (a discrepant response). Becoming aware of this discrepancy in her actions, Virginia will feel guilty. In turn, this guilt will motivate her to heighten her self-awareness and search her memory for the situations that trigger these prejudiced responses (Monteith et al., 1993; Zuwerink et al., 1996). Through such attentiveness, Virginia will slowly be able to monitor and control her prejudicial responding (Monteith, 1993; Monteith et al., 1998).

The lesson to be learned here is that you can avoid prejudiced responding if low-prejudiced standards are central to your self-concept and you bring these standards to mind before acting (Macrae et al., 1998; Monteith, 1996). Thus, although automatic stereotype activation makes nonprejudiced responding difficult, you can inhibit such intolerance by consciously and carefully paying attention to what you are thinking. The crucial factor here is the strength of your motivation: How committed are you to thinking and acting in a nonprejudiced manner?

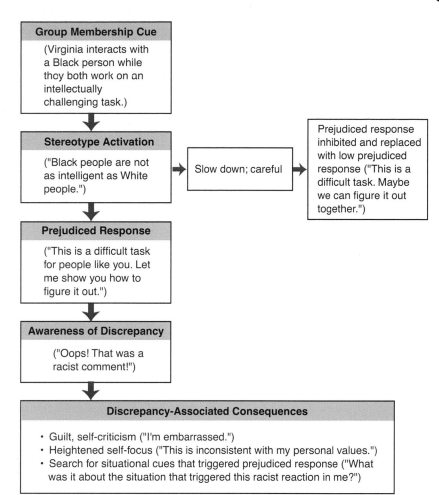

Group Membership Cue

(Virginia interacts with a Black person while they both work on an intellectually challenging task.)

↓

Stereotype Activation

("Black people are not as intelligent as White people.")

→ Slow down; careful → Prejudiced response inhibited and replaced with low prejudiced response ("This is a difficult task. Maybe we can figure it out together.")

↓

Prejudiced Response

("This is a difficult task for people like you. Let me show you how to figure it out.")

↓

Awareness of Discrepancy

("Oops! That was a racist comment!")

↓

Discrepancy-Associated Consequences

• Guilt, self-criticism ("I'm embarrassed.")
• Heightened self-focus ("This is inconsistent with my personal values.")
• Search for situational cues that triggered prejudiced response ("What was it about the situation that triggered this racist reaction in me?")

FIGURE 16-1
Reducing Prejudiced Responding through Self-Regulation

When low prejudiced persons first begin to try to respond in a nonprejudiced manner toward previously denigrated outgroup members, stereotype activation often spontaneously triggers a discrepant (that is, prejudiced) response, which subsequently triggers a series of discrepancy-associated consequences. This cognitive process is depicted by the vertical arrows on the left side of the figure. Over time, through careful self-regulation of one's thoughts and attention to one's nonprejudiced standards, low prejudiced people break the "prejudice habit" and respond as depicted by the horizontal arrows. If this model accurately describes how prejudiced behavior can be eliminated, what would be the first step you would need to take to reduce your own prejudiced responding?

Source: From "Self-Regulation of Prejudiced Responses: Implications for Progress in Prejudice-Reduction Efforts" by J. J. Monteith in *Journal of Personality and Social Psychology* 65, 1993, pp. 469–485. Copyright © 1993 by the American Psychological Association. Adapted with permission.

Nonverbal behavior:
The communication of feelings and intentions without words.

16-1e Nonverbal Behavior Shapes Social Judgments

When we form first impressions, they are based not only on stereotypes but also on the more dynamic and fluid aspects of nonverbal behavior. **Nonverbal behavior** involves a communication of feelings and intentions without words. One of the more important nonverbal channels of communication is the face. In fact, evolutionary theorist Charles Darwin (1872) proposed that certain facial expressions are inborn and thus are understood throughout the world. Studies conducted during the past 30 years provide strong support for Darwin's assertions (Ekman, 1993, 1994; Izard, 1994). For example, as was previously discussed in chapter 11, section 11-5b, people from very different cultures manifest similar facial expressions when experiencing certain emotions (Ekman & Friesen, 1971; Keating et al., 1981). The seven primary emotions that are universally recognized are happiness, surprise, anger, sadness, fear, disgust, and contempt (Buck, 1984; Ekman et al., 1987; Matsumoto, 1992).

Evolutionary psychologists believe that this ability to recognize emotion from facial expressions is genetically programmed into our species and has survival value for us. How might this ability aid in survival? One possibility is that being able to read others' emotions by attending to facial expressions not only allows us to better predict their intentions ("Do they mean to harm me?"), but also helps us to understand others' interpretations of the world ("Why are they afraid? Are we all in danger here?"). In support of this "survival value" hypothesis, research indicates that we are most attentive to facial expressions that signal potential danger, namely fear and anger (Hansen & Hansen, 1988; Öhman et al., 2001).

Besides facial cues, the body as a whole can convey a wealth of information. For example, people who walk with a good deal of hip sway, knee bending, loose-jointedness, and body bounce are perceived to be younger and more powerful than those who walk with less pronounced gaits (Montepare & Zebrowitz-McArthur, 1988). If the body can convey rich information of this sort, think back to your walk down the dark city sidewalk. Imagine that the man walking toward you is a mugger. As he draws near, he may pay close attention to your body movements to determine whether you will be an easy or difficult target. Research indicates that people with an organized quality to their body movements are less likely to be picked out as "easy" victims by would-be muggers, while those with inconsistent or "jerky" movements are more likely to be chosen (Grayson & Stein, 1981). Thus, similar to the way wounded animals invite attack from predators in the wild (Tinbergen, 1969), potential victims of crime may unwittingly and nonverbally communicate a sense of vulnerability to criminals.

16-1f Most People Are Poor at Detecting Deception

Because of the wealth of information that can be gleaned from nonverbal behavior, when we believe others are trying to deceive us, we pay close attention to these nonverbal gestures (Ekman & O'Sullivan, 1991; Mehrabian, 1972). Why? Apparently, we assume that nonverbal information is more likely to reveal others' true feelings because it is less likely to be consciously controlled than is verbal information. Consistent with this assumption, a number of studies indicate that when people are trying to deceive, they fidget—that is, they touch, scratch, and rub various parts of their bodies (Harrigan, 1985; Harrigan et al., 1991).

Despite the numerous nonverbal deception signals available to us, studies—and everyday experience—indicate that we frequently make mistakes in judging others' truthfulness (Vrij & Semin, 1996). Deceivers fool us regardless of our sex, race, cultural background, socioeconomic status, or educational level. Indeed, the best-known professional deception detectors, namely Secret Service officers, are successful only about 70 percent of the time (Ekman & O'Sullivan, 1991).

One of the biggest mistakes we make is placing too much importance on the face to reveal deception. For example, we tend to believe that others do not smile when they lie, when in fact, smiling is a common device used by deceivers to hide their true feelings (Ekman et al., 1988). We also tend to be fooled by the structure of people's faces, falsely assuming that baby-faced individuals (large eyes and symmetrical facial features) and physically attractive persons are more honest than those with mature-looking and less attractive faces (Zebrowitz & Montepare, 1992; Zebrowitz et al., 1996). Further, confidence doesn't predict accuracy. A meta-analysis of 17 studies involving almost 2,800 participants found that people's confidence in detecting deception does not predict their accuracy in distinguishing liars from nonliars (DePaulo et al., 1997). This suggests that if deceivers closely monitor their nonverbal behavior, even well-trained deception-detectors will have a difficult time separating truths from lies (DePaulo, 1992; Tucker & Riggio, 1988).

16-1g Explaining People's Behavior Hinges on Either Internal or External Attributions

Beyond trying to understand others on the basis of physical appearance, group membership, and nonverbal behavior, we also try to understand why they behave the way they do. The process by which we use information to make inferences about the causes of behavior or events is called *attribution*. Why are we so interested in making attributions about

---

INFO-BIT: Research by Bella DePaulo and her colleagues indicates that, during an average week, American college students lie to about one-third of all of those with whom they interact (DePaulo et al., 1996; Kashy & DePaulo, 1996). On average, young adults tell about 10 lies per week, with the greatest lying committed by those who are more sociable, manipulative, and concerned about creating favorable impressions than others. Do you or does anyone you know fit this college student profile?

> *She (Lady Desborough) tells enough white lies to ice a wedding cake.*
> —Margo Asquith, English socialite, 1864–1945

other people's behavior? Put simply, if we think we know why people behave the way they do, we will be much more likely to view the world as coherent and controllable than if we have no clue to their intentions and dispositions (Heider, 1958).

Primary Dimensions of Causal Experience

In making attributions, the most important judgment concerns whether we will attribute a given action either to internal qualities of the person or external factors of the situation. An **internal attribution** consists of any explanation that locates the cause as being inside the person, such as personality traits, moods, attitudes, abilities, or effort. An **external attribution** consists of any explanation that locates the cause as being outside the person, such as the actions of others, the nature of the situation, or luck. When a clerk at a store doesn't smile at you, you may infer that he is rude and unfriendly (an internal attribution), or you may infer that he is distracted or having a bad day (an external attribution). The attribution you make will guide your future actions toward this person. Discovery Box 16-2 discusses how culture can influence how we make attributions about others' actions.

Internal attribution:
An attribution that locates the cause of an event to factors internal to the person, such as personality traits, moods, attitudes, abilities, or effort.

External attribution:
An attribution that locates the cause of an event to factors external to the person, such as luck, or other people, or the situation.

SECTION SUMMARY

- Social perception can be classified into two areas: impression formation and attribution.

- Impression formation is often based on rapid assessments of easily observable qualities and behaviors in others.

- We group people into different social categories and develop beliefs about them, known as stereotypes.

- Stereotyping can bring greater speed and efficiency to our social judgments; it also inhibits thought and can promote prejudice and discrimination.

- According to the physical attractiveness stereotype, what is beautiful is good.

- Beauty often conforms to the standards of a culture's dominant social group; it also may be partly based on some universal beauty standards.

- Women are judged more attractive when they have youthful or immature facial features.

- Male attractiveness is increased with mature facial characteristics related to social dominance.

- The seven primary universally recognized emotions are happiness, surprise, anger, sadness, fear, disgust, and contempt.

- Attention to facial expressions and body movements can provide useful information about others' level of emotional arousal and their truthfulness.

- We tend to attribute others' actions either to internal or external causes.

- People from individualist cultures often underestimate the influence of the situation, a judgmental bias known as the fundamental attribution error.

16-2 ATTITUDES

Thus far, we have discussed how we form impressions and how we try to explain others' actions. Through our observations of people and events, we also develop **attitudes,** which are positive or negative evaluations of objects (Schuman, 1995; Zanna & Rempel, 1988). "Objects" include people, things, events, and issues. When we use such words as *like, dislike, love, hate, good,* and *bad,* we are describing our attitudes.

Attitudes: Positive or negative evaluations of an object.

DISCOVERY BOX 16-2

How Universal Is the Fundamental Attribution Error?

When explaining others' actions, people from individualist cultures tend to make internal attributions rather than external attributions, a bias known as the **fundamental attribution error** (Ross, 1977). In a study that documented these cultural differences in attributional style, Joan Miller (1984) asked groups of American and Asian-Indian citizens of varying ages to explain the causes of positive and negative behaviors they had seen in their own lives. As figure 16-2 shows, in the youngest children of the two cultures (8- to 11-year-olds), there were no significant attribution differences. However, as the age of the participants increased, Americans made more internal attributions, and the Asian Indians made more external attributions. This study and others strongly suggest that the fundamental attribution error is more common in individualist cultures than in those that are collectivist and is learned through socialization (Lee et al., 1996; Norenzayan & Nisbett, 2000).

Why do you think the fundamental attribution error is more common in individualist cultures than in those that are collectivist? Research findings indicate that collectivists are just as likely as individualists to take into account people's dispositions when explaining their behavior (Krull et al., 1999). Where they differ is in their awareness of the power of the situation. Collectivists are more attentive to how situational factors may influence people's behavior, and that is apparently why they are less susceptible to the fundamental attribution error (Choi & Nisbett, 1998; Choi et al., 1999). This cultural difference appears to be rooted in different views of the self. As stated in chapter 4, section 4-2e, individualists view the self as internally driven and relatively uninfluenced by situational forces. In contrast, collectivists view the self as dependent upon the group and strongly influenced by social obligations. The collectivist self-view seems to foster a greater appreciation of how personal and situational factors interact in shaping behavior, which is essentially how social psychology understands social behavior. Based on these findings, some social psychologists suggest the "rules" that members of collectivist cultures develop in making social judgments about other people often lead to more accurate attributions than what is typically developed in individualist cultures (Choi et al., 1999).

16-2a Two Common Attitude Shapers Are Repeated Exposure and Conditioning

We seem to develop positive attitudes naturally toward those things that are repeatedly presented to us, be they the unknown students we regularly see in class or the soft drink advertised on television (Zajonc, 1968). One of the more interesting experimental demonstrations of this **mere exposure effect** was conducted by Theodore Mita and his colleagues (1977). They reasoned that people are more exposed to their mirrored facial images than they are to their true facial images and thus should have more positive attitudes toward the former than the latter. To test this hypothesis, they photographed students on campus and later showed them and their close friends their picture along with a mirror image print. When asked to indicate which of the two prints they "liked better,"

Mere exposure effect: The tendency to develop more positive feelings toward objects and individuals the more frequently we are exposed to them.

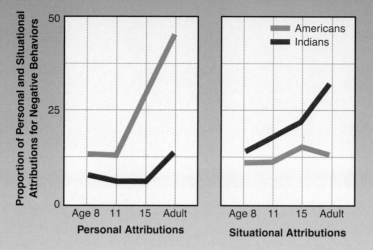

Personal Attributions   **Situational Attributions**

FIGURE 16-2

Is the Fundamental Attribution Error Only an Individualist Bias?

Asian-Indian and American participants of varying ages explained the causes of positive and negative behaviors they had seen in their own lives. Consistent with the fundamental attribution error, the individualist American adults made more dispositional than situational attributions for both positive and negative events. The exact opposite was true for the collectivist Asian-Indian adults. Among the younger children, no attribution differences were found. Why do you think there were differences between adults but not children in these two cultures?

Source: From J. G. Miller, "Culture and the Development of Everyday Social Explanation," *Journal of Personality and Social Psychology*, 46 (1987): 961–978.

The fundamental attribution error can have significant social consequences. Attributing the behavior of others to internal factors often leads us to brush off people's attempts to deny responsibility for negative events with which they are associated (Inman et al., 1993). For example, the tendency to disregard situational forces in explaining the plight of victims within our society (for example, rape victims, street people, disadvantaged minorities) can result in an unsympathetic response because we hold them responsible for their condition due to "bad" personalities or choices.

Even if we respond with sympathy, where we locate the cause of social problems will shape the type of solutions we seek (Sampson, 1991). That is, if we attribute the difficulties of unfortunate others to personal defects rather than to their circumstances, it is likely that the treatment programs we devise will focus on changing individuals, while ignoring social conditions. Yet, if the people in these treatment programs are members of social groups in which failure is often partly due to poverty and discrimination, our attempted interventions will likely be unsuccessful and may even be psychologically damaging.

Fundamental attribution error: The tendency to make internal attributions over external attributions in explaining the behavior of others.

the students preferred the mirror print, while their close friends preferred the actual picture. Overall, the significance of the mere exposure effect is that it illustrates how attitudes sometimes develop outside the realm of conscious awareness.

Other ways in which attitudes can be formed are through operant and classical conditioning, both of which we considered in chapter 7, sections 7-1 and 7-2. Regarding operant conditioning, if you are praised and encouraged when learning how to dance, for example, you are likely to develop a positive attitude toward this activity. However, if others tease and make fun of your initial awkwardness, you are likely to form a negative attitude. In a similar vein regarding classical conditioning, attitudes may form by pairing a previously neutral stimulus with another stimulus that naturally evokes a positive or negative response in a person. For example, children may develop prejudicial attitudes toward certain groups because the children listen to their parents continuously using negatively

Think about the mere exposure effect the next time you gaze into a mirror. You're probably the only person who knows you well who prefers that image of your face staring back at you!

evaluated words such as *stupid, lazy, dishonest,* and *dirty* when referring to these people (Cacioppo et al., 1992; Staats & Staats, 1958). By repeatedly pairing the social group's previously neutral name (the conditioned stimulus) with these negative adjectives (the unconditioned stimulus), children can acquire prejudicial attitudes (the conditioned response) toward these people.

16-2b Attitude Change Can Occur with or without Comprehension of the Persuasive Message

Not only do we form attitudes, but we also change attitudes. In fact, every day we are inundated with attempts to change our attitudes. Turn on the television and commercial spokespersons will try to convince you that their products are better than all others. Go in for your annual physical exam and your doctor may try to change your attitudes toward salt, fatty foods, and exercise. This process of consciously attempting to change attitudes through the transmission of some message is known as **persuasion** (Petty & Wegener, 1996).

One of the most influential persuasion theories is Richard Petty and John Cacioppo's (1986) **elaboration likelihood model.** The term *elaboration likelihood* refers to the probability that a person who receives a persuasive message will elaborate on—that is, carefully analyze and attempt to comprehend—the information contained in the message. According to the model, we tend to engage in either high or low elaboration when processing persuasive messages. When motivated and able to think carefully about the message content (high elaboration), we take the central route to persuasion and are influenced by the strength and quality of the arguments. When unable or unwilling to analyze the message, we take the peripheral route to persuasion, where we pay attention to cues that are irrelevant to the content or quality of the communication (low elaboration), such as the attractiveness of the communicator or the sheer amount of information presented. By attending to these peripheral cues, we can evaluate a message (for example, "Does the persuader look honest?" "Does she sound knowledgeable?") without engaging in any extensive thinking about the actual issues under consideration. What this means is that it isn't necessary when you take the peripheral route to comprehend the message: Attitude change can occur without comprehension. Figure 16-3 depicts these two different persuasion routes.

Research indicates that although attitude change can occur through either the thoughtful mode of central processing or the lazy mode of peripheral processing, attitudes

Persuasion: The process of consciously attempting to change attitudes through the transmission of some message.

Elaboration likelihood model: A theory that there are two ways in which persuasive messages can cause attitude change, each differing in the amount of cognitive effort or elaboration they require.

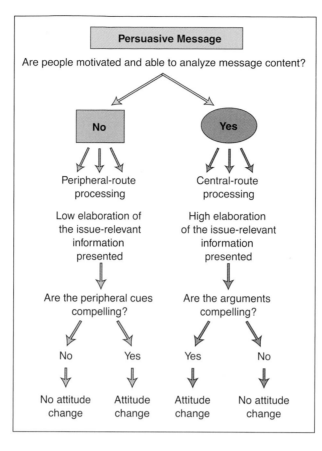

FIGURE 16-3
Two Routes to Persuasion

The elaboration likelihood model describes how people evaluate a persuasive message based on their ability and motivation to analyze its contents. As the likelihood of thinking about the attitude object increases, the processes specified by the central route become more likely determinants of attitudes, and those specified by the peripheral route become less likely determinants. This process is reversed as the likelihood of thinking about the attitude object decreases. In central-route processing, message contents are carefully scrutinized before they are accepted. However, in peripheral-route processing, evaluation of the message is based on a more shallow analysis of incidental cues, such as the communicator's credibility, status, or likability. Of the two routes to persuasion, which do you think secures the most enduring attitude change?

formed via the lazy route are weaker, less resistant to counterarguments, and less predictive of actual behavior than those formed through the thoughtful route (Haugtvedt & Petty, 1992; Petty et al., 1995). An analogy might be that if attitudes are like houses, then attitudes changed by the peripheral route are like houses made from straw or sticks; they require little effort to develop and are extremely vulnerable to destruction. In contrast, attitudes changed by the central route are like houses made of bricks—they take a good deal of effort to construct and are strong and durable. This is the reason why our psychological journey of discovery has placed so much importance on critical thinking: Such thinking results in a stronger foundation for our knowledge about the world.

16-2c Cognitive Dissonance Theory Explains How the Need for Consistency Can Lead to Attitude Change

Besides changing our attitudes due to others' persuasive messages, sometimes we are motivated by an internal desire to keep our attitudes and behavior consistent. For example, suppose that young Jack tells his grade school friends that he dislikes girls, but later he is seen walking up a hill with Jill. How might Jack respond to this inconsistency between his attitude ("I don't like girls") and his behavior (walking with Jill)? According to Leon Festinger's (1957) cognitive dissonance theory, when aware of an inconsistency between our attitudes and actions, we experience an unpleasant psychological state, called *cognitive dissonance* (refer back to chapter 2, section 2-3a). **Cognitive dissonance** is a feeling of discomfort caused by performing an action that is inconsistent with one's attitudes. To relieve this feeling of discomfort, we will often change our attitudes so that they are in line with our behavior (Elliot & Devine, 1994). Thus, if no one forced Jack to walk up the hill with Jill, then he should experience discomfort due to his dissonant thoughts ("I dislike girls, but I walked with a girl") and could be motivated to change his attitude ("Gee, maybe girls aren't that bad after all").

Cognitive dissonance: A feeling of discomfort caused by performing an action that is inconsistent with one's attitudes.

Consistency, madam, is the first of Christian duties.

—Charlotte Brontë, American author, 1816–1855

Consistency is the last refuge of the unimaginative.

—Oscar Wilde, Irish author, 1854–1900

An initial assumption underlying cognitive dissonance theory was that everyone has an equal desire to think and act consistently. More recent research, however, suggests that this desire for consistency is more common in individualist cultures than in those that have a collectivist orientation (Heine & Lehman, 1997; Kashima et al., 1992). That is, because people from collectivist cultures are socialized to think of group needs before their own needs, it is more acceptable for them to behave in a manner inconsistent with their attitudes than it is for individualists. As a result, they are less concerned about maintaining cognitive consistency. Thus, what many North Americans and other "individualists" consider to be discrepant and psychologically aversive—namely, believing one thing but saying something else—may not be as troubling to people from other cultures with a collectivist orientation.

If you are from an individualist culture, you might be thinking to yourself, "I don't often get upset with acting inconsistently. Why is this so?" One possibility is that beyond cultural considerations, research also indicates that some of us generally tolerate cognitive inconsistencies better than others. Spend a few minutes completing the Preference for Consistency Scale in Discovery Box 16-3. Robert Cialdini and his colleagues (1995) have found that people who score high on this scale are highly motivated to behave consistent with their attitudes, as predicted by cognitive dissonance theory. In contrast, those who score low on this preference for consistency scale are not bothered much by inconsistent actions and instead appear open and oriented to flexibility in their behavior.

This research suggests that when we consider the universality of the cognitive consistency motive, at least two factors can derail expected cognitive dissonance effects: A person's cultural upbringing may make attitude-discrepant behavior an appropriate and acceptable option, and a person's underlying psychological needs may reduce the aversiveness of attitude-discrepant acts.

SECTION SUMMARY

- Attitudes are formed by various means, including mere exposure, operant conditioning, and classical conditioning.

- The elaboration likelihood model describes how attitudes can be changed either through effortful or lazy thinking; attitudes changed via the lazy route are weaker, less resistant to counterarguments, and less likely to predict later behavior.

- Cognitive dissonance theory explains how attitudes can be changed as a means to maintain cognitive consistency.

- Individualists desire to keep attitudes and behavior consistent.

- Collectivists more likely to tolerate cognitive inconsistencies.

16-3 SOCIAL INFLUENCE

Social influence: The exercise of social power by a person or group to change the attitudes or behavior of others in a certain direction.

Social influence involves the exercise of social power by a person or group to change the attitudes or behavior of others in a certain direction. *Social power* refers to the force available to the influencer to motivate this change. This power can originate from having access to certain resources (for example, rewards, punishments, information), or from being liked and admired by others (French & Raven, 1959; Tyler, 1997). The three main behavioral consequences of social influence are conformity, compliance, and obedience.

DISCOVERY   BOX 16-3

Do You Have a Preference for Consistency?

Instructions: The extent to which people have a preference for consistency is measured by items on the Preference for Consistency Scale (PCS; Cialdini et al., 1995). To take the PCS, read each item that follows and then indicate how well each statement describes you, using the following scale:

1 = Strongly disagree
2 = Disagree
3 = Somewhat disagree
4 = Slightly disagree
5 = Neither agree nor disagree
6 = Slightly agree
7 = Somewhat agree
8 = Agree
9 = Strongly agree

____ 1. It is important to me that those who know me can predict what I will do.

____ 2. I want to be described by others as a stable, predictable person.

____ 3. The appearance of consistency is an important part of the image I present to the world.

____ 4. An important requirement for any friend of mine is personal consistency.

____ 5. I typically prefer to do things the same way.

____ 6. I want my close friends to be predictable.

____ 7. It is important to me that others view me as a stable person.

____ 8. I make an effort to appear consistent to others.

____ 9. It doesn't bother me much if my actions are inconsistent.

Directions for scoring: The last PCS item (#9) is reverse-scored; that is, for this item, a lower rating actually indicates a higher level of consistency preference. Before summing the items, recode item 9 so that 1 = 9, 2 = 8, 3 = 7, 4 = 6, 6 = 4, 7 = 3, 8 = 2, 9 = 1. To calculate your preference for consistency score, add up your responses to the 9 items.

When Cialdini and his colleagues developed the PCS in 1995, the mean score for college students was about 48. The higher your score is above this value, the greater is your preference for consistency. The lower your score is below this value, the less of this preference you probably possess.

Source: From "Preference for consistency: The development of a valid measure and the discovery of surprising behavioral implications" by R. Cialdini, M. Trost and J. Newsom in JOURNAL OF PERSONALITY AND SOCIAL PSYCHOLOGY, 1995, 69, 318–328 (Appendix, p. 328). Copyright © 1995 by the American Psychological Association. Adapted with permission.

16-3a Asch's Research Demonstrates the Power of Conformity Pressure

Can you recall incidents from your past where you behaved a certain way because everyone else was behaving that way? For instance, did you ever join in on Halloween pranks simply because it was "the thing to do"? If not, perhaps you cut classes, took drugs, or volunteered for a local charity drive because others did so. If you engaged in these activities due to perceived group pressure, you were conforming. In **conformity,** our behavior or beliefs become more similar to those of the group. Conformity is not necessarily a bad thing. In fact, if we didn't abide by most of the formal and informal rules of the social groups to which we belong, there would be social chaos.

Conformity: A yielding to perceived group pressure.

Asch's Line Judgment Studies

In a set of classic conformity studies, Solomon Asch (1951, 1952, 1956) had male college students take part in what was described as a group visual perception experiment. Over a series of trials, six to eight men told Asch which of three comparison lines were equal in length to a standard line (see figure 16-4). Although this may seem like an easy task, there was a catch. Only one person in each group was an actual participant—the rest were confederates of Asch who had been given prior instructions to pick the wrong line. The students made a total of 18 different line judgments and announced them out loud with the actual participant giving his opinion second to last. What would the participant do when faced with this dilemma? Would he conform to the group's incorrect judgment or would he stick with what his eyes told him? If you were in his place, what would you do?

Overall, participants conformed by naming the same incorrect line as the confederates on one-third of the critical trials. In contrast, when participants in a control condition made their judgments privately, less than 1 percent conformed (Asch, 1951). What Asch's research and other studies (Tanford & Penrod, 1984) demonstrate is that we often find it easier to conform rather than challenge the unanimous opinions of others.

Factors That Influence Conformity

To more fully understand the nature of conformity, we need to identify the types of social settings and personal characteristics that make us more or less susceptible to others' influence. Some of the more important factors that affect conformity are listed next:

FIGURE 16-4
Asch's Line Judgment Task

This is an example of the stimulus lines used in Asch's classic conformity experiments. Participants were asked to judge which of the three comparison lines were equal in length to the standard line.

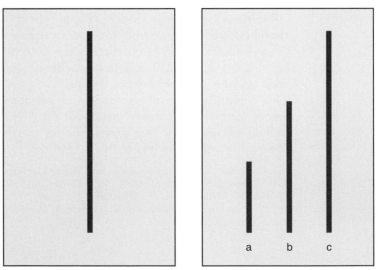

Standard line   Comparison lines

Group size—As group size increases, so does conformity, but only up to a point. After the number of people exerting conformity pressure goes beyond three or four, the tendency to yield to the group doesn't increase (Asch, 1955).

Group cohesiveness—In general, groups with a strong sense of togetherness elicit greater conformity than less cohesive groups (Hogg, 1992; Nowak et al., 1990). For example, we are more likely to accept our friends' influence than that of others due to our respect for their opinions, our desire to please them, and our fear of rejection (Crandall, 1988).

Social support—A social supporter greatly reduces conformity by diminishing the social influence of the group (Allen & Levine, 1969, 1971). In the line judgment studies, Asch (1956) found that when one of the confederates picked the correct line, conformity dropped dramatically—to one-fourth the level shown by participants faced with a unanimous majority.

Desire for personal control—Sometimes we resist social influence in order to feel that we control our own actions (Brehm, 1966; Brehm & Brehm, 1981). Individuals with a high desire for personal control resist conformity more than those who have a low desire for control (Burger, 1987).

Culture—People from collectivist cultures are more concerned than individualists with gaining the approval of their group and feel shameful if they fail to get it (Hui & Triandis, 1986; Triandis, 1989). A person from an individualist culture, on the other hand, has a higher desire for personal control (see last point) and a need to feel unique. As a result of these different orientations, people from collectivist cultures are more conforming to their own group than individualists (Bond & Smith, 1996). This yielding to the group by collectivists is not considered to be a sign of weakness, as it is often perceived in individualist cultures, but rather is believed to indicate self-control, flexibility, and maturity (Kumagai, 1981; White & LeVine, 1986).

16-3b Compliance Is Influenced by Mood, Reciprocity, and Reason-Giving

In trying to "get our way" with others, the most direct route is to simply ask them to do what we desire. **Compliance** is publicly acting in accord with a direct request. Establishing the correct atmosphere is especially important to secure compliance.

> **Compliance:** Publicly acting in accord with a direct request.

One factor that can build the proper atmosphere for compliance is mood alteration. Others are more likely to comply to requests when they are in a good mood, especially if the request is prosocial in nature, such as helping someone in need (Forgas, 1998; Isen, 1987). Because of this general awareness that good moods aid compliance, we often try to flatter people before making a request (Liden & Mitchell, 1988). Although those we "butter up" in this manner may be suspicious of our motives after receiving our requests, the preceding flattery is still often effective in securing compliance (Kacmar et al., 1992).

A second factor that can increase compliance is appealing to a powerful social norm that people in all cultures follow, namely the **reciprocity norm.** This norm states that one should return a favor or a good deed, and it is based on maintaining fairness in social relationships (Gouldner, 1960; Howard, 1995). Although this norm helps to ensure that social exchanges will be roughly equitable between two parties, it can also be used to exert influence over others. For example, how often have you had someone come up to you in a public place and offer you a small gift such as a flower, pencil, or flag, and then ask you to donate money to their organization? In such instances, the gift-giver is hoping that the small token will make you feel obligated to return the favor and give them money (Burger et al., 1997).

> **Reciprocity norm:** The expectation that one should return a favor or a good deed.

Finally, compliance can also be secured by simply providing a reason why the request should be granted. Ellen Langer and her colleagues (1978) found evidence for the power of reason-giving when they had confederates try to cut in line ahead of others at a photocopying machine. In one condition the confederates gave no reason, merely asking, "May I use the photocopying machine to make five copies?" Sixty percent of those waiting complied with this "no reason" request. Interestingly, when confederates provided a pseudoreason that provided no explanation at all but merely restated their desire to make copies ("May I use the photocopying machine to make five copies because I have to make copies?"), 94 percent complied, identical to the compliance when an actual reason was given ("I'm in a hurry"). Langer (1989) believes that such pseudoreasons work because we often mindlessly assume the requester would not ask if the request was illegitimate. When my daughter, Lillian, was 2 years old, she had already learned the importance of giving reasons when seeking compliance from her parents. In asking to go outside she would say, "Can I go outside? . . . Because I have to go outside." Based on Langer's findings, when it comes to securing compliance, Lillian had already developed sufficient social skills to do quite nicely in the adult world.

16-3c Milgram's Research Demonstrates That People Often Can Be Induced to Obey Destructive Orders

Obedience: The performance of an action in response to a direct order.

Unlike the rather subtle social pressures of compliance, **obedience,** which is the performance of an action in response to a direct order, is easily recognized as an exercise of power. Usually the order comes from a person of high status or authority. Due to the fact that people are often instructed from a very young age to respect and obey those who are in positions of authority (for example, parents, teachers, and police officers), obedience to those of higher status is common and is often perceived as a sign of proper socialization. To understand how situational factors increase or decrease obedience to authority, let's explore the most discussed social psychological study ever conducted.

Milgram's Obedience Research

Imagine that you volunteer to participate in an experiment investigating the effects of punishment on the learning of word pairs. You will be the teacher and a 50-year-old man will be the learner. The experimenter explains that you will deliver increasing levels of electrical shock each time the learner makes a mistake. Once the study begins, the learner in an adjacent room makes many mistakes. Starting at 75 volts, you hear through the intercom system the learner grunting and moaning in pain whenever you deliver the shocks. At 150 volts he demands to be released, shouting that his heart is bothering him. Would you stop participating in the study at this point?

Let's imagine that you continue. At 180 volts the learner shouts that he can no longer stand the pain. Would you now stop delivering the shocks? Why or why not?

Let's imagine that you don't stop. At 300 volts the learner says that he absolutely refuses to provide any more answers. Now the experimenter turns to you and orders you to treat the absence of a response as equivalent to an error and to deliver the appropriate level of shock. Would you do so?

Let's imagine that you obey the experimenter's commands and continue. Now, even though the learner no longer gives answers to your questions, from the adjoining room you continue to hear his screams of agony whenever your finger flips the shock generator switch. Would these developments now be sufficient for you to stop participating in the experiment?

Let's imagine that you continue, despite his pleas to stop. When you surpass the 330-volt switch, the learner falls silent, not to be heard from again. As you continue to increase the shock intensity, you realize that you are getting closer to the last switch, the 450-volt switch. If you hesitate in delivering a shock, the experimenter first tells you, "Please continue," then "The experiment requires that you continue," then "It is absolutely essential that you go on," and finally, "You have no other choice; you must go on!" What would you do?

The person who never submits to anything will soon submit to a burial mat.

—Nigerian proverb

In imagining your responses in this hypothetical situations, when do think you would have disobeyed the experimenter's commands? Would it have been following the learner's first protest? Second? Third? Is it possible that you would have continued, despite the intensity of the learner's pleas?

I would hazard a guess that your prediction would be that you would have disobeyed the experimenter's orders well before the 450-volt limit was reached. If this is the case, you are in good company, for widespread disobedience is exactly what was predicted by college students, middle-class adults, and psychiatrists who were presented with this hypothetical scenario (Milgram, 1963).

When Stanley Milgram conducted this research in the early 1960s, no one actually received electrical shocks. The learner was a confederate of the experimenter. Even the learner's screams of protest and pain were prerecorded so that all participants heard exactly the same thing. To Milgram's surprise, 65 percent of the participants (26 out of 40) obeyed the experimenter completely, despite the convincing cries of agony from the learner (Milgram, 1965).

Because the findings were so unexpected, Milgram carried out a number of variations of his experiment to better understand the conditions under which obedience and disobedience would be most likely. As illustrated in figure 16-5, these studies found that obedience increased as the distance between the teacher and the learner increased, or as the distance between the teacher and experimenter decreased. In addition, when college students and women served as participants, the same level of destructive obedience was found (Milgram, 1974). Different researchers also obtained similar results in several other countries, suggesting that these high levels of obedience were not solely an American phenomenon (Kilham & Mann, 1974; Mantell, 1971; Shanab & Yahya, 1977). The participants in these studies were not closet sadists who enjoyed their destructive obedience—in fact, their actions caused them a good deal of stress, although no enduring psychological damage (Elms, 1995; Elms & Milgram, 1966).

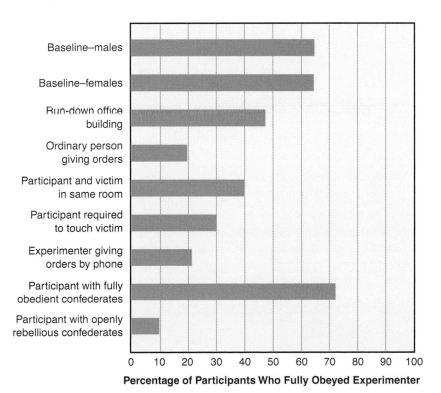

Percentage of Participants Who Fully Obeyed Experimenter

FIGURE   16-5
Some Factors That Influence Obedience and Disobedience to Authority

To determine what factors increase or decrease obedience beyond the baseline 5 percent, Milgram varied the location of the experiment, the participant's proximity to the victim and the experimenter, and the presence of obedient or disobedient confederates. As you can see, all of these factors influenced obedience levels.

Source: Data from S. Milgram, OBEDIENCE TO AUTHORITY: AN EXPERIMENTAL VIEW, Harper and Row, Publishers, Inc., 1974; and S. Milgram, THE INDIVIDUAL IN A SOCIAL WORLD: ESSAYS AND EXPERIMENTS, Addison-Wesley Publishing Company, 1992.

In schools all over the world, little boys learn that their country is the greatest in the world, and the highest honor that could befall them would be to defend it heroically someday. The fact that empathy has traditionally been conditioned out of boys facilitates their obedience to leaders who order them to kill strangers.

—Myriam Miedzian, U.S. author, 1991

Recently, François Rochot and his coworkers (2000) analyzed the audio recordings of one of Milgram's obedience studies to better understand how participants behaved over the course of the experiment. Results indicated that all participants were initially cooperative toward the experimenter, but this changed as the learner began complaining. What predicted obedience versus disobedience was the timing of participants' first firm opposition to the shocks they were told to administer to the learner. Those who firmly verbally opposed the experimenter by 150 volts all ended up defying his authority by disobeying. In contrast, only about half of the participants who began their verbal challenges after 150 volts ever disobeyed. Further, no disobedience ever occurred among those who never took a firm verbal stance against the experimenter. This reanalysis of one of Milgram's classic studies provides additional insights into the social psychological process of obedience and disobedience. It appears that a crucial factor in resisting the destructive commands of authority figures is an early and firm statement of opposition to what is transpiring.

Underestimation of Situational Factors

When describing the situation confronting these participants, I asked whether or not you would have fully obeyed the commands of the experimenter. Most people, when presented with this scenario, believe that they would resist the destructive commands and openly rebel. How do we reconcile these beliefs with the actual experimental findings?

To answer this question, let me remind you about the fundamental attribution error described earlier in the chapter. This tendency to assume that others' actions are caused by internal dispositions rather than external forces results in an underestimation of the power of the situation to shape behavior. Such misrepresentation of how the social world actually operates leaves us vulnerable to being manipulated by the very social forces we underestimate. If we developed a greater appreciation of how we can be influenced by the wishes, desires, and dictates of others, we might be better able to recognize when we are in danger of falling prey to social manipulation.

SECTION SUMMARY

- Social influence is the exercise of social power to change the attitudes or behavior of others in a certain direction.
- Conformity increases as group size and group togetherness increase; it decreases when you have a social supporter.
- Individualists are less conforming to their own groups than are collectivists.
- Compliance is more likely to be secured if you put a person in a good mood, do them a favor, or give them a reason for granting your request.
- Milgram's experiments on obedience demonstrated that we will often obey the destructive commands of an authority figure.
- Underestimating situational pressures make you more susceptible to its power.

16-4 HURTING AND HELPING OTHERS

Although obedience doesn't necessarily result in harm to others, the concept of aggression is directly associated with pain and destruction. *Aggression* is any form of behavior intended to harm another living being (Björkqvist & Niemelä, 1992; Geen, 1996). In contrast, *helping* entails voluntary behavior that is carried out to benefit another person (Batson, 1998). Let us examine these two fundamental aspects of human behavior.

16-4a Aggression Involves the Intention to Harm Another Living Being

Social psychologists have traditionally distinguished two different types of aggression. **Instrumental aggression** is the intentional use of harmful behavior so that one can achieve some other goal, while **hostile aggression** is the intentional use of harmful behavior simply to cause injury or death to the victim.

> **Instrumental aggression:**
> The intentional use of harmful behavior so that one can achieve some other goal.
>
> **Hostile aggression:**
> The intentional use of harmful behavior where the goal is simply to cause injury or death to the victim.

Instrumental aggression is motivated by the anticipation of rewards or the avoidance of punishment. In that sense, it can be thought of as being relatively deliberate and rational. In most robbery attempts, thieves employ aggression as an instrument to achieve their real goal, which is obtaining the victim's money. The aggression that occurs in a military context is also often instrumental. Here, the principal goal may be to either defend one's own territory or to confiscate the enemy's land. On the other hand, hostile aggression is not really motivated by the anticipation of rewards or the avoidance of punishments, even though these may indeed be ultimate consequences of the aggressive act. Instead, this type of aggression is often impulsive and irrational. We are more apt to engage in hostile aggression when we are very angry.

Although the distinction between instrumental and hostile aggression has been useful in helping researchers understand human aggression, there are many aggressive actions that cannot be neatly placed into only one of the categories (Bushman & Anderson, 2001). For example, a child may angrily hit another child who has taken his favorite toy, and then he may retrieve the toy while the victim cries. The motives underlying this aggression are both the infliction of pain (hostile aggression) and the recovery of the favored toy (instrumental aggression). In such instances, no clear distinctions can be made between hostile and instrumental aggression. In other instances, aggression might start out instrumentally, yet then turn hostile. For example, a soldier's "cool" and methodical firing of a weapon at a hidden enemy may turn into impulsive rage when one of her comrades is killed. Because of this problem of multiple motives, in the coming years social psychologists will likely revise this classic distinction to better represent the often complex motivational nature of aggression.

16-4b There Are Gender Differences in Styles of Aggression

There is a widespread belief in our culture that men are more aggressive than women. Does research support this cultural belief? Would it surprise you to learn that the answer is both yes and no?

Men and women do differ in one important kind of aggression: physical aggression. That is, men (and boys) are more likely than women (and girls) to engage in aggression that produces pain or physical injury (Bartholow & Anderson, 2002; Eagly & Steffen, 1986). They are also more likely than women and girls to be physically aggressive against others without being provoked (Bettencourt & Miller, 1996). However, in situations where people are provoked, gender differences tend to shrink or even disappear.

Not only do men and women typically differ in their level of physical aggression, they also appear to experience physical aggression differently (Campbell & Muncer, 1987). Among North Americans, women tend to view their physical aggression as being stress-induced, precipitated by a loss of self-control, and a negative experience. Men, in

> *No man can think clearly when his fists are clenched.*
>
> —George Jean Nathan, American critic and writer, 1882–1958

contrast, tend to perceive this type of aggression as an exercise of control over others, provoked by challenges to their self-esteem or integrity, and a positive experience (see the discussion of sexual aggression in chapter 11, section 11-2a). A similar gender difference pattern has been found in Poland (Fraczek, 1992). These results suggest that when discussing physical aggression, the more spontaneous and unplanned behaviors typical of hostile aggression are more descriptive of the antisocial actions of women, while the more planned and calculated actions of instrumental aggression are more descriptive of male hostility (Campbell et al., 1992).

One form of aggression largely ignored by researchers is *indirect aggression*—a form of social manipulation in which the aggressor attempts to harm another person without a face-to-face encounter (Björkqvist et al., 1992). Gossiping, spreading bad or false stories about someone, telling others not to associate with a person, and revealing someone's secrets are all examples of indirect aggression. Field studies among adolescents in Europe and North America (see figure 16-6) find that girls are more likely than boys to use indirect aggression (Björkqvist et al., 1992; Fry, 1992). One explanation for this gender difference is that girls tend to be discouraged more than boys from engaging in direct acts of aggression. As a result, they may employ indirect aggression simply because it is more socially acceptable. This research further indicates that, whereas male physical aggression decreases significantly during adolescence, teenage girls continue to exhibit higher levels of indirect aggression at all age levels. Can you think why this might be so? One possibility is that indirect aggression is harder to detect and punish than physical aggression.

When discussing gender differences in aggression, it is natural to ask what accounts for these differences. In most cases, social psychologists search for social or cultural explanations (see Discovery Box 16-4). However, besides these causes, some evidence indicates that biological factors also play a role in the heightened physical aggression among males. For example, men with higher levels of testosterone (an important male sex hormone) in their blood tend to be more physically aggressive than those with lower levels (Berman et al., 1993; Gladue, 1991). This finding is reversed for women: The higher the testosterone levels, the lower their levels of aggression. This evidence suggests that, in addition to social and cultural factors, biological factors may also help account for gender differences in aggression.

FIGURE 16-6
Gender Comparisons in Aggressive Strategies

When studying aggressive styles used by adolescents in Finland, Björkqvist and his colleagues (1992) found that verbal aggression (for example, yelling, insulting, name-calling) is the most used by both boys and girls. Boys display more physical aggression (hitting, kicking, shoving), whereas girls utilize more indirect forms of aggression (gossiping, writing nasty notes about another, telling bad or false stories).

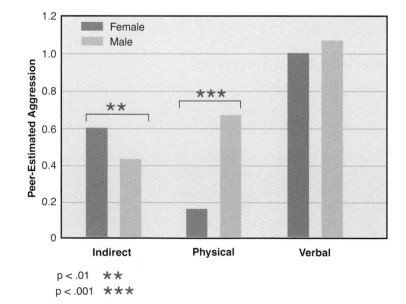

DISCOVERY   BOX 16-4

Can the "Culture of Honor" Explain Certain Types of Male Violence?

Cross-cultural research indicates that societies in which the economy is based on the herding of animals have more male violence than farming societies. Social psychologists Richard Nisbett and Dov Cohen (1996) believe that the greater violence exhibited by herding people is due to their **culture of honor,** which is a belief system that prepares men to protect their reputation by resorting to violence. In cultures that place a high value on honor, males learn from childhood that it is important to project a willingness to fight to the death against insults and to vigorously protect their property—specifically, their animals—from theft. Nisbett and Cohen hypothesize that this culture of honor is more necessary in herding than in farming societies because herders' assets (animals) are more vulnerable to theft—and thus, more in need of aggressive protection—than are the assets of farmers (land).

How does this culture of honor theory relate to contemporary violence in the United States? First, in an analysis of crime statistics in this country, Nisbett and Cohen found that the southern and western states, which were settled by people whose economy was originally based on herding, have higher levels of current violence related to honor than the northern states, which were originally settled by farmers (Cohen, 1996; Cohen & Nisbett, 1994). Honor-related violence involves arguments, brawls, and lovers' triangles where a person's public prestige and honor have been challenged. Second, in a series of experimental studies, Nisbett and Cohen also found that, when insulted, young White men from the South not only became more stressed and angry than young White men from the North, but they also were more prepared to respond to insults with aggression (Cohen et al., 1996).

These studies suggest that southern White males tend to be more physically aggressive than northern White males in certain situations because they have been socialized to live by a code of honor that requires them to quickly respond violently to threats to their property or personal integrity (Cohen, 1998). Although the vast majority of these southern men no longer depend on herding for their livelihood, Nisbett and Cohen contend that they still live by the culture of honor of their ancestors.

A similar regional difference in violence is not found among young African-American males. Thus, the culture of honor in the South is unique to White males. Having stated this, however, Nisbett and Cohen note that the higher incidence of violence among inner-city African-American males than among African-American males in rural or suburban areas may be partly related to a similar honor code (Nisbett & Cohen, 1996). Thus, just as a culture of honor may exist among southern White men, in the inner-city "street" culture there may also be a culture of honor that makes violent outbursts more likely. That is, in the inner city, where it is extremely difficult to pull oneself out of poverty by legal means, and where police provide little protection from crime and physical attack, young Black males may strive to gain and maintain respect by responding violently to any perceived insults (Anderson, 1994).

Culture of honor: A belief system in which males are socialized to protect their reputation by resorting to violence.

Although males appear to be more physically aggressive than females, research suggests that females may engage in more indirect aggression, such as spreading bad or false stories about others, or revealing someone's secrets. What might explain these gender differences?

INFO-BIT: There is a common belief that people can purge themselves of aggressive urges by punching a pillow or playing some aggressive game. However, numerous studies (Bushman, 2002; Bushman et al., 1999) clearly indicate that "letting off steam" in this manner does not reduce aggressive urges, it increases them!

Journey of Discovery Question

"Road rage" has become an all-too-familiar term describing violent outbursts by people driving cars on our nation's highways. Would this type of aggression typically be instrumental or hostile in nature? Why? Beyond harsh penalties, what strategies might public officials employ to reduce road rage?

16-4c Helping Others Is Largely a Learned Response

Just as all of us have had personal experiences with aggression, we too have helped and been helped by others. Although this inclination to help those in need may have a genetic basis (especially if they are blood relatives), its strength is substantially strengthened or weakened by our upbringing (McAndrew, 2002). As we mature, parents, teachers, and peers are extremely influential in shaping our personal norms for helping. If helping others becomes an important self-defining value, we will feel proud when responding to others' suffering and ashamed when ignoring them (Schwartz & Howard, 1981, 1982). In this regard, observational learning or modeling (refer back to chapter 7, section 7-3) can have a powerful effect on our willingness to help (Eisenberg & Valiente, 2002; Rushton, 1980). For example, an international study of people who rescued Jews in Nazi-occupied territory during World War II revealed that the rescuers were more likely than nonrescuers to say that they learned generosity and caring from their parents (Oliner & Oliner, 1988). Similar findings have been obtained in studies of civil rights activists in the United States. Strongly committed activists had parents who had been excellent prosocial models when they were children, whereas less committed activists had parents who tended to be inconsistent models, often preaching prosocial action but not actually practicing it (Rosenhan, 1970). These studies suggest that parents who try to instill prosocial values only by preaching and not by modeling helping will likely raise children who are only weakly helpful. Yet, parents who not only preach helping, but also let their prosocial actions serve as guidelines for their children's behavior, are more likely to foster helping responses in the next generation.

The power of our social environment in shaping helping behavior may well explain gender differences in lending assistance. Research indicates that men are more likely than

Many of you will be—or currently are—parents. Based on what you have learned about help-ing, what sort of cultural role models might influence the "helping habits" of boys and girls? How might greater gender role flexibility influence male and female helping tendencies?

women to help when the situation involves an element of danger, and when there is an audience (Eagly & Crowley, 1986). In addition, men provide more frequent help to women than men, especially if the women are attractive (West & Brown, 1975). These findings suggest that the help men typically offer is consistent with the male gender role: It is heroic and chivalrous and generally directed toward the benefit of female victims. Women helpers, in contrast, do not show a gender bias in whom they help. Further, although men help more in dangerous situations, women appear to be more helpful than men when assistance is consistent with the female gender role; that is, when the situation involves empathy and devotion. For example, women are more likely than men to pro-vide social and emotional support to others (Shumaker & Hill, 1991), are more likely to volunteer for community service (Trudeau & Devlin, 1996), and also are more likely to take on the caretaking role for children and elderly people (Unger & Crawford, 1992).

16-4d Deciding to Help Often Involves a Series of Decisions

As discussed in chapter 2, section 2-2a, the 1964 murder of Kitty Genovese in New York City prompted social psychologists John Darley and Bibb Latané (1968) to study the con-ditions that inhibit bystanders from helping in emergencies. Their subsequent *bystander intervention model* contended that being helpful during an emergency involves not just one decision, but a series of five decisions. As you can see from figure 16-7, at each point in this five-step process of deciding whether or not to help, one decision results in no help being given, while the other decision takes the person one step closer to helping.

According to this model, the first thing that you must do as a potential helper is notice that something unusual is happening. Unfortunately, in many social settings, you are distracted by countless sights and sounds, and thus, a cry for help may go unnoticed. This is one of the possible reasons why there is a negative correlation between population density and helping (Levine et al., 1994). That is, because of all the distracting sights and sounds of a crowded city, residents are less likely to notice when someone needs help than those who live in less densely populated urban centers.

As a bystander to an emergency, if you do indeed notice that something unusual is happening, Latané and Darley (1968, 1970) contend that you move to the second step in the decision-making process; namely, deciding whether something is wrong and help is needed. For instance, if you pass an unconscious man lying on the grass in a park, you may ask yourself, "Did he suffer a heart attack, or is he merely sleeping?" This is an extremely important decision because if you decide he is merely sleeping you will continue on your way, having defined this as a nonemergency. Yet, what if you are mistaken?

When you define the situation as an emergency, the bystander intervention model states that the third decision you must make is determining the extent to which you have responsibility to help. Failure to assume responsibility results in no helping, while feeling a sense of obligation moves you to the fourth step in Latané and Darley's model.

If you assume responsibility for helping, your next decision is to settle on the appro-priate form of assistance to render. Yet, in the heat of the moment, what if you aren't sure what to do? You may become paralyzed with uncertainty. Unable to decide, you may not offer any help at all. If you are able to make a choice in step 4, in the final step, you must decide to carry out the helpful behavior.

As you can see, Latané and Darley believe that the decision to intervene in a possi-ble emergency involves a rather complex set of decisions. If we, as bystanders, make an incorrect decision at any point in this process, we will not intervene.

FIGURE 16-7
The Model of Bystander Intervention: A Five-Step Decision Process

As outlined by Latané and Darley (1970), the decision to help someone involves a five-step process. At any step, a bystander's decision could lead to either further analysis of the situation or to nonintervention.

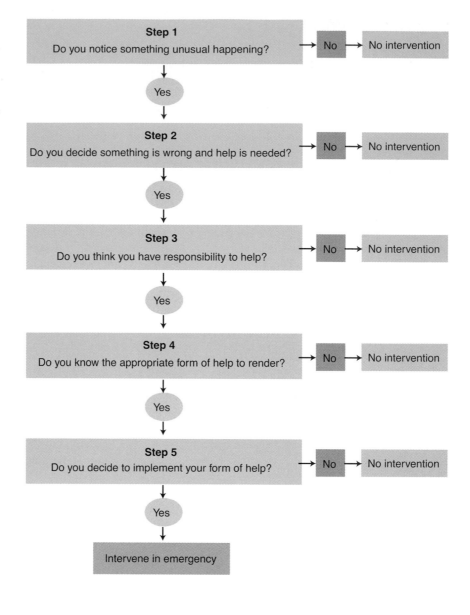

Step 1
Do you notice something unusual happening? → No → No intervention
↓ Yes

Step 2
Do you decide something is wrong and help is needed? → No → No intervention
↓ Yes

Step 3
Do you think you have responsibility to help? → No → No intervention
↓ Yes

Step 4
Do you know the appropriate form of help to render? → No → No intervention
↓ Yes

Step 5
Do you decide to implement your form of help? → No → No intervention
↓ Yes

Intervene in emergency

Journey of Discovery Question

There is a strong likelihood that at some point in your life you will need help in an emergency. Based on what you now know about the bystander intervention model, how could you increase the probability of receiving aid?

Because many emergency situations are not clearly defined as such, when a possible emergency is witnessed by a group of people, each person's reactions will be based partly or exclusively on the reaction of others. Unfortunately, due to our concern with how others might evaluate us, we often pretend to be calm while witnessing a possible emergency. Acting cool and calm, we then observe others' behavior as a clue as how to define what we all are witnessing. Yet, because everyone else is also acting cool and nonchalant, we tend to underestimate the seriousness of the situation and to define it as a nonemergency. In ambiguous emergency situations, then, the fear of being negatively evaluated, combined with the tendency to look to others for further information, results in the **audience inhibition effect.**

Inhibition in seeking information due to fear of embarrassment is one reason why we sometimes don't help in emergencies, but what about those situations where someone clearly needs help yet no one intervenes? Darley and Latané believe that the realization

Audience inhibition effect: People are inhibited from helping due to a fear of being negatively evaluated by other bystanders if they intervene and it is not an emergency.

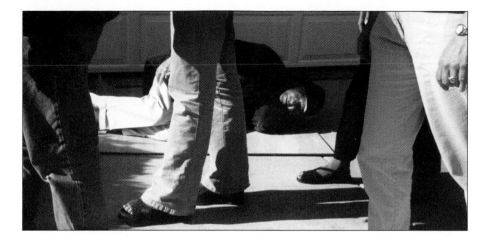

If bystanders define a situation as an emergency, how might the presence of others inhibit intervention?

that others could also help diffuses bystanders' feelings of individual responsibility (step 3 in the model). They call this response to others' presence the **diffusion of responsibility**—the belief that the presence of other people in a situation makes one less personally responsible for events that occur in that situation.

Over 50 laboratory and naturalistic studies have confirmed this effect (Latané & Nida, 1981). On average, in studies where participants believed they were the only bystander to an emergency, 75 percent of them helped, compared with only 53 percent who were in the presence of others. Despite the clear evidence that the presence of others influences our decisions to help, most of us deny that other bystanders have any effect on our actions (or inactions). As discussed earlier, this underestimation of the effect that others have on our own behavior makes it all the more likely that we will fall prey to their influence. After all, how can we guard against being unhelpful when we don't recognize how the simple presence of others not only can inhibit our ability to identify emergencies accurately, but also can change our feelings of personal responsibility for helping?

The good news for you, the reader of this textbook, is that knowledge really is power. Research indicates that people are less likely to fall victim to these bystander effects in emergencies if they have previously learned about them in a psychology course (Beaman et al., 1978). What this finding suggests is that simply knowing about the social barriers to helping can free one from their antisocial effects.

> **Diffusion of responsibility:** The belief that the presence of others in a situation makes one less personally responsible for events that occur in that situation.

SECTION SUMMARY

- Instrumental aggression is the intentional use of harmful behavior so that one can achieve some other goal.

- Hostile aggression is the intentional use of harmful behavior simply to cause injury or death to the victim.

- Men are more likely than women to engage in physical aggression.

- Women are more likely than men to engage in indirect aggression.

- Culture of honor refers to the willingness to fight to the death against insults and vigorously protect one's property from theft.

- Observational learning has a powerful effect on the willingness to help.

- Men are more likely than women to help in dangerous situations.

- Women are more helpful than men in situations requiring empathy and devotion.

- The bystander intervention model contends that being helpful during an emergency involves a series of five decisions; if bystanders make incorrect decisions at any point in this process, they will not intervene.

- Two factors that make helping less likely when others are present are the audience inhibition effect and the diffusion of responsibility.

16-5 INTERPERSONAL ATTRACTION AND LOVE

Now that we have examined the psychology of harming and helping others, let's turn our attention to friendships and intimate relationships. What determines our attraction to others? Social scientists have identified a number of factors that increase the likelihood that close relationships will take root.

16-5a Proximity and Similarity Often Lead to Attraction

One of the most powerful factors in determining whether you develop a relationship with another person is his or her proximity to you (Ebbesen et al., 1976; Festinger et al., 1950). For example, spend a minute or two thinking about who you played with as a child. Chances are, most of your friends were neighbors living nearby. Why does proximity promote liking? As your own childhood experiences suggest, it's easier to develop friendships with those who live close to you simply because they are more accessible. Yet, another reason has to do with the mere exposure effect discussed earlier in the chapter: Proximity tends to be associated with repeated exposure, and such familiarity leads to greater liking.

Beyond proximity, another ingredient in attraction is similarity. Numerous studies indicate that we choose as friends and lovers those who are similar to us in race, age, social class, education, and attitudes (Kandel, 1978; Whitbeck & Hoyt, 1994). Our belief that similarity attracts is the principal reason why, when trying to match others up as potential friends, we pay close attention to their shared characteristics (Chapdelaine et al., 1994). This tendency to be attracted to similar others is known as the **matching hypothesis** (Berscheid et al., 1971).

One reason why we might seek the company of similar others is because of our desire for social comparison (Festinger, 1954; Goethals, 1986). That is, we are drawn to those with whom we can compare ourselves. The more similar they are to us, the more likely that the resulting comparison will provide information that we can use in better understanding ourselves and our future plans (Goethals & Darley, 1987; Miller, 1984). For example, imagine that you are deciding whether to take a certain college course. You know three people who were previously enrolled in the course: Juan, who always is the top student in every course he takes; Vanessa, who usually receives similar grades as you; and Sarah, who always seems to be on academic probation. Who would you seek out for information about the course? Most likely, you would go to Vanessa because of her academic similarity to you. Her opinions and observations about the course—and her actual final grade—will be more useful in predicting your own performance than information obtained from Juan and Sarah.

Another possible explanation for our attraction to similar others is found in Fritz Heider's (1946, 1958) **balance theory.** Heider proposed we desire consistency or "balance" in our thoughts, feelings, and social relationships. Because of this desire for consistency, balanced relationships should be rewarding, while imbalanced relationships—those in which a person holds inconsistent or discrepant thoughts—should be unpleasant. Between two people, balance is created when both parties value the same things—that is, they have similar attitudes.

16-5b Romantic Love Consists of Both Passionate and Companionate Love

Just knowing that proximity and similarity may attract us to one another does not tell us about the psychological nature of romantic love. What can psychologists tell us that poets have not already revealed?

Matching hypothesis: The proposition that people are attracted to others who are similar to them in certain characteristics, such as attitudes and physical attractiveness.

Balance theory: A theory that people desire cognitive consistency or "balance" in their thoughts, feelings, and social relationships.

To like and dislike the same things, that is indeed true friendship.

—Gaius Crispus, 34 B.C.

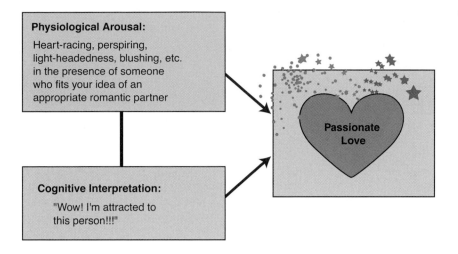

Physiological Arousal:
Heart-racing, perspiring, light-headedness, blushing, etc. in the presence of someone who fits your idea of an appropriate romantic partner

Cognitive Interpretation:
"Wow! I'm attracted to this person!!!"

Passionate Love

FIGURE 16-8
Two-Factor Theory of Emotion and Passionate Love

According to the two-factor theory of emotion, when we experience physiological arousal in the presence of someone who fits our idea of a suitable romantic partner, we are likely to interpret this arousal as romantic and sexual attraction. This is the beginning of passionate love.

Some psychologists consider romantic love as consisting of passionate love and companionate love. **Passionate love** is a state of intense longing for union with another that we typically experience most intensely during the early stages of a romantic relationship (Hatfield, 1988). It is a type of love that we feel with our bodies—a warm-tingling, body-rush, stomach-in-a-knot kind of love. According to Ellen Berscheid and Elaine Hatfield (1974), passionate love is produced, or at least enhanced, during these first romantic encounters due to a rather interesting transference of arousal from one stimulus to another. Drawing on Schachter's (1964) two-factor theory of emotion described in chapter 11, section 11-5f, Berscheid and Hatfield (1974) contend that passionate love is likely to occur when the following three conditions are met:

1. You must learn what love is and come to expect that you will eventually fall in love.

2. You must meet someone who fits your preconceived beliefs of an appropriate lover.

3. While in this person's presence, you must experience a state of physiological arousal.

How does the arousal that develops under these conditions become passionate love? Recall that Schachter's theory of emotion, discussed in chapter 11, section 11-5f, asserts that we use external cues to label our arousal states. According to this two-factor explanation, when arousal occurs in the presence of an appropriate love object, we may well interpret this arousal as romantic and sexual attraction (see figure 16-8).

One reason the emotional roller coaster ride of early love slows over time to a more smooth and steady experience is because passion generally burns less intensely as a relationship matures (Fletcher, 2002). As we settle into a romantic relationship, the emotional freshness and uncertainty of passionate love is replaced by a more certain and dependable type of love—if love survives at all. Some social scientists explain this lowering of passion as being genetically predetermined. According to this perspective, passion is adaptive early in a relationship because it frequently results in children, yet once born, the infants' survival is aided by the parents becoming less obsessed with one another (Kenrick & Trost, 1987).

This less impassioned, more enduring **companionate love** is the affection we feel for those with whom our lives are deeply entwined (Hatfield, 1988). Companionate love exists between close friends as well as between lovers. It develops out of a sense of certainty in one another's love and respect, and a feeling of genuine mutual understanding (Hatfield & Rapson, 1996; Singelis et al., 1996; Sprecher, 1999).

Passionate love: A state of intense longing for union with another that we typically experience most intensely during the early stages of a romantic relationship.

Companionate love: The affection we feel for those with whom our lives are deeply entwined.

Love and eggs are best when they are fresh.

—Russian proverb

DISCOVERY BOX 16-5

Does the Relationship between Love and Marriage Differ across Cultures?

Conceptions of love differ cross-culturally. For example, a study by Robert Levine and his colleagues (1995) examined the importance of love as a basis for marriage in both individualist and collectivist cultures. Results indicate that there are strong cross-cultural differences in the perceived importance of love. Individualist countries such as the United States, England, and Australia placed great importance on love in marriage, while collectivist countries such as India, Pakistan, Thailand, and the Philippines rated it as much less important. These beliefs appear to have behavioral consequences as well. Those countries placing great importance on love had higher marriage rates, lower fertility rates, and higher divorce rates. Other studies indicate that collectivists tend to select mates who will best "fit in" to the extended family, while individualists are more likely to select a mate who is physically attractive or has an "exciting" personality. This doesn't mean, however, that love is not a part of a collectivist marriage. Instead, it means that in collectivist cultures it is more common for people to get married, and then to fall in love.

One question the researchers raised was whether there isn't an inherent conflict between individualist values and the interdependence necessary to maintain romantic love. That is, if you were raised to be autonomous and independent, wouldn't you tend to have difficulty maintaining an intimate relationship that is defined by partners depending on each other? The curious irony is that although individualists are more likely to marry due to romantic love, the way they've been socialized may make it less likely that their marriages will survive and their love will be nurtured.

Another difference between passionate love and companionate love is in the beliefs that you have about your partner. In the early stages of romantic relationships, when passions run high, we tend to see our partners through rose-colored glasses (Brehm, 1988). They are "perfect," the "ideal man or woman," our "dream come true." As passion fades and we develop companionate love, this idealization of our beloved gives way to a more realistic view. In addition, culture affects our approach to romantic love, as depicted in Discovery Box 16-5.

16-5c Homosexual and Heterosexual Romantic Relationships Are Psychologically Similar

Until recently, virtually all research on romantic relationships focused on heterosexual dating and marriage. However, as discussed in chapter 11, section 11-2c, some adolescents and adults are primarily or exclusively attracted to their own sex (Gonsiorek & Weinrich, 1991; Hatfield, 1989). The lack of research on homosexual love has allowed cultural stereotypes to foster myths about the gay lifestyle (Herek, 1991). One myth is that gay people are unsuccessful in developing enduring, committed romantic relationships. Actual surveys, however, indicate that between 40 and 60 percent of gay men and between 45 and 80 percent of lesbians are currently in a steady relationship (Peplau, 1991). How long do these relationships last? Studies that have examined heterosexual and homosexual couples' happiness and longevity have found few, if any, differences

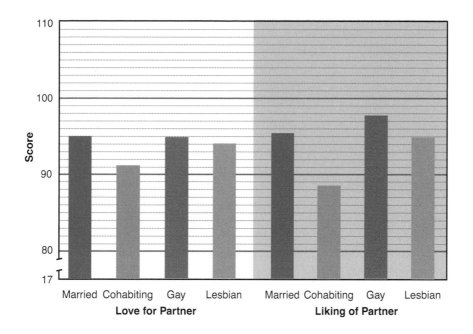

FIGURE 16-9
Expressed Love and Liking in Homosexual and Heterosexual Romantic Relationships

In a study of married, heterosexual cohabiting, gay, and lesbian monogamous couples, Kurdek and Schmitt (1986) obtained a liking and a loving score from each partner, ranging from a low of 17 to a high of 177. Higher scores indicated greater liking/loving. They found no differences in expressed love for one's partner between any of the different types of romantic relationships. Further, the married, gay, and lesbian relationships expressed equally high amounts of liking of their partners. In contrast, heterosexual cohabiting couples had lower liking scores than the other couples. This study and others of its kind have dispelled the myth that gay couples are less capable of developing satisfying romantic relationships than are heterosexual couples.

Source: Data from L. A. Kurdek and J. P. Schmitt, "Relationship Quality of Partners in Heterosexual Married, Heterosexual Cohabiting, and Gay and Lesbian Relationships," in *Journal of Personality and Social Psychology,* 51:711–720, American Psychological Association, 1986.

(Kurdek, 1991b, 1994). Many lesbians and gay men establish lifelong partnerships, despite the fact that they cannot legally marry. As you can see in figure 16-9, lesbians, gay men, and heterosexuals involved in monogamous romantic relationships all tend to score high on scales that evaluate liking and love for one's partner (Kurdek & Schmitt, 1986), and all tend to be equally well adjusted and satisfied (Eldridge & Gilbert, 1990; Kurdek & Schmitt, 1987).

These findings indicate that if you are a gay man or a lesbian, you are no more prone to relationship dissatisfactions and difficulties than if you are a heterosexual man or woman. In addition, this research suggests that the psychological theories used to describe heterosexual romantic relationships can also describe romance among gay men and lesbians and, most likely, among bisexual couples as well (Kurdek, 1991a; Peplau et al., 1996). Regardless of whether you are "straight," "gay," or "bisexual," and despite the turmoil that love often brings to your life, you very likely yearn for romance even after experiencing romantic failure. While some call this persistence a form of addiction, others describe the desire for romantic intimacy as an expression of one of our most basic needs, the desire to share ourselves as completely as possible with those who have become integral parts of our self-concepts.

SECTION SUMMARY

- Two factors determining interpersonal attraction are proximity and similarity.
- Possible reasons that similarity leads to liking include: social comparison, shared genes, and a balanced relationship.
- Passionate love is often experienced during the early stages of romance; it is associated with an idealized perception of one's romantic partner.
- Companionate love is a more enduring kind of love that exists between lovers, as well as between close friends; it is associated with a more realistic view of one's romantic partner.
- Both heterosexual or homosexual romantic relationships follow a similar psychological course.

SUGGESTED WEBSITES

Note: These websites were functional when we went to press. Please access the online text for the most up-to-date URLs.

stanleymilgram.com
http://www.stanleymilgram.com/

This website is a source of accurate information about the life and work of one of the most outstanding social scientists of our time, social psychologist Stanley Milgram. His untimely death at the age of 51 on December 20, 1984, ended a life of scientific inventiveness and controversy.

What Makes Kids Care?
http://www.apa.org/pubinfo/altruism.html

This American Psychological Association site offers suggestions on how to raise children to be more altruistic and supports the suggestions with relevant theories.

Controlling Anger—Before It Controls You
http://www.apa.org/pubinfo/anger.html

This American Psychological Association site provides recommendations on how to control anger before it leads to aggression.

Prejudice and Discrimination
http://www.colorado.edu/conflict/peace/problem/prejdisc.htm

The International Online Training Program on Intractable Conflict at the University of Colorado offers a website on prejudice and discrimination around the world and possible solutions to these social problems.

PSYCHOLOGICAL APPLICATIONS
How Can You Cope with Jealousy?

"O! Beware my lord, of jealousy; It is the green-eyed monster which doth mock."

—William Shakespeare, Othello

What Is Jealousy?
One emotion that threatens love is jealousy. **Jealousy** is the negative emotional reaction you feel when a real or imagined rival threatens a relationship that is important to your self-concept (Hupka, 1991; Parrott & Smith, 1993). In most cases, the threat is another person, but you can also feel jealous about your partner's involvement with work, hobbies, and family obligations (Buunk & Bringle, 1987; Hansen, 1985). Although some people believe that jealousy is a healthy sign in romantic relationships, it is actually related to strong feelings of dependence and relationship insecurity (Bringle & Buunk, 1986; White, 1981). It also triggers many negative feelings and behaviors and tends to lower self-esteem (Mathes et al., 1985; Pines & Aronson, 1983).

Ways to Reduce Jealousy
Because jealousy is so destructive to intimate relationships, social scientists and mental health therapists have sought to develop strategies that we can use to cope constructively with the "green-eyed monster." What we do know is that people most susceptible to jealousy are those who are highly dependent on the relationship and have few alternative avenues to express intimacy (White & Mullen, 1989).

What type of coping strategies—both of the constructive and destructive variety—do we employ in contending with jealousy? All jealousy coping strategies boil down to two major goals: (1) trying to maintain the relationship; and (2) trying to maintain self-esteem.

As you can see from table 16-1, these two goals can either be present or absent in the coping strategy adopted. If you are jealous and desire to maintain both the relationship and your self-esteem, you will probably try to reach a mutually satisfying solution with

TABLE 16-1

Different Ways of Coping with Jealousy

		Relationship-Maintaining Behaviors	
		Yes	**No**
Self-Esteem-Maintaining Behaviors	**Yes**	Negotiating a mutually acceptable solution	Verbal/physical attacks against the partner or rival
	No	Clinging to the relationship	Self-destructive behaviors

Source: Adapted from J. B. Bryson, "Situational Determinants of the Expression of Jealousy" in H. Sigall (chair), Sexual Jealousy symposium presented at the annual meeting of the American Psychological Association, San Francisco, 1977.

your partner. However, if you desire to maintain your romantic relationship regardless of any harm to your self-esteem, you may swallow your pride and put up with your partner's behavior that elicits the jealousy. In contrast to these relationship-maintaining strategies, verbal and physical attacks against your partner or your rival are often used when you are more concerned with maintaining self-esteem than with maintaining the relationship. Likewise, when you are not principally attempting to either maintain the relationship or bolster your self-esteem, you may engage in self-destructive behavior.

In commenting on these different coping strategies, Sharon Brehm (1992) brings up a good point: When jealous, you should think about both the short-term and long-term consequences of your coping responses before acting. For example, verbally or physically attacking partners may temporarily intimidate them into not leaving, but this strategy will most likely hasten their exit from the relationship. Similarly, begging and pleading with a partner to end

another romance may succeed in the short run, but such emotional clinging will not only threaten self-esteem, it will probably also reduce the partner's attraction to the relationship.

The best antidotes to the "green-eyed monster" are to contain emotional outbursts, maintain daily routines, and reevaluate the importance of the relationship (Salovey & Rodin, 1988). Further, to reduce your depression and anger, you should also engage in self-bolstering, which involves thinking positively about yourself and doing nice things for yourself. Making new friends and pursuing positive goals in other areas of your life is all part of the self-bolstering process, and such activities will increase self-esteem, which in turn, will reduce jealousy (Hatfield & Rapson, 1993).

Jealousy: The negative emotional reaction experienced when a real or imagined rival threatens a relationship that is important to one's self-concept.

KEY TERMS

attitudes (p. 491)
audience inhibition effect (p. 508)
balance theory (p. 510)
cognitive dissonance (p. 495)
companionate love (p. 511)
compliance (p. 499)
conformity (p. 498)
culture of honor (p. 505)
diffusion of responsibility (p. 509)
discrimination (p. 486)
elaboration likelihood model (p. 494)

external attribution (p. 491)
fundamental attribution error (p. 493)
hostile aggression (p. 503)
impression formation (p. 484)
instrumental aggression (p. 503)
internal attribution (p. 491)
jealousy (p. 515)
matching hypothesis (p. 510)
mere exposure effect (p. 492)
nonverbal behavior (p. 489)
obedience (p. 500)

passionate love (p. 511)
persuasion (p. 494)
physical attractiveness stereotype (p. 486)
prejudice (p. 486)
reciprocity norm (p. 499)
social influence (p. 496)
social perception (p. 484)
social psychology (p. 484)
stereotypes (p. 485)

REVIEW QUESTIONS

1. Social perception processes involved in categorizing people
   a. do not explain how stereotyping occurs.
   b. emphasize physical characteristics of others far less than internal characteristics.
   c. are shortcuts that decrease the efficiency with which we make social judgments.
   d. are highly complex and effortful processes that enable us to think more critically.
   e. involve combining various sources of information about a person into an overall judgment.

2. Stereotyping influences information processing through all of the following *except*
   a. activation of ethnic stereotypes, which limit critical thinking.
   b. increasing the amount of attention and rehearsal to stereotype-consistent information.
   c. increasing attention to new information rather than old information.
   d. decreasing attention to stereotype-inconsistent information.
   e. decreasing reliance on false information.

3. Stereotypes that favor physical attractiveness
   a. are based on universal standards of beauty rather than cultural standards.
   b. are explained better by evolution than by cultural influences.
   c. exist only in individualistic cultures.
   d. can be found in all age groups and across all cultures.
   e. affect only young adults of child-bearing age.

4. Stereotypes associated with particular groups of people
   a. persist because they tend to be global and undefined.
   b. rarely lead to violence, even when they are negative.
   c. involve discriminating attitudes and prejudicial behavior.
   d. involve prejudicial attitudes and discriminating behavior.
   e. consist of subcategories that are less flattering and desirable than global stereotypes.

5. Research on stereotypes and prejudice has found that
   a. prejudice is easier to change than discrimination.
   b. reducing prejudice involves self-awareness and thought monitoring.
   c. efforts to reduce prejudicial responding are a waste of time.
   d. the strength of automatic associations is more important than motivation in reducing one's prejudices.
   e. efforts to change one's prejudiced responding result in eliminating the prejudice from memory.

6. Nonverbal communication, an important aspect of impression formation,
   a. often provides important clues to others' "real" intent.
   b. is the most reliable sign relied on to detect deception.
   c. is 95 percent accurate when used by trained law enforcement to detect honesty.
   d. is more consciously controlled than verbal communication.
   e. is most accurately "read" through facial expressions.

7. According to researchers, the fundamental attribution error
   a. is learned at an early age, even before age 5.
   b. is more widespread in collectivist cultures.
   c. is the tendency for people from individualistic cultures to attribute others' behavior to internal causes.
   d. causes Americans to make more situational than dispositional attributions for negative events.
   e. is associated with interactions between dispositional and situational factors.

8. Research by Mita on attitude formation indicates that
   a. only your close friends prefer mirror images of your face.
   b. mere exposure plays an important role in the development of prejudice.
   c. repeated exposure to TV commercials leads to negative attitudes toward the product.
   d. close friends consistently prefer actual images of each other, whereas mere acquaintances prefer mirror images of each other.
   e. attitudes may be formed unconsciously.

9. One of your friends has strong political beliefs, and your persuasive arguments do little to change her mind. Your friend's political attitudes have likely been formed through
   a. attending to the credibility of political speakers.
   b. the central route to persuasion.
   c. low elaboration of political arguments.
   d. the peripheral route to persuasion.
   e. the elaboration likelihood model.

10. According to Festinger's theory of cognitive dissonance,
   a. people from collectivist cultures are more prone to feelings of cognitive dissonance than people from individualist cultures.
   b. cognitive dissonance is shaped by conditioning.
   c. people in individualistic cultures are generally motivated to be consistent in their attitudes and behaviors.
   d. someone who exhibits a great deal of flexibility in his or her behavior is bothered by cognitive dissonance.
   e. saying one thing while believing something else is not aversive to individualists.

11. When you arrive at a party, you see that everyone is drinking dark ale, which you dislike. When your host brings you a bottle of ale, you accept graciously, exhibiting
   a. conformity.
   b. obedience.
   c. compliance.
   d. personal consistency.
   e. cognitive dissonance.

12. If you interpret going along with the group in question 11 as flexibility or maturity, you
   a. have a high need for personal control.
   b. will experience cognitive dissonance.
   c. are complying with the reciprocity norm.
   d. may be from a collectivist culture.
   e. are respecting the authority of your host.

13. The results of Milgram's research were shocking primarily because
   a. only 10 percent of the participants obeyed the experimenter.
   b. proximity to the learner had no effect on participants' conformity.
   c. participants were found to be closet sadists, feeling no negative effects from their actions.
   d. they showed the power of the situation in determining behavior.
   e. they emphasized the power of dispositional factors.

14. An individual's willingness to conform may be influenced by all of the following *except*
   a. group size.
   b. the presence of a dissenter.
   c. cultural norms.
   d. desire for personal control.
   e. being given a small gift.

15. Indirect aggression is often associated with
   a. a culture of honor.
   b. being motivated by the anticipation of rewards.
   c. a tendency to be impulsive when angry.
   d. a desire to hurt others.
   e. gossiping about others.

16. The model of bystander intervention describes a five-step decision-making process involving all of the following *except*
   a. deciding if help is needed.
   b. assuming a sense of personal responsibility.
   c. fear of being hurt.
   d. observing how others respond.
   e. the audience inhibition effect.

Appendix

Possible Answers to Journey of Discovery Questions

CHAPTER 1

Journey of Discovery Question: At the beginning of the twentieth century, Hermann Ebbinghaus (1850–1909), one of psychology's pioneers, stated that "Psychology has a long past, but only a short history." What do you think he meant by this statement?

Possible answer: Ebbinghaus meant that well before there was a science of psychology, philosophers wrote extensively about the human condition. Indeed, the study of the mind was once the exclusive domain of philosophers, and many of the issues discussed and analyzed in psychology were originally raised in philosophical circles.

Journey of Discovery Question: Consider the five early perspectives in psychology. What contribution did each make to our understanding of thinking and behavior?

Possible answer: Perhaps you could say that the contribution that structuralism made to our understanding of thinking and behavior is that this psychological perspective, led by Wilhelm Wundt, was instrumental in launching the scientific discipline. Wundt is generally credited with establishing the first institute for research in experimental psychology, and he trained many of those who went on to make a lasting mark in the field. William James and the functionalists attempted to steer the young science away from the reductionism of Wundt and to instead emphasize how the mind affects what people *do* and how the mind *functions*. Of course, Freud and psychoanalysis alerted us to the importance of examining and attending to the unconscious mind. Like Freud, John Watson and behaviorism put psychology "on the map" in people's minds, but for different reasons. Whereas Freud outraged and titillated many people with his emphasis on sex as a primary motive, the behaviorists demonstrated how the findings of psychology could be put to practical use in the real world, such as in conditioning new behavior. Finally, perhaps the gestaltists' most significant contribution was proposing that our perceptions are not to be understood as the mind passively responding to a simple combination of individual elements, but rather, as actively organizing stimuli into coherent wholes.

CHAPTER 2

Journey of Discovery Question: For every dog or cat used in a laboratory experiment, 10,000 dogs and cats are abandoned by their owners (Miller, 1985). When these abandoned animals are brought to local humane societies and are not adopted, should they be made available as subjects for scientific research? Upon what values would you base your decision?

Possible answer: For many people, this is a very personal and individual judgment. After arriving at a basis for your judgment, examine Lawrence Kohlberg's theory of moral development in chapter 4, section 4-4a. Can you identify on what level of Kohlberg's theory of moral development your judgment is based?

CHAPTER 3

Journey of Discovery Question: You have probably heard the following statement many times: "We use only 10 percent of our brain." Based on what you have learned about brain functioning, do you think that this statement is true? In pondering the merits of this expression, consider another type of human functioning: athletic performance. Do athletes use only 10 percent of their muscles when competing?

Possible answer: Here we have an example of an oft-repeated statement of seeming scientific fact that has absolutely no scientific basis. Just as it would seem absurd to suggest that athletes competing in sporting events only use 10 percent of their muscles, it is also foolish to suggest such a thing about our everyday thinking. It is likely that this 10 percent figure was simply pulled out of thin air by someone and gained credence through simple repetition. In reality, there is absolutely no evidence to suggest that only 10 percent of our neurons are active at any given moment. There is also no evidence to suggest that we could remotely behave normally if only 10 percent of any brain area was functioning. Perhaps those who make this statement simply mean to assert that we all have untapped cognitive potential and that there is always something that we can do to improve our everyday thinking.

Journey of Discovery Question: In the case of limbs that have been amputated, amputees often feel excruciating pain in the area of their lost limb. How might the brain's plasticity play a role in this pain?

Possible answer: Recent studies suggest that the often-intense pain that amputees experience, known as phantom pain, is due to the brain's capacity for growth. For example, when the nerve of one finger is severed, brain areas associated with that nerve do not wither away. Instead, neurons activated by nearby fingers take over some of the function of the now nonexistent neurons in the severed finger, and they fool the brain into thinking that the lost finger is still there. The more collateral growth that occurs, the more phantom pain the amputee feels (Flor et al., 1995).

CHAPTER 4

Journey of Discovery Question: If you were to tell someone to "just be yourself," what would that mean to them, depending upon whether they were from an individualist or a collectivist culture?

Possible answer: When Chie Kanagawa and his colleagues (2001) asked U.S. and Japanese college students this question, they received very different responses. For the individualist Americans, this question suggested a self comprised of personal attributes that were not influenced by the situation they happened to be in at the time. Further, these attributes reflected the Americans unique qualities, and these qualities were mostly positive. In contrast, for the collectivist Japanese, this question called to mind a self that was defined by their social relationships in their group. Here, "being yourself" meant constructing a self-presentation that was fairly self-critical and would help one fit into the group. This research suggests that, for individualists, "being yourself" assumes a relatively fixed and stable self-concept made up of generally positive personal attributes. For collectivists, "being yourself" assumes a self that changes according to the situation to better fit in with the group.

Journey of Discovery Question: Why do you think it might be easier to encourage women to expand their gender roles to include work outside the household than it is to encourage men to expand their gender roles to include domestic childcare responsibilities?

Possible answer: One possibility is that North American culture places considerably higher value on tasks traditionally defined as masculine rather than those defined as feminine. Thus, when women work outside the household, they often reap the rewards that have traditionally been reserved for men (wages and jobs that increase one's social status in the larger culture). In contrast, when men take on the domestic task of childcare—a role traditionally assigned to women—there are few tangible rewards doled out by the larger culture. Until we value traditionally defined feminine tasks at the same level as traditionally defined masculine tasks, it will be difficult to encourage men to expand their gender roles to a comparable level as that exhibited by women.

CHAPTER 6

Journey of Discovery Question: Because daydreaming involves thinking about internal thoughts and imaginary situations, what effect do you think television viewing might have on daydreaming? Do you think people who watch a lot of television would daydream more or less than those who watch little television? Why?

Possible answer: Because the content of many television shows involves a great deal of new information and vivid images to viewers, it's possible that people who watch a lot of television might daydream more than infrequent viewers because they are provided with a lot of raw imaginative material from which to construct daydreams. However, due to the fact that television viewing often involves rather passive reception of information, it's also possible that people who watch a lot of television would daydream less because this passive reception of information may stifle their ability to actively construct their own compelling internal images and storylines. Of these two possibilities, research suggests that television viewing does lead to increased daydreaming by providing vivid images that form the content of later fantasies (Valkenburg & van der Voort, 1994). However, this same research also suggests that greater television viewing is related to lower creative imagination. Thus, television viewing may encourage people to more often withdraw into their own inner world, but it doesn't appear to encourage much creative thinking in this state of consciousness.

Journey of Discovery Question: Have you ever had a dream that later seemed to come true? Many people who have had this experience, or who hear of it from a close friend or family member, believe that dreams can predict the future. What other potential explanations could there be for a dream that comes true?

Possible answer: Precognitive dreams may appear real for many possible reasons. One potential explanation lies in what criteria we use to judge whether the dream is "true." If you are in college now and dream that you will graduate some day, it does not necessarily demonstrate psychic ability as much as an awareness of the laws of

probability and the logical consequences of completing your requirements. More specific details of the day—what the weather is like, who the speaker is, what you eat for lunch—would be a much more stringent test, a test that most "predictive" dreams are likely to fail.

Another explanation has to do with the sheer number of dreams you have. Over the course of your life, you will experience thousands upon thousands of dreams. Each dream, in turn, will have many elements. If one element from one dream comes true—for instance, in dreaming about your college graduation, you dream that it rains, and in fact it does rain on your graduation day—that striking occurrence may cause you to believe you have predicted the future. What you have forgotten is the many times you have dreamed of rain when the day has turned out to be sunny, or that in your dream of graduation day, you also "predicted" that your brother would be late, when in fact he was on time. The tendency to see relationships where there is only coincidence is called *illusory correlation* (Berndsen et al., 1996) and is especially common when people are faced with unusual events—such as seeming to predict the future.

Finally, as you will see in Chapter 8, human memory is not a perfect recording device. Our current circumstances influence our recall of events, and dreams are often difficult to recall completely even when they are fresh in our minds. It is difficult to know, looking back across months or years, whether you truly dreamed of rain, or whether the fact that it is now raining is changing your recollection of the dream.

CHAPTER 7

Journey of Discovery Question: Every year, thousands of drug users die from overdoses. Those who have narrowly survived such overdoses tend to report that the setting in which they took the drug that caused the problem was different from their normal drug-taking environment (Siegel, 1984). How might classical conditioning principles explain why these different settings were more likely to be associated with drug overdoses?

Possible answer: It's possible that when drug users repeatedly take drugs in a particular environment, that environment becomes a conditioned stimulus. Whenever drug users enter that drug-associated environment, they experience a conditioned response: Their bodies become prepared ahead of time for the drug injection. When the injected drug is an overdose, this prior-occurring conditioned response may partially counteract the effects of the lethal injection. This conditioned response, however, does not occur in an environment where drug users do not normally take drugs, and thus, their bodies are less prepared to handle an overdose in those unusual settings.

Support for this classical conditioning explanation comes from an actual drug overdose experiment in which rats received injections of either a placebo or heroin on alternating days and in alternating environments (Siegel et al., 1982). Then half of them received a potentially high lethal dose of heroin in the setting in which they normally received the heroin, while the other rats received the drug in their normal placebo-associated environment. More rats died of the overdose when they received it in the setting not normally associated with drug injections.

Journey of Discovery Question: Many of the studies that have explored the principles of classical conditioning and operant conditioning were performed on animals, such as rats and pigeons. How can scientists make generalizations about the way people behave based on these studies? Why not just study people?

Possible answer: It is clear that humans differ from other animals in a variety of ways that would seem to pose a challenge to these studies. In some cases, it is possible to study people, and psychologists have tested behaviorist principles using human participants. In other cases, ethical concerns make the use of human participants impossible. For example, can you imagine conducting the electrical-shock learned helplessness study using college students as participants? In such cases, animal participants provide important information in a rigorously controlled experimental setting. Also remember that the behaviorist perspective is largely concerned with what organisms do, and not with what they think or feel. Once our conscious awareness is removed from the equation, humans appear more similar to non-human animals. Thus animals become a simplified model or analogy of human behavior. This simplification of the model is an asset, not a liability, when scientists are attempting to wrestle with a complex phenomenon; it allows researchers to remove extraneous variables and concentrate on the important theoretical issues. Scientists are also able to argue that, because they are seeking universal principles of behavior, any principle that can be demonstrated in diverse species is a good candidate to be considered universal.

Journey of Discovery Question: Why are the studies on observational learning now mostly based on human populations? And why does observational learning make evolutionary sense for human beings?

Possible answer: The most obvious difference between observational learning and the other types of learning covered in this chapter is that observational learning requires cognition; the more complex the relationship between the observed behavior and the observed consequences, the greater sophistication of thought required to learn from it. Because cognition is relevant to this type of learning, then, it makes sense to study populations with sophisticated cognitive abilities.

Observational learning provides several advantages from an evolutionary standpoint. On a basic level, the ability to learn from your neighbor's errors means that your neighbor, not you, takes the risks. Thus, if, as your mother used to say, all of your friends jumped off a cliff, you at least have the opportunity to see what happens to them before deciding to join in. In a primitive and hostile environment, the capacity for that kind of learning could easily enhance reproductive success. In addition, observational learning can result in cumulative cultural evolution, wherein members of societies exhibit behavior that no individual could invent on her or his own (Boyd & Richerson, 1996), leading to increasingly complex adaptive behaviors.

CHAPTER 8

Journey of Discovery Question: The finding that deep processing leads to more effective encoding and better retention of new information has many practical applications for you as a student. In your own studying, how can you process new information at a deep, rather than a shallow, level?

Possible answer: You could use a number of possible cognitive strategies. The general strategy would be to make connections between information that you already know and new information. One of the most effective forms of retaining information is to associate it with something that has a lot of personal meaning—you. Also, actively question new information and try to think of relevant examples of the concepts under study.

Journey of Discovery Question: Do you think you could falsely reconstruct a childhood memory based on your *beliefs* about how memory works? That is, do you think that your beliefs about how memory works could affect your recollection of past events?

Possible answer: The findings from one recent study raise the possibility that our beliefs about how memory works can indeed affect our recollection of past events. Piotr Winkielman and Norbert Schwarz (2001) asked participants to recall either 4 childhood events (which most people experience as an easy task) or 12 childhood events (which most people experience as a difficult task). Based on past memory studies, Winkielman and Schwarz knew that most people would find that recalling 4 childhood events was rather easy, but that recalling 12 events was rather difficult. Following this either easy or difficult memory task, the researchers manipulated participants' beliefs about how memory works by telling them that either pleasant or unpleasant periods of one's life fade from memory. When the recall task was difficult (12 events recalled), participants who were led to believe that memories from unpleasant periods fade away rated their childhood as less happy than participants who were led to believe that memories from pleasant periods fade away. The opposite pattern of findings was obtained when the recall task was easy (4 events recalled).

Of what practical importance are these findings that people's memories of past events may be shaped by their beliefs about how memory works? Consider clients in psychotherapy who are asked to recall a large number of childhood events. They are likely to experience recall difficulty. It is also likely that they will be told by their therapists that unpleasant childhood memories tend to be repressed and difficult to remember (Garry et al., 1997). The findings from Winkielman and Schwarz's study suggest that clients who both experience recall difficulty and share the popular belief that negative events are difficult to remember may incorrectly conclude that their childhood was unhappy!

CHAPTER 9

Journey of Discovery Question: Research indicates that infants have an inborn ability to detect phoneme sounds that are not a part of their culture's language repertoire. Given that you cannot ask infants questions, how do you think psychologists tested this ability in newborns? That is, how did they design an experiment to test children's inborn ability to detect phoneme sounds?

Possible answer: Janet Werker and her colleagues (1988) tested infants' inborn capacity to detect phonemes by first using operant conditioning principles to condition infants to turn their heads toward a sound source when they detected a change from one phoneme sound to another. The reward that infants received was seeing a clapping and drumming toy animal. The researchers measured infants' ability to differentiate between nonoverlapping English and Hindi phonemes. Using this conditioning technique, they discovered that infants, regardless of which language they were learning, could detect the differences until the age of 8 months. After 8 months, infants could no longer detect phonemes that were not a part of their native language.

Journey of Discovery Question: In Olympic competition, athletes who win an event receive the gold medal, those who come in second place receive a silver medal, and third-place finishers get a bronze medal. Fourth-place finishers receive nothing. Researchers discovered that during the 1992 Olympics, bronze medalists (third-place finishers) exhibited more joy than silver medalists (second-place finishers) after their events (Medvec et al., 1995). How could this finding be explained by the availability heuristic?

Possible answer: When thinking about where they finished in the competition, the second-place finishers are more likely to think about just missing out on winning their event. For them, the most available memory is just missing out on glory, and thus, they don't feel very happy. In contrast, third-place finishers are more likely to think about just beating out the fourth-place finisher for the last medal. Due to this more available memory, they feel joyful.

CHAPTER 10

Journey of Discovery Question: Women who go to college after their midtwenties receive better grades than what you would predict based upon their SAT scores taken just before entering college. Why might this be the case?

Possible answer: There are a number of possible reasons. First, they might initially score lower on the SATs because their test-taking skills are a bit rusty or they are unduly anxious. It may also be the case that these women, being more mature and focused, have greater motivation than younger students, and, thus, they work harder for their grades in college. Finally, given that these women are older, they may be able to rely more upon useful life experiences in managing the stress produced in seeking academic achievement.

Journey of Discovery Question: Imagine that you wanted to develop your own intelligence test. What are some of the pitfalls in early intelligence testing you would want to avoid?

Possible answer: Early intelligence tests were developed using one population but then were incorrectly used to test other populations. So one thing you would need to do in developing an intelligence test is establish a uniform procedure for administering a test and for interpreting its scores so that such bias did not occur. Because intelligence is assumed to be relatively stable, you would want to make sure that your new test yielded consistent results when taken at different times. Also, to what degree does your test measure what it is designed to measure? Early tests often measured things other than intelligence. Thus, you would need to establish your test's validity. Does your test predict other observable behaviors related to intelligence? If so, you have predictive validity.

Journey of Discovery Question: Stereotype threat in the academic area can also occur among members of privileged groups, such as White middle-class men. Can you guess what ethnic group might cause White middle-class men to experience stereotype threat in academia?

Possible answer: Stereotype threat can occur among members of privileged groups, such as White middle-class men. In one study, White male undergraduates who were proficient in math performed poorly on a difficult math test when they were told beforehand that the test was one on which Asians outperformed Whites (Aronson et al., 1999). This and other research suggests that negative stereotypes can create damaging self-fulfilling prophecies among members of many different social groups by inducing stereotype threat.

CHAPTER 11

Journey of Discovery Question: Sometimes, when athletes are paid large sums of money to play their sport, they seem to lose their "love

for the game" and become less motivated. How could this change in athletic motivation be explained by intrinsic and extrinsic motivation?

Possible answer: When playing their sport as amateurs, athletes undoubtedly perceive their actions as being intrinsically motivated. However, after receiving large sums of money to play the sport that they previously played for nothing, some athletes may begin to perceive that they are playing for the money rather than for the "love of the game." This thinking causes a shift from intrinsic to extrinsic motivation. Now, believing that their actions are being controlled by external sources (the money), the athletes do not enjoy playing the sport as much as they did previously.

Journey of Discovery Question: Imagine that you are going out on a date with someone and you would like this person to fall in love with you. Up to this point in your relationship, this person only likes you "as a friend." Based on your knowledge of the two-factor theory of emotions, what sort of activities might you plan for the date to increase the likelihood that the object of your affections will experience a similar emotion toward you?

Possible answer: You could take a cue from the Dutton and Aron "bridge" study and bring your date somewhere in which she or he will become physiologically aroused by the situation. The situation could be a scary movie, a fast ride at an amusement park, or an exciting sporting event. While she or he is experiencing this physiological arousal, you should position yourself nearby so that the arousal is more likely to be attributed to you ("Gee, I am romantically attracted to this person!" your date suddenly realizes.). Good luck!!!

CHAPTER 12

Journey of Discovery Question: An increasing number of contemporary personality theorists pay attention to how culture and evolutionary forces shape personality. Is there any evidence in Freud's theory of personality that he considered the impact that culture and evolution had on personality?

Possible answer: Like many thinkers of his day, Freud was influenced by Charles Darwin's theory of evolution. Freud's emphasis on the sexual and aggressive instincts of the id is compatible with evolutionary explanations of the role that these two behaviors play in adaptation and survival. There is much less evidence that Freud took into account the impact that culture has on personality development. His explanation that the superego develops by the child internalizing the values of his or her parents perhaps represents some small consideration of cultural factors, but he does not explicitly develop this idea.

Journey of Discovery Question: If people with low self-esteem reject attempts to increase their feelings of self-worth by others lavishly praising them, what strategy might you employ to satisfy their self-enhancement needs without triggering their need for self-verification?

Possible answer: Self-verification needs are most likely to override self-enhancement needs when low self-esteem people are presented with positive feedback that, if accepted, would require a major change in their self-concepts. However, research suggests that these same people will engage in direct forms of self-enhancement when the positive feedback is not related to a highly important aspect of their self-concepts (Seta & Donaldson, 1999). Based on this information, one thing you might try is to provide them with positive feedback that is not so lavish and not directly associated with a negative belief that you know they hold about themselves. Subtle praise and positive feedback stretched over long periods of time might be effective in slowly nudging low self-esteem people into gradually changing their self-beliefs so that they develop more positive attitudes and beliefs about themselves.

Journey of Discovery Question: How do you think Freud would describe the highly conscientious person?

Possible answer: Highly conscientious people would, from Freud's perspective, be seen as having a highly developed superego. Freud warned that this has drawbacks as well as advantages. Highly conscientious people may be inflexible, self-righteous, stubborn, stingy, and perfectionist in addition to being successful at work. Low conscientiousness people may be less reliable but are much more fun to be with as they are constantly thinking of new and exciting things to do.

Journey of Discovery Question: Is self-efficacy the same thing as self-esteem?

Possible answer: Self-efficacy is not the same thing as self-esteem. Instead, it is most like what we commonly refer to as self-confidence, but self-confidence related to specific activities. People who have high self-efficacy for many different activities tend to have high self-esteem, but this is not always the case.

CHAPTER 13

Journey of Discovery Question: How might the *confirmation bias*, which was a topic of discussion in chapter 9, section 9-2c, explain the decision-making process of the hospital personnel in the Rosenhan study?

Possible answer: As discussed in chapter 9, the confirmation bias is the tendency to seek only information that verifies our beliefs. Unfortunately, this selective information gathering often prevents us from realizing that our judgments may be incorrect. In forming first impressions of others, research suggests that the questions we ask them tend to be biased in the direction of our initial expectations (Snyder & Swann, 1978). In regard to diagnosing mental illness, these findings suggest that hospital personnel in the Rosenhan study were more likely to ask the pseudopatients questions indicative of mental illness than those indicative of mental health. In this case, such confirmation seeking led to mistakes in diagnosing healthy individuals as psychologically disordered.

Journey of Discovery Question: How could you explain seasonal affective disorder and its treatment using light therapy from an evolutionary perspective?

Possible answer: From an evolutionary perspective, it makes sense that human physiology would have evolved to awaken at fairly low ambient light levels corresponding to the imminent rising of the sun and the beginning of the daylight hours for which humans are best adapted. The effectiveness of light therapy in alleviating the depressive symptoms of seasonal affective disorder suggests the existence of biological pathways in which genetic variation is likely to affect susceptibility to the disorder and its treatment.

CHAPTER 14

Journey of Discovery Question: Suppose a male college student seeks therapy because he is shy and has been unsuccessful in his attempts to talk to women. He reports that he stammers and has trouble thinking of anything to say. He does not initiate conversations with women classmates, even to make small talk. When he starts to make a phone call to ask someone out, he hesitates and talks himself out of making the call. How might a behavioral psychotherapist use modeling and social skills training to treat this student's shyness?

Possible answer: A behavioral psychotherapist might begin by modeling different and more effective social behaviors (how to initiate a conversation, how to make small talk). The therapist may also model ways of managing the anxiety that occurs when the client attempts to talk to women. These anxiety management techniques may include both physiological and cognitive exercises. For example, physiological anxiety management may include slow breathing exercises, while cognitive anxiety management may include telling oneself to "calm down, speak slowly," and "don't anticipate the worst possible outcome." The client would learn these social and coping skills by imitating the therapist and then by practicing them, in the therapy session under the therapist's guidance and throughout the week.

Journey of Discovery Question: Besides effective psychotherapeutic techniques being the cause for people improving during the course of therapy, what are some other factors that might explain the reduction and/or alleviation of psychological disorders?

Possible answer: One possible cause of mental health improvement during psychotherapy is the power of *belief* in a treatment, called the *placebo effect* (see chapter 5, *Psychological Applications* section). That is, if you think a treatment is going to help you, it just may do so through the power of your mind in persuading you to become well. A second possibility has to do with *regression toward the mean*, which is the tendency for unusual events to "regress" or return toward their average state. Thus, extraordinary psychological states, such as feeling very depressed or very anxious, tend to be followed by more ordinary psychological states. When this regression toward the mean occurs, people suffering from a psychological disorder may inaccurately attribute it to the therapy's effectiveness instead of to this naturally occurring tendency.

CHAPTER 15

Journey of Discovery Question: It is generally thought that problem-focused coping is maladaptive in situations when a person has no personal control. Yet, a situation that appears on its surface to be uncontrollable may still have controllable aspects. Consider people caring for loved ones with terminal illnesses. During the weeks leading up to death, what sort of problem-focused coping might caregivers engage in to increase their positive moods and lower stress?

Possible answer: Research by Judith Moskowitz and Susan Folkman found that when people were caring for loved ones with AIDS-related terminal illnesses, many of them created "to-do" lists made up of seemingly mundane tasks, such as getting a prescription filled, buying groceries, and changing the person's bed linens. These lists served at least two positive functions: (1) they provided caregivers opportunities to feel effective and in control, thereby decreasing feelings of helplessness; and (2) successfully completing these tasks provided real benefits to the loved one, whose subsequent positive feedback elevated caregivers' moods. Such problem-focused coping increased positive moods of caregivers during the weeks leading up to death (Moskowitz et al., 1996).

Journey of Discovery Question: Based on your readings, what tactics can you employ to manage your stress and reduce stress-related ailments?

Possible answer: A stress management program could include healthy eating habits, combined with aerobic exercise and progressive relaxation. In addition, if you tend to have a Type A behavior pattern, it would be important for you to slow down and relax. We also know that social support helps people cope with stressors, so maintaining family ties, friendships, and romantic relationships will also prove beneficial to your health. Finally, looking on the positive side of life by developing an optimistic explanatory style will help you deal with uncontrollable negative events.

CHAPTER 16

Journey of Discovery Question: "Road rage" has become an all-too-familiar term describing violent outbursts by people driving cars on our nation's highways. Would this type of aggression typically be instrumental or hostile in nature? Why? Beyond harsh penalties, what strategies might public officials employ to reduce road rage?

Possible answer: In many reported cases of road rage, it appears that the motive underlying the aggression is simply to harm people whom aggressors believe have frustrated their driving goals. The aggression is fueled by anger and, thus, most clearly fits the category of hostile aggression. Possible strategies to reduce road rage would be to try to induce incompatible responses in potentially angry drivers. Brooklyn, New York, has recently employed this strategy by posting signs along the highway containing "knock-knock" jokes. You could also encourage radio stations with "happy" programming formats to advertise their dial numbers on billboards so that drivers would be more likely to tune in to these stations. Another way to use billboards would be to use the insights of social learning theory: Remind adults driving vehicles on the highway that they are role models for children and how they behave while driving will be observed and learned by younger passengers and drivers. This strategy might prompt drivers to think twice before acting upon their frustration, so that their anger doesn't precipitate aggression.

Journey of Discovery Question: Many of you will be—or currently are—parents. Based on what you have learned about helping, what sort of cultural role models might influence the "helping habits" of boys and girls? How might greater gender role flexibility influence male and female helping tendencies?

Possible answer: Social modeling studies suggest that children are most likely to imitate the behavior of people with whom they strongly identify, and for most children, this means same-sex adults. Thus, to foster helping habits in children, existing cultural role models for boys and girls could be enlisted to convey prosocial messages in public service announcements.

In Hollywood movies, most leading-male actors play the traditional masculine role of helping people in dangerous situations, while being rather unwilling or ineffective in providing commonplace, long-term help, such as caring for children and the elderly. The underlying message in many of these movies is that this kind of assistance is unmanly.

In contrast, most leading-female actors play characters who have less traditional gender roles, and they are often depicted as being willing to intervene in both dangerous situations and in those requiring nurturance and long-term care to needy others. This greater flexibility in helping responses reflects the greater gender flexibility available to women in contemporary culture. For instance, girls are generally allowed to engage in more nontraditional gender behavior than boys. As a result, you might expect that girls will learn to help in a wider variety of situations than boys.

Journey of Discovery Question: There is a strong likelihood that at some point in your life you will need help in an emergency. Based on what you now know about the bystander intervention model, how could you increase the probability of receiving aid?

Possible answer: One thing to keep in mind is that deciding to intervene in a possible emergency often involves a complex set of decisions. If bystanders make an incorrect decision at any point in this process, they will not intervene. As the victim, you must attack and neutralize the psychological factors that cause nonintervention. The first psychological hurdle is the *audience inhibition effect*, in which the fear of being negatively evaluated, combined with the tendency to look to others for further information, leads bystanders to identify emergencies as nonemergencies. You can eliminate this inhibition by clearly letting everyone know that this is an emergency and you need help. Yet, even after clearing this hurdle, you must next attack the *diffusion of responsibility*, which is bystanders' tendency to believe they are less personally responsible for helping when others are present. Here, you should implore specific people to help you because it's hard to deny assistance when singled out. Finally, because some people may want to help but are unsure what to do, you can overcome this last hurdle by specifically giving them instructions. Using your most authoritative voice will further increase obedience. And obedience is exactly what you are seeking here.

Glossary

A

Absolute threshold: The lowest level of intensity of a given stimulus that a person can detect half the time.

Accommodation: The process of changing existing schemas in order to absorb new information.

Acetylcholine (ACh): A neurotransmitter involved in muscle contractions and memory information.

Achievement test: A test designed to assess what a person has learned.

Acquaintance rape: Forced sexual intercourse that occurs either on a date or between people who are acquainted or romantically involved. Also known as date rape.

Acquisition: The initial stage of classical conditioning, during which a previously neutral stimulus begins to acquire the ability to elicit a conditioned response.

Action potential: The brief shift in a neuron's electrical charge that travels down the axon.

Activation-synthesis theory: A theory that dreaming is a by-product of random brain activity, which the forebrain weaves into a somewhat logical story.

Adolescence: The transition period between childhood and adulthood.

Adrenal glands: Two glands, located near the kidneys, that secrete *epinephrine* and *norepinephrine,* which activate the sympathetic nervous system.

Aerobic exercise: Sustained exercise that increases heart and lung fitness.

Afterimage: A visual image that persists after a stimulus has been removed.

Aging: The progressive deterioration of the body that culminates in death.

Agoraphobia: A fear of going out to public or open spaces.

Alcoholism: The occurrence of tolerance and physical dependence due to the prolonged abuse of alcohol.

Algorithm: A problem-solving strategy that involves following a specific rule or step-by-step procedure until you inevitably produce the correct solution.

Alpha waves: Fast, low-amplitude brain waves associated with a relaxed, wakeful state.

Altered state of consciousness: An awareness of oneself and one's environment that is noticeably different from the normal state of consciousness.

Amplitude: The height of a sound wave; corresponds to the psychological experience of loudness.

Anal stage: In Freud's theory, the second stage of psychosexual development during which the child derives pleasure from defecation.

Anorexia nervosa: An eating disorder in which a person weighs less than 85 percent of her or his expected weight, but still expresses an intense fear of gaining weight or becoming fat.

Anterograde amnesia: The inability to form long-term memories due to physical injury to the brain.

Antianxiety drugs: Drugs that have an immediate calming effect by facilitating the inhibitory action of the GABA neurotransmitter, thereby reducing nerve impulse transmission.

Antidepressant drugs: Drugs that relieve depression by increasing the supply of norepinephrine and/or serotonin at the neuron's receptor sites.

Antipsychotic drugs: A group of medications that are effective in treating the delusions, hallucinations, and loose associations of schizophrenia by blocking dopamine receptors and thereby reducing dopamine activity.

Antisocial personality disorder: A personality disorder characterized by a persistent pattern of disregard for and violation of the rights of others.

Anxiety disorders: Disorders characterized by distressing, persistent anxiety or maladaptive behavior.

Aphasia: The inability to recognize or express language as a result of damage to brain tissue, such as after a stroke.

Applied psychologists: Psychologists who use existing psychological knowledge to solve and prevent problems.

Aptitude test: A test designed to predict a person's capacity for learning.

Archetypes: In Jung's personality theory, inherited images that are passed down from our prehistoric ancestors and that reveal themselves as universal symbols in dreams, religion, and art.

Assimilation: The process of absorbing new information into existing schemas.

Attachment: The strong emotional bond a young child forms with its primary caregiver.

Attitudes: Positive or negative evaluations of an object.

Audience inhibition effect: People are inhibited from helping due to a fear of being negatively evaluated by other bystanders if they intervene and it is not an emergency.

Audition: The sense of hearing.

Autonomic nervous system: A division of the peripheral nervous system that controls movement of nonskeletal muscles, such as the heart and lung muscles, over which people have little or no voluntary control.

Availability heuristic: The tendency to judge the frequency or probability of an event in terms of how easy it is to think of examples of that event.

Aversive conditioning: A counterconditioning technique in which a classically conditioned aversive response is conditioned to occur in response to a stimulus that has previously been associated with an undesired behavior.

Axon: An extension of the soma that sends information in the form of electrochemical impulses to other neurons.

B

Balance theory: A theory that people desire cognitive consistency or "balance" in their thoughts, feelings, and social relationships.

Basilar membrane: A membrane that runs down the middle of the cochlea that contains the auditory receptor.

Behavior genetics: The study of how the genotype and the environment of an organism influence the organism's behavior.

Behavioral medicine: An interdisciplinary field of science that integrates behavioral and medical knowledge and then applies it to health and illness.

Behavioral perspective: An approach to psychology that focuses on observable behavior, rather than hidden mental processes.

Behavioral therapies: Psychotherapies that apply learning principles to the elimination of unwanted behaviors.

Behaviorism: An approach to psychology that studies observable behavior, rather than hidden mental processes.

Beta waves: Very fast, low-amplitude brain waves associated with an active, alert state of mind.

Binocular cues: Depth cues that require information from both eyes.

Biological perspective: An approach to psychology that attempts to understand behavior by examining physiological processes, especially those occurring in the brain.

Biomedical therapies: The treatment of psychological disorders by altering brain functioning with physical or chemical interventions.

Biopsychosocial model: An interdisciplinary model that assumes that health and overall wellness is caused by a complex interaction of biological, psychological, and sociocultural factors.

Bipolar disorder: A mood disorder characterized by swings between the emotional extremes of mania and depression.

Bisexuality: The sexual orientation in which a person is sexually attracted to members of both sexes.

Blind spot: The area on the retina where the optic nerve leaves the eye and that contains no receptor cells.

Bulimia: An eating disorder in which a person engages in recurrent episodes of binge eating followed by drastic measures to purge the body of the consumed calories.

C

Cannon-Bard theory: A theory that emotion-provoking events simultaneously induce both physiological responses and subjective states that are labeled as emotions.

Case study: A descriptive scientific method involving an in-depth analysis of a single subject, usually a person.

Catatonic schizophrenia: A subtype of schizophrenia characterized by some extreme level of motor activity.

Categorization: The process of forming concepts.

Central nervous system: That portion of the nervous system located in the bony central core of the body and consisting of the brain and spinal cord.

Cerebellum: A part of the hindbrain that regulates and coordinates basic motor activities and may also play a role in learning.

Cerebral cortex: The thin, outer surface of the cerebrum, containing about 80 percent of the brain's total mass; largely responsible for higher-order mental processes.

Cerebral hemispheres: The two main parts of the cerebral cortex.

Cerebral lateralization: The degree to which the right or left hemispheres control various cognitive and behavioral functions.

Cerebrospinal fluid: A clear, cushioning fluid secreted by the brain and circulated inside and around the brain and spinal cord.

Cerebrum: The uppermost portion of the forebrain, which is the "thinking" center of the brain.

Chromosomes: Threadlike structures carrying genetic information and found in every cell of the body.

Chunking: Organizing items of information into a meaningful unit, or chunk, that can be stored in short-term memory.

Circadian rhythms: Internally generated behavioral and physiological changes that occur on a daily basis.

Classical conditioning: A type of learning in which a neutral stimulus acquires the capacity to elicit a response after being paired with another stimulus that naturally elicits that response.

Client-centered therapy: A humanistic therapy in which the client and not the therapist directs the course of therapy.

Cochlea: The coiled, fluid-filled tube in the inner ear that contains the hairlike auditory receptors.

Cognition: The mental activity of knowing and the processes through which knowledge is acquired and problems are solved.

Cognitive dissonance: A feeling of discomfort caused by performing an action that is inconsistent with one's attitudes.

Cognitive perspective: An approach to psychology that attempts to understand behavior by studying how the mind organizes perceptions, processes information, and interprets experiences.

Cognitive therapies: Psychotherapies that focus on identifying and then modifying dysfunctional patterns of thought.

Cognitive-behavior therapy (CBT): The cognitive therapy of Aaron Beck that identifies and then changes negative thinking and behavior by using both cognitive and behavioral principles.

Collective unconscious: In Jung's personality theory, the part of the unconscious mind containing inherited memories shared by all human beings.

Color blindness: A deficiency in the ability to distinguish among colors.

Color constancy: Perceiving objects as having consistent color under different conditions of illumination.

Communication: The sending and receiving of information.

Companionate love: The affection we feel for those with whom our lives are deeply entwined.

Complexity: The extent to which a sound is composed of waves of different frequencies; corresponds to the psychological experience of *timbre*.

Compliance: Publicly acting in accord with a direct request.

Computerized axial tomograph (CAT) scan: A brain-imaging technique in which thousands of X-ray photographs of the brain are taken and then combined to construct a cross-sectional brain picture.

Concept: A mental grouping of objects, ideas, or events that share common properties.

Concrete operational stage: The third stage in Piaget's theory of cognitive development (ages 7 to 11), a time in which children can perform mental operations on tangible objects or events and gradually engage in logical reasoning.

Conditional positive regard: An attitude of acceptance toward another person only when she or he meets your standards.

Conditioned response (CR): In classical conditioning, the learned response to a previously neutral conditioned stimulus.

Conditioned stimulus (CS): In classical conditioning, a previously neutral stimulus that, after repeated pairings with an unconditioned stimulus, comes to elicit a conditioned response.

Cones: Receptor neurons in the eye located near the center of the retina that mediate color vision.

Confirmation bias: The tendency to seek information that supports our beliefs, while ignoring disconfirming information.

Conformity: A yielding to perceived group pressure.

Conscious mind: According to Freud, the relatively small part of our mind that we are aware of at the moment.

Consciousness: Awareness of ourselves and our environment.

Conservation: The understanding that certain physical properties of an object remain unchanged despite superficial changes in its appearance.

Content validity: The degree to which the items on a test are related to the characteristic the test supposedly measures.

Continuous reinforcement: A schedule of reinforcement in which every correct response is followed by a reinforcer.

Control condition: The condition in an experiment where participants are not exposed to the independent variable.

Conventional morality: The second level of moral reasoning in Kohlberg's theory of moral development, characterized by conforming to societal norms and laws.

Conversion disorder: A somatoform disorder characterized by a specific sensory or motor symptom that has a psychological rather than a physical basis.

Cornea: A clear membrane covering the front of the eyeball that aids in visual acuity by bending light that falls on its surface.

Corpus callosum: A thick band of nerve fibers connecting the right and left cerebral hemispheres that transmits information between them.

Correlation coefficient (r): A statistical measure of the direction and strength of the linear relationship between two variables, which can range from −1.00 to +1.00.

Correlational research: Research designed to examine the nature of the relationship between two or more naturally occurring variables.

Counterconditioning: A behavior therapy procedure based on classical conditioning that involves conditioning new responses to stimuli that trigger unwanted behaviors.

Countertransference: Feelings the therapist develops for the client that are presumed to reflect feelings the therapist had for others early in life.

Couples therapy: Therapy designed to help couples improve the quality of their relationship.

Critical thinking: The process of deciding what to believe and how to act based on a careful evaluation of the evidence.

Cryptomnesia: A memory illusion in which people believe that some work they have done is a novel creation, when, in fact, it is not original.

Culture: The total lifestyle of people from a particular social grouping, including all the ideas, symbols, preferences, and material objects that they share.

Culture of honor: A belief system in which males are socialized to protect their reputation by resorting to violence.

D

Daydreaming: A relatively passive state of waking consciousness that involves turning attention away from external stimuli to internal thoughts and imaginary situations.

Decay: Forgetting due to the passage of time.

Defense mechanisms: In Freud's theory, the ego's methods of keeping threatening and unacceptable material out of consciousness and thereby reducing anxiety.

Déjà vu: A memory illusion in which people feel a sense of familiarity in a situation that they know they have never encountered before.

Delta waves: Slow, high-amplitude brain waves most typical of stage 4 deep sleep.

Dendrites: Branchlike extensions of the soma that receive information from other neurons.

Deoxyribonucleic acid (DNA): The complex molecular strands of a chromosome that contains thousands of different genes, located at fixed positions.

Dependent variable: The experimental variable that is measured because it is believed to depend on the manipulated changes in the independent variable.

Depressants: Psychoactive drugs that slow down—or depress—the nervous system and decrease mental and physical activity.

Depression: A mood disorder characterized by sad mood and the inability to experience pleasure from activities one previously enjoyed.

Depth perception: The ability to perceive objects three-dimensionally.

Descriptive statistics: Numbers that summarize and describe the behavior or characteristics of a particular sample of participants in a study.

Development: The systematic physical, cognitive, and social changes in the individual occurring between conception and death.

Diagnosis: The process of distinguishing one disorder from another.

Diagnostic and Statistical Manual of Mental Disorders (DSM): Manual of psychological disorders published by the American Psychiatric Association and used for descriptive diagnoses.

Diathesis-stress model: A predisposition to a given disorder (diathesis) that combines with environmental stressors to trigger a psychological disorder.

Diffusion of responsibility: The belief that the presence of others in a situation makes one less personally responsible for events that occur in that situation.

Discrimination: A negative action toward members of a specific social group.

Disorganized schizophrenia: A rare subtype of schizophrenia characterized by a variety of unrelated hallucinations and delusions, incoherent speech, and strange facial grimaces.

Displacement: A defense mechanism that diverts people's sexual or aggressive urges toward objects that are more acceptable than those that actually stimulate their feelings.

Dissociative amnesia: A dissociative disorder characterized by a sudden loss of memory of one's identity and other personal information.

Dissociative disorders: Psychological disorders characterized by disruptions in consciousness, memory, sense of identity, or perception.

Dissociative fugue: A dissociative disorder characterized by a sudden departure from home or work, combined with loss of memory of identity and the assumption of a new identity.

Dissociative identity disorder (DID): A dissociative disorder characterized by the presence of two or more distinct identities or personalities, which take turns controlling the person's behavior (also known as multiple personality disorder).

Dopamine (DA): A neurotransmitter that promotes and facilitates movement, as well as influencing thought and emotion.

Down syndrome: A form of mental retardation caused by an extra chromosome in one's genetic makeup.

Dreams: Storylike sequences of vivid visual images experienced during sleep.

Drive: A physiological state of arousal that moves an organism to meet a need.

Drive-reduction theory: The idea that an imbalance in homeostasis creates a physiological need, which produces a drive that motivates the organism to satisfy the need.

Drug abuse: Persistence in drug use even when impaired behavior or social functioning results.

E

Eardrum: A thin, flexible membrane at the end of the auditory canal that vibrates in sequence with sound waves.

Ego: The part of our minds that includes our consciousness and that balances the demands of the id, superego, and reality.

Egocentrism: The tendency to view the world from one's own perspective without recognizing that others may have different points of view.

Elaboration likelihood model: A theory that there are two ways in which persuasive messages can cause attitude change, each differing in the amount of cognitive effort or elaboration they require.

Elaborative rehearsal: Rehearsal that involves thinking about how new information relates to information already stored in long-term memory.

Electroconvulsive therapy (ECT): A physiological treatment for severe depression in which a brief electric shock is administered to the brain of an anesthetized patient.

Electroencephalograph (EEG): An instrument that records "waves" of electrical activity in the brain using metal electrodes placed on a person's scalp.

Embryonic stage: The second stage of prenatal development that lasts from the third week through the eighth week of pregnancy.

Emotion: A positive or negative feeling state that typically includes some combination of physiological arousal, cognitive appraisal, and behavioral expression.

Emotional intelligence: The ability to recognize and regulate our own and others' emotions.

Emotion-focused coping: A coping strategy designed to manage the emotional reactions to stressors rather than trying to change the stressors themselves.

Empty-chair technique: A Gestalt technique in which clients engage in emotional expression by imagining that the person to whom they would like to speak is sitting in an empty chair facing them.

Encoding: The first memory process, in which information is organized and transformed so that it can be entered into memory.

Encoding specificity principle: A retrieval rule stating that retrieving information from long-term memory is most likely when the conditions at retrieval closely match the conditions present during the original learning.

Endocrine system: A network of glands in various parts of the body that manufactures and secretes hormones directly into the bloodstream.

Endorphins: A family of neurotransmitters that are similar to morphine and that play an important role in the experience of pleasure and the control of pain.

Episodic memory: Memory for factual information acquired at a specific time and place.

Ethnic identity: A person's sense of personal identification with a particular ethnic group.

Etiology: The initial cause that led to the development of the disorder.

Eugenics: The practice of encouraging supposedly superior people to reproduce, while discouraging or even preventing those judged inferior to do so.

Evolution: The genetic changes that occur in a species over generations due to natural selection.

Evolutionary psychology: An approach to psychology based on the principle of natural selection.

Existential therapy: A philosophical approach to treating clients who are experiencing distress principally related to a lack of meaning in their lives.

Experimental condition: The condition in an experiment where participants are exposed to different levels of the independent variable.

Experimental research: Research designed to test cause-effect relationships between variables.

Explicit memory: Memory of previous experiences that one can consciously recollect.

External attribution: An attribution that locates the cause of an event to factors external to the person, such as luck, or other people, or the situation.

Extinction: In classical conditioning, the gradual weakening and disappearance of the conditioned response when the conditioned stimulus is repeatedly presented without being paired with the unconditioned stimulus.

Extrasensory perception (ESP): The ability to perceive events without using normal sensory receptors.

Extraverts: People who are focused on the external world and tend to be confident and socially outgoing.

Extrinsic motivation: Motivation to engage in a behavior or an activity because of the external rewards it can provide.

F

Factor analysis: A statistical technique that allows researchers to identify clusters of variables or test items that correlate with one another.

Family systems therapy: A form of family therapy in which the family is treated as a dynamic system, with each member being an important interacting element in that system.

Family therapies: Therapies designed to constructively modify the dysfunctional relationships among family members.

Fantasy-prone personality: A person who has regular, vivid fantasies and who sometimes cannot separate fantasy from reality.

Feature detectors: Cells in the visual cortex that respond only to a highly specific feature of a visual stimulus, such as a straight edge, an angle, movement of a spot, or brightness.

Fetal alcohol syndrome: Physical and cognitive abnormalities in children caused by pregnant women consuming large quantities of alcohol.

Fetal stage: The last and longest stage in prenatal development that extends from the ninth week after conception until birth.

Figure-ground relationship: The Gestalt principle that when people focus on an object in their perceptual field, they automatically distinguish it from its surroundings.

Five-Factor Model: A trait theory that asserts that personality consists of five traits (neuroticism, extraversion, openness, agreeableness, and conscientiousness).

Fixation: A tendency to persist in pleasure-seeking behaviors associated with an earlier psychosexual stage where conflicts were unresolved.

Fixed-interval schedules: Partial reinforcement schedules that reinforce the first response after a fixed time interval has elapsed.

Fixed-ratio schedules: Partial reinforcement schedules that reinforce a response after a specified number of nonreinforced responses.

Flashbulb memories: Detailed and vivid memories of surprising and emotion-provoking events.

Flynn effect: The tendency for people's performance on IQ tests to improve from one generation to the next.

Forebrain: Region of the brain above the midbrain that contains the thalamus, hypothalamus, and limbic system.

Form perception: The process by which sensations are organized into meaningful shapes and patterns.

Formal operational stage: The fourth and final stage in Piaget's theory of cognitive development (ages 11 or beyond), during which a person is able to reason abstractly and make predictions about hypothetical situations.

Fovea: The retina's area of central focus.

Framing: The way in which choices are structured.

Fraternal twins: Twins who develop in the womb from the union of two separate sperms and eggs (also known as dizygotic twins).

Free association: A psychodynamic therapy technique developed by Freud, in which clients say whatever comes to mind, without making any effort to inhibit their speech.

Frequency: The number of sound waves that pass a given point in one second; corresponds to the psychological experience of pitch.

Frequency theory: A theory that pitch is determined by the frequency with which the basilar membrane vibrates.

Frontal lobes: One of the four major sections of the cerebral cortex, situated in the front of the cerebral hemispheres and behind the forehead, that is involved in the coordination of movement and higher mental processes.

Functional fixedness: The tendency to think of objects as functioning in fixed and unchanging ways and ignoring other less obvious ways in which they might be used.

Functional magnetic resonance imaging (fMRI): A brain-imaging technique that measures over a few seconds the average neural activity in different brain regions by showing fluctuations in blood oxygen levels.

Functionalism: An approach to psychology that studied how the conscious mind helps humans survive and successfully adapt to their environment.

Fundamental attribution error: The tendency to make internal attributions over external attributions in explaining the behavior of others.

G

Gate-control theory: A theory of pain perception that proposes that small and large nerve fibers open and close "gateways" for pain in the spinal cord.

Gender identity: The knowledge that one is a male or a female and the internalization of this fact into one's self-concept.

Gene: The basic biochemical unit of inheritance that is located on and transmitted by chromosomes.

General adaptation syndrome (GAS): Selye's model of stress in which an event that threatens an organism's well-being (a stressor) leads to a three-stage bodily response: alarm, resistance, and exhaustion.

General intelligence (g): A general intelligence factor that Spearman and other researchers believed underlies all mental abilities.

Generalized anxiety disorder (GAD): An anxiety disorder characterized by a constant state of moderate anxiety.

Generic masculine: The use of masculine nouns and pronouns to refer to all people, instead of just males.

Genital stage: In Freud's theory, the last stage of psychosexual development during which mature sexual feelings toward others begin to emerge, and the ego learns to manage and direct these feelings.

Genotype: The underlying genetic composition of an organism.

Gestalt: An organized and coherent whole.

Gestalt psychology: An approach to psychology that studies how the mind actively organizes stimuli into coherent wholes.

Gestalt therapy: A humanistic psychotherapy that stresses awareness of feelings in the here and now.

Glial cells: Non-neuron cells that supply the neurons with support, nutrients, and insulation.

Gonads: The two sex glands, called ovaries in females and testes in males.

Grammar: The system of rules that determines the proper use and combination of language symbols.

Group therapy: The simultaneous treatment of several clients under the guidance of a therapist.

Gustation: The sense of taste.

H

Hallucinogens: Psychoactive drugs that distort perception and generate sensory images without any external stimulation.

Happiness: A predominance of positive over negative affect (emotion), and satisfaction with life as a whole.

Health psychologists: Psychologists who study the effects of behavior and mental processes on health and illness.

Heritability coefficient: A statistical coefficient, ranging from 0 to 1, that estimates the degree to which heredity determines intelligence within a particular human group.

Heterosexism: A system of cultural beliefs, values, and customs that exalts heterosexuality and denies, denigrates, and stigmatizes any nonheterosexual form of behavior or identity.

Heterosexuality: The sexual orientation in which a person is sexually attracted primarily to members of the other sex.

Heuristic: A problem-solving strategy that involves following a general rule of thumb to reduce the number of possible solutions.

Hierarchy of needs: Maslow's progression of human needs, in which those that are the most basic, namely physiological needs, must be sufficiently satisfied before higher-level safety needs and then psychological needs become activated.

Higher-order conditioning: A classical conditioning procedure in which a neutral stimulus becomes a conditioned stimulus after being paired with an existing conditioned stimulus.

Hindbrain: Region of the brain above the spinal cord that contains the medulla, pons, and cerebellum.

Hindsight bias: The tendency, once an event has occurred, to overestimate our ability to have foreseen the outcome.

Homeostasis: The tendency for organisms to keep physiological systems internally balanced by adjusting them in response to change.

Homosexuality: The sexual orientation in which a person is sexually attracted primarily to members of the same sex.

Hormones: Chemical signals manufactured and secreted into the blood in one part of the body and that affect other parts of the body.

Hostile aggression: The intentional use of harmful behavior where the goal is simply to cause injury or death to the victim.

Humanistic perspective: An approach to psychology that emphasizes human beings' innate capacity for personal growth and their ability to consciously make choices.

Humanistic therapies: Psychotherapies that help people get in touch with their feelings, with their "true selves," and with their purpose in life.

Hypnosis: A psychological state of altered attention and awareness in which a person is unusually receptive to suggestions.

Hypnotizability: The degree to which a person can enter a deep hypnotic state.

Hypochondriasis: A somatoform disorder characterized by excessive preoccupation with or fear of developing some physical condition.

Hypothalamus: A part of the forebrain involved in regulating basic biological processes, such as eating, drinking, sexual activity, emotion, and a stable body temperature.

Hypotheses: Specific propositions or expectations about the nature of things derived from a theory.

I

Id: An entirely unconscious part of the mind that contains our sexual and aggressive drives.

Identical twins: Twins who develop from the union of the same egg and sperm, and thus, share exactly the same genotype (also known as monozygotic twins).

Imaginary audience: Adolescents' belief that their thoughts, feelings, and behavior are constantly being focused on by other people.

Immune system: A complex surveillance system of specialized cells, tissues, and organs that is the body's primary defense against disease.

Implicit memory: Memory of previous experiences without conscious recollection.

Implicit personality theory: Assumptions or naive belief systems people make about which personality traits go together.

Impression formation: The process of integrating various sources of information about a person into an overall judgment.

Incentive: A positive or negative environmental stimulus that motivates behavior.

Incentive theory: A theory of motivation stating that behavior is directed toward attaining desirable stimuli, called positive incentives, and avoiding undesirable stimuli, called negative incentives.

Independent variable: The experimental variable that the researcher manipulates.

Induced movement: The illusory movement of a stationary object caused by the movement of another nearby object.

Infantile amnesia: The inability to remember events that occurred during the early part of life (usually, before the age of 3).

Inferential statistics: Mathematical analyses that move beyond mere description of research data to make inferences about the larger population from which the sample was drawn.

Information-processing model: A memory model concerning the sequential processing and use of information, involving *encoding*, *storage*, and *retrieval*.

Insight: A problem-solving strategy that involves a sudden realization of how a problem can be solved.

Insomnia: A common sleep disorder involving the chronic inability to fall or stay asleep.

Instinct: An unlearned, relatively fixed pattern of behavior that is essential to a species' survival.

Instinctive drift: Species-specific behavior patterns that interfere with operant conditioning.

Instrumental aggression: The intentional use of harmful behavior so that one can achieve some other goal.

Intelligence: The mental abilities necessary to adapt to and shape the environment.

Intelligence quotient (IQ): Originally, the ratio of mental age to chronological age multiplied by 100 (MA/CA × 100). Today, it is calculated by comparing how a person's performance deviates from the average score of her or his same-age peers, which is 100.

Interactionism: The study of the combined effects of both the situation and the person on human behavior.

Internal attribution: An attribution that locates the cause of an event to factors internal to the person, such as personality traits, moods, attitudes, abilities, or effort.

Internalization: A process of cognition in which people absorb knowledge from their social surroundings.

Intrinsic motivation: Motivation to engage in a behavior or an activity because one finds it interesting or enjoyable for its own sake.

Introverts: People who are preoccupied with their inner world and tend to be hesitant and cautious when interacting with people.

Iris: A ring of muscles that range in color from light blue to dark brown.

J

James-Lange theory: A theory that emotion-provoking events induce specific physiological changes in the autonomic nervous system that our brain automatically interprets as specific emotions.

Jealousy: The negative emotional reaction experienced when a real or imagined rival threatens a relationship that is important to one's self-concept.

Just-noticeable difference (JND): The smallest difference in the amount of stimulation that a specific sense can detect.

K

Kinesthetic sense: A type of proprioceptive sense that provides information about the movement and location of body parts with respect to one another.

L

Language: A systematic way of communicating information using symbols and rules for combining them.

Language acquisition device: According to Chomsky's linguistic theory, an innate mechanism that facilitates the learning of language.

Latency stage: In Freud's theory, the fourth stage of psychosexual development during which the child is relatively free from sexual desires and conflict.

Latent content: The true meaning of the dream that is concealed from the dreamer through the symbols that make up the manifest dream content.

Latent learning: Learning that occurs without apparent reinforcement and is not demonstrated until sufficient reinforcement is provided.

Law of effect: A basic principle of learning that states that behavior becomes more or less likely based on the *effect* it has in producing desirable or undesirable consequences.

Learned helplessness: The passive resignation produced by repeated exposure to aversive events that cannot be avoided.

Lens: An elastic, disc-shaped structure that focuses light.

Limbic system: A part of the forebrain consisting of structures that influence fear and aggression (*amygdala*) and the acquisition and consolidation of new information in memory (*hippocampus*).

Linguistic relativity hypothesis: The proposal that the structure of language determines the structure of thought, meaning that people who speak different languages also think differently.

Locus of control: The degree to which we expect that outcomes in our lives depend on our own actions and personal characteristics versus the actions of uncontrollable environmental forces.

Longitudinal study: Research in which the same people are restudied and retested over time.

Long-term memory: A durable memory system that has an immense capacity for information storage.

Long-term potentiation: The long-lasting strengthening of synaptic transmission along a specific neural circuit, which is believed to be the neural basis for long-term memory.

LSD: The most potent of the hallucinogens, which is synthesized and induces hallucinations, distortions, and a blending of sensory experiences.

Lucid dreams: Dreams in which the dreamer is aware of dreaming and is often able to change the plot of the dream.

M

Magnetic resonance imaging (MRI): A brain-imaging technique that produces three-dimensional images of the brain's soft tissues by detecting magnetic activity from nuclear particles in brain molecules.

Maintenance rehearsal: The process of repetitively verbalizing or thinking about information to either extend the usual 18-second duration of short-term memory or transfer the rehearsed information to long-term memory.

Managed care system: A system of insured health care in which the insurance company may determine such issues as which therapists clients may choose, the number of sessions permitted, and which drugs are prescribed.

Mania: An excessively elated, active emotional state.

Manifest content: The dream that is remembered by the dreamer.

Marijuana: A mild hallucinogen derived from the leafy material of the hemp, or *Cannabis,* plant that often induces a sense of giddiness or euphoria, as well as a heightened sensitivity to various stimuli.

Matching hypothesis: The proposition that people are attracted to others who are similar to them in certain characteristics, such as attitudes and physical attractiveness.

Meditation: A variety of mental exercises that alter the normal flow of consciousness in order to enhance self-knowledge.

Medulla: A part of the hindbrain that controls breathing, heart rate, swallowing, and digestion, as well as allowing us to maintain an upright posture.

Memory: The mental process by which information is encoded and stored in the brain, and later retrieved.

Menarche: The first menstrual period.

Menopause: The ending of menstruation.

Mental retardation: A diagnostic category used for people who not only have an IQ score below 70, but also have difficulty adapting to the routine demands of independent living.

Mental set: The tendency to continue using solutions that have worked in the past, even though better alternatives may exist.

Mere exposure effect: The tendency to develop more positive feelings toward objects and individuals the more frequently we are exposed to them.

Meta-analysis: The use of statistical techniques to sum up a body of similar studies in order to objectively estimate the reliability and overall size of the effect.

Metacognition: An awareness and understanding of one's own cognitive processes.

Midbrain: Region of the brain above the hindbrain that contains the reticular formation.

Minnesota Multiphasic Personality Inventory (MMPI): An objective personality test consisting of true-false items that measure various personality dimensions and clinical conditions such as depression.

Misinformation effects: Distortions and alterations in witnesses' memories due to them receiving misleading information during questioning.

Mnemonics: Strategies to make it easier to encode, store, and/or retrieve information.

Modeling: A behavioral method of psychotherapy in which desirable behaviors are demonstrated as a way of teaching them to clients.

Monocular cues: Depth cues that require information from only one eye.

Mood disorders: Psychological disorders characterized by emotional extremes that cause significant disruption in daily functioning.

Moon illusion: A perceptual illusion in which the moon appears larger when near the horizon than when high in the sky.

Morphemes: The smallest units of language that carry meaning.

Motivated forgetting: Forgetting due to a desire to eliminate awareness of some unpleasant or disturbing memory.

Motivation: An inner state that energizes behavior toward the fulfillment of a goal.

Müeller-Lyer illusion: A perceptual illusion in which the perceived length of a line is influenced by placing inward or outward facing wings on the ends of lines.

Multiple intelligences: Gardner's theory contends that there are at least seven distinct and relatively independent intelligences (linguistic, logical-mathematical, spatial, musical, bodily-kinesthetic, interpersonal, intrapersonal), all of which are differently developed in each of us.

Myelin sheath: A protective coating of fatty cells around an axon that hastens the transmission of the electrochemical charge.

N

Narcolepsy: A sleep disorder characterized by uncontrollable REM sleep attacks during normal waking hours.

Natural selection: The process by which organisms with inherited traits best suited to the environment reproduce more successfully than less well-adapted organisms over a number of generations. Natural selection leads to evolutionary changes.

Naturalistic observation: A descriptive scientific method that investigates behavior in its usual natural environment.

Nature-nurture debate: The question of whether individual differences in behavior are primarily due to inborn biological processes or environmental factors.

Need for achievement (n-Ach): A desire to overcome obstacles and to meet high standards of excellence.

Need for cognition: A person's preference for and tendency to engage in effortful cognitive activities.

Negative reinforcers: Stimuli that strengthen a response by *removing* an aversive or unpleasant stimulus after a response.

Neodissociation theory: A theory that hypnotized persons enter an altered state in which two streams of consciousness operate simultaneously, one actively responding to suggestions and the other passively observing what is going on.

Nerve: A bundle of axons from many neurons that are routed together in the peripheral nervous system.

Neurons: Specialized cells in the nervous system that send and receive information.

Neurotransmitters: Chemical messengers released by the synaptic vesicles that travel across the *synaptic cleft* and either excite or inhibit adjacent neurons.

Night terrors: A sleep disorder involving panic attacks that occur during early night stage 4 NREM sleep.

Nonverbal behavior: The communication of feelings and intentions without words.

Normal distribution: The bell-shaped appearance of standardized tests when individual scores are placed in a graph. Most scores cluster around the average test score, and fewer scores are found far from the average score.

O

Obedience: The performance of an action in response to a direct order.

Obesity: The excessive accumulation of body fat. Medically, a person with a body mass index over 30 is considered obese.

Object permanence: The realization that an object continues to exist even if you can't see it or touch it.

Objective tests: Personality tests that ask direct, unambiguous questions about a person's thoughts, feelings, and behavior.

Observational learning: Learning a behavior by observing and imitating the behavior of others (models).

Obsessive-compulsive disorder (OCD): An anxiety disorder characterized by repetitive, unwanted, and distressing actions and/or thoughts.

Occipital lobes: One of the four major sections of the cerebral cortex, located at the back of the cerebral hemispheres, that is primarily responsible for visual processing.

Off-line dream theory: A theory that the cognitive process of dreaming consolidates and stores information gathered during the day, thus allowing us to maintain a smaller and more efficient brain.

Olfaction: The sense of smell.

Olfactory epithelium: A thin layer of tissue at the top of the nasal cavity that contains the olfactory receptor cells.

Operant conditioning: A type of learning in which behavior is strengthened if followed by reinforcement and weakened if followed by punishment.

Opiates: A category of depressant drugs, including opium, morphine, and heroin, that depress the nervous system, temporarily relieve pain, and produce a relaxed, dreamlike state.

Opponent-process theory: (1) A theory of emotion suggesting that every emotion triggers an opposite emotion. (2) A theory proposing that color perception depends on receptors that make opposing responses to three pairs of colors.

Optic nerve: The bundle of nerve cells that carries information from the retina to the brain.

Optimistic explanatory style: The habitual tendency to explain uncontrollable negative events as being caused by temporary factors external to oneself that do not affect other aspects of one's life. This optimistic style is associated with good health and longevity.

Oral stage: In Freud's theory, the first stage of psychosexual development during which the child derives pleasure by engaging in oral activities.

P

Panic disorder: An anxiety disorder characterized by episodes of intense fear and dread that usually occur suddenly and unexpectedly.

Papillae: Taste receptors on the tongue.

Parallel distributed processing models: Models of memory in which a large network of interconnected neurons, or processing units, distributed throughout the brain simultaneously work on different memory tasks.

Paranoid schizophrenia: A subtype of schizophrenia characterized by hallucinations and delusions of persecution or grandeur that can sometimes lead to violence.

Parapsychology: The field that studies ESP and other paranormal phenomena.

Parasympathetic nervous system: The part of the autonomic nervous system that acts to conserve and maintain the body's energy resources.

Parietal lobes: One of the four major sections of the cerebral cortex, situated in front of the occipital lobes, that is involved in touch sensation and in monitoring the body's position in space.

Partial reinforcement: A schedule of reinforcement in which correct responses are followed by reinforcers only part of the time.

Participant observation: A descriptive scientific method where a group is studied from within by a researcher who records behavior as it occurs in its usual natural environment.

Passionate love: A state of intense longing for union with another that we typically experience most intensely during the early stages of a romantic relationship.

Peak experiences: Fleeting but intense moments when a person feels happy, absorbed, and extremely capable.

Perception: The process that organizes sensations into meaningful objects and events.

Perceptual constancy: The tendency to perceive objects as relatively stable despite continually changing sensory information.

Perceptual illusion: A misperception of physical reality often due to the misapplication of perceptual principles.

Perceptual sets: Expectations that create a tendency to interpret sensory information in a particular way.

Peripheral nervous system: That portion of the nervous system containing all the nerves outside the brain and spinal cord.

Personal fable: The tendency for adolescents to believe that their experiences and feelings are unique.

Personality: The consistent and distinctive thoughts, feelings, and behaviors in which an individual engages.

Personality disorders: Psychological disorders characterized by general styles of living that are ineffective and that lead to problems.

Personality styles: Collection or constellation of traits that describes the functioning of the person across situations and settings.

Persuasion: The process of consciously attempting to change attitudes through the transmission of some message.

Pessimistic explanatory style: The habitual tendency to explain uncontrollable negative events as being caused by one's own stable personal qualities that affect all aspects of one's life. This pessimistic style is associated with health problems and premature death.

Phallic stage: In Freud's theory, the third stage of psychosexual development during which the child derives pleasure from masturbation.

Phenotype: The visible and measurable traits of an organism.

Phobic disorder: An anxiety disorder characterized by strong, irrational fears of specific objects or situations.

Phonemes: The smallest significant sound units in speech.

Phonology: The rules used in language to combine basic sounds into words.

Physical attractiveness stereotype: The belief that physically attractive individuals possess socially desirable personality traits and lead happier, more fulfilling lives than less attractive persons.

Pituitary gland: The body's "master" gland, located in the base of the brain, whose hormones stimulate and regulate the rest of the endocrine system.

Place theory: A theory that pitch is determined by which place along the cochlea's basilar membrane is most activated.

Placebo effect: A situation where people experience some change or improvement from an empty, fake, or ineffectual treatment.

Play therapy: A therapeutic technique in which the therapist provides children with toys and drawing materials, on the assumption that whatever is troubling them will be expressed in their play.

Pleasure principle: The process by which the id seeks to immediately satisfy whatever desire is currently active.

Polygraph: A machine that measures several of the physiological responses accompanying emotion (such as respiration, heart rate, blood pressure, and palm perspiration).

Pons: A part of the hindbrain that is concerned with sleep and arousal.

Ponzo illusion: A perceptual illusion in which the perceived length of horizontal lines are influenced by being placed between vertical converging lines that serve as distance cues.

Population: All of the members of an identifiable group from which a sample is drawn.

Positive psychology: A relatively new scientific approach to studying optimal human functioning that asserts that the normal functioning of human beings cannot be accounted for within purely negative (or problem-focused) frames of reference.

Positive reinforcers: Stimuli that strengthen a response by presenting a positive stimulus after a response.

Positron emission tomography (PET) scan: A brain-imaging technique that measures over several minutes the average amount of neural activity in different brain regions by showing each region's consumption of sugar glucose, the brain's chemical fuel.

Postconventional morality: The third and final level of moral reasoning in Kohlberg's theory of moral development, characterized by making moral judgments based on abstract universal principles.

Post-traumatic stress disorder (PTSD): An anxiety disorder characterized by flashbacks and recurrent thoughts of life-threatening or other traumatic events.

Preconscious mind: According to Freud, those mental processes that are not currently conscious but could become so at any moment.

Preconventional morality: The first level of moral reasoning in Kohlberg's theory of moral development, characterized by avoiding punishment and seeking rewards.

Predictive validity: The degree to which a test predicts other observable behavior related to the characteristic the test supposedly measures. (Also known as *criterion validity*.)

Prejudice: A negative attitude directed toward people because they are members of a specific social group.

Prenatal development: The many changes that transform a fertilized egg into a newborn baby.

Preoperational stage: The second stage in Piaget's theory of cognitive development (ages 2 to 7), marked by the full emergence of representational thought.

Primacy effect: The increased memory for the first bits of information presented in a string of information.

Primary reinforcers: Stimuli that are innately reinforcing because they satisfy some biological need.

Primary sex characteristics: The body organs that make sexual reproduction possible.

Priming: A method of activating implicit memories in which a recently presented bit of information facilitates—or "primes"—responses in a subsequent situation.

Private speech: Overt language that is not directed to others but, rather, is self-directed.

Proactive interference: Forgetting due to interference from previously learned information.

Problem solving: The thought process employed to overcome obstacles.

Problem-focused coping: A coping strategy designed to reduce the stress by overcoming the source of the problem.

Problem-solving theory: A theory that dreams provide people with the opportunity to creatively solve their everyday problems.

Procedural memory: Memory of how to perform skilled motor activities.

Prodigies: Individuals who easily master skills in one intellectual area.

Prognosis: A prediction about the likely course of a disorder.

Progressive relaxation: A stress-reducing technique that involves the successive tensing and relaxing of each of the major muscle groups of the body.

Projection: A powerful defense mechanism in which people perceive their own aggressive or sexual urges not in themselves, but in others.

Projective tests: Psychological tests that ask people to respond to ambiguous stimuli or situations in ways that will reveal their unconscious motives and desires.

Prototypes: The most representative members of a concept.

Psychiatry: A branch of medicine concerned with the diagnosis and treatment of psychological disorders. The roughly comparable specialty area in psychology is known as *clinical psychology*.

Psychoactive drugs: Chemicals that modify mental processes and behavior.

Psychoanalysis: An approach to psychology that studies how the unconscious mind shapes behavior.

Psychodynamic perspective: A diverse group of theories descended from the work of Sigmund Freud that assert that behavior is controlled by unconscious forces.

Psychodynamic therapies: A diverse group of psychotherapies based on the work of Sigmund Freud that assert that psychological disorders stem primarily from unconscious forces.

Psychological disorder: A pattern of atypical behavior that results in personal distress or a significant impairment in a person's social or occupational functioning.

Psychology: The scientific study of mental processes and behavior.

Psychometrics: The measurement of intelligence, personality, and other mental processes.

Psychophysics: The study of how physical stimuli are translated into psychological experience.

Psychophysiological disorders: Physical conditions, such as high blood pressure and migraine headaches, that are caused or aggravated by psychological factors such as stress.

Psychosexual stages: The fixed sequence of childhood developmental stages during which the id primarily seeks sexual pleasure by focusing its energies on distinct erogenous zones.

Psychosurgery: A rarely used surgical procedure to treat psychological disorders in which brain tissue thought to be the cause of the disorder is destroyed.

Psychotherapy: The treatment of psychological disorders by employing psychological methods that include a personal relationship between a trained therapist and a client.

Puberty: The growth period of sexual maturation, during which a person becomes capable of reproducing.

Punishment: The process by which a stimulus *decreases* the probability of the behavior that it follows.

Pupil: A hole in the center of the iris that regulates how much light enters the eye.

R

Random assignment: Placement of research participants into experimental conditions in a manner that guarantees that all have an equal chance of being exposed to each level of the independent variable.

Rape myth: The false belief that deep down, women enjoy forcible sex and find it sexually exciting.

Rational-emotive behavior therapy (REBT): The cognitive therapy of Albert Ellis, in which people are confronted with their irrational beliefs and persuaded to develop a more realistic way of thinking.

Rationalization: A defense mechanism in which people offer logical self-justifying explanations for their actions in place of the real, more anxiety-producing, unconscious reasons.

Reaction formation: A defense mechanism allowing people to express unacceptable feelings or ideas by consciously expressing their exact opposite.

Reaction range: The extent to which genetically determined limits on IQ may increase or decrease due to environmental factors.

Reality principle: The process by which the ego seeks to delay gratification of id desires until appropriate outlets and situations can be found.

Recall: A measure of explicit memory in which a person must retrieve and reproduce information from memory.

Recency effect: The increased memory for the last bits of information presented in a string of information.

Reciprocal determinism: The social-cognitive belief that personality emerges from an ongoing mutual interaction among people's cognitions, their actions, and their environment.

Reciprocity norm: The expectation that one should return a favor or a good deed.

Recognition: A measure of explicit memory in which a person need only decide whether or not something has been previously encountered.

Reflex: An automatic, involuntary response to sensory stimuli, many of which are facilitated by the spinal nerves.

Regression: A defense mechanism in which people faced with intense anxiety psychologically retreat to a more infantile developmental stage, where some psychic energy remains fixated.

Reinforcement: The process by which a stimulus *increases* the probability of the behavior that it follows.

Reinforcer: Any stimulus or event that *increases* the likelihood that the behavior preceding it will be repeated.

Reliability: The degree to which a test yields consistent results.

REM (rapid eye movement) sleep: A relatively active phase in the sleep cycle, characterized by rapid eye movements, in which dreaming occurs.

Representativeness heuristic: The tendency to make decisions based on how closely an alternative matches (or represents) a particular prototype.

Repression: In Freud's theory, a very basic defense mechanism in which people move anxiety-arousing thoughts from the conscious mind into the unconscious mind.

Resistance: Anything the client does to interfere with therapeutic progress.

Response prevention: A counterconditioning technique commonly used in the treatment of obsessive-compulsive disorder, in which clients are exposed to the situation in which they previously exhibited a compulsive behavior and are not permitted to engage in the ritual.

Resting potential: The stable, negative charge of an inactive neuron.

Reticular formation: A part of the midbrain involved in the regulation and maintenance of consciousness.

Retina: A light-sensitive surface at the back of the eye.

Retrieval: The third memory process, which involves recovering stored information from memory so that it can be used.

Retrieval cue: A stimulus that allows us to more easily recall information from long-term memory.

Retroactive interference: Forgetting due to interference from newly learned information.

Retrograde amnesia: The loss of information previously stored in long-term memory due to physical injury to the brain.

Rods: Receptor neurons in the eye located at the edges of the retina that are sensitive to the brightness of light.

Rorschach Inkblot Test: A projective personality test in which people are shown ten symmetrical inkblots and asked what each might be depicting.

S

Sample: A group of subjects who are selected to participate in a research study.

Satiety: Being full to satisfaction, in this case, by food.

Savants: Mentally retarded individuals who demonstrate exceptional ability in one specific intellectual area.

Schema: An organized cluster of knowledge that people use to understand and interpret information.

Schizophrenia: Psychological disorder characterized by severe impairment in thinking, such as hallucinations, delusions, or loose associations.

Scientific method: A set of procedures used in science to gather, analyze, and interpret information in a way that minimizes error and leads to dependable generalizations.

Seasonal affective disorder (SAD): A subtype of depression characterized by depressive symptoms at particular times of the year, usually during winter, when daylight is minimal.

Secondary reinforcers: Stimuli that are learned and become reinforcing by being associated with primary reinforcers.

Secondary sex characteristics: The nonreproductive physical features that distinguish the two sexes from one another.

Selective attention: The ability to focus awareness on a single stimulus to the exclusion of all others.

Self-actualization: The ultimate goal of growth, being the realization of one's full potential.

Self-awareness: A psychological state where you take yourself as an object of attention.

Self-concept: The "theory" or "story" that a person constructs about herself or himself through social interaction.

Self-efficacy: A person's belief about his or her ability to perform behaviors that should bring about a desired outcome.

Self-esteem: A person's evaluation of his or her self-concept.

Self-help group: Several people regularly meeting and discussing their problems with one another without the guidance of a therapist.

Self-monitoring: A personality trait involving the tendency to use cues from other people's self-presentations in controlling one's own self-presentations.

Self-serving bias: The tendency to bolster and defend self-esteem by taking credit for positive events while denying blame for negative events.

Semantic memory: Memory for general knowledge about the world that is not associated with a time and place when the information was learned.

Semantic network model: A theory that describes concepts in long-term memory organized in a complex network of associations.

Semantics: The rules used in language to communicate the meaning of words, phrases, and sentences.

Sensation: The process that detects stimuli from our bodies and our environment.

Sensorimotor stage: The first stage in Piaget's theory of cognitive development (birth to age 2) in which infants develop the ability to coordinate their sensory input with their motor actions.

Sensory adaptation: The tendency for our sensory receptors to have decreasing responsiveness to stimuli that continue without change.

Sensory memory: A memory system that very briefly stores the sensory characteristics of a stimulus.

Separation anxiety: The fear and distress that infants display when separated from their primary caregiver.

Set point: A level of weight that the body works to maintain.

Sex chromosome: One of 23 pairs of chromosomes that determines whether someone is male or female.

Sexual orientation: The degree to which a person is sexually attracted to persons of the other sex and/or to persons of the same sex.

Sexual response cycle: The four stages of sexual responding—excitement, plateau, orgasm, and resolution—first identified by Masters and Johnson.

Sexual script: A learned preconception about how a series of events, perceived as being sexual, are likely to occur.

Shape constancy: The form of perceptual constancy in which there is a tendency to perceive an object as the same shape no matter from what angle it is viewed.

Shaping (or the *method of successive approximations*): In operant conditioning, the process of teaching a new behavior by reinforcing closer and closer approximations to the desired behavior.

Short-term memory: A limited-capacity memory system where we actively "work" with information.

Signal-detection theory: The theory that explains how detection of a stimulus is influenced by observers' expectations.

Size constancy: The form of perceptual constancy in which there is a tendency to perceive objects as stable in size despite changes in the size of their retinal images when they are viewed from different distances.

Sleep: A nonwaking state of consciousness characterized by minimal physical movement and minimal responsiveness to one's surroundings.

Sleep apnea: A sleep disorder in which a person repeatedly stops breathing during sleep.

Sleep spindles: Bursts of rapid, rhythmic electrical activity in the brain characteristic of stage 2 sleep.

Sleepwalking: A sleep disorder in which a person arises and wanders about while remaining asleep.

Slips of the tongue: Inadvertent speech errors that occur when sounds or words are rearranged.

Social influence: The exercise of social power by a person or group to change the attitudes or behavior of others in a certain direction.

Social learning theory: A theory that contends that people learn social behaviors mainly through observation and cognitive processing of information.

Social perception (also known as social cognition): The way we seek to know and understand other persons and events.

Social psychology: The scientific discipline that attempts to understand and explain how the thoughts, feelings, and behavior of individuals are influenced by others.

Social skills training: A behavioral method of psychotherapy in which clients are taught how to interact with others more comfortably and effectively.

Social support: The helpful coping resources provided by friends and other people.

Social-cognitive perspective: A psychological perspective that examines how people interpret, analyze, remember, and use information about themselves, others, social interactions, and relationships.

Sociocultural perspective: An approach to psychology that emphasizes social and cultural influences on behavior.

Soma: The cell body of the neuron that contains the nucleus and other components that preserve and nourish it.

Somatic nervous system: A division of the peripheral nervous system that transmits commands to the voluntary skeletal muscles and receives sensory information from the muscles and the skin.

Somatization disorder: A somatoform disorder characterized by a series of numerous physical complaints that have a psychological rather than a physical basis.

Somatoform disorders: Psychological disorders involving some bodily symptom, even though there is no actual physical cause of the symptom.

Sound localization: The ability to locate objects in space solely on the basis of the sounds they make.

Sound waves: Pressure changes in a medium (air, water, solids) caused by the vibrations of molecules.

Speech: The oral expression of language.

Spinal cord: The slender, tube-shaped part of the central nervous system that extends from the base of the brain, down the center of the back, and is made up of a bundle of nerves.

Spontaneous recovery: The reappearance of an extinguished response after a period of nonexposure to the conditioned stimulus.

Standardization: The process of establishing uniform procedures for administering a test and for interpreting its scores.

Stanford-Binet Intelligence Test: The widely used American revision of the original French Binet-Simon intelligence test.

State-dependent memory: The tendency for retrieval from memory being better when our state of mind during retrieval matches our state during encoding.

Stereotype threat: The realization that your performance on some task might confirm a negative stereotype associated with your social group.

Stereotypes: Fixed ways of thinking about people that puts them into categories and doesn't allow for individual variation.

Stimulants: Psychoactive drugs that speed up—or stimulate—the nervous system and increase mental and physical activity.

Stimulus discrimination: In classical conditioning, the tendency for a conditioned response not to be elicited by stimuli similar to the conditioned stimulus.

Stimulus generalization: In classical conditioning, the tendency for a conditioned response to be elicited by stimuli similar to the conditioned stimulus.

Storage: The second memory process, in which information is entered and maintained in memory for a period of time.

Stranger anxiety: The fear and distress that infants often display when approached by an unfamiliar person.

Stress: Our response to events that disturb, or threaten to disturb, our physical or psychological equilibrium.

Stressors: External or internal events that challenge or threaten us.

Stroboscopic movement: The illusion of movement produced by a rapid pattern of stimulation on different parts of the retina.

Structuralism: An early theory in psychology that sought to identify the components of the conscious mind.

Subliminal stimulation: Stimulation just below the absolute threshold for conscious awareness.

Superego: The part of our minds that includes our conscience and counterbalances the more primitive demands of the id.

Superstitious behavior: A behavior learned simply because it happened to be followed by a reinforcer, even though this behavior was not the cause of the reinforcer.

Suppression: Motivated forgetting that occurs consciously.

Surveys: Structured sets of questions or statements given to a group of people to measure their attitudes, beliefs, values, or behavioral tendencies.

Sympathetic nervous system: The part of the autonomic nervous system that activates the body's energy resources to deal with threatening situations.

Symptom: A sign of a disorder.

Synapse: The entire area composed of the terminal button of one neuron, the synaptic cleft, and the dendrite of another neuron.

Syntax: The rules used in language to combine words into sentences.

Systematic desensitization: A counterconditioning technique commonly used to treat phobias in which the client is gradually exposed to the feared object, while remaining relaxed.

T

Telegraphic speech: An early speech phase in which children use short, multiple-word sentences that leave out all but the essential words, like in a telegrammed message.

Temporal lobes: One of the four major sections of the cerebral cortex, located below the parietal lobes and near the temples, that is important in audition and language.

Teratogen: Any disease, drug, or other noxious agent that causes abnormal prenatal development.

Testosterone: A male sex hormone found in both men and women that has a positive influence on sexual desire. The additional testosterone in males stimulates the growth of the male sex organs in the fetus and the development of the male sex characteristics during puberty.

Thalamus: A part of the forebrain that is the brain's sensory relay station, sending messages from the senses to higher parts of the brain.

THC: The major psychoactive ingredient in marijuana.

Thematic Apperception Test (TAT): A test in which people "project" their inner feelings and motives through the stories they make up about ambiguous pictures.

Theory: An organized system of ideas that seeks to explain why two or more events are related.

Theory of mind: A theory of other people's mental states—their beliefs, feelings, and desires—that allows them to predict how these people will behave in specific situations.

Theta waves: Irregular, low-amplitude brain waves associated with stage 1 sleep.

Thyroid gland: The gland, located just below the larynx in the neck, that controls metabolism.

Tip-of-the-tongue phenomenon: The temporary inability to remember something you know, accompanied by the feeling that it is just beyond your conscious state.

Token economy: A technique often used to modify the behavior of severely disturbed people in institutional settings that involves reinforcing desirable behaviors with tokens that can be exchanged for other forms of reinforcement, such as snacks or television privileges.

Tolerance: An effect of drug abuse in which greater amounts of the drug are necessary to produce the same effect once produced by a smaller dose.

Trait: A relatively stable tendency to behave in a particular way across a variety of situations.

Trait perspective: A descriptive approach to personality that identifies stable characteristics that people display over time and across situations.

Transference: Feelings the client develops for the therapist that are presumed to reflect the client's feelings for significant others early in life.

Trial and error: A problem-solving strategy that involves trying one possible solution after another until one works.

Triarchic theory of intelligence: Sternberg's theory that there are three sets of mental abilities making up human intelligence: analytic, creative, and practical.

Trichromatic theory: A theory of color perception that proposes that there are three types of color receptors in the retina that produce the primary color sensations of red, green, and blue.

Two-factor theory: A theory of emotion suggesting that our emotional states are sometimes determined by experiencing physiological arousal and then attaching a cognitive label to the arousal.

Type A behavior pattern: A complex pattern of behaviors and emotions characterized by competitiveness, impatience, ambition, hostility, and a hard-driving approach to life.

Type B behavior pattern: A pattern of behaviors and emotions characterized by a patient, relaxed, easygoing approach to life, with little hurry or hostility.

U

Unconditional positive regard: An attitude of complete acceptance toward another person regardless of what she or he has said or done; it is based on the belief in that person's essential goodness.

Unconditioned response (UCR): In classical conditioning, the unlearned, automatic response to an unconditioned stimulus.

Unconditioned stimulus (UCS): In classical conditioning, a stimulus that naturally and automatically elicits an unconditioned response.

Unconscious mind: According to Freud, the thoughts, desires, feelings, and memories that are not consciously available to us but that nonetheless shape our everyday behavior.

Undifferentiated schizophrenia: A catchall category for cases that do not fall neatly into any single kind of schizophrenia.

V

Validity: The degree to which a test measures what it is designed to measure.

Variable-interval schedules: Partial reinforcement schedules that reinforce the first response after a variable time interval has elapsed.

Variable-ratio schedules: Partial reinforcement schedules that reinforce a response after a variable number of nonreinforced responses.

Vestibular sense (or *equilibrium*): A type of proprioceptive sense that provides information on the position of the body—especially the head—in space.

Vicarious conditioning: The process by which one learns the consequences of an action by observing its consequences for someone else.

Volley theory: A theory of pitch that neurons work in groups and alternate firing, thus achieving a combined frequency corresponding to the frequency of the sound wave.

W

Wavelength: The distance between two peaks of adjacent waves.

Weber's law: The principle that a weak or small stimulus does not require much change before a person notices that the stimulus has changed, but a strong or large stimulus requires a proportionately greater change before the change is noticed.

Wechsler Intelligence Scales: The most widely used set of intelligence tests, containing both verbal and performance (nonverbal) subscales.

Working memory: The term used to describe short-term memory as an active memory system that contains a "central executive" processor and two subsystems for temporarily storing auditory and visual-spatial input.

Z

Zone of proximal development (ZPD): The cognitive range between what a child can do on her or his own and what the child can do with the help of adults or more-skilled children.

Zygote stage: The first two weeks of prenatal development, from conception until the zygote implants itself in the wall of the uterus.

References

A

Abou-Hatab, F. A.-L. H. (1997). Psychology from Egyptian, Arab, and Islamic perspectives: Unfulfilled hopes and hopeful fulfillment. *European Psychologist, 2*, 356–365.

Abramov, I., & Gordon, J. (1994). Color appearance: On seeing red, or yellow, or green, or blue. *Annual Review of Psychology, 45*, 451–485.

Abrams, R. (1993). ECT technique: Electrode placement, stimulus type, and treatment frequency. In C. E. Coffey (Ed.), *The clinical science of electroconvulsive therapy*. Washington, DC: American Psychiatric Press.

Ackard, D., & Neumarck-Sztainer, D. (2001). *Date violence and date rape among adolescents: Associations with disordered eating behaviors and psychological health.* Presented at the 109th Annual Convention of the American Psychological Association, San Francisco, CA.

Ackerman, N. (1966). *Treating the troubled family*. New York: Basic Books.

Adams, J. (1995). *Sellout: Aldrich Ames and the corruption of the CIA.* New York: Viking.

Adams, M. J. (1986). *Odyssey: A curriculum for thinking.* Watertown, MA: Mastery Education Corporation.

Adams, P. R., & Adams, G. R. (1984). Mount Saint Helen's ashfall: Evidence for a disaster stress reaction. *American Psychologist, 39*, 252–260.

Adams, R. D., & Victor, M. (1993). *Principles of neurology* (5th ed.). New York: McGraw-Hill.

Adler, J. (June 17, 1996). Building a better dad. *Newsweek*, pp. 58–64.

Ahlering, R. F. (1987). Need for cognition, attitudes, and the 1984 presidential election. *Journal of Research in Personality, 21*, 100–102.

Aiken, L. R. (1996). *Assessment of intellectual functioning* (2nd ed.). New York: Plenum.

Ainslie, G. (1975). Specious reward: A behavioral theory of impulsiveness and impulse control. *Psychological Bulletin, 82*, 463–496.

Ainsworth, M. D. S., Blehar, M., Waters, E., & Wall, S. (1978). *Patterns of attachment.* Hillsdale, NJ: Erlbaum.

Akerstedt, T. (1991). Sleepiness at work: Effects of irregular work hours. In T. M. Monk (Ed.), *Sleep, sleepiness, and performance* (pp. 129–152). New York: Wiley.

Akil, L. (1982). On the role of endorphins in pain modulation. In A. L. Beckman (Ed.), *The neural bases of behavior* (pp. 311–333). New York: Spectrum.

Al-Ansari, E. M. (2002). Effects of gender and education on the moral reasoning of Kuwait university students. *Social Behavior & Personality, 30*, 75–82.

Alcock, J. E. (1989). *Science and supernature: A critical appraisal of parapsychology.* Buffalo, NY: Prometheus Books.

Alegria, M., McGujire, T., Vera, M., Canino, G., Matias, L., & Calderon, J. (2001). Changes in access to mental health care among the poor and nonpoor: Results from health care reform in Puerto Rico. *American Journal of Public Health, 91*, 1431–1434.

Alexander, C. N., Chandler, H. M., Langer, E. J., Newman, R. I., & Davies, J. L. (1989). Transcendental meditation, mindfulness, and longevity: An experimental study with the elderly. *Journal of Personality and Social Psychology, 57*, 950–964.

Alexander, J. F., & Parsons, B. (1973). Short-term behavioral intervention with delinquent families: Impact on family process and recidivism. *Journal of Abnormal Psychology, 81*, 219–225.

Alexander, J. M., & Schwanenflugel, P. J. (1994). Strategy regulation: The role of intelligence, metacognitive attributions, and knowledge base. *Developmental Psychology, 30*, 709–723.

Alicke, M. D., Yurak, T. J., & Vredenburg, D. S. (1996). Using personal attitudes to judge others: The roles of outcomes and consensus. *Journal of Research in Personality, 30*, 103–119.

Alksnis, C., Desmarais, S., & Wood, E. (1996). Gender differences in scripts for types of dates. *Sex Roles, 34*, 321–336.

Allen, L. S., & Gorski, R. A. (1992). Sexual orientation and the size of the anterior commisure in the human brain. *Proceedings of the National Academy of Sciences of the United States of America, 89*, 7199–7202.

Allen, R. E., & Oliver, J. M. (1982). The effects of child maltreatment on language development. *Child Abuse and Neglect, 6*, 299–305.

Allen, V. L., & Levine, J. M. (1969). Consensus and conformity. *Journal of Experimental Social Psychology, 5*, 389–399.

Allen, V. L., & Levine, J. M. (1971). Social support and conformity: The role of independent assessment of reality. *Journal of Experimental Social Psychology, 7*, 48–58.

Alley, T. R., & Cunningham, M. R. (1991). Averaged faces are attractive, but very attractive faces are not average. *Psychological Science, 2*, 123–125.

Allison, D., Heshka, S., Neale, M., Lykken, D., & Heymsfield, S. (1994). A genetic analysis of relative weight among 4,020 twin pairs, with an emphasis on sex effects. *Health Psychology, 13*, 362–365.

Allison, J. A., & Wrightsman, M. R. (1993). *Rape: The misunderstood crime.* Newbury Park, CA: Sage.

Allison, P. D., & Furstenberg, F. F., Jr. (1989). How marital dissolution affects children: Variation by age and sex. *Developmental Psychology, 25*, 540–549.

Alloy, L. B., Abramson, L. Y., & Francis, E. L. (1999). Do negative cognitive styles confer vulnerability to depression? *Current Directions in Psychological Science, 8*, 128–132.

Allport, G. W. (1937). *Personality: A psychological interpretation.* New York: Henry Holt.

Allport, G. W. (1961). *Pattern and growth in personality.* New York: Holt Rinehart & Winston.

Allport, G. W. (1967). Gordon W. Allport. In E. G. Boring & G. Lindzey (Eds.), *A history of psychology in autobiography* (Vol. 5). New York: Appleton-Century-Crofts.

Allport, G. W., & Odbert, H. S. (1936). Trait-names: A psycholexical study. *Psychological Monographs, 47* (Whole No. 211).

Allport, G. W., & Postman, L. (1945). The basic psychology of rumor. *Transactions of the New York Academy of Sciences, 11,* 61–81.

Allport, G. W., & Postman, L. (1947). *The psychology of rumor.* New York: Henry Holt.

Almagor, U. (1987). The cycle and stagnation of smells: Pastoralists-fishermen relationships in an East African society. *RES, 14,* 106–121.

Almeida, O. P., Tamai, S., & Garrido, R. (1999). Sleep complaints among the elderly: Results from a survey in a psychogeriatric outpatient clinic in Brazil. *International Psychogeriatrics, 11,* 47–56.

Aloise-Young, P. A., Graham, J. W., & Hansen, W. B. (1994). Peer influence on smoking initiation during early adolescence: A comparison of group members and group outsiders. *Journal of Applied Psychology, 79,* 281–287.

Amabile, T. M. (1996). *The context of creativity.* Boulder, CO: Westview.

Amabile, T. M., & Hennessey, B. A. (1992). The motivation for creativity in children. In A. K. Boggiano & T. S. Pittman (Eds.), *Achievement and motivation: A social-developmental perspective.* New York: Cambridge University Press.

Amato, P. R., & Keith, B. (1991). Parental divorce and the well-being of children: A meta-analysis. *Psychological Bulletin, 110,* 26–46.

Ambady, N., Shih, M., Kim, A., & Pittinsky, T. L. (2001). Stereotype susceptibility in children: Effects of identity activation on quantitative performance. *Psychological Science, 12,* 385–390.

American Psychiatric Association (1994). *Diagnostic and statistical manual of mental disorders* (4th ed.). Washington, DC: American Psychiatric Press.

American Psychiatric Association. (1980). *Diagnostic and statistical manual of mental disorders* (3rd ed.), Washington, DC: American Psychiatric Press.

American Psychiatric Association. (2000). *Diagnostic and statistical manual of mental disorders* (4th ed., Text Revision), Washington, DC: American Psychiatric Press.

American Psychological Association. (1992). Ethical principles of psychologists and code of conduct. *American Psychologist, 47,* 1597–1611.

Amsterdam, B. (1972). Mirror self-image reactions before age two. *Developmental Psychobiology, 5,* 297–305.

Anch, A. M., Browman, C. P., Mitler, M. M., & Walsh, J. K. (1988). *Sleep: A scientific perspective.* Englewood Cliffs, NJ: Prentice Hall.

Anderson, C. A., & Bushman, B. J. (2001). Effects of violent video games on aggressive behavior, aggressive cognition, aggressive affect, physiological arousal, and prosocial behavior: A meta-analytic review of the scientific literature. *Psychological Science, 12,* 353–359.

Anderson, E. (1994). The code of the streets. *Atlantic Monthly, 5,* 81–94.

Anderson, J. L., Crawford, C. B., Nadeau, J., & Lindberg, T. (1992). Was the Duchess of Windsor right? A cross-cultural review of the socioecology of ideals of female body shape. *Ethology and Sociobiology, 13,* 197–227.

Anderson, J. R. (1993). Problem solving and learning. *American Psychologist, 48,* 35–44.

Anderson, J. R. (1983). Retrieval of information from long-term memory. *Science, 220,* 25–30.

Anderson, J. R. (1990). *The adaptive nature of thought.* Hillsdale, NJ: Erlbaum.

Anderssen, N. (2002). Does contact with lesbians and gays lead to friendlier attitudes? A two year longitudinal study. *Journal of Commujnity & Applied Social Psychology, 12,* 124–136.

Andersson, J., & Rönnberg, J. (1997). Cued memory collaboration: Effects of friendship and type of retrieval cue. *European Journal of Cognitive Psychology, 9,* 273–287.

Ando, K., Kripke, D. F., Cole, R. J., & Elliott, J. A. (1999). Light mask 500 lux treatment for delayed sleep phase syndrome. *Progress in Neuro-Psychopharmacology & Biological Psychiatry, 23,* 15–24.

Andrews, P. (1986). Molecular evidence for catarrhine evolution. In B. Wood, L. Martin, & P. Andrews (Eds.), *Major topics in primate and human evolution* (pp. 107–129). Cambridge, UK: Cambridge University Press.

Angst, J., & Marneros, A. (2001). Bipolarity from ancient to modern times: Conception, birth and rebirth. *Journal of Affective Disorders, 67,* 3–19.

Annett, M. (1985). *Left, right, hand and brain: The right shift theory.* Hillsdale, NJ: Erlbaum.

Anstis, S. M. (1978). Apparent movement. In R. Held, H. W. Leibowitz, & H. L. Teuber (Eds.), *Handbook of sensory physiology: Vol. 8. Perception* (pp. 655–673). Berlin: Springer-Verlag.

Antrobus, J. (1987). Cortical hemisphere asymmetry and sleep mentation. *Psychological Review, 94,* 359–368.

Antrobus, J. (1991). Dreaming: Cognitive processes during cortical activation and high afferent thresholds. *Psychological Review, 98,* 96–121.

Appel, J. (1963). Aversive effects of a schedule of positive reinforcement. *Journal of the Experimental Analysis of Behavior, 6,* 423–428.

Argyle, M. (2000). *Psychology and religion: An introduction.* London: Routledge.

Arkin, A. M., & Antrobus, J. S. (1991). The effects of external stimuli applied to and during sleep on sleep experience. In S. J. Ellman & J. S. Antrobus (Eds.), *The mind in sleep: Psychology and psychopathology* (2nd ed., pp. 265–307). New York: Wiley.

Armony, J. L., & LeDoux, J. E. (2000). How danger is encoded: Toward a systems, cellular, and computational understanding of cognitive-emotional interactions in fear. In M. S. Gazzaniga (Ed.), *The new cognitive neurosciences* (2nd ed., pp. 1067–1080). Cambridge, MA: MIT Press.

Armstrong, B. G., & Greenberg, B. S. (1990). Background television as an inhibitor of cognitive processing. *Human Communication Research, 16,* 355–386.

Aron, E. N., & Aron, A. (1982). An introduction to Maharishi's theory of creativity: Its empirical base and description of the creative process. *Journal of Creative Behavior, 16,* 29–49.

Aronoff, S. R., & Spilka, B. (1984–1985). Patterning of facial expressions among terminal cancer patients. *Omega, 15,* 101–108.

Aronow, E., Reznikoff, M., & Moreland, K. L. (1995). The Rorschach: Projective technique or psychometric test? *Journal of Personality Assessment, 64,* 213–228.

Aronson, J., Lustina, M.J., Good, C., Keough, K., Steele, C.M., & Brown, J. (1999). When White men can't do math: Necessary and sufficient factors in stereotype threat. *Journal of Experimental Social Psychology, 35,* 29–46.

Arvidson, K., & Friberg, U. (1980). Human taste response and taste bud number in fungiform papillae. *Science, 209,* 807–808.

Asch, S. E. (1946). Forming impressions of personality. *Journal of Abnormal and Social Psychology, 41,* 258–290.

Asch, S. E. (1951). Effects of group pressure upon the modification and distortion of judgments. In H. Guetzkow (Ed.), *Groups, leadership, and men.* Pittsburgh, PA: Carnegie Press.

Asch, S. E. (1952). *Social psychology.* New York: Prentice Hall.

Asch, S. E. (1955, November). Opinions and social pressure. *Scientific American,* pp. 31–35.

Asch, S. E. (1956). Studies of independence and conformity: A minority of one against a unanimous majority. *Psychological Monographs, 70* (Whole No. 416).

Aserinsky, E., & Kleitman, N. (1953). Regularly occurring periods of eye motility and concomitant phenomena during sleep. *Science, 118,* 273–274.

Ash, M. G. (2002). Cultural contexts and scientific change in psychology: Kurt Lewin in Iowa. In W. E. Pickren, & D. A. Dewsbury (Eds.), *Evolving perspectives on the history of psychology* (pp. 385–406). Washington, DC: American Psychological Association.

Ashton, G. S. (1982). Handedness: An alternative hypothesis. *Behavior Genetics, 12,* 125–148.

Atkinson, A. (1995). What makes love last. In K. R. Gilbert (Ed.), *Marriage and the family 95/96* (Annual Editions). Guilford, CT: Dushkin/Brown & Benchmark.

Atkinson, D. R., Brown, M. T., Parham, T. A., & Matthews, L. G. (1996). African American client skin tone and clinical judgments of African Americans and European American psychologists. *Professional Psychological Research Practice, 27,* 500–505.

Atkinson, J. (1957). Motivational determinants of risk-taking behavior. *Psychological Review, 64,* 359–372.

Atkinson, J. W. (1977). Motivation for achievement. In T. Blass (Ed.), *Personality variables in social behavior.* Hillsdale, NJ: Erlbaum.

Au, T. K., Knightly, L. M., Jun, S.-A., & Oh, J. S. (2002). Overhearing a language during childhood. *Psychological Science, 13,* 238–243.

Auerbach, S., M. & Gramling, S. (1998). *Stress management: Psychological foundations.* Upper Saddle River, NJ: Prentice Hall.

Australian Bureau of Statistics. (2000). *Apparent consumption of foodstuffs: Australia* (www.abs.gov.au).

Auwerx, J., & Staels, B. (1998). Leptin. *The Lancet, 351,* 737–742.

Axline, V. M. (1947). *Play therapy.* Boston: Houghton Mifflin.

Ayllon, T., & Azrin, N. H. (1968). *The token economy: A motivational system for therapy and rehabilitation.* New York: Appleton-Century-Crofts.

B

Babad, E., Hills, M., & O'Driscoll, M. (1992). Factors influencing wishful thinking and predictions of election outcomes. *Basic and Applied Social Psychology, 13,* 461–476.

Babyak, M., Blumenthal, J., Herman, S., Khatri, P., Doraiswamy, M., et al. (2000). Exercise treatment for major depression: Maintenance of therapeutic benefit at 10 months. *Psychosomatic Medicine, 62,* 633–638.

Bach-y-Rita, P. (1990). Brain plasticity as a basis for recovery in humans. *Neuropsychologia, 28,* 547–554.

Baddeley, A. D. (1992). Working memory. *Science, 255,* 556–559.

Bahrick, H. P, Bahrick, L. E., Bahrick, A. S., & Bahrick, P. E. (1993). Maintenance of foreign vocabulary and the spacing effect. *Psychological Science, 4,* 316–321.

Bahrick, H. P, Bahrick, P. O., & Wittlinger, R. P. (1975). Fifty years of memory for names and faces: A cross-sectional approach. *Journal of Experimental Psychology: General, 104,* 54–75.

Bailey, J., & Pillard, R. (1991). A genetic study of male homosexual orientation. *Archives of General Psychiatry, 48,* 1089–1097.

Bailey, J., & Pillard, R. (1995). Genetics of human sexual orientation. *Annual Review of Sex Research, 6,* 126–150.

Bailey, J., Pillard, R., Neale, M., & Agyei, Y. (1993). Heritable factors influence sexual orientation in women. *Archives of General Psychiatry, 50,* 217–223.

Bailey, J. M., & Zucker, K. J. (1995). Childhood sex-typed behavior and sexual orientation: A conceptual analysis and quantitative review. *Developmental Psychology, 31,* 43–55.

Bailey, J. M., Bobrow, D. Wolfe, M., & Mikach, S. (1995). Sexual orientation of adult sons of gay fathers. *Developmental Psychology, 31,* 124–129.

Baillargeon, R., & DeVos, J. (1991). Object permanence in young infants: Further evidence. *Child Development, 62,* 1227–1246.

Baker, R. A. (1990). *They call it hypnosis.* Buffalo, NY: Prometheus Books.

Baldwin, E. (1993). The case for animal research in psychology. *Journal of Social Issues, 49,* 121–131.

Balleine, B., & Dickinson, A. (1994). Role of cholecystokinin in the motivational control of instrumental action in rats. *Behavioral Neuroscience, 108,* 590–605.

Balsam, P. D. (1988). Selection, representation, and equivalence of controlling stimuli. In R. C. Atkinson, R. J. Hernstein, G. Lindzey, & R. D. Luce (Eds.), *Stevens' handbook of experimental psychology.* New York: Wiley.

Bandura, A. (1965). Influences of models' reinforcement contingencies on the acquisition of initiative responses. *Journal of Personality and Social Psychology, 1,* 589–593.

Bandura, A. (1979). The social learning perspective: Mechanism of aggression. In H. Toch (Ed.), *Psychology of crime and criminal justice.* New York: Holt, Rinehart & Winston.

Bandura, A. (1986). *Social foundations of thought and action: A social-cognitive theory.* Englewood Cliffs, NJ: Prentice-Hall.

Bandura, A. (1999). A sociocognitive analysis of substance abuse: An agentic perspective. *Psychological Science, 10,* 214–218.

Bandura, A., Ross, D., & Ross, S. A. (1961). Transmission of aggression through imitation of aggressive models. *Journal of Abnormal and Social Psychology, 63,* 575–582.

Bandura, A., Ross, D., & Ross, S. A. (1963). Vicarious reinforcement and imitative learning. *Journal of Abnormal and Social Psychology, 67,* 601–607.

Banich, M. T. (1998). Integration of information between the cerebral hemispheres. *Current Directions in Psychological Science, 7,* 32–37.

Bankston, C. L. III., & Caldas, S. J. (1997). The American school dilemma: Race and scholastic performance. *The Sociological Quarterly, 38,* 423–429.

Banyai, E. I., & Hilgard, E. R. (1976). A comparison of active-alert hypnotic induction with traditional relaxation induction. *Journal of Abnormal Psychology, 85,* 218–224.

Barbaro, N. M. (1988). Studies of PAG/PVG stimulation for pain relief in humans. *Progress in Brain Research, 77,* 165–173.

Barber, B. L., & Eccles, J. S. (1992). Long-term influence of divorce and single parenting on adolescent family- and work-related values, behaviors, and aspirations. *Psychological Bulletin, 111,* 108–126.

Barber, T. X. (1979). Suggested ("hypnotic") behavior: The trance paradigm versus an alternative paradigm. In E. Fromm & R. E. Shor (Eds.), *Hypnosis: Developments in research and new perspectives.* New York: Aldine.

Barber, T. X. (2000). A deeper understanding of hypnosis: Its secrets, its nature, its essence. *American Journal of Clinical Hypnosis, 42,* 208–272.

Bard, P. (1934). On emotional expression after desortication with some remarks on certain theoretical views. *Psychological Review, 41,* 309–328.

Barinaga, M. (1997, June 27). New imaging methods provide a better view into the brain. *Science, 276,* 1974–1976.

Barlow, D., & Rapee, R. (1991). *Mastering stress: A lifestyle approach.* Dallas, TX: American Health.

Barlow, D. H., & Lehman, C. L. (1996). Advances in the psychological treatment of anxiety disorders: Implications for national health care. *Archives of General Psychiatry, 53,* 727–735.

Barnes, S., Gutfreund, M., Satterly, D., & Wells, G. (1983). Characteristics of adult speech which predict children's language development. *Journal of Child Language, 10,* 65–84.

Barnlund, D. C. (1989). *Communicative styles of Japanese and Americans.* Belmont, CA: Wadsworth.

Bar-On, R. (2001). Emotional intelligence and self-actualization. In J. Ciarrochi & J. P. Forgas (Eds.), *Emotional intelligence in everyday life: A scientific inquiry* (pp. 82–97). Philadelphia: Psychology Press.

Baron, R. A. (1973). Threatened retaliation from the victim as an inhibitor of physical aggression. *Journal of Research in Personality, 7,* 103–115.

Baron, R. A. (1983). The control of human aggression: An optimistic perspective. *Journal of Social and Clinical Psychology, 1,* 97–119.

Baron, R. A., & Kepner, C. R. (1970). Model's behavior and attraction toward the model as determinants of adult aggressive behavior. *Journal of Personality and Social Psychology, 14,* 335–344.

Barr, C. L. (2001). Genetics of childhood disorders: XXII. ADHD, Part 6: The dopamine D4 receptor gene. *Journal of the American Academy of Child & Adolescent Psychiatry, 40,* 382.

Barr, H. M., Streissguth, A. P., Darby, B. L., & Sampson, P. D. (1990). Prenatal exposure to alcohol, caffeine, tobacco, and aspirin: Effects on fine and gross motor performance in 4-year-old children. *Developmental Psychology, 26,* 339–348.

Barrett, L., Dunbar, R., & Lycett, J. (2002). *Human evolutionary psychology.* Princeton, NJ: Princeton University Press.

Barrett, P. T., & Eysenck, H. J. (1992). Brain evoked potentials and intelligence: The Hendrickson paradigm. *Intelligence, 16,* 361–381.

Barrick, M. R., & Mount, M. K. (1991). The Big Five personality dimensions and job performance: A meta-analysis. *Personnel Psychology, 44,* 1–26.

Bartholow, B. D., & Anderson, C. A. (2002). Effects of violent video games on aggressive behavior: Potential sex differences. *Journal of Experimental Social Psychology, 38,* 283–290.

Bartlett, F. C. (1932). *Remembering: A study in experimental and social psychology.* London: Cambridge University Press.

Bartoshuk, L. M. (1991). Taste, smell, and pleasure. In R.C. Bolles (Ed.), *The hedonics of taste.* Hillsdale, NJ: Erlbaum.

Bartoshuk, L. M., & Beauchamp, G. K. (1994). Chemical senses. *Annual Review of Psychology, 45,* 419–449.

Bartusiak, M. (1980, November). Beeper man. *Discover,* p.57.

Bass, B. M. (2002). Cognitive, social, and emotional intelligence of transformational leaders. In R. E. Riggio & S. E. Murphy (Eds.), *Multiple intelligences and leadership. LEA's organization and management series* (pp. 105–118). Mahwah, NJ: Erlbaum.

Basson, R. (2002). Women's sexual desire: Disordered or misunderstood? *Journal of Sex and Marital Therapy, 28,* 17–28.

Batejat, D. M., & Lagarde, D. P. (1999). Naps and modafinil as countermeasures for the effects of sleep deprivation on cognitive performance. *Aviation Space & Environmental Medicine, 70,* 493–498.

Bates, E., & Dick, F. (2002). Language, gesture, and the developing brain. *Developmental Psychobiology, 40,* 293–310.

Bates, E., & MacWhinney, B. (1982). Functionalist approaches to grammar. In E. Wanner & L. Gleitman (Eds.), *Language acquisition: The state of the art* (pp. 173–218). Cambridge: Cambridge University Press.

Bates, E., Beeghly-Smith, M., Bretherton, I., & McNew, S. (1983). Social basis of language development: A reassessment. In H. Reese & L. Lipsitt (Eds.), *Advances in child development and behavior* (Vol. 16, pp. 8–75). New York: Academic Press.

Bateson, G., Jackson, D. D., Haley, J., & Weakland, J. (1956). Toward a history of schizophrenia. *Behavioral Science, 1,* 252–264.

Batson, C., Schoenrade, P., & Ventis, W. (1993). *Religion and the individual: A social-psychological perspective.* New York: Oxford.

Batson, C. D. (1998). Prosocial behavior and altruism. In D.T. Gilbert, S.T. Fiske, & G. Lindzey (Eds.), *The handbook of social psychology* (4th ed., pp. 282–316). New York: McGraw-Hill.

Battle, E. K., & Brownell, K. D. (1996). Confronting a rising tide of eating disorders and obesity: Treatment vs. prevention and policy. *Addictive Behaviors, 21,* 755–765.

Battro, A. M. (2001). *Half a brain is enough: The story of Nico.* New York: Cambridge University Press.

Bauer, P. J. (2002). Long-term recall memory: Behavioral and neurodevelopmental changes in the first 2 years of life. *Current Directions in Psychological Science, 11,* 137–141.

Baum, A., & Posluszny, D. M. (1999). Health psychology: Mapping biobehavioral contributions to health and illness. *Annual Review of Psychology, 50,* 137–163.

Baum, A., Gatchel, R., & Krantz, D. (1998). *An introduction to health psychology* (3rd ed.) New York: McGraw-Hill.

Baumeister, R.F. (1998). The self. In D. T. Gilbert, S. T. Fiske, & G. Lindzey (Eds.), *The handbook of social psychology* (4th ed., pp. 680–740). New York: McGraw-Hill.

Baumeister, R. F., & Leary, M. R. (1995). The need to belong: Desire for interpersonal attachments as a fundamental human motivation. *Psychological Bulletin, 117,* 497–529.

Baumrind, D. (1986). Sex differences in moral reasoning: Response to Walker's (1984) conclusion that there are none. *Child Development, 57,* 511–521.

Baumrind, D. (1991). Parenting styles and adolescent development. In J. Brooks-Gunn, R. Lerner, & A. C. Petersen (Eds.), *The encyclopedia of adolescence.* New York: Garland.

Bayley, N. (1949). Consistency and variability in the growth of intelligence from birth to eighteen years. *Journal of Genetic Psychology, 75,* 165–196.

Beach, S. R. H., Whisman, M. A., & O'Leary, K. D. (1994). Marital therapy for depression: Theoretical foundation, current status, and future directions. *Behavior Therapy, 25,* 345–371.

Beaman, A. L., Barnes, P. J., Klentz, B., & McQuirk, B. (1978). Increasing helping rates through information dissemination: Teaching pays. *Personality and Social Psychology Bulletin, 9,* 181–196.

Beatty, J. (2001). *The human brain: Essentials of behavioral neuroscience.* Thousand Oaks, CA: Sage.

Becht, M. C., & Vingerhoets, J. J. M. (2002). Crying and mood change: A cross-cultural study. *Cognition & Emotion, 16,* 87–101.

Beck, A. T. (1967). *Depression: Clinical, experimental, and theoretical aspects.* New York: Harper & Row.

Beck, A. T. (1991). Cognitive therapy: A 30-year retrospective. *American Psychologist, 46,* 368–375.

Beck, A. T. (1997). Cognitive therapy: Reflections. In J. K. Zeig (Ed.), *The evolution of psychotherapy: The third conference.* New York: Brunner/Mazel.

Beck, A. T., & Emery, G. (1985). *Anxiety disorders and phobias: A cognitive perspective.* New York: International Universities Press.

Beck, A. T., Rush, A. J., Shaw, B. F., & Emery, G. (1979). *Cognitive therapy of depression.* New York: Guilford Press.

Beck, C., Silverstone, P., Glor, K., & Dunn, J. (1999). Psychostimulant prescriptions by psychiatrists higher than expected: A self-report survey. *Canadian Journal of Psychiatry, 44,* 680–684.

Beckwith, J., & Alper, J. S. (2002). Genetics of human personality: Social and ethical implications. In J. Benjamin & R. P. Ebstein (Eds.), *Molecular genetics and the human personality* (pp. 315–331). Washington, DC: American Psychiatric Publishing.

Begg, I. M., Anas, A., & Farinacci, S. (1992). Dissociation of processes in belief: Source recollection, statement familiarity, and the illusion of truth. *Journal of Experimental Psychology: General, 121,* 446–458.

Beilin, H., & Pufall, P. (Eds.). (1992). *Piaget's theory.* Hillsdale, NJ: Erlbaum.

Békésy, G. von. (1947). The variation of phase along the basilar membrane with sinusoidal vibrations. *Journal of the Acoustical Society of America, 19,* 452–460.

Békésy, G. von. (1957, August). The ear. *Scientific American,* pp. 66–78.

Békésy, G. von. (1960). *Experiments in hearing.* New York: McGraw-Hill.

Bell, A. P., Weinberg, M. S., & Hammersmith, S. K. (1981). *Sexual preference: Its development in men and women.* Bloomington: Indiana University Press.

Bellack, A. S., & Mueser, K. T. (1993). Psychosocial treatment for schizophrenia. *Schizophrenia Bulletin, 19,* 317–336.

Belle, D. (1982). The stress of caring: Women as providers of social support. In L. Goldberger & S. Breznitz (Eds.), *Handbook of stress: Theoretical and clinical aspects* (pp. 496–505). New York: Free Press.

Bellingham, K., & Gillies, P. (1993). Evaluation of an AIDS education programme for young adults. *Journal of Epidemiology and Community Health, 47,* 134–138.

Bellus, S. B., Vergo, J. G., Kost, P. P., Stewart, D., & Barkstrom, S. R. (1999). Behavioral rehabilitation and the reduction of aggressive and self-injurious behaviors with cognitively impaired, chronic psychiatric inpatients. *Psychiatric Quarterly, 70,* 27–37.

Belsky, J. (1990). Parental and nonparental child care and children's socioemotional development: A decade in review. *Journal of Marriage and the Family, 52,* 885–903.

Belsky, J., & Cassidy, J. (1994). Attachment: Theory and evidence. In M. Rutter & D. Hay (Eds.), *Development through life: A handbook for clinicians* (pp. 373–402). Oxford, England: Blackwell.

Belsky, J., & Rovine, M. J. (1988). Nonmaternal care in the first year of life and the security of infant-parent attachment. *Child Development, 59,* 157–167.

Bem, S. L. (1983). Gender schema theory and its implications for child development: Raising gender-aschematic children in a gender-schematic society. *Signs, 8,* 598–616.

Ben-Amos, I. K. (1994). *Adolescence and youth in early modern England.* New Haven: Yale University Press.

Benassi, V. A., Sweeney, P. D., & Dufour, C. L. (1988). Is there a relation between locus of control orientation and depression? *Journal of Abnormal Psychology, 97,* 357–367.

Benbadis, S. R., Perry, M. C., Sundstad, L. S., & Wolgamuth, B. R. (1999). Prevalence of daytime sleepiness in a population of drivers. *Neurology, 52,* 209–210.

Benbow, C. P., & Stanley, J.C. (1983). Sex differences in mathematical reasoning ability: Fact or artifact? *Science, 222,* 1029–1031.

Bender, R., Trautner, C., Spraul, M., & Berger, M., (1998). Assessment of excess mortality in obesity. *American Journal of Epidemiology, 147,* 42–48.

Benjamin, L. T., Jr., & Crouse, E. M. (2002). The American Psychological Association's response to *Brown v. Board of Education:* The case of Kenneth B. Clark. *American Psychologist, 57,* 38–50.

Ben-Nathan, D., & Feuerstein, G. (1990). The influence of cold or isolation stress on resistance of mice to West Nile virus encephalitis. *Experientia, 46,* 285–290.

Ben-Nathan, D., Lustig, S., & Kobiler, D. (1996). Cold stress-induced neuroinvasiveness of attenuated arboviruses is not solely mediated by corticosterone. *Archives of Virology, 141,* 1221–1229.

Benson, H. (1975). *The relaxation response.* New York: Morrow.

Benson, H., & Klipper, M. Z. (1988). *The relaxation response.* New York: Avon.

Benson, H., & Stuart, E. M. (Eds.). (1992). *The wellness book.* New York: Simon & Schuster.

Beren, S. E., Hayden, H. A., Wilfley, D. E., & Striegel-Moore, R. H. (1997). Body dissatisfaction among lesbian college students. *Psychology of Women Quarterly, 21,* 431–445.

Bergeman, C. S., Chiuer, H. M., Plomin, R., Pedersen, N. L., McClearn, G. E., Nesselroade, J. R., Costa, P. T., Jr., & McCrae, R. R. (1993). Genetic and environmental effects on openness to experience, agreeableness, and conscientiousness: An adoption/twin study. *Journal of Personality, 61,* 159–179.

Bergin, A. E., & Garfield, S. L. (1994). *Handbook of psychotherapy and behavior change* (4th ed.). New York: John Wiley & Sons.

Berk, L. E. (1994). Why children talk to themselves. *Scientific American, 271,* 78–83.

Berkman, L., & Syme, S. L. (1979). Social networks, host resistance, and mortality: A nine-year follow-up study of Alameda County residents. *American Journal of Epidemiology, 109,* 186–204.

Berkowitz, L., & Macaulay, J. (1971). The contagion of criminal violence. *Sociometry, 34,* 238–260.

Berlyne, D. E. (1974). *Studies in the new experimental aesthetics: Steps toward an objective psychology of aesthetic appreciation.* Washington, DC: Hemisphere.

Berman, M., Gladue, B., & Taylor, S. (1993). The effects of hormones, Type A behavior pattern and provocation on aggression in men. *Motivation and Emotion, 17,* 182–199.

Berndsen, M., Spears, R., & Van Der Pligt, J. (1996). Illusory correlation and attitude-based vested interest. *European Journal of Social Psychology, 26,* 247–264.

Berninger, V. W., Abbott, R. D., Abbott, S. P., Graham, S., & Richards, T. (2002). Writing and reading: Connections between language by hand and language by eye. *Journal of Learning Disabilities, 35,* 39–56.

Bernstein, D. A., Borkovec, T. D., & Hazlette-Stevens, H. (2000). *Progressive relaxation training: A manual for the helping professions* (rev. ed.). Westport, CT: Greenwood.

Bernstein, I. L. (1978). Learned taste aversions in children receiving chemotherapy. *Science, 200,* 1302–1303.

Bernstein, J. G. (1995). *Handbook of drug therapy in psychiatry* (3rd ed.). St. Louis, MO: Mosby.

Berridge, K. C. (2001). Reward learning: Reinforcement, incentives, and expectations. In D. L. Douglas (Ed.), *The psychology of learning and motivation: Advances in research and theory, Vol. 40* (pp. 223–278). San Diego, CA: Academic Press.

Berscheid, E., & Hatfield (Walster), E. (1974). A little bit about love. In T. Huston (Ed.), *Foundations of interpersonal attraction* (pp. 355–381). New York: Academic Press.

Berscheid, E., Dion, K., Hatfield (Walster), E., & Walster, G. W. (1971). Physical attractiveness and dating choice: A test of the matching hypothesis. *Journal of Experimental Social Psychology, 7,* 173–189.

Berube, A. (1990). *Coming out under fire: The history of gay men and women in World War II.* New York: Free Press.

Best, C. T., & Avery, R. A. (1999). Left-hemispheric advantage for click consonants is determined by linguistic significance and experience. *Psychological Science, 10,* 65–70.

Bettencourt, B. N., & Miller, N. (1996). Gender differences in aggression as a function of provocation: A meta-analysis. *Psychological Bulletin, 119,* 422–447.

Beyer, C., Caba, M., Banas, C., & Komisaruk, B. R. (1991). Vasoactive intestinal polypeptide (VIP) potentiates the behavioral effect of substance P intrathecal administration. *Pharmacology, Biochemistry and Behavior, 39,* 695–698.

Beyerstein, B., & Beyerstein, D. (Eds.). (1992). *The write stuff: Evaluations of graphology.* Buffalo, NY: Prometheus Books.

Bidlack, W. R. (1996). Interrelationships of food, nutrition, diet, and health: The National Association of State Universities and Land Grant Colleges White Paper. *Journal of the American College of Nutrition, 15,* 422–433.

Bieliauskas, L. A., Counte, M. A., & Glandon, G. L. (1995). Inventorying stressing life events as related to health change in the elderly. *Stress Medicine, 11,* 93–103.

Bierut, L. J., Dinwiddie, S. H., Begleiter, H., Crowe, R. R., Hesselbrook, V., Nurnberger, J. I. Jr., Porjesz, B., Schuckit, M. A., & Reich, T. (2002). "Familial transmission of substance dependence: Alcohol, marijuana, cocaine, and habitual smoking: A report from the collaborative study on the genetics of alcoholism": Erratum. *Archives of General Psychiatry, 59,* 153.

Billett, E. A., Richter, M. A., & Kennedy, J. L. (1998). Genetics of obsessive-compulsive disorder. In R. P. Swinson & M. M. Antony (Eds.), *Obsessive-compulsive disorder: Theory, research, and treatment* (pp. 181–206). New York: Guilford Press.

Billy, J. O. G., Tanfer, K., Grady, W. R., & Klepinger, D. H. (1993, March/April). The sexual behavior of men in the United States. *Family Planning Perspectives, 25,* 52–60.

Binet, A., & Simon, T. (1905; reprinted 1916). New methods for the diagnosis of the intellectual level of subnormals. In A. Binet & T. Simon, *The development of intelligence in children.* Baltimore: Williams & Wilkins.

Biondi, M. (2001). Effects of stress on immune functions: An overview. In R. Ader, D. Felten, & N. Cohen (Eds.), *Psychoneuroimmunology* (Vol. 2, 3rd ed., pp. 189–226). San Diego, CA: Academic Press.

Birenbaum, M., & Pinku, P. (1997). Effects of test anxiety, information organization, and testing situation on performance on two test formats. *Contemporary Educational Psychology, 22,* 23–38.

Bishop, G. D. (1991). Understanding the understanding of illness: Lay disease representations. In J. A. Skelton & R. T. Croyle (Eds.), *Mental representation in health and illness.* New York: Springer-Verlag.

Björkqvist, K., & Niemelä, P. (1992). New trends in the study of female aggression. In K. Björkqvist & P. Niemelä (Eds.), *Of mice and women: Aspects of female aggression* (pp. 3–16). San Diego: Harcourt Brace Jovanovich.

Björkqvist, K., Lagerspetz, K. M. J., Kaukiainen, A. (1992). Do girls manipulate and boys fight? Developmental trends regarding direct and indirect aggression. *Aggressive Behavior, 18.*

Björkqvist, K., Österman, K. & Kaukiainen, A. (1992). The development of direct and indirect aggressive strategies in males and females. In K. Björkqvist & P. Niemelä (Eds.), *Of mice and women: Aspects of female aggression* (pp. 51–64). San Diego: Harcourt Brace Jovanovich.

Black, J. E., Isaacs, K. R., Anderson, B. J., Alcantara, A. A. & Greenough, W. T. (1990). Learning causes synaptogenesis, whereas motor activity causes angiogenesis in cerebellar cortex of adult rats. *Proceedings of the National Academy of Science, 87,* 5568–5572.

Blacker, D., & Tsuang, M. T. (1999). Classification and DSM-IV. In A. M. Nichols (Ed.), *The Harvard guide to psychiatry.* Cambridge, MA: Harvard University Press.

Blair, S. N., Kohl, H. W., Paffenbarger, R. S., Clark, D. G., Cooper, K. H., & Gibbons, L. W. (1989). Physical fitness and all-cause mortality: A prospective study of healthy men and women. *Journal of the American Medical Association, 262,* 2395–2401.

Blass, T. (Ed.). (2000). *Obedience to authority: Current perspectives on the Milgram paradigm.* Mahwah, NJ: Erlbaum.

Blazer, D. G. (1997). Generalized anxiety disorder and panic disorder in the elderly: A review. *Harvard Review of Psychiatry, 5,* 18–27.

Bliwise, D. L. (1989). Normal aging. In M. H. Kryger, T. Roth, & W. C. Dement (Eds.), *Principles and practice of sleep medicine.* Philadelphia: Saunders.

Block, (1971). *Lives through time.* Berkeley, CA: Bancroft Books.

Bloom, B. S. (1985). *Developing talent in young people.* New York: Ballantine.

Bloom, S., & Polak, J. (Eds.). (1981). *Gut hormones* (2nd ed.). Edinburgh: Churchill-Livingstone.

Blumenthal, A. L. A. (2002). A reappraisal of Wilhelm Wundt. In W. E. Pickren, & D. A. Dewsbury (Eds.), *Evolving perspectives on the history of psychology* (pp. 65–78). Washington, DC: American Psychological Association.

Bodenhausen, G. V. (1988). Stereotypic biases in social decision making: Testing process models of stereotype use. *Journal of Personality and Social Psychology, 55,* 726–737.

Bogen, J. E. (2000). Split-brain basics: Relevance for the concept of one's other mind. *Journal of the American Academy of Psychoanalysis, 28,* 341–369.

Bok, S. (1978). *Lying: Moral choice in public and private life.* New York: Vintage.

Bolles, R. (1980). Some functionalistic thoughts about regulation. In F. Toates & T. Halliday (Eds.), *Analysis of motivational processes* (pp. 63–75). London: Academic Press.

Bond, R., & Smith, P. B. (1996). Culture and conformity: A meta-analysis of studies using Asch's (1952b, 1956) line judgment task. *Psychological Bulletin, 119,* 111–137.

Bond, S., & Cash, T. F. (1992). Black beauty: Skin color and body images among African-American college women. *Journal of Applied Social Psychology, 22,* 874–888.

Bonneau, R., Padgett, D., & Sheridan, J. (2001). Psychoneuroimmune interactions in infectious disease: Studies in animals. In R. Ader, D. Felten, & N. Cohen (Eds.), *Psychoneuroimmunology* (Vol. 2, 3rd ed., pp. 483–497). San Diego, CA: Academic Press.

Bonson, K. R., Grant, S. J., Contoreggi, C. S., Links, J. M., Metcalfe, J., Weyl, H. L., Kurian, V., Ernst, M., & London, E. D. (2002). Neural systems and cue-induced cocaine craving. *Neuropsychopharmacology, 26,* 376–386.

Booth, C. L., Clarke-Stewart, K. A., Vandell, D. L., McCartney, K., & Owen, M. T. (2002). Child-care usage and mother-infant "quality time." *Journal of Marriage & the Family, 64,* 16–26.

Boring, E. G. (1923). Intelligence as the tests test it. *New Republic, 35,* 35–37.

Borkenau, P., Riemann, R., Angleitner, A., & Spinath, F. M. (2001). Genetic and environmental influences on observed personality: Evidence from the German observational study of adult twins. *Journal of Personality and Social Psychology, 80,* 655–668.

Borkovec, T., Ray, W., & Stoeber, J. (1998). A cognitive phenomenon intimately linked to affective, physiological, and interpersonal behavioral processes. *Cognitive Therapy & Research, 22,* 561–576.

Bornstein, R. F., Leone, D. R., & Galley, D. J. (1987). The generalizability of subliminal mere exposure effects: Influence of stimuli perceived without awareness on social behavior. *Journal of Personality and Social Psychology, 53,* 1070–1079.

Boss, P. (1999). *Ambiguous loss: Learning to live with unresolved grief.* Cambridge, MA: Harvard University Press.

Boswell, J. (1980). *Christianity, social tolerance and homosexuality.* Chicago: University of Chicago Press.

Botha, R. P. (1997). Neo-Darwinian accounts of the evolution of language: a. Questions about their explanatory focus. *Language & Communication, 17,* 249–267.

Bouchard, T. J., & McGue, M. (1981). Familial studies of intelligence: A review. *Science, 212,* 1055–1059.

Bouchard, T. J., Jr., Lykken, D. T., McGue, M., Segal, N. L., & Tellegen, A. (1990). Sources of human psychological differences: The Minnesota study of twins reared apart. *Science, 250,* 223–228.

Boudreaux, E., Carmack, C. L., Scarinci, I. C., & Brantley, P. J. (1998). Predicting smoking stage of change among a sample of low socioeconomic status, primary care outpatients: Replication and extension using decisional balance and self-efficacy theories. *International Journal of Behavioral Medicine, 5,* 148–165.

Bougrine, S., Mollard, R., Ignazi, G., & Coblentz, A. (1995). Appropriate use of bright light promotes a durable adaptation to night-shifts and accelerates readjustment during recovery after a period of night-shifts. *Work & Stress, 9,* 314–326.

Bousfield, W. A. (1953). The occurrence of clustering in the recall of randomly arranged associates. *Journal of General Psychology, 49,* 229–240.

Bovbjerg, D. H., Redd, W. H., Maier, L. A., Holland, J. C., Lesko, L. M., Niedzwiecki, D., Rubin, S. C., & Hakes, T. B. (1990). Anticipatory immune suppression in women receiving cyclic chemotherapy for ovarian cancer. *Journal of Consulting and Clinical Psychology, 58,* 153–157.

Bowen, M. (1960). A family concept of schizophrenia. In D. D. Jackson (Ed.), *The etiology of schizophrenia* (pp. 346–388). New York: Basic Books.

Bowen, M. (1966). The use of family therapy in clinical practice. *Comprehensive Psychiatry, 7,* 345–374.

Bower, B. (1994, October 8). Images of the intellect: Brain scans may colorize intelligence. *Science News, 46,* 236–237.

Bower, B. (1995). Moods and the muse. *Science News, 147,* 378–380.

Bower, G. H., & Hilgard, E. R. (1981). *Theories of learning* (5th ed.). Englewood Cliffs, NJ: Prentice Hall.

Bower, G. H., & Mayer, J. D. (1991). In search of mood-dependent retrieval. In D. Kuiken (Ed.), *Mood and memory.* Newbury Park, CA: Sage.

Bower, G. H., Clark, M. C., Lesgold, A. M., & Winzenz, D. (1969). Hierarchical retrieval schemes in recall of categorized word lists. *Journal of Verbal Learning and Verbal Behavior, 8,* 323–343.

Bowers, K. S., & Woody, E. Z. (1996). Hypnotic amnesia and the paradox of intentional forgetting. *Journal of Abnormal Psychology, 105,* 381–390.

Bowers, K. S., Farvolden, P., & Mermigis, L. (1995). Intuitive antecedents of insight. In S. M. Smith, T. M. Ward, & R. A. Finke (Eds.), *The creative cognition approach* (pp. 27–52). Cambridge, MA: MIT Press.

Bowers, T. (1997). Supporting special needs in the mainstream classroom: Children's perceptions of the adult role. *Child: Care, Health and Development, 23,* 217–232.

Bowes, D. E., Tamlyn, D., & Butler, L. J. (2002). Women living with ovarian cancer: Dealing with an early death. *Health Care for Women International, 23,* 135–148.

Bowlby, J. (1969). *Attachment and loss*. Vol. I. *Attachment*. New York: John Wiley.

Bowlby, J. (1988). *A secure base: Parent-child attachment and healthy human development*. New York: Basic Books.

Bowman, C., & Brownell, P. (2000). Prelude to contemporary Gestalt therapy. *Gestalt Journal, 4*, 118–129.

Boyce, T. E., & Geller, E. S. (2002). An instrumented vehicle assessment of problem behavior and driving style: Do younger males really take more risks? *Accident Analysis & Prevention, 34*, 51–64.

Boyd, R. & Richerson, P. J. (1996). Why culture is common, but cultural evolution is rare. In W. G. Runciman, J. M Smith, et al. (Eds.), *Evolution of social behavior patterns in primates and man. Proceedings of The British Academy, Vol. 88* (pp. 77–93). Oxford, England: Oxford University Press.

Bracken, B. A., Howell, K. K., & Crain, M. R. (1993). Prediction of Caucasian and African-American preschool children's fluid and crystallized intelligence: Contributions of maternal characteristics and home environment. *Journal of Clinical Child Psychology, 22*, 455–463.

Bradburn, N. M., & Sudman, S. (1988). *Polls and surveys: Understanding what they tell us*. San Francisco: Jossey-Bass.

Bradley, R. H., & Caldwell, B. M. (1984). 174 children: A study of the relationship between home environment and cognitive development during the first 5 years. In A. W. Gottfried (Ed.), *Home environment and early cognitive development: Longitudinal research*. Orlando, FL: Academic Press.

Brainerd, C. J., Reyna, V. F., & Brandse, E. (1995). Are children's false memories more persistent than their true memories? *Psychological Science, 6*, 359–364.

Brandimonte, M. A., Hitch, G. J., & Bishop, D. V. M. (1992). Influence of short-term memory codes on visual image processing: Evidence from image transformation tasks. *Journal of Experimental Psychology: Learning, Memory, and Cognition, 18*, 157–165.

Brannon, L., & Feist, J. (2000). *Health psychology: An introduction to behavior and health* (4th ed.) Belmont, CA: Wadsworth/Thomson Learning.

Branscombe, N. R., Schmidt, M. T., & Harvey, R. D. (in press). Perceiving pervasive discrimination among African-Americans: Implications for group identification and well-being. *Journal of Personality and Social Psychology*.

Bransford, J. D., & Johnson, M. K. (1972). Contextual prerequisites for understanding: Some investigations of comprehension and recall. *Journal of Verbal Learning and Verbal Behavior, 11*, 717–726.

Bray, G. (1992). Pathophysiology of obesity. *American Journal of Clinical Nutrition, 55*, 488S–494S.

Breedlove, S. M. (1997). Sex on the brain. *Nature, 389*, 801.

Breggin, P. R. (1979). *Electroshock: Its disabling effects*. New York: Springer-Verlag.

Breggin, P. R. (1991). *Toxic psychiatry*. New York: St. Martin's Press.

Brehm, J. (1966). *A theory of psychological reactance*. New York: Academic Press.

Brehm, S. S. (1988). Passionate love. In R. J. Sternberg & M. L. Barnes (Eds.), *The psychology of love* (pp. 232–263). New Haven, CT: Yale University Press.

Brehm, S. S. (1992). *Intimate relationships*. New York: McGraw-Hill.

Brehm, S. S., & Brehm, J. W. (1981). *Psychological reactance: A theory of freedom and control*. New York: Academic Press.

Breland, K., & Breland, M. (1961). The misbehavior of organisms. *American Psychologist, 16*, 681–684.

Brems, C. (1995). Women and depression: A comprehensive analysis. In E. E. Beckham & W. R. Leber (Eds.), *Handbook of depression* (2nd ed., pp. 539–566). New York: Guilford Press.

Brennan, P. A., Grekin, E. R., & Mednick, S. A. (1999). Maternal smoking during pregnancy and adult male criminal outcomes. *Archives of General Psychiatry, 56*, 215–219.

Bretherton, I. (1985). Attachment theory: Retrospect and prospect. In I. Bretherton & E. Waters (Eds.), Growing points of attachment theory and research. *Monographs of the Society for Research in Child Development, 50*(1–2, Serial No. 209), 3–35.

Breuer, J., & Freud, S. (1955). Studies on hysteria. In J. Strachey (Ed. And Trans.), *The standard edition of the complete psychological works of Sigmund Freud* (Vol. 2, pp. 1–251). London: Hogarth. (original work published in 1893–1895)

Brewer, M. B. (1988). A dual process model of impression formation. In T. K. Srull & R. S. Wyer, Jr. (Eds.), *Advances in social cognition, Vol. 1: A dual process model of impression formation* (pp. 1–36). Hillsdale, NJ: Erlbaum.

Brewer, M. B., & Brown, R. J. (1998). Intergroup relations. In D. T. Gilbert, S. T. Fiske, & G. Lindzey (Eds.), *The handbook of social psychology* (4th ed.). New York: McGraw-Hill.

Brewin, C. R., Dalgleish, T., & Joseph, S. (1996). A dual representation theory of posttraumatic stress disorder. *Psychological Review, 103*, 670–686.

Brickman, P., Coates, D., & Janoff-Bulman, R. J. (1978). Lottery winners and accident victims: Is happiness relative? *Journal of Personality and Social Psychology, 36*, 917–927.

Bridges, J. S., & Etaugh, C. (1994). Black and White college women's perceptions of early maternal employment. *Psychology of Women Quarterly, 18*, 427–431.

Briere, J., & Lanktree, C. (1983). Sex-role related effects of sex bias in language. *Sex Roles, 9*, 625–632.

Bril, B. (1986). Motor development and cultural attitudes. In H. T. A. Whiting & M. G. Wade (Eds.), *Themes in motor development*. Dordrecht, Netherlands: Martinus Nijhoff.

Bringle, R. G., & Buunk, B. (1986). Examining the causes and consequences of jealousy: Some recent findings and issues. In R. Gilmour & S. Duck (Eds.), *The emerging field of personal relationships* (pp. 225–240). Hillsdale, NJ: Erlbaum.

Brislin, R. (1993). *Understanding culture's influence on behavior*. Fort Worth, TX: Harcourt Brace Jovanovich.

Broberg, D. J., & Bernstein, I. L. (1987). Candy as a scapegoat in the prevention of food aversions in children receiving chemotherapy. *Cancer, 60*, 2344–2347.

Brody, L. R., & Hall, J. A. (1993). Gender and emotion. In M. Lewis & J. M. Haviland (Eds.), *Handbook of emotions* (pp. 447–460). New York: Guilford.

Brody, N. (1992). *Intelligence* (2nd ed.). San Diego, CA: Academic Press.

Brody, N. (2000). History of theories and measurements of intelligence. In R. J. Sternberg (Ed.), *Handbook of intelligence* (pp. 16–33). Cambridge: Cambridge University Press.

Bromet, E. J., & Havenaar, J. M. (2002). Mental health consequences of disasters. In N. Sartorius & W. Gaebel (Eds.), *Psychiatry in society* (pp. 241–261). New York: Wiley.

Brooner, R. K., Schmidt, C. W., Jr., & Herbst, J. H. (2002). Personality trait characteristics of opioid abusers with and without comorbid personality disorders. In P. T. Costa, Jr., & T. A. Widiger (Eds.), *Personality disorders and the five-factor model of personality* (2nd ed., pp. 249–268). Washington, DC: American Psychological Association.

Bruehl, S. (2002). A case of borderline personality disorder. In P. T. Costa, Jr., & T. A. Widiger (Eds.), *Personality disorders and the five-factor model of personality* (2nd ed., pp. 283–291). Washington, DC: American Psychological Association.

Broughton, R., De Konick, J., Gagnon, P., Dunham, W., & Stampi, C. (1990). Sleep-wake biorhythms and extended sleep in man. In J. Montplaisir & R. Godbout (Eds.), *Sleep and biological rhythms: Basic mechanisms and applications to psychiatry* (pp. 25–41). New York: Oxford University Press.

Brown, A. D., & Murphy, D. R. (1989). Cryptomnesia: Delineating inadvertent plagiarism. *Journal of Experimental Psychology: Learning, Memory, & Cognition, 15,* 432–442.

Brown, A. S. (1991). A review of the tip-of-the-tongue experience. *Psychological Bulletin, 109,* 204–223.

Brown, G. M. (1994). Light, melatonin, and the sleep-wake cycle. *Journal of Psychiatry and Neuroscience, 19,* 345–353.

Brown, J. (1958). Some tests of the decay theory of immediate memory. *Quarterly Journal of the Behavioral Sciences, 11,* 342–349.

Brown, P., & Levinson, S. (1987). *Politeness: Some universals in language usage.* Cambridge, England: Cambridge University Press.

Brown, P. K., & Wald, G. (1964). Visual pigments in single rods and cones of the human retina. *Science, 144,* 45–52.

Brown, R. (1973). *A first language: The early stages.* Cambridge, MA: Harvard University Press.

Brown, R. (1986). Linguistic relativity. In S. H. Hulse & B. F. Green, Jr. (Eds.), *One hundred years of psychological research in America.* Baltimore: John Hopkins University Press.

Brown, R., & Kulik, J. (1977). Flashbulb memories. *Cognition, 5,* 73–99.

Brown, S. R. (2000). Tip-of-the-tongue phenomena: An introductrory phenomenological analysis. *Consciousness & Cognition: An International Journal, 9,* 516–537.

Brownell, K. D. (1991). Dieting and the search for the perfect body: Where physiology and culture collide. *Behavior Therapy, 22,* 1–12.

Brownell, K. D., & Rodin, J. (1994). Medical, metabolic, and psychological effects of weight cycling. *Archives of Internal Medicine, 154,* 1325–1330.

Brownell, K. D., & Wadden, T. (1991). The heterogeneity of obesity: Fitting treatments to individuals. *Behavior Therapy, 22,* 153–177.

Brownell, K. D., & Wadden, T. (1992). Etiology and treatment of obesity: Understanding a serious, prevalent, and refractory disorder. *Journal of Consulting and Clinical Psychology, 60,* 505–517.

Bruch, H. (1973). *Eating disorders. Obesity, anorexia nervosa, and the person within.* New York: Basic Books.

Bruch, H. (1982). Anorexia nervosa: Therapy and theory. *American Journal of Psychiatry, 139,* 1531–1538.

Brudzynski, S. M. (2001). Pharmacological and behavioral characteristics of 22 kHz alarm calls in rats. *Neuroscience & Biobehavioral Reviews, 25,* 611–617.

Bryant, R. A., Barnier, A. J., Mallard, D., & Tibbits, R. (1999). Posthypnotic amnesia for material learned before hypnosis. *International Journal of Clinical and Experimental Hypnosis, 47,* 46–64.

Bryden, M. P. (1979). Evidence for sex-related differences in cerebral organization. In M. A. Whiting & A. Peterson (Eds.), *Sex-related differences in cognitive functioning* (pp. 121–143). New York: Academic Press.

Bryson, S. E. (1990). Autism and anomalous handedness. In S. Coren (Ed.), *Left-handedness: Behavioral implications and anomalies.* Amsterdam: North-Holland.

Buck, L., & Axel, R. (1991). A novel multigene family may encode odorant receptors: A molecular basis for odor recognition. *Cell, 65,* 175–187.

Buck, R. (1984). *The communication of emotion.* New York: Guilford Press.

Buhusi, C. V., & Schmajuk, N. A. (1999). Timing in simple conditioning and occasion setting: A neural network approach. *Behavioural Processes, 45,* 33–57.

Bullough, V. (1980). The Kinsey scale in historical perspective. In D. P. McWhirter, S. A. Sanders, & J. M. Reinisch (Eds.), *Homosexuality/heterosexuality: Concepts of sexual orientation.* New York: Oxford University Press.

Burger, J. M. (1987). Desire for control and conformity to a perceived norm. *Journal of Personality and Social Psychology, 53,* 355–360.

Burger, J. M., Horita, M., Kinoshita, L., Roberts, K., & Vera, C. (1997). Effects of time on the norm of reciprocity. *Basic and Applied Social Psychology, 19,* 91–100.

Burling, R. (1986). The selective advantage of complex language. *Ethology & Sociobiology, 1,* 1–16.

Burt, M. (1980). Cultural myths and supports for rape. *Journal of Personality and Social Psychology, 38,* 217–230.

Busch, C. M., Zonderman, A. B., & Costa, P. T. (1994). Menopausal transition and psychological distress in a nationally representative sample: Is menopause associated with psychological distress? *Journal of Aging and Health, 6,* 209–228.

Bushman, B. J. (2002). Does venting anger feed or extinguish the flame? Catharsis, rumination, distraction, anger, and aggressive responding. *Personality and Social Psychology Bulletin, 28,* 724–731.

Bushman, B. J., & Anderson, C. A. (2001). Is it time to pull the plug on the hostile versus instrumental aggression dichotomy? *Psychological Review, 108,* 273–279.

Bushman, B. J., Baumeister, R. F., & Stack, A. D. (1999). Catharsis, aggression, and persuasive influence: Self-fulfilling or self-defeating prophecies. *Journal of Personality and Social Psychology, 76,* 367–376.

Buske-Kirschbaum, A., Kirschbaum, C., Stierle, H., Jabaij, L., & Hellhammer, D. (1994). Conditioned manipulation of natural killer (NK) cells in humans using a discriminative learning protocol. *Biological Psychology, 38,* 143–155.

Buss, A. H., & Plomin, R. (1984). *Temperament: Early developing personality traits.* Hillsdale, NJ: Erlbaum.

Buss, D. H. (1999). *Evolutionary psychology.* Boston: Allyn & Bacon.

Buss, D. H., & Kenrick, D. (1998). Evolutionary social psychology. In D. Gilbert, S. Fiske, & G. Lindzey (Eds.), *The handbook of social psychology* (Vol. 2, 4th ed., pp. 982–1026). New York: Oxford University Press.

Buss, D. M. (1987). Sex differences in human mate selection criteria: An evolutionary perspective. In C. Crawford, M. Smith, & D. Krebs (Eds.), *Sociobiology and psychology: Ideas, issues and applications* (pp. 335–351). Hillsdale, NJ: Erlbaum.

Buss, D. M. (1988). The evolution of human intrasexual competition: Tactics of mate attraction. *Journal of Personality and Social Psychology, 54,* 616–628.

Buss, D. M. (1989). Sex differences in human mate preferences: Evolutionary hypotheses tested in 37 cultures. *Behavioral and Brain Sciences, 12,* 1–49.

Buss, D. M. (1990). Evolutionary social psychology: Prospects and pitfalls. *Motivation and Emotion, 14,* 265–286.

Buss, D. M. (1995). Evolutionary psychology: A new paradigm for psychological science. *Psychological Inquiry, 6,* 1–31.

Buss, D. M. (1999). *Evolutionary psychology: The new science of mind.* Boston, MA: Allyn & Bacon.

Buss, D. M. (1999). Human nature and individual differences: the evolution of human personality. In L. A. Pervin & O. P. John (Eds.), *Handbook of personality: Theory and research* (pp. 31–56). New York: Guilford Press.

Buss, D. M., & Schmitt, D. P. (1993). Sexual strategies theory: An evolutionary perspective on human mating. *Psychological Review, 100,* 204–232.

Buss, D. M., Haselton, M. G., Shackelford, T. K., Bleske, A. L., & Wakefield, J. (1998). Adaptations, exaptations, and spandrels. *American Psychologist, 53,* 533–548.

Butcher, J. N., & Rouse, S. V. (1996). Personality: Individual differences and clinical assessment. *Annual Review of Psychology, 47,* 87–111.

Butcher, J. N., & Williams, C. L. (2000). *Essentials of MMPI-2 and MMPI-A interpretation.* Minneapolis, Minnesota: University of Minnesota Press.

Butcher, J. N., Dahlstrom, W. G., Graham, J. R., Tellegen, A., & Kaemmer, B. (1989). *Manual for administration and scoring: The Minnesota Multiphasic Personality Inventory–2.* Minneapolis, Minnesota: University of Minnesota Press.

Butterworth, G. (1992). Origins of self-perception in infancy. *Psychological Inquiry, 3,* 103–111.

Buunk, B., & Bringle, R.G. (1987). Jealousy in love relationships. In D. Perlman & S. Duck (Eds.), *Intimate relationships: Development, dynamics, and deterioration* (pp. 123–147). Newbury Park, CA: Sage.

Bybee, J., & Fleischman, S. (Eds.). (1995). *Modality in grammar and discourse.* Philadelphia: Benjamins Publishing.

Byrne, R. W. (1995). The ape legacy: The evolution of Machiavellian intelligence and anticipatory interactive planning. In E. N. Goody (Ed.), *Social intelligence and interaction: Expressions and implications of the social bias in human intelligence* (pp. 37–52). Cambridge, England: Cambridge University Press.

C

Cabeza, R., & Nyberg, L. (1997). Imaging cognition: An empirical review of PET studies with normal subjects. *Journal of Cognitive Neuroscience, 9,* 1–26.

Cacioppo, J. T., & Petty, R. E. (1982). The need for cognition. *Journal of Personality and Social Psychology, 42,* 116–131.

Cacioppo, J. T., Hawkley, L. C., Berntson, G. G., Ernst, J. M., Gibbs, A. C., Stickgold, R., & Hobson, A. (2002). Do lonely days invade the nights? Potential social modulation of sleep efficiency. *Psychological Science, 13,* 384–387.

Cacioppo, J. T., Marshall-Goodell, B. S., Tassinary, L. G., & Petty, R. E. (1992). Rudimentary determinants of attitudes: Classical conditioning is more effective when prior knowledge about the attitude stimulus is low than high. *Journal of Experimental Social Psychology, 28,* 207–233.

Cacioppo, J. T., Petty, R. E., Feinstein, J. A., & Jarvis, W. B. G. (1996). Dispositional differences in cognitive motivation: The life and times of individuals varying in need for cognition. *Psychological Bulletin, 119,* 197–253.

Cacioppo, J. T., Petty, R. E., Kao, C. F., & Rodriguez, R. (1986). Central and peripheral routes to persuasion: An individual differences perspective. *Journal of Personality and Social Psychology, 51,* 1032–1043.

Cahill, L., Haier, R. J., Fallon, J., Alkire, M. T., Tang, C., Keator, D., Wu, J., & McGaugh, J. L. (1996). Amygdala activity at encoding correlated with long-term free recall of emotional information. *Proceedings of the National Academy of Sciences, USA, 93,* 8016–8021.

Cain, W. S. (1978). The odoriferous environment and the application of olfactory research. In E. C. Carterette & M. P. Friedman (Eds.), *Handbook of perception* (pp. 277–304). New York: Academic Press.

Cairns-Smith, A. G. (1996). *Evolving the mind: On the nature of matter and the origin of consciousness.* Cambridge: Cambridge University Press.

Caldwell, D. F., & O'Reilly, C. A. III. (1982). Boundary spanning and individual performance: The impact of self-monitoring. *Journal of Applied Psychology, 67,* 124–127.

Caldwell, J. D. (2002). A sexual arousability model involving steroid effects at the plasma membrane. *Neuroscience & Biobehavioral Reviews, 26,* 13–30.

Callahan, C. M. (2000). Intelligence and giftedness. In R. J. Sternberg (Ed.), *Handbook of intelligence* (pp. 159–175). Cambridge: Cambridge University Press.

Calle, E. E., Thun, M. J., Petrelli, J. M., Rogriguez, C., & Health, C. W., Jr. (1999). Body-mass index and mortality in a prospective cohort of U.S. adults. *New England Journal of Medicine, 341,* 1097–1105.

Calvin, W. H., & Ojemann, G. A. (1994). *Conversations with Neil's brain: The neural nature of thought and language.* Reading, MA: Addison-Wesley.

Campbell, A. (1981) *The sense of well-being in America.* New York: McGraw-Hill.

Campbell, A., & Muncer, S. (1987). Models of anger and aggression in the social talk of women and men. *Journal of the Theory of Social Behaviour, 17,* 489–511.

Campbell, A., Muncer, S., & Coyle, E. (1992). Social representation of aggression as an explanation of gender differences: A preliminary study. *Aggressive Behavior, 18,* 95–108.

Campbell, D. M., Hall, M. H., Barker, D. J. P., Cross, J., Shiell, A. W., & Godfrey, K. M. (1996). Diet in pregnancy and the offspring's blood pressure 40 years later. *British Journal of Obstetrics & Gynecology, 104,* 663–667.

Campbell, F. A., & Ramey, C. T. (1994). Effects of early intervention on intellectual and academic achievement: A follow-up study of children from low-income families. *Child Development, 65,* 684–698.

Campbell, F. A., & Ramey, C. T. (1995). Cognitive and school outcomes for high risk students at middle adolescence: Positive effects of early intervention. *American Educational Research Journal, 32,* 743–772.

Campbell, K. L., & Wood, J. W. (Eds.). (1994). Human reproductive ecology: Interactions of environment, fertility, and behavior. *Annals of the New York Academy of Sciences, 709.* New York: New York Academy of Sciences.

Campbell, W. K., & Sedikides, C. (1999). Self-threat magnifies the self-serving bias: A meta-analytic integration. *Review of General Psychology, 3,* 23–43.

Campos, J. L., Langer, A., & Krowitz, A. (1970). Cardiac responses on the visual cliff in prelocomotor human infants. *Science, 170,* 196–197.

Canli, T., Desmond, J. E., Zhao, A., & Gabrieli, J. D. E. (2002). Gender and memory. *Proceedings of the National Academy of Sciences, 10,* 1073.

Cannon, W. (1927). The James-Lange theory of emotion: A critical examination and an alternative theory. *American Journal of Psychology, 39,* 106–124.

Cannon, W., & Washburn, A. (1912). An explanation of hunger. *American Journal of Physiology, 29,* 441–454.

Cantfort, T. V., Rimpau, J. B. (1982). Sign language studies with children and chimpanzees. *Sign Language Studies, 34,* 15–72.

Capaldi, E. (Ed.) (1996). *Why we eat what we eat: The psychology of eating.* Washington, DC: American Psychological Association.

Caprara, G. V., Barbaranelli, C., & Zimbardo, P. G. (1996). Understanding the complexity of human aggression: Affective, cognitive, and social dimensions of individual differences in propensity toward aggression. *European Journal of Personality, 10,* 133–155.

Caprara, G. V., Perugini, M., & Barbaranelli, C. (1994). Studies of individual differences in aggression. In M. Potegal & J. F. Knutson (Eds.), *The dynamics of aggression: Biological and social processes in dyads and groups* (pp. 123–153). Hillsdale, NJ: Erlbaum.

Capron, C., & Duyme, M. (1989). Assessment of effects of socioeconomic status on IQ in a full cross-fostering study. *Nature, 340,* 552–553.

Carli, L. L. (1990). Gender, language, and influence. *Journal of Personality and Social Psychology, 59,* 941–951.

Carli, L. L., LaFleur, S. J., & Loeber, C. C. (1995). Nonverbal behavior, gender, and influence. *Journal of Personality and Social Psychology, 68,* 1030–1041.

Carlin, A. S., Hoffman, H. G., & Weghorst, S. (1997). Virtual reality and tactile augmentation in the treatment of spider phobia: A case report. *Behavioral Research and Therapy, 35,* 153–158.

Carmelli, D., Swann, G., Robinette, D., & Fabsitz, R. (1992). Genetic influence on smoking: A study of male twins. *New England Journal of Medicine, 327,* 829–833.

Carpenter, S. (2001). Everyday fantasia: The world of synesthesia. *Monitor on Psychology, 32,* 26–29.

Carroll, J. B. (1993). *Human cognitive abilities: A survey of factor-analytic studies.* Cambridge, England: University of Cambridge Press.

Carroll, J. B. (1997). The three-stratum theory of cognitive abilities. In D. P. Flanagan, J. L. Genshaft, & P. L. Harrison (Eds.), *Contemporary intellectual assessment: Theories, tests, and issues* (pp. 122–130). New York: Guilford Press.

Carroll, K. M. (1997). Listening to smoking researchers: Negative affect and drug abuse treatment. *Psychological Science, 8,* 190–193.

Cartwright, R. D. (1977). *Night life: Explorations in dreaming.* Englewood Cliffs, NJ: Prentice Hall.

Cartwright, R. D. (1989). Dreams and their meaning. In M. H. Dryger, T. Roth, & W. C. Dement (Eds.), *Principles and practice of sleep medicine.* San Diego: Harcourt Brace Jovanovich.

Cartwright, R. D. (1991). Dreams that work: The relation of dream incorporation to adaptation to stressful events. *Dreaming, 1,* 3–9.

Carver, C. S., & Baird, E. (1998). The American dream revisited: Is it what you want or why you want it that matters? *Psychological Science, 9,* 289–292.

Caryl, P. G. (1994). Early event-related potentials correlate with inspection time and intelligence. *Intelligence, 18,* 15–46.

Case, R. (1985). *Intellectual development: Birth to adulthood.* New York: Academic Press.

Case, R. (1991). *The mind's staircase: Exploring the conceptual underpinnings of children's thought and knowledge.* Hillsdale, NJ: Erlbaum.

Case, R. (1992). Neo-Piagetian theories of child development. In R. J. Sternberg & C. A. Berg (Eds.), *Intellectual development* (pp. 161–196). New York: Cambridge University Press.

Cash, T. (1996). The treatment of body image disturbances. In J. Thompson (Ed.), *Body image, eating disorders, and obesity* (pp. 83–108). Washington, DC: American Psychological Association.

Cash, T., & Henry, P. (1995). Women's body images: The results of a national survey in the U.S.A. *Sex Roles, 33,* 19–28.

Caspi, A., Bem, D. J., & Elder, G. H., Jr. (1989). Continuities consequences of interactional styles across the life course [Special issue]. *Journal of Personality, 57,* 375–406.

Cassel, R. N. (2000). Third force psychology and person-centered theory: From ego-status to ego-ideal. *Psychology: A Quarterly Journal of Human Behavior, 37,* 44–48.

Cassidy, J., & Shaver, P. R. (1999). *Handbook of attachment.* New York: Guilford.

Catania, J., Coates, T., Kegeles, S., Thompson-Fullilove, M., Peterson, J., Marin, B., Siegel, D., & Hully, S. (1992). Condom use in multi-ethnic neighborhoods of San Francisco: The population-based AMEN study. *American Journal of Public Health, 82,* 284–287.

Cattell, R. B. (1965). *The scientific analysis of personality.* Chicago: Aldine.

Cattell, R. B. (1986). The 16 PF personality structure and Dr. Eysenck. *Journal of Social Behavior and Personality, 1,* 153–160.

Cazden, C. (1972). *Child language and education.* New York: Holt.

Ceci, S. J. (1995). False beliefs: Some developmental and clinical considerations. In D. L. Schacter (Ed.), *Memory distortion: How minds, brains, and societies reconstruct the past* (pp. 91–125). Cambridge, MA: Harvard University Press.

Ceci, S. J., & Bruck, M. (1993). Suggestibility of the child witness: A historical review and synthesis. *Psychological Bulletin, 113,* 403–439.

Ceci, S. J., & Bruck, M. (1995). *Jeopardy in the courtroom: A scientific analysis of children's testimony.* Washington, DC: American Psychological Association.

Ceci, S. J., Crotteau, M. L., Smith, E., & Loftus, E. F. (1995). Repeatedly thinking about a non-event: Source misattributions among preschoolers. *Consciousness and Cognition: An International Journal, 3,* 388–407.

Ceci, S. J., Loftus, E. F., Leichtman, M., & Bruck, M. (1994). The role of source misattributions in the creation of false beliefs among preschoolers. *International Journal of Clinical and Experimental Hypnosis, 42,* 304–320.

Centers for Disease Control (2000). *Obesity epidemic increases dramatically in the United States.* http://www.cdc.gov/nccdphp/dnpa/obesity-epidemic.htm.

Cervantes, R. C. (1987). Hispanics in psychology. In P. J. Woods & C. S. Wilkinson (Eds.), *Is psychology the major for you?* Washington, DC: American Psychological Association.

Cervone, D. & Mischel, W. (2002). Personality science. In D. Cervone & W. Mischel (Eds.), *Advances in personality science* (pp. 1–26). New York: Guilford Press.

Cervone, D., & Shoda, Y. (Eds.). (1999). *The coherence of personality: Social-cognitive bases of consistency, variability, and organization.* New York: Guilford Press.

Chait, L. D., & Pierri, J. (1992). Effects of smoked marijuana on human performance: A critical review. In L. Murphy & A. Bartke (Eds.), *Marijuana/cannabinoids: Neurobiology and neurophysiology* (pp. 387–423). Boca Rayon, FL: CRC Press.

Chalmers, I., Hedges, L. V., & Cooper, H. (2002). A brief history of research synthesis. *Evaluation & the Health Professions, 25,* 12–37.

Chambless, D. L. (1990). Spacing of exposure sessions in the treatment of agoraphobia and simple phobia. *Behavior Therapy, 21,* 217–229.

Chang, F. I. F., Isaacs, K. R., & Greenough, W. T. (1991). Synapse formation occurs in association with the induction of long-term potentiation in two-year-old rat hippocampus in vitro. *Neurobiology of Aging, 12,* 517–522.

Chao, R. K. (1992). Beyond parental control and authoritarian parenting style: Understanding Chinese parenting through the cultural notion of training. *Child Development, 65,* 1111–1119.

Chapdelaine, A., Kenny, D. A., & LaFontana, K. M. (1994). Matchmaker, matchmaker, can you make me a match? Predicting liking between two unacquainted persons. *Journal of Personality and Social Psychology, 67,* 83–91.

Chase, M. H., & Morales, F. R. (1983). Subthreshold excitatory activity and motorneuron discharge during REM periods of active sleep. *Science, 221,* 1195–1198.

Chase, W. G., & Simon, H. A. (1973). The mind's eye in chess. In W. G. Chase (Ed.), *Visual information processing.* New York: Academic Press.

Chase-Lansdale, P. L., Cherlin, A. J., & Kiernan, K. E. (1995). The long-term effects of parental divorce on the mental health of young adults: A developmental perspective. *Child Development, 66,* 1614–1634.

Chaves, J. F. (1999). Applying hypnosis in pain management: Implications of alternative theoretical perspectives. In E. Kirsch & A. Capafons (Eds.), *Clinical hypnosis and self-regulation: Cognitive-behavioral perspectives. Dissociation, trauma, memory, and hypnosis book series* (pp. 227–247). Washington, DC: American Psychological Association.

Chedrnoff, N. N. (2002). NIMH study: Blacks mentally healthier. *Observer, 15,* No. 4, 21.

Cheer, S. M., & Goa, K. L. (2001). Fluoxetine: Review of its therapeutic potential in the treatment of depression associated with physical illness. *Drugs, 61,* 81–110.

Chemers, M. M., Hu, L., & Garcia, B. F. (2001). Academic self-efficacy and first year student performance and adjustment. *Journal of Educational Psychology, 93,* 55–64.

Chen, J.-Y. (2000). Syllable errors from naturalistic slips of the tongue in Mandarin Chinese. *Psychologia:An International Journal of Psychology in the Orient, 43,* 15–26.

Chen, N. Y., Shaffer, D. R., & Wu, C. (1997). On physical attractiveness stereotyping in Taiwan: A revised sociocultural perspective. *Journal of Social Psychology, 137,* 117–124.

Cheney, D. L., & Seyfarth, R.M. (1985). Vervet monkey alarm calls: Manipulation through shared information? *Behavior, 94,* 150–166.

Cherlin, A. J., Furstenberg, F. F., Jr., Chase-Lansdale, P. L., Kiernan, K. E., Robins, P. K., Morrison, D. R., & Teitler, J. O. (1991). Longitudinal studies of effects of divorce on children in Great Britain and the United States. *Science, 252,* 1386–1389.

Cherry, E. C. (1953). Some experiments on the recognition of speech, with one and with two ears. *Journal of the Acoustical Society of America, 25,* 975–979.

Chesney, M., & Coates, T. (1990). Health promotion and disease prevention: AIDS put the models to the test. In S. Petro, P. Franks, & T. Wolfred (Eds.), *Ending the HIV epidemic: Community strategies in disease prevention and health promotion* (pp. 48–62). Santa Cruz, CA: ETR Associates.

Chess, S., & Thomas, A. (1987). *Origins and evolution of behavior disorders: From infancy to early adult life.* Cambridge, MA: Harvard University Press.

Choi, I., & Nisbett, R. E. (1998). Situational salience and cultural differences in the correspondence bias and in the actor-observer bias. *Personality and Social Psychology Bulletin, 24,* 949–960.

Choi, I., Nisbett, R. E., & Norenzayan, A. (1999). Causal attribution across cultures: Variation and universality. *Psychological Bulletin, 125,* 47–63.

Chomsky, N. (1957). *Syntactic structures.* The Hague: Mouton.

Chomsky, N. (1965). *Aspects of the theory of syntax.* Cambridge, MA: Harcourt Brace Jovanovich.

Christensen, K. A., Stephens, M. A. P., & Townsend, A. L. (1998). Mastery in women's multiple roles and well-being: Adult daughters providing care to impaired parents. *Health Psychology, 17,* 163–171.

Christensen, L. (1988). Deception in psychological research: When is its use justified? *Personality and Social Psychology Bulletin, 14,* 664–675.

Cialdini, R., Trost, M., & Newsom, J. (1995). Preference for consistency: The development of a valid measure and the discovery of surprising behavioral implications. *Journal of Personality and Social Psychology, 69,* 318–328.

Cialdini, R. B., Eisenberg, N., Green, B. L., Rhoads, K., & Bator, R. (1998). Undermining the undermining effect of reward on sustained interest. *Journal of Applied Social Psychology, 28,* 249–263.

Cicchetti, D. (2002). How a child builds a brain: Insights from normality and psychopathology. In W. Hartup, & R. A. Weinberg (Eds.), *Child psychology in retrospect and prospect: In celebration of the 75th anniversary of the Institute of Child Development. The Minnesota symposia on child psychology, Vol. 32* (pp. 23–71). Mahwah, NJ: Erlbaum.

Clark, D. C. (1995). Epidemiology, assessment, and management of suicide in depressed patients. In E. E. Beckham & W. R. Leber (Eds.), *Handbook of depression* (2nd ed., pp. 526–538). New York: Guilford Press.

Clark, K., Friedman, H., & Martin, L. (1999). A longitudinal study of religiosity and mortality risk. *Journal of Health Psychology, 4,* 381–391.

Clark, K. B., & Clark, M. P. (1939). The development of self and the emergence of racial identification in Negro preschool children. *Journal of Social Psychology, 10,* 591–599.

Clarke-Stewart, K. A., & Allhusen, V. D. (2002) Nonparental caregiving. In M. H. Bornstein (Ed.). *Handbook of parenting: Vol. 3: Being and becoming a parent* (2nd ed., pp. 215–252). Mahwah, NJ: Erlbaum.

Clarkin, J. F., & Carpenter, D., (1995). Family therapy in historical perspective. In B. M. Bongar, & L. E. Beutler (Ed.). *Comprehensive textbook of psychotherapy: Theory and practice. Oxford textbooks in clinical psychology, Vol. 1* (pp. 205–227). New York: Oxford University Press.

Classen, C. (1993). *Worlds of sense: Exploring the senses in history and across cultures.* New York: Routledge.

Classen, C., Howes, D., & Synnott, A. (1994). *Aroma: The cultural history of smell.* London: Routledge.

Clayton, N. S. (1998). Memory and the hippocampus in food-storing birds: A comparative approach. *Neuropharmacology, 37,* 441–452.

Clayton, N. S., & Dickinson, A. (1998). Episodic-like memory during cache recovery by scrub jays. *Nature, 395,* 272–274.

Clement, R. W., & Krueger, J. (2002). Social categorization moderates social projection. *Journal of Experimental Social Psychology, 38,* 219–231.

Cloninger, G. B., Dinwiddie, S. H., & Reich, T. (1989). Epidemiology and genetics of alcoholism. *Annual Reviews of Psychiatry, 8,* 331–346.

Cloud, J. (2000, June 5). The lure of ecstasy. *Time,* pp. 62–68.

Coates, J. (1992). *Women, men, and language* (2nd ed.). New York: Longman.

Coates, T. (1990). Strategies for modifying sexual behavior for primary and secondary prevention of HIV disease. *Journal of Consulting and Clinical Psychology, 58,* 57–69.

Coates, T., Stall, R., Catania, J., & Kegeles, S. (1988). Behavioral factors in HIV infection. *AIDS 1988, 2*(Suppl.1), S239–S246.

Coates, T. J., & Collins, C. (1998). Preventing HIV infection. *Scientific American, 279* (1), 96–97.

Cochran, W., & Tesser, A. (1996). The "what the hell" effect: Some effects of goal proximity and goal framing on performance. In L. Martin & A. Tesser (Eds.), *Striving and feeling: Interactions among goals, affect, and self-regulation* (pp. 99–120). Mahwah, NJ: Erlbaum.

Coffey, C. E. (1993). *Clinical science of electroconvulsive therapy.* Washington, DC: American Psychiatric Press.

Cogan, J. C., Bhalla, S. K., Sefa-Dedeh, A., & Rothblum, E. D. (1996). A comparison study of United States and African students on perceptions of obesity and thinness. *Journal of Cross-Cultural Psychology, 27,* 98–113.

Cohen, A. G., & Gutek, B. A. (1991). Differences in the career experiences of members of two APA divisions. *American Psychologist, 46,* 1292–1298.

Cohen C. (1994). The case for the use of animals in biomedical research. In E. Erwin, S. Gendin, & L. Kleiman (Eds.), *Ethical issues in scientific research: An anthology* (pp. 253–266). New York: Garland.

Cohen, D. (1996). Law, social policy, and violence: The impact of regional cultures. *Journal of Personality and Social Psychology, 70,* 961–978.

Cohen, D. (1998). Culture, social organization, and patterns of violence. *Journal of Personality and Social Psychology, 75,* 408–419.

Cohen, D., & Nisbett, R. E. (1994) Self-protection and the culture of honor: Explaining southern violence. *Personality and Social Psychology Bulletin, 20,* 551–567.

Cohen, D., & Nisbett, R. E. (1997). Field experiments examining the culture of honor: The role of institutions in perpetuating norms about violence. *Personality and Social Psychology Bulletin, 23,* 1188–1199.

Cohen, D., Nisbett, R. E., Bowdle, B., & Schwarz, N. (1996). Insult, aggression, and the southern culture of honor: An "experimental ethnography." *Journal of Personality and Social Psychology, 70,* 945–960.

Cohen, D., Taieb, O., Flament, M., Benoit, N., Chevret, S., Corcos, M., Fossati, P., Jeammet, P., Allilaire, J. F., & Basquin, M. (2000). Absence of cognitive impairment at long-term follow-up in adolescents treated with ECT for severe mood disorder. *American Journal of Psychiatry, 157,* 460–462.

Cohen, K. M. (2002). Relationships among childhood sex-atypical behavior, spatial ability, handedness, and sexual orientation in men. *Archives of Sexual Behavior, 31,* 129–143.

Cohen, L. B., Diehl, R. L., Oakes, L. M., & Loehlin, J. L. (1992). Infant perception of /aba/versus/apa/: Building a quantitative model of infant categorical discrimination. *Developmental Psychology, 28,* 261–272.

Cohen, S., & Miller, G. (2001). Stress, immunity, and susceptibility to upper respiratory infection. In R. Ader, D. Felten, & N. Cohen (Eds.), *Psychoneuroimmunology* (Vol. 2, 3rd ed., pp. 499–509). San Diego, CA: Academic Press.

Cohen, S., Underwood, L. G., & Gottlieb, B. H. (Eds.). (2000). *Social support measurement and intervention: A guide for health and social scientists.* New York: Oxford University Press.

Cole, M. (1992). Culture in development. In M. H. Bornstein & M. E. Lamb (Eds.), *Developmental psychology: An advanced textbook* (3rd ed.). Hillsdale, NJ: Erlbaum.

Cole, M., & Cole, S. R. (1993). *The development of children* (2nd ed.). New York: Freeman.

Cole, S., & Kemeny, M. (2001). Psychosocial influences on the progression of HIV infection. In R. Ader, D. Felten, & N. Cohen (Eds.), *Psychoneuroimmunology* (Vol. 2, 3rd ed., pp. 583–612). San Diego, CA: Academic Press.

Colligan, J. (1983). Musical creativity and social rules in four cultures. *Creative Child and Adult Quarterly, 8,* 39–47.

Collins, A. M., & Loftus, E. F. (1975). A spreading-activation theory of semantic processing. *Psychological Review, 82,* 407–428.

Colombo, J. (1995). Cost, utility, and judgments of institutional review boards. *Psychological Science, 6,* 318–319.

Coltheart, M., Hull, E., & Slater, D. (1975). Sex differences in imagery and reading. *Nature, 253,* 438–440.

Comey, G., & Kirsch, I. (1999). Intentional and spontaneous imagery in hypnosis: The phenomenology of hypnotic responding. *International Journal of Clinical and Experimental Hypnosis, 47,* 65–85.

Conrad, R. (1964). Acoustic confusions in immediate memory. *British Journal of Psychology, 55,* 75–84.

Conway, M. (1995). *Flashbulb memories.* East Sussex: Erlbaum.

Cooney, T. M., Pedersen, F. A., Indelicato, S., & Palkovitz, R. (1993). Timing of fatherhood: Is "on-time" optimal? *Journal of Marriage and the Family, 55,* 205–215.

Cooper, B. Y., Vierck, C. J., Jr., & Yeomans, D. C. (1986). Selective reduction of second pain sensations by systemic morphine in humans. *Pain, 24,* 93–116.

Cooper, D. B. (Ed.). (2000). *Alcohol use.* Oxford: Radcliffe Medical Press.

Cooper, J. R., Bloom, F. E., & Roth, R. H. (1991). *The biochemical basis of neuropharmacology* (6th ed.). New York: Oxford University Press.

Cooper, M. L., Shapiro, C. M., & Powers, A. M. (1998). Motivations for sex and risky sexual behavior among adolescents and young adults. *Journal of Personality and Social Psychology, 75,* 1528–1558.

Coppola, K. M., & Trotman, F. K. (2002). Dying and death: Decisions at the end of life. In F. K. Trotman, C. M. Brody, & M. Claire (Eds.), *Psychotherapy and counseling with older women: Cross-cultural, family, and end-of-life issues. Springer series, focus on women* (pp. 221–238). New York: Springer.

Corballis, M. C. (1999). Are we in our right minds? In S. D. Sala (Ed.), *Mind myths: Exploring popular assumptions about the mind and brain* (pp. 25–41). London: Wiley.

Corbitt, E. M. (2002). Narcissism from the perspective of the five-factor model. In P. T. Costa, Jr., & T. A. Widiger (Eds.), *Personality disorders and the five-factor model of personality* (2nd ed., pp. 293–298). Washington, DC: American Psychological Association.

Coren, S. (1989). Left-handedness and accident-related injury risk. *American Journal of Public Health, 79,* 1–2.

Coren, S. (1989). The many moon illusions: An integration through analysis. In M. Hershenson (Ed.), *The moon illusion* (pp. 351–370). Hillsdale, NJ: Erlbaum.

Coren, S. (1992). *The left-hander syndrome: The causes and consequences of left-handedness.* New York: Free Press.

Coren, S. (1996). *Sleep thieves: The A to ZZZs on sleep.* New York: Free Press.

Coren, S., & Aks, D. J. (1990). Moon illusion in pictures: A multimechanism approach. *Journal of Experimental Psychology: Human Perception and Performance, 16,* 365–380.

Coren, S., & Halpern, D. F. (1991). Left-handedness: A marker for decreased survival fitness. *Psychological Bulletin, 109,* 90–106.

Coren, S., Porac, C., & Theodor, L. H. (1987). Set and subjective contour. In S. Petry & G. E. Meyer (Eds.), *The perception of illusory contours* (pp. 237–245). New York: Springer-Verlag.

Corkin, S. (1984). Lasting consequences of bilateral medial temporal lobectomy: Clinical course and experimental findings in H. M. *Seminars in Neurology, 4,* 249–259.

Cornejo, C. (2001). Piaget, Vigotski and Maturana: Three voices, two constructivisms. *Psykhe: Revista de la Escuela de Psicologia, 10,* 87–96.

Corsini, R. J. (Ed.). (1981). *Handbook of innovative psychotherapies.* New York: Wiley.

Cosmides, L., & Tooby, J. (2002). Unraveling the enigma of human intelligence: Evolutionary psychology and the multimodular mind. In R. J. Sternberg & J. C. Kaufman (Eds.). (2002). *The evolution of intelligence* (pp. 145–198). Mahwah, NJ: Erlbaum.

Costa, P. T., Jr., & McCrae, R. R. (1992). *Revised NEO Personality Inventory (NEO PI-R) and NEO Five-Factor Inventory (NEO-FFI). Professional Manual.* Odessa, FL: Psychological Assessment Resources.

Costa, P. T., Jr., McCrae, R. R., and Arenberg, D. (1980). Enduring dispositions in adult males. *Journal of personality and social psychology, 38,* 793–800.

Costa, P. T., Jr., McCrae, R. R., and Dembroski, T. M. (1989). Agreeableness versus antagonism; Explication of a potential risk factor for CHD. In A. Siegman & T. M. Dembroski (Eds.), *In search of coronary-prone behavior* (pp. 41–63). New York: Oxford University Press.

Cotman, C. W. (1990). Synaptic plasticity, neurotropic factors, and transplantation in the aged brain. In E. L. Schneider & J. W. Rowe (Eds.), *Handbook of the biology of aging* (3rd ed.). San Diego: Academic Press.

Courage, M. L., & Adams, R. J. (1990). Visual acuity assessment from birth to three years using the acuity card procedures: Cross-sectional and longitudinal samples. *Optometry and Vision Science, 67,* 713–718.

Covington, M. & Omelich, C. (1987). "I knew it cold before the exam": A test of the anxiety-blockage hypothesis. *Journal of Educational Psychology, 79,* 393–400.

Cowan, C. P., & Cowan, P. (2000). *When partners become parents: The big life change for couples.* Mahwah, NJ: Erlbaum.

Cowan, N. (1995). *Attention and memory: An integrated framework.* New York: Oxford University Press.

Cowan, N., Lichty, W., & Grove, T. R. (1990). Properties of memory for unattended spoken syllables. *Journal of Experimental Psychology: Learning, Memory, & Cognition, 16,* 258–269.

Cowart, B. J. (1981). Development of taste perception in humans: Sensitivity and preference through the lifespan. *Psychological Bulletin, 90,* 43–73.

Crabtree, B. F., & Miller, W. L. (Eds.). (1992). *Doing qualitative research: Multiple strategies.* Thousand Oaks, CA: Sage.

Craig, J. C., & Rollman, G. B. (1999). Somesthesis. *Annual Review of Psychology, 50,* 305–331.

Craik, F. I. M., & Lockhart, R. S. (1972). Levels of processing: A framework for memory research. *Journal of Verbal Learning and Verbal Behavior, 11,* 671–684.

Cramer, P. (1999). Future directions for the Thematic Apperception Test. *Journal of Personality Assessment, 72,* 74–92.

Crandall, C. S. (1994). Prejudice against fat people: Ideology and self-interest. *Journal of Personality and Social Psychology, 66,* 882–894.

Crandall, C. S. (1988). Social contagion of binge eating. *Journal of Personality and Social Psychology, 55,* 588–598.

Crano, W. D., & Brewer, M. B. (2002). *Principles and methods of social research* (2nd ed.). Mahwah, NJ: Erlbaum.

Craske, M. G. (1999). *Anxiety disorders: Psychological approaches to theory and treatment.* Boulder, CO: Westview Press.

Craske, M. G., & Barlow, D. H. (1993). Panic disorder and agoraphobia. In D. H. Barlow (Ed.), *Clinical handbook of psychological disorders: A step-by-step treatment manual* (2nd ed., pp. 1–47). New York: Guilford.

Crawford, H. J., & Gruzelier, J. H. (1992). A midstream view of the neuropsychology of hypnosis: Recent research and future directions. In E. Fromm & M. R. Nash (Eds.), *Contemporary hypnosis research* (pp. 227–266). New York: Guilford Press.

Crawford, M., Chaffin, R., & Fitton, L. (1995). Cognition in social context. Special Issue: Psychological and psychobiological perspectives on sex differences in cognition: I. Theory and research. *Learning and Individual Differences, 7,* 341–362.

Crews, F. C. (1998). *Unauthorized Freud: Doubters confront a legend.* New York: Viking Penguin, Inc.

Criqui, M. H., & Ringel, B. L. (1994). Does diet or alcohol explain the French paradox? *Lancet, 344,* 1719–1723.

Crocker, J., & Major, B. (1989). Social stigma and self-esteem: The self-protective properties of stigma. *Psychological Review, 96,* 608–630.

Crocker, J., Major, B., & Steele, C. (1998). Social stigma. In D. T. Gilbert, S. T. Fiske, & G. Lindzey (Eds.), *The handbook of social psychology* (4th ed.). New York: McGraw-Hill.

Crook, J. H. (1980). *The evolution of human consciousness.* Oxford: Clarendon Press.

Cross, S. E., & Madson, L. (1997). Models of the self: Self-construals and gender. *Psychological Bulletin, 122,* 5–37.

Cross, S. E., Bacon, P. L., & Morris, M. L. (2000). The relational-interdependent self-construal and relationships. *Journal of Personality and Social Psychology, 78,* 791–808.

Croyle, R. T. (1992). Appraisal of health threats: Cognition, motivation, and social comparison. *Cognitive Therapy and Research, 16,* 165–182.

Crystal, D. S., Chen, C., Fuligni, A.J., Stevenson, H. J., Hsu, C-C., Ko, H-J., Kitamura, S., & Kimura, S. (1994). Psychological maladjustment and academic achievement: A cross-cultural study of Japanese, Chinese, and American high school students. *Child Development, 65,* 738–753.

Culp, R. E., Appelbaum, M. I., Osofsky, J. D., & Levy, J. A. (1988). Adolescent and older mothers: Comparison between maternal variables and newborn interaction measures. *Infant Behavior and Development, 11,* 353–362.

Culp, R. E., Watkins, R. V., Lawrence, H., & Letts, D. (1991). Maltreated children's language and speech development: Abused, neglected, and abused and neglected. *First Language, 11,* 377–389.

Cummings, E. M., & Cummings, J. S. (2002). Parenting and attachment. In M. H. Bornstein (Ed.), *Handbook of parenting: Vol. 3: Being and becoming a parent* (2nd ed., pp. 35–58). Mahwah, NJ: Erlbaum..

Cunningham, M. R., Barbee, A. P., & Philhower, C. L. (2002). Dimensions of facial physical attractiveness: The intersection of biology and culture. In G. Rhodes & L. A. Zebrowitz (Eds.), *Facial attractiveness: Evolutionary, cognitive, and social perspectives. Advances in visual cognition* (Vol. 1, pp. 193–238). Westport, CT: Ablex.

Cunningham, M. R., Roberts, A. R., Barbee, A. P., Druen, P. B., & Wu, C.-H. (1995). "Their ideas of beauty are, on the whole, the same as ours": Consistency and variability in the cross-cultural perception of female physical attractiveness. *Journal of Personality and Social Psychology, 68,* 261–279.

Curtiss, S., de Bode, S., & Mathern, G. W. (2001). Spoken language outcomes after hemispherectomy: Factoring in etiology. *Brain & Language, 79,* 379–396.

Cutrona, C. E. (1996). *Social support in couples.* Thousand Oaks, CA: Sage.

Cutrona, C. E., & Suhr, J. A. (1994). Social support communication in the context of marriage: An analysis of couples' supportive interactions. In B. B. Burleson, T. L., Albrecht, & I. G. Sarason (Eds.), *Communication of social support: Messages, relationships, and community* (pp. 113–135). Thousand Oaks, CA: Sage.

Czeisler, C. A., Johnson, M. P., Duffy, J. F., Brown, E. N., Ronda, J. M., & Kronauer, R. E. (1990). Exposure to bright light and darkness to treat physiologic maladaptation to night work. *New England Journal of Medicine, 322,* 1253–1259.

Czeisler, C. A., Moore-Ede, M. C., & Coleman, R. M. (1982). Rotating shift work schedules that disrupt sleep are improved by applying circadian principles. *Science, 217,* 460–463.

D

d'Ydewalle, G. (2000). Sensation/pderception, information processing, attention. In K. Pawlik & M. R. Rosenzweig (Eds.), *International handbook of psychology* (pp. 79–99). London: Sage.

d'Ydewalle, G., & Rosselle, H. (1978). Text expectations in text learning. In M. M. Gruneberg, P. E. Morris, & R. N. Sykes (Eds.), *Practical aspects of memory.* Orlando, FL: Academic Press.

Dade, L. A., Zatorre, R. J., & Jones-Gotman, M. (2002). Olfactory learning: Convergent findings from lesion and brain imaging studies in humans. *Brain, 125,* 86–101.

Dakof, G., & Taylor, S. (1990). Victims' perceptions of social support: What is helpful from whom? *Journal of Personality and Social Psychology, 58,* 80–89.

Dalbert, C., & Yamauchi, L. (1994). Belief in a just world and attitudes toward immigrants and foreign workers: A cultural comparison between Hawaii and Germany. *Journal of Applied Social Psychology, 24,* 1612–1626.

Dallenbach, K. M. (1927). The temperature spots and end organs. *American Journal of Psychology, 54,* 431–433.

Damasio, A. R. (1994). *Descartes' error: Emotion, reason, and the human brain.* New York: Grosset/Putnam.

Damasio, H., Grabowski, T., Frank, R., Galaburda, A. M., & Damasio, A. R. (1994). The return of Phineas Gage: The skull of a famous patient yields clues about the brain. *Science, 264,* 1102–1105.

Daneman, M., & Hannon, B. (2001). Using working memory theory to investigate the construct validity of multiple-choice reading. *Journal of Experimental Psychology: General, 130,* 208–223.

Daniell, H. W. (1971). Smoker's wrinkles: A study in the epidemiology of "Crow's feet." *Annals of Internal Medicine, 75,* 873–880.

Darley, J. M., & Latané, B. (1968). Bystander intervention in emergencies: Diffusion of responsibility. *Journal of Personality and Social Psychology, 8,* 377–383.

Darwin, C. (1859). *On the origin of species.* New York: New York University Press, 1988.

Darwin, C. (1871). *The descent of man.* London: John Murray.

Darwin, C. (1872). *The expression of the emotions in man and animals.* London: John Murray.

Dasen, P. R. (1994). Culture and cognitive development from a Piagetian perspective. In W. J. Lonner & R. Malpass (Eds.), *Psychology and culture* (pp. 145–149). Boston: Allyn & Bacon.

Daum, I., Ackermann, H., Schugens, M. M., Reimold, C., Dichgans, J., & Birbaumer, N. (1993). The cerebellum and cognitive functions in humans. *Behavioral Neuroscience, 104,* 411–419.

Davidson, I., & Noble, W. (1989). The archeology of depiction and language. *Current Anthropology, 30,* 125–156.

Davidson, R. (1992). Anterior cerebral asymmetry and the nature of emotion. *Brain and Cognition, 20,* 125–151.

Davidson, R. J., Pizzagalli, D., Nitschke, J. B., & Putnam, K. (2002). Depression: Perspectives from affective neuroscience. *Annual Review of Psychology, 53,* 545–574.

Davies, I. R. L. (1998). A study of colour grouping in three languages: A test of linguistic relativity hypothesis. *British Journal of Psychology, 89,* 433–452.

Davies, M. F. (1997). Positive test strategies and confirmatory retrieval processes in the evaluation of personality feedback. *Journal of Personality and Social Psychology, 73,* 574–583.

Davis, M. H. (1996). *Empathy: A social psychological approach.* Boulder, CO: Westview Press.

Davis, S. (1990). Men as success objects and women as sex objects: A study of personal advertisements. *Sex Roles, 23,* 43–50.

Davison, G. C., & Neale, J. M. (2001). *Abnormal psychology* (8th ed.). New York: Wiley.

Davison, K. P., Pennebaker, J. W., & Dickerson, S. S. (2000). Who talks? The social psychology of illness support groups. *American Psychologist, 55,* 205–217.

Dawson, T. L. (2002). New tools, new insights: Kohlberg's moral judgement stages revisited. *International Journal of Behavioral Development, 26,* 154–166.

De Pascalis, V. (1999). Psychophysiological correlates of hypnosis and hypnotic susceptibility. *International Journal of Clinical and Experimental Hypnosis, 47,* 117–143.

de Valois, R. L., & Jacobs, G. H. (1984). Neural mechanisms of color vision. In I. Darian-Smith (Ed.), *The nervous system* (Vol. 3). Baltimore: Williams & Wilkins.

de Valois, R. L., Abramov, I., & Jacobs, G. H. (1966). Analysis of response patterns of LGN cells. *Journal of the Optical Society of America, 56,* 966–977.

De Waal, F. B. M. (2000). Primates—A natural heritage of conflict resolution. *Science, 289,* 586–590.

Deacon, T. W. (1989). The neural circuitry underlying primate calls and human language. *Human Evolution,* 367–401.

DeAngelis, T. (1996). Women in psychology: Women's contributions large; recognition isn't. *The APA Monitor, 27*(3), 12–13.

DeAngelis, T. (2002). Binge-eating disorder: What's the best treatment? *Monitor, 33, No. 3,* 30.

DeAngelis, T. (2002, February). New data on lesbian, gay and bisexual mental health. *Monitor on Psychology, 33,* 46–47.

Deaux, K., Winton, W., Crowley, M., & Lewis, L. L. (1985). Levels of categorization and content of gender stereotypes. *Social Cognition, 3,* 145–167.

deBoysson-Bardies, B., Halle, P., Sagart, L., & Durand, C. (1989). A cross linguistic investigation of vowel formats in babbling. *Journal of Child Language, 16,* 1–17.

DeCasper, A. J., & Fifer, W. P. (1980). Of human bonding: Newborns prefer their mothers' voices. *Science, 208,* 1174–1176.

DeCasper, A. J., & Sigafoos, A. D. (1983). The intrauterine heartbeat: A potent reinforcer for newborns. *Infant Behavior and Development, 6,* 19–25.

DeCasper, A. J., & Spence, M. J. (1986). Prenatal maternal speech influences newborns' perception of speech sounds. *Infant Behavior and Development, 9,* 133–150.

DeCatanzaro, D. A. (1998). *Motivation and emotion: Evolutionary, physiological, developmental, and social perspectives.* Upper Saddle River, NJ: Prentice Hall.

Deci, E. (1975). *Intrinsic motivation.* New York: Plenum.

Deci, E. L., Driver, R. E., Hotchkiss, L., Robbins, R., J., & Wilson, I. M. (1993). The relation of mothers' controlling vocalizations to children's intrinsic motivation. *Journal of Experimental Child Psychology, 55,* 151–162.

Deci, E., & Ryan, R. (1985). *Intrinsic motivation and self-determination in human behavior.* New York: Plenum.

Deci, E., Koestner, R., & Ryan, R. (1999). A meta-analytic review of experiments examining the effects of extrinsic rewards on intrinsic motivation. *Psychological Bulletin, 125,* 627–668.

Deepak, K. K., Manchanda, S. K., & Maheshwari, M. C. (1994). Meditation improves clinicoelectroencephalographic measures in drug-resistant epileptics. *Biofeedback and Self Regulation, 19,* 25–40.

Deikman A. J. (2000). A functional approach to mysticism. In J. Andresen & R. K. C. Forman (Eds.), *Cognitive models and spiritual maps: Interdisciplinary explorations of religious experience* (pp. 75–91). Thorverton, England: Imprint Academic.

Delgado-Gaitan, C. (1994). Socializing young children in Mexican-American families: An intergenerational perspective. In P. M. Greenfield & R. R. Cocking (Eds.), *Cross-cultural roots of minority child development* (pp. 55–86). Hillsdale, NJ: Erlbaum.

Dell, G. S. (1986). A spreading activation theory of retrieval in sentence production. *Psychological Review, 93,* 283–321.

Dell, G. S. (1988). The retrieval of phonological forms in production: Tests of predictions from a connectionist model. *Journal of Memory and Language, 27,* 124–142.

Dembroski, T., MacDougall, J., Williams, R., Haney, T., & Blumenthal, J. (1985). Components of Type A, hostility, and anger-in: Relationship to angiographic findings. *Psychosomatic Medicine, 47,* 219–233.

Dement, W. (1960). The effect of dream deprivation. *Science, 131,* 1705–1707.

Dement, W. C. (1999). *The promise of sleep.* New York: Delacorte Press.

Dement, W. C. (1978). *Some must watch while some must sleep.* New York: Norton.

Dement, W. C., & Wolpert, E. (1958). The relation of eye movements, body motility, and external stimuli to dream content. *Journal of Experimental Psychology, 55,* 543–553.

Dement, W. C., Greenberg, S., & Klein, R. (1966). The effect of partial REM sleep deprivation and delayed recovery. *Journal of Experimental Psychology, 53,* 339–346.

Demetriou, A. (Ed.) (1988). *The neo-Piagetian theories of cognitive development: Toward an integration.* Amsterdam: Elsevier.

DeNeve, K. M. (1999). Happy as an extraverted clam? The role of personality for subjective well-being. *Current Directions in Psychological Science, 124,* 197–229.

Dennett, D. C. (1991). *Consciousness explained.* Boston: Little, Brown.

Dennett, D. C. (1994). Real consciousness. In A. Revonsuo & M. Kamppinen (Eds.), *Consciousness in philosophy and cognitive neuroscience* (pp. 55–63). Hillsdale, NJ: Erlbaum.

DePaulo, B. M. (1992). Nonverbal behavior and self-presentation. *Psychological Bulletin, 111,* 230–243.

DePaulo, B. M., Charlton, K., Cooper, H. M., Lindsay, J. J., & Muhlenbruck, L. (1997). The accuracy-confidence correlation in the detection of deception. *Personality and Social Psychology Review, 1,* 346–357.

DePaulo, B. M., Kashy, D. A., Kirkendol, S. E., Wyer, M. M., & Epstein, J. A. (1996). Lying in everyday life. *Journal of Personality and Social Psychology, 70,* 979–995.

Deregowski, J. B. (1989). Real space and represented space: Cross-cultural perspectives. *Brain and Behavioral Sciences, 12,* 51–119.

Detterman, D. K., Gabriel, L. T., & Ruthsatz, J. M. (2000). Intelligence and mental retardation. In R. J. Sternberg (Ed.), *Handbook of intelligence* (pp. 141–158). Cambridge: Cambridge University Press.

Devine, P. G. (1989). Stereotypes and prejudice: Their automatic and controlled components. *Journal of Personality and Social Psychology, 56,* 5–18.

Devine, P. G., & Baker, S. M. (1991). Measurement of racial stereotype subtyping. *Personality and Social Psychology Bulletin, 17,* 44–50.

DeVoe, M. W. (1977). Cooperation as a function of self-concept, sex, and race. *Educational Research Quarterly, 2,* 3–8.

DeVries, R. (2000). Vygotsky, Piaget, and education: A reciprocal assimilation of theories and educational practices. *New Ideas in Psychology, 18,* 187–213.

Dewsbury, D. A. (1992). Triumph and tribulation in the history of American comparative psychology. *Journal of Comparative Psychology, 1067,* 3–19.

Diamond, A. (1985). The development of the ability to use recall to guide action, as indicated by infants' performance on AB. *Child Development, 56,* 868–883.

Diamond, J. (1966). Classification system of primitive people. *Science, 151,* 1102–1104.

Diamond, M. C. (1988). *Enriching heredity: The impact of environment on the anatomy of the brain.* New York: Free Press.

Diaz-Guerrero, R., Diaz-Loving, R., & Rodriguez de Diaz, M. L. (2001). In L. L. Adler & U. P. Gielen (Eds.), *Cross-cultural topics in psychology* (2nd ed., pp. 171–184). Westport, CT: Praeger.

Dick, C. L., Bland, R. C., & Newman, S. C. (1994). Panic disorder. *Acta Psychiatrica Scandinavica, 89,* 45–53.

Dick, D. M., & Rose, R. J. (2002). Behavior genetics: What's new? What's next? *Current Directions in Psychological Science, 11,* 70–74.

Diehl, W. (1993). *Primal fear.* New York: Villard.

Diener, E. (1984). Subjective well-being. *Psychological Bulletin, 95,* 542–575.

Diener, E., & Diener, M. (1995). Cross-cultural correlates of life-satisfaction and self-esteem. *Journal of Personality and Social Psychology, 68,* 653–663.

Diener, E., & Lucas, R. E. (1999). Personality and subjective well-being. In D. Kahneman, E. Diener, & N. Schwarz (Eds.). *Well-being: The foundations of hedonic psychology* (pp. 213–229). New York: Russell Sage.

Diener, E., & Lucas, R. E. (2000). Explaining differences in societal levels of happiness: Relative standards, need fulfillment, culture and evaluation theory. *Journal of Happiness Studies, 1,* 41–78.

Diener, E., & Lucas, R. E. (2000). Subjective emotional well-being. In M. Lewis & J. M. Haviland (Eds.), *Handbook of emotions* (2nd ed., pp. 325–337). New York: Guilford.

Diener, E., & Seligman, E. P. (2002). Very happy people. *Psychological Science, 13,* 81–84.

Diener, E., Sandvik, E., Seidlitz, L., & Diener, M. (1993). The relationship between income and subjective well-being: Relative or absolute? *Social Indicators Research, 28,* 195–223.

Diener, E., Suh, E. M., Lucas, R. E., & Smith, H. L. (1999). Subjective well-being: Three decades of progress. *Psychological Bulletin, 125,* 276–302.

Dietz, W., Jr., & Gortmaker, S. (1985). Do we fatten our children at the television set? Obesity and television viewing in children and adolescents. *Pediatrics, 75,* 807–812.

Dijker, A. J., & Koomen, W. (1996). Stereotyping and attitudinal effects under time pressure. *European Journal of Social Psychology, 26,* 61–74.

Dijksterhuis, A., & Knippenberg, A. V. (1996). The knife that cuts both ways: Facilitated and inhibited access to traits as a result of stereotype activation. *Journal of Experimental Social Psychology, 32,* 271–288.

DiLalla, L. F., Kagan, J., Reznick, J. S. (1994). Genetic etiology of behavioral inhibition among 2-year-old children. *Infant Behavior & Development, 17,* 405–412.

Dilsaver, S. C., Chen, Y. R., Shoaib, A. M., & Swann, A. C. (1999). Phenomenology of mania: Evidence for distinct depressed, dysphoric, and euphoric presentations. *American Journal of Psychiatry, 156,* 426–430.

Dinges, D. F., Pack, F., Williams, K., Gillen, K. A., Powell, J. W., Ott, G. E., Aptowicz, C., & Pack, A. I. (1997). Cumulative sleepiness, mood vigilance performance decrements during a week of sleep restricted to 4–5 hours per night. *Sleep, 20,* 267–273.

Dinges, N. G., & Hull, P. (1992). Personality, culture, and international studies. In D. Lieberman (Ed.), *Revealing the world: An interdisciplinary reader for international studies.* Dubuque, IA: Kendall-Hunt.

Dion, K. K., Berscheid, E., & Walster (Hatfield), E. (1972). What is beautiful is good. *Journal of Personality and Social Psychology, 24,* 285–290.

Docherty, J. P. (1999). Cost of treating mental illness from a managed care perspective. *Journal of Clinical Psychiatry, 60,* 49–53.

Dodson, C., & Reisberg, D. (1991). Indirect testing of eyewitness memory: The (non)effect of misinformation. *Bulletin of the Psychonomic Society, 29,* 333–336.

Dodwell, P. (2000). *Brave new mind: A thoughtful inquiry into the nature and meaning of mental life.* New York: Oxford University Press.

Doi, T. (1973). *The anatomy of dependence.* (Trans., J. Bester). New York: Kodansha International.

Domino, G., Short, J., Evans, A., & Romano, P. (2002). Creativity and ego defense mechanisms: Some exploratory empirical evidence. *Creativity Research Journal, 14,* 17–25.

Dong, Q., Wang, Y., & Ollendick, T. H. (2002). Consequences of divorce on the adjustment of children in China. *Journal of Community Psychology, 31,* 101–110.

Dorfman, D. D. (1995). Soft science with a neoconservative agenda. *Contemporary Psychology, 40,* 418–421.

Dorfman, J., Shames, V. A., & Kihlstrom, J. F. (1996). Intuition, incubation, and insight: Implicit cognition in problem solving. In G. Underwood (Ed.), *Implicit cognition* (pp. 257–296). Oxford: Oxford University Press.

Doty, R. L., Green, P. A., Ram, C., & Tandeil, S. L. (1982). Communication of gender from human breath odors: Relationship to perceived intensity and pleasantness. *Hormones and Behavior, 16,* 13–22.

Dovidio, J. F., Kawakami, K., & Beach, K. R. (2001). Implicit and explicit attitudes: Examination of the relationship between measures of intergroup bias. In R. Brown & S. L. Gaertner (Eds.), *Blackwell handbook of social psychology* (Vol. 4, *Intergroup Relations,* pp. 175–197). Oxford, England: Blackwell.

Dowling, J. E. (1992). *Neurons and networks: An introduction to neuroscience.* Cambridge, MA: Harvard University Press.

Drachman, D. A. (1997). Aging and the brain: A new frontier. *Annals of Neurology, 42,* 819–828.

Duberman, M. B., Vicinus, M., & Chauncey, G., Jr. (1989). *Hidden from history: Reclaiming the gay and lesbian past.* New York: New American Library.

Duckworth, K., & Borus, J. F. (1999). Population-based psychiatry in the public sector and managed care. In A. M. Nicholi (Ed.), *The Harvard guide to psychiatry.* Cambridge, MA: Harvard University Press.

Dunbar, R. I. M. (1993). Coevolution of neocortical size, group size and language in humans. *Behavioral and Brain Sciences, 16,* 681–735.

Duncan, J., Seitz, R. J., Kolodny, J., Bor, D., Herzog, H., Ahmed, A., Newell, F. N., & Emslie, H. (2000). A neural basis for general intelligence. *Science, 289,* 457–460.

Duncker, K. (1945). On problem solving. *Psychological Monographs, 58* (5, No. 270).

Dunkel-Schetter, C., Blasband, D., Feinstein, L., & Herbert, T. (1992). Elements of supportive interactions: When are attempts to help effective? In S. Spacapan & S. Oskamp (Eds.), *Helping and being helped: Naturalistic studies* (pp. 83–114). Newbury Park, CA: Sage.

Dunning, D., Leuenberger, A., & Sherman, D.A. (1995). A new look at motivated inference: Are self-serving theories of success a product of motivational forces? *Journal of Personality and Social Psychology, 69,* 58–68.

Dursan, S. M., & Devarajan, S. (2001). When treating patients with schizophrenia, what clinical points should be considered if lamotrigine is chosen to augment clozapine? *Journal of Psychiatric Neuroscience, 26,* 168.

Durso, F. T., Rea, C. B., & Dayton, T. (1994). Graph-theoretic confirmation of restructuring during insight. *Psychological Science, 5,* 94–98.

Dutton, D. G., & Aron, A. (1974). Some evidence for heightened sexual attraction under conditions of high anxiety. *Journal of Personality and Social Psychology, 30,* 510–517.

Dweck, C. S. (1990). Toward a theory of goals: Their role in motivation and personality. In R. A. Dienstbier (Ed.), *Nebraska Symposium on Motivation* (Vol. 38). Lincoln: University of Nebraska Press.

Dweck, C. S. (1992). The study of goals in psychology [Commentary to feature review]. *Psychological Science, 3,* 165–167.

Dywan, J., & Bowers, K. S. (1983). The use of hypnosis to enhance recall. *Science, 222,* 184–185.

E

Eagly, A. H., & Crowley, M. (1986). Gender and helping behavior: A meta-analytic review of the social psychological literature. *Psychological Bulletin, 100,* 283–308.

Eagly, A. H., & Steffen, V. J. (1986). Gender and aggressive behavior: A meta-analytic review of the social psychological literature. *Psychological Bulletin, 100,* 309–330.

Earleywine, M. (2002). *Understanding marijuana: A new look at the scientific evidence.* New York: Oxford University Press.

Ebbesen, E. B., Kjos, G. L., & Konecni, V. J. (1976). Spatial ecology: Its effects on the choice of friends and enemies. *Journal of Experimental Social Psychology, 12,* 505–518.

Ebbinghaus, H. (1885). *Über das gedächtnis: Untersuchugen zur experimentellen psychologie.* Leipzig: Dunker & Humbolt. Translated by H. A. Ruger & C. E. Byssenine as *Memory: A contribution to experimental psychology.* Mew York: Dover, 1913.

Eccles, J. C. (1989). *Evolution of the brain: Creation of the self.* London: Routledge.

Echterling, L. G., & Whalen, J. (1995). Stage hypnosis and public lecture effects on attitudes and beliefs regarding hypnosis. *American Journal of Clinical Hypnosis, 38,* 13–21.

Eckensberger, L. H. (1994). Moral development and its measurement across cultures. In W. J. Lonner & R. Malpass (Eds.), *Psychology and culture.* Boston: Allyn & Bacon.

Edwards, D. C. (1999). *Motivation & emotion: Evolutionary, physiological, cognitive, and social influences.* Thousand Oaks, CA: Sage.

Edwards, K., & Smith, E. E. (1996). A disconfirmation bias in the evaluation of arguments. *Journal of Personality and Social Psychology, 71,* 5–24.

Edwards, W. (1977). How to use multiattribute utility measurement for social decision making. *IEEE Transactions in Systems Man and Cybernetics, 17,* 326–340.

Egan, D., & Schwartz, B. (1979). Chunking in recall of symbolic drawings. *Memory & Cognition, 7,* 149–158.

Egas Moñiz, A. (1948). How I came to perform prefrontal leucotomy. *Proceedings of the First International Congress of Psychosurgery* (pp. 7–18). Lisbon: Edicos Atica.

Egeland, J. D., & Sussex, J. N. (1985). Suicide and family loading for affective disorders. *Journal of the American Medical Association, 254,* 915–918.

Ehrlichman, H., & Halpern, J. N. (1988). Affect and memory: Effects of pleasant and unpleasant odors on retrieval of happy and unhappy memories. *Journal of Personality and Social Psychology, 55,* 769–779.

Eible-Eibesfeldt, I., & Sutterlin, C. (1990). Fear, defense and aggression in animals and man: Some ethological perspectives. In P. Brain & S. Parmigiani (Eds.), *Fear and defense.* London: Harwood.

Eich, J. E. (1989). Theoretical issues in state dependent memory. In H. L. Roediger III & F. I. M. Craik (Eds.), *Varieties of memory and consciousness: Essays in honour of Endel Tulving* (pp. 331–354). Hillsdale, NJ: Erlbaum.

Eisenberg, N., & Valiente, C. (2002). Parenting and children's prosocial and moral development. In M. H. Bornstein (Ed.), *Handbook of parenting: Vol. 5: Practical issues in parenting* (2nd ed., pp. 111–142). Mahwah, NJ: Erlbaum.

Eisenberger, R., & Cameron, J. (1996). Detrimental effects of reward: Reality or myth? *American Psychologist, 51,* 1153–1166.

Ekman, P. (1970). Universal facial expressions of emotion. *California Mental Health Research Digest, 8,* 151–158.

Ekman, P. (1973). *Darwin and facial expression: A century of research in review.* New York: Academic Press.

Ekman, P. (1993). Facial expression and emotion. *American Psychologist, 48,* 384–392.

Ekman, P. (1994). Strong evidence for universals in facial expressions: A reply to Russell's mistaken critique. *Psychological Bulletin, 115,* 268–287.

Ekman, P., & Friesen, W. V. (1971). Constants across cultures in the face and emotion. *Journal of Personality and Social Psychology, 17,* 124–129.

Ekman, P., & O'Sullivan, M. (1991). Who can catch a liar? *American Psychologist, 46,* 913–920.

Ekman, P., Friesen, W. V., & O'Sullivan, M. (1988). Smiling when lying. *Journal of Personality and Social Psychology, 54,* 414–420.

Ekman, P., Friesen, W. V., O'Sullivan, M., Chan, A., Diacoyanni-Tarlatzis, I., Heider, K., Krause, R., LeCompte, W. A., Pitcairn, T., Ricci-Bitti, P. E., Scherer, K., Tomita, M., & Tzavaras, A. (1987). Universals and cultural differences in the judgments of facial expressions of emotion. *Journal of Personality and Social Psychology, 53,* 712–717.

Elbedour, S., Shulman, S., & Kedem, P. (1997). Adolescent intimacy: A cross-cultural study. *Journal of Cross-Cultural Psychology, 28,* 5–22.

Eldridge, N. S., & Gilbert, L. A. (1990). Correlates of relationship satisfaction in lesbian couples. *Psychology of Women Quarterly, 14,* 43–62.

Elkin, I., Shea, M. T., Watkins, J. T., Imber, S. D., Sotsky, S. M., Collins, J. F., Glass, D. R., Pilkonis, P. A., Leber, W. R., Docherty, J. P., Fiester, S. J., & Parloff, M. B. (1989). National Institute of Mental Health Treatment of Depression Collaborative Research Program: General effectiveness of treatments. *Archives of General Psychiatry, 46,* 971–982.

Elkind, D. (1985). Egocentrism redux. *Developmental Review, 5,* 218–226.

Elkind, D., & Bowen, R. (1979). Imaginary audience behavior in children and adolescents. *Developmental Psychology, 15,* 38–44.

Ellenberger, H. (1970). *The discovery of the unconscious.* New York: Basic Books.

Elliot, A. J., & Devine, P. G. (1994). On the motivational nature of cognitive dissonance: Dissonance as psychological discomfort. *Journal of Personality and Social Psychology, 67,* 382–394.

Ellis, A. (1962). *Reason and emotion in psychotherapy.* New York: Lyle Stuart.

Ellis, A. (1999). Why rational emotive therapy to rational emotive behavior therapy? *Psychotherapy, 36,* 154–159.

Ellis, H. C., & Hunt, R. R. (1993). *Fundamentals of cognitive psychology* (5th ed.). Dubuque, IA: Wm. C. Brown.

Elman, J. L. (1999). The emergence of language: A conspiracy theory. In B. MacWhinney (Ed.), *The emergence of language* (pp. 1–27). Mahwah, NJ: Erlbaum.

Elmquist, J. K. (2001). Hypothalamic pathways underlying the endocrine, autonomic, and behavioral effects of leptin. *Physiology & Behavior, 74,* 703–708.

Elms, A. C. (1995). Obedience in retrospect. *Journal of Social Issues, 51,* 21–31.

Elms, A. C., & Milgram, S. (1966). Personality characteristics associated with obedience and defiance toward authoritative command. *Journal of Experimental Research in Personality, 1,* 282–289.

Embretson, S. E., & McCollam, K. M. S. (2000). Psychometric approaches to understanding and measuring intelligence. In R. J. Sternberg (Ed.), *Handbook of intelligence* (pp. 423–444). Cambridge: Cambridge University Press.

Emmelkamp, P. M. G. (1986). Behavior therapy with adults. In S. L. Garfield & A. E. Bergin (Eds.), *Handbook of psychotherapy and behavior change* (3rd ed., pp. 385–442). New York: Wiley.

Empson, J. (1993). *Sleep and dreaming* (2nd ed.). New York: Harvester Wheatsheaf.

Endler, N. S., & Speer, R. L. (1998). Personality psychology: Research trends for 1993–1995. *Journal of Personality, 66,* 621–669.

Engels, G. L., Garnefski, N., & Diekstra, R. (1993). Efficacy of rational-emotive therapy: A quantitative analysis. *Journal of Consulting and Clinical Psychology, 61,* 1083–1090.

Epstein, S. (1979). The stability of behavior: I. On predicting most of the people much of the time. *Journal of Personality and Social Psychology, 37,* 1097–1126.

Epstein, S. (1980). The stability of behavior: II. Implications for psychological research. *American Psychologist, 35,* 790–806.

Epstein, S. (1998). Cognitive-experiential self-theory. In D. F. Barone & M. Hersen (Eds.), *Advanced personality: The Plenum series in social/clinical psychology* (pp. 211–238). New York: Plenum.

Epstein, S. (1999). The interpretation of dreams from the perspective of cognitive-experiential self-theory. In J. A. Singer & P. Salovey (Eds.), *At play in the fields of consciousness: Essays in honor of Jerome L. Singer* (pp. 51–82). Mahwah, NJ: Erlbaum.

Erford, B. T. (1999). A modified time-out procedure for children with noncompliant or defiant behaviors. *Professional School Counseling, 2,* 205–210.

Erickson, B., Lind, E. A., Johnson, B. C., & O'Barr, W. M. (1978). Speech style and impression formation in a court setting: The effects of "powerful" and "powerless" speech. *Journal of Experimental Social Psychology, 14,* 266–279.

Ericsson, K. A., & Kintsch, W. (1995). Long-term working memory. *Psychological Review, 102,* 211–245.

Erikson, E. H. (1950). *Childhood and society.* New York: W. W. Norton.

Erikson, E. H. (1968). *Identity: Youth and crisis.* New York: W. W. Norton.

Erikson, E. H. (1980). *Identity: Youth and crisis.* New York: W. W. Norton.

Erwin, E., Gendin, S., & Kleiman, L. (1994). (Eds.). *Ethical issues in scientific research: An anthology.* New York: Garland.

Erwin, P. G. (1994). Effectiveness of social skills training with children: A meta-analytic study. *Counseling Psychology Quarterly, 7,* 305–310.

Esterson, A. (1993). *Seductive mirage: An exploration of the work of Sigmund Freud.* Chicago: Open Court.

Etaugh, C., & Liss, M. B. (1992). Home, school, and playroom: Training grounds for adult gender roles. *Sex Roles, 26,* 129–147.

Everson, S., Kauhanen, J., Kaplan, G., Goldberg, D., Julkunen, J., Tuomilehto, J., & Salonen, J. (1997). Hostility and increased risk of mortality and acute myocardial infarction: The mediating role of behavioral risk factors. *American Journal of Epidemiology, 146,* 142–152.

Exner, J. E. (1993). *The Rorschach: A comprehensive system.* (Vol. 1, 3rd ed.). New York: John Wiley.

Eyeferth, K. (1961). Leistungen vershiedener Gruppen von Besatzungskindern in Hamburg-Wechsler Intelligenztest für Kinder (HAWIK). *Archir für die Gesamte Psychologie, 113,* 224–241.

Eysenck, H. J. (1952). The effects of psychotherapy: An evaluation. *Journal of Consulting Psychology, 16,* 319–324.

Eysenck, H. J. (1973). *Eysenck on extraversion.* New York: Wiley.

Eysenck, H. J. (2000). Personality as a risk factor in cancer and coronary heart disease. In D. T. Kenny & J. G. Carlson (Eds.), *Stress and health: Research and clinical applications* (pp. 291–318). Amsterdam: Harwood Academic.

Eysenck, H. J., & Eysenck, S. B. G. (1983). Recent advances: The cross-cultural study of personality. In Butcher, J. N. and Spielberger, C. D. (Eds.), *Advances in personality assessment* (Vol. 2, pp. 41–72). Hillsdale, NJ: Erlbaum.

Eysenck, H. J., Wakefield, J. A., Jr., & Friedman, A. F. (1983). Diagnosis and clinical assessment: The DSM-III. *Annual Review of Psychology, 34,* 167–193.

Eysenck, S. B. G., & Eysenck, H. J. (1963). The validity of questionnaire and rating assessments of extraversion and neuroticism, and their factorial stability. *British Journal of Psychology, 54,* 51–62.

F

Fagan, J. F. (1992). Intelligence: A theoretical viewpoint. *Current Directions in Psychological Science, 1,* 82–86.

Fagot, B. I., Leinbach, M. D., & Hagan, R. (1986). Gender labeling and the adoption of sex-typed behaviors. *Developmental Psychology, 17,* 24–35.

Fairburn, C. G., Welch, S. L., Doll, H. A., Davies, B. A., & O'Connor, M. E. (1997). Risk factors for bulimia nervosa. *Archives of General Psychiatry, 54,* 509–511.

Falk, D. (1991). 3.5 million years of hominid brain evolution. *Seminars in the Neurosciences, 3,* 409–416.

Farrell, P. (1997). The integration of children with severe learning difficulties: A review of the recent literature. *Journal of Applied Research in Intellectual Disabilities, 10,* 1–14.

Farwell, L., & Donchin, E. (1991). The truth will out: Interrogative polygraphy ("lie detection") with event-related potentials. *Psychophysiology, 28,* 531–547.

Faust, M. S. (1977). Somatic development of adolescent girls. *Monographs of the Society for Research in Child Development, 42* (Whole No. 169).

Fava, M., & Rosenbaum, J. F. (1995). Pharmacotherapy and somatic therapies. In E. E. Beckham & W. R. Leber (Eds.), *Handbook of depression* (2nd ed., pp. 280–301). New York: Guilford Press.

Faw, H. W. (1990). Memory for names and faces: A fair comparison. *American Journal of Psychology, 103,* 317–326.

Feather, N. (1994). Values and culture. In W. Lonner & R. Malpass (Eds.), *Psychology and culture.* Boston: Allyn & Bacon.

Fechner, G. T. (1966). *Elements of psychophysics* (H. E. Alder, Trans.). New York: Holt, Rinehart & Winston. (Original work published 1860.)

Federmeier, K. D., & Kutas, M. (2002). Picture the difference: Electrophysiological investigations of picture processing in the two cerebral hemispheres. *Neuropsychologia, 40,* 730–747.

Feinberg, T. E. (2001). *Altered egos: How the brain creates the self.* Oxford: Oxford University Press.

Feingold, A. (1992). Cognitive gender differences: A developmental perspective. *Sex Roles, 29,* 91–112.

Feingold, A. (1992). Good-looking people are not what we think. *Psychological Bulletin, 111,* 304–341.

Feingold, A., & Mazzella, R. (1998). Gender differences in body image are increasing. *Psychological Science, 9,* 190–195.

Feldman, D. H. (1999). The development of creativity. In R. Sternberg (Ed.), *Handbook of creativity* (pp. 169–186). Cambridge, England: Cambridge University Press.

Felmlee, D. H. (1999). Social norms in same- and cross-gender friendships. *Social Psychology Quarterly, 62,* 53–67.

Felmlee, D. H., & Sprecher, S. (2000). Close relationships and social psychology: Intersections and future paths. *Social Psychology Quarterly, 63,* 365–376.

Fenigstein, A., Scheier, M. F., & Buss, A. H. (1975). Public and private self-consciousness: Assessment and theory. *Journal of Consulting and Clinical Psychology, 43,* 522–527.

Fenton, W., & McGlashan, T. (1991). Natural history of schizophrenia subtypes: I. Longitudinal study of paranoia, hebephrenic, and undifferentiated schizophrenia. *Archives of General Psychiatry, 48,* 969–977.

Fenwick, P. (1987). Meditation and the EEG. In M. A. West (Ed.), *The psychology of meditation.* Oxford: Clarendon Press.

Fenwick, P. (2001). The neurophysiology of religious experience. In I. Clarke (Ed.), *Psychosis and spirituality: Exploring the new frontier* (pp. 15–26). London: Whurr Publishers.

Fernandez, E., & Turk, D. C. (1989). The utility of cognitive coping strategies for altering pain perception: A meta-analysis. *Pain, 38,* 123–135.

Fernberger, S. W. (1933). Wundt's doctorate students. *Psychological Bulletin, 30,* 80–83.

Ferrari, J. R., & Dovidio, J. F. (2001). Behavioral information search by indecisives. *Personality and Individual Differences, 30,* 1–12.

Ferrari, J. R., & Tice, D. M. (2000). Procrastination as a self-handicap for men and women: A task avoidance strategy in a laboratory setting. *Journal of Research in Personality, 34,* 73–83.

Ferster, C. S., & Skinner, B. F. (1957). *Schedules of reinforcement.* New York: Appleton-Century-Crofts.

Festinger, L. (1954). A theory of social comparison processes. *Human Relations, 7,* 117–140.

Festinger, L. (1957). *A theory of cognitive dissonance.* Stanford, CA: Stanford University Press.

Festinger, L., Riecken, H. W., & Schachter, S. (1956). *When prophecy fails.* Minneapolis: University of Minnesota Press.

Festinger, L., Schachter, S., & Back, K. (1950). *Social pressures in informal groups: A study of a housing community.* New York: Harper.

Fetzer, J. H. (Ed.). (2002). *Advances in consciousness research.* Amsterdam: John Benjamins.

Field, T. (1996). Attachment and separation in young children. In J. T. Spence, J. M. Darley, & D. J. Foss (Eds). *Annual review of psychology* (Vol. 47, pp. 541–561). Palo Alto, CA: Annual Reviews.

Field, T. M. (1982). Individual differences in the expressivity of neonates and young infants. In R. S. Feldman (Ed.), *Development of nonverbal behavior in children.* New York: Springer-Verlag.

Field, T. M., Cohen, D., Garcia, R., & Greenberg, R. (1984). Mother-stranger face discrimination by the newborn. *Infant Behavior and Development, 7,* 19–25.

Fields, J. I. (1997). Measuring giftedness in young children: A comparative study in Malaysia. *Early Development and Care, 131,* 93–106.

Findley, M. J., & Cooper, H. M. (1983). Locus of control and academic achievement: A literature review. *Journal of Personality and Social Psychology, 44,* 419–427.

Fink, J. (1999a). *How to use computers and cyberspace in the clinical practice of psychotherapy.* Northvale, NJ: Jason Aronson, Inc.

Fink, M. (1999b). *Electroshock: Restoring the mind.* New York: Oxford University Press.

Finn, P. R., Justus, A. N., Mazas, C., Rorick, L., & Steinmetz, J. E. (2001). Constraint, alcoholism, and electrodermal response to aversive classical conditioning and mismatch novelty paradigms. *Integrative Physiological & Behavioral Science, 36,* 154–167.

Finucane, M. L., Slovic, P., Hibbard, J. H., Peters, E., Mertz, C. K., & MacGregor, D. G. (2002). Aging and decision-making competence: An analysis of comprehension and consistency skills in older versus younger adults considering health-plan options. *Journal of Behavioral Decision Making, 15,* 141–164.

Fischoff, B. (1977). Perceived informativeness of facts. *Journal of Experimental Psychology, 3,* 349–358.

Fishbach, G. D. (1992, September). Mind and brain. *Scientific American, 267,* 48–57.

Fisher, J., & Fisher, W. (1992). Changing AIDS-risk behavior. *Psychological Bulletin, 111*, 455–474.

Fisher, W. (1993). Confessions of a sexual scientist. In G. Brannigan and M. Merrens (Eds.), *The undaunted psychologist: Adventures in research* (pp. 13–29). Philadelphia, PA: Temple University Press.

Fisher, W., Byrne, D., White, L., & Kelley, K. (1988a). Erotophobia-erotophilia as a dimension of personality. *Journal of Sex Research, 25*, 123–151.

Fisher, W., et al. (1979). Psychological and situation-specific correlates of contraceptive behavior among university women. *Journal of Sex Research, 15*, 38–55.

Fisher, W., Fisher, J., & Byrne, D. (1977). Consumer reactions to contraceptive purchasing. *Personality & Social Psychology Bulletin, 3*, 293–296.

Fisher, W., Grenier, G., Watters, W., Lamont, J., et al. (1988b). Students' sexual knowledge, attitudes toward sex, and willingness to treat sexual concerns. *Journal of Medical Education, 63*, 379–385.

Fiske, S. T., & Neuberg, S. L. (1990). A continuum model of impression formation, from category-based to individuating processes: Influence of information and motivation on attention and interpretation. In M. P. Zanna (Ed.), *Advances in experimental social psychology* (Vol. 23). New York: Academic Press.

Fiske, S. T., & Taylor, S. E. (1991). *Social cognition* (2nd ed.). New York: McGraw-Hill.

Flanagan, O. (1996). Deconstructing dreams: The spandrels of sleep. In S. R. Hameroff, A. W. Kaszniak, & A. C. Scott (Eds.), *Toward a science of consciousness: The first Tucson discussions and debates* (pp. 67–88), Cambridge, MA: MIT Press.

Flavell, J. (1982). Structures, stages, and sequences in cognitive development. In W. Collins (Ed.), *The concept of development* (pp. 1–28). Hillsdale, NJ: Erlbaum.

Flavell, J. H. (1992). Cognitive development: Past, present, and future. *Developmental Psychology, 28*, 998–1005.

Flavell, J. H. (1996). Piaget's legacy. *Psychological Science, 7*, 200–203.

Flavell, J. H. (1999). Cognitive development: Children's knowledge about the mind. *Annual Review of Psychology, 50*, 21–45.

Flavell, J. H., Beach, D. R., & Chinsky, J. M. (1966). Spontaneous verbal rehearsal in a memory task as a function of age. *Child Development, 37*, 283–299.

Fletcher, G. (2002). *The new science of intimate relationships.* Malden, MA: Blackwell

Flor, H., Elbert, T., Knecht, S., & Wienbruch, C. (1995). Phantom-limb pain as a perceptual correlate of cortical reorganization following arm amputation. *Nature, 375*, 482–484.

Flynn, J. R. (1987). Massive IQ gains in 14 nations: What IQ tests really measure. *Psychological Bulletin, 101*, 171–191.

Flynn, J. R. (1990). Massive IQ gains on the Scottish WISC: Evidence against Brand et al.'s hypothesis. *Irish Journal of Psychology, 11*, 41–51.

Flynn, J. R. (1996). *What environmental factors affect intelligence: The relevance of IQ gains over time.* Norwood, NJ: Ablex.

Foertsch, J., & Gernsbacher, M. A. (1997). In search of gender neutrality: Is singular *they* a cognitively efficient substitute for generic *he*? *Behavior Therapy, 16*, 292–302.

Folkman, S., & Lazarus, R. (1980). An analysis of coping in a middle-aged community sample. *Journal of Health and Social Behavior, 21*, 219–239.

Folkman, S., & Moskowitz, J. T. (2000). Positive affect and the other side of coping. *American Psychologist, 55*, 647–654.

Folkman, S., Lazarus, R. S., Gruen, R. J., & DeLongis, A. (1986). Appraisal, coping, health status, and psychological symptoms. *Journal of Personality and Social Psychology, 50*, 571–579.

Ford, C. S., & Beach, F. A. (1951). *Patterns of sexual behavior.* New York: Harper & Brothers.

Ford, D. Y. (1996). *Reversing underachievement among gifted Black students: Promising practices and programs.* New York: Teachers College Press.

Ford, M. (1979). The construct validity of egocentrism. *Psychological Bulletin, 86*, 1169–1188.

Fordham, S., & Ogbu, J. U. (1986). Black students' school success: Coping with the "burden of 'acting white'." *The Urban Review, 18*, 176–206.

Forer, B. R. (1949). The fallacy of personal validation: A classroom demonstration of gullibility. *Journal of Abnormal and Social Psychology, 44*, 118–123.

Foreyt, J., Walker, S., Poston, C. II, & Goodrick, G. (1996). Future directions in obesity and eating disorders. *Addictive Behaviors, 21*, 767–778.

Forgas, J. P. (1998). Asking nicely? The effects of mood on responding to more or less polite requests. *Personality and Social Psychology Bulletin, 24*, 173–185.

Forgays, D. G., & Forgays, D. K. (1994). The use of flotation isolation to modify important Type A components in young adults. *Journal of Environmental Psychology, 14*, 47–55.

Forstmeier, W., & Balsby, T. J. S. (2002). Why mated dusky warblers sing so much: Territory guarding and male quality announcement. *Behaviour, 139*, 89–111.

Fouts, R. (1997). *Next of kin: What chimpanzees have taught me about who we are.* New York: Morrow.

Fowles, D. (1992). Schizophrenia: Diathesis-stress revisited. *Annual Review of Psychology, 43*, 303–336.

Fox, B. (1998). Psychosocial factors in cancer incidence and progression. In J. Holland (Ed.), *Psycho-oncology.* New York: Oxford University Press.

Fox, B. A. (1988). *Cognitive and interactional aspects of correction in tutoring* (Tech. Rep. No. 88-2). Boulder: University of Colorado, Institute of Cognitive Science.

Fox, D. R. (1985). Psychology, ideology, utopia, and the commons. *American Psychologist, 40*, 48–58.

Fox, N., & Davidson, R. (1991). Hemispheric specialization and attachment behaviors: Developmental processes and individual differences in separation process. In J. Gewirtz & W. Kurtines (Eds.), *Interactions with attachment.* Hillsdale, NJ: Erlbaum.

Fraczek, A. (1992). Patterns of aggressive-hostile behavior orientation among adolescent boys and girls. In K. Björkqvist & P. Niemelä (Eds.), *Of mice and women: Aspects of female aggression* (pp. 107–112). San Diego: Harcourt Brace Jovanovich.

Frank, L. R. (2002). Electroshock: A crime against the spirit. *Ethical Human Sciences & Services, 4*, 63–71.

Frankenhaeuser, M. (1975). The experimental psychology research unit. *Man-Environment Systems, 5*, 193–195.

Frankenhauser, M., Myrsten, A., & Post, B. (1970). Psychophysiological reactions to cigarette smoking. *Scandinavian Journal of Psychology, 11*, 237–245.

Frankl, V. (1963). *Man's search for meaning: An introduction to logotherapy.* New York: Vintage Books.

Frankl, V. (1969). *The will to meaning.* New York: World Publishing.

Franzoi, S. L. (1985). Personality characteristics of the cross-country hitchhiker. *Adolescence, 29*, 655–668.

Franzoi, S. L. (1995). The body-as-object versus the body-as-process: Gender differences and gender considerations. *Sex Roles, 33,* 417–437.

Franzoi, S. L., & Chang, Z. (2000). The sociocultural dynamics of the physical self: How does gender shape body esteem? In J. A. Holstein & G. Miller (Eds.), *Perspectives on social problems* (Vol. 12, pp. 179–201). Stamford, CT: JAI Press.

Franzoi, S. L., & Chang, Z. (2002). The body esteem of Hmong and Caucasian young adults. *Psychology of Women Quarterly, 26,* 89–91.

Franzoi, S. L. & Shields, S. A. (1984). The Body-Esteem Scale: Multidimensional structure and sex differences in a college population. *Journal of Personality Assessment, 48,* 173–178.

Franzoi, S. L., Davis, M. H., & Young, R. D. (1985). The effects of private self-consciousness and perspective-taking on satisfaction in close relationships. *Journal of Personality and Social Psychology, 48,* 1584–1594.

Fredrickson, B. L. (2001). The role of positive emotions in positive psychology. *American Psychologist, 56,* 218–226.

Fredrickson, B. L., Maynard, K. E., Helms, M. J., Haney, T. L., Siegler, I. C., & Barefoot, J. C. (2000). Hostility predicts magnitude and duration of blood pressure response to anger. *Journal of Behavioral Medicine, 23,* 229–243.

Fredrickson, B. L., Roberts, T., Noll, S. M., Quinn, D.M., & Twenge, J. M. (1998). That swimsuit becomes you: Sex differences in self-objectification, restrained eating, and math performance. *Journal of Personality and Social Psychology, 75,* 269–284.

Freedman, M. (1971). *Homosexuality and psychological functioning.* Belmont, CA: Brooks/Cole.

Fremouw, W. J., de Perczel, M., & Ellis, T. E. (1990). *Suicide risk: Assessment and response guidelines.* New York: Pergamon Press.

French, J. R. P., & Raven, B. H. (1959). The bases of social power. In D. Cartwright (Ed.), *Studies in social power.* Ann Arbor: University of Michigan Press.

Freud, A. (1936). *The writings of Anna Freud: The ego and the mechanics of defense.* New York: International Universities Press.

Freud, S. (1900). *The interpretation of dreams.* In Vols. 4 and 5 of the *Standard edition.* London: Hogarth Press.

Freud, S. (1900/1953). The interpretation of dreams. In J. Strachey (Ed.), *The standard edition of the complete psychological works of Sigmund Freud* (Vols. 4 and 5). London: Hogarth Press.

Freud, S. (1917). Introductory lectures on psychoanalysis. Part III. General theory of the neurosis. In J. Strachey (Ed. & Trans.), *The standard edition of the complete psychological works of Sigmund Freud* (Vol. 16, pp. 243–496). London: Hogarth Press, 1959.

Freud, S. (1926). Inhibitions, symptoms, and anxiety. In J. Strachey (Ed. & Trans.), *The standard edition of the complete psychological works of Sigmund Freud* (Vol. 20, pp. 89–174). London: Hogarth Press, 1959.

Freud, S. (1946). *The ego and the mechanisms of defense.* New York: International Universities Press.

Freud, S. (1949). *A general introduction to psychoanalysis.* New York: Penguin.

Freud, S. (1950/1895). Project for a scientific psychology. In J. Strachey (Ed. & Trans.), *The standard edition of the complete psychological works of Sigmund Freud* (Vol. 1, pp. 282–398). London: Hogarth Press, 1966.

Freud, S. (1963). Analysis of a phobia in a five-year-old boy. In J. Strachey (Ed. and Trans.), *The standard edition of the complete psychological works of Sigmund Freud* (Vol. 10, pp. 3–149). London: Hogarth. (original work published in 1909)

Friedman, H., Hawley, P., Tucker, J. (1994). Personality, health, and longevity. *Current Directions in Psychological Science, 3,* 37–41.

Friedman, H. S., & Schustack, M. W. (1999). *Personality: Classic theories and modern research.* Boston: Allyn & Bacon.

Friedman, J. M. (2000). Obesity in the new millennium. *Nature, 404,* 632–634.

Friedman, L. J. (2001). Erik Erikson on identity, generativity, and pseudospeciation: A biographer's perspective. *Psychoanalysis & History, 3,* 179–192.

Friedman, M., & Ulmer, D. (1984). *Treating Type A behavior—and your heart.* New York: Knopf.

Frieze, I. H., Olson, J. E., & Russell, J. (1991). Attractiveness and income for men and women in management. *Journal of Applied Social Psychology, 21,* 1039–1057.

Frisch, K. von. (1950). *Bees: Their vision, chemical senses, and language.* Ithaca: Cornell University Press.

Frisch, K. von. (1962). Dialects in the language of the bees. *Scientific American, 207,* 78–87.

Frisch, K. von. (1967). *The dance language and orientation of bees.* Cambridge, MA: Harvard University Press.

Fromm, E., & Shor, R. E. (Eds.). (1979). *Hypnosis: Developments in research and new perspectives* (2nd ed.). Hawthorne, NY: Aldine.

Fry, D. P. (1992). Female aggression among the Zapotec of Oaxaca, Mexico. In K. Björkqvist & P. Niemelä (Eds.), *Of mice and women: Aspects of female aggression* (pp. 187–199). San Diego: Harcourt Brace Jovanovich.

Fuchs, C. S., Stampfer, M. J., Colditz, G. A., et al. (1995). Alcohol consumption and mortality among women. *New England Journal of Medicine, 332,* 1245–1250.

Fuhriman, A., & Burlingame, G. M. (1994). Group psychotherapy: Research and practice. In A. Fuhriman & G. M. Burlingame (Eds.), *Handbook of group psychotherapy.* New York: Wiley.

Fuligni, A. J., & Stevenson, H. W. (1995). Time use and mathematics achievement among American, Chinese, and Japanese high school students. *Child Development, 66,* 830–842.

Funder, D. C. (2001). Personality. *Annual Review of Psychology, 52,* 197–221.

Furio, C., Calatayud, M. L., Barcenas, S. L., & Padilla, O. M. (2000). Functional fixedness and functional reduction as common sense reasonings in chemical equilibrium and in geometry and polarity of molecules. *Science & Education, 84,* 545–565.

Furnham, A., Shahidi, S., & Baluch, B. (2002). Sex and culture differences in perceptions of estimated multiple intelligence for self and family: A British-Iranian comparison. *Journal of Cross-Cultural Psychology, 33,* 270–285.

Furumoto, L. (1992). Joining separate spheres—Christine Ladd-Franklin, Woman-scientist (1847–1930). *American Psychologist, 47,* 174–182.

Furumoto, L., & Scarborough, E. (2002). Placing women in the history of psychology: The first American women psychologists. In W. E. Pickren & D. A. Dewsbury (Eds.), *Evolving perspectives on the history of psychology* (pp. 527–543). Washington, DC: American Psychological Association.

Fuster, J. M. (1989). *The prefrontal cortex: Anatomy, physiology, and neuropsychology of the frontal lobe* (2nd ed.). New York: Raven Press.

G

Gabiano, C., Tovo, P. A., de Martino, M., Galli, L., Giaquinto, C., Loy, A., Schoeller, M. C., Giovannini, M., Ferranti, G., Rancilio, L., Caselli, D., Segini, G., Livadiotti, S., Conte, A., Rizzi, M., Viggiano, D., Mazza, A., Ferrazzin, A., Tozzi, A. E., & Cappello, N. (1992). Mother-to-child transmission of human immunodeficiency virus type 1: Risk of infection and correlates of transmission. *Pediatrics, 90,* 369–374.

Gabrieli, J. D. E. (1998). Cognitive neuroscience of human memory. *Annual Review of Psychology, 49,* 87–115.

Gabrieli, J. D. E. (1999). The architecture of human memory. In J. K. Foster & M. Jelicic (Eds.), *Memory: Systems, process, or function?* (pp. 205–231). Oxford: Oxford University Press.

Gabrieli, J. D. E., Desmond, J. E., Demb, J. B., Wagner, A. D., Stone, M. V., Vaidya, C. J., et al. (1996). Functional magnetic resonance imaging of semantic memory processes in the frontal lobes. *Psychological Science, 7,* 278–283.

Gagliese, L., & Katz, J. (2000). Medically unexplained pain is not caused by psychopathology. *Pain Research & Management, 5,* 251–257.

Galanter, E. (1962). Contemporary psychophysics. In R. Brown (Ed.), *New directions in psychology.* New York: Holt, Rinehart & Winston.

Gallagher, J., Harradine, C. C., & Coleman, M. R. (1997). Challenge or boredom? Gifted students' views on their schooling. *Roeper Review, 19,* 132–141.

Galotti, K. M., Kozberg, S. F., & Farmer, M. C. (1991). Gender and developmental differences in adolescents conceptions of moral reasoning. *Journal of Youth and Adolescence, 20,* 13–30.

Galton, F. (1869). *Hereditary genius: An inquiry into its laws and consequences.* New York: Appleton.

Gandevia, S. C., McCloskey, D. I., & Burke, D. (1992). Kinesthetic signals and muscle contraction. *Trends in Neurosciences, 15,* 62–65.

Gangestad, S. W., & Snyder, M. (2000). Self-monitoring: Appraisal and reappraisal. *Psychological Bulletin, 126,* 530–555.

Garcia, J., & Koelling, R. A. (1966). Relation of cue to consequence in avoidance learning. *Psychonomic Science, 4,* 123–124.

Garcia, J., Rusniak, K. W., & Brett, L. P. (1977). Conditioning food-illness aversions in wild animals: Caveat Canonici. In H. Davis & H. M. B. Hurwitz (Eds.), *Operant-Pavlovian interactions.* Hillsdale, NJ: Erlbaum.

Gardner, H. (1983). *Frames of mind: The theory of multiple intelligences.* New York: Basic Books.

Gardner, H. (1991). *The unschooled mind: How children think and how schools should teach.* New York: Basic Books.

Gardner, H. (1993). *Creating minds: An anatomy of creativity seen through the lives of Freud, Einstein, Picasso, Stravinsky, Eliot, Graham, and Gandhi.* New York: Basic Books.

Gardner, H. (1993). *Multiple intelligences: The theory in practice.* New York: Basic Books.

Gardner, H., Kornhaber, M. L., & Wake, W. K. (1996). *Intelligence: Multiple perspectives.* Ft. Worth, TX: Harcourt Brace.

Gardner, R. A., & Gardner, B. T. (1969). Teaching sign language to a chimpanzee. *Science, 165,* 664–672.

Gardner, R. J. M., & Sutherland, G. R. (1996). *Chromosomal abnormalities and genetic counseling.* New York: Oxford University Press.

Garfinkel, D., Laudon, M., Of, D., & Zisapel, N. (1995). Improvement of sleep quality in elderly people by controlled-release melatonin. *Lancet, 146,* 541–544.

Garry, M., Loftus, E. F., Brown, S. W., & DuBreuil, S. C. (1997). Womb with a view: Memory beliefs and memory-work experiences. In D. G. Payne & F. G. Conrad (Eds.), *Intersections in basic and applied memory research* (pp. 233–255). Mahwah, NJ: Erlbaum.

Gatchel, R. J., & Turk, D. C. (Eds.). (1999). *Psychosocial factors in pain: Critical perspectives.* New York: Guilford Press.

Gay, P. (1998). *Freud: A life for our time.* New York: Norton.

Gazzaniga, M. S. (1967). The split brain in man. *Scientific American, 217,* 24–29.

Gazzaniga, M. S. (1970). *The bisected brain.* New York: Appleton-Century-Crofts.

Gazzaniga, M. S. (1988). *Mind matters: How mind and brain interact to create our conscious lives.* Boston: Houghton Mifflin.

Gazzaniga, M. S. (1989). Organization of the human brain. *Science, 245,* 947–952.

Gazzaniga, M. S. (Ed.). (2000). *The new cognitive neuroscience* (2nd ed.). Cambridge, MA: The MIT Press.

Gazzaniga, M. S., & Miller, M. B. (2000). Testing Tulving: The split-brain approach. In E. Tulving (Ed.), *Memory, consciousness, and the brain: The Tallinn Conference* (pp. 307–318). Philadelphia, PA: Psychology Press.

Gedo, J. E. (2001). The enduring scientific contributions of Sigmund Freud. In J. A. Winer & J. W. Anderson (Eds.), *The annual of psychoanalysis volume XXIX: Sigmund Freud and his impact on the modern world* (pp. 105–115). Hillsdale, NJ: Analytic Press.

Geen, R. G. (1996). Aggression and antisocial behavior. In D. T. Gilbert, S. T. Fiske, & G. Lindzey (Eds.), *The handbook of social psychology* (4th ed.). New York: McGraw-Hill.

Gelderloos, P., Walton, K. G., Orme-Johnson, D. W., & Alexander, C. N. (1991). Effectiveness of the Transcendental Meditation program in preventing and treating substance misuse: A review. *The International Journal of Addictions, 26,* 293–325.

Gelfand, S. A. (1981). *Hearing.* New York: Marcel Dekker.

Geller, J. (2002). Estimating readiness for change in anorexia nervosa: Comparing clients, clinicians and research assessors. *International Journal of Eating Disorders, 31,* 251–260.

Georgopoulos, A. P., Whang, K., Georgopoulos, M.-A., Tagaris, G. A., Amirikan, B., Richter, W., Kim, S.-G., & Ugurbil, K. (2001). Functional magnetic resonance imaging of visual object construction and shape discrimination: Relations among task, hemispheric lateralization, and gender. *Journal of Cognitive Neuroscience, 13,* 72–89.

Gerbner, G., & Signorielli, N. (1990). *Violence profile 1967 through 1988–89: Enduring patterns.* Unpublished manuscript, Annenberg School of Communications, University of Pennsylvania.

Gerhart, K. A., Koziol-McLain, J., Lowenstein, S. R., & Whiteneck, G. G. (1994). Quality of life following spinal cord injury: Knowledge and attitudes of emergency care providers. *Annals of Emergency Medicine, 23,* 807–812.

Gerra, G., Zaimovic, A., Ferri, M., Zambelli, U., Timpano, M., Neri, E., Marzocchi, G. F., Delsignore, R., & Brambilla, F. (2000). Long-lasting effects of (+–)3,4-Methylenedioxymethamphetamine (Ecstasy) on serotonin system function in humans. *Biological Psychiatry, 47,* 127–136.

Gerschwind, N., & Galaburda, A. (1987). *Cerebral lateralization: Biological mechanisms, association and pathology*. Cambridge, MA: Bradford/MIT Press.

Gesheider, G. A. (1985). *Psychophysics: Method and theory*. Hillsdale, NJ: Erlbaum.

Ghazvini, A., & Mullis, R. L. (2002). Center-based care for young children: Examining predictors of quality. *Journal of Genetic Psychology, 163*, 112–125.

Giambra, L. M. (1989). Task-unrelated-thought frequency as a function of age: A laboratory study. *Psychology and Aging, 4*, 136–143.

Giambra, L. M. (2000). Daydreaming characteristics across the lifespan: Age differences and seven to twenty year longitudinal changes. In R.G. Kunzendorf & B. Wallace (Eds.), *Individual differences in conscious experience: Advances in consciousness research* (Vol. 20, pp. 147–206). Amsterdam: John Benjamins.

Gibson, E. J., & Walk, R.D. (1960, April). The "visual cliff." *Scientific American*, pp. 64–71.

Gibson, H. B. (1991). Can hypnosis compel people to commit harmful, immoral, and criminal acts? A review of the literature. *Contemporary Hypnosis, 8*, 129–140.

Gilbert, D. T., Pinel, E. C., Wilson, T. D., Blumberg, S. J., & Wheatley, T. P. (1998). Immune neglect: A source of durability bias in affective forecasting. *Journal of Personality and Social Psychology, 75*, 617–638.

Gilbert, L. A. (1994). Reclaiming and returning gender to context: Examples from studies of heterosexual dual-earner families. *Psychology of Women Quarterly, 18*, 539–584.

Gill, J. H. (1997). *If a chimpanzee could talk: And other reflections on language acquisition*. Tucson: University of Arizona Press.

Gillett, G. R. (2001). Free will and events in the brain. *Journal of Mind & Behavior, 22*, 287–310.

Gilligan, C. (1982). *In a different voice: Psychological theory and women's development*. Cambridge, MA: Harvard University Press.

Gilligan, C. (1990). Teaching Shakespeare's sister. In C. Gilligan, N. Lyons, & T. Hanmer (Eds.), *Making connections: The relational worlds of adolescent girls at Emma Willard School*. Cambridge, MA: Harvard University Press.

Gilligan, C., & Attanucci, J. (1988). Two moral orientations: Gender differences and similarities. *Merrill-Palmer Quarterly, 34*, 223–237.

Gillin, J. C. (1993). Clinical sleep-wake disorders in psychiatric practice: Dyssomnias. In D. L. Dunner (Ed.), *Current psychiatric therapy*. Philadelphia: Saunders.

Gilman, S. L. (2001). Karen Horney, M.D., 1885–1952. *American Journal of Psychiatry, 158*, 1205.

Ginsburg, G., & Bronstein, P. (1993). Family factors related to children's intrinsic/extrinsic motivational orientation and academic motivation orientation and performance. *Child Development, 64*, 1461–1474.

Gladue, B.A. (1991). Aggressive behavioral characteristics, hormones, and sexual orientation in men and women. *Aggressive Behavior, 17*, 313–326.

Glaser, R., Kiecolt-Glaser, J., Bonneau, R., Malarkey, W., Kennedy, S., & Hughes, J. (1992). Stress-induced modulation of the immune response to recombinant hepatitis B vaccine. *Psychosomatic Medicine, 54*, 22–29.

Glass, D., & Singer, J. (1972). *Urban stress: Experiments on noise and social stressors*. New York: Academic Press.

Gleason, J. B. (1997). *The development of language*. Boston: Allyn & Bacon.

Gleaves, D. H. (1996). The sociocognitive model of dissociative identity: A reexamination of evidence. *Psychological Bulletin, 120*, 42–59.

Glick, P. Gottesman, D., & Jolton, J. (1989). The fault is not in the stars: Susceptibility of skeptics and believers in astrology to the Barnum effect. *Personality and Social Psychology Bulletin, 15*, 417–429.

Glover, S., & Dixon, P. (2002). Dynamic effects of the Ebbinghaus illusion in grasping: Support for a planning/control model of action. *Perception & Psychophysics, 64*, 266–278.

Gluck, M. A., & Myers, C. E. (2001). *Gateway to memory: An introduction to neural network modeling of the hippocampus and learning*. Cambridge, MA: MIT Press.

Glucksberg, S., & Danks, J. (1968). Effects of discriminative labels and of nonsense labels upon availability of novel function. *Journal of Verbal Learning and Verbal Behavior, 7*, 72–76.

Glucksberg, S., & Weisberg, R. W. (1966). Verbal behavior and problem solving: Some effects of labeling in a functional fixedness problem. *Journal of Experimental Psychology, 71*, 659–664.

Godbout, R., Montplaisir, J., Bédard, M.-A., Doivan, D., & LaPierre, O. (1990). Fundamental and clinical neuropharmacology of sleep disorders: Restless legs syndrome with periodic movements in sleep and narcolepsy. In J. Montplaisir & R. Godbout (Eds.), *Sleep and biological rhythms: Basic mechanisms and applications to psychiatry* (pp. 219–236). New York: Oxford University Press.

Godby, K. E. (2002). Mystical experience: Unveiling the veiled. *Pastoral Psychology, 50*, 231–242.

Goddard, H. H. (1913). The Binet tests in relation to immigration. *Journal of Psycho-Asthenics, 18*, 105–107.

Goddard, H. H. (1919). *Psychology of the normal and subnormal*. New York: Dodd, Mead.

Goebel, B., & Brown, D. (1981). Age differences in motivation related to Maslow's needs hierarchy. *Developmental Psychology, 17*, 809–817.

Goetestam, K. G. (2002). One session group treatment of spider phobia by direct or modeled exposure. *Cognitive Behaviour Therapy, 31*, 18–24.

Goethals, G. R. (1986). Social comparison theory: Psychology from the lost and found. *Personality and Social Psychology Bulletin, 12*, 261–278.

Goethals, G. R., & Darley, J. M. (1987). Social comparison theory: Self-evaluation and group life. In B. Mullen & G. R. Goethals (Eds.), *Theories of group behavior*. New York: Springer-Verlag.

Goffman, E. (1959). *The presentation of self in everyday life*. Garden City, NY: Doubleday.

Goh, V. H.-H., Tong, Y.-Y., Lim, C.-L., Low, E. C.-T., & Lee, L. K.-H. (2000). Circadian disturbances after night-shift work aboard a naval ship. *Military Medicine, 165*, 101–105.

Goldberg, B. (1995). Slowing down the aging process through the use of altered states of consciousness: A review of the medical literature. *Psychology: A Quarterly Journal of Human Behavior, 32*, 19–21.

Goldberg, E. (2001). *The executive brain: Frontal lobes and the civilized mind*. New York: Oxford University Press.

Goldberg, J., Lyons, M. J., Eisen, S. A., True, W. R., & Tsuang, M. (1993). Genetic influence on drug use: A preliminary analysis of 2674 Vietnam era veteran twins. [Abstract.] *Behavioral Genetics Society*.

Goldenberg, I., & Goldenberg, H. (1995). Family therapy. In R. J. Corsini & D. Wedding (Eds.), *Current psychotherapies* (5th ed.). Itasca, IL: Peacock.

Goldman, J., & Coté, L. (1991). Aging of the brain: Dementia of the Alzheimer's type. In E. R. Kandel, J. H. Schwartz, & T. M. Jessell (Eds.), *Principles of neural science* (3rd ed.). New York: Elsevier.

Goldman-Rakic, P. S. (1992). Working memory and the mind. *Scientific American, 267,* 110–117.

Goldman-Rakic, P. S. (1995). Cellular basis of working memory. *Neuron, 14,* 477–485.

Goldner, E., & Birmingham, C. (1994). Anorexia nervosa: Methods of treatment. In L. Alexander-Mott & D. Lumsden (Eds.), *Understanding eating disorders: Anorexia nervosa, bulimia nervosa, and obesity* (pp. 135–157). Washington, DC: Taylor & Francis.

Goldstein, R. B., Wickramaratne, P. J., Horwath, E., & Weissman, M. M. (1997). Familial aggregation and phenomenology of "early"-onset (at or before age 20 years) panic disorder. *Archives of General Psychiatry, 54,* 271–278.

Goleman, D. (1995). *Emotional intelligence.* New York: Bantam.

Golombok, S., & Tasker, F. (1996). Do parents influence the sexual orientation of their children? Findings from a longitudinal study of lesbian families. *Developmental Psychology, 32,* 3–11.

Gonsiorek, J. C. (1982). Results of psychological testing on homosexual populations. *American Behavioral Scientist, 25* (4), 385–396.

Gonsiorek, J. C. (1991). The empirical basis for the demise of the illness model of homosexuality. In J. Gonsiorek & J. Weinrich (Eds.), *Homosexuality: Research implications for public policy* (pp. 115–136). Thousand Oaks, CA: Sage.

Gonsiorek, J. C., & Weinrich, J. D. (1991). The definition and scope of sexual orientation. In J. C. Gonsiorek & J. D. Weinrich (Eds.), *Homosexuality: Research implications for public policy* (pp. 1–12). Newbury Park, CA: Sage.

Goode, E. (1999, February 16). Tales of midlife crisis found greatly exaggerated. *The New York Times* (www.nytimes.com).

Goodnow, J. J. (1988). Children's household work: Its nature and function. *Psychological Bulletin, 103,* 5–26.

Gopnik, A. (1996). The post-Piaget era. *Psychological Science, 7,* 221–225.

Gopnik, J. J., Meltzoff, A. N., & Kuhl, P. K. (1999). *The scientist in the crib: Minds, brains, and how children learn.* New York: Morrow.

Gorassini, D. R. (1996). Conviction management: Lessons from hypnosis research about how self-images of dubious validity can be willfully sustained. In N. P. Spanos & B. Wallace (Eds.), *Hypnosis and imagination: Imagery and human development series* (pp. 177–198). Amityville, NY: Baywood.

Gordon, P. (1990). Learnability and feedback. *Developmental Psychology, 26,* 217–220.

Gorman, C. (2002, June 10). The science of anxiety. *Time,* pp. 46–54.

Gortmaker, S. L., Must, A., Perrin, J. M., Sobol, A. M., & Dietz, W. H. (1993). Social and economic consequences of overweight in adolescence and young adulthood. *New England Journal of Medicine, 329,* 1008–1012.

Gosling, S. D. (2001). From mice to men: What can we learn about personality from animal research? *Psychological Bulletin, 127,* 45–86.

Gosling, S. D., & John, O. P. (1999). Personality dimensions in nonhuman animals: A cross-species review. *Current Directions in Psychological Science, 8,* 69–75.

Gottesman, I. I. (1991). *Schizophrenic genesis: The epigenetic puzzle.* New York: Cambridge University Press.

Gottfried, A. W., Gottfried, A. E., Bathurst, K., & Guerin, D. W. (1994). *Gifted IQ: Early developmental aspects: The Fullerton longitudinal study.* New York: Plenum Press.

Gottfried, A., Fleming, J., & Gottfried, A. (1994). Role of parental motivational practices in children's academic intrinsic motivation and achievement. *Journal of Educational Psychology, 86,* 104–113.

Gottlieb, G. (2002a). Developmental-behavioral initiation of evolutionary change. *Psychological Review, 109,* 211–218.

Gottlieb, G. (2002b). Origin of species: The potential significance of early experienced for evolution. In W. Hartup & R. A. Weinberg (Eds.), *Child psychology in retrospect and prospect: In celebration of the 75th anniversary of the Institute of Child Development. The Minnesota Symposia on Child Psychology, vol. 32* (pp. 1–22). Mahwah, NJ: Erlbaum.

Gould, E., Reeves, A. J., Graziano, M. S., & Gross, C. G. (1999). Neurogenesis in the neocortex of adult primates. *Science, 286,* 548–552.

Gould, J. L., & Marler, P. (1987). Learning by instinct. *Scientific American, 256,* 74–75.

Gould, S. J. (1991). *Bully for Brontosaurus: Reflections in natural history.* New York: W. W. Norton.

Gould, S. J. (1996). *The mismeasure of man.* New York: Norton.

Gould, S. K. (1993). Mozart and modularity. In S. K. Gould (Ed.), *Eight little piggies: Reflections in natural history* (pp. 249–261). New York: Norton.

Gouldner, A. W. (1960). The norm of reciprocity: A preliminary statement. *American Sociological Review, 25,* 161–178.

Gouras, P. (1991). Color vision. In E. R. Kandel, J. H. Schwartz, & T. M. Jessell (Eds.), *Principles of neural science* (3rd ed., pp. 467–480). New York: Elsevier.

Graffin, N. F., Ray, W. J., & Lundy, R. (1995). EEG concomitants of hypnosis and hypnotic susceptibility. *Journal of Abnormal Psychology, 104,* 123–131.

Grayson, B., & Stein, M. W. (1981). Attracting assault: Victims' nonverbal cues. *Journal of Communication, 31,* 68–75.

Graziano, W. G., & Eisenberg, N. (1997). Agreeableness: A dimension of personality. In R. Hogan, J. Johnson, & S. Briggs (Eds.), *Handbook of personality psychology* (pp. 795–824). San Diego: Academic Press.

Graziano, W. G., Jensen-Campbell, L. A., & Hair, E. C. (1996). Perceiving interpersonal conflict and reacting to it: The case for agreeableness. *Journal of Personality and Social Psychology, 70*(4).

Green, B., & Saenz, D. (1995). Tests of a mediational model of restrained eating: The role of dieting self-efficacy and social comparisons. *Journal of Social and Clinical Psychology, 14,* 1–22.

Green, M. F. (1998). *Schizophrenia from a neurocognitive perspective: Probing the impenetrable darkness.* Boston: Allyn & Bacon.

Green, R. (1987). *The "sissy boy syndrome" and the development of homosexuality.* New Haven, CT: Yale University Press.

Green, R. A., Cross, A. J., & Goodwin, G. M. (1995). Review of the pharmacology and clinical pharmacology of 3,4-methylenedioxymethamphetamine (MDMA or "ecstacy"). *Psychopharmacology, 119,* 247–260.

Greenberg, L. S., & Johnson, S. M. (1988). *Emotionally focused therapy for couples.* New York: Guilford Press.

Greenberg, M., & Frisch, D. (1972). Effects of intentionality on willingness to reciprocate a favor. *Journal of Experimental Social Psychology, 21,* 61–72.

Greenfield, P. M. (1994). Independence and interdependence as developmental scripts: Implications for theory, research, and practice. In P. M. Greenfield & R. R. Cocking (Eds.), *Cross-cultural roots of minority child development* (pp. 1–37). Hillsdale, NJ: Erlbaum.

Greenfield, P. M., & Lave, J. (1982). Cognitive aspects of informal education. In D. A. Wagner & H. W. Stevenson (Eds.), *Cultural perspectives on child development.* San Francisco: W. H. Freeman.

Greenwald, A. G., McGhee, D. E., & Schwartz, J. L. K. (1998). Measuring individual differences in implicit cognition: The implicit association test. *Journal of Personality and Social Psychology, 74,* 1464–1480.

Greenwald, A. G., Spangenberg, E. R., Pratkanis, A. R., & Eskenazi, J. (1991). Double-blind tests of subliminal self-help audiotapes. *Psychological Science, 2,* 119–122.

Greenwald, D. F., & Harder, D. W. (1997). Fantasies, coping behavior, and psychopathology. *Journal of Clinical Psychology, 53,* 91–97.

Greenwood, M. R. C. (1989). Sexual dimorphism and obesity. In A. J. Stunkard & A. Baum (Eds.), *Perspectives in behavioral medicine: Eating, sleeping, and sex.* Hillsdale, NJ: Erlbaum.

Gregory, R. L. (1998). *Eye and brain: The psychology of seeing* (5th ed.). Princeton, NJ: Princeton University Press.

Greif, E. B., & Ulman. K. J. (1982). The psychological impact of menarche on early adolescent females: A review of the literature. *Child Development, 53,* 1413–1430.

Griffiths, R. R., & Mumford, G. K. (1995). Caffeine—A drug of abuse? In F. E. Bloom & D. J. Kupfer (Eds.), *Psychopharmacology: The fourth generation* (pp. 1699–1713). New York: Raven Press.

Grigorenko, E. L. (2000). Heritability and intelligence. In R. J. Sternberg (Ed.), *Handbook of intelligence* (pp. 53–91). Cambridge: Cambridge University Press.

Grinker, J. A. (1982). Physiological and behavioral basis for human obesity. In D. W. Pfaff (Ed.), *The physiological mechanisms of motivation.* New York: Springer-Verlag.

Gripps, C. (2002). Sociocultural perspectives on assessment. In G. Wells & G. Claxton (Eds.), *Learning for life in the 21st century: Sociocultural perspectives on the future of education* (pp. 73–83). Malden, MA: Blackwell.

Grohol, J. M. (1998). Future clinical directions: Professional development, pathology, and psychotherapy on-line. In J. Gackenbach (Ed.), *Psychology and the internet: Interpersonal, intrapersonal, and transpersonal implications* (pp. 111–140). San Diego, CA: Academic Press.

Grolnick, W. S., & Ryan, R. M. (1989). Parent styles associated with children's self-regulation and competence in school. *Journal of Educational Psychology, 81,* 143–154.

Gross, A., & Latané, J. (1974). Receiving help, reciprocating, and interpersonal attraction. *Journal of Applied Social Psychology, 4,* 210–223.

Grossman, J. B., & Kaufman, J. C. (2002). Evolutionary psychology: Promise and perils. In R. J. Sternberg, & J. C. Kaufman (Eds.), *The evolution of intelligence* (pp. 9–25). Mahwah, NJ: Erlbaum.

Groth-Marnat, G. (1997). *Handbook of psychological assessment* (3rd ed.). New York: Wiley.

Grotzer, T. A., & Perkins, D. N. (2000). Teaching intelligence: A performance conception. In R. J. Sternberg (Ed.), *Handbook of intelligence* (pp. 492–515). Cambridge: Cambridge University Press.

Gruzelier, J. (2002). A Janusian perspective on the nature, development and structure of schizophrenia and shizotypy. *Schizophrenia Research, 54,* 95–103.

Guilleminault, C. (1976). Cataplexy. In C. Guilleminault, W. C. Dement, & P. Passouant (Eds.), *Narcolepsy* (pp. 125–143). New York: Spectrum.

Gulick, W. L., Gescheider, G. A., & Frisina, R. D. (1989). *Hearing: Physiological acoustics, neural coding, and psychoacoustics.* New York: Oxford University Press.

Gumperz, J. J., & Levinson, S. C. (Eds.). (1996). *Rethinking linguistic relativity.* Cambridge: Cambridge University Press.

Gur, R. C., Turetsky, B. I., Matsui, M., Yan, M., Bilker, W., Hughett, P., & Gur, R. E. (1999). Sex difference in gray and white matter in healthy young adults: Correlations with cognitive performance. *Journal of Neuroscience, 19,* 4065–4072.

Gustafson, C. R., Garcia, J., Hawkins, W., & Rusniak, K. (1974). Coyote predation control by aversive conditioning. *Science, 184,* 581–583.

Guthrie, J. P., Ash, R. A., & Bendapudi, V. (1995). Additional validity evidence for a measure of morningness. *Journal of Applied Psychology, 80,* 186–190.

Guthrie, R. (1976). *Even the rat was white: A historical view of psychology.* New York: Harper & Row.

H

Haaga, D., & Davison, G. C. (1993). An appraisal of rational-emotive therapy. *Journal of Consulting and Clinical Psychology, 61,* 215–220.

Haggerty, J. J., Stern, R., Mason, G., & Beckwith, J. (1993). Subclinical hypothyroidism: A modifiable risk factor for depression? *American Journal of Psychiatry, 150,* 508–510.

Haier, R. J., Chueh, D., Touchette, P., Lott, I., Buchsbaum, M. S., MacMillan, D., Sandman, C., LaCasse, L., & Sosa, E. (1995). Brain size and cerebral glucose metabolic rate in nonspecific mental retardation and Down syndrome. *Intelligence, 20,* 191–210.

Haier, R. J., Siegel, B. V, Tang, C., Abel, L., & Buchsbaum, M. S. (1992). Intelligence and changes in regional cerebral glucose metabolic rate following learning. *Intelligence, 16,* 415–426.

Haight, W. L. (2002). *African-American children at church: A sociocultural perspective.* New York: Cambridge University Press.

Haines, B. A., Metalsky, G. I., Cardamone, A. L., & Joiner, T. (1999). Interpersonal and cognitive pathways into the origins of attributional style: A developmental perspective. In T. Joiner and J. C. Coyne, *The interactional nature of depression: Advances in interpersonal approaches* (pp. 65–92). Washington, DC: American Psychological Association.

Hall, D. T., & Nougaim, K. E. (1968). An examination of Maslow's need hierarchy in an organizational setting. *Organizational Behavior and Human Performance, 3,* 12–35.

Hall, S., & Brannick, M. T. (2002). Comparison of two random-effects methods of meta-analysis. *Journal of Applied Psychology, 87,* 377–389.

Hall, Z. W. (1992). *Introduction to molecular neurobiology.* Sunderland, MA: Sinauer.

Hallman, R. J. (1970). Toward a Hindu theory of creativity. *Educational Theory, 20*, 368–376.

Halonen, J. (1995). Demystifying critical thinking. *Teaching of Psychology, 22*, 75–81.

Halpern, D. (1995). *Thought and knowledge: An introduction to critical thinking* (3rd ed.). Hillsdale, NJ: Erlbaum.

Halpern, D. F. (1996). *Thinking critically about critical thinking*. Mahwah, NJ: Erlbaum.

Halpern, D. F. (2000). *Sex differences in cognitive abilities* (3rd ed.). Mahwah, NJ: Erlbaum.

Hamann, S. B., Ely, T. D., Hoffman, J. M., & Kilts, C. D. (2002). Ecstasy and agony: Activation of the human amygdala in positive and negative emotion. *Psychological Science, 13*, 135–141.

Hamer, D. H. (2002). Genetics of sexual behavior. In J. Benjamin, & R. P. Ebstein (Eds.). *Molecular genetics and the human personality* (pp. 257–272). Washington, DC: American Psychiatric Publishing.

Hamilton M. E., Voris, J. C., Sebastian, P. S., Singha, A. K., Krejci, L. P., Elder, I. R., Allen, J. E., Beitz, J. E., Covington, K. R., Newton, A. E., Price, L. T., Tillman, E., & Hernandez, L. L. (1997). Money as a tool to extinguish conditioned responses to cocaine in addicts. *Journal of Clinical Psychology, 54*, 211–218.

Hampson, S. E. (1988). The dynamics of categorization and impression formation. In T. K. Srull & R. S Wyer, Jr. (Eds.), *Advances in social cognition, Vol. 1: A dual process model of impression formation* (pp. 77–82). Hillsdale, NJ: Erlbaum.

Handen, B. L. (1997). Mental retardation. In E. J. Mash & L. G. Terdal (Eds.), *Assessment of childhood disorders* (3rd ed., pp. 369–407). New York: Guilford Press.

Hansen, C. H., & Hansen, R. D. (1988). Finding the face in the crowd: An anger superiority effect. *Journal of Personality and Social Psychology, 54*, 917–924.

Hansen, G. L. (1985). Dating jealousy among college students. *Sex Roles, 12*, 713–721.

Hanshaw, J. B., Dudgeon, J. A., & Marshall, W. C. (1985). *Viral diseases of the fetus and newborn*. Philadelphia: Saunders.

Hanson, R. K., Cadsky, O., Harris, A., & Lalonde, C. (1997). Correlates of battering among 997 men: Family, history, adjustment, and attitudinal differences. *Violence and Victims, 12*, 191–208.

Harackiewicz, J. M., & Sansone, C. (2000). Rewarding competence: The importance of goals in the study of motivation. In C. Sansone & J. M. Harackiewicz (Eds.), *Intrinsic and extrinsic motivation: The search for optimal motivation and performance* (pp. 79–103). San Diego, CA: Academic Press.

Harder, D., Maggio, J., & Whitney, G. (1989). Assessing gustatory detection capabilities using preference procedures. *Chemical Senses, 14*, 547–564.

Hardin, C., & Banaji, M. R. (1993). The influence of language on thought. *Social Cognition, 11*, 277–308.

Harlow, H. F., & Zimmermann, R. R. (1959). Affectional responses in the infant monkey. *Science, 130*, 421–432.

Harlow, H. F., Harlow, M. K. (1962). Social deprivation in monkeys. *Scientific American, 200*, 68–74.

Harnish, R. M. (2002). *Minds, brains, computers: An historical introduction to the foundations of cognitive science*. Malden, MA: Blackwell.

Harpur, T. J., Hart, S. D., & Hare, R. D. (2002). Personality of the psychopath. In P. T. Costa, Jr., & T. A. Widiger (Eds.), *Personality disorders and the five-factor model of personality* (2nd ed., pp. 299–324). Washington, DC: American Psychological Association.

Harrigan, J. A. (1985). Self touching as an indicator of underlying affect and language processing. *Social Science and Medicine, 20*, 1161–1168.

Harrigan, J. A., Lucic, K. S., Kay, D., McLaney, A., & Rosenthal, R. (1991). Effect of expresser role and type of self-touching on observers' perceptions. *Journal of Applied Social Psychology, 21*, 585–609.

Harriot, J., & Ferrari, J. R. (1996). Prevalence of procrastination among samples of adults. *Psychological Bulletin, 78*, 611–616.

Harris, B. (2002). What ever happened to little Albert? In W. E. Pickren & D. A. Dewsbury (Eds.), *Evolving perspectives on the history of psychology* (pp. 237–254). Washington, DC: American Psychological Association.

Harris, M. (1999). *Theories of culture in postmodern times*. Walnut Creek, CA: Alta Mira Press.

Harris, S. (1995). Family, self, and sociocultural contributions to body-image attitudes of African-American women. *Psychology of Women Quarterly, 19*, 129–145.

Harrison, P. L., Flanagan, D. P., & Genshaft, J. L. (1997). An integration and synthesis of contemporary theories, tests, and issues in the field of intellectual assessment. In D. P. Flanagan, J. L. Genshaft, & P. L. Harrison (Eds.), *Contemporary intellectual assessment: Theories, tests, and issues* (pp. 533–561). New York: Guilford Press.

Harte, J. L., Eifert, G. H., & Smith, R. (1995). The effects of running and meditation on beta-endorphin, corticotropin-releasing hormone and cortisol in plasma, and on mood. *Biological Psychology, 40*, 251–265.

Harter, S. (1988). Developmental processes in the construction of the self. In T. D. Yawkey & J. E. Johnson (Eds.), *Integrative processes and socialization: Early to middle childhood*. Hillsdale, NJ: Erlbaum.

Hartley, W. S. (1970). *Manual for the twenty statements problem*. Kansas City, MO: Department of Research, Greater Kansas City Mental Health Foundation.

Hartshorne, H., & May, M. A. (1928). *Studies in deceit*. New York: Macmillan.

Harvey, E. (1999). Short-term and long-term effects of early parental employment on children of the National Longitudinal Survey of Youth. *Developmental Psychology, 35*, 445–459.

Harvey, J. H., & Martin, R. (1995). Celebrating the story in social perception, communication, and behavior. In R. S. Wyer & T. K. Srull (Eds.), *Knowledge and memory: Advances in social cognition* (Vol. 8). Hillsdale, NJ: Erlbaum.

Harwood, R. L., Miller, J. G., & Irizarry, N. L. (1995). *Culture and attachment: Perceptions of the child in context*. New York: Guilford Press.

Haslam, N. (1997). Evidence that male sexual orientation is a matter of degree. *Journal of Personality and Social Psychology, 73*, 862–870.

Hasselmo, M. E., & Bower, J. M. (1993). Acetylcholine and memory. *Trends in Neurosciences, 16*, 218–222.

Hatfield, E. (1988). Passionate and companionate love. In R. J. Sternberg & M. L. Barnes (Eds.), *The psychology of love* (pp. 191–217). New Haven, CT: Yale University Press.

Hatfield, E., & Rapson, R. (1996). *Love and sex: Cross-cultural perspectives*. Boston: Allyn & Bacon.

Hatfield, E., & Rapson, R. L. (1993). *Love, sex, and intimacy: Their psychology, biology, and history*. New York: HarperCollins.

Hatfield, L. (1989, June 5). Method of polling. *San Francisco Examiner*, p. A–20.

Hatzidimitriou, G., McCann, U. D., & Ricaurte, G. A. (1999). Altered serotonin innervation patterns in the forebrain of monkeys treated with (+–)3,4,-methylenedioxymethamphetamine seven years previously: Factors influencing abnormal recovery. *Journal of Neuroscience, 19,* 506–517.

Haugtvedt, C. P., & Petty, R. E. (1992). Personality and persuasion: Need for cognition moderates the persistence and resistance of attitude changes. *Journal of Personality and Social Psychology, 63,* 308–319.

Hauri, P. J. (1992). *Sleep disorders.* Kalamazoo, MI: Upjohn.

Hauser, R. M. (1998). Trends in Black-White test-score differentials: I. Uses and misuses of NAEP/SAT data. In U. Neisser (Ed.), *The rising curve* (pp. 219–249). Washington, DC: American Psychological Association.

Hawkins, D. R. (1986, March). The importance of dreams. *Harvard Medical School Mental Health Letter,* pp. 5–7.

Hawkins, J. D., Catalano, R. F., & Miller, J. Y. (1992). Risk and protective factors for alcohol and other drug problems in adolescence and early adulthood: Implications for substance abuse prevention. *Psychological Bulletin, 112,* 64–105.

Hawkins, S. A., & Hastie, R. (1990). Hindsight: Biased judgments of past events after the outcomes are known. *Psychological Bulletin, 107,* 311–327.

Hayes, C. (1951). *The ape in our house.* New York: Harper.

Hayes, N. (2002). *Psychology in perspective* (2nd ed.). Basingstoke, England: Palgrave.

Hazan, C., & Shaver, P. (1987). Romantic love conceptualized as an attachment process. *Journal of Personality and Social Psychology, 52,* 511–524.

Hazelrigg, M. D., Cooper, H. M., & Borduin, C. M. (1987). Evaluating the effectiveness of family therapies: An integrative review and analysis. *Psychological Bulletin, 101,* 428–442.

Healy, A. F., & Bourne, L. E., Jr. (Eds.). (1995). *Learning and memory of knowledge and skills: Durability and specificity.* Thousand Oaks, CA: Sage.

Heatherton, T. F., & Vohs, K. D. (2000). Interpersonal evaluations following threats to self: Role of self-esteem. *Journal of Personality and Social Psychology, 78,* 725–736.

Heatherton, T., Herman, C., & Polivy, J. (1991). Effects of physical threat and ego threat on eating behavior. *Journal of Personality and Social Psychology, 60,* 138–143.

Hebb, D. (1955). Drives and the C.N.S.—conceptual nervous system. *Psychological Review, 62,* 245–254.

Hebl, M. R., Foster, J. B., Mannix, L. M., & Dovidio, J. F. (2002). Formal and interpersonal discrimination: A field study of bias toward homosexual applicants. *Personality and Social Psychology Bulletin, 28,* 815–825.

Heffernan, D. D., Harper, S. M., & McWilliam, D. (2002). Women's perceptions of the outcome of weight loss diets: A signal detection approach. *International Journal of Eating Disorders, 31,* 339–343.

Heider, F. (1946). Attitudes and cognitive organization. *Journal of Psychology, 21,* 107–112.

Heider, F. (1958). *The psychology of interpersonal attraction.* New York: Wiley.

Heinberg, L. (1996). Theories of body image disturbance: Perceptual, developmental, and sociocultural factors. In J. Thompson (Ed.), *Body image, eating disorders, and obesity* (pp. 23–26). Washington, DC: American Psychological Association.

Heine, S. J., & Lehman, D. R. (1997). Culture, dissonance, and self-affirmation. *Personality and Social Psychology Bulletin, 23,* 389–400.

Heine, S. J., & Lehman, D. R. (1999). Culture, self-discrepancies, and self-satisfaction. *Personality and Social Psychology Bulletin, 25,* 915–925.

Held, J. D., Alderton, D. E., Foley, P. P., & Segall, D. O. (1993). Arithmetic reasoning gender differences: Explanations found in the Armed Services Vocational Aptitude Battery (ASVAB). *Learning and Individual Differences, 5,* 171–186.

Hellige, J. B. (1990). Hemispheric asymmetry. *Annual Review of Psychology, 41,* 55–80.

Hellige, J. B. (1993). *Hemispheric asymmetry: What's right and what's left?* Cambridge, MA: Harvard University Press.

Helmholtz, H. von. (1863). *On the sensations of tone as a physiological basis for the theory of music* (A. J. Ellis, Trans.). New York: Dover.

Helms, J. E. (1990). *Black and white racial identity: Theory, research, and practice.* New York: Greenwood Press.

Hembree, R. (1988). Correlates, causes, effects, and treatment of test anxiety. *Review of Educational Research, 58,* 47–77.

Henningfield, D. R., Schuh, L. M., & Jarvik, M. E. (1995). Pathophysiology of tobacco dependence. In F. E. Bloom & D. J. Kupfer (Eds.), *Psychopharmacology: The fourth generation* (pp. 1715–1729). New York: Raven Press.

Henningfield, J. E., Clayton, R., & Pollin, W. (1990). Involvement of tobacco in alcoholism and illicit drug use. *British Journal of Addiction, 85,* 279–292.

Henriques, J. B. & Davidson, R. J. (1990). Regional brain electrical asymmetries discriminate between previously depressed and healthy control subjects. *Journal of Abnormal Psychology, 99,* 22–31.

Henry, K. R. (1984). Cochlear damage resulting from exposure to four different octave bands of noise at three different ages. *Behavioral Neuroscience, 1,* 107–117.

Hepper, P. G., Shahidullah, S., & White, R. (1990). Origins of fetal handedness. *Nature, 347,* 431.

Hepworth, J. T., & West, S. G. (1988). Lynchings and the economy: A time-series reanalysis of Hovland and Sears (1940). *Journal of Personality and Social Psychology, 55,* 239–247.

Herek, G. M. (1990). The context of anti-gay violence: Notes on cultural and psychological heterosexism. *Journal of Interpersonal Violence, 5*(3), 316–333.

Herek, G. M. (1991). Myths about sexual orientation: A lawyer's guide to social science research. *Law and Sexuality: A Review of Lesbian and Gay Legal Issues, 1,* 133–172.

Herek, G. M., Kimmel, D. C., Amaro, H., & Melton, G. B. (1991). Avoiding heterosexist bias in psychological research. *American Psychologist, 46,* 957–963.

Herman, C. P., & Polivy, J. (1980). Restrained eating. In A. J. Stunkard (Ed.), *Obesity.* Philadelphia: Saunders.

Herman, L. M., & Uyeyama, R. K. (1999). The dolphin's grammatical competency: Comments on Kako (1999). *Animal Learning & Behavior, 27,* 18–23.

Heron, W. (1957). The pathology of boredom. *Scientific American, 196,* 52–56.

Herrenkohl, E. C., Herrenkohl, R. C., & Toedter, L. J. (1983). Perspectives on the intergenerational transmission of abuse. In D. Finkelhor, R. J. Gelles, G. T. Hotaling, & M. A. Straus (Eds.), *The dark side of families* (pp. 305–316). Beverly Hills, CA: Sage.

Herrera, R. S., & DelCampo, R. L. (1995). Beyond the superwoman syndrome: Work satisfaction and family functioning among working-class Mexican American women. *Hispanic Journal of Behavioral Sciences, 17,* 49–60.

Herrnstein, R. J., & Murray, C. (1994). *The bell curve: Intelligence and class structure in American life.* New York: Free Press.

Herrnstein, R. J., Nickerson, R. S., de Sanchez, M., & Swets, J. A. Teaching thinking skills. (1986). *American Psychologist, 41,* 1279–1286.

Hersen, M., & Bellack, A. S. (Eds.). (1999). *Handbook of comparative interventions for adult disorders* (2nd ed.). New York: Wiley.

Hertel, P. T., & Rude, S. S. (1991). Depressive deficits in memory: Focusing attention improves subsequent recall. *Journal of Experimental Psychology: General, 120,* 301–309.

Hess, E. H. (1975, November). The role of pupil size in communication. *Scientific American,* pp. 110–112, 116–119.

Hetherington, A. W., & Ranson, S. W. (1942). The spontaneous activity and food intake of rats with hypothalamic lesions. *American Journal of Physiology, 136,* 609–617.

Hetherington, E. M., & Stanley-Hagen, M. (2002). Parenting in divorced and remarried families. In M. H. Bornstein (Ed.), *Handbook of parenting: Vol. 3: Being and becoming a parent* (2nd ed., pp. 287–315). Mahwah, NJ: Erlbaum.

Hewson-Bower, B., & Drummond, P. D. (1996). Secretory immunoglobulin A increases during relaxation in children with and without recurrent upper respiratory tract infections. *Journal of Developmental and Behavioral Pediatrics, 17,* 311–316.

Hewstone, M., Macrae, C. N., Griffiths, R., Milne, A. B., & Brown, R. (1994). Cognitive models of stereotype change: (5). Measurement, development, and consequences of subtyping. *Journal of Experimental Social Psychology, 30,* 505–526.

Heyman, R. E., Chaudhry, B. R., Treboux, D., Crowell, J., Lord, C., Vivian, D., & Waters, E. B. (2001). How much observational data is enough? An empirical test using marital interaction coding. *Behavior Therapy, 32,* 107–122.

Hicks, D. (1968). Short- and long-term retention of affectively-varied modeled behavior. *Psychonomic Science, 11,* 369–370.

Hilgard, E. R., Leary, D. E., & McGuire, G. R. (1991). History of psychology: A survey and critical assessment. *Annual Review of Psychology, 42,* 79–107.

Hilgard, E. R. (1965). *Hypnotic susceptibility.* New York: Harcourt Brace Jovanovich.

Hilgard, E. R. (1986). *Divided consciousness: Multiple controls in human thought and action.* New York: Wiley.

Hilgard, E. R. (1992). Dissociation and theories of hypnosis. In E. Fromm & M. R. Nash (Eds.), *Contemporary hypnosis research* (pp. 69–101). New York: Guilford Press.

Hill, P. (1993). Recent advances in selected areas of adolescent development. *Journal of Child Psychology and Psychiatry, 34,* 69–99.

Hille, B. (1984). *Ionic channels of excitable membranes.* Sunderland, MA: Sinauer.

Hilton, H. (1986). *The executive memory guide.* New York: Simon & Schuster.

Hilton, J. L., & Hippel, W. V. (1996). Stereotypes. *Annual Review of Psychology, 47,* 237–271.

Hilts, P. J. (1995). *Memory's ghost: The strange tale of Mr. M. and the nature of memory.* New York: Simon & Schuster.

Hines, M. (1982). Prenatal gonadal hormones and sex differences in human behavior. *Psychological Bulletin, 92,* 56–80.

Hines, T. (1988). *Pseudoscience and the paranormal.* Buffalo, NY: Prometheus Books.

Hirsch, H. V. B., & Spinelli, D. N. (1970). Visual experience modifies distribution of horizontally and vertically oriented receptive fields in cats. *Science, 168,* 869–871.

Hirsch, J., Fried, S. K., Edens, N. K., & Leibel, R. L. (1989). The fat cell. *Medical Clinics of North America, 73,* 83–96.

Hirsh-Pasek, K., & Golinkoff, R. (1993). Skeletal supports for grammatical learning: What the infant brings to the language learning task. In C. Rovee-Collier & L. Lipsitt (Eds.), *Advances in infancy research* (Vol. 8). Norwood, NJ: Ablex.

Hirt, E. R. (1990). Do I see only what I expect? Evidence for an expectancy-guided retrieval model. *Journal of Personality and Social Psychology, 58,* 937–951.

Hoberman, H. M., & Lewinsohn, P. M. (1985). The behavioral treatment of depression. In E. E. Beckham & W. R. Leber (Eds.), *Handbook of depression: Treatment, assessment, and research* (pp. 39–81). Homewood, IL: Dorsey.

Hoberman, J. (1997). *Darwin's athletes: How sport has damaged Black America and preserved the myth of race.* Boston: Houghton Mifflin.

Hobson, J. A. (1989). *Sleep.* New York: Scientific American Library.

Hobson, J. A. (1994). *The chemistry of conscious states: How the brain changes its mind.* Boston: Little, Brown.

Hobson, J. A., & McCarley, R. W. (1977). The brain as a dream state generator: An activation-synthesis hypothesis of the dream process. *The American Journal of Psychiatry, 134,* 1335–1348.

Hock, R. R. (1992). *Forty studies that changed psychology: Explorations into the history of psychological research.* Englewood Cliffs, NJ: Prentice Hall.

Hockett, C. F. (1960). The origins of speech. *Scientific American, 203,* 89–96.

Hockett, C. F., & Altmann, S. A. (1968). A note on design features. In T. A. Sebeok (Ed.), *Animal communication: Techniques of study and results of research.* Bloomington: Indiana University Press.

Hodapp, V., & Benson, J. (1997). The multidimensionality of test anxiety: A test of different models. *Anxiety, Stress, and Coping, 10,* 219–244.

Hodos, W., & Butler, A. B. (2001). Sensory system evolution in vertebrates. In G. Roth (Ed.), *Brain evolution and cognition* (pp. 113–133). New York: John Wiley.

Hofferth, S. L. (1996). Effects of public and private policies on working after childbirth. *Work and Occupations, 23,* 378–404.

Hoffman, C., Lau, I., & Johnson, D. R. (1986). The linguistic relativity of person cognition: An English-Chinese comparison. *Journal of Personality and Social Psychology, 51,* 1097–1105.

Hoffman, L. W. (1989). Effects of maternal employment in the two-parent family. *American Psychologist, 44,* 283–292.

Hofstede, C. (1980). *Culture's consequences: International differences in work-related values.* Beverly Hills, CA: Sage.

Hogan, R., & Smither, R. (2001). *Personality: Theories and applications.* Boulder, CO: Westview.

Hogg, M. A. (1992). *The social psychology of group cohesiveness: From attraction to social identity.* London: Harvester-Wheatsheaf.

Holahan, C. K., & Sears, R. R. (1955). *The gifted group in later maturity.* Palo Alto, CA: Stanford University Press.

Holcomb, W. R., & Anderson, W. P. (1983). Alcohol and drug abuse in accused murderers. *Psychological Reports, 52,* 159–164.

Holden, C. (1993). Wake-up call for sleep research. *Science, 259,* 305.

Holland, R. L., Musch, B. C., & Hindmarch, I. (1999). Specific effects of benzodiazepines and tricyclic antidepressants in panic disorder: Comparisons of clomipramine with alprazolam SR and adinazolam SR. *Human Psychopharmacology: Clinical and Experimental, 14,* 119–124.

Hollander, E., Simon, D., & Gorman, J. M. (1999). Anxiety disorders. In R. E. Hales, S. C. Yudofsky, & J. A. Talbot (Eds.), *American Psychiatric Press textbook of psychiatry.* Washington, DC: American Psychiatric Press.

Hollander, E., Zohar, J., & Marazziti, D. (2002). Introduction: Exploring the foundations of obsessive-compulsive disorder and other anxiety disorders. *Journal of Clinical Psychiatry, 63,* 3–4.

Hollis, K. L. (1997). Contemporary research on Pavlovian conditioning: A "new" functional analysis. *American Psychologist, 52,* 956–965.

Hollon, S. D., & Kendall, P. C. (1980). Cognitive self-statements in depression: Development of an Automatic Thoughts Questionnaire. *Cognitive Therapy and Research, 4,* 383–395.

Holloway, R. L. (1983). Human brain evolution. *Canadian Journal of Anthropology, 3,* 215–230.

Holm, N. G. (1991). Pentecostalism: Conversion and charismata. *International Journal for the Psychology of Religion, 1,* 135–151.

Holm, N. G. (1995). Role theory and religious experience. In R. W. Hood (Ed.), *Handbook of religious experience* (pp. 397–420). Birmingham, AL: Religious Education Press.

Holman, W. D. (2001). Reaching for integrity: An Eriksonian life-cycle perspective on the experiences of adolescents being raised by grandparents. *Child & Adolescent Social Work Journal, 18,* 21–35.

Holmes, T., & Rahe, R. (1967). The Social Readjustment Rating Scale. *Journal of Psychosomatic Research, 11,* 213–218.

Holtgraves, T. (1997). Styles of language use: Individual and cultural variability in conversational indirectness. *Journal of Personality and Social Psychology, 73,* 624–637.

Holtgraves, T., & Yang, J. N. (1992). Interpersonal underpinnings of request strategies: General principles and differences due to culture and gender. *Journal of Personality and Social Psychology, 62,* 246–256.

Holtgraves, T. M. (1992). The linguistic realization of face management: Implications for language production and comprehension, person perception, and cross-cultural communication. *Social Psychology Quarterly, 55,* 141–159.

Hong, L. K., & Duff, R. W. (2002). Modulated participant-observation: Managing the dilemma of distance in field research. *Field Methods, 14,* 190–196.

Honts, C., & Perry, M. (1992). Polygraph admissibility: Changes and challenges. *Law and Human Behavior, 16,* 357–379.

Hood, R. W., Jr. (1991). Holm's use of role theory: Empirical and hermeneutical considerations of sacred text as a source of role adoption. *International Journal for the Psychology of Religion, 1,* 153–159.

Hood, R. W., Jr. (1995). The facilitation of religious experience. In R. W. Hood (Ed.), *Handbook of religious experience* (pp. 568–597). Birmingham, AL: Religious Education Press.

Hooker, E. (1957). The adjustment of the male overt homosexual. *Journal of Projective Techniques, 21,* 18–31.

Hopko, D. R., McNeil, D. W., Zvolensky, M. J., & Eifert, G. H. (2001). The relation between anxiety and skill in performance-based anxiety disorders: A behavioral formulation of social phobia. *Behavior Therapy, 32,* 185–207.

Hoppe, R. B. (1988). In search of a phenomenon: Research in parapsychology. [Review of *Foundations of parapsychology.*] *Contemporary Psychology, 33,* 129–130.

Hoptman, M. J., & Davidson, R. J. (1994). How and why do the two cerebral hemispheres interact? *Psychological Bulletin, 116,* 195–219.

Horn, J. M. (1983). The Texas adoption project: Adopted children and their intellectual resemblance to biological and adoptive parents. *Child Development, 54,* 268–275.

Horney, K. (1926/1967). *Feminine psychology.* New York: Norton.

Horney, K. (1945). *Our inner conflicts.* New York: Norton.

Hornyak, L. M., & Green, J. P. (Eds.). (2000). *Healing from within: The use of hypnosis in women's health care.* Washington, DC: American Psychological Association.

Hosman, L. A. (1997). The relationship between locus of control and the evaluative consequences of powerful and powerless speech styles. *Journal of Language and Social Psychology, 16,* 70–78.

Hothersall, D. (1995). *History of psychology.* New York: McGraw-Hill.

House, J., Landis, K., & Umberson, D. (1988). Social relationships and health. *Science, 241,* 540–545.

Howard, A., Pion, G. M., Gottfredson, G. D., Flattau, P. E., Oskamp, S., Pfafflin, S. M., Bray, D. W., & Burnstein, A. G. (1986). The changing face of American Psychology. *American Psychologist, 41,* 1311–1327.

Howard, D. J. (1995). "Chaining" the use of influence strategies for producing compliance behavior. *Journal of Social Behavior and Personality, 10,* 169–185.

Howard, P. J., & Howard, J. M. (2000). *The owner's manual for personality at work.* Austin, TX: Bard Press.

Hubel, D. H. (1996). A big step along the visual pathway. *Nature, 380,* 197–198.

Hubel, D. H., & Wiesel, T. N. (1965a). Receptive fields and functional architecture in two non-striate visual areas (18 and 19) of the cat. *Journal of Neurophysiology, 28,* 229–289.

Hubel, D. H., & Wiesel, T. N. (1965b). Binocular interaction in striate cortex of kittens reared with artificial squint. *Journal of Neurophysiology, 28,* 1041–1059.

Huesmann, L. R., & Hasbrouck, J. E. (1996). Television violence: Implications for violence prevention. *School Psychology Review, 25,* 134–151.

Huesmann, L. R., & Miller, L. S. (1994). Long-term effects of repeated exposure to media violence in childhood. In L. R. Huesmann (Ed.), *Aggressive behavior: Current perspectives* (pp. 153–186). New York: Plenum.

Huff, R., & Kline, M. (Eds.). (1999). *Promoting health in multicultural populations: A handbook for practitioners.* Thousand Oaks, CA: Sage.

Huffman, S., Zehner, E., Harvey, P., Martin, P., Piwoz, E., Ndure, K., Combest, C., Mwadime, R., & Quinn, V. (2001, April). *The LINKAGES Project.* http://www.linkagesproject.org/FAQ_Html/EHS/tbrief.htm.

Hughes, J., Smith, T. W., Kosterlitz, H. W., Fothergill, L. A., Morgan, B. A., & Morris, H. R. (1975). Identification of two related pentapeptides from the brain with the potent opiate agonist activity. *Nature, 258,* 577–579.

Hui, C. H., & Triandis, H. C. (1986). Individualism-collectivism, a study of cross-cultural researchers. *Journal of Cross-Cultural Psychology, 17,* 225–248.

Hulit, L. M., & Howard, M. R. (1993). *Born to talk: An introduction to speech and language development.* Needham, MA: Macmillan.

Hull, C. L. (1943). *Principles of behavior: An introduction to behavior theory concerning the individual organism.* New Haven, CT: Yale University Press.

Humphrey, N. K. (1992). *A history of the mind.* New York: Simon & Schuster.

Humphreys, L. G. (1939). Acquisition and extinction of verbal expectations in a situation analogous to conditioning. *Journal of Experimental Psychology, 25,* 294–301.

Hunn, E. (1982). The utilitarian factor in folk biological classification. *American Anthropologist, 84,* 830–847.

Hunn, E. (1990). *Nch'i-Wana "The Big River": Mid-Columbia Indians and their land.* Seattle: University of Washington Press.

Hunsley, J., & Bailey, J. M. (1999). The clinical utility of the Rorschach: Unfulfilled promises and an uncertain future. *Psychological Assessment, 11,* 266–277.

Hunt, M. (1982). *The universe within.* New York: Simon & Schuster.

Hunter, R. S., & Kilstrom, N. (1979). Breaking the cycle in abusive families. *American Journal of Orthopsychiatry, 56,* 142–146.

Hupka, R. B. (1991). The motive for the arousal of romantic jealousy: Its cultural origin. In P. Salovey (Ed.), *The psychology of jealousy and envy* (pp. 252–270). New York: Guilford Press.

Hutchings, B., & Mednick, S. A. (1977). Criminality in adoptees and their adoptive and biological parents: A pilot study. In S. A. Mednick & K. O. Christiansen (Eds.), *Biosocial bases of criminal behavior* (pp. 127–141). New York: Plenum Press.

Hutnik, N. (1991). *Ethnic minority identity: A social psychological perspective.* New York: Oxford University Press.

Hyde, J. S., Fennema, E., & Lamon, S. J. (1990). Gender differences in mathematics performance: A meta-analysis. *Psychological Bulletin, 107,* 139–155.

Hyman, R. (1994). Anomaly or artifact? Comments on Bem and Honorton. *Psychological Bulletin, 115,* 19–24.

Hyman, R. (1996, March/April). Evaluation of the military's twenty-year program on psychic spying. *The Skeptical Inquirer, 27,* 21–23.

I

Iaccino, J. F. (1993). *Left brain-right brain differences: Inquiries, evidence, and new approaches.* Hillsdale, NJ: Erlbaum.

Iacono, W., & Lykken, D. (1997). The validity of the lie detector: Two surveys of scientific opinion. *Journal of Applied Psychology, 82,* 426–433.

Ichikawa, M., & Saida, S. (2002). Integration of motion parallax with binocular disparity specifying different surface shapes. *Japanese Psychological Research, 44,* 34–44.

Ingbar, D. H., & Gee, J. B. L. (1985). Pathophysiology and treatment of sleep apnea. *Annual Review of Medicine, 36,* 369–395.

Inglehart, R. (1990). *Culture shift in advanced industrial society.* Princeton, NJ: Princeton University Press.

Ingram, D. M. (2001). The Hofgeismar lectures: A contemporary overview of Horneyan psychoanalysis. *American Journal of Psychoanalysis, 60,* 113–141.

Inhelder, B., & Piaget, J. (1958). *The growth of logical thinking from childhood to adolescence.* New York: Basic Books.

Inman, M. L., Reichl, A. J., & Baron, R. S. (1993). Do we tell less than we know or hear less than we are told? Exploring the teller-listener extremity effect. *Journal of Experimental Social Psychology, 29,* 528–550.

Innis, N. K. (1992). Animal psychology in America as revealed in APA presidential addresses. *Journal of Experimental Psychology: Animal Behavior Processes, 18,* 3–11.

Intons-Peterson, M. J., & Newsome, G. L. (1992). External memory aids: Effects and effectiveness. In D. J. Herrmann, H. Weingartner, A. Searleman, & C. L. McEvoy (Eds.), *Memory improvement: Implications for memory theory* (pp. 101–121). New York: Springer-Verlag.

Ioannides, A. A., Kostopoulos, G. K., Laskaris, N. A., Liu, L., Shibata, T., Schellens, M., Poghosyan, V., & Khurshudyan, A. (2002). Timing and connectivity in the human somatosensory cortex from single trial mass electrical activity. *Human Brain-Mapping, 15,* 231–246.

Ironson, G., Taylor, C., Boltwood, M., et al. (1992). Effects of anger on left ventricular ejection fraction in coronary artery disease. *American Journal of Cardiology, 70,* 281–285.

Irvine, J. (1990). *Disorders of desire: Sex and gender in modern American sexology.* Philadelphia: Temple University Press.

Isaac, G. L. (1983). Aspects of human evolution. In D. S. Bendall (Ed.), *Evolution from molecules to men.* Cambridge: Cambridge University Press.

Isada, N. B., & Grossman, J. H., III. (1991). Perinatal infections. In S. G. Gabbie, J. R. Niebyl, & J. L. Simpson (Eds.), *Obstetrics: Normal and problem pregnancies.* New York: Churchill Livingstone.

Isen, A. M. (1987). Positive affect, cognitive processes, and social behavior. In L. Berkowitz (Ed.), *Advances in experimental social psychology* (Vol. 20, pp. 203–253). New York: Academic Press.

Ito, T. A., Miller, N., & Pollock, V. E. (1996). Alcohol and aggression: A meta-analysis on the moderating effects of inhibitory cues, triggering effects, and self-focused attention. *Psychological Bulletin, 120,* 60–82.

Iversen, I. (1992). Skinner's early research: From reflexology to operant conditioning. *American Psychologist, 47,* 1318–1328.

Izard, C. (1989). The structure and functions of emotions: Implications for cognition, motivation, and personality. In I. S. Cohen (Ed.), *The G. Stanley Hall Lecture Series* (Vol. 9, pp. 39–73). Washington, DC: American Psychological Association.

Izard, C. E. (1994). Innate and universal facial expressions: Evidence from developmental and cross-cultural research. *Psychological Bulletin, 115,* 288–299.

Izard, C. E., Fantauzzo, C. A., Castle, J. M., Haynes, O. M., Rayias, M. F., & Putnam, P. H. (1995). The ontogeny and significance of infants' facial expressions in the first 9 months of life. *Developmental Psychology, 31,* 997–1013.

J

Jackson, L. A., Hunter, J. E., & Hodge, C. N. (1995). Physical attractiveness and intellectual competence: A meta-analytic review. *Social Psychology Quarterly, 58,* 108–122.

Jacobs, B., Schall, M., & Scheibel, A. B. (1993). A quantitative dendritic analysis of Wernicke's area in humans: II. Gender, hemispheric, and environmental factors. *Journal of Comparative Neurology, 327,* 97–106.

Jacobs, B. L. (1994). Serotonin, motor activity, and depression-related disorders. *American Scientist, 82,* 456–463.

Jacobs, R. A. (2002). Visual cue integration for depth perception. In R. P. N. Rao & B. A. Bruno (Eds.), *Probabilistic models of the brain: Perception and neural function. Neural information processing series* (pp. 61–76). Cambridge, MA: The MIT Press.

Jacobson, E. (1924). The technique of progressive relaxation. *Journal of Nervous and Mental Disease, 60,* 568–578.

Jacobson, N. S., & Margolin, G. (1979). *Marital therapy: Strategies based on social learning and behavior exchange principles.* New York: Brunner/Mazel.

Jacobson, S. W., & Jacobson, J. L. (2001). Alcohol and drug-related effects on development: A new emphasis on contextual factors. *Infant Mental Health Journal, 22,* 416–430.

Jaffe, J. H. (1990). Drug addiction and drug abuse. In A. G. Gilman, T. W. Rall, A. S. Nies, & P. Taylor (Eds.), *Goodman and Gilman's The pharmacological basis of therapeutics* (8th ed.). New York: Pergamon.

James, J. E. (1997). *Understanding caffeine: A biobehavioral analysis.* Newbury Park, CA: Sage.

James, L. E., & Burke, D. M. (2000). Phonological priming effects on word retrieval and tip-of-the-tongue experiences in young and older adults. *Journal of Experimental Psychology: Learning, Memory, & Cognition, 26,* 1378–1391.

James, S. (1990). *Normal language acquisition.* Austin, TX: Pro-Ed.

James, W. (1884). What is an emotion? *Mind, 9,* 188–205.

James, W. (1890). *The principles of psychology* (2 vols.). New York: Henry Holt.

James, W. (1899). *Talks to teachers on psychology and to students on some of life's ideals.* New York: Henry Holt.

James, W. (1902/1985). *The varieties of religious experience.* Cambridge, MA: Harvard University Press.

Jameson, D. (1985). Opponent-colors theory in light of physiological findings. In D. Ottoson & S. Zeki (Eds.), *Central and peripheral mechanisms of color vision* (pp. 8–102). New York: Macmillan.

Jamieson, D. W., Lydon, J. E., & Zanna, M. P. (1987). Attitude and activity preference similarity: Differential bases of interpersonal attraction for low and high self-monitors. *Journal of Personality and Social Psychology, 53,* 1052–1060.

Jamison, K. R. (1995). Manic-depressive illness and creativity. *Scientific American (2),* 62–67.

Jang, K. L., Hu, S., Livesley, W. J., Angleitner, A., Riemann, R., Ando, J., Ono, Y., Vernon, P. A., & Hamer, D. H. (2001). Covariance structure of neuroticism and agreeableness: A twin and molecular genetic analysis of the role of the serotonin transporter gene. *Journal of Personality and Social Psychology, 81,* 295–304.

Janoff-Bulman, R. (1992). *Shattered assumptions: Towards a new psychology of trauma.* New York: Free Press.

Janos, P. M., & Robinson, N. M. (1985). Psychosocial development in intellectually gifted children. In F. D. Horowitz & M. O'Brien (Eds.), *The gifted and talented: Developmental perspectives* (pp. 149–195). Washington, DC: American Psychological Association.

Jaramillo, D. (1999). *The effect of culture on the body esteem of adolescent females.* Unpublished dissertation, Wisconsin School of Professional Psychology, Inc., US.

Jarvis, E. D., Ribeiro, S., da Silva, M. L., Ventura, D., Vielliard, J., & Mello, C. V. (2000). Behaviourally driven gene expression reveals song nuclei in hummingbird brain. *Nature, 406,* 628–632.

Jarvis, W. B. G., & Petty, R. E. (1996). The need to evaluate. *Journal of Personality and Social Psychology, 70,* 172–194.

Jaschinski, U., & Wentura, D. (2002). Misleading postevent information and working memory capacity: An individual differences approach to eyewitness memory. *Applied Cognitive Psychology, 16,* 223–231.

Jayakar, K. (1994). Women of the Indian Subcontinent. In L. Comas-Diaz & B. Greene (Eds.), *Women of color.* New York: Guilford Press.

Jeffrey, R., & Wing, R. (1983). Recidivism and self-cure of smoking and obesity: Data from population studies. *American Psychologist, 38,* 852.

Jemmott, J. III, & Magloire, K. (1988). Academic stress, social support, and secretory immunoglobulin A. *Journal of Personality and Social Psychology, 55,* 803–810.

Jenkins, J. G., & Dallenbach, K. M. (1924). Oblivescence during sleep and waking. *American Journal of Psychology, 35,* 605–612.

Jensen, A. R. (1969). How much can we boost IQ and scholastic achievement? *Harvard Educational Review, 39,* 1–123.

Jensen, A. R. (1973). *Educability and group differences.* New York: Harper & Row.

Jensen, A. R. (1985). The nature of the black-white difference on various psychometric tests: Spearman's hypothesis. *Behavioral and Brain Sciences, 8,* 193–263.

Jensen, A. R. (1992). Understanding g in terms of information processing. *Educational Psychology Review, 4,* 271–308.

Jensen, A. R., & Johnson, F. W. (1994). Race and sex differences in head size and IQ. *Intelligence, 18,* 309–333.

Jensen, J. K., & Neff, D. L. (1993). Development of basic auditory discrimination in preschool children. *Psychological Science, 4,* 104–107.

Jensvold, M. L. A., & Gardner, R. A. (2000). Interactive use of sign language by cross-fostered chimpanzees (Pan troglodytes). *Journal of Comparative Psychology, 114,* 335–346.

Jerison, H. J. (1975). Fossil evidence of the evolution of the human brain. *Annual Review of Anthropology, 16,* 403–426.

Jerison, H. J. (1991). Brain size and the evolution of mind. *Fifty-ninth James Arthur Lecture.* American Museum of Natural History.

Jiang, Y., Luo, Y. J., & Parasuraman, R. (2002). Neural correlates of perceptual priming of visual motion. *Brain Research Bulletin, 57,* 211–219.

John, D., Shelton, B.A., & Luschen, K. (1995). Race, ethnicity, gender, and perceptions of fairness. *Journal of Family Issues, 16,* 357–379.

John, O. P., & Srivastava, S. (1999). The big five trait taxonomy: History, measurement, and theoretical perspectives. In L. A. Pervin & O. P. John (Eds.), *Handbook of personality* (2nd ed., pp. 102–138). New York: Guilford Press.

John, O. P., Cheek, J. M., & Klohnen, E. C. (1996). On the nature of self-monitoring: Construct explication with Q-sort ratings. *Journal of Personality and Social Psychology, 71,* 763–776.

Johnson, J.D., Noel, N.E. & Sutter-Hernandez, J. (2000). Alcohol and male acceptance of sexual aggression: The role of perceptual ambiguity. *Journal of Applied Social Psychology, 30,* 1186–1200.

Johnson, M. E., & Brems, C. (1991). Comparing theoretical orientations of counseling and clinical psychologists: An objective approach. *Professional Psychology: Research and Practice, 22,* 133–137.

Johnson, M. K., & Raye, C. L. (2000). Cognitive and brain mechanisms of false memories and beliefs. In D. L. Schacter & E. Scarry (Eds.), *Memory, brain, and belief* (pp. 35–86). Cambridge, MA: Harvard University Press.

Johnston, J. H., Driskell, J. E., & Salas, E. (1997). Vigilant and hypervigilant decision making. *Journal of Applied Psychology, 82,* 614–622.

Johnston, T. D., & Edwards, L. (2002). Genes, interactions, and the development of behavior. *Psychological Review, 109,* 26–34.

Jones, M. C. (1924). A laboratory study of fear: The case of Peter. *Pedagogical Seminary and Journal of Genetic Psychology, 31,* 308–315.

Julien, R. M. (1992). *A primer of drug action: A concise, nontechnical guide to the actions, uses, and side effects of psychoactive drugs.* New York: W. H. Freeman.

Julien, R. M. (1998). *A primer of drug action: A concise nontechnical guide to the actions, uses, and side effects of psychoactive drugs* (8th ed.). New York: Freeman.

Julien, R. M. (2001). *A primer of drug action: A concise nontechnical guide to the actions, uses, and side effects of psychoactive drugs* (9th ed.). New York: Freeman.

Jung, C. G. (1921). *Psychological types.* New York: Harcourt, Brace.

Just, M. A., & Carpenter, P. A. (1987). *The psychology of reading and language comprehension.* Newton, MA: Allyn & Bacon.

K

Kacmar, K. M., Delery, J. E., & Ferris, G. R. (1992). Differential effectiveness of applicant impression management tactics on employment interview decisions. *Journal of Applied Social Psychology, 22,* 1250–1272.

Kaelber, C. T., Moul, D. E., & Farmer, M. E. (1995). Epidemiology of depression. In E. E. Beckham & W. R. Leber (Eds.), *Handbook of depression* (2nd ed., pp. 3–35). New York: Guilford Press.

Kafka, J. S. (2002). History of psychoanalysis: Freud and dream contributing to and celebrating the centenary of "The Interpretation of Dreams" as the origin of the psychoanalytic method. *International Journal of Psycho-Analysis, 83,* 483–486.

Kagan, J., Snidman, N., & Arcus, D. M. (1992). Initial reactions to unfamiliarity. *Current Directions in Psychological Science, 1,* 171–174.

Kagan, S., & Knight, G. P. (1979). Cooperation-competition and self-esteem: A case of cultural relativism. *Journal of Cross-Cultural Psychology, 10,* 457–467.

Kâğitçibasi, C. (1994). A critical appraisal of individualism and collectivism: Toward a new formulation. In U. Kim, H. C. Triandis, C. Kâğitçibasi, S. Choi, & G. Yoon (Eds.), *Individualism and collectivism: Theory, method, and applications* (pp. 52–65). Thousand Oaks, CA: Sage.

Kahn, D., & Hobson, J. A. (1993). Self-organization theory of dreaming. *Dreaming: Journal of the Association for the Study of Dreams, 3,* 151–178.

Kahn, E., Fisher, C., & Edwards, A. (1991). Night terrors and anxiety dreams. In S. J. Ellman & J. S. Antrobus (Eds.), *The mind in sleep: Psychology and psychopathology* (2nd ed., pp. 437–447). New York: Wiley.

Kail, R. (1991). Processing time declines exponentially during childhood and adolescence. *Developmental Psychology, 27,* 259–266.

Kalat, J. (1998). *Biological psychology* (6th ed.). Pacific Grove, CA: Brooks/Cole.

Kalish, R. (1981). *Death, grief, and caring relationships.* Monterey, CA: Brooks-Cole.

Kalish, R. (1985). The social context of death and dying. In R. H. Binstock & E. Shanas (Eds.), *Handbook of aging and the social sciences* (2nd ed.). New York: Van Nostrand Reinhold.

Kamarck, T., & Jennings, R. (1991). Biobehavioral factors in sudden cardiac death. *Psychological Bulletin, 109,* 42–75.

Kanagawa, C., Cross, S. E., & Markus, H. R. (2001). "Who am I?" The cultural psychology of the conceptual self. *Personality and Social Psychology Bulletin, 27,* 90–103.

Kandel, D. B. (1978). Similarity in real-life adolescent friendship pairs. *Journal of Personality and Social Psychology, 36,* 306–312.

Kandel, E. R. (1995). Cellular mechanisms of learning and memory. In E. R. Kandel, J. H. Schwartz, & T. M. Jessell (Eds.), *Essentials of neural science and behavior.* Norwalk, CT: Appleton & Lange.

Kandel, E. R., & Schwartz, J. H. (1982). Molecular biology of learning: Modulation of transmitter release. *Science, 218,* 433–443.

Kanner, A., Coyne, J., Schaefer, C., & Lazarus, R. (1981). Comparison of two modes of stress measurement: Daily hassles and uplifts versus major life events. *Journal of Behavioral Medicine, 4,* 1–39.

Karni, A., Tanne, D., Rubenstein, B. S., Askenazy, J. J. M., & Sagi, D. (1994). Dependence on REM sleep of overnight improvement of a perceptual skill. *Science, 265,* 679–682.

Karno, M., Golding, J. M., Sorenson, S. B., & Burnam, M. A. (1988). The epidemiology of obsessive-compulsive disorder in five U.S. communities. *Archives of General Psychiatry, 45,* 1094–1099.

Karraker, K. H., & Stern, M. (1990). Infant physical attractiveness and facial expression: Effects on adult perceptions. *Basic and Applied Social Psychology, 11,* 371–385.

Kasamatsu, M., & Hirai, T. (1969). An electroencephalographic study of the Zen meditation (zazen). In C. Tart (Ed.), *Altered states of consciousness* (pp. 489–501). New York: Wiley.

Kashima, Y., Siegel, M., Tanaka, K., & Kashima, E. S. (1992). Do people believe behaviours are consistent with attitudes? Towards a cultural psychology of attribution processes. *British Journal of Social Psychology, 31,* 111–124.

Kashy, D. A., & DePaulo, B. M. (1996). Who lies? *Journal of Personality and Social Psychology, 70,* 1037–1051.

Kasser, T., & Ryan, R. M. (1996). Further examining the American dream: Differential correlates of intrinsic and extrinsic goals. *Personality and Social Psychology Bulletin, 22,* 20–287.

Kassin, S. M., Tubb, V. A., Hosch, H. M., & Memon, A. (2001). On the "general acceptance" of eyewitness testimony research: A new survey of the experts. *American Psychologist, 56,* 405–416.

Katigbak, M. S., Church, A. T., Guanzon-Lapena, M. A., Carlota, A. J., & del Pilar, G. H. (2002). Are indigenous personality dimensions culture specific? Philippine inventories and the five-factor model. *Journal of Personality and Social Psychology, 82,* 89–101.

Katz, P. (1986). Gender identity: Development and consequences. In R. Ashmore & F. Del Boca (Eds.), *The social psychology of female-male relations* (pp. 21–67). Orlando, FL: Academic Press.

Katz, R., & McGuffin, P. (1993). The genetics of affective disorders. In D. Fowles (Ed.), *Progress in experimental personality and psychopathology research*. New York: Springer.

Katzenberg, D., Young, T., Finn, L., Lin, L., King, D. P., Takahashi, J. S., & Mignot, E. (1998). A CLOCK polymorphism associated with human diurnal preference. *Sleep, 21,* 569–576.

Kaufman, A. S. (1990). *Assessing adolescent and adult intelligence.* Boston: Allyn & Bacon.

Kaufman, A. S. (2000). Tests of intelligence. In R. J. Sternberg (Ed.), *Handbook of intelligence* (pp. 445–476). Cambridge: Cambridge University Press.

Kaufman, L., & Rock, I. (1962). The moon illusion (Vol. 1). *Science, 136,* 953–961.

Kaufman, M. H. (1997). The teratogenic effects of alcohol following exposure during pregnancy, and its influence on the chromosome constitution of the pre-ovulatory egg. *Alcohol & Alcoholism, 32,* 113–128.

Kaye, W., Klump, K., Frank, G., & Strober, M. (2000). Anorexia and bulimia nervosa. *Annual Review of Medicine, 51,* 299–313.

Kayumov, L., Rotenberg, V., Buttoo, K., Auch, C., Pandi-Perumal, S. R., & Shapiro, C. M. (2000). Interrelationships between nocturnal sleep, daytime alertness, and sleepiness: Two types of alertness proposed. *Journal of Neuropsychiatry & Clinical Neurosciences, 12,* 86–90.

Kazdin, A. E. (1982). The token economy: A decade later. *Journal of Applied Behavior Analysis, 15,* 431–445.

Keating, C. F., Mazur, A., Segall, M. H., Cysneiros, P. G., DiVale, W. T., Kilbride, J. E., Komin, S., Leahy, P., Thurman, B., & Wirsing, R. (1981). Culture and the perception of social dominance from facial expression. *Journal of Personality and Social Psychology, 40,* 601–614.

Keefauver, S. P., & Guilleminault, C. (1994). Sleep terrors and sleepwalking. In M. Kryger, T. Roth, & W. C. Dement (Eds.), *Principles and practices of sleep medicine* (2nd ed., pp. 567–573). Philadelphia: Saunders.

Keen, C. L., Bendich, A., & Willhite, C. C. (Eds.). (1993). Maternal nutrition and pregnancy outcome. *Annals of the New York Academy of Sciences, 678.* New York: New York Academy of Sciences.

Keen, C., & Howard, A. (2002). Experiential learning in Antioch College's work-based learning program as a vehicle for social and emotional development for gifted college students. *Journal of Secondary Gifted Education, 13,* 130–140.

Keenan, J. P., Nelson, A., O'Connor, M., & Pascual-Leone, A. (2001). Self-recognition and the right hemisphere. *Nature, 409,* 305.

Keesey, R. E. (1995). A set-point model of weight regulation. In K. D. Brownell & C. G. Fairburn (Eds.), *Eating disorders and obesity* (pp. 46–50). New York: Guilford Press.

Keith, J. R., & McVety, K. M. (1988). Latent place learning in a novel environment and the influences of prior training in rats. *Psychobiology, 16,* 146–151.

Keller, H. (1903). *The story of my life.* New York: Doubleday.

Keller, S., Shiflett, S., Schleifer, S., & Bartlett, J. (1994). Stress, immunity, and death. In R. Glaser & J. Kiecolt-Glaser (Eds.), *Handbook of human stress and immunity* (pp. 217–244). New York: Cambridge University Press.

Kellogg, W. N., & Kellogg, L. A. (1933). *The ape and the child.* New York: McGraw-Hill.

Kelly, A. E. (1999). Revealing personal secrets. *Current Directions in Psychological Science, 8,* 105–109.

Kelly, G. (2001). *Sexuality today: The human perspective* (7th ed.) Boston: McGraw-Hill.

Kelly, I. W. (1997). Modern astrology: A critique. *Psychological Reports, 81,* 1035–1066.

Kelly, L. (1997). Skills training as a treatment for communication problems. In J. A. Daly, J. C. McCroskey, J. Ayres, T. Hopf, & D. M. Ayres (Eds.), *Avoiding communication: Shyness, reticence, and communication apprehension* (2nd ed., pp. 331–365). Creskill, NJ: Hampton Press.

Kelman, H. C. (1998). The place of ethnic identity in the development of personal identity: A challenge for the Jewish family. *Studies in contemporary Jewry: An annual* (pp. 3–26). New York: Oxford University.

Kempermann, G., & Gage, F. H. (1999). Experienced-dependent regulation of adult hippocampal neurogenesis: Effects of long-term stimulation and stimulus withdrawal. *Hippocampus, 9,* 321–332.

Kempermann, G., & Gage, F. H. (1999, May). New nerve cells for the adult brain. *Scientific American,* pp. 48–53.

Kempler, W. (1974). *Principles of Gestalt family therapy.* Salt Lake City, UT: Desert.

Kendler, K. S., Karkowski, L. M., & Prescott, C. A. (1999). Fears and phobias: Reliability and heritability. *Psychological Medicine, 29,* 539–553.

Kendler, K. S., Myers, J., & Prescott, C. A. (2002). The etiology of phobias: An evaluation of the stress-diathesis model. *Archives of General Psychiatry, 59,* 242–248.

Kendler, K. S., Neale, M. C., Thornton, L. M., Aggen, S. H., Gilman, S. E., & Kessler, R. C. (2002). Cannabis use in the last year in a U.S. national sample of twin and sibling pairs. *Psychological Medicine, 32,* 551–554.

Kenrick, D. T., & Trost, M. R. (1987). A biosocial theory of heterosexual relationships. In K. Kelly (Ed.), *Females, males, and sexuality.* Albany: State University of New York Press.

Kenrick, D. T., & Trost, M. R. (1989). Reproductive exchange model of heterosexual relationships: Putting proximate relationships in ultimate perspective. In C. Henrick (Ed.), *Review of personality and social psychology* (Vol. 10). Newbury Park, CA: Sage.

Keppel-Benson, J. M., Ollendick, T. H., & Benson, M. J. (2002). Post-traumatic stress in children following motor vehicle accidents. *Journal of Child Psychology & Psychiatry & Allied Disciplines, 43,* 203–212.

Kessler, R. C., McGonagle, K. A., Zhao, S., Nelson, C. B., Hughes, M., Eshleman, S., Wittchen, H. U., & Kendler, K. S. (1994). Lifetime and 12-month prevalence of *DSM-III-R* psychiatric disorders in the United States. *Archives of General Psychiatry, 51,* 8–19.

Kessler, R. C., Sonnega, A., Bromet, E., Hughes, M., & Nelson, C. B. (1995). Post traumatic stress disorder in the National Comorbidity Study. *Archives of General Psychiatry, 52,* 1048–1060.

Kessner, D. M. (1973). *Infant death: An analysis by maternal risk and health care.* Washington, DC: National Academy of Sciences.

Ketter, T. A., & Wang, P. W. (2002). Predictors of treatment response in bipolar disorders: Evidence from clinical and brain imaging studies. *Journal of Clinical Psychiatry, 63,* 21–25.

Key, W. B. (1973). *Subliminal seduction.* Englewood Cliffs, NJ: Signet.

Key, W. B. (1989). *The age of manipulation.* New York: Holt.

Keys, A., Brozek, J., Henschel, A., Mickelsen, O., & Taylor, H. (1950). *The biology of human starvation* (Vols. I and II). Minneapolis: University of Minnesota Press.

Khaleque, A. (1999). Sleep deficiency and quality of life of shift workers. *Social Indicators Research, 46,* 181–189.

Khalid, R. (1991). Personality and academic achievement: A thematic apperception perspective. *British Journal of Projective Psychology, 36,* 25–34.

Kiecolt-Glaser, J. K., Glaser, R. (1992). Psychoneuroimmunology: Can psychological interventions modulate immunity? *Journal of Consulting and Clinical Psychology, 60,* 569–575.

Kiecolt-Glaser, J. K., Glaser, R., Williger, D., Stout, J., Messick, G., Sheppard, S., Ricker, D., Romisher, S. C., Briner, W., Bonnell, G., & Donnerberg, R. (1985). Psychosocial enhancement of immunocompetence in a geriatric population. *Health Psychology, 4,* 25–41.

Kihlstrom, J. F. (1985). Hypnosis. *Annual Review of Psychology, 36,* 385–418.

Kihlstrom, J. F. (1989). On what does mood-dependent memory depend? *Journal of Social Behavior and Personality, 4,* 23–32.

Kilham, W., & Mann, L. (1974). Level of destructive obedience as a function of transmitter and executant roles in the Milgram obedience paradigm. *Journal of Personality and Social Psychology, 29,* 696–702.

Kilpatrick, D. G., & Resnick, H. S. (1993). Posttraumatic stress disorder associated with exposure to criminal victimization in clinical and community populations. In J. R. T. Davidson & E. B. Foa (Eds.), *Posttraumatic stress disorder: DSM-IV and beyond* (pp. 113–143). Washington, DC: American Psychiatric Press.

Kimble, D. L., Covell, N. H., Weiss, L. H., Newton, K. J., & Fisher, J. D. (1992). College students use implicit personality theory instead of safer sex. *Journal of Applied Social Psychology, 22,* 921–933.

Kimmel, E. B. (1992). Women's contributions to psychology. *Contemporary Psychology, 37,* 201–202.

Kimura, D. (1987). Are men's and women's brains really different? *Canadian Journal of Psychology, 28,* 133–147.

Kimura, D. (1992). Sex differences in the brain. *Scientific American, 267,* 81–87.

Kimura, D., & Hampson, E. (1994). Cognitive pattern in men and women is influenced by fluctuations in sex hormones. *Current Directions in Psychological Science, 3,* 57–61.

King, S. A., & Moreggi, D. (1998). Internet therapy and self-help groups—The pros and cons. In J. Gackenbach (Ed.), *Psychology and the internet: Interpersonal, intrapersonal, and transpersonal implications* (pp. 77–109). San Diego, CA: Academic Press.

Kingery, P. M., Alford, A. A., & Coggeshall, M. B. (1999). Marijuana use among youth: Epidemiologic evidence from the US and other nations. *School Psychology International, 20,* 9–21.

Kingsbury, S. J. (1987). Cognitive differences between clinical psychologists and psychiatrists. *American Psychologist, 42,* 152–156.

Kinsey, A., Pomeroy, W., & Martin, C. (1948). *Sexual behavior in the human male.* Philadelphia: Saunders.

Kinsey, A., Pomeroy, W., Martin, C., & Gebhard, P. (1953). *Sexual behavior in the human female.* Philadelphia: Saunders.

Kiple, K. F., & Ornelas, K. C. (2001). Experimental animals in medical research: A history. In E. F. Paul & J. Paul (Eds.), *Why animal experimentation matters: The use of animals in medical research. New studies in social policy* (pp. 23–48). New Brunswick, NJ: Transaction Publishers.

Kirchner, M. (2000). Gestalt therapy theory: An overview. *Gestalt Journal, 4,* 200–210.

Kish, S. J. (2002). How strong is the evidence that brain serotonin neurons are damaged in human users of ecstasy? *Pharmacology, Biochemistry, & Behavior, 71,* 845–855.

Kite, M. E., & Deaux, K. (1987). Gender belief systems: Homosexuality and the implicit inversion theory. *Psychology of Women Quarterly, 11,* 83–96.

Kjaer, T. W., Bertelsen, C., Piccini, P., Brooks, D., Alving, J., & Lou, H. C. (2002). Increased dopamine tone during meditation-induced change of consciousness. *Cognitive Brain Research, 13,* 255–259.

Klayman, J., & Ha, Y-W. (1987). Confirmation, disconfirmation, and information in hypothesis testing. *Psychological Review, 94,* 211–228.

Kleese, D. A. (2001). Nature and nature in psychology. *Theoretical & Philosophical Psychology, 21,* 61–79.

Klein, G. (1996). The effect of acute stressors on decision making. In J. Driskell & E. Salas (Eds.), *Stress and human performance* (pp. 49–88). Mahwah, NJ: Erlbaum.

Klein, M. (1932). *The psycho-analysis of children.* London: Hogarth.

Kleinknecht, R. A. (1991). *Mastering anxiety: The nature and treatment of anxious conditions.* New York: Plenum.

Kleinmuntz, B., & Szucko, J. (1984). Lie detection in ancient and modern times: A call for contemporary scientific study. *American Psychologist, 39,* 766–776.

Klerman, G. (1987). Clinical epidemiology of suicide. *Journal of Clinical Psychiatry, 48,* 33–38.

Kline, S., & Groninger, L. D. (1991). The imagery bizarreness effect as a function of sentence complexity and presentation time. *Bulletin of the Psychonomic Society, 29,* 25–27.

Klinger, E. (1990). *Daydreaming: Using waking fantasy and imagery for self-knowledge and creativity.* Los Angeles: Tarcher.

Klinger, E. (1999). Thought flow: Properties and mechanisms underlying shifts in content. In J. A. Singer & P. Salovey (Eds.), *At play in the fields of consciousness: Essays in honor of Jerome L. Singer* (pp. 29–50). Mahwah, NJ: Erlbaum.

Klump, K., Kaye, W., & Strober, M. (2001). The evolving genetic foundations of eating disorders. *Psychiatric Clinics of North America. Special Issue: Eating Disorders, 24* (2), 215–225.

Koester, J. (1995). Membrane potential. In E. R. Kandel, J. H. Schwartz, & T. M. Jessell (Eds.), *Essentials of neural science and behavior.* Norwalk, CT: Appleton & Lange.

Kohlberg, L. (1981). *Essays on moral development.* New York: Harper & Row.

Kohlberg, L. (1984). The psychology of moral development: The nature and validity of moral stages. In *Essays on moral development* (Vol. 2). New York: Harper & Row.

Kohn, A. (1993). *Punished by rewards: The trouble with gold stars, incentive plans, A's, praise, and other bribes.* New York: Houghton Mifflin.

Kolb, B. (1989). Brain development, plasticity, and behavior. *American Psychologist, 44,* 1203–1212.

Kolb, B., & Whishaw, I. Q. (1990). *Fundamentals of human neuropsychology* (3rd ed.). New York: Freeman.

Kolb, B., & Whishaw, I. Q. (1998). Brain plasticity and behavior. *Annual Review of Psychology, 49,* 43–64.

Korn, J. H., Davis, R., & Davis, S. F. (1991). Historians' and chairpersons' judgments of eminence among psychologists. *American Psychologist, 46,* 789–792.

Koss, M. (1993). Rape: Scope, impact, interventions, and public policy responses. *American Psychologist, 48,* 1062–1069.

Kotzer, A. M. (2000). Factors predicting postoperative pain in children and adolescents following spine fusion. *Issues in Comprehensive Pediatric Nursing, 23,* 83–102.

Koutsaal, W., Schacter, D. L., Johnson, M. K., & Gallucio, L. (1999). Facilitation and impairment of event memory produced by photographic review. *Memory & Cognition, 27,* 478–493.

Kozulin, A. (1990). *Vygotsky's psychology: A biography of ideas.* Cambridge, MA: Harvard University Press.

Kramer, A. F., Larish, J. F., & Strayer, D. L. (1995). Training for attentional control in dual task settings: A comparison of young and old adults. *Journal of Experimental Psychology: Applied, 1,* 50–76.

Kramlinger, K. (Ed.). (2001). *Mayo clinic on depression.* Rochester, MN: Mayo Clinic Health Information.

Kramrisch, S., Otto, J., Ruck, C., & Wasson, R. (1986). *Persephone's quest: Etheogens and the origins of religion.* New Haven, CT: Yale University Press.

Krantz, D. S., Contrada, R. J., Hill, D. R., & Fiedler, E. (1988). Environmental stress and biobehavioral antecedents of coronary heart disease. *Journal of Consulting and Clinical Psychology, 56,* 333–341.

Krantz, D. S., Kop, W., Santiago, H., & Gottdiener, J. (1996). Mental stress as a trigger of myocardial ischemia and infarction. *Cardiology Clinics of North America, 14,* 271–287.

Krantz, D., & Manuck, S. (1984). Acute psychophysiologic reactivity and risk of cardiovascular disease: A review and methodologic critique. *Psychological Bulletin, 96,* 435–464.

Kravitz, E. A. (1988). Hormonal control of behavior: Amines and the biasing of behavioral output in lobsters. *Science, 241,* 1775–1782.

Kreitler, S. (1999). Consciousness and meaning. In J. A. Singer & P. Salovey (Eds.), *At play in the fields of consciousness: Essays in honor of Jerome L. Singer* (pp. 207–224). Mahwah, NJ: Erlbaum.

Kribbs, N. B. (1993). Siesta. In M. A. Carskadon (Ed.), *Encyclopedia of sleep and dreaming.* New York: Macmillan.

Kristeller, P. O. (1983). "Creativity" and "tradition." *Journal of the History of Ideas, 44,* 105–114.

Kroger, J. (1996). *Identity in adolescence: The balance between self and other.* London: Routledge.

Kroll, N. E. A., Yonelinas, A. P., Dobbins, I. G., & Frederick, C. M. (2002). Separating sensitivity from response bias: Implications of comparisons of yes-no and forced-choice tests for models and measures of recognition memory. *Journal of Experimental Psychology: General, 131,* 241–254.

Krosnick, J. A., Betz, A. L., Jussim, L. J., & Lynn, A. R. (1992). Subliminal conditioning of attitudes. *Personality and Social Psychology Bulletin, 18,* 152–162.

Kruglanski, A. W., & Freund, T. (1983). The freezing and unfreezing of lay inferences: Effects on impressional primacy, ethnic stereotyping, and numerical anchoring. *Journal of Experimental Social Psychology, 19,* 448–468.

Krull, D. S., Loy, M. H.-M., Lin, J., Wang, C.-F., Chen, S., & Zhao, X. (1999). The fundamental attribution error: Correspondence bias in individualist and collectivist cultures. *Personality and Social Psychology Bulletin, 25,* 1208–1219.

Kübler-Ross, E. (1969). *On death and dying.* New York: Macmillan.

Kübler-Ross, E. (1981). *Living and dying.* New York: Macmillan.

Kuczmarski, R. J., Flegal, K. M., Campbell, S. M., & Johnson, C. L. (1994). Increasing prevalence of overweight among U.S. adults: The National Health and Nutrition Examination Surveys, 1960 to 1991. *Journal of the American Medical Association, 272,* 205–211.

Kuhn, T. (1977). *The essential tension.* Chicago: University of Chicago Press.

Kulik, J. A., Bangert-Downs, R. L., & Kulik, C. (1984). Effectiveness of coaching for aptitude tests. *Psychological Bulletin, 95,* 179–188.

Kumagai, H. A. (1981). A dissection of intimacy: A study of "bipolar posturing" in Japanese social interaction—amaeru and amayakasu, indulgence and deference. *Culture, Medicine, and Psychiatry, 5,* 249–272.

Kumar, V. K., Pekala, R. J., & Cummings, J. (1996). Trait factors, state effects, and hypnotizability. *International Journal of Clinical and Experimental Hypnosis, 44,* 232–249.

Kunda, Z., & Oleson, K. C. (1995). Maintaining stereotypes in the face of disconfirmation: Constructing grounds for subtyping deviants. *Journal of Personality and Social Psychology, 68,* 565–579.

Kuo, Y-Y. (1996). Taoistic psychology of creativity. *Journal of Creative Behavior, 30,* 197–212.

Kurdek, L. A. (1991a). The dissolution of gay and lesbian couples. *Journal of Social and Personal Relationships, 8,* 265–278.

Kurdek, L. A. (1991b). Sexuality in homosexual and heterosexual couples. In K. McKinney & S. Sprecher (Eds.), *Sexuality in close relationships* (pp. 177–191). Hillsdale, NJ: Erlbaum.

Kurdek, L. A. (1994). Areas of conflict for gay, lesbian, and heterosexual couples: What couples argue about influences relationship satisfaction. *Journal of Marriage and the Family, 56,* 923–934.

Kurdek, L. A. (1994). Conflict resolution styles in gay, lesbian, heterosexual non-parent, and heterosexual parent couples. *Journal of Marriage and the Family, 56,* 705–722.

Kurdek, L.A. (1995). Lesbian and gay couples. In A.R. D'Augelli & C.J. Patterson (Eds.), *Lesbian, gay, and bisexual identities over the lifespan: Psychological perspectives* (pp. 243–261). New York: Oxford University Press.

Kurdek, L. A. (1998). Relationship outcomes and their predictors: Longitudinal evidence from heterosexual married, gay cohabiting, and lesbian cohabiting couples. *Journal of Marriage and the Family, 60,* 553–568.

Kurdek, L. A., & Schmitt, J. P. (1986). Relationship quality of partners in heterosexual married, heterosexual cohabiting, and gay and lesbian relationships. *Journal of Personality and Social Psychology, 51,* 711–720.

Kurdek, L. A., & Schmitt, J. P. (1987). Partner homogamy in married, heterosexual cohabiting, gay, and lesbian couples. *Journal of Sex Research, 23,* 212–232.

Kutash, I. L., & Wolf, A. (1990). Object relational groups. In I. L. Kutash & A. Wolf (Eds.), *The group psychotherapist's handbook: Contemporary theory and technique* (pp. 99–115). New York: Columbia University Press.

Kutchins, H., & Kirk, S. A. (1997). *Making us crazy: DSM—The psychiatric Bible and the creation of mental disorders.* New York: Free Press.

L

LaBerge, S. P. (1992). *Physiological studies of lucid dreaming.* Hillsdale, NJ: Erlbaum.

Labov, W. (1973). The boundaries of words and their meanings. In C. J. N. Bailey & R. W. Shiny (Eds.), *New ways of analyzing variation in English* (Vol. 1). Washington, DC: Georgetown University Press.

Lachman, M. E., & Weaver, S. L. (1998). The sense of control as a moderator of social class differences in health and well-being. *Journal of Personality and Social Psychology, 74,* 763–773.

Ladd-Franklin, C. (1929), *Colour and colour theories.* New York: Harcourt, Brace & Company.

LaGrenade, L., Graham, D., & Trontell, A. (2001). Myocarditis and cardiomyopathy associated with clozapine use in the United States. *New England Journal of Medicine, 345,* 224–225.

Laing, D. G., Prescott, J., Bell, G. A., & Gillmore, R. (1993). A cross-cultural study of taste discrimination with Australians and Japanese. *Chemical Senses, 18,* 161–168.

Laing, R. D. (1967). *The politics of experience.* New York: Pantheon.

Laitmann, J. T. (1983, August). The anatomy of human speech. *Natural History,* 20–27.

Lakkis, J., Ricciardelli, L. A., & Williams, R. J. (1999). Role of sexual orientation and gender-related traits in disordered eating. *Sex Roles, 31,* 1–16.

Lakoff, R. T. (1975). *Language and woman's place.* New York: Harper & Row.

Lakoff, R. T. (1990). *Talking power: The politics of language in our lives.* New York: Basic Books.

Lal, S. (2002). Giving children security: Mamie Phipps Clark and the racialization of child psychology. *American Psychologist, 57,* 20–28.

Lamb, M. E. (Ed.). (1987). *The father's role: Cross-cultural perspectives.* Hillsdale, NJ: Erlbaum.

Lamb, M. E., Pleck, J. H., Charnov, E. L., & Levine, J. A. (1987). A biosocial perspective on paternal behavior and involvement. In J. B. Lancaster, A. Rossi, J. Altmann, & L. R. Sherrod (Eds.), *Parenting across the lifespan: Biosocial perspectives.* Hawthorne, NY: Aldine de Gruyter.

Lamb, M., Sternberg, K. J., & Prodromidis, M. (1992). Nonmaternal care and the security of the infant-mother attachment: A reanalysis of the data. *Infant Behavior and Development, 15,* 71–83.

Lambert, A. J. (1995). Stereotypes and social judgment: The consequences of group variability. *Journal of Personality and Social Psychology, 68,* 388–403.

Laming, D. (1985). Some principles of sensory analysis. *Psychological Review, 92,* 462–485.

Lamprecht, F., & Sack, M. (2002). Posttraumatic stress disorder revisited. *Psychosomatic Medicine, 64,* 222–237.

Land, E. H. (1986). Recent advances in retinex theory. *Vision Research, 26,* 7–21.

Landolt, H.-P., Werth, E., Borbely, A. A., Dijk, D.-J. (1995). Caffeine intake (200 mg) in the morning affects human sleep and EEG power spectra at night. *Brain Research, 675,* 67–74.

Landrine, H. (1988). Revising the framework of abnormal psychology. In P. Bronstein & K. Quina (Eds.), *Teaching a psychology of people.* Washington, DC: American Psychological Association.

Lang, P. (1995). The emotion probe: Studies of motivation and attention. *American Psychologist, 50,* 372–385.

Langer, E. J. (1989). Minding matters: The consequences of mindlessness-mindfulness. In L. Berkowitz (Ed.), *Advances in experimental social psychology* (Vol. 22, pp. 137–173). San Diego: Academic Press.

Langer, E. J., Blank, A., & Chanowitz, B. (1978). The mindlessness of ostensibly thoughtful action. *Journal of Personality and Social Psychology, 36,* 635–642.

Langer, L. M., Warheit, G. J., & McDonald, L. P. (2001). Correlates and predictors of risky sexual practices among a multiracial/ethnic sample of university students. *Social Behavior and Personality, 29,* 133–144.

Larsen, R. J., & Kasimatis, M. (1990). Individual differences in entrainment of mood to the weekly calendar. *Journal of Personality and Social Psychology, 58,* 164–171.

Lashley, K. S. (1950). In search of the engram. *Symposium of the Society for Experimental Biology, 4,* 454–482.

Latané, B., & Darley, J. M. (1968). Group inhibition of bystander intervention in emergencies. *Journal of Personality and Social Psychology, 10,* 216–221.

Latané, B., & Darley, J. M. (1970). *The unresponsive bystander: Why doesn't he help?* Englewood Cliffs, NJ: Prentice Hall.

Latané, B., & Nida, S. (1981). Ten years of research on group size and helping. *Psychological Bulletin, 89,* 308–324.

Lau, C. W., & Hoosain, R. (1999). Working memory and language difference in sound duration: A comparison of mental arithmetic in Chinese, Japanese, and English. *Psychologia: An International Journal of Psychology in the Orient, 42,* 139–144.

Laumann, E., & Gagnon, J. (1995). A sociological perspective on sexual action. In R. Parker & J. Gagnon (Eds.), *Conceiving sexuality: Approaches to sex research in a postmodern world.* New York: Routledge.

Laumann, E., Gagnon, J., Michael, R., & Michaels, S. (1994). *The social organization of sexuality: Sexual practices in the United States.* Chicago: University of Chicago Press.

Lavrakas, P. J. (1993). *Telephone survey methods: Sampling, selection, and supervision* (2nd ed.). Newbury Park, CA: Sage.

Law, D. J., Pellegrino, J. W., & Hunt, E. B. (1993). Comparing the tortoise and the hare: Gender differences and experience in dynamic spatial reasoning tasks. *Psychological Science, 4,* 35–40.

Lazarus, R., & Cohen, J. (1977). Environmental stress. In I. Altman & J. Wohlwill (Eds.), *Human behavior and the environment: Current theory and research* (Vol. 2, pp. 89–127). New York: Plenum.

Lazarus, R., & Folkman, S. (1984). *Stress, appraisal, and coping.* New York: Springer.

Lazarus, R. S. (1993). From psychological stress to the emotions: A history of changing outlooks. *Annual Review of Psychology, 44,* 1–21.

Lazarus, R. S., & Lazarus, B. N. (1994). *Passion and reason: Making sense of our emotions.* New York: Oxford University Press.

Leahey, T. H. (1991). *A history of modern psychology.* Englewood Cliffs, NJ: Prentice-Hall.

Leary, D. E. (2002). William James and the art of human understanding. In W. E. Pickren, & D. A. Dewsbury (Eds.), *Evolving perspectives on the history of psychology* (pp. 101–120). Washington, DC: American Psychological Association.

Leary, M. R., Nezlek, J. B., Downs, D., Radford-Davenport, J., Martin, J., & McMullen, A. (1994). Self-presentation in everyday interactions: Effects of target familiarity and gender composition. *Journal of Personality and Social Psychology, 67,* 664–673.

Leck, K., & Simpson, J. (1999). Feigning romantic interest: The role of self-monitoring. *Journal of Research in Personality, 33,* 69–91.

Leckman, J. F., & Herman, A. E. (2002). Maternal behavior and developmental psychopathology. *Biological Psychiatry, 51,* 27–43.

LeDoux, J. (1995). Emotion: Clues from the brain. *Annual Review of Psychology, 46,* 209–235.

LeDoux, J. (1998). *The emotional brain.* New York: Simon & Schuster.

Lee, F., Hallahan, M., & Herzog, T. (1996). Explaining real-life events: How culture and domain shape attributions. *Personality and Social Psychology Bulletin, 22,* 732–741.

Lehman, A. F., Steinwachs, D. M., Dixon, L. B., Goldman, H. H., Osher, F., Postrado, L., Scott, J. E., Thompson, J. W., Fahey, M., Fischer, P., Kasper, J. A., Lyles, A., Skinner, E. A., Buchanan, R., Carpenter, W. T., Jr., Levine, J., McGlynn, E. A., Rosenheck, R., & Zito, J. (1998). Translating research into practice: The schizophrenia patient outcomes research team (PORT) treatment recommendations. *Schizophrenia Bulletin, 24,* 1–10.

Lehman, D. R., Lempert, R. O., & Nisbett, R. E. (1988). The effects of graduate training on reasoning. *American Psychologist, 43,* 431–442.

Leiner, H. C., Leiner, A. L., & Dow, R. S. (1989). Reappraising the cerebellum: What does the hindbrain contribute to the forebrain? *Behavioral Neuroscience, 103,* 998–1008.

Leippe, M. R., & Elkin, R. A. (1987). When motives clash: Issue involvement and response involvement as determinants of persuasion. *Journal of Personality and Social Psychology, 52,* 269–278.

Leitenberg, H., & Henning, K. (1995). Sexual fantasy. *Psychological Bulletin, 117,* 469–496.

Lemonick, M., & Dorfman, A. (2002, July 22). Father of us all? *Time,* pp. 40–47.

Lenton, A. P., Blair, I. V., & Hastie, R. (2001). Illusions of gender: Stereotypes evoke false memories. *Journal of Experimental Social Psychology, 37,* 3–14.

Leonard, C. M, Lombardino, L. J., Mercado, L. R., Browd, S. R., Brier, J. I., & Agee, O. F. (1996). Cerebral asymmetry and cognitive development in children: A magnetic resonance imaging study. *Psychological Science, 7,* 89–95.

Lepper, M., Greene, D., & Nisbett, R. (1973). Undermining children's intrinsic interest with extrinsic rewards: A test of the overjustification hypothesis. *Journal of Personality and Social Psychology, 23,* 129–137.

Lerner, M. J. (1980). *The belief in a just world: A fundamental delusion.* New York: Plenum.

Levant, R. F. (1984). *Family therapy: A comprehensive overview.* Englewood Cliffs, NJ: Prentice-Hall.

LeVay, S. (1991). A difference in hypothalamic structure between heterosexual and homosexual men. *Science, 253,* 1034–1037.

LeVay, S. (1996). *Queer science: The use and abuse of research into homosexuality.* Cambridge, MA: MIT Press.

Levenson, R. W. (1992). Autonomic nervous system differences among emotions. *Psychological Science, 3,* 23–27.

Levenson, R. W., Carstensen, L. L., & Gottman, J. M. (1993). Long-term marriage: Age, gender, and satisfaction. *Psychology and Aging, 8,* 301–313.

Levenson, R. W., Ekman, P., Heider, K., & Friesen, W. V. (1992). Emotion and autonomic nervous system activity in the Minangkabau of West Sumatra. *Journal of Personality and Social Psychology, 62,* 972–988.

Levi, L. (1974). Psychological stress and disease: A conceptual model. In E. Gunderson & R. Rahe (Eds.), *Life stress and illness.* Springfield, IL: Charles C Thomas.

Levin, H. S., Papanicolaou, A., & Eisenberg, H. (1984). Observations on amnesia after nonmissle head injury. In L. R. Squire & N. Butters (Eds.), *Neuropsychology of memory.* New York: Guilford Press.

Levin, I. P., & Gaeth, J. (1988). How consumers are affected by the framing of attribute information before and after consuming the product. *Journal of Consumer Research, 15,* 374–378.

Levine, H. G. (1992). Temperance cultures: Alcohol as a problem in Nordic and English-speaking cultures. In M. Lader, G. Edwards, & D. Drummond (Eds.), *The nature of alcohol and drug-related problems* (pp. 16–36). New York: Oxford University Press.

Levine, R. V., Martinez, T. S., Brase, G., & Sorenson, K. (1994). Helping in 36 U.S. cities. *Journal of Personality and Social Psychology, 67,* 69–82.

Levine, R. V., Sata, S., Hashimoto, T., & Verma, J. (1995). Love and marriage in eleven cultures. *Journal of Cross-Cultural Psychology, 26,* 554–571.

Levine, R., & Norenzayan, A. (1999). The pace of life in 31 countries. *Journal of Cross-Cultural Psychology, 26,* 554–571.

Levitan, I. B., & Kaczmarek, L. K. (1991). *The neuron: Cell and molecular biology.* New York: Oxford University Press.

Levy, J. (1969). Possible basis for the evolution of lateral specialization of the human brain. *Nature, 224,* 614–615.

Levy, J. (1972). Lateral specialization of the human brain: Behavioral manifestations and possible evolutionary basis. In J. A. Kiger (Ed.), *The biology of behavior.* Corvallis: Oregon State University.

Levy, J., Heller, W., Banich, M., & Burton, L. A. (1983). Asymmetry of perception in free viewing of chimeric faces. *Brain and Cognition, 2,* 404–419.

Lewandowsky, S., & Murdock, B. B., Jr. (1989). Memory for serial order. *Psychological Review, 96,* 25–57.

Lewin, R. (1993a). *Human evolution: An illustrated introduction.* Boston: Blackwell Scientific Publications.

Lewin, R. (1993b). *The origin of modern humans.* New York Scientific American Library.

Lewinsohn, P. M., & Gotlib, I. H. (1995). Behavioral theory and treatment of depression. In E. E. Beckham & W. R. Leber (Eds.), *Handbook of depression* (2nd ed., pp. 352–375). New York: Guilford Press.

Lewinsohn, P. M., & Rosenbaum, M. (1987). Recall of parental behavior by acute depressives, remitted depressives, and nondepressives. *Journal of Personality and Social Psychology, 52,* 611–619.

Lewis, M., & Brooks, J. (1978). Self-knowledge in emotional development. In M. Lewis & L. Rosenblum (Eds.), *The development of affect* (pp. 205–226). New York: Plenum.

Lewis, M., & Weintraub, M. (1979). Origins of early sex-role development. *Sex Roles, 5,* 135–153.

Lewontin, R. (1982). *Human diversity.* New York: Scientific American Library.

Leyens, J.-P. (Ed.). (1991). Prolegomena for the concept of implicit theories of personality. *European Bulletin of Cognitive Psychology, 11,* 131–136.

Lichtenberg, J. D. (1989). *Psychoanalysis and motivation.* Hillsdale, NJ: The Analytic Press.

Lichtenstein, E., & Brown, R. A. (1980). Smoking cessation methods: Review and recommendations. In W. R. Miller (Ed.), *The addictive behaviors: Treatment of alcoholism, drug abuse, smoking, and obesity* (pp. 169–206). New York: Pergamon.

Liden, R. C., & Mitchell, T. R. (1988). Ingratiatory behaviors in organizational settings. *Academy of Management Review, 13,* 572–587.

Lieberman, M. A. (1990). A group therapist perspective on self-help groups. *International Journal of Group Psychotherapy, 40,* 251–278.

Lieberman, P. (1984). *The biology and evolution of language.* Cambridge: Harvard University Press.

Liebert, R., & Morris, L. (1967). Cognitive and emotional components of test anxiety: A distinction and some initial data. *Psychological Reports, 20,* 975–978.

Liebert, R. M., & Sprafkin, J. (1988). *The early window* (3rd ed.). New York: Pergamon Press.

Lilienfeld, S. O., Kirsch, I., Sarvin, T. R., Lynn, St. J., Chaves, J. F., Ganaway, G. K., & Powell, R. A. (1999). Dissociative identity disorder and the sociocognitive model: Recalling the lessons of the past. *Psychological Bulletin, 125,* 507–523.

Lilienfeld, S. O., Wood, J. M., & Garb, H. N. (2000). The scientific status of projective techniques. *Psychological Science in the Public Interest, 1,* 27–66.

Lin, C. (1998). Comparison of the effects of perceived self-efficacy on coping with chronic cancer pain and coping with chronic low back pain. *Clinical Journal of Pain, 14,* 303–310.

Linden, D. R., Savage, L. M., & Overmier, J. B. (1997). General learned irrelevance: A Pavlovian analog to learned helplessness. *Learning and Motivation, 28,* 230–247.

Linehan, M. M. (1993). *Cognitive-behavioral treatment of borderline personality disorder.* New York: Guilford Press.

Lipkus, I. M., Dalbert, C., & Siegler, I. C. (1996). The importance of distinguishing the belief in a just world for self versus for others: Implications for psychological well-being. *Personality and Social Psychology Bulletin, 2,* 666–677.

Lipman, J. J., Miller, B. E., Mays, K. S., & Miller, M. N. (1990). Peak B endorphin concentration in cerebrospinal fluid: Reduced in chronic pain patients and increased during the placebo response. *Psychopharmacology, 102,* 112–116.

Lippa, R. A. (2002). Gender-related traits of heterosexual and homosexual men and women. *Archives of Sexual Behavior, 21,* 83–98.

Littleton, J. M., & Little, H. J. (1989). Adaptation in neuronal calcium channels as a common basis for physical dependence on central depressant drugs. In A. J. Goudie & M. W. Emmett-Oglesby (Eds.), *Psychoactive drugs: Tolerance and sensitization* (pp. 461–518). Clifton, NJ: Human Press.

Locke, E., & Latham, G. (1990). *A theory of goal setting and task performance.* Englewood Cliffs, NJ: Prentice Hall.

Lockhart, R. S., & Craik, F. I. (1990). Levels of processing: A retrospective commentary on a framework for memory research. *Canadian Journal of Psychology, 44,* 87–112.

Loehlin, J. C., Horn, J. M., & Willerman, L. (1989). Modeling IQ change: Evidence from the Texas Adoption Project. *Child Development, 60,* 993–1004.

Loehlin, J. C., Horn, J. M., & Willerman, L. (1997). Heredity, environment, and IQ in the Texas Adoption Project. In R. J. Sternberg & E. L. Grigorenko (Eds.), *Intelligence, heredity, and environment* (pp. 105–125). Cambridge, England: Cambridge University Press.

Loehlin, J. C., Vandenberg, S., & Osborne, R. (1973). Blood group genes and negro-white ability differences. *Behavior Genetics, 3,* 263–270.

Loftus, E. F. (1992). When a lie becomes memory's truth: Memory distortion after exposure to misinformation. *Current Directions in Psychological Science, 1,* 121–123.

Loftus, E. F. (1993). The reality of repressed memories. *American Psychologist, 48,* 518–537.

Loftus, E. F., & Coan, D. (1995). The construction of childhood memories. In D. Peters (Ed.), *The child witness in context: Cognitive, social and legal perspectives.* New York: Kluwer.

Loftus, E. F., & Palmer, J. C. (1974). Reconstruction of automobile destruction: An example of the interaction between language and memory. *Journal of Verbal Learning and Verbal Behavior, 13,* 585–589.

Loftus, E. F., Feldman, J., & Dashiell, R. (1995). The reality of illusory memories. In D. L. Schacter (Ed.), *Memory distortion: How minds, brains, and societies reconstruct the past* (pp. 47–68). Cambridge, MA: Harvard University Press.

Logvinenko, A. D., & Epelboim, J., & Steinman, R. M. (2002). The role of vergence in the perception of distance: A fair test of Bishop Berkeley's claim. *Spatial Vision, 15,* 77–97.

LoLordo, V. M., & Droungas, A. (1989). Selective associations and adaptive specializations: Taste aversions and adaptive specializations: Taste aversions and phobias. In S. B Klein & R. R. Mower (Eds.), *Contemporary learning theories: Instrumental conditioning and the impact of biological constraints on learning.* Hillsdale, NJ: Erlbaum.

Long, G. M, & Beaton, R. J. (1982). The case for peripheral persistence: Effects of target and background luminance on a partial-report task. *Journal of Experimental Psychology: Human Perception and Performance, 8,* 383–391.

Lonsway, K. A., Klaw, E. L., Berg, D. R., Waldo, C. R., Kothari, C., Mazurek, C. J., & Hegeman, K. E. (1998). Beyond "no means no": Outcomes of an intensive program to train peer facilitators for campus acquaintance rape education. *Journal of Interpersonal Violence, 13,* 73–92.

Looren de Jong, H. (2000). Genetic determinism: How not to interpret behavioral genetics. *Theory & Psychology, 10,* 615–637.

Loring, D. W., Meador, K., Lee, G., Murro, A., Smith, J., Flanigin, H., Gallagher, B., & King, D. (1990). Cerebral language lateralization: Evidence from intracarotid amobarbital testing. *Neuropsychologia, 28,* 831–838.

Lott, B. (2002). Cognitive and behavioral distancing from the poor. *American Psychologist, 57,* 100–110.

Lourenço, O., & Machado, A. (1996). In defense of Piaget's theory: A reply to 10 common criticisms. *Psychological Review, 103,* 143–164.

Lowe, G., Bland, R., Greenman, J., Kirkpatrick, N., & Lowe, G. (2001). Progressive muscle relaxation and secretory immunoglobulin A. *Psychological Reports, 88,* 912–914.

Lowery, C. R., & Settle, S. A. (1985). Effects of divorce on children: Differential impact of custody and visitation patterns. *Family Relations: Journal of Applied Family and Child Studies, 34,* 455–463.

Lu, L., Gilmour, R., & Kao, S. (2001). Culture values and happiness: An East-West dialogue. *Journal of Social Psychology, 141,* 111–141.

Lu, L., Gilmour, R., Kao, S., Weng, T., Hu, C., Chern, J., Huang, S., & Shih, J. (2001). Two ways to achieve happiness: When the East meets the West. *Personality and Individual Differences, 30,* 1161–1174.

Lubart, T. I. (1999). Creativity across cultures. In R. J. Sternberg (Ed.), *Handbook of creativity* (pp. 339–350). Cambridge, England: Cambridge University Press.

Lubart, T. I., & Sternberg, R. J. (1994). An investment approach to creativity. In R. J. Sternberg (Ed.), *Thinking and problem solving* (pp. 289–332). San Diego, CA: Academic Press.

Lubinski, D., Webb, R. M., Morelock, M. J., & Benbow, C. P. (2001). Top 1 in 10,000: A 10-year follow-up of the profoundly gifted. *Journal of Applied Psychology, 86*, 718–729.

Luchins, A. S. (1942). Mechanization in problem solving. *Psychological Monographs, 54* (6, No. 248).

Luchins, A. S., & Luchins, E. H. (1994). The water jar experiments and Einstellung effects: II. Gestalt psychology and past experience. *Gestalt Theory, 16*, 205–259.

Lucy, J. A. (1992). *Language diversity and thought: A reformulation of the linguistic relativity hypothesis.* New York: Cambridge University Press.

Lucy, J. A. (1997). Linguistic relativity. *Annual Review of Anthropology, 26*, 291–312.

Luria, A. R. (1968). *The mind of a mnemonist: A little book about a vast memory.* (Trans. L. Solotaroff). New York: Basic Books.

Lyddon, W. J., & Chatkoff, D. K. (2001). Empirically supported treatments: Recent trends, current limitations, and future promise. In W. J. Lyddon, & J. V. Jones, Jr. (Eds.), *Empirically supported cognitive therapies: Current and future application* (pp. 235–246). New York: Springer.

Lykken, D. (1984). Polygraph interrogation. *Nature, 307*, 681–684.

Lykken, D. (1998). *A tremor in the blood: Uses and abuses of the lie detector.* New York: Plenum.

Lykken, D., & Tellegen, A. (1996). Happiness is a stochastic phenomenon. *Psychological Science, 65*, 56–68.

Lynch, G., & Staubli, U. (1991). Possible contributions of long-term potentiation to the encoding and organization of memory. *Brain Research Reviews, 16*, 204–206.

Lynch, M. (1994). Developmental psychology. In D. Matsumoto (Ed.), *People: Psychology from a cultural perspective* (pp. 65–81). Pacific Grove, CA: Brooks/Cole.

Lyness, S. A. (1993). Predictors of differences between Type A and Type B individuals in heart rate and blood pressure reactivity. *Psychological Bulletin, 114*, 266–295.

Lynn, R. (1994). Sex differences in intelligence and brain size: A paradox resolved. *Personality and Individual Differences, 17*, 257–271.

Lynn, R. (1996). Racial and ethnic differences in intelligence in the U.S. on the Differential Ability Scale. *Personality and Individual Differences, 20*, 271–273.

Lynn, S. J., & Neufeld, V. A. (1996). Fantasy styles, hypnotic dreaming, and fantasy proneness. *Contemporary Hypnosis, 12*, 4–12.

Lynn, S. J., & Ruhe, J. W. (1986). The fantasy-prone person: Hypnosis, imagination, and creativity. *Journal of Personality and Social Psychology, 51*, 404–408.

Lynn, S. J., Neufeld, V. A., Green, J. P., Sandberg, D., et al. (1996). Daydreaming, fantasy, and psychopathology. In R. G. Kunzendorf, N. P. Spanos, & B. Wallace (Eds.), *Hypnosis and imagination. Imagery and human development series.* Amityville, NY: Baywood.

Lyons, I. C., & Woods, P. J. (1991). The efficacy of rational-emotive therapy: A quantitative review of outcome research. *Clinical Psychology Review, 11*, 357–369.

Lyons, M. J., True, W. R., Eisen, S. A., Goldberg, J., Meyer, J. M., Faraone, S. V., Eaves, L. J., & Tsuang, M. T. (1995). Differential heritability of adult and juvenile antisocial traits. *Archives of General Psychiatry, 52*, 906–915.

Lytton, H., & Gallagher, L. (2002). Parenting twins and the genetics of parenting. In M. H. Bornstein (Ed.), *Handbook of parenting: Vol. 1: Children and parenting* (2nd ed., pp. 227–253). Mahwah, NJ: Erlbaum.

M

Ma, H. K. (1988). The Chinese perspective on moral judgment and development. *International Journal of Psychology, 23*, 201–227.

Maas J. B. (1998). *The sleep advantage: Preparing your mind for peak performance.* New York: Villard.

Maccoby, E. E. (1990). Gender and relationships: A developmental account. *American Psychologist, 45*, 513–520.

Maccoby, E. E., & Jacklin, C. N. (1987). Gender segregation in childhood. In H. W. Reese (Ed.), *Advances in child development and behavior* (Vol. 20, pp. 239–288). New York: Academic Press.

Maccoby, E. E., & Martin, J. A. (1983). Socialization in the context of the family: Parent-child interaction. In E. M. Hetherington (Ed.), *Handbook of child psychology: Vol. 4. Socialization, personality, and social development* (4th ed.). New York: Wiley.

MacDonald, D. A., & Holland, D. (2002). Examination of the psychometric properties of the Temperament and Character Inventory self-transcendence dimension. *Personality & Individual Differences, 32*, 1013–1027.

MacDonald, K. (1998). Evolution, culture, and the five-factor model. *Journal of Cross-Cultural Psychology, 29*, 119–149.

MacDonald, T. K., & Martineau, A. M. (2002). Self-esteem, mood, and intentions to use condoms: When does low self-esteem lead to risky health behaviors? *Journal of Experimental Social Psychology, 38*, 299–306.

Macfarlane, A. (1975). Olfaction in the development of social preferences in the human neonate. *CIBA Foundation Symposium 33: Parent-infant interaction.* Amsterdam, The Netherlands: Elsevier.

MacFarlane, J. G., Cleghorn, J. M., Brown, G. M., & Streiner, D. L. (1991). The effects of exogenous melatonin on the total sleep time and daytime alertness of chronic insomniacs: A preliminary study. *Biological Psychiatry, 30*, 371–376.

MacLeod, C. M. (1988). Forgotten but not gone: Savings for pictures and words in long-term memory. *Journal of Experimental Psychology: Learning, Memory, and Cognition, 14*, 195–212.

Macrae, C. N., Bodenhausen, G. V., & Milne, A. B. (1998). Saying no to unwanted thoughts: Self-focus and the regulation of mental life. *Journal of Personality and Social Psychology, 74*, 578–589.

Macrae, C. N., Milne, A. B., & Bodenhausen, G. V. (1994). Stereotypes as energy-saving devices: A peek inside the cognitive toolbox. *Journal of Personality and Social Psychology, 66*, 37–47.

Madden, D. J. (1992). Adult age differences in attentional selectivity and capacity. *European Journal of Cognitive Psychology, 2*, 229–252.

Madden-Derdich, D. A., & Leonard, S. A. (2002). Shared experiences, unique realities: Formerly married mothers' and fathers' perceptions of parenting and custody after divorce. *Family Relations: Interdisciplinary Journal of Applied Family Studies, 51*, 37–45.

Madigan, S., & O'Hara, R. (1992). Short-term memory at the turn of the century. *American Psychologist, 47,* 170–174.

Maestripieri, D. (1997). The evolution of communication. *Language & Communication, 17,* 269–277.

Magnavita, J. J. (2002). *Theories of personality: Contemporary approaches to the science of personality.* New York: John Wiley & Sons.

Magnusson, D. and Endler, N. S. (1977). Interaction psychology: Present status and future prospects. In Magnusson, D., and Endler, N. S. (Eds.), *Personality at the crossroads* (pp. 3–31). New York: Wiley.

Maher, W. B., & Maher, B. A. (1985). Psychopathology: II. From the eighteenth century to modern times. In G. A. Kimble & K. Schlesinger (Eds.), *Topics in the history of psychology* (pp. 295–329). Hillsdale, NJ: Erlbaum.

Maheu, M. M., & Gordeon, B. L. (2000). Counseling and therapy on the Internet. *Professional Psychology-Research & Practice, 31,* 484–489.

Mahoney, D. J., & Restak, R. M. (1998). *The longevity strategy: How to live to 100 using the brain-body connection.* New York: Wiley.

Maier, S. F., Seligman, M. E. P., & Solomon, R. L. (1969). Pavlovian fear conditioning and learned helplessness: Effects on escape and avoidance behavior of (a) the CS-US contingency, and (b) the independence of the US and voluntary responding. In B. A. Campbell & R. M. Church (Eds.), *Punishment and aversive behavior.* New York: Appleton-Century-Crofts.

Major, B., & Gramzow, R. H. (1999). Abortion as stigma: Cognitive and emotional implications of concealment. *Journal of Personality and Social Psychology, 77,* 735–745.

Major, B., Spencer, S., Schmader, T., Wolfe, C., & Crocker, J. (1998). Coping with negative stereotypes about intellectual performance: The role of psychological disengagement. *Personality and Social Psychology Bulletin, 24,* 34–50.

Makin, J. W., & Porter, R. H. (1989). Attractiveness of lactating females' breast odors to neonates. *Child Development, 60,* 803–810.

Makoul, G. (1998). Perpetuating passivity: Reliance and reciprocal determinism in physician-patient interaction. *Journal of Health Communication, 3,* 233–259.

Malik, M. L., & Beutler, L. E. (2002). The emergence of dissatisfaction with the DSM. In L. E. Beutler, & M. L. Malik (Eds.). (2002). *Rethinking the DSM: A psychological perspective. Decade of behavior* (pp. 3–15). Washington, DC: American Psychological Association.

Malnic, B., Hirono, J., Sato, T., & Buck, L. B. (1999). Combinatorial receptor codes for odors. *Cell, 96,* 713–723.

Malone, J. C., & Cruchon, N. M. (2001). Radical behaviorism and the rest of psychology: A review/précis of Skinner's "About Behaviorism." *Behavior & Philosophy, 29,* 31–57.

Malt, B. C. (1995). Category coherence in cross-cultural perspective. *Cognitive Psychology, 29,* 85–148.

Manabe, T., Noda, Y., Mamiya, T., Katagirl, H., Houtani, T., Nishi, M., Noda, T. Takahashi, T., Sugimoto, T., Nabeshima, T., & Takeshima, H. (1998). Facilitation of long-term potentiation and memory in mice lacking nociceptin receptors. *Nature, 394,* 577–581.

Mancia, M. (1981). On the beginning of mental life in the foetus. *International Journal of Psycho-Analysis, 62,* 351–357.

Mandler, G., & Pearlstone, Z. (1966). Free and constrained concept learning and subsequent recall. *Journal of Verbal Learning and Verbal Behavior, 5,* 126–131.

Mann, C.C. (1994). Behavioral genetics in transition. *Science, 264,* 1686–1689.

Mantell, D. M. (1971). The potential for violence in Germany. *Journal of Social Issues, 27,* 101–112.

Mantyla, T. (1986). Optimizing cue effectiveness: Recall of 500 and 600 incidentally learned words. *Journal of Experimental Psychology: Learning, Memory, and Cognition, 12,* 66–71.

Marcus, B., et al. (1999). "Commit to Quit" study. *Archives of Internal Medicine,* June issue.

Marcus, G. F. (1996). Why do children say "breaked"? *Current Directions in Psychological Science, 5,* 81–85.

Margalit, M. (1995). Effects of social skills training for students with an intellectual disability. *International Journal of Disability, Development and Education, 42,* 75–85.

Margolskee, R. (1995). Receptor mechanisms in gustation. In R. L. Doty (Ed.), *Handbook of olfaction and gustation.* New York: Marcel Dekker.

Marín, G. (1994). The experience of being a Hispanic in the United States. In W. J. Lonner & R. Malpass (Eds.), *Psychology and culture.* Boston: Allyn & Bacon.

Markman, A. B. (1999). *Knowledge representation.* Mahwah, NJ: Erlbaum.

Marks, S. B. (1997). Reducing prejudice against children with disabilities in inclusive settings. *International Journal of Disability, Development and Education, 44,* 117–131.

Markus, H., & Kitayama, S. (1991). The cultural psychology of personality. *The Journal of Cross-Cultural Psychology, 29,* 63–87.

Marsh, H. W., Craven, R. G., & Debus, R. (1991). Self-concepts of young children 5 to 8 years of age: Measurement and multidimensional structure. *Journal of Educational Psychology, 83,* 377–392.

Marshall, S. P. (1995). *Schemas in problem solving.* Cambridge: Cambridge University Press.

Martens, R. (1969). Effects of an audience on learning and performance of a complex motor skill. *Journal of Personality and Social Psychology, 12,* 252–260.

Martin, B. R. (1995). Marijuana. In F. E. Bloom & D. J. Kupfer (Eds.), *Psychopharmacology: The fourth generation* (pp. 1757–1765). New York: Raven Press.

Martin, E. (Ed.). (2000). *Dictionary of medicines.* New York: Market House Books.

Martin, P., & Bateson, P. (1993). *Measuring behaviour: An introductory guide* (2nd ed.). Cambridge, England: Cambridge University Press.

Martindale, C. (1991). *Cognitive psychology: A neural-network approach.* Pacific Grove, CA: Brooks/Cole.

Marx, E. (1999). Gender processing in speech production: Evidence from German speech errors. *Journal of Psycholinguistic Research, 28,* 601–621.

Maslow, A. H. (1970). *Motivation and personality* (2nd ed.). New York: Harper and Row.

Maslow, A. H. (1971). *The farther reaches of human nature.* New York: Viking Press.

Mason, J. (1975). A historical review of the stress field. *Journal of Human Stress, 1,* 22–36.

Mason, W. A. (1997). Discovering behavior. *American Psychologist, 52,* 713–720.

Masson, J. M. (1999). *The emperor's embrace: Reflections on animal families and fatherhood.* New York: Pocket Books.

Masten, A. S. (2001). Ordinary magic: Resilience, processes in development. *American Psychologist, 56,* 227–238.

Masters, M. S., & Sanders, B. (1993). Is the gender difference in mental rotation disappearing? *Behavior Genetics, 23,* 337–341.

Masters, R. E. L., & Houston, J. (1966). *The varieties of psychedelic experience.* New York: Delta.

Masters, W., & Johnson, V. (1966). *Human sexual response.* Boston: Little, Brown.

Mathes, E. W., Adams, H. E., & Davies, R. M. (1985). Jealousy: Loss of relationship rewards, loss of self-esteem, depression, anxiety, and anger. *Journal of Personality and Social Psychology, 48,* 1552–1561.

Mathies, H. (1989). Neurobiological aspects of learning and memory. *Annual Review of Psychology, 40,* 381–404.

Matsumoto, D. (1992). American-Japanese cultural differences in the recognition of universal facial expressions. *Journal of Cross-Cultural Psychology, 23,* 72–84.

Matsumoto, D. (1994). *People: Psychology from a cultural perspective.* Pacific Grove, CA: Brooks/Cole.

Matsumoto, D., Kudoh, J., Scherer, K., & Wallbott, H. (1988). Antecedents and reactions to emotions in the United States and Japan. *Journal of Cross-Cultural Psychology, 19,* 267–286.

Matthews, K. A. (1992). Myths and realities of the menopause. *Psychosomatic Medicine, 54,* 1–9.

Matusov, E., & Hayes, R. (2000). Sociocultural critique of Piaget and Vygotsky. *New Ideas in Psychology, 18,* 215–239.

Matute, H. (1995). Human reactions to uncontrollable outcomes: Further evidence for superstitions rather than helplessness. *Quarterly Journal of Experimental Psychology: Comparative and Physiological Psychology, 48,* 142–157.

Mavromatis, A. (1991). *Hypnagogia: The unique state of consciousness between wakefulness and sleep.* London: Routledge.

Mawhinney, V. T., Boston, D. E., Loaws, O. R., Blumenfeld, G. T., & Hopkins, B. L. (1971). A comparison of students' studying behavior produced by daily, weekly, and three-week testing schedules. *Journal of Applied Behavior Analysis, 4,* 257–264.

May, J., & Kline, P. (1987). Measuring the effects upon cognitive abilities of sleep loss during continuous operations. *The British Psychological Society, 78,* 443–455.

May, R. (1959). *The discovery of being: Writings in existential psychology.* New York: Norton.

May, R. (1990). Will, decision, and responsibility. *Review of Existential Psychiatry, 20,* 269–278.

Mayer, E. L. (2002). Freud and Jung: The boundaried mind and the radically connected mind. *Journal of Analytical Psychology, 47,* 91–99.

Mayer, J. D., & Salovey, P. (1997). What is emotional intelligence? In P. Salovey & D. Sluyter (Eds.), *Emotional development, emotional literacy, and emotional intelligence.* New York: Basic Books.

Mayer, J. D., Salovey, P., & Caruso, D. (2000). In R. J. Sternberg (Ed.), *Handbook of intelligence* (pp. 396–420). Cambridge: Cambridge University Press.

Mayrhauser, R. T. V. (2002). The mental testing community and validity: A prehistory. In W. E. Pickren, & D. A. Dewsbury (Eds.), *Evolving perspectives on the history of psychology* (pp. 303–324). Washington, DC: American Psychological Association.

McAdams, D. P. (1988). Personal needs and personal relationships. In S. Duck (Ed.), *Handbook of personal relationships: Theory, research and interventions* (pp. 7–22). New York: Wiley.

McAdoo, H. P. (2002). The village talks: Racial socialization of our children. In H. P. McAdoo (Ed.), *Black children: Social, educational, and parental environments* (2nd ed., pp. 47–55). Thousand Oaks, CA: Sage.

McAndrew, F. T. (2002). New evolutionary perspectives on altruism: Multilevel-selection and costly-signaling theories. *Current Directions in Psychological Science, 11,* 79–82.

McArthur, L. Z. (1982). Judging a book by its cover: A cognitive analysis of the relationship between physical appearance and stereotyping. In A. H. Hastorf & A. M. Isen (Eds.), *Cognitive social psychology* (pp. 149–211). New York: Elsevier/North Holland.

McAuliffe, S. P., & Knowlton, B. J. (2001). Hemispheric differences in object identification. *Brain & Cognition, 45,* 119–128.

McBride, R. E., Xiang, P. & Wittenburg, D. (2002). Dispositions toward critical thinking: The preservice teacher's perspective. *Teachers & Teaching: Theory & Practice, 8,* 29–40.

McCabe, R., & Quayle, E. (2002). Knowing your own mind. *Psychologist, 15,* 14–16.

McCall, R. B., & Carriger, M. S. (1993). A meta-analysis of infant habituation and recognition memory performance as predictors of later IQ. *Child Development, 64,* 57–79.

McCarthy, G. (1995). Functional neuroimaging of memory. *The Neuroscientist, 1,* 155–163.

McCarthy, R. E. (1992). *Secrets of Hollywood: Special effects.* Stoneham, MA: Focal Press.

McCaul, K. D., & Malott, J. (1984). Distraction and coping with pain. *Psychological Bulletin, 95,* 516–533.

McClearn, G. E. (1993). Behavioral genetics: The last century and the next. In R. Plomin & G. E. McClearn (Eds.), *Nature, nurture, and psychology.* Washington, DC: American Psychological Association.

McClelland, D. C. (1985). *Human motivation.* Glenview, IL: Scott, Foresman.

McClelland, D. C. (1995). Achievement motivation in relation to achievement-related recall, performance, and urine flow, a marker associated with release of vasopressin. *Motivation and Emotion, 19,* 59–76.

McClelland, D. C., Atkinson, J., Clark, R., & Lowell, E. (1953). *The achievement motive.* New York: Appleton-Century-Crofts.

McClelland, J. L. (1994). The organization of memory: A parallel distributed processing perspective. *Revue Neurologique, 150,* 570–579.

McClelland, J. L., & Rumelhart, D. E. (1981). An interactive activation model of context effects in letter perception: Part I. An account of basic findings. *Psychological Review, 102,* 375–407.

McConkey, K. M. (1992). The effects of hypnotic procedures on remembering: The experimental findings and their implications for forensic hypnosis. In E. Fromm & M. R. Nash (Eds.), *Contemporary hypnosis research* (pp. 405–426). New York: Guilford Press.

McConnell, A. R., & Fazio, R. H. (1996). Women as men and people: Effects of gender-marked language. *Personality and Social Psychology Bulletin, 22,* 1004–1013.

McCrae, R. R. (1994). Openness to experience: Expanding the boundaries of Factor V. *European Journal of Personality, 13,* 39–55.

McCrae, R. R. (1996). Social consequences of experiential openness. *Psychological Bulletin, 52,* 509–516.

McCrae, R. R., & Costa, P. T., Jr. (1990). Personality trait structure as a human universal. *American Psychologist, 52,* 509–516.

McCrae, R. R., & Costa, P. T., Jr. (1997a). Conceptions and correlates of openness to experience. In R. Hogan, J. Johnson, & S. Briggs (Eds.). *Handbook of personality psychology* (pp. 825–847). San Diego: Academic Press.

McCrae, R. R., & Costa, P. T., Jr. (1997b). Personality structure as a human universal. *American Psychologist, 52,* 509–516.

McCrae, R. R., and Costa, P. T., Jr. (1987). Validation of a five-factor model of personality across instruments and observers. *Journal of Personality and Social Psychology, 52,* 81–90.

McCrae, R. R., & John, O. P. (1992). An introduction to the five-factor model and its applications. *Journal of Personality, 60,* 175–215.

McCrae, R. R., Costa, P. T., Jr., de Lirna, M. P., Simoes, A., Ostendorf, F., Angleitner, A., Marusic, I., Bratko, D., Caprara, G. V., Barbaranelli, G., Chae, J-H., & Piedmont, R. L. (1999). Age differences in personality across the adult life span: Parallels in five cultures. *Developmental Psychology, 35,* 466–477.

McCrae, R. R., Costa, P. T., Jr., del Pilar, G. H., Rolland, J. P., & Parker, W. D. (1998). Cross-cultural assessment of the five-factor model: The revised NEO personality inventory. *Journal of Cross-Cultural Psychology, 29,* 171–188.

McDougall, W. (1908). *Introduction to social psychology.* London: Methuen & Co.

McGarry-Roberts, P. A., Stelmack, R. M., & Campbell, K. B. (1992). Intelligence, reaction time, and event-related potentials. *Intelligence, 16,* 289–313.

McGee, M. T. (1989). *Beyond ballyhoo: Motion picture promotion and gimmicks.* Jefferson, NC: McFarland.

McGeoch, J. A., & McDonald, W. T. (1931). Meaningful relation and retroactive inhibition. *American Journal of Psychology, 43,* 579–588.

McGlone, J. (1978). Sex differences in functional brain asymmetry. *Cortex, 14,* 122–128.

McGue, M., Bouchard, T. J., Jr., Iacono, W. G., & Lykken, D. T. (1993). Behavioral genetics of cognitive ability: A life-span perspective. In R. Plomin & G. E. McClearn (Eds.), *Nature, nurture and psychology.* Washington, DC: American Psychological Association.

McGue, M., Pickens, R. W., & Svikis, D. S. (1992). Sex and age effects on the inheritance of alcohol problems: A twin study. *Journal of Abnormal Psychology, 202,* 3–17.

McHugh, P. R. (1995). Witches, multiple personalities, and other psychiatric artifacts. *Nature Medicine, 1,* 110–114.

McKinnon, J. W. (1976). The college student and formal operations. In J. W. Renner, D. G. Stafford, A. E. Lawson, J. W. McKinnon, F. E. Friot, & D. H. Kellog (Eds.), *Research training and learning with the Piaget model* (pp. 110–129). Norman: University of Oklahoma Press.

McKinnon, J. W., & Renner, J. W. (1971). Are colleges concerned with intellectual development? *American Journal of Psychology, 39,* 1047–1052.

McLean, J. H., & Shipley, M. T. (1992). Neuroanatomical substrates of olfaction. In M. J. Serby & K. L. Chobor (Eds.), *Science of olfaction* (pp. 126–171). New York: Springer-Verlag.

McMullin, E. (1983). Values in science. In P. D. Asquith & T. Nickles (Eds.), *Proceedings of the 1982 Philosophy of Science Association* (Vol. 2, pp. 3–23). East Lansing, MI: Philosophy of Science Association.

McNeil, B. J., Pauker, S. G., Sox, H. C., Jr., & Tversky, A. (1982). On the elicitation of preferences for alternative therapies. *New England Journal of Medicine, 306,* 1259–1262.

McShane, D. A. (1987). American Indians and Alaska natives in psychology. In P. J. Woods & C. S. Wilkinson (Eds.), *Is psychology the major for you?* Washington, DC: American Psychological Association.

McShane, D. A., & Plas, J. M. (1984). The cognitive functioning of American Indian children: Moving from the WISC to the WISC-R. *School Psychology Review, 13,* 61–73.

Mebert, C., & Michel, G. (1980). Handedness in artists. In J. Herron (Ed.), *Neuropsychology of left handedness.* New York: Academic Press.

Medin, D. L. (1989). Concepts and conceptual structure. *American Psychologist, 44,* 1469–1481.

Mednick, S. A. (1958). A learning theory approach to research in schizophrenia. *Psychological Bulletin, 55,* 316–327.

Medvec, V. H., Madley, S. F., & Gilovich, T. (1995). When less is more: Counterfactual thinking and satisfaction among Olympic medallists. *Journal of Personality and Social Psychology, 69,* 603–610.

Mehrabian, A. (1972). *Nonverbal communication.* Chicago: Aldine-Atherton.

Meichenbaum, D., & Turk, D. (1976). The cognitive-behavioral management of anxiety, anger, and pain. In P. O. Davidson (Ed.), *The behavioral management of anxiety, depression and pain* (pp. 1–34). New York: Brunner/Mazel.

Meins, E. (1999). Sensitivity, security, and internal working models: Bridging the transmission gap. *Attachment and Human Development, 1,* 325–342.

Melis, M. R., & Argiolas, A. (1993). Nitric oxide synthase inhibitors prevent apomorphine- and oxytocin-induced penile erection and yawning in male rats. *Brain Research Bulletin, 32,* 71–74.

Mellinger, G. D., Balter, M. B., & Uhlenhuth, E. H. (1985). Insomnia and its treatment: Prevalence and its correlates. *Archives of General Psychiatry, 42,* 225–232.

Melton, A. W. (1963). Implications of short-term memory for a general theory of memory. *Journal of Verbal Learning and Verbal Behavior, 2,* 1–21.

Meltzer, H. Y. (1979). Biochemical studies in schizophrenia. In L. Bellak (Ed.), *Disorders of the schizophrenic syndrome* (pp. 45–135). New York: Basic Books.

Meltzer, H. Y. (2000). Genetics and etiology of schizophrenia and bipolar disorder. *Biological Psychiatry, 47,* 171–173.

Meltzoff, A. N., & Moore, M. K. (1977). Imitation of facial and manual gestures by human neonates. *Science, 198,* 75–78.

Meltzoff, A. N., & Moore, M. K. (1989). Imitation in newborn infants: Exploring the range of gestures imitated and the underlying mechanisms. *Developmental Psychology, 25,* 954–962.

Melzack, R. (1973). *The puzzle of pain.* New York: Basic Books.

Melzack, R. (1986). Neurophysiological foundations of pain. In R. A. Sternbach (Ed.), *The psychology of pain* (pp. 1–24). New York: Raven Press.

Melzack, R. (1992, April). Phantom limbs. *Scientific American, 266,* pp. 120–126.

Melzack, R., & Wall, P. D. (1982a). *The challenge of pain.* Harmondsworth, England: Penguin.

Melzack, R., & Wall, P.D. (1982b). Pain mechanisms: A new theory. *Science, 13,* 971–979.

Menson, V., Boyett-Anderson, J. M., Schatzberg, S. F., & Reiss, A. L. (2002). Relating semantic and episodic memory systems. *Cognitive Brain Research, 13,* 261–265.

Menzel, R., & Backhaus, W. (1989). Color vision in honey bees: Phenomena and physiological mechanisms. In D. G. Stavenga & R. C. Hardie (Eds.), *Facets of vision* (pp. 281–297). Berlin: Springer-Verlag.

Mesquita, B., & Frijda, N. (1992). Cultural variations in emotions: A review. *Psychological Bulletin, 112,* 179–204.

Messer, W. S., & Griggs, R. A. (1989). Student belief and involvement in the paranormal and performance in introductory psychology. *Teaching of Psychology, 16,* 187–191.

Michael, R., Gagnon, J., Laumann, E., & Kolata, G. (1994). *Sex in America.* New York: Little, Brown.

Middlebrooks, J. C., & Green, D. M. (1991). Sound localization by human listeners. *Annual Review of Psychology, 42,* 135–159.

Mikulincer, M., & Erev, I. (1991). Attachment style and the structure of romantic love. *British Journal of Social Psychology, 30,* 273–291.

Miley, W. M. (1999). *The psychology of well being.* Westport, CN: Praeger.

Milgram, S. (1963). Behavioral study of obedience. *Journal of Abnormal and Social Psychology, 67,* 371–378.

Milgram, S. (1965). Some conditions of obedience and disobedience to authority. *Human Relations, 18,* 57–76.

Milgram, S. (1974). *Obedience to authority: An experimental view.* New York: Harper & Row.

Miller, C., & Swift, K. (1991). *Words and women.* New York: HarperCollins.

Miller, E. M. (1994). Intelligence and brain myelination: A hypothesis. *Personality and Individual Differences, 17,* 803–832.

Miller, G. A. (1956). The magical number seven, plus or minus two: Some limits on our capacity to process information. *Psychological Review, 63,* 81–97.

Miller, G. A., & Gildea, P. M. (1987). How children learn words. *Scientific American, 257,* 94–99.

Miller, I. J., Jr. (1995). Anatomy of the peripheral taste system. In R. L. Doty (Ed.), *Handbook of olfaction and gustation.* New York: Marcel Dekker.

Miller, J. G. (1984). Culture and the development of everyday social explanation. *Journal of Personality and Social Psychology, 46,* 961–978.

Miller, J. G. (1987). "Culture and the Development of Everyday Social Explanation," *Journal of Personality and Social Psychology, 46,* pp. 961–978.

Miller, J. G. (1994). Cultural diversity in the morality of caring: Individually-oriented versus duty-oriented interpersonal codes. *Cross-Cultural Research, 28,* 3–39.

Miller, J. J., Fletcher, K., & Kabat-Zinn, J. (1995). Three-year follow-up and clinical implications of a mindfulness meditation-based stress reduction intervention in the treatment of anxiety disorders. *General Hospital Psychiatry, 17,* 192–200.

Miller, L. C., Berg, J. H., & Archer, R. L. (1983). Openers: Individuals who elicit intimate self-disclosure. *Journal of Personality and Social Psychology, 44,* 1234–1244.

Miller, N. E. (1985). The value of behavior research on animals. *American Psychologist, 40,* 423–440.

Miller, R. S. (1997). We always hurt the ones we love: Aversive interactions in close relationships. In R. M. Kowalski (Ed.), *Aversive interpersonal behaviors* (pp. 11–29). New York: Plenum Press.

Miller, W. C. (1999). Fitness and fatness in relation to health: Implications for a paradigm shift. *Journal of Social Issues, 55,* 207–220.

Miller, W. I. (1997). *The anatomy of disgust.* Cambridge, MA: Harvard University Press.

Miller, W. R., & Hester, R. K. (1980). Treating the problem drinker. In W. R. Miller (Ed.), *The addictive behaviors: Treatment of alcoholism, drug abuse, smoking, and obesity* (pp. 111–141). New York: Pergamon.

Mills, M., & Stunkard, A. (1976). Behavioral changes following surgery for obesity. *American Journal of Psychiatry, 133,* 527–531.

Milner, B., Corkin, S., & Teuber, H. L. (1968). Further analysis of the hippocampal amnesic syndrome: 14-year follow-up study of H.M. *Neuropsychologia, 6,* 317–338. *Developmental Psychobiology, 40,* 266–277.

Mindell, J. A. (1999). Sleep disorders. In A. J. Goreczny, M. Hersen, et al. (Eds.), *Handbook of pediatric and adolescent health psychology* (pp. 371–386). Boston, MA: Allyn & Bacon.

Mineka, S., & Zinbarg, R. (1995). Conditioning and ethological models of anxiety disorders: Stress-in-Dynamic-Context models. In D. A. Hope (Ed.), *Nebraska symposium on motivation, 1995: Perspectives of anxiety, panic, and fear. Current theory and research in motivation, Vol. 43* (pp. 135–210). Lincoln, NE: University of Nebraska Press.

Minturn, L., Grosse, M., & Haider, S. (1969). Cultural patterning of sexual beliefs and behavior. *Ethnology, 8,* 301–313.

Mintz L. B., & Kashubeck, S. (1999). Body image and disordered eating among Asian American and Caucasian college students: An examination of race and gender differences. *Psychology of Women Quarterly, 23,* 781–796.

Mischel, W. (1968). *Personality and assessment.* New York: Wiley.

Mischel, W. (1984). Convergences and challenges in the search for consistency. *American Psychologist, 39,* 351–364.

Mischel, W., & Shoda, Y. (1999). Integrating dispositions and processing dynamics within a unified theory of personality: The cognitive-affective personality system. In L. A. Pervin & O. P. John (Eds.), *Handbook of personality: Theory and research* (2nd ed., pp. 197–218). New York: Guilford Press.

Miserandino, M. (1991). Memory and the seven dwarfs. *Teaching of Psychology, 18,* 169–171.

Mistry, J., & Rogoff, B. (1994). Remembering in a cultural context. In W. J. Lonner & R. S. Malpass (Eds.), *Psychology and culture.* Boston: Allyn & Bacon.

Mita, T. H., Dermer, M., & Knight, J. (1977). Reversed facial images and the mere-exposure hypothesis. *Journal of Personality and Social Psychology, 35,* 597–601.

Mitchell, C. M., Novins, D. K., & Holmes, T. (1999). Marijuana use among American Indian adolescents: A growth curve analysis from ages 14 through 20 years. *Journal of the American Academy of Child & Adolescent Psychiatry, 38,* 72–78.

Mitchell, D. E. (1980). The influence of early visual experience on visual perception. In C. S. Harris (Ed.), *Visual coding and adaptability.* Hillsdale, NJ: Erlbaum.

Mittleman, M., Maclure, M., Sherwood, J., et al. (1995). Triggering of acute myocardial infarction onset by episodes of anger. Determinants of myocardial infarction onset study investigators. *Circulation, 92,* 1720–1725.

Moely, B. E., Olson, F. A., Halwes, T. G., & Flavell, J. H. (1969). Production deficiency in young children's clustered recall. *Developmental Psychology, 1,* 26–34.

Mogg, K., & Bradley, B. P. (1999). Orienting of attention to threatening facial expressions presented under conditions of restricted awareness. *Cognition and Emotion, 12*, 713–740.

Mokdad, A., Serdula, M., Dietz, W., Bowman, B., Marks, J., & Koplan, J. (1999). The spread of obesity epidemic in the United States, 1991–1998. *Journal of the American Medical Association, 282*, 1519–1522.

Mollon, J. D. (1990). The club-sandwich mystery. *Nature, 343*, 16–17.

Monane, M. (1992). Insomnia in the elderly. *Journal of Clinical Psychiatry, 53* (6, Suppl.), 23–28.

Mondloch, C. J., Lewis, T. L., Budreau, D. R., Maurer, D., Dannemiller, J. L., Stephens, B. R., & Kleiner-Gathercoal, K. A. (1999). Face perception during early infancy. *Psychological Science, 10*, 419–422.

Monk, T. H. (2000). What can the chronobiologist do to help the shift worker? *Journal of Biological Rhythms, 15*, 86–94.

Monk, T. M., & Folkard, S. (1992). *Making shift work tolerable.* London: Taylor & Francis.

Monroe, S. M., & Simons, A. D. (1991). Diathesis-stress theories in the context of life stress research: Implications for the depressive disorders. *Psychological Bulletin, 110*, 406–425.

Monteith, M. J. (1993). Self-regulation of prejudiced responses: Implications for progress in prejudice-reduction efforts. *Journal of Personality and Social Psychology, 65*, 469–485.

Monteith, M. J. (1996). Affective reactions to prejudice-related discrepant responses: The impact of standard salience. *Personality and Social Psychology Bulletin, 22*, 48–59.

Monteith, M. J., Devine, P. G., & Zuwerink, J. R. (1993). Self-directed versus other-directed affect as a consequence of prejudice-related discrepancies. *Journal of Personality and Social Psychology, 64*, 198–210.

Monteith, M. J., Sherman, J. W., & Devine, P. G. (1998). Suppression as a stereotype control strategy. *Personality and Social Psychology Review, 2*, 63–82.

Montepare, J. M., & Zebrowitz-McArthur, L. (1988). Impressions of people created by age-related qualities of their gaits. *Journal of Personality and Social Psychology, 55*, 547–556.

Moore, B. E., & Fine, B. D. (Eds.). (1990). *Psychoanalytic terms and concepts.* New Haven: The American Psychoanalytic Association and Yale University Press.

Moore, K. L., & Persaud, T. V. N. (1993). *Before we are born* (4th ed.). Philadelphia: Saunders.

Moore, R. Y. (1990). The circadian system and sleep-wake behavior. In J. Montplaisir & R. Godbout (Eds.), *Sleep and biological rhythms: Basic mechanisms and applications to psychiatry* (pp. 3–10). New York: Oxford University Press.

Moran, M. G., & Stoudemire, A. (1992). Sleep disorders in the medically ill patient. *Journal of Clinical Psychiatry, 53* (6, Suppl.), 29–36.

Morgan, D. L., & Morgan, R. K. (2001). Single-participant research design. *American Psychologist, 56*, 119–127.

Morgan, J. (1986). *From simple input to complex grammar.* Cambridge, MA: MIT Press.

Morgan, J., & Travis, L. (1989). Limits on negative information in language input. *Journal of Child Language, 16*, 531–532.

Morganstern, J., Labouvie, E., McGrady, B. S., Kahler, C. W., & Frey, R. M. (1997). Affiliation with Alcoholics Anonymous after treatment: A study of its therapeutic effects and mechanism of action. *Journal of Consulting and Clinical Psychology, 65*, 768–777.

Morin, A. (2001). The split-brain debate revisited: On the importance of language and self-recognition for right hemispheric consciousness. *Journal of Mind and Behavior, 22*, 107–118.

Morin, C. M., Mimeault, V., & Gagne, A. (1999). Nonpharmacological treatment of late-life insomnia. *Journal of Psychosomatic Research, 46*, 103–116.

Morley, J. (1998). The private theater: A phenomenological investigation of daydreaming. *Journal of Phenomenological Psychology, 29*, 116–134.

Morley, J., Levine, A., Bartness, T., Nizielski, S., Shaw, M., & Hughes, J. (1985). Species differences in the response to cholecystokinin. *Annals of the New York Academy of Sciences, 448*, 413–416.

Morling, B., & Epstein, S. (1997). Compromises produced by the dialectic between self-verification and self-enhancement. *Journal of Personality and Social Psychology, 73*, 1268–1283.

Morris, C. D., Bransford, J. D., & Franks, J. J. (1977). Levels of processing versus transfer appropriate processing. *Journal of Verbal Learning and Verbal Behavior, 16*, 519–533.

Morton, J., & Johnson, M. H. (April, 1991). CONSPEC and CONLEARN: A two-process theory of infant face recognition. *Psychological Review, 98*, 164–181.

Moses, L. J., Chandler, M. J. (1992). Traveler's guide to children's theories of mind. *Psychological Inquiry, 3*, 286–301.

Moses, P., & Stiles, J. (2002). The lesion methodology: Contrasting views from adult and child studies.

Moss, D. (1999). Abraham Maslow and the emergence of humanistic psychology. In D. Moss (Ed.), *Humanistic and transpersonal psychology: A historical and biographical sourcebook* (pp. 24–37). Westport, CT: Greenwood Press.

Motley, M. T. (1985). Slips of the tongue. *Scientific American, 253*, 116–127.

Motley, M. T., & Baars, B. J. (1979). Effects of cognitive set upon laboratory-induced verbal (Freudian) slips. *Journal of Speech and Hearing Research, 22*, 421–432.

Mowrer, O. H. (1947). On the dual nature of learning—a reinterpretation of "conditioning" and "problem-solving." *Harvard Education Review, 17*, 102–148.

Moynihan, J., & Stevens, S. (2001). Mechanisms of stress-induced modulation of immunity in animals. In R. Ader, D. Felten, & N. Cohen (Eds.), *Psychoneuroimmunology* (Vol. 2, 3rd ed., pp. 227–250). San Diego, CA: Academic Press.

Mozell, M. M., Smith, B. P., Smith, P. E., Sullivan, R. L., & Swender, P. (1969). Nasal chemoreception in flavor identification. *Archives of Otolaryngology, 90*, 131–137.

Muchinsky, (2000). *Psychology applied to work* (6th ed.). Pacific Grove, CA: Brooks-Cole.

Mulac, A., & Lundell, T. L. (1986). Linguistic contributors to the gender-linked language effect. *Journal of Language and Social Psychology, 5*, 81–101.

Muller, J., Abela, G., Nestro, R., & Tofler, G. (1994). Triggers, acute risk factors, and vulnerable plaques: The lexicon of a new frontier. *Journal of the American College of Cardiology, 23*, 809–813.

Murray, C. J., & Lopez, A. D. (Eds.). (1996). *The global burden of disease: A comprehensive assessment of mortality and disability from diseases, injuries, and risk factors in 1990 and projected to 2020.* Cambridge, MA: Harvard University Press.

Murray, H. (1938). *Explorations in personality.* New York: Oxford University Press.

Murray, H. A. (1938). *Explorations in personality: A clinical and experimental study of fifty men of college age, by the workers at the Harvard Psychological Clinic.* New York: Oxford University Press.

Murray, H. A. (1948). *Assessment of men.* New York: Science Editions.

Murray, J. B. (1980). *Television and youth: 25 years of research and controversy.* Boys Town, NE: Boys Town Center for the Study of Youth Development.

Must, A., Spadano, J., Coakley, E., Field, A., Colditz, G., & Dietz, W. (1999). The disease burden associated with overweight and obesity. *Journal of the American Medical Association, 282,* 1523–1529.

Myers, D. (1993). *The pursuit of happiness.* New York: Avon Books.

Myers, D., & Diener, E. (1995). Who is happy? *Psychological Science, 6,* 10–19.

Myers, H. F., Wohlford, P., Guzman, L. P., & Echemendia, R. J. (Eds.). (1991). *Ethnic minority perspectives on clinical training and services in psychology.* Washington, DC: American Psychological Association.

N

Nabuzoka, D., & Ronning, J. A. (1997). Social acceptance of children with intellectual disabilities in an integrated school setting in Zambia: A pilot study. *International Journal of Disability, Development and Education, 44,* 105–115.

Nadeau, S. N. (2001). Phonology: A review and proposals from a connectionist perspective. *Brain & Language, 79,* 511–579.

Nadel, L., & Zola-Morgan, S. (1984). Infantile amnesia: A neurobiological perspective. In M. Moscovitch (Ed.), *Infant memory.* New York: Plenum Press.

Nair, K. U., & Ramnarayan, S. (2000). Individual differences in need for cognition and complex problem solving. *Journal of Research in Personality, 34,* 305–328.

Nakajima, M., Nakajima, S., & Imada, H. (2000). General learned irrelevance and its prevention. *Learning and Motivation, 30,* 265–280.

Nash, J. M. (1997, May 5). Addicted: Why do people get hooked? Mounting evidence points to a powerful brain chemical dopamine. *Time,* pp. 68–76.

Nash, M. (1987). What, if anything, is regressed about hypnotic age regression? A review of the empirical literature. *Psychological Bulletin, 102,* 42–52.

Nathan, P. (1982). *The nervous system* (2nd ed.). Oxford: Oxford University Press.

Nathan, P. E., & Gorman, J. M. (Eds.). (2002). *A guide to treatments that work* (2nd ed.). London: Oxford University Press.

National Academy of Sciences. (1999). Marijuana and medicine: Assessing the science base (by J. A. Benson, Jr., and S. J. Watson, Jr.). Washington, DC: National Academy Press.

National Institutes of Health. (2000). Clinical guidelines on the identification, evaluation, and treatment of overweight and obesity in adults. *Executive Summary, Obesity Education Initiative, National Heart, Lung, and Blood Institute.* Washington, DC: U.S. Government Printing Office.

National Science Foundation. (1994). *Characteristics of doctoral scientists and engineers in the United States: 1991* (pp. 94–307). Arlington, VA: NSF.

National Sleep Foundation. (2002). *2001 Sleep in America Poll.* Retrieved July 30, 2002, from http://www.sleepfoundation.org/img/2002sleepInAmericaPoll.pdf.

Naveh-Benjamin, M. (1990). The acquisition and retention of knowledge: Exploring mutual benefits to memory research and the educational setting. *Applied Cognitive Psychology, 4,* 295–320.

Neal, A. M., & Wilson, M. L. (1989). The role of skin color and features in the Black community: Implications for Black women and therapy. *Clinical Psychology Review, 9,* 323–333.

Neher, A. (1996). Jung's theory of archetypes: A critique. *Journal of Humanistic Psychology, 36,* 61–91.

Neisser, U. (1982). Snapshots or benchmarks? In U. Neisser (Ed.), *Memory observed* (pp. 43–48). San Francisco: Freeman.

Neisser, U., & Harsch, N. (1992). Phantom flashbulbs: False recollections of hearing the news about *Challenger.* In E. Winograd & U. Neisser (Eds.), *Affect and accuracy in recall: Studies of "flashbulb" memories* (pp. 9–31). New York: Cambridge University Press.

Neisser, U., Boodoo, G., Bouchard, T. J., Jr., Boykin, A. W., Brody, N., Ceci, S. J., Halpern, D. F., Loehlin, J. C., Perloff, R., Sternberg, R. J., & Urbina, S. (1996). Intelligence: Knowns and unknowns. *American Psychologist, 51,* 77–101.

Nelson, C. A. (1999). Neural plasticity and human development. *Current Directions in Psychological Science, 8,* 42–45.

Nelson, D. L., Schreiber, T. A., & McEvoy, C. L. (1992). Processing implicit and explicit representations. *Psychological Review, 99,* 322–348.

Nelson, E. S., Karr, K. M., & Coleman, P. K. (1995). Relationships among daily hassles, optimism and reported physical symptoms. *Journal of College Student Psychotherapy, 10,* 11–26.

Nelson, K. (1981). Acquisition of words by first-language learners. In H. Winitz (Ed.), *Annals of the New York Academy of Sciences, 379,* 148–160.

Nelson, R. (2000). *An introduction to behavioral endocrinology* (2nd ed.). Sunderland, MA: Sinauer Associates.

Nelson, T. E., Acker, M., & Manis, M. (1996). Irrepressible stereotypes. *Journal of Experimental Social Psychology, 32,* 13–28.

Nemeroff, C. B. (1998, June). The neurobiology of depression. *Scientific American,* pp. 42–49.

Neugarten, B. L., Wood, V., Kraines, R. J., & Loomis, B. (1963). Women's attitudes toward the menopause. *Vita Humana, 6,* 140–151.

Neumeister, A., Praschak-Rieder, N., Hebelmann, B., Rao, M.-L, Glück, J., & Kasper, S. (1997). Effects of tryptophan depletion on drug-free patients with seasonal affective disorder during a stable response to bright light therapy. *Archives of General Psychiatry, 54,* 133–138.

Neville, B., & Parke, R. D. (1997). Waiting for paternity: Interpersonal and contextual implications of the timing of fatherhood. *Sex Roles, 37,* 45–59.

Newcombe, N. S., Drummey, A. B., Fox, N. A., Lie, E., & Ottinger-Alberts, W. (2000). Remembering early childhood: How much, how, and why (or why not). *Current Directions in Psychological Science, 9,* 55–58.

Newman, A. W., & Thompson, J. W., Jr. (1999). Constitutional rights and hypnotically elicited testimony. *Journal of the American Academy of Psychiatry & the Law, 27,* 149–154.

NICHD Early Child Care Research Network. (2002). Parenting and family influences when children are in child care: results from the NICHD study of early child care. In J. G. Borkowski, & S. L. Ramey (Eds.), *Parenting and the child's world: Influences on academic, intellectual, and social-emotional development. Monographs in parenting* (pp. 99–123). Mahwah, NJ: Erlbaum.

Nicholson, A. N., Pascoe, P. A., Spencer, M. B., Stone, B. M., Roehis, T., & Roth, T. (1986). Sleep after transmeridian flights. *Lancet, 2*, 1205–1208.

Nicholson, I. A. M. (2002). Gordon Allport, character, and the "Culture of Personality." In W. E. Pickren, & D. A. Dewsbury (Eds.), *Evolving perspectives on the history of psychology* (pp. 325–345). Washington, DC: American Psychological Association.

Nickell, J. A. (1996, May/June). Fantasy proneness in the thirteen cases of alleged encounters in John Mack's *Abduction. Skeptical Inquirer, 54*, 18–20.

Nickerson, R. S. (2000). Null hypothesis significance testing: A review of an old continuing controversy. *Psychological Methods, 5*, 241–301.

Nickerson, R. S., & Adams, M. J. (1979). Long-term memory for a common object. *Cognitive Psychology, 11*, 287–307.

Nicolaus, L. K., & Nellis, D. W. (1987). The first evaluation of the use of conditioned taste aversion to control predation by mongooses upon eggs. *Applied Animal Behaviour Science, 17*, 329–346.

Nielsen, C. (1995). *Animal evolution: Interrelationships of the living phyla*. Oxford, England: Oxford University Press.

Nielsen, L. L., & Sarason, I. G. (1981). Emotion, personality, and selective attention. *Journal of Personality and Social Psychology, 41*, 945–960.

Niemi, R., Mueller, J., & Smith, T. (1989). *Trends in public opinion: A compendium of survey data*. New York: Greenwood Press.

Nietzel, M. T., Speltz, M. L., McCauley, E. A., & Bernstein, D. A. (1998). *Abnormal psychology*. Boston: Allyn & Bacon.

Nigg, J. T., & Goldsmith, H. H. (1994). Genetics of personality disorders: Perspectives from personality and psychopathology research. *Psychological Bulletin, 115*, 346–380.

Nijhawan, R. (1991). Three-dimensional Müeller-Lyer illusion. *Perception & Psychophysics, 49*, 333–341.

Nisbett, R. (1995). Race, IQ, and scientism. In S. Fraser (Ed.), *The Bell Curve wars: Race, intelligence and the future of America* (pp. 36–57). New York: Basic Books.

Nisbett, R. E., & Cohen, D. (1996). *Culture of honor: The psychology of violence in the south*. Boulder, CO: Westview Press.

Nisbett, R. E., & Wilson, T. D. (1977). Telling more than we can know: Verbal reports on mental processes. *Psychological Review, 84*, 231–259.

Nock, M. K., & Kazdin, A. E. (2002). Examination of affective, cognitive, and behavioral factors and suicide-related outcomes in children and young adolescents. *Journal of Clinical Child & Adolescent Psychology, 31*, 48–58.

Nogrady, H., McConkey, K., & Perry, C. (1985). Enhancing visual memory: Trying hypnosis, trying imagination, and trying again. *Journal of Abnormal Psychology, 94*, 195–204.

Noice, T., & Noice, H. (2002). Very long-term recall and recognition of well-learned material. *Applied Cognitive Psychology, 16*, 259–272.

Nolen-Hoeksma, S., Girgus, J. S., & Seligman, M. E. P. (1992). Predictors and consequences of childhood depressive symptoms: Five year longitudinal study. *Journal of Abnormal Psychology, 101*, 405–422.

Noll, K. M., Davis, J. M., & DeLeon-Jones, F. (1985). Medication and somatic therapies in the treatment of depression. In E. E. Beckham & W. R. Leber (Eds.), *Handbook of depression: Treatment, assessment, and research* (pp. 220–315). Homewood, IL: Dorsey.

Norden, K. A., Klein, D. N., Donaldson, S. K., Popper, C. M., & Klein, L. M. (1995). Reports of the early home environment in DSM-III-R personality disorders. *Journal of Personality Disorders, 9*, 213–223.

Norenzayan, A., & Nisbett, R.E. (2000). Culture and causal cognition. *Current Directions in Psychological Science, 9*, 132–135.

Norris, J. E., & Tinsdale, J. A. (1994). *Among generations: The cycle of adult friendships*. New York: Freeman.

North, M. M., North, S. M., & Coble, J. R. (2002). Virtual reality therapy: An effective treatment for phobias. In K. M. Stanney (Ed.), *Handbook of virtual environments: Design, implementation, and applications. Human factors and ergonomics* (pp. 1065–1078). Mahwah, NJ: Erlbaum.

Norwich, K. H. (1987). On the theory of Weber fractions. *Perception & Psychophysics, 42*, 286–298.

Nowak, A., Szamrej, J., & Latané, B. (1990). From private attitude to public opinion: A dynamic theory of social impact. *Psychological Review, 97*, 362–376.

Nyberg, L., Forkstam, C., Petersson, K. M., Cabeza, R., & Ingvar, M. (2002). Brain imaging of human memory systems: Between-systems similarities and within-system differences. *Cognitive Brain Research, 13*, 281–292.

O

O'Brien, C. P., Eckardt, M. J., & Linnoila, M. I. (1995). Pharmacotherapy of alcoholism. In F. E. Bloom & D. J. Kupfer (Eds.), *Psychopharmacology: The fourth generation* (pp. 1745–1755). New York: Raven Press.

O'Connor, N., Cowan, R., & Samella, K. (2000). Calendrical calculation and intelligence. *Intelligence, 28*, 31–48.

O'Connor, P. (1997). Overtraining and staleness. In W. Morgan (Ed.), *Physical activity and mental health* (pp. 145–160). Washington, DC: Taylor & Francis.

O'Farrell, T., & Murphy, C. M. (1995). Marital violence before and after alcoholism treatment. *Journal of Consulting and Clinical Psychology, 63*, 256–262.

O'Keeffe, M., Nesselhof-Kendall, S., & Baum, A. (1990). Behavior and prevention of AIDS: Bases of research and intervention. *Personality and Social Psychology Bulletin, 16*, 166–180.

O'Leary, A. (1990). Stress, emotion, and human immune function. *Psychological Bulletin, 108*, 363–382.

O'Leary, K. D., Vivian, D., & Malone, J. (1992). Assessment of physical aggression in marriage: The need for multimodal assessment. *Behavioral Research and Therapy, 14*, 1–10.

O'Mahony, J. F. (1986). Development of person description over adolescence. *Journal of Youth and Adolescence, 15*, 389–403.

O'Sullivan, C., & Yeager, C. P. (1989). Communicative context and linguistic competence: The effects of a social setting on a chimpanzee's conversational skill. In R. A. Gardner, B. T. Gardner, & T. E. Van Cantfort (Eds.), *Teaching sign language to chimpanzees*. New York: State University of New York Press.

Oatley, K., & Jenkins, J. (1996). *Understanding emotions*. Cambridge, MA: Blackwell.

Ochse, R. (1990). *Before the gates of excellence: The determinants of creative genius*. Cambridge, England: Cambridge University Press.

Oda, R. (2001). Lemur vocal communication and the origin of human language. In T. Matsuzawa (Ed.), *Primate origins of human cognition and behavior* (pp. 115–134). New York: Springer-Verlag.

Oehman, A. (2002). Automaticity and the amygdala: Nonconscious responses to emotional faces. *Current Directions in Psychological Science, 11,* 62–66.

Oetting, E. R., & Beauvais, F. (1987). Peer cluster theory: Socialization characteristics, and adolescent drug use: A path analysis. *Journal of Counseling Psychology, 34,* 205–213.

Oetting, E. R., & Beauvais, F. (1990). Adolescent drug use: findings of national and local surveys. *Journal of Consulting and Clinical Psychology, 58,* 385–394.

Ogbu, J. U. (1986). Class stratification, racial stratification and schooling. In L. Weis (Ed.). *Race, class and schooling: Special studies in comparative education* (Vol. 17, pp. 6–35). New York: Comparative Education Center, State University of New York at Buffalo.

Ogbu, J. U. (1993). Differences in cultural frame of reference. *International Journal of Behavioral Development, 16,* 483–506.

Ohayon, M. M., Guilleminault, C., & Priest, R. G. (1999). Night terrors, sleepwalking, and confusional arousals in the general population: Their frequency and relationship to other sleep and mental disorders. *Journal of Clinical Psychiatry, 60,* 268–276.

Öhman, A., Lundqvist, D., & Esteves, F. (2001). The face in the crowd revisited: A threat advantage with schematic stimuli. *Journal of Personality and Social Psychology, 80,* 381–396.

Oishi, S., Diener, E. F., Lucas, R. E., & Suh, E. M. (1999). Cross-cultural variations in predictors of life satisfaction: Perspectives from needs and values. *Personality and Social Psychology Bulletin, 25,* 980–990.

Oldfield, R. C. (1971). The assessment and analysis of handedness: The Edinburgh Inventory. *Neuropsychologia, 9,* 97–114.

Oliner, S. P., & Oliner, P. M. (1988). *The altruistic personality: Rescuers of Jews in Nazi Europe.* London: Free Press.

Oliver, M. B., & Hyde, J. S. (1993). Gender differences in sexuality: A meta-analysis. *Psychological Bulletin, 114,* 29–51.

Oller, D. K., & Eilers, R. E. (1988). The role of audition in infant babbling. *Child Development, 59,* 441–449.

Olweus, D. (1980). Familial and temperamental determinants of aggressive behavior in adolescent boys: A causal analysis. *Developmental Psychology, 16,* 644–666.

Orlinsky, D. E., & Howard, K. I. (1987). The relation of process to outcome in psychotherapy. In S. L. Garfield & A. E. Bergin (Eds.), *Handbook of psychotherapy and behavior change* (3rd ed., pp. 311–381). New York: Wiley.

Ostatnikova, D., Laznibatova, J., Putz, Z., Mat-aseje, A., Dohnanyiova, M., & Pastor, K. (2000). Salivary testosterone, handedness, allergy and cognition in children. *Homeostasis in Health and Disease, 40,* 121–123.

Ouellet, C., Le Norman, M.-T., & Cohen, H. (2001). Language evolution in children with cochlear implants. *Brain & Cognition, 46,* 231–235.

Ouimette, P. C., Finney, J. W., & Moos, R. H. (1997). Twelve-step and cognitive behavioral treatment for substance abuse: A comparison of treatment effectiveness. *Journal of Consulting and Clinical Psychology, 65,* 230–240.

Overmier, J. B., & Leaf, R. C. (1965). Effects of discriminative Pavlovian fear conditioning upon previously or subsequently acquired avoidance responding. *Journal of Comparative and Physiological Psychology, 60,* 213–218.

Oyserman, D., Coon, H. M., & Kemmelmeier, M. (2002). Rethinking individualism and collectivism: Evaluation of theoretical assumptions and meta-analyses. *Psychological Bulletin, 128,* 3–72.

P

Paffenbarger, R. S., Jr., Hyde, R. T., Wing, A. L., & Hsieh, C. (1986). Physical activity, all-cause mortality, and longevity of college alumni. *New England Journal of Medicine, 314,* 605–613.

Pagel, J. F. (1994). Treatment of insomnia. *American Family Physician, 49,* 1417–1421.

Pahnke, W. N. (1970). Drugs and mysticism. In B. Aarson & H. Osmond (Eds.), *Psychedelics.* New York: Anchor.

Paivio, S. C., & Greenberg, L. S. (1995). Resolving "unfinished business": Efficacy of experiential therapy using empty-chair dialogue. *Journal of Consulting and Clinical Psychology, 63,* 419–425.

Pakkenberg, B., & Gundersen, H. J. G. (1997). Neocortical neuron number in humans: Effect of sex and age. *The Journal of Comparative Neurology, 384,* 312–320.

Palazzo-Craig, J. (1986). *The upside-down boy.* Mahwah, NJ: Troll Associates.

Parham, T. A., & Helms, J. E. (1985). Attitudes of racial identity and self-esteem in Black students: An exploratory investigation. *Journal of College Student Personnel, 26,* 143–147.

Paris, J. (1997). Childhood trauma as an etiological factor in the personality disorders. *Journal of Personality Disorders, 11,* 34–49.

Park, B. (1986). A method for studying the development of impressions of real people. *Journal of Personality and Social Psychology, 51,* 907–917.

Park, D. C., Smith, A. D., & Cavanaugh, J. C. (1990). Metamemories of memory researchers. *Memory & Cognition, 18,* 321–327.

Parke, R. D., & Buriel, R. (1998). Socialization in the family: Ethnic and ecological perspectives. In W. Damon & N. Eisenberg (Eds.), *Handbook of child psychology: Vol. 3. Social, emotional, and personality development* (5th ed., pp. 463–552). New York: Wiley.

Parkes, C. M. P., & Weiss, R. S. (1983). *Recovery from bereavement.* New York: Basic Books.

Parkinson Study Group. (2002). Dopamine transporter brain imaging to assess the effects of pramipexole vs. levodopa on Parkinson disease progression. *JAMA: Journal of the American Medical Association, 287,* 1653–1661.

Parrott, W. G., & Smith, R. H. (1993). Distinguishing the experiences of envy and jealousy. *Journal of Personality and Social Psychology, 64,* 906–920.

Pasch, L. A., Bradbury, T. N., & Sullivan, K. T. (1997). Social support in marriage: An analysis of intraindividual and interpersonal components. In G.R. Pierce, B. Lakey, I.G. Sarason, & B.R. Sarason (Eds.), *Sourcebook of social support and personality* (pp. 229–256). New York: Plenum.

Pashler, H. (1992). Attentional limitations in doing two tasks at the same time. *Current Directions in Psychological Science, 1,* 44–48.

Pashler, H., Johnston, J. C., & Ruthruff, E. (2000). Attention and performance. *Annual Review of Psychology, 52,* 629–651.

Passman, R. H., & Weisberg, P. (1975). Mothers and blankets as agents for promoting play and exploration by young children in a novel environment: The effects of social and nonsocial attachment objects. *Developmental Psychology, 11,* 170–177.

Pate, R., Pratt, M., Blair, S., Haskell, W., Macera, C. et al. (1995). Physical activity and public health: A recommendation from the Centers for Disease Control and Prevention and the American College of Sports Medicine. *Journal of the American Medical Association, 273,* 402–407.

Pato, M. T., Pato, C. N., & Pauls, D. L. (2002). Recent findings in the genetics of OCD. *Journal of Clinical Psychiatry, 63,* 30–33.

Patterson, F. (1978, October). Conversations with a gorilla. *National Geographic*, pp. 438–465.

Pauls, D. L., Alsobrook, J. P., Goodman, W., Rasmussen, S., & Leckman, J. F. (1995). A family study of obsessive-compulsive disorder. *American Journal of Psychiatry, 152*, 76–84.

Paunonen, S. V., & Ashton, M. C. (2001). Big five factors and facets and the prediction of behavior. *Journal of Personality and Social Psychology, 81*, 524–539.

Pavlides, C., & Winson, J. (1989). Influences of hippocampal place cell firing in the awake state on the activity of these cells during subsequent sleep episodes. *Journal of Neuroscience, 9*, 2907–2918.

Pavlov, I. P. (1927). *Conditioned reflexes* (G.V. Anrep, Trans.). London: Oxford University Press.

Pavlov, I. P. (1997). Excerpts from *The work of the digestive glands. American Psychologist, 52*, 936–940. (Original work published in 1897).

Pearson, J., Brandeis, L., & Cuello, A. C. (1982). Depletion of substance P-containing axons in substantia gelatinosa of patients with diminished pain sensitivity. *Nature, 295*, 61–63.

Pedersen, C., & Boccia, M. L. (2002). Oxytocin maintains as well as initiates female sexual behavior: Effects of a highly selective oxytocin antagonist. *Hormones & Behavior, 4*, 170–177.

Pedersen, W. C., Miller, L. C., Putcha-Bhagavatula, A. D., & Yang, Y. (2002). Evolved sex differences in the number of partners desired? The long and the short of it. *Psychological Science, 13*, 157–161.

Pederson, D. R., Moran, G., Sitko, C., Campbell, K., Ghesquire, K., & Acton, H. (1990). Maternal sensitivity and the security of infant-mother attachment: A q-sort study. *Child Development, 61*, 1974–1983.

Peele, S. (1993). The conflict between public health goals and the Temperance mentality. *American Journal of Public Health, 83*, 805–810.

Peele, S. (1996). Utilizing culture and behaviour in epidemiological models of alcohol consumption and consequences for Western nations. *Alcohol & Alcoholism, 32*, 51–64.

Pekkanen, J. (1982, June). Why do we sleep? *Science, 82*, 86.

Penfield, W. W. (1958). *The excitable cortex in conscious man.* Springfield, IL: Charles Thomas.

Pennebaker, J. W., & Beall, S. (1986). Confronting a traumatic event: Toward an understanding of inhibition and disease. *Journal of Abnormal Psychology, 95*, 274–281.

Pennebaker, J. W., Colder, M., & Sharp, L. K. (1990). Accelerating the coping process. *Journal of Personality and Social Psychology, 58*, 528–537.

Penny, L. (1996). *The Whorf theory complex: A critical reconstruction.* Philadelphia: John Benjamins.

Peoples, C. E., Fagan, J. F., III, & Drotar, D. (1995). The influence of race on 3-year-old children's performance on the Stanford-Binet: Fourth Edition. *Intelligence, 21*, 69–82.

Peplau, L. A. (1991). Lesbian and gay relationships. In J. C. Gonsiorek & J. Dweinrich (Eds.), *Homosexuality: Research implications for public policy* (pp. 177–196). Newbury Park, NJ: Sage.

Peplau, L. A., & Taylor, S. E. (Eds.). (1997). *Sociocultural perspectives in social psychology: Current readings.* Upper Saddle River, NJ: Prentice-Hall.

Peplau, L. A., Veniegas, R. C., & Campbell, S. M. (1996). Gay and lesbian relationships. In R. C. Savins-Williams & K. M. Cohen (Eds.), *The lives of lesbians, gays, and bisexuals: Children to adults* (pp. 250–273). Ft. Worth, TX: Harcourt Brace.

Pepperberg, I. M. (2002). Cognitive and communicative abilities of grey parrots. *Current Directions in Psychological Science, 11*, 83–87.

Percy, W. (1976). *The message in the bottle.* New York: Farrar, Straus & Giroux.

Perkins, D. (1995). *Outsmarting IQ: The emerging science of learnable intelligence.* New York: The Free Press.

Perls, F. S. (1969). *Gestalt therapy verbatim.* Lafayette, CA: Real People Press.

Perls, F. S., Heffertine, R. F., & Goodman, P. (1951). *Gestalt therapy.* New York: Julian Press.

Perris, E. E., Myers, N. A., & Clifton, R. K. (1990). Long-term memory for a single infancy experience. *Child Development, 61*, 1796–1807.

Persky, H. (1983). Psychosexual effects of hormones. *Medical Aspects of Human Sexuality, 17*, 74–101.

Pert, C. B. (1999). *Molecules of emotion.* New York: Simon & Schuster.

Pert, C. B., & Snyder, S. H. (1973). Opiate receptor: Demonstration in nervous tissue. *Science, 179*, 1011–1014.

Pervin, L. A. (1996). *The science of personality.* New York: Wiley.

Peters, M. F. (2002). Racial socialization of young Black children. In H. P. McAdoo (Ed.). *Black children: Social, educational, and parental environments* (2nd ed., pp. 57–72). Thousand Oaks, CA: Sage.

Peterson, B. D., West, J., Pincus, H. A., & Kohout, J. (1996). An update on human resources in mental health. In R. W. Manderscheid & M. A. Sonnenschein (Eds.), *Mental Health, United States 1996* (DHHS Publication No. SMA 96-3098). Washington, DC: U.S. Department of Health and Human Services.

Peterson, C., & Park, C. (1998). Learned helplessness and explanatory style. In D. F. Barone, M. Hersen, & V. B. Van Hasselt (Eds.), *Advanced personality.* New York: Plenum.

Peterson, C., & Seligman, M. E. (1984). Causal explanations as a risk factor for depression: Theory and evidence. *Psychological Review, 91*, 347–374.

Peterson, C., & Seligman, M. E. P. (1987). Explanatory style and illness. *Journal of Personality, 55*, 237–265.

Peterson, C., Maier, S. F., & Seligman, M. E. P. (1993). *Learned helplessness: A theory for the age of personal control.* New York: Oxford University Press.

Peterson, L. R., & Peterson, M. J. (1959). Short-term retention of individual verbal items. *Journal of Experimental Psychology, 58*, 193–198.

Peto, R., Lopez, A. D., Boreham, J., & Thun, M. (1992). Mortality from tobacco in developed countries: Indirect estimation from national vital statistics. *Lancet, 339*, 1268–1278.

Petrill, S. A., Luo, D., Thompson, L. A., & Detterman, D. K. (1996). The independent prediction of general intelligence by elementary cognitive tasks: Genetic and environmental influences. *Behavior Genetics, 26*, 135–147.

Petty, R. E., & Cacioppo, J. T. (1986). *Communication and persuasion: Central and peripheral routes to attitude change.* New York: Springer-Verlag.

Petty, R. E., & Wegener, D. T. (1996). Attitude change: Multiple roles for persuasion variables. In D. Gilbert, S. Fiske, & G. Lindzey (Eds.), *The handbook of social psychology* (4th ed.). New York: McGraw-Hill.

Petty, R. E., Haugtvedt, C. P., & Smith, S. M. (1995). Elaboration as a determinant of attitude strength: Creating attitudes that are persistent, resistant, and predictive of behavior. In R. E. Petty & J. A. Krosnick (Eds.), *Attitude strength: Antecedents and consequences.* Hillsdale, NJ: Erlbaum.

Pfaffmann, C. (1978). The vertebrate phylogeny, neural code, and integrative process of taste. In C. Carteerette & M. P. Friedman (Eds.), *Handbook of perception* (Vol. 6A). New York: Academic Press.

Pfaffmann, C., Frank, M., & Norgren, R. (1979). Neural mechanisms and behavioral aspects of taste. *Annual Review of Psychology, 30,* 283–325.

Phelps, J. A., Davis, J. O., & Schartz, K. M. (1997). Nature, nurture, and twin research strategies. *Current Directions in Psychological Science, 6,* 117–121.

Phillips, D. P. (1983). The impact of mass media violence on U.S. homicides. *American Sociological Review, 48,* 560–568.

Phillips, D. P. (1986). Natural experiments on the effects of mass media violence on fatal aggression: Strengths and weaknesses of a new approach. In L. Berkowitz (Ed.), *Advances in experimental social psychology* (Vol. 19, pp. 207–250). Orlando, FL: Academic Press.

Phillips, D. P., & Brugge, J. F. (1985). Progress in neurophysiology of sound localization. *Annual Review of Psychology, 36,* 245–274.

Phillips, M. R., Li, S., & Zhang, Y. (2002). Suicide rates in China: 1995–99. *Lancet, 359,* 835–840.

Phillips, R. D., Wagner, S. H., Fells, C. A., & Lynch, M. (1990). Do infants recognize emotion in facial expressions? Categorical and "metaphorical" evidence. *Infant Behavior and Development, 13,* 71–84.

Phinney, J. S. (1993). A three-stage model of ethnic identity development. In M. Bernal & G. Knight (Eds.), *Ethnic identity: Formation and transmission among Hispanics and other minorities* (pp. 61–79). Albany: State University of New York Press.

Phinney, J. S., Cantu, C. L., & Kurtz, D. A. (1997). Ethnic and American identity and self-esteem. *Journal of Youth and Adolescence, 26,* 165–185.

Phinney, J., & Kohatsu, E. (1997). Ethnic and racial identity and mental health. In J. Schulenberg, J. Maggs, & K. Hurrelmann (Eds.), *Health risks and developmental transitions during adolescence* (pp. 420–443). New York: Cambridge University Press.

Phinney, V. G., Jensen, L. C., Olsen, J. A., & Cundick, B. (1990). The relationship between early development and psychosexual behaviors in adolescent females. *Adolescence, 25,* 321–332.

Piaget, J. (1972a). Development and learning. In C. S. Lavatelli & F. Stendler (Eds.), *Readings in child behavior and development* (3rd ed.). New York: Harcourt Brace Jovanovich.

Piaget, J. (1972b). Intellectual evolutions from adolescence to adulthood. *Human Development, 15,* 1–12.

Piaget, J., & Inhelder, B. (1956). *The child's conception of space.* (F. J. Langdon & J. L. Lunzer, Trans.). London: Routledge & T. K. Paul.

Piaget, J., & Inhelder, B. (1969). *The psychology of the child.* New York: Basic Books.

Piasecki, T. M., Kenford, S. L., Smith, S. S., Fiore, M. C., & Baker, T. B. (1997). Listening to nicotine: Negative affect and the smoking withdrawal conundrum. *Psychological Science, 8,* 184–189.

Piccione, C., Hilgard, E. R., & Zimbardo, P. G. (1989). On the degree of stability of measured hypnotizability over a 25-year period. *Journal of Personality and Social Psychology, 56,* 289–295.

Pickens, R. W., Svikis, D. S., McGue, M., Lykken, D. T., Heston, L. L., & Clayton, P. J. (1993). Heterogeneity in the inheritance of alcoholism: A study of male and female twins. *Archives of General Psychiatry, 48,* 19–28.

Pike, K. M., & Rodin, J. (1991). Mothers, daughters, and disordered eating. *Journal of Abnormal Psychology, 100,* 198–204.

Pillemer, D. B. (1984). Flashbulb memories on the assassination attempt on President Reagan. *Cognition, 14,* 709–715.

Pine, F. (1990). *Drive, ego, object, and self: A synthesis for clinical work.* New York: Basic Books.

Pinel, J. (1997). *Biopsychology.* Boston: Allyn & Bacon.

Pinel, J., Assanand, S., & Lehman, D. (2000). Hunger, eating, and ill health. *American Psychologist, 55,* 1105–1116.

Pinel, J. P. J., Lehman, D. R., & Assanand, S. (2002). "Eating for optimal health: How much should we eat?": Comment. *American Psychologist, 57,* 372–373.

Pines, A., & Aronson, E. (1983). Antecedents, correlates, and consequences of sexual jealousy. *Journal of Personality, 51,* 108–136.

Pines, A. M. (1993). Burnout. In L. Goldberger & S. Breznitz (Eds.), *Handbook of stress: Theoretical and clinical aspects.* New York: Free Press.

Pinker, S. (1994). *The language instinct: How the mind creates language.* New York: Morrow.

Piotrowski, C., Belter, R. W., & Keller, J. W. (1998). The impact of "managed care" on the practice of psychological testing: Preliminary findings. *Journal of Personality Assessment, 70,* 441–447.

Pittman, T. (1998). Motivation. In D. Gilbert, S. Fiske, & G. Lindzey (Eds.), *The handbook of social psychology* (Vol. 1, 4th ed., pp. 549–590). New York: Oxford University Press.

Plaut, D. C., & Kello, C. T. (1999). The emergence of phonology from the interplay of speech comprehension and production: A distributed connectionist approach. In B. MacWhinney (Ed.), *The emergence of language* (pp. 381–415). Mahwah, NJ: Erlbaum.

Plomin, R. (1984). Childhood temperament. In B. Lahey & A. Kazdin (Eds.), *Advances in clinical child psychology* (Vol. 6). New York: Plenum.

Plomin, R., & Crabbe, J. (2000). DNA. *Psychological Bulletin, 125,* 806–828.

Plomin, R., & McClearn, G. E. (1993). (Eds.). *Nature-nurture and psychology.* Washington, DC: American Psychological Association.

Plomin, R., DeFries, J. C., McClearn, G. E., & Rutter, M. (1997). *Behavioral genetics* (3rd ed.). New York: Freeman.

Plous, S. (1996a). Attitudes toward the use of animals in psychological research and education: Results from a national survey of psychologists. *American Psychologist, 51,* 1167–1180.

Plous, S. (1996b). Attitudes toward the use of animals in psychological research and education: Results from a national survey of psychology majors. *Psychological Science, 7,* 352–358.

Plous, S. (1998). Signs of change within the animal rights movement: Results from a follow-up survey of activists. *Journal of Comparative Psychology, 112,* 48–54.

Plutchik, R. (1994). *The psychology and biology of emotion.* New York: HarperCollins.

Pokorny, J., Shevell, S. K., & Smith, V. C. (1991). Colour appearance and colour constancy. In P. Gouras (Ed.), *The perception of colour: Vol. 6. Vision and visual dysfunction* (pp. 43–61). Boca Raton, FL: CRC.

Polivy, J., Herman, C., & McFarlane, T. (1994). Effects of anxiety on eating: Does palatability moderate distress-induced overeating of dieters? *Journal of Abnormal Psychology, 103,* 505–510.

Pomerantz, J. M. (2002). Is social phobia a serious medical disorder? *Drug Benefit Trends, 14,* 5.

Pomerantz, S. C. (1979). Sex differences in the relative importance of self-esteem, physical self-satisfaction and identity in predicting adolescent satisfaction. *Journal of Youth and Adolescence, 8,* 51–61.

Pope, K. S., & Vasquez, M. J. T. (2001). *Ethics in psychotherapy and counseling: A practical guide* (2nd ed.). San Francisco: Jossey-Bass.

Porac, C., & Coren, S. (1981). *Lateral preferences and human behavior.* New York: Springer-Verlag.

Porter, F. L., Porges, S. W., & Marshall, R. E. (1988). Newborn pain cries and vagal tone: Parallel changes in response to circumcision. *Child Development, 59,* 495–505.

Porter, R. H., & Moore, J. D. (1981). Human kin recognition by olfactory cues. *Physiology and Behavior, 27,* 493–495.

Posavac, H. D., & Posavac, S. S. (1998). Exposure to media images of female attractiveness and concern with body weight among young women. *Sex Roles, 38,* 187–201.

Posner, M. I. (2002). Convergence of psychological and biological development. *Developmental Psychobiology, 40,* 339–343.

Povinelli, D. J., & Bering, J. M. (2002). The mentality of apes revisited. *Current Directions in Psychological Science, 11,* 115–119.

Powers, D. E. (1993). Coaching for the SAT: A summary of the summaries and an update. *Educational Measurement Issues and Practice, 12,* 24–30.

Pratkanis, A. R. (1989). The cognitive representation of attitudes. In A. R. Pratkanis, S. J. Breckler, & A. G. Greenwald (Eds.), *Attitude structure and function* (pp. 71–98). Hillsdale, NJ: Erlbaum.

Pratkanis, A. R., & Aronson, E. (1992). *Age of propaganda: The everyday use and abuse of persuasion.* New York: W. H. Freeman.

Pratt, D. D. (1991). Conceptions of self within China and the United States: Contrasting foundations for adult education. *International Journal of Intercultural Relations, 15,* 285–310.

Premack, D., & Premack, A. (1983). *The mind of an ape.* New York: Norton.

Presson, P. K., & Benassi, V. A. (1996). Locus of control and depressive symptomatology: A meta-analysis. *Journal of Social Behavior and Personality, 11,* 201–212.

Pritchard, R. (1991). The effects of cultural schemata on reading processing strategies. *Reading Research Quarterly, 24,* 273–293.

Prochiantz, A. (1992). *How the brain evolved.* New York: McGraw-Hill.

Provins, K.A. (1997). Handedness and speech: A critical reappraisal of the role of genetic and environmental factors in the cerebral lateralization of function. *Psychological Review, 104,* 544–571.

Pugh, E. N., Jr. (1988). Vision: Physics and retinal physiology. In R. C. Atkinson, R. J. Herrnstein, G. Lindzey, & R. D. Luce (Eds.), *Stevens' handbook of experimental psychology* (Vol. 1). New York: Wiley.

Putnam, S. P., Sanson, A. V., & Rothbart, M. K. (2002). Child temperament and parenting. In M. H. Bornstein (Ed.). *Handbook of parenting: Vol. 1: Children and parenting* (2nd ed., pp. 255–277). Mahwah, NJ: Erlbaum.

Pyryt, M. C. (1993). The fulfillment of promise revisited: A discriminant analysis of factors predicting success in the Terman study. *Roeper Review, 15,* 178–179.

Pytlik Zillig, L. M., Hemenover, S. H., & Dienstbier, R. A. (2002). What do we assess when we assess a Big 5 trait? A content analysis of the affective, behavioral and cognitive processes represented in the Big 5 personality inventories. *Personality and Social Psychology Bulletin, 28,* 847–858.

R

Rabin, M. D., & Cain, W. S. (1986). Determinants of measured olfactory sensitivity. *Perception & Psychophysics, 39,* 281–286.

Raffone, A., & Leeuwen, C. V. (2001). Activation and coherence in memory processes: Revisiting the parallel distributed processing approach to retrieval. *Connection Science: Journal of Neural Computing, Artificial Intelligence & Cognitive Research, 13,* 349–382.

Ramachandran, V. S. (1992, May). Blind spots. *Scientific American,* pp. 102–109.

Ramirez-Amaya, V., & Bermudez-Rattoni, F. (1999). Conditioned enhancement of antibody production is disrupted by insular cortex and amygdala but not hippocampal lesions. *Brain, Behavior, and Immunity, 13,* 46–60.

Ramus, F., Hauser, M. D., Miller, C., Morris, D., & Mehler, J. (2001). Language discrimination by human newborns and by cotton-top tamarin monkeys. In M. Tomasello (Ed.), *Language development: The essential readings. Essential readings in developmental psychology* (pp. 34–41). Malden, MA: Blackwell.

Randi, J. (1980). *Flim-flam!* New York: Lippincott.

Rao, S. M., Huber, S. J., & Bornstein, R. A. (1992). Emotional changes with multiple sclerosis and Parkinson's disease. *Journal of Consulting and Clinical Psychology, 60,* 369–378.

Rapee, R. M. (1995). Psychological factors influencing the affective response to biological challenge procedures in panic disorder. *Journal of Anxiety Disorders, 9,* 59–74.

Ratcliff, R., & McKoon, G. (1994). Retrieving information from memory: Spreading-activation theories versus compound-cue theories. *Psychological Review, 101,* 177–184.

Rathunde, K. (2001). Toward a psychology of optimal human functioning: What positive psychology can learn from the "experiential turns" of James, Dewey, and Maslow. *Journal of Humanistic Psychology, 41,* 135–153.

Ratliff-Crain, J., Donald, K., & Ness, J. (1999). The relative impact of knowledge, beliefs, peer norms, and past behaviors on current risky sexual behaviors among college students. *Psychology and Health, 14,* 625–641.

Ravasia, S. (2001). Risperidone-induced edema. *Canadian Journal of Psychiatry, 46,* 453–454.

Raven, P. H., & Johnson, G. B. (1999). *Biology* (5th ed.). New York: McGraw-Hill.

Raz, A., & Shapiro, T. (2002). Hypnosis and neuroscience: A cross talk between clinical and cognitive research. *Archives of General Psychiatry, 59,* 85–90.

Raz, S., & Raz, N. (1990). Structural brain abnormalities in the major psychoses: A quantitative review of the evidence from computerized imaging. *Psychological Bulletin, 108,* 93–108.

Reed, C. F. (1989). Terrestrial and celestial passage. In M. Hershenson (Ed.), *The moon illusion* (pp. 267–280). Hillsdale, NJ: Erlbaum.

Reed, G. (1979). Everyday anomalies of recall and recognition. In J. F. Kihlstrom & F. J. Evans (Eds.), *Functional disorders of memory* (pp. 1–28). Hillsdale, NJ: Erlbaum.

Reed, S. K. (1996). *Cognition: Theory and applications* (4th ed.). Pacific Grove, CA: Brooks/Cole.

Reese, F. L., Kliewer, W., & Suarez, T. (1997). Control appraisals as moderators of the relationship between intrusive thoughts and coping. *Journal of Applied Social Psychology, 27,* 1131–1145.

Reeve, J. (1992). *Understanding motivation and emotion.* Fort Worth, TX: Harcourt Brace.

Regan, D., & Beverley, K. I. (1984). Figure-ground segregation by motion contrast and by luminance contrast. *Journal of the Optical Society of America A, 1,* 433–442.

Regan, P. C. (1996). Sexual outcasts: the perceived impact of body weight and gender on sexuality. *Journal of Applied Social Psychology, 26,* 1803–1815.

Reichel-Dolmatoff, G. (1971). *Amazonian cosmos: The sexual and religious symbolism of the Tukano Indians.* Chicago: University of Chicago Press.

Reichman J. (1998). *I'm not in the mood: What every woman should know about improving her libido.* New York: Morrow.

Reinisch, J., Hill, C., Sanders, S., & Ziemba-Davis, M. (1995). High-risk sexual behavior at a Midwestern university: A confirmatory survey. *Family Planning Perspectives, 27,* 79–82.

Reissland, N. (1988). Neonatal imitation in the first hour of life: Observations in rural Nepal. *Developmental Psychology, 24,* 464–469.

Remington, G., Shammi, C. M., Sethna, R., & Lawrence, R. (2001). Antipsychotic patterns for schizophrenia in three treatment settings. *Psychiatric Services, 52,* 96–98.

Reneman, L., Booij, J., Schmand, B., van den Brink, W., & Gunning, B. (2000). Memory disturbances in "Ecstacy" users are correlated with an altered brain serotonin neurotransmission. *Psychopharmacology, 148,* 322–324.

Renner, J. W., Abraham, M. R., Grzybowski, E. B., & Marek, E. A. (1990). Understandings and misunderstandings of eighth graders of four physics concepts found in textbooks. *Journal of Research in Science in Teaching, 27,* 35–54.

Rescorla, R. A. (1968). Probability of shock in the presence and absence of CS in fear conditioning. *Journal of Comparative and Physiological Psychology, 66,* 1–5.

Rescorla, R. A. (1992). Hierarchical associative relations in Pavlovian conditioning and instrumental training. *Current Directions in Psychological Science, 1,* 66–70.

Rescorla, R. A., & Wagner, A. R. (1972). A theory of Pavlovian conditioning: Variations in the effectiveness of reinforcement and nonreinforcement. In A. H. Black & W. F. Perokasy (Eds.), *Classical conditioning II: Current theory.* New York: Appleton-Century-Crofts.

Ressler, K. J., Sullivan, S. L., & Buck, L. B. (1994). A molecular dissection of spatial patterning in the olfactory system. *Current Opinion in Neurobiology, 4,* 588–596.

Reuter-Lorenz, P. A., & Miller, A. C. (1998). The cognitive neuroscience of human laterality: Lessons from the bisected brain. *Current Directions in Psychological Science, 7,* 15–20.

Revonsuo, A., Kamppinen, M., & Sajama, S. (1994). General introduction: The riddle of consciousness. In A. Revonsuo & M. Kamppinen (Eds.), *Consciousness in philosophy and cognitive neuroscience* (pp. 1–23). Hillsdale, NJ: Erlbaum.

Rexrode, K., Carey, V., Hennekens, C., Walters, E., Colditz, G., Stampher, M., Willett, W., & Manson, J. (1997). A prospective study of body mass index, weight change, and risk of stroke in women. *Journal of the American Medical Association, 277,* 1539–1545.

Riccio, D. C., Rabinowitz, V. C., & Axelrod, S. (1994). Memory: When less is more. *American Psychologist, 49,* 917–926.

Rice, G., Anderson, C., Risch, N., & Ebers, G. (1999). Male homosexuality: Absence of linkage to microsatellite markers at Xq28. *Science, 284,* 665–667.

Richardson, J. (1993). The curious case of coins: Remembering the appearance of familiar objects. *The Psychologist: Bulletin of the British Psychological Society, 6,* 360–366.

Richardson, J. T. E., & Zucco, G. M. (1989). Cognition and olfaction: A review. *Psychological Bulletin, 105,* 352–360.

Richardson, J. T. E., Engle, R. W., Hasher, L., Logie, R. H., Stoltzfus, E. R., & Zacks, R. T. (Eds.). (1996). *Working memory and human cognition.* New York: Oxford University Press.

Rickman, R., Lodico, M., DiClemente, R., Morris, R., Baker, C., & Huscroft, S. (1994). Sexual communication is associated with condom use by sexually active incarcerated adolescents. *Journal of Adolescent Health, 15,* 383–388.

Rieves, L., & Cash, T. (1996). Social developmental factors and women's body-image attitudes. *Journal of Social Behavior and Personality, 11,* 63–78.

Riger, S. (1992). Epistomological debates, feminist voices: Science, social values, and the study of women. *American Psychologist, 47,* 730–740.

Riley, L. R. (1987). *Psychology of language development: A primer.* Toronto: C. J. Hogrefe.

Rimberg, H., & Lewis, R. (1994). Older adolescents and AIDS: Correlates of self-reported safer sex practices. *Journal of Research on Adolescence, 4,* 453–464.

Rimmelle, C. T., Howard, M. O., & Hilfrink, M. L. (1995). Aversion therapies. In R. K. Hester & W. R. Miller (Eds.), *Handbook of alcoholism treatment approaches: Effective alternatives* (2nd ed., pp. 134–147). Boston: Allyn & Bacon.

Roazen, P. (1975). *Freud and his followers.* New York: Knopf.

Roberts, B. W., & DelVecchio, W. F. (2000). The rank-order consistency of personality traits from childhood to old age: A quantitative review of longitudinal studies. *Psychological Bulletin, 126,* 3–25.

Roberts, J. V., & Herman, C. P. (1986). The psychology of height: An empirical review. In C. P. Herman, M. P. Zanna, & E. T. Higgins (Eds.), *Physical appearance, stigma, and social behavior: The Ontario symposium* (Vol. 3, pp. 113–140). Hillsdale, NJ: Erlbaum.

Roberts, R. E., Phinney, J. S., Masse, L. C., Chen, Y., Roberts, C. R., & Romero, A. (1999). The structure of ethnic identity of young adolescents from diverse ethno cultural groups. *Journal of Early Adolescence, 19,* 301–322.

Robins, R. W., Norem, J. K., & Cheek, J. M. (1999). Naturalizing the self. In L. A. Pervin & O. P. John (Eds.), *Handbook of personality: Theory and research* (pp. 443–477). New York: Guilford Press.

Robinson, E. L., & Nagel, R. J. (1992). The comparability of the test of cognitive skills with the Wechsler Intelligence Scale for Children-Revised and the Stanford-Binet: Fourth edition with gifted children. *Psychology in School, 29,* 107–112.

Robinson, T. (1999). Reducing children's television viewing to prevent obesity: A randomized controlled trial. *Journal of the American Medical Association, 282,* 1561–1567.

Robinson, T. N., Wilde, M. L., Navracruz, L. C., Haydel, K. F., & Varady, A. (2001). Effects of reducing children's television and video game use on aggressive behavior: A randomized controlled trial. *Archives of Pediatrics and Adolescent Medicine, 155,* 17–23.

Rochot, F., Maggioni, O., & Modigliani, A. (2000). The dynamics of obeying and opposing authority: A mathematical model. In T. Blass, (Ed.). *Obedience to authority: Current perspectives on the Milgram paradigm* (pp. 161–192). Mahwah, NJ: Erlbaum.

Rodin, J. (1981). Understanding obesity: Defining the samples. *Personality and Social Psychology Bulletin, 7,* 147–151.

Rodin, J. (1986). Aging and health: Effects of the sense of control. *Science, 233,* 1271–1276.

Rodin, J., & Wing, R. R. (1988). Behavioral factors in obesity. *Diabetes/Metabolism Reviews, 4,* 701–725.

Roediger, H. L., III (1990). Implicit memory: Retention without remembering. *American Psychologist, 45,* 1043–1056.

Roehling, M. V. (2000). Weight-based discrimination in employment: Psychological and legal aspects. *Personnel Psychology, 52,* 969–1016.

Roehrs, T., Papineau, K., Rosenthal, L., & Roth, T. (1999). Sleepiness and the reinforcing and subjective effects of methylphenidate. *Experimental and Clinical Psychopharmacology, 7,* 145–150.

Rogers, C. R. (1951). *Client-centered therapy: Its current practice, implications, and theory.* Boston: Houghton Mifflin.

Rogers, C. R. (1959). A theory of therapy, personality, and interpersonal relationships as developed in the client-centered framework. In S. Koch (Ed.), *Psychology: A study of a science* (Vol. 3, pp. 184–256). New York: McGraw-Hill.

Rogers, C. R. (1961). *On becoming a person.* Boston: Houghton Mifflin.

Rogers, L. (2001). *Sexing the brain.* London: Weidenfeld & Nicolson.

Rogers, R. G. (1995). Marriage, sex, and mortality. *Journal of Marriage and the Family, 57,* 515–526.

Rogers, T. B., Kuiper, N. A., & Kirker, W. S. (1977). Self-reference and the encoding of personal information. *Journal of Personality and Social Psychology, 35,* 677–688.

Rogoff, B. (1984). *Children's learning in the "zone of proximal development."* San Francisco: Jossey-Bass.

Rogoff, B. (1990). *Apprenticeship in thinking: Cognitive development in a social context.* New York: Oxford University Press.

Rolls, A., & Deco, G. (2002). *Computational neuroscience of vision.* London: Oxford University Press.

Rolls, B. (1986). Sensory-specific satiety. *Nutrition Reviews, 44,* 93–101.

Rolls, B., Rolls, E., Rowe, E., & Sweeney, K. (1981). Sensory specific satiety in man. *Physiology and Behavior, 27,* 137–142.

Rorschach, H. (1921). *Psychodiagnostics.* Bern: Bircher (Transl. Hans Huber Verlag, 1942).

Rosch, E. H. (1973). Natural categories. *Cognitive Psychology, 4,* 328–350.

Rosch, E. H. (1978). Principles of categorization. In E. Rosch & B. L. Lloyd (Eds.), *Cognition and categorization.* Hillsdale, NJ: Erlbaum.

Rose, R. J., & Ditto, W. B. (1983). A developmental-genetic analysis of common fears from early adolescence to early adulthood. *Child Development, 54,* 361–368.

Rosen, K. S., & Rothbaum, F. (1993). Quality of parental caregiving and security of attachment. *Developmental Psychology, 29,* 358–367.

Rosenberg, M. (1965). *Society and the adolescent self-image.* Princeton, NJ: Princeton University Press.

Rosenberg, M. (1979). *Conceiving the self.* New York: Basic Books.

Rosenberg, M. L., & Mercy, J. A. (1991). Assaultive violence. In M. L. Rosenberg & M. A. Fenley (Eds.), *Violence in America: A public health approach* (pp. 14–50). New York: Oxford University Press.

Rosenhan, D. L. (1970). The natural socialization of altruistic autonomy. In J. Macaulay & L. Berkowitz (Eds.), *Altruism and helping behavior.* New York: Academic Press.

Rosenhan, D. L. (1971). On being sane in insane places. *Science, 179,* 250–258.

Rosenman, R. H. (1993). Relationships of the Type A behavior pattern with coronary heart disease. In L. Goldberger & S. Breznitz (Eds.), *Handbook of stress: Theoretical and clinical aspects* (2nd ed.). New York: Free Press.

Rosenman, R. H., Brand, R. J., Jenkins, C. D., Freidman, M., Straus, R., & Wurm, M. (1975). Coronary heart disease on the Western collaborative group study: Final follow-up experience of 8 1/2 years. *Journal of the American Medical Association, 233,* 872–877.

Rosenthal, R. (1994). Science and ethics in conducting, analyzing, and reporting psychological research. *Psychological Science, 5,* 127–134.

Rosenthal, R. (1995). Ethical issues in psychological science: Risk, consent, and scientific quality. *Psychological Science, 6,* 322–323.

Rosenzweig, M. R. (1984). Experience, memory, and the brain. *American Psychologist, 47,* 718–722.

Rosenzweig, M. R., Breedlove, S. M., & Leiman, A. L. (2002). *Biological psychology: An introduction to behavioral, cognitive, and clinical neuroscience* (3rd ed.). Sunderland, MA: Sinauer Associates.

Ross, C. A. (1991). Epidemiology of multiple personality disorder and dissociation. *Psychiatric Clinics of North America, 14,* 503–516.

Ross, C. A., Norton, G. R., & Wozney, K. (1989). Multiple personality disorder: An analysis of 236 cases. *Canadian Journal of Psychiatry, 34,* 413–418.

Ross, H. E. (2000). Sensation and perception. In D. S. Gupta, & R. M. Gupta (Eds.), *Psychology for psychiatrists* (pp. 20–40). London: Whurr Publishers.

Ross, L. (1977). The intuitive psychologist and his shortcomings: Distortions in the attribution process. In L. Berkowitz (Ed.), *Advances in experimental social psychology* (Vol. 10, pp. 174–221). New York: Academic Press.

Ross, R., & Glomset, J. (1976). The pathogenesis of atherosclerosis. *New England Journal of Medicine, 295,* 369–377.

Rossini, P. M., & Pauri, F. (2000). Neuromagnetic integrated methods tracking human brain mechanisms of sensorimotor areas "plastic" reorganization. *Brain Research Reviews, 33,* 131–154.

Roszak, T. (1975). *The unfinished animal.* New York: Harper & Row.

Roth, G. (2001). The evolution of consciousness. In G. Roth (Ed.), *Brain evolution and cognition* (pp. 555–582). New York: John Wiley.

Rothbart, M. K. (1989). Biological process in temperament. In G. A. Kornstramm, J. Bates, & M. K. Rothbart (Eds.), *Handbook of temperament in childhood* (pp. 77–110). Sussex, England: Wiley.

Rothbaum, B. O., Hodges, L. F., Kooper, R., Opdyke, D., Williford, J., & North, M. M. (1995). Effectiveness of computer-generated (virtual reality) graded exposure in the treatment of acrophobia. *American Journal of Psychiatry, 152,* 626–628.

Rothkopf, J. S., & Blaney, P. H. (1991). Mood congruent memory: The role of affective focus and gender. *Cognition and Emotion, 5,* 53–64.

Rothstein, H. R., McDaniel, M. A., & Borenstein, M. (2002). Meta-analysis: A review of quantitative cumulation methods. In F. Drasgow & N. Schmitt (Eds.), *Measuring and analyzing behavior in organizations: Advances in measurement and data analysis. The Jossey-Bass business & management series.* San Francisco: Jossey-Bass.

Rotter, J. (1966). Generalized expectancies for internal versus external control of reinforcement. *Psychological Monographs, 80* (Whole No. 609).

Rotter, J. (1990). Internal versus external control of reinforcement: A case history of a variable. *American Psychologist, 45,* 489–493.

Rowatt, W. C., Cunningham, M. R., & Druen, P. B. (1998). Deception to get a date. *Personality and Social Psychology Bulletin, 24,* 1228–1242.

Rowe, D. C. (1997). Genetics, temperament, and personality. In R. Hogan, J. Johnson, & S. Briggs (Eds.), *Handbook of personality psychology* (pp. 267–286). San Diego, CA: Academic Press.

Rowe, J. W., & Kahn, R. L. (1998). *Successful aging.* New York: Pantheon Books.

Rowland, D. L., & Burnett, A. L. (2000). Pharmacotherapy in the treatment of male sexual dysfunction. *Journal of Sex Research, 37,* 226–243.

Roy-Byrne, P. P., & Cowley, D. S. (2002). Pharmacological treatments for panic disorder, generalized anxiety disorder, specific phobia, and social anxiety disorder. In P. E. Nathan, & J. M. Gorman (Eds.), *A guide to treatments that work* (2nd ed., pp. 337–365). London: Oxford University Press.

Rozin, P., Dow, S., Moscovitch, M., Rajaram, S. (1998). What causes humans to begin and end a meal? A role for memory for what has been eaten, as evidenced by a study of multiple meal eating in amnesic patients. *Psychological Science, 9,* 392–396.

Rubin, D. C., & Wallace, W. T. (1989). Rhyme and reason: Analyses of dual retrieval cues. *Journal of Experimental Psychology: Learning, Memory, and Cognition, 15,* 698–709.

Rubin, E. (1915/1958). Synoplevede Figurer (Figure and ground). In D. C. Beardslee & M. Wertheimer (Eds.), *Readings in perception* (pp. 194–203). Princeton, NJ: Von Nostrand.

Rucker, C. III, & Cash, T. (1992). Body images, body-size perceptions, and eating behaviors among African-American and White college women. *International Journal of Eating Disorders, 12,* 291–299.

Ruggerio, V. R. (1988). *Teaching thinking across the curriculum.* New York: Harper & Row.

Rumbaugh, D. M. (1990). Comparative psychology and the great apes: Their competency in learning, language, and numbers. *Psychological Record, 40,* 15–39.

Rumbaugh, D. M., & Savage-Rumbaugh, S. (1986). Reasoning and language in chimpanzees. In R. J. Hoage & L. Goldman (Eds.), *Animal intelligence.* Washington, DC: Smithsonian Institution Press.

Rushton, J. P. (1980). *Altruism, socialization, and society.* Englewood Cliffs, NJ: Prentice Hall.

Rushton, J. P. (1995). *Race, evolution, and behavior.* New Brunswick, NJ: Transaction.

Rushton, K. P., & Ankney, C. D. (1996). Brain size and cognitive ability: Correlations with age, sex, social class, and race. *Psychonomic Bulletin and Review, 3,* 21–36.

Russell, J. A., & Yik, S. M. (1996). Emotion among the Chinese. In M. H. Bond (Ed.), *The handbook of Chinese psychology.* Hong Kong, China: Oxford University Press.

Russell, J. D., & Roxanas, M. (1990). Psychiatry and the frontal lobes. *Australian & New Zealand Journal of Psychiatry, 24,* 113–132.

Russell, W. R. (1971). *The traumatic amnesics.* London: Oxford University Press.

Russo, P., Persegani, C. M., Papeschi, L. L., & Trimarchi, M. (2001). Sex differences in EEG correlates of a self-reported measure of hemisphere preference. *International Journal of Neuroscience, 106,* 109–121.

Rutman, E. M. (1990). Studies of attention development in ontogenesis. *Voprosy Psikhologii, 4,* 161–167.

Rutter, M. (2002). Nature, nurture, and development: From evangelism through science toward policy and practice. *Child Development, 73,* 1–21.

Ryan, R. M., & Deci, E. L. (2000). When rewards compete with nature: The undermining of intrinsic motivation and self-regulation. In C. Sansone & J. M. Harackiewicz (Eds.), *Intrinsic and extrinsic motivation: The search for optimal motivation and performance* (pp. 13–78). San Diego, CA: Academic Press.

Ryan, R. M., & Deci, E. L. (2001). On happiness and human potentials: A review of research on hedonic and eudaimonic well-being. *Annual Review of Psychology, 52,* 141–166.

Ryan, R. M., Chirkov, V. I., Little, T. D., Sheldon, K. M., Timoshina, E., & Deci, E. L. (1999). The American dream in Russia: Extrinsic aspirations in two cultures. *Personality and Social Psychology Bulletin, 25,* 1509–1524.

Rymer, R. (1993). *Genie: An abused child's flight from silence.* New York: HarperCollins.

Rzewnicki, R., & Forgays, D. (1987). Recidivism and self-cure of smoking and obesity: An attempt to replicate. *American Psychologist, 42,* 97–100.

S

Saarni, C. (1999). *The development of emotional competence.* New York: Guilford.

Sachs, J. (1989). Communication development in infancy. In J. Berko-Gleason (Ed.), *The development of language.* Columbus, OH: Merrill/Macmillan.

Sachs, J., Bard, B., & Johnson, M. L. (1981). Language learning with restricted input: Case studies of two hearing children of deaf parents. *Applied Psycholinguistics, 2,* 33–54.

Sackheim, H. A., Prudic, J., Devanand, D. P., Nobler, M. S., Lisanby, S. H., Peyser, S., Fitzsimons, L., Moody, B. J., & Clark, J. (2000). A prospective, randomized, double-blind comparison of bilateral and right unilateral electroconvulsive therapy at different stimulus intensities. *Archive of General Psychiatry, 57,* 425–434.

Sagi, A., Lamb, M. E., Lewkowicz, K. S., Shoman, R., Dvir, R., & Estes, D. (1985). Security of infant-mother, -father, and metapelet attachment among kibbutz-reared Israeli children. *Monographs of the Society for Research in Child Development, 50* (1–2, Serial No. 209).

Saks, E. R., Jeste, D. V., Granholm, E., Palmer, B. W., & Schneiderman, L. (2002). Ethical issues in psychosocial intrerventions research involving controls. *Ethics & Behavior, 12,* 87–101.

Salmon, P. (2001). Effects of physical exercise on anxiety, depression, and sensitivity to stress: A unifying theory. *Clinical Psychology Review, 21,* 33–61.

Salovey, P., & Mayer, J. (1994). Some final thoughts about personality and intelligence. In R. J. Sternberg & P. Ruzgis (Eds.), *Personality and intelligence* (pp. 303–318). New York: Cambridge University Press.

Salovey, P., & Rodin, J. (1988). Coping with envy and jealousy. *Journal of Social and Clinical Psychology, 7,* 15–33.

Sameroff, A., Seifer, R., Baldwin, A., & Baldwin, C. (1993). Stability of intelligence from preschool to adolescence: The influence of social and family risk factors. *Child Development, 64,* 80–97.

Sampson, E. E. (1991). *Social worlds, personal lives: An introduction to social psychology.* San Diego: Harcourt Brace Jovanovich.

Sandage, S. J., & Hill, P. C. (2001). The positive virtues of positive psychology: The rapproachment and challenges of an affirmative postmodern perspective. *Journal for the Theory of Social Behaviour, 31,* 241–260.

Sanders, G., Sjodin, M., & de Chastelaine, M. (2002). On the elusive nature of sex differences in cognition: Hormonal influences contributing to within-sex variation. *Archives of Sexual Behavior, 31,* 145–152.

Sandfort, T. G. M., de Graaf, R., Bijl, R. V., & Schnabel, P. (2001). Same-sex sexual behavior and psychiatric disorders. *Archives of General Psychiatry, 58,* 85–91.

Sansone, C., & Harackiewicz, J. M. (2000). Controversies and new directions—Is it déjà vu all over again? In C. Sansone & J. M. Harackiewicz (Eds.), *Intrinsic and extrinsic motivation: The search for optimal motivation and performance* (pp. 443–453). San Diego, CA: Academic Press.

Sappington, A. A. (1990). Recent psychological approaches to the free will versus determinism issue. *Psychological Bulletin, 108,* 19–29.

Sarason, I. (1984). Stress, anxiety, and cognitive interference: Reactions to tests. *Journal of Personality and Social Psychology, 46,* 929–938.

Sarason, I., Sarason, B., & Pierce, G. (1990). Anxiety, cognitive interference, and performance. *Journal of Social Behavior and Personality, 5,* 1–18.

Sarris, V., & Wertheimer, M. (2001). Max Wertheimer's research on aphasia and brain disorders: A brief account. *Gestalt Theory, 23,* 267–277.

Saudino, K. J., Plomin, R., Pedersen, N. L., & McClearn, G. E. (1994). The etiology of high and low cognitive ability during the second half of the life span. *Intelligence, 19,* 359–371.

Saufley, W. H., Otaka, S. R., & Bavaresco, J. L. (1985). Context effects: Classroom tests and context independence. *Memory & Cognition, 13,* 522–528.

Savage-Rumbaugh, S., Shanker, S. G., & Taylor, T. J. (1998). *Apes, language, and the human mind.* New York: Oxford University Press.

Scarr, S., & Weinberg, R. A. (1976). IQ test performance of black children adopted by white families. *American Psychologist, 31,* 726–739.

Scarr, S., & Weinberg, R. A. (1983). The Minnesota adoption studies: Genetic differences and malleability. *Child Development, 54,* 260–267.

Scarr, S., Pakstis, A. J., Katz, S. H., & Barker, W. B. (1977). The absence of a relationship between degree of white ancestry and intellectual skills within a black population. *Human Genetics, 39,* 69–86.

Schachter, S. (1959). *The psychology of affiliation: Experimental studies of the sources of gregariousness.* Stanford, CA: Stanford University Press.

Schachter, S. (1964). The interaction of cognitive and physiological determinants of emotional state. In L. Berkowitz (Ed.), *Advances in experimental social psychology* (Vol. 1, pp. 49–80). New York: Academic Press.

Schachter, S. (1966). The interaction of cognitive and physiological determinants of emotional state. In C. Spielberger (Ed.), *Anxiety and behavior.* New York: Academic Press.

Schachter, S., & Singer, J. (1962). Cognitive, social, and physiological determinants of emotional state. *Psychological Review, 69,* 379–399.

Schacter, D. L. (1992). Understanding implicit memory: A cognitive neuroscience approach. *American Psychologist, 47,* 559–569.

Schacter, D. L. (1996). *Searching for memory.* New York: Basic Books.

Schacter, D. L., & Badgaiyan, R. D. (2001). Neuroimaging of priming: New perspectives on implicit and explicit memory. *Current Directions in Psychological Science, 10,* 1–4.

Schacter, D. L., & Scarry, E. (Eds.). (2000). *Memory, brain, and belief.* Cambridge, MA: Harvard University Press.

Schacter, D. L., Chiu, C.-Y. P., & Ochsner, K. N. (1993). Implicit memory: A selective review. *Annual Review of Neuroscience, 16,* 159–182.

Schafer, D. W. (1996). *Relieving pain: A basic hypnotherapeutic approach.* Northvale, NJ: Jason Aronson.

Schafer, W. (Ed.). (1992). *Stress management for wellness* (2nd ed.). New York: Holt, Rinehart.

Schaller, M. (1997). Beyond "competing," beyond "compatible." *American Psychologist, 52,* 1379–1380.

Scharf, B. (1983). Loudness. In J. V. Tobias & E. D. Schubert (Eds.), *Hearing research and theory* (pp. 1–56). New York: Academic Press.

Scharff, C. (2000). Chasing fate and function of new neurons in adult brains. *Current Opinion in Neurobiology, 10,* 774–783.

Scharfstein, B.-A. (1973). *Mystical experience.* Indianapolis, IN: Bobbs-Merrill.

Schatzberg, A. F., & Nemeroff, C. B. (Eds.). (1995). *The American Psychiatric Press textbook of psychopharmacology.* Washington, DC: American Psychiatric Press.

Scheier, M., & Carver, C. (2000). Optimism, coping, and health: Assessment and implications of generalized outcome expectancies. *Health Psychology, 4,* 219–247.

Schenck, C. H., & Mahowald, M. W. (2002). REM sleep behavior disorder: Clinical, developmental, and neuroscience perspectives 16 years after its formal identification in sleep. *Sleep: Journal of Sleep & Sleep Disorders Research, 25,* 120–138.

Schiff, M., Duyme, M., Dumaret, A., Steward, J., Tomkiewicz, S., & Feingold, J. (1978). Intellectual status of working class children adopted early into upper middle-class families. *Science, 200,* 1503–1504.

Schiffman, S. S. (1997). Taste and smell losses in normal aging and problem disease. *Journal of the American Medical Association, 278,* 1357–1363.

Schlesinger, K. (1985). A brief introduction to a history of psychology. In G. A. Kimble & K. Schlesinger (Eds.), *Topics in the history of psychology* (Vol. 1, pp. 1–20). Hillsdale, NJ: Erlbaum.

Schluter, N. D., Krams, M., Rushworth, M. F. S., & Passingham, R. E. (2001). Cerebral dominance for action in the human brain: The selection of actions. *Neuropsychologia, 39,* 105–113.

Schmidt, L. A., & Fox, N. A. (2002). Molecular genetics of temperamental differences in children. In J. Benjamin, & R. P. Ebstein (Eds.), *Molecular genetics and the human personality* (pp. 245–255). Washington, DC: American Psychiatric Publishing.

Schmitter-Edgecombe, M., & Nissley, H. M. (2002). Effects of aging on implicit covariation learning. *Aging Neuropsychology & Cognition, 9,* 61–75.

Schmolck, H., Buffalo, E. A., & Squire, L. R. (2000). Memory distortions develop over time: Recollections from the O. J. Simpson trial verdict after 15 and 32 months. *Psychological Science, 11,* 39–45.

Schmuck, P., & Sheldon, K. M. (Eds.). (2001). *Life goals and well-being: Towards a positive psychology of human striving.* Kirkland, WA: Hogrefe & Huber.

Schmuck, P., Kasser, T., & Ryan, R. M. (2000). The relationship of well-being to intrinsic and extrinsic goals in Germany and the U.S. *Social Indicators Research, 50,* 225–241.

Schnaitter, R. (1987). American practicality and America's psychology [Review of *The origins of behaviorism: American psychology, 1870–1920*]. *Contemporary Psychology, 32,* 736–737.

Schneider, B. (1985). Organizational behavior. *Annual Review of Psychology, 36,* 573–611.

Schneider, D. J., Hastorf, A. H., & Ellsworth, P. C. (1979). *Person perception* (2nd ed.). Reading, MA: Addison-Wesley.

Schneider, F., Weiss, U., Kessler, C., Mueller-Gaertner, H.-W., Posse, S., Salloum, J. B., Grodd, W., Himmelmann, F., Gaebel, W., & Birbaumer, N. (1999). Subcortical correlates of differential classical conditioning of aversive emotional reactions in social phobia. *Biological Psychiatry, 45,* 863–871.

Schneider, M. L., Moore, C. F., Kraemer, G. W., Roberts, A. D., & DeJesus, O. T. (2002). The impact of prenatal stress, fetal alcohol exposure, or both on development: Perspectives from a primate model. *Psychoneuroendocrinology, 27,* 285–298.

Schooler, J. W., Gerhard, D., & Loftus, E. F. (1986). Qualities of the unreal. *Journal of Experimental Psychology: Learning, Memory, and Cognition, 12,* 171–181.

Schulz, R., & Alderman, D. (1974). Clinical research and the stages of dying. *Omega, 5,* 137–143.

Schulze, C., Karie, T., & Dickens, W. (1996). *Does the bell curve ring true?* Washington, DC: Brookings Institution.

Schuman, H. (1995). Attitudes, beliefs, and behavior. In K. S. Cook, G. A. Fine, & J. S. House (Eds.), *Sociological perspectives on social psychology* (pp. 68–89). Boston: Allyn & Bacon.

Schunk, D. H. (1996). *Learning theories* (2nd ed.). Englewood Cliffs, NJ: Merrill.

Schwartz, B., & Robbins, S. J. (1995). *Psychology of learning and behavior.* New York: W. W. Norton.

Schwartz, B. L. (2001). The relation of tip-of-the-tongue states and retrieval time. *Memory and Cognition, 29,* 117–126.

Schwartz, B. L. (2002). *Tip-of-the-tongue states: Phenomenology, mechanism, and lexical retrieval.* Mahwah, NJ: Erlbaum.

Schwartz, J. H. (1995). The neuron. In E. R. Kandel, J. H. Schwartz, & T. M. Jessell (Eds.), *Essentials of neural science and behavior.* Norwalk, CT: Appleton & Lange.

Schwartz, R. H. (1993). Chronic marihuana smoking and short-term memory impairment. In G. G. Nahas & C. Latour (Eds.), *Cannabis: Physiopathology, epidemiology, detection* (pp. 61–71). Boca Raton, FL: CRC Press.

Schwartz, S. & Maquet, P. (2002). Sleep imaging and the neuropsychological assessment of dreams. *Trends in Cognitive Sciences, 6,* 23–30.

Schwartz, S. H., & Howard, J. A. (1981). A normative decision-making model of altruism. In J. P. Rushton & R. M. Sorrentino (Eds.), *Altruism and helping behavior: Social, personality, and developmental perspectives* (pp. 189–211). Hillsdale, NJ: Erlbaum.

Schwartz, S. H., & Howard, J. A. (1982). Helping and cooperation: A self-based motivational model. In V. J. Derlega & J. Grzelak (Eds.), *Cooperation and helping behavior: Theories and research* (pp. 327–353). New York: Academic Press.

Schwarz, B. E. (1960). Ordeal by serpents, fire and strychnine: A study of some provocative psychosomatic phenomena. *Psychiatry Quarterly, 34,* 405–429.

Schwarz, N., Bless, H., Strack, F., Klumpp, G., Rittenauer-Schatka, & Simons, A. (1991). Ease of retrieval as information: Another look at the availability heuristic. *Journal of Personality and Social Psychology, 61,* 195–202.

Scott, A. J. (1994). Chronobiological considerations in shiftworker sleep and performance and shiftwork scheduling. *Human Performance, 7,* 207–233.

Scott, W. A., Scott, R., & McCabe, M. (1991). Family relationships and children's personality: A cross-cultural, cross-source comparison. *British Journal of Social Psychology, 30,* 1–20.

Sealey, A. (2000). *Childly language: Children, language and the social world.* Harlow, England: Pearson.

Searle, J. R. (1994). The problem of consciousness. In A. Revonsuo & M. Kamppinen (Eds.), *Consciousness in philosophy and cognitive neuroscience* (pp. 93–104). Hillsdale, NJ: Erlbaum.

Searle, J. R. (1995). Ontology is the question. In P. Baumgartner & S. Payr (Eds.), *Speaking minds: Interviews with twenty eminent cognitive scientists* (pp. 202–213). Princeton, NJ: Princeton University Press.

Searleman, A., & Herrmann, D. (1994) *Memory from a broader perspective.* New York: McGraw-Hill.

Sears, L. L., Finn, P.R., & Steinmetz, J. E. (1994). Abnormal classical eye-blink conditioning in autism. *Journal of Autism and Developmental Disorders, 24,* 737–751.

Sedgwick, J. (1995). Inside the Pioneer Fund. In R. Jacoby & N. Glauberman (Eds.), *The bell curve debate: History, documents, opinions* (pp. 144–161). New York: Random House.

Sedikides, C., & Strube, M. J. (1997). Self-evaluation: To thine own self be good, to thine own self be sure, to thine own self be true, and to thine own self be better. In M. P. Zanna (Ed.) *Advances in experimental social psychology* (Vol. 29, pp. 209–269). San Diego: Academic Press.

Seeman, P., Guan, H., & Hubert, H. (1993). Dopamine D4 receptors elevated in schizophrenia. *Nature, 365,* 441–445.

Segall, M. H., Campbell, D. T., & Herskovits, M. J. (1966). *The influence of culture on visual perception.* Indianapolis, IN: Bobbs-Merrill.

Segall, M. H., Dasen, P. R., Berry, J. W., & Poortinga, Y. H. (1990). *Human behavior in global perspective: An introduction to cross-cultural psychology.* New York: Pergamon.

Segerstrom, S., Taylor, S., Kemeny, M., & Fahey, J. (1998). Optimism is associated with mood, coping, and immune change in response to stress. *Journal of Personality and Social Psychology, 74,* 1646–1655.

Seifer, R., Schiller, M., Sameroff, A. J., Resnick, S., & Riordin, A. J. (1996). Attachment, maternal sensitivity, and infant temperament during the first year of life. *Developmental Psychology, 32,* 12–25.

Seipp, B. (1991). Anxiety and academic performance: A meta-analysis of findings. *Anxiety Research, 4,* 27–41.

Sekuler, R., & Blake, R. (1994). *Perception* (3rd ed.). New York: McGraw-Hill.

Seligman, M. E. P. (1970). On the generality of laws of learning. *Psychological Review, 77,* 406–418.

Seligman, M. E. P. (1971). Phobias and preparedness. *Behavior Therapy, 2,* 307–321.

Seligman, M. E. P. (1975). *Helplessness: On depression, development, and death.* San Francisco: Freeman.

Seligman, M. E. P. (1994). *What you can change and what you can't: The complete guide to successful self-improvement.* New York: Knopf.

Seligman, M. E. P. (1995). The effectiveness of psychotherapy: The *Consumer Reports* study. *American Psychologist, 50,* 965–974.

Seligman, M. E. P., & Maier, S. F. (1967). Failure to escape traumatic shock. *Journal of Experimental Psychology, 74,* 1–9.

Selkoe, D. J. (1992). Aging brain, aging mind. *Scientific American, 267,* 135–142.

Selye, H. (1936). A syndrome produced by nocuous agents. *Nature, 138,* 32.

Selye, H. (1956). *The stress of life.* New York: McGraw-Hill.

Senior, C., Ward, J., & David, A. S. (2002). Representational momentum and the brain: An investigation into the functional necessity of V5/MT. *Visual Cognition, 9,* 81–92.

Seppa, N. (1996, May). A multicultural guide to less spanking and yelling. *APA Monitor,* p. 37.

Serbin, L. A., & Sprafkin, C. (1986). The salience of gender and the process of sex typing in three- to seven-year-old children. *Child Development, 57,* 1188–1199.

Serpell, R. (2000). Intelligence and culture. In R. J. Sternberg (Ed.), *Handbook of intelligence* (pp. 549–577). Cambridge: Cambridge University Press.

Servan-Schreiber, E., & Anderson, J. R. (1990). Learning artificial grammars with competitive chunking. *Journal of Experimental Psychology: Learning, Memory, & Cognition, 16,* 592–608.

Seta, J. J., & Donaldson, S. (1999). Self-relevance as a moderator of self-enhancement and self-verification. *Journal of Research in Personality, 33,* 442–462.

Sevy, S., Mendlewicz, J., & Mendelbaum, K. (1995). Genetic research in bipolar illness. In E. E. Beckham & W. R. Leber (Eds.), *Handbook of depression* (2nd ed., pp. 203–212). New York: Guilford Press.

Seyfarth, R. M., & Cheney, D. L. (1992). Meaning and mind in monkeys (vocalizations and intent). *Scientific American, 267,* 122–128.

Shadish, W. R., Montgomery, L. M., Wilson, P., Wilson, M. R., Bright, I., & Okwumabua, T. (1993). Effects of family and marital psychotherapies: A meta-analysis. *Journal of Consulting and Clinical Psychology, 61,* 992–1002.

Shaffer, D., & Greenberg, T. (2002). Suicide and suicidal behavior in children and adolescents. In D. Shaffer & B. D. Waslick (Eds.), *The many faces of depression in children and adolescents. Review of psychiatry* (Vol. 21, no. 2., pp. 129–178). Washington, DC: American Psychiatric Association.

Shakow, D. (2002). Clinical psychology seen some 50 years later. In W. E. Pickren & D. A. Dewsbury (Eds.), *Evolving perspectives on the history of psychology* (pp. 433–451). Washington, DC: American Psychological Association.

Shalev, A., & Munitz, H. (1986). Conversion without hysteria: A case report and review of the literature. *British Journal of Psychiatry, 148,* 198–203.

Shanab, M. E., & Yahya, K. A. (1977). A behavioral study of obedience in children. *Journal of Personality and Social Psychology, 35,* 530–536.

Shanahan, T. L., Kronauer, R. E., Duffy, J. F., Williams, G. H., & Czeisler, C. A. (1999). Melatonin rhythm observed throughout a three-cycle bright-light stimulus designed to reset the human circadian pacemaker. *Journal of Biological Rhythms, 14,* 237–253.

Shapiro, D. H., Jr. (1987). Implications of psychotherapy research for the study of meditation. In M. A. West (Ed.), *The psychology of meditation.* Oxford: Clarendon Press.

Shapiro, S. L., Schwartz, G. E., & Bonner, G. (1998). Effects of mindfulness-based stress reduction on medical and premedical students. *Journal of Behavioral Medicine, 21,* 581–599.

Sharfstein, S. S. (2001). The President's Advisory Commision on Consumer Protection and Quality in the Health Care Industry. In B. Dickey & L. I. Sederer (Eds.), *Improving mental health care: Commitment to quality* (pp. 5–20). Washington, DC: American Psychiatric Publishing.

Sharp, S. E. (1898). Individual psychology: A study of psychological method. *American Journal of Psychology, 10,* 329–391.

Shaywitz, B. A., Shaywitz, S. E., Pugh, K. R., Constable, R. T., Skudlarski, P., Fulbright, R. K., Bronen, R. A., Fletcher, J. M., Shankweiler, D. P., Katz, L., & Gore, J. C. (1995). Sex differences in the functional organization of the brain for language. *Nature, 373,* 607–609.

Sheikh, A. A. (Ed.). (2002). *Handbook of therapeutic imagery, techniques. Imagery and human development series* (pp. 351–353). Amityville, NY: Baywood Publishing.

Shekim, W. O., Bylund, D. B., Frankel, F., Alexson, J., Jones, S. B., Blue, L. D., Kirby, J., & Corchoran, C. (1989). Platelet MAO activity and personality variations in normals. *Psychiatry Research, 27,* 81–88.

Sheldon, K. M., & King, L. (2001). Why positive psychology is necessary? *American Psychologist, 56,* 216–217.

Shepperd, J. A., Ouellette, J. A., & Fernandez, J. K. (1996). Abandoning unrealistic optimism: Performance estimates and the temporal proximity of self-relevant feedback. *Journal of Personality and Social Psychology, 70,* 844–855.

Sher, L. (2002a). Genetics of seasonal affective disorder. *Lancet, 359,* 803–804.

Sher, L., (2002b). Suicidal behaviour and seasonality. *Nordic Journal of Psychiatry, 56,* 67.

Sherman, S. J., Presson, C. C., Chassin, L., Corty, E., & Olshavsky, R. (1983). The false consensus effect in estimates of smoking prevalence: Underlying mechanisms. *Personality and Social Psychology Bulletin, 9,* 197–208.

Shestowsky, D., Wegener, D. T., & Fabrigar, L. R. (1998). Need for cognition and interpersonal influence: Individual differences in impact on dyadic decisions. *Journal of Personality and Social Psychology, 74,* 1317–1328.

Shields, S. A. (1987). Women, men, and the dilemma of emotion. In P. R. Shaver & C. Hendrick (Eds.), *Sex and gender (Review of Personality and Social Psychology, 7,* 229–250). Beverly Hills, CA: Sage.

Shields, S. A. (1995). The role of emotion beliefs and values in gender development. In N. Eisenberg (Ed.), *Review of personality and social psychology, Vol. 15* (pp. 212–232). Thousand Oaks, CA: Sage.

Shneidman, E. (1992). *Death: Current perspectives* (3rd ed.). Mountain View, CA: Mayfield.

Shumaker, S. A., & Hill, D. R. (1991). Gender differences in social support and physical health. *Health Psychology, 10,* 102–111.

Shweder, R. A. (1984). Preview: A colloquy of culture theorists. In R. A. Shweder & R. A. LeVine (Eds.), *Cultural theory: Essays on minds, self, and emotion* (pp. 1–24). Cambridge, England: Cambridge University Press.

Shweder, R. A., Mahapatra, M., & Miller, J. G. (1990). Culture and moral development. In J. W. Stigler, R. A. Shweder, & G. Herdt (Eds.), *Cultural psychology* (pp. 130–204). New York: Cambridge University Press.

Sicotte, N. L., Woods, R. P., & Mazziotta, J. C. (1999). Handedness in twins: A meta-analysis. *Laterality, 4,* 265–286.

Siegel, J. M. (1990). Stressful life events and use of physician services among the elderly: The moderating role of pet ownership. *Journal of Personality and Social Psychology, 58,* 1081–1086.

Siegel, S. (1984). Pavlovian conditioning and heroin overdose: Reports by overdose victims. *Bulletin of the Psychonomic Society, 22,* 428–430.

Siegel, S., Hinson, R. E., Krank, M. D., & McCully, J. (1982). Heroin "overdose" death: The contribution of drug-associated environmental cues. *Science, 216,* 436–437.

Siegler, R. S. (1996). *Emerging minds: The process of change in children's thinking.* New York: Oxford University Press.

Siegler, R. S. (1998). *Children's thinking* (3rd ed.). Upper Saddle River, NJ: Prentice-Hall.

Siegler, R. S., & Ellis, S. (1996). Piaget on childhood. *Psychological Science, 7,* 211–215.

Siegman, A., Anderson, R., Herbst, J., Boyle, S., & Wilkinson, J. (1992). Dimensions of anger-hostility and cardiovascular reactivity in provoked and angered men. *Journal of Behavioral Medicine, 15,* 257–272.

Sigelman, L., & Tuch, S. A. (1997). Metastereotypes: Blacks' perceptions of whites' stereotypes of blacks. *Public Opinion Quarterly, 61,* 87–101.

Sigvardsson, S., von Knorring, A. L., Bohman, M., & Cloninger, C. R. (1984). An adoption study of somatoform disorders I. The relationship of somaticization to psychiatric disability. *Archives of General Psychiatry, 41,* 853–859.

Silva, C. E., & Kirsch, I. (1992). Interpretive sets, expectancy, fantasy proneness, and dissociation as predictors of hypnotic response. *Journal of Personality and Social Psychology, 63,* 847–856.

Silverman, J., Raj, A., Mucci, L., & Hathaway, J. (2001). Dating violence against adolescent girls and associated substance use, unhealthy weight control, sexual risk behavior, pregnancy, and suicide. *Journal of the American Medical Association, 286,* 572–579.

Silverstein, L. B. (1996). Fathering is a feminist issue. *Psychology of Women Quarterly, 20,* 3–37.

Simcock, G., & Hayne, H. (2002). Breaking the barrier? Children fail to translate their preverbal memories into language. *Psychological Science, 13,* 225–231.

Simkins, L. (1995). Risk of HIV transmission in sexual behaviors of college students. *Psychological Reports, 76,* 787–799.

Simmons, R. G., Blyth, D. A., Van Cleave, E. F., & Bush, D. M. (1979). Entry into adolescence: The impact of school structure, puberty, and early dating on self-esteem. *American Sociological Review, 44,* 948–967.

Simon, H. A. (1957). *Models of man.* New York: Wiley.

Simon, H. B. (1991). Exercise and human immune function. In R. Ader, D. E. Felton, & N. Cohen (Eds.), *Psychoneuroimmunology* (2nd ed., pp. 869–895). New York: Academic Press.

Simons, R. C., & Hughes, C. C. (1993). Culture-bound syndromes. In A. C. Gaw (Ed.), *Culture, ethnicity, and mental illness* (pp. 75–99). Washington, DC: American Psychological Association.

Simonton, D. K. (1992). The social context of career success and course for 2,026 scientists and inventors. *Personality and Social Psychology Bulletin, 18,* 452–463.

Simonton, D. K. (2000a). Creativity: Cognitive, personal, developmental, and social aspects. *American Psychologist, 55,* 151–158.

Simonton, D. K. (2000b). Creative development as acquired expertise: Theoretical issues and an empirical test. *Developmental Review, 20,* 283–318.

Sims, E. (1974). Studies in human hyperphagia. In G. Bray & J. Bethune (Eds.), *Treatment and management of obesity.* New York: Harper & Row.

Sims, E., & Horton, E. (1968). Endocrine and metabolic adaptation to obesity and starvation. *American Journal of Clinical Nutrition, 21,* 1455–1470.

Singelis, T., Choo, P., & Hatfield, E. (1996). Love schemas and romantic love. *Journal of Social Behavior and Personality, 10,* 15–36.

Singelis, T. M., Triandis, H. C., Bhawuk, D. S., & Gelfand, M. (1995). Horizontal and vertical dimensions of individualism and collectivism: A theoretical and measurement refinement. *Cross-Cultural Research, 29,* 240–275.

Singer, J. A., & Salovey, P. (1988). Mood and memory: Evaluating the network theory of affect. *Clinical Psychology Review, 8,* 211–251.

Singhal, R., & Misra, G. (1994). Achievement goals: A situational-contextual analysis. *International Journal of Intercultural Relations, 18,* 239–258.

Skinner, B. F. (1938). *The behavior of organisms.* New York: Appleton-Century-Crofts.

Skinner, B. F. (1948a). *Walden two.* New York: Macmillan.

Skinner, B. F. (1948b). "Superstition" in the pigeon. *Journal of Experimental Psychology, 38,* 168–172.

Skinner, B. F. (1957). *Verbal behavior.* New York: Appleton-Century-Crofts.

Skinner, B. F. (1979). *The shaping of a behaviorist.* New York: Knopf.

Skinner, B. F. (1990). Can psychology be a science of the mind? *American Psychologist, 45,* 1206–1210.

Skokal, M. M. (2002). Origins and early years of the American Psychological Association. In W. E. Pickren, & D. A. Dewsbury (Eds.), *Evolving perspectives on the history of psychology* (pp. 141–167). Washington, DC: American Psychological Association.

Slade, L. A., & Rush, M. C. (1991). Achievement motivation and the dynamics of task difficulty choices. *Journal of Personality and Social Psychology, 60,* 165–172.

Slaughter, M. (1990). The vertebrate retina. In K. N. Leibovic (Ed.), *Science of vision.* New York: Springer-Verlag.

Slavney, P. R. (1990). *Perspectives on hysteria.* Baltimore: Johns Hopkins University Press.

Slay, H., Hayaki, J., Napolitano, M., & Brownell, K. (1998). Motivations for running and eating attitudes in obligatory versus nonobligatory runners. *International Journal of Eating Disorders, 23,* 267–275.

Slife, B. D., & Fisher, A. M. (2000). Modern and postmodern approaches to the free will/determinism dilemma in psychotherapy. *Journal of Humanistic Psychology, 40,* 80–107.

Slobin, D. I. (1985). *A cross linguistic study of language acquisition.* Hillsdale, NJ: Erlbaum.

Smith, C. T. (1985). Sleep states and learning: A review of the animal literature. *Neuroscience & Biobehavioral Reviews, 9,* 157–168.

Smith, C. T. (1995). Sleep states and memory processes. *Behavioural Brain Research, 69,* 137–145.

Smith, C. T., & Lapp, L. (1986). Prolonged increase in both PS and number of REMS following a shuttle avoidance task. *Physiology & Behavior, 36,* 1053–1057.

Smith, D. (1982). Trends in counseling and psychotherapy. *American Psychologist, 37,* 802–809.

Smith, D. V. (1985). Brainstem processing of gustatory information. In D. W. Pfaff (Ed.), *Taste, olfaction, and the central nervous system* (pp. 151–177). New York: Rockefeller University Press.

Smith, E. J., Partridge, J. C., Parsons, K. N., White, E. M., Cuthill, I. C., Bennett, A. T. D., & Chjurch, S. C. (2002). Ulraviolet vision and mate choice in the guppy (Poecilia reticulata). *Behavioral Ecology, 13,* 1–19.

Smith, J. M., & Szathmáry, E. (1995). *The major transitions in evolution.* Oxford, England: Freeman.

Smith, L., Totterdell, P., & Folkard, S. (1995). Shiftwork effects in nuclear power workers: A field study using portable computers. *Work & Stress, 9,* 235–244.

Smith, L. D. (2002). On prediction and control: B. F. Skinner and the technological ideal of science. In W. E. Pickren, & D. A. Dewsbury (Eds.), *Evolving perspectives on the history of psychology* (pp. 255–272). Washington, DC: American Psychological Association.

Smith, M. L., & Glass, G. V. (1977). Meta-analysis of psychotherapy outcome studies. *American Psychologist, 32,* 752–760.

Smith, P., & Bond, M. (1994). *Social psychology across cultures.* Boston: Allyn & Bacon.

Smith, R. A. (2002). *Challenging your preconceptions: Thinking critically about psychology* (2nd ed.). Belmont, CA: Wadsworth/Thomson Learning.

Smith, S. M., & Petty, R. E. (1992). Personality moderators of mood congruency effects on cognitions: The role of self-esteem and negative mood regulation. *Journal of Personality and Social Psychology, 68,* 1092–1107.

Smith, S. M., Glenberg, A. M., & Bjork, R. A. (1978). Environmental context and human memory. *Memory & Cognition, 6,* 342–355.

Smith, S. S., & Richardson, D. (1983). Amelioration of deception and harm in psychological research: The important role of debriefing. *Journal of Personality and Social Psychology, 44,* 1075–1082.

Smith, T. (1992). Hostility and health: Current status of a psychosomatic hypothesis. *Health Psychology, 11,* 139–150.

Smith, T. L. (1994). *Behavior and its causes: Philosophical foundations of operant psychology.* Dordrecht, The Netherlands: Kluwer Academic Publishers.

Smolensky, P. (1995). On the proper treatment of connectionism: In C. Macdonald, & G. Macdonald (Eds.), *Connectionism: Debates on psychological explanation.* Cambridge, USA: Blackwell.

Smyth, J. M. (1998). Written emotional expression: Effect sizes, outcome types, and moderating variables. *Journal of Consulting and Clinical Psychology, 66,* 174–184.

Snarey, J. R. (1985). Cross-cultural universality of social-moral development: A critical review of Kohlbergian research. *Psychological Bulletin, 97,* 202–233.

Sno, H. N. (2000). Deja vu and jamais vu. In G. E. Berrios & J. R. Hodges (Eds.), *Memory disorders in psychiatric practice* (pp. 338–347). New York: Cambridge University Press.

Snow, C. E. (1999). Social perspectives on the emergence of language. In B. MacWhinney (Ed.), *The emergence of language* (pp. 257–276). Mahwah, NJ: Erlbaum.

Snowden, L. R., & Hu, T. W. (1996). Outpatient service use in minority-serving mental health programs. *Administration and Policy in Mental Health, 24,* 149–159.

Snyder, C. R. (2000). The past and possible futures of hope. *Journal of Social and Clinical Psychology, 19,* 11–28.

Snyder, M. (1974). The self-monitoring of expressive behavior. *Journal of Personality and Social Psychology, 30,* 526–537.

Snyder, M. (1987). *Public appearances/private realities: The psychology of self-monitoring.* New York: Freeman.

Snyder, M., & Copeland, J. (1989). Self-monitoring processes in organizational settings. In R. A. Giacalone & P. Rosenfeld (Eds.), *Impression management in the organization* (pp. 7–19). Hillsdale, NJ: Erlbaum.

Snyder, M., & Gangestad, S. (1982). Choosing social situations: Two investigations of self-monitoring processes. *Journal of Personality and Social Psychology, 43,* 123–135.

Snyder, M., & Simpson, J. A. (1984). Self-monitoring and dating relationships. *Journal of Personality and Social Psychology, 47,* 1281–1291.

Snyder, M., & Swann, W. B. (1978). Hypothesis-testing processes in social interaction. *Journal of Personality and Social Psychology, 36,* 1202–1212.

Solanto, M. V. (2002). Dopamine dysfunction in AD/HD: Integrating clinical and basic neuroscience research. *Behavioural Brain Research, 130,* 65–71.

Solomon, R. L. (1980). The opponent-process theory of acquired motivation: The costs of pleasure and the benefits of pain. *American Psychologist, 35,* 691–712.

Solomon, R. L., & Corbit, J. D. (1974). An opponent-process theory of motivation: I. Temporal dynamics of affect. *Psychological Review, 81,* 119–145.

Sommers, S. R., & Kassin, S. M. (2001). On the many impacts of inadmissible testimony: Selective compliance, need for cognition, and the overcorrection bias. *Personality and Social Psychology Bulletin, 27,* 1368–1377.

Sonnert, G., & Holton, G. (1995). *Gender differences in science careers: The Project Access Study.* New Brunswick, NJ: Rutger University Press.

Sorokin, A. A., Maksimov, A. L., & Jermain, J. (2000). Human circadian rhythm synchronization by social timers: The role of motivation: IV. Individual features of the free-running 24-hour sleep-wake cycle under simulated conditions of vital activity. *Human Physiology, 26,* 41–47.

Sorrentino, R., & Hewitt, E. (1984). The uncertainty-reducing properties of achievement tasks revisited. *Journal of Personality and Social Psychology, 47,* 884–899.

Spangler, W. D. (1992). Validity of questionnaire and TAT measures of need for achievement: Two meta-analyses.

Spanos, N. P. (1986). Hypnosis and the modification of hypnotic susceptibility: A social psychological perspective. In P. L. N. Naish (Ed.), *What is hypnosis? Current theories and research* (pp. 85–120). Philadelphia: Open University Press.

Spanos, N. P., & Chaves, J. F. (1989). The cognitive-behavioral alternative to hypnosis research. In N. P. Spanos & J. F. Chaves (Eds.), *Hypnosis: The cognitive-behavioral perspective* (pp. 9–16). Buffalo, NY: Prometheus Books.

Spanos, N. P., & Coe, W. C. (1992). A social-psychological approach to hypnosis. In E. Fromm & M. R. Nash (Eds.), *Contemporary hypnosis research* (pp. 102–130). New York: Guilford Press.

Spanos, N. P., Flynn, D. M., & Niles, J. (1989–1990). Rapport and cognitive skill training in the enhancement of hypnotizability. *Imagination, Cognition, and Personality, 9,* 245–262.

Spear, N. E. (1979). Experimental analysis of infantile amnesia. In J. F. Kihlstrom & F. J. Evans (Eds.), *Functional disorders of memory* (pp. 75–102). Hillsdale, NJ: Erlbaum.

Spearman, C. E. (1927). *The abilities of man.* London: Macmillan.

Speier, P. L., Sherak, D. L., Hirsch, S., & Cantwell, D. P. (1995). Depression in children and adolescents. In E. E. Beckham & W. R. Leber (Eds.), *Handbook of depression* (2nd ed., pp. 467–493). New York: Guilford Press.

Spelke, E. S., Breinlinger, K., Macomber, J., & Jacobson, K. (1992). Origins of knowledge. *Psychological Review, 99,* 605–632.

Spence, C., Shore, D. I., Gazzaniga, M. S., Soto-Faraco, S., & Kingstone, A. (2001). Failure to remap visuotactile space across the midline in the split-brain. *Canadian Journal of Experimental Psychology, 55,* 133–140.

Spencer, S. J., Steele, C. M., & Quinn, D. M. (1999). Stereotype threat and women's math performance. *Journal of Experimental Social Psychology, 35,* 4–28.

Sperling, G. (1960). The information available in brief visual presentation. *Psychological Monographs: General and Applied, 74,* 1–29.

Sperry, R. W. (1964). The great cerebral commissure. *Scientific American, 210,* 42–52.

Sperry, R. W. (1968). Hemisphere deconnection and unity in conscious experience. *American Psychologist, 23,* 723–733.

Spiegel, D. (1999). Healing words. Emotional expression and disease outcome. *Journal of the American Medical Association, 281,* 1328–1329.

Spielman, A., & Herrera, C. (1991). Sleep disorders. In S. J. Ellman & J. S. Antrobus (Eds.), *The mind in sleep: Psychology and psychopathology* (2nd ed., pp. 437–447). New York: Wiley.

Spitzer, R. L., Forman, J. B. W., & Nee, J. (1979). DSM-III field trials: II. Initial experience with the multiaxial system. *American Journal of Psychiatry, 136,* 815–817.

Sprecher, S. (1999). "I love you more today than yesterday": Romantic partners' perceptions of changes in love and related affect over time. *Journal of Personality and Social Psychology, 76,* 46–53.

Sprecher, S., Metts, S., Burleson, B., Hatfield, E., & Thompson, A. (1995). Domains of expressive interaction in intimate relationships: Associations with satisfaction and commitment. *Family Relations, 44,* 1–8.

Springer, S. P., & Deutsch, G. (1998). *Left brain, right brain: Perspectives from cognitive neuroscience* (5th ed.). New York: W. H. Freeman.

Squire, L. R. (1992). Memory and the hippocampus: A synthesis from findings with rats, monkeys, and humans. *Psychological Review, 99,* 195–231.

Squire, L. R., & Kandel, E. R. (1999). *Memory: From mind to molecules.* New York: Scientific American Library.

Squire, L. R., & Knowlton, B. J. (1995). Memory, hippocampus, and brain systems. In M. S. Gazzaniga (Ed.), *The cognitive neurosciences.* Cambridge, MA: MIT Press.

Staats, A. W., & Staats, C. K. (1958). Attitudes established by classical conditioning. *Journal of Abnormal and Social Psychology, 57,* 37–40.

Staddon, J. E. R., & Simmelhag, V. L. (1971). The "superstition" experiment: A reexamination of its implications for the principles of adaptive behavior. *Psychological Review, 78,* 3–43.

Stamps, A. E., III. (2002). Meta-analysis. In R. B. Bechtel & A. Churchman (Eds.), *Handbook of environmental psychology* (pp. 222–232). New York: John Wiley & Sons.

Stanley, B., Kyrkouli, S., Lampert, S., & Leibowitz, S. (1986). Neuropeptide Y chronically injected in the hypothalamus: A powerful neurochemical inducer of hyperphagia and obesity. *Peptides, 7,* 1189–1192.

Stanley, J. (1993). Boys and girls who reason well mathematically. In G. R. Bock & K. Ackrill (Eds.), *The origins and development of high ability.* Chichester, England: Wiley.

Stanovich, K. (1996). *How to think straight about psychology.* New York: HarperCollins.

Stark, R. (1965). A taxonomy of religious experience. *Journal for the Scientific Study of Religion, 3,* 3–21.

Statistics Canada. (1999). *Statistical report.*

Stebbins, W. C. (1980). The evolution of hearing in the mammals. In A. N. Popper & R. R. Fay (Eds.), *Comparative studies of hearing in vertebrates* (pp. 421–436). New York: Springer-Verlag.

Steele, C. M. (1992). Race and the schooling of Black Americans. *The Atlantic Monthly,* April, 68–78.

Steele, C. M. (1997). A threat in the air: How stereotypes shape intellectual identity and performance. *American Psychologist, 52,* 613–629.

Steele, C. M., & Aronson, J. (1995). Stereotype threat and the intellectual test performance of African Americans. *Journal of Personality and Social Psychology, 69,* 797–811.

Steele, C., & Josephs, R. (1990). Alcohol myopia: Its prized and dangerous effects. *American Psychologist, 45,* 921–933.

Steele, C. M., & Josephs, R. A. (1988). Drinking your troubles away. I: The psychology of drunken excess. *Journal of Personality and Social Psychology, 48,* 18–34.

Steil, J. M. (1994). Equality and entitlement in marriage. In M. J. Lerner & G. Mikula (Eds.), *Entitlement and the affectional bond: Justice in close relationships* (pp. 229–258). New York: Plenum Press.

Stein, D. G., Brailowsky, S., & Will, B. (1995). *Brain repair.* New York: Oxford University Press.

Steinberg, L. (1999). *Adolescence* (5th ed.). New York: McGraw-Hill.

Steinberg, L., Dornbusch, S. M., & Brown, B. B. (1992). Ethnic differences in adolescent achievement: An ecological perspective. *American Psychologist, 47,* 723–729.

Steiner, J. E. (1979). Human facial expressions in response to taste and smell stimulation. In H. E. Reese & L. Lipsitt (Eds.), *Advances in child development and behavior* (Vol. 13). New York: Academic Press.

Steinmetz, J. E. (1999). A renewed interest in human classical eyeblink conditioning. *Psychological Science, 10,* 24–25.

Steketee, G. S. (1993). *Treatment of obsessive-compulsive disorder.* New York: Guilford.

Stellar, E. (1954). The physiology of motivation. *Psychological Review, 61,* 5–22.

Stemberger, R. T., Turner, S. M., Beidel, D. C., & Calhoun, K. S. (1995). Social phobia: An analysis of possible developmental factors. *Journal of Abnormal Psychology, 104,* 526–531.

Stephan, W., Stephan, C., & de Vargas, M. (1996). Emotional expression in Costa Rica and the United States. *Journal of Cross-Cultural Psychology, 27,* 147–160.

Steriade, M., Ropert, N., Kitsikis, A., & Oakson, G. (1980). Ascending activating neuronal networks in midbrain reticular core and related rostral systems. In S. A. Hobson & A. M. Brazier (Eds.), *The reticular formation revisited: Specifying function for a nonspecific system.* New York: Raven.

Stern, D. (1985). *The interpersonal world of the infant: A view from psychoanalysis and developmental psychology.* New York: Basic Books.

Stern, W. (1914). *The psychological methods of testing intelligence.* Baltimore: Warwick & York.

Sternbach, H. (1998). Age-associated testosterone decline in men: Clinical issues for psychiatry. *American Journal of Psychiatry, 155,* 1310–1318.

Sternbach, R. A. (1963). Congenital insensitivity to pain: A review. *Psychological Bulletin, 60,* 252–264.

Sternberg, R. J. (1985). *Beyond IQ: A triarchic theory of human intelligence.* New York: Cambridge University Press.

Sternberg, R. J. (1996). *Successful intelligence: How practical and creative intelligence determine success in life.* New York: Penguin Books.

Sternberg, R. J. (1997a). The concept of intelligence and its role in lifelong learning and success. *American Psychologist, 52,* 1030–1037.

Sternberg, R. J. (1997b). The triarchic theory of intelligence. In D. P. Flanagan, J. L. Genshaft, & P. L. Harrison (Eds.), *Contemporary intellectual assessment: Theories, tests, and issues* (pp. 92–104). New York: Guilford Press.

Sternberg, R. J., & Davidson, J. E. (1999). Insight. In M. A. Runco & S. R. Pritzker (Eds.), *Encyclopedia of creativity* (Vol. 2). San Diego: Academic Press.

Sternberg, R. J., & Kaufman, J. C. (Eds.). (2002). *The evolution of intelligence.* Mahwah, NJ: Erlbaum.

Sternberg, R. J., & Lubart, T. I. (1995). *Defying the crowd: Cultivating creativity in a culture of conformity.* New York: The Free Press.

Sternberg, R. J., & Lubart, T. I. (1996). Investing in creativity. *American Psychologist, 51,* 677–688.

Sternberg, R. J., & O'Hara, L. A. (2000). Intelligence and creativity. In R. J. Sternberg (Ed.), *Handbook of intelligence* (pp. 611–630). Cambridge: Cambridge University Press.

Sternberg, R. J., Wagner, R. K., Williams, W. M., & Horvath, J. A. (1995). Testing common sense. *American Psychologist, 50,* 913–927.

Stevens, J. C. (1989). Food quality reports from noninstitutionalized aged. *Annals of the New York Academy of Sciences, 561,* 87–93.

Stevens, S. S. (1955). The measurement of loudness. *Journal of the Acoustical Society of America, 27,* 815–819.

Stevenson, H. W., Chen, C., & Lee, S. (1993). Mathematics achievement of Chinese, Japanese, and American children: Ten years later. *Science, 259,* 53–58.

Stevenson, H. W., Lee, S., & Stigler, J. W. (1986). Mathematics achievement of Chinese, Japanese, and American children. *Science, 231,* 693–699.

Stewart, K. T., Hayes, B. C., & Eastman, C. I. (1995). Light treatment for NASA shiftworkers. *Chronobiology International, 12,* 141–151.

Stone, M. H. (2002). Treatment of personality disorders from the perspective of the five-factor model. In P. T. Costa, Jr., & T. A. Widiger (Eds.), *Personality disorders and the five-factor model of personality* (2nd ed., pp. 405–430). Washington, DC: American Psychological Association.

Storms, M. D. (1983). *Development of sexual orientation.* Washington, DC: Office of Social and Ethical Responsibility, American Psychological Association.

Strausfeld, N. J. (2001). Insect brain. In G. Roth & M. F. Wullimann (Eds.), *Brain evolution and cognition* (pp. 367–400). New York: Wiley.

Street, L. L., & Luoma, J. B. (2002). Control groups in psychosocial intervention research: Ethical and methodological issues. *Ethics & Behavior, 12,* 1–30.

Streissguth, A. P., Bookstein, F. L., Sampson, P. D., & Barr, H. M. (1993). *The enduring effects of prenatal alcohol exposure on child development: Birth through seven years, a partial least squares solution.* Ann Arbor: University of Michigan.

Stricker, G. (1996). Empirically validated treatment, psychotherapy manuals, and psychotherapy integration. *Journal of Psychotherapy Integration, 6,* 217–226.

Strigini, P., Sansone, R., Carobbi, S., & Pierluigi, M. (1990). Radiation and Down's syndrome. *Nature, 347,* 717.

Strobel, A., Issad, T., Camoin, L., Ozata, M., & Strosberg, A. (1998). A leptin missense mutation associated with hypogonadism and morbid obesity. *Natural Genetics, 18,* 213–215.

Strober, M. (1992). Family-genetic studies. In K. Halmi (Ed.), *Psychobiology and treatment of anorexia nervosa and bulimia nervosa* (pp. 61–76). Washington, DC: American Psychiatric Press.

Stunkard, A. J., Harris, J. R., Pedersen, N. L., & McClearn, G. E. (1990). The body-mass index of twins who have been reared apart. *New England Journal of Medicine, 322,* 1483–1487.

Subotnik, R. F., Karp, D. E., & Morgan, E. R. (1989). High IQ children at midlife: An investigation into the generalizability of Terman's genetic studies of genius. *Roeper Review, 11,* 139–144.

Suddath, R. L., Christison, G. W., Torrey, E. F., Casanova, M. F., & Weinberger, D. R. (1990). Anatomical abnormalities in the brains of monozygotic twins discordant for schizophrenia. *The New England Journal of Medicine, 322,* 789–794.

Sue, S. (1991). Ethnicity and culture in psychological research and practice. In J. D. Goodchilds (Ed.), *Psychological perspectives on human diversity.* Washington, DC: American Psychological Association.

Suler, J. (August 1, 2001). The future of online psychotherapy and clinical work. In *The psychology of cyberspace.* www.rider.edu/users.suler/psycyber/psycyber.html

Super, C. W. (1981). Behavioral development in infancy. In R. H. Munroe, R. L. Munroe, & B. B. Whiting (Eds.), *Handbook of cross-cultural human development* (pp. 181–269). Chicago: Garland.

Surgeon General. (1999). *Mental health: A report of the Surgeon General.* Rockville, MD: U.S. Department of Health and Human Services.

Susan, T. A. (1990). How to handle the process litigation effectively under the Education for All Handicapped Children Act of 1975. *Journal of Reading, Writing, and Learning Disabilities International, 6,* 63–70.

Sutton, S. K., & Davidson, R. J. (1997). Prefrontal brain symmetry: A biological substrate of the behavioral approach and inhibition systems. *Psychological Science, 8,* 204–210.

Swann, W. B., Jr. (1997). The trouble with change: Self-verification and allegiance to the self. *Psychological Science, 8,* 177–183.

Swayze, V. W. (1995). Frontal leucotomy and related psychosurgical procedures in the era before antipsychotics (1935–1954): A historical overview. *American Journal of Psychiatry, 152,* 505–515.

Swerdlow, J. L. (1995). Quiet miracles of the brain. *National Geographic, 187* (6), 2–41.

Swets, J. A. (1992). The science of choosing the right decision threshold in high-stakes diagnostics. *American Psychologist, 47,* 522–532.

Symons, C. S., & Johnson, B. T. (1997). The self-reference effect in memory: A meta-analysis. *Psychological Bulletin, 121,* 371–394.

Szasz, T. (1961). *The myth of mental illness: Foundations of a theory of personal conduct.* New York: Harper.

Szasz, T. (1990). *Insanity: The idea and its consequences.* New York: John Wiley.

Szeto, H. H., Wu, D. L., Decena, J. A., & Cheng, Y. (1991). Effects of single and repeated marijuana smoke exposure on fetal EEG. *Pharmacology, Biochemistry, and Behavior, 40,* 97–101.

T

Tacey, D. (2001). *Jung and the new age.* Philadelphia: Brunner-Routledge.

Takeshige, C. (1985). Differentiation between acupuncture and non-acupuncture points by association with analgesia inhibitory system. *Acupuncture and Electro-Therapeutics Research, 10,* 195–202.

Tanford, S., & Penrod, S. (1984). Social influence model: A formal integration of research on majority and minority influence. *Psychological Bulletin, 95,* 189–225.

Tang, T.-P., Shimizu, E., Dube, G. R., Rampon, C., Kerchner, G. A., Zhuo, M., Liu, G., & Tsien, J. Z. (1999). Genetic enhancement of learning and memory in mice. *Memory, 401,* 63–69.

Tanner, J. M. (1990). *Foetus into man: Physical growth from conception to maturity* (rev. and enlarged ed.). Cambridge, MA: Harvard University Press.

Tansley, K. (1965). *Vision in vertebrates.* London: Chapman & Hall.

Tart, C. T. (1988). From spontaneous event to lucidity: A review of attempts to consciously control nocturnal dreaming. In J. Gackenbach & S. LaBerge (Eds.), *Conscious mind, sleeping brain: Perspectives on lucid dreaming.* New York: Plenum.

Tashkin, D. P. (1999). Effects of marijuana on the lung and its defenses against infection and cancer. *School Psychology International, 20,* 23–37.

Taylor, F. K. (1965). Crypomnesia and plagiarism. *British Journal of Psychiatry, 111,* 1111–1118.

Taylor, S. E. (1981). A categorization approach to stereotyping. In D. L. Hamilton (Ed.), *Cognitive processes in stereotyping and intergroup behavior.* Hillsdale, NJ: Lawrence Erlbaum.

Taylor, S. E. (1999). *Health psychology* (4th ed.). New York: McGraw-Hill.

Taylor, S. E., Klein, L. C., Lewis, B. P., Gruenewald, T. L., Gurung, R. A. R., & Updegraff, J. A. (2000). Biobehavioral responses to stress in females: Tend-and-befriend, not fight-or-flight. *Psychological Review, 107,* 411–429.

Teasdale, T. W., & Owen, D. R. (1984). Heredity and familial environment in intelligence and educational level: A sibling study. *Nature, 309,* 620–622.

Teigen, K. H. (1994). Yerkes-Dodson: A law for all seasons. *Theory and Psychology, 4,* 525–547.

Tellegen, A., Lykken, D. T,. Bouchard, T. J., Jr., Wilcox, K. J., Segal, N. L., & Rich, S. (1988). Personality similarity in twins reared apart and together. *Journal of Personality and Social Psychology, 54,* 1020–1030.

Teri, L., & Lewinsohn, P. M. (1985). Group intervention for unipolar depression. *Behavior Therapist, 8,* 109–111.

Terman, L. M. (1916). *The measurement of intelligence.* Boston: Houghton Mifflin.

Terman, L. M. (1925). *Genetic studies of genius: Vol. 1. Mental and physical traits of a thousand gifted children.* Stanford, CA: Stanford University Press.

Terman, L. M., & Oden, M. H. (1947). *Genetic studies of genius: Vol. 4. The gifted child grows up: Twenty-five years' follow-up of a superior group.* Stanford, CA: Stanford University Press.

Terr, L. C. (1988). What happens to early memories of trauma? A study of 20 children under age five at the time of documented traumatic events. *Journal of the American Academy of Child and Adolescent Psychiatry, 27,* 96–104.

Terrace, H. S. (1979). *Nim: A chimpanzee who learned sign language.* New York: Washington Square Press.

Terrace, H. S., Petitto, L. A., Saunders, R. J., & Bever, T. G. (1979). Can an ape create a sentence? *Science, 206,* 891–902.

Teti, D. M., Nakagawa, M., Das, R., & Wirth, O. (1991). Security of attachment between pre-schoolers and their mothers: Relations among social interaction, parenting stress, and mothers' sorts of the Attachment Q-Set. *Developmental Psychology, 27,* 440–447.

Thase, M. E. (2000). Relapse and recurrence of depression: An updated practical approach for prevention. In K. J. Palmer (Ed.), *Drug treatment issues in depression* (pp. 35–52). Kwai Chung, Hong Kong: Adis International Publications.

Thase, M. E., & Howland, R. H. (1995). Biological processes in depression: An updated review and integration. In E. E. Beckham & W. R. Leber (Eds.), *Handbook of depression* (2nd ed., pp. 213–279). New York: Guilford Press.

Thayer, R. (2001). *Calm energy: How people regulate mood with food and exercise.* Oxford University Press.

Thayer, R., Newman, J., & McClain, T. (1994). Self-regulation of mood: Strategies for changing a bad mood, raising energy, and reducing tension. *Journal of Personality and Social Psychology, 67,* 910–925.

Thigpen, C. H., & Cleckley, H. M. (1957). *The three faces of Eve.* New York: McGraw-Hill.

Thoma, S. J. (1986). Estimating gender differences in the comprehension and preference of moral issues. *Developmental Review, 6,* 165–180.

Thoman, E. B. (1999). Morningness and eveningness: Issues for study of the early ontogeny of these circadian rhythms. *Human Development, 42,* 206–212.

Thomas, D. R. (1992). Discrimination and generalization. In L. R. Squire (Ed.), *Encyclopedia of learning and memory.* New York: Macmillan.

Thomas, R. M. (2001). *Recent theories of human development.* Thousand Oaks, CA: Sage.

Thomis, M. A., Vlietnick, R. F., Maes, H. H., Limkie, C. J., van Leemputte, M., Claessens, A. L., Marchal, G., & Beunen, G. P. (2000). Predictive power of individual genetic and environmental factor scores. *Twin Research, 3,* 99–108.

Thompson, J. (1996). Introduction: Body image, eating disorders, and obesity: An emerging synthesis. In J. Thompson (Ed.), *Body image, eating disorders, and obesity* (pp. 1–22). Washington, DC: American Psychological Association.

Thompson, R. F. (2000). *The brain: A neuroscience primer* (3rd ed.). New York: Freeman.

Thompson, R. F., Bao, S., Chen, L., Cipriano, B. D., Grethe, J. S., Kim, J. J., Thompson, J. K., Tracy, J. A., Weninger, M. S., & Krupa, D. J. (1997). Associative learning. In R. J. Bradley, R. A. Harris, & P. Jenner (Series Eds.) & J. D. Schahmann (Vol. Ed.), *International review of neurobiology: Vol. 41. The cerebellum and cognition* (pp. 152–189). San Diego: Academic Press.

Thompson, S. H., Sargent, R. G., & Kemper, K. A. (1996). Black and White adolescent males' perceptions of ideal body size. *Sex Roles, 34,* 391–406.

Thorndike, E. L. (1898). Animal intelligence: An experimental study of the associative processes in animals. *Psychological Review Monograph Supplement, 2* (No. 8).

Thorndike, E. L. (1911). *Animal intelligence: Experimental studies.* New York: Macmillan.

Thorndike, E. L. (1914). *The psychology of learning.* New York: Teachers College.

Thurman, D. W. (1985). Effectiveness of cognitive-behavioral treatments in reducing Type A behavior among university faculty one year later. *Journal of Counseling Psychology, 32,* 445–448.

Thurstone, L. L. (1938). Primary mental abilities. *Psychometric Monographs, Vol. 1.* Chicago: Chicago University Press.

Tice, D., & Baumeister, R. F. (1993). Anger control. In D. Wegner & J. Pennebaker (Eds.), *Handbook of mental control.* Englewood Cliffs, NJ: Prentice Hall.

Tice, D. M., & Baumeister, R. F. (1997). Longitudinal study of procrastination, performance, stress, and health: The costs and benefits of dawdling. *Psychological Science, 8,* 454–458.

Tice, D. M., Butler, J. L., Muraven, M. B., & Stillwell, A. M. (1995). When modesty prevails: Differential favorability of self-presentation to friends and strangers. *Journal of Personality and Social Psychology, 69,* 1120–1138.

Tilley, A. J., & Empson, J. A. (1978). REM sleep and memory consolidation. *Biological Psychology, 6,* 293–300.

Timmers, M., Fischer, A.H., & Manstead, A.S.R. (1998). Gender differences in motives for regulating emotions. *Personality and Social Psychology Bulletin, 24,* 974–985.

Tinbergen, N. (1969). *The study of instinct.* Oxford, England: Clarendon Press.

Ting-Toomey, S., Gao, G., Trubisky, P., Yang, Z., Kim, H.S., Lin, S., & Nishida, T. (1991). Culture, face maintenance, and styles of handling interpersonal conflict: A study in five cultures. *International Journal of Conflict Management, 2,* 275–296.

Tinker, M. A. (1932). Wundt's doctorate students and their theses, 1875–1920. *American Journal of Psychology, 44,* 630–637.

Titone, D. A. (2002). Memories abound: The neuroscience of dreams. *Trends in cognitive Sciences, 6,* 4–5.

Todes, D. P. (1997). From the machine to the ghost within: Pavlov's transition from digestive physiology to conditional reflexes. *American Psychologist, 52,* 947–955.

Toga, A. W., & Mazziota, J. C. (Eds.). (1999). *Brain mapping.* New York: Morgan Kaufman.

Tolman, E. C. (1922). A new formula for behaviorism. *Psychological Review, 29,* 44–53.

Tolman, E. C. (1932). *Purposive behavior in animals and men.* New York: Appleton-Century-Crofts.

Tolman, E. C., & Honzik, C. H. (1930). Insight in rats. *University of California Publications in Psychology, 4,* 215–232.

Tomarken, A. J., Davidson, R. J., & Henriques, J. B. (1990). Resting frontal brain asymmetry predicts affective responses to films. *Journal of Personality and Social Psychology, 59,* 791–801.

Tonigan, J. S., Miller, W. R., & Connors, G. J. (2000). Project MATCH client impressions about Alcoholics Anonymous: Measurement issues and relationship to treatment outcome. *Alcoholism Treatment Quarterly, 18,* 25–41.

Torgersen, S. (1983). Genetic factors in anxiety disorders. *Archives of General Psychiatry, 40,* 1085–1089.

Torrey, E. F. (1997). *Out of the shadows: Confronting America's mental illness crisis.* New York: Wiley.

Torrey, E. F., Bowler, A. F., Rawlings, R., & Yolken, R. H. (1997). Seasonality of births in schizophrenia and bipolar disorder: A review of the literature. *Schizophrenia Research, 28* (1), 1–38.

Torvik, A., Lindhoe, C., & Rogde, S. (1982). Brain lesions in alcoholics—a neuropathological study with clinical correlations. *Journal of Neurological Science, 75,* 43–51.

Tower, R. K., Kelly, C., & Richards, A. (1997). Individualism, collectivism and reward allocation: A cross-cultural study in Russia and Britain. *British Journal of Social Psychology, 36,* 331–345.

Travis, J. (1994). Glia: The brain's other cells. *Science, 266,* 970–972.

Treffert, D. A. (1989). *Extraordinary people: Understanding savant syndrome.* New York: Ballantine Books.

Treffert, D. A. (1992). Savant syndrome. In L. R. Squire (Ed.), *Encyclopedia of learning and memory* (pp. 573–574). New York: Macmillan.

Triandis, H. C. (1989). The self and social behavior in differing cultural contexts. *Psychological Review, 96,* 506–520.

Triandis, H. C. (1995). *Individualism & collectivism.* Boulder, CO: Westview Press.

Triandis, H. C., & Suh, E. M. (2002). Cultural influences on personality. *Annual Review of Psychology, 53,* 133–160.

Trimpop, R., & Kirkcaldy, B. (1997). Personality predictors of driving accidents. *Personality & Individual Differences, 23,* 147–152.

Trovillo, P. (1939). A history of lie detection. *American Journal of Political Science, 29,* 848–881.

Truax, C. B., & Carkhuff, R. R. (1967). *Toward effective counseling and psychotherapy: Training and practice.* Chicago: Aldine.

Trudeau, K. J., & Devlin, A. S. (1996). College students and community service: Who, with whom, and why? *Journal of Applied Social Psychology, 26,* 1867–1888.

Tryon, G., (1980). The measurement and treatment of test anxiety. *Review of Educational Research, 50,* 343–372.

Tsuang, M. (2000). Schizophrenia: Genes and environment. *Biological Psychiatry, 47,* 210–220.

Tucker, J. S., & Riggio, R. E. (1988). The role of social skills in encoding of posed and spontaneous facial expressions. *Journal of Nonverbal Behavior, 12,* 87–97.

Tulving, E. (1962). Subjective organization in free-recall of "unrelated" words. *Psychological Review, 69,* 344–354.

Tulving, E. (1997). Human memory. In M. S. Gazzaniga (Ed.), *Conversations in the cognitive neurosciences*. Cambridge, MA: MIT Press.

Tulving, E. (1999). Study of memory: Processes and systems. In J. K. Foster & M. Jelicic (Eds.), *Memory: Systems, process, or function?* (pp. 11–30). Oxford: Oxford University Press.

Tulving, E., & Lepage, M. (2000). Where in the brain is the awareness of one's past? In D. L. Schacter & E. Scarry (Eds.), *Memory, brain, and belief* (pp. 208–228). Cambridge, MA: Harvard University Press.

Tulving, E., & Schacter, D. L. (1990). Priming and human memory systems. *Science, 247*, 301–306.

Tulving, E., & Thomson, D. M. (1973). Encoding specificity and retrieval processes in episodic memory. *Psychological Review, 80*, 352–373.

Turkheimer, E. (1991). Individual and group differences in adoption studies of IQ. *Psychological Bulletin, 110*, 392–405.

Turnbull, C. (1989). *The mountain people*. London: Paladin.

Turner, H. S., & Watson, T. S. (1999). Consultant's guide for the use of time-out in the preschool and elementary classroom. *Psychology in the Schools, 36*, 135–148.

Turner, J., Meyer, D., Cox, K., Logan, C., DiCintio, M., & Thomas, C. (1998). Creating contexts for involvement in math. *Journal of Educational Psychology, 90*, 730–745.

Turner-Cobb, J., Sephton, S., & Spiegel, D. (2001). Psychosocial effects on immune function and disease progression in cancer: Human studies. In R. Ader, D. Felten, & N. Cohen (Eds.), *Psychoneuroimmunology* (Vol. 2, 3rd ed., pp. 565–582). San Diego, CA: Academic Press.

Tversky, A., & Kahneman, D. (1973). Availability: A heuristic for judging frequency and probability. *Cognitive Psychology, 5*, 207–232.

Tversky, A., & Kahneman, D. (1974). Judgment under uncertainty: Heuristics and biases. *Science, 185*, 1124–1131.

Tversky, A., & Kahneman, D. (1981). The framing of decisions and the psychology of choice. *Science, 211*, 453–458.

Tygart, C. E. (2000). Genetic causation attribution and public support of gay rights. *International Journal of Public Opinion Research, 12*, 259–275.

Tyler, T. R. (1997). The psychology of legitimacy: A relational perspective on voluntary deference to authorities. *Personality and Social Psychology Review, 1*, 323–345.

Tyrrell, R. A., & Leibowitz, H. W. (1990). The relation of vergence effort to reports of visual fatigue following prolonged near work. *Human Factors, 32*, 341–357.

U

Uchino, B. N., Cacioppo, J. T., & Kiecolt-Glaser, J. K. (1996). The relationship between social support and physiological processes: A review with emphasis on underlying mechanisms and implications for health. *Psychological Bulletin, 119*, 488–531.

Uhl, G. R., Elmer, G. I., LaBuda, M. C., & Pickens, R. W. (1995). Genetic influences in drug abuse. In F. E. Bloom & D. J. Kupfer (Eds.), *Psychopharmacology: The fourth generation* (pp. 1793–1806). New York: Raven Press.

Ujike, H., & Ono, H. (2001). Depth thresholds of motion parallax as a function of head movement velocity. *Vision Research, 41*, 2835–2843.

Ukrainetz, T. A., & Blomquist, C. (2002). The criterion validity of four vocabulary tests compared to a language sample. *Child Language Teaching & Therapy, 18*, 59–78.

Ulfberg, J., Carter, N., & Edling, C. (2000). Sleep-disorder breathing and occupational accidents. *Scandinavian Journal of Work, Environment, & Health, 26*, 237–242.

Ullman, S. E., & Brecklin, L. R. (2002). Sexual assault history, PTSD, and mental health service seeking in a national sample of women. *Journal of Community Psychology, 30*, 261–279.

Underwood, G., & Bright, J.E.H. (1996). Cognition with and without awareness. In G. Underwood (Ed.), *Implicit cognition* (pp. 1–40). Oxford: Oxford University Press.

Unger, R. K., & Crawford, M. (1992). *Women and gender: A feminist psychology*. New York: McGraw-Hill.

University of California (1993, December). The new American body. *University of California at Berkeley Wellness Letter*, pp. 1–2.

Urdan, T., & Maehr, M. (1995). Beyond a two-goal theory of motivation and achievement: A case for social goals. *Review of Educational Research, 65*, 213–243.

Uribe, F. M. T., LeVine, R. A., & LeVine, S. E. (1994). Maternal behavior in a Mexican Community: The changing environments of children. In P. M. Greenfield, & R. R. Cocking (Eds.), *Cross-cultural roots of minority child development* (pp. 41–54). Hillsdale, NJ: Erlbaum.

U.S. Bureau of the Census. (2001). *Statistical abstract of the United States, 2001*. Washington, DC: U.S. Government Printing Office.

V

Vahtera, J., Kivimaeki, M., Uutela, A., & Pentti, J. (2000). Hostility and ill health: Role of psychosocial resources in two contexts of working life. *Journal of Psychosomatic Research, 48*, 89–98.

Valentine, T., Brennen, T., & Brédart, S. (1996). *The cognitive psychology of proper names: On the importance of being Ernest*. London: Routledge.

Valkenburg, P. M., & van der Voort, T. H. A. (1994). Influence of TV on daydreaming and creative imagination: A review of research. *Psychological Bulletin, 116*, 316–339.

Vallerand, R. J., Fortier, M. S., & Guay, F. (1997). Self-determination and persistence in a real-life setting: Toward a motivational model of high school dropout. *Journal of Personality and Social Psychology, 72*, 1161–1176.

Valleroy, L. A., Harris, J. R., & Way, P. O. (1990). The impact of HIV infection on child survival in the developing world. *AIDS, 4*, 667–672.

Van Bakel, H. J. A., & Riksen-Walraven, J. M. (2002). Quality of infant-parent attachment as reflected in infant interactive behaviour during instructional tasks. *Journal of Child Psychology & Psychiatry & Allied Disciplines, 43*, 387–394.

van den Heuvel, H., Tellegen, G., & Koomen, W. (1992). Cultural differences in the use of psychological and social characteristics in children's self-understanding. *European Journal of Social Psychology, 22*, 353–362.

Van der Heijden, A. H. C. (1981). *Short-term visual information forgetting*. London: Routledge & Kegan Paul.

Van der Zee, K., Oldersma, F., Buunk, B. P., & Bos, D. (1998). Social comparison preferences among cancer patients as related to neuroticism and social comparison orientation. *Journal of Personality and Social Psychology, 75*, 801–810.

van Doornen, L., de Geus, E., & Orlebeke, J. (1988). Aerobic fitness and physiological stress response: A critical evaluation. *Social Science and Medicine, 26,* 303–307.

VanderVoort, D. J., & Fuhriman, A. (1991). The efficacy of group therapy for depression: A review of the literature. *Small Group Research, 22,* 320–338.

Varela, F. J., Palacios, A. G., & Goldsmith, T. H. (1993). Color vision of birds. In H. P. Ziegler & H-J. Bishof (Eds.), *Vision, brain and behavior in birds* (pp. 77–98). Cambridge: MIT Press.

Vasquez, C. I. (1991). A training program for Hispanic psychologists at New York University—Bellevue Hospital Center. In H. F. Myers, P. Wohlford, L. P. Guzman, & R. J. Echemendia. (Eds.). *Ethnic minority perspectives on clinical training and services in psychology* (pp. 143–148). Washington, DC: American Psychological Association.

Vaughn, B. E., & Langlois, J. H. (1983). Physical attractiveness as a correlate of peer status and social competence in preschool children. *Developmental Psychology, 19,* 561–567.

Vein, A. M., Sidorov, A. A., Martazaev, M. S., & Karlov, A. V. (1991). Physical exercise and nocturnal sleep in healthy humans. *Human Physiology, 17,* 391–397.

Veniegas, R. C., & Peplau, L. A. (1997). Power and the quality of same-sex friendships. *Psychology of Women Quarterly, 21,* 279–297.

Vernon, P. A., & Mori, M. (1992). Intelligence, reaction times, and peripheral nerve conduction velocity. *Intelligence, 16,* 273–288.

Vernon, P. A., Wickett, J. C., Bazana, P. G., & Stelmack, R. M. (2000). The neuropsychology and psychophysiology of human intelligence. In R. J. Sternberg (Ed.), *Handbook of intelligence* (pp. 245–264). Cambridge: Cambridge University Press.

Vgontzas, A. N., & Kales, A. (1999). Sleep and its disorders. *Annual Review of Medicine, 50,* 387–400.

Vigliocco, G. V., Vinson, D. P., Martin, R. C., & Garrett, M. F. (1999). Is "count" and "mass" information available when the noun is not? An investigation of tip of the tongue states and anomia. *Journal of Memory & Language, 40,* 534–558.

Viken, R. J., Rose, R. J., Kapiro, J., & Koskenvuo, M. (1994). A developmental genetic analysis of adult personality: Extraversion and neuroticism from 18 to 59 years of age. *Journal of Personality and Social Psychology, 66,* 722–730.

Vines, G. (1995, July 22). Fight fat with feeling. *New Scientist,* pp. 14–15.

Vingerhoets, A. (1985). The role of the parasympathetic division of the autonomic nervous system in stress and the emotions. *International Journal of Psychosomatics, 32* (3), 28–34.

Vining, E. P. G., Freeman, J. M., Pillas, D. J., Uematsu, S., Carson, B. S., Brandt, J., Boatman, D., Pulsifer, M. B., & Zukerberg, A. (1997). Why would you remove half a brain? The outcome of 58 children after hemispherectomy—The Johns Hopkins Experience: 1968 to 1996. *Pediatrics, 100,* 163–171.

Vinokur, A. D., & Vinokur-Kaplan, D. (1990). In sickness and in health: Patterns of social support and undermining in older married couples. *Journal of Aging and Health, 2,* 215–241.

Vitaterna, M. H., King, D. P., Chang, A. M., Kornhauser, J. M., Lowrey, P. L., McDonald, J. D., Dove, W. F., Pinto, L. H., Twek, F. W., & Takahashi, J. S. (1994). Mutagenesis and mapping of a mouse gene, Clock, essential for circadian behavior. *Science, 264,* 719–725.

Vives, F., & Oltras, C. M. (1992). Plasma levels of beta-endorphin, ACTH, glucose, free fatty acids and lactata in athletes after running races of different distances. *Medical Science Research, 20,* 67–69.

Voegtlin, W. L. (1940). The treatment of alcoholism by establishing a conditioned reflex. *American Journal of the Medical Sciences, 199,* 802–810.

Vogt, E. Z. (1976). *Tortillas for the gods: A symbolic analysis of Zinacanteco rituals.* Cambridge, MA: Harvard University Press.

Vohs, K. D., Heatherton, T. F., & Herrin, M. (in press). Disordered eating and the transition to college: A prospective study. *International Journal of Eating Disorders.*

Vonk, R., & Kippenberg, A. van. (1995). Processing attitude statements from ingroup and outgroup members: Effects of within-group and within-person inconsistencies on reading times. *Journal of Personality and Social Psychology, 68,* 215–227.

Vrij, A., & Semin, G. R. (1996). Lie experts' beliefs about nonverbal indicators of deception. *Journal of Nonverbal Behavior, 20,* 65–80.

Vygotsky, L. S. (1986). *Thought and language* (A. Kozulin, Trans.). Cambridge, MA: MIT Press. (Original work published 1934).

W

Wade, N. (1999, September 23). Number of human genes is put at 140,000, a significant gain. *The New York Times,* p. 86.

Wagenaar, W. A., & Groeneweg, J. (1990). The memory of concentration camp survivors. *Applied Cognitive Psychology, 4,* 77–87.

Wagner, H. (2001). Hunting in barn owls: Peripheral and neurobiological specializations and their general relevance in neural computation. In G. Roth (Ed.), *Brain evolution and cognition* (pp. 205–235). New York: John Wiley.

Wagner, R. K. (2000). Practical intelligence. In R. J. Sternberg (Ed.), *Handbook of intelligence* (pp. 380–395). Cambridge: Cambridge University Press.

Wahlbeck, K., Cheine, M., Essali, A., & Adams, C. (1999). Evidence of clozapine's effectiveness in schizophrenia: A systematic review and meta-analysis of randomized trials. *American Journal of Psychiatry, 156,* 990–999.

Wald, G. (1964). The receptors of human color vision. *Science, 145,* 1007–1017.

Waldman, I. D., Weinberg, R. A., & Scarr, S. (1994). Racial-group differences in IQ in the Minnesota transracial adoption study: A reply to Levin and Lynn. *Intelligence, 19,* 29–44.

Walk, R. D. (1981). *Perceptual development.* Monterey, CA: Brooks/Cole.

Walk, R. D., & Gibson, E. J. (1961). A comparative and analytical study of visual depth perception. *Psychological Monographs,* No.75.

Walker, E. F., & Diforio, D. (1998). Schizophrenia: A neural diathesis-stress model. *Psychological Review, 104,* 667–685.

Walker, L. J. (1989). A longitudinal study of moral reasoning. *Child Development, 60,* 157–166.

Wall, P. (2000). *Pain: The science of suffering.* New York: Columbia University Press.

Wallace, B. (1993). Day persons, night persons, and variability in hypnotic susceptibility. *Journal of Personality and Social Psychology, 64,* 827–833.

Wallace, P. (1977). Individual discrimination of humans by odor. *Physiology and Behavior, 19,* 577–579.

Wallace, R. K., & Benson, H. (1972). The physiology of meditation. *Scientific American, 226,* 84–90.

Walsh, R. (1996). Meditation research: The state of the art. In B. W. Scotton, A. B. Chinen, & J. R. Battista (Eds.), *Textbook of transpersonal psychiatry and psychology* (pp. 167–175). New York: Basic Books.

Walsh, S. (1993). Cited in Toufexis, A. (1993, February 15), *Time*, pp. 49–51.

Walsh, V. (2000). Hemispheric asymmetries: A brain in two minds. *Current Biology, 10,* 460–462.

Walters, J. M., & Gardner, H. (1986). The theory of multiple intelligences: Some issues and answers. In R. Sternberg & R. Wagner (Eds.), *Practical intelligences* (pp. 163–183). New York: Cambridge University Press.

Wanberg, C. R., Kenfer, R., & Rotundo, M. (1999). Unemployed individuals: Motives, job-search constraints as predictors of job seeking and reemployment. *Journal of Applied Psychology, 54,* 897–910.

Wardhaugh, R. (1993). *Investigating language: Central problems in linguistics.* Oxford: Blackwell Publishers.

Warren, R. M. (1970). Perceptual restoration of missing speech sounds. *Science, 167,* 392–393.

Wason, P. C. (1960). On the failure to eliminate hypotheses in a conceptual task. *Quarterly Journal of Experimental Psychology, 12,* 129–140.

Wass, H., Christian, M., Myers, J., & Murphey, M. (1978–1979). Similarities and dissimilarities in attitudes toward death in a population of older persons. *Omega, 9,* 337–354.

Wasserman, D., Lempert, R. O., & Hastie, R. (1991). Hindsight and causality. *Personality and Social Psychology Bulletin, 17,* 30–35.

Wasserman, E. A., & Miller, R. R. (1997). What's elementary about associative learning? *Annual Review of Psychology, 48,* 573–607.

Watkins, M. J., & Tulving, E. (1975). Episodic memory: When recognition fails. *Journal of Experimental Psychology: General, 104,* 5–29.

Watson, D. & Clark, L. A. (1997). Extraversion and its positive emotional core. In R. Hogan, J. Johnson, & S. Briggs (Eds.), *Handbook of personality psychology.* San Diego: Academic Press.

Watson, D., Wiese, D., Vaidya, J., & Tellegen, A. (1999). The two general activation systems of affect: Structural findings, evolutionary considerations, and psychobiological evidence. *Journal of Personality and Social Psychology, 76,* 820–838.

Watson, J. B. (1913). Psychology as the behaviorist sees it. *Psychological Review, 20,* 158–177.

Watson, J. B. (1924). *Behaviorism.* New York: Norton.

Watson, J. B., & Rayner, R. (1920). Conditioned emotional reactions. *Journal of Experimental Psychology, 3,* 1–14.

Watson, J. B., & Rayner, R. (1920). Conditioned emotional responses. *Journal of Experimental Psychology, 3,* 1–14.

Waxman, S. G. (Ed.). (2001). *Form and function in the brain and spinal cord: Perspectives of a neurologist.* Cambridge, MA: MIT Press.

Way, N., Cowal, K., Gingold, R., Pahl, K., & Bissessar, N. (2001). Friendship patterns among African American, Asian American, and Latino adolescents from low-income families. *Journal of Social and Personal Relationships, 18,* 29–53.

Wearden, A. J., Tarrier, N., Barrowclough, C., Zastowny, T. R., & Rahill, A. A. (2000). A review of expressed emotion research in health care. *Clinical Psychology Review, 20,* 633–666.

Webb, W. B. (1992). *Sleep: The gentle giant.* Bolton, MA: Anker Publishing.

Weber, E. H. (1834). *De pulen, resorptione, auditu et tactu: Annotationes anatomicae et physiologicae.* Leipzig: Koehler.

Wegner, D. M., Erber, R., & Raymond, P. (1991). Transactive memory in close relationships. *Journal of Personality and Social Psychology, 61,* 923–929.

Weick, K. E. (1985). Systematic observational methods. In G. Lindzey & E. Aronson (Eds.), *Handbook of social psychology* (Vol. 1, pp. 567–634). New York: Random House.

Weinberg, R. A., Scarr, S., & Waldman, I. D. (1992). The Minnesota Transracial Adoption Study: A follow-up of IQ test performance at adolescence. *Intelligence, 16,* 117–135.

Weiner, T., Johnston, D., & Lewis, N. (1995). *Betrayal: The story of Aldrich Ames, an American spy.* New York: Random House.

Weingardt, K. R., Loftus, E. F., & Lindsay, D. S. (1995). Misinformation revisited: New evidence on the suggestibility of memory. *Memory and Cognition, 23,* 72–82.

Weisenberg, M. (1977). Pain and pain control. *Psychological Bulletin, 84,* 1008–1044.

Weiss, C. S. (1992). Depression and immuno-competence: A review of the literature. *Psychological Bulletin, 111,* 475–489.

Weissman, M. M., Bland, R. C., Canino, G. J., Faravelli, C., Greenwald, S., & Hwu, H-G. (1997). The cross-national epidemiology of panic disorder. *Archives of General Psychiatry, 54,* 305–309.

Weissman, M. M., Bland, R. C., Canino, G. J., Faravelli, C., Greenwald, S., Hwu, H-G., Joyce, P. R., Karam, E. G., Lee, C-K., Lellouch, J., Lepine, J-P., Newman, S. C., Rubio-Stepic, M., Wells, J. E., Wickramaratne, P. J., Wittchen, H-U., & Yeh, E-K. (1996). Cross-national epidemiology of major depression and bipolar disorder. *Journal of the American Medical Association, 276,* 293–299.

Weissman, M. M., Bruce, M., Leaf, P., Florio, L., & Holzer, C. (1991). Affective disorders. In L. N. Robins & D. A. Regier (Eds.), *Psychiatric disorders in America* (pp. 53–80). New York: Free Press.

Weisz, J. R., Weiss, B., & Donenberg, G. R. (1992). The lab versus the clinic: Effects of child and adolescent psychotherapy. *American Psychologist, 47,* 1578–1585.

Weldon, M. S. (1999). The memory chop shop: Issues in the search for memory systems. In J. K. Foster & M. Jelicic (Eds.), *Memory: Systems, process, or function?* (pp. 162–205). Oxford: Oxford University Press.

Wellman, H. M. (1990). *The child's theory of mind.* Cambridge, MA: MIT Press.

Welsh, D. K. (1993). Timing of sleep and wakefulness. In M. A. Carskadon (Ed.), *Encyclopedia of sleep and dreaming.* New York: Macmillan.

Wertsch, J. V., & Tulviste, P. (1992). L. S. Vygotsky and contemporary developmental psychology. *Developmental Psychology, 28,* 548–557.

West, S. G., & Brown, T. J. (1975). Physical attractiveness, the severity of the emergency and helping: A field experiment and interpersonal simulation. *Journal of Experimental Social Psychology, 11,* 531–538.

Westen, D. (1998). The scientific legacy of Sigmund Freud: Toward a psychodynamically informed psychological science. *Psychological Bulletin, 124,* 333–371.

Westen, D., & Gabbard, G. O. (1999). Psychoanalytic approaches to personality. In L. A. Pervin & O. P. John (Eds.), *Handbook of personality: Theory and research* (pp. 57–101). New York: Guilford Press.

Westen, D., & Morrison, K. (2001). A *meta-analytic investigation of empirically supported treatments for depression, anxiety, and generalized anxiety disorder.* Unpublished manuscript, Boston University.

Wever, E. G. (1949). *Theory of hearing.* New York: Wiley.

Wever, E. G., & Bray, C. W. (1937). The perception of low tones and the resonance-volley theory. *Journal of Psychology, 3,* 101–114.

Wever, R. A. (1979). *The circadian system in man.* Berlin: Springer-Verlag.

Wheeler, L., & Kim, Y. (1997). What is beautiful is culturally good: The physical attractiveness stereotype has different content in collectivist cultures. *Personality and Social Psychology Bulletin, 23,* 795–800.

Whitbeck, L. B., & Hoyt, D. R. (1994). Social prestige and assortive mating: A comparison of students from 1956 and 1988. *Journal of Social and Personal Relationships, 11,* 137–145.

Whitbourne, S. K. (1985). *The aging body: Physiological changes and psychological consequences.* New York: Springer-Verlag.

White, G. L. (1981). Some correlates of romantic jealousy. *Journal of Personality, 49,* 129–147.

White, G. L., & Mullen, P. E. (1989). *Jealousy: Theory, research, and clinical strategies.* New York: Guilford Press.

White, J. R., Froeb, H. F., & Kulik, J. A. (1991). Respiratory illness in nonsmokers chronically exposed to tobacco smoke in the workplace. *Chest, 100,* 39–43.

White, L., Katzman, R., & Losonczy, K. (1994). Association of education with incidence of cognitive impairment in three established populations for epidemiologic studies of the elderly. *Journal of Clinical Epidemiology, 47,* 363–371.

White, M., & LeVine, R. A. (1986). What is an Ii ko (good child)? In H. Stevenson, H. Azuma, & K. Hakuta (Eds.), *Child development and education in Japan* (pp. 55–62). New York: Freeman.

Whitehead, W., III, & Kuhn, W. F. (1990). Chronic pain: An overview. In T. W. Miller (Ed.), *Chronic pain* (Vol. 1, pp. 5–48). Madison, CT: International Universities Press.

Whitehurst, G. J., Arnold, D. S., Epstein, J. N., Angell, A. L., Smith, M., & Gischel, J. E. (1994). A picture book reading intervention in day care and home for children from low-income families. *Developmental Psychology, 30,* 679–689.

Whorf, G. L. (1956). Science and linguistics. In J. B. Carroll (Ed.), *Language, thought, and reality: Selected writings of Benjamin Lee Whorf.* Cambridge, MA: MIT Press.

Wich, S. A., Assink, P. R., Becher, F., & Sterck, E. H. M. (2002). Playbacks of loud calls to wild Thomas langurs (primates; Presbytis thomasi): The effect of familiarity. *Behaviour, 139,* 79–87.

Wickelgren, W. A. (1965). Acoustic similarity and intrusion errors in short-term memory. *Journal of Experimental Psychology, 70,* 102–108.

Wickens, C. D. (1992a). Virtual reality and education. In *Proceedings of the IEEE International Conference on Systems, Man and Cybernetics.* New York: IEEE.

Wickens, C. D. (1992b). *Engineering psychology and human performance* (2nd ed.). New York: HarperCollins.

Wierzbicki, M. (1993). *Issues in clinical psychology: Subjective versus objective approaches.* Boston: Allyn & Bacon.

Wierzbicki, M. (1997). *Introduction to clinical psychology: Scientific foundations to clinical practice.* Boston: Allyn & Bacon.

Wierzbicki, M., & Bartlett, T. S. (1987). The efficacy of group and individual cognitive therapy for mild depression. *Cognitive Therapy and Research, 11,* 337–342.

Wierzbicki, M., & Pekarik, G. (1993). A meta-analysis of psychotherapy dropout. *Professional Psychology: Research and Practice, 24,* 190–195.

Wierzbicki, M., & Rexford, L. (1989). Cognitive and behavioral correlates of depression in clinical and nonclinical populations. *Journal of Clinical Psychology, 45,* 872–877.

Wiesel, T. N. (1982). Postnatal development of the visual cortex and the influence of environment. *Nature, 299,* 583–591.

Wiggins, J. S. (Ed.). (1996). *The five factor model of personality: Theoretical perspectives.* New York: Guilford Press.

Willerman L., & Cohen, D. B. (1990). *Psychopathology.* New York: McGraw-Hill.

Williams, R. W., & Herrup, K. (1988). The control of neuron number. *Annual Review of Neuroscience, 11,* 423–453.

Williams, W. L. (1992). The relationship between male-male friendship and male-female marriage. In P. M. Nardi (Ed.), *Men's friendships* (pp. 186–200). Newbury Park, CA: Sage.

Williamson, D. (1993). Descriptive epidemiology of bodyweight and weight change in U.S. adults. *Annals of Internal Medicine, 119,* 646–649.

Willis, W. D. (1985). *The pain system: The neural basis of nociceptive transmission in the mammalian nervous system.* Basel: Karger.

Wilson, B. (1970). *Religious sects.* London: Weidenfeld & Nicolson.

Wilson, B. J., Donnerstein, E., Linz, D., Kunkel, D., Potter, J., Smith, S. L., Blumenthal, E., & Gray, T. (1998). Content analysis of entertainment television: The importance of context. In J. T. Hamilton (Ed.), *Television violence and public policy* (pp. 13–53). Ann Arbor, MI: University of Michigan Press.

Wilson, E. O. (1997). *In search of nature.* Washington, DC: Island Press.

Wilson, S. C., & Barber, T. X. (1983). The fantasy-prone personality: Implications for understanding imagery, hypnosis, and parapsychological phenomena. In A. A. Sheikh (Ed.), *Imagery: Current theory, research, and applications.* New York: Wiley.

Windschitl, P. D. (1996). Memory for faces: Evidence of retrieval-based impairment. *Journal of Experimental Psychology: Learning, Memory, and Cognition, 22,* 1101–1122.

Winkielman, P., & Schwarz, N. (2001). How pleasant was your childhood? Beliefs about memory shape inferences from experienced difficulty of recall. *Psychological Science, 12,* 176–179.

Winn, P. (1995). The lateral hypothalamus and motivated behavior: An old syndrome reassessed and a new perspective gained. *Current Directions in Psychological Science, 4,* 182–187.

Winner, E. (1997). Exceptionally high intelligence and schooling. *American Psychologist, 52,* 1070–1081.

Winograd, E., & Killinger, W. A. (1983). Relating age at encoding in early childhood to adult recall: Development of flashbulb memories. *Journal of Experimental Psychology: General, 112,* 413–422.

Winson, J (1990, November). The meaning of dreams. *Scientific American,* pp. 86–96.

Wissler, C. (1901). The correlation of mental and physical tests. *Psychological Review Monograph Supplement 3,* No. 6.

Wixted, J. T., & Ebbesen, E. B. (1991). On the form of forgetting. *Psychological Science, 2,* 409–415.

Wolf, A., & Colditz, G. (1996). Social and economic effects of weight in the United States. *American Journal of Nutrition, 63* (Suppl. 3), 466S–469S.

Wolpe, J. (1958). *Psychotherapy by reciprocal inhibition.* Stanford, CA: University Press.

Wolpe, J., & Plaud, J. J. (1997). Pavlov's contributions to behavior therapy: The obvious and the not-so-obvious. *American Psychologist, 52,* 966–972.

Wood, D. J., & Middleton, D. (1975). A study of assisted problem-solving. *British Journal of Psychology, 66,* 181–191.

Wood, D. J., Bruner, J. S., & Ross, G. (1976). The role of tutoring in problem solving. *Journal of Child Psychology and Psychiatry, 17,* 89–100.

Wood, J. M., Lilienfeld, S. O., Garb, H. N., & Nezworski, M. T. (2000). The Rorschach Test in clinical diagnosis: A critical review, with a backward look at Garfield (1947). *Journal of Clinical Psychology, 56,* 395–430.

Wood, J. M., Nezworski, M. T., & Stejskal, W. J. (1996). The comprehensive system for the Rorschach: A critical examination. *Psychological Science, 7,* 3–10.

Wood, N., & Cowan, N. (1995). The cocktail party phenomenon revisited: How frequent are attention shifts to one's name in an irrelevant auditory channel? *Journal of Experimental Psychology: Learning, Memory, and Cognition, 21,* 255–260.

Wood, W., Wong, F. Y., & Chachere, J. G. (1991). Effects of media violence on viewers' aggression in unconstrained social interaction. *Psychological Bulletin, 109,* 371–383.

Woodruff, M. L. (1993). Report: Electroencephalograph taken from Pastor Liston Pack, 4:00 P.M., 7 Nov. 1985. In T. Burton, *Serpent-handling believer* (pp. 142–144). Knoxville: University of Tennessee Press.

Woods, S. (1991). The eating paradox: How we tolerate food. *Psychological Review, 98,* 488–505.

Woods, S., Schwartz, M., Baskin, D., & Seeley, R. (2000). Food intake and the regulation of body weight. *Annual Review of Psychology, 51,* 255–277.

Wright, I. C., Rabe, H. S., Woodruff, P. W. R., David, A. S., Murray, R. M., & Bullmore, E. T. (2000). Meta-analysis of regional brain volumes in schizophrenia. *American Journal of Psychiatry, 157,* 16–25.

Wright, K., & Flemons, D. (2002). Dying to know: Qualitative research with terminally ill persons and their families. *Death Studies, 26,* 255–271.

Wu, T-C., Tashkin, D. P., Djahed, B., & Rose, J. E. (1988). Pulmonary hazards of smoking marijuana as compared with tobacco. *New England Journal of Medicine, 318,* 347–351.

Wyatt, F., & Teuber, H. L. (1944). German psychology under the Nazi system, 1933–1940. *Psychological Review, 51,* 229–247.

Wyche, K. F. (1993). Psychology and African American women: Findings from applied research. *Applied & Preventive Psychology, 2,* 115–121.

Y

Yalom, I. D. (1995). *The theory and practice of group psychotherapy* (4th ed.). New York: Basic Books.

Yamane, D., & Polzer, M. (1994). Ways of seeing ecstasy in modern society: Experimental-expressive and cultural-linguistic views. *Sociology of Religion, 55,* 1–25.

Yang, J., Dai, X., Yao, S., Cai, T., Gao, B., McCrae, R. R., & Costa, P. T., Jr. (2002). Personality disorders and the five-factor model of personality in Chinese psychiatric patients. In P. T. Costa, Jr., & T. A. Widiger (Eds.), *Personality disorders and the five-factor model of personality* (2nd ed., pp. 215–221). Washington, DC: American Psychological Association.

Yanovski, J., & Yanovski, S. (1999). Recent advances in basic obesity research. *Journal of the American Medical Association, 282,* 1504–1506.

Yapko, M. D. (1994). Suggestibility and repressed memories of abuse: A survey of psychotherapists' beliefs. *American Journal of Clinical Hypnosis, 36,* 163–171.

Yeargin-Allsopp, M., Murphy, C. C., Cordero, J. F., & Decoufle, P. (1997). Reported biomedical causes and associated medical conditions for mental retardation among 10-year-old children. *Developmental Medicine & Child Neurology, 39,* 142–149.

Yelena, P., Leo, M. A., Kroll, W., & Lieber, C. S. (2002). Effects of alcohol consumption on eight circulating markers of liver fibrosis. *Alcohol & Alcoholism, 37,* 256–260.

Yoder, J. D., & Schleicher, T. L. (1996). Undergraduates regard deviation from occupational gender stereotypes as costly for women. *Sex Roles, 34,* 171–188.

Young, L. J. (2002). The neurobiology of social recognition: Approach, and avoidance. *Biological Psychiatry, 51,* 18–26.

Yu, B., Zhang, W., Jing, Q., Peng, R., Zhang, G., & Simon, H. A. (1985). STM capacity for Chinese and English language materials. *Memory and Cognition, 13,* 202–207.

Yule, G. (1996). *The study of language.* Cambridge: Cambridge University Press.

Yzerbyt, V. Y., Rocher, S., & Schadron, G. (1996). Stereotypes as explanations: A subjective essentialistic view of group perception. In R. Spears, P. J. Oakes, N. Ellemers, & S. A. Haslam (Eds.), *The social psychology of stereotyping and group life.* Cambridge: Blackwell.

Z

Zajonc, R. B. (1968). Attitudinal effects of mere exposure. *Journal of Personality and Social Psychology Monograph Supplement, 9* (2, Part 2), 1–27.

Zamansky, H. S., & Bartis, S. P. (1985). The dissociation of an experience: The hidden observer observed. *Journal of Abnormal Psychology, 94,* 243–248.

Zanna, M. P., & Rempel, J. K. (1988). Attitudes: A new look at an old concept. In D. Bar-Tal & A. W. Kruglanski (Eds.), *The social psychology of knowledge* (pp. 315–334). New York: Cambridge University Press.

Zanot, E. J., Pincus, J. D., & Lamp, E. J. (1983). Public perceptions of subliminal advertising. *Journal of Advertising, 12,* 37–45.

Zaragoza, M. S., & Mitchell, K. J. (1996). Repeated exposure to suggestion and the creation of false memories. *Psychological Science, 7,* 294–300.

Zatzick, D. F. (1999). Managed care and psychiatry. In R. E. Hales, S. C. Yudofsky & J. A. Talbott (Eds.), *American Psychiatric Press textbook of psychiatry.* Washington, DC: American Psychiatric Press.

Zebrowitz, L. A., & Montepare, J. M. (1992). Impressions of baby-faced individuals across the life span. *Developmental Psychology, 28,* 1143–1152.

Zebrowitz, L. A., & Rhodes, G. (2002). Nature let a hundred flowers bloom: The multiple ways and wherefores of attractiveness. In G. Rhodes & L. A. Zebrowitz (Eds.), *Facial attractiveness: Evolutionary, cognitive, and social perspectives. Advances in visual cognition* (Vol. 1, pp. 261–293). Westport, CT: Ablex.

Zebrowitz, L. A., Voinescu, L., Collins, M. A. (1996). "Wide-eyed" and "crooked-faced": Determinants of perceived and real honesty across the life span. *Personality and Social Psychology Bulletin, 22,* 1258–1269.

Zhou, L., Yang, W., Liao, S., & Zou, H. (1999). Experimental study of lie detection with P300 in simulated crime. *Chinese Journal of Clinical Psychology, 7,* 31–33.

Zhyan, T., & Singer, J. L. (1997). Daydreaming styles, emotionality and the Big Five personality dimensions. *Imagination, Cognition & Personality, 16,* 399–414.

Zimmerman, R., & Olson, K. (1994). AIDS-related risk behavior change in a sexually active, heterosexual sample: A test of three models of prevention. *AIDS Education and Prevention, 6,* 189–205.

Zipursky, R. B., & Schulz, S. C. (Eds.). (2002). *The early stages of schizophrenia* (pp. 191–204). Washington, DC: American Psychiatric Publishing, Inc.

Zola-Morgan, S., & Squire, L. R. (1993). Neuroanatomy of memory. *Annual Review of Neuroscience, 16,* 547–563.

Zorick, F. (1989). Overview of insomnia. In M. H. Dryger, T. Roth, & W. C. Dement (Eds.), *Principles and practice of sleep medicine.* San Diego: Harcourt Brace Jovanovich.

Zrenner, E., Abramov, I. Akita, M., Cowey, A., Livingstone, M., & Valberg, A. (1990). Color perception: Retina to cortex. In L. Spillman & J. S. Werner (Eds.), *Visual perception: The neurophysiological foundations.* San Diego: Academic Press.

Zuckerman, M. (1984). Sensation seeking: A comparative approach to a human approach. *The Behavioral and Brain Sciences, 7,* 413–471.

Zuckerman, M. (1999). *Vulnerability to psychopathology: A biosocial model.* Washington, DC: American Psychological Association.

Zuwerink, J. R., Devine, P. G., Monteith, M. J., & Cook, D. A. (1996). Prejudice toward Blacks: With and without compunction? *Basic and Applied Social Psychology, 18,* 131–150.

Zwislocki, J. J. (1981). Sound analysis in the ear: A history of discoveries. *American Scientist, 69,* 184–192.

Name Index

Subject Index

Page numbers in italics identify an illustration. An italic *t* next to a page number (e.g., 177*t*) indicates information that appears in a table.

A

Absolute thresholds, 117–18
Abstract reasoning, 99
Acceleration, 300
Accommodation, 96, 259
Acetylcholine (ACh), 46
Achieved ethnic identity, 94
Achievement motivation, 336–38
Achievement tests, 283
Acoustic encoding, 216, 220
Acquaintance rape, 326–27
Acquired immune deficiency
    syndrome (AIDS). *See* HIV/AIDS
Acquisition, 188
Acronyms, 244
Acrostics, 244
Action potential, 43–44
Activation-synthesis theory, 165, 166*t*
Active training in hypnosis, 169
Activity level, 472–73
Actual self, 367
Acupuncture, 47
Adaptation to sensory stimuli, 118–19
Adler, Alfred
    differences with Freud, 5–6, 364
    general theoretical approach, 364–65
    therapeutic approach, 428
Adolescence
    cognitive development, 99, 106–7
    drug use factors, 177–78
    identity versus role confusion stage, 92–93
    physical development, 51, 105–6
    social development, 107
Adolescent growth spurt, 51
Adoption studies, 302–3, 305
Adrenal glands, 51*t*, 52
Adult development, 107–11
Aerial perspective, 139
Aerobic exercise, 476–77
Afterimages, 124–25
Age
    influence on memory, 234, 235, 236
    relation to intelligence, 282, 296–97
    sleep needs and, 159
Aggression
    Bobo doll studies, 34–35, 207–8
    effects of punishment on, 202–3
    expressions of, 503–6
    observational learning of, 207–8
Aging
    brain development and, 66
    effects on attention, 153
    effects on vision, 120
    general physical effects, 75, 108–10
Agoraphobia, 402
Agreeableness (in Five-Factor Model),
    373*t*, 374, 375
AIDS. *See* HIV/AIDS
Alarm stage (GAS), 456
Alcohol
    as early anxiety treatment, 444
    effects on consciousness, 174
    effects on prenatal development, 76
    temperance cultures, 178
    unsafe sex and, 469
Alcoholics Anonymous (AA), 440
Alcoholism, 174, 431, 440

Algorithms, 265
All-or-none law, 43
"All-or-none" thinking, 434
Allport, Gordon, 370, 371
Alpha waves, 158
Alprazolam, 444, 445*t*
Altered memories, 233–36
Altered states of consciousness, 166
Alternate-forms reliability, 287
Alzheimer's disease, 46
Amnesia, 168, 242–43, 410
Amphetamines, 175
Amplitude of sound waves, 128
Amygdala
    basic functions, 56
    role in emotion, 344, 345, 346
Anal stage, 361
Analytical intelligence, 292
Analytical psychology, 365
Anaximander, 12
Anesthetics, 55
Angell, James, 5
Anger, punishment and, 202
Animal magnetism, 167
Animal research
    biological perspective and, 10
    ethical guidelines, 26, 27*t*
    taste aversion, 192–93
Animal rights, 26
Anna O., 417
Anorexia nervosa, 476
Antabuse, 431
Anterograde amnesia, 242
Antianxiety drugs, 444, 445*t*
Antibiotics, 76*t*
Anticipation, role in hunger, 334
Anticonvulsants, 76*t*
Antidepressant drugs, 443–44, 445*t*
Antigens, 460
Antipsychotic drugs, 414, 442–43, 445*t*
Antisocial personality disorder, 418–19
Anxiety
    about tests, 189, 307–9, 351
    defense mechanisms, 363–64
    disorders, 401–5, 429–30, 444, 445*t*
    superstitious behavior for coping with, 201
Ape language ability, 251–53
Aphasia, 61
Aplysia, 242
Apparent-distance theory, 142–44
Appearance stereotypes, 486, 487
Appetite, 333–35
Applied psychology, 15
Aptitude tests, 283
Aqueous humor, 120
Archetypes, 365
Archival information, 27
Aristotle, 11, 12
Arousal
    motivation and, 318–19
    role in emotion, 346–47
    as romantic attraction, 511
Asian children, achievement
    motivation, 309–10
Aspirin, 76*t*
Assimilation, 96, 259
Ativan, 444, 445*t*
Attachment, 82–86

Attention
    divided, 153
    during hypnosis, 167
    memory and, 244
    selective, 152–53
Attention-deficit hyperactivity
    disorder (ADHD), 153, 176
Attitudes, 491–96
Attribution, 491, 492–93
Attributive self-descriptions, 87*t*
Atypical behavior, 394
Audience inhibition effect, 508
Audition. *See* Hearing
Auditory canal, 128
Auditory nerve, 129
Authoritarian parents, 87
Authoritative parents, 87
Authority, 102–3, 500–502
Automatic Thoughts Questionnaire, 407*t*
Autonomic nervous system, 48–49, 341, 342
Autonomy versus shame and doubt, 91*t*, 92
Availability heuristic, 271–72
Aversive conditioning, 431
Avoidance behavior, 202*t*, 205
Axons, 41–42

B

Babbling, 259
Babies. *See* Infants
Babinski reflex, 79*t*
Backward conditioning, 188
Balance theory, 510
Barnum effect, 356
Base-rate fallacy, 271
Basilar membrane, 129, 130
B cells, 460
Beauty standards, 486, 487
Beck, Aaron, 434
Bee dances, 250, 251
Behavior. *See also* Learning; Motivation
    attachment, 82–83
    common research methods, 28–35
    disordered, 394–96
    free will versus determinism, 3
    genetic influences, 66–68, 317
    health and, 467–78
    nonverbal, 489–90
    traits versus, 376–78
Behavioral medicine, 454
Behaviorism
    association with Watson, 6
    language acquisition theory, 257
    Skinner's contributions, 9
    therapies, 429–33
    views of mental illness, 396–97, 404,
        414–15, 417
Behaviorism, 184
Behavior modification, 432
The Bell Curve, 305–6
Belongingness and love needs, 320
Benzodiazepines, 444, 445*t*
Beta waves, 158
Binet, Alfred, 282
Binet-Simon Test, 282, 283
Binocular cues, 138
Biological basis of memory, 240–43
Biological constraints on learning, 203–4